İstanbul TO Kathmandu

A CLASSIC OVERLAND ROUTE

D1245411

Paul Harding
Simon Richmond

LONELY PLANET PUBLICATIONS
Melbourne | Oakland | London | Paris

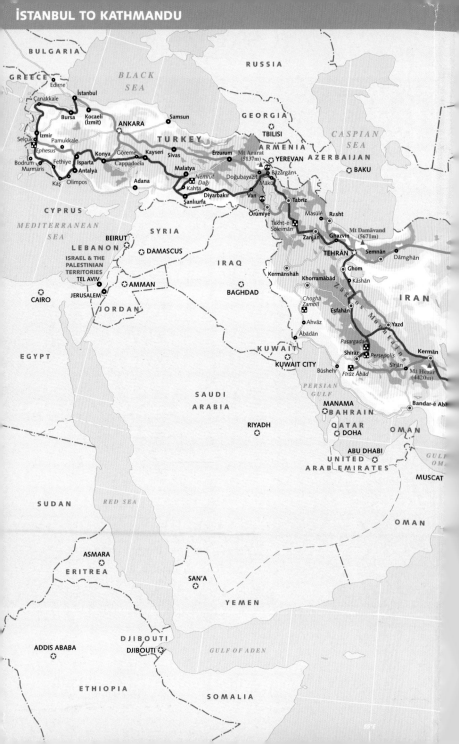

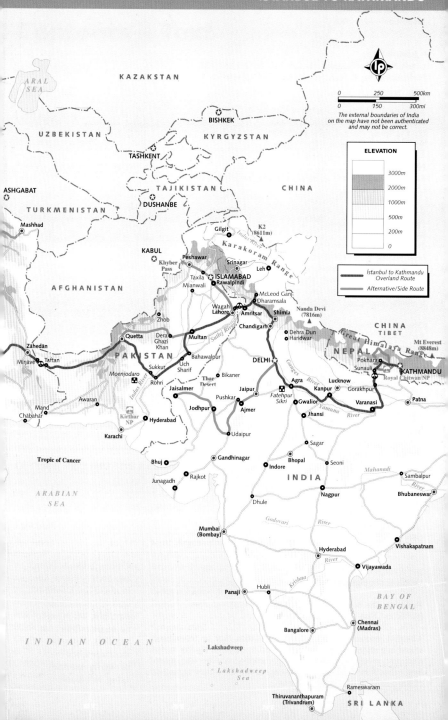

2 Contents – Text

Around Antalya 216
Inland to Central Anatolia ..217
Sagalassos 217
Eğirdir 217
Konya 218
Cappadocia 222
Nevşehir 224
Göreme 224
Çavuşin & Zelve 228
Avanos 229
Around Avanos 229
Uçhisar & Ortahisar 229
Ürgüp 230
Mustafapaşa 230
Gülşehir & Hacıbektaş 231

Soğanlı 231
Ihlara Gorge 231
Underground Cities 232
Niğde 232
Around Niğde 232
Kayseri 233
Around Kayseri 234
Kayseri to Şanlıurfa 234
Malatya 235
Adıyaman 236
Kahta 236
Kahta to Nemrut Dağı 237
Nemrut Dağı 238
Şanlıurfa (Urfa) 240
Harran & Around 244

Şanlıurfa to Doğubayazıt ..244
Diyarbakır 245
Mardin & Midyat 248
Bitlis 249
Tatvan 249
Van Gölü 249
Van 251
Around Van 253
Doğubayazıt 254
İstanbul to Iran Via
Ankara & Erzurum 257
Ankara 257
Erzurum 262

IRAN   265

The Route 265
Bāzārgān to Tehrān 266
Bāzārgān 266
Mākū 267
Ghara Kelīsā 267
Tabrīz 267
Around Tabrīz 270
Takht-é Soleimān 270
Soltānīyé 271
Ghazvīn 271
Alamūt & the Castles
of the Assassins 273

Māsūlé 273
Tehrān 274
Around Tehrān 287
Alborz Mountains 287
Holy Shrine Of Emām Khomeinī
& Behesht-é Zahrā 287
Mashhad 288
Tehrān to Esfahān 291
Ghom 291
Kāshān 291
Around Kāshān 293
Esfahān 293

Around Esfahān 300
Esfahān to Shīrāz 301
Shīrāz 301
Around Shīrāz 305
Persepolis 306
Yazd 310
Yazd to Mīrjāvé 313
Kermān 313
Around Kermān 316
Bam 316
Zāhedān 318
Mīrjāvé 319

PAKISTAN   321

The Route 322
Taftan to Lahore 323
Taftan 323
Dalbandin 323
Quetta 325
Around Quetta 331
Quetta to Bahawalpur 332

Bahawalpur 332
Around Bahawalpur 335
Multan 336
Lahore 340
Lahore Fort & Badshahi
Mosque 346
Lahore to Peshawar 356

Lahore to Rawalpindi 356
Rawalpindi 356
Islamabad 363
Around Islamabad 368
Peshawar 371
Around Peshawar 381

INDIA   385

The Route 385
Wagah to Amritsar 387
Wagah 387
Amritsar 387
Golden Temple 392
Northern India 397
Dharamsala 397
McLeod Ganj 398
Around Dharamsala 409
Shimla 409
Around Shimla 415

Shimla to Kalka 416
Chandigarh 416
Delhi 420
The Rajasthan Route 446
Jaipur 446
Around Jaipur 455
Jaipur to Pushkar 456
Pushkar 457
Udaipur 462
Around Udaipur 470
Jodhpur 470

Jaisalmer 475
Around Jaisalmer 482
Agra to Sunauli 483
Agra 483
Fatehpur Sikri 493
Varanasi 495
Sarnath 507
Gorakhpur 508
Kushinagar 510
Sunauli 510

NEPAL 513

The Route 513
Sunauli & Around 514
Sunauli 514
Lumbini 516

Pokhara 516
Royal Chitwan NP 529
Sauraha 532
Kathmandu 534

Around Kathmandu Valley 561
Temples of the Kathmandu
Valley 564

LANGUAGE 573

Farsi 573-6
Hindi & Urdu 577-81

Nepali 581-4
Turkish 584-7

Gazeteer 587-8

GLOSSARY 589

INDEX 601

Text 601

Boxed Text 607

MAP LEGEND back page

METRIC CONVERSION inside back cover

Contents – Maps

TURKEY

Turkey 146-7
Greater İstanbul 149
İstanbul 150-1
Sultanahmet & Around ..154-5
Topkapı Palace Museum 158
Beyoğlu & Taksim 163
Princes Islands (Kızıl Adalar) ..173
Central Bursa 174-5
Anzac Battlefields 179

Çanakkale 181
İzmir 186
Selçuk 189
Ephesus (Efes) 193
Bodrum 197
Marmaris 201
Fethiye 206-7
Kaş 210
Antalya (Kaleiçi) 214

Konya 219
Cappadocia (Kapadokya) ..223
Göreme 225
Nemrut Dağı Area 238
Şanlıurfa (Urfa) 241
Diyarbakır 246
Van 251
Doğubayazıt 255
Ankara 259

IRAN

Iran 266
Tabrīz 268
Ghazvīn 272
Greater Tehrān 275
Central Tehrān 280-1

Mashhad 289
Kāshān 292
Esfahān 294
Meidūn-é Emām Khomeinī 296
Shīrāz 302

Persepolis (Takht-é Jamshīd) ..307
Yazd 311
Kermān 314
Bam 317
Zāhedān 319

PAKISTAN

Pakistan 323
Quetta 327
Bahawalpur 333
Multan 337
Lahore 341
Central Lahore 342-3
Lahore Fort 347

Rawalpindi 357
Rajah Bazaar, Committee
Chowk & Liaquat Chowk ..359
Rawalpindi – Saddar
Bazaar & Cantonment 360
Islamabad 364-5
Taxila 369

Peshawar 372
Peshawar – Old City 375
Peshawar Cantonment &
Saddar Bazaar 378

INDIA

India 386
Amritsar 389
Dharamsala 397
McLeod Ganj 399
Shimla 410
Chandigarh 417
Delhi 422-3

Old Delhi 427
New Delhi 429
Paharganj 435
Connaught Place 436
Jaipur 447
Pushkar 458
Udaipur 463

Jodhpur 471
Jaisalmer 476
Agra 484
Taj Ganj 489
Varanasi 497
Godaulia & the Old City 502
Gorakhpur 509

NEPAL

Nepal 514-5
Pokhara 517
Pokhara Lakeside 521
Sauraha 533

Kathmandu 536-7
Durbar Square
(Kathmandu) 541
Walking Tour 543

Greater Thamel 550-1
Kathmandu Valley 562
Bodhnath 565
Swayambhunath 567

The Authors

Paul Harding

Paul was coordinating author for this book. He researched and wrote the introductory chapters – with help from Dan Goldberg on Facts about the Region – and the Pakistan, India and Nepal chapters.

Born in Melbourne, Paul grew up mostly in country Victoria and started working life as a reporter on a local newspaper. He spent three years backpacking in Europe and Asia, stopping briefly to work as editor of a London travel magazine – among assorted (other) low-paying, menial jobs – before landing at Lonely Planet's Melbourne office as an editor in 1996. Reading travel guidebook manuscripts all day long only made his itchy feet worse, so he swapped his red pen for a blue one and now works as a full-time writer and researcher. Travelling overland trails is Paul's latest passion. He has worked on Lonely Planet's *South-East Asia*, *India*, *South India*, *Australia*, *New South Wales* and *Read this First: Europe*.

Simon Richmond

Veteran of several transcontinental overland jaunts, including New York to LA by Greyhound, and London to Hong Kong by train, Simon Richmond thought himself well prepared for covering the İstanbul to Kathmandu route. Little did he realise that he'd end up tipping out of a kayak into the Mediterranean, consorting with security honchos in eastern Turkey at a footy cup final, breaking up a fracas and nursing a septic toe in Iran, dodging dacoits in an air-con Volvo in Pakistan, sweating it out in India and enduring garrulous guides in Kathmandu – but that's another story. Thankfully, the skills he's honed on several books for Lonely Planet, including *Central Asia*, *Walking in Australia* and the *Out to Eat* guides to Sydney and London, plus assorted travel books and features for other publishers, magazines and newspapers, came in handy.

FROM THE AUTHORS

Paul Harding

When Lonely Planet suggested an overland guide from İstanbul to Kathmandu, my hand was firmly in the air, so thanks to Geoff Stringer and Sharan Kaur for their continuing faith. Thanks also to Adriana Mammarella for her support during the research and writing and to the editors and designers at Lonely Planet Melbourne who put the book together.

To my partner in crime, Simon Richmond, thanks for your work and support and a much needed night out on the town in Lahore.

In Nepal thanks to Stan Armington, Brandon Korht and Martin Eckhardt. In India, Ramesh and his lovely family in Agra, Rajendra Kumar in Delhi, Joe Hawk in McLeod Ganj, and Sonu and Monu in Amritsar for an enjoyable night out in the pool hall. In Pakistan, Lahore was made easy thanks to Rana Salah, and thanks also to Jeremy Frankel and James and Gail (for a fun night out). Andy Hill and Jackie Ashworth were a mine of knowledge in Islamabad, as were Sarah Austin and her friends in Quetta. Thanks to Bonnie and Miyaki for company in Iran, and Pat Yale in Turkey. Big thanks to Kylie for keeping me company for the first part of the trip. Finally, thanks to Nigel Croft and Sue Cooper for their valuable contributions on driving and cycling.

Simon Richmond

I can't think of a better person to travel and write about the overland route with than Paul Harding, even though we went in opposite directions – at least we had those beers together in Lahore. Cheers, Paul! Also thanks to Geoff Stringer for putting me up to it in the first place and Adriana Mammarella for her fine organisational efficiency.

Cheers to all the other fellow overlanders I met along the way: Drew and Ruth; Trevor McDonald; Nigel Croft; all at Bougainville Travel in Kaş; Kyle and Jackie in Kayseri; Toby and Deano on Nemrut Dağı; Simon, Nadia and Alia on the leg from Khata to Doğubayazıt; Jean Yves Clemenzo; Edmund Blair; Ken Twyford and Gerald Smewing; super-cyclist Sue Cooper; Bettina Stollar and the architects from Barcelona; Christer Gerlach; the Dragoman team in Taftan and the Exodus Crew in Lahore and Amritsar.

Others who generously gave their time and knowledge, all much appreciated, include: Nasrin Harris; Dominic Whiting; Kate Clow; Andrew Humphreys; Ken Dakan; Etienne Le Roux; Verity Campbell; Pat Yale; Ruth Lockwood; Arhan Işın in Ankara; Korhan, his mate Ali and Nafiz Tanir, all of whom made Diyarbakır truly memorable; Saim from Murat Camping (thanks for trusting me with your 4WD!); Nasser and Mansour Khan and fellow guide Fereydoon in Tabrīz; Serge and Marie Laure Michel; Jim Muir, Koulak and Maryam Amanpour; Ali and Maryam Ghanbari; Iraj Jahanbakhsh; Jane Modaressi; Natasha Shahidi, Douglas Tunn and all at the British Embassy, Tehrān; Zarinfar Jamshid who got us to Persepolis and back; Komeil Noofeli; Dinyar Shahzadi and Hussein in Yazd; Mr Javaid and Jeremy Franklin in Lahore; Simon, Anara and baby Sebastian Forrester in Kathmandu.

This Book

For this first edition of *İstanbul to Kathmandu*, Paul Harding wrote the introductory chapters and the Pakistan, India and Nepal chapters; Simon Richmond wrote the Turkey and Iran chapters and contributed material to the introductory chapters.

From the Publisher

This edition of İstanbul to Kathmandu was edited in Lonely Planet's Melbourne office by Jenny Mullaly, with assistance from Bruce Evans, Adam Ford, Justin Flynn, John Hinman, Susan Holtham, Rowan McKinnon, Hilary Rogers, Julia Taylor and Isabelle Young.

Shahara Ahmed coordinated the mapping, with assistance from Sarah Sloane and Jody Whiteoak. She also prepared the climate charts and did additional research for the health section. Sarah Sloane coordinated the design and layout. Andrew Weatherill designed the cover and Lachlan Ross created the back-cover map. Margie Jung designed the country highlights colour sections, and Annie Horner and Brett Pascoe from Lonely Planet Images assisted with the photographs.

Quentin Frayne and Emma Koch compiled the Language chapter and Dan Goldberg compiled material for the Facts about the Region chapter. Sharan Kaur and Andrew Humphreys helped to get the project off the ground. For their expert guidance and support from start to finish, thank you to Hilary Ericksen, senior editor, and Adriana Mammarella, senior designer. And of course, thanks to authors Paul and Simon for their hard work, both during their travels from İstanbul to Kathmandu and thereafter.

Foreword

ABOUT LONELY PLANET GUIDEBOOKS

The story begins with a classic travel adventure: Tony and Maureen Wheeler's 1972 journey across Europe and Asia to Australia. Useful information about the overland trail did not exist at that time, so Tony and Maureen published the first Lonely Planet guidebook to meet a growing need.

From a kitchen table, then from a tiny office in Melbourne (Australia), Lonely Planet has become the largest independent travel publisher in the world, an international company with offices in Melbourne, Oakland (USA), London (UK) and Paris (France).

Today Lonely Planet guidebooks cover the globe. There is an ever-growing list of books and there's information in a variety of forms and media. Some things haven't changed. The main aim is still to help make it possible for adventurous travellers to get out there – to explore and better understand the world.

At Lonely Planet we believe travellers can make a positive contribution to the countries they visit – if they respect their host communities and spend their money wisely. Since 1986 a percentage of the income from each book has been donated to aid projects and human rights campaigns.

Updates Lonely Planet thoroughly updates each guidebook as often as possible. This usually means there are around two years between editions, although for more unusual or more stable destinations the gap can be longer. Check the imprint page (following the colour map at the beginning of the book) for publication dates.

Between editions up-to-date information is available in two free newsletters – the paper *Planet Talk* and email *Comet* (to subscribe, contact any Lonely Planet office) – and on our Web site at www.lonelyplanet.com. The *Upgrades* section of the Web site covers a number of important and volatile destinations and is regularly updated by Lonely Planet authors. *Scoop* covers news and current affairs relevant to travellers. And, lastly, the *Thorn Tree* bulletin board and *Postcards* section of the site carry unverified, but fascinating, reports from travellers.

Correspondence The process of creating new editions begins with the letters, postcards and emails received from travellers. This correspondence often includes suggestions, criticisms and comments about the current editions. Interesting excerpts are immediately passed on via newsletters and the Web site, and everything goes to our authors to be verified when they're researching on the road. We're keen to get more feedback from organisations or individuals who represent communities visited by travellers.

Lonely Planet gathers information for everyone who's curious about the planet – and especially for those who explore it first-hand. Through guidebooks, phrasebooks, activity guides, maps, literature, newsletters, image library, TV series and Web site we act as an information exchange for a worldwide community of travellers.

Research Authors aim to gather sufficient practical information to enable travellers to make informed choices and to make the mechanics of a journey run smoothly. They also research historical and cultural background to help enrich the travel experience and allow travellers to understand and respond appropriately to cultural and environmental issues.

Authors don't stay in every hotel because that would mean spending a couple of months in each medium-sized city and, no, they don't eat at every restaurant because that would mean stretching belts beyond capacity. They do visit hotels and restaurants to check standards and prices, but feedback based on readers' direct experiences can be very helpful.

Many of our authors work undercover, others aren't so secretive. None of them accept freebies in exchange for positive write-ups. And none of our guidebooks contain any advertising.

Production Authors submit their raw manuscripts and maps to offices in Australia, USA, UK or France. Editors and cartographers – all experienced travellers themselves – then begin the process of assembling the pieces. When the book finally hits the shops, some things are already out of date, we start getting feedback from readers and the process begins again...

WARNING & REQUEST

Things change – prices go up, schedules change, good places go bad and bad places go bankrupt – nothing stays the same. So, if you find things better or worse, recently opened or long since closed, please tell us and help make the next edition even more accurate and useful. We genuinely value all the feedback we receive. Julie Young coordinates a well-travelled team that reads and acknowledges every letter, postcard and email and ensures that every morsel of information finds its way to the appropriate authors, editors and cartographers for verification.

Everyone who writes to us will find their name in the next edition of the appropriate guidebook. They will also receive the latest issue of *Planet Talk*, our quarterly printed newsletter, or *Comet*, our monthly email newsletter. Subscriptions to both newsletters are free. The very best contributions will be rewarded with a free guidebook.

Excerpts from your correspondence may appear in new editions of Lonely Planet guidebooks, the Lonely Planet Web site, *Planet Talk* or *Comet*, so please let us know if you *don't* want your letter published or your name acknowledged.

Send all correspondence to the Lonely Planet office closest to you:

Australia: Locked Bag 1, Footscray, Victoria, 3011
USA: 150 Linden St, Oakland, CA 94607
UK: 10a Spring Place, London NW5 3BH
France: 1 rue du Dahomey, 75011 Paris

Or email us at: talk2us@lonelyplanet.com.au

For news, views and updates see our Web site: www.lonelyplanet.com

HOW TO USE A LONELY PLANET ROUTE GUIDE

The best way to use a Lonely Planet route guide is any way you choose. At Lonely Planet we believe that the most memorable travel experiences are often those that are unexpected, and the finest discoveries are those that you make yourself. Route guides, like any guidebooks, are not intended to be used as though they contain an infallible set of instructions!

Contents All Lonely Planet route guides follow roughly the same format. The Facts about the Region chapter gives background information ranging from history to weather. The Regional Facts for the Visitor chapter gives practical information on issues like visas and health. Getting There & Away gives a brief starting point for researching travel to and from the region. Getting Around the Region gives an overview of transport along the route.

The peculiar demands of each route determine how subsequent chapters are broken up, but some things remain constant. We begin at the starting point, and all other destinations are ordered in the sequence they will be encountered by someone following the described route. For each major destination we always start with background, then proceed to sights, places to stay, places to eat, entertainment, getting there and away, and getting around information – in that order.

Heading Hierarchy Lonely Planet headings are used in a strict hierarchical structure that can be visualised as a set of Russian dolls. Each heading (and its following text) is encompassed by any preceding heading that is higher on the hierarchical ladder.

Entry Points Although route guides are ordered from specific beginning to specific end points, they are also written so that the route can be travelled in reverse. We also assume that some people will not be travelling the whole route but visiting only one or more specific areas or countries. In this case, the traditional entry points are the table of contents and the index.

The Regional Facts for the Visitor chapter begins with highlights, suggested itineraries and route details. Each chapter covering a geographical region also begins with a locator map, further route details and another list of highlights.

Maps Maps play a crucial role in Lonely Planet guidebooks, and include a huge amount of information. A legend is printed on the back page. We seek to have complete consistency between maps and text, and to have every important place in the text captured on a map. Map key numbers usually start in the top left corner.

Although inclusion in a guidebook usually implies a recommendation we cannot list every good place. Exclusion does not necessarily imply criticism. In fact there are a number of reasons why we might exclude a place – sometimes it is simply inappropriate to encourage an influx of travellers.

Introduction

İstanbul to Kathmandu: The names alone inspire images of an exotic overland adventure. There's something undeniably irresistible about starting a journey at the gateway to Asia, among the minarets, bazaars and Turkish teahouses, and ending up surrounded by the snowy peaks of the Nepal Himalaya, picking your way through the cobbled backstreets and durbar squares of Kathmandu. Or vice versa, because you don't have to travel from west to east. This is a two-way street, and many people travel from Kathmandu to İstanbul and on to Europe – the essence is the exactly the same. In between you plot a course through five very diverse countries.

This journey has a great deal of history. Long before anyone had thought of travelling for fun, Alexander the Great was plundering his way towards India. Many of the regions covered by this route were visited by him on his empire-building march eastwards. Well before the birth of Christ, important trade routes were being carved out through Central Asia and the Middle East. The so-called Silk Road from China passed through present-day Iran and Turkey, while nomadic traders' caravans criss-crossed in both directions between Europe, China and India, swapping everything from salt, silk and spices to tea, jewels and wine. Much later, this route was made famous by the Italian traveller Marco Polo, who set the standard for European explorers heading east in search of different cultures and untold riches.

In more recent times, this route has been the domain of the overlanding hippy, that new breed of youthful wanderer who took off just for the sake of travel – spurred on in a quest for Indian-style spirituality and cheap pot in Kabul. Those days are pretty much over, inasmuch as the stereotype of the hippy traveller has faded and Afghanistan is off the itinerary. Modern-day hippies, however, still hit the trail, and in India and Nepal you'll still see the odd one who doesn't seem to have made it out of the 1970s. In fact, İstanbul to Kathmandu is part of Lonely Planet's roots. It was along here

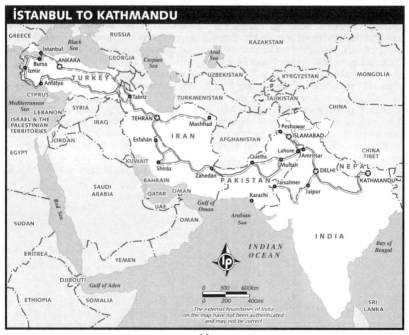

in 1972 that Tony and Maureen Wheeler first blazed a trail by car, bus and train on their way from London to Australia.

While travel has opened up to the masses since then – and parts of the world are groaning under the weight of tourism – the overland trail is still relatively unbeaten. It's still an incredible adventure. You might not be able to escape the holidaying summer crowds in western Turkey, but as you drift east you'll notice the change. There are fewer familiar voices and sun-loving individuals in shorts and T-shirts. You begin to chat with the locals more and notice traditional dress and customs. Before you know it you're crossing the border (always a period of great trepidation and anticipation) into Iran, where new experiences of local hospitality, new heights of bargain-basement travel and, above all, wonderful teahouses await. Further still, you can go for days on end in Pakistan without seeing another westerner, even travelling on the standard route.

By the time you get to India you won't be alone. Apart from a billion or so locals (who all seem to be attempting to board the same train as you), India draws curious visitors from all over the world like a magnet. It's an intoxicating and at times frustrating fusion of spirituality, poverty, belching vehicles and colourful saris, but travel here always comes with a healthy dose of the unexpected.

Crossing the border into Nepal is a bit like being sucked out of a vortex. The chaos of India is replaced by the positively laid-back demeanour of the Nepalis and the dry, dusty plains give way to green hills, deep valleys and, eventually, a stunning unbroken chain of the world's highest peaks.

Of course, travelling the overland trail is not just about getting from A to B (or, in this case, I to K) and feeling intrepid. There are plenty of experiences to be had along the way. You can swim and sail (or just laze) on the Mediterranean coast, explore ancient Roman and Persian ruins, ski and hike in the mountains, raft some of the world's best rapids, study Tibetan Buddhism at the home of the Dalai Lama, ponder the Taj Mahal at dawn and ride off into the desert on a camel.

Some of your most memorable experiences will be more personal: Attending Friday prayers at a monumental mosque, observing teahouse life over an aromatic hubble-bubble, being invited to a traditional wedding or simply picking your way through ancient bazaars and meeting local characters.

It's a long way from Istanbul to Kathmandu – over 10,000km – but it's a surprisingly easy journey. With Iran and Pakistan opening up to tourism, many of the obstacles that dogged overland travellers in the past are beginning to disappear. If you haven't travelled in this region before, you're probably feeling a bit apprehensive. Is it safe in Pakistan and eastern Turkey? Will I get ripped off in India or thrown into jail in Iran? Will I succumb to malaria or heat exhaustion? The simple answer is that this is not a difficult or hazardous trip. You'll need to be wary and occasionally thick-skinned, dress appropriately and respect local sensibilities. But provided you carry a bit of common sense – and a healthy sense of adventure – you'll love it. It's also very cheap by Western standards, so you can afford to enjoy yourself. This book will hopefully smooth the way a little and provide the answers to all your nagging questions. So read on.

When you're sitting back in a bar in the Thamel district of Kathmandu, swapping overland stories over a cold beer and some gourmet food, you'll know you've made it.

Facts about the Region

HISTORY

Spanning the Middle East, parts of Asia and the Indian subcontinent, the five countries crossed in this route share little common history. While Turkey and Iran fall within the Middle Eastern domain, Pakistan, India and Nepal straddle the borders of Asia and the subcontinent.

Three historical events affected most (but not all) of the countries on this route: the conquest of Alexander the Great; the birth and spread of Islam; and the expansion of British power in the Indian subcontinent.

A brief account of the general history of the region follows.

Early Civilisation

The earliest civilisation in the region dates back millennia. Archaeological evidence suggests there was a Stone Age city in Turkey some 7,500 years ago. In Iran, excavations point to the settlement of hunter gatherers living in caves around the Zagros and Alborz Mountains during the Neolithic Age.

Over in the East, the seeds of Indian and Pakistani civilisation were planted in the Indus Valley. India's first major civilisation flourished there in 2500 BC though it is thought to date back much further; recorded history in Nepal begins with the Kiratis around the 7th or 8th centuries BC.

Alexander The Great

In 336 BC Philip of Macedon, a warlord who had conquered much of mainland Greece, was murdered. His son Alexander assumed the throne and began a series of conquests that would eventually encompass Persia, most of Asia Minor, the Middle East and north-western India. By the time he died in 323 BC, with an empire stretching from Greece to India, he was considered the greatest general who ever lived.

By 327 BC, Alexander came over the Hindukush to mop up the eastern bits of the Persian Empire he had defeated. Two years later his troops decided they'd had enough of foreign travel, and mutinied near present-day Amritsar. So Alexander built several thousand boats and everybody went down the Indus River, some to sail away, some to plod

MICK WELDON

Alexander the Great's conquests covered much of the territory making up this route.

back through Baluchistan and Persia, leaving a few generals to keep things together.

Following Alexander's death, his empire was carved up by his generals, who spent the next 40 years fighting each other. The eastern Mediterranean splintered into an array of local dynasties with fluctuating borders as different parts were conquered and lost. Eventually the entire region fell to the Romans, who conquered most of Asia Minor in 188 BC and, later, the whole of the Mediterranean.

The Birth of Islam

In AD 570, not long after Christianity spread across the Roman Empire, Mohammed was born in the Arabian town of Mecca. He began to preach three years after the first revelation, which he received from God (Allah) at around the age of 40. His teachings challenged the pagan religion of the Meccans, who worshipped many gods represented by idols. As a result, in 622 Mohammed and his followers (known as Muslims) were forced to flee to Medina, an oasis town some 360km to the north. This Hejira, or migration, is taken to mark the start of the new Muslim era.

In Medina, Mohammed rose to become a successful religious, political and military leader. He brought all the region's tribes into his fold and eventually gathered an army of 10,000 troops and conquered his home town of Mecca.

Mohammed died in 632 but under his successors, known as caliphs (from the Arabic word for 'follower'), the new religion continued its rapid spread throughout all of Arabia by 634. In 711, the same year the Arabs landed in Spain, they sent dhows down the Indus River to India and by the 12th century all of India fell into Muslim hands. Islam was then spread by Indian traders into South-East Asia, reaching as far afield as Indonesia and Malaysia.

When the Prophet died in 632 leaving no sons, there was a major dispute over the line of succession. This dispute over the caliphate eventually opened a rift in Islam that grew into today's divide between Sunni and Shi'ite Muslims. Competing for power were Abu Bakr, the father of Mohammed's second wife, and Ali, Mohammed's cousin and the husband of his daughter. Initially, the power was transferred to Abu Bakr, who became the first caliph.

Subsequent civil war ended with the rise to power of Mu'awiyah, the Muslim military governor of Syria, who was also a distant relative of the Prophet. Mu'awiyah moved the capital of the caliphate from Medina to Damascus and established the first great Muslim dynasty – the Umayyad (or Omayyad) dynasty. The Umayyad dynasty rose to rule the vast majority of the Muslim world, marking the start of the Sunni sect. Those who continued to support the claims of the descendants of Ali became known as Shi'ites.

In 750 the Umayyads were toppled in a revolt fuelled by accusations of impiety. Their successors, and the strong arm behind the revolt, were a dynasty called the Abbasids.

The Abbasid caliphate created a new capital in Baghdad and the early centuries of its rule constituted what has been remembered ever since as the golden age of Islamic culture and society. The most famous of the Abbasid caliphs was Haroun ar-Rashid (reigned 786–809), a warrior king who led one of the most successful early Muslim invasions of Byzantium, almost reaching Constantinople. After Haroun's death the empire was effectively divided between two of his sons. Predictably, civil war ensued. In 813 one son, Al-Ma'mun, emerged triumphant and reigned as caliph for the next 20 years. But Al-Ma'mun's hold on power remained insecure and he felt compelled to surround himself with Turkish mercenaries. Over time the caliph's Turkish bodyguards became the real rulers of an empire that itself was rapidly shrinking.

The Seljuks

By the middle of the 10th century the Abbasid caliphs were the prisoners of their Turkish guards, who spawned a dynasty of their own, the Seljuks (1038–1194). The Seljuks extended their reach throughout Persia, Central Asia and Afghanistan. They also took control of Armenia, Azerbaijan and a large part of Anatolia, where the Seljuk Sultanate of Rum made its capital at Konya. The resulting pressure on the Byzantine Empire was intense enough to cause the emperor and the Greek Orthodox Church to swallow their pride and appeal to the Roman Catholic pope for help.

The Mongols

In the wake of the Seljuks came the rampaging Mongols, who eventually conquered the area stretching from China to Turkey in the early 13th century. They destroyed many of the cities they conquered and massacred anyone who stood in their way. Their rout came to an abrupt end when they simply ran out of effective rulers after the death of Sultan Abu Said in 1335.

The Rise of the Ottomans

In 1258, just eight years after the Mamluks first seized power in Cairo and began their bloody dynasty, a boy named Osman was born to the chief of a pagan Turkish tribe in western Anatolia. Osman, the first ruler of what would become the Ottoman Empire, converted to Islam in his youth. He began his military career by hiring out his tribe's army as mercenaries in the civil wars then plaguing what was left of the Byzantine Empire. Payment came in the form of land.

Rather than taking on the Byzantines directly, Osman's successors patiently scooped up the bits and pieces of the empire that Constantinople could no longer control.

The Ottoman Empire reached its peak during the reign of Süleyman the Magnificent.

By the end of the 14th century the Ottomans had conquered Bulgaria, Serbia, Bosnia, Hungary and the majority of the territory that makes up present-day Turkey. They had also moved their capital across the Dardanelles to Adrianople, today the Turkish city of Edirne. In 1453 Sultan Mehmet II took Constantinople, the hitherto unachievable object of innumerable Muslim wars almost since the 7th century.

The empire reached its peak, both politically and culturally, under Süleyman the Magnificent (reigned 1520–66), who led the Ottoman armies west to the gates of Vienna. After Süleyman's reign, the empire dwindled slowly in a long period of decline.

Expansion of British Power

In the East, the British were carefully moving into the Indian subcontinent. They were not the first to arrive, nor were they the last to leave – both those honours go to the Portuguese. In 1498, Vasco da Gama arrived on the coast of modern-day Kerala, having sailed around the Cape of Good Hope. Pioneering this route gave the Portuguese a century of uninterrupted monopoly over Indian and Far Eastern trade with Europe. In 1510, they captured Goa, the Indian enclave they controlled until 1961. In the long term, however, the Portuguese did not have the resources to maintain a worldwide empire and they were quickly eclipsed after the arrival of the British, French and Dutch.

In 1600, Queen Elizabeth I granted a charter to a London trading company giving it a monopoly on British trade with India. In 1612, the East India Company's representatives established their first trading post at Surat in Gujarat. Further trading posts were established at Madras (present-day Chennai), Bengal and Bombay (Mumbai). Strange as it seems now, for nearly 250 years a commercial trading company (and not the British government) 'ruled' British India.

The transformation of the British from traders to governors began almost by accident. Having been granted a licence to operate in Bengal by the Great Mughal, and following the establishment of a new trading post, Calcutta (Kolkata), in 1690, business began to expand rapidly. Eventually the nawab (the local ruler) decided that British power had grown far enough. In June 1756 he attacked and took Calcutta.

Six months later, Robert Clive led a relief expedition to retake Calcutta and overthrew the nawab in June 1757 at the Battle of Plassey. During the period that followed, with the British effectively in control of Bengal, the company's agents engaged in unbridled profiteering. When a subsequent nawab finally took up arms to protect his own interests, he was defeated at the Battle of Baksar in 1764. This victory confirmed the British as the paramount power in east India.

In the early 19th century, following a brief series of battles between the British and the Gurkhas (Nepali soldiers) in 1814, the borders of Nepal were delineated. The Gurkhas were initially victorious but, two years later, were forced to sue for peace as the British marched on Kathmandu. As part of the price for peace, the Nepalis were forced to cede the provinces of Kumaon and Shimla, but mutual respect for each other's military prowess prevented Nepal's incorporation into the Indian empire and led to the establishment of the Gurkha regiments of the British army.

British India By the early 19th century, India was effectively under British control. The country remained a patchwork of states, many nominally independent and governed by their own rulers, the maharajas and nawabs. While these 'princely states' administered their own territories, a system of central government was developed. British organisation was replicated in the Indian government and civil service – a legacy which still exists today.

The British also established English as the local language of administration. While this may have been useful in a country with so many different languages, and even today fulfils a very important function in nationwide communication, it also kept the new rulers at arm's length from the Indians.

The Indian Uprising In 1857, half a century after having established firm control of India, the British suffered a serious setback: the Indian Uprising (known at the time as the 'Indian Mutiny' and subsequently labelled by nationalist historians as a 'War of Independence'). The causes of the uprising are still the subject of debate. The key factors included the influx of cheap goods, such as textiles, from Britain, which destroyed many livelihoods, the dispossession of many rulers of their territories and taxes imposed on landowners.

During the uprising, 47 Indian battalions of the Bengal army mutinied. The soldiers and peasants rallied around the ageing Great Mughal in Delhi, but there was never any clear idea of what they hoped to achieve. They held Delhi for four months and besieged the British Residency in Lucknow for five months, before they were finally suppressed, leaving deep scars on both sides.

Almost immediately, the East India Company was wound up and direct control of the country was assumed by the British government, which announced its support of the existing rulers of the princely states – as long as they remained loyal to the British.

Road to Independence Opposition to British rule in India began to increase at the turn of the 20th century. The Indian National Congress met for the first time in 1885 and soon began to push for a measure of participation in the government of the country.

Despite a number of hints and promises in return for India's immense effort in WWI, no such rewards emerged and disillusionment soon followed. Disturbances were particularly noticeable in the Punjab.

The 1919 massacre at Amritsar, in which a British army contingent opened fire into a crowd of unarmed protesters, causing well in excess of 1000 casualties, turned huge numbers of otherwise apolitical Indians into Congress supporters.

At this time, the Congress movement also found a new leader in Mohandas Gandhi. Gandhi, who subsequently became known as the Mahatma, or Great Soul, adopted a policy of *satyagraha* (passive resistance) to British rule.

As the mass movement led by Gandhi gained momentum, Muslims began to look to their own interests. The large Muslim minority realised that an independent India would also be a Hindu-dominated India. By the 1930s Muslims were raising the possibility of a separate Muslim state.

Partition During WWII, large numbers of Congress supporters were jailed to prevent disruption to the war effort. Meanwhile, support grew among Muslims for an independent state of their own. Mohammed Ali Jinnah, the leader of the Muslim League declared that he wished to have 'India divided or India destroyed'. Gandhi, the father figure of Congress, urged reconciliation, but his voice was drowned out by others.

In early 1946, a British mission failed to bring the two sides together and the country slid closer towards civil war. In February 1947, faced by a growing crisis, the British government made the momentous decision that Independence would come by June 1948. Lord Louis Mountbatten replaced Lord Wavell as viceroy.

Mountbatten made a last-ditch attempt to convince the rival factions that a united India was a more sensible proposition, but they remained intransigent. Reluctantly, the decision was then made to divide the country. Only Gandhi stood firmly against the division.

Faced with increasing civil violence, Mountbatten decided to follow a breakneck pace to Independence and announced that it would come on 14 August 1947.

The most important decision to be made was the actual location of the dividing line. Neatly slicing the country in two proved to be an impossible task. Although some areas were clearly Hindu or Muslim, others had evenly mixed populations, and there were isolated 'islands' of communities in areas predominantly settled by other religions. Moreover, the two overwhelmingly Muslim regions were on opposite sides of the country and therefore Pakistan would inevitably have an eastern and western half divided by a hostile India. The instability of this arrangement was self-evident, but it took 25 years before the predestined split finally came and East Pakistan became Bangladesh.

An independent British referee was given the task of drawing the borders. The dividing line became known as the Radcliffe Line (after British jurist Sir Cyril Radcliffe), and it was a disaster.

The problem was particularly acute in the Punjab, where intercommunity antagonisms were already running at fever pitch. The Punjab was one of the most fertile and affluent regions of the country, and had large Muslim, Hindu and Sikh communities. The Sikhs had already campaigned unsuccessfully for their own state, and now saw their homeland divided down the middle. The new border ran straight between the Punjab's two major cities – Lahore and Amritsar.

Huge exchanges of population took place. Trains full of Muslims fleeing westward were held up and slaughtered by Hindu and Sikh mobs. Hindus and Sikhs fleeing to the east suffered the same fate. The army sent to maintain order proved totally inadequate and, at times, all too ready to join the partisan carnage. By the time the Punjab chaos had run its course, over 10 million people had changed sides and even the most conservative estimates calculate that 250,000 people had lost their lives. The true figure may well have been over half a million. Prior to Independence, Lahore's total population of 1.2 million included approximately 500,000 Hindus and 100,000 Sikhs. When the dust had finally settled, Lahore had a Hindu and Sikh population of only 1000.

The final stages of Independence saw one last tragedy played out. On 30 January 1948, Gandhi, deeply disheartened by the Partition and its subsequent bloodshed, was assassinated by a Hindu fanatic.

The independently adjudicated border between India and Pakistan failed to prevent disputes. The issue was complicated by the fact that the 'princely states' in British India were nominally independent. As part of the process, local rulers were asked which country they wished to belong to. In all but three cases the matter was solved relatively simply.

Kashmir, however, was a predominantly Muslim state with a Hindu maharaja who, by October 1948, had still not opted for India or Pakistan when a rag-tag Pathan (Pakistani) army crossed the border, intent on racing to Srinagar and annexing Kashmir. The Pathans, inspired to mount their invasion by the promise of plunder, did so much plundering en route that India had time to rush troops to Srinagar and prevent the town's capture. The indecisive maharaja finally opted for India, provoking the first, albeit brief, India-Pakistan war.

The United Nations eventually stepped in, but the issue of Kashmir has remained a central cause of disagreement and conflict between the two countries ever since. With its overwhelming Muslim majority and its geographic links to Pakistan, many people were inclined to support Pakistan's claims to the region. To this day, India and Pakistan are divided in this region by a demarcation line (known as the Line of Actual Control), yet neither side agrees that this constitutes the official border.

The Turkish Republic

Following Turkey's defeat in WWI, Mustafa Kemal later dubbed Atatürk, 'Father Turk'), the heroic general who'd repelled the Anzacs (Australian and New Zealand Army Corps) at Gallipoli, out-manoeuvred the weak Ottoman rulers and Allied forces in the War of Independence. Victory came in 1923 at Smyrna (present-day İzmir) where the invading Greeks were pushed out of Anatolia for good. The treaties of WWI, which had left the Turks with almost no country, were renegotiated and a new Turkish republic, comprising Anatolia and part of Thrace, was born.

Atatürk, considered the father of modern Turkey, embarked on a rapid modernisation program, including the establishment of a secular democracy, the introduction of Latin script and European dress and the theoretical adoption of equal rights for women. The capital was also moved from İstanbul to Ankara. Such sweeping changes didn't come easily and some battles are still being fought today (eg, over women's rights) as Islamic fundamentalism gains popularity.

The Iranian Revolution

Across the border in Iran, Islam would have a far more decisive role in the formation of the modern nation. Like Atatürk, the all-powerful Shāh Mohammed Rezā Pahlavī had aimed to be a modernising force, reducing illiteracy, emancipating women, redistributing land holdings and embarking on a major industrialisation program. At the same time his government was repressive and corrupt.

The 1974 oil price revolution was the shāh's undoing: He allowed US arms merchants to persuade him to squander Iran's vast new wealth on huge arsenals of useless weapons. The flood of petrodollars lined the pockets of a select few, while galloping inflation made the majority worse off than before. As the economy went from bad to worse, the growing opposition made its presence felt with sabotage and massive street demonstrations. The shāh introduced martial law, and hundreds of demonstrators were killed in street battles in Tehrān. The shāh finally fled the country in January 1979, and died a year later.

The revolution underway, Āyatollāh Khomeinī returned to Iran on 1 February 1979 from France, where he had been in exile, to be greeted by adoring millions. His fiery brew of nationalism and Muslim fundamentalism had been at the forefront of the revolt, but few realised how much deep-rooted support he had and how strongly he reflected the beliefs and ideals of millions of Iranians.

Khomeinī's intention was to set up a clergy-dominated Islamic republic – the first true Islamic state in modern times. He went about achieving this with brutal efficiency: opposition disappeared; executions took place after meaningless trials; minor officials took the law into their own hands; and policies were implemented that were confrontationist and unashamedly designed to promote similar Islamic revolutions elsewhere.

The main opponent was (and continues to be) the USA, the country which provided support to the Pahlavīs and then later to Iraq, the instigator of the Iran-Iraq War. The USA also continues to support the state of Israel and Zionism, and is responsible for trade embargoes against Iran. Relations between the USA and Iran reached a nadir when students seized the US embassy in Tehrān along with 52 staff in 1979, and held them hostage for 444 days.

In 1980, Saddam Hussein made an opportunistic land grab in south-west Iran, taking advantage of Iran's domestic chaos, on the pretext that the oil-rich province of Khūzestān was historically part of Iraq. Although Iraq was better equipped, Iran drew on a larger population and a fanaticism fanned by the rhetoric of the mullahs (Muslim teachers). For the first time since WWI the world witnessed the hideous spectre of trench warfare and poison gas. A cease-fire was finally negotiated in mid-1988, with neither side achieving its objectives.

Nepal

Recorded history in Nepal begins with the Kiratis, Mongoloid people who arrived in Nepal from the east around the 7th or 8th century BC. Buddhism was embraced in the birthplace of the Buddha during Kirati rule.

However, Hinduism reasserted itself with the Licchavis, Indo-Ayran people who invaded from north India in about AD 300 and overthrew the last Kirati king. They brought with them the caste divisions that continue in Nepal to this day, but also ushered in a golden age of Nepali art and architecture.

The illustrious Malla dynasty of Nepal was founded in the 13th century. According to legend, King Ari-deva was wrestling when news came of the birth of his son. He instantly awarded his son the title *malla* or 'wrestler'. This golden age saw great wealth flow to the Kathmandu Valley and the kingdom's architects constructed many of the wonderful buildings that can be seen in Nepal today. The Hindu Mallas were followers of Shiva but were considered to be incarnations of the god Vishnu, and their tolerance of Buddhism allowed the Himalayan Tantric form of the religion to continue to flourish.

By the 18th century constant squabbling among the Malla kingdoms of Nepal opened the door to a new dynasty, the Shahs. The Shah kings gradually strengthened and extended their power. In 1768, Prithvi Narayan Shah, ninth of the Shah kings, moved his capital to Kathmandu. The Shah dynasty, which continues to this day, was established.

A palace revolt in 1846 saw leadership change into the hands of a ruthless young noble from western Nepal named Jung Bahadur, who initiated a decisive coup. His soldiers massacred several hundred of the most important men in the kingdom, and Bahadur took the title of prime minister, and changed his family name to the more prestigious Rana. Later the title was changed to maharaja, and became hereditary. For over a century, the family of Rana prime ministers held power. Nepal was never ruled by a colonial power, but was almost completely isolated right through the Rana period. Only on rare occasions were visitors allowed into Nepal, and even then they were only permitted access to a very limited part of the kingdom.

As it had managed to resist British colonisation, Nepal was not directly affected by the events surrounding Independence in the late 1940s. However, wedged between India and China, Nepal became a buffer zone between the two Asian giants.

In 1950 King Tribhuvan managed to reassert the monarchy, overthrowing the Ranas, with the backing of India.

The Region Today

Turkey Since Atatürk's death in 1938, Turkey has experienced three military coups (the last was in 1980) and considerable political turbulence. For the past couple of decades it has been wracked by violent conflict with the PKK (Kurdistan Workers Party), which has been agitating for the creation of a Kurdish state in Turkey's southeast corner. An estimated 30,000 have died during these troubles which have also caused huge population shifts inside the country, and wreaked havoc on the economy. In 1999, the PKK leader Abdullah Öcalan was captured and put on trial for treason. He was condemned to death, but the death sentence has yet to be carried out and his case is currently on appeal to the European Court of Human Rights.

Modern Turkey is suffering from an identity crisis. It is desperate to become part of Europe, but full membership of the European Union remains elusive while the country continues to grapple with its poor human rights record and territorial disputes with the Kurds and in Cyprus. Turkey is also looking to the East as a place it can do business and have an influence. The PKK called off its armed rebellion in 1999 and

tensions have eased considerably in the volatile east of the country. Another positive step was the unanimous election of a new president – the refreshingly outspoken Ahmet Necdet Sezer, former chief justice of the Constitutional Court – by all the major political parties.

A terrible blow came in August 1999 when a major earthquake struck in the Sea of Marmara, near İstanbul, killing thousands (there were 30,000 deaths according to some estimates) and causing major destruction of towns along the coast, where decades of shoddy building practices took their toll.

Iran Khomeinī died in 1989, leaving an uncertain legacy to the country he had dominated for a decade. Āyatollāh Alī Khameneī was appointed his successor as Iran's spiritual leader for life, but inherited little of his popular appeal and commanding political power. Two months later, Hojjat-ol-Eslām Rafsanjānī was elected as president, a post that had previously been largely ceremonial.

In 1997, the moderate and more visionary Hojjat-ol-Eslām Seyed Mohammed Khatamī easily beat another candidate (who was backed by the Iranian parliament) to become president. Khatamī attracted a large vote from women and youth, both hoping

Āyatollāh Alī Khameneī's black turban signifies that he descended from the Prophet.

he will change many of the more stern impositions of the Islamic Republic.

However, liberalism has been very limited since Khatamī came to power, because hardline factions, dedicated to the Islamic Revolution, remain powerful within the government. In 1998, several liberal Iranian writers were murdered by persons linked to the Iranian Ministry of Interior (ie, security forces). The murderers were eventually caught, and their actions made public, thereby indicating that Khatamī is not entirely helpless.

The Iranian parliamentary elections in spring 2000 gave another heavy endorsement to Khatamī's more open brand of Islam, sweeping many of the old guard Islamists out of government in favour of reformists. However, the president sat on the sidelines as the reactionary judiciary shut down more than 20 reformist newspapers in the wake of this victory. Street clashes in Tehrān between right and left wing groups also continue.

Meanwhile, Iran's economic outlook appears bleak. It is still struggling to recover from the economic devastation caused by the Iran-Iraq War, which ended more than 10 years ago. Another major hurdle to improving the economy is the trade embargo imposed by the US in 1995. Iran can no longer afford to carry the heavy burden of the subsidies it provides to its populace, but the reduction or abolition of these subsidies could cause political and social unrest.

Pakistan Since Partition, Pakistan has alternated between martial law (under the control of the military) and parliamentary democracy. In 1996, Benazir Bhutto, the first female prime minister of an Islamic nation, was dismissed from office by President Farooq Leghari (who himself resigned a year later). Nawaz Sharif was elected prime minister in 1997, but was deposed in a bloodless coup led by military chief General Pervez Musharraf on 12 October 1999. He is now in exile in Saudi Arabia after being freed from prison.

General Musharraf cited a ruined economy and corrupt government as the main reasons for his move, but the fact that Sharif was planning to dump him as army chief at the time probably had a bit to do with it. General Musharraf has promised to honour a Supreme Court ruling to return the country to democratic civilian rule by October 2002.

The reaction within the country was mixed following the coup and there is still plenty of tension surrounding the shift in power. Many believed Sharif to have been corrupt. General Musharraf's early move to introduce a general sales tax didn't impress the nation's traders though. They promptly went on Pakistan's longest ever strike, which saw shops closed for three weeks.

India India stepped into the 21st century with a population topping one billion, a change, or at least reformation of government, and continuing tensions with Pakistan over Kashmir.

Following the assassination of Prime Minister Indira Gandhi by her Sikh bodyguards in 1984, her son Rajiv led the Congress Party into power. Rajiv was killed in a bomb blast during election campaigns in 1989 but the Gandhi political dynasty may well continue. His wife, Sonia, became president of the Congress Party, now in opposition, in 1997 and despite the stronghold of a coalition party led by the Hindu-fundamentalist Bharatiya Janata Party (BJP), and her Italian heritage, she is tipped as a future prime minister.

The past decade has been marked by renewed conflict with Pakistan over Kashmir, wobbly political alliances, and communal violence which was so tragically demonstrated at Ayodhya in 1992. This small town in Uttar Pradesh, which is revered by Hindus as the birthplace of Rama, has come to symbolise the tension between religious groups, particularly Hindus and Muslims. In 1992, fundamentalist Hindus destroyed a mosque that they claimed was on the site of the original Rama Temple. Rioting followed in cities across north India and several hundred people were killed.

India's decision to test five nuclear weapons in the Rajasthani desert in 1998 brought about international condemnation and economic sanctions, but it was widely supported within the country.

Nepal In 1990, King Birenda was forced by a 'people's movement' to abandon the *panchayat* system under which the king enjoyed virtually sole power. A new constitution was adopted in November 1990,

The Conflict in Kashmir

During his 2000 visit to India, US President Bill Clinton described Kashmir as 'the most dangerous place in the world'. Beautiful, tragic Kashmir has been the splinter between India and Pakistan since Partition in 1947.

The two countries' first act upon Independence was to go to war over Kashmir, and in the five decades since – during which they have fought two more wars – neither they nor the United Nations have resolved the question of who, if anyone, it belongs to.

Most Pakistanis feel that the predominantly Muslim Jammu & Kashmir was unfairly snatched from them by its Hindu maharajah at Partition, and has been held illegally by India ever since.

Since 1989, military activity has increased substantially in Kashmir and it's estimated that as many as 20,000 Kashmiris have died in fighting. Both countries have thousands of troops in the region, and they almost went to war again in 1999 when India claimed Pakistani militants had crossed the Line of Actual Control at Kargil, although neither side agrees that this military demarcation line constitutes an actual border.

Since 1988 a third party has entered the fray: Kashmiri separatists agitating for their own state on the Indian-held side. Here India is accused of routine atrocities and Pakistan of training Kashmiri guerrillas.

Some concessions have been won over the years. Direct rule from Delhi ended in 1996 following democratic elections in Jammu and Kashmir which were won by the National Conference Party, but this has failed to bring about a resolution. A faint glimmer at the end of the diplomatic tunnel came with the opening of dialogue in 1997 between the then Pakistani prime minister Nawaz Sharif and the then Indian prime minister Inder Kumar Gujral in (Pakistani) Punjab. Again in 1999, both sides agreed to peace talks over the issue. However, with both sides having conducted tit-for-tat underground nuclear tests in 1998 and Pakistan's government being overthrown by a military coup in 1999, Clinton's observation seems accurate.

The threat of all-out war aside, the conflict in Kashmir has meant that the Himalayan beauty spot is all but off limits to travellers. Despite government warnings (there are no official restrictions), quite a few travellers still venture up to the Kashmir Valley, famous for its houseboat holidays on Dal Lake and for superb hiking. In 1995 six foreign tourists were kidnapped from a resort near Srinagar and never seen again (although in February 2000 police discovered a body they believed to be one of the six). In August 2000, a German traveller was shot dead by Islamic militants, apparently after he had hitched a lift while hiking near Kargil. Tourists are rarely the targets of militants, but indiscriminate bomb blasts on buses and trains and in public places around Srinagar occur all too frequently.

For the time being, the Kashmir issue seems intractable and will continue to make relations between India and Pakistan tense. However, this should not affect travellers on the route described in this book.

---

featuring a constitutional monarchy and a multi-parliamentary system.

In the May 1991 elections, the Nepali Congress won 110 seats and formed government. Over the next six years political instability was prevalent and governments came and went with startling regularity (four times in 1998 alone). After the May 1999 elections, stability again seemed achievable – the Nepali Congress won a majority, with Krishna Bhattarai as prime minister, although he was ousted by Girija Prasad Koirala 10 months later.

The biggest threat to the stability and security in Nepal is from the 'people's war' against the constitutional monarchy and democratic system. Led by a Maoist faction of the Communist Party, insurgency and rioting have consumed Nepal since 1996. In the three years following the beginning of the insurgency, more than 600 people were killed. In early 2000 a series of *bandhs* (strikes) succeeded in bringing the country, including Kathmandu, to a standstill. Tourists haven't yet been targeted by the rebels, although tourism has declined in recent years.

GEOGRAPHY

Travellers on this route will traverse some 10,000km on the road between İstanbul and Kathmandu, from the lowlands of the Indus Plain in Pakistan to the heady heights of the Himalaya in Nepal.

Turkey

Geographically, Turkey lies at the crossroads between East and West. Western Turkey is dominated by low hills with rich soil for agriculture, and the Aegean coast comprises fertile plains and river valleys dotted with olive, fig and fruit orchards. In contrast, the Mediterranean coast is mountainous, while central Anatolia perches on a high plateau.

Iran

Three times the size of France, Iran dwarfs its neighbours: Iraq, Turkey, Armenia, Azerbaijan, Turkmenistan, Afghanistan and Pakistan. Around half of the country is covered by mountains. To the east and north-east are two great deserts: Dasht-é Kavīr and Dasht-é Lūt. To the north, stretching from the Azerbaijani border towards Turkmenistan is the Alborz range, home to Kūh-é Damāvand, Iran's highest mountain at 5671m.

Pakistan

Only a quarter the size of India, Pakistan is still a large country wedged between Iran, Afghanistan, China and India, with the Arabian Sea washing onto its southern shores. To the north is one of the densest concentrations of high peaks in the world, including K2 (8611m), second only to Mt Everest. Much of the southern part of the country is dominated by desert, in particular the Baluchistan and Cholistan Deserts. The Indus Plain – where most of the population lives – constitutes about one-third of the country's territory.

India

A colossus of a country, India covers a land mass of 3,287,263 sq km. The north of the country is scored by the magnificent Himalayan range, the foothills of which run through Himachal Pradesh. The northern plains slope gradually from Delhi eastwards where the delta of the holy Ganges opens out like a fan and pours into the Bay of Bengal. West of Delhi, the land becomes increasingly arid, until you find yourself in the remote and baking Thar Desert which stretches up to and beyond the Pakistan border.

Nepal

Tiny in length and breadth, Nepal is massive in height. No prizes for the name of the world's tallest peak, Everest at 8848m, but there are another seven peaks above 8000m in Nepal's mighty Himalayan range. The Annapurnas, north of Pokhara, are among the most spectacular mountains in the world.

Nepal is also home to the Terai in the south – a montage of paddy fields, mango groves, bamboo stands and villages, only 100m or so above sea level.

CLIMATE

There are dramatic variations in climate across this route, depending on altitude and the time of year. You will almost certainly experience some extremely high temperatures (40°C plus) in India, Pakistan and Iran if you visit anytime between March and September. At the same time, you'll encounter snow and ice in eastern Turkey, Nepal, northern India and the high altitude areas of Pakistan between December and February.

High rainfall can be a problem in India and Nepal (and to a lesser extent in eastern Pakistan) roughly between July and September, when the monsoon sweeps across the subcontinent.

It's worth timing your travel to avoid the worst extremes of weather and temperature. See Planning in the Regional Facts for the Visitor chapter.

Turkey

The Aegean and Mediterranean coasts have mild, rainy winters and hot, dry summers. The Black Sea Coast in the north is considerably cooler (even in summer the water temperature in the Black Sea is icy). Mountainous eastern Turkey is bitterly cold and subject to snow in winter, when freezing winds blow down from the Russian steppes. Between May and August, the south-east, stretching down to the Syrian border, is baking hot, with 45°C-plus temperatures not uncommon.

Iran

Being flat, expansive and desert-like, most of Iran is hot and dry in summer and cold and dry in winter. In the south, the summer heat of the Gulf can surpass a debilitating 40°C. The far north and north-west are the coolest parts of the country and also have the highest rainfall.

Pakistan

Pakistan has three seasons: cool (October– February), hot (March–June) and wet (July–September). During the wet season the tail end of the south-west monsoon dumps steady rain across the central and eastern plains interspersed with heat and heavy sauna-like humidity. The Northern Areas and the high altitude town of Quetta are at their best in the warmer season (April to September), while the desert areas and the Punjabi plains are unbelievably hot at this time. Places such as Multan, Bahawalpur and the Baluchistan Desert can hit 50°C at times!

India

India is so vast that the climate in the north bears little relation to that in the south. Like Pakistan, India has three seasons. During the hot season (March to June) the mercury tops 40°C in central India. From July to October the monsoon rains flood parts of the country, especially in the south. By October the cool season arrives in the wake of the monsoon. The air is clear in the north and the mountain peaks of the Himalaya are visible. The Indian Himalaya is at its best from March to June and September to November. From December to March it gets very cold at altitude.

Nepal

Nepal has a typical monsoonal two-season year: the dry season from October to May and the wet season from June to September. The Kathmandu Valley can get quite hot in summer and even winter has bright sunny days. Surprisingly, it never snows either. Pokhara lies at a lower altitude and is consequently slightly warmer than Kathmandu. The lowland Terai is quite hot and humid from April to September.

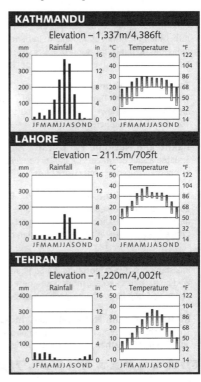

ECOLOGY & ENVIRONMENT
Turkey
The aftershock of Turkey's devastating 1999 earthquake continues to take its toll on the nation, its people and the environment. The Tupras oil refinery, set ablaze by the quake, emitted huge amounts of pollution into the air. Concern has also been expressed by the environment movement over plans to build a nuclear power plant on the Mediterranean coast to meet the country's burgeoning energy needs.

Iran
One of the great tragedies of modern Iran is the almost complete lack of consideration for the environment. Natural beauty spots are invariably ruined with litter, an appalling situation most noticeable along the hiking trails of the Alborz Mountains, near Tehrān.

Air pollution in Tehrān has reached such alarmingly high levels that the Environmental Protection Department has been forced to issue a warning to children as well as heart and asthma patients to stay indoors. In this city of 10 million, the proliferation of vehicles is the major contributing factor to the pall of smoke that hovers above the cityscape.

The contamination of the Gulf by oil spills from rigs and tankers has also had devastating effects; untreated sewage and unrestrained development on the islands of Kīsh and Gheshm abound. Similar pollution problems are being experienced along the Caspian Sea coast, and will only get worse as oil production gears up in this region.

Some efforts have been mounted to re-forest and preserve native flora and fauna but it is frankly too little – but, hopefully, not too late.

National Parks

There are numerous national parks and wildlife reserves scattered across the countries en route – India alone has some 560 protected areas, including 80 national parks. Many of the national parks in Turkey are designated for their historical value (such as the Mt Nimrod National Park) rather than their flora and fauna. In Iran, designated national parks have no rangers or fenced areas and no public transport or tours so you'll need to arrange private transport and possibly a guide. Only those national parks on or close to our route are listed here.

Termessos National Park, Turkey
The ancient city of Termessos is set high in the mountains, 34km inland from Antalya. The area is lush, the views are excellent and there are some very good walks around the park. You can also camp here.

Bakhtegān National Park, Iran
Situated about 80km east of Shīrāz, between Bakhtegān and Tashk Lakes, this park has been established to protect migratory birds.

Hazarganji-Chiltan National Park, Pakistan
Only 20km from Quetta, this park is home to a wide range of flora and fauna, including the native Chiltan markhor (a large wild goat). You need a permit from the Divisional Forestry Office in Quetta to visit (see the Pakistan chapter for details).

La Suhanra National Park, Pakistan
Pakistan's only listed biosphere, La Suhanra is 36km from Bahawalpur. Wildlife here includes wild boars, hares, jackals, mongooses, desert foxes, porcupines, larks, owls, hawks, nilgai, and ravine and hog deer. There's accommodation available inside the park.

Keoladeo Ghana National Park, India
This magnificent World Heritage-listed bird sanctuary is located at Bharatpur, between Agra and Jaipur in Rajasthan. Around 350 species of birds have been identified here, including the

Pakistan

Prior to the 1990s little attention was paid to environmental issues in Pakistan, where human waste is the main source of water pollution and the cause of widespread disease.

Air pollution is also a severe problem in urban areas, largely due to vehicle emissions, and deforestation is causing soil erosion, water pollution and flooding. However, the Environmental Protection Council has created a National Conservation Strategy (NCS) with three objectives: promotion of sustainable development; conservation of natural resources; and improved efficiency in their use.

India

India's growing population is putting increasing pressure on the fragile environment. Rapid industrialisation, ongoing deforestation and heavy reliance on chemical fertilisers, pesticides and herbicides are but a few of the issues. While there is no shortage of legislation designed to protect the environment, it can be rendered ineffective by corruption and flagrant abuses of power.

While the increase in tourism has boosted the local economy, it has come at a price to the environment. A UN report estimates that over a 30 year-period (1950–80) a staggering 40% of the Himalayan watershed was destroyed due to deforestation. In addition, inadequate access to clean drinking water and proper sanitation are huge concerns.

With 25 million vehicles on the road, air pollution is at hazardous levels due to continuing diesel usage and little progress in attempts to control emissions. However, the Indian Supreme Court has moved to ban commercial vehicles more than eight years

National Parks

endangered Siberian crane. The best time to visit is between October and February, and there's plenty of accommodation in the town of Bharatpur.

Corbett Tiger Reserve, India

This is probably the most accessible of India's famous tiger reserves on our route. In the newly formed state of Uttaranchal, it's around a seven-hour bus or train ride from Delhi. Corbett (named, ironically, after a British hunter) is renowned for its diverse wildlife and was the first national park to be designated under the Project Tiger program in 1973. Spotting a tiger is entirely dependent on chance, as the animals are no longer tracked here. The best sightings are late in the season (April to mid-June). Accommodation is available at Ramnagar and Dhikala, both within the reserve.

Other places to spot tigers, more or less within striking distance of our route, include Bandhavgarh and Kanha National Parks in Madhya Pradesh. Both can be reached by train and bus from Varanasi, although you'll need to allow two days just to get there. Kanha is regarded as the best place in India (if not the world) to see a tiger in the wild.

Royal Chitwan National Park, Nepal

Royal Chitwan is the place to ride an elephant and spot a rhinoceros in the wild. A stop here on the way to Kathmandu is a must. Chitwan is easily reached from Kathmandu, Pokhara and Sunauli and there's plenty of cheap 'jungle' accommodation at Sauraha, just outside the park. As well as elephants and rhinos, you can expect to see numerous types of deer (including the chital and sambar). What you probably won't see (but which live in the park) are Bengal tigers, leopards and jackals. A boat ride on the Rapti River will probably result in some crocodile sightings. See the Nepal chapter for details.

Also in Nepal, but requiring a considerable deviation into the west of the country, Royal Bardia National Park offers a less touristy experience. In this virtually untouched wilderness, chances are you and your guide may be the only ones walking or riding an elephant at dawn. Rhino numbers are fewer than at Chitwan, but you stand a better chance of spotting a tiger here.

old from Delhi, which would put an estimated 20,000 autorickshaws, buses and taxis off the road. Whether this can be achieved is another matter.

Nepal

Deforestation, along with the resultant erosion and flooding of the lowlands, is a major problem in Nepal. The burgeoning trekking market adds to the pressure on the fragile environment, with the average trekker consuming as much fuel wood in a day as an entire Nepali household does in one week. The build-up of discarded plastic water bottles is another imported environmental disaster.

Kathmandu's air pollution is among the worst in the world, but the government recently moved to curb the problem by banning diesel-powered tempos (large passenger autorickshaws) and replacing them with electric models.

The Impact of Tourism

Greenpeace considers tourism to be one of the major causes of coastal destruction in Turkey. It cites the dozens of marinas, 'land reclamation' projects and hotels that have been established illegally along the coast.

Problems also arise when destinations cannot cope with the number of tourists they attract, so that natural and social environments quickly become damaged. The prime example of this is in the Himalayan villages en route to Everest base camp and the Annapurna Circuit.

Responsible Tourism

A British organisation called Tourism Concern (☎ 020-7753 333) at Stapleton House, 177–281 Holloway Rd, London N7 8NN has come up with some guidelines for travellers who wish to minimise any negative impact they may have on the countries they visit. These guidelines include:

- Save precious natural resources.
- Try not to waste water (by taking long showers, for instance).
- Switch off lights and air-conditioning when you go out.
- Avoid establishments that clearly consume limited resources such as water and electricity at the expense of local residents.
- Use locally owned hotels and restaurants and support trade and craft workers by buying locally made souvenirs.

To which we would add:

- Leave it as you found it: Consider the irreparable damage you inflict upon sites when you climb to the top of them or take home an unattached sample of carved masonry.
- Don't litter. Resist the local tendency of indifference to littering and bin your rubbish or, if there are no bins, carry it with you until you can dispose of it properly.
- When trekking, use fuel stoves and patronise only teahouses that do the same; also, take your own water bottle and either boil water or use purifiers such as iodine.

FLORA & FAUNA
Flora

Once cloaked in dense forest, Anatolia is now largely denuded after thousands of years of woodcutting. The government encourages reforestation but the great forests will never return. Nevertheless, Turkey's temperate climate allows domesticated plants (apples, citrus, bananas, cherries, cotton, dates, and tobacco) to thrive.

Despite its expansive deserts, Iran hosts more than 10,000 species of flora. The north has densely concentrated forests while the south and east are largely bare. The Iranian National Flora Research Garden in Paykanshahr, between Tehrān and Karaj, is one of the biggest in the region.

Pakistan, however, is not renowned for its flora. Natural vegetation in the lowlands is sparse, though parts of the Himalaya are heavily forested. Across the border in India there are some 15,000 flowering plants and 16 major forest types (which can be subdivided into 221 minor types). In Nepal, there are 6500 known species of trees, shrubs and wild flowers in Nepal, including over 300 species of wild orchids.

Fauna

Turkey has similar animal life to that in the Balkans and much of Europe (bears, deer, jackals, lynx, wild boars and wolves). Desert regions are full of small rodents such as the desert foxes, sand rats, hares and jerboas but most of these are nocturnal.

Of the 100 or so mammals found in Iran, about one-fifth are endemic. The larger species, such as wolves, jackals, wild boars, hyenas and lynx, are more common in the depths of the Māzandarān Province. Two of the more fascinating creatures are the huge ibex-like Alborz red sheep with its black 'beard' and spiralling horns and the Oreal ram, with a white 'beard' and enormous horns, found near Turkmenistan. Iran is also home to the Caspian seal, flamingoes, sturgeons and turtles. Camels are fairly prevalent in desert areas.

Among the animals found in Pakistan (mainly in the south) are wild or feral cats, jackals, foxes, hares, small rodents and reptiles, bats and common birds like kites, crows and magpies. Sharks, shellfish and two species of sea turtles can be found along the coastal wetlands as well as around 200 species of fish. However, half the wildlife species known to have lived in Pakistan are now either extinct or considered endangered.

The Himalaya harbours a hardy range of creatures. In the freezing altitudes, the yak, a shaggy horned wild ox, survives alongside a wild sheep called the Ladakh urial, the Tibetan antelope and the Himalayan ibex among others. When it comes to mystique none of the above match the snow leopard, of which there are fewer than 5000 left in the world. They reside in the Indian states of Sikkim and Arunachal Pradesh. In the eastern Himalaya you may encounter the endearing red panda. The one-horned Indian rhino and the elephant can still be found roaming the northern grasslands.

GOVERNMENT & POLITICS
Turkey
In theory, Turkey is a multiparty democracy on the Western European model, though in practice it has proved to be a semidemocracy with the military wielding considerable power behind the scenes. In the 1999 elections the MHP (Nationalist Action Party) took a share of the spoils for the first time ever, a shock result possibly reflecting increasing Turkish nationalism as a reaction to Kurdish nationalism. Three parties, with little in common, are now sharing power, under veteran left-winger Prime Minister Bulent Ecevit and newly appointed President Ahmet Necdet Sezer, a former chief justice of the Constitutional Court.

Iran
After the Islamic Revolution in 1979, 98% of the population apparently voted to implement a unique form of Islamic government, with three levels of political power. Firstly, there's a parliament, the Majlis, which comprises Islamic experts and revered Islamic leaders from around the country, and includes a representative from the Jewish and Zoroastrian communities, and two from the Armenian Christians. The Majlis approves (but does not instigate, in theory) laws and economic decisions, but under the constitution it can 'investigate and examine all affairs of the country'.

The Majlis is dominated by the *velayat-é faqih*, or Supreme Leader, currently Āyatollāh Alī Khameneī, who has enormous power: He can select (and sack) the commander of the armed forces; declare war or peace; and veto the election of (and dismiss) the president. The Majlis is elected by the Iranian people every four years, but the candidates are carefully vetted before the elections.

The second level of power, the Council of the Guardians, 'safeguards the Islamic Ordinances and Constitution', and comprises 12 Islamic jurists and religious experts, all selected by the Supreme Leader. The Council's main purposes are to uphold Islamic values, ensure that the parliament remains free of corruption and approve the handful of presidential candidates.

Thirdly, the president manages (and elects himself) a cabinet, although final control always rests with the Majlis. The president is elected every four years (and is only allowed two terms), but the people normally have only a few candidates to choose from.

As promised by President Khatamī, Iran held its first municipal elections in February 1999. A high percentage of Iranians, particularly youth and women, again voted for candidates who support the liberalisation espoused by Khatamī. The vote was mostly free of incident and violence, and some candidates from banned, but tolerated, opposition parties were allowed to participate.

Parliamentary elections in February and April 2000 again saw reformists swept to power behind President Khatamī, ousting many of the old guard Islamists from the Majlis. Iran has, ostensibly, paved the way for a less fundamentalist era. The reality is that many of the old guard still control the vital organs of power, and the reformists need to proceed cautiously – as the closure of 20 pro-reform newspapers and periodicals since the elections has shown. But the lifting by the US of some sanctions against Iran does seem to illustrate that the positive overtures Iran has made have been registered, and even welcomed, by the West.

Pakistan

In theory Pakistan is governed by a parliamentary democracy, but the military is never far from politics and in parts of the country, tribal rule still prevails. In 1997 the Pakistani parliament passed the 13th Amendment to the Constitution. The president and provincial governors were stripped of their power to dissolve their assemblies and the country shifted from presidential back to parliamentary government.

The military coup of 1999 was Pakistan's fourth experience of martial law since the nation was formed in 1947.

When under civil rule, Parliament has two houses: the Senate and the National Assembly. The Senate is mainly advisory; the National Assembly does most of the work, and has sole responsibility for fiscal bills. The 217 members of the National Assembly (MNAs) are directly elected for five-year terms; 20 of these seats are set aside for women and 10 for non-Muslims. The president is the head of state and is elected jointly by the Senate and Assembly for a five-year term. The prime minister is the head of government and is elected by the Assembly, to whom he and his cabinet are responsible. Both must be Muslims.

In reality old ways of governing prevail in much of Pakistan. In most rural areas people do not go to their MNA but directly to their *zamindar* (powerful landowner) or tribal chief to get problems sorted out. If something needs to be settled officially, he will pass the matter onto the relevant MNA – if he isn't one himself – who will most probably have relied on feudal patronage to get elected in the first place.

India

India is a constitutional democracy made up of 28 states and seven union territories. The parliament is bicameral and elections are held every five years. The lower house is known as the Lok Sabha (House of the People) and the upper house is known as the Rajya Sabha (Council of States). The president (whose duties are largely ceremonial) is elected by both houses and the state legislatures every five years. The president acts on the advice of a council of ministers, chosen by the prime minister. The president may dissolve the lower house but not the upper.

In May 1996, the Congress Party, which had ruled India for all but four years since Independence in 1947, lost its majority. The Hindu-nationalist Bharatiya Janata Party (BJP) formed another coalition government after the 1998 elections. The following year was a turbulent one politically. The coalition crumbled and Prime Minister Atal Behari Vajpayee lost a vote of no confidence. Italian-born Congress Party president Sonia Gandhi resigned her post following a government smear campaign, but returned to the leadership a short time later.

Elections in 2000 saw the ruling BJP returned to government as part of the 20-party National Democratic Alliance. The victory was not so much won by Vajpayee and the BJP as lost by the opposing parties and their inability to control the fractured monster that is Indian politics.

Nepal

In April 1990, the Jana Andolan, or People's Movement, forced King Birendra to abandon the panchayat system that had been established by his father, under which the king enjoyed virtually sole power. A new constitution was adopted in November 1990, which provided for a constitutional monarchy and a multiparty parliamentary system.

Members of the 205-seat Pratinidhi Sabha (House of Representatives) are elected every five years according to a first-past-the-post system.

In the May 1991 elections, the Nepali Congress won 110 seats, giving it a simple majority, and formed the government with Girija Prassad Koirala as prime minister. Mid-term elections in 1994 were inconclusive, and a coalition government was formed. Since May 1996 the government has changed a number of times. Elections in May 1999 resulted in a majority for the Nepal Congress Party, ending many years of minority government. The current prime minister, GP Koirala, ousted his predecessor Krishna Prasad Bhattarai in a party-led revolt in March 2000.

ECONOMY

Though Turkey has traditionally relied on agriculture (it's the biggest wool producer in Europe), tourism has become one of its most lucrative earners, bringing in billions of dollars to the economy. No wonder the country reeled from the combined effects of the 1999 earthquake coming hot on the heels of PKK terrorism scares, which kept tourists away in droves. Still, Turkey has seen impressive leaps in the export of manufactured goods (cheap labour keeps prices down) and its annual growth rate of around 4% puts it in the top ten of developing countries, according to the United Nations Development Programme.

The same cannot be said for Iran which, after the excesses of the Islamic Revolution followed by the Iran-Iraq War, has still not fully recovered. To add to its economic woes, Iran has suffered from the trade embargo imposed by the USA (though this was eased in August 2000), in addition to a high inflation rate and fluctuations in oil prices. Nevertheless, its economy has survived, though tourism remains negligible. The authorities are beginning to market the country as a tourist destination in an attempt to revive the Old Silk Road and promote ancient Persian archaeological sites and cities. Oil exports continue to prop up the economy, accounting for 40% of all government income, but they won't last forever. Iran produces one-third of all traditional carpets and rugs made worldwide. Persian carpets are an increasingly vital part of trade, earning the country over US$2 billion per year.

Likewise, Pakistan's economy has not received the shot in the arm that tourism injected into Turkey's economy. The biggest sector of the local economy is agriculture, the major crops being cotton, wheat, rice and sugar cane.

India, too, relies heavily on agriculture as the mainstay of its economy, accounting for 29% of GDP and employing some 64% of the workforce. In 1997 India became the world's top milk producer (72 million tonnes) and, unsurprisingly, its cattle population leads the world too, at some 193 million head (many of which seem to be feeding off garbage in Delhi and Calcutta!).

Judged by Western standards, Nepal is one of the poorest countries on earth, with an estimated GDP of around US$210 per person. Subsistence farmers make up more than 90% of the population, with agriculture accounting for 41% of GDP.

POPULATION & PEOPLE

India's population topped a billion in early 2000, making it the second most populous country in the world after China, with an annual growth rate of 2%. With a population tipped to exceed China's in the 21st century, birth control is a perennial matter for concern. Moves to introduce birth control gained notoriety in the 1970s especially during the 'Emergency' when sterilisation squads moved into the countryside and terrorised villagers. In the 1980s Prime Minister Rajiv Gandhi instituted an ambitious sterilisation target of 1.3 billion Indians by 2050. Widespread media coverage in support of birth control has promoted the ideal of the two-child family, and the use of contraceptives, especially condoms.

Pakistan conducted a census in 1998, although the results were widely disputed with claims that it was 'fixed' to reflect lower population figures in certain parts of the country. Officially the population is 130.58 million with the vast majority (over 72 million) living in the Punjab. The annual growth rate is 2.3%.

Iran and Turkey are relatively sparse, with 70 million and 63 million people respectively. Nepal, the smallest of the five countries geographically, is also the smallest in terms of population, at approximately 23 million, with some 700,000 living in the Kathmandu Valley.

You will encounter many ethnic groups along this route, including some that have been transplanted from neighbouring countries, such as the Afghans in Pakistan and the Tibetans in India and Nepal.

Turks

The Turkish peoples originated in Central Asia where they ruled several vast empires before being pushed westwards by the Mongols. At first they were shamanist nomads but at one time or another these early Turks followed each of the great religions of the region including Buddhism, Nestorian Christianity and Judaism. During their western migrations they became familiar with Islam and it stuck. The Turks kept their own language even after conversion. During the

400-year Ottoman Empire, when the Turks ruled most of the Middle East, they became known as the Shimaliyya, or Northerners, throughout the Arab world.

Armenians

The Armenians are thought by some to be descended from the Urartians (518–330 BC), whose kingdom was based near Lake Van, but others think they arrived from the Caucasus area after the Urartian state collapsed. Armenians have lived in eastern Anatolia for a thousand years, almost always as subjects of some greater state such as the Alexandrine empire, or of the Romans, Byzantines, Persians, Seljuks or Ottomans.

They lived with their Kurdish and Turkish neighbours in relative peace and harmony under the Ottoman *millet* system of distinct religious communities. But, when this system gave way to modern ethnic nationalism, they suffered one of the greatest tragedies in their history. Between 1915 and 1923 an estimated 1.5 million Armenians were slaughtered at the hands of the Turks. Today there are about 70,000 Armenians living in Turkey, mainly in İstanbul and around Lake Van.

Kurds

Kurds are spread across a large area of the Middle East, including a substantial part of eastern Turkey (where there are approximately 10 million Kurds). Although they have been around longer than any other people in the region (at least since the 2nd millennium BC), Kurds have never enjoyed the status of nationhood. There are also some 4.5 million Kurds living in western Iran, mainly around the province of Kordestān. Kurds predominantly follow the Sunni sect of Islam.

Persians

More than 65% of the inhabitants of Iran can be called Persians, or Fārsīs. They are the descendants of the Elamite and Aryan races who first set up camp in the central plateau back in the 2nd millennium BC and gave Persia its name.

Punjabis

Punjabis are the clear majority in Pakistan. They are descendants of the Indo-Aryans who arrived in the 15th to 12th centuries BC. Punjabis have historically identified themselves according to their tribe and still do, particularly in rural areas.

Baluchis

Crossing from Iran into Pakistan, travellers will enter Baluchistan, a dry, barren expanse of land inhabited largely by nomads. Some Baluchis claim origin in pre-Christian Syria, though most are probably Turko-Iranian. Sometime between the 6th and 14th centuries they migrated to present-day Baluchistan. Baluchis speak Baluchi, a derivation of Persian. Most are Sunni Muslims. There are also Baluchis in southeastern Iran near the Pakistani border.

Pashtuns

The Pashtuns, also known as Pathans, are closely identified with the North-West Frontier Province (NWFP) in Pakistan, but also form the largest group in Baluchistan. Like Punjabis, the Pashtuns are Indo-Aryans and mainly herders and farmers. Historically they've also been known as ferocious fighters. Nowadays they're recognised as shrewd traders, and have also virtually taken over Pakistan's commercial transportation network. Pashtuns are nearly all Sunni, religiously conservative and proud of their early conversion to Islam. Pashtuns in the NWFP belong to around two dozen tribes, and, within these, to clans, each named for an early arrival in the area to whom they trace their ancestry.

Tibetans

Tibetans have been fleeing Tibet since China overpowered the Tibetan army in 1950. Some 2000 refugees brave the 6000m passes between Tibet and India or Nepal each year, following in the footsteps of the Dalai Lama who fled in 1959. Nepal is home to about 12,000 Tibetans (mostly in Pokhara and Kathmandu). There is also a sizeable Tibetan population of about 100,000 in northern India, notably around Dharamsala. Tibetans are devout Buddhists.

Other Ethnic Groups

In India, you may encounter Gujar people in Himachal Pradesh and some parts of Uttarakhand. They converted to Islam from Hinduism and initially settled in Kashmir before migrating east.

Nepal is home to a mosaic of ethnic peoples. Its population includes at least a dozen major ethnic groups. Nepal is the crossroads between the Indo-Aryan people of India and the Tibeto-Burmese of the Himalaya. In the Himalaya, the people are largely Mongoloids of Tibetan descent. These include the Sherpa of the Everest region, the Manangpa of the region north of Annapurna and the Lopa of the Mustang region. With few exceptions these people are Buddhists. The Newars, who are thought by some to be Kirati people who believe in shamanism, live around the Kathmandu Valley.

Elsewhere on the overland route you'll also come across Bedouin, Nomads, Āzarīs, Adivasis (tribal groups), Sindhis, Jews and many more.

ARTS
Visual Arts

The arts of this region cross the boundary between East and West. Artistic tradition in the Western sense of painting and sculpture has historically been largely absent in the Middle East, as Islam has always regarded the depiction of living beings as idolatrous. There have been exceptions, however. The long-standing figurative art traditions in Asia Minor and farther east were never completely extinguished by Islam, and the Turks continued to produce beautiful illuminated manuscripts.

With the pervasive influence of Europe in the region from the 19th century onwards, Western-style painting and sculpture have become part of the Middle Eastern artistic repertoire. However, few artists

More Than Just a Floor Covering

The Persian carpet is Iran's best-known cultural export. It is a display of wealth, an investment and an integral part of religious and cultural festivals. It is also used in everyday life, eg, as a prayer mat.

Historians know that by the 7th century AD Persian carpets made of wool or silk had become famous in court circles throughout the region. Carpets were exported as far away as China, though for many centuries they must have remained a great luxury in their country of production, with the finest pieces being the preserve of royalty. The early patterns were usually symmetrical with geometric and floral motifs designed to evoke the beauty of the classical Persian garden.

After the Arab Conquest, Quranic verses were incorporated into some carpet designs, and prayer mats began to be produced on a grand scale; secular carpets also became a major industry and were highly prized in European courts.

The reign of Shāh Abbās I (1587–1629) marks the peak of Persian carpet production, when the quality of the raw materials and all aspects of the design and weaving were brought to a level never seen before or since, perhaps anywhere.

Towards the end of the 17th century, as demand for Persian carpets grew, standards of production began to fall and designs tended to lack inspiration. A long period of stagnation followed, although the finest Persian carpets of the 18th century and later still often led the world in quality and design. The reputation of modern Persian carpets has still not entirely recovered from the near-sacrilegious introduction of artificial fibres and dyes earlier in the 20th century.

Persian carpets are a huge export earner for Iran, but there are problems: Loom weaving is being supplanted by modern factories; young Iranians are not interested in learning the traditional methods of weaving; and cheaper, often blatantly copied, versions of 'Persian' carpets are being produced in India and Pakistan (where child labour is sometimes used, but not in Iran).

Iran is heavily promoting the prestige that the term 'Persian carpets' still evokes, and has recently recaptured a large slice of the world's trade in carpets and rugs. While some authorities hope that the export of Persian carpets and rugs from Iran will top US$17 billion per year by 2020, pragmatists concede that the production costs of genuine hand-made Persian carpets and rugs will increase to a point where consumers (mainly westerners) will be more happy admiring them in a local museum than forking out good money to buy them.

have been able to reconcile these mediums with their heritage, and all too often the results rely heavily on poorly appropriated European models.

Islamic art has a cultural heritage of unsurpassable richness, however, in the areas of calligraphy, manuscript illumination, metalwork, ceramics, glass blowing, carpets and textiles. Favourite motifs include geometrical shapes and patterns and complex floral patterns. This decorative aspect of Islamic art has in turn had great influence on the West. Middle Eastern artisans and crafts people (Armenians, Christians and Jews as well as Muslims) have for over 1200 years applied complex and sumptuous decorations to often very practical objects to create items of extraordinary beauty. You will see such items in the region's museums such as the Topkapı Sarayı (Topkapı Palace) in İstanbul.

In the East almost all Himalayan art is religious in both motivation and subject. The whole Kathmandu Valley is one enormous art gallery. Woodcarving and sculpture are often the best part of a building. A temple is not a temple without its finely carved roof struts. Crafts also reflect the unique Nepali melting pot with their Tantric Hindu and Buddhist overtones.

Music

There's a huge diversity of music across this region, too much to cover adequately in such a brief space. In the broadest of terms, traditional (and contemporary) music can be split between the Middle East and the Indian subcontinent.

Middle East Tonality and instrumentation aside, classical Arabic music differs from that of the West in one big respect – in the Middle East the orchestra is there primarily to back the singer.

The kind of orchestra that backs such a singer is a curious cross-fertilisation of East and West. Western-style instruments (such as violins and many of the wind and percussion instruments) predominate, next to local instruments such as the oud and tabla. The overall effect is anything but Western. There is all the mellifluous seduction of Asia in the backing melodies, the vaguely melancholic, languid tones you would expect from a sun-drenched and heat-exhausted Middle Eastern summer.

Subcontinent Indian classical music traces its roots back to Vedic times, when religious poems chanted by priests were first collated in an anthology called the *Rigveda*. Over the millennia it has been shaped by many influences. The two main forms today are Carnatic (characteristic of south India) and Hindustani (the classical style of north India).

With common origins, both forms share a number of features. They both use the raga (the melodic shape of the music) and tala (the rhythmic meter characterised by the number of beats) as a basis for composition and improvisation. Both are performed by small ensembles comprising about half a dozen musicians and have many instruments in common. A striking difference is that Carnatic makes greater use of voice, while Hindustani music has more purely instrumental compositions.

Classical music, however, is enjoyed by a relatively small section of society. Most people are more familiar with their own local folk forms, popular during festivities and important village ceremonies – or with popular music. Musicians may be professional or semiprofessional. But music is not the exclusive domain of those who call themselves musicians. Wandering magicians, snake charmers and storytellers may also use song to entertain their audiences; the storyteller often sings the tales from the great epics.

Radio and cinema have played a large role in broadcasting popular music to the remotest corners of India. Bollywood's latest musical offerings are never far away thanks to the proliferation of cassette players throughout the country.

Pakistan's classical music is almost identical to Hindustani music. Where Pakistan comes into its own is in the devotional sufi music performed at shrines, usually on Thursday nights.

Qawwali is a mesmeric traditional form of music with minimal accompaniment. It's a kind of mystical Islamic version of gospel and is popular not only at sufi celebrations, but also as secular entertainment. The greatest exponent of qawwali was Nusrat Fateh Ali Khan (1948–97). Born in Faisalabad, he became a superstar in his own country and was acclaimed as 'Pakistan's Pavarotti' in the West. He made many recordings, the best of which include *Shahen Shah* (The Brightest Star) and *Night Song*.

Traditional Nepali music can still be heard, despite the pervasiveness of Western music in Kathmandu. The folk music of rural Nepal still has a strong following and the *gaines* (traditional professional musicians) are often as much storytellers as musicians. The *damais* are modern professional musicians, all drawn from the tailor caste, who form the backbone of wedding bands. This music can definitely be hard on Western ears, falling uncomfortably close to the painful standards of Indian video-bus music.

Literature

Turkey Turkey's best-known contemporary writer is probably Yaşar Kamal, winner of the 1998 Nobel Prize for Literature. His famous and very readable *Mehmet My Hawk* deals with near-feudal life in the villages of the eastern Mediterranean. Author of the moment is Orhan Pamuk whose books are walking out of the bookshops in record numbers. *The Black Book* is the Kafkaesque tale of an abandoned husband's search for his wife in İstanbul, but it's pretty heavy going.

Iran While no-one knows the exact date of origin of the *Avesta*, the first example of Persian literature, it is known that Persian poetry first blossomed in the 9th century AD. With influences from nearby empires, various forms of Persian poetry developed, such as the *mathnavi*, with its unique rhyming couplets, and the *ruba'i*, similar to the quatrain (a stanza of four lines).

These styles later developed into the long and detailed 'epic poems', the first of which was Ferdōsī's *Shah-nama* finished in AD 1010 – with 50,000 couplets! Many epic poems regaled the glories of the old Persia before whichever foreigners had invaded and occupied the country at the time. The last truly great 'epic poem', *Zafar-nam*, covered the history of Islam from the birth of Mohammed to the early 14th century.

The next major form of Persian poetry to develop is known as *ghasidas*, poems of more than 100 couplets which do not rhyme. Famous exponents were Anvarī and Sanjar. Moral and religious poetry became famous following the success of Sa'dī's poems, such as *Bustan* and *Golestān*.

By the 14th century, smaller *ghazal* poems, which ran to about 10 non-rhyming couplets, were used for love stories. Ghazal poetry was made famous by Hāfez, and is still practised today. Persian poetry rarely produced anything exceptional after the Timurid dynasty (1380–1502).

Iranians still venerate their poets, often because the poets promoted Islam, and protected the Persian language and culture during times of occupation. Also, the crackdown on literature that came in the wake of the revolution largely spared the classics. Many poets have large mausoleums, and streets and squares named after them. Ferdōsī and Omar Khayyām are buried in huge (separate) gardens near Mashhad and the two famous poets from Shīrāz, Sa'dī and Hāfez, each have tombs set in pleasant gardens.

Pakistan & India Pakistan's earliest literature was not 'literary' but sacred. The *Rigveda* and other Vedic (early Brahminical Hindu) books of hymns to the Aryan gods in the 2nd millennium BC were the forerunners of India's Sanskrit literary tradition.

From the Delhi sultans onwards, rulers patronised the Islamic literature – both scholarly and mystical – of Persia and Central Asia. Most appeared in regional languages such as Punjabi, Sindhi, Baluchi, Pashto and Urdu, rather than Sanskrit.

The richest traditions are poetic. Sufis considered poetry and music as means to reach union with God. The 16th to 18th centuries saw a large output of devotional poetry in all regional languages. The warlike Pashtuns were also great lovers of poetry and their best poets are folk heroes.

Hindi literature began in the 12th century, mostly in the form of religious works. The best known are by the Sufi poet Kabir, who sought to reconcile Hinduism and Islam.

Urdu arose in the 16th century as a military lingua franca under the Mughals, based on Hindi but borrowing from Arabic and Persian. It was associated with open-air poetry recitals called *mushairah*, still held today in Pakistan and northern India, and often as well attended as sports events. Urdu poetry's most beloved form is the short lyric poem called *ghazal*, typically dealing with devotional or erotic love.

Modern Urdu literature is heavy on reformism. The greatest modern Urdu poet was Dr Allama Mohammed Iqbal who in the 1930s first proposed a separate Muslim state within India.

A separate Punjabi literature appeared in the 17th century, its first and best-known work being the *Adi Granth*, the collected poems of Sikhism's founder, Guru Nanak. Modern Punjabi works include poetry, prose and drama.

India has a long tradition of Sanskrit literature, although works in the vernacular have contributed to a particularly rich legacy. In fact, it's claimed that there are as many literary traditions as there are written languages.

For most visitors, the only accessible literature is that written in (or translated into) English. Prominent authors include Mul Raj Anand, whose work focuses on the downtrodden *(Cooli, Untouchable)*; Raja Rao *(Kanthapura, The Serpent and the Rope, The Cat* and *Shakespeare)*; Vikram Seth *(A Suitable Boy)*; Shashi Tharoor *(The Great Indian Novel)*; and the widely translated novelist Amitav Ghosh *(The Circle of Reason)*.

Keralan-born Arundhati Roy grabbed the headlines in 1997 by winning the Booker Prize for her novel *The God of Small Things*. The story, set in Kerala, centres on the fate of seven-year-old twins.

One of India's best-known writers, RK Narayan, hails from Mysore and many of his stories centre on the fictitious south Indian town of Malgudi. Well-known works by Narayan include *Swami & His Friends, The Financial Expert, The Guide, Waiting for the Mahatma* and *Malgudi Days*.

Kushwant Singh, one of India's most published contemporary authors and journalists, seems to have as many detractors as fans. One of his more recent offerings, *Delhi*, spans 600 years and brings to life various periods in Delhi's history through the eyes of poets, princes and emperors. Singh has also written the harrowing *Train to Pakistan* about the Partition, the humorous *India – An Introduction* and a collection of short stories.

Although educated in England, Salman Rushdie was born in Bombay in 1947 to a Muslim family and many of his works are set in India or Pakistan, including *Midnight's Children* (1981), *Shame* (1983) and *The Moor's Last Sigh* (1995). Just don't carry a copy of *The Satanic Verses* on your trip.

Prominent Indian poets include Nissam Ezekiel; AK Ramanujan *(The Striders, Relations)*; Arun Kolatkar *(Jejuri)*; and Kamala Das, one of the best-known women poets.

Nepal Nepal does not have a long literary tradition. It dates back to the 19th century to the works of Bhanubhakta Acharya (1814–68). He was the first to break away from the Indian influence and compose truly Nepali verse.

Further development of Nepali literature was hindered by the fact that until the 20th century very little written Nepali was actually published. The Rana regime sought to promote Nepali literature early in the 20th century with the establishment of the Ghorkha Language Publication Committee in 1913. This body basically had a monopoly over Nepali publishing. Due to its heavy censorship local writers and poets regarded it with suspicion and chose to have their work published in India. It was only in the 1930s that Nepal's first journal, *Sharada*, was published. Important Nepali writers and poets include Lekhnath Paudyal, Balkrishna Sama, Lakshmiprasad Devkota, Daulat Bikrram Bishtha and Gurtuprasad Mainali.

Temple Architecture

From the magnificent mosques of Islamic Turkey and Pakistan, to the pagoda temples of Nepal, you'll encounter varying styles of temple architecture throughout this region.

Mosque Architecture Islamic architecture is typified in the minds of the non-Muslim by exotic curves and arabesques, and by intricate geometric patterning. Mosques are the mainstay of Islamic architecture.

They are generally built around an open courtyard, off which lie one or more *iwan* (covered halls). The iwan facing Mecca is the focal point of prayer – it's indicated by a niche in the wall, called a mihrab. Beside the mihrab is often a free-standing pulpit and narrow stair, known as a *minbar.* It's from here that the *imam* gives the Friday *khutba* (sermon). Some of these minbars are ornately decorated.

The two most distinctive architectural components of the mosque are the dome and the minaret. In open-courtyard mosques, the dome is usually above the mihrab area; in

Ottoman-Turkish style mosques it covers the whole prayer hall. The minaret is the tower from which, traditionally, the call to prayer is made. In the past a muezzin would climb the stairs to the top of the minaret to perform the call; nowadays it's more than likely to be a tape recording broadcast into loudspeakers.

Stupas The Buddhist stupas of the Kathmandu Valley – particularly the stupas of Swayambhunath and Bodhnath – are among the most impressive and most visited monuments in Nepal.

The earliest stupas in India were merely domed burial mounds, but they have evolved over the centuries to become complex structures which represent the Buddha and Buddhist philosophy. The lowest level of the stupa is the plinth, which may be simply a square platform, but may also be terraced, as at Bodhnath. On top of the plinth is the hemispherical dome or *kumbha* (meaning 'pot'), and this is usually whitewashed each year.

Atop the dome is a spire which always consists of a number of elements. Immediately on top of the dome is a square-based *harmika,* and usually painted on each side is a pair of eyes, which most people believe represent the all-seeing nature of the Buddha.

Topping the harmika is a tapering section of 13 stages, which are said to represent the 13 stages of perfection. At the very peak is a gilt parasol, which symbolises royalty.

Shikhara Temples The most common form of Hindu temple in north India is the shikhara temple (known as vimana in the south). The tapering tower of these temples resembles a mountain peak (*shikhara* in Sanskrit). The shikhara style developed in India during the Gupta period in the 6th century, and first appeared in Nepal in the late Licchavi period (9th century).

The main feature is the tapering, pyramidal tower, which is often surrounded by four similar but smaller towers, and these may be on porches over the shrine's entrances. The tower is usually built on a square stepped plinth. Occasionally the shikhara temple follows the same basic design but is much more elaborate, with porches and small turrets seemingly all over the place. The Krishna Mandir and octagonal Krishna

Temple, both in Patan's Durbar Square, are excellent examples.

All temples provide shelter for a deity and are thus sacred. At the centre is an unadorned space, the *garhagriha* (inner sanctum) which provides a residence for the deity to which the temple is dedicated. A Shiva temple will contain a lingam, others contain statues or images of a particular god. Many temples also feature an entrance porch and a *mandapa* (hall) which leads to the inner sanctum. Temple decorations range from simple to the remarkably detailed sculptures you'll find in south India and at the famous temples in Khajuraho.

Newar Pagoda Temples The distinctive Newar pagoda temples are a major feature of the Kathmandu Valley skyline. While strictly speaking they are neither wholly Newari nor pagodas, the term has been widely adopted to describe the temples of the Kathmandu Valley.

The temples are generally square in design, and may be either Hindu or Buddhist (or both in the case of mother-goddesses). The major feature of the temples is the tiered roof, which may vary from one to five tiers, with two or three being the most common. The sloping roofs are usually covered with distinctive baked clay tiles or *jhingati,* although richer temples will often have one roof of gilded copper. The pinnacle or *gajur* of the temple is usually bell-shaped and made of baked clay or gilded copper.

The temples are usually built on a stepped plinth, which may be as high or even higher than the temple itself. In some cases the number of steps on the plinth corresponds with the number of roofs on the temple. The temple building itself has just a small sanctum housing the deity. The only people permitted to actually enter the sanctum are the temple priests or *pujari.*

Perhaps the most interesting feature of these temples is the detailed decoration which is only evident when close up. Under each roof there are often brass or metal decorations, such as rows of small bells or embossed metal banners or *kinkinimala.* Another major decorative element is the wooden struts which support the roofs. The intricate carvings are usually of deities associated with the temple deity or the deity's vehicle or *vahana.*

Cinema

Turkey It's a shame that the best-known film about Turkey is the American-made *Midnight Express*, when Turkish directors have produced much better and more interesting portrayals of the country. Nor are these particularly uncritical. Yılmaz Güney's *Yol* (The Road), which won the Palme d'Or at Cannes, has only recently been shown in Turkish cinemas; its portrait of what happens to five prisoners out of a week's release was too grim for the authorities to take. Güney's *The Herd* has also been shown in the West.

Other Turkish directors whose films are worth looking out for are Tunç Başaran, Zülfü, Halit Refiğ and Ömer Kavur. About the best forum for modern Turkish cinema is the İstanbul International Film Festival held each April (films are subtitled in English).

Iran Despite serious straitjacketing by the authorities regarding content, Iranian directors have been turning out some extremely sophisticated and beautifully made films that have won great plaudits internationally. Their accent on character and story stands in refreshing contrast to bubblegum Hollywood cinema. A mark of how widely this work is hailed is the fact that at the time of writing, London's National Film Theatre was holding a festival of Iranian cinema with screenings of over 50 different films.

Names to look out for are Abbas Kiaorastami, regarded as Iran's pre-eminent film maker, whose *The Taste of Cherry* won the Palm d'Or at Cannes in 1997 and Mohsen Makhmalbaf and Jafar Panahi, whose charming *The White Balloon* is widely available in an English-subtitled video. Makhmalbaf's daughter Samira's film *Blackboard* was also highly praised in competition at the 2000 Cannes Film Festival.

India When India's first (silent) epic-based feature film *Raja Harischandra* was released in 1913 few would have anticipated the enormous industry that would emerge in the following decades. The fruits of India's film makers up to 1931 barely fill six video cassettes in the National Film Archives of India. But by the 1980s India's output had eclipsed Hollywood's, earning it the moniker 'Bollywood'. But even Bollywood (otherwise known as Mumbai) has found a challenger in the burgeoning southern cinema industry, fuelled by gigantic studios in Chennai and Hyderabad and a similarly huge demand from Tamil- and Telugu-speaking audiences.

To date India has produced some 28,000 feature films and thousands more short films and documentaries. Well-known to Western audiences is Satyajit Ray's 1955 Bengali classic *Patter Piangil* (Song of the Road) in which the protagonist, Pa, is torn between an individualistic urban existence and a yearning for the familiarity and security of traditional country ways, evoked by nostalgic footage of the Bengali countryside. For 40 years Ray turned out consistently excellent work, and in 1992, shortly before he died, he was awarded an Oscar. His best films include *Patter Pantile, Appear Sandra, Ashani Sanket* and *Jana Aranya*.

The excellent *Salaam Bombay* by Mira Nair was shot on the streets of Mumbai and depicts the plight of the street children in Mumbai. It won the Golden Camera Prize at Cannes in 1989. Mira Nair also directed *Kama Sutra* (1997). Its theme of sensuality and sexuality in 16th century India shocked the Bollywood establishment, which until very recently prohibited the depiction of even chaste kisses between romantic protagonists.

Mani Ratnam's 1993 film *Roja*, in which a young Tamil couple is posted to strife-torn Kashmir was dubbed into Hindi and proved a national success. Other southern films have since been similarly dubbed.

Controversy certainly focused on Deepa Mehta's film *Fire* in 1998. The Shiv Sainaks (supporters of Shiv Sena, a Hindu fundamentalist party) smashed cinemas in Delhi and Mumbai where the film was being screened. Critics claimed the film denigrated Indian culture while others supported it in the name of free speech.

SOCIETY & CONDUCT
Family Structure & the Status of Women

Turkey, Iran & Pakistan Islamic societies allot very different social space to men and to women. Women are seen as subordinate to men, and judged by their abilities as wives, mothers and housekeepers. At the same time they're the standard-bearers of the family's honour, to be shielded from disgrace at all costs.

In the Islamic countries on this route – Turkey, Iran and Pakistan – this aspect of Islamic culture is manifested in different ways and to different extents.

The segregation of men and women was a feature of traditional Turkish society. With the spread of liberal Western attitudes, born of Atatürk's reforms, this situation has changed dramatically in the big towns and along the coast, especially in western Turkey. Rural areas and eastern Turkey are more conservative, traditional and religious and it's still unusual to find men and women mixing.

In Iran, there is absolute segregation of men and women (including separate queues for men and women) and there are strict dress requirements for women.

In orthodox communities in Pakistan, women past the age of puberty observe *purdah* (the Persian word for 'curtain'), ie, they're kept away from all men outside the inner family. To the extent that the family can afford not to have them employed outside, they're kept at home. When they must go out they're veiled, often covered from head to toe in the tent-like *burqah*.

When she marries, a woman joins her husband's family, and that may mean moving in with them. Once all the daughters have married into other families, the inner household 'matures' as a hierarchy of mother and daughters-in-law. The older women are in charge, involved not only in routine household decisions but often in wider ones, eg, about marriages and children's education. The younger women are responsible for child rearing, household chores and light farming work.

India Problems for Indian women often begin before birth. Such is the desire to have male children that the government has legislated to prohibit the abortion of healthy foetuses, the modern equivalent of the practice of female infanticide. 'Sex determination' clinics are also banned but abortions continue. Girls are often seen as a burden on the family, not only because they leave the family when married (traditionally boys remain in their parent's house even after marriage), but also because an adequate dowry must be supplied. Consequently, girls may get less food and their education is often neglected.

Arranged marriages are still the norm rather than the exception. A village girl may well find herself married off while still in her early teens to a man she has never met. She then goes to live in his village, where she is expected not only to do manual labour (at perhaps half the wages that a man would receive for the same work), but also raise children and keep house. This might involve a daily trek of several kilometres to fetch water, as much again to gather firewood, and a similar amount again to gather fodder for domestic animals. She has no property rights if her husband owns land, and domestic violence is common; a man often feels it is his right to beat his wife. In many ways, her status is little better than that of a slave.

For the urban, middle-class woman, life is materially much more comfortable, but pressures still exist. She is much more likely to be given an education, but only because this will improve her marriage prospects. Once married, she is still expected to be mother and homemaker above all else. Like her village counterpart, if she fails to live up to expectations – even if it is just not being able to give her in-laws a grandson – the consequences can be dire, as the practice of 'bride burning' is not uncommon. On a daily basis, newspapers report women having burned to death in kitchen fires, usually caused by 'spilt' kerosene. The majority of these cases, however, are either suicides – desperate women who could no longer cope with the pressure from their in-laws – or outright murders by parents-in-law who want their son to remarry someone they consider to be a better prospect.

In the past decade or so, the women's movement has had some successes in improving the status of women. Although the professions are still very much male dominated, women are making inroads – in 1993, the first women were inducted into the armed forces. In addition, they also account for around 10% of all parliamentarians. Although attitudes towards women are slowly changing, it will be a long time before they gain even a measure of equality with men. For the moment, their power lies in their considerable influence over family affairs and so remains largely invisible to outsiders.

Hospitality

In Islam, a guest – Muslim or not – has a position of honour not understood in the West. If someone visits you and you don't have much to offer, as a Christian you are urged to share what you have; as a Muslim you're urged to give it all away. Traditionally, guests are seated higher than the head of the household.

Most people have little to offer *but* their hospitality, and a casual guest could drain a host's resources and never hear a word about it. It's tactful to very politely refuse gifts or invitations once or twice before accepting them. Someone who doesn't persist with an offer after you decline probably can't afford it anyway. Pulling out your own food or offering to pay someone for a kindness may well humiliate them. All you can do is enjoy it, and take yourself courteously out of the picture before you become a burden.

If you're invited to someone's house, always arrive with a small gift, like postcards from home or sweets for the kids. Don't be surprised if you aren't thanked for it. Gifts are taken more as evidence of God's mercy than of your generosity. If you're going for a meal, something for the table might do (eg, fruit from the market), but don't expect to see it again as some consider it bad form to offer guests food they have brought themselves.

Traditional homes are divided into women's quarters and guest quarters. Most visiting men will never see anything but guest rooms, while women may be coaxed further into the house.

You'll probably be showered with snacks. In this case a refusal would be rude, although meat for a vegetarian or a glass of water from an unknown source can be a problem. Try to present your excuses *before* it's put in front of you; a useful one for drinks is a bad stomach and doctor's orders to drink only hot tea.

If you are to be given food, especially in rural areas, you may first be offered an ewer of water with which to wash your hands before and after the meal; always accept.

Eating with Your Right Hand

The left hand is considered unclean, mainly because it is used for washing after using the bathroom. Eating with your left hand or handling food with it is disagreeable, if not revolting, to Muslims and Hindus. It's an acquired skill to break off bits of chapati with only the right hand, and not everybody bothers, but few Muslims raise food to their mouth with the left hand. Many westerners recoil at the thought of eating with *either* hand; cutlery is usually available and many travellers use a fork. But in any case, even the grottiest cafe usually has a wash stand somewhere for use before and after eating.

You should also avoid passing anything with your left hand or touching people with it.

Talking with Hands & Head

Turks say 'yes' by nodding forward and down. To say 'no', nod your head up and back, lifting your eyebrows at the same time. Or just raise your eyebrows, which is 'no'. When a Turkish person seems to be giving you an arch look, they're only saying 'no'. They may also make the sound 'tsk', which also means 'no'. By contrast, wagging your head from side to side doesn't mean 'no'; it means 'I don't understand'.

Between Pakistani men a handshake is as essential to conversation as eye contact in the West. A common – and oddly appealing – way Indians and Pakistanis say 'yes' is by a sideways tilt of the head; foreigners often mistake this for 'I don't care'. They may say 'no' with a single *'tsp'* or *'tut'*, often with raised eyebrows or a slight backwards flick of the head. It's neither rude nor does it necessarily imply disapproval or surprise. A mere raising of the eyebrows has the same meaning: You may see taxi drivers and rickshaw-wallahs give it when refusing a fare.

A twist of the wrist with fingers outspread seems to be a generalised question, eg, 'What's going on here?' or 'Where are you going?'. The gestures thumbs up and thumbs down are either rude or likely to be misunderstood.

Another gesture that you'll observe on this route is a flat hand extended and waved downward; this means that the person wants you to come over or to follow.

Other Body Language

Public physical contact between men and women – holding hands or kissing, whether with fellow travellers or with local people – is a 'touchy' matter, very often offensive to locals. Holding hands in public is acceptable only between members of the same sex (and is not a sign of homosexuality).

Male tourists have been known to wink at local women or otherwise seek out eye contact, but this is as offensive (and potentially risky) as more overt approaches.

Never point the sole of your shoe or foot at a Muslim, step over any part of someone's body or walk in front of someone praying to Mecca.

Inquiries

Avoid phrasing questions that seek 'yes' or 'no' replies, because people will say anything rather than admit to not knowing the answer. For example, don't ask 'Is this the bus to Lahore?' but rather 'Which bus goes to Lahore?' – and don't believe the answer unless several more people give the same answer!

Visiting Mosques

With few exceptions, non-Muslims are quite welcome to visit mosques at any time other than during noon prayers on Friday. You must dress modestly. For men that means no shorts; for women that means no shorts, tight pants, shirts that aren't done up, or anything else that may be considered immodest. Some of the more frequently visited mosques provide wraparound cloaks for anyone who is improperly dressed. Shoes have to be removed; some mosques will provide slip-on covers for a small fee.

Visiting Temples

Always walk clockwise around Buddhist stupas, chörtens or mani walls. Always remove your shoes before entering a Buddhist or Hindu temple or sanctuary. You may also have to remove any items made from leather, such as belts and bags. Many Hindu and Jain temples do not permit foreigners to enter.

It's the custom to give a white scarf or *khata* to a Buddhist abbot when you are introduced. The honorific title *Rimpoche* (which means 'precious one') is usually bestowed on abbots. The scarves can easily be found in Tibetan shops.

RELIGION
Islam

Turkey, Pakistan and Iran are predominantly Muslim countries. More than 11% of India's population is Muslim, making it the largest minority religion in the country. Nepal also has a small Islamic population.

Muslims believe that their holy book, the Quran, or Koran (Kur'an-i Kerim in Turkish), contains the final revelations of God. The Quran is also believed to clarify points not made clear by the earlier prophets of Judaism and Christianity.

Islam was founded in the early 7th century by the Prophet Mohammed who was born around AD 570 in the city of Mecca. At the age of 40 Mohammed began to receive revelations containing the words of God (Allah) from the archangel Gabriel. The revelations continued for the rest of Mohammed's life and were written down in the Quran (from the Arabic word for 'recitation') in a series of suras (verses). The Quran is said to be the direct word of Allah and since its transcription, not one dot has been altered.

Islam is derived from the Arabic word for submission. This submission is signified by observance of the five pillars of the faith:

Shahada Muslims must publicly declare that 'there is no God but God and Mohammed is his Prophet' (in Arabic, *ha il allah Mohammed ar rasul allah*).

Salat Praying five times a day: at sunrise, noon, mid-afternoon, sunset and night. It's acceptable to pray at home or elsewhere, except for Friday noon prayers, which are traditionally performed at a mosque. The act of praying consists of a series of predefined movements of the body and recitals of prayers and passages of the Quran. Before praying, the believer washes to indicate a willingness to be purified – there are ablution fountains in mosques for this purpose.

Zakat Giving alms to the poor to the value of one-fortieth of the believer's annual income. This used to be the responsibility of the individual but zakat now usually exists as a state-imposed welfare tax administered by a ministry of religious affairs.

Ramadan Fasting during daylight hours during the month of Ramadan (Ramazan in Turkey and Iran). During this month, Muslims abstain from eating, drinking, smoking and sexual intercourse from sunrise to sunset. The purpose of fasting is to bring people closer to God. (For more details on Ramadan see Public Holidays in the Regional Facts for the Visitor chapter.)

Haj Every Muslim capable of affording it should perform the haj, or pilgrimage, to the holiest of cities, Mecca, at least once in his or her lifetime. The reward is considerable: The forgiving of all past sins.

Muslims also believe in the angels who brought God's messages to humans, in the prophets who received these messages, in the books in which the prophets expressed these revelations, and in the last day of judgement. The Quran mentions 28 prophets, 21 of whom are also mentioned in the Bible: Adam, Noah, Abraham, David, Jacob, Joseph, Job, Moses and Jesus are given particular honour, although the divinity of Jesus is strictly denied. The Quran also recognises the Scriptures of Abraham, the Torah of Moses, the Psalms of David and the Gospels of Jesus as God's revelation.

An early dynastic rivalry led to the divide between Shi'ite Islam and Sunni Islam (see The Birth of Islam earlier in this chapter). Sunnism is the orthodox strain of Islam. Sunnis comprise some 90% of the world's total of more than 800 million Muslims. Shi'ites believe that only imams (exemplary leaders) are able to reveal the hidden and true meaning of the Quran. The orthodox view is that there have been 12 imams, the last of them being Mohammed. Shi'ites constitute a clear majority in Iran.

Hinduism

Hinduism is one of the oldest extant religions with firm roots extending back to beyond 1000 BC. It is the largest religion in Asia in terms of the number of adherents, although India, Nepal, Bali, Mauritius and possibly Fiji are the only places where Hindus predominate.

The Indus Valley civilisation, which flourished from about the 23rd to 18th centuries BC, developed a religion which shows a close relationship to Hinduism in many ways. It was further developed on the subcontinent through the combined religious practices of the Dravidians and the Aryan invaders who arrived in northern India around 1500 BC. Around 1000 BC, the Vedic scriptures were introduced and gave the first loose framework to the religion.

Hinduism has a number of holy books, the most important being the four *Vedas*, or 'Divine Knowledge', which are the foundation of Hindu philosophy. The *Upanishads* are contained within the *Vedas* and delve into the metaphysical nature of the universe and soul. Another of the sacred texts of Hinduism is the *Mahabharata*, an epic poem describing the battles between the Kauravas and Pandavas. It contains the story of Rama, and it is likely that the most famous Hindu epic, the *Ramayana*, was based on this. The *Bhagavad Gita* is a famous episode of the *Mahabharata* in which Krishna relates his philosophies to Arjuna.

Hinduism postulates that we will all go through a series of rebirths or reincarnations that eventually lead to moksha, the spiritual salvation which frees one from the cycle of rebirths. With each rebirth you can move closer to or further from eventual *moksha*; the deciding factor is your karma, which is literally a law of cause and effect. Bad actions during your life result in bad karma, which ends in reincarnation on a lower level. Conversely, if your deeds and actions have been good you will be reincarnated on a higher level and be a step closer to eventual freedom from rebirth.

Dharma is the natural law which defines the total social, ethical and spiritual harmony in a Hindu's life. There are three categories of dharma: the eternal harmony that involves the whole universe; the castes and the relations between castes; and the moral code which an individual should follow.

The Hindu religion has three basic practices: puja or worship; cremation of the dead; and the rules and regulations of the caste system. The four main castes are the Brahmin (priests); the Kshatriya (soldiers and governors); the Vaishyas (tradespeople and farmers); and the Sudras (menial workers and craftspeople). Beneath all the castes are the Dalits or Untouchables, the casteless class for whom all the most menial and degrading tasks are reserved.

Westerners may have trouble understanding Hinduism because of its vast pantheon of gods. These different gods can be seen simply as pictorial representations of the many attributes of one god. This one omnipresent god usually has three physical representations: Brahma (the creator), Vishnu (the preserver) and Shiva (the destroyer and reproducer).

All three gods are usually shown with four arms. Brahma also has four heads. Each god has an associated animal or 'vehicle' on which they ride, as well as a consort with certain attributes and abilities. Generally each god also holds symbols. You can often work out which god is represented by the vehicle or the symbols.

Most temples are dedicated to one or other of the gods, but most Hindus profess to be either Vaishnavites (followers of Vishnu) or Shaivites (followers of Shiva). A variety of lesser gods and goddesses also crowd the scene. The cow is, of course, the holy animal of Hinduism.

Hinduism is not a proselytising religion. The orthodox view is that you can't be converted; to be a Hindu you must be born one. The strictly orthodox maintain that only a person born in India of Hindu parents can truly claim to be Hindu. Similarly, once you are a Hindu you cannot change your caste – you're born into it and are stuck with it for the rest of that lifetime. Nevertheless, the spiritual nature of Hinduism holds a great attraction for many westerners and India's 'export gurus' are numerous and successful.

A guru is not so much a teacher as a spiritual guide, somebody who by example or simply by their presence indicates what path you should follow. In a spiritual search one always needs a guru. A sadhu is an individual on a spiritual search. They're an easily recognised group, usually wandering around half-naked, smeared in dust with matted hair and beards.

Sikhism

There are some 16 million Sikhs in India, mostly in the Punjab, where the Sikh religion was founded by Guru Nanak in the late 15th century. Sikhism had its inception in the Hindu bhakti movement that started in South India as a reaction against the caste system and Brahmin domination of ritual. It was conceived at a time of great social unrest and was an attempt to fuse the best of Islam and Hinduism. The Sikh's holy text, the *Granth Sahib*, was completed by the fifth Sikh guru and declared by the 10th to be a guru in its own right, capable of providing leadership to the community.

Sikhs believe in one god and reject the worship of idols. Like Hindus and Buddhists, they accept samsara (the cycle of rebirth) and karma, and believe that only a human birth offers the chance for salvation. Fundamental to Sikhs is the concept of khalsa, or belief in a chosen race of soldier-saints who abide by strict codes of moral conduct (abstaining from alcohol, tobacco and drugs) and engage in a crusade for *dharmayudha* (righteousness). There is no as-

cetic or monastic tradition ending the eternal cycles of death and rebirth in Sikhism.

There are five emblems associated with khalsa: the kesh (turban); kangha (comb); the kacch (drawers, worn by soldiers); the kirpan (sabre or dagger); and the kara (steel bracelet usually worn on the right wrist). The kara is usually said to be a charm against evil; some claim it's to remind believers that they are shackled to god. A khalsa must not cut his hair, hence the Sikh turban. This rule is said to stem from a yogic practice for preserving vitality and drawing it upward.

Zoroastrianism

Zoroastrianism had its inception in Persia and was known to the ancient Greeks. It influenced the evolution of Judaism and Christianity. Zoroaster (Zarathustra) was a priest but little is known of him, except that he was probably born in about 550 BC and lived in eastern Persia. The religion that bears his name, however, became the state religion of the region now known as Iran and remained so for some 1200 years.

Zoroastrianism was eclipsed in Persia by the rise of Islam in the 7th century, and its followers, many of whom openly resisted this, suffered persecution. In the 10th century some emigrated to India, where they became known as Parsis (Persians). They settled in Gujarat and later formed a prosperous community in Mumbai. There are 85,000 or so Parsis left in India. An estimated 30,000 Zoroastrians still live in and around Yazd in Iran.

Zoroastrianism has a dualistic nature; good and evil are locked in continuous battle, with good always triumphing. It leans towards monotheism, but it isn't quite: good and evil entities are believed to co-exist, although believers are enjoined to honour only the good. Humanity has a choice; purity is achieved by avoiding contamination with dead matter and things pertaining to death. Unlike Christianity, there is no conflict between body and soul; both are believed to be united in the struggle of good versus evil. Zoroastrianism rejects fasting and celibacy except in purely ritualistic circumstances.

Perhaps the most famous Zoroastrian practice is the towers of silence. Corpses were placed within the towers, naked and exposed to vultures, who picked the bones clean. In Iran, the practice is rarely undertaken today. Instead, deceased Zoroastrians are usually buried in graves lined with concrete, to prevent 'contamination' of the earth.

Buddhism

Strictly speaking, Buddhism is not a religion, since it is not centred on a god, but a system of philosophy and a code of morality. Bud-

dhism was founded in northern India about 500 BC when Siddhartha Gautama, born a prince, achieved enlightenment. According to some, Gautama Buddha was not the first Buddha but the fourth, and neither is he expected to be the last 'enlightened one'. Buddhists believe that the achievement of enlightenment is the goal of every being, so eventually we will all reach Buddhahood.

The Buddha Trail

For anyone with more than a passing interest in Buddhism, parts of this route provide a fascinating historical chronology of this ancient faith. The route passes through or close to the four most important places in the life of the Buddha himself, Siddhartha Gautama. It also crosses the region of Gandhara (Pakistan), where Buddhism flourished and from where it was believed to have spread into China.

Lumbini, Nepal

This is believed to have been the birthplace of Gautama Buddha in the 6th century BC. There are numerous ancient ruins here and a pillar inscribed by the great Buddhist emperor, Ashoka (3rd century BC). Close to the Nepal-India border town of Sunauli, and hardly disturbed by tourists, it is a peaceful and, dare we say, enlightening, place to spend a day.

Bodhgaya, India

This is quite a way off our route, but it can be reached fairly easily by bus or train from Varanasi. Bodhgaya is where Buddha is said to have attained enlightenment at the age of 35, after giving up his material world (he was a prince) in a quest to end world suffering. This is a working Buddhist centre, rather than just an archaeological site, and it's the most important Buddhist pilgrimage site in the world. The focal point is the Mahabodhi Temple.

Sarnath, India

A short ride from Varanasi, Sarnath is where Budhha first came to preach his message of the 'middle way' to nirvana after attaining enlightenment at Bodhgaya. There are numerous temples, the huge Dhamekh Stupa, and the remains of monasteries, shrines and an Ashoka Pillar.

Kushinagar, India

This is where Buddha is said to have died, after breathing his last words: 'Decay is inherent in all things.' Kushinagar is another site of pilgrimage and is easily reached from Gorakhpur, 55km away.

Rawalpindi to Peshawar, Pakistan

This region was historically known as Gandhara. From the 3rd century BC Gandhara was ruled by the Indian Mauryan dynasty whose emperor, Ashoka, opened it up to Buddhism. It was from here that Buddhism thrived and spread into Central Asia and China. From the 1st to the 3rd centuries AD this was a centre for Mahayana Buddhism under the Kushan empire and the birthplace of Graeco-Buddhist (Gandharan) art, which you can see in the museums at Lahore, Taxila and Peshawar. Swat, further north, is thought to have been the birthplace of Vajrayana, or Tantric (Tibetan) Buddhism.

Dharamsala, India

The home of the Tibetan Government in Exile, Upper Dharamsala (McLeod Ganj) has few historical links to Buddhism but now has a thriving Tibetan culture and is a good place to study Tibetan Buddhism.

The Buddha never wrote down his dharma, or teachings, and a schism later developed so that today there are two major Buddhist schools. The Theravada school holds that the path to nirvana (final release from the cycle of rebirth), the eventual aim of all Buddhists, is an individual pursuit. In contrast, the Mahayana school holds that the combined belief of its followers will eventually be great enough to encompass all of humanity and bear it to salvation. To some, the less austere and ascetic Mahayana school is considered a 'soft option'. Today it is chiefly practised in Vietnam, Japan and China, while the Theravada school is followed in Sri Lanka, Myanmar (Burma) and Thailand. There are still other, sometimes more esoteric, divisions of Buddhism, including the Hindu-Tantric Buddhism of Tibet, which is the version found in Nepal.

The Buddha renounced his material life to search for enlightenment but, unlike other prophets, found that starvation did not lead to discovery. Therefore he developed his rule of the 'middle way', meaning moderation in all things. The Buddha taught that all life is suffering, but that suffering comes from our sensual desires and the illusion that they are important. By following the 'eightfold path', these desires will be extinguished and a state of nirvana will be reached. This process requires going through a series of rebirths until the goal is eventually reached and no more rebirths into the world of suffering are necessary. The path that takes you through this cycle of births is karma, but this is not simply fate. Karma is a law of cause and effect; your actions in one life determine the role you will play and what you will have to go through in your next life.

In India, Buddhism developed rapidly when it was embraced by the great emperor Ashoka. As his empire extended over much of the subcontinent, so Buddhism was carried forth. Later, however, Buddhism began to contract in India because it had never really taken a hold on the great mass of people. As Hinduism revived, Buddhism in India was gradually reabsorbed into the older religion.

LANGUAGE

In 1928, Kemal Atatürk abolished the Arabic alphabet in Turkey and replaced it with the modern Latin-based Turkish alphabet. The change was so drastic that most Turks today cannot read old Ottoman texts which were written in Arabic script. As a traveller you will find English quite widely spoken in tourist areas, particularly along the Mediterranean and Aegean coast and in İstanbul. Outside the big cities, and certainly in the east of the country, English speakers are much harder to find. Many Turks know at least a little German and you may well be asked if you are *Alman* (German).

Turks don't expect foreigners to know their language, but learning a few words and phrases in Turkish is not difficult and will go a long way towards earning a little respect.

Iran's national language is Persian, also known as Fārsī. The Arabic script was adapted to Persian after the introduction of Islam. Classical Persian, such as that found in text books, is not the language of everyday speech. There is no standard method of transliterating Fārsī into English so that English speakers can pronounce it.

Urdu was chosen as Pakistan's national language because it was the lingua franca of the Muslim Mughal empire, but only about 8% of Pakistanis speak it as a first language. The rest speak over 300 dialects of some two dozen languages, including Sindhi, Punjabi, Pashto and Baluchi. You will find, however, that most Pakistanis in cities and large towns speak and understand Urdu. English is still the language of the ruling elite (in government, military, business and higher education), so you shouldn't have trouble speaking with students, shop owners and officials in cities. In rural areas few people speak fluent English.

Hindi is India's national language, but again no single language holds a true majority. Eighteen languages are recognised by the constitution, though a mind-bending 1600 minor languages and dialects were listed in the latest census. English is widely spoken 50 years after the British left and is still regarded as the language of the judiciary and higher education. Years of tourism has meant that shopkeepers, hotel owners, rickshaw-wallahs and touts have developed at least a basic understanding of English in cities and popular areas. In rural areas and mountain villages you'll find it harder to communicate. Hindi, which has many similarities with Urdu, is particularly widespread in central and northern India, though each region has its own specific language (Kashmiri, Gujarati, Punjabi etc).

Along the main tourist trails in Nepal (in the Kathmandu Valley, Pokhara and along the Annapurna Circuit), English is widely understood. In the Thamel district of Kathmandu you probably won't find a local who can't speak English! Nepali is not dissimilar to Hindi and is quite easy to pick up.

Numerous other minority languages – including Tibetan – are spoken in Nepal.

For an introductory guide to Turkish, Fārsī, Urdu, Hindi and Nepali, see the Language chapter at the back of this book. For a more comprehensive guide to each of these languages, get a copy of the Lonely Planet phrasebooks for *Turkish*, *Farsi, Hindi & Urdu* and *Nepali*.

Regional Facts for the Visitor

HIGHLIGHTS

It's tough to pick the best of a trip spanning five such diverse countries and, in any case, one traveller's highlight could be another's disappointment. Often it's the atmosphere of a place and the people you meet that make it more special and memorable than the sights you go there to see. You could whip through the main attractions of Lahore's Old City in half a day, but getting lost in the bazaar or attending a devotional qawwali concert is much more fun.

With that in mind, you could have a memorable trip along this route without seeing any of our highlights. In fact, some travellers may want to avoid these places precisely because they are in this book.

We list here a few of the more impressive or interesting sights along the route and there are more highlights given at the start of each country chapter.

Natural Attractions

The **Mediterranean coast** of Turkey might not have many golden sandy beaches (Patara is an exception), but its blue waters and dramatic rocky and pine-clad inlets are so seductive you might never get to Kathmandu. Equally beguiling is the extraordinary landscape of **Cappadocia** in central Turkey, the result of centuries of natural erosion. The alpine and volcanic scenery around **Lake Van** is fantastic, while across the border in Iran, the mountainous region of **Alamūt**, lair of the Castles of the Assassins, has the feel of Shangri-la about it.

The Rajasthani **desert** features Saharan-style dunes and wonderful golden sunsets. The Himalaya, in India and Nepal, provide some of the most spectacular mountain scenery in the world. **Pokhara** has a wonderful lakeside setting with the snow-covered mountains of the Annapurna range forming a superb backdrop. Although there are few mountain views from Kathmandu city itself, a short trip to **Nagarkot** on the valley rim offers one of the finest views in Nepal.

Also in Nepal, **Royal Chitwan National Park** is a fine place to tramp through the jungle and see some wildlife, particularly the one-horned Indian rhinoceros.

Cities & Towns

Apart from the obvious highlights of İstanbul and Kathmandu, there are many smaller cities and towns that are worth lingering in for their culture, vibrancy and atmosphere alone.

In Iran, **Esfahān** is a definite highlight with its wonderful blue-and-white tiled mosques and exotic teahouses hidden in the pillars of ancient bridges. In Pakistan, **Peshawar** has a rough and ready mix of tribal cultures, Afghan refugees and cross-border smuggling.

McLeod Ganj, home of the exiled Dalai Lama, has a large Tibetan community and a cool Himalayan climate – a great place to hang out in the warmer months. **Udaipur**, in Rajasthan, is perhaps the most romantic city on the route, even if you don't stay in the magnificent Lake Palace Hotel. Finally, **Varanasi**, on the banks of the holy Ganges River, is a fascinating microcosm of Hindu India.

Museums & Galleries

The **Topkapı Palace** in İstanbul should be seen for its architecture and decoration rather than any of the exhibits; visit the **Carpet Museum** in Tehrān if you're interested in looking at, or thinking of buying, Persian carpets or rugs. The **National Museum of Iran** together with the **Islamic Arts Museum**, also in Tehrān, is the country's best all-round museum, and the **Decorative Arts Museum of Iran**, in Esfahān, is also well worth a look.

The **Lahore Museum** has the finest collection of art, sculpture and antiquities in Pakistan, though the **Taxila Archaeological Museum** is not far behind. The **National Museum** in Delhi and the **Patan Museum** near Kathmandu showcase some of the rich heritage of India and Nepal respectively.

Monuments & Ancient Sites

Turkey is chock-a-block with classical ruins, but the one site you shouldn't miss is **Ephesus**. The hilltop statues at **Nemrut Dağı** in eastern Turkey are also remarkable. Ancient Persia is best summed up by a visit to **Persepolis**, near Shīrāz, and the mud-brick citadel **Arg-é Bam** in Bam, both in Iran.

To Follow or Not to Follow

Guidebooks are sometimes criticised for dragging travellers in the same direction to see the same things and stay at the same hotels. But there's enough variety in these pages that this need not be the case. There's a lot of road between İstanbul and Kathmandu and not everyone will want to travel the same bits. Independent travellers all think differently and will make their own decisions on where they eat, sleep, drink and travel, using this book's recommendations as a guide.

We've tried to fit the best of the areas the route passes into this guide, but that doesn't mean you have to stick to our path. There are literally hundreds of detours you could possibly make from the route outlined in this book – even if it's not mentioned here, don't be afraid to deviate if there's something you particularly want to see. And you don't have to go blindly. Talk to other travellers, beg, borrow or buy other guidebooks to cover the information you need, or visit tourist offices whose staff can advise on transport, accommodation and things to see.

A simple way of getting off the beaten track is to leave the main towns and cities and head to the country. A side trip to a small village, into a national park or hiking in the hills will not only help you 'escape' from other travellers (if that's your aim), but also allow you to discover a purer version of a country's culture, traditions and people that is so often lacking in the cities. Some ideas…

- The Black Sea Coast in Turkey, particularly Trabzon and the Sumela Monastery. Also check out the Ottoman houses of Safranbolu, the Georgian Valleys and the ruins of Ani near Kars.
- Syria, particularly Aleppo and Damascus (you'll need a visa).
- The Caucasus – travel the route from Turkey via Georgia and Azerbaijan to Iran (again you'll need visas).
- In western Iran you could visit the Alī Sadr Caves near Hamadān, the ruins of ancient Susa (Shūsh) and Choghā Zambīl for its Elamite architecture. Also consider the resort towns of the Caspian Sea and the Persian Gulf, particularly Hormoz and Kīsh Islands.
- Cross over into Turkmenistan from Iran and work your way through the Central Asian states to China and the north end of the Karakoram Highway to rejoin our route in Pakistan – a major detour!
- The Northern Areas of Pakistan, particularly the Swat Valley, Chitral and Gilgit – this area is regarded by many as the most beautiful part of Pakistan. You can continue up the Karakoram Highway into China if you have a visa.
- Manali and the Kullu Valley in India – superb Himalayan hiking, spectacular scenery and a great place to hang out. Manali is easily reached from Dharamsala or Shimla.
- Just south of Agra, Gwalior and Jhansi in India are interesting historical cities with imposing forts, while Khajuraho's erotic temple architecture is one of India's finest sights. Near Jhansi, Orchha is a remarkable collection of virtually forgotten palaces and temples.
- Trekking in Nepal – we touch on some trekking areas, but you could venture farther out on the Langtang and Helambu treks and the famous Everest Base Camp trek. Also check out the Mustang region and the Royal Bardia National Park.

Another option is to take an organised tour from a base along the route. There are cycling and sailing tours on the Mediterranean coast in Turkey; tours into the Swat Valley and Northern Areas from Islamabad or Peshawar in Pakistan; extended desert camel safaris in India; and 4WD trips up to Lhasa in Tibet from Kathmandu. See the relevant sections in each chapter for more information.

In Pakistan, not many travellers get to **Uch Sharif** but it has a fine collection of mausoleums and Sufi shrines, while **Taxila**, near Rawalpindi, is an ancient reminder of the Buddhist Gandharan dynasty.

The **Taj Mahal,** masterpiece of Mughal architecture and monument to love, is an unmissable sight in India, and nearby is the haunting, abandoned city of **Fatehpur Sikri,** also well worth a visit.

Architecture & Forts

The finest Turkish architecture is on display in İstanbul, home of **Aya Sofia** and the **Blue Mosque**. For something more modern, check out **Anıtkabir**, the grand, yet elegant mausoleum in Ankara of Mustafa Kemal Atatürk, the founder of modern Turkey. On the Turkey/Iran border, the **İshak Paşa Sarayı** in Doğubayazıt may be a mishmash of architectural styles but it's still a real beauty, and stunningly situated.

The finest collection of buildings in Iran is in **Esfahān**, where Emām Khomeinī Square, ringed by magnificent mosques, palaces and the bazaar is one of the world's great plazas. The city also has several graceful bridges crossing the Rūd-é Zāyandé (Zāyandé River). In terms of visual splendour, Esfahān is run a close second by the dazzling Holy Shrine of Emām Rezā in **Mashhad**.

Pakistan and northern India boast many impressive forts, among them the great Mughal strongholds in Lahore and Delhi. **Derawar Fort** in Pakistan is not terribly accessible but it's an impressive structure. The ruined **Rohtas Fort** is also isolated but easier to reach and worth a day's exploration. In Rajasthan, don't miss the spectacular **Jodhpur Fort**, with its commanding view over the blue city. There are also impressive forts in Jaisalmer and at Amber, near Jaipur.

Finally, in Kathmandu, the palaces and pagodas in the **Durbar Squares** at Patan and Bhaktapur are superb examples of Nepali and Newari architecture.

Adventure Activities

Paragliding near Ölüdeniz is one of the most exciting thing you can do in Turkey. **Skiing** is also possible; beginners will appreciate the gentle slopes of Turkey's ski resorts, such as Uludağ, while those with more experience will find the Alborz mountain resorts in Iran a more suitable challenge.

Kaş is the adventure sports mecca of Turkey's Turquoise Coast, with opportunities for **diving**, **kayaking** and **mountain biking**. At Bodrum, Marmaris and Fethiye you can also arrange to go **sailing** on a *gulet* (traditional Turkish yacht).

A desert **camel safari** is a must if you visit Rajasthan, and Jaisalmer is the most popular place to do it. You don't have to walk to Everest Base Camp to enjoy trekking in Nepal. The Annapurnas near Pokhara and the Kathmandu Valley provide excellent hiking opportunities. The areas around Dharamsala and Shimla in Himachal Pradesh also offer good hiking.

White-water rafting is superb in Nepal and you can combine a trip on the Bhote Kosi with a death-defying **bungee jump** into a stunning gorge.

For details on other outdoor pursuits, see the Activities section later in this chapter.

Nightlife

Enjoy the after-dark delights of **İstanbul** – they're the most sophisticated you'll find on the trip to Kathmandu, spanning everything from cinemas showing the latest Western movies to *Türkü* (traditional folk music) bars and a thriving gay club scene. Mediterranean resorts such as **Bodrum**, **Marmaris** and **Fethiye** have a raucous nightlife during the package tourist season.

In Iran, go on a teahouse crawl in **Esfahān**. In Pakistan, a night at a mesmerising qawwali performance in Lahore is a real cultural experience. In India and Nepal there's always the chance of a group of travellers getting together for a night out, regardless of the local scene. **McLeod Ganj** is particularly good, and **Kathmandu** has a growing local nightclub scene to complement the numerous travellers/trekkers bars.

Seeing the ghostly **Taj Mahal** on a full-moon night is worth the expense if you happen to be there at the right time.

See Entertainment later in this chapter for more information.

THE ROUTE

As the title suggests, this book is organised from west to east, the classic direction of Asian overland travel from the days when Marco Polo first ventured east in search of a good cuppa. But there's no reason why the route can't be travelled in the opposite direction and many will choose to do it that way. This book was researched in both directions.

If you're planning this route as part of a bigger trip, your starting point will depend on where you want to end up – Europe or Asia. If this is a stand alone journey, the biggest factor in your decision may be the time of year you intend to start. Working on a three-month trip, late August/early September is

İstanbul to Kathmandu & the Lonely Planet Story

The ferry chugged across the Bosphorus, carrying us not just from one side of İstanbul to the other but from one continent (Europe) to another (Asia). There was an unmistakable feeling of going somewhere, of making a major transition, of, let's admit it, embarking on an adventure.

That was back in 1972, only a year before the first Bosphorus bridge was completed, linking the two continents. We were on the Hippy Trail, the route that, for a brief spell in the ' ' '60s and '70s, lured countless backpackers, before they were even known as backpackers, on a winding route across Asia. It was the era of the Magic Bus, kicking off from somewhere near the Dam Square in Amsterdam and ending up in New Delhi or Kathmandu. The Beatles had paid their obligatory ashram call on the Maharishi Mahesh Yogi, Goa was becoming *the* place to spend Christmas, the shāh was still in power in Iran and Afghanistan was years away from crumbling into anarchy and thereby inviting the Russians to march in and turn a small mess into a really big one. It was a very interesting time to be in Asia.

We remember that long haul across Asia as a series of transitions, starting with that first dramatic change – leaving Europe behind and entering Asia. Then there was the transition from Turkey to Iran and, farther east, the much more dramatic shift as we crossed the border into Afghanistan, a curious mixture of chaos and somnolence. From Herat we went south to Kandahar and then north to Kabul, over surprisingly smooth and well-kept roads; they've since been destroyed by 25 years of war and neglect.

The Khyber Pass into Pakistan brought another transition, from the relatively uncrowded open spaces of Central Asia to the teeming crowds of the subcontinent. The brief war with India after the civil war between West and East Pakistan had occurred less than a year before and the new nation of Bangladesh, which arose out of the ensuing chaos, had only come into existence at the beginning of the year. It was hardly surprising that relations between Pakistan and India were not very good (and little has changed on that front in the past 30 years). As a result the border between Lahore and Amritsar was open for only a few hours once a week, and we duly queued up to file across into India.

Eventually our wanderings took us to Birganj, a miserable little dump just across the border into Nepal. From there we spent a day on a bus, roller coasting over the Himalayan foothills before winding down into the Kathmandu Valley just as dusk fell across the city and the lights came on. It was a magical image that has stuck with us ever since. We hung around in Kathmandu for awhile, staying in a dollar-a-day dive on Freak St (the shift north to the Thamel district was yet to take place) before retracing our steps down to the plains and continuing east to Calcutta, then Bangkok, Singapore, Jakarta, Bali and, eventually, Australia.

Even today much of that trip seems as fresh as yesterday, hardwired into our brains like some read-only computer file. And of course it was to have a lasting effect on our lives, and on those of a lot of other people, much more so than we could ever have imagined. Less than a year later we wrote and published *Across Asia on the Cheap*, the very first Lonely Planet guidebook. Every subsequent book, including the one in your hands right now, is descended from that first little foray from İstanbul to Kathmandu.

Tony & Maureen Wheeler

---

the ideal time to start from İstanbul, but February/early March is the best time to start from Kathmandu. See the When to Go section later for more details.

The route itself is fairly logical and straightforward. Travelling south along the coast from İstanbul, it heads inland from Antalya and takes you through Cappadocia and east towards the Iranian border (if you're in a hurry, we also describe the direct route via Ankara). In Iran it heads towards the capital, Tehrān, then south through Esfahān towards Shirāz, before turning east across the desert to Pakistan. Through Pakistan, the route crosses the country heading north-east towards Lahore.

The main roads (or train line) on this route are safe for travel, but due to travel restrictions there's little scope to head off into the wilderness here. From Lahore there's the option to travel to Peshawar via the capital Islamabad and Rawalpindi. Onwards to India, we describe a northern route into Himachal Pradesh then down to Delhi, with the option to forge deep into Rajasthan or simply continue east to Agra and then Varanasi. The route then turns due north to Nepal and on to Kathmandu via Pokhara and Royal Chitwan National Park. Each country chapter begins with a section called 'The Route', which gives more detail.

SUGGESTED ITINERARIES

This book covers a set route but we've tried to branch out a bit to include the best of the areas it passes through. As a result you probably won't stop at every place en route but will make choices along the way. You might want to spend more time lounging on the Mediterranean beaches in Turkey or trekking in the mountains of Nepal.

But does a side trip to Jaisalmer mean there's no time for the Annapurna Circuit? Is it best to chill out for a few days on the Turkish beaches and leave the classical monuments until next time? There are some tough decisions to be made. Most travellers will, we hope, actually make it from İstanbul to Kathmandu (or vice versa), for which you should allow at least 10 to 12 weeks. Of course, it can be done in less time, particularly if you skip some of the side routes and make long hops between cities, but you risk turning your trip into a frustrating succession of bus stations and passing landscapes.

If you don't have that much time, consider travelling only part of the route. You can easily finish your trip in Tehrān, Lahore or Delhi. It would be a shame to see hardly anything of any country in a headlong rush to see a little bit of each. As a rule of thumb you should allow three weeks for the route covered in Turkey and India and two each for Iran, Pakistan and Nepal (more for Nepal if you intend to do any serious trekking). With Pakistan and Nepal you could conceivably cut back to one week for each if you intend to travel straight through, spending time at only Quetta, Lahore and, say, Peshawar in Pakistan, and foregoing trekking or adventure activities in Nepal.

At the other end of the scale you could easily spend many months covering the route at your leisure.

The following trip breakdowns are based on a three-month complete trip. Even though one day has been added to each itinerary to account for transit time, you'll almost certainly find that you need to add more.

That said, these itineraries mean travelling at breakneck speed, visiting highlights and major sites only. Cutting out some of these places and allowing longer at others will probably suit most travellers.

Turkey (21 days)

İstanbul (3 days), Çanakkale (1 day), Selçuk (2 days), then 4 days along the Mediterranean coast. A night in either Eğirdir or Konya, followed by 3 days in Cappadocia (Göreme), Malatya or Khata (1 day) for Nemrut Dağı, Şanlıurfa and Harran (2 days), Diyarbakır (1 day), Van (2 days), Doğubayazıt (1 day)

Iran (17 days)

Mākū or Tabrīz (1 day), Takāb (for Takht-é Soleimān, 1 day), Ghazvīn/Alamūt (2 days), Tehrān (2 days), Mashhad (1 day), Kāshān (1 day), Esfahān (3 days), Shīrāz (2 days), Yazd (1 day), Kermān (1 day), Bam (1 day)

Pakistan (13 days)

Quetta (2 days), Bahawalpur or Multan (2 days), Lahore (3 days), Islamabad/Rawalpindi (3 days), Peshawar (2 days)

India (22 days)

Amritsar (1 day), Dharamsala/McLeod Ganj (3 days), Shimla (1 day), Delhi (2 days), Jaipur (2 days), Pushkar (2 days), Udaipur (2 days), Jodhpur (1 day), Jaisalmer (3–4 days, with camel safari), Agra (1 day), Varanasi (2 days)

Nepal (12 to 21 days)

The amount of time that you spend in Nepal will depend largely on whether or not you intend to go trekking and/or rafting. Allow at least a week for the shortest of treks into the Himalaya and two to three weeks for the Annapurna Circuit. You should also allow another four days minimum in the Kathmandu Valley and two days in Royal Chitwan National Park.

Warning: Overland Dangers!

Aussie travel writer Peter Moore travelled the overland trail to research his book *The Wrong Way Home*. Here he lists the five overland 'dangers' he wishes he'd been warned about...

1. Turkish Tea Poisoning

It is considered rude to refuse a cup of tea in Turkey. And in the east, you won't be able to go 200m without being dragged in for a cuppa. Decide to buy a carpet and your chances of a tannin overdose increase tenfold.

2. Your Very Own Iranian Hostage Crisis

The Iranian people are pathologically hospitable and you'll soon lose count of the number of times you are dragged off to people's homes to meet the family and share a meal. Don't even try to leave before the third helping!

3. Pakistani Cricket Stats

Don't like cricket? Well, in Pakistan you better learn to love it. The average person on the street will regale you with the stats on every player in the national team, and in all probability the number of runs David Boon, the ex-Australian opener, scored on Sundays.

4. Indian Film Tunes

From Amritsar to Sunauli, you won't be able to escape the hit tune from the latest Bollywood epic. Worse, you'll soon find yourself singing it. Years later I'm still humming the chorus from a song called 'Sexy, sexy, sexy' with the unforgettable line of 'Pantaloons, be sexy!'

5. Kathmandu Clothing

Finally, when you reach Kathmandu, you will be overwhelmed with the urge to buy outrageously colourful clothing. Just remember this: Yes, you do look ridiculous!

Remember! Forewarned is forearmed. Happy overlanding!

Peter Moore

PLANNING
When to Go

There's a lot of climatic variation between İstanbul and Kathmandu, so it's very important to consider not only when and where you will start the journey, but how long you will take to complete it. You don't want to be stuck in the Baluchistan Desert in July (believe us) or in eastern Turkey in December. Nor is it much fun being at a Mediterranean beach resort in winter or trying to trek in the Himalaya during the monsoon.

On the other hand, in some popular areas you'll probably want to avoid the absolute peak travel times – July and August in western Turkey, December and January in Rajasthan, and October in Nepal. It's also worth factoring in religious holidays that you should try to avoid, or festivals that you might want to attend. See Public Holidays and Special Events later in this chapter for more information.

The Weather Factor Because of differences in climate and altitude across the five countries on this route, enjoying ideal weather conditions throughout the trip is not going to be easy. Turkey and Iran are at their best in spring (March to June) and autumn (fall; September to November). Turkey is bearable in summer, particularly in the east, but Iran's desert climate may be a bit oppressive, particularly as the Islamic dress code means you have to stay well covered.

Pakistan is simply too hot for comfort between April and September, unless you journey right up into the Northern Areas around Chitral and Gilgit (not covered on this route). The exception is Quetta, which, at an altitude of almost 2000m, is at its best in summer but very cold in winter. The tail-end of the monsoon comes from late July to September, dumping rain from Lahore to Peshawar but not reaching much farther west.

It's a similar situation in India. The northern plains, including Delhi, all of Rajasthan and Varanasi, are like a furnace from May to July. The monsoon kicks in around mid-July and continues through to September, bringing relief from the heat but (naturally) a lot of rain. However, up in Himachal Pradesh the climate is perfect from March to July and very cold (usually with snowfall) from November to February.

The best time to visit Nepal is from October to March. The air is still and clear, the mountain views are at their best, and it's not as cold as you might expect (until you start trekking into the mountains, where it gets very cold in December and January). Kathmandu is only 1300m above sea level and is actually farther south in latitude than Delhi. From April to June it can get quite hot, especially on the lowland Terai, and the monsoon brings heavy rain from June to September.

So what does all this mean?

You need to take into account where you will be starting the journey, how long you wish to take, and which areas are of most interest to you – beaches, mountains, deserts, cities, or a mixture of everything. Starting from İstanbul and working on a three-month journey, late August/early September is an ideal time to start. You can enjoy fine coastal weather in western Turkey and cooler late-summer weather in eastern Turkey. The worst of the summer heat will be over by the time you travel through Iran and Pakistan. It will be post-monsoon in India, and you arrive in Nepal around November/December, a good time for mountain viewing and trekking.

Starting in April (as we did) is the perfect time to travel in Turkey and Iran, but it will be very hot in Pakistan and India, and the monsoon starts in Nepal around July. A third option, if you're not interested in beaches or the backpacker circuit, is to start early, say in February, and arrive in Kathmandu around April/May. Unfortunately you'll experience very cold weather in Turkey, particularly in the east where there will almost certainly be snow around (and consequently fewer tourists). The climate in Iran will be milder, and it won't be too hot in Pakistan and India. April in Nepal is still good, although it starts to get hot and hazy in May.

If you start from Kathmandu, the best month is probably February, which brings you to İstanbul around April/May. You'll experience near-perfect weather for most of the trip. January would also be OK but if you start any earlier you'll arrive in Turkey before the start of the tourist season. If you start later (say April), you'll run into very hot weather in India and Pakistan.

If your trip is to be shorter than three months, you'll have a better chance of timing fine weather. A longer trip gives you the chance to take it slower and hang out in the places where the weather is more suitable.

Religious Holidays & Festivals The most important Islamic festival to watch out for (and perhaps avoid) in Turkey, Iran and Pakistan is **Ramadan** (one month) in the ninth month of the Islamic calendar. (See Public Holidays and Special Events later in this chapter for further details and for dates.) During this time, Muslims must fast between sunrise and sunset (only water is allowed) and many aspects of daily life grind to a halt. Although non-Muslims are not bound by the fasting, most restaurants and cafes throughout the region (with the exception of those in hotels catering to tourists) will be closed. Transport and office hours are erratic. In addition, going all day without food or drink doesn't improve many people's mood. However, it does offer an insight into a unique religious festival and there's some great feasting to be had after dark.

Kurban Bayramı, which lasts a full week in Turkey, is another interesting one. Hotels are jam-packed, banks close and transport is booked up weeks ahead, but it's another event worth seeing if you can (and if you're not too squeamish about livestock being sacrificed on the streets). The equivalent festival in Pakistan is called **Eid-ul-Adha** (spelled Eid al-Adha generally in the Middle East). The other big Muslim feasts only last a day or two and shouldn't prove too disruptive to most travel plans. In fact, if at all possible it is well worth trying to time your visit to tie in with something like **Eid al-Kebir** or the Prophet's Birthday, as these are wonderfully colourful occasions.

In Iran it's exceptionally difficult to find hotel accommodation throughout **Nō Rūz**, the Iranian New Year (about 10 days around the Spring equinox in the middle of March). All forms of public transport are heavily booked. Most businesses, including restaurants, will close for about five days from about March 21 to March 25 inclusive. If you're not going to be staying with Iranian friends, it's best to avoid travel in Iran at this time.

Diwali (five days, usually in November) and **Dussehra** (10 days around September/October) are the big events in India and, again, accommodation can be tight when these are on, but usually only in places popular with Indian holiday-makers. The big problem is transport – trains will be overcrowded (more so than usual) and traffic will be horrendous as Indians move en masse to visit family and friends. School holidays in India (late December/early January and April/May) can also be tricky times to travel, particularly trying to get a seat on a train.

The **Pushkar Camel Fair** in November is one of many colourful Indian events worth looking out for.

October (and late September) is the busiest time in Nepal thanks to **Dasain**, the most important of all Nepali celebrations. Village life can be vibrant at this time but transport will be heavily booked as Nepalis hit the road.

See the Public Holidays and Special Events sections later in this chapter for further details and for dates.

What Kind of Trip

Whatever you may be thinking, travelling independently overland from Istanbul to Kathmandu is not difficult. Bus and train services are good (you won't need to hitchhike), cheap accommodation is generally easy to find, costs are low, crime is minimal, English is widely spoken (there are exceptions in eastern Turkey, Iran and Pakistan – see the Language section in the Facts about the Region chapter) and the locals are, for the most part, very friendly and hospitable.

If you prefer to go it alone or simply don't have anyone to travel with, solo travel is one of the best ways to meet and get to know local people. You'll also meet many other travellers along the way with whom you can hook up for a while. The beauty is that you're not stuck with a travelling partner or partners that you may not get along with. Women travelling alone in this part of the world are relatively rare but certainly not unknown. A lone woman traveller may be regarded as something of an oddity by local people in Asia and unwanted attention is likely to be unavoidable, but don't let that put you off. You can still enjoy the region, provided you're not too thin-skinned and keep certain conditions in mind – see the Women Travellers section later in this chapter.

Travelling as a couple, or with a friend or two, is a more attractive proposition for most people, particularly first-time travellers. It means you'll never be lonely but it can also cut you off a bit from local people (you'll talk to each other rather than to other people). A big advantage of group travel is that it's cheaper and makes bargaining easier – you can share hotel rooms as well as costs such as hiring guides or taxis. With a small group the option also opens up of hiring a car for a few days to explore areas that are more problematic or time consuming by public transport. It's also safer in that you won't find yourself alone and nervous when you arrive late at night in a strange town, and it's easier to manage when you're weighed down with bags – one can mind the luggage while another goes off on a fact-finding mission.

Finally there's the organised tour, arranged in your home country. It frees you from time-consuming hassles such as getting visas and the inevitable hotel run-around that comes with each new town. This could be anything from a short adventure tour to an extended overland trip, where you and up to a dozen like-minded others trundle across Asia in a big truck, doing your own shopping, sharing the cooking and maybe camping out. One advantage of the organised overland tour, particularly for first-time travellers, is that you will be assured of travelling companions (which you hope will be a good thing). See the Organised Tours section in the Getting There & Away chapter for more information.

Budgeting

Travel in this part of the world is cheap, with Turkey being about the most expensive country en route. Real shoestringers can get by on no more than US$10 to US$15 a day, staying in cheap hotels and hostel dormitories and existing on a street food diet with maybe one moderately priced restaurant meal a day. No doubt travellers will write to tell us how they managed it on US$5 a day.

Although you probably want to make your money stretch as far as possible, you have spent quite a lot just to get there and who knows when you'll be back, so you also want to get as much out of the trip as possible. Don't be too cheap. Too many travellers turn up at museums or famous sights with the intention of going in, see the admission price and decide to skip it. The Taj Mahal now costs a day or two's budget to enter, but can you afford to miss it? Of course, travelling is not only about spending money. There are plenty of free sights and experiences to seek out along the way.

A more realistic budget of US$20 to US$25 a day allows for site admissions, a varied diet and an improved chance of getting hot water or a private bathroom at the hotel. This breaks down to an average of US$5 for a room in a hotel or guesthouse (a dorm bed in Turkey), US$5 for one decent meal a day, US$2 for a couple of street food snacks, with around US$8 to US$10 left over for transport, admissions and incidentals. Some days you won't spend this much, other times you'll blow two or three days' money in one afternoon. On a budget of around US$150 a week, you should be able to see and do an awful lot.

Other things you should prepare your budget for are entertainment activities. Alcohol is relatively expensive in India and Nepal and nights spent partying in Turkey will really make a dent in your funds. Organised tours or adventure activities such as rafting, diving or camel safaris will also add to your expenses. Do keep money aside for visa fees (which can top US$50 depending on where you get them and what your nationality is) and unusual travel expenses (such as baksheesh). Shopping is another matter, and should probably figure separately from your daily travel budget.

Finally, despite what many backpackers expound (and what many of our own recommendations encourage), it's not always best to take the cheapest possible option. Staying a night in a mid-range hotel, taking the first-class train or more comfortable bus, and splurging at a decent restaurant are all good ways to make yourself feel more human again after weeks or months of budget travel. Allow room in your budget for a few treats and you'll feel better about the trip.

See the Money section later in this chapter for more details on the costs you can expect in each country.

Maps

If you're using public transport and following our route, the country and city maps in this book will be sufficient for most travellers. If you're driving, cycling, walking or otherwise getting by under your own steam, or if you want to get off the beaten path, more detailed maps will be required. Locally produced maps can be picked up along the way at tourist offices (often free but varying in quality from useless to marginally useful) and bookshops.

For Turkey we'd go with the Bartholomew *Euromap*, which comes in two sheets at a scale of 1:800,000 and is excellent. Nowhere near as detailed, but free and useful enough if you're using public transport, is the *Turkey Camping* map produced by the Ministry of Tourism and available from Turkish Tourist Offices. Lonely Planet's *İstanbul City Map* is up-to-date and fully indexed with walking tours.

For Iran, Gita Shenasi (☎ 21-679 335, fax 675 782), 15 Kheyābūn-é Ostad Shahrīvar, Tehrān, PO Box 14155/3441, publishes an impressive array of maps of the country and all major cities. Some are sold at bookshops throughout Iran, but the better maps are only available at Gita Shenasi's office. Its *General Map of Iran* (1:1,000,000), published in English, is the best; and the new *A Tourist Guide to Tehrān* is the best map of that mammoth metropolis. The best dual-language map (ie, Fārsī and English) is the *Tourist Map of the Islamic Republic of Iran* (1:2,500,000), published by the Ministry of Culture & Islamic Guidance, although it's not widely available in Iran. The best English-language map probably available in your home country is *Iran* (1:2,000,000) published by GeoCenter.

The Survey of Pakistan is the main publisher of maps in that country. They're widely available from large city bookshops as well as the Survey of Pakistan office in Islamabad. Its 1:2,000,000 *Road Map of Pakistan* is pretty good and there are various maps of provinces and cities. Outside Pakistan, Nelles publishes a good 1:1,500,000 of the country. These maps are printed in Germany but are available from book and map shops worldwide. Maps handed out by the Pakistan tourist offices are colourful but of little use.

For following this route you really only need a map of northern India. Lonely Planet publishes a comprehensive India Road Atlas which covers the entire country at 1:1,250,000 and is completely indexed. Nelles also produces maps to this area. The

Survey of India produces a comprehensive series, while the TTK Discover India series covers each state, many cities, as well as road and rail maps (from INRs 40).

All the trekking and city maps you'll need for Nepal are available within the country, mostly in Kathmandu. If you want something before you get there Nelles produces a good map of Nepal. Locally produced Mandala Trekking Maps are cheap and adequate for most trekkers. Topographic map sheets at 1:25,000 are available from the Topographic Department of the Survey Ministry in Kathmandu. The Himalayan Map House and Nepamap also produce a range of colourful trekking and city maps.

What to Bring

The standard advice on any overland trip is to travel light – pack as little as possible. You'd be surprised how little you can get by on in the way of clothes and gear and you'll really appreciate the freedom of a light bag when walking through crowded streets or getting on and off trains and buses. Some travellers take all they need in a backpack small enough to pass as hand luggage on the plane, although that really puts restrictions on what you can wear! The duration of your journey should make little difference to the amount of kit you need.

Most travellers go for a medium-sized backpack (about three-quarters full – allow room for purchases along the way) and a small day-pack, and watch their belongings magically expand as the trip progresses.

Clothes You'll probably experience some extremes of temperature on this trip, but don't let that fool you into packing an entire wardrobe of summer and winter gear. You can pack one item for both extremes and then pick up what you need along the way. You'll have no problem buying clothes anywhere and you can have them cheaply tailor-made in Pakistan, India and Nepal. Many travellers (men and women) pick up a *salwar kameez* (outfit comprising a long tunic over a pair of baggy trousers) in Pakistan.

If Nepal is your final destination, there's no need to lug fleeces and Gore-Tex jackets all the way there – all sorts of cold weather and trekking gear is available cheaply in Kathmandu and Pokhara. You can even rent gear for next to nothing,

including all the trekking equipment you would need.

The best advice is to pack loose fitting, lightweight clothing: A couple of cotton shirts or T-shirts, a pair of shorts, a pair of trousers or a skirt, a light sweater and a waterproof jacket should be sufficient (the jacket mightn't get a lot of use depending on when you make the trip, but you can always send it home). Remember to have at least one long-sleeve shirt or a lightweight sweater – in Iran and Pakistan it's best to be covered. Women will need a headscarf and a baggy shawl for Iran (see Women Travellers later in this chapter). Jeans are OK but can get uncomfortably hot and don't dry easily after washing. Loose pants are generally more comfortable.

Note that in most places, especially in cities, local people dress smartly if they can afford to, so it might be worth taking a decent shirt and a pair of pants or a skirt that you can keep clean and wear when the occasion demands it. They will be useful when it comes to visa applications or other official encounters, or if you are invited to somebody's home. Also, a lot of hotel bars and nightclubs have some kind of loose dress code. Military-style clothing or baggage is definitely not a good idea, but cargo-style pants are fine (the ones with the zip-off legs are particularly handy).

Equipment Outside Turkey, there aren't many camping grounds on the route, so unless you are cycling or driving it's not worth lugging around a tent and camping gear. A sleeping bag is useful in the cooler months, particularly if you're planning on trekking in the Himalaya, but is really not necessary unless you're camping. Again, these can be hired very cheaply in Nepal. Bring some sort of sheet liner, though, to put something between you and the occasional dodgy hotel bed.

Other useful items include a basic medical kit, mosquito repellent, sun block, a torch (flashlight) and several passport-sized photos for visa applications or extensions (you can get these very cheaply along the way). A universal washbasin plug is a good idea, as are a few small padlocks to secure the contents of your pack from opportunistic riflers, a compact travel alarm clock, a Swiss Army-style knife, and a length of cord for hanging out clothes. Also consider bringing some earplugs for bus journeys and for hostels adjacent to the local mosque/bar/nightclub. A compass is incredibly handy for orientating yourself in cities and essential for trekking, and a walkman and some tapes will ease those long bus trips. Women should bring preferred tampons or pads – you can't always find what you want and, when you do, it will be pricey.

Outside big cities, tourist resorts and traveller haunts, English-language reading matter can be hard to come by so bring a book – one is usually enough since you should be able to keep swapping it at book exchanges or with other travellers along the way.

TOURIST OFFICES
Local Tourist Offices

All the countries in this book have tourist offices in major towns and cities, but they vary in usefulness. Sometimes they can be a wonderful source of local information and a place to have a cup of tea with enthusiastic English-speaking tourism officials. They may be able to arrange guides, book hotels or transport and give advice on local festivals. Other times the blank expression on the face of the person behind the empty desk tells you there's no point even asking directions.

In Turkey it's usually worth calling at one of the Ministry of Tourism offices (Turizm Bakanlığı) for their sometimes excellent town maps (free). You might well find hostels and backpacker guesthouses more clued up on local info, though.

With the exception of Esfahān, official tourist offices in Iran are a waste of time and thin on the ground anyway – the capital, Tehrān, doesn't even have one. Backpacker-oriented guesthouses are often the best source of information here.

The Pakistan Tourism Development Corporation (PTDC) is very active in promoting tourism within the country and some of the offices can be very helpful, particularly those in Lahore, Islamabad and Peshawar. There are no less than three offices in Islamabad.

In India, the Government of India Tourist Office in Delhi is useful and every town or city along the route has its representative state tourist office which can supply local and statewide brochures and information. For example, McLeod Ganj has an office of the Himachal Pradesh Tourism Development Corporation (HPTDC), Jaipur has an office of the Rajasthan Tourism Development Corporation (RTDC) and so on. These definitely vary in friendliness and usefulness, depending on who's behind the desk.

The Nepal Tourism Board in Kathmandu is worth a visit but tourist offices are generally not much use in Nepal. Trekking information is available from various sources (see the Nepal chapter for details).

Tourist Offices Abroad

Turkey has overseas tourist offices in many major international cities. These places usually have an incredible amount of information and are good for picking up thick glossy brochures that will give you a first glimpse of the countries you intend visiting. You may also be able to get free maps.

Iran has no offices abroad, although you may be able to pick up some leaflets from its embassies. Pakistan's PTDC doesn't maintain any official tourist offices overseas, but there are some travel agents that act as tourist offices, notably in Canada, Japan and Europe. You're better off searching the Internet for information on these places (see Internet Resources later in this chapter).

The Government of India Tourist Office has overseas offices in the UK, USA, Canada, Australia, Japan and several European countries. Again, these are a good place for glossy brochures and basic planning. The Nepal Tourism Board does not operate any offices abroad, but travel and trekking agencies can provide information.

VISAS & DOCUMENTS
Passport

Everyone needs a valid passport to travel – if you don't have one yet, apply immediately. Some countries require your passport to be valid for at least six months beyond the time you plan staying in their country, so get a new one if it's near the end of its lifespan. Make sure it has plenty of blank pages, too – at least two for every country you intend visiting (one for the visa, one for the entry and exit stamps).

Visas

Visas are annoying, expensive and time-consuming pieces of red tape, but you can't travel without them. A visa is a sticker or stamp placed in your passport allowing you to visit a particular country for a specified period of time. You can get them before you go, or try to get them at consulates along the way. Generally it's better to apply for the visa in your home country, but this may not always be practical. Getting a tourist visa for Iran is not easy at the best of times. Even if you do get one it's only valid for three months from the time of issue so there's no point applying too early. For Turkey and Nepal, visas are available at the border or airport without any hassle and Pakistan now issues 30-day 'landing permits' to tourists at any land border or airport. It pays to get your Indian and Pakistani visas before you leave home.

Some visas are free but most require forms, photos and cash. Some embassies ask for a confirmed travel itinerary or a return plane ticket. This may be impossible for an overland traveller to supply, but if you explain your travel plans in writing and give the dates you intend to enter and leave the country, there shouldn't be a problem. If you're applying abroad, some embassies request a letter of introduction from your embassy (eg, if you're an Australian applying for an Iranian visa in Delhi, the Iranian consulate requires a letter of introduction from the Australian embassy *in Delhi* – for which you will have to pay). Iran may not issue a transit visa unless you already have a visa for Pakistan in your passport – another reason to get this one early.

Turkey Nationals of the following countries (a partial list) can enter Turkey for up to three months with just a valid passport and no visa: Denmark, Finland, France, Germany, Japan, Malaysia, New Zealand, Norway, Sweden and Switzerland.

Nationals of Australia, Austria, Belgium, Canada, Holland, Ireland, Israel, Italy, the UK and the USA need a multiple-entry sticker visa that can be obtained at the border or airport. UK citizens pay UK£10 in cash, Australians US$20 and US citizens US$45. On arrival at the airport make sure you queue to pay this fee before joining the second queue for immigration.

Visa Extensions If you are staying in Turkey for more than three months you can apply for an *ikamet tezkeresi* (residence permit). Contact a tourist office or tourism police office.

It's probably easier to hop across the border into Greece for a day and get a new three-month visa on re-entry.

Iran Getting a visa for Iran is where things get tricky for the overland traveller. The different application of rules (which basically don't exist) makes definitive advice on this subject impossible. General tips are to apply well in advance of your departure, preferably in your home country, and don't give up if you're rejected.

Only visitors from Slovenia, Macedonia (ie, the Former Yugoslav Republic of...) and Turkey can get a three-month tourist visa on arrival. Everyone else needs a visa prior to arrival. If you plan to spend more than a week in Iran, it's best to apply for a tourist visa; in some countries, eg, UK, you'll almost certainly be rejected by applying independently for a transit visa. Check first with the embassy or consulate whether it's best to apply through an agent. Agents can charge hefty fees – anything from £45 to over £100 for those in the UK – but given sufficient time they can practically guarantee to get you the visa you require.

Among the most reliable, and cheapest, agents in the UK, highly recommended by travellers we met, is Travcour (☎ 020-7223 7662), Tempo House Falcon Rd, Battersea, London, SW11 2PJ, which charges £45 for arranging a visa. If you're on the road, they can arrange for you to pick up your visa from whichever mission you nominate. Similarly professional (though more costly) services are offered by Persian Voyages (☎ 01306-885894, e info@persianvoyages.com), 12D Rothes Rd, Dorking, Surrey, RH4 1JN, and Magic Carpet Travel (☎ 01344-622832), 1 Field House Close, Ascot, Berkshire, SL5 9LT. The latter's Web site is at www.magic-carpet-travel.com. Also consider contacting a travel agency in Iran (see the Tehrān section in the Iran chapter) to act as your sponsor.

Ask for as many days as you think you'll need, but remember that all visas are extendable in Iran and that it's much easier to get longer extensions on a tourist than a transit visa. If you're planning on passing quickly through Iran then a transit visa (also extendable) for a week to 10 days should be fine. Multiple entry visas are only issued to foreign workers and diplomats.

If you can't get a tourist visa in your home country, don't give up. Drop in at every Iranian mission on your way to Iran. In Turkey there are missions in Ankara, İstanbul and Erzurum. Word of mouth is that in İstanbul there's a 10% chance of your application being rejected. The Ankara embassy told us that they issue only transit visas to non-resident foreigners, but we met travellers who'd received tourist visas from them anyway. In Erzurum, transit visas are available (except for US citizens), and can be arranged in five days (possibly less), but again, we met travellers who had been given a tourist visa here.

When applying for a visa, you must complete two or three application forms (in English); provide up to four passport-sized photos – complete with the *hejāb* (head covering) for women; and pay a fee. This usually varies according to nationality; for example UK citizens pay £40 in London for a tourist visa, Australians A\$77/47 in Canberra for a tourist/transit visa. However, in İstanbul and Ankara, UK, US, Australian and Japanese citizens all pay US\$50, Germans US\$30 for a tourist visa, while transit visas are US\$30 across the board. If you're applying overseas you'll also be asked to provide a 'letter of introduction' from your embassy, which will also cost an extortionate amount.

Processing times for visas vary. In İstanbul it seems to take an average of 10 working days, while in Ankara, five working days or less is possible. In Delhi (if you're coming the other way) it takes two weeks for UK and US citizens, but only four days for Australians. At consulates in the UK and Australia expect the process to take at least two weeks. Handily, you don't need to leave your passport with a mission while your application is being processed – just take it in once the visa has been granted and you can usually pick it up the next day.

Some other important points: All visas are valid for only three months, ie, you must enter Iran within three months of the date of visa issue; every part of every day counts towards the length of your visa; and passport stamps issued on entry, and for visa extensions, often use the Islamic calendar, so make sure you know the expiry date in the Gregorian (Western) calendar.

If you have an Israeli stamp in your passport or any other evidence of a visit to Israel, you will be refused a visa and denied entry into the country.

Visa Extensions On a tourist visa you can get one or two extensions of up to two weeks each without too much hassle, but don't expect extensions totalling more than one month. For transit visas, you'll be lucky if you get more than six days at a go.

You should apply for an extension two or three days before the visa is due to expire, bearing in mind that on Thursday afternoon, Friday, and public holidays, nothing will get done. The best places to get extensions are Tabrīz, Esfahān, Kermān, Shīrāz and, if you're really stuck, Tehrān. The locations of the visa offices are provided in the relevant sections.

To get an extension you'll need to fill out a form from the visa office, and take the form to a nominated Bank Melli branch for the relevant stamp (10,000 rials, plus 2,500 rials for the administration). In Esfahān you can pay the fee directly at the visa office. They will also want one or two photocopies of your passport and original Iranian visa, and possibly two passport-sized photos. (Remember, women must be photographed in hejāb.) Once accepted, you can usually collect your passport (and, hopefully, visa extension) the next day.

Pakistan Just about everybody needs a visa to enter Pakistan although landing permits are available at the border (see below). With a single-entry tourist visa you can normally enter up to six months from the date of issue, and stay for up to three months from the date of entry. In the UK a single entry three-month visa costs £40, Australians pay A\$40 (A\$80 for an urgent visa, which takes only a few days) and US citizens pay US\$45. You can go almost anywhere except sensitive border areas, certain tribal areas and remote or high-elevation places where you'd need a trekking or mountaineering permit. Pakistan may refuse entry to nationals of Israel.

Late in 2000, Pakistan's ruling military decided tourism was a good thing for the country and relaxed border regulations. Tourists can now receive a 30-day landing permit at any land border (eg, Taftan or Wagah) or airport. Although we haven't been able to personally check the situation on the road (the rules changed after our research trip), our information is that the permit is free, so if you don't intend to stay longer than 30 days in Pakistan, this is the way to go. If you do intend to stay longer, however, it's better to get a visa in advance. The rules may well change suddenly, so check with a Pakistani embassy or consulate before you travel.

Places to apply for a Pakistani visa en route include Istanbul, Ankara, Tehrān and Zāhedān, where one can be issued within the hour. If you're coming the other way, Delhi is the best place to apply.

Visa Extensions Islamabad is officially the only place to extend a visa, although travellers have reported being able to do so at the passport offices in Lahore and Peshawar. If you're somewhere else with time running out, local police might provide a letter of authorisation giving you a few extra days to get to Islamabad or to the border. The Civil Secretariat in provincial capitals can do the same.

Foreigners' Registration If you intend to stay longer than 30 days in Pakistan you become a 'resident' (even if you have a three-month tourist visa), which means you must register at a Foreigners' Registration Office (FRO) before the 30 days is up. What follows is a complicated process of bureaucratic form-filling that will probably make you want to leave Pakistan on day 29.

First you must go with passport photos and photocopies of relevant passport pages to the FRO in the district where you're staying. Fill out the Certificate of Registration (Form B), which entitles you to a Residential Permit. If you go to a new district and stay more than a week you're expected to transfer your registration by reporting to the FRO there within 24 hours.

When you're ready to leave Pakistan, go to the FRO in the town where you're registered, surrender your Certificate of Registration and Residential Permit, and apply for a Travel Permit. This is a permit to get from that town to the specified border crossing, and is valid for seven days. As with anything like this, travellers have reported staying longer than 30 days, not registering, and leaving the country with no hassles. If you intend to stay longer than 30 days, check out the current situation.

Given the relaxed tourist entry regulations, this registration process may not apply – check when you arrive at the border.

India You must have a valid visa for India before you arrive at the border. Six-month multiple-entry visas (valid from the date of issue) are now issued to most nationals regardless of whether you intend staying that long or re-entering the country. Visas cost A$55 for Australians, UK£20 for Britons, US$50 for US citizens, and C$47 for Canadians. US passport holders may also apply for one-year and 10-year multiple-entry visas, the latter, at the time of writing, only available from Indian embassies in the USA, Japan and Hong Kong. A 12-month multiple-entry visa costs US$70, while a 10-year multiple-entry visa costs US$120.

Visa Extensions Extensions on six-month tourist visas are no longer available in India, so there's little point in visiting the local Foreigners' Registration Office. Even in dire emergencies authorities are instructed to direct you to Delhi where a two-week extension may be issued (US$40). You can get another six-month visa by leaving the country and applying for a new visa at the Indian consulate of a neighbouring country. However, some travellers have reported difficulty getting another visa in Nepal, even though the Indian embassy in Kathmandu claims to issue visas within seven days.

Nepal Visas for Nepal are easily available at land border crossings with India or at Tribhuvan airport in Kathmandu, so many travellers choose not to apply in advance. Single entry tourist visas are valid for 60 days and cost US$30. Single re-entry visas cost US$55, double re-entry visas cost US$70, while multiple-entry visas are US$90.

At the airport, and usually at border crossings, officials will insist on payment in US cash dollars; keep aside the correct amount. One passport photo is also required.

If you want to avoid queues at immigration (particularly at the airport) and get your visa in advance, bear in mind that it is only valid for three months from the date of issue. This is fine if you're starting the trip in Kathmandu, but not much good if it's your final destination. Outside your home country, visas can be obtained in Bangkok (Thailand), Islamabad (Pakistan), Delhi and Kolkata (formerly Calcutta, India).

Visa Extensions Tourist visas can be extended for 30 days at a cost of US$50, and one photo is required. The maximum stay period is 150 days in any calendar year. If a visitor has previously entered Nepal within the last 150 days, they can obtain a 30-day visa at a cost of US$50. Again this visa can be obtained from a Royal Nepalese Embassy abroad or upon arrival at the international airport.

Visas for Neighbouring Countries

There's a chance that you, as an independent, free-thinking traveller, will want to change course during this trip and enter a neighbouring country, or travel on to another country at the end of the trip. If so, you'll probably need to pick up more visas. Although we can't give detailed advice on how and where to obtain visas for every possible country, the following is a start:

Eastern Europe If you are travelling via Bulgaria or Romania, nationals of the USA are admitted without a visa for stays of less than 30 days; and European Union (EU) nationals are admitted to Bulgaria without a visa. Bulgarian transit visas cost a steep US$68 at the border. Visas are available at the border or airport or the respective consulates in your home country. Citizens of the US and EU don't need a visa to enter Hungary, but others do. Everyone needs a visa to travel through Yugoslavia.

Syria All foreigners entering Syria must obtain a visa in advance. The easiest and safest way to do this is to apply for the visa in your home country. At most embassies and consulates the visa takes from four days to two weeks to issue.

If you have an Israeli stamp in your passport or any other evidence of a visit to Israel, you will be refused a visa and denied entry into the country.

In Turkey, you can get Syrian visas in both Ankara and İstanbul without too much of a problem. Australians and Canadians pay nothing, New Zealanders pay US$6; UK nationals pay a whopping US$60. You'll also need a letter of recommendation

from your embassy, for which you may be charged. Visas in Turkey take one working day to issue.

Central Asia You will need a visa if you plan to visit any of the Central Asian countries – Turkmenistan, Uzbekistan, Kazakstan, Tajikistan or Kyrgyzstan – and you will need to get them in advance. It's possible to travel overland from Turkmenistan into Iran or vice versa (see the Getting There & Away chapter for details).

Visas for Georgia are available from the consulate in Trabzon in Turkey, located off the north side of the main square at Gazipaşa Caddesi 20. They're issued on the spot and cost US$20 for 15 days, US$25 for 30 days.

China If you want to divert into China from Pakistan via the Karakoram Highway, or if you want to visit Tibet after Nepal, you'll need a Chinese visa. These are fairly easy to get in your home country, but when filling out the visa form, *don't* include Tibet as part of your intended itinerary. The standard 30-day single entry visa costs around A$30 in Australia, UK£25 in the UK and US$30 in the USA. The visas are valid for three months from the date of issue and the 30 days begins when you enter the country.

It's possible to get a Chinese visa en route, but not at the border between Pakistan and China. The Chinese embassy in Islamabad is worth a try but it's extremely busy. It's virtually impossible to get a Chinese visa in Kathmandu because the Nepal-Tibet border at Kodari is theoretically closed to independent travellers. One option is to join a tour to Lhasa (see the Nepal chapter for more information). Another option is to apply for a Chinese visa elsewhere, eg, Delhi.

Afghanistan Afghanistan, still struggling with a bitter and protracted civil war, is not recommended for tourists. There is little infrastructure and the safety of independent travellers cannot be guaranteed. But it's not impossible to visit and a few curious souls do go in. At the time of writing, the border between Iran and Afghanistan remained closed to foreigners, because of Iran's refusal to recognise the ruling Taliban.

The best place en route to obtain a visa and enter Afghanistan is Peshawar in Pakistan – see the Pakistan chapter for details.

Bangladesh It's theoretically possible to get a visa at Dhaka's Zia International Airport if you're flying into Bangladesh, but it's much better to get one in advance. A three-month visa is usually valid for six months from the date of issue. You can either apply for this in your home country, or at the Bangladeshi embassy in Delhi (see the India chapter for the address). In Delhi, visas are normally issued without fuss on the same day.

Visa fees vary depending on your nationality: Americans and Australians pay US$21, Canadians US$37, and Britons a hefty £40. See the Getting There & Away chapter for overland routes into Bangladesh from India.

Travel Insurance

The importance of travel insurance – to protect you against loss or theft and to cover you for medical assistance – can't be stressed enough. Usually you can be covered for both under one policy, but work out what you need and then shop around. You may not want to insure that grotty old backpack, but it's worth covering camera gear, expensive hiking boots and other specialist equipment. Everyone should be covered for the worst possible scenario: An accident, for example, that will require expensive hospital treatment and an emergency flight home.

There is a wide variety of policies and your travel agent will have recommendations. The policies handled by STA or other student travel organisations are usually good value. Some policies offer options for lower and higher medical expenses but the higher one is chiefly for countries like the USA which have extremely high medical costs. Check the small print.

Some policies specifically exclude 'dangerous activities' which can include scuba diving, motorcycling, white-water rafting (grade 3 rapids or above), and even trekking. If such activities are on your agenda you don't want that sort of policy, or you may have to pay a slightly higher premium. You may prefer a policy that pays doctors or hospitals directly rather than requiring you to pay on the spot and claim later. If you have to claim later make sure you keep all documentation. Some policies ask you to call back (reverse charges) to a centre in your home country where an

immediate assessment of your problem is made. If you are planning a long trip, the insurance may seem very expensive but if you can't afford it, you won't be able to afford to deal with a medical emergency en route.

Check if the policy covers ambulances or an emergency flight home. If you have to stretch out you will need two seats and somebody has to pay for them!

You should make two copies of your policy, but keep one with you and the other at home in case the original is lost.

Finally, in recent years we have received reports from India of scams where travellers have been encouraged to collude with a doctor in making a false medical expenses claim. The doctor pays the traveller, then claims back a much higher amount from the insurance company. Obviously this is fraudulent and illegal for both parties, and it only pushes insurance premiums up for other travellers. Don't get sucked into any quick-money schemes. Even more disturbing is reports of travellers actually being mildly poisoned in order to get them into hospital for what then becomes a genuine expense claim. See Dangers & Annoyances later in this chapter for details.

Student Cards

An International Student Identity Card (ISIC) can be useful. Turkey has student discounts on flights and rail travel and reduced admissions at museums, archaeological sites and monuments of anything between 25% and 33% for card holders. Recently, however, some operators in Turkey were refusing to honour the ISIC card because of the number of fakes floating around.

In Iran, a 50% discount applies at some major tourist sites, which takes some of the sting out of the relatively high admission prices. Pakistan offers a 50% student discount to rail travellers, although predictably it's not as simple as showing up at the ticket counter with your card (see the Getting Around chapter).

You'll get virtually no mileage out of student cards in India and Nepal, although Indian Airlines offers a 25% discount to students on domestic airfares.

If you have a student card issued by your own university or college, or a letter of confirmation that you're enrolled there, take it along as a backup to the ISIC.

Driving Licence & Permits

An International Driving Permit (IDP) is easily and cheaply issued in your home country, usually by a major motoring organisation (the AA in Britain, the AAA in the US or the RAC in Australia). It's very useful when you're driving in countries where your own licence may not be recognised (you'll need it in Pakistan, India and Nepal) and has the added advantage of being written in several languages, with a photo and lots of stamps so it looks much more impressive when presented to car rental clerks or police.

If you plan to take your own car you will need a *carnet de passage* and third-party insurance or a 'green card' (see Car & Motorcycle in the Getting Around the Region chapter for more information).

Restricted Area Permits

In Pakistan you'll need a special permit to leave the main roads and enter Tribal Areas around Quetta (Baluchistan) and Peshawar (North-West Frontier Province). Assuming these are available, you can get them from the Civil Secretariat in those towns. You'll also need to hire an armed tribal escort to accompany you. The only time you'll probably need to use this is to visit the Khyber Pass. See the Peshawar and Quetta sections in the Pakistan chapter for details. Also in Pakistan, certain treks in the Northern Areas require a permit. You can only get these from the Ministry of Tourism in Islamabad.

Trekking permits are no longer required for the main ranges in Nepal (the Annapurnas and Everest) but you do need to pay a park entry fee. See the Nepal chapter for details.

Copies

All important documents (passport data page and visa pages, credit cards, travel insurance policy, air/bus/train tickets, driving licence, purchase slips and numbers of travellers cheques etc) should be photocopied before you leave home. Leave one copy with someone at home and keep another with you, separate from the originals.

EMBASSIES & CONSULATES
Foreign Embassies Abroad

The following is a list of the embassies or consulates of the countries en route, in your home country:

Australia
India
> *Embassy:* (☎ 02-6273 3999, fax 6273 3328) 3–5 Moonah Place, Yarralula, ACT 2600
> *Consulate:* (☎ 02-9223 9500) Level 27, 25 Bligh St, Sydney, NSW 2000

Iran
> *Embassy:* (☎ 02-6290 2421, fax 6290 2431) 25 Culgoa Crt, O'Malley, ACT 2606

Nepal
> (☎/fax 02-9328 7062) Level 1, 17 Castlereagh St, Sydney, NSW 2000

Pakistan
> *High Commission:* (☎ 02-6290 1676, fax 6290 1073) PO Box 684, Mawson, ACT 2607
> *Consulate:* (☎ 02-9299 3250) Level 10, 49 York St, Sydney, NSW 2000
> Web site: www.pakistan.org.au

Turkey
> *Embassy:* (☎ 02-6295 0227, fax 6239 6592) 60 Mugga Way, Red Hill, ACT 2603
> *Consulate:* (☎ 02-9328 1155, fax 9362 4533) 66 Ocean St, Woollahra, Sydney, NSW 2025

Canada
India
> *High Commission:* (☎ 613-744 3751, fax 744 0913) 10 Springfield Rd, Ottawa, Ontario K1M 1C9
> Web site: www.docuweb.ca/India

Iran
> *Embassy:* (☎ 613-235 4726, fax 232 5712) 245 Metcalfe St, Ottawa, Ontario K2P 2K2

Nepal
> (☎ 416-226 8722, fax 226 8878) 2 Sheppard Ave, East, Suite 1700, Toronto, Ontario M2N 5Y7

Pakistan
> (☎ 613-238 7881, fax 238 7296) 151 Slater St, Suite 608, Ottawa K1P 5H3

Turkey
> *Embassy:* (☎ 613-232 1577, fax 789 3442) 197 Wurtemburg St, Ottawa, Ontario KIN 8L9

France
India
> *Embassy:* (☎ 01 40 50 70 70, fax 01 40 50 09 96) 15 rue Alfred Dehodencq, 75016 Paris

Iran
> *Embassy:* (☎ 01 47 20 30 95, fax 40 70 01 57) 4 Ave d'Iena, 75016 Paris

Nepal
> (☎ 01 46 22 48 67, fax 01 42 27 08 65) 45 bis Rue des Acacias, 75017 Paris

Pakistan
> (☎ 01 45 62 23 32) 18 Rue Lord Byron, Paris 75008

Turkey
> (☎ 01 45 24 52 24) 16 Ave de Lamballe, 75016 Paris

Germany
India
Embassy: (☎ 228-54050, fax 540 5153)
Adenauerallee 262–264, 53113 Bonn 1 & 11
Embassy branch: (☎ 30-800178, fax 482
7034) Majakowskiring 55, 13156 Berlin
Iran
Embassy: (☎ 30-841 9180) Podbielskialle 67,
D-14195, Berlin
Consulate: (☎ 69-560 0070, fax 560 0071)
Guiollettstrasse 56, Frankfurt
Nepal
(☎ 228-343097, fax 856747) Im Hag 15,
53179 Bonn
Pakistan
(☎ 228-95530) Rheinalee 24, 53173 Bonn
Turkey
(☎ 228-34 60 52) Ute str 47, 5300 Bonn 2

Ireland
India
Embassy: (☎ 01-497 0483, fax 497 8074) 6
Leeson Park, Dublin 6
Iran
Embassy: (☎ 01-885 881, fax 834 246) 72
Mount Merrion Ave, Blackrock, Dublin
Pakistan
See the embassy in France listed earlier for
all consular services.
Turkey
(☎ 01-668 5240) 11 Clyde Rd, Ballsbridge,
Dublin 4

New Zealand
India
High Commission: (☎ 04-473 6390, fax 499
0665) 180 Molesworth St, Wellington
Iran
Embassy: (☎ 04-862 976, fax 863 065) 151
Te Anau Rd, Roseneath, Wellington
Turkey
(☎ 04-472 1290) 15–17 Murphy St, Level 8,
Wellington

UK
India
High Commission: (☎ 020-7836 8484, fax
836 4331) India House, Aldwych, London
WC2B 4NA
Web site: www.hcilondon.org
Consulate General: (☎ 021-212 2782, fax
212 2786) 20 Augusta St, Jewellery Quarters,
Hockley, Birmingham B18 6JL
Iran
(☎ 020-7937 5225, fax 7938 1615) 50
Kensington Court, London, W8 5DB
Nepal
(☎ 020-7229 1594, fax 7792 9861) 12A
Kensington Palace Gardens, London W8 4QU
Pakistan
(☎ 020-7664 9200, *recorded visa information*
☎ 0891-880880) 36 Lowndes Square,

London SW1X 9JN
Web site: http://212.106.96.110
Turkey
Embassy: (☎ 020-7393 0202) 43 Belgrave
Square, London SW1X 8PA

USA
India
Embassy: (☎ 202-939 7000, fax 939 7027)
2107 Massachusetts Ave NW, Washington,
DC 20008
Web site: www.indianembassy.org
Iran
The Iranian Interests Section is in the Em-
bassy of Pakistan (☎ 202-965 4990) 2209
Wisconsin Ave, NW, Washington, 20007
Nepal
Embassy: (☎ 202-667 4550, fax 667 5534)
2131 Leroy Place NW, Washington, DC
20008
Consulate: (☎ 415-434 1111, fax 434 3130)
Suite 400, 909 Montgomery St, San Francisco,
California 94133
Pakistan
Embassy: (☎ 202-939 6200, fax 387 0484)
2315 Massachusetts Ave NW, Washington,
DC 20008
Web site: www.pakistan-embassy.com
Turkey
(☎ 202-659 8200) 1714 Massachusetts Ave
NW, Washington, DC 20036

Embassies & Consulates on the Route

It's important to know what your own embassy abroad can and can't do. It won't bail
you out of trouble if you are at fault or have
broken the laws of the country you are in; it
won't lend you money if you run out; it will
not hold mail for you; and its newspapers
are more than likely to be out of date. In
genuine emergencies you should receive
some assistance but only if all other channels have been exhausted. For example, if
all of your documents and money stolen are
stolen your embassy will arrange a new
passport but a loan for an air ticket home is
out of the question.

However, in some cases it's worth registering with your embassy, which means simply going in and giving your name, passport
and address details and a rough travel itinerary. This can also be done over the phone
or by fax or email. Embassies in Islamabad
actively encourage this, particularly for travellers intending to go up to Peshawar and the
surrounding tribal areas, or those going
trekking in the Northern Areas. If you plan

on going trekking in Nepal you should consider registering with your embassy in Kathmandu. The same applies for travel in eastern Turkey and Iran. Remember to let the embassy know when you've safely returned and are ready to leave the country.

Some embassies also post useful warning notices about local dangers, unsafe areas or potential problems. The US embassies are particularly good (well, particularly paranoid) at providing this information. Check their notice boards. Of course, it's very difficult to get into a US embassy unless you hold a US passport.

Finally, if you plan on applying for visas en route, you'll have to visit the embassies or consulates of those countries. Always go early (most open for business around 9 am), make sure you have the necessary paperwork (eg, letters of introduction if required) and expect long queues and bureaucratic hassles. For the addresses and contact details of embassies and consulates in the countries of this book, see the relevant city sections.

CUSTOMS

There are no customs checks as such at the land borders (other than vehicle searches and occasional bag searches). Customs regulations vary between countries but in most cases they aren't much different from what you'd expect in the West – a couple of hundred cigarettes and a couple of bottles of booze (but no alcohol in Iran or Pakistan).

It's best to avoid bringing in any foreign magazines because there is bound to be a picture in one of them that will be seen to 'promote moral and ideological perversion'. Surprisingly, though, customs checks on Western tourists coming into Iran at the Turkey and Pakistan land borders range from lax to nonexistent.

Officials in Pakistan are very sharp eyed about pen guns and other disguised firearms, eg, those from Darra Adam Khel in the North-West Frontier Province. Foreigners have been busted and penalties are stiff.

Duty Free

In Turkey you can bring in up to 5L of liquor and 400 cigarettes. In Iran the limit is 200 cigarettes, 200 cigars or 200g of tobacco and a 'reasonable quantity' of perfume, but no alcohol.

There are no significant entry restrictions into Pakistan, and no apparent limits on carrying rupees in or out of the country.

If you are entering India from Nepal you are not entitled to import anything free of duty.

Declarations on Entry

In all countries along the route you may well need to declare items of exceptional value, eg, computers, expensive photographic gear and video cameras. In Turkey this information could be entered in your passport but elsewhere you are likely to receive a Disembarkation Card and possibly a Customs Declaration. Do not lose such documents as you will have to surrender them to immigration when you leave.

Declarations on Exit

There are definite restrictions on exporting antiquities in all countries on this route.

You may officially take out of Iran handicrafts up to the value of 150,000 rials (so keep a receipt handy); two Persian carpets or rugs; and 150g of gold and 3kg of silver (but no gemstones). If you exceed the stated values or quantities you need an export permit from the local customs office. Foreigners are normally given some leeway and are allowed to take home a reasonable amount of souvenirs but must not take out more than 200,000 rials in cash.

In Turkey anything more than 100 years old is barred from export; similarly in Pakistan you are not allowed to take antiquities out of the country. Despite the claims of vendors, any souvenir you purchase in India or Nepal is unlikely to be antique. If you are in any doubt when in Nepal your souvenirs should be cleared by, and a certificate obtained from, the Department of Archaeology (π 215358) in the National Archives building on Ram Shah Path, Kathmandu. These controls also apply to the export of precious and semiprecious stones.

MONEY
Currencies

Currencies in use in the countries on this route are the Turkish lira (TL), Iranian rial, Pakistani rupee (PKRs), Indian rupee (INRs) and Nepali rupee (NPRs). Exchange rates for each are given at the start of each chapter. In most cases you'll want to exchange some of your cash or travellers cheques into local currency as soon as you arrive, although US dollars cash can work wonders in most places.

When you first arrive in each country, take some time to become familiar with the new currency. With a wad of strange notes in hand it's very easy to hand over a Rs 100 note instead of a Rs 10. Also separate small bills from big ones and keep them aside for tips, bus fares etc. Large denomination notes can be very hard to change at small shops or museums, so try to use them in restaurants or hotels. Turkey suffers from out of control inflation and the lira is constantly being devalued (which is why we list all prices in that chapter in US dollars). On changing US$100, you'll walk away with about 600,000,000 lira! The likelihood of getting confused by large denomination notes is clearly there, and it won't always be an honest shopkeeper or taxi driver you hand the wrong money to.

Iran has a peculiar problem. The currency is called the rial and is usually written in this way, but in everyday situations most Iranians use the term *toman*, which is 10 rials. So when you're asking for or bargaining a price and the taxi driver says '6000', make sure you know whether he means rials or toman (which would be 60,000 rials). At times it seems as if Iranian taxi drivers use this point of confusion to dupe tourists.

Exchanging Money

Although most major international currencies, including Australian, Canadian and New Zealand dollars, can be changed at some major banks in cities throughout the region, the US dollar is without doubt the best cash to carry followed closely by pounds sterling. In Iran, particularly, and smaller towns in Pakistan, India and Nepal, you won't have any luck changing anything other than US dollars and UK pounds. At the very least, carry an emergency stash of about US$150 for visas and unexpected situations.

Check around when exchanging cash or travellers cheques as rates can vary quite a bit and some places charge an exchange fee or commission (or both) while others charge neither. Moneychangers and forex (foreign exchange) bureaus usually offer better deals than the banks and they are

invariably quicker with the paperwork. Anyone who has tried changing a travellers cheque at any branch of the State Bank of India will know to take a good book and a lot of patience in with them. Exchange offices at airports generally offer poor rates (although that's not the case in Istanbul). At land border crossings you'll encounter mobile (black market) moneychangers clutching wads of cash. You should exercise caution when dealing with these guys but usually they're as good a place as any to offload your excess local currency – for example, you can change your Iranian rials into Pakistani rupees at the border. It's best not to change a large amount of cash at the border since the rates are rarely as good as at the next sizeable town, but it's fine to change a small amount to tide you over. Remember to bargain up on their rates as they will always start low. Ask travellers coming in the other direction what the going rate is.

Throughout the region avoid accepting torn or particularly tatty notes as you will have difficulty disposing of them. This is especially true in India, where notes seem to remain in circulation until they have almost completely disintegrated – and somehow they all end up in your possession.

Exchange rates are given in the 'At a Glance' boxes at the beginning of each country chapter.

Cash & Travellers Cheques It's worth carrying a mix of cash and travellers cheques and, for that matter, a plastic card. Cash (US dollars or UK pounds) is quicker to deal with, can be exchanged almost anywhere and gets better rates, but it can't be replaced if you lose it. Travellers cheques are accepted in most banks in major towns and cities throughout the region (except Iran) and if they're lost or stolen you can get them replaced. When you buy your cheques, make sure you understand what to do when the worst happens. Most companies have a 24-hour international phone number, which you should contact as soon as you discover the cheques are missing, even if you're nowhere near a replacement office. Well-known brands such as American Express and Thomas Cook are the best: They're the most widely accepted, the easiest to replace and have offices in major cities throughout the region. Because of the US trade embargo, American Express cheques are useless in Iran.

In Iran, don't rely on travellers cheques at all. The only banks where you can reliably change them are Bank Melli branches in the major cities, but you may well have to wait an hour for the paperwork, the exchange rate will be far less than the 'street rate' and you may be charged up to 10% commission. The legal money exchange office on Kheyābūn-é Sepāh in Esfahān changes travellers cheques with no waiting, but at a significantly lower rate than for cash. Major branches of most banks will change US dollars cash (and often Deutschmarks and UK pounds), but at rates lower than on the street. Legal money exchange offices have better rates, very close to those of black market traders, who only accept US dollars. See the Black Market section below for more information. Top-end hotels will change money at the bank rate, while some mid-range hotels, and a few budget places, will change money at the 'street rate', if you ask discreetly.

It can be a hassle getting travellers cheques exchanged at banks in Pakistan (outside the major cities), but private moneychangers usually take them and offer rates as good as the banks. In India and Nepal you won't have trouble changing cheques in major towns, but make sure you have enough local currency if you head out trekking or into small villages.

It's worth carrying a mix of high and low denomination notes and cheques so if you're about to leave a country you can change just enough for a few days and not have loads of spare currency to get rid of. The high denomination cheques are useful if you find yourself having to pay commission per cheque.

ATMs Automatic Teller Machines (ATMs) are extremely handy. They dispense cash at market rates 24 hours a day, but you can only use the ones that are linked to international networks (eg, MasterCard/Cirrus, Visa/Plus or GlobalAccess systems) and you'll find these in Turkey, Pakistan and major cities in India and Nepal, but not in Iran.

In Turkey, it's more or less possible to travel around exclusively on your plastic card. Most of the larger banks now have ATMs linked to one of the international networks. So if your home bank card is linked to Cirrus or Plus or GlobalAccess (and most cards these days are), all you need to know is your PIN number to withdraw money (in local currency) straight from your home bank account while on the road. You can also make withdrawals on your credit card (Visa or MasterCard) via most ATMs, but these cash advances are subject to immediate (and high) interest. Even using your debit card will attract banking charges that can be extremely high (the Commonwealth Bank in Australia charges A$4 per withdrawal and Lloyds Bank charges a similarly outrageous £1.50). For this reason it's better to make one or two large withdrawals rather than lots of small ones. You could also shop around among your home banks and if you find one with low withdrawal charges, open up a separate travelling account.

Since some banks are linked to either Visa/Plus or MasterCard/Cirrus, but not both, you can cover all bases by carrying two cards.

There are no ATMs accepting foreign-issued cards in Iran. In Pakistan, the unassuming Muslim Commercial Bank (MCB) has branches with ATMs accepting Cirrus/Maestro (but not Visa/Plus) in Quetta, Multan, Lahore, Islamabad, Rawalpindi and Peshawar. Citibank in Lahore also has ATMs accepting most international cards.

In India (on this route), Delhi is the main place for ATMs, which can be found at the large Standard Chartered Grindlays Bank (SCB Grindlays; formerly ANZ Grindlays) and Citibank branches, but you'll also find ATMs in Chandigarh, Amritsar and Jaipur (banks in the latter two accept only Master-Card/Cirrus).

Recently, Nepal Grindlays Bank opened several ATMs that accept foreign cards, see the Nepal chapter for details.

Credit Cards Credit cards are fairly widely accepted in the region (Visa and Master-Card being the most popular), although in some places their use is restricted to top-end hotels. In major cities you can use them to book plane tickets, hire cars, buy carpets or other pricey souvenirs and pay for meals at many mid-range restaurants.

In Iran some mid-range hotels, all top-end hotels, major souvenir shops, larger travel agencies and some airline offices accept Visa and/or MasterCard – but not AmEx. However, if your Visa or Master-Card has been issued in the USA, it may not be accepted because of the US trade embargo. Before you use a credit card, find out which exchange rate the bank(s) will use – you may be far better off paying in cash. You can also use Visa or MasterCard for cash advances (in rials) at the central branches of Bank Melli at most major cities. However, banks usually charge up to 5% commission, you may have to wait an hour or two for authorisation, and the exchange rate will be unfavourable compared to the 'street rate'.

You can get cash advances over the counter using your credit card at banks throughout Turkey. Visa cash advances are possible at SC Grindlays branches in Pakistan (Quetta, Lahore, Rawalpindi and Peshawar), India (Amritsar, Shimla, Delhi) and Nepal Grindlays Bank (Pokhara, Kathmandu) but the commission charges are invariably high (around 5% with a minimum charge). The Bank of Baroda in India gives cash advances on MasterCard and usually Visa card, and is the place to go in Dharamsala, Shimla, Varanasi and most cities in Rajasthan.

International Transfers Bank-to-bank transfers are possible, but unless your home bank has links with a banking group in the country you're travelling in it is a very complicated, time-consuming and expensive business, especially when you get outside the major capitals. Unless you are going to be in one place for at least a couple of weeks don't attempt it. A cash advance on a credit card is much simpler.

Alternatively, you could use a transfer company such as Western Union (www .westernunion.com), which has agents spread throughout the region (except in Iran). Through them you can have money (usually limited to about US$200) wired from your home bank account, or have someone send money to you find via Western Union, within a few minutes – for a fee, of course.

Black Market Iran and parts of Pakistan and Nepal are the only places you'll find a true black market, where the difference between the rates set by the banks and by the open market is significant.

In Iran the difference between government exchange rates and street rates is so great that the only sensible option is to use the black market, or at least the licensed moneychangers who offer similar rates. In Pakistan you'll get slightly better rates on the street in Quetta and Peshawar than you will at any bank. In Kathmandu there are street moneychangers lurking in Thamel but what they offer is not much greater than the banks. Cash is obviously the most welcome object of illicit exchange, and the US dollar is the preferred currency. Treat the black market like any other transaction and bargain.

It's not hard to find people with whom to change money. If you want to change and have not been approached, jewellery stalls or carpet shops in the bazaars are a good place to start. Be aware that changing money in this way is illegal and you must exercise caution. Double-check the rates with the dealer and count your money carefully before leaving the transaction.

Security

The safest place to carry your money is next to your skin, under your clothing. A money belt or pouch, or an extra pocket inside your jeans, will help to keep things with their rightful owner.

Always wear your moneybelt. Don't leave it in your daypack because it's uncomfortable, or leave it in a dorm room when you go for a shower. It should contain everything of value on this trip (passport, travellers cheques etc), so look after it.

Remember that if you lose cash you have lost it forever, so don't go overboard on the convenience of cash versus the safety of cheques. It's a good idea to keep a small, totally separate emergency stash of cash – say US$50 to US$100, to tide you over if everything else disappears. Some travellers hide this in (or even sew it into the lining of) their main pack, which, being full of smelly old clothes, is usually the last thing to get stolen.

Costs

Costs will vary slightly from country to country as you progress along this route. In Turkey things will seem very cheap if

Dual Pricing

An unfortunate but unavoidable aspect of travelling in Iran and India is the dual-pricing policy for foreigners.

In Iran this mainly applies to visiting tourist sights and museums and staying at some hotels (though not all). If you have a student card you may be able to get some discount on entrance prices, but otherwise resign yourself to typically paying 10 times the price paid by an Iranian. Such relatively high entrance fees can be particularly galling at mosques (where you'd think entrance should be free) and means that if you're on a limited budget, you must be especially choosy as to what you see.

The upshot of this is that a few unscrupulous Iranians think nothing of jacking prices for their services or goods to foreigners, too. So expect sometimes to be slugged by inflated bills in restaurants, shops and – most typically – taxis.

The recent decision by the Indian government to increase the foreigners' entry fee to all heritage-listed monuments to US$10 and many lesser monuments to US$5 seems to be a serious case of shooting itself in the foot, at least as far as budget travellers are concerned. This rise has, in some cases (such as Fatehpur Sikri) increased the admission fee almost 100-fold. On this route the area mainly affected is Agra, with a visit to the Taj Mahal, Agra Fort and Fatehpur Sikri costing over US$40!

Top-end hotels throughout the region and airlines on the subcontinent will quote prices in US$, and in Iran payment in US$ is often expected. This can work in your favour, depending on the exchange rate being offered. But most of the time it's just another ploy for getting more money from foreigners. In hotels, the best thing to do is ask to see a room first and if you don't think it worth the price and the management is not prepared to bargain, go elsewhere.

Dual pricing occurs to a lesser extent in Pakistan – where several museums charge foreigners five to 10 times the local price – and in Nepal, most notably in museums in the Kathmandu Valley.

you've just come from Europe, but they get much cheaper as you head east.

You could expect to get by on about US$15 a day in Turkey, but not if you like a few beers in the evening or a room to yourself. Transport costs on the deluxe buses are about US$2 for each hour of travel. In Iran, food and transport are dirt cheap (a one-hour flight costs only US$12, and the equivalent distance by bus – say eight hours – is around US$2) and budget accommodation is inexpensive, but tourist site admissions – including mosques – are a real killer. Changing money at the street rate, you can easily get by on US$15 a day or less.

In Pakistan and India, getting by on US$10 a day isn't hard. You can get a room with private bathroom and free cockroaches for as little as US$2 (even less with shared bathroom), a street snack for US$0.50 and a 14-hour bus ride for US$5! However, there's plenty of good shopping to be done in India, and taking the occasional luxury option, such as a comfortable bed, fancy meal or air-con sleeper train won't go astray. Nepal is also very cheap, although it's hard to resist the bars and restaurants of Pokhara and Kathmandu, which can push your budget up. If you're trekking (without a porter or guide) and subsisting on basic Nepali food along the way, count on spending as little as US$5 a day. In Kathmandu it will probably be closer to US$15 or more. See the 'Comparative Costs' table for details.

Tipping

Tipping in this region is more than just a reward for having rendered a service. Salaries and wages are much lower than in Western countries, so tipping is regarded as an often essential means of supplementing income. To a cleaner in a cheap hotel who might earn the equivalent of US$50 per month (much less in India and Nepal), the accumulated daily tips given by guests can constitute the mainstay of his or her salary.

In Pakistan, India and Nepal, the concept of baksheesh is slightly different. It can mean anything from simply tipping for a service rendered or giving alms to beggars, to ensuring that a little miracle actually gets performed. For example, Rs 20 offered to a porter at a crowded Indian railway station *before* you attempt to board the train could mean the difference between you getting a

Comparative Costs

The following table is approximate, as costs can vary within a country (eg, accommodation in cities is more expensive than in villages) but it will give you an idea of what things will cost and what the comparative costs are between countries. For that reason, prices are given in US dollars.

	Turkey	Iran	Pakistan	India	Nepal
hostel dorm/cheap hotel	5	2–4	2–3	1–3	1–3
mid-range hotel (double)	15	15	12	10–12	15–20
street food snack	1	0.50	0.30–0.50	0.30–0.50	0.80
a beer in restaurant/bar	1.25	n/a	2–3	1.50–3	1.50
Big Mac	2.50	n/a	2	2	n/a
mid-range restaurant meal	4–5	6	3–4	3	4
packet of local cigarettes	1.25	1	0.50	0.50	0.75
two-hour bus ride	4	0.50	1	1	0.80
200km train ride (sleeper)	n/a	1.50	2	2.50	n/a
museum entrance*	3	2	0.20–1	0.11–3.20	0.20–3
36-exposure film (100ASA)	3.50	2	2.50	2	1.50

* Note that the Taj Mahal in India costs around US$21 and the Durbar Squares of Patan and Bhaktapur in Kathmandu cost US$3 to enter, but these are exceptions. Many museums throughout the region are free.

seat in an economy carriage or standing up all the way. Baksheesh can also be seen as a bribe for getting out of difficult situations, but this should be used judiciously and only as a last resort.

For Western travellers who are not used to continually tipping, demands for baksheesh for doing anything from opening doors to pointing out the obvious in museums can be quite irritating. Generally, if someone provides a service, payment will be expected. If you don't want a guide in a museum or at an archaeological site, firmly say so. If you do, establish a price. Some people make their living from giving unsolicited service to tourists. Don't be intimidated into paying when you don't think the service warrants it, but remember that more things warrant tips here than anywhere in the West. At the same time, don't assume that all attempts to help you come with a price tag. In Iran and Pakistan in particular, people will often want to help you out of hospitality or to practice their English.

One important tip to remember is to carry lots of small change, but keep it separate from bigger bills, so that you can offer a reasonable tip without having to ask for change or showing off how much money you have.

Tipping too much only leads people to demand bigger tips from future travellers.

Bargaining

Throughout the Middle East and subcontinent you'll be expected to bargain for all sorts of goods and services. This not only applies in markets and bazaars, but also for private transport such as rickshaws, anything sold by street vendors, and even for accommodation. Remember, though, that not every vendor is starting at an outrageous price and not every transaction is subject to a discount just because you're a hard-up backpacker. Avoid the temptation to go around thinking you're constantly being ripped off or overcharged. See the boxed text 'The Fine Art of Bargaining' for more information.

Taxes & Refunds

A value-added tax of 15% to 20% is included in the price of most items and services in Turkey: It's known as *KDV dahil* (VAT included). A few hotels and shops give discounts if you agree not to request an official receipt; this way they don't have to pay the tax and you save. It's illegal but not unusual.

The Fine Art of Bargaining

Bargaining – or haggling – is the name of the game when shopping in the Middle East and subcontinent (remember Monty Python's *Life of Brian*?). It's not so much a matter of beating poor vendors down to a pittance for your souvenirs, but a game played out between buyer and seller.

Visitors from the West often feel uncomfortable with this idea since they are used to things having a fixed value, but here commodities are often worth whatever their seller can get for them. It can get annoying having to bargain for everything from a rickshaw ride to a piece of fruit, but you'll soon get used to it and, while tourists may face a higher starting price, remember that locals do this as well. At the same time, many vendors won't jack their prices up for things like fresh produce, so don't automatically assume you have to get everything cheaper than the initial price.

Generally, in markets and bazaars throughout the region, goods don't have fixed prices. You will be invited to offer a price or (and this is easier), you can ask a vendor how much he or she wants for it. The starting price will usually be twice – but sometimes up to four times – what the vendor is willing to accept. And so the game begins. Your aim is to establish the price below which the vendor will not sell, so start at about half what you're willing to pay and work up. You good-naturedly remark that it's too expensive and counter with a lower offer. The vendor appears hurt and comes back with a counter offer. You go to walk away but are summoned back. Eventually you will hopefully reach a mutually agreeable price.

There are three rules to remember with market bargaining. Firstly, be fair. As much as you want to get a good price, the five or 10 rupees you're trying to get it down is nothing to you, but it may be a lot to a struggling trader. Number two, don't get angry or aggressive. Bargaining is supposed to be a friendly and spirited exchange, not a battle to the death. If you don't like the price, don't buy it. Finally, if you make an offer, you should go through with the deal when the vendor meets your price.

Of course, Western tourists are often seen as having more money than sense, and it can be very difficult to bargain down to local prices these days, especially in India and Nepal. It helps enormously to know roughly what the local price is (otherwise you won't even know you've been ripped off). After a few days in a country you'll get a feeling for the prices of everyday items like fruits and vegetables. For handicrafts you could try browsing in fixed-price shops such as government emporiums (although bazaars are usually cheaper). Finally, asking local people who have no vested interest should give you a good idea of local prices.

Another sure-fire advantage is to know the local phrase for 'How much?' and to be able to count to at least 100 in the local language. This takes a bit of work, particularly over five countries, but you'll be surprised how much you pick up in just a few days if you keep trying to use it. Even just learning 'How much?' (*kach lira?* in Turkish; *chande?* in Fārsī; *kitna?* in Hindi and Urdu, and *kati?* in Nepali) is a good start, as a pen and paper or calculator can be used to show the price.

If you buy an expensive item (eg, a carpet or some leather apparel) that you want to export, ask the shopkeeper for a *KDV iade özel fatura* (special VAT refund receipt). Get the receipt stamped as you clear customs, then get your refund at a bank branch in the airport departure lounge (which is usually not open); or you can mail the receipt and be sent a cheque (be patient...and ever-hopeful).

In Pakistan there's a 12.5% service charge at most restaurants and hotels. Top-end hotels charge an additional 8% bed tax and possibly a 5% service charge. Cheap hotels and cafes usually won't charge this, or may simply build it into the price.

In India you might find mysterious taxes added to hotel or restaurant bills. Hotels sometimes use a 'tax' to add to your bill the commission they have paid an autorickshaw driver. Cheap hotels, guesthouses and restaurants tend not to bother with taxes. If you stay in India longer than 120 days you're supposed to have a tax clearance certificate to leave the country. To get it you have to go to the Income Tax Department in Delhi, Kolkata (Calcutta), Chennai or Mumbai with your passport and a handful or foreign exchange receipts (to prove you've been exchanging your foreign currency into rupees officially), fill out a form and wait. We've never heard of anyone who has actually been asked for this document on departure.

In Nepal most hotels above the budget range charge a 10% to 12% tax, plus a 2% Tourism Service Charge.

POST & COMMUNICATIONS

Post and telephone services are quite reliable throughout the region, though in rural areas (such as in Nepal) the service can range from slow to nonexistent – it pays to make your calls or send your mail from the main centres.

Receiving Mail on the Road

If you need to receive mail on the road, you can use the poste restante service. This is where letters are sent to a post office and held for you to collect. Although post offices in small towns may offer this service, it's always wise to stick to main post offices in the capital or major towns or cities. Letters should be addressed in the following form:

SMITH, Jane
Poste Restante
General Post Office
Kathmandu
Nepal

Your surname should come first in capital letters. For letters to Turkey, substitute 'Merkez Postane' for 'General Post Office'.

To collect your mail, go to the main post office in that town and show your passport. Sometimes letters will be filed under your first name rather than your last, so check there if you can't find it. Other places have no filing system and you'll simply have to sort through a great pile of letters yourself. Mail sometimes take a few weeks to work through the system, so have it sent to a place where you're going to be for a while, or have it sent well in advance. Some post offices will only hold mail for one month (who

knows where it goes after that), others will hold it from two to six months. Note that post restante office hours are often shorter than the hours of the post office itself – it's best to go in early for collection.

In Iran the most reliable poste restante services are at the post office at Meidūn-é Emām Khomeinī (Tehrān) and at the main post offices in Shīrāz and Esfahān. Poste restante mail is normally held indefinitely, despite requests for it to be forwarded. There is a nominal collection fee and you need to take your passport.

In Pakistan, most cities along the route offer post restante (except Multan). The same applies in India – New Delhi and Varanasi are reliable places. Kathmandu and Pokhara are the best places to have mail sent in Nepal.

Sending Mail

The safest way to send mail is to go to the post office yourself and have the letter, postcard or parcel franked (cancelled) in front of you, rather than buying stamps and posting letters in post boxes. This is especially true in Pakistan, India and Nepal and it's partly to ensure your stamps aren't stolen and the letters thrown away. Another reason is that many post boxes are for local mail only. Post offices can be busy places, though, so take plenty of patience and ask around to ensure that you're queuing at the correct counter.

Turkey Turkish post offices were once called PTT (Posta, Telefon, Telegraf). This has been changed to Posta Telegraf (PT) as the telephone system has now been privatised, but few of the old black-on-yellow signs have changed.

Letters sent from major cities take about a week to reach most parts of Europe, and anything between a week and two weeks to reach North America or Australasia. Stamps are best purchased at the main post offices, which are also the best places to send your mail from – don't trust post boxes. Alternatively, postal boxes at the five-star hotels are emptied at least once a day.

If you have urgent/important mail then the post office offers APS (*acele posta servisi*), an express courier-type service, and *kayıtlı* (registered mail). Alternatively, DHL and/or Federal Express have offices in major cities.

Iran The Iranian international postal service is generally reliable and reasonably swift; the domestic service is reliable but slow. Some of the Iranian stamps are very colourful – worth collecting as well as putting on your postcards.

Sending parcels is a major exercise in form shuffling. Take your unwrapped package to the daftar-é amānāt-é postī (parcel post counter) at the postkhūné-yé markazī (head post office) in any provincial capital. The package will be checked, wrapped and signed for in triplicate. Major post offices offer an express mail and parcel service.

Pakistan International service is adequate for letters and parcels from big towns and cities, but they can take a week or more just to exit the country from remote places.

Except for printed matter, outgoing parcels must be sewn into cloth bags; a tailor in the bazaar can make quick work of it. It will need a customs declaration and postal inspection, so leave it open and finish the job yourself.

Avoid posting out any purchase with a declared value of over PKRs 500, as you'll need an export permit, which can be a headache to get. Registration costs a few rupees extra, but it is a good idea for letters and parcels.

India Indian postal and poste restante services are generally excellent. Expected letters are almost always there and letters you send almost invariably reach their destination, although they may take up to three weeks. If you use the more expensive EMS Speedpost service, available at all large post offices, airmail parcels generally take only four days to anywhere in the world.

If sending parcels, you have to have them sewn up in white cloth. Often there will be a tailor or parcel-stitching wallah outside the post office to do this for you – if not, postal staff should be able to direct you to one. Negotiate a price in advance, but it should-n't cost more than INRs 40. Back at the post office, be sure to state that the value of the parcel is under INRs 1000 (to avoid the need for a bank clearance certificate) and, if asked, specify that the contents are a gift.

Books or printed matter can go by book-post (maximum 5kg), which is considerably cheaper than parcel post and the contents don't have to be sewn up. These parcels must be sent by 'open packet' mode, meaning they must be able to be easily opened and inspected. The packaging technique is best left to the professionals either at the post office or through one of the major bookshops.

Be cautious with places that offer to mail things to your home address after you have bought them. Government emporiums are usually OK. In most other places it pays to do the posting yourself.

Nepal The postal service to and from Nepal is erratic and can be extremely slow, but just to surprise you, things can also be amazingly efficient. Most articles do finally arrive, but they can take weeks.

The contents of parcels must be inspected by officials before it is wrapped so do not take it to the post office already wrapped. There are packers at the Kathmandu foreign post office who will package it for a small fee.

Telephone

You can make direct international calls from public phones on the new cardphone systems that are slowly being introduced, but these phones can be hard to find. In Turkey you'll nearly always find a bank of them at telephone or post offices, which is where you can also buy your phonecards (*telekarts*).

In Pakistan, India and Nepal there's usually a government-run telephone office in cities and larger towns (often called the Central Telegraph Office or similar). From here you can make local, STD and international calls at fixed rates that may or may not be cheaper than private offices. Making international calls from these countries is very expensive, even by Western standards. Some telephone offices have direct dial, while in others you'll have to give the number to an operator who will dial it and put it through to your phone.

Private phone offices are much more widespread and thus a lot more convenient. They're also easier to use and, if you shop around, you should be able to get reasonable rates. In Pakistan these offices are usually marked 'PCO' (Public Call Office), in India and Nepal they're marked 'STD/ISD'. These days they often have fax, photocopy and Internet facilities as well. Most places have private booths that you can go into and an electronic display that ticks over, telling you how many rupees the call is costing.

You can dial abroad from some hotel phones (rarely direct dial), but these calls cost a fortune.

Taking along an international phonecard is an option, although the concept of making a toll free call from private phone office will not be understood and you'll probably still end up paying for it.

Turkey You pay for a call on Türk Telekom's network with a telekart debit card, a credit card or, in a few older phones, a *jeton* (token). Telephone debit cards are sold in shops and kiosks near public phones.

Rates for local and intercity domestic calls are moderate, but international calls can be quite expensive. If you make an international call from a Türk Telekom telephone centre, be sure to get a receipt. Fiddling the bills is common as you see no meter and can't tell what a call will cost.

Iran Making telephone calls in Iran, including international calls, is fairly easy. In Tehrān, you can buy a *kard telefon*, but very few telephones accept these cards. Most public telephone boxes are only good for local calls. They only accept 5 or 10 rial coins, but because these are almost impossible to find, locals usually use private telephones in shops. Local calls are so cheap that your hotel will probably let you make a few for nothing. Airports and major bus stations usually have at least one free public telephone.

International calls can be made at a *markazī-é telefon* or *edāre-yé koll-yém okhābarāt* (telephone office), or from a smaller, private telephone office, in any town – but it's far easier from major cities. Long-distance calls can also be made from most hotels for an additional fee. International calls are charged a minimum period of three minutes, plus each subsequent minute (or part thereof).

Pakistan Pakistan has two kinds of telephone cards. One sort you can insert into a public phone, but finding one of these phones might not be easy, especially outside Lahore and Islamabad, and they're really only good for local calls. The other type allows you to call a toll-free or local number, dial in the

number on the card and then make your call using the credit on the card. Again you'll have to find a public or private phone that will allow you to do this. The cards are available from general stores in the main cities.

Telephone offices (PCOs) are more convenient, but are not cheap for international calls.

India & Nepal Government-run telegraph offices (usually close to or attached to the main post office) and private STD/ISD offices are the best places for making long distance calls in India and Nepal. In India the charge is worked out by a pulse rate, and calls are cheaper after 11 pm.

The latest hi-tech fad to hit is Internet calling, but at the time of writing this was only available to the US. Several call offices in Kathmandu have this facility where you can make a long distance call via the Internet using dialpad.

eKno Communication Service

Lonely Planet's eKno global communication service provides low-cost international calls – for local calls you're usually better off with a local phonecard. The service has just become available in Turkey. eKno also offers free messaging services, email, travel information and an online travel vault, where you can securely store all your important documents. These services can be used anywhere on the route where you can access the Internet. You can join online at www.ekno.lonelyplanet.com, where you will find the local-access numbers for the 24-hour customer-service centre. Once you have joined, always check the eKno Web site for the latest access numbers for each country and updates on new features.

Fax

Faxes can be sent from telephone offices and Internet cafes and sometimes from businesses such as travel agents or hotels. A single page usually works out to cost roughly the same as a three minute phone call, ie, it's expensive.

Email & Internet Access

The Netsurfing bug has bitten almost everywhere, with the exception of Iran, where the Internet exists but public online facilities are relatively scarce, expensive and, unsurprisingly, frowned upon by the authorities. Everywhere else along the route you'll find plenty of busy Internet cafes (or Internet clubs as they're often called in India and Pakistan) – enough to allow you to check your email virtually every day if you really need to. A growing number of hostels, hotels and pensions are also getting in on the act and starting to provide online terminals for their guests' use.

The easiest way to keep in touch by email on the road is to open up a free Internet-based account before you go. There are plenty around and all you need to do is go to their site and follow instructions for registering. Hotmail (www.hotmail.com) is plagued by junk mail these days, but try Lonely Planet's eKno (www.ekno.lonelyplanet.com), Yahoo! (www.yahoo.com), Excite (www.excite.com) or one of countless others. If you have an ISP and email account at home, you can access it via these Internet based account using your POP or IMAP address and password. Another option is to use www.mailstart.com, which can access your home account – just type in your user name and the password you use to log on to your ISP, and it loads up your new messages.

Internet Cafes Internet cafes, Cyber cafes, Internet clubs, or just plain public libraries – the Internet has become so commonplace that you'll find yourself accessing the Net in a variety of settings. Sometimes it's a single terminal in a hostel, phone office or tourist office, other times (usually where travellers congregate) there are banks of machines humming away to the incessant clicking of keyboards.

Online costs vary, even within countries, so unless you have urgent messages to send it's worth saving up your email time for the cheapest places. For example, you'll find eastern Turkey is cheaper than western Turkey; Kathmandu is much cheaper than elsewhere in Nepal; Delhi has the cheapest Internet access in the region (less than US$0.50 an hour); and Islamabad, Rawalpindi and Peshawar are all cheaper than Lahore in Pakistan (around US$0.70 an hour). Of course, connection times, modem speeds and reliability also vary.

You'll be able to find Internet access easily at the following places en route (see the Information sections for the relevant towns and cities in the country chapters for locations):

India Amritsar, McLeod Ganj, Shimla, Chandigarh, Delhi (cheapest in Paharganj), Agra, Jaipur, Pushkar, Udaipur, Jodhpur, Jaisalmer, Varanasi. Online time varies from INRs 20 an hour in Delhi to INRs 80 an hour (US$0.50 to US$2).

Iran Esfahān, Kermān, Tehrān, Yazd. Online time costs around 25,000 rials (US$3.50).

Nepal Pokhara, Sauhara, Kathmandu. Online time is around NPRs 3 per minute in Kathmandu, NPRs 7 per minute in Pokhara (US$2.50/US$5.50 per hour).

Pakistan Bahawalpur, Islamabad, Lahore, Multan, Peshawar, Quetta, Rawalpindi. Online time costs from PKRs 30 to PKRs 60 an hour (US$0.75 to US$1.50).

Turkey Ankara, Antalya, Ayvalık, Çanakkale, Bodrum, Bursa, Doğubayazıt, Eğirdir, Fethiye, Göreme, İstanbul, İzmir, Kayseri, Kaş Konya, Köyceğiz, Kuşadası, Malatya, Marmaris, Şanlıurfa, Selçuk, Van. Online time is generally charged per minute, with rates around US$1.80 per hour (US$1 in eastern Turkey).

INTERNET RESOURCES

The World Wide Web is a rich source for travellers. You can research your trip, hunt down bargain air fares, book hotels or chat with locals and other travellers about the best places to visit (or avoid). Some Web sites that may be of interest to travellers to the region are listed below.

The Lonely Planet Web site (www.lonely planet.com) is a good place to start looking. Here you'll find succinct summaries on travelling to most places on earth, postcards from other travellers and the Thorn Tree bulletin board, where you can ask questions before you go or dispense advice when you get back. You can also find travel news as well as Upgrades (containing regular postings of all the latest travel information) on all the countries covered in this book. There's also the subWWWay section which has links to the most useful travel resources elsewhere on the Web.

A list of useful sites follows.

General

www.1001sites.com This link site is organised by country and by topic. It's strong on arts and culture, plus plenty of travel; best link: 'Islamic City in Cyberspace'.

www.bootsnall.com This is a handy site for independent travellers, full of travel tales, advice, and general information-sharing.

www.go-overland.com This site is dedicated to overland travel; it is mainly intended for those travelling in a vehicle (independently or with a tour), but a lot of the information is relevant for any overlanders.

www.travel-finder.com This is a good site for digging up all sorts of travel-related Web resources. You can search by category or country.

www.world66.com/asia This is a good site for looking up world travel and background country information.

Turkey

www.mfa.gov.tr This lists all the embassies in Turkey and has some interesting cultural information as well.

www.turkey.org This official Turkish government site has visa, passport, consular and economic information, email addresses of Turkish diplomatic missions, and useful links to other sites related to Turkey.

www.turkishdailynews.com This *Turkish Daily News* Web site has current information, weather and, in the classifieds section, ads for rental apartments and jobs as English teachers and translators etc.

Iran

www.iranmania.com This is an excellent search-engine for topics ranging from Iranian history to its arts and architecture.

www.IranVision.com The Iran Culture & Information Centre (Canada) has excellent informantion on Iranian history and culture plus many links to other sites.

www.neda.net This well-organised site from Iran has a useful travel section and access to a comprehensive weekly press digest, available on subscription.

Pakistan

www.dawn.com This is the online version of *Dawn* newspaper.

www.pak.gov.pk This is the official government site.

www.tourism.gov.pk The Web site of the Pakistan Tourism Development Corporation (PTDC) offers advice on travel, accommodation and transport.

India

www.gadnet.com/india This has lots of links to tour and travel companies in India.

www.indiagov.org/ This site contains embassy addresses and *Discover India* magazine.

www.tibet.com This Web site of the office of the Dalai Lama has information on Tibet and the Tibetan government in exile and a miniguide to Dharamsala.

Nepal

www.info-nepal.com This has excellent links to various Web sites with good information on Nepal.

www.kathmandu.com While mostly concerned with booking treks and tours in Nepal, this site does have some useful travel information.

www.nepalnews.com.np/ktmpost This is the site of the capital's daily English-language newspaper.

www.wowadventure.com/html/nplcontents This site contains eclectic information on Nepal, including maps of the Everest region.

BOOKS

Reading just a little bit on the history, culture and art of this region will add an enormous amount to your experience. There's no one book that is absolutely essential reading, instead try to dip into a few of the following before you go.

Lonely Planet

In addition to this book, Lonely Planet also publishes books devoted to each country on the route: *Turkey*, *Iran*, *Pakistan*, *India* and *Nepal*. There are also city guides for *İstanbul* and *Delhi* and the *Turkish*, *Farsi*, *Hindu & Urdu* and *Nepali* phrasebooks. There's also the *Karakoram Highway* guide, *Trekking in the Indian Himalaya* and *Trekking in Nepal*. Most of these can be picked up in major bookshops along the way.

Travel

In Xanadu, William Dalrymple's impressive literary debut, is the most appropriate book for the whole overland experience, covering territory from Turkey to Pakistan and beyond. His subsequent books, *City of Djinns*, *From the Holy Mountain* and *The Age of Kali*, an excellent collection of essays on the Indian subcontinent, are entertaining and informative and all appropriate to parts of the journey.

In a much lighter vein, *The Wrong Way Home* by Peter Moore is a droll account of the highs and lows of the author's overland trip from London to Sydney.

Although the rail route east from İstanbul has been relegated to history, Paul Theroux's *The Great Railway Bazaar* remains an engrossing read from the world's most obnoxious but talented travel writer, and follows his journey through Turkey, Iran, Afghanistan, Pakistan and India.

In Lonely Planet's Journeys travel literature series, Ana M Briongos' *Black on Black* shines a brilliant light on everyday corners of Iran and shouldn't be missed. *A Season in Heaven*, an account of the hippy trail told by its survivors and compiled by David Tomory, is less successful but accurately conveys the druggy chaos and charm of it all. *On the Road Again* by Simon Dring is out of print now, but you should be able to pick up a copy somewhere. It follows the writer's return journey on the overland trail to India 30 years after his original trip.

Hand to Mouth to India by Tom Thumb, is a recent offering (2000) of the author's effort to hitchhike from London to India with no money. It's no literary masterpiece but if you want some tips on rock bottom budget travel it might be worth flicking through.

Robert Byron's *The Road to Oxiana*, widely acknowledged as one of the great travel books, is a vividly observed and often hilarious diary of a trip from England to the River Oxus (Amu Darya) in Afghanistan. (See the boxed text 'An Englishman Abroad'.)

Kulu: The End of the Habitable World by Penelope Chetwoode is an entertaining story about a woman who travels on horseback throughout the region.

A Fez of the Heart by Jeremy Seal is about the author's recent journeys throughout Turkey in search of Turks still wearing the fez. Despite its unfortunate title, it's a witty and entertaining inquiry into the resurgence of Islam and what it means to be a modern Turk.

History & Politics

John Simpson's *Behind Iranian Lines* is an informed account of life after the Islamic Revolution. He shared Khomeinī's fateful flight from Paris in 1979 and took full advantage of an invitation to return in 1987.

If you're interested in archaeology, Sylvia Matheson's *Persia: An Archaeological Guide* is an essential companion, scholarly yet very readable.

VS Naipaul's *Among the Believers*, about the impact of Islam outside Arab lands, and its follow up, *Beyond Belief*, contain insightful and lucid chapters on both Iran and Pakistan.

An Englishman Abroad

The archetype of the eccentric Englishman travelling abroad was never more perfectly realised than in the intellectual, exuberant and whimsical charm of Robert Byron. His classic travelogue *The Road to Oxiana* (1937) traces the overland route from Turkey through Persia and Afghanistan. A history of travel through this region would be incomplete without an appreciation of Byron and the influence he continues to exude over those who have followed in his footsteps.

Educated at Eton and Oxford, Byron had written a travelogue and two seminal works on Byzantine art and architecture before embarking on his journey in search of the origins of Islamic architecture. Written in the form of a diary, and giving the impression of having been written in no time at all, *The Road to Oxiana* spans a period of 11 months and took three years to write. With camp irreverence, and a mysterious friend called Christopher in tow, this impressionistic work moves effortlessly from farcical humour to artistic, architectural and cultural observation and insight. Byron's precocious intellect and pompous Englishness cloak a self-parody and ability to laugh at himself and everyone around him.

While sailing to Egypt in 1941, the banana boat carrying Byron was torpedoed off the north coast of Scotland. Robert Byron died at the age of 36.

Of the many writers influenced by Byron, Bruce Chatwin, who referred to *The Road to Oxiana* as his Bible, stands alone. Chatwin's impressive knowledge of art and architecture, skill as a raconteur, self-assuredness and low threshold to boredom are all reminiscent of Byron. At the age of 18, and with *The Road to Oxiana* in mind, Chatwin made the first of three trips to Afghanistan. Although he never produced a published work centred on the region, his travels there were to be the foundation of his travel writing career.

David McClymont

Freedom at Midnight by Larry Collins & Dominique Lapierre is a well-researched documentary of the months preceding Partition and Gandhi's assassination.

Fatalism & Development – Nepal's Struggle for Modernisation by Dor Bahadur Bista is an often controversial analysis of Nepali society and its dynamics. It has a very good historical introduction, and the author looks critically at the role of the caste system.

General

Afzalur Rahman's *Islam: Ideology and the Way of Life* is a good introduction for any non-Muslim wanting a guide to Islam. Sarah Hobson's *Through Persia in Disguise* is an intriguing book about a woman who travelled through Islamic countries in the early seventies disguised as a boy.

Nepal – the Kingdom in the Himalaya by Toni Hagen is one of the most complete studies of Nepal's people, geography and geology. One of the best and most up-to-date references.

Travels Through Sacred India by Roger Housden provides a very readable account of popular and classical traditions.

There are plenty of books on travel in Nepal, mostly about trekking and mountaineering. Maurice Herzog's *Annapurna* is a mountaineering classic. Herzog led the first group to reach the top of an 8000m peak, but the descent turned into a frostbitten nightmare taking them to the outer edges of human endurance.

NEWSPAPERS & MAGAZINES

There are no English-language daily or weekly newspapers covering the whole of the region, although the *International Herald Tribune* has Middle-Eastern and Asian editions that can be picked up in major cities or tourist areas in most countries (at a price). However, all the countries have their own English-language press, which are cheap and quite often a good read. Most of these newspapers are also on the Internet, so you can check out local news before you get there.

The Turkish Daily News is published in Ankara and is available across much of the country. The *Iran Daily, Iran News, Tehrān Times* and *Kayhan International* are Iran's four daily English-language papers, but you'll be hard pressed to find current editions, or any at all, outside Tehrān.

Dawn, the *Pakistan Times* and the *Morning News* are some of Pakistan's English-language offerings, based either in Lahore, Karachi or Islamabad, while the *Frontier Post* is based in Peshawar.

Times of India, Hindustan Times, Indian Express and the *Statesman* are among the publications in India. In Nepal, pick up the *Kathmandu Post,* the *Rising Nepal* and the weekly *Independent.*

In the capitals and the main coastal resorts and western cities of Turkey you'll be able to track down day-old or weekly editions of European and US newspapers but they cost a fortune compared to their face value. *Time, Newsweek* and the *Economist* can often be found at newsagents throughout the region. India has a wide range of English-language weekly news magazines, including *India Today.*

RADIO & TV

International radio stations can be vital if you want to keep abreast of world events while travelling. Voice of America (for information on broadcast frequencies see its Web site www.voa.gov) and the BBC World Service (www.bbc.co.uk/worldservice) can be picked up on various frequencies but you'll need a good short-wave or international band radio.

Many top end and mid-range hotels have satellite TV and receive CNN, BBC or EuroNews. However, having a TV in your room is often meaningless in cheaper hotels as they only broadcast local stations.

PHOTOGRAPHY & VIDEO
Film & Equipment

Most types of film, including black & white and slide, are available in the region, though they may not be easily found outside big cities. Colour-print processing is available in all large towns and cities and the results are usually perfectly adequate. Professional black-and-white processing is difficult to find, and the quality of slide processing varies considerably. If you value your precious photographs enough to use slide film, you're probably better off waiting until you get home before getting them developed. For print film you usually pay a small cost for developing, then an additional cost per print. With slide, you pay for the processing, then an amount per frame if you want them mounted.

Film prices are generally cheaper than you'll find them at home, but if you use a particular type or brand you may want to bring your own supply. Fuji and Kodak slide film is difficult to find in Iran (most places stock only Konica) and anything faster than 100ASA can be hard to find anywhere. Basic 100ASA print film (Fuji, Kodak, Agfa, Konica and other brands), Fuji Sensia and Kodak Ektachrome are available in major cities in Turkey, Pakistan, India and in Kathmandu and Pokhara. In some places, film may have been stored for ages and in less than ideal conditions, so always check the 'use by' date. See the Comparative Costs table earlier in this chapter for comparative prices of film and processing.

Remember that cameras and lenses collect dust quickly in desert areas, and lens paper and cleaner can be difficult to find in some countries, so bring your own. A dust brush is also useful.

For tips on taking decent photos, *Travel Photography: A Guide to Taking Better Pictures* is written by internationally renowned travel photographer, Richard I'Anson and published by Lonely Planet. It's full colour throughout and has been designed to take on the road.

Properly used, a video camera can give a fascinating record of your holiday. As well as videoing the obvious things – sunsets, spectacular views – remember to record some of the ordinary everyday details of life in the country. Often the most interesting things occur when you're actually intent on filming something else. Remember too that, unlike still photography, video 'flows' – so, for example, you can shoot scenes of countryside rolling past the train window, to give an overall impression that isn't possible with ordinary photos.

In most countries, it is possible to obtain video cartridges easily in large towns and cities, but make sure you buy the correct format. It's usually worth buying at least a few cartridges duty free at the start of your trip. Make sure you keep the batteries charged and have the necessary charger, plugs and transformer for the country you are visiting.

Restrictions

In most countries en route, but especially Iran and Pakistan, it is forbidden to photograph anything even vaguely military in nature (bridges, railway stations, airports and other public works). The definition of what is 'strategic' differs from one country to another, and signs are not always posted, so err on the side of caution.

In some cases, if you want to take a camera into a museum you must pay a fee (or surrender it at the cloakroom or ticket office). Higher fees are charged in many places for the use of video cameras. If there are no signs posted, ask first before taking photographs or filming in museums, galleries, forts or palaces.

Photography is usually allowed inside religious and archaeological sites, unless there are signs indicating otherwise. As a rule, however, do not photograph inside mosques during prayers and don't photograph people worshipping inside churches or temples without permission.

Many people are sensitive about the negative aspects of their country, so exercise discretion when taking photos in poorer areas.

Photographing People

As a matter of courtesy, do not photograph or video people without asking their permission first. Show them your camera and make it clear that you want to take a picture of them. This is particularly important when the potential subject is a woman. In Pakistan it's positively risky taking photographs of any woman older than a child (in public), and if you ask you will probably be refused. Pakistani men, on the other hand, will fall over themselves to have you take their picture. Children will almost always say yes, but their parents or other adults may say no. In Turkey, India and Nepal subjects are much more open to photography. Even in Iran, you'll find both men and women willing to be photographed.

Always err on the side of discretion and don't invade people's privacy in sensitive situations such as funerals, protests and prayer times. Never photograph people bathing.

Sometimes your subjects will demand payment if you take their photograph. This is a popular ploy in Kathmandu where children shriek 'ten rupees!' or 'one pen!' after happily posing for the camera, and clown-like sadhus wave you over and pull all sorts of photogenic faces then get stroppy when you only proffer NPRs 20 in baksheesh. In other countries, particularly at tourist attractions, you may wish to photograph people dressed in colourful traditional costumes but find that they want payment for being photographed. Whether you give baksheesh to sadhus or people who make a living out of posing for the camera is up to you, but you should firmly discourage children from seeing this as a way of making money.

Often you may be asked by the subject if you will send them a copy of the photograph. If you take their address and promise to send one, you should follow through with this. It's all too easy to forget or not bother once you're home.

TIME

Turkey is two hours ahead of Greenwich Mean Time (or Universal Time Coordinated; GMT/UTC), except in the summer months when clocks are turned ahead one hour. It usually begins at 1 am on the last Sunday in March and ends at 2 am on the last Sunday in September.

Time throughout Iran is 3½ hours ahead of GMT/UTC, so when it's noon in Tehrān it's 8.30 am in London.

Pakistan has a single time zone, five hours ahead of GMT and does not have daylight saving. So, when it's noon in Pakistan, it's 7 or 8 am in London depending on daylight saving there.

Indian Standard Time (IST) is 5½ hours ahead of GMT/UTC. Nepal is curiously 15 minutes ahead of India – 5¾ hours ahead of GMT – just to make it abundantly clear that this is a separate country!

Thus, when travelling from west to east, if it's noon in İstanbul, it's 1.30 pm in Tehrān, 3 pm in Lahore, 3.30 pm in Delhi and 3.45 pm in Kathmandu. So one more thing to remember at border crossings is to adjust your watch.

Time is something that the people of this region always seem to have plenty of – something that should take five minutes will invariably take an hour. Trying to speed things up will only lead to frustration. It is better to take it philosophically than try to fight it.

ELECTRICITY

The electric current in most of the countries is 220V AC, 50Hz, though in India it's 230–240V. Most plug sockets have the two/three round pin variety. In Turkey, there are two sizes of plug pin: most common is the small-diameter prong; the other is the large-diameter, grounded plug used in Germany and Austria. Adaptors can usually be found locally without too much trouble.

WEIGHTS & MEASURES

Officially, all the countries in this book use the metric system (see the standard conversion table at the back of this book) though many regions still refer to previous systems. In India and Pakistan, imperial weights and measures are still used in some areas of commerce. You will often hear people refer to lakhs (one lakh = 100,000) and crore (one crore = 10 million) of cars, apples or whatever. Similarly, in Pakistan, short distances may be measured in furlongs (one furlong = one-eighth of a mile or about 200m). Cloth merchants and tailors still use yards. Some traditional Pakistani weights still in use are the *tola* (about 11.7kg), *pao* (250g) and *seer* (0.933kg).

In Iran, you may still come across the *sīr* (about 75g) and the *chārak* (10 sīr) in some remote places. Gold and other precious metals are still often measured by the *mesghāl*, equal to 4.7g. The *farsang* is an old Persian measure of distance that used to differ from place to place but is about 6km.

If asking distances in Pakistan and India, make sure you know whether the answer is in miles or kilometres, as both may be used. All distances given in this book are in kilometres.

LAUNDRY

You'll have no problems finding a laundry service in most places you go, but usually it's easiest to ask at your hotel/hostel; they'll either have their own service or send it out for a minimal charge. You can often get a list of charges, ie, pair of trousers INRs 30, socks INRs 5, so you know how much you're up for. It's a good idea to know exactly what you've handed over anyway, so you can ensure you get it all back (and not half of someone else's laundry).

Getting your laundry done is generally very cheap and your clothes are returned spotlessly clean (if a little faded) and neatly folded. In India the work of the dhobi-wallahs (washer persons) is legendary. However, you can do your own washing in the sink or bath at your hotel. Remember to carry a small bag of washing powder, a universal sink plug and a length of line to hang your washing on. Be aware too that many hotel and hostel managers detest this practice.

TOILETS

Public toilets, and Asian toilets in general, can be the bane of many travellers' lives. Public toilets are either impossible to find, or are fly-infested, dirty and smelly. Most are 'squats' – holes in the floor with footrests on either side. The custom is to wash yourself with water (from a jug or small pipe attached to the toilet) using the left hand. Doesn't appeal? Then always carry toilet paper with you, but don't put it in the toilet, it will only clog the system. As difficult as the concept may seem, put it in the bin that should be provided. Many travellers find that when they get used to the local hand-and-water system, it's clean, effective and environmentally friendly. The biggest problem is working out how to dry yourself and to avoid getting your clothes wet.

In Iran, Turkey and Pakistan, the best place to look for decent public toilets is in a mosque; all have toilets attached and they're invariably clean, if spartan. There are usually separate toilets for men and women. You'll rarely find public toilets in India but that doesn't stop locals (mostly men) relieving themselves whenever they get the urge!

In better restaurants and hotels you'll find Western-style seated toilets, although rarely is toilet paper provided. In cities, it's a good idea to make a mental note of all Western-style fast food joints (McDonald's and KFC) and five-star hotels, as these are the places where you'll find the most sanitary facilities.

Toilets in cheap hotels and guesthouses vary from country to country. Modern places often have Western-style toilets, and you'll find them practically everywhere in Pakistan, India and Nepal. Iran mostly uses the squat toilet.

HEALTH

Travel health depends on your predeparture preparations, your daily health care while travelling and how you handle any medical problem that does develop. While the potential dangers can seem quite frightening, in reality few travellers experience anything more than an upset stomach, or, as it is known in India, 'Delhi belly'.

Predeparture Planning

Immunisations Plan ahead for getting your vaccinations: some of them require more than one injection, while some vaccinations should not be given together. Note that some vaccinations should not be given during pregnancy or to people with allergies – discuss with your doctor.

It is recommended you seek medical advice at least six weeks before travel. Be aware that there is often a greater risk of disease with children and during pregnancy.

Discuss your requirements with your doctor, but vaccinations you should consider for this trip include the following (for more details about the diseases themselves, see the individual disease entries later in this section). Carry proof of your vaccinations, especially yellow fever, as this is sometimes needed to enter some countries.

Cholera The current injectable vaccine against cholera is poorly protective and has many side effects, so it is not generally recommended for travellers. However, in some situations it may be necessary to have a certificate as travellers are very occasionally asked by immigration officials to present one, even though all countries and the World Health Organization (WHO) have dropped cholera immunisation as a health requirement for entry.

Diphtheria & Tetanus Vaccinations for these two diseases are usually combined and are recommended for everyone. After an initial course of three injections (usually given in childhood), boosters are necessary every 10 years.

Hepatitis A The vaccine for Hepatitis A (eg, Avaxim, Havrix 1440 or VAQTA) provides long-term immunity (possibly more than 10 years) after an initial injection and a booster at six to 12 months. Alternatively, an injection of gamma globulin can provide short-term protection against hepatitis A – two to six months, depending on the dose given. It is not a vaccine, but is ready-made antibody collected from blood donations. It is reasonably effective and, unlike the vaccine, it is protective immediately, but because it is a blood product, there are concerns about its long-term safety. Hepatitis A vaccine is also available in a combined form, Twinrix, with hepatitis B vaccine. Three injections over a six-month period are required, the first two providing substantial protection against hepatitis A.

Hepatitis B Travellers who should consider vaccination against hepatitis B include those on a long trip, as well as those visiting countries where there are high levels of hepatitis B infection – all the countries on this route – where blood transfusions may not be adequately screened or where sexual contact or needle sharing is a possibility. Vaccination involves three injections, with a booster at 12 months. More rapid courses are available if necessary.

Japanese B Encephalitis Consider vaccination against this disease if spending a month or longer in a high risk area (eg, the Indian subcontinent), making repeated trips to a risk area or visiting during an epidemic. It involves three injections over 30 days.

Meningococcal Meningitis Vaccination is recommended for travellers to India and Nepal. A single injection gives good protection against the major epidemic forms of the disease for three years. Protection may be less effective in children under two years.

Polio Everyone should keep up to date with this vaccination, which is normally given in childhood. A booster every 10 years maintains immunity.

Rabies Vaccination should be considered by those who will spend a month or longer in a country where rabies is common, especially if they are cycling, handling animals, caving or travelling to remote areas, and for children (who may not report a bite). Pretravel rabies vaccination involves having three injections over 21 to 28 days. If someone who has been vaccinated is bitten or scratched by an animal, they will require two booster injections of vaccine; those not vaccinated require more.

Tuberculosis The risk of TB to travellers is usually very low, unless you will be living with or closely associated with local people in high risk areas. Vaccination against TB (BCG) is recommended for children and young adults living in these areas for three months or more.

Typhoid Vaccination against typhoid is recommended as typhoid is present in all countries on this route. It is now available either as an injection or as capsules to be taken orally. A combined hepatitis A/typhoid vaccine was launched recently but its availability is still limited – check with your doctor to find out its status in your country.

Yellow Fever A yellow fever vaccine is now the only vaccine that is a legal requirement for entry into certain countries, including Iran, Pakistan, India and Nepal, usually only enforced when coming from an infected area. You may have to go to a special yellow fever vaccination centre.

Malaria Medication Antimalarial drugs do not prevent you from being infected but kill the malaria parasites during a stage in their development and significantly reduce the risk of becoming very ill or dying. Expert advice on medication should be sought, as there are many factors to consider, including the area to be visited, the risk of exposure to malaria-carrying mosquitoes, the side effects of medication, your medical history and whether you are a child or an adult or pregnant. Travellers to isolated areas in high-risk countries (see Malaria under Insect-Borne Diseases later in this section) may wish to carry a treatment dose of medication for use if symptoms occur.

Health Insurance Make sure that you have adequate health insurance. See Travel Insurance under Visas & Documents in this chapter for details.

Travel Health Guides Lonely Planet's *Healthy Travel: Asia & India* by Dr Isabelle Young is a handy pocket-size guide to illness-free travel in Pakistan, India and Nepal, although much of the information applies generally.

There are a number of other books on travel health, including:

CDC's Complete Guide to Healthy Travel, Open Road Publishing, 1997. The US Centers for Disease Control & Prevention recommendations for international travel.

Staying Healthy in Asia, Africa & Latin America, by Dirk Schroeder, Moon Publications, 1994. Probably the best all-round guide to carry, as it's compact but very detailed and well-organised.

Travellers' Health, by Dr Richard Dawood, Oxford University Press, 1995. Comprehensive, easy to read, authoritative and highly recommended, although it's too large to lug around.

Where There is No Doctor, by David Werner, Macmillan, 1994. A very detailed guide intended for someone, such as a Peace Corps worker, going to work in an underdeveloped country, rather than for the average traveller.

There are also a number of sites on the Internet that have excellent travel health information. From the Lonely Planet home page there are links at www.lonelyplanet .com/weblinks/wlheal.htm to the World Health Organization and the US Centers for Disease Control & Prevention.

Other Preparations Make sure you're healthy before you start travelling. If you are going on a long trip make sure your teeth are OK. If you wear glasses take a spare pair and your prescription.

If you require a particular medication take an adequate supply, as it may not be available locally. Take part of the packaging showing the generic name rather than the brand, which will make getting replacements easier. It's a good idea to have a legible prescription or letter from your doctor to show that you legally use the medication in order to avoid any problems.

Basic Rules

Food There is an old colonial adage which says: 'If you can cook it, boil it or peel it you can eat it…otherwise forget it'. Vegetables and fruit should be washed with purified water or peeled where possible. Beware of ice cream which is sold in the street or anywhere it might have been melted and refrozen; if there's any doubt (eg, a power cut in the last day or two), steer well clear. Shellfish such as mussels, oysters and clams should be avoided as well as undercooked meat, particularly in the form of mince. Steaming does not make shellfish safe for eating.

If a place looks clean and well run and the vendor also looks clean and healthy, then the food is probably safe. In general, places that are packed with travellers or locals will be fine, while empty restaurants are questionable. The food in busy restaurants is cooked and eaten quite quickly with little standing around and is probably not reheated.

Water The number one rule is be careful of the water and especially ice. If you don't know for certain that the water is safe, assume the worst. Reputable brands of bottled water or soft drinks are generally fine, although in some places bottles may be refilled with tap water. Only use water from containers with a serrated seal – not tops or corks. Take care with fruit juice, particularly if water may have been added. Milk should be treated with suspicion as it is often unpasteurised, though boiled milk is fine if it is kept hygienically. Tea or coffee should also be OK, since the water should have been boiled.

Water Purification The simplest way of purifying water is to boil it thoroughly. Vigorous boiling should be satisfactory; however, at high altitude water boils at a lower temperature, so germs are less likely to be killed. Boil it for longer in these environments.

Consider purchasing a water filter for a long trip. There are two main kinds of filter. Total filters take out all parasites, bacteria and viruses and make water safe to drink. They are often expensive, but they can be more cost effective than buying bottled water. Simple filters (which can even be a nylon mesh bag) take out dirt and larger foreign bodies from the water so that chemical solutions work much more effectively; if water is dirty, chemical solutions may not work at all. It's very important when buying a filter to read the specifications, so that you know exactly what it removes from the water and what it doesn't. Simple filtering will not remove all dangerous organisms, so if you cannot boil water

Nutrition

If your diet is poor or limited in variety, if you're travelling hard and fast and therefore missing meals or if you simply lose your appetite, you can soon start to lose weight and place your health at risk.

Make sure your diet is well balanced. Cooked eggs, tofu, beans, lentils (dhal in India) and nuts are all safe ways to get protein. Fruit you can peel (bananas, oranges or mandarins, for example) is usually safe and a good source of vitamins. Melons can harbour bacteria in their flesh and are best avoided. Try to eat plenty of grains (including rice) and bread. Remember that although food is generally safer if it is cooked well, overcooked food loses much of its nutritional value. If your diet isn't well balanced or if your food intake is insufficient, it's a good idea to take vitamin and iron pills.

In hot climates make sure you drink enough – don't rely on feeling thirsty to indicate when you should drink. Not needing to urinate or voiding small amounts of very dark yellow urine is a danger sign. Always carry a water bottle with you on long trips. Excessive sweating can lead to loss of salt and therefore muscle cramping. Salt tablets are not a good idea as a preventative, but in places where salt is not used much, adding salt to food can help.

Everyday Health

Normal body temperature is up to 37°C (98.6°F); more than 2°C (4°F) higher indicates a high fever. The normal adult pulse rate is 60 to 100 per minute (children 80 to 100, babies 100 to 140). As a general rule the pulse increases about 20 beats per minute for each 1°C (2°F) rise in fever.

Respiration (breathing) rate is also an indicator of illness. Count the number of breaths per minute: Between 12 and 20 is normal for adults and older children (up to 30 for younger children, 40 for babies). People with a high fever or serious respiratory illness breathe more quickly than normal. More than 40 shallow breaths a minute may indicate pneumonia.

it should be treated chemically. Chlorine tablets will kill many pathogens, but not some parasites like giardia and amoebic cysts. Iodine is more effective in purifying water and is available in tablet form. Follow the directions carefully and remember that too much iodine can be harmful.

Medical Problems & Treatment

Self-diagnosis and treatment can be risky, so you should always seek medical help. An embassy, consulate or five-star hotel can usually recommend a local doctor or clinic. Although we do give drug dosages in this section, they are for emergency use only. Correct diagnosis is vital. In this section we have used the generic names for medications – check with a pharmacist for brands available locally.

Note that antibiotics should ideally be administered only under medical supervision. Take only the recommended dose at the prescribed intervals and use the whole course, even if the illness seems to be cured earlier. Stop immediately if there are any serious reactions and don't use the antibiotic at all if you are unsure that you have the correct one. Some people are allergic to commonly prescribed antibiotics such as penicillin; carry this information (eg, on a bracelet) when travelling.

Environmental Hazards

Air Pollution Pollution is something you'll become very aware of in urban environments on this route. Air pollution can be

a health hazard, particularly if you suffer from a lung disease such as asthma. It can also aggravate coughs, colds and sinus problems and cause eye irritation. Consider avoiding badly polluted areas, especially if you have asthma, or you could invest in a surgical mask.

Air pollution can be a problem in Ankara and İstanbul, especially in winter, but in general the pollution in Turkey is no worse than in other big cities around the world. Air pollution is a major problem in Tehrān, most of all in summer. Esfahān and Kermān also record high levels, especially in winter when fuel burned for heating compounds the normal problems created by traffic and industrial waste. Air pollution is also a problem in urban environments in the Indian subcontinent, especially in Delhi, where the air pollution poses grave risks for inhabitants.

Altitude Sickness Lack of oxygen at high altitudes (over 2500m) affects most people to some extent. The effect may be mild or severe and occurs because less oxygen reaches the muscles and the brain at high altitude. This requires the heart and lungs to compensate by working harder. Symptoms of Acute Mountain Sickness (AMS) usually develop during the first 24 hours at altitude but may be delayed by up to three weeks. Mild symptoms include headache, lethargy, dizziness, difficulty sleeping and loss of appetite. AMS may become more severe without warning and can sometimes be fatal. Severe symptoms include breathlessness, a dry, irritative cough (which may progress to the production of pink, frothy sputum), severe headache, lack of coordination and balance, confusion, irrational behaviour, vomiting, drowsiness and unconsciousness. There is no hard-and-fast rule as to what is too high: AMS has been fatal at 3000m, although 3500 to 4500m is the usual range.

Mild symptoms are treated by resting at the same altitude until recovery, usually a day or two. Paracetamol or aspirin can be taken for headaches. If symptoms persist or become worse, however, immediate descent is necessary; even going down 500m can help. Drug treatments should never be used to avoid descent or to enable further ascent.

Medical Kit Check List

Following is a list of items you should consider including in your medical kit – consult your pharmacist for brands available in your country.

☐ **Aspirin or paracetamol (acetaminophen in the USA)** – for pain or fever

☐ **Antihistamine** – for allergies, eg, hay fever; to ease the itch from insect bites or stings; and to prevent motion sickness

☐ **Cold and flu tablets, throat lozenges and nasal decongestant**

☐ **Multivitamins** – consider for long trips, when dietary vitamin intake may be inadequate

☐ **Antibiotics** – consider including these if you're travelling well off the beaten track; see your doctor, as they must be prescribed, and carry the prescription with you

☐ **Loperamide or diphenoxylate** –'blockers' for diarrhoea

☐ **Prochlorperazine or metaclopramide** – for nausea and vomiting

☐ **Rehydration mixture** – to prevent dehydration, which may occur, for example, during bouts of diarrhoea; particularly important when travelling with children

☐ **Insect repellent, sunscreen, lip balm and eye drops**

☐ **Calamine lotion, sting relief spray or aloe vera** – to ease irritation from sunburn and insect bites or stings

☐ **Antifungal cream or powder** – for fungal skin infections and thrush

☐ **Antiseptic (such as povidone-iodine)** – for cuts and grazes

☐ **Bandages, Band-Aids (plasters) and other wound dressings**

☐ **Water purification tablets or iodine**

☐ **Scissors, tweezers and a thermometer** – note that mercury thermometers are prohibited by airlines

☐ **Sterile kit** – sealed medical kit containing syringes and needles in case you need injections and are in a country where there are medical hygiene problems; discuss with your doctor

Some doctors recommend acetazolamide and dexamethasone for prevention of AMS, but their use is controversial. They can reduce the symptoms, but may also mask warning signs; severe and fatal AMS has occurred in people taking these drugs. In general we do not recommend them for travellers.

To prevent acute mountain sickness:

• Ascend slowly – have frequent rest days, spending two to three nights at each rise of 1000m. If you reach a high altitude by trekking, acclimatisation takes place gradually and you are less likely to be affected than if you fly directly to high altitude.

• It is always wise to sleep at a lower altitude than the greatest height reached during the day if possible. Also, once above 3000m, care should be taken not to increase the sleeping altitude by more than 300m per day.

• Drink extra fluids. The mountain air is dry and cold and moisture is lost as you breathe. Evaporation of sweat may occur unnoticed and result in dehydration.

• Eat light, high-carbohydrate meals for more energy.

• Avoid alcohol as it may increase the risk of dehydration.

• Avoid sedatives.

Heat Exhaustion Dehydration and salt deficiency can cause heat exhaustion. Take time to acclimatise to high temperatures, drink sufficient liquids and do not do anything too physically demanding.

Salt deficiency is characterised by fatigue, lethargy, headaches, giddiness and muscle cramps; salt tablets may help, but adding extra salt to your food is better.

Anhidrotic heat exhaustion is a rare form of heat exhaustion that is caused by an inability to sweat. It tends to affect people who have been in a hot climate for some time, rather than newcomers. It can progress to heatstroke. Treatment involves removal to a cooler climate.

Heatstroke This serious, occasionally fatal, condition can occur if the body's heat-regulating mechanism breaks down and the body temperature rises to dangerous levels. Long, continuous periods of exposure to high temperatures and insufficient fluids can leave you vulnerable to heatstroke.

The symptoms are feeling unwell, not sweating very much (or at all) and a high body temperature (39°C to 41°C or 102°F to 106°F). Where sweating has ceased, the skin becomes flushed and red. Severe, throbbing headaches and lack of coordination will also occur, and the sufferer may be confused or aggressive. Eventually the victim will become delirious or convulse. Hospitalisation is essential, but in the interim get victims out of the sun, remove their clothing, cover them with a wet sheet or towel and then fan continually. Give fluids if they are conscious.

Hypothermia Too much cold can be just as dangerous as too much heat. If you are trekking at high altitudes or simply taking a long bus trip over mountains, particularly at night, be prepared. In Nepal's mountain regions you should always be prepared for cold, wet or windy conditions even if you're just out walking or hitching.

Hypothermia occurs when the body loses heat faster than it can produce it and the core temperature of the body falls. It is surprisingly easy to progress from very cold to dangerously cold due to a combination of wind, wet clothing, fatigue and hunger, even if the air temperature is above freezing. It is best to dress in layers; silk, wool and some of the new artificial fibres are all good insulating materials. A hat is important, as a lot of heat is lost through the head. A strong, waterproof outer layer (and a 'space' blanket for emergencies) is essential. Carry basic supplies, including food containing simple sugars to generate heat quickly and fluid to drink.

Symptoms of hypothermia are exhaustion, numb skin (particularly toes and fingers), shivering, slurred speech, irrational or violent behaviour, lethargy, stumbling, dizzy spells, muscle cramps and violent bursts of energy. Irrationality may take the form of sufferers claiming they are warm and trying to take off their clothes.

To treat mild hypothermia, first get the person out of the wind and/or rain, remove their clothing if it's wet and replace it with dry, warm clothing. Give them hot liquids – not alcohol – and some high-kilojoule, easily digestible food. Do not rub victims: instead, allow them to slowly warm themselves. This should be enough to treat the early stages of hypothermia. The early recognition and treatment of mild hypothermia is the only way to prevent severe hypothermia, which is a critical condition.

Prickly Heat Prickly heat is an itchy rash caused by excessive perspiration trapped under the skin. It usually strikes people who have just arrived in a hot climate. Keeping cool, bathing often, drying the skin and using a mild talcum or prickly heat powder or resorting to air-conditioning may help.

Sunburn In the desert or at high altitude you can get sunburnt surprisingly quickly, even through cloud. Use a sunscreen, a hat, and a barrier cream for your nose and lips. Calamine lotion or a commercial after sun preparation are good for mild sunburn. Protect your eyes with good quality sunglasses, particularly if you will be near water, sand or snow.

Infectious Diseases

Diarrhoea Simple things like a change of water, food or climate can all cause a mild bout of diarrhoea, but a few rushed toilet trips with no other symptoms is not indicative of a major problem.

Dehydration is the main danger with any diarrhoea, particularly in children or the elderly as dehydration can occur quite quickly. Under all circumstances *fluid replacement* (at least equal to the volume being lost) is the most important thing to remember. Weak black tea with a little sugar, soda water, or soft drinks allowed to go flat and diluted 50% with clean water are all good. With severe diarrhoea a rehydrating solution is preferable to replace minerals and salts lost. Commercially available oral rehydration salts (ORS) are very useful; add them to boiled or bottled water. In an emergency you can make up a solution of six teaspoons of sugar and a half teaspoon of salt to a litre of boiled or bottled water. You need to drink at least the same volume of fluid that you are losing in bowel movements and vomiting. Urine is the best guide to the adequacy of replacement – if you have small amounts of concentrated urine, you need to drink more. Keep drinking small amounts often. Stick to a bland diet as you recover.

Gut-paralysing drugs such as loperamide or diphenoxylate can be used to bring relief from the symptoms, although they do not actually cure the problem. Only use these drugs if you do not have access to toilets, eg, if you *must* travel. Note that these drugs are not recommended for children under 12 years.

In certain situations antibiotics may be required: diarrhoea with blood or mucus (dysentery), any diarrhoea with fever, profuse watery diarrhoea, persistent diarrhoea not improving after 48 hours and severe diarrhoea. These suggest a more serious cause of diarrhoea and in these situations gut-paralysing drugs should be avoided.

In these situations, a stool test may be necessary to diagnose what bug is causing your diarrhoea, so you should seek medical help urgently. Where this is not possible the recommended drugs for bacterial diarrhoea (the most likely cause of severe diarrhoea in travellers) are norfloxacin 400mg twice daily for three days or ciprofloxacin 500mg twice daily for five days. These are not recommended for children or pregnant women. The drug of choice for children would be co-trimoxazole with dosage dependent on weight. A five-day course is given. Ampicillin or amoxycillin may be given in pregnancy, but medical care is necessary.

Two other causes of persistent diarrhoea in travellers are giardiasis and amoebic dysentery.

Giardiasis is caused by a common parasite, *Giardia lamblia*. Symptoms include stomach cramps, nausea, a bloated stomach, watery, foul-smelling diarrhoea and frequent gas. Giardiasis can appear several weeks after you have been exposed to the parasite. The symptoms may disappear for a few days and then return; this can go on for several weeks.

Amoebic dysentery, caused by the protozoan *Entamoeba histolytica,* is characterised by a gradual onset of low-grade diarrhoea, often with blood and mucus. Cramping abdominal pain and vomiting are less likely than in other types of diarrhoea, and fever may not be present. It will persist until treated and can recur and cause other health problems.

You should seek medical advice if you think you have giardiasis or amoebic dysentery, but where this is not possible, tinidazole or metronidazole are the recommended drugs. Treatment is a 2g single dose of tinidazole or 250mg of metronidazole three times daily for five to 10 days.

Fungal Infections These occur more commonly in hot weather and are usually found on the scalp, between the toes (athlete's foot) or fingers, in the groin and on the body (ringworm). You get ringworm (which is a fungal infection, not a worm) from infected animals or other people. Moisture encourages these infections.

To prevent fungal infections wear loose, comfortable clothes, avoid artificial fibres, wash frequently and dry yourself carefully. If you do get an infection, wash the infected area at least daily with a disinfectant or medicated soap and water, and rinse and dry well. Apply an antifungal cream or powder like tolnaftate. Try to expose the infected area to air or sunlight as much as possible and wash all towels and underwear in hot water, change them often and let them dry in the sun.

Hepatitis This is a general term for inflammation of the liver. It is a common disease worldwide. There are several different viruses that cause hepatitis, and they differ in the way that they are transmitted. The symptoms are similar in all forms of the illness, and include fever, chills, headache, fatigue, feelings of weakness and aches and pains, followed by loss of appetite, nausea, vomiting, abdominal pain, dark urine, light-coloured faeces, jaundiced (yellow) skin and yellowing of the whites of the eyes. People who have had hepatitis should avoid alcohol for some time after the illness, as the liver needs time to recover.

Hepatitis A is transmitted by contaminated food and drinking water. You should seek medical advice, but there is not much you can do apart from resting, drinking lots of fluids, eating lightly and avoiding fatty foods. Hepatitis A is found in all countries on this route. Hepatitis E is transmitted in the same way as hepatitis A; it can be particularly serious in pregnant women. It is found in all countries on this route except Turkey.

There are almost 300 million chronic carriers of hepatitis B in the world. The disease exists in all countries on this route. It is spread through contact with infected blood, blood products or body fluids, for example through sexual contact, unsterilised needles and blood transfusions, or contact with blood via small breaks in the skin. Other risk situations include having a shave, tattoo or body piercing with contaminated equipment. The symptoms of hepatitis B may be more severe than type A and the disease can lead to long-term problems such as chronic liver damage, liver cancer or a long-term carrier state. Hepatitis C and D are spread in the same way as hepatitis B and can also lead to long-term complications.

There are vaccines against hepatitis A and B, but there are currently no vaccines against the other types of hepatitis. Following the basic rules about food and water (hepatitis A and E) and avoiding risk situations (hepatitis B, C and D) are important preventative measures.

HIV & AIDS Infection with the human immunodeficiency virus (HIV) may lead to acquired immune deficiency syndrome (AIDS), which is a fatal disease. Any exposure to blood, blood products or body fluids may put the individual at risk. The disease is often transmitted through sexual contact or dirty needles – vaccinations, acupuncture, tattooing and body piercing can be potentially as dangerous as intravenous drug use. HIV/AIDS can also be spread through infected blood transfusions; some developing countries cannot afford to screen blood used for transfusions.

If you do need an injection, ask to see the syringe unwrapped in front of you, or take a needle and syringe pack with you.

That said, fear of HIV infection should never preclude treatment for serious medical conditions.

Intestinal Worms These parasites are most common in rural, tropical areas. The different worms have different ways of infecting people. Some (eg, tapeworms) may be ingested on food such as undercooked meat and some (eg, hookworms) enter through your skin. Infestations may not show up for some time, and although they are generally not serious, if left untreated some can cause severe health problems later. Consider having a stool test when you return home to check for these and determine the appropriate treatment.

Meningococcal Meningitis This serious disease can be fatal. There are recurring epidemics in northern India and Nepal.

A fever, severe headache, sensitivity to light and neck stiffness which prevents forward bending of the head are the first symptoms. There may also be purple patches on the skin. Death can occur within a few hours, so urgent medical treatment is required.

Trekkers to rural areas of Nepal should be particularly careful, as the disease is spread by close contact with people who carry it in their throats and noses and spread it through coughs and sneezes; they may not be aware that they are carriers. Lodges in the hills where travellers spend the night are prime spots for the spread of infection.

Treatment is large doses of penicillin given intravenously, or chloramphenicol injections.

Sexually Transmitted Infections HIV/AIDS and hepatitis B can be transmitted through sexual contact – see the relevant sections earlier for more details. Other STIs include gonorrhoea, herpes and syphilis; sores, blisters or rashes around the genitals and discharges or pain when urinating are common symptoms. In some STIs, such as wart virus or chlamydia, symptoms may be less marked or not observed at all, especially in women. Chlamydia infection can cause infertility in men and women before any symptoms have been noticed. Syphilis symptoms eventually disappear completely but the disease continues and can cause severe problems in later years. While abstinence from sexual contact is the only 100% effective prevention, using condoms is also effective. The treatment of gonorrhoea and syphilis is with antibiotics. The different sexually transmitted diseases each require specific antibiotics.

Typhoid This fever is a dangerous gut infection caused by contaminated water and food. Medical help must be sought.

In its early stages sufferers may feel they have a bad cold or flu on the way, as early symptoms are a headache, body aches and a fever which rises a little each day until it is around 40°C (104°F) or more. The victim's pulse is often slow relative to the degree of fever present – unlike a normal fever where the pulse increases. There may also be vomiting, abdominal pain, diarrhoea or constipation.

In the second week the high fever and slow pulse continue and a few pink spots may appear on the body; trembling, delirium, weakness, weight loss and dehydration may occur. Complications such as pneumonia, perforated bowel or meningitis may occur.

Insect-Borne Diseases

Filariasis, leishmaniasis and typhus are all insect-borne diseases, but they do not pose a great risk to travellers. Protecting yourself against mosquito bites is an important preventative measure. For more information on them see Less Common Diseases at the end of this health section.

Malaria This serious and potentially fatal disease is spread by mosquito bites. If you are travelling in endemic areas it is extremely important to avoid mosquito bites and to take tablets to prevent this disease.

Overall, the risk of malaria in Turkey is very small, and most travellers will not need to take precautions. Officially, the benign form of malaria is present in south-eastern Anatolia from Mersin on the Mediterranean coast eastward to the Iraqi border, but the highest danger is in the muggy agricultural area called Çukurova north of Adana, and in the newly irrigated areas around Şanlıurfa.

If you just pass through these areas, or spend most of your time in cities, the danger is lower; but if you plan to spend lots of time in rural areas and camp out in this region, you're at significant risk and should take appropriate precautions – consult your doctor.

In Iran, there is a limited risk of catching malaria in areas north of the Zagros Mountains and in the western and south-western regions in the summer months. This includes the areas around Shīrāz and Kermān, and also in Zāhedān in the east.

In Pakistan and India, there is a risk of catching malaria throughout the country in areas below 2000m. Malaria is not found in the tourist areas of Nepal – the Kathmandu Valley, Pokhara and the Himalaya – but the benign form does exist in the lowland Terai region throughout the year, as well as along the Indian border.

Symptoms range from fever, chills and sweating, headache, diarrhoea and abdominal pains to a vague feeling of ill-health. Seek medical help immediately if malaria is suspected. Without treatment malaria can rapidly become more serious and can be fatal.

If medical care is not available, malaria tablets can be used for treatment. You need to use a malaria tablet which is different from the one you were taking when you contracted malaria. The standard treatment dose of mefloquine is two 250mg tablets and a further two six hours later. For Fansidar, it's a single dose of three tablets. If you were previously taking mefloquine and cannot obtain Fansidar, then other alternatives are Malarone (atovaquone-proguanil; four tablets once daily for three days), halofantrine (three doses of two 250mg tablets every six hours) or quinine sulphate (600mg every six hours). There is a greater risk of side effects with these dosages than in normal use if used with mefloquine, so medical advice is preferable. Be aware also that halofantrine is no longer recommended by the WHO as emergency standby treatment, because of side effects, and should only be used if no other drugs are available.

Travellers are advised to prevent mosquito bites at all times. The main messages are:

• Wear light-coloured clothing.
• Wear long trousers and long-sleeved shirts.
• Use mosquito repellents containing the compound DEET on exposed areas (prolonged overuse of DEET may be harmful, especially to children, but its use is considered preferable to being bitten by disease-transmitting mosquitoes).
• Avoid perfumes or aftershave.
• Use a mosquito net impregnated with mosquito repellent (permethrin) – it may be worth taking your own.
• Impregnating clothes with permethrin effectively deters mosquitoes and other insects.

Dengue Fever This viral disease, found in Pakistan and India, is transmitted by mosquitoes and is fast becoming one of the top public health problems in the tropical world. Unlike the malaria mosquito, the *Aedes aegypti* mosquito, which transmits the dengue virus, is most active during the day, and is found mainly in urban areas, in and around human dwellings.

Signs and symptoms of dengue fever include a sudden onset of high fever, headache, joint and muscle pains (hence its old name, 'breakbone fever') and nausea and vomiting. A rash of small red spots sometimes appears three to four days after the onset of fever. In the early phase of illness, dengue may be mistaken for other infectious diseases, including malaria and influenza. Minor bleeding such as nose bleeds may occur in the course of the illness, but this does not necessarily mean that you have progressed to the potentially fatal dengue haemorrhagic fever (DHF). This is a severe illness, characterised by heavy bleeding, which is thought to be a result of second infection due to a different strain (there are four major strains) and usually affects residents of the country rather than travellers. Recovery even from simple dengue fever may be prolonged, with tiredness lasting for several weeks.

You should seek medical attention as son as possible if you think you may be infected. A blood test can exclude malaria and indicate the possibility of dengue fever. There is no specific treatment for dengue. Aspirin should be avoided, as it increases the risk of haemorrhaging. There is no vaccine against dengue fever. The best prevention is to avoid mosquito bites at all times by covering up, using insect repellents containing the compound DEET and mosquito nets – see the Malaria section earlier for more advice on avoiding mosquito bites.

Japanese B Encephalitis This viral infection of the brain is transmitted by mosquitoes. It exists in Pakistan, India and Nepal. Most cases occur in rural areas as the virus exists in pigs and wading birds. Symptoms include fever, headache and alteration in consciousness. Hospitalisation is needed for correct diagnosis and treatment. There is a high mortality rate among those who have symptoms; of those who survive many are intellectually disabled.

Cuts, Bites & Stings

See Less Common Diseases for details of rabies, which is passed through animal bites.

Cuts & Scratches Wash well and treat any cut with an antiseptic such as povidone-iodine. Where possible avoid bandages and Band-Aids, which can keep wounds wet. Coral cuts are notoriously slow to heal and if they are not adequately cleaned, small pieces of coral can become embedded in the wound.

Bedbugs & Lice Bedbugs live in dirty mattresses and bedding, evidenced by spots of blood on bedclothes or on the wall. Bedbugs leave itchy bites in neat rows. Calamine lotion or a sting relief spray may help.

All lice cause itching and discomfort. They make themselves at home in your hair (head lice), your clothing (body lice) or in your pubic hair (crabs). You catch lice through direct contact with infected people or by sharing combs, clothing and the like. Powder or shampoo treatment will kill the lice and infected clothing should then be washed in very hot, soapy water and left in the sun to dry.

Bites & Stings Bee and wasp stings are usually painful rather than dangerous. However, in people who are allergic to them severe breathing difficulties may occur and require urgent medical care. Calamine lotion or a sting relief spray will give relief and ice packs will reduce the pain and swelling. There are some spiders with dangerous bites but antivenins are usually available. Scorpion stings are notoriously painful and in some parts of Asia can actually be fatal. Scorpions often shelter in shoes or clothing.

Leeches & Ticks Leeches may be present in damp conditions; they attach themselves to your skin to suck your blood. Trekkers often get them on their legs or in their boots. Salt or a lighted cigarette end will make them fall off. Do not pull them off, as the bite is then more likely to become infected. Clean and apply pressure if the point of attachment is bleeding. An insect repellent may keep them away.

You should always check all over your body if you have been walking through a potentially tick-infested area as ticks can cause skin infections and other more serious diseases. If a tick is found attached, press down around the tick's head with tweezers, grab the head and gently pull upwards. Avoid pulling the rear of the body as this may squeeze the tick's gut contents through the attached mouth parts into the skin, increasing the risk of infection and disease. Smearing chemicals on the tick will not make it let go and is not recommended.

Snakes To minimise your chances of being bitten always wear boots, socks and long trousers when walking through undergrowth where snakes may be present. Don't put your hands into holes and crevices, and be careful when collecting firewood.

Snake bites do not cause instantaneous death and antivenins are usually available. Immediately wrap the bitten limb tightly, as you would for a sprained ankle, and then attach a splint to immobilise it. Keep the victim still and seek medical help, if possible with the dead snake for identification. Don't attempt to catch the snake if there is a possibility of being bitten again. Tourniquets and sucking out the poison are now comprehensively discredited.

Women's Health

Gynaecological Problems Antibiotic use, synthetic underwear, sweating and contraceptive pills can lead to fungal vaginal infections, especially when travelling in hot climates. Thrush or vaginal candidiasis is characterised by a rash, itch or discharge. Nystatin, miconazole or clotrimazole pessaries or vaginal cream are the usual treatment, but some people use a more traditional remedy involving vinegar or lemon-juice douches, or yogurt. Maintaining good personal hygiene and wearing loose-fitting clothes and cotton underwear may help prevent these infections.

Sexually transmitted diseases are a major cause of vaginal problems. Symptoms include a smelly discharge, painful intercourse and sometimes a burning sensation when urinating. Medical attention should be sought and male sexual partners must also be treated. For more details see the section on Sexually Transmitted Infections earlier. Besides abstinence, the best thing is to practise safer sex using condoms.

Pregnancy It is not advisable to travel to some places while pregnant as some vaccinations normally used to prevent serious diseases are not advisable during pregnancy (eg, yellow fever). In addition, some diseases are much more serious for the mother (and may increase the risk of a stillborn child) in pregnancy (eg, malaria).

Most miscarriages occur during the first three months of pregnancy. Miscarriage is not uncommon and can occasionally lead to severe bleeding. The last three months should also be spent within reasonable distance of good medical care. A baby born as early as 24 weeks stands a chance of survival, but only in a good modern hospital. Pregnant women should avoid all unnecessary medication, although vaccinations and malarial prophylactics should still be taken where needed. Additional care should be taken to prevent illness and particular attention should be paid to diet and nutrition. Alcohol and nicotine, for example, should be avoided.

Less Common Diseases

The following diseases pose a small risk to travellers, and so are only mentioned in passing. Seek medical advice if you think you may have any of these diseases.

Cholera This is the worst of the watery diarrhoeas and medical help should be sought. Outbreaks of cholera are generally widely reported, so you can avoid such problem areas. *Fluid replacement is the most vital treatment* – the risk of dehydration is severe as you may lose up to 20L a day. If there is a delay in getting to hospital, then begin taking tetracycline. The adult dose is 250mg four times daily. It is not recommended for children under nine years nor for pregnant women. Tetracycline may help shorten the illness, but adequate fluids are required to save lives.

Filariasis This is a mosquito-transmitted parasitic infection found in all countries on this route. Possible symptoms include fever, pain and swelling of the lymph glands; inflammation of lymph drainage areas; swelling of a limb or the scrotum; skin rashes; and blindness. Treatment is available to eliminate the parasites from the body, but some of the damage already caused may not be reversible. Medical advice should be obtained promptly if the infection is suspected.

Leishmaniasis This is a group of parasitic diseases transmitted by sandflies, which are found in many parts of the Middle East, India and the Mediterranean. Cutaneous leishmaniasis, which exists in Iran, Pakistan, India (Rajasthan only) and Nepal, affects the skin tissue causing ulceration and disfigurement. Visceral leishmaniasis affects the internal organs. It is found in south-east Anatolia in Turkey, Iran, northern Pakistan, India and Nepal. Seek medical advice, as laboratory testing is required for diagnosis and correct treatment. Avoiding sandfly bites is the best precaution. Bites are usually painless, itchy and yet another reason to cover up and apply repellent.

Rabies This fatal viral infection is found in all countries on this route. Many animals can be infected (such as dogs, cats, bats and monkeys) and it is their saliva which is infectious. Any bite, scratch or even lick from an animal should be cleaned immediately and thoroughly. Scrub with soap and running water, and then apply alcohol or iodine solution. Medical help should be sought promptly to receive a course of injections to prevent the onset of symptoms and death.

Tetanus This disease is caused by a germ which lives in soil and in the faeces of horses and other animals. It enters the body via breaks in the skin. The first symptom may be discomfort in swallowing, or stiffening of the jaw and neck; this is followed by painful convulsions of the jaw and whole body. The disease can be fatal. It can be prevented by vaccination.

Tuberculosis (TB) This is a bacterial infection that is usually transmitted from person to person by coughing. It may also be transmitted through the consumption of unpasteurised milk. Milk that has been boiled is safe to drink, and the souring of milk to make yogurt or cheese also kills the bacilli. Travellers are usually not at great risk because close household contact with the infected person is usually required before the disease is passed on. You may need to have a TB test before you travel as this can help diagnose the disease later if you become ill.

Typhus This disease is spread by ticks, mites or lice. It begins with fever, chills, headache and muscle pains followed a few days later by a body rash. There is often a large painful sore at the site of the bite and nearby lymph nodes are swollen and painful. Typhus can be treated under medical supervision. Seek local advice on areas where ticks pose a danger and always check your skin carefully for ticks after walking in a danger area such as a tropical forest. An insect repellent can help, and walkers in tick-infested areas should consider having their boots and trousers impregnated with benzyl benzoate and dibutylphthalate.

WOMEN TRAVELLERS

Attitudes towards women are generally conservative in this region – especially about matters concerning sex.

An entire book could be written from the comments and stories of women travellers about their adventures and misadventures in the region. However, most of the incidents are nonthreatening nuisances. Invariably the biggest complaint from female travellers is of the constant staring and occasional jeering. Curious local males will stop whatever they are doing to gawk at any passing female who is not from their country. On trains and buses it's not uncommon to be surrounded by a dozen staring faces and this can go on, quite literally, for hours. It's very unnerving and even humiliating, but local people don't see this as being rude or confronting in the way that we do.

Travel in Pakistan can be hard work for women, though plenty of women have done the country solo and reported few problems. While it is a conservative Muslim country, Western attitudes are common, especially in the big cities. Female expatriates living in Lahore, Islamabad and Quetta report few hassles, although there was a disturbing incident involving an apparently unprovoked attack on a group of young Dutch women in Lahore during our visit. Dress conservatively at all times, but especially in tribal areas and places like Peshawar, where you should ensure that your arms and legs are covered, and preferably wear a headscarf.

Iran is not the place to make a feminist statement, although attitudes under the reformist leadership of President Khatamī are loosening up. The main hassle for foreign women is wearing the appropriate clothing and reports from women who have travelled through Pakistan and Turkey suggest that most women will have a far more comfortable experience in Iran.

India is particularly bad for unwanted attention, including groping on crowded buses or in the street. The concept of personal space in India is one you have to get used to doing without but don't be afraid to make a scene if someone is physically putting their hands on you.

Avoid trekking alone in Nepal or India and only trek with reputable companies. It's also better to stick with a group on things like camel safaris or if you hire a car and driver.

Tampon-users may want to pack enough to get them through their trip. Tampons are not only almost impossible to find, but if you do manage to track them down you might find that two packets cost as much as a flight from, for example, Tehrān to Esfahān.

Attitudes Towards Women

Some of the biggest misunderstandings between easterners and westerners occur over the issue of women. Half-truths and stereotypes abound; many westerners assume all women in this region are veiled, repressed victims, while many locals see Western women as sex-obsessed and immoral.

For many easterners, the role of a woman is specifically defined: She is mother and matron of the household. The man is the provider. However, generalisations can be misleading and the reality is far more nuanced. There are thousands of middle and upper-middle class professional women in the region who, like their counterparts in the West, juggle work and family responsibilities. Among the working classes, where adherence to tradition is strongest, the ideal may be for women to concentrate on home and family, but economic reality means that millions of women are forced to work (but are still responsible for all domestic chores).

The issue of sex is where the differences between Western and Eastern women are most apparent. Premarital sex (or, indeed, any sex outside marriage) is taboo. For women the issue is serious; they are expected to be virgins when they get married and a family's reputation can rest upon this point. In such a context, the restrictions placed on a young girl – no matter how onerous they may seem to a westerner – are intended to protect her and her reputation from the potentially disastrous attentions of men.

The presence of foreign women presents, in the eyes of some eastern men, a chance to get around these norms with ease and without consequences. That this is even possible is heavily reinforced by distorted impressions gained from Western TV and, it has to be said, by the behaviour of some foreign women in the country.

So, as a woman traveller you can at least expect some verbal harassment. Sometimes it will go as far as pinching bottoms or brushing breasts but serious physical harassment and rape are not significant threats.

Reducing the Hassle

There are a number of things that you can do to lessen harassment but top of the list is to dress modestly. The woman wearing short pants and a tight T-shirt on the street confirms, in some locals' eyes, the worst views of Western women. Generally, if you're alone or with other women, the amount of harassment you get will be directly related to how you dress: the more skin that is exposed, or the tighter the clothing, the more harassment you'll get. In some places nothing you can do short of garbing yourself in full Saudi-style chādor will completely leave you free of unwanted attention. For more on the dress issue see the following What to Wear section.

Other helpful tips include:

- If you are unmarried but travelling in male company say you are married rather than girlfriend and boyfriend or just friends.
- It's better not to let on if you are travelling alone or just in the company of another female friend – always say that you are with a group.
- Wearing a wedding ring may help (generally married women are shown more respect), but only if local men understand that the ring signifies marriage, which is not always the case.
- Avoid direct eye contact with local men; dark sunglasses help.
- Don't respond to any obnoxious comments – act as if you didn't hear them. However, if you are being touched or feel threatened (in public) it will probably help to make a scene by reacting angrily and vocally (which will probably be a very natural reaction!).
- Be careful in crowds and other situations where you are crammed between people, as it is not unusual for opportunistic groping to occur, particular if the offender thinks he can get away with it unnoticed.
- Don't sit in the front seat of a taxi unless the driver is a woman (which will be rare).
- On public transport, sit next to a woman if possible.
- Be very careful about behaving in a flirtatious or suggestive manner; it could create more problems than you ever imagined.
- If you need help for any reason (eg, directions), ask a woman first. That said, local women are less likely than men to have had an education that included English – you'll find this a major drawback in getting to meet and talk with them. One traveller in Pakistan said she would always ask directions from children rather than approach a man. Children often speak a little English and can be very helpful.
- Be wary when horse or camel riding, especially at touristy places. Riding in front of a man on the same camel is simply asking for trouble.

One other bit of advice is that if you're hassled on buses or have men show up at your hotel door, then complain to the driver or manager. You are paying for these services and have a right to be allowed to use them without hassle, and if you don't complain it adds to the belief that foreign women don't mind.

What to Wear

As with anywhere, take your cues from those around you: If you're in a rural area and all the women are in long, concealing dresses, you should be conservatively dressed, too.

Outside of the beach resorts and cosmopolitan cities of western Turkey, it's better to ensure that legs, arms, shoulders and neckline are covered. Baggy T-shirts and loose cotton trousers or long skirts won't make you sweat as much as you think and will protect your skin from the sun as well as from unwanted comments. Wearing a bra will avoid countless unwelcome confrontations, and a hat or headscarf is also a good idea. If you have long hair it's preferable to tie it back.

In India and Nepal, dress restrictions tend to relax but too many travellers see this as an opportunity to peel off the clothing. Local sensibilities and beliefs still should be respected. Dress conservatively in religious areas such as the old cities of Amritsar and Varanasi and in Dharamsala.

GAY & LESBIAN TRAVELLERS

This region is not a good place for gay and lesbian travellers to be overt about their sexuality. Homosexuality is prohibited by law in Pakistan and Iran and subject to corporal punishment or worse (though foreigners are more likely to get deported). In Nepal, it's also illegal. This should not deter gays from visiting these countries, but, just as with heterosexual couples, you should refrain from overt signs of affection in public.

Check postings on the Lonely Planet Web site's Gay & Lesbian branch of the Thorn Tree (www.lonelyplanet.com/thorn). Requests for specific information posted here sometimes yield good results.

The International Lesbian & Gay Association (ILGA) is a worldwide federation of groups and individuals, representing almost 70 countries, dedicated to achieving equal rights for lesbians and gay men. You can contact it for general information (☎/fax 32-2-502 2471; @ ilga@ilga.org) at 81 Kolenmarkt, 1000 Brussels, Belgium. Another general resource is Amnesty International Members for Lesbian & Gay Concerns (AIMLGC), c/o Amnesty International (@ aimlgc@igc.apc.org), 304 Pennsylvania Ave SE, Washington, DC 20003, USA.

Turkey

Of all the countries along the route, Turkey has the most accepting attitude to homosexuality, but the farther east you go the more conservative it becomes. There are several gay organisations in Turkey, the most visible being Lambda İstanbul (☎ /fax 212-256 1150), PK 103, Göztepe, İstanbul. Its Web site is at www.qrd.org/qrd/www /world/europe/turkey. It also has a gay guide to Turkey in English.

India

Homosexual relations for men are illegal in India. The law forbids 'carnal intercourse against the order of nature' (that is, anal intercourse). The penalties for transgression can be up to life imprisonment. Take care to avoid situations where locals could attempt to blackmail you. There is no law against lesbian relations.

While overt displays of affection between members of the opposite sex, such as cuddling and hand-holding, are frowned upon in India, it is not unusual to see Indian men holding hands. This doesn't necessarily suggest that they are gay. The gay movement in India is confined almost exclusively to larger cities and Mumbai is really the only place where there's a gay 'scene'. Since marriage is seen as very important, to be gay is a particular stigma – most gays stay in the closet or risk being disowned by their families.

Khush is a San Fransisco-based mailing list for gay, lesbian and bisexual south Asians and friends. Its Web site adress is: (www.qrd.org/qrd/orgs/TRIKONE/khush).

DISABLED TRAVELLERS

Generally speaking, scant regard is paid to the needs of disabled travellers in the region. Steps, high kerbs and other assorted obstacles are everywhere, streets are often badly rutted and uneven, roads are made virtually uncrossable by heavy traffic, while many doorways are low and narrow. Ramps and specially equipped lodgings and toilets are an extreme rarity. You will have to plan your trip carefully and probably be obliged to restrict yourself to luxury-level hotels and private, hired transport.

Before setting off for the region disabled travellers could get in touch with their national support organisation (preferably with the travel officer, if there is one). In the UK, contact Radar (☎ 020-7250 3222), 250 City Rd, London EC1V 8AF, or see its Web site at www.radar.org.uk, or the Holiday Care Service (☎ 01293-774 535). In the US, contact Mobility International USA (☎ 1-541-343-1284), PO Box 10767, Eugene, Oregon, USA 97440, or see its Web site at www.miusa.org. In Australia, contact Nican (02-6285 3713), PO Box 407, Curtin, ACT 2605, or see its Web site at www.nican.com.au.

TRAVEL WITH CHILDREN

Taking the kids can add another dimension to any trip, let alone an overland experience! There are a few things to consider. Firstly, it's a good idea to avoid travel in summer as extreme heat can be uncomfortable and energy sapping for you, more so for children. With infants, another problem may be hygiene. It's impractical to carry more than about half a dozen washable nappies around with you, but disposable ones are not always that easy to come by. Powdered milk is widely available, as is bottled water. As for hotels, you are going to want something with a (clean) private bathroom and hot water, which precludes a lot of budget accommodation. The good news is that children are made a big fuss of in the region. They'll help break the ice and open doors to closer contact with locals.

For more comprehensive advice on the dos and don'ts of taking the kids in your luggage, check out Lonely Planet's *Travel with Children* by Maureen Wheeler.

DANGERS & ANNOYANCES

Travelling along this route is not dangerous as such. Reports of westerners – occasionally tourists – disappearing or being kidnapped surface from time to time, but the trouble spots that fill international news slots are usually well defined, and as long as you keep track of political developments, you are unlikely to come to any harm. Political insurgency has been a problem in eastern Turkey, parts of Pakistan and in Nepal in recent years but tourists are not targets of these groups. From time to time foreigners disappear while trekking in Nepal and in the Kullu region of Himachal Pradesh. Avoid trekking alone and let someone know where you're going and when you'll be back.

Before heading off the beaten track, always ask local advice from someone you can (or should be able to) trust, such as staff at a tourist office, embassy or at your hotel. Police in the region tend not to have much time or patience for doling out advice to travellers, so they're best left alone. Registering with your embassy (see Embassies & Consulates earlier in this chapter) is one way of maintaining peace of mind.

There are, various minor frustrations, irritations and hazards to be aware of. These include the scams and con men you'll almost certainly encounter, particularly in cities and touristy areas, and the behaviour of some local males towards women, particularly in Turkey and India – see the Women Travellers section earlier in this chapter.

Drugs

You don't have to have seen *Midnight Express* (even if it was a scandalously biased film) to know that possession, use or smuggling of drugs will land you a lengthy jail term in Turkey, and the same can be said for Iran, Pakistan and India.

There was a time, back in the hazy, heady days of the late 1960s and 1970s, when the Asian overland trail was, for many, a chance to indulge in cheap drugs – mainly marijuana and hashish – with Kathmandu providing the ultimate destination for 'freaks'. But the party is over. Drug use is no longer free and easy and the penalties are enough to put anyone off.

Of course, this doesn't mean that drugs are not available. Together with Afghanistan, Pakistan is second only to the South-East Asian Golden Triangle in theproduction and export of heroin. Drug smuggling is big business along the Afghan border and the Baluchistan coast. Nudged by the US, the government has tried to curtail the cultivation of opium poppies, but

Is it Safe?

The relative safety of travel in this region is quite a subjective issue. Asked if they would consider Pakistan or south-eastern Turkey safe places to travel, many westerners would say 'No'. And that view would probably be the result of news headlines describing drive-by shootings, kidnappings, drug cartels, smugglers and the terrorist activities of separatists or fundamentalists. Stories of buses plunging over cliffs in Nepal and of riots in India also pop up from time to time.

But imagine a person whose image of the United States was built solely on CNN reports of gang violence in Los Angeles, Waco-style incidents or Jerry Springer shows. Or someone whose knowledge of the British came only from the behaviour of football hooligans abroad.

Daily life in this region rarely involves guns, bombs or other elements of terror, and as a traveller you're likely to see very few ugly incidents. Of course, parts of the region are unstable and there are trouble spots to be avoided. Always pay close heed to local advice, local media and information from other travellers. Nothing beats getting the latest news on the ground. This applies particularly if you're driving through sensitive areas such as south-eastern Turkey and Baluchistan or the North-West Frontier Province in Pakistan. Steer clear of troubled areas, avoid large gatherings of people – which can potentially turn into angry mob scenes – and avoid walking alone after dark unless you know the area is safe.

For official travel advice, try the following sources, which you can phone or look up on the Internet. They tend to be a bit paranoid at times, but are good for getting the latest information on trouble spots and incidents:

British Foreign & Commonwealth Office Travel Advice Unit
(☎ 020-7008 0232/0233) www.fco.gov.uk
Australian Department of Foreign Affairs & Trade
(☎ 02-6261 3305) www.dfat.gov.au
US State Department
(☎ 202-647 5225) travel.state.gov/travel_warnings.html

---

state influence is negligible in tribal areas, and enforcement agencies are riddled with corruption. Hashish is widely available in places like Lahore, Islamabad and Peshawar – in Islamabad you may actually notice cannabis plants growing on the side of the road! At Thursday night qawwali gatherings in Lahore the air is thick with hashish smoke.

Penalties for possession, use or smuggling of drugs are strictly enforced, with long jail sentences and large fines frequently imposed. Several westerners presently languish in Pakistani jails over drug offences. Legislation passed in 1994 makes drug smuggling punishable by death. Be wary of absolutely anyone, local or tourist, who approaches you with drugs for sale. Some dealers are in cahoots with the police, and will set you up in exchange for a cut of the fine or bribe. We've received several reports of travellers openly being offered heroin in Peshawar.

For a long time India was a place where you could indulge in all sorts of illegal drugs (again, mostly grass and hashish) with relative ease – they were cheap, readily available and the risks were minimal. Although dope is still widely available, particularly in the Himalaya, the risks have certainly increased. Penalties for possession, use, or trafficking in illegal drugs are strictly enforced. The sentence for anything the judge believes is not personal use is a *minimum* of 10 years, even for minor offences, and there is no remission or parole. Several westerners are currently sitting in Goa's jail at Fort Aguada for drug-related offences.

Bhang, a derivative of marijuana, is available legally from government bhang shops in Rajasthan and Varanasi, and you can order it (discreetly) mixed in a lassi at travellers' restaurants just about anywhere. But take care – the effects can be very strong and can leave you confused and vulnerable to other dangers. See the India chapter for details.

Theft & Violence

In general, theft is not a problem in these countries and robbery (mugging) even less so. The exception, ironically, is in heavily touristed areas – the very places in which you, as a traveller, may end up spending a lot of time. Lonely Planet has received many letters reporting thefts from hotel and hostel rooms and, more alarmingly, items and cash missing from hotel safes – the only conclusion to draw here is that it is the hotel management responsible for the thefts. This problem seems particularly prevalent in Olimpos in Turkey. Cheap hotels in Lahore also have a reputation for theft. Always keep valuables with you – never leave them in your room, not even while you just nip out to the toilet or for breakfast. Use a moneybelt, or a pouch under your clothes. If you leave items or money in a hotel safe insist on a receipt. We also met several travellers who'd fallen foul of bag snatching thieves (typically riding in pairs on motorbikes) in normally scrupulously honest Iran – the places to be on your guard are Tehrān, Esfahān and Bam.

It pays to be vigilant in India. It only takes a second in a crowded railway station to turn around and find your bag is gone. Never leave valuables in your hotel room and always keep an eye on your gear on trains, especially if you're travelling second class. On overnight sleepers you could chain your pack to the seat and use your day-pack as a pillow. Certain trains are notorious for theft, especially those going in and out of Delhi, Agra and Varanasi, so take particular care.

Also, beware of your fellow travellers; there are more than a few backpackers who make their money go further by helping themselves to other people's.

It's uncommon for foreigners to get involved in violent incidents but you should certainly avoid public demonstrations, protests or political gatherings.

Scams

A common problem you'll come across in the region – practically anywhere in the world for that matter – is the various hustlers, touts and con men who prey on tourists. Turkey and India have particularly high hassle factors. Predictably, most of the action is in large cities and areas frequented by tourists, such as beach resorts or places like Agra in India. Although these guys are not necessarily dangerous, some awareness and suitable precautions are advisable. Following are a few examples of the scams that hustlers commonly run.

Hotel Commission Scam This is the one in which a local convinces the newly arrived traveller that the hotel they are heading for is closed, horrible or very expensive and then leads them off to another 'better' place, for which they earn a commission. The main culprits are the taxi and rickshaw drivers. They receive fixed commission from hotels and hostels in touristed areas and will take you to the one offering them the best rate – which, of course, you pay for.

The simple rule is do not be swayed by anyone who tries to dissuade you from going to the hotel of your choice. And if you pick up a new 'friend' walking you to your hotel, stop them at the door: If they begin to protest, then bear in mind that no decent, ordinary person would ever dream of accompanying a foreigner into their hotel.

The Colossal Commission Rip-Off In a similar vein, the practice of paying commissions to anyone who brings in business has gotten completely out of hand in Turkey and on the subcontinent in recent years. If a tout leads you to a carpet shop, he gets a commission. If your pension owner books you on a tour, she gets a commission.

Commissions, or finder's fees, are a normal part of doing business in most parts of the world. But in Turkey the fee is at least 20% and often as high as 50% or more. This money comes directly out of your pocket but buys you almost nothing. What to do? It's simple: Don't go into a shop accompanied by anyone. Make your own reservations for special activities and events. Buy your own tickets. Sign up for a tour at the tour operator's office, not at your pension or hotel. Don't let anyone 'claim' you as their commission bait.

The Turkish Taxi Sting The following tale is not the only one we received about the practice of some Turkish taxi drivers taking tourists for a ride in more than one sense:

While catching a taxi in İstanbul, my wife and I came across a sting we'd heard about before but never experienced first-hand. Arriving back at our hotel we paid the metered fare of TL1.6Mil with a TL5Mil note. Before our very eyes, the taxi driver boldly switched the TL5Mil note for a TL100,000 from his top pocket and turned to us saying that we must have got confused by the currency and that TL100,000 wasn't enough. We demanded to be taken to the tourist police and, maybe hoping to call our bluff, he complied. After two hours explaining what had happened and being able to back this up with an ATM withdrawal receipt for the TL5Mil, the police finally came down on the side of the driver. To add to the indignity, on top of the lost TL5Mil we were also obliged to pay the original TL1.6Mil fare.

Stuart & Catherine Murphy

The Turkish Knockout In Turkey there is a small but significant danger of theft by drugging. Thieves befriend travellers, usually single men, and offer them drinks containing powerful drugs which cause the victims to lose consciousness quickly. When the victims awake hours later, they've been stripped of everything except their clothes and a terrible hangover.

A variation was described by a female reader who claims that an over-friendly local in the village of Tevfikiye (next to Troy) drugged her husband in the course of a 'friendly' evening of drinking with them, in order to get her alone and pressure her for sex.

The best way to avoid this is not to accept drinks or food from strangers, the problem being that most offers are genuine and refusal sometimes offends.

Iran Dangers We've had reports of thieves on motorbikes snatching bags from travellers in Tehrān and Esfahān; be aware that this could happen and take appropriate measures.

In three separate incidents between June and September 1999, groups of European travellers were kidnapped in the south-east of Iran, near Bam. All were released unharmed several weeks later. These incidents were perpetrated by Iranian drug traffickers seeking money or the release of colleagues from prison. There is no evidence that foreigners are being targeted (almost all drug-related crime is against locals), but it pays to be aware of the situation. Security has

been tightened in the area and it's highly likely that if you're travelling with your own transport you'll be given an escort by the army; there are increased police checks on buses too.

Our advice is to spend as little time as possible travelling between Bam and the Pakistan border (it's a desolate, scorching area anyway), and to travel during daylight. Also keep your embassy informed of your whereabouts. Avoid anywhere near the Afghanistan border, where most of the drug running happens.

Food Poisoning Scam A disturbing scam that came to light in India in 1998 appeared to be a joint venture between some unscrupulous doctors and hotel/restaurant owners (or staff). It went something like this: A traveller staying at a hotel is targeted, and when they eat at the restaurant their food is deliberately adulterated. The victim becomes quickly and violently ill with a stomach complaint. The hotel calls a particular doctor, or arranges for the victim to go to a certain clinic where the victim is treated (at high cost) and a tidy profit is made, usually from the insurance company. The doctor will usually insist the victim be hospitalised and undergo extensive – sometimes unnecessary – treatment. The scam first appeared in the backpacker areas of Agra and Varanasi when travellers complained to authorities (shortly before that it had become widely known on the backpacker grapevine) and two Irish travellers allegedly died as a result of it. When we visited in 2000, the scam seemed to have faded, but these things have a habit of going quiet for a while, and then starting up again.

You may also be approached to fraudulently sign for medical treatment you didn't receive, in exchange for part of the profits. Apart from being highly illegal, this only results in medical insurance premiums going up.

Gem Scams It seems difficult to believe, but we still get a steady trickle of letters from travellers who have fallen prey to various gem scams. Agra and Jaipur in India are two places where you're likely to meet the smooth-talking con men who convince you to buy gems 'cheaply' so that you can sell them back home for many times the price. Invariably, if you get the gems at all, they will be almost worthless. Any offer to get involved in export and sales is invariably a scam, so (unless you're a gem expert) resist the temptation to make a quick buck and don't hand over any money.

A variation on this is the carpet scam, which you might encounter in Turkey or Iran. Again the shop owner insists you can get around export duties and sell the carpets for a huge profit at home.

Other Scams If you are stopped in the street by people claiming to be police or immigration officials, ask to see ID. Never hand over your passport or money and if they insist, offer to accompany them back to the police station.

BUSINESS HOURS

The end-of-week holiday in Iran is Friday (although some shops open again on Friday evening). In addition most embassies and government offices are also closed on Thursday afternoon. Many shops and businesses (in particular those in the bazaar) close during the afternoon for a 'siesta' (from about 1 to 3 or 4 pm) and then open again in the evenings.

In India and Nepal Saturday is the weekly holiday and in Pakistan and Turkey Sunday is the day of rest. In Pakistan most business close at noon on Friday, and all day on Sunday.

In many countries, shops have different hours at different times of the year, depending on the seasons (they tend to work shorter hours in summer). During Ramadan, the month-long fast for Muslims, almost everything shuts down in the afternoon.

PUBLIC HOLIDAYS
Islamic Holy Days

Turkey, Iran and Pakistan nationally observe the main Islamic holidays of Ramadan, Eid al-Fitr, Eid al-Adha and the Prophet's Birthday. India's minority Muslim population also observes these occasions.

All Islamic holidays are celebrated within the framework of the Muslim calendar. The Muslim year is based on the lunar cycle and is divided into 12 lunar months, each with 29 or 30 days. Consequently, the Muslim year is 10 or 11 days shorter than the Christian reckoning, and the Muslim

festivals gradually move around the Gregorian calendar year, completing the cycle in roughly 33 years.

Year 0 in the Muslim calendar was when Mohammed and his followers fled from Mecca to Medina (which occurred in AD 622 in the Christian calendar). This Hejira, or migration, is taken to mark the start of the new Muslim era, much as Christ's birth marks year 0 in the Christian calendar.

Most of the countries in this book also observe both the Gregorian and the Islamic New Year holidays.

Islamic New Year Known as Ras as-Sana, literally 'the head of the year', this is usually just a one-day holiday.

The Prophet's Birthday Also known as Moulid an-Nabi, 'the feast of the Prophet', this is a one-day holiday marked by the consumption of lots of dolls and horses made from sugar.

Ramadan The ninth month of the Muslim calendar is Ramadan (Ramazan in Turkey, Ramazān in Iran), when Muslims fast during daylight hours. How strictly the fast is observed depends on the country but most Muslims conform to some extent. Foreigners are not expected to follow suit, but it is impolite to smoke, drink or eat in public during Ramadan. Business hours tend to become more erratic and usually shorter, and in out-of-the-way places in Turkey, Iran and Pakistan you may find it hard to find a street food stall, cafe or restaurant open during daylight hours. Every evening is, in a sense, a celebration. *Iftar*, the breaking of the day's fast, is a time of animated activity when the people of the local community come together to eat, drink and pray. Enough food is usually consumed to compensate for the previous hours of abstinence.

Eid al-Fitr Eid means feast and this one marks the end of Ramadan fasting. Possibly the biggest event in the Muslim calendar, it's traditionally celebrated by the sacrifice of sheep – which you'll see tethered on balconies and in courtyards during the run up to the event. It's not a festival for the squeamish. The celebrations officially last for either two or three days depending on the country. In Turkey this feast is known as Şeker Bayramı.

Major Islamic Holidays

Islamic Year	New Year	Prophet's Birthday	Ramadan Begins	Eid al-Fitr	Eid al-Adha
1422	26 Mar 01	3 Jun 01	16 Nov 01	16 Dec 01	23 Feb 02
1423	15 Mar 02	23 May 02	5 Nov 02	5 Dec 02	12 Feb 03
1424	5 Mar 03	14 May 03	27 Oct 03	27 Nov 03	31 Jan 04
1425	22 Feb 04	2 May 04	15 Oct 04	15 Nov 04	20 Jan 05

Eid al-Adha Also known as Eid al-Kebir (the Great Feast), or in Turkey as Kurban Bayramı, this feast marks the time that Muslims make the pilgrimage to Mecca. It also celebrates the Old Testament story of Abraham's willingness to sacrifice his son in order to prove his loyalty to God. At the last minute God instructed him to sacrifice a ram instead. It's very much a rerun of Eid al-Fitr, except in Turkey, where this is the more important feast and the whole country grinds to a halt for four days and sheep and cattle are sacrificed en masse. Travellers beware!

Hindu Holy Days

Hindu festivals are widely celebrated in India and Nepal. Dates are not fixed as most follow the complex Indian lunar calendar.

Shivratri This day of fasting in the Hindu month of Phalguna (February/March) is dedicated to Lord Shiva; his followers believe that it was on this day he danced the *tandava* (the dance of destruction). Processions to the temples are followed by the chanting of mantras and anointing of lingams. This is known as Maha Shivaratri in Nepal and is marked by big celebrations at Pashupatinath.

Holi Also in the month of Phalguna, this is one of the most exuberant Hindu festivals, with people marking the end of winter by throwing coloured water and red powder at one another. On the night before Holi, bonfires are built to symbolise the destruction of the evil demon Holika.

Ramanavami The birth of Rama, an incarnation of Vishnu, is celebrated in the week leading up to Ramanavami, and the *Ramayana* is widely read and performed. This festival takes place in the month of Chaitra (March/April).

Shravan Purnima In Bhadra (August/September), after a day-long fast, high-caste Hindus replace the sacred thread that they always wear looped over their left shoulder.

Dussehra Dussehra is celebrated by Hindus to celebrate the victory of Rama over Ravana, the demon king of Lanka. This 10-day festival in September/October (Asvina) is the most popular of all Hindu events; it's particularly big in Delhi.

Diwali (Deepavali) This is the happiest festival of the Hindu calendar, celebrated on the 15th day of Kartika (October/November). At night countless oil lamps are lit to show Rama the way home from his period of exile. The festival runs over five days. On the first day, houses are thoroughly cleaned and doorsteps are decorated with intricate *rangolis* (chalk designs). Day two is dedicated to Krishna's victory over Narakasura, a legendary tyrant. Day three is spent in worshipping Lakshmi, the goddess of fortune. Traditionally, this is the beginning of the new financial year for companies. Day four commemorates the visit of the friendly (but uppity) demon Bali whom Vishnu put in his place. On the fifth day men visit their sisters to have a *tika* placed on their forehead.

In Nepal this festival is called Tihar and takes place over five days in late October or early November.

Dasain Celebrated only in Nepal, the biggest of all Nepali festivals is similar to Diwali in India. The celebrations last for 15 days during Kartik, finishing on the full-moon day of late September or early October. It's very much a family affair (like Christmas in the West) but there are several important festive days. Nepalis travel at this time to be with family and friends, so getting around can be difficult.

Govardhana Puja This Hindu festival during Kartika is dedicated to that holiest of animals, the cow.

Janmashtami This national holiday celebrates the anniversary of Krishna's birth. Agra is one of the main centres of celebration. It takes place in August/September (Bhadra).

Sikh, Tibetan & Buddhist Holy Days

Sikh holy days are observed mainly in the Punjab regions of India and Pakistan, Buddhist holy days are observed in India and Nepal, while Tibetan religious events are celebrated mainly in Nepal and the Dharamsala region of India.

Baisakhi This Sikh festival commemorates the day Guru Govind Singh founded the Khalsa, the Sikh brotherhood, which adopted the five *kakkars* (the means by which Sikh men recognise each other), as part of their code of behaviour. The *Granth Sahib*, the Sikh holy book, is read through at gurdwaras (Sikh temples).

Nanak Jayanti In October/November, this celebrates the birthday of Guru Nanak, founder of the Sikh religion.

Losar Tibetan New Year falls in either February or March according to the Tibetan lunar calendar. Colourful local festivals celebrate the commencement of the new year, and this is a good time to be in a Tibetan centre.

Buddha Jayanti Buddha's birth, enlightenment and attainment of nirvana (final release from the cycle of existence), are all commemorated on this day. Buddha experienced each of these on the same day but in different years. The festival falls on the full moon on the fourth lunar month and is known as Saga Darwa in Tibetan. This is a big event in the Kathmandu Valley, particularly at Swayambhunath, Bodhnath and Patan.

Drukpa Teshi This festival celebrates the first teaching given by the Buddha. It is held on the fourth day of Bhadra (August/September).

Secular Holidays

Every country also has its own national days and other public holidays, which are secular holidays and follow the Gregorian (Christian) calendar.

New Year's Day (Regional) 1 January – every country in the region has a day off

Republic Day (India) 26 January – celebrates the anniversary of India's establishment as a republic in 1950

Magnificent Victory of the Islamic Revolution (Iran) 20 March – marks the anniversary of Khomeinī's coming to power

Pakistan Day 23 March – the date of the 1956 resolution proclaiming the Pakistan republic

Islamic Republic Day (Iran) 1 April – the anniversary of the establishment of the Islamic Republic of Iran in 1979

Nepali New Year mid-April – starts at the beginning of the month of Baisakh

National Sovereignty Day (Turkey) 23 April – celebrates the first republican parliament in Ankara in 1920

Dalai Lama's Birthday 6 July – Buddhist celebrations in Nepal and at the home of the Tibetan leader in McLeod Ganj

Independence Day (Pakistan) 14 August – the anniversary of the birth of Pakistan in 1947

Independence Day (India) 15 August – celebrates the anniversary of India's independence from Britain in 1947

Victory Day (Turkey) 30 August – celebrates the victory over the invading Greek armies at Dumlupınar in 1922

Jinnah's Death (Pakistan) 11 September – the *urs* (death anniversary) of Mohammed Ali Jinnah, regarded as the founder of Pakistan

Gandhi Jayanti (India) 2 October – celebration of Gandhi's birthday

Republic Day (Turkey) 29 October – marks the proclamation of the republic in 1923

Queen's Birthday (Nepal) 7 November

Atatürk's Death (Turkey) 10 November – a minute's silence at 9.05 am commemorates Atatürk's death in 1938

King's Birthday (Nepal) 29 December

In addition to the main Islamic holidays, Iran observes:

Ghadir-é Khom 18 Zu-l-Hejjé (variable) – the day that the Prophet Mohammed appointed Emām Alī as his successor

Ashura 9 & 10 Moharram (variable) – anniversary of the martyrdom of Hussein, the third emām of the Shi'ites; celebrated with religious dramas and sombre parades

International Qods Day Last Friday of Ramadan (variable) – many Iranians take to the streets to protest against the Israeli 'occupation' of Palestine

Arbaeen 20 & 21 Safar (variable) – the 40th day after 9 & 10 Moharram (Ashura)

Anniversary of Khomeinī's rise to power 11 February (22 Bahman)

Oil Nationalisation Day 20 March (29 Esfand)

Nō Rūz (Iranian New Year) around 21 to 24 March (1 to 4 Farvardīn)

Islamic Republic Day 1 April (12 Farvardīn) – the anniversary of the establishment of the Islamic Republic of Iran in 1979

Sīzdah Bedar 2 April (13 Farvardīn) – 13th day after the Iranian New Year, when most Iranians leave their houses for the day

Death of Emām Khomeinī 4 June (14 Khordād) – particularly chaotic in Tehrān and Qom

Arrest of Emām Khomeinī 5 June (15 Khordād)

Anniversary of a bomb blast in 1980 8 June (7 Tīr) – marks a bomb blast that happened at a meeting of the Islamic Republic Party

Day of the Martyrs of the Revolution 8 September (17 Shahrīvar)

SPECIAL EVENTS

There are dozens of festivals and events held annually throughout the region; some are religious (most of which are mentioned earlier), others are aimed at attracting tourists and others are traditional events dating back centuries. Tourist offices can usually give exact dates for the coming year. Some events worth looking out for on this route include:

January

Camel-Wrestling Festival (Turkey) Held on 1 January in the village of Selçuk, south of İzmir.

February

Basant (Pakistan) The kite festival of Lahore. People have picnics on their rooftops and the sky is full of kites. Many kite fliers coat their strings with ground glass, suitable for cutting another's string, and battles go on all day. This spring festival is also celebrated in parts of India.

Taj Mahotsava (India) A festival of music and dance in Agra, the home of the Taj Mahal.

Jaisalmer Desert Festival (India) This is a somewhat touristy event but the setting and upbeat atmosphere make it worthwhile. Three days of folk music, cultural shows and camel races.

March

Ghodejatra (Nepal) Festival of horses in Kathmandu.

Nō Rūz (Iran) The New Year period is celebrated for about 10 days by all Iranians. The best place is Yazd, home of Iran's Zoroastrian community, and the nearby fire temple at Chak Chak.

Rose Festival (Pakistan) The first of several annual flower shows in the Rose & Jasmine Garden at Islamabad.

April

Anzac Day (Turkey) On 25 April, this day is commemorated with a dawn ceremony at Gallipoli.

Shoton Festival (India) This festival of opera singing and dance is performed at the Tibetan Institute of Performing Arts in McLeod Ganj near Dharamsala.

Mewar Festival (India) A colourful Rajasthani folk festival held in Udaipur during the state wide Gangaur Festival. As well as music and dancing, the festival concludes with a procession of boats on the lake.

May

Selçuk Festival (Turkey) Held in the first week of May. Features folk dances and concerts, some using the ancient Roman theatre at Ephesus.

Bari Imam (Pakistan) A carnival-like celebration of the urs of Bari Shah Latif, patron saint of Islamabad.

June

International İstanbul Festival of the Arts (Turkey) A world-class festival held from late June to early July, with top performers in music and dance, and special exhibitions.

Armenian Christian festival of St Thaddaeus (Iran) The place to be is the Ghara Kelīsā near Mākū.

July

Gaijatra (Cow Festival) (Nepal) Eight-day carnival with singing, dancing and comedy.

International Mango Festival (India) A three-day event in Delhi celebrating this sticky, sweet fruit with mango eating and cooking competitions, dancing, music and a cultural program.

August

Çanakkale Troy Festival (Turkey) Held 15–18 August with folk dances and music.

Indrajatra (Nepal) Celebrated in the Kathmandu Valley, this is the festival of Indra, Goddess of Rain. Lasting eight days, the highlight is when the chariot of Kumari, the Living Goddess, is paraded through the streets.

Teej Fair (India) Most notably celebrated in Jaipur, this marks the onset of the monsoon and honours the marriage of Shiva and Parvati. It's also known as the Festival of Swings.

September

Dasain (Nepal) The most important of all Nepali festivals is held in late September/October. It celebrates the victory of the goddess Durga over the forces of evil in the guise of the buffalo demon Mahisasura.

November

Pushkar Camel Fair (India) One of India's largest non-religious events, this is one not to be missed if you're in Rajasthan at the time. Primarily a trade fair, it has grown into a huge carnival – see the India chapter for more details.

December

Mevlâna Festival (Turkey) Held in the town of Konya from 10 to 17 December. The whirling dervishes go through their paces.

ACTIVITIES

Although much of this region is not generally associated with activities or adventure sports, its wide variety of terrain – from deserts to beaches to snow-capped mountains – offers quite a few opportunities for adventure-seekers. Turkey and Nepal in particular have plenty of scope for challenging the great outdoors. This section offers an overview of some of the possible activities en route – details on how to get involved are in the relevant country chapters.

Beaches & Water Sports

If the beach is your scene, this route may not be for you. Beaches can only be found in Turkey on the Mediterranean coast and, Ölüdeniz and Patara aside, they're not particularly alluring. The rest of the route is strictly inland and any beach excursions would involve a major detour.

Turkey is, however, a great place for water sports such as diving, windsurfing, sea kayaking and yachting. See the Turkey chapter for more information.

Skiing

At the right time of year it's possible to ski in Turkey and Iran, and even in Pakistan and India, though the resorts at the latter are not well developed. In Turkey there is OK skiing for beginners and intermediates on Uludağ, near Bursa, at a few resorts in the Beydağları mountain range near Antalya, at Erciyes Dağı near Kayseri and at Palendöken on the outskirts of Erzurum. Ski

facilities are basic by European or US standards but the snow can be good and sometimes lasts until spring.

In Iran, skiing is popular among the middle and upper classes (and foreigners who appreciate that Iran is one of the least expensive skiing destinations in the world). The season is long (between January and May), the snow is often like powder and there are several downhill skiing areas, with resorts, within an hour or two by road from Tehrān. It's also possible to ski near Tabrīz at Mt Sahand. Regulations that require men and women to ski on different slopes and use different lifts are being relaxed. Women must still wear appropriate attire, but often something baggy over your ski clothes will suffice.

One of the very few recognised ski agencies in Iran is Iran Khudro (☎ 21-276 701, fax 265 555), 33 Sadābād St, Tajrish Square, Tehrān; PO Box 19615/519.

In Pakistan, there are very simple skiing facilities accessible from our route at Kalabagh near Murree. A much bigger ski resort is at Malam Jabba in the Swat Valley. The season is from December to March. In India there is an equally basic ski resort at Narkanda near Shimla, and better facilities at Solang Nullah, north of Manali. India's best ski resort is at Auli in Uttaranchal (formerly the northern part of Uttar Pradesh). The season lasts from January to April.

Despite the existence of all those mountains, there are no ski resorts in Nepal.

Cycling

You don't have to ride all the way from İstanbul to Kathmandu to enjoy some cycling along this route. In Turkey and Nepal in particular there is plenty of opportunity to hire bikes for day rides or to join a short cycling tour. In India, where thousands of people are always riding around on bicycles, you can hire old rattlers for around INRs 25 a day – but don't expect to find many state-of-the-art mountain bikes.

The concept of bicycle hire has not caught on in Pakistan. We tried asking at a few second-hand bicycle shops, but the owners wanted a deposit equal to the full value of a brand new bike! Come to think of it, you can buy a brand new Chinese-built bicycle freshly smuggled in from Afghanistan for about PKRs 1000. You'd have to go up to

Gilgit in the Northern Areas to find a tour operator organising cycling trips.

Iran is not well suited to leisurely cycling and Iranians don't do much of it – powered transport is far too cheap. Bikes can be rented from the Y@zd Internet Cafe in Yazd (see the Iran chapter for details), but rental is not common elsewhere.

In Turkey, bikes can be hired on Büyükada, the largest of the Kızıl Adalar (Princes' Islands) near İstanbul, and in Göreme, in Cappadocia. It's possible to buy a fairly good bike in İstanbul for around US$400 to US$500 at Asli Bisiklet (☎ 212-527 3563), Hamidiye Caddesi, Eski Duyunu Umumiye Sokak No 2/2, Sirkeci, or Bahar Hirduvat (☎ 212-244 4715), Yuksekkarldirim Galip Dede Caddesi 181, Taksim. Both of these shops also have accessories and good quality spares. Mountain biking excursions are also organised out of Kaş.

Nepal is where mountain biking comes into its own and there are several professional outfits in Kathmandu offering tours from one day to a few weeks. See the Nepal chapter for details. You can also hire ageing Indian bicycles very cheaply in Kathmandu and Pokhara.

Information on bringing your own bicycle for a more extensive tour of the region is given in the Getting Around chapter.

Desert Safaris

Rajasthan, in India, is the place for desert safaris, either by camel or 4WD. The most popular starting point is Jaisalmer, way out on the edge of the Thar Desert, where dozens of operators compete fiercely for business. You can go on anything from an afternoon camel ride on the fringes of the dunes to a week-long, bum-wearying safari, camping out under the stars. There are also camel safaris from Jodhpur and Pushkar, which aren't quite as romantic but have the advantage of being less touristy. November to March is the best time to go, with the peak season being in December and January.

It's also possible to head off into the desert in Pakistan. Camel trips to Derawar Fort in the Cholistan Desert can be arranged from Bahawalpur or Multan if you give the local tourist office enough notice.

There's plenty of desert in Iran but it's not all terribly accessible. For a short trip,

Y@zd Internet Cafe in Yazd organises 'breakfast-in-the-desert' tours that include visits to Zoroastrian temples and towns. Longer excursions into the Dasht-é Kavīr and Dasht-é Lūt can also be organised out of Tehrān; you'll need a reputable guide, sturdy transport and plenty of supplies.

Hamams (Turkish Baths)

Enjoying a steam-clean and massage is a quintessential Middle Eastern thing to do and one that shouldn't be missed. The best place to do this is in Turkey, although there are also traditional baths in the bazaars in Kāshān and Kermān in Iran. See the 'Bath Time' boxed text in the Turkey chapter.

Hiking & Trekking

Parts of this route were made for walking, with a wealth of opportunities from leisurely strolls to strenuous overnight treks – and not just in Nepal.

Turkey Hiking and mountain trekking are becoming increasingly popular in Turkey, particularly in the north-east and in the Cappadocia region. Turkey's first marked long distance walk, the Lycian Way, links Fethiye with Antalya, taking in ancient sites, deserted beaches, high passes and nomad camps. It can be walked in several stages – see the boxed text 'The Lycian Way' in the Turkey chapter.

Iran In Iran, there are many trails from Tehrān heading up into the Alborz Mountains – favourite spots close to the city include Darband and the starker slopes of Tōchāl. More serious climbers will want to tackle the country's highest mountain Damāvand (5671m). Māsūlé, a delightful village on the lush slopes near the Caspian province city of Rasht, is the perfect place to be based for easy trekking. On the other side of the mountain range, the villages of Alamūt, holding the ruins of the Castles of the Assassins, are also great places for hiking with plenty of trails.

Pakistan There are leisurely walking options around Quetta and the Ziarat Valley, as well as in the Margalla Hills around Islamabad. Murree hill station and the nearby *galis* (villages), easily accessible from Islamabad, have some good summer walking trails. However, the best of the hiking in Pakistan is found in the Swat Valley and the Northern Areas, which are beyond the scope of this route. Hiking and mountain tours can be organised from Peshawar, Islamabad and Lahore.

India Northern India's best hiking is to be found in the Himalayan regions of Himachal Pradesh and farther north in the sensitive areas of Jammu and Kashmir. There are several excellent hikes around Dharamsala, including the trek over the Indrahar Pass into the Chamba Valley, and the Kullu Valley is also a superb hiking area. We describe the trek from McLeod Ganj to Ilaqa in the India chapter. The pleasant hill station of Shimla is surrounded by forests crisscrossed with walking trails. March to July is the best time for walking in these areas.

Nepal Nepal is, of course, a trekker's paradise. No matter how tired you feel when you get there, the stunning mountain views and cool, clear air (outside of Kathmandu, that is) will seduce you every time. Try to allow some time to get out of the Kathmandu Valley and into the mountains proper. Short treks can easily be made from Pokhara. The full Annapurna Circuit takes two to three weeks but if you fly into Jomson and walk back on the western side it can be done in five days. The Royal Trek (also known as Annapurna Skyline) takes only about three days, while the walk to the Annapurna Base Camp and back takes about 11 days. There are many more short day walks around Pokhara from where you can still enjoy the unmatched panorama of the Annapurna range.

Walking to or from the rim of the Kathmandu Valley is a must, and Nagarkot is a favourite destination. See the Nepal chapter for more details. The more adventurous can strike out on the Helambu or Langtang treks or the famous Everest Base Camp trek. The best time for trekking is October to March, although it gets extremely cold at altitude from December to February. You must be prepared for all conditions – the weather in the mountains can change in the blink of an eye. If trekking above 3000m, you should be fully aware of the need to acclimatise and what to do if you or a trekking partner shows signs of altitude sickness. See the Health section earlier in this chapter for more details.

White-Water Rafting & Kayaking

In Turkey, rafting is run on a few rivers but the sport has not really been developed as it has in Nepal and is also being hampered by the wholesale damming of rivers. Along the Mediterranean coast the Dalaman and Köprülü Rivers offer one-day rafting trips. Rivers that are regularly rafted are the Çoruh and Findikli in Eastern Turkey and the Firat (Euphrates) in central Turkey near Erzincan.

The dam being built on the Çoruh River will flood the river up to Yusufeli but this will take at least five years to complete. Rafting is also possible on the Zamanti River in Cappadocia; it can be arranged through tour agencies in Göreme.

In Iran there is commercial kayaking down the Dez River from Dorud to Telle Zange with days in Esfahān before and after the trip. The Dez is not suitable for rafting. Contact Dave Manby, 12 Mayfield Park, Shrewsbury, SY2 6PD, UK, or see his Web site at www.dmanby.demon.co.uk.

In Pakistan, several NWFP and Northern Areas rivers have stretches of rapids suitable for commercial rafting and kayaking. These include the Indus (Jaglot to Thakot in Indus Kohistan), Kunhar (Naran to Kaghan in the Kaghan Valley), Swat (Madyan to Saidu Sharif), Gilgit (from Punial to the Indus confluence), lower Ishkoman, Shyok (from Khapalu to Gol in Baltistan), and Hunza (Sost to Passu and Aliabad to Gilgit). Although these are north of our route, travel agents and tour operators in major cities and in Gilgit can organise trips with transport and accommodation. The season is approximately from May to late June and late September through November.

With the waters cascading off the Himalayan peaks, it should come as no surprise that Nepal has some of the world's finest white-water rafting. There are many outfits offering trips from two to eight days out of Kathmandu and Pokhara. The Bhote Kosi, Sun Kosi, Kali Gandaki and Karnali have some of Nepal's best rapids, while the Trisuli is good for beginners. Kayaking is also popular on most of these rivers. See the Nepal chapter for more details

COURSES
Language Courses
Turkish One of our authors spent a month studying Turkish for four hours a day, five days a week at Tömer in İstanbul (☎ 252 5154), İnönü Caddesi, Prof Dr Tarık Zafer Tunaya Sokak 18, Taksim for US$250. Morning, afternoon and evening classes are available at a variety of different levels. There are other branches at İzmir and Antalya. Another possibility is International House (☎ 282 9064, fax 282 3218), Nispetiye Caddesi, Güvercin Durayı, Erdölen İşhani38, Kat 1, Levent, İstanbul.

The *Turkish Daily News* carries ads for private tutors, as does *ISTANbullshit*, a freebie available at the Orient hostel in İstanbul, or see the Web site (www.istanbullshit.net).

Hindi & Tibetan At McLeod Ganj it's possible to learn Tibetan either at the Library of Tibetan Works & Archives or from private teachers. Hindi classes are also given here.

Nepali Nepali is not a difficult language to learn, and there are a number of courses available. You will often see signs and notices around Kathmandu advertising language courses, many of them conducted by ex-Peace Corps workers. Embassies should be able to recommend somewhere that they themselves use.

Most schools offer courses (often around two weeks long) or individual tuition. Places to try in Kathmandu include the Speed Language Institute (☎ 220999) in Bagh Bazaar; Insight Nepal (☎ 418963); the Bud Language Institute (☎ 249576); or the School of International Languages (☎ 211713) at Kathmandu University. Expect to pay about US$50 for a two week course, around US$3 for private hourly tuition.

Other Courses
Meditation, Yoga & Philosophy In India, McLeod Ganj is a popular centre for Tibetan Buddhism, yoga and meditation courses. Delhi also has many yoga and meditation schools, while Varanasi is India's spiritual heartland and a popular place for travellers to zone out.

In Nepal, courses are centred around the Kathmandu Valley, and there are a number of places and options. Check the notice boards in Thamel for up-to-date information about yoga and Buddhism courses. The Arogya Ashram near the Pashupatinath Temple teaches yoga. Arogya also has a branch in Kathmandu.

WORK
It is quite possible to pick up work in the region in order to extend your stay and stretch out your savings but you have to know where to look and what you are looking for.

Teaching English
The first option is teaching English. Teaching centres – both the respectable kind and cowboy outfits – can be found throughout the region. The latter are often desperate for teachers and will take on people whose only qualification is that their mother tongue is English. Pay is minimal and you'll probably have to stay on a tourist visa, which you'll have to renew, but many long-termers finance their stays this way. Try English Fast at Altiyol, Yogurtcu Sukru Sokak 29 in the Kadikoy district of İstanbul or visit the British Council.

If you have a Certificate in English Language Teaching to Adults (CELTA) your chances of getting a job are greatly improved. To get the qualification, you need to attend a one-month intensive course, which you can do in your home country via an English-language training centre. In the UK, contact International House (☎ 020-7491 2598), which runs more than a dozen courses a year. IH has 110 affiliated schools in 30 countries worldwide, including İstanbul, and once you've completed the course you can apply for any advertised positions.

The other big employer of English-language teachers is the British Council. Its overseas teaching centres do most of their recruiting in the UK; contact the Information Centre (☎ 0161-957 7755, fax 957 7762) to find out, but you may pick up some part time work on spec. Check out its Web site (www.britishcouncil.org) for more information.

In Pakistan there is a growing demand for English teachers. You may be offered free room and board with a local family and possibly a small salary. Teaching is usually in private primary schools. In McLeod Ganj you can teach English to newly arrived Tibetan refugees, although this work is usually voluntary. There is also plenty of scope for teaching English in Nepal, usually at private schools in the Kathmandu region. Many of these positions are filled from abroad, ie, you line the job up through an agency in your home country (often at great personal expense), but if you ask around there may be something available on the spot.

Working at Hostels

In Turkey (particularly İstanbul, Selçuk, Bodrum, Fethiye and Cappadocia) it's usually possible to pick up work in a hostel, typically cleaning rooms or looking after reception. It doesn't pay much but it will usually get you free accommodation, a meal or two a day plus some beer money. The only way to find this kind of work is to ask around. If you're looking for casual work in Turkey, the best bet is to ask around at bars and restaurants in the main resort towns.

Tourism

Everywhere that tourists gather there is a huge array of jobs on offer. In İstanbul, for example, foreigners are often hired as middle agents by carpet shops on the theory that other visitors respond more positively to non-Turkish sales people. You get paid about 20% commission for each sale.

Similarly, some travellers are employed in travel agencies as a first point of contact between other travellers and the agency. Many work on commission, others work on a fixed rate of about US$400 per year. There's a lot of work for travellers over in Göreme of the bar staff, carpet seller, hostel-minder type.

Often hostels carry notices of employment but otherwise it's not difficult to find out where the job opportunities are. More likely than not a couple of people at your hostel will be 'long-termers' in some kind of employment and you can ask them for advice.

This sort of employment doesn't tend to apply on the subcontinent. Except in Kathmandu, it's rare to see westerners working in tourist-related industries or hospitality.

Volunteer Work

If you're planning on staying in the region for some time – at either end of your journey – the following organisations offer either one- or two-year skills-based placements or shorter-term opportunities.

Action Without Borders Inc (☎ 212-843-3973, fax 564-3377) 50 Fifth Avenue, Suite 6614, New York, NY 10118
  Web site: www.idealist.org
Australian Volunteers International (☎ 03-9279 1788, fax 9419 4280, ⓔ ozvol@ozvol.org.au) PO Box 350, Fitzroy Victoria 3065, Australia
  Web site: www.ozvol.org.au
Co-ordinating Committee for International Voluntary Service (☎ 01 45 68 27 31, ⓔ ccivs@zcc.net) Unesco House, 1 rue Miollis, 75732 Paris Cedex, France
  Web site: www.unesco.org/cciivs
Global Volunteers (☎ 800-487 1073, fax 651-482 0915, ⓔ email@globalvolunteers.org) 375 East Little Canada Rd, St Paul, MN 55117-1627, USA
  Web site: www.globalvolunteers.org
Peace Corps of the USA (☎ 1800-424 8580, fax 202-692 2201, ⓔ webmaster@peacecorps.gov) 1111 20th St NW, Washington DC 20526, USA
  Web site: www.peacecorps.gov
Voluntary Service Overseas, VSO (☎ 020-8780 7200, fax 8780 7370, ⓔ enquiry@vso.org.uk) 317 Putney Bridge Rd, London SW15 2PN, UK
  Web site: www.vso.org.uk
Volunteer Work Information Service, VWIS (☎ /fax 22-366 16 51, ⓔ info@workingabroad.com) Case Postale 90, 1268 Begnins, Vaud, Switzerland
  Web site: www.workingabroad.com

ACCOMMODATION

Most overlanders are travelling on a tight budget and although travel through these countries is cheap, accommodation is still going to represent a major portion of your funds. Our coverage concentrates on the budget and mid-range options (which are still budget by Western standards), with a few interesting top-end places thrown in for a splurge.

Even staying at the cheapest places, the range of accommodation you'll encounter in the region is wide and can be memorable, if not always comfortable – from treehouses on the Mediterranean coast of Turkey to teahouses on trekking routes in Nepal.

Most of the time, though, you'll be staying in a fairly standard, cheapo hotel. Wherever there's a backpacker scene – from Sultanahmet in İstanbul to Thamel in

Kathmandu – you'll find decent, cheap hotels or guesthouses, understanding management (sometimes) and plenty of other travellers. Elsewhere, there are cheap local hotels in varying states of cleanliness with management ranging from indifferent to unpleasant. These places are typically (though not always) run-down and frequented by shady characters. We try to avoid the real dives – for the sake of a few rupees it's worth going for something safe and half-clean. In any case many cheap hotels in India and Pakistan are simply not interested in having foreigners stay (they are required to register all foreign guests with the local police station). Hotels close to train and bus stations are convenient but they're usually the seediest of the lot.

In Turkey the cheapest rooms are dormitories that accommodate anything from four to 10 people and cost around US$5. There are shared bathroom facilities that can get pretty crowded at times. You'll also find dormitories at backpacker places in Iran and at a handful of YHAs and YWCAs in Pakistan. In India you'll find dormitories at railway retiring rooms, state-run tourist bungalows and the occasional YHA, but they're usually not much cheaper than a budget single room.

Even cheap hotel rooms in Pakistan and India usually have an attached bathroom with toilet (often of the squat variety) and running water. Hot water is not always available, though hotels accustomed to dealing with tourists now make a point of advertising 24-hour hot water. If you want it, ask if there's *garam pani*. when you check the room. Some hotels in India and Nepal have either geyser hot water, which is just a tap by which you fill a bucket, or they don't have running hot water at all and you have to ask for a bucket of it to be brought to your room.

Always ask to see the room before checking in, and inquire about other rooms as you won't always be shown the best option first. Mid-range hotels offer affordable relief from basic rooms, especially in Pakistan, India and Nepal. They might have carpeting, a TV with cable, room service, clean bathrooms and even air-conditioning (although you pay considerably more for the latter).

Some hotel managers might ask to hold your passport. This is generally to ensure payment but they have no right to it and you shouldn't acquiesce – tell them you need it to change money at the bank. If you want to hang on to it, the hotel may insist on advance payment for the room.

You don't always have to head for the nearest hotel or hostel. Following are some of the more interesting places to stay en route:

Treehouses in Olimpos (Turkey) A favourite among travellers, you can hang out in a tree for US$6 a night.

Caves in Cappadocia (Turkey) Göreme is famous for its surreal lunar landscape and 'fairy chimneys' and here you can actually stay in one of the caves cut into the soft rock, again for around US$6.

Golden Temple at Amritsar (India) The Sikh religion has a code of hospitality towards travellers and pilgrims. As a result you can stay for free at most Sikh gurdwaras (temples). The best is the magnificent Golden Temple in Amritsar.

Palaces & Forts (India) In Rajasthan you can stay in luxurious former maharaja's palaces, more modest havelis, or inside the fort at Jaisalmer. The cost can be anything from a couple of dollars to US$500 a night!

Ashrams & Spiritual Centres (India) There are several ashrams in Varanasi's old city where you can stay very cheaply and receive spiritual education to boot. In McLeod Ganj there are a couple of residential courses in meditation and Buddhist philosophy where you stay for free or for a small donation.

Teahouses (Nepal) These are often no different from any small, family-run guesthouse, but it's the location – in a tiny village or along a trail 3000m up – that makes them special. The view when you get up for breakfast can't be beaten.

Camping

There are plenty of camp sites in Turkey, particularly along the Aegean and Mediterranean coasts. However, by Turkish standards they are not particularly cheap and the facilities are not that great. Instead, it's quite possible to pitch your tent in a discreet spot.

Elsewhere in the region camping is possible but it's always better to stick to officially sanctioned camping sites (of which there are few) because many areas that are military or restricted zones aren't always marked as such. And in India, especially, you'll find it's impossible to pitch a tent with any sort of privacy or solitude. There are camping grounds catering to overland travellers in İstanbul, Islamabad and Delhi.

FOOD

The quality of food and the local staples varies, but you'll never go hungry. Local-style food is usually safer than Western-style food because it's cooked longer (sometimes all day) and the ingredients are invariably fresh. What's more, Eastern attempts at Western food rarely seem to come out as you'd expect! Kathmandu is an exception, relatively speaking. After subsisting on thalis (all-you-can-eat vegetarian meals) and kebabs for months, the 'international' restaurants of Thamel will blow you away.

Street food in the region is good, cheap and usually safe enough to eat, although you take your chances with meat in Pakistan, India and Nepal. The scope of street food can become quite limited so it's always good to dine out at a decent restaurant occasionally. Vegetarians will have a hard time of things in some areas – especially Turkey, Iran and Pakistan where kebabs (*kebaps* in Turkey, *kabābs* in Iran) rule. India offers the ubiquitous thali, *dosas* (lentil pancakes) and other vegetarian treats, although the best vegetarian food comes from the south.

Self-catering is a possibility, although you'll rarely find accommodation where you can use the kitchen in the style of youth hostels. Fresh fruit and vegetables are available at markets throughout the region. In larger cities and towns you'll also find Western-style supermarkets or grocery stores. Buying local staples such as rice and lentils will never be a problem.

Turkey

It is worth travelling to Turkey just to eat. For those on an adventurer's low budget, the Turkish *pideci* (pizza place) is a godsend. At a pideci, the dough for flat bread is patted out and shaped something like a boat, then dabbed with butter and other toppings, baked in a wood-fired oven, and served at once. It's fresh, delicious, inexpensive and nutritious. Then there's the *kebapçi* where you get thin strips of meat loaded into a loaf of bread the size of a football – filling and cheap. The meat is either lamb or chicken – ground or in chunks. There are many types of kebaps and preparation, spices and extras (onions, peppers, sauces, bread) make all the difference. Some may be ordered *yoğurtlu*, with a side-serving of yogurt.

If you fancy other cheap snacks, there are millions of little stands and quick-lunch places known as *büfe* (buffet). These serve sandwiches, often grilled, puddings, portions of *börek*, flaky pastries, and perhaps *lahmacun*, an Arabic soft pizza made with chopped onion, lamb and tomato sauce. *Pastane* are pastry shops that are good for breakfast and sweet snacks.

In restaurants it's possible to make an entire meal of *meze* (appetisers). Often you will be brought a tray from which you choose what you want: *zeytin* (olives), *turşu* (pickled vegetables), *patates tava* (french fries/chips) or light potato fritters called *patates köfte*.

Turkish desserts tend to be very sweet. Many are baked, such as crumpets, biscuits or shredded wheat. Baklava comes in several varieties: *cevizli* is with chopped walnut stuffing; *fıstıklı* is with pistachio nuts; *kaymaklı* is with clotted cream. Sometimes you can order *kuru baklava*, 'dry' baklava that has less syrup. True baklava is made with honey, not syrup, and though the home-made stuff may contain honey, the store-bought stuff rarely does. Little need be said about Turkish delight, the soft, gummy sweet that's available everywhere.

Iran

There is some excellent Iranian cuisine but, unless you get invited to an Iranian home, your chance of finding it is limited. More often than not the choice for the budget traveller is a kebāb, a hamburger or fried sausage (made from totally mysterious ingredients) sandwich or pizza from a fast food cafe or kabābī. The standard is not bad but it gets boring quickly.

In restaurants, fluffy white rice (*berenji*) and flat bread *nūn* are the staples, along with salad and the standard *kabāb*, made either from chicken, lamb or mutton, beef and very occasionally veal or fish. When served with rice – lots of it – the meal is known as *chelō kabāb*; chicken with rice is *chelō morgh*. Kebabs are usually accompanied by raw onion, a pat of butter and a bowl of yogurt to stir into the rice.

A more interesting dish is *ābgūsht* (also called *dīzī*), a hearty stew of mutton, fat, chickpeas, potato and tomato, all mashed up in a bowl; this is a lunchtime standard in teashops and is always served with plenty of bread that you break up and soak in the stew's sauce. At better places the bread will be served with a basket of fresh herbs and maybe some goats' cheese – combined they make a great appetiser.

Khōresht is a blanket term for stew and makes a pleasant change from kebabs, if it's on the menu; vegetarians should be on the lookout for *sabzī khōresht* (vegetable stew). One of the most delicious stews is *fesenjān*, traditionally poultry, but sometimes beef or lamb, in a rich sauce of pomegranate juice and walnuts.

Iranian ice cream (*bastanī*) is totally addictive, especially when flavoured with saffron. Another refreshing iced dessert to look out for is *fālūdé*, vermicelli in rosewater syrup served with a dash of lime juice. The local *bāghlavā* is not as sweet as the Turkish version and often filled with delicious pistachio nuts.

Pakistan

Pakistani food is similar to that of northern India – *Mughlai*, cuisine of the Mughals – but with Middle Eastern influences via Afghanistan. It tends to be spicy (but not to Indian extremes) and oily. On the whole, budget travellers won't remember Pakistan for good eating but there are exceptions. The Pakistani diet is based largely on meat, although Tuesday (and sometimes Wednesday) is a 'meatless' day everywhere. On such days mutton and beef are not supposed to be sold or served in public places (chicken is allowed); the reasons are economic, not religious. Pork is taboo to Muslims, so you won't find it anywhere.

The general term for bread is roti. Most varieties are made from unleavened wheat flour. No eatery in the land is without chapatis, flat rounds cooked on a dry griddle. They also serve for grabbing, spooning or soaking up all the bits and juices. Dhal (lentil gravy) is commonly found on menus and is handy for vegetarians. *Paratha* is like a chapati but thicker, and fried. It's common breakfast fare with an egg; sometimes it has a vegetable filling. *Puri* is a light, deep-fried pastry that puffs up when cooked; with the orange confection called *halwa*, it's the subcontinent's continental breakfast. Naan is a soft Middle Eastern-style round or oblong baked bread with thick edges, wonderful when it's hot out of the tandoor. Meat

(*gosht*) eaten in Pakistan is usually mutton (also *gosht*, or *bakri*) or chicken (*murgi*) and sometimes beef (*gayka gosht*).

Qorma is a braised meat curry in gravy. *Qofta* are lamb meatballs (or sometimes vegetable versions); *nargasi qofta* is minced beef and egg. *Qeema* is minced mutton or beef in a sauce. Middle Eastern influence is evident in *seekh kebabs*, mutton or chicken bits or meatballs barbecued on a skewer, and *shami kebabs*, 'pancakes' of lentils and minced mutton. A delicious Pashtun variation is *chapli kebabs*, spicy 'mutton burgers' shaped like the sole of a *chappal* (sandal).

A delicious, protein-potent dish is braised chicken livers, *karai kaleji*. Others, if you can bear the thought, are *gurda* (kidneys), *kapureh* (testicles) and *maghaz* or *bheja* (brains). To rescue your taste buds from a mouthful of chillies, keep a dish of *dai* (plain yogurt) or *raita* (curd with cumin and vegetable bits) nearby.

Among spicy street snacks are samosas (deep-fried pastry triangles filled with potatoes, chickpeas or other vegetables), tasty tikkas (spiced and barbecued beef, mutton or chicken bits) and pakoras (floured, deep-fried vegetables). 'Crispy Nimco' (known elsewhere as 'Bombay Mix') is crispy-spicy fried bits of lentils or chickpeas.

India

Many of the dishes available are explained above in the Pakistan section. In smaller towns there is not a wide choice and you'll soon get bored with *chaval* (rice), *sabzi* (mushy vegetables) and dhal, but in Delhi you can get pretty much anything you want.

Strict vegetarianism is widespread throughout the country. For those who do eat meat (known on most menus as 'non-veg'), it is not always a pleasure to do so in India – the quality tends to be low (most chickens give the impression that they died from starvation) and the hygiene is not all that it might be. Beef, from the holy cow, is strictly taboo, and pork is quite rare.

In the most basic Indian restaurants and eating places, known as *dhabas*, the cooking is usually done right out the front so you can see exactly what is going on and how it is done. Vegetables will be on the simmer all day and tend to be overcooked and mushy to Western tastes. In these basic places you can get a vegetable dish, dhal and a few chapatis for around INRs 20. If you order half-plates of the various dishes brewing out the front you get half the quantity at half the price and get a little more variety. With chutneys and a small plate of onions, which come free, you can put together a reasonable vegetarian meal for INRs 30, or nonvegetarian for INRs 40. The best Indian rice, it is generally agreed, is found in the north where Basmati rice grows in the Dehra Dun Valley. It has long grains, is yellowish and has a slightly sweetish or '*bas*' smell.

Indian breads are varied but always delicious. Simplest is the chapati/roti, which is a mixture of flour and water (no yeast) cooked on a hotplate griddle known as a *tawa*. Direct heat blows them up but how well that works depends on the gluten content of the wheat. In restaurants featuring Punjabi cuisine, a roti is called *phulka/fulka*. A paratha (or parantha) is also cooked on the hotplate but ghee (clarified butter) is used and the bread is rolled in a different way. Deep-fried bread that puffs up is known as a *puri*. Bake the bread in a clay (tandoori) oven and you have naan, usually thicker and more filling than a chapati. It's fascinating to watch the bakers in the dhabas and bakeries, especially early in the morning – the best time to buy your Indian bread.

A thali is the all-purpose blue collar Indian meal. The name 'thali' is taken from the dish in which the meal is served. This consists of a metal plate with a number of small metal bowls known as *katoris* on it: a variety of curry vegetable dishes, relishes, a couple of pappadams, puris or chapatis and a mountain of rice. Often the thali is 'bottomless' and a waiter will periodically come around to top up your plate until you've had enough. All this for about INRs 20!

Nepal

Real Nepali food is distinctly dull. Most of the time it consists of *dal bhat tarkari,* lentil soup, rice and curried vegetables. The occasional dal bhat tarkari, prepared to tourist tastes in Kathmandu restaurants, can be just fine. If you're trekking you'll probably eat quite a lot of it, although teahouses on popular routes now prepare various Western-style dishes with their limited ingredients.

Of course Indian cuisine has had a major influence on Nepal and many Tibetan dishes have come over the border, along with the many Tibetan refugees.

Many of the 'international' restaurants use large quantities of imported food. Cows, for instance, are theoretically not killed in Hindu Nepal, so beef is imported frozen from Kolkata or Delhi. In Kathmandu and Pokhara you'll find Chinese, Thai, Italian, French and Mexican restaurants in the tourist areas, pumping out reasonable imitations of their chosen cuisine. You'll have to search, but in among these are some very good Nepali and Tibetan restaurants.

DRINKS
Tea & Coffee

From the moment you're lured into your first carpet shop in İstanbul, to the time you watch the sun rise over the Himalaya from the rim of the Kathmandu Valley, there's one thing you can be sure of – tea will be close at hand.

In Turkey, those tulip-shaped thimbles of tea *(çay)* are part of the very fabric of social life and are the focus of offers of hospitality. Sweet apple tea will be served copiously while you're politely haggling over goods, while black tea is served in more serious teahouses. Iran's passion for tea *(chāy)* is legendary and a visit to a teahouse (the best are in Esfahān) is mandatory. In Pakistan, milky tea *(dudh chai)* is popular, although in Pashtun areas green or black tea imported from China and Sri Lanka are preferred. India goes for the mixed *chai*, where tea, milk and sugar are brewed together to form a sickly sweet brew whether you like it that way or not! It's nicely described by William Sutcliffe in *Are You Experienced?* as 'sweeter than Coke and only marginally less milky than milk'. Tea purists may not like it, but it's really quite good once you've acquired a taste. At hotels or restaurants you can always ask for black tea with milk and sugar separate. In Nepal and Dharamsala (India) you'll find Tibetan butter tea – another acquired taste.

Coffee is really only popular in Turkey, where it's served strong and sweet in small cups. If you want less sugar ask for it *mazboota*; without sugar ask for *sada* (plain). Iranian coffee is the same but is rarely seen.

Throughout the region, Western-style instant coffee is often known as 'Nescafe' (whether it is or not). It's usually relatively expensive, especially compared with tea. You shouldn't have any trouble getting this type of coffee at decent hotels and restaurants.

Juices & Other Drinks

Juice stalls selling delicious freshly squeezed or blended fruit juice are common throughout the region. Popular juices include mango, orange, banana, apple, pineapple, rock melon and watermelon. Steer clear of stalls that add milk to their drinks (it's probably not pasteurised), or ask for your juice without milk. Also, particularly in Nepal, ensure that they don't dilute your juice with water.

In Turkey, *ayran* is a tangy, refreshing drink made from yogurt and water. In Iran, *dugh* is similar but also contains sour milk and is very bitter. Lassi, made from curd (yogurt) is popular on the subcontinent, particularly in India where it has achieved the level of art form. You'll see lassi-wallahs in street-side stalls preparing the curd in huge wok-like saucers, then putting it into an urn where they mix in sugar and ice to create the delicious sweet, cool taste. In restaurants you can also order lassis salted or mixed with fruit (usually banana).

Soft drinks are widely available throughout the region. Competing titans Coke and Pepsi are gradually taking over the market, but local brands such as Coffy-Cola in Iran and Limca (lemon and lime) in India are still going strong. Soft drinks are dirt cheap everywhere – typically around US$0.20 for a small bottle. If you buy a bottle from a street vendor you'll have to stand there and drink it, because he'll want the empty bottle back.

Water & Ice

Tap water is generally safe to drink in Turkey and Iran, particularly in the cities, but not so in Pakistan, India and Nepal. The quickest way to a stomach ailment and three days on the toilet is to consume dubious water in these countries. Having said that, many travellers use tap water in hotels to clean their teeth with no ill effects, and others seem to be able to drink local water without problems.

In any case, bottled mineral water is widely available throughout the region and is usually pretty cheap (though not as cheap as soft drinks) Tests carried out on bottled water brands in India over the years have indicated that they're not all as pure as they claim, but at least they've been treated in some way. Make sure the plastic seal on the top of the bottle is intact when you buy it.

Boiling water is a 100% guaranteed way of ensuring it is safe; many hotels claim to boil their drinking water, but most only filter it. Ice can be a problem – make sure any water used for ice has been boiled or purified. Ice used by street vendors and dhabas to cool drinks in India and Pakistan is made commercially and distributed in huge blocks. As there's no refrigeration, these are kept cool under dirty hessian bags and crushed into usable blocks with a mallet. Again, you can take your chances with this – one of the authors on this book could barely walk past a fruit juice stand in Pakistan (in May) or a lassi-wallah in India without plunging in and gulping down a drink packed with ice.

In Nepal and northern India (and elsewhere), discarded plastic water bottles are causing a huge environmental problem, particularly on trekking routes. A better option is to take your own water bottle and either boil tap water or purify it with iodine.

Alcoholic Drinks

Even though two thirds of this trip is through Islamic territory, you won't be completely denied alcohol.

Turkey is very Western in this regard: There are several locally brewed beers including Efes, Tuborg and Tiger; imported spirits; and the local aniseed-based *rakı*. The national passion, rakı is clear but is usually mixed with water, which turns it milky white. A large bottle of beer costs about US$1.50 in a bar, but less than US$1 in a supermarket. Alcohol is strictly banned in Iran and no alcohol can be taken into the country – one of the first things you see at the border when crossing from Iran into Turkey is a duty-free liquor shop!

Likewise, you cannot take alcohol into Pakistan and Pakistani Muslims (almost the entire population) are forbidden from drinking alcohol. Foreigners (non-Muslims) can, however, indulge. To do so you have to go through a tedious process of obtaining a permit from the Excise & Tax Department in whichever town you're staying, which you can then use to purchase alcohol from permit rooms at top-end hotels in Lahore, Islamabad and Rawalpindi. The exceptions to this are Quetta, which has a surprisingly open black market trade in alcohol, and Peshawar, which has Pakistan's only 'bar' at the Pearl Continental Hotel. Murree beer is brewed in Rawalpindi and Cossack vodka is produced at the Quetta distillery.

In India you can just about return to your normal drinking habits, although it's not cheap by local standards. A 650ml bottle of beer purchased at a restaurant costs between US$2 and US$3. Considering alcohol is often frowned upon by the Hindu and Muslim elite, and is out of the range of affordability for many Indians, a surprising number of beers are brewed here and some are quite good (if you can get them cold). Kingfisher is the most popular, but you'll also find Golden Eagle, Haywards 5000, Hakkebeck, Golden Peacock and the odd-tasting Mona Lisa among others. These are regarded as 'light' beers (around 5% alcohol). Strong beers, including Haywards 10000, Thunderbolt, Torpedo, Charger and Godfather, are around 8%, which really packs a punch. Beer can be more difficult (or impossible) to obtain in small towns and religious centres such as Varanasi's old city or in Pushkar. In addition to beer there's a range of locally produced spirits such as Honeybee brandy as well as Indian versions of scotch, gin and others.

You'll have no problems getting a beer in Pokhara and Kathmandu, and here the heady travellers scene gives extra incentive to go out and party. And why not? You're at the end of a long trip. You can even get a beer while trekking if you're on a popular route such as the Jomsom Trek. You'll pay a bit more, but then a porter has to carry all those bottles of beer up into the mountains, and he'll carry the empty bottles back down!

ENTERTAINMENT
Middle Eastern and Asian people are a social and gregarious lot. Local entertainment often involves simply hanging out with friends or visiting each others' homes. The cinema is a popular form of evening entertainment throughout the region, and in Turkey bars are part of the nightlife scene

among young people (older men can be seen hunched over a table with a bottle of rakı).

Locals, particularly men, can often be found socialising at teahouses and cafes and this is a good place for travellers to meet with them, or simply observe daily life.

Teahouses
Teahouses, or chai shops, are common throughout the region, but in Iran the *chāykhāné* (teahouse) is a great institution that should not be missed. Teahouses are normally an all-male retreat (certainly in Turkey and Pakistan, but not so in Iran); foreign women are often allowed in but if you're a solo traveller you may well feel more comfortable visiting in company.

In Turkey and Iran, the teahouses have a Middle Eastern atmosphere (probably because they're in the Middle East). Regulars sit all day drinking pot after pot of tea (çay in Turkey, chāy in Iran) sipping the tea through sugar lumps and pausing to puff on a traditional water pipe or hubble-bubble (known as a *nargileh* in Turkey and a *qalyan* in Iran). You can try regular or fruit *(mīvé)* tobacco, which comes in several flavours and is as sensuous as tasting sherbet. The best teahouses are beautifully decorated in old Persian style, with carpeted platforms and pillows to lounge on and sometimes even live music or a storyteller as entertainment. In Iran, teahouses can be found built into ancient bridges (Esfahān) or in a refurbished hamam (Yazd).

In Pakistan the best teahouses, or chai shops, are in the bazaars of Peshawar, where fat samovars (urns) boil the water and locals sit around cross-legged on mats or on miniature stools clutching tin cups. The Pashtuns of this area have taken Chinese green tea to an art-form – none of this milky chai for them. In India and Nepal, chai shops are less of a social venue – more often than not the chai-wallah prepares his tea on a mobile cart.

Bars & Clubs
Nightlife, in the sense of going out partying in bars and clubs, is pretty limited on the overland trail, which in many ways is a good thing.

In Turkey you'll certainly be able to let your hair down in İstanbul – either in the budget travellers' bars of Sultanahmet or the trendier nightclub district of Taksim. The resort towns of the Mediterranean and Aegean have a vibrant and sometimes over-the-top scene, with package holiday-makers and backpackers spilling out of bars at all hours of the night. Even tiny Göreme in Cappadocia has some decent bars, open until as late as 4 am and frequented by locals and tourists alike. Farther east of here, however, bars generally become limited to smoky all-male haunts (although there are a couple of more relaxing places in Diyarbakır).

Places to catch live music in Turkey include the backstreet bars of Taksim in İstanbul, Safran Restaurant in Bursa, İzmir, Ankara and any of the major Aegean and Mediterranean resorts in the summer.

Alcohol is completely prohibited in Iran, and illegal for Muslims in Pakistan, so you won't find any bars or clubs in a Western sense. There is an austere bar in the Pearl Continental Hotel in Peshawar, Pakistan, where foreign visitors can sign a form and drink away, but elsewhere you can only purchase alcohol from permit rooms (once you've obtained a permit) and consume it in a private place such as your hotel room. Another possibility is to try to tap into the local expatriate community. Quetta has a sociable bunch and the International Club in Lahore, although notionally open only to members and guests, is worth a try.

It's easy enough to get a drink in northern India, but you won't find too many bars or clubs other than in Delhi and places frequented by young tourists. McLeod Ganj has a reasonably lively travellers' scene for such a small place, and it even has a weekly disco! Shimla has several restaurant-bars, and Delhi has a variety of theme pubs around Connaught Place, as well as several expensive discos in top-end hotels. In Rajasthan the government is phasing out 'beer bars', but you can still drink freely in many restaurants and guesthouses. Chandigarh is an anomaly (in more ways than one): Hardly any travellers spend a night here, but with a strong, middle-class university population, it has some lively local bars.

Cinema

Most major towns and cities along the route have at least a couple of cinemas, and the capitals all have a dozen or more. While many of the cinemas screen local-language films, there are always a few that show the latest mainstream Western releases (except in Iran). You won't have to look hard to find a cinema in Pakistan and India – massive hand-painted hoardings advertise the latest films in dramatic and colourful style.

English-language films are usually subtitled rather than dubbed, although this is not always so in Turkey: Check at the box office. Having to read rather than listen frees local patrons to carry on their own conversations. Indian cinema-goers in particular are also big on audience participation, which can be great fun if it's a no-brain adventure flick, but the whooping, cheering and applause can be a bit distracting if you're trying to settle into something a bit more subtle. Catching a Hindi or Urdu film in India or Pakistan is worthwhile for the cultural experience – you don't really need to be able to follow the dialogue!

Foreign films are almost always subject to censorship. How heavy-handed this is depends on the mood of the moment, but even seemingly innocuous movies often arrive on screen with tell-tale hiccups indicating the cut of the censors.

Dance & Music

Traditional 'folkloric shows' are often put on for tourists, sometimes at five-star hotels and top-end restaurants. In Turkey there are also numerous folkloric festivals – see the Special Events section earlier in this chapter.

Ankara is a good place to see opera, ballet or a classical music performance. The Mevlâna Festival is held in Konya in mid-December and is the only time you'll be able to see the dance of the whirling dervishes in this city. You'll need to book accommodation in advance, since the festival is popular.

An easier opportunity to witness whirling dervishes in action is at the Galata Mevlevihanesi in İstanbul, on the last Sunday of each month (see the Turkey chapter for details).

Teahouses in Iran sometimes have live performances of folk or devotional music.

In Pakistan, the most accessible live music is at the qawwali concerts that you may get to see in Lahore and at Sufi centres such as Multan and Uch Sharif. Qawwali singing is a form of devotional chanting accompanied by drums and dancing. It takes place on Thursday nights and often continues through till dawn. See the Lahore section the Pakistan chapter for more information.

In India and Nepal you can often see traditional dance and music performed at restaurants or other venues specifically for tourists. Udaipur and Jaipur in Rajasthan are good places for this, as is Kathmandu. Delhi is the best place in India to see traditional performers and there are a number of venues hosting regular shows. See the Delhi section of the India chapter for details.

Weddings

Visitors often find themselves invited by locals to weddings, which are always raucous affairs with troupes of drummers and undulating women. Weddings are also a good opportunity to see traditional dance and music. But you don't necessarily need an invitation. If you see a procession in the street or a lot of activity around a hotel, hang around and see if you can join in. The success of weddings in India and Pakistan is often judged by the number of people in attendance.

Spectator Sports

Football Turks and Iranians are football (soccer) crazy, the Turks especially so with the recent success of European Cup winners Galatasaray. Try to score a ticket for one of their matches or that of the other two İstanbul biggies, Fenerbahçe or Beşiktaş. If you don't attend in person, you can rock up to a cafe or pub when a game is being televised and share in the audience's loudly voiced enthusiasm.

Iranians are not quite so demonstrative, although the country celebrated on the streets when Iran qualified for the 1998 World Cup (Aussie travellers, the losers in that particular match, will not be allowed to forget this). The national competition lasts from about October to June, and games are played throughout the country on Thursday and Friday.

Cricket In Pakistan and India, cricket reigns supreme. Travellers not from a colonial cricketing nation may find this obsession a bit extreme. If you are from England, Australia, New Zealand or South Africa, however, cricket is a great conversation-starter – just about every male in Pakistan and India could happily converse for hours on the subject (although recent match-fixing scandals have tainted many players and made Indians and Pakistanis less willing to praise some of their heroes).

Everywhere you go you'll see impromptu cricket matches taking place on dusty pitches, with makeshift equipment. If there's a big match being televised, hundreds of people will crowd around any available TV set. If there happens to be a test match or one-day international being played in town while you are on the road, it's worth going along to see just for the atmosphere and crowd participation. International matches are played in Lahore, Rawalpindi, Peshawar and Delhi. Tickets (if there are any left) can be bought at the ground, or the local paper should carry an advertisement telling you where to buy tickets.

Other Sports Wrestling is popular in Turkey and Iran. In Turkey the combatants are smothered in oil – the place to go to check this 'oiled wrestling' out is Edirne in June. In Iran, the wrestling sport of *zurkhané* has developed more into a kind of tai chi with strenuous exercise combined with Islamic praises; it's easy to attend practice sessions in Esfahān and Yazd and other cities if you ask around.

A more unusual form of wrestling is that between camels; catch the bouts near Selçuk, in Turkey. In Iran's Sīstān va Balūchestān Province, the camels are used for more traditional racing; the most likely place to see this is in Zāhedān.

For unbridled aggression check out the drag races at Āzādī Stadium in Tehrān. Most visitors will appreciate the extreme irony of paying good money to witness hundreds of Iranian cars scream around in a frenzied circle.

Buzkashi is the national sport of the Afghans but you may be lucky enough to see a match in Quetta or Peshawar in Pakistan. Literally meaning 'goat grabbing', this wild sport is played on horseback and involves two teams of horsemen attempting to grab a goat or calf carcass and deliver it to their scoring circle. Meanwhile everyone else is trying to stop the carcass-carrier. It's like primitive rugby on horseback!

SHOPPING

A highlight of travel in Turkey and Iran is exploring the covered bazaars. Nothing beats the excitement of going up and down the hectic, vaulted alleyways, past pungent barrels of basil and cloves, through to medieval caravanserais. Have a sense of humour and curiosity, and if you want to buy, be prepared to bargain – see the boxed text 'The Fine Art of Bargaining' earlier in this chapter.

On the subcontinent the bazaars tend to be open, often with stalls, merchandise, vendors and livestock scattered in all directions. Traders have been setting up in the old parts of many towns for centuries. In Pakistan, the mix of tribal cultures and ancient trade routes has given Peshawar's old city a fascinating bazaar. Quetta, Multan and Lahore also have wonderful markets. In India and Nepal you'll often find specialist markets, such as the silk bazaars in Varanasi, marble shops in Agra and the craft markets of Kathmandu.

Sending a lot of stuff home can be expensive, especially if you use courier services like DHL or TNT. But it's also not viable to backpack with heavy purchases. And on a trip like this, it doesn't work to wait until the journey's end and buy everything then. That Persian rug you saw in Esfahān, or the hand-painted camel skin lamp in Multan, won't be found sitting in a Kathmandu bazaar. The bottom line is that if you like something – and you can afford it – you should buy it, especially if it's unique to that region.

Surface mail (sea mail) can be sent from major post offices at relatively low cost. Air mail costs several times more. Reputable merchants can also arrange shipping as part of the purchase price, and will ensure that it is properly packed. Make sure you get all the necessary receipts and the contact details of the shop.

Of course, small purchases along the way make great souvenirs, gifts or mementos and can easily be stuffed in your pack.

Buyer Beware!

In touristy places, take extreme care with the commission merchants. These guys hang around waiting to pick you up and cart you off to their favourite dealers where whatever you pay will have a hefty margin built into it to pay their commission. Stories about 'my family's place', 'my brother's shop' and 'special deal at my friend's place' are just stories and nothing more.

Whatever you might be told, if you are taken by a rickshaw/taxi driver or tout to a place, be it a hotel, craft shop or market, the price you pay will be inflated. This can be by as much as 50%, so try to visit these places on your own. And don't underestimate the persistence of these guys. We heard of one ill traveller who virtually collapsed into a cycle-rickshaw in India and asked to be taken to a doctor only to end up at a marble workshop, with the rickshaw driver insisting that, yes, indeed a doctor did work there. The high pressure sales techniques of both the runners and the owners is the best in the world. Should you get up and leave without buying anything, the feigned anger is just that. Next time you turn up (alone), it will be all smiles – and the prices will have dropped dramatically.

Another trap that many foreigners fall into occurs when using a credit card. You may well be told that if you buy the goods, the merchant won't forward the credit slip for payment until you have received the goods, even if it is in three months' time – this is total bullshit. No trader will be sending you as much as a postcard until they have received the money, in full, for the goods you are buying. What you'll find in fact is that within 48 hours of you signing the credit slip, the merchant has telexed the bank in Delhi and the money will have been credited to their account.

Also beware of any shop that takes your credit card out the back and comes back with the slip for you to sign. Sometimes while out of sight, the vendor will imprint a few more forms, forge your signature, and you'll be billed for items you haven't purchased. Have the slip filled out right in front of you.

While it is certainly a minority of traders who are actually involved in dishonest schemes, virtually all are involved in the commission racket, so you need to shop with care – take your time, be firm and bargain hard. Good luck!

I've Just Got To Have *That!*

There's nothing like wandering around in strange, exotic bazaars – or in touristy haunts – for turning up all sorts of unusual souvenirs. Try a few of these for the folks back home...

Troglodyte Pottery
Avanos is the pottery hotspot of Cappadocia, but for true masterpieces in clay, including stubby fairy chimneys and baying wolves springing out of maps of Turkey, go shopping in Ürgüp.

Nemrut Dağı Heads
After marvelling at the 2m tall originals, snap up a pocket sized copy of this monument to megalomania. From the gift shacks at the summit of Nemrut Dağı.

Atatürk Memorabilia
Over 60 years after his death, there's still no escaping the frozen gaze of Mustafa Kemal. The most extensive collection of Atatürk goodies – everything from paperweights to CD-Roms – is found at the souvenir shop at his mausoleum, Anıtkabir, in Ankara.

Wall Carpets
Napoleon, lusty Persian courtiers, Mickey Mouse, even the Last Supper – you name it, you can find it on carpet wall hangings. Search through the bazaars in Tabrīz, Tehrān, Esfahān and Shīrāz.

Camel Skin Lamps & Zases
A speciality of Multan in Pakistan, the camel skin is stretched over a mould, dried and then painted. Go shopping in Multan's hectic bazaar.

Pen Guns & Knives
No, we _DON'T_ advise that you buy a pen gun. No bigger than a fat biro – and lethal – they are sold in Darra, Pakistan, but the penalties for possessing one, let alone trying to take one out of the country, are harsh. A safer option is one of the Afghan pocket knives sold on the street in Peshawar. They come with handles inland with semi-precious stone such as lapis lazuli.

Mini Taj Mahals
Agra is the place for kitsch souvenirs in India and most involve cheap soapstone carvings (occasionally passed off as marble) of the Taj Mahal or little elephants, usually with a second elephant inside. Marble chess boards, plates and jewellery inlaid in *pietra dura* style are popular and a nice souvenir if you get can the price down to something realistic.

Gandhi Family Dolls
Ceramic caricatures of the Gandhi family – Indira, Rajiv and Sonia – can be found skulking in Jaipur bazaars.

Hindu Paraphernalia
With such a vast pantheon of gods, Hinduism has plenty of scope for merchandising and very little of this stuff is aimed at Western tourists. You can get a Ganesh keyring, a Krishna calendar or dolls featuring characters from the *Ramayana*.

Wooden Ties
Wooden neck ties are just one of the bizarre wooden items produced by the craftsmen at Bhaktapur in the Kathmandu Valley. Perfect for looking smart for your next visa application.

Everest Snow Domes
Inevitably, Mt Everest features in one of those collectable snow domes. Shake it up and watch the blizzard. Available in Kathmandu.

Paul Harding & Simon Richmond

Getting There & Away

While many travellers will start this route in either İstanbul or Kathmandu, it's quite possible to fly into or out of one of the other major gateways along the way – such as Tehrān, Lahore or Delhi – or to arrive overland from Europe, China or elsewhere.

This chapter covers getting to points on the route by land, sea and air, and outlines onward travel from the region. For details of travel within the region, including travelling between countries covered in this book, see the Getting Around chapter.

AIR
If this is a self-contained trip, you'll most likely arrive at your starting point by air, flying into and out of İstanbul or Kathmandu.

Airports & Airlines
The major international airports on the route are at İstanbul (Atatürk International Airport), Tehrān (Mehrābād International Airport), Lahore, Islamabad, Delhi (Indira Gandhi International Airport) and Kathmandu (Tribhuvan International Airport). İstanbul and Delhi are the busiest, and as a

result you can often hunt down some very good fares to these two places. The majority of international flights into Pakistan arrive in Karachi.

If you're flying from Europe, it's worth looking out for cheap charter flight packages to destinations such as Bodrum, Antalya and Dalaman in Turkey and even to Goa in India – although it's well off our route, it's not difficult to get from there up to Delhi. Some flight and accommodation packages work out cheaper than a regular return flight, although probably not cheaper than a one-way flight to İstanbul or Delhi. With the national airline of each of the countries on this route, you can fly direct from many European, Asian and North American cities.

Major airlines flying into either İstanbul or Kathmandu include:

Air India
www.airindia.com
Austrian Airlines
www.austrianair.com
Biman Bangladesh
www.bangladeshonline.com/biman
British Airways
www.britishairways.com
Emirates Air
www.emirates.com
Gulf Air
www.gulfairco.com
Iran Air
www.iranair.com
Lauda Air
www.laudaair.com
Pakistan International Airlines
www.fly-pia.com
Qatar Airways
www.qatarairways.com
Royal Nepal Airlines Corporation (RNAC)
www.royalnepal.com
Sabena
www.sabena.com
Thai Airways
www.thaiair.com
Turkish Airlines (Türk Hava Yolları; THY)
www.thy.com
Virgin Atlantic
www.virgin-atlantic.com

Buying Tickets
The plane ticket will probably be the single most expensive item in your budget, and buying it can be an intimidating business.

There is likely to be a multitude of airlines and travel agents hoping to separate you from your money. Given that you're going to want to get the best deal possible, it's always worth putting aside time to research the current state of the market. Start early, because some of the cheapest tickets have to be bought months in advance and some popular flights sell out quickly. Look at the advertisements in newspapers and magazines (it's also worth looking at the press of the ethnic group whose country you plan to visit), and watch out for special offers. You should then phone around travel agencies for the best prices. Airlines can supply information on routes and timetables; however, except at times of inter-airline warfare, they do not supply the cheapest tickets. Travel agencies buy tickets in discounted blocks and pass some of the savings on to consumers.

You may discover that those impossibly cheap flights are 'fully booked, but we have another one that costs a bit more...' or that the flight is on an airline notorious for its poor safety standards and leaves you in the world's least favourite airport in mid-journey for 14 hours. Or else they may claim that only two seats remain available for that country for the whole of July, which they will hold for you for a maximum of two hours. Don't panic – keep ringing around.

Use the fares quoted in this book as a guide only. They are approximate and based on the rates advertised by travel agencies at the time of going to press. Quoted airfares do not necessarily constitute a recommendation for the carrier.

If you are travelling from the UK or the USA (or Hong Kong or Bangkok for that matter) you will probably find that the cheapest flights are being advertised by obscure 'bucket shops' whose names haven't yet reached the telephone directory. Many such firms are honest and solvent, but there are a few rogues who will take your money and disappear, only to reopen elsewhere a month or two later under a new name. If you feel suspicious about a firm, don't hand over all the money at once – leave a deposit of 20% or so and pay the balance when you get the ticket. If they insist on cash in advance, go somewhere else. Once you have the ticket, ring the airline to confirm that you are actually booked on the flight.

You may decide to pay more than the rock-bottom fare by opting for the safety and reliability of a better-known travel agency. Firms such as STA, who have offices worldwide, Council Travel in the USA or Travel CUTS in Canada are not going to disappear overnight, leaving you clutching a receipt for a nonexistent ticket, but they do offer good prices to most destinations.

Once you have your ticket, write down its number, together with the flight number and other details, and keep the information separate from your ticket. If the ticket is lost or stolen, this will help you get a replacement.

Open-Jaw Tickets These are return tickets where you fly out to one destination but return from another, which saves you backtracking to your arrival point. It's unlikely that you'll find a return ticket into İstanbul and out of Kathmandu (or vice versa) with the same airline, but travel agencies will certainly be able to put together two one-way tickets with different airlines. This gives you peace of mind and something to show immigration officials, but it takes away some of that fly-by-the-seat-of-your-pants flexibility. It means you have to be at the other end on a certain date, or go through the hassle of changing your flight en route. Also, it won't be any cheaper to do it this way as one-way tickets to major destinations can be purchased quite cheaply and at short notice in Kathmandu, İstanbul, Delhi and elsewhere. Generally, you will be better off buying a one-way ticket into your destination and another one-way ticket out when you finish the trip.

Buying Tickets Online The Internet has thrown up a whole new world of travel options. There are many Web sites specifically aimed at selling flights, where you can look up fares and timetables by selecting your departure point and destination, then book a ticket online using your credit card. Your ticket will (hopefully) be mailed out to you, or it may be an 'electronic ticket' that you claim at the airport before checking in for your flight.

Sometimes these fares are cheap, often they're no cheaper than those sold at a standard travel agency, and occasionally they're

Air Travel Glossary

Cancellation Penalties If you have to cancel or change a discounted ticket, there are often heavy penalties involved; insurance can sometimes be taken out against these penalties. Some airlines impose penalties on regular tickets as well, particularly against 'no-show' passengers.

Courier Fares Businesses often need to send urgent documents or freight securely and quickly. Courier companies hire people to accompany the package through customs and, in return, offer a discount ticket which is sometimes a phenomenal bargain. However, you may have to surrender all your baggage allowance and take only carry-on luggage.

Full Fares Airlines traditionally offer 1st class (coded F), business class (coded J) and economy class (coded Y) tickets. These days there are so many promotional and discounted fares available that few passengers pay full economy fare.

Lost Tickets If you lose your airline ticket an airline will usually treat it like a travellers cheque and, after inquiries, issue you with another one. Legally, however, an airline is entitled to treat it like cash and if you lose it then it's gone forever. Take good care of your tickets.

Onward Tickets An entry requirement for many countries is that you have a ticket out of the country. If you're unsure of your next move, the easiest solution is to buy the cheapest onward ticket to a neighbouring country or a ticket from a reliable airline which can later be refunded if you do not use it.

Open-Jaw Tickets These are return tickets where you fly out to one place but return from another. If available, this can save you backtracking to your arrival point.

Overbooking Since every flight has some passengers who fail to show up, airlines often book more passengers than they have seats. Usually excess passengers make up for the no-shows, but occasionally somebody gets 'bumped' onto the next available flight. Guess who it is most likely to be? The passengers who check in late.

Promotional Fares These are officially discounted fares, available from travel agencies or direct from the airline.

Reconfirmation If you don't reconfirm your flight at least 72 hours prior to departure, the airline may delete your name from the passenger list. Ring to find out if your airline requires reconfirmation.

Restrictions Discounted tickets often have various restrictions on them – such as needing to be paid for in advance and incurring a penalty to be altered. Others are restrictions on the minimum and maximum period you must be away.

Round-the-World Tickets RTW tickets give you a limited period (usually a year) in which to circumnavigate the globe. You can go anywhere the carrying airlines go, as long as you don't backtrack. The number of stopovers or total number of separate flights is decided before you set off and they usually cost a bit more than a basic return flight.

Transferred Tickets Airline tickets cannot be transferred from one person to another. Travellers sometimes try to sell the return half of their ticket, but officials can ask you to prove that you are the person named on the ticket. On an international flight tickets are compared with passports.

Travel Periods Ticket prices vary with the time of year. There is a low (off-peak) season and a high (peak) season, and often a low-shoulder season and a high-shoulder season as well. Usually the fare depends on your outward flight – if you depart in the high season and return in the low season, you pay the high-season fare.

way too expensive – but it's a convenient way of researching flights from the comfort of your own home or office. Many large travel agencies also have Web sites, but not all allow you to look up fares and schedules.

Web sites worth checking out include:

www.cheapestflights.co.uk This site really does post cheap flights (out of the UK only) but you have to get in early to get the bargains.

www.dialaflight.com This site offers worldwide flights out of Europe and the UK.

www.expedia.msn.com A good site for checking worldwide flight prices.

www.flifo.com This is the site of OneTravel.Com

www.lastminute.com This site deals mainly in European flights but does have worldwide flights, mostly package returns. There's also an Australian version.

www.statravel.com STA Travel's US Web site. There are also sites for the UK (www.sta travel.co.uk) and Australia (www.statravel .com.au).

www.travel.com.au A good site for Australians to find cheap flights, although some prices may turn out to be too good to be true.

www.travelonline.co.nz A good site for New Zealanders to find worldwide fares from their part of the world.

The UK & Europe

In London, one of the bucket-shop capitals of the world, you'll probably find the cheapest deals. There are also flights to İstanbul and points along the route from other European hubs, eg, Paris, Brussels, Amsterdam and Frankfurt.

Newspapers and magazines such as London's *Time Out* and *TNT Magazine* regularly advertise very low fares to İstanbul, Delhi and Kathmandu, but often when you call up these deals have 'sold out' or are restricted to particular dates. A good place to start shopping for fares is with the major student or backpacker-oriented travel agencies, eg, Usit Campus Travel, STA and Trailfinders. You can then get an idea of what's available and how much you're going to pay – although a bit of ringing around to the smaller agencies afterwards will often turn up cheaper fares. Addresses of agencies in London include:

Bridge the World (☎ 7911 0900) 45–47 Chalk Farm Rd, London NW1 8AJ

STA Travel (☎ 020-7361 6262) 74–88 Old Brompton Rd, London SW7; plus branches in Bristol, Manchester and most big university cities

Trailfinders (☎ 020-7938 3366) 42–48 Earls Court Rd, London W8; plus branches in Bristol and Manchester

Usit Campus Travel (☎ 0870-240 1010) 52 Grosvenor Gardens, London SW1W OAG; plus offices elsewhere in London and at universities and colleges around the country

Charter flights (ie, nonscheduled flights) to İstanbul make this a very cheap destination from London – you can get there for as little as UK£90. Scheduled flights start at around UK£115 one way, with many European airlines to choose from. Flights from İstanbul to London and other European cities cost about the same.

One-way fares from London to Kathmandu are frequently advertised for around UK£250, but with taxes you'll probably pay a bit more. Flights to Delhi are slightly cheaper and more frequent, typically starting at around UK£200. Most flights to Kathmandu from London go via the Middle East (Dubai, Qatar, Bahrain etc) or somewhere like Karachi or Dhaka, depending on the carrier. Royal Nepal Airlines has direct flights from Frankfurt.

The USA & Canada

There are more flights to the region from the USA than from Canada but still not that many. Prices depend largely on whether you fly the Atlantic route via Europe, or the South-East Asian route.

There are no nonstop direct flights from North America to Kathmandu, but Thai Airways flies daily from Los Angeles from around US$850 (via Bangkok and Osaka) and from New York (via Bangkok or Frankfurt) for a whopping US$3170. You can fly from New York to Kathmandu with Air India and RNAC for as little as US$1020, or you could consider flying into Delhi (around US$880) and on from there.

A cheap way to get from North America, particularly the east coast, to İstanbul might be to fly to London and then buy another ticket from a bucket shop there, but this would depend on the fare to London and the time spent in London waiting for a flight out. Otherwise, Delta Airlines flies direct from New York to İstanbul for around US$550, or from Los Angeles (via New York) from US$680.

Discount travel agencies can be found through the *Yellow Pages* or the major daily newspapers. The *New York Times,* the *Los Angeles Times,* the *Chicago Tribune* and the *San Francisco Examiner* all produce weekly travel sections filled with travel agency ads. Council Travel, America's largest student travel organisation, has around 60 offices in the USA; its head office (☎ 800-226 8624) is at 205 E 42 St, New York, NY 10017. Call it for the office nearest you or visit its Web site at www.ciee.org. STA Travel (☎ 800-777 0112) has offices in Boston, Chicago, Miami, New York, Philadelphia, San Francisco and other major cities. Call the tollfree 800 number for office locations or visit its Web site at www.statravel.com.

In Canada, the *Toronto Star,* Toronto's *Globe & Mail,* the *Montreal Gazette* and the *Vancouver Sun* carry travel agency ads and are good places to look for cheap fares. Travel CUTS (☎ 800-667 2887) is Canada's national student travel agency and has offices in all major cities. Its Web address is www.travelcuts.com.

From the east coast (Toronto), you can fly to İstanbul one way for around C$1398 but flights to Kathmandu are much more expensive – around C$2035 – and to Delhi it is C$2479. From Vancouver you're looking at around C$1158 to İstanbul and C$1842 to Delhi around C$1464 to Kathmandu.

Australia & New Zealand
Long-haul flights from Australia and New Zealand are usually routed through South-East Asia and/or the Middle East. Many travellers actually buy tickets to Kathmandu from Bangkok, where you can pick them up for around US$250 in a bucket shop. Malaysian Airlines and Singapore Airlines have flights from Australia (Melbourne or Sydney) to İstanbul for around A$1600 one way, while Gulf Air, Egypt Air and Emirates Air are among the cheapest at A$1535 for low-season return fares. At the time of research one of the cheapest deals was one way from Sydney to İstanbul on Olympic for A$776. Japan Airlines, Egypt Air and Lauda Air all had one-way fares for around A$900 or less. It might also be worth considering a flight on a combination of Qantas or British Airways and Turkish Airlines via Bangkok, because Turkish Airlines will add on two free domestic flights within Turkey and offer a 50% discount on any additional domestic flights.

One-way fares from Sydney to Kathmandu are more expensive, with the cheapest deal being on a combination of Qantas and Royal Nepal for A$976. Thai International has a fare for A$1042, while Singapore Airlines charges A$1284. All airlines, though, have some sort of fare deal going at most times of the year. From the west coast (ie, from Perth) most fares are around A$200 cheaper.

Sometimes it might pay to pick up a bargain one-way fare to London (Britannia Airways has charter flights from as low as A$500 between November and February) and then pick up a cheap ticket (or travel overland) to İstanbul from there, but again that depends on whether or not you actually want to go to London.

Good places to go for cheap fares are STA Travel and Flight Centre. STA Travel (☎ 03-9349 2411) has its main office at 224 Faraday St, Carlton, Melbourne, and has offices in all major cities and on many university campuses. Flight Centre (☎ 131 600 Australia-wide) has a central office at 82 Elizabeth St, Sydney, and there are dozens of offices throughout Australia. Its Web address is www.flightcentre.com.au.

In New Zealand, the *New Zealand Herald* has a travel section in which travel agencies advertise fares. Flight Centre (☎ 09-309 6171) has a large central office in Auckland at National Bank Towers (on the corner of Queen and Darby Sts) and many branches throughout the country. STA Travel (☎ 09-309 0458) has its main office at 10 High St, Auckland, and has other offices in Auckland as well as in Hamilton, Palmerston North, Wellington, Christchurch and Dunedin.

Travelling on by Air
Once you get to the end of the route – or to any gateway city along the way – you shouldn't have too much trouble getting a cheap (or reasonably priced) ticket to wherever you want to go. For information on departing gateway cities en route, see the city sections of the relevant chapters for more information.

If you're flying on from Kathmandu, you can get cheap fares out of Nepal through the travel agencies around Thamel and Durbar Marg. There are plenty of airlines flying into and out of Nepal. Royal Nepal Airlines has flights to Bangkok (US$220), Dubai (US$260), Frankfurt (US$605), Hong Kong (US$310), Singapore (US$310), London (US$630) and Paris (US$575). Singapore Airlines flies to London (US$670), Los Angeles (US$669), New York (US$780), Sydney (US$676) and many Asian destinations.

If you're flying out of Kathmandu, it's imperative to reconfirm your flight and to get to the airport early. There's a Rs 1000 international departure tax payable at the Nepal Arab Bank in the airport terminal.

If you've travelled the route from east to west and are looking for an onward ticket in İstanbul, you'll find plenty of reasonable fares. As well as discounts on tickets to Western Europe and North America, the İstanbul agencies have cheap deals to Moscow (US$90), Mumbai/Dehli (from US$299), Tokyo (from US$395), Singapore/Bangkok (from US$335) and San Francisco (from US$350).

There are a small but rapidly growing number of flights from İstanbul to destinations in Central Asia and the Caucasus. There are now regular flights between İstanbul and Almaty (Turkish Airlines, three times weekly, US$180 one way), Bishkek (Kyrgystan Airlines, twice weekly, US$280 one way), Baku (Turkish Airlines, three times weekly, US$240 one way) and Tashkent (Uzbekistan Airways, twice weekly, US$510 one way). There are also daily flights between İstanbul and Ashgabat (Turkmenistan Airlines, US$250, one way).

Turkey levies a tax of about US$12 on visitors departing by air. The tax is customarily included in the cost of your ticket.

LAND

If you are travelling overland to begin or join up with this route, there are several directions from which you can come.

Heading in to İstanbul by bus, train or car, Europe is the obvious starting point. You can also travel via the Caucasus (from Georgia or Azerbaijan) into eastern Turkey or north-western Iran, or up from Syria into south-eastern Turkey.

Pakistan can be approached or exited from China (via the spectacular Karakoram Highway linking Pakistan and China); India can be reached from the east via Bangladesh; and it's possible to enter Nepal via China and Tibet.

The UK & Europe

The easiest and most travelled overland route to Turkey and the Middle East is by bus, train or car via Greece or Bulgaria (ferries from Greece are described under Sea later in this chapter). Unless you're travelling from somewhere relatively nearby such as Eastern Europe, taking the bus or train won't work out any cheaper than flying, particularly as you may need an expensive transit visa (see Visas & Documents in the Facts for the Visitor chapter).

Bus To İstanbul, buses run from many European cities. One of the main operators is Eurolines (www.eurolines.com), which sells tickets through various agencies. Two of the best Turkish companies – Ulusoy and Varan – operate big Mercedes buses on European routes and they are also reliable. For details get in touch with the booking office at any international bus station or with any travel agency dealing in bus tickets.

During the summer there are bus services to İstanbul from the following cities: Bucharest, Tirano, Rome, Turin, Bregenz, Graz, Innsbruck, Salzburg, Vienna, Wiener Neustadt, Paris Strasbourg, Basel, Zurich, Amsterdam, and Brussels. Eurolines does not operate direct from London to İstanbul, but with flights to İstanbul costing less than the London-Rome bus, why go through the torture? Sample one-way fares to İstanbul are DM216 from Frankfurt, DM185 from Munich, and 670FF from Paris. Round-trip fares are discounted by about 20%. Ask about student, youth and child discounts.

In Greece, a bus to İstanbul departs from Athens' Peloponnese train station at 7 pm from Friday to Tuesday. The journey costs US$58 and takes about 22 hours – slightly less than the train and a somewhat more pleasant prospect. Try to book your seat a day ahead. You can also pick up the bus in Thessalonika (US$37) on the train-station forecourt at 2.30 am (except Thursday) and at Alexandroupolis (US$14) at 8.30 am Friday to Wednesday.

Alternatively, you can make your own way to Alexandroupolis and take a service from the intercity bus station to the border town of Kipi (three departures a day, US$2.40). You can't walk across the border but it's easy enough to hitch – you may be lucky and get a lift all the way to İstanbul.

Otherwise, take a bus to Ipsala (5km beyond the border) or Keşan (30km beyond the border) from where there are many buses on to the capital.

From Bulgaria there are regular daily buses from Sofia to İstanbul (US$25). They may also pick up in Plovdiv and Svilengrad.

Train There are no through trains from northern Europe to Turkey, but with a change of trains it is possible to get to İstanbul from most European cities. The *Balkan Express* runs from Budapest (Hungary) via Sofia (Bulgaria) to İstanbul (US$37, 30 hours). The *Bosfor Express* runs between Bucharest (Romania) and İstanbul once a day (US$25, 16½ hours).

Another option is to go via Greece – a must for masochists. The daily service departs Thessalonika at 10.20 pm (although bear in mind that the timetable is subject to seasonal change) and the 1400km trip is supposed to take 16 hours. However, delays of more than five or six hours at the border are common, especially on the eastbound leg. The train can get uncomfortably crowded and, despite being an overnight international journey, only 2nd-class seats are available (US$38).

Car & Motorcycle The two border posts between Greece and Turkey are at Kastanies and Kipi. If you're lucky you may get through in an hour or two.

Bulgaria's main road crossing with Turkey (open 24 hours a day) is at Kapitan-Andreevo on the E5 road from Svilengrad; over the fence lies the Turkish border post of Kapikule, 18km west of Edirne. The second is at Malko Târnovo, 92km south of Burgas. Motorists in transit through Bulgaria may only be allowed to cross at Kapitan-Andreevo, depending on the current regulations.

Central Asia
Afghanistan Until the Soviet invasion of Afghanistan in 1979, the most popular route with overland travellers was east from Mashhad in Iran to Herat in Afghanistan, through Kabul then over the Khyber Pass to Peshawar in Pakistan. This neat little shortcut is virtually impossible now since the Iran-Afghanistan border crossing is not open to travellers. At the time of writing,

hostile relations between Afghanistan's conquering Taliban and neighbouring Iran meant that borders remained firmly closed. In the last 20 years only journalists, aid workers and a handful of the most intrepid travellers have ventured into Afghanistan at all, but it is possible to enter via Pakistan, notably from Peshawar. To do so you'll need Taliban assistance and a lot of luck – we don't recommend it!

See the Around Peshawar section of the Pakistan chapter for details on getting to the Khyber Pass.

Turkmenistan Sarakhs, 178km north-east of Mashhad in Iran, is the main border crossing from Iran into Turkmenistan. Several buses travel daily from Mashhad to Sarakhs (5000 rials, three hours). You'll need to catch a taxi or minibus from the town to the border crossing and the same on the other side.

To enter Turkmenistan here you will need a visa specifying Saraghs (the Turkmenistan town 5km from the border) as your entry point. Visas are not available at the border – sort one out in Tehrān, or preferably in your home country. The border is open from 8 am to 5 pm daily. There's not much in the way of public transport onwards from Saraghs with only one daily bus to both Ashgabat and Mary, both travelling via Tejen.

South Caucasus
Georgia From Turkey, a bus to Batumi in Georgia departs from Trabzon's Russian bazaar at 7 pm daily, but it arrives in Batumi in the middle of the night. You may prefer to take a morning minibus to Rize or Hopa and pick up another one heading for the border at Sarp. On the other side of the border, taxis will be waiting to run you to Batumi. Ask to be dropped near the train station.

Armenia At present it is not possible to cross into Armenia from Turkey. As far as crossing from Iran goes, while the fighting continues between Armenia and Azerbaijan over disputed land near the Iranian border, it's unwise to attempt it. Some intrepid travellers have recently succeeded but we don't recommend that anyone try to follow in their footsteps. At present, it's even unclear where the current border crossing is between Iran and Armenia.

Azerbaijan Some of the buses from İstanbul/Trabzon to Tbilisi (Georgia) continue on to Baku (US$75, plus a further US$10 'tip' payable on the bus if you're going to Tbilisi; US$25 for Baku). It's a fairly gruelling journey with a three- to four-hour delay at the Sarp border crossing from Turkey into Georgia – mainly because the Georgians and Azeris buy up half of Turkey to take home. Trabzon to Tbilisi takes the best part of 19 hours.

The border at Astara (Iran) and Astara (Azerbaijan) is currently closed to foreigners, although it is open to Iranians and Azaris. Check the current situation with the Russian embassy in Tehrān.

China & Tibet
A popular way to enter and exit Pakistan is from China via the Karakoram Highway (KKH), which crosses the Khunjerab Pass (4730m) on the Pakistan-China border and is said to be the world's highest public international highway. The pass is usually only open in summer (from May to September), when there are regular bus and 4WD services from Kashgar in China (Xinjiang) and Gilgit in Pakistan. Long-distance buses also operate along the length of the KKH, from Islamabad/Rawalpindi to Kashgar. See Lonely Planet's *Karakoram Highway* for more information.

Many travellers enter Tibet from China (the main route is via Golmund on the Qinghai-Tibet Highway) and then continue on into Nepal from Lhasa to Kathmandu on the Friendship Highway. However, there are no public buses from Lhasa to the border town of Zhangmu. There are occasional minibuses that operate to pick up tour groups, or you can hire a private 4WD. Going from Kathmandu to Tibet, it's easy enough to get a public bus up to Kodari but after that things get difficult. Even with a valid visa, Chinese border officials won't let you leave the Tibetan border town of Zhangmu unless you hire a costly 4WD – which is why many travellers take a tour from Kathmandu to Lhasa (see the Nepal chapter for details).

Bangladesh
It's possible to cross overland from India to Bangladesh or vice versa. The main overland route is at Benapol in Bangladesh (Haridispur in India). You can reach Benapol by bus from Jessore (which, in turn, is connected to Dhaka), cross the border on foot or by rickshaw, then take a train from Haridispur to Kolkata (Calcutta).

A more important route for travellers who have come from Kathmandu and continued eastwards to Darjeeling (India) is the northern crossing from Hemkumari in India to Chilahati in Bangladesh. There are several less-popular border crossing points on the eastern border with India.

If you arrived in Bangladesh by air and are leaving by land, you need to get a road permit from the Passport & Immigration office in Dhaka. It's free but the process usually takes at least 24 hours.

SEA
Few sea routes will concern travellers on the İstanbul to Kathmandu route, with the exception of using Mediterranean ferries to reach Turkey from Greece, Italy or Cyprus.

There are a few others, but they require more planning than can be covered by the scope of this book, and they're generally not cheap. These include ferries from the Gulf states to Bandar-é Abbās in Iran and from Baku in Azerbaijan to Iran's Caspian Sea coast (fortnightly in summer); and a passenger ferry from Dubai to Karachi in Pakistan.

Mediterranean
There are many Mediterranean ferries connecting Turkey with Greece and Italy, although none go direct to İstanbul. Thomas Cook's annually published *Greek Island Hopping* covers most domestic and international services in the east Mediterranean, not just those between the Greek islands. It includes summaries of sights and budget accommodation in most ports. You can also contact the carrier or its nearest agency in advance for timetables and fares. This is important if your itinerary depends on catching a particular ferry, or if you intend to ship your vehicle. In summer you won't have too much trouble getting a ferry, but they run to drastically reduced timetables – or cease altogether – out of season, which could cause a problem.

Although vehicles can be shipped on most routes, bookings may have to be made some time in advance. The charge usually depends on the length or volume of the vehicle and should be checked with the carrier. As a rule, motorcycles cost almost nothing to ship and bicycles go free.

Local services include ferries connecting the Greek islands of Lesbos, Chios, Samos, Kos and Rhodes with the Turkish coastal towns of Ayvalık, Çeşme, Kuşadası, Bodrum and Marmaris, respectively. Timetables and fares are notoriously fickle and the few dependable services generally vary according to demand. For further details see the individual town sections in the Turkey chapter.

Turkish Maritime Lines (TML) runs weekly car ferries between Venice and İzmir from May to mid-October. The charge is US$236 to US$286 one way, with reclining seat; mid-price cabins cost US$386 to US$493 per person. Greek and Italian lines also visit İzmir and İstanbul.

Black Sea

Russia Karden Line ferries run between Trabzon in north-east Turkey and Sochi in Russia, departing Trabzon at 6 pm on Monday and Thursday and returning from Sochi at 6 pm on Tuesday and Friday. Cabin tickets (US$60) are available in Trabzon from Navi Tour (☎ 462-326 4484), at Iskele Caddesi Belediye Duükkanlari. At the time of writing, most people would have to obtain a visa from a Russian consulate in their home country in order to use this service, but that may change.

ORGANISED TOURS

Three main sorts of tours are available: package tours, overland tours and inclusive tours. Package tours mainly deal with the resort areas of Turkey, or Goa in India, and are offered by virtually every high-street travel agency; they fall outside the scope of this book.

Overland tours are most likely to interest readers of this book. On these trips – which may last from 15 days to three months or more – you share a truck with a bunch of other travellers and hit the overland trail covering one or more of the countries in this book.

On an inclusive tour you fly to your destination and spend time touring in a single country, or a combination of countries. This could mean a trekking tour to Nepal, a desert safari in India or a cultural tour of Iran.

Overland Tours

If the idea of independent travel scares you to death, these trips are ideal. They cover a variety of overland routes, including the İstanbul to Kathmandu trip, in a specially adapted 'overland truck'. On board will be anything from 10 to 24 other passengers and your group leader-cum-driver/navigator/mechanic/nurse/guide/fixer/entertainer – much of the success of your trip rests on this person's shoulders, and on the group dynamics. Accommodation is usually a mix of camping and budget hotels. Food is bought along the way and the group cooks and eats together. You are very much expected to muck in; cooking and shopping is done on a roster system and everyone is expected to lend a hand when it comes to digging the truck out of sand or setting up camp. Although the itinerary is fixed, there is usually some flexibility built into the schedule that allows for seeing and doing things that aren't otherwise written into the program.

Advantages of this sort of trip are that many of the time-consuming hassles such as waiting around for public transport and finding decent accommodation each night are taken care of, maximising time for exploring and sightseeing. There's also the security that comes with being in a large group, which allows for camping out in the desert, exploring off the beaten track or activities that might be unsafe for individuals or couples. Disadvantages include a fairly rigid itinerary and the possibility of having to spend large amounts of time with a bunch of other people, not all of whom you will necessarily get along with.

Companies & Routes The overland tour market is dominated by British companies, although passengers come from all over the world. The standard Asian overland route, similar to the one in this book, is commonly followed, but there are lots of variations. Many of them start from London but move quickly through Europe so that the 'real' overland experience can begin. Some divert from Pakistan northwards into China, others head down from Turkey through the Middle East to Africa.

When considering an overland tour, find out exactly what the price includes. Does it include visa fees? Site admission fees? Food?

Often a food kitty is paid on top of the trip cost. Flights are generally not included in the package, so you have to make your own way to and from the start and end points. However, some companies can get discounted group bookings. Also, the quality of the trucks and camping and cooking equipment varies greatly. All in all, it's very much a case of you get what you pay for.

Some of the major companies operating on this route include:

Dragoman (☎ 01728-861 133, fax 861 127) 96 Camp Green, Kent Rd, Debenham, Suffolk IP14 6LA. Overland specialists with numerous itineraries through the Middle East and subcontinent, as well as Africa. Trips include London to Kathmandu (15 weeks, UK£2780) and İstanbul to Kathmandu (nine weeks, UK£1680).
Web site: www.dragoman.co.uk

Encounter Overland (☎ 020-7370 6845, fax 7244 9737, e adventure@encounter.co.uk) 267 Old Brompton Rd, London SW5 9JA. Extensive overland tours are offered, crossing all parts of our route from Turkey to Nepal as well as the Middle East and Africa. There are also many shorter tours covering specific areas such as Nepal and India. The Classic Overland trip from London to Kathmandu takes 11 weeks and costs around US$41 a day.
Web site: www.encounter.co.uk

Exodus (☎ 020-8673 0859, fax 8673 0779) 9 Weir Rd, London SW12 0LT. A major company offering a London to Kathmandu trip (15 weeks, UK£2390 plus UK£180 kitty) as well as various shorter trips including London to Islamabad (nine weeks, UK£1560) and Islamabad to Kathmandu via China (seven weeks, UK£1690) or via India (six weeks, UK£960).
Web site: www.exodustravels.co.uk

New Frontier Expeditions (☎ 01702-307 848, fax 305 367, e travel@new-frontier.co.uk) 96B West Road, Westcliff-on-Sea, Essex SS0 9DB. Trips with this company include London to Kathmandu (16 weeks, UK£1300 plus UK£180 food kitty); İstanbul to Islamabad (nine weeks, UK£770 plus UK£130 kitty), from where you can pick up a KKH trip (three weeks, UK£990); and Islamabad to Kathmandu (five weeks, UK£540 plus UK£55 kitty). Numerous shorter trips in the region are also available.
Web site: www.first48.com

In North America and Australasia overland companies are represented by specialist travel agencies – see the following Inclusive Tours section and check the advertisements in travel magazines and weekend papers.

Inclusive Tours

You can reach various parts of the region from your home country on a tour that includes your international flight, internal transport, accommodation, food, local guide and so on. These range from 'highlights' tours of India, such as the Wonders of Rajasthan, to trekking tours into the Nepali Himalaya.

The following lists give some idea of what's available but nothing beats your own research – checking travel magazines and travel supplements in the national newspapers, and requesting brochures and itineraries from suitable agencies.

As with the overland companies, most of the inclusive tours seem to be offered by UK companies:

Crusader Travel (☎ 020-8744 0474, fax 8744 0574) 57 Church St, Twickenham TW1 3NR. This company runs seven-day jeep safaris through the Bozburun peninsula in Turkey, with trekking in Lycia and rafting on the Çoruh.

Explore Worldwide (☎ 01252-319 448, fax 343 170) 1 Fredrick St, Aldershot, Hampshire GU11 1LQ. This company offers small group exploratory holidays in India, Nepal and Pakistan, including overland trips such as the Silk Road.

High Places (☎ 0114-275 7500, fax 275 3870, e highpl@globalnet.co.uk) Globe Works, Penistone Rd, Sheffield S6 3AE. High Places offers small group (maximum 12) trekking tours in Turkey, Pakistan, India and Nepal.

The Imaginative Traveller (☎ 020-8742 8612, fax 8742 3045) 14 Barley Mow Passage, Chiswick, London W4 4PH. This company offers small group tours.

Top Deck (☎ 020-7244 8641, fax 7373 6201, e topdeck@dial.pipex.com) 131–35 Earls Court Rd, London SW5 9RH. Top Deck offers an 11-week London to Kathmandu overland trip as well as Middle East and Asian tours.

In Australia most of the companies act as agents for the UK packages, although there are a few interesting homegrown firms:

Adventure World (☎ 02-9956 7766, 1300-363 055, fax 9956 7707) Level 3, 73 Walker St, North Sydney, NSW 2060; also in Perth. Agents for the UK's Explore Worldwide.

Intrepid Travel (☎ 1300-360 667, fax 03-9419 4426, e info@intrepidtravel.com.au) 11–13 Spring St, Fitzroy, Melbourne, Victoria 3065. Intrepid is mainly involved in adventure trips in South-East Asia, but it also has a wide range of tours through India, including a 15-day Delhi to

Kathmandu overland trip. It represents The Imaginative Traveller for trips in Turkey. Group sizes are no bigger than 12.

Web site: www.intrepidtravel.com.au

Passport Travel (☎ 03-9867 3888, fax 9867 1055, e passport@travelcentre.com.au) suite 11A, 401 St Kilda Rd, Melbourne, Victoria 3004. This Middle East and Indian subcontinent specialist assists in arranging itineraries for individuals or groups.

Web site: www.travelcentre.com.au

Peregrine (☎ 02 9290 2770, 1300-85 44 40, fax 9290 2155, e enq4@peregrine.net.au) Level 5, 38 York St, Sydney; also in Brisbane, Melbourne, Adelaide and Perth. Peregrine offers all Exodus tours as well as their own small-group adventure tours in the region.

Web site: www.peregrine.net.au

Sundowners (☎ 03-9600 1934, 1800-337 089, fax 9642 5838, e silk@sundowners.com.au) Suite 15, Lonsdale Court, 600 Lonsdale St, Melbourne, Victoria 3000. This is a small-group journey and independent adventure specialist for Middle East and Central Asia, with several packages covering most of the overland route and the Silk Road.

Web site: www.sundowners.com.au

World Expeditions (☎ 02-9264 3366, fax 9261 1974, e enquiries@worldexpeditions.com.au) Level 3, 441 Kent St, Sydney; also in Melbourne, Brisbane, Auckland, London and San Francisco. It offers trips within the region that include India, Nepal, Pakistan, Iran and Central Asia.

Web site: www.worldexpeditions.com.au

Agencies in North America include:

Adventure Center (☎ 1800-227 8747, fax 510-654 4200, e tripinfo@adventure-center.com) 1311 63rd St, Suite 200, Emeryville, CA 94608. The Adventure Center is the agent for the UK's Dragoman and Encounter.

Cross Cultural Adventurers (☎ 703-237 0100, fax 237 2558) Box 3285, Arlington, VA 22203.

GAP Adventures (☎ 1-800-465 5600, e adventure@gap.ca) 19 Duncan St, Suite 401, Toronto, Ontario M5H 3H1. Agents for Exodus.

Himalayan Travel (☎ 203-359 3711, fax 359 3669, e himalayantravel@cshore.com) 110 Prospect St, Stamford, CT 06901. Agents for The Imaginative Traveller.

Wilderness Travel (☎ 800-368 2794, fax 510-558 2489) 1102 Ninth St, Berkeley, CA 94710.

Getting Around the Region

Travelling overland from İstanbul to Kathmandu will almost certainly involve using a combination of bus, train, car – perhaps even plane – as well as various means of local transport. Then there are those who will get by under their own steam, whether it be by car, van, bicycle or even simply walking.

Among the modes of transport used by travellers in recent years are a London black cab, an Indian autorickshaw, bicycles, Enfield Bullet motorcycles, hitching…and then there are those rumoured to be getting around on roller skates, pushing airport trolleys…you name it, someone will try it!

However you decide to travel, getting from A to B will be at times an adventure, and at others it will be a long, boring and uncomfortable ride. Planning ahead, particularly with long train journeys on popular routes, can save a lot of hassle and frustrations.

For information on organised tours see the Getting There & Away chapter.

AIR

Although overland purists might regard taking a domestic flight as tantamount to cheating, a short hop within the region can save the time and discomfort of a long bus or train journey.

In certain circumstances flying may be the best option. For instance, flights in Iran are so cheap that it seems absurd not to take advantage of them for side-trips to, say, Mashhad or Shīrāz. In Pakistan, a short US$50 flight can save you a torturous 24-hour bus ride such as the one between Quetta and Peshawar. In northern India and Nepal, flying is reasonably cheap and what's more, has the added bonus of superb mountain views.

Domestic airlines throughout the region are generally reliable (some would argue that point when it comes to, say, Indian Airlines or Pakistan International Airlines – PIA) and have decent safety records. Ticket prices are usually fixed, whether you book directly through the airline or through a travel agent. Booking through a travel agent is generally easier and they often deal with more than one carrier, so they can offer a choice of fares and schedules. But beware of shonky backstreet operators, particularly in Delhi – just because you're issued with a ticket doesn't necessarily mean you're on the plane. It's certainly possible to get a seat on domestic flights at short notice, but if you know when you want to go it's definitely worth booking as far ahead as possible, especially during holiday periods and on popular routes.

You can pick up comprehensive timetables from airline offices in most cities. For more information on the location of airline offices see the Getting There & Away sections of each country chapter.

Turkey

Turkish Airlines (Türk Hava Yolları, THY) links all the country's major cities. There's heavy demand for seats on many routes so book in advance.

Get to the airport at least 45 minutes before departure to allow for security checks. You'll also be expected to identify your luggage just before you board the plane – if you don't do this, the bag is unlikely to be loaded and may well be destroyed.

You can look up THY's fares and schedules at www.thy.com.

Sample routes and fares from İstanbul include: Ankara US$106, İzmir US$106, Konya US$89, Antalya US$112, Diyarbakır US$112, Kayseri US$89, Şanlıurfa US$117 and Van US$123.

Iran

Iran is one of the cheapest countries in the world for domestic flights and you'd be mad not take advantage of this while travelling there.

Unless you're on a very tight schedule, don't bother booking the flights from home – you may well have to pay far more than you would in Iran. It's usually possible with a few days notice to get on the flight of your choice, but if you want to be safe book your tickets early during your trip – this is especially important around the major holiday of Nō Rūz (Iranian New Year) in mid-March. Even if flights are said to be full by travel agents or the airline offices, you can take your chances for a stand-by seat at the airport. Popular routes are Tehrān-Mash-had, Tehrān-Shīrāz and Esfahān-Shīrāz.

The main domestic airline, Iran Air, has regular services to just about anywhere you'd want to go in the country. The airline is reliable, safe, efficient and fully comput-erised. Ask for the very useful pocket-sized timetables from an Iran Air office. Of the myriad other small airlines, Iran Asseman has the widest range of services and is the most reliable. There is no price competition between the airlines.

Some sample routes and fares are: Tehrān-Tabrīz 113,000 rials; Tehrān-Mashhad 150,000 rials; Tehrān-Shīrāz 138,000 rials; Tehrān-Esfahān 91,000 rials; Esfahān-Shīrāz 91,000 rials; Tehrān-Yazd 111,000 rials; Tehrān-Kermān 165,000 rials; Tehrān-Zāhedān 205,000 rials.

Pakistan

Pakistan International Airlines (PIA) is the national carrier, although there are a num-ber of smaller private operators such as Karachi-based Bhoja Air, Aero Asia and the new airline, Safe Air.

PIA has an extensive network of services to all major cities, particularly out of Lahore, Karachi and Islamabad. While not as rock bottom as Iran, fares are still very cheap here. Sample routes and approximate fares include: Quetta-Peshawar US$50; Lahore-Peshawar US$35; Lahore-Islamabad US$26; Karachi-Lahore US$58. Any town or city that has an airport will have at least one PIA booking office. Their Web site lets you look up domestic fares and schedules (www.fly-pia.com).

India

Indian Airlines is the national domestic air-line. It has an extensive network covering most of the Indian towns and cities on this route. Although it tends to have frequent delays Indian Airlines is reasonably reli-able, but its fares are not as cheap as com-parable flights in Iran or Pakistan. If you're aged under 30 or are a foreign student (with a valid ISIC card) you can get a 25% discount.

Sample routes and fares include: Delhi-Amritsar US$100; Delhi-Varanasi US$125; Delhi-Shimla US$110, Delhi-Mumbai US$135. You can look up fares and sched-ules at indian-airlines.nic.in.

Jet Airways (asp.jetairways.com) is India's second-largest domestic carrier and flies the Delhi-Varanasi and Delhi-Udaipur routes. Its fares are generally slightly cheaper than those of Indian Airlines.

Nepal

If you plan to trek in the Everest region of Nepal, you might want to save a three-week hike and fly straight into Lukla airport (US$91 from Kathmandu).

Royal Nepal Airlines Corporation or RNAC is the national carrier for domestic and international flights, but there are no fewer than 17 private airlines operating in this tiny kingdom. Recommended airlines include Buddha Air, Necon Air and Cosmic Air. Your best option for buying a ticket is through a travel agent in Kathmandu or Pokhara. The Kathmandu-Pokhara flight (with spectacular views thrown in) costs around US$67.

BUS

Bus travel is the one form of transport you will certainly use on this trip unless you have your own vehicle. Buses range from luxury, air-con coaches with on-board host, movies and refreshments, to the most dilapidated, crowded, uncomfortable and potentially life-threatening piles of junk you could ever imagine being allowed on a road.

The beauty of buses is that they go al-most everywhere, departures are frequent (often overnight on long journeys), you don't always need to book, and they are very cheap – in Iran you will pay as little as US$0.20 for every hour travelled by bus. Long-distance buses are invariably packed, so it's worth booking ahead for these ser-vices – at least a day in advance. For shorter trips (anything up to five hours) or for the real economy services, especially on the subcontinent, it's a case of first-come-first-served, so turn up early. In Pak-istan, India and Nepal, buses rarely go anywhere until they are completely full, so timetables don't mean a great deal. One of the oddities of travel in this region is that you can get on a long-distance bus that is virtually empty until minutes before its in-tended departure, then suddenly 60 people appear from nowhere and crowd on. It's as if they've collectively had a sudden inspiration to take a 12-hour bus journey to any-where.

There are some interesting aspects to bus travel along the route. In Turkey the on-board attendant periodically comes around and offers lemon-scented cologne, which is poured into your cupped hands. It certainly freshens the place up. Pakistan's older-style buses are cigar-shaped contraptions painted up like mobile kaleidoscopes. In Nepal, mountain buses are so crowded that dozens of people usually travel upper class – on the roof!

A common problem on long distance buses throughout the region is the famous on-board video. The local passengers seem to love it, but listening to the wailing of a Hindi or Urdu film at two o'clock in the morning on an all-night bus ride is not most tourists' idea of fun. There's not a lot you can do about it except look for a bus service without video, or take ear plugs and put it down as a cultural experience. And if you don't sleep well on buses anyway, it can provide a mildly interesting distraction.

Another thing to consider is the temper-ature on board, particularly on overnight trips. Air-con buses can get cold enough to require a light blanket or jacket at night. Overnight bus travel in winter, particularly in eastern Turkey, Nepal, or the desert re-gions of Pakistan and India, can get ex-tremely cold, so be prepared. At the other end of the scale, travelling on non air-con buses in summer can be an uncomfortable and dehydrating experience. Take plenty of water and a towel or bandanna that you can soak and put on your head.

If you buy your ticket on board the bus, make sure you actually get a ticket with the price written on it, which will hopefully dis-courage the conductor from overcharging and pocketing the difference.

For more information on buses within each country, see National Networks later in this chapter.

International Buses

Bus travel between countries in this region is easy and mostly preferable to taking the train. Generally the best option is to take a bus to the border, pass through immigration and customs, then catch another bus to the near-est major town and continue on from there.

Border Crossings

The inevitable border crossings, with their bureaucratic hassles, queue-jumping, long waits and occasional demands for baksheesh can be nerve-racking and tir-ing. But they're also part of the excitement and adventure that is overland travel. Few travellers can approach the Indo-Pakistan border without a sense of trepidation, and watching the closing of the border gates there each day is truly an event not to be missed! (See the boxed text 'Showtime at the Border' in the India chapter.)

The reality is that most of the crossings are quite painless (provided of course you have the correct visas, carnets and whatever other documents you require). To smooth the way, we've provided detailed border crossing sections (in both directions) at the end of each country chapter. The table below is for quick reference and gives the relevant page numbers.

from-to	border crossing	visa/permit at border	further details
Turkey-Iran	Doğubayazıt/Bāzārgān	no	p 264
Iran-Turkey	Bāzārgān/Doğubayazıt	yes	p 264
Turkey-Iran	Esendere/Serō	no	p 254
Iran-Pakistan	Mīrjāvé/Taftan	yes	p 320
Pakistan-Iran	Taftan/ Mīrjāvé	no	p 320
Pakistan-India	Wagah	no	p 384
India-Pakistan	Wagah	yes	p 384
India-Nepal	Sunauli	yes	p 512
Nepal-India	Sunauli	no	p 512

However, there are some international buses that connect major cities in neighbouring countries:

İstanbul-Tehrān There are direct buses from İstanbul via Ankara to Tehrān. In İstanbul they depart at around 1 pm from Laleli area, and cost US$33 for a journey of around 40 hours, depending on how quickly the passengers are processed through the border. Tickets can be bought from travel agencies in Sultanahmet. There are also buses between Baku in Azerbaijan and Tabrīz in Iran, although you'll need to have a visa with permission to cross the border at Jolfa to use this service.

Zāhedān-Quetta There are no buses on this route between Iran and Pakistan but there is a painfully slow train service. See the boxed text 'Iran Border Crossings' in the Iran chapter.

Lahore-Delhi The new Lahore-Delhi direct bus service is something of a minor breakthrough in cross-border relations between these two countries. The air-con bus departs from Faletti's Hotel in Lahore on Tuesday, Wednesday, Friday and Saturday at 6 am (PKRs 950, 12 hours). From Delhi, it leaves from the Delhi Transport Corporation Terminal on the same days at 6 am (INRs 800).

Delhi-Kathmandu It's possible to get a direct bus all the way from Delhi to Kathmandu (agents in Paharganj sell tickets), but it's a pretty rugged 40- to 50-hour trip (INRs 850). It's better to take a train as far as Gorakhpur and then take buses from there.

Varanasi-Kathmandu Again there are plenty of agents advertising direct bus tickets from Varanasi to Kathmandu or Pokhara (around INRs 500), but there are *no* direct tourist buses on this route. You will have to change buses at the border and will probably need to stay a night in Sunauli (which may be included in your ticket). It's easy to do the trip yourself in two stages. The journey takes about 20 hours but will inevitably take longer with border delays and bus changes.

National Networks

Turkey Travelling on buses in Turkey spoils you for anywhere else. Not only do services go practically everywhere (frequently and cheaply) but they are also generally very comfortable and include on-the-road service from a conductor offering complimentary refreshments and a splash of cologne.

The major operators are Kamil Koç, Metro, Pamukkale, Ulusoy and Varan, all of which have better safety records than most. The *otogar* (bus terminal) is usually on the outskirts of town, but bigger bus companies generally offer free *servis* buses to and from their city centre offices.

Tickets for long-distance services should be reserved in advance. On local routes you can pay on the bus. When you book, make sure you have a seat number written on your ticket. Do try to get to the terminal early because some companies have a habit of over-booking, leaving stragglers without a seat.

All Turkish bus services are officially smoke-free, but you may want to avoid the front seats near the driver and the conductor – they're allowed to puff away freely.

Iran Thanks to government subsidies and the low cost of fuel the bus fares in Iran are the cheapest you'll find on the overland route. On top of this the services are regular, go almost everywhere, and the buses are comfortable, with individual cushioned seats (standing isn't normally allowed). The best companies, with the most extensive networks, are TBT and Cooperative Bus Company No 1, while Sayro Safar has the most modern fleet.

If you're taking a long overnight journey, consider paying extra for the more comfortable and faster Volvo bus services. For short distances, the difference is marginal. Don't count on averaging more than 60km/h on most routes. It's difficult to sleep well on buses, although it's a good idea to travel at night in summer, because the daytime heat can be unbearable and few buses are air-conditioned.

You can generally buy tickets up to one week in advance at the bus terminal, or at a bus company office (assuming there is one) in town. From one major city to another, such as Shīrāz to Esfahān, a bus from one company or another leaves every 15 minutes or so, but departures are less frequent in more remote places or between smaller towns.

Minibuses are often used for shorter distances and between less populated places. These are often faster than buses, and carry fewer passengers, so they spend less time dropping off and picking up. However, minibuses are not as comfortable – you can't pre-book a ticket, they usually only leave when full, and as many bodies as possible are squeezed on board.

No 1 Network vs the Fez Bus

The battle for backpacking travellers in Turkey has heated up with the recent introduction of the No 1 Accommodation and Travel Network to compete against the established Fez Bus company. Both offer hop-on, hop-off bus services (No 1's using local bus companies, Fez using their own minibuses) around the most popular parts of Turkey: namely from İstanbul along the Aegean coast and the Mediterranean coast as far as Antalya, then inland to Eğirdir, Konya, Cappadocia and back to İstanbul via Ankara.

Operated by an association of hostels, the No 1 network deal covers both accommodation and transport for US$12 a day – vouchers or tickets can only be bought at the Yücelt Interyouth Hostel in İstanbul, or Savos Hotel & TJ Hostel in Eceabat, and then exchanged at another eight participating hostels (Artemis Guest House in Selçuk, Meltem Motel Backpackers Inn in Pamukkale, Interyouth Hostel in Marmaris, İdeal Pension in Fethiye, Ateş Pension in Kaş, Bayram's in Olimpos, Backpackers Cave in Göreme and Lale Pension in Eğirdir).

Some of the hostels in the association are very good, others leave a little to be desired, so check out the individual reviews in the Turkey chapter. Fez is just a bus service (running from June to October), but with the services of a rep (called an 'off-sider') to help sort out hostels and onward transport at each stop. Accommodation is recommended but you're essentially free to stay where you want. The cost for the full circuit of travel is £108 in June rising to £120 in August; shorter sections (say İstanbul to Selçuk) are cheaper as are fares for students and those under 26.

Fez Bus can be contacted in İstanbul (☎ 212-516 9024, fax 518 5085, e feztravel@feztravel.com), at Akbiyik Caddesi 15, Sultanahmet, or via their Web site (www.feztravel.com). Bookings can be made through STA Travel in the UK and Australia. For information on the No 1 network contact Yücelt Interyouth Hostel in İstanbul (www.yucelthostel.com) or any of the other participating hostels.

The advantage of using Fez is that you're taken door-to-door and can get help and advice from the off-sider. The minus is that you're trapped within a backpacking travellers cocoon. By using local buses the No 1 network at least puts you in contact with ordinary people, but the downside is that to take full advantage of it you must use their fixed accommodation options.

Pakistan Once you pass from the Middle East to the subcontinent, things generally start to get more chaotic. However, Pakistan has a surprisingly well-organised, efficient and comfortable bus service.

The old state-run bus system is no more, but most major routes are served by one or more private operators with comfortable air-con coaches. There's also the beaten-up old Bedford buses, usually hand-painted in a riot of colour and further decorated with shiny tassels, buttons, badges and chrome-sequined fixtures. These might look good but they're not so comfortable – there's little leg room, the windows are either stuck open, stuck shut, or there are no windows, and they are typically overcrowded. But they're very cheap and a great way to meet local people.

The most extensive bus services (and best roads) are between Lahore, Islamabad/Rawalpindi and Peshawar. Here you'll find the country's only motorway – a six-lane toll road practically devoid of traffic. Numerous private companies operate deluxe buses on this route, the main ones being New Khan Road Runners, Daewoo Express, Skyways, and New Abasin. These buses are frequent, reasonably quick, and it's usually not necessary to book in advance. It costs less than US$1 per hour of travel. There are also regular buses between Lahore and Multan or Bahawalpur, but getting through the vast interior of Pakistan is another story. There are no direct buses from Quetta to Lahore, which makes the train a better option.

On regional routes or short trips of three hours or less, you'll find 15-seat minivans or 21-seat Coasters run more frequently than the large buses. They cost a bit more and are pretty cramped, but they're usually quicker. On the Coasters, special fold-away seats in the aisle ensure that every available bit of space is occupied. You don't pay any less for this uncomfortable position, so try to get on early.

Pakistan's bus stands are usually chaotic, dusty affairs with no central ticket or information office. Private companies sometimes have a desk set up (near where their bus departs) where you can buy tickets or attempt to extract timetable information. The easiest way to get where you're going, however, is simply to ask around for a bus to your destination and you'll be led in the right direction. There may be more than one bus stand in a town or city (serving different destinations) and they are often quite a way out of town.

One thing that you should be aware of about Pakistan's buses is the segregation of women. On most buses, women (and families) are seated separately towards the front. Men should not sit in seats reserved for women, even if there are no women on board (you may be asked to move). Foreign mixed couples will often be asked to rearrange themselves so that a Muslim man is not seated next to a strange woman. This becomes more obvious in conservative rural areas.

India India is perhaps the exception on the Istanbul to Kathmandu route as far as buses go. Bus services here are as extensive and frequent as elsewhere (if not more so), but India's excellent rail system makes the train a much better – and safer – mode of travel.

In the north of India there are very few luxury public buses (although anything with a reclining seat and on-board video will be called 'deluxe'), and the ageing hulks that regularly lumber out of India's bus stations are driven frighteningly fast on shocking roads. Because trains don't go everywhere (or may be infrequent or overbooked), bus travel fills the gaps, and in some cases the bus is actually quicker than the train because it's more direct. The mountainous region of Himachal Pradesh is best served by bus, in this case the Amritsar-Dharamsala-Shimla route. Rajasthan has a reasonably good bus service that can make a good alternative to the train, especially getting from Udaipur to Jodhpur and Jodhpur to Jaisalmer.

Classes of bus include 'ordinary', 'express', 'semi-deluxe', 'deluxe' and the relatively rare 'super-deluxe' (further south in India they even have deluxe sleeper buses!). Ordinary buses have hard bench seats with five people squeezed into the space of three, along with livestock, furniture and whatever else needs moving. They're dirt cheap, leave when full and stop to pick up more passengers every few minutes (or so it seems). They also tend to simply stop, frequently and for no apparent reason, and thus take a frustratingly long time to get anywhere. Travelling on these buses can be an interesting local experience and they're fine for short trips. Express buses are similar but don't stop as often. Semi-deluxe and deluxe buses are more organised, with set departure times (in theory), more comfortable seats and less stopping. Deluxe buses have two seats (usually reclining) on each side of the aisle, while semi-deluxe has five seats (three and two). These buses are not as crowded since the higher fare tends to discourage locals who can afford only the cheapest transport. Finally, super-deluxe should have air-conditioning and other 'luxury' features – you'll find these on a few routes out of Delhi, including to Agra and Jaipur.

There are state-run companies operating in most states, as well as private operators that vary in reliability and safety. Most city bus stands, while every bit as confusing as you would expect in India, have a central ticket and information office where you should be able to get assistance in English. Seat reservations can usually be made on semi-deluxe and deluxe buses (and are essential on super-deluxe) or with private bus companies. Otherwise, just turn up at the bus stand and get ready to join the rugby scrum for a seat. Buses leave frequently on popular routes – sometimes once very 15 minutes – so don't despair if you miss the first one.

Finally, keep an eye on your baggage and always take your day pack on board with you. If, for space reasons, your main pack ends up on the roof, check on it at chai stops and, if you have a chain or bicycle lock, secure it to the roof-rack.

Nepal Bus is the main form of land transport in Nepal and trips here will be some of the bumpiest you'll experience anywhere along the route. Since most of Nepal's roads are in a terrible state of repair, there's no reason for the buses to be any better!

The Kathmandu-Pokhara route is the country's main highway. Plenty of buses ply this reasonably well-maintained road. Getting from the Indian border to Pokhara or Kathmandu is also straightforward. Tourist buses in Pokhara and Kathmandu can (and should) be booked through agents. Long distance local buses can be booked at the bus stand, but for shorter trips, such as around the Kathmandu Valley, just turn up and squeeze on board. For many – locals and tourists alike – riding on the roof is part of the Nepali experience. You'll commonly see buses lumbering along mountain roads with 30 people clinging to the roof-rack. It's a safe enough practice as long as you hold on tight and preferably position yourself firmly in among your bags. In fact, there's an argument that travelling on the roof is safer than being inside – because you can jump off if the bus goes careering off the road into a gorge!

TRAIN

In the days of the hippy overland trail you could travel by train all the way from İstanbul across Turkey, Iran, Afghanistan and Pakistan to India. Sadly, such an epic rail journey is no longer possible, but the romance of the rails lives on and you can still squeeze a lot of train travel out of the İstanbul to Kathmandu route.

There are a limited number of train routes in Turkey and Iran, more extensive routes in Pakistan and India, and none in Nepal. There's talk of through services from Turkey to Iran restarting but don't hold your breath.

Turkey

Turkey's state railway company, Türkiye Cumhuriyeti Devlet Demiryollari (TCDD or DDY), has a hard time competing with the best long-distance buses for speed and comfort. Only on special-express trains such as the *mavi tren* and the İstanbul to Ankara *Fatih Ekspresi* and *Başkent Ekspresi* can you get some places faster and in more luxury than by bus. Sleeping-car trains linking İstanbul, İzmir and Ankara are good value; the cheaper *örtülü kuşetli* carriages have four simple beds per compartment.

At the time of research, the *Vangölü Ekspresi* was only running as far as Elazığ, stopping at Ankara, Kayseri, Malatya. If it does resume travelling to Tatvan, on the western shore of Lake Van, then the 1900km trip will take around 48 hours.

Iran

Iran has a comfortable, efficient and cheap train system, though it's nowhere near as extensive as the bus service.

Travelling first class sleeper on an Iranian train is a comfortable and easily affordable experience that you should really try to fit in somewhere on the trip. The best overnight routes are Tabrīz-Tehrān and Tehrān-Mashhad. Tehrān-Esfahān is a useful daytime service.

The downside of trains is that schedules are infrequent to popular places like Esfahān and Kermān (and nonexistent to places like Shīrāz), buying a ticket can be difficult, and departure and arrival times for some places along a route are often lousy.

All trains have two classes; some have three. It's always worth paying a little more for 1st-class compartments, but if you buy a ticket from any town along a route (ie, not at the starting or finishing point), you may only be able to buy a 2nd-class ticket (but you can probably upgrade to 1st class along the way). On trains that travel overnight, 1st class has sleepers: four or six bunks in a small compartment, as in India, Pakistan and Turkey. There are also decent restaurant cars.

In Tehrān, Esfahān, Tabrīz and Mashhad, tickets are available up to 15 days in advance for a 20% surcharge, but it's often not possible to book a return ticket.

Pakistan

Pakistan's rail system is reasonably comprehensive – you could easily travel between the main cities on our route without using the bus. The train is quite comfortable (provided you have a seat) and offers sleeper class for overnight travel. Train stations are usually centrally located and are nowhere near as chaotic and busy as those in India.

The main classes are unreserved economy, for which you buy a ticket (very cheaply) but are not guaranteed a seat; reserved economy, in an open carriage;

1st-class sleeper, which has enclosed sleeper compartments but is not air-conditioned; and air-con sleeper. Not all trains have all classes, and the sleeper classes should be booked at least a day or two in advance.

The main trains of interest to travellers on this route are the Quetta-Lahore services (via Bahawalpur and Multan) and Lahore-Peshawar (via Rawalpindi). You can pick up a copy of Pakistan Railways' comprehensive *Time & Fare Table* from bookstalls in major railway stations. It's not essential reading but it's certainly worth the Rs 10.

Fares are calculated by distance travelled. A 1st-class sleeper is a bit more than double the economy fare, and air-con travel is about 2½ times more than 1st class. If you're a student (with valid ISIC card) you can get a whopping 50% discount, and all foreign tourists are eligible for a 25% discount. To get these takes a bit of work though. For the tourist concession you first have to go to the tourist office and get a letter confirming that you are, in fact, a tourist (PTDC offices have these letters already typed up). You then take the letter (or your student ID) to the Commercial Department at the train station, which is in a separate building from the ticket office. With luck, the appropriate person will be there to exchange your letter for a voucher, which you then take to the ticket window. Expect all this to take a couple of hours.

India

Rail travel is the classic way to get around India. The British legacy has given India the world's fourth largest rail system and Indians love to travel on it – sometimes it seems like half the country is on the move and train stations are like cities within cities.

If you intend to make any use at all of trains in India, it's worth investing in *Trains at a Glance* (Rs 25), an easy-to-follow set of timetables for every train in the country. It gives you not only routes, times and frequency of departures, but the train name and number (essential for filling out reservation forms) and the distance in kilometres, which allows you to work out the fare. You can buy it at bookstalls in most large stations (you should be able to pick up a copy when you first arrive in Amritsar or Varanasi).

Except on very short trips, try to avoid 'Passenger' trains. These are local services that stop everywhere and anywhere for interminable periods and are very slow. Mail and Express trains are the ones to use – you'll find many of these running on major routes throughout the day and night. Indian trains have numerous classes but not all trains will have all classes. Second class is the basic unreserved seating and it's invariably very crowded. Second-class sleeper is a better bet. It's crowded during the day and you may find your reserved seat has been taken over by a crowd of locals, but after 9 pm a conductor comes around to make sure everyone is in their allocated seats, which fold down into three-tier sleeper berths.

Most long distance (and overnight) trains have air-con sleeper carriages that come in three-tier (six beds in a compartment), two-tier (four beds) and 1st class (four beds). Bedding is usually provided and, although not luxurious, this is a perfectly comfortable way to travel. Air-con chair is available on flash trains such as the *Shatabdi Express*. Standard fares are cheap: on the Delhi-Varanasi route (13 to 16 hours) 2nd class costs INRs 149 (about US$3); sleeper class is INRs 231 (US$5); air-con three-tier is INRs 671 (US$15); and air-con two-tier is INRs 1073 (US$25).

Because of the volume of passengers on Indian trains, making a reservation for anything above 2nd class (and especially for overnight travel) is essential. This can only be done in person at a train station (agents will do it for you for a fee, but they simply send someone down to the station in your place) and should be done as early as possible. An entire morning can easily be spent booking a train ticket. Before you join any queues, get a reservation form – these are either sitting on a counter or available from a special window. Fill it out with train name, number, class etc, then join the queue at the booking window that corresponds to the class and train you want. Also check if there's a special queue for tourists (there's one at Agra and Jaipur stations for instance). In Delhi there are entire booking offices set aside for tourists, which takes away some of the pain. Popular trains also have a tourist quota – a number of tickets set aside for tourists – so if the train you want is booked, ask about this.

Women should ask about the Ladies' Compartments that are available on some trains and which can provide respite from the crowds and staring men in other compartments.

CAR & MOTORCYCLE
Car
Few people would bother with the hassle of bringing their own car into any of the countries on this route purely to travel within the country. But every year hundreds of travellers set off in their own vehicle on the great overland journey from Europe to the subcontinent, and few have any regrets about their chosen means of transport.

. The advantages of having your own vehicle are obvious. You aren't tied to schedules, you can choose your own company, set your own pace, take the scenic route, and you won't be at the mercy of dishonest taxi drivers or have to fight for a place on a bus. And you can avoid all the hassles that go with carrying your world on your back.

But there are also distinct disadvantages to taking your own car across five countries (not to mention Europe if you're coming from the UK or elsewhere on the Continent). Number one is the bureaucracy involved – you are going to face mountains of paperwork and red tape before you leave home in order to obtain the necessary carnets de passage and other documents (see Carnets later in this section). The documents usually take a month or more to obtain, and just finding out the current regulations can be difficult. It's best to get in touch with your automobile association (eg, the AA or RAC in the UK) at least three months in advance. Note that the rules and conventions given here may not apply if you stay more than three months in any one country, or if you're going for any purpose but tourism. None of these documents come cheap – the more expensive your vehicle, the more you'll have to put up. On top of that there is also the expense of the insurance charged by some countries at the border, and the hassle of having your vehicle thoroughly searched at every crossing.

There is also the question of which route to take and what to do with the vehicle at the other end. If you intend to drive only from İstanbul to Kathmandu, you possibly have to be prepared to do it twice – once again in reverse to get your car back out of the region. Selling or dumping a temporar-

ily imported vehicle in Nepal is more or less ruled out by customs regulations. It's at least theoretically possible to have it put under a customs seal in one country and to return for it later, but this is a hassle to arrange, requires backtracking and somewhat negates the point of bringing a vehicle in the first place.

Motorcycle
The overland trail is a challenge that quite a few motorcycling enthusiasts undertake –

Braving the Baluchistan Desert

In November 1999, Steve Long drove a black taxi cab from his home in Kent to India. With just one day off in İstanbul, 'Taxi Steve' made the whole journey in 17 days so he could meet his family, who flew into Bombay. In April 2000 he set off back home again, having given rides to two Czech guys, an Indian who idolised the Queen, two Sikhs, the High Commissioner of the Maharashtra police, an Iranian soldier with a machine gun, a mad Scotsman called John, a Japanese guy called Zen and his bicycle, and a dog called Nipper that nipped him.

Taxi Steve is therefore well qualified to offer the following tips on driving across Pakistan's notorious Baluchistan desert:

'Some travellers say that the road from Bam to Quetta is boring, but I don't agree, as it gave me time to think about the meaning of life and what the hell I was doing this trip for'. When you get tired of this, try:

1. Spot the train
2. Spot the cloud
3. Spot the camel
4. Spot the white camel (these tend to be baby camels)
5. Hold your arm straight out the window and use the wind to make it aerodynamic
6. Exchange cassette tapes with the truck drivers that overtake you
7. Read your Lonely Planet while driving (We don't recommend this)
8. Play chicken with an Iranian 40-tonne truck (We REALLY don't recommend this)

Simon Richmond

many of them carry on all the way from London to Australia! Again you'll face the problems of bureaucracy. Most of the same rules apply to motorcycles as to cars or vans.

India is a favourite destination of motorcyclists. The idea of flying in and buying an old Enfield Bullet to tour the country is so common it's almost cliched. Delhi, in particular the Karol Bagh markets, is a popular place to pick up new or second-hand Enfields or other machines. The problem with the Enfield is that many travellers find them unreliable. You have to carry a lot of spares, trust the work of local mechanics and you risk not being able to get it repaired outside India.

A good Web site to try is www.indiabikes.com. It features travel information, you can chat with other bikers and you can even order an Enfield over the Net in the 'Bike Bazaar'! You can also check out what trips other people are doing around the world on www.adventuremotorcycling.com.

Carnets

A carnet de passage is like a visa for your vehicle. Essentially it's a booklet that is stamped on arrival in and departure from a country to ensure that you export the vehicle again after you've imported it. It can be issued by a motoring organisation in the country where the vehicle is registered (eg, the AA in Britain), although you may have to join the organisation if you're not already a member. The situation on carnets changes frequently but at the time of writing, carnets were required for every country on this route.

The big problem with a carnet is that you have to lodge a deposit or bank guarantee to secure it. If you default on the carnet – that is, you don't have an export stamp to match the import one – then the country in question can claim your deposit, and that can be up to 300% of the new value of the vehicle. You can get around this problem with carnet insurance but this requires a hefty, non-refundable premium from an insurance company.

Should the worst occur and your vehicle is irretrievably damaged in an accident or catastrophic breakdown, you'll have to argue it out with customs officials. Having a vehicle stolen can be even worse, as you may be suspected of having sold it.

Other Documents & Expenses

An International Driving Permit (IDP) is compulsory for foreign drivers and motorcyclists in Pakistan, India and Nepal, and very useful in Turkey and Iran.

For the vehicle you'll need the registration documents. Check with your insurer whether you're covered for the countries you intend to visit and whether third party cover is included. You'll also need a 'green card', issued by insurers. Insurance for some countries is only obtainable at the border.

Breakdowns & Spare Parts

Mechanical failure can be a problem, since spare parts – or at least official ones – are often unobtainable. Fear not: Ingenuity often compensates for the paucity of factory parts.

Generally, Land Rovers, Volkswagens, Range Rovers and Mercedes-Benz are the cars for which spare parts are most likely to be available, though in Iran and Pakistan you'll see quite a few Japanese models such as Toyotas. One tip is to ask your vehicle manufacturer for a list of any authorised service centres it has in the countries you plan to visit. The length of this list is likely to be a pretty good reflection of how easy it is to get spare parts on your travels.

Road Rules & Conditions

One of the enduring memories of your trip will undoubtedly be the driving standards, which are appalling by Western norms. India generally wins the prize for the most hair-raising – time is money for Indian truck drivers. And in Islamic countries fatalism rules supreme – Muslim motorists tend to trust that Allah is looking after them so they feel they can afford to take risks! Many regulations are, in practice, purely cautionary. Car horns, used at the slightest provocation, take the place of caution and courtesy. Obviously city driving is the biggest nightmare. Traffic is gridlocked, finding your way is confusing (a good city map is essential) and competing with local drivers takes nerves of steel. Overlanders rate Delhi and Lahore as two of the most difficult cities en route. By contrast, countryside driving can be a breeze.

In Turkey and Iran, driving is on the right; in Pakistan, India and Nepal driving is on the left (as in Britain). You're unlikely even to know what the speed limit is on a particular road, let alone be forced to keep to it. As a rule few locals wear motorcycle helmets or car safety belts, but you definitely should!

In Turkey, speed limits are 130km/h on motorways, 90km/h on major roads, and 50km/h in built-up areas. The main roads are good or at least reasonable in Turkey and Iran, although there are plenty of unsurfaced roads, and the roads crossing borders are generally narrow and crowded.

Distances across Iran are great, the countryside is often boring, and the traffic is truly horrendous – nearly 14,000 people die on Iranian roads each year. Road surfaces throughout Iran are generally excellent, but expect them to be poor or unpaved in remote desert and mountainous regions. Just about every road sign you'll ever need is in English. Never drive off the main road near the Pakistani, Iraqi or Afghani borders. In theory the speed limits are 110km/h on motorways, 80km/h during the day and 70km/h at night in built-up areas – you'd be wise to stick to these even if others don't.

In Pakistan the highway begins to deteriorate and there are plenty of 'main' roads that will barely take two passing vehicles, but the main Lahore to Peshawar highway is excellent. India's roads are generally rough and congested – most motorists agree this is the least pleasant place to drive a vehicle. In Nepal you will again find poor roads but you'll probably stick to the main highways between the border and Kathmandu, which are in reasonable condition.

Remember that an accident in the more remote parts of the region isn't always handled by your friendly insurance company. 'An eye for an eye' is likely to be the guiding principle of the other party and his or her relatives. Don't hang around to ask questions or gawp. Of course, we're not saying that you shouldn't report an accident, but it may be more prudent to head for the nearest police station than to wait at the scene. In India you may well be pressured into a serious baksheesh situation. Except in well-lit urban areas, try to avoid driving at night, as you may find your vehicle is the only thing on the road with lights.

A warning triangle is required for vehicles (except motorcycles) in some countries; in Turkey two triangles and a first-aid kit are compulsory.

Petrol & Diesel

Usually two grades are available; if in doubt get the more expensive one. Petrol stations are few and far between on many desert roads, particularly through Pakistan and parts of Iran – make inquiries before setting out. Away from the main towns, it's advisable to fill up whenever you get the chance. Locally produced maps sometimes indicate the locations of petrol stations. Diesel is fairly widely available and quite cheap (most of the overland tour operators use diesel trucks). Lead-free petrol is not as common as super, but is certainly available in Turkey, Iran and Pakistan.

Petrol prices vary but, apart from Iran, they are by no means cheap compared with North American and Australian prices. In Turkey you'll pay around US$0.82/0.55 for super/diesel. At the time of research, leaded petrol in Iran cost around 350 rials per litre (just over four US cents a litre if you're changing money at the street rate). Unleaded petrol is rarely available, or leaded fuel is sold as 'unleaded'. You also need to be careful not fill up with diesel by mistake. Petrol stations are open daily in, or just outside of, every major town. The outskirts of every city, town and village have filthy shops where you can arrange repairs. In Pakistan leaded/unleaded petrol costs PKRs 30/18; in India INRs 26/15; and NPRs 40/23 in Nepal. Petrol stations in India and Pakistan have widely been accused of diluting their product, but there's not a lot you can do about this.

Rental

In most large cities on the route there are car rental agencies, but other than in Turkey and Iran, these are rarely self-drive. In India, Pakistan and Nepal it's simply not worth trying to drive yourself around and, other than a handful of places in Pakistan, it's not possible anyway. Hiring a car and driver is a much better option. This is slightly different from hiring a taxi. There are no meters and the cost is calculated by the amount of kilometres travelled, plus an additional amount for overnight stays. In India, costs are roughly INRs 4 per kilometre and INRs 100 per day if you're staying overnight. Bear in mind that if you are travelling only one way, you'll be charged for twice the distance to cover the driver's return trip. Also check if you are expected to pay for the driver's meals and/or accommodation (he will usually sleep in the car) and set aside some money for a tip.

A couple of car rental agencies in Tehrān advertise in the *Tehrān Times* and *Iran News*. Don't bother – you can hire a taxi *and* a driver for about 90,000 rials (US$10) per day, and the driver can cope with the appalling traffic.

The news isn't so good in Pakistan. The cost of a car and driver is calculated at around PKRs 9 per kilometre plus about PKRs 70 an hour, so it's quite expensive for long trips. There are self-drive car-hire places in Lahore and Rawalpindi, but you'll pay even more for these.

BICYCLE

To anyone not familiar with long-distance cycling, the idea of riding a bicycle from Istanbul to Kathmandu seems distinctly nutty.

Even if you took a direct route it's roughly 8000km. You have to pass through several deserts, ride up mountains, battle some of the world's worst traffic and drivers, deal with extremes in temperature – and all this with your luggage balanced on the bicycle. Sounds like a challenge? A surprising number of travellers tackle the overland route – or at least part of it – in this way. On our research trip we met several cyclists en route, including Brit Sue Cooper, who was riding from Kathmandu back to London (see the boxed text 'Sue's Long Ride). Others cycling around the same time were Cass Gilbert and Mark Eskdale, both riding (independently of each other) from London to Australia via Turkey, Iran and Pakistan. Clearly, cycling from Istanbul to Kathmandu (or vice versa) is a viable proposition, provided you're fit and well-prepared.

Most riders say the best cycling is in Turkey, the eastern (and northern) parts of Pakistan, rural parts of India (as long as you're away from the horrendous traffic) and Nepal. Although hilly, the scenery in Turkey is particularly fine and accommodation is fairly easy to come by even in the smallest villages. Iran involves a lot of very long, very boring rides through the desert, while the section of Pakistan from the Taftan border to Quetta is not only long and boring, but unsafe as well.

By far the major difficulty cited by all cyclists is the heat. This is at its worst from

Sue's Long Ride

After two years working on the UK's Voluntary Service Overseas (VSO) program in Nepal, Sue Cooper decided to cycle back to Britain from Kathmandu, starting on Christmas Eve 1999.

Riding a second-hand Giant mountain bike with two back panniers and a front kit bag, she carried around 25kg of gear including a spare tyre and three pairs of cycling shorts. She didn't take a tent and didn't camp at all during the trip, feeling safer to stay in hotels. As a safety precaution, before heading out Sue wrote to all the British embassies en route. The letter included her passport details and outlined her plans with a rough itinerary indicating when she would be in each country.

The journey from Kathmandu to London took around seven months, of which Sue estimated 110 days (almost half the total) was actually spent pedalling, the rest sightseeing or resting. The distance travelled was roughly 12,000km, averaged out at around 110km a day in the hills, 140km on flat roads. The only repairs required along the way were five punctures and four snapped spokes. Sue took public transport once (the bus from Quetta in Pakistan to Bam in Iran, for safety reasons), and accepted two lifts from motorists, both in Iran. Other than a few rides in England, Sue had never previously done a long-distance cycling trip, but as big a challenge as it was, she was surprised at how easy and natural the trip seemed. She's now planning to ride the length of South America.

The accounts of Sue's ride, together with advice on road conditions and routes, appear as boxed texts throughout this guide. The information is presented in the east to west direction she was riding, but it also applies in the reverse direction.

June to August in Turkey, and from March to September further east on the route. Cycling in these months is definitely not recommended. September through to February is the best time for two-wheel touring if you're setting out from İstanbul; October through to May or June is better if you leave from Kathmandu (see When to Go in the Facts for the Visitor chapter for more information). Most cyclists still find it's best to make an early morning start and be done with most of the pedalling by early afternoon.

Whatever pace it's taken at, the consensus is that if you are considering cycling this route, go for it. You'll have a ball. We've included some route-specific cycling information provided by readers throughout this book.

For information on cycling tours and bicycle hire within the region see Activities in the Facts for the Visitor chapter.

Road Rules & Hazards

Motorised vehicles take priority on the roads. They will make little allowance for cyclists and expect you to give way, so when a vehicle comes up behind you, pull right over to the side of the road. Cyclists en route reported that India was particularly dangerous in this regard. Cyclists are truly an oppressed caste on Indian roads – one step up from pedestrians. Not only do trucks and buses make no room, but cyclists have reported unnerving experiences such as being jeered, surrounded by curious people or even vehicles trying to push them off the road.

Transporting a Bicycle

Most airlines have a 20kg baggage allowance, while an average bicycle weighs in at 15kg. Get an old bicycle box from a bicycle shop and pack your partly dismantled bicycle in it along with another 5kg of bulky baggage. If you then carry your heaviest equipment as cabin luggage, you should, if you are travelling light (as you should be), be able to transport your bicycle by air for nothing.

In Turkey, if you get tired of pedalling it's no problem to have your bicycle transported in the luggage hold of the big modern buses they have there. In Pakistan and India, bicycles can usually be put on trains as freight or luggage.

Practicalities

The following is a basic list of things it would be a good idea to have with you on the ride:

- a couple of extra chain links
- a chain breaker
- spare spokes
- spoke key
- at least two inner tubes
- tyre levers
- repair kit
- flat-head and Phillips screwdrivers
- Allen keys and spanners to fit all the bolts on your bicycle (check the bolts daily and carry spares)
- as many water bottles as you can fit to your bicycle – staying hydrated is very important

Make sure the bicycle's gearing will get you over the hills, and confine the load in your panniers to 15kg to 20kg maximum. You could also carry a two-person tent (weighing about 1.8kg) that can accommodate the bicycle when security is a concern,

Gosh! Lots of luggage. Where's your bike? In there... somewhere!

DON HATCHER

but it's possible to do the trip without ever needing to camp, so decide whether you really need it. Other possible items include a good sleeping bag, inflatable sleeping mat, water filter, and a torch (flashlight). Wear cycling shorts (under other suitable clothing) with a chamois or silicon-gel bum and cleated cycling shoes. You won't need to take food – it will be plentiful and fresh along the route.

Contacts

If you are considering cycling this route but have a few pressing questions that first need answering, one place to go is the Thorn Tree on Lonely Planet's Web site (www.lonelyplanet.com). Post your query on the Activities branch (in the Lobby) and there's a strong likelihood somebody will respond with the information you're looking for.

Alternatively, you could contact the Cyclists' Touring Club (CTC ☎ 01483-417 217, fax 426 994, ⓔ cycling@ctc.org.uk), a UK-based organisation that, among other things, produces information sheets on cycling in different parts of the world. As well as maintaining its Web site (www.ctc.org.uk), the club also publishes a good, glossy bimonthly magazine that always carries one or two travel-type cycling pieces.

HITCHING

Hitching in this part of the world is not common and we don't recommend it. There is certainly nowhere along this route that would be regarded as safe for lone women to hitch in.

Hitching as commonly understood in the West hardly exists in the Middle East and subcontinent. Although in most countries you'll often see people standing by the road hoping for a lift, they will nearly always expect (and be expected) to pay. The going rate is usually roughly the equivalent of the bus or shared taxi fare, but may be more if a driver takes you somewhere off his or her route, and the demands may be much more if the driver (understandably) feels he can get more out of a Western tourist. In Iran and Turkey you may well be offered free lifts from time to time but you won't get very far if you set out deliberately to avoid paying for transport.

In the Middle East a raised thumb is a vaguely obscene gesture, and it won't be understood on the subcontinent. A common way of signalling that you want a lift is to extend your right hand, palm down.

LOCAL TRANSPORT

There are loads of interesting ways of getting around town, or between towns, as the locals do. Crowded minivans and local buses, cycle-rickshaws and taxis are just some of the options. In most cities and towns on the route there are plenty of local bus services, though it can be confusing to work out which one is going to your destination and they're often full to bursting. Printed timetables or route maps are generally nonexistent. Try to have small change on hand with you when you board local transport – nothing annoys a conductor more than being proffered a Rs 100 note for a Rs 5 fare.

Minibus

There are various names for the little minibuses or pick-ups that shuttle around towns throughout the region, constantly loading and unloading passengers. They're usually very cheap, very crowded and a bit of fun once you get the hang of them.

In Turkey, the *dolmuş* is usually a Toyota van with a sliding door at the side, which carries about 12 passengers. A dolmuş departs as soon as every seat (or nearly every seat) is taken. You can catch one from point to point in a city, or from village to village, and in some cases from town to town. Though dolmuşes on some routes operate like buses by selling tickets in advance, the true dolmuş does not. Rather, it is parked at the point of departure (a town square, city otogar or beach) and waits for the seats to fill up. You pay on board, usually with everyone passing money to the front, which gives you a chance to see what the locals are paying. The dolmuş route may be painted on the side of the minibus, or on a sign posted next to the dolmuş, or in its window; or a hawker may call out the destination. When the driver is satisfied with the load, the dolmuş heads off.

In Pakistan you'll find similar minibuses (called wagons) doing short trips around and between towns, as well as the more unique Suzukis. These colourful little pickups are open at the back; you wave the vehicle down, jump aboard (often while it's still moving) and climb in. There are also Suzuki stops at strategic points around town as they run on fixed routes and have fixed fares (about Rs 5). Rawalpindi is the place you're most likely to find these.

Taxi

Taxis, like everywhere else in the world, are expensive by local standards and are rarely a necessary form of around-town transport. The exception is getting to or from an airport that may be some distance out of town and that may not be serviced by any other public transport.

Another exception is Iran, where shared taxis (and even private taxis) are a cheap and much-used form of local transport. Shared taxis – often referred to as *savari* – can normally be taken between any major town less than four hours away by car. Speed is the main advantage, because shared taxis are generally more uncomfortable than the bus (but better than the minibus). Two people are expected to squeeze into the front passenger seat, so never sit there unless you have no choice. Three people will share the back of the taxi, which is not too uncomfortable unless you're built like a wrestler.

Shared taxis need less people to fill them, so they usually depart fairly quickly. However, shared taxies never leave with an empty seat unless a passenger agrees to pay for it.

As a general rule, shared taxis cost about three times more than a typical bus fare. This may seem like a lot in rials, but if you work it out in your own currency shared taxis are still cheap, and worth using for quick trips, especially through dull stretches of countryside. If you wish to speed up a departure, or if you crave a little extra comfort you can pay for an empty seat or charter the entire vehicle.

Shared taxis normally leave from inside, or just outside, the relevant bus terminal, though occasionally there are special terminals for shared taxis heading in particular directions. You can't prebook a seat in a shared taxi; they leave when they are full.

In Pakistan you'll probably find you won't use taxis much. They're always cruising around if you need them and there are plenty at airports and train stations. In India, the Ambassador taxis (usually off-white in colour) are similarly common but charge typically two or three times the equivalent autorickshaw fare. In Nepal, larger towns such as Kathmandu and Pokhara have taxis. Metered taxis have black licence plates; private cars often operate as taxis, particularly on long-distance routes or for extended periods, and have red plates.

Taxis usually have a meter, but whether you can convince the driver to use it or not is another matter. If he won't, either look for another taxi or bargain for a fare before getting in.

Taxis come in useful if you have a group and want to take a short trip out of town at your own pace. You can hire a taxi to visit the Khyber Pass from Peshawar, the Sam sand dunes near Jaisalmer or to vantage points around the Kathmandu Valley in Nepal. With a little bargaining and a round trip (if you only go one way the driver will charge for the return trip anyway) it can work out quite economical.

Autorickshaws

Noisy, polluting but extremely handy, autorickshaws can be found around the main cities and towns of Pakistan, India and in Kathmandu. These three-wheel, two-stroke taxis, like a squat motorbicycle with an open-sided cabin and canopy, buzz around cities and towns searching for customers. They're painted yellow and black in India, often with colourful designs added. They're coloured blue in Pakistan.

Autorickshaws (often just called autos) provide reasonably cheap, quick transport around town, hold three people (two in comfort) and can carry a bit of luggage. When distances are too great to walk, this is the way to go. The ride can be pretty bumpy though – every pothole will have you instantly airborne – and hair-raising. Few Indian drivers are as crazy as these guys and, although these machines are pretty manoeuvrable, glancing blows and near misses with oncoming traffic are not uncommon!

There are no emission standards on the subcontinent and belching autorickshaws are responsible for much of the pollution that plagues cities like Delhi and Kathmandu. Many travellers choose not to use them for this reason, taking cycle-rickshaws or other environmentally friendly transport instead.

The British Autorickshaw Overland Expedition

In early 2000, Kenneth Twford and Gerald Smewing drove 'Ricky' the autorickshaw home to the UK from India. We caught up with them in Doğubayazıt, just after they'd crossed the border from Iran.

Why do it?

Ken: It was partly the challenge of getting an autorickshaw back that attracted us. They have small engines, only 150cc, so it's pretty well underpowered and we didn't know what the roads would be like en route. Also for the sense of fun.

Gerald: One of the problems of flying home from India is that the trip ends very abruptly after the 10-hour flight. We thought this would a great way of linking it up, passing through several countries, landscapes and cultures.

Done anything like this before?

Gerald: We'd cycled and motorbiked in Asia and in particular India, where we travelled on a scooter for 15,000km in 1988, but never anything like this. We've often stayed in the Delhi Tourist Camp, mainly used by overlanders and heard their stories.

What route have you taken?

Ken: We spent three months touring southern India, testing Ricky out on all kinds of roads. From there we drove north to Amritsar. Then through Pakistan to Quetta and across the desert of Baluchistan into Iran. Straight through Iran, pretty much on the tourist route to here in Turkey.

Had any problems?

Ken: A few minor ones, because it's three years old and things are wearing out on it. We've replaced all the seals on the break system and the clutch. Wires have cracked as well.

Another downside is that you'll find yourself constantly haggling with the drivers, a novelty that soon wears off. A few days in Delhi can seem like one big autorickshaw bargaining session. Although they are supposed to have meters, these will either be broken, nonexistent or out of date – fares are adjusted upwards faster than meters can be recalibrated, in which case the driver should have a card showing the fare adjustment. In any case, the drivers simply won't use the meters for tourists, knowing they can extract a higher fare.

The golden rule (if you didn't know it already) is to agree on the fare before getting in, otherwise the driver *will* charge an outrageous sum when you get to your destination, and trying to argue your way out of it then can create an uncomfortable and threatening crowd scene. When bargaining, it helps to know approximately what the local fare is, but at the very most offer two-thirds of the asking price and keep things cordial. If there are other autos around, you

have a pretty good chance of playing them off. After a while you get an idea of what a fair price is.

To combat the problem of rapacious auto drivers, several Indian cities have set up pre-paid autorickshaw (and taxi) booths at bus and railway stations. These are operated by the police and have fixed fares. You pay your money directly at the booth, jump in an auto from the queue and give the driver your ticket at the end. Even then some drivers will demand a 'tip', but you don't have to give one. When you see the prices of these pre-paid journeys, you'll realise how much lower the odds you've been paying elsewhere!

In Pakistan, auto drivers are much more reasonable than in India (where they're more accustomed to moneyed tourists), so you shouldn't have too much trouble getting a reasonable fare there, particularly outside Lahore. In Kathmandu you can generally convince them to use the meters.

The other problem with autorickshaws (or taxis) is that of commission. Any time

The British Autorickshaw Overland Expedition

Where did you buy Ricky?
Gerald: We went to a garage in Hyderabad. They had this one that had been used privately – it's never been a taxi. If it had, it would've been knackered.

Did you make any special changes to Ricky for the journey?
Ken: We had it painted and put a big horn on the front. We also attached front indicators and grab handles at the front in case we had to pick it up and pull it. So far, we've only had to push it out of soft sand once. We also put spare wheels on either side to make it look like a Land Rover.

How much did it cost?
Gerald: £600 but the carnet is £2000, a sizeable chunk to lose if it doesn't make it. We went to the Bajaj (the rickshaw's manufacturer) factory in Pune and got kitted out with a couple of T-shirts, baseball caps and the all-important service manual.

Would you recommend overlanding in a rickshaw?
Gerald: I would if you have time. We only average about 45km an hour. But you're exposed to people, the elements and so on.
Ken: It's also very comfortable, when you're in the back and it's a boring piece of landscape you can just sit and read a book or listen to music, which you can't do on the back of a motorcycle.

What's the reaction at borders?
Gerald: They're very relaxed. I think they assume you're fairly innocent if you're driving around in a rickshaw. You're not likely to be doing any heavy duty crimes – you won't get very far down the road before someone catches up.

Simon Richmond

you're taken to a hotel or shop, the driver gets commission and you pay extra for it on your room bill or purchase. See Scams under Dangers & Annoyances in the Facts for the Visitor chapter for more information.

Cycle-rickshaws

Cycle-rickshaws are basically three-wheeled bicycles with a seat between the rear wheels, a fold-down concertina canopy, and the driver pedalling furiously up front.

You'll find these in most Indian cities (although only in the old part of Delhi these days). Cycle-rickshaws are common in the old part of Kathmandu and can be a good way of making short trips through the crowded and narrow streets. They're cheaper than autorickshaws or taxis, easier to bargain with, don't emit any noxious gas, and are a fun way to cover short distances when walking becomes too much.

Again, the rule here is to agree on the fare before you get in and to act like you don't care whether you take this particular rickshaw or not. Don't get sucked in by the frequently uttered line, 'As you like', accompanied by a warm smile. The driver is hoping that you will overpay (and will probably insist on it at the end of the ride), or he will take you to a carpet/gem shop instead of your preferred destination. A trip of two or three kilometres shouldn't cost any more than Rs 20. However, even agreeing on a fare may not be the end of the story – there's generally more chance of post-travel fare disagreement with cycle-rickshaws than with other forms of transport.

Other Transport

Tempos are ungainly looking three-wheel shared taxis that look a lot like a large autorickshaw. You'll find them in a handful of Indian cities and all over Kathmandu. They run on set routes and the fares are very cheap, but unless you're in town for a while it can be difficult to work out which ones are going where. Most of the new tempos in Kathmandu are electric, and therefore not contributing to the city's chronic pollution.

The tonga is a form of transport still used in some cities and tourist areas in Pakistan and India. This is a two-wheeled horse-drawn carriage that will take you short distances for a little more than that charged by cycle-rickshaws.

In Tehrān and Kathmandu you'll find trolleybus lines (well, one in each city). These are a cross between a tram (powered by electricity via overhead wires) and a bus, ie, running on the normal road.

Turkey has trams in Konya and Antalya. İstanbul has the short Tünel underground train and there are longer metro lines in Ankara. Tehrān in Iran also has a metro line.

TURKEY

İstanbul

Ephesus   Göreme

PETER PTSCHELINZEW

Aya Sofya, İstanbul

PETER PTSCHELINZEW

Ephesus

SIMON RICHMOND

Castle of St Peter, Bodrum

SIMON RICHMOND

Cappadocia

PETER PTSCHELINZEW

İshak Paşa Sarayı, Doğubayazıt

TURKEY
highlights

Aya Sofya, İstanbul
An awe-inspiring interior, with ancient mosaics and a stupendous dome, belies an unremarkable exterior.

Gallipoli
An essential pilgrimage for Aussies and Kiwis, the pine-dotted Gelibolu (Gallipoli) peninsula is also an evocative place in which to walk or cycle.

Ephesus
A megastar among Turkey's many classical ruins, Ephesus is where you really get an idea of what a Roman city looked like.

Bodrum
Nestled in a crease of the Aegean Coast, Bodrum is home to the magnificent Castle of St Peter, across which the Crusaders once strode.

Cappadocia
A unique crumbling landscape with 'fairy chimneys', cave churches and dwellings and remarkable underground cities.

Nemrut Dağı
The giant tumulus, with its enigmatic carved rock heads, provides a stunning vista of the surrounding mountains.

Van
The ruined fortress Van Kalesi stands by the shores of the lovely mountain-surrounded Van Gölü (Lake Van), while the beautiful Armenian church Akdamar Kilisesi perches on an island in the lake.

İshak Paşa Sarayı, Doğubayazıt
Close to the Iranian border, this restored but swooningly romantic palace is a marvellous introduction or farewell to Turkey.

Anıtkabir, Ankara
At the heart of Turkey's capital is the impressive mausoleum of Atatürk, the man who created the modern Turkish republic.

Turkish Bath
Bathing at a *hamam* is a must no matter where you are in Turkey.

Turkey

Turkey is the bridge between Europe and the Middle East, both physically and culturally. The Ottoman sultans ruled the entire Middle East for centuries, and traces of Turkish influence remain in all of the countries once controlled from İstanbul. Turkey was the first formerly Ottoman Muslim land to establish a republic and to achieve democracy, as well as the first to look to Europe and North America for cultural models. The tourism boom of the 1990s brought even more European influence, from rock music to topless bathing.

Still, Turkey is no imitation Europe. With more accessible ancient ruins than any other country on the overland trail, 4000km of warm-water coastline, varied countryside and excellent food, Turkey has lots to offer. In addition, accommodation is plentiful, prices are cheap and travel to all points is simplified by an incredibly efficient bus system which rivals Swiss railways for punctuality. Insistent hotel and carpet-shop touts aside, Turks are mostly very friendly and hospitable, especially in the east of the country.

THE ROUTE

Our main route starts in historic İstanbul, then heads across the Sea of Marmara to the old Silk Road outpost and hot-springs resort of Bursa. It follows the coast south, passing the battlefields of Gallipoli, legendary Troy, the remarkable ancient city of Ephesus, picturesque Aegean and Mediterranean towns and resorts, the ruins of Olimpos and the flames of the Chimaera. From Antalya we head inland to the idyllic lakeside town of Eğirdir, the dervish capital of Konya, and on to one of the world's greatest scenic wonders, Cappadocia.

Going beyond the backpacker circuit, the next pit stop is Nemrut Dağı (not to be confused with the mountain of the same name on the shores of Lake Van), to see the toppled giant stone heads of gods and kings. Şanlıurfa, close to the Syrian border, offers a first taste of the Middle Eastern pleasures to come. The cessa-

Turkey at a Glance

Capital: Ankara (population 4 million)

Population: 69.7 million

Area: 788,695 sq km

Head of state: President Necdet Sezer

Country telephone code: ☎ 90

Exchange rates: The Turkish lira is subject to rapid devaluation. Check exchange rates before you visit Turkey.

country	unit		Turkish lira (TL)
Australia	A$1	=	372,829
EU	€1	=	629,685
UK	£1	=	992,500
USA	US$1	=	673,507

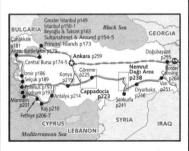

tion of Kurdish insurgency in eastern Anatolia has opened up the route to the fascinating medieval city of Diyarbakır and onward towards Lake Van (Van Gölü), where the landscape takes on an alpine grandeur more usually associated with Switzerland.

There are two border crossings into Iran from Turkey. The main one is between Gürbulak (Turkey) and Bāzārgān (Iran), near the town of Doğubayazıt at the foot of twin-peaked Mt Ararat. You can approach Doğubayazıt via the route described in the previous paragraph, or, more directly, via Ankara and Erzurum. For information on this border crossing, see the 'Turkey Border

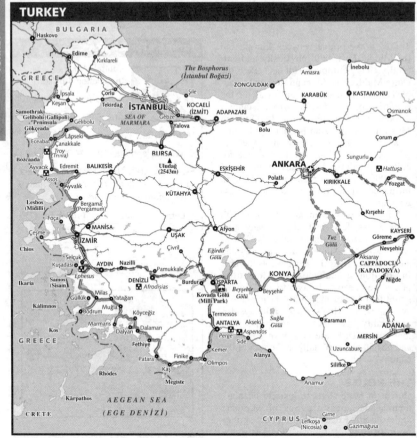

Crossings' boxed text at the end of this chapter. The other border crossing is between Esendere (Turkey) and Serō (Iran), for details see the 'Van to Orūmīye' boxed text in the Van section later in this chapter.

İstanbul

☎ 212 (European İstanbul)
☎ 216 (Asian İstanbul) • pop 12 million

Can there be a better place to start or finish your overland journey than İstanbul? The city formerly known as Constantinople is a dream destination: Spend your days wandering around the mosques, ruins and tangled streets where empires have risen and fallen. It was here, five and a half centuries ago, that the final fragment of the Roman Empire crumbled. Through Europe's Dark Ages the city carried European civilisation on from its Greek and Roman origins.

At night, lose yourself in the hedonistic dining and drinking pleasures of Taksim, where modern İstanbul goes to party. Or you can just sit back and soak up the East-meets-West atmosphere from a ferry plying the Bosphorus or from the roof of a Sultanahmet hostel.

HISTORY

Legend has it that Byzas, an invader from Magaria (a Greek state), founded the city in the 6th century BC, although there's evidence of occupation as early as the 9th century BC. He's said to have given the name

Byzantium to what was previously a collection of fishing villages on the Bosphorus.

Late in the 2nd century AD, Rome conquered the small city-state, but it wasn't until AD 324, when Emperor Constantine reached Byzantium (chasing away his rival Licinius), that its fortunes really took off. Constantine moved his capital there from Rome and renamed the city after himself.

When the Roman Empire divided in 395 BC, the sons of the emperor Theodosius left Constantinople as the capital of the eastern part of the empire. Christianity became more strongly entrenched and monuments and churches such as Aya Sofya were built.

For nearly a thousand years the stout Roman walls of Constantinople kept invaders pretty much at bay, while the rest of the Byzantine Empire crumbled away. The Crusaders breached the defences in 1204 and took control, but when the Byzantines regained the city 57 years later, it was a shadow of its former glory.

In 1453, after a long and bitter siege of seven weeks, the Ottoman Turks breached the city walls just north of Topkapı gate on the city's western side. Sultan Mehmet II, known as Mehmet Fatih or Mehmet the Conqueror, marched to Aya Sofya and converted the church to a mosque. The Byzantine Empire had ended. In 1463 Mehmet II had his builders commence İstanbul's first imperial mosque, the Fatih Camii.

As the capital of the Ottoman Empire, the city entered a new golden age. During the glittering reign of Süleyman the Magnificent

(1520–66), the city acquired many new buildings of great beauty, some by the brilliant architect Mimar Sinan.

Wanting a new capital for his new republic, Atatürk chose Ankara over Constantinople. İstanbul (its new name), however, remains the economic and cultural centre of Turkey.

ORIENTATION

The Bosphorus strait (Boğaziçi), between the Black Sea and the Sea of Marmara, divides Europe from Asia. On its western shore, European İstanbul is divided by the Golden Horn (Haliç) into Old İstanbul (Stamboul or Eski İstanbul) in the south and Beyoğlu in the north. Sultanahmet, the heart of Old İstanbul, is where the vast majority of visitors stay, and where most of the main tourist sites are.

The international airport (Yeşilköy Atatürk Hava Limanı, or just Atatürk airport) is 25km west of Sultanahmet; there is a suburban train to Sirkeci (near Sultanahmet) from Yeşilköy station near the airport. Sirkeci station is where European trains arrive, while Haydarpaşa, on the Asian shore, is the terminus for services heading east. The International İstanbul Bus Terminal (Uluslararası İstanbul Otogarı), usually just called the otogar, is at Esenler, 10km west of Sultanahmet.

In Beyoğlu you'll find Taksim, the city's modern centre, with the best shopping and nightlife. Further north are fashionable suburbs including Beşiktaş near the Dolmabahçe Palace and Ortaköy in the shadow of the Bosphorus Bridge, the first bridge linking Europe to Asia across the Bosphorus.

INFORMATION
Tourist Offices

The Ministry of Tourism has offices in the international arrivals hall at Atatürk airport (☎ 663 0793); in the international maritime terminal, Yolcu Salonu (☎ 249 5776), at Karaköy; in Sirkeci train station (☎ 511 5888); near the UK consulate in Beyoğlu at Meşrutiyet Caddesi 57 (☎ 245 6875); in Taksim Square (☎ 245 6876) on İstiklal Caddesi; and in the İstanbul Hilton arcade on Cumhuriyet Caddesi (☎ 233 0592), four long blocks north of Taksim Square. There is a tourist booth (☎ 518 8754) open 9 am to 5 pm daily near the toilets at the north-east end of the Hippodrome in Sultanahmet.

The free maps – one sponsored by the bank Yapı Kredi, the other by the Ministry of Tourism – are useful, as is İstanbul: The Guide, a monthly listings guide (US$3). Also grab a copy of Fez Travel's free Fark etmez magazine; it has good travel tips and amusing articles and is available from most of the budget accommodation places.

Consulates

Opening hours for visa applications at consulates are generally from 9 to 11 am. (For information on visa requirements for this route, see the Facts for the Visitor chapter.)

The Iranian consulate is within walking distance of all points in Sultanahmet, and is open for visa applications from 9 am to 11.30 pm Monday to Thursday. The Indian, Nepali and Pakistani consulates are spread across a wide area north of Taksim; you'll need to take a bus or taxi between them.

Consulates in İstanbul include the following:

Australia (☎ 257 7050, fax 257 7601) Tepecik Yolu 58, 80630 Etiler
Bulgaria (☎ 269 2216) Ahmet Adnan Saygun Caddesi 2, Levent
Canada (☎ 272 5174, fax 272 3427) Büyükdere Caddesi 107/3, Gayrettepe
Egypt (☎ 263 6038, fax 257 4428) Bebek Sarayı, Cevdetpaşa Caddesi 173, Bebek
France (☎ 293 2460, fax 249 4895) İstiklal Caddesi 8, Taksim
Germany (☎ 251 5404, fax 249 9920) İnönü Caddesi, Selim Hatun Camii Sokak 46, Ayazpaşa, Taksim
Greece (☎ 245 0596, fax 252 1365) Turnacıbaşı Sokak 32, Ağahamam, Beyoğlu
India (☎ 296 2132, fax 296 2130) Cumhuriyet C Dörtler 18/7, Harbiye
Iran (☎ 513 8230/1) Ankara Caddesi 1/2, Cağaloğlu
Japan (☎ 251 7605, fax 252 5864) İnönü Caddesi 24, Taksim
Nepal (☎ 246 6104, fax 240 2199) Iş Hani Valikonaği Kat 44, Nişantaşı
Netherlands (☎ 251 5030, fax 251 9289) İstiklal Caddesi 393, Beyoğlu
Pakistan (☎ 233 5801) Abide-i Hürriyet Caddesi 11, Hacionbaşi Bldg, 6th floor, Şişli
Russia (☎ 244 2610, fax 249 0507) İstiklal Caddesi 443, Beyoğlu
Syria (☎ 232 7110) Hüsrev Gerede Caddesi 75/3, Mecidiyeköy
UK (☎ 293 7540, fax 245 4989) Meşrutiyet Caddesi 34, Tepebaşı, Beyoğlu
USA (☎ 251 3602, fax 251 3218) Meşrutiyet Caddesi 104–108, Tepebaşı, Beyoğlu

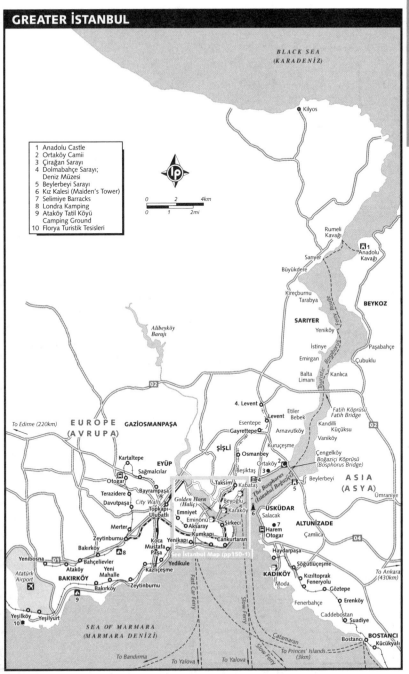

GREATER İSTANBUL

1 Anadolu Castle
2 Ortaköy Camii
3 Çirağan Sarayı
4 Dolmabahçe Sarayı;
   Deniz Müzesi
5 Beylerbeyi Sarayı
6 Kız Kalesi (Maiden's Tower)
7 Selimiye Barracks
8 Londra Kamping
9 Ataköy Tatil Köyü
   Camping Ground
10 Florya Turistik Tesisleri

BLACK SEA
(KARADENİZ)

Kilyos

Rumeli
Kavağı

Anadolu
Kavağı

Sarıyer

Büyükdere

BEYKOZ

Kireçburnu
Tarabya

SARIYER

Yeniköy

Paşabahçe

İstinye

Emirgan

Çubuklu

Balta
Limanı

Kanlıca

Alibeyköy
Barajı

4. Levent

Etiler

Fatih Köprüsü
Fatih Bridge

Levent

Bebek

Kandilli

To Edirne (220km)

EUROPE
(AVRUPA)

GAZİOSMANPAŞA

Esentepe

Arnavutköy

Küçüksu

Gayrettepe

ŞİŞLİ

Kuruçeşme

Vaniköy

Osmanbey

Çengelköy

Boğaziçi Köprüsü
(Bosphorus Bridge)

Kartaltepe

EYÜP

Ortaköy

Sağmalcılar

Beşiktaş

ASIA
(ASYA)

Otogar

Taksim

Kabataş

Beylerbeyi

Bayrampaşa

Beyoğlu

Terazidere

Ümraniye

Davutpaşa

City Walls

Golden Horn
(Haliç)

Karaköy

ÜSKÜDAR

Topkapı-
Ulubatlı

Emniyet

Salacak

ALTUNİZADE

Eminönü

Merter

Aksaray

Sirkeci

Çamlıca

Zeytinburnu

Koca
Mustafa
Paşa

Yenikapı

Kumkapı

Cankurtaran

Harem
Otogar

Bakırköy

Yenibosna

Bahçelievler

Yedikule

Haydarpaşa

Ataköy

Yeni
Mahalle

Kazlıçeşme

Söğütlüçeşme

To Ankara
(430km)

Atatürk
Airport

BAKIRKÖY

Bakırköy

Zeytinburnu

KADIKÖY

Kızıltoprak
Feneryolu

Moda

Göztepe

Yeşilköy

Yeşilyurt

Fenerbahçe

Erenköy

Caddebostan

Suadiye

SEA OF MARMARA
(MARMARA DENİZİ)

Bostancı

BOSTANCI

Küçükyalı

To Bandırma

To Yalova

To Yalova

To Princes' Islands
(3km)

See İstanbul Map (pp150-1)

The Bosphorus İstanbul Boğazı

Bosphorus Ferry Route

TURKEY

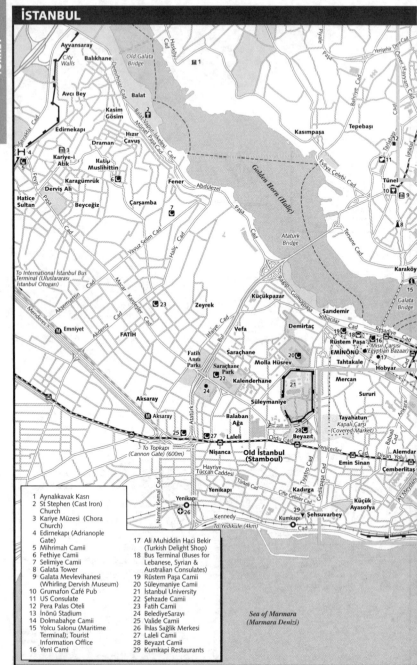

İSTANBUL

1 Aynalıkavak Kasrı
2 St Stephen (Cast Iron) Church
3 Kariye Müzesi (Chora Church)
4 Edirnekapı (Adrianople Gate)
5 Mihrimah Camii
6 Fethiye Camii
7 Selimiye Camii
8 Galata Tower
9 Galata Mevlevihanesi (Whirling Dervish Museum)
10 Grumafon Café Pub
11 US Consulate
12 Pera Palas Oteli
13 İnönü Stadium
14 Dolmabahçe Camii
15 Yolcu Salonu (Maritime Terminal); Tourist Information Office
16 Yeni Cami

17 Ali Muhiddin Haci Bekir (Turkish Delight Shop)
18 Bus Terminal (Buses for Lebanese, Syrian & Australian Consulates)
19 Rüstem Paşa Camii
20 Süleymaniye Camii
21 İstanbul University
22 Şehzade Camii
23 Fatih Camii
24 BelediyeSarayı
25 Valide Camii
26 İhlas Sağlik Merkesi
27 Laleli Camii
28 Beyazıt Camii
29 Kumkapi Restaurants

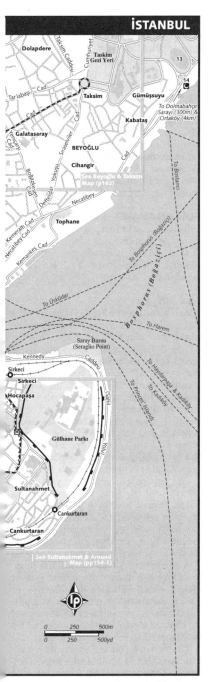

Money

Divan Yolu in Sultanahmet is lined with foreign exchange offices and travel agencies offering speedy, hassle-free exchange facilities at good rates (open from 9 am to 9 pm daily).

There are ATMs all over the city which take all major credit and cash cards; among the easiest to find are the Yapı Kredi ones because they're marked on the free city maps available from tourist offices.

Post & Telephone

The central post office *(merkez posthane)* is on Yeni Posthane Caddesi, just west of Sirkeci station. It's open from 8.30 am to 8 pm daily. There are branch offices in Aksaray and in the Kapalı Çarşı (Grand Bazaar), and in Beyoğlu at Galatasaray and Taksim, as well as in the departure areas at Atatürk airport. Post offices are also known as PTTs.

For poste restante at the central post office, bring your passport for identification. The counter is closed from 12.30 to 1.30 pm for lunch and shuts for the day at 5.30 pm. For mailing parcels, go round the back to the entrance on Aşirefendi Caddesi. This is open from 8.30 am to 12.30 pm and 1.30 to 4.30 pm daily.

Email & Internet Access

There are plenty of Internet cafes across İstanbul. The major Sultanahmet and Cankurtaran hostels all have Internet facilities and you'll find several places around İstiklal Caddesi and Taksim in Beyoğlu. One handy and reliable place (with English keyboards) is the Backpackers Internet Cafe (☎ 638 6343, e backpackers@turk.net), Akbıyık Caddesi 22, Sultanahmet (part of the Backpackers Travel Agency). Expect to pay about US$1 per half hour. If the keyboard is in Turkish, ask the manager to change the operating system to English and touch-type as normal.

İstanbul Telephone Area Codes

İstanbul has two area codes: ☎ 212 for the European side and ☎ 216 for the Asian side. Throughout the İstanbul section of this book, assume that phone numbers take the area code 212 unless stated otherwise.

Travel Agencies

Divan Yolu in Sultanahmet is lined with travel agencies, all of them selling cheap air and bus tickets; they can also arrange train tickets. Shop around for the best deals. Most also offer speedy foreign exchange facilities and minibus transport to the airport. The New Deal Travel Agency (☎/fax 511 3023) at Divan Yolu 42 has been fine in the past, though this is no recommendation. The Backpackers Travel Agency (☎ 638 6343) at Akbıyık Caddesi 22 in Sultanahmet is also OK.

Bookshops

The most convenient bookshops include Aypa at Mimar Mehmet Ağa Caddesi 19, Sultanahmet, just down the hill from Aya Sofya, which has guides, maps and magazines in English, French and German, and the No Name Book Exchange upstairs at Bayram Fırını Sokak. Galeri Kayseri (☎ 512 0456) at Divan Yolu 58, Sultanahmet, has a good selection but is expensive. Robinson Crusoe, at İstiklal Caddesi 389, and Pandora (☎ 243 3503), at Büyükparmakkapı Sokak 3 off İstiklal Caddesi, are two good options over in Beyoğlu. Remzi Kitabevi (☎ 234 5475), Rumeli Caddesi 44, Nişantaşı, is a top-quality general English-language bookshop.

Photography

All types of film, even specialist slide film, are available in İstanbul; the best place to go is Yeni Posthane Caddesi, not far east of the central post office, where there are several photography shops. It's a good idea to stock up here before heading off to the coast or to eastern Turkey.

Laundry

Most hostels and hotels will do your laundry, but you may need to negotiate the cost. Otherwise try the Hobby Laundry at Caferiye Sokak 6/1, Sultanahmet, by the Yücelt Interyouth Hostel, or Star Laundry, opposite the Orient Youth Hostel at Aykbılık Caddesi 18, Sultanahmet, which charges about US$1 per kilo.

Medical Services

For hospitals, the Amerikan Admiral Bristol (☎ 311 2000) at Güzelbahçe Sokak, Nişantaşı (2km north-west of Taksim Square), and the International (☎ 663 3000) at Çınar Oteli Yanı, İstanbul Caddesi 82, in Yeşilköy near the airport, have both been recommended. İhlas Sağlik Merkesi (☎ 632 0506), a health clinic near Yenikapı train station, south of Aksaray, has English-speaking doctors. It will deal with most health concerns, including dental and optical matters.

Emergency

The Tourist Police (☎ 527 4503) are at Yerebatan Caddesi 6, Sultanahmet, across the street from the Sunken Palace Cistern (Yerebatan Sarnıçı). The ordinary police (☎ 155 in an emergency) are less experienced in dealing with foreigners.

SULTANAHMET & AROUND

Sultanahmet is the first place to explore. All the major sights are ranged within walking distance of the Hippodrome and, at a squeeze, you could see most within a couple of days.

Aya Sofya

The construction of what was intended to be the grandest, finest house of worship in the world, the Church of the Divine Wisdom (Hagia Sofia in Greek, Sancta Sophia in Latin), began under the Byzantine emperor Justinian in AD 532. The resulting edifice was for almost 1000 years the largest church in the Christian world (later superseded by St Peter's in Rome). However, a good 100 years before St Peter's was built, Sancta Sophia had stopped being a church because the Muslim commander Mehmet II had the building converted into a mosque immediately after he took İstanbul in 1453.

The unattractive pink paint job on the exterior belies the stunning interior that lies within. It must have been doubly stunning centuries ago when it was covered in gilded mosaics. Inside, you cannot help but gasp at the audacity of the early engineers who made the dome seemingly hang there in space.

A number of Aya Sofya's features relate to its time as a mosque: the mihrab (prayer niche), which indicates the direction of Mecca; the alabaster urns, which once provided water for worshippers' ablutions; and the elevated kiosk (or Sultan's Loge), added by Ahmet III so he could pray unseen.

The mosaics you see everywhere have had something of a turbulent history. They survived the Iconoclastic Controversy of

AD 726–843, when images other than the cross were banned, but not the conquest of Constantinople by the Turks; fortunately they were plastered over rather than destroyed by the conquering Turks. The best mosaics can be seen in the southern gallery.

On the way to the exit you pass a small bookshop on your left. Pause and turn around to see a superb 10th-century mosaic of the Madonna and child. To her left, Constantine offers her the city of Constantinople. Emperor Justinian, on the right, offers her a model of Aya Sofya.

Aya Sofya is open from 9.30 am to 4.30 pm (7 pm in summer) daily except Monday. Admission is US$5.

Haseki Hürrem Hamamı

Near Aya Sofya, east of the park with the fountain, are the Haseki Hürrem Hamamı (Baths of Lady Hürrem), built in 1556 by Sinan for what was then a mosque – all mosques had baths nearby. Now a government-run carpet shop, this place is open from 9.30 am to 5 pm daily, except Tuesday; admission is free.

Blue Mosque

Compared with Aya Sofya, the Blue Mosque, also known as Sultan Ahmet Camii or the Mosque of Sultan Ahmet I, is a light, delicate thing, graced by a form that seems to bubble up from the ground in a froth of domes, half-domes and six spindly minarets.

Only Muslim worshippers are allowed through the main door; tourists enter through a door on the north side. Once inside you'll see where the 'Blue' of its name comes from: the luminous İznik tiled interior. The main dome is supported by four pillars, which isn't half as daring structurally as Aya Sofya, despite being built over 1000 years later (1609–19). There is no admission charge but you are expected to make a small donation.

Rent from the **Arasta** (row of shops) on the street behind the mosque provides support for the mosque's upkeep. Along the Arasta is the entrance to the **Mosaic Museum** (Büyüksaray Mozaik Müzesi), where a portion of ancient Byzantine pavement showing marvellous scenes of nature and the hunt is worth seeing. It's open from 9.30 am to 4.30 pm daily except Monday. Admission is US$1.25.

Don't miss the free **sound-and-light show** at the mosque on summer evenings. It's in different languages on different nights; ask at the Hippodrome tourist information booth for the schedule.

Hippodrome

In front of the Blue Mosque is the Hippodrome, or Atmeydanı (Horse Grounds). Dating back to AD 203, it was once used for chariot races. The three ancient monuments here are the **Obelisk of Theodosius**, a Pharaonic column from the Temple of Karnak in Egypt; the 10m-high **Obelisk of Constantine Porphyrogenitus** (AD 913–59), which was once covered in bronze plates (later stolen by the Crusaders); and the remains of a **spiral column** of intertwined snakes. Erected at Delphi by the Greeks to celebrate their victory over the Persians, the column was later transported to the Hippodrome. (All that remains of the snakes' heads is one upper jaw in the Archaeological Museum). At the north-east end of the Hippodrome is a **fountain** built to commemorate Kaiser Wilhelm's visit in 1901.

On the west side of the Hippodrome, the **Turkish & Islamic Arts Museum** (Türk ve İslam Eserleri Müzesi) is housed in the former palace (1524) of İbrahim Paşa, grand vizier and son-in-law of Süleyman the Magnificent. A video of a potted history of Turkey is shown on the 1st floor and it makes a good introduction for recently arrived travellers. On the lower floor there is an excellent ethnographic collection with a good explanation of nomadic life in eastern Turkey. The museum is open from 10 am to 4.30 pm daily, except Monday; admission is US$2.

Yerebatan Sarnıçı

Across Divan Yolu from the north-east end of the Hippodrome is a small park; on its north side is the entrance to the wonderfully atmospheric Yerebatan Sarnıçı, the Sunken Palace Cistern. Built by Constantine and later enlarged by Justinian, this vast, columned cistern, some 70m wide and 140m long, held water not only for regular summer use but also for times of siege. The entrance to the cistern is in Yerebatan Caddesi. It's open from 9 am to 5 pm daily, sometimes later in summer when concerts

[Continued on page 160]

TURKEY

SULTANAHMET & AROUND

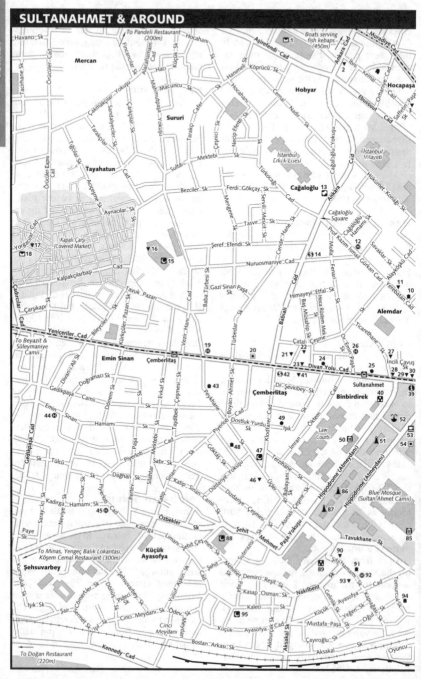

Havancı Sk
To Pandeli Restaurant (200m)
Boats serving fish kebaps (450m)
Aşirefendi Cad
Muradiye Cad
Ankara Cad
Ibni Kemal
Omaniye Cad
☑ 1
2
Hocapaşa
Mercan
Hacı
Küçük Sk
Hammeli
Köprücü Sk
Hobyar
Cemal Nadir Sk
Ebussut Cad
Selfehin Paşa
3
Fincancılar Sk
Nahmaşağ Sk
Macuncu
Sururi
Tarakçı
Cafer
Necip Efendi Sk
İstanbul Erkek Lisesi
Hocahanı
Çağaloğlu Yokuşu
İstanbul Vilayeti
İstanbul Vilayeti
Sultan
Mektebi
Sk
Türkocağı Cad
Cağaloğlu 13
Hükümet Konağı Sk
Tayahatun
Cad
Açeşeme Sk
Bezciler-Sk
Ferdi Gökçay Sk
Cağaloğlu Square
12
Cağaloğlu Hamamı
Ankara
Savaklar Sk
Aynacılar-Sk
Mengene-Sk
Tasvır Sk
Cerıde-Hane Sk
Prof Kazım İsmail Gürkan Cad
Alayköşkü Cad
Kapalı Çarşı (Covered Market)
16
Şeref Efendi Sk
Nuruosmaniye Cad
14
Molla
Fenarı Sk
11
10
Yerebatan Cad
☑18
17
15
Kalpçılarbaşı Cad
Tavuk Pazarı
Gazi Sinan Paşa Sk
Baba Türbesi Sk
Himayeyi Etfal Sk
Baş Müşahip Sk
Hoca Rüstem Mek
Alemdar
Çarşıkapı Sk
Bileyici
Kürkçüler Pazarı
Vezir Hanı
Türbedar Sk
Babıali Cad
Ticarethane Sk
To Beyazıt & Süleymaniye Camii
Yeniçeriler Cad
Çatal Sk
Çeşme
Dr Emin Paşa Sk
Incili Çavuş Sk
19
20
21▼
22
26
27
Emin Sinan
Çemberlitaş
▼41
23▼ 24
25
28
29▼ 30
42
Divan Yolu Cad
Sultanahmet
39
Divan-ı Ali Sk
Doğramacı Sk
43
Dr Şevkibey Sk
Binbirdirek
40
Gedikpaşa Camii
Dönem Sk
Evkaf Sk
Çeşmesi Sk
Peykhane
Çemberlitaş
52
44
Emin Sinan
Hamamı
Taşdibek Sk
Piyerloti Boyacı Ahmet Sk
Klodfarer Cad
49
İşık
Law Courts
50
53
51
54
Tülcü
Piyerloti Cad
Dağhan Sk
Satır Sk
Silahtar Sk
Gökçak Sk
Dizdariye Camii Sk
47
46▼
İmran
Öktem Cad
Ople
Terzihane
Babayanı
Hippodrome (Atmeydanı)
86
Kadırga Hamamı Sk
45
Katip Sinan Sk
Dizdariye Çeşmesi
Armalı Çeşme Sk
Hippodrome (Atmeydanı)
87
Blue Mosque (Sultan Ahmet Camii)
Paye Sk
Özbekler Sk
Kadırga Limanı Cad
Şehit Çeşmesi Sk
Şehit
Mehmet Paşa Yokuşu
88
Suterazısı Sk
Tavukhane Sk
85
To Minas, Yengeç Balık Lokantası, Köşem Cemal Restaurant (300m)
Küçük Ayasofya
Şehit
Mehmet Paşa Yokuşu
Demirci Reşit Sk
91
Şifa Hamamı Sk
92
Şehsuvarbey
Işık Sk
Şair Sk
Sermet Sk
Donus Sk
Pidea Sk
Odev Sk
Şehsuvarbey Sk
Yusuf Aşkın Sk
Kasap Osman Sk
Nakilbent
89
Cinci Meydanı Sk
Çardaklı
Mustafa-Paşa Sk
93▼
Gelinlik Sk
Küçük Ayasofya Cad
Yeğen Sk
94
Cinci Meydanı
95
Kaleci
Küçük Ayasofya Cad
Akburak Cad
Aksakal Cad
Oğul Sk
Tomruk Sk
Mimar Mehmet Ağa Cad
To Doğan Restaurant (220m)
Kennedy Cad
Bostan Arkası Sk
Çayıroğlu Sk
Aksakal
Oyuncu

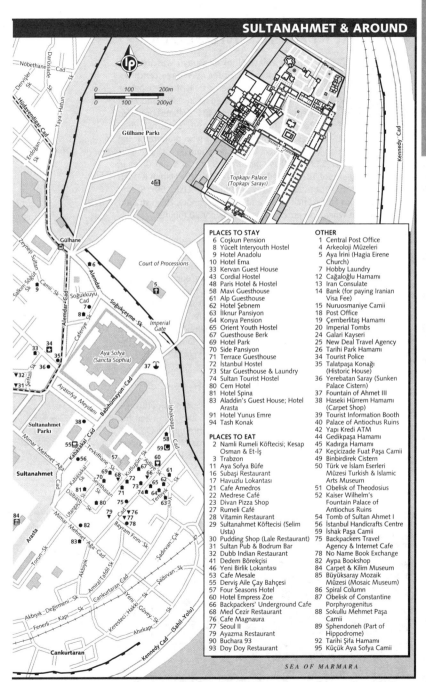

SULTANAHMET & AROUND

TURKEY

PLACES TO STAY
6 Coşkun Pension
8 Yücelt Interyouth Hostel
9 Hotel Anadolu
10 Hotel Ema
33 Kervan Guest House
43 Cordial Hostel
48 Paris Hotel & Hostel
58 Mavi Guesthouse
61 Alp Guesthouse
62 Hotel Şebnem
63 İlknur Pansiyon
64 Konya Pension
65 Orient Youth Hostel
67 Guesthouse Berk
69 Hotel Park
70 Side Pansiyon
71 Terrace Guesthouse
72 İstanbul Hostel
73 Star Guesthouse & Laundry
74 Sultan Tourist Hostel
80 Cem Hotel
81 Hotel Spina
83 Aladdin's Guest House; Hotel Arasta
91 Hotel Yunus Emre
94 Tash Konak

PLACES TO EAT
2 Namli Rumeli Köftecisi; Kesap Osman & Et-İş
3 Trabzon
11 Aya Sofya Büfe
16 Subaşi Restaurant
17 Havuzlu Lokantası
21 Cafe Amedros
22 Medrese Café
23 Divan Pizza Shop
27 Rumeli Café
28 Vitamin Restaurant
29 Sultanahmet Köftecisi (Selim Usta)
30 Pudding Shop (Lale Restaurant)
31 Sultan Pub & Bodrum Bar
32 Dubb Indian Restaurant
41 Dedem Börekçisi
46 Yeni Birlik Lokantası
53 Cafe Mesale
55 Derviş Aile Çay Bahçesi
57 Four Seasons Hotel
60 Hotel Empress Zoe
66 Backpackers' Underground Cafe
68 Med Cezir Restaurant
76 Cafe Magnaura
77 Seoul II
79 Ayazma Restaurant
90 Buchara 93
93 Doy Doy Restaurant

OTHER
1 Central Post Office
4 Arkeoloji Müzeleri
5 Aya İrini (Hagia Eirene Church)
7 Hobby Laundry
12 Cağaloğlu Hamamı
13 Iran Consulate
14 Bank (for paying Iranian Visa Fee)
15 Nuruosmaniye Camii
18 Post Office
19 Çemberlitaş Hamamı
20 Imperial Tombs
24 Galari Kayseri
25 New Deal Travel Agency
26 Tarihi Park Hamamı
34 Tourist Police
35 Talatpaşa Konağı (Historic House)
36 Yerebatan Saray (Sunken Palace Cistern)
37 Fountain of Ahmet III
38 Haseki Hürrem Hamamı (Carpet Shop)
39 Tourist Information Booth
40 Palace of Antiochus Ruins
42 Yapı Kredi ATM
44 Gedikpaşa Hamamı
45 Kadırga Hamamı
47 Keçicizade Fuat Paşa Camii
49 Binbirdirek Cistern
50 Türk ve İslam Eserleri Müzesi Turkish & Islamic Arts Museum
51 Obelisk of Theodosius
52 Kaiser Wilhelm's Fountain Palace of Antiochus Ruins
54 Tomb of Sultan Ahmet I
56 İstanbul Handicrafts Centre
59 İshak Paşa Camii
75 Backpackers Travel Agency & Internet Cafe
78 No Name Book Exchange
82 Aypa Bookshop
84 Carpet & Kilim Museum
85 Büyüksaray Mozaik Müzesi (Mosaic Museum)
86 Spiral Column
87 Obelisk of Constantine Porphyrogenitus
88 Sokullu Mehmet Paşa Camii
89 Sphendoneh (Part of Hippodrome)
92 Tarihi Şifa Hamamı
95 Küçük Aya Sofya Camii

SEA OF MARMARA

TOPKAPI PALACE MUSEUM

Topkapı Palace (Topkapı Sarayı) was the residence of the sultans for over three centuries. Mehmet the Conqueror built the first palace shortly after the Conquest in 1453 and lived here until his death in 1481. Sultans continued to live here until the 19th century, when Mahmut II (1808–39) was succeeded by sultans who preferred living in new European-style palaces built on the Bosphorus.

Topkapı (☎ 212-512 0480) is open from 9 am to 5 pm (later in summer) daily except Tuesday (admission is US$6); the Harem is open from 9.30 am to 4 pm (admission is an additional US$2.50). Seeing Topkapı requires at least half a day, and preferably more. Head straight for the Harem when you enter; tours leave every 30 minutes.

Court of Processions

Topkapı grew and changed over time, but its basic four-courtyard plan remained the same. The Ottomans followed the Byzantine practice of secluding the monarch from the people: the First Court was open to all; the Second Court only to people on imperial business; the Third Court only to the imperial family, important personages and palace staff; and the Fourth Court was the 'family quarters'.

As you pass through the great **Imperial Gate**, behind Aya Sofya, you enter the Alay Meydanı, the Court of Processions. On your left is the former **Aya İrini Kilisesi**, or Church of Divine Peace (☎ 212-520 6952), Sarayiçi 35, which is now a concert hall.

Ortakapı & Second Court

The Ortakapı (Middle Gate) leads to the palace's Second Court, once used for the business of running the empire. Only the sultan and the *valide sultan* (mother of the sultan) were allowed through the Ortakapı on horseback. The gate was constructed by Süleyman the Magnificent in 1524, utilising architects and workers brought back from his conquest of Hungary.

Inset: Detail from the Ortakapı, or Middle Gate (Photo by Tom Brosnahan)

Bottom: Beautiful Delft tiles line the interior of the Hünkar Sofası (Emperor's Chamber).

EDDIE GERALD

The **palace kitchens**, on the right-hand side of the court, now hold part of the palace's vast collection of Chinese celadon porcelain, as well as fine European and Ottoman porcelain and glassware. The **Helvahane** is the kitchen in which all the palace sweets were once made. Imagine the staff preparing food for the 5000 palace inhabitants!

On the left side of the Second Court is the ornate **Kubbealtı**, or Imperial Council Chamber. Also called the Divan Salonu, this is where the Imperial Divan (Imperial Council) met to discuss matters of state, while the sultan eavesdropped through a grille- high on the wall.

The Harem

An object of legend and romance, the Harem is usually imagined as a place where the sultan could engage in debauchery at will. In fact, these were the imperial family quarters, and every detail of Harem life was governed by tradition, obligation and ceremony.

The women of the Harem had to be foreigners, as Islam forbade enslaving Muslims, Christians and Jews (although with some exceptions). Besides prisoners of war, girls were bought as slaves (often sold by their parents), or received as gifts from nobles and potentates. Upon entering the Harem, the girls would be schooled in Islam and Turkish culture and language, the arts of make-up, dress, comportment, music, reading and writing, embroidery and dancing. Ruling the Harem was the mother of the reigning sultan, the valide sultan, who often owned large estates in her own name and whose influence on the sultan, on the selection of his wives and concubines and on matters of state was often profound.

Bottom: The gilded entrance to the Harem, a place steeped in romance and mystery that in reality was probably a lot more prosaic than many foreigners imagine.

The entrance to the Harem – open by guided tour only – is through the Carriage Gate beneath the distinctive **Adalet Kulesi** (Tower of Justice). Many of the Harem's 300-odd rooms were constructed during the reign of Süleyman the Magnificent (1520–66), but the Harem has been added to and reconstructed over the years. In 1665 a disastrous fire destroyed much of the complex, which was rebuilt by Mehmet IV and later sultans.

Most Harem tours are given in Turkish and English, and in other languages during summer. Plaques in Turkish and English have been placed at some points around the Harem. Highlights of the Harem tour include the narrow **Ağalar Taşlığı** (Black Eunuchs' Courtyard), decorated in Kütahya tiles from the 17th century; the **Cariye ve Kadınefendi Taşlığı** (Concubines' & Consorts' Courtyard); the **Valide Sultan's Quarters & Courtyard**; and the ornate **Hünkar Sofası** (Emperor's Chamber), among the Harem's largest and most splendid rooms and decorated in Delft tiles. Don't miss the **Privy Chamber of Murat III** (1578), one of the most sumptuous rooms in the palace. The **Dining Room of Ahmet III** (1706) was built by Ahmet I's successor.

GREG ELMS

TOPKAPI PALACE MUSEUM

SECOND COURT
38 Kubbealtı
39 Enderun Hazinesi; Arms
   (Inner Treasury; Arms &
   Armour Display)
40 Helvahane
41 Palace Kitchens
   (Porcelain & Glass Display)
42 Ortakapı

THIRD COURT
7 Mukaddes Emanetler Dairesi
8 Treasury Barracks
9 Hazine

10 Seferli Koğuşu
11 Library of Ahmet III
12 Arz Odası
13 Bab-üs Saade

FOURTH COURT
1 Mecidiye Köşkü
2 Hayat Balkonu
   (Balcony of Life)
3 Bağdat Köşkü
4 Marble Terrace & Pool
5 Sünnet Odası
   (Circumcision Room)
6 Revan Köşü

THE HAREM
14 Favourites' Courtyard
15 Double Kiosk with Stained Glass
16 Privy Chamber of Murat III
17 Library of Ahmet I
18 Dining Room of Ahmet III
19 Hünkar Sofası
20 Room with Hearth;
   Room with Fountain
21 Valide Sultan's Hamam
22 Sultan's Hamam
23 Chamber of Abdül Hamit I
24 Valide Sultan's Quarters
25 Valide Sultan's Courtyard

26 Altınyol
   (Golden Road)
27 Birdcage Gate
28 Main Gate
29 Chief Black Eunuch's Room
30 Concubines' Corridor
31 Cariye ve Kadınefendi Taşlığı
32 Women's Dormitory
33 Black Eunuchs' Dormitory
34 Ağalar Taşlığı
35 Guard Room
36 Carriage Gate
   (Tourist Entrance)
37 Adalet Kulesi

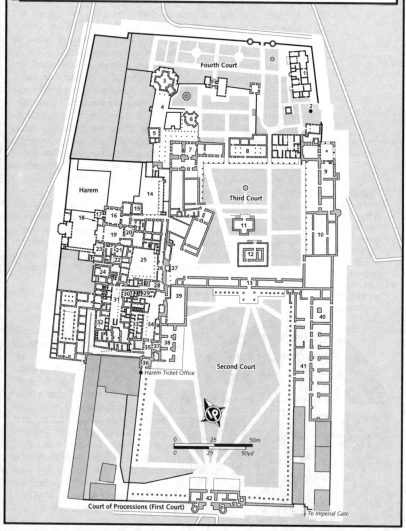

Third Court

For full effect, enter the Third Court through the main gate, the **Babüs Saade** (Gate of Felicity) rather than through the Harem. Sometimes called the **Akağalar Kapısı** (Gate of the White Eunuchs), this was the entrance into the sultan's private domain.

Just inside the Bab-üs Saade is the **Arz Odası** (Audience Chamber), constructed in the 16th century but refurbished in the 18th century. Important officials and foreign ambassadors were brought to this little kiosk to conduct the high business of state.

Walk to the right as you leave the Arz Odası and enter the rooms of the **Seferli Koğuşu** (Dormitory of the Expeditionary Force), which now house the rich collections of imperial robes, kaftans and uniforms (follow the signs for 'Padişah Elbiseleri').

Nearby, the **Hazine** (Imperial Treasury) is packed with a wondrous collection of objects made from or decorated with gold, silver and gems. The Kaşıkçının Elması, or Spoonmaker's Diamond, is an 86-carat rock surrounded by several dozen smaller stones; it is the world's fifth-largest diamond. There's also an uncut emerald weighing 3.26kg, and a golden dagger set with three large emeralds that was the object of Peter Ustinov's criminal quest in the movie *Topkapi*.

Opposite the treasury is the holy relics in the Hırka-i Saadet, or Suite of the Felicitous Cloak, now called the **Mukaddes Emanetler Dairesi** (Sacred Safe-Keeping Rooms). These rooms, sumptuously decorated with İznik *faïence* (coloured tiles), constitute a holy of holies within the palace. While only the chosen could enter the Third Court, entry into the Hırka-i Saadet rooms was for the chosen of the chosen, and only on ceremonial occasions.

To the right (north) is a room containing the cloak of the Prophet Mohammed and other relics. Sometimes an *imam* (prayer leader) is seated here, chanting passages from the Quran. The 'felicitous cloak' itself resides in a golden casket in a special alcove along with the battle standard. Although anyone, prince or commoner, faithful or infidel, can enter the rooms now, remember that it is a sacred place.

Fourth Court

Four imperial pleasure domes occupy the north-easternmost part of the palace, sometimes called the gardens. The **Mecidiye Köşkü**, built by Abdül Mecit (1839–61), was designed according to 19th-century European models.

Up the stairs at the end of the tulip garden are two of the most enchanting kiosks. Sultan Murat IV (1623–40) built the **Revan Köşkü** (Erivan Kiosk) in 1635 after reclaiming the city of Yerevan (now in Armenia) from Persia. He also built the **Bağdat Köşkü** (Baghdad Kiosk) in 1638 to commemorate his victory over that city.

Tom Brosnahan

Bottom: A detail of the geometric pattern decorating one of the ceilings in the palace.

[Continued from page 153]

are held inside the cistern (check with a tourist office); admission is US$2.

Archaeological Museums

Sandwiched between Gülhane Parkı and Topkapı Palace is a complex of three museums.

The **Arkeoloji Müzesi** (Archaeological Museum) has an outstanding collection of Greek and Roman statuary and a sarcophagus once thought to be that of Alexander the Great. Check out the mock-up of the facade of the Temple of Athena at Behramkale (Assos), especially if you intend visiting that site later. There are pieces of the original frieze, but, like many of Turkey's treasures, the rest was whisked overseas by 19th-century plunderers. The museum is open from 9.30 am to 4.30 pm Tuesday to Sunday.

The **Eski Şark Eserleri Müzesi** (Museum of the Ancient Orient) is dedicated to the pre-Islamic and pre-Byzantine civilisations. The main reason to visit is to see the gates of ancient Babylon, dating from the time of Nebuchadnezzar II (604–562 BC). Also here are cuneiform tablets bearing Hammurabi's legal code (the world's first) and other interesting artefacts from the Hittite and Assyrian Empires. The museum is open from 9.30 am to 4.30 pm on Wednesday, Friday and Sunday.

The **Çinili Köşk** (Tiled Pavilion), built for Mehmet the Conqueror in 1472, is among the very oldest Turkish buildings in the city. It is now a museum of Turkish tilework. It is open from 9.30 am to 4.30 pm on Tuesday, Thursday and Saturday.

One ticket to all three museums costs US$3.

Gülhane Parkı

Down the slope west of the museums is Gülhane Parkı, formerly the park where the sultan would review his troops on parade. It now has a small zoo, restaurants and amusements. Head for the tea garden at the northern end of the park for fantastic views of the Bosphorus. The park is open from 9 am to 6 pm daily; there's a token admission charge.

Kapalı Çarşı

Dating from the time of Mehmet the Conqueror (1451–81), the Kapalı Çarşı (Grand

A Walk Between the Bazaars

A great walk that takes in the quintessential İstanbul begins at the Kapalı Çarşı. Find Yaçılar Caddesi near the western end of Kalpakçılarbaşı Caddesi and follow it north (Şark Kahvesi is on your left). Pass the small Ağa Camii on your left and continue up and across Mercan Caddesi/Çakmakçılar Yokuşu; you are now in Uzunçarşı Caddesi (Longmarket Street). Follow this street, full of all manner of shops, to where it ends at the small Rüstem Paşa Camii. To your right (east) is the market district of Tahtakale, Mısır Çarşısı (Egyptian Bazaar) and Yeni Cami (New Mosque). From here you can catch the tram back to Sultanahmet or extend your walk through the backstreets of Sirkeci or across the Golden Horn to Karaköy and Galata.

Bazaar or Covered Market) is an enormous medieval shopping mall. Although most stalls have been converted into modern, glassed-in spaces, it's still fun to wander among the 65 streets and 4400 shops. It's a great place to get lost in, as you almost certainly will.

The market is divided into areas selling specific things, such as carpets, jewellery, clothing, silverware. West of the market proper, across Çadırcılar Caddesi, beside the Beyazıt Camii, is the Sahaflar Çarşısı (Old Book Market) with many stalls selling second-hand books, most of them in Turkish.

You will be asked continually to look, buy, take tea, change money; it may be annoying at first, but realise that business is business. This one place where you should be on your guard against pickpockets.

Even if you don't want to buy anything, you can attend the auctions in the Sandal Bedesteni at 1 pm (ornaments and furniture on Tuesday, carpets on Wednesday and jewellery on Thursday); watch artisans at work (jewellery in Zincirli Han, carpet repairers in Mercan Ali Paşa Han and silversmiths in Kalcılar Han); or sip tea or coffee at the old, atmospheric Şark Kahvesi at the end of Fesçiler Caddesi.

The market is open from 9 am to 7 pm Monday to Saturday.

Travelling by boat is an ideal way to experience Turkey's stunning Aegean and Mediterranean Coasts.

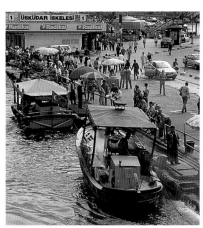
Fish sandwich boats at Eminönü, İstanbul

All aboard the Taksim tram, İstanbul.

Tea to go.

Gulets (yachts) moored in picturesque Bodrum harbour, with the Castle of St Peter in the background.

Bus travel is ubiquitous and cheap in Turkey.

Europe ends and Asia begins at the Bosphorus.

İstanbul's ferries gather at Karaköy Harbour, below the splendid Süleymaniye Camii.

Beyazıt & Süleymaniye

Beyazıt takes its name from the graceful mosque **Beyazıt Camii**, built in 1506 on the orders of Sultan Beyazıt II, son of Mehmet the Conqueror. This plaza, laid out in AD 393, was the Forum of Theodosius in Byzantine times. The great portal on the north side of the square is that of İstanbul University.

Behind the university, to the north-west, rises İstanbul's grandest mosque complex, the **Süleymaniye**. Construction was completed in 1557 on the orders of Süleyman the Magnificent; he and his wife Roxelana are buried in a **mausoleum** behind the mosque to the south-east. Süleyman's great architect, Sinan, is entombed near the sultan.

To the south of Süleymaniye Camii, Yeniçericiler Caddesi becomes Ordu Caddesi. As you continue on down the hill you enter the busy Aksaray Square, where a mass of concrete overpasses obscures the ornate **Valide Camii** on its north-west side.

Turkish Baths (Hamams)

Although they are housed in interesting and well-maintained buildings, İstanbul's most historic baths are now touristy and poor value for money. The elegant **Çemberlitaş Hamamı**, off Divan Yolu near the Kapalı Çarşı, is, on balance, the best place for your first Turkish bath experience. Designed in 1584 by Sinan for Nurbanu Sultan, the wife of Sultan Selim II, there are sections for both men and women and it operates from

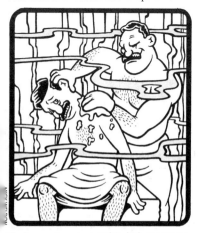

The hamam is an essential Turkish experience – although perhaps not for the faint hearted!

6 am to midnight. The cost is US$8 to wash yourself or US$15 for the full works.

The **Cağaloğlu Hamamı** at Yerebatan Caddesi 34, just a short stroll north-west of Sultanahmet, has separate entrances for men (on the main street) and women (around the corner to the right). The prices here would be outrageous anywhere else in Turkey, starting at US$15 and rising to US$30 for a bath with full massage, supposedly inclusive of tips. Men's hours are from 7 am to 9.30 pm daily, while for women they're 8 am to 9 pm.

Slightly cheaper, though not as fancy as the Çemberlitaş or Cağaloğlu, is the **Gedikpaşa Hamamı**, on Emin Sinan Hamamı Sokak. It was built in 1457 and certainly looks its age. A bath here is US$7 (US$10 with a massage).

CITY WALLS

Stretching for 7km from the Golden Horn to the Sea of Marmara, the city walls date back to about AD 420. They are also known as the Byzantine Walls or the Theodosian Walls. Many parts of the walls have been restored during the past decade, particularly the gates at Topkapı, Mevlanakapı and Belgrat Kapısı.

If you're thinking of walking alongside the walls, note there are some unsafe areas (eg, between Silvrikapı and Belgrat Kapısı in the south, and near the Topkapı Bit Pazarı or Flea Market in the centre).

The best view of the walls is at **Yedikule**, near the Sea of Marmara – you'll see this imposing fortress if you arrive in İstanbul by train or ride in by taxi from the airport. Here obstreperous diplomats and inconvenient princes were held in squalor and despair. The fortress is open from 9.30 am to 5 pm daily, except Monday; admission is US$0.75. The best way to get here is by train from Sirkeci.

Near the Edirnekapı (Adrianople Gate) is the marvellous **Chora Church** (Kariye Müzesi), a Byzantine building with impressive 14th-century mosaics. Built in the 11th century, it was later restored and converted to a mosque. It is now a museum called Kariye Müzesi. Opening hours are from 9.30 am to 4.30 pm Thursday to Tuesday (closed Wednesday); admission is US$3. To get here, take an Edirnekapı bus along Fevzipaşa Caddesi.

TURKEY

Bath Time

A grim-faced masseur leans with the full bulk of his body on my back, and does his best to rip my contorted arm from its socket. 'Is it good?' he keeps asking. I clench my teeth, focus on the marble and the soaring dome through the steam, and remind myself that this near torture is what I paid US$15 for.

Whether you're at a swanky, tourist-driven joint or a more workaday *hamam*, the Turkish bath experience follows a set pattern. On entering, you'll be shown to a private changing room where you can lock up your belongings and retire to relax after the bath. Men will be given a *peştamal*, a thin towel, which should be worn at all times in the hamam. Take care walking to and from the bath in the wooden sandals provided – they have a tendency to act as ice skates.

In the steam room, your first task is to wash. Fill a basin from one of the taps around the *göbek taşı*, the central heated dais on which you'll later poach. While sluicing yourself down, take care not to splash your neighbours, who may be going through a ritual ablution prior to prayer. Afterwards, lean back on the göbek taşı and relax.

If you've paid extra for the full works, the *tellâk* (masseur) will turn up after around 15 minutes. First will come the rub down with an abrasive *kese* (mitt), stripping away the grimy top layer of skin. Next a pillowcase of soap will be lathered over your body in cascades of foam. The massage follows, and is likely to leave you feeling as if you've just done 10 rounds in a wrestling match with your hands tied behind your back.

As you limp out of the bath, the attendants will wrap you in fresh towels. If you're offered a drink, it will cost you extra (it's a good idea to have one since the bath will have dehydrated you). Some masseurs may try to tap you for a tip, too.

Traditionally, men and women bathe separately, but baths in tourist areas often accept both sexes at the same time for higher than usual prices. For safety and comfort's sake, women should know at least some of the men in the bath with them, and women might want to avoid male masseurs (a Turkish woman would only accept a female masseur).

Not all baths accept women. Smaller baths in small towns accommodate men and women on different days or at different times of the day.

Lonely Planet has received a number of letters from women and men about unwelcome behaviour by male masseurs in Turkish baths. Let the masseur know the limits and kick up a fuss if he oversteps the boundaries.

Simon Richmond

EMINÖNÜ

At the southern end of Galata Bridge (Galata Köprüsü) is the bustling, chaotic district known as Eminönü. Its narrow streets are crammed with stevedores, merchandise and gaping holes in the footpath through which merchandise is lowered for storage in underground rooms.

Above the area looms the large **Yeni Cami** (New Mosque), built between 1597 and 1663. Only in İstanbul could a 400-year-old mosque be called 'new'!

Beside the mosque is the **Mısır Çarşısı** (Egyptian or Spice Bazaar), which is not to be missed. The market was originally established in the 1660s to support the upkeep of Yeni Cami through rental income. There

are great photographic opportunities such as colourful displays of Turkish delight and conical piles of spices. You can buy *pestil* (sheets of dried and pressed fruit), *lokum* (Turkish delight) and what some enterprising Turkish merchants refer to as 'local Viagra' – *incir* (dried figs).

The original shop of the inventor of Turkish delight, Ali Muhiddin Hacı Bekir, is on the corner of Şeyhülislam Hayri Efendi Caddesi and Hamidiye Caddesi. Point to the variety that takes your fancy and ask if you can try it.

Emerging from the bazaar, walk across the **Galata Bridge**; the view from here is one of İstanbul's greatest free attractions. During the day, join the many fishermen who dangle their lines hopefully into the Golden Horn; at dusk, come to admire the sunset.

BEYOĞLU

Beyoğlu (and its vibrant centre Taksim) is home to İstanbul's best nightlife, but there is still a bit to see during the day. Although Beyoğlu is considered the 'new' side of İstanbul, it is anything but – there was a settlement here before the birth of Christ. Beyoğlu was a suburb of Constantinople in the time of Theodosius II (AD 408–50), who called it Galata because there were many Galatians (from north-west Turkey) living there.

The following description of Beyoğlu starts at the Galata Bridge. To the right of the bridge is Karaköy, where there are docks for ferries and cruise ships, and a small fish market. To the left is the entrance to the Tünel, a short underground railway built in 1875 to save the long haul up the hill; it costs US$0.40, and runs every five minutes.

Galata Tower

The tower dates from 1216, when Galata was a Genoese trading colony. It has also served as a prison and an observatory from which, during the 17th century, an intrepid local 'birdman' launched himself from the top in a (failed) attempt at the first intercontinental flight. Later the tower served as a fire lookout before it went up in flames itself in 1835. It was restored in 1967. The observation deck is an excellent place for

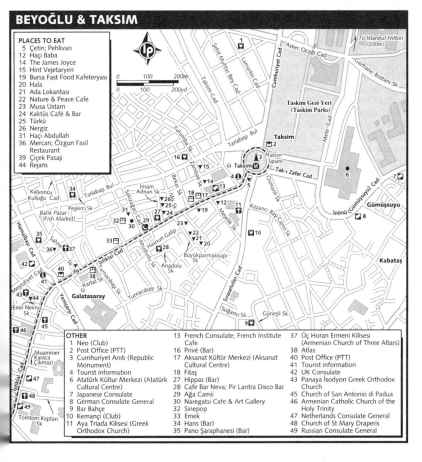

BEYOĞLU & TAKSIM

PLACES TO EAT
5 Çetin; Pehlivan
12 Haçi Baba
14 The James Joyce
15 Hint Vejetaryen
19 Bursa Fast Food Kafeteryası
20 Hala
21 Ada Lokantası
22 Nature & Peace Cafe
23 Musa Ustam
24 Kaktüs Café & Bar
25 Türkü
26 Nergiz
31 Haçi Abdullah
36 Mercan; Özgun Fasil Restaurant
39 Çiçek Pasaji
44 Rejans

OTHER
1 Neo (Club)
2 Post Office (PTT)
3 Cumhuriyet Anıtı (Republic Monument)
4 Tourist information
6 Atatürk Kültür Merkezi (Atatürk Cultural Centre)
7 Japanese Consulate
8 German Consulate General
9 Bar Bahçe
10 Kemançi (Club)
11 Aya Triada Kilisesi (Greek Orthodox Church)
13 French Consulate; French Institute Cafe
16 Privé (Bar)
17 Aksanat Kültür Merkezi (Aksanat Cultural Centre)
18 Fitaş
27 Hippas (Bar)
28 Cafe Bar Neva; Pir Lantra Disco Bar
29 Ağa Camii
30 Naregatsi Cafe & Art Gallery
32 Sinepop
33 Emek
34 Hans (Bar)
35 Pano Şaraphanesi (Bar)
37 Üç Horan Ermeni Kilisesi (Armenian Church of Three Altars)
38 Atlas
40 Post Office (PTT)
41 Tourist information
42 UK Consulate
43 Panaya İsodyon Greek Orthodox Church
45 Church of San Antonio di Padua
46 Armenian Catholic Church of the Holy Trinity
47 Netherlands Consulate General
48 Church of St Mary Draperis
49 Russian Consulate General

views and photos. It's open from 9 am to 6 pm daily (7 pm in summer); admission is US$3, or US$1.50 on Monday.

İstiklal Caddesi & Taksim

İstiklal Caddesi starts where the Tünel terminates. Once called the Grand Rue de Péra, İstiklal Caddesi is now a pedestrian way served by a restored tram (US$0.50). Not far from Tünel Square is the **Galata Mevlevihanesi** or Whirling Dervish Hall (☎ 245 4141), originally a meeting place of the Sufic mystics and officially called the Museum of Court Literature (Divan Edebiyatı Müzesi). It's open from 9.30 am to 5 pm daily (admission US$1.25) and is best visited on the last Sunday of each month when you can see the *sema* (ceremony), involving whirling dances, chants and music.

Turn down **Asmalımescit Caddesi**, a typical Beyoğlu street with its budget hotels (for rent by the hour) and antique shops, to reach the famed **Pera Palas Oteli** (☎ 251 4560), which opened in the 1890s as the last stop for travellers on the Orient Express. The atmosphere inside has hardly changed since Agatha Christie checked in, and it's worth the detour and even lingering over an overpriced coffee. If you want to treat yourself to a room, it costs US$140/220 per single/double.

Back on İstiklal Caddesi you'll pass a number of grand consulates (they were embassies in Ottoman times). Buildings to look out for include the Russian consulate general (1837), the Church of St Mary Draperis (1678), the Palazzo di Venezia, the Palais de France, the Netherlands consulate general and the Church of St Antonio di Padua (1725).

At Galatasaray Square, İstiklal Caddesi swings to the north-east. Just before the kink, on the western side, is the Greek Orthodox **Church of Panaya Isodyon**. Just north of the square is Sahne Sokak, the heart of the colourful **Balık Pazar** (Fish Market). A little further north is the **Çiçek Pasajı** (Flower Passage), an assortment of generally overpriced fish-and-beer restaurants (but worth strolling through).

The next section of İstiklal, to Taksim Square, is wall-to-wall fast-food outlets, designer clothing shops and banks (with ATMs). You only have to step off the main streets, however, to discover a plethora of more traditional Turkish restaurants, clubs,

seedy hotels and bars. **Taksim Square**, with its huge hotels and the Atatürk Cultural Centre (also known as the Opera House), surrounding a lacklustre park, is the hub of modern İstanbul.

THE BOSPHORUS

The Bosphorus, 32km long and from 500m to 3km wide, divides European from Asian İstanbul. In Turkish, the straits are known as Boğaziçi. The expanse was not bridged until 1973, when the Bosphorus Bridge (Boğaziçi Köprüsü) was built. A second bridge, the Fatih Köprüsü, has since been built and a third is planned.

If you follow Gümüşsuyu Caddesi from Taksim down to the Bosphorus you'll pass the İnönü Stadium and come to the waterfront Dolmabahçe Camii and Dolmabahçe Palace (Dolmabahçe Sarayı) – the last palace of the Ottoman sultans. Further up the Bosphorus is the **Çırağan Sarayı**, a less ostentatious palace restored as a luxury hotel. Not far away, the small but well-formed **Ortaköy Camii** nestles beneath the Bosphorus Bridge, providing a magnificent backdrop to the faintly bohemian waterside restaurants and bars of Ortaköy. It's a fine spot to while away a balmy evening. There's a **craft market** on Sunday, which adds to the bohemian air.

A ferry ride further up the Bosphorus is *de rigueur* for all İstanbul tourists. There are frequent commuter services between Eminönü, Beşiktaş, Ortaköy and further up the Bosphorus.

Dolmabahçe Palace

The ridiculously rococo Dolmabahçe Palace (Dolmabahçe Sarayı) was built between 1843 and 1856 in the 'European style'. The interior decor is eye-boggling, but the rushed tour costs US$14 (US$8 if you are prepared to skip the harem) and you might well feel that it's better value for money to instead visit Topkapı Palace and fit in a few extra sights with the change. If you do visit, go early, since tours get booked up later in the day. Inside the palace all the clocks are stopped at 9.05 am, the time at which Atatürk died here on 10 November 1938. The palace is open from 9 am to noon and 1.30 to 4 pm daily except Monday and Thursday.

Near the palace on Beşiktaş Caddesi is the much more interesting **Deniz Müzesi**

(Maritime Museum), which contains, along with boats and giant carved figureheads, a monstrous 21-tonne cannon from the time of Selim the Grim. The museum is open from 9 am to 12.30 pm and 1.30 to 5 pm Friday to Tuesday; admission is US$2.

Any bus heading out of Karaköy along the Bosphorus shore road will take you to Dolmabahçe. Get off at the Kabataş stop. Just north is Dolmabahçe Camii, and beyond it, the palace.

Asian Shore

A highlight of a visit to İstanbul is 'ferry hopping' across the Bosphorus to the eastern shore or taking a cruise up the full length of the strait.

Üsküdar is a lively, bustling city and a major dormitory suburb for İstanbul. Just offshore is the **Kız Kulesi** (Maiden's or Leander's Tower), which had a starring role in the Bond flick *The World is Not Enough*.

South of Üsküdar is the grand 19th-century **Haydarpaşa train station**, for train departures to all points east, and the large **Selimiye Barracks**. Here you'll find a small **museum** (☎ 216-343 7310) dedicated to Florence Nightingale's work at the barracks when it served as a military hospital during the Crimean War. It's open from 9 am to 4 pm Saturday only or by appointment.

If you are on the Asian shore at night go up to the top of **Çamlıca**, the high point behind Üsküdar. You can dine by candlelight here; alternatively the view itself is free. **Salacak**, across from Kız Kulesi, is another good spot to watch the sunset; it's 10 minutes' walk from the ferry terminal.

The grandest palace on the Asian shore is the white marble **Beylerbeyi**, a few kilometres north of Üsküdar, built by Abdülaziz between 1861 and 1876. The last sultan, Abdülahmid II, spent his final years here (1913–18). The palace is open from 9.30 am to 5 pm daily except Monday and Thursday; admission is US$3 and the guided tour is a fast affair.

To get to the Asian shore, catch the Üsküdar ferry from Dock No 2 in Eminönü (US$0.40, every 20 minutes from 6 am to midnight); ferries also run from Kabataş. A similar service runs from Beşiktaş to Üsküdar. To get to Beylerbeyi Palace, take a bus or *dolmuş* (shared taxi) from Üsküdar's main square.

Near the Black Sea end of the Bosphorus, the charming village of **Anadolu Kavaği** is the ultimate stop for the sightseeing ferries from Sirkeci. The medieval castle above the town is a good spot for a picnic and trekking.

If you're planning on going to Anadolu Kavağı, the best option is the twice-daily tourist cruise that leaves Dock No 3 in Eminönü at 10.35 am and 1.35 pm. The return journeys are at 3 pm and 5 pm. There are more services in the summer. The trip takes 1½ hours each way and the cost is around US$2.50 return.

PLACES TO STAY – BUDGET

The most convenient areas to base yourself, with the widest range of accommodation, are in and around Sultanahmet, including Çemberlitas and Cankurtaran. Hostels charge between US$7 and US$8 for a dorm bed in summer, less in winter. For a basic single/double room with its own bathroom, you're looking at US$15/30. In high summer, even the hostels fill up (with the inevitable problems of noise and overstretched facilities) and roof space in hostels and at some pensions becomes available for around US$5.

Camping

This is a bit of a waste of time as the camping grounds are miles away from the attractions and cost about as much as cheap hotel rooms (around US$10). *Londra Kamping (☎ 560 4200)* is a truck stop with a large camping area attached, on the south side of the Londra Asfaltı between Sultanahmet and the airport. *Ataköy Tatil Köyü (☎ 559 6000)*, south-east of the airport, and the *Florya Turistik Tesisleri (☎ 663 1000)* nearby in Florya, are both beachside holiday complexes with bungalow and hotel accommodation and camping facilities. To get here, take the *banliyö treni* (suburban train) from Sirkeci train station.

Hostels

In a prime spot opposite Aya Sofya, *Yücelt Interyouth Hostel (☎ 513 6150, fax 512 7628, e info@yucelthostel.co, Caferiye Sokak 6/1)* is a large, institutional place, but with plenty of facilities and a good terrace cafe. Dorm beds are US$7, beds in three- or four-bed rooms cost US$8 and doubles with toilet cost US$18.

The newer hostels are clustered in Cankurtaran. *İstanbul Hostel* (☎ 516 9380, fax 516 9384, e info@valide.com, Kutlugün Sokak 35), across the street from the Four Seasons Hotel, near the corner of Tevkifhane Sokak, has fine dorm beds for US$10, doubles for US$25, and a popular restaurant and rooftop bar.

The *Sultan Tourist Hostel* (☎ 516 9260, fax 517 1626, e bookings@sultanhostel .com, Terbıyık Sokak) is patronised by 'Fezzies' (people who travel on the Fez Bus) and other first-time travellers. Dorms beds are $7, singles/doubles are US$8.50/17. It has a cafeteria, information and travel office, laundry, international telephones, TV (Sky and cable), luggage room, safekeeping facilities and a great rooftop terrace.

The big and bright *Orient Youth Hostel* (☎ 517 9493, fax 518 3894, e orienthostel@ superonline.com, Akbıyık Caddesi 13) is a party place, so don't expect any early nights if you're in the noisy dorms at the front. Dorms are US$7 to US$8, while standard doubles with sink and shared bathroom are US$18. There are also deluxe doubles with private bathroom and TV for US$35. This hostel too has the obligatory rooftop terrace bar.

In Çemberlitaş, the *Cordial Hostel* (☎ 518 0576, fax 516 4108, e cordial@ dominet.in.com.tr, Peykhane Sokak 29), two minutes' walk south-east of the Çemberlitaş tram station off Divan Yolu, is a quiet, clean place. The cost is US$6 for a dorm bed or US$20 for a double room. This place will also arrange shuttles to the airport (US$4).

The nearby *Paris Hotel & Hostel* (☎ 518 9820, fax 518 9918, Dizdariye Medresese Sokak 9/11) is more old-fashioned, but has beds, not bunk beds, in its dorms for US$7 to US$8, and reasonable singles/doubles for US$15/25. There's also a small terrace with a good sea view.

Pensions & Hotels

Some pensions also have dorm beds. In Cankurtaran, *Mavi Guesthouse* (☎ 516 5878, fax 517 7287, e mavipans@hotmail .com, Kutlugün Sokak 3) is friendly and quiet. Four-bed dorm rooms are US$6 to US$8 per person; doubles without bathroom cost US$16 to US$20 including breakfast. A spot on the roof in summer costs US$5.

The small *Konya Pension* (☎ 638 3638, Terbıyık Sokak 15) is one of the cheapest places, with dorm beds from US$5 (even cheaper if you're prepared to sleep in the lobby). There's a kitchen for guests' use. Opposite is *İlknur Pension* (☎ 517 6833, Terbıyık Sokak 22), but only come here if you're desperate or broke. The attic dorm with 12 beds is stuffy and costs US$3; tiny double rooms cost US$6.

One of the best cheap hotels, and a fine mid-range option too, is *Side Pansiyon* (☎ 517 6590, fax 517 6590, e info@sid ehotel.com). Rooms with shared bathroom start at US$15 per person including breakfast, which is served on a delightful roof terrace. The adjoining Side Hotel has the same friendly owners, and comfy rooms for US$30/40 a single/double.

The *Star Guest House* (☎ 638 2302, fax 516 1827, Akbıyık Caddesi 18) has good rooms with shower, TV and fridge for US$20/35 including breakfast.

There are a couple of reasonable options just off Yerebatan Caddesi. *Hotel Ema* (☎ 511 7166, fax 512 4878, Salkım Söğüt Sokak 18) has doubles for US$15 (US$20 with private bathroom). *Hotel Anadolu* (☎ 512 1035), down the street on the right, has shabbier doubles but a pleasant front terrace for US$20 (US$25 with private bathroom).

The *Hotel Yunus Emre* (☎ 638 4562, fax 517 4389, e yunusemrehotel@superonline. com, Şifa Hamamı Sokak 30), across from the Doy Doy Restaurant, comes highly recommended by readers. It has friendly owners, a lovely terrace and fine rooms for US$15/30 including breakfast.

PLACES TO STAY – MID-RANGE

Coşkun Pension (☎/fax 526 1311, e chieko@ atlas.net.tr, Soğukçeşme Sokak 40) has bags of character, clean rooms and no bunk beds, and is on possibly the nicest street in Sultanahmet. The owners are friendly and there's a rooftop cafe. Doubles go for US$30.

The *Kervan Guest House* (☎ 528 2949, fax 527 2390, Şeftali Sokak 10) off Yerebatan Caddesi in Sultanahmet is a reliable place worth the US$30/45 including breakfast for singles/doubles with wooden floors, comfy beds and spacious bathrooms.

In a quiet quarter of Cankurtaran, *Tash Konak* (☎ 518 2882, Tomurcuk Sokak 5) has comfy singles/doubles for US$30/40 including a buffet breakfast. It also has a very pretty garden terrace.

The *Hotel Park* (☎ *517 6596, fax 518 9602,* e *hotelpark@ihlas.net.tr, Utangaç Sokak 26)*, opposite the Four Seasons Hotel, charges US$35/40 for a room with shared bathroom, or US$45 for a double with private bathroom, including breakfast.

The *Cem Hotel* (☎ *516 5041, fax 517 6576, Kutlugün Sokak 30)* is a good choice for US$25/50 including breakfast; all rooms have bathroom, telephone and heating in winter. There's also a TV room, a kitchen and a rooftop with panoramic views.

The *Terrace Guesthouse* (☎ *638 9733, fax 638 9734,* e *terrace@escortnet.com, Kutlugün Sokak 30)* has only a handful of rooms but they're very tidy and appealing; doubles/ triples with bathroom cost US$35/45.

Around the corner on Adliye Sokak, two fine options are *Hotel Şebnem* (☎ *517 6623, fax 638 1056,* e *sebnemhotel@su peronline.com)*, with singles/doubles/triples for US$35/50/60, and the family-run *Alp Guesthouse* (☎ *517 9570, fax 518 5728,* e *alpguesthouse@turk.net)* with doubles (all with bathroom) for US$40 to US$50.

Aladdin's Guest House (☎ *516 2330, fax 638 6059, Mimar Mehmet Ağa Caddesi)* and the neighbouring *Hotel Arasta* (☎ *516 1817, fax 638 3104)* are both excellent value, with single/double rooms for US$25/ 35 including breakfast.

A couple of pricier options with sound reputations are the homely *Guesthouse Berk* (☎ *516 9671, fax 517 7715,* e *reser vations@berkguesthouse.com, Kutlugün Sokak 27)* which has standard doubles for US$50, and *Hotel Spina* (☎ *638 1727, fax 638 742, Utangaç Sokak 19)* which has well-appointed rooms (US$55 for a double) and a lift (a rarity in Cankurtaran) to take you to the rooftop terrace.

PLACES TO EAT
Sultanahmet & Around
Sultanahmet Any overland guide to eating in İstanbul is obliged to start with the *Pudding Shop* (officially known as *Lale Restaurant)*, at the foot of Divan Yolu, and once a legend among hippy travellers. It's now just one in a string of medium-priced restaurants. Typical meals cost US$4 to US$6; drop by for a coffee and pudding at the very least. The nearby *Sultanahmet Köftecisi* (also known as *Selim Usta)* is unpretentious and serves delicious grilled meatballs *(köfte)* with salad, bread and a drink for US$3.50 or less.

Further up the road, *Vitamin Restaurant* was undergoing a facelift when we visited; we get mixed reviews about this place, but it's undoubtedly popular. Classier but more expensive is the *Sultan Pub* (☎ *526 6347, Divan Yolu 2)*. There is a cafe downstairs and a much more expensive restaurant upstairs. A 'location' fee is added to your bill.

Round the corner, İncili Çavuş Sokak is a narrow alley lined with a good range of generally pricier options. Making a pleasant change from the Turkish staples is *Dubb Indian Restaurant*, a stylish place with a reasonable selection of vegetarian dishes. A meal here is around US$6. At the top of the alley, *Rumeli Cafe* (*Ticarethane Sokak 8)* is a class act, with a meal averaging US$15.

İstanbul is a self-caterer's paradise; even in touristy Sultanahmet there are several *halk pazari* (small supermarkets) and corner shops where you can buy all the essentials, even wine.

Çemberlitaş Heading towards Çemberlitaş up Divan Yolu, the excellent *Divan Pizza Shop* serves up large Turkish-style pizza for US$3 and Italian-style pizza for US$4. Opposite is *Dedem Börekçisi* (*Divan Yolu 21)* a street-side booth selling *börek* (flaky pastry) filled with sheep's milk cheese for US$2, drink included.

Just off Divan Yolu, *Cafe Amedros* (*Hora Rüstem Sokak 7)* is a trendy cafe and bar with Western music, friendly service and beer for US$2.50. Meals such as a very hearty moussaka are around US$7.

Subaşi Restaurant (*Nuruosmaniye Caddesi 48)* near one of the entrances to the Kapalı Çarsı is an authentic *lokanta* (restaurant) that's an ideal lunch choice. Inside the market, search out *Havuzlu Lokantası* (☎ *527 3346, Gani Çelebi Sokak 3)* which has an appealing setting and does a mixed meze plate for US$6; it's near the post office (PTT).

Yeni Birlik Lokantası (☎ *517 6465, Peykhane Sokak 46)*, not far from the Hippodrome, serves light fast food and is favoured by lawyers from the nearby law courts. It's only open from 11 am to 4 pm on weekdays, and meals cost from US$2.50 to US$4.

Aya Sofya Büfe (Yerebatan Caddesi) is a friendly, inexpensive place for breakfast, lunch or a snack, with pavement tables and a comfy carpeted upstairs room.

There are a number of *teahouses* with outdoor tables around the Hippodrome that are pleasant, but pricey, places to rest up and revive over *çay* (tea) and a *nargileh* (hubble-bubble); good ones are *Cafe Mesale* and the nearby *Derviş Aile Çay Bahçesi*. Also try *Medrese Cafe (Hora Rüstem Sokak)*, which is cheaper and has tables in the cool inner courtyard of an old theological college, now a centre for contemporary writers.

Cankurtaran *Doy Doy (Şifa Hamamı 13)*, down behind the Blue Mosque, is renowned for serving some of the best-value Turkish food around. It is a simple place, and cheap, with a good range of kebaps, *pide* (Turkish pizza) and salads for around US$2.50 a plate. Nearby is the sunny *Buchara 93 (Nakilbent Sokak 15/A)*, which also has fine food at reasonable prices.

In the thick of the backpacker quarter on Akbıyık Caddesi, *Cafe Magnaura* and *Ayazma Restaurant* have excellent food in nice surroundings. Although these places are generally pricey, cheaper set menus are available. *Seoul II* serves reasonable Korean and Chinese food for around US$10 a meal.

Uphill from Akbıyık Caddesi is the congenial *Med Cezir (Tevkifhane Sokak)*. It's a popular spot for breakfast, pizza or coffee. If you fancy splashing out, the opulent *Four Seasons Hotel* is opposite; a coffee is US$5 before tax.

Kumkapı This neighbourhood, which follows the shoreline south of Beyazıt and includes Tiyatro Caddesi, boasts many seafood restaurants clustered around a square. In fair weather the whole place is one big party. You can eat meat for US$8 or US$10, but are more likely to spend from US$12 to US$20 on fish dishes (eg, swordfish kebaps) and *rakı* (aniseed-flavoured brandy).

Tried and tested are *Minas (Samsa Sokak 7)*, *Yengeç Balık Lokantası (Telli Odalar Sokak 6)*, *Doğan Restaurant (Kennedy Caddesi)*, and *Köşem Cemal Restaurant (Samsa Sokak 1)*.

Eminönü

Join the locals for a cheap lunch at the *boats* that dish out filling fish sandwiches and kebaps near the Galata Bridge for just US$1.

Just off Hüdavendigar Caddesi, *Trabzon (Safettin Paşa Sokak)* is a fine lokanta with very friendly staff; look for the fish sign.

Nearby on pedestrianised İbni Kemal Caddesi there are several cheap places with outdoor tables – try the *Namli Rumeli Köftecisi* for lamb meatballs and *piyaz* (white bean salad) and the *Kasap Osman* for İskender kebap (grilled meat topped with tomato sauce and browned butter). *Et-İş (Hocapaşa Sokak 25)* has fresh, tasty food, cheap at US$2 to US$4 for a meal; there is a spotless *aile salonu* (family room) upstairs.

The upmarket choice is *Pandeli (☎ 527 3909)* over the main entrance of the Mısır Çarsısı. It serves magnificent seafood lunches from Monday to Saturday, and charges in accordance with its fame.

The *Mısır Çarşısı* in Eminönü has a lot more than just spices, and there are several other shops nearby selling all manner of foodstuffs.

Beyoğlu & Taksim

For cheap eats such as *döner* (spit-roasted meat) sandwiches (US$1) go to the *büfes* (snack bars) between Sıraselviler and İstiklal Caddesi.

Heading down İstiklal from Taksim Square, restaurants to check out include the *Çetin* and *Pehlivan*, the more expensive *Hacı Baba*, which has a terrace overlooking the Aya Triada Kilisesi (Greek Orthodox Church), and the *Bursa Fast Food Kafeteryası*, which serves beer along with kebaps and ice cream.

Also worth a look is the *French Institute Cafe*, inside the French consulate, serving *salade Niçoise* and *tarte tatin* at reasonable prices. On Zambak Sokak *The James Joyce* serves Irish food for breakfast, lunch and dinner, while further down the road is the 2nd-floor *Hint Vejetaryen*, a funkily decorated Indian restaurant with good curries and vegetarian options for around US$6.

Further down İstiklal Caddesi to the left is Büyükparmakkapı Sokak, where you'll find *Nature & Peace*, a good vegetarian place, with divine lentil köfte, and the cheap and reliable *Ada Lokantası*. At the top of the alley turn left to find *Hala (Çukurlu*

Çeşmesi Sokak), a traditional *mantı* (Turkish-style ravioli) joint. Another rustic option in the area is *Musa Ustam (Küçük Par-makkapı Sokak 14)*, great for spicy hot Adana kebaps.

İmam Adnan Sokak, to the right off İstiklal, has several cafes and live music joints (see Entertainment later) – try the reliable *Nergiz*, *Türkü* and *Kaktüs*. Another bunch of cheap eateries, with just about every variety of Turkish food, can be found in Ahududu Sokak on the south side of İstiklal. The restaurants in the *Çiçek Pasajı* (Flower Passage) tend to be overpriced and pushy; you'll do better just around the corner in Sahne Sokak (near the Balık Pazar) and in nearby side streets. The *Özgün Fasil Restaurant* is one of the best in the area; köfte and *tavuk şiş* (grilled chicken) are around US$3, and beer is around US$1.50. At *Mercan* try a great cheap snack – the *midye tavası* (mussels deep-fried on a skewer). There are plenty of other shops here where you can put together a cheap picnic, and this is a good area to try for hard-to-get Western items; the pickings are particularly rich around Sahne and Dudu Odaları Sokaks.

A couple of Beyoğlu institutions that justify their higher price tags are *Rejans* (☎ 444 1610, Emir Nevruz Sokak 17), which still serves dishes such as borscht that were adored by the Russians who came here in the 1930s; and *Hacı Abdullah* (☎ 293 8561, Sakızağacı Caddesi 17), a stylish purveyor of Ottoman cuisine. Expect to spend around US$15 for a full meal.

ENTERTAINMENT
Cafes, Bars & Nightclubs
Sultanahmet & Around Sultanahmet is not where the night-time action is, but with the Bosphorus as a backdrop, there are few better ways to spend an evening than enjoying a *picnic* on the roof of your pension. Don't miss the free *sound-and-light show* at the Blue Mosque – the setting is unbelievable and few travellers come away without being awestruck. A trip to a *hamam* (Turkish bath) is also a great way to wind down or prepare for a night on the town.

There are several bars around Divan Yolu in Sultanahmet, including the buzzing *Bodrum Bar* and the nearby *Sultan Pub*. The budget crowd tends to congregate around the *cafes* on Akbıyık Caddesi – the

Backpackers' Underground Cafe keeps raging late into the night. A more sophisticated option is the rooftop bar of the chichi *Hotel Empress Zoe* (☎ 518 2504, 518 4360, fax 518 5699, Adliye Sokak 10). The hostels all have bars, usually on their roofs.

The *Orient Youth Hostel* offers a cheesy Turkish cultural evening, complete with nargilehs and belly dancers. You can do better than this – try the backstreets of Beyoğlu or the cafes in Üsküdar on the eastern shore of the Bosphorus for a more authentic experience.

Beyoğlu & Taksim Left and right of İstiklal Caddesi, across the Golden Horn from Sultanahmet, are alleys packed with plenty of drinking, dining and clubbing options. İmam Adnan Sokak is a good place to start; here you'll find *Hippas* and the cool *Kaktüs*.

On Zambak Sokak, *The James Joyce* has live music every night (Latin and tango on Tuesday night) and cheaper drinks until 8 pm. The atmosphere is very Dublin, but the beer is pricey. On Friday and Saturday after 9 pm, entry is US$8, which includes a couple of free drinks.

There are a string of places along Büyükparmakkapı Sokak, mostly dishing out Turko pop (a pleasant blend of familiar rock and roll in an unfamiliar language, sans grunge) – *Açk Sahne Taxim Music Bar*, *Gayfe Cafe Bar & Restaurant*, *Mojo Live* and *Barabar*. The *Cafe Bar Neva* and *Pir-lanta Disco Bar* in Anadolu Sokak are a little wilder; *Caravan* near Sahne Sokak is rock only; and the *Gramofon Cafe Pub* near the Galata Mevlevihanesi at the south end of İstiklal Caddesi is a jazz joint.

A good wine bar is *Pano Şaraphanesi* near the UK consulate on Hamalbaşı Caddesi. Another alternative to the beer scene is the surreal pop-art *Naregatsi Cafe & Art Gallery (1st floor, Sakızağacı Sokak 3)*. You can drink various coffees and nibble at waffles in the shape of Mickey Mouse while admiring the Day-Glo decoration, and perhaps playing one of the many board games.

Among the dance clubs, the three-level *Kemancı (Sıraselviler Caddesi)*, near Taksim Square, is primarily for Goths. *Switch (Muammer Karaca Çikmazi 3)* is more contemporary and has a '70s and '80s disco on Wednesday. Entry to such clubs is around US$5, which usually includes one drink.

On no account should you follow a street tout to the 'best night venue in İstanbul'. They get commission and you'll get fleeced by the local Mafia, often in a rough manner. These places are dives. If you're male and a 'Natasha' (Russian prostitute) sits at your side, you'll have trouble getting out of the place anything less than penniless.

Gay & Lesbian Venues

İstanbul has Turkey's most open gay scene, and a surprisingly wide range of venues. Tucked north off Taksim Square on Lamartin Caddesi is *Neo*, downstairs opposite the Golden Age Hotel. The decor is a mix of pseudo Tom of Finland paintings and silver milk-bottle tops, but looks sophisticated beside the likes of *Hans* on Tarlabaşi Bulvarı, a brick barn where Turko pop rules. Further up Tarlabaşi Bulvarı towards Taksim, you'll also find the metallic *Privé*, next to a Japanese restaurant. The best option is the chic *Bar Bahçe (Soğancı Sokak)* on the ground floor of the Blisak Building, where the bartenders bop around to the groovy tunes and canapes are served into the small hours. There's a decent bar and restaurant on the 5th floor of this building, too.

Folk Dance & Music

Turks are enthusiastic folklore fans and many know their regional dances well enough to jump in and dance along at a performance. University groups, good amateur companies and professionals all schedule performances throughout the year.

Look for news of performances and concerts in the weekend supplement to the Friday edition of the *Turkish Daily News*, and in its Arts & Culture section on Sunday. There are regular concerts of Turkish traditional music at the *Cemal Reşit Rey Konser Salonu*, near the İstanbul Hilton north of Taksim.

Cinema

There are plenty of cinemas along İstiklal Caddesi in Beyoğlu, many showing the latest big Hollywood releases. Cinemas include *Fitas*, *Sinepop*, *Emek* and *Atlas*. For all movie listings, see the *Turkish Daily News* and heed its warning about starting times constantly changing.

Ask at the box office to see if the film is in the *orijinal* (original) language or dubbed in *Türkçe* (Turkish). When possible, buy your tickets a few hours in advance. Tickets cost from US$3 to US$5.

The İstanbul International Film Festival, held annually from mid-April to early May, is a good opportunity to see many local films with English subtitles. Tickets are sold at the Atatürk Cultural Centre (Atatürk Kültür Merkezi) in Beyoğlu.

Night Cruises

One of the cheapest, yet most enjoyable, night-time activities is to take a Bosphorus ferry. It doesn't really matter where, as long as you don't end up stranded on the southern coast of the Sea of Marmara or on the Princes' Islands (Kızıl Adalar). Catch one over to Üsküdar or any town up the Bosphorus and enjoy the view, the twinkling lights, the fishing boats bobbing on the waves, and the powerful searchlights of the ferries sweeping the sea lanes. Have a glass of tea (a waiter will offer you some). Get off anywhere, and take a taxi back to your hotel if you can't catch a ferry or a bus back directly.

The easiest ferry to catch for this purpose is the one from Eminönü to Üsküdar. Buy two *jetons* (metal tokens) for the voyages out and back. From Üsküdar, just come back; or wait for one of the frequent ferries to Beşiktaş or Kabataş, from where you can catch a bus or dolmuş back to your part of town.

A similar ride is the one from Karaköy to Haydarpaşa or Kadıköy. Return boats bring you right back to Karaköy. The voyage takes 20 minutes in each direction and costs US$1 for a round trip.

SPECTATOR SPORTS

If you can score tickets, attend a match involving one of İstanbul's top soccer teams – Fenerbahçe, Galatasaray or Beşiktaş. The next best thing is to check out the bars on Türkeli Caddesi, five streets south of Beyazıt tram station, where hundreds of Turkish men gather on weekends to watch football on TV. It's football mania at its best and worst – people cry, sing, jump on tables, yell at the referee and drink heaps of beer.

GETTING THERE & AWAY
Air

İstanbul is Turkey's airline hub. Most foreign airlines have their offices near Taksim, or north of it, along Cumhuriyet Caddesi. You can buy Turkish Airlines tickets in Taksim at

Cumhuriyet Caddesi 10, or at any travel agency. For reservations call ☎ 522 8888.

Bus

The International İstanbul Bus Terminal (Uluslararası İstanbul Otogarı, ☎ 658 0036), usually just called 'the otogar', is at Esenler, about 10km west of the city. It has 170-plus ticket offices and buses leaving for all parts of Turkey and beyond. When you book your ticket with an agency ensure that it includes a service bus to the bus terminal; this saves a considerable sum. Otherwise you can get to the terminal via metro train from Aksaray; get out at the station called Otogar.

Buses depart for Ankara (US$8 to US$18, seven hours; express US$12 to $US20, six hours) roughly every 15 minutes, both day and night, and to most other cities in Turkey at least every hour. Major destinations include Cappadocia (US$15 to US$20, 10 to 12 hours), Çanakkale (US$10, six hours), Selçuk and Ephesus (US$16, 10 hours); and İzmir (US$15 to US$20, eight hours).

Train

Sirkeci (☎ 527 0050) is the station for trains heading west to Edirne, Greece and Europe. Haydarpaşa (☎ 216-336 0475), on the Asian shore, is the terminus for trains to Anatolia. From Sirkeci there is a daily express train to Edirne (US$4, five hours), but the bus is faster (three hours). From Haydarpaşa there are seven daily express trains to Ankara (US$11 to US$30, 7½ to 11 hours).

From the Saray Burnu dock, just north of Topkapı Palace, ships depart each morning and evening (except Friday and Saturday) for Bandırma, from where you continue to İzmir on the *Marmara Express* (US$10, 10½ to 12 hours).

Boat

Ferries and hydrofoils depart from Kabataş dock, east of Taksim and south of Dolmabahçe, for the Princes' Islands (Kızıl Adalar) and Yalova, half a dozen times daily in summer. From Yalova buses run to İznik and Bursa.

İstanbul to İzmir

Day 1:	İstanbul to Gemlik	95km	Day 5:	Biga to Çanakkale	80km
Day 2:	Gemlik to Bursa	40km	Day 6:	Çanakkale to Ayvacık	80km
Day 3:	Bursa to Bandırma	90km	Day 7:	Ayvacık to Ayvalık	90km
Day 4:	Bandırma to Biga	70km	Day 8:	Ayvalık to İzmir	110km

Cycling out of İstanbul is possible but not easy, the dense traffic on all the main exit roads making it a bit of a nightmare. The best way out is to go to Yenikapı and take the ferry across the Sea of Marmara to Yalova.

From Yalova follow the scenic road along the Çınarcık Peninsula, with a sea view on one side and forests on other. The road up to Gemlik is a hard climb reaching about 600m above sea level. Forestry workers will be eager to provide you with food, tea and water. The road from Gemlik to Bursa starts with another steep climb (from sea level to 230m within a few kilometres). The traffic is also busy on the road and gets busier as you pass the otogar and enter Bursa.

Depart Bursa for Bandırma in the early morning to avoid the traffic – the same holds true for all big cities. The road to Bandırma is undulating but not particularly taxing. After Bandırma it's hilly for about 15km but reverts to rolling countryside as you approach the Dardanelles. There are plenty of opportunities for rough camping; just avoid military areas.

In Çanakkale take your bike over to explore the Gallipoli Peninsula. Cycling is also an ideal way to get round Gökçeada and Bozcaada, the two Turkish islands off the Aegean coast.

The road from Çanakkale to Troy is a relatively easy peddle, with a steep hill about 15km out. There are a few steep climbs both before and after Ayvacık until you reach the coastal road through Edremit to Ayvalık. About 50km from Ayvalık is the turn-off to Bergama. Follow the road over undulating terrain from Bergama to İzmir and try to find a spot for rough camping just outside the city. Cycle out at first light to avoid the traffic.

Etienne Le Roux & Simon Richmond

There are ferries from Sirkeci to İzmir, leaving Friday at 2 pm and arriving Saturday at 9 am (US$14 for a reclining Pullman seat, US$27 for the cheapest cabin).

GETTING AROUND
To/From the Airport
Atatürk airport is 25km west of Sultanahmet. Airport buses depart from the airport's international terminal about every 30 minutes, stopping at the domestic terminal, Bakırköy and Aksaray before terminating in Taksim Square (get out at Aksaray for Sultanahmet). The trip takes 30 to 45 minutes and costs US$3. The metro is cheaper but less convenient; Dünya Ticaret Merkezi stop is the closest to the airport and you will need to take a taxi from there. City buses from the airport to Sultanahmet are infrequent and slow.

An airport taxi costs about US$12 for the 23km trip to Sultanahmet, and US$15 to Beyoğlu; it costs 50% more at night. Many of the travel agencies along Divan Yolu in Sultanahmet, and the Sultanahmet hostels, book minibus transport to the airport for US$4.

Bus
Destinations and intermediate stops are indicated at the front and side of the bus. On many (but not all) buses you must have a ticket (US$0.50) before boarding; some long routes require that you put two tickets into the ticket box (to the right of the driver). You can buy tickets from booths near major stops or from nearby shops.

Train
To get to Sirkeci train station, take the tram from Aksaray or Sultanahmet, or any bus

heading for Eminönü. Haydarpaşa train station is connected by ferry to Karaköy (US$0.50, at least every 30 minutes). *Banliyö tren* (suburban trains) run every 20 minutes along the southern walls of Old İstanbul and west along the Marmara shore; the fare is US$0.40.

Tram
The tramway between Sirkeci and Aksaray via Divan Yolu and Sultanahmet is useful, and costs just US$0.30; buy a ticket before boarding from the booths near the stops. The Hızlı tramway is a light railway system that runs west from Aksaray via Adnan Menderes Bulvarı through the city walls to the otogar (US$0.50). A third tramway trundles along İstiklal Caddesi to Taksim (US$0.30).

Underground
The Tünel (İstanbul's underground train) climbs the hill from Karaköy to Tünel Square and İstiklal Caddesi (US$0.35, every 10 or 15 minutes).

Taxi
İstanbul has 60,000 yellow taxis, all with digital meters; some are driven by lunatics who will really take you for a ride. A trip from Sultanahmet to Taksim costs US$4 to US$5; to the otogar costs around US$10.

For information on taxi rip-offs, see the Dangers & Annoyances section of the Regional Facts for the Visitor chapter.

Around İstanbul

PRINCES' ISLANDS (KIZIL ADALAR)
☎ 216

The Princes' Islands or Kızıl Adalar are one of the best day trips you can make from İstanbul, and are even worth considering as an overnight stop. They are called the Princes' Islands because this is where out-of-favour Ottoman nobles were once banished to. Four out of the nine islands are easily accessible by ferry, with Büyükada, the largest, the one you'll want to make the most time for.

One of the pleasures of the islands is the almost complete absence of motorised transport. You get around Büyükada either by horse-drawn carriage (*fayton*) or by bicycle,

---

Akbil

If you're staying in İstanbul a few days, consider using Akbil, the electronic transit pass. You buy a metal Akbil 'button' with an initial *şarj* (charge) of US$5.50 or more. When you enter the underground, tram, bus or ferry, you touch the button to the Akbil contact point and the fare is deducted from your button. You recharge your button from Akbil machines at major transit points by inserting money into the machine.

TURKEY

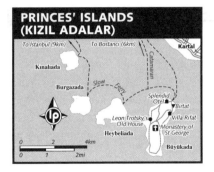

PRINCES' ISLANDS (KIZIL ADALAR)

To İstanbul (9km)   To Bostancı (6km)   Kartal

Kınalıada

Catamaran

Burgazada   Slow   Ferry

Splendid
Otel   Birtat
Leon Trotsky's   Villa Rifat
Old House   Monastery of
Heybeliada   St George
Büyükada

0   2   4km
0   1   2mi

the latter being the most fun. A 45-minute tour by carriage costs around US$10; the 70-minute version costs US$12. Bike hire, available from near the ferry landing, is less than US$2 per hour.

Apart from the verdant scenery, Büyükada's main attraction is the hilltop **Monastery of St George**, which commands spectacular views and has a rather good restaurant. You can also search out the crumbling house that Leon Trotsky once lived in, and picnic in the pleasant **Dil Burnu Park** (entry US$1), a pine-dotted peninsula from where you can climb down to some pebbly beaches.

Places to Stay & Eat

In summer you must book accommodation in advance because the islands are very popular with locals. In the winter most hotels are closed. The following places are all on Büyükada.

The congenial *Villa Rifat* (☎ 382 6068, 382 3081), on the coast road east of the ferry landing, has doubles for US$30-plus. *Splendid Otel* (☎ 382 6950, fax 382 6775), up the hill west of the ferry landing, is a late Ottoman beauty that has had a recent face-lift. Prices for large singles/doubles start at US$40/60 including breakfast, and rise during the peak July to August season.

There are plenty of fish restaurants along Gülistan Caddesi by the ferry landing – a good one is *Birtat* – but always check prices when ordering. The restaurant at the *monastery* does great köfte and salad for around US$5 and also serves wine.

Getting There & Away

Ferries (US$2) and *deniz otobüsü* (hydrofoils; US$3.50) depart the dock at Eminönü

in İstanbul. The trips can take a couple of hours if the ferry stops at a number of Asian terminals. From Bostancı to Büyükada takes 25 minutes. There are regular ferries between the main islands, Büyükada, Burgazada, Heybeliada and Kınalıada.

İstanbul to the Dardanelles

Instead of following the road through Thrace to reach the Gelibolu (Gallipoli) peninsula, our route crosses the Sea of Marmara by ferry or hydrofoil and heads towards Bursa, a pivotal city on the old Silk Route and a delightful stopover offering hot springs, old caravanserai, ancient mosques and even the chance to ski. From Bursa the route heads along the coast to the top end of the Dardanelles, the strait between the Aegean Sea and the Sea of Marmara, then follows the narrow channel to Çanakkale, the base for trips to the war graves of Gallipoli and the ruins of Troy (Truva).

BURSA
☎ 224 • pop 1 million
Sprawled at the base of Uludağ (2543m), Turkey's biggest winter sports centre, Bursa was the Ottoman capital before the conquest of İstanbul. There are few tourists here, which adds to the charm of the place. It is a complete contrast to the coastal regions and has a very Turkish feel.

Bursa developed some importance in the early centuries of Christianity when the silk trade was being established. The suburb of Çekirge grew in popularity after Justinian (527–65) developed bathhouses there. In 1326 Bursa became the Ottoman capital after a siege by Osman Gazi, and it was from here that he expanded the Ottoman Empire. Even when Bursa was replaced as capital of the empire in 1402 by Adrianople, it remained a revered Ottoman city.

Bursa's big attraction, still, is the thermal springs at Çekirge. The city is also famous as the place where the İskender kebap (grilled meat topped with savoury tomato sauce and browned butter) was invented, and as the home of Karagöz shadow puppets. The name for these puppets, which are made of painted translucent camel hide,

CENTRAL BURSA

TURKEY

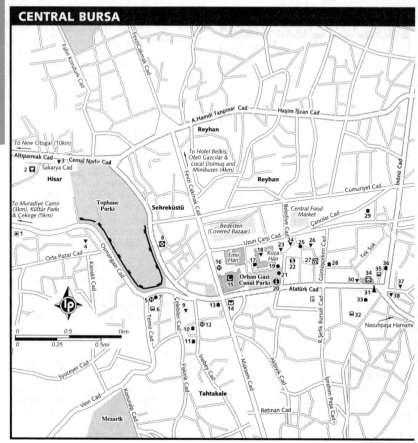

comes from a legendary character Karagöz (Black Eye), who helped build Bursa's Orhan Gazi Camii. He and his co-worker used to distract their colleagues with humorous antics – many recreated in today's puppet shows.

Orientation & Information

The city centre is along Atatürk Caddesi between the Ulu Cami (Grand Mosque) to the west and the main square, Cumhuriyet Alanı, commonly called Heykel (meaning 'statue'), to the east. The post office (PTT) is on Atatürk Caddesi across from the Ulu Cami. Çekirge is about 6km west of Heykel.

You can get maps and brochures at the helpful tourist office (☎/fax 220 1848) in

the Orhan Gazi Altgeçidi subway, Orhan Gazi Camii Parkı, opposite the Koza Han. For Internet access try Internet House Cafe on Oman Sokak. There are plenty of banks and ATMs along Atatürk Caddesi.

Things to See & Do

Start by exploring the **Bedesten** (Covered Bazaar), with its evocative caravanserai, particularly **Koza Han**, which is still the headquarters for Bursa's silk merchants, and a great place to chill out at one of the alfresco teahouses. The adjacent 20-domed **Ulu Cami** (1399), the largest of Bursa's mosques, has beautiful interior decoration and a central pool. Across the square you'll also see the Orhan Gazi Camii, Bursa's second-oldest mosque, dating from 1336.

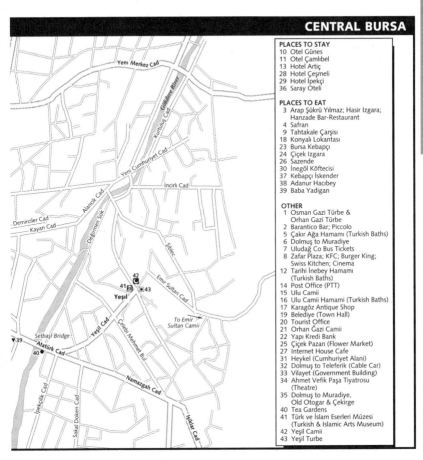

CENTRAL BURSA

PLACES TO STAY
10 Otel Güneş
11 Otel Çamlıbel
13 Hotel Artiç
28 Hotel Çeşmeli
29 Hotel İpekçi
36 Saray Oteli

PLACES TO EAT
3 Arap Şükrü Yılmaz; Hasir Izgara; Hanzade Bar-Restaurant
4 Safran
9 Tahtakale Çarşısı
18 Konyalı Lokantası
23 Bursa Kebapçı
24 Çiçek Izgara
26 Sazende
30 İnegöl Köftecisi
37 Kebapçı Iskender
38 Adanur Hacıbey
39 Baba Yadigan

OTHER
1 Osman Gazi Türbe & Orhan Gazi Türbe
2 Barantico Bar; Piccolo
5 Çakır Ağa Hamamı (Turkish Baths)
6 Dolmuş to Muradiye
7 Uludağ Co Bus Tickets
8 Zafar Plaza; KFC; Burger King; Swiss Kitchen; Cinema
12 Tarihi İnebey Hamamı (Turkish Baths)
14 Post Office (PTT)
15 Ulu Camii
16 Ulu Camii Hamamı (Turkish Baths)
17 Karagöz Antique Shop
19 Belediye (Town Hall)
20 Tourist Office
21 Orhan Gazi Camii
22 Yapı Kredi Bank
25 Çiçek Pazarı (Flower Market)
27 Internet House Cafe
31 Heykel (Cumhuriyet Alanı)
32 Dolmuş to Teleferik (Cable Car)
33 Vilayet (Government Building)
34 Ahmet Vefik Paşa Tiyatrosu (Theatre)
35 Dolmuş to Muradiye, Old Otogar & Çekirge
40 Tea Gardens
41 Türk ve İslam Eserleri Müzesi (Turkish & Islamic Arts Museum)
42 Yeşil Camii
43 Yeşil Turbe

About 1km east of Heykel, across the Gök Deresi River, is Yeşil, a pedestrian zone of attractive Islamic architecture. The star attraction is the early Ottoman **Yeşil Camii** (Green Mosque, 1424). The striking turquoise-tiled Yeşil Türbe (Green Tomb) is opposite and the **Türk ve İslam Eserleri Müzesi** (Turkish & Islamic Arts Museum), with its pretty courtyard, is worth a look. It's open from 8 am to noon and 1 to 5 pm daily except Monday; admission costs US$1. Around 300m east of Yeşil is the rococo **Emir Sultan Camii** (1805), usually thronged by believers. To get here, take bus No 1A, 6A or 36A, or a *dolmuş* (shared taxi), from Heykel.

Uphill and west of the Ulu Cami, on the way to Çekirge, are the **Osman Gazi Türbe** and the **Orhan Gazi Türbe**, dating from the 14th century. These tombs of the first Ottoman sultans are missable but the surrounding park with views across the city is pleasant enough, as are the Ottoman houses of the nearby **Hisar** area. One kilometre beyond is the **Muradiye Camii** complex with decorated tombs dating from the 15th and 16th centuries and a couple of interesting restored Ottoman mansions. There's also a lively **street market** here on Tuesdays.

To save the expense of a bath in Çekirge, there are several cheaper options in downtown Bursa, including the historic **Çakır Ağa Hamamı** at the foot of the Hisar, **Tarihi İnebey Hamamı** on İnebey Caddesi and **Nasuhpaşa Hamamı** on Hamamı Sokak just off Namazgah Caddesi. Expect to pay around US$6 for a bath and massage at these places.

Go to **Çekirge** to indulge yourself at one of the ancient bathhouses. The best is the **Eski Kaplıca**, next to the Kervansaray Termal Hotel. Originally built in Roman times (but more recently restored), the soaring brick-domed edifice is very impressive. You can bathe amid the splendour of marble and Byzantine columns and soak in a piping hot pool of mineral water for around US$6 (bath only), or pay US$18 for the full works.

The **Karagöz Antique Shop**, in the arcade between the Koza and Emir Hans in Bursa, sells Karagöz puppets and a wide range of local crafts and dusty relics. The owners can also direct you to Çekirge's **Karagöz Art House**. Here you can learn about the city's famed camel-leather puppets and of the unfortunate fate of the satirists Karagöz and Hacıvat, who were executed for distracting workers building the Orhan Gazi Camii. They are the two characters you see silhouetted in the small shadow-puppet-theatre illustrations seen all over Turkey. The Karagöz Art House is open from 11 am to 5 pm daily except Sunday; take a Çekirge dolmuş there for US$0.50.

On the way to Çekirge, is the vast **Kültür Parkı**. Here you'll find an unexceptional **archaeological museum**. It's also a pleasant place for a stroll or to take tea.

MICK WELDON

Karagöz shadow-puppet theatre, seen all over Turkey, originated in Bursa.

Places to Stay

Otel Güneş (☎ 222 1404, İnebey Caddesi) is a cheap, central and friendly place, with small but spotless and brightly painted singles/doubles for US$8/16 with shared bathroom.

Up the road, the rooms at the mid-range *Otel Çamlıbel* (☎ 221 2565, fax 223 4405, İnebey Caddesi 71) have better facilities and cost US$16/23.

Saray Oteli (☎ 221 2820, İnönü Caddesi 1) is in a noisy spot; the bedrooms and toilets are clean and reasonable value for US$13/25. It's a better bet than *Hotel İpekçi* (☎ 221 1935, Çancılar Caddesi 38), which is in a quieter location near the bazaar. A grungy room is US$12/18 (US$16/21 with a hot shower).

There are a few cheap but unsavoury options near the old Santral Garaj around 4km north of the Ulu Cami, including *Hotel Belkis* (☎ 254 8322, Gazcılar Caddesi 168) which has rooms with sink for US$6.50/10; showers are extra. *Oteli Gazcılar* (☎ 251 8118, Gazcılar Caddesi 156) is reasonable and charges about US$20 for a clean double with shower.

Hotel Çeşmeli (☎/fax 224 1511, Gümüşçeken Caddesi 6) just north of Heykel is a decent mid-range option. Comfy rooms with fridge and TV cost US$34/44 including breakfast. Also consider the amenable *Hotel Artiç* (☎ 224 5505, fax 224 5509, Atatürk Caddesi) with rooms for US$20/30 including breakfast.

Staying in Çekirge, you pay more but get mineral baths thrown in. The dated *Otel Öz Hayat* (☎ 236 5105, Hamamlar Caddesi) is one of the cheaper options, with rooms for US$15/26. *Yeşil Yayla Oteli* (☎ 236 8026, Çekirge Caddesi), behind the Yıldız Hotel at the upper end of the village, charges US$15 a double for a room with sink.

A fine mid-range choice is *Atlas Termal Hotel* (☎ 234 4100, fax 236 4605) with modern, well-appointed rooms for US$25/40 including breakfast.

Places to Eat
Restaurants Bursa is renowned for İskender kebap, and *the* place to try it is *Kebapçı İskender (Ünlü Caddesi)* just east of Heykel. Kebaps are all that is served at this stylish restaurant, which dates back to 1867, but the prices are low – about US$6 with a soft drink.

Adanur Hacıbey (Ünlü Caddesi 7), opposite, is less fancy, but slightly cheaper and it also offers *pide* (pizza). Near the Koza Han is the reliable *Bursa Kebapçı*.

If you would rather eat İnegöl köfte (mincemeat balls made with a mixture of beef, lamb and onion) then the aptly named *İnegöl Köftecisi* on Atatürk Caddesi will give you a full plate for around US$4.

Çiçek Izgara (Belediye Caddesi 15), just north of the half-timbered belediye (town hall), in the Çiçek Pazarı (Flower Market), is bright, modern and packed with families and couples. Expect to queue. It's open from 11 am to 3.30 pm and 5.30 to 9 pm daily. For lunch, also check out *Konyalı Lokantası* in the Koza Han. *Sazende (Hamamlar Caddesi 37)*, tucked behind the Çiçek Pazarı, is pricey, but has bags of Ottoman ambience.

If you're hankering after fast food, dive into the swanky new shopping centre *Zafar Plaza* on Cemal Nadir Caddesi. It has a lively food court with the usual suspects (KFC, Burger King etc) and a few others including *Swiss Kitchen*, which offers schnitzel for US$1.50.

The chic restaurant at *Safran* (☎ 224 7216, Kale Sokak), a classy pension in an Ottoman house, serves good mixed meze plates for US$3 and has beer. Also well worth a splurge is *Daruzzifaye* (☎ 224 6439, Murat Caddesi 36), set in a converted *medrese* (theological school) in Muradiye. Try the local creamy soup *Muradiye çorbası* for US$1, and the köfte (US$3) served sizzling on an iron platter in a rich sauce.

Sakarya Caddesi, down the hill from Zafar Plaza, is an alley lined with restaurants (many specialising in fish) and bars. Try the buzzy bar/restaurant *Hasir Izgara* or the more upmarket *Hanzade Bar-Restaurant* and *Arap Şükrü Yılmaz* .

Baba Yadigan (Namazgah Caddesi 73), near the bridge, is a convivial cafe serving a good range of cakes and teas; it has live music Wednesday to Saturday.

Self-Catering Kepekli (bran loaves), one of the culinary delights of Bursa, can be found at most bakeries. There are plenty of stores selling cheese and olives around the *Tahtakale Çarşısı*, the market area just off Atatürk Caddesi. Finish off the meal with some of the chestnut-based sweets for which the region is famous.

The central *food market* is just off Belediye Caddesi. Here you'll find cheese for your bran loaves, lots of fruit, and nuts. There's also the Tuesday *street market* in Muradiye.

Entertainment

Join the night-time crowds strolling around the **Kültür Parkı**, which is on the way to Çekirge; you could even stop for a meal and listen to the cabaret singers.

If you fancy a drink, Sakarya Caddesi is the place to go. **Barantico Bar** and **Piccolo** are both popular joints along here.

Safran (see Places to Eat) has a lively traditional band to entertain dinner guests on Friday and Saturday.

There's a **cinema** complex in Zafar Plaza (US$4 a ticket) and a couple more down Altıparmak Caddesi.

Getting There & Away

The best way to get here from İstanbul is by hydrofoil to Yalova (US$6.50, one hour, five daily), then connecting bus to Bursa (US$3, 70 minutes).

Buses to places all over Turkey leave from the new **otogar** (bus station), which is 10km north of the old Santral Garaj on Yeni Yalova Yolu. Leaving Bursa for İstanbul, buses designated *feribot ile* (by ferry boat) use the Topçular-Eskihisar ferry, which is quicker (2½ hours) than the *karayolu ile*

(land route) round the Marmara (US$9, four hours).

From Bursa, it is 300km to Çanakkale (US$10, five hours) and 400km to Ankara (US$12, 5½ hours).

Getting Around

The No 90 bus runs between Heykel and the new otogar (US$0.50). A taxi is around US$10.

The city bus company is called BOI. You can buy BOI city bus tickets (US$0.50) at kiosks and shops. Bursa dolmuşes with little 'D' plates on top charge US$0.45 or more for a seat. Those marked 'SSK Hastanesi' go to Çekirge. Dolmuş stops are dotted around Heykel – the most useful one is the underground station south of the square.

GELIBOLU (GALLIPOLI) PENINSULA & DARDANELLES

The ramparts either side of the Dardanelles, the strait between the Aegean Sea and the Sea of Marmara, have been strategically important since time immemorial. Today the towns of the Gelibolu (Gallipoli) peninsula are home to a different sort of invasion.

Anzac Day

April 25 is Anzac Day. It's a public holiday in Australia and New Zealand but I had been guilty of shrugging it off as just another holiday. That all changed when I travelled around Turkey. Undoubtedly the highlight was a trip to the battlefields of Gallipoli.

I stood on the beach at Kabatepe where the Anzacs were supposed to have landed. The sea was calm and the land was flat, a perfect place for an amphibious landing. Then I went to the beach where the Anzacs did land, at Anzac Cove several kilometres to the north-east. Steep cliffs confronted the Anzacs here, with Turkish soldiers at the top. Our men didn't stand a chance.

It was an eerie feeling standing at the site where the Anzac soldiers sacrificed their lives for our countries. We visited the trenches, the tunnels and the beautiful memorials built in tribute to our hero soldiers. I was very proud to be an Australian that day.

Turkey's national hero, Atatürk, had a memorial built at Anzac Cove to honour our fallen soldiers. His words left a lump in my throat:

Those heroes that shed their blood and lost their lives...you are now lying in the soil of a friendly country...you the mothers who sent their sons from faraway countries, wipe away your tears; your sons are now lying in our bosom and are in peace. After having lost their lives on this land, they have become our sons as well.

I was not embarrassed by my tears, nor were my tour companions. It is impossible to describe how much I learned that day, how proud I was, and how lucky I feel. April 25 isn't just another day. April 25 is Anzac Day.

Justin Flynn

MICK WELDON

TURKEY

Australians and New Zealanders flock here to see where their ancestors fought during WWI, particularly around April 25, Anzac Day, which commemorates the Allied landings on the peninsula in 1915. Even if this history doesn't interest you, you will almost certainly be moved by the vast cemeteries and memorials that scatter this scenic peninsula, which is now covered with pine forests. It's a hauntingly beautiful place to walk or cycle. The former battlefields are most easily reached from Çanakkale on the eastern side of the Dardanelles, or from Eceabat (Maidos) on the peninsula.

Anzac Battlefields

If you've not got your own transport, bear in mind that walking around the Gallipoli sites involves covering a fair distance (from Kabatepe to Chunuk Bair and back, for example, is 12km). Wear appropriate footwear and take plenty of water.

Make your first stop the **Kabatepe Information Centre and Museum**, around 9km from Eceabat. It's open from 8.30 am to 5 pm daily and entry is US$0.50. The centre sells a booklet that describes a walking tour of the main sites. (Anzac House in Çanakkale also has useful free maps, produced by the Commonwealth War Graves Commission.)

The road uphill to Lone Pine begins 750m west of the information centre, but many people start by heading 3.5km north along the coastal road to **Anzac Cove**, where the ill-fated Allies landed to meet fierce resistance from the Turks under the command of Mustafa Kemal, Turkey's future leader Atatürk. There is a memorial bearing Atatürk's famous eulogy for the Anzac troops on this beach (see the boxed text 'Anzac Day') and there are various cemeteries nearby, including Arıburnu.

About two-thirds of the way up the beach towards Anzac Cove you'll come to a track curling through a valley up to the **Lone Pine Cemetery**, the largest and perhaps most poignant of all the Anzac cemeteries, containing graves and memorials of unknown soldiers or those lost at sea. This area saw the most bitter fighting of the campaign. From here, a sealed road leads 2km uphill to the **Mehmet Çavuş** and the **Nek** cemeteries. It was at the Nek on 7 August 1915 that Australian regiments of the Third Light

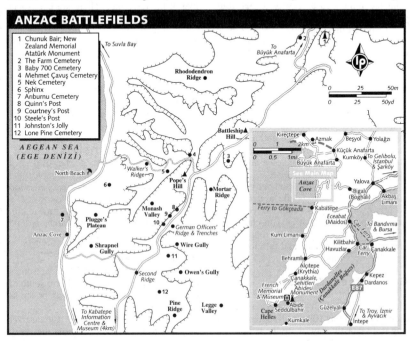

ANZAC BATTLEFIELDS

1 Chunuk Bair; New Zealand Memorial Atatürk Monument
2 The Farm Cemetery
3 Baby 700 Cemetery
4 Mehmet Çavuş Cemetery
5 Nek Cemetery
6 Sphinx
7 Arıburnu Cemetery
8 Quinn's Post
9 Courtney's Post
10 Steele's Post
11 Johnston's Jolly
12 Lone Pine Cemetery

To Suvla Bay

Rhododendron Ridge

AEGEAN SEA
(EGE DENİZİ)

North Beach

Walker's Ridge

Pope's Hill

Monash Valley

Plugge's Plateau

Anzac Cove

Shrapnel Gully

Second Ridge

To Kabatepe Information Centre & Museum (4km)

Mortar Ridge

German Officers' Ridge & Trenches

Wire Gully

Owen's Gully

Pine Ridge

Legge Valley

Battleship Hill

Kireçtepe

Azmak

Beşyol   Yolağzı

Küçük Anafarta

To Büyük Anafarta

Büyük Anafarta

Kumköy   To Gelibolu, İstanbul & Şarköy

See Main Map

Anzac Cove

Yalova

Bigalı (Boghali)

Akbaş Limanı

Ferry to Gökçeada   Kabatepe

Eceabat (Maidos)   To Bandırma & Bursa

Kum Limanı

Kilitbahir Havuzlar   Çanakkale

Behramlı

Alçitepe (Krythia)

French Memorial & Museum

Çanakkale, Şehitleri Abidesi Monument

Abide

Cape Helles   Seddülbahir

Kumkale

Güzelyalı

Kepez   Dardanos

E87

To Troy, İzmir & Ayvacık

Intepe

Horse Brigade vaulted out of their trenches into certain death – doomed but utterly courageous.

Chunuk Bair was the first objective of the Allied landings and is now the site of the New Zealand memorial. The peaceful pine grove there today makes it difficult to image the blasted wasteland of almost a century ago. The many trenches nearby, some no more than a few metres apart, give an idea of how ferocious and deadly the fighting was.

There's a good swimming beach at **Kum Limanı**, 5km south of Kabatepe. It's also possible to **camp** here. Head towards Alçitepe (Krythia) if you want to tour the cemeteries and battle sites of the southern cape, culminating at **Cape Helles**, where the British naval obelisk marks land's end. There are fine views of the straits. If you head around Morto Bay, you'll pass the **French Memorial and Museum** and arrive at the giant stone table that is the **Çanakkale Şehitleri Abidesi**, the memorial to the Turkish soldiers.

Organised Tours

An easy way to tour the spread-out sites (and recommended as a way to get your bearings) is to take a minibus tour. These are organised in Çanakkale by Hassle Free (☎ 286-213 5969, e hasslefree@anzachouse.com) at Anzac House and also sold through Troy Anzac Tours (☎ 286-217 5849) and Down Under Travel Agency (☎ 286-814 2431, e d.under@mailexcite.com) for US$21 per person. Two-day trips offered by Hassle Free out of İstanbul, Selçuk or Kuşadası (US$55), with an overnight stay in Çanakkale and a visit to Troy (Truva), are worth considering if you're travelling along this route and don't want to stop off anywhere else.

Bursts of fierce competition occasionally erupt among the Çanakkale and Eceabat hostels over Gallipoli tours, so you may find cheaper deals on offer. But check exactly what's included in any tour before handing over your cash, and talk to fellow travellers about their experiences.

Getting There & Away

If you're staying in Çanakkale, take the regular ferry (US$0.50, 30 minutes) to Eceabat, then take a dolmuş 10km to Kabatepe. Cycling is a fantastic way to see the peninsula;

bicycles and motorbikes can be hired from Varol Bisiklet (☎ 286-213 1737) at Tekke Sokak 37 in Çanakkale.

ÇANAKKALE

☎ 286 • pop 60,000

Çanakkale, a hub for transport to Troy (Truva) and across the Dardanelles to Gelibolu (Gallipoli), is a pleasant and lively seaside base. It was here, according to Greek legend, that Leander swam what was then called the Hellespont to his lover Hero, and here too that Lord Byron did his romantic bit and duplicated the feat. The defence of the strait during WWI led to a Turkish victory over the French and British navies on 18 March 1915, now a big local holiday. Anzac Day (25 April) brings a 10,000-strong influx of Aussies and Kiwis.

Orientation & Information

The restored Ottoman clock tower Saat Kulesi acts as the town's central landmark. The otogar is around 1km east of the clock tower. The nearby helpful tourist office (☎ 217 1187), all the cheap hotels and a range of good cafes are all within a block or two of the ferry pier. There are banks and ATMs along Cumhuriyet Bulvarı. Internet cafes around town include Efe Cafe and Millennium Internet, and there's one terminal at Anzac House and one at Yellow Rose Pension.

Things to See & Do

Çimenlik Kale, an Ottoman castle built by Mehmet the Conqueror in 1452, is south of the ferry docks near the river (entry US$1.50). In the surrounding park are the interesting **Askeri Müzesi** (Military Museum) and **Deniz Müzesi** (Naval Museum). Just over 2km south-east of the ferry pier, the **Arkeoloj Müzesi** (Archaeological Museum) has artefacts from Troy and Assos and is worth a quick look if you've got time to kill.

The **Tarihi Yalı Hamamı** charges around US$7 for a scrub and massage.

Places to Stay

Camping for around US$2 per person is possible at Güzelyalı Beach, 15km south of town, off the road to Troy (Truva), or across the Dardanelles in Eceabat.

Anzac House (☎ 213 5969, Cumhuriyet Meydanı 61) is geared to handle the many

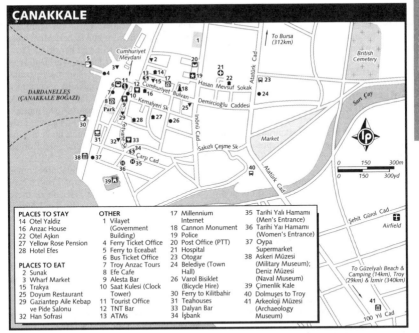

ÇANAKKALE

PLACES TO STAY	OTHER	17 Millennium	35 Tarihi Yalı Hamamı
14 Otel Yaldiz	1 Vilayet	Internet	(Men's Entrance)
16 Anzac House	(Government	18 Cannon Monument	36 Tarihi Yaı Hamamı
22 Otel Aşkın	Building)	19 Police	(Women's Entrance)
27 Yellow Rose Pension	4 Ferry Ticket Office	20 Post Office (PTT)	37 Oypa
28 Hotel Efes	5 Ferry to Eceabat	21 Hospital	Supermarket
	6 Bus Ticket Office	23 Otogar	38 Askeri Müzesi
PLACES TO EAT	7 Troy Anzac Tours	24 Belediye (Town	(Military Museum);
2 Sunak	8 Efe Cafe	Hall)	Deniz Müzesi
3 Wharf Market	9 Alesta Bar	26 Varol Bisiklet	(Naval Museum)
15 Trakya	10 Saat Kulesi (Clock	(Bicycle Hire)	39 Çimenlik Kale
25 Doyum Restaurant	Tower)	30 Ferry to Kilitbahir	40 Dolmuşes to Troy
29 Gaziantep Aile Kebap	11 Tourist Office	31 Teahouses	41 Arkeoloji Müzesi
ve Pide Salonu	12 TNT Bar	33 Dalyan Bar	(Archaeology
32 Han Sofrasi	13 ATMs	34 İşbank	Museum)

visiting Aussies and Kiwis and it provides good tours of the peninsula. Cramped but clean singles are US$9 with shared bathroom; doubles are more roomy and few have bathrooms. The licensed restaurant is good value, and the travel agency is well run. This place regularly screens the excellent Peter Weir film *Gallipoli* (starring a young Mel Gibson) and a crackly documentary, *The Fatal Shore*.

Hotel Efes (☎ 217 3256, Aralık Sokak 5) is a fine option, with light, modern single/doubles, all with bathrooms, for US$8/10. It has a quiet courtyard garden and a friendly owner. The owner's brother runs the colourfully decorated *Yellow Rose Pension* (☎/fax 217 3343, Yeni Sokak 5), which we get mixed reports on. It has plenty of facilities but the dorm (US$3 a bed) would get pretty stuffy in summer. Singles/doubles are US$6/10.

Otel Aşkın (☎/fax 217 4956, Hasan Mevsuf Sokak 53), near the otogar, charges US$12/24 for single/doubles with shower and TV. A recommended mid-range option is *Otel Yaldiz* (☎ 217 1793, fax 212 6704, Kızılay Sokak 20), which has good rooms in

two buildings opposite each other, for US$12/20 including breakfast.

Places to Eat

The *Gaziantep Aile Kebap ve Pide Salonu* behind the clock tower serves good cheap pide and more substantial kebaps.

Sunak has a comfy coffee-shop atmosphere and does a fine range of good-value dishes; a kebap, *pilav* (rice dish) and drink here shouldn't set you back more than US$3.

Trakya on the main square specialises in soups and a range of ready cooked meals with plenty of options for vegetarians.

The *Doyum Restaurant* (Demircioğlu Caddesi) serves fantastic Turkish food — the İskender kebap for US$2.50 and the kaşarlı pide (cheese pide) for US$1.75 are excellent.

Han Sofrasi (Fetvane Sokak) is a charming old caravanserai draped with wisteria, turned into a restaurant and bar with alfresco tables covered with check cloths. There's also a craft shop here.

Before eating at the fancier waterfront fish restaurants, check the prices. A sardine sandwich from the stalls in the *wharf market* will be much cheaper (about US$0.70) than

TURKEY

some of the small dishes from more upmarket places.

Self-caterers should check out the ramshackle wharf market near the ferry ticket office, and the *Oypa supermarket* next to the Askeri Müzesi.

Entertainment

Being a student town, as well as a backpacker haven, Çanakkale is not short of a bar or two. The licensed restaurant in *Anzac House* is a popular meeting spot. Around the corner is the spacious *TNT Bar*, which often has live music on weekends; it charges US$1.75 for a large beer. Just south of the clock tower is the cramped but popular *Alesta Bar*, a good place to meet locals.

Along Fetvane Sokak you could try *Dalyan Bar*, but far more pleasant is *Han Sofrasi* (see Places to Eat earlier).

The *teahouses* down towards the Askeri Müzesi are great places to relax on a sunny afternoon – sit back and watch the sea traffic plying the Dardanelles.

There's a *cinema* in the shopping complex by the cannon on Cumhuriyet Bulvarı.

Getting There & Away

From the otogar there are several buses daily to Ankara (US$15, 10 hours), Bursa (US$8, five hours), İstanbul (US$13, six hours), İzmir (US$10, six hours) and Ayvalık (US$8, three hours).

ECEABAT
☎ 286

Much quieter than Çanakkale across the strait, Eceabat is another possible base for visits to the Gelibolu (Gallipoli) peninsula.

Accommodationwise, *Savos Hotel & TJ Hostel* (☎ 814 1065, fax 814 1900, Cumhuriyet Caddesi 5) is a large and somewhat gloomy place (especially out of season), but does have singles for US$5. It's part of the No 1 network of hostels and pensions. A bit more upmarket is *Eceabat Hotel* (☎/fax 814 2458, İskele Meydanı), facing the ferry dock, with clean double rooms for US$15, some with sea views, balconies and TV.

The *Vegemite Bar*, around 1km south of the ferry dock, has a happy hour between 8 and 9 pm, and cooks a decent burger. You could also try the *Boomerang Bar* around 500m north of the Savos Hotel & TJ Hostel along Cumhuriyet Caddesi.

TROY (TRUVA)

According to Homer, Paris abducted the beautiful Helen from her father, Menelaus, king of Sparta, and whisked her off to Troy, thus precipitating the Trojan War. But Troy was a thriving city long before the Spartans supposedly beat the Trojans by means of a wooden horse secretly filled with soldiers. Troy I goes back to the Bronze Age. Homer's Troy is thought to be Troy VI by some, Troy VII by others. Most of the ruins, including the prominent Temple of Athena, are Roman ones from Troy IX (maybe Troy VIII).

Confused? A guide or guidebook comes in really handy at the ruins of Troy, 32km south-west of Çanakkale. That said, there are excellent interpretative signs in English around the site, which is compact and commands a sweeping view of the Dardanelles. If nothing else grabs your imagination, then the giant replica wooden horse beside the entrance will; when we visited it wasn't possible to climb inside. The site is open from 8 am to 5 pm daily (7 pm in summer) and admission costs US$3.

In Tevfikiye, the farming village 1km before the site, there are a few small *pensions* charging US$10 to US$14 a double. There's also a restaurant by the site entrance but, inevitably, it's pricey.

The guided tours of Troy run from Çanakkale by Hassle Free (☎ 286-213 5969, e hasslefree@anzachouse.com) are worth considering; they are pricey (US$14) but well organised.

Frequent dolmuşes leave Çanakkale for Troy (US$2, 30 minutes). From the Çanakkale ferry pier, walk straight inland to Atatürk Caddesi and turn right at the second traffic lights towards Troy (the southern road); the dolmuş station is at the bridge.

North Aegean Coast

The idyllic fishing villages, majestic ruins and picturesque olive groves of the north Aegean coast are enough to sidetrack many an overland traveller. You could do far worse than to hole up at the coastal resort of Ayvalık for a day or two, close to the impressive ruins at Bergama (Pergamum). The metropolis of İzmir, en route to Selçuk, can easily be avoided, but does offer the usual big-city facilities if you need them.

If you really do have time on your hands, you could consider stopping off at charming Behramkale (Assos) for a day or two, or hopping over to the Turkish islands of Gökçeada and Bozcaada – both nowhere near as busy in summer as their neighbouring Greek counterparts.

AYVALIK
☎ 266 • pop 30,000

This compact, pleasant fishing port and beach resort is the departure point for ferries to Lesbos (Midilli in Turkish). It's worth pausing here for the chance to stay in one of coastal Turkey's most charming pensions (see Places to Stay). You could also use Ayvalık as a base for visiting Bergama (Pergamum) before continuing south.

İnönü Caddesi, which becomes Atatürk Caddesi when it hits the seafront, is the town's main artery. The tourist office (☎/fax 312 2122) is 1km south of the town centre, opposite the marina. There's an Internet cafe in the Nazar Pasaji arcade on İnönü Caddesi, not far from the main post office.

Things to See & Do
Back from the waterfront, lose yourself in the picturesque cobbled streets lined with decaying but still handsome Ottoman buildings and dotted with Greek Orthodox churches.

Alibey Adası (also known as Cunda) is an island across the bay, with open-air restaurants and a host of hideous condos. It's linked to the mainland by ferries (US$0.40/$0.80 one way/return) and a causeway; take the red 'Ayvalık Belediyesi' bus north from İskele Meydanı, opposite the tour boat berth.

Some 6km south of Ayvalık is the 12km **Sarımsaklı Plaj** (*plaj* means beach), also called Plajlar. To get there take a blue 'Sarımsaklı Belediyesi' bus from İskele Meydanı.

It only takes around an hour to hike to the top of **Şeytan Sofrası** (Devil's Dinner Table), a hilltop south of town. In summer you'll be able to catch a dolmuş.

Places to Stay
Taksiyarhis Pansiyon (☎ 312 1494, Maraşal Çakmak Caddesi 71) is a real gem – it gets our vote for the prettiest pension in Turkey. Characterful rooms in this renovated

Ottoman house cost a bargain US$9 per person (less off season). There are lovely verandas, the breakfasts are delicious and the kitchen is available for self-caterers.

Some 400m south of the centre is the *Turistik Çiçek Pansiyon (☎ 312 1201)*, which has clean, quiet singles/doubles with shower for US$11/14.

The *Hotel Kaptan (☎ 312 8834, Balıkhane Sokak 2)* is a popular mid-range option. All the spacious, light rooms have private bathroom and some have balconies with sea views. It's good value with rooms at US$17/30 including breakfast.

Places to Eat
Off Atatürk Bulvarı near the market are several good, cheap places such as the *Ayvalık* and the *Anadolu Döner ve Pide Salonu*. The nameless places in the market, east of the main road, are more atmospheric.

You'll get a warm welcome at *Hüsnünün Yeri (Tenekeciler Sokaği)* and even though some of the seafood meze on offer looks a bit dodgy, it's all good stuff and fairly inexpensive. This place serves beer, too.

The *Öz Canlı Balık* and *Kardesler* restaurants on the waterfront are pricier, but good for seafood. Alternatively you could make the trip over to the fish restaurants of Cunda.

Clustered near the Atatürk statue are a few other cheap options, including the *Cenk Büfe* and *Sofra Pizza*. The *Sakarija Klub* near İşbank is a great place for coffee, cake and views. The *Gözde Büfe*, nearby, has excellent köfte for US$3.50.

Ayvalık Gücü 3 and *Barbaros* are two harbourside teahouses at which you can while away an hour or so watching the boats come and go.

Getting There & Away
Bus The otogar is 1.5km north of the town centre.There are plenty of buses passing through Ayvalık, but take note that they will probably drop you off on Atatürk Bulvarı rather than pay the otogar fee. Some buses will drop you out on the highway, from where there are infrequent service buses into town; you're often better off hitching.

Bergama is 75km south-east; catch the bus (US$2, 45 minutes) from the stop on the harbour side of the Atatürk statue.

Boat In high season there are tourist boats between Ayvalık and Behramkale.

For Lesbos (Midilli), boats leave Ayvalık at 9 am each morning, arriving in Lesbos at 11 am; the return departure from Lesbos is at 4 pm, arriving in Ayvalık at 6 pm. The fare isn't cheap: US$50 one way, or US$65 same-day return. The boats operate daily from late May to September.

BERGAMA (PERGAMUM)
☎ 232 • pop 50,000

From the 3rd century BC to the 1st century AD, Bergama (Pergamum) was a powerful, wealthy kingdom, one of the most cultured in the Middle East. Some highly impressive ruins from Bergama's classical age remain, despite prize lots having been carted off to Berlin in the late 19th century, although you'll have to travel out of the modern, unimpressive city centre to find them.

The friendly tourist office (☎ 631 2851) on Cumhuriyet Meydanı, next to the Arkeoloji Müzesi in the town centre, will provide you with all the information you need. It's open from 8.30 am to 5.30 pm daily.

Things to See
The dramatically sited **acropolis** should not be missed. It is on a hill-top site 6km by twisting road from the city centre. If you are walking, there is a short cut up through the ruins; it is a bit of a slog which enters the ruins proper at the 10,000-seat theatre, among the steepest and narrowest in the classical world. Below the stage are the remains of the Temple of Dionysus. From the back row of the theatre a concealed passageway takes you up to the temples of Athena and Trajan. The latter features reconstructed marble columns that suggest how grand this place once was. The site is open from 9 am to 5 pm daily (to 7 pm in summer); admission is US$2.

After the acropolis, Bergama's other major ruin, the **Asclepion** (Medical School), 2km west of the town centre, is a bit of a letdown, even though its library once rivalled that of Alexandria in Egypt. A Roman bazaar street leads up to the main complex, where you can still make out bas-reliefs of the snake and staff of Asclepius, god of medicine (now the symbol of modern medicine). The Asclepion is open from 8.30 am to 5.30 pm daily (until 7 pm in summer); entry costs US$2.

At the foot of the acropolis is the 2nd-century **Red Basilica** (Kızıl Avlu, Red Courtyard). This large red-brick ruin was originally built as a temple to Serapis, a Graeco-Roman god worshipped in Egypt; it was later converted to a Christian basilica by the Byzantines, and now holds a small mosque. It's open from 8.30 am to 5.30 pm daily and entry is US$2.

The excellent **Arkeoloji Müzesi** (Archaeology & Ethnography Museum) in the city centre is where you can see a model of the amazing Altar of Zeus. The original was once part of the acropolis and is now in a Berlin museum. The museum is open from 8.30 am to 5.30 pm daily and entry is US$2.

Taxis waiting here charge US$5 one way to the acropolis, or US$7 if they wait and bring you back down. A taxi tour of the acropolis, the Asclepion and museum costs around US$20.

Places to Stay
Bergama Camping (☎ 633 3902) charges US$2.50 per person and is 2km outside of town on the way to the coast.

The friendly *Böblingen Pension* (☎ 633 2153, Asklepion Caddesi 2) is a family-run place on the road to the Asclepion that's well set up for travellers. Singles/doubles cost US$7/15 (US$9/18 with private bathroom), including breakfast. There's also a terrace roof bar.

The *Pergamon Pension* (☎ 632 3492, Bankalar Caddesi 5) near the Çarşı Hamamı is in a 250-year-old Greek house and has a range of slowly decaying rooms for US$5 to US$10.

The *Sayın Pension* (☎ 633 2405, İzmir Caddesi 12), 100m south-west of the otogar, is a better choice in the centre of town; it's friendly, it has a restaurant and the clean rooms are good value at US$5/10.

At the northern end of town, handy for the acropolis, are two good pensions. The *Nike* (☎ 633 3901) is across and uphill from the old stone bridge. This is an atmospheric place and the rooms (with adjoining courtyard) are worth the US$12 for doubles.

The admirable *Athena* (☎ 633 3420, İmam Çıkmazı 5), south of the stone bridge and reasonably well signposted, is in an old Ottoman house; rooms with shared bathroom are US$5 per person and breakfast is US$2. Its motto: 'We are not the best but trying to get there'.

Places to Eat

Meydan Restaurant is about 150m south-west of the Red Basilica on the main street by the square; it charges US$5 or US$6 for a three-course meal out on the shaded terraces.

The *Pergamon Pension* serves good food, and the eggplant and meatballs are recommended (US$2). The *Sarmaşık Lokantası* is simpler and has no outdoor seating, but is much cheaper.

The *Gözde Yemek ve Kebap Salonu* next to the Çarşı Hamamı is also good.

Opposite the museum are three restaurants worth checking out – *Zeus*, *Dostlar* and *Zikkim*. Near the otogar are the tempting *pastanes* (pastry shops) *Manolya* and *Simge*, serving all types of baked goods including baklava.

If you crave a baked potato, the *cafe* next to the Sayın Pension serves them with a choice of toppings for US$1.50 to US$2.

Getting There & Away

The otogar is around 300m south of the centre, just off İzmir Caddesi.

Buses shuttle between Bergama and İzmir every 30 minutes in summer (US$3.50, two hours). Several buses go to Ayvalık daily (US$2). If nothing is available, try hitching the 7km to the highway and catching a passing bus there.

İZMİR

☎ 232 • pop 2.5 million

With over two million inhabitants, İzmir, a sprawling concrete metropolis choked with traffic and spewing its smelly pollution out into the bay, is Turkey's third-largest city and not a place to linger. In fact, it's quite easy to roll into the enormous out-of-town otogar and roll straight out again, onwards to Selçuk for the ruins at Ephesus, or any other major destination.

However, this city, 100km south of Bergama, is not entirely without redeeming features. There's a cosmopolitan atmosphere to parts of İzmir, with correspondingly good shopping, dining and nightlife. There's an airport with international flights, and the car ferry from Venice docks here. It's also convenient to visit by train from Selçuk (a day trip is easy), since the terminus is right in the city centre.

Once named Smyrna, İzmir was the birthplace of Homer (about 800 BC). It was continually taken and retaken by opposing forces over the years and it lay in ruins until Alexander the Great rebuilt it. Disaster struck again in 1923 when, in the wholesale mayhem that accompanied the defeat of the Greek army, three-quarters of the city was burned to the ground. Out of these ashes has sprung a much more modern city than most others in Turkey.

Orientation & Information

Central İzmir is a web of *meydan* (plazas) linked by streets that aren't at right angles to each other. Instead of having names, the back streets have numbers. You'd go mad without a map (and you'll probably go mad with one).

The main otogar is 13km east of the city centre, while there are two central train stations – Basmane and Alasancak. Budget hotels can be found near the Basmane train station.

To the south-west, Anafartalar Caddesi twists and turns through the venerable bazaar to the waterfront at Konak, the commercial and political centre. Atatürk Caddesi, also called Birinci Kordon, runs north-east from Konak along the waterfront to the ritzy area of Alsancak. Cumhuriyet Meydanı, midway along Atatürk Caddesi, is the square around which you'll find the main post office, luxury hotels, airline offices, and the main tourist office (☎ 489 9278), at Gaziosmanpaşa 1, which is open from 8.30 am to 5 pm daily. There's also a tourist office at the Adnan Menderes Airport, 25km south of the city centre.

To glide into İzmir on the ferry is to see the city at its best.

Things to See & Do

There's little of architectural interest in the sprawling **bazaar**, but it's an atmospheric area to explore, guaranteed to throw up a few surprises. History buffs should check out the 2nd-century Roman **agora**, then walk up to the hill-top **Kadifekale** fortress, preferably to catch the sunset.

On the waterfront at Konak check out the ornate **Saat Kulesi**, a turn-of-the-century clock tower that's one of the city's favourite meeting places, and the pretty tiled **Konak Camii**. South of here you'll find the Atatürk Cultural Centre, the State Opera and Ballet Theatre and the **archaeology** and **ethnographic museums**, in Bahri Baba Park, on

TURKEY

İZMİR

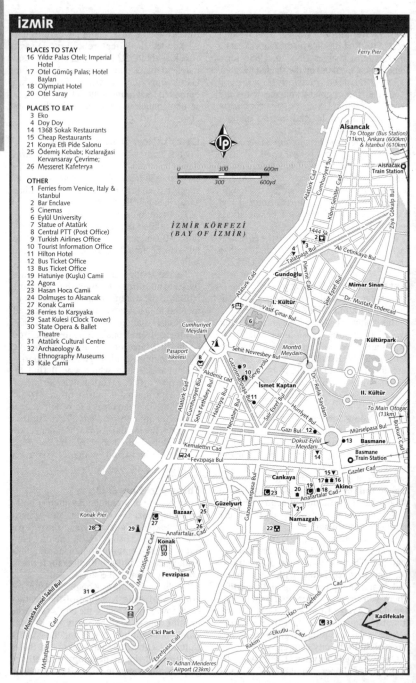

PLACES TO STAY
16 Yıldız Palas Oteli; Imperial Hotel
17 Otel Gümüş Palas; Hotel Baylan
18 Olympiat Hotel
20 Otel Saray

PLACES TO EAT
3 Eko
4 Doy Doy
14 1368 Sokak Restaurants
15 Cheap Restaurants
21 Konya Etli Pide Salonu
25 Ödemiş Kebabı; Kızlarağası Kervansaray Çevrime;
26 Messeret Kafeterya

OTHER
1 Ferries from Venice, Italy & Istanbul
2 Bar Enclave
5 Cinemas
6 Eylül University
7 Statue of Atatürk
8 Central PTT (Post Office)
9 Turkish Airlines Office
10 Tourist Information Office
11 Hilton Hotel
12 Bus Ticket Office
13 Bus Ticket Office
19 Hatuniye (Kuşlu) Camii
22 Agora
23 Hasan Hoca Camii
24 Dolmuşes to Alsancak
27 Konak Camii
28 Ferries to Karşıyaka
29 Saat Kulesi (Clock Tower)
30 State Opera & Ballet Theatre
31 Atatürk Cultural Centre
32 Archaeology & Ethnography Museums
33 Kale Camii

İzmir to Antalya

Day 1:	İzmir to Selçuk	60km	Day 5:	Fethiye to Kaş	90km
Day 2:	Selçuk to Aydın	55km	Day 6:	Kaş to Olimpos	90km
Day 3:	Aydın to Muğla	90km	Day 7:	Olimpos to Antalya	70km
Day 4:	Muğla to Fethiye	70km			

İzmir to Selçuk offers a good run on a decent highway, although it reaches 780m at its highest point. Your bike will be handy for getting to Ephesus or for a run to Pamucak Beach or Kuşadası. Also, if you take the meandering coastal route to Bodrum, you can easily visit the ancient sites of Priene, Miletus and Didyma.

Staying inland, the cycle to Aydın is hard work with several tough climbs. The road to Muğla is also up and down and there is more hard work to Köyceğiz or Dalyan – a good spot to relax. Again, a bike is useful for day trips. From here to Fethiye is a good day's ride. It's harder between here and Antalya to find a good spot for rough camping, because of the terrain. The cycle over to Ölüdeniz is enjoyable, but you have to drop the gears to get back out.

Fethiye to Kaş starts with a good, hard climb but there are great views. The big problem is the never-ending succession of buses, so be careful. In Kaş, carry your bike down to the beach and camp there. There is another tough climb just out of Demre (Kale). Keep your eyes peeled for the turn-off to Olimpos and note the road is unsealed in many spots; yep, it's a tough climb back out. From the main road it's undulating all the way to Antalya.

Etienne Le Roux & Simon Richmond

---

the way to Kadifekale. They're open from 9 am to noon and 1 to 5 pm daily except Monday; admission to each is US$3.50.

If you fancy a quick boat trip, catch a ferry (US$1) from Konak across to **Karşıyaka** on the other side of the bay.

Places to Stay

There are plenty of cheap hotels (many quiet unsavoury) south of Fevzipaşa Bulvarı in the region known as Akıncı (or Yenigün).

The best budget option is *Otel Saray* (☎ 483 6946, Anafartalar Caddesi 635), near the Hatuniye (Kuşlu) Camii. It's been popular with travellers for years. Get a spotless room on the upper floor (it's quieter there) for US$5 per person for a room with sink.

Closer to Basmane train station, *Yıldız Palas Oteli* (☎ 425 1518, 1296 Sokak 50) and *Otel Gümüş Palas* (1299 Sokak) around the corner are both pretty cruddy, but acceptable if you can only scrape up US$6 or less per person. The *Imperial Hotel* (☎ 425 6883, 1296 Sokak 54) is one of the slightly better choices in this part of town, but overcharges at US$20/30 for singles/doubles.

The budget *Olympiat* (☎ 425 1269, 945 Sokak 2) has basic rooms (around US$12) but charges extra for hot showers.

A good mid-range choice is *Hotel Baylan* (☎ 483 1426, 1299 Sokak 8) where the housekeeping standards are high. Single/doubles with bathroom and TV are US$35/50 including breakfast.

Places to Eat

Restaurants Immediately opposite Basmane train station, there are heaps of places offering quick, cheap meals; the touts will find you before you get a whiff of the cooking (meatballs cost about US$1.30). The restaurants on 1368 and 1369 Sokaks, just north of Fevzipaşa Bulvarı, are much more pleasant and some serve alcohol. The *Dört Mevsim Et Lokantası* (1369 Sokak 51/A) specialises in meat. It will fill you up for about US$5 or US$6, and also serves alcohol.

On Anafartalar Caddesi, near the Otel Saray, try the *Konya Etli Pide Salonu* for good Turkish pizza. Dive into the bazaar to locate *Messeret Kafeterya*, İzmir's answer to a food court, where you can get Western pizza and burgers for around US$1. More atmospheric are the pretty kebap restaurants, including *Çevrime* and *Ödemiş Kebabı* around the Kızlarağası Kervansaray.

The upmarket restaurants are along Atatürk Caddesi by the sea (although at the time of research, building work on the promenade made outdoor dining here less than appealing). A couple of popular haunts a block inland in the Gundoğdu area are *Eko* and *Doy Doy*, both good for beers and snacks too.

Self-Catering Mussels are worth trying when they're in season (avoid them from late May to early September). Within spitting distance of the bazaar and Anafartalar Caddesi are several shops where you can get all you need to fashion yourself a hearty meal.

Entertainment
For nightlife, head to Alsancak where there are lots of chic cafes and restaurants and a host of *clubs* featuring good music; you'll find plenty of options along the western pedestrianised portion of Ali Çetinkaya Bulvarı, particularly along 1444 Sokak.

For movies, try the *cinemas* on Cumhuriyet Bulvarı opposite Eylül University. Music lovers can check out what's happening at the *Atatürk Cultural Centre*, where the local symphony orchestra plays regularly, and at the Art Deco *State Opera and Ballet Theatre*, on Milli Kütüphane Caddesi.

Getting There & Away
Air Turkish Airlines (☎ 484 1220), Gaziosmanpaşa Bulvarı 1/F, in the Büyük Efes Oteli, has flights to İstanbul and Ankara, with connections to other points.

Bus Many bus companies have ticket offices around Dokuz Eylül Meydanı, just north of Basmane train station, west along Gazi Bulvarı and near the tourist information centre on Gaziosmanpaşa Bulvarı. Some provide a free *şehiriçi servis* (minibus shuttle service) to the otogar (13km east of the city centre). There are plenty of services heading to İstanbul (US$15 to US$20, eight hours), Selçuk (US$2 to US$3, one hour, 75km) and Ankara (US$10, eight hours).

Train Most intercity trains arrive at Basmane train station (☎ 484 8638), including services from Selçuk (US$1, 1¾ hours) and Ankara (US$5 to US$7, 14 hours). For İstanbul, take the Marmara Ekspresi to Bandırma, then a ferry (US$9 for train and ferry).

Boat Car ferry services to and from İstanbul and Venice depart from the pier in Alsancak.

Getting Around
To/From the Airport An airport bus (US$3, 30 minutes) departs from the Turkish Airlines office at the Büyük Efes Oteli several times daily for Adnan Menderes Airport (25km). Trains (US$0.50) run hourly from Alsancak train station to the airport, and some Denizli-bound trains from Basmane also stop at the airport. From Montrö Meydanı, 700m north of Basmane, south-bound 'Adnan Menderes Belediyesi' buses go near the airport during the day for about US$1. A taxi to the airport costs about US$20.

Bus & Dolmuş From the new otogar you should be able to get a service bus to Basmane train station. Dolmuşes are the best way to get around the city.

Ephesus Region & South Aegean Coast

Some people come to Turkey just to see the splendid Roman ruins at Ephesus, considered one of the best preserved ancient cities in this part of Asia. Many are shocked by the crowds. You are now entering tourist territory, home to the 'packagee' hoping to snap up Turkey in a week or day-tripping from a cruise ship anchored off Kuşadası.

SELÇUK
☎ 232
Almost everybody comes to Selçuk, 80km south of İzmir, on their way to Ephesus, but the town itself has some interesting sights, not least those that attract legions of Christian pilgrims. The town also has some of the best cheap accommodation in Turkey and is quiet at night when the tour buses have returned to the coastal resorts. Swimming is possible at the nearby Pamucak Beach, and you can also use Selçuk as a base from which to visit the Pamukkale hot springs and the ruins of Hierapolis.

Orientation & Information
Selçuk is relatively small, and finding your way around is easy. On the east side of the central highway (Atatürk Caddesi) are restaurants, some pensions and hotels, and

TURKEY

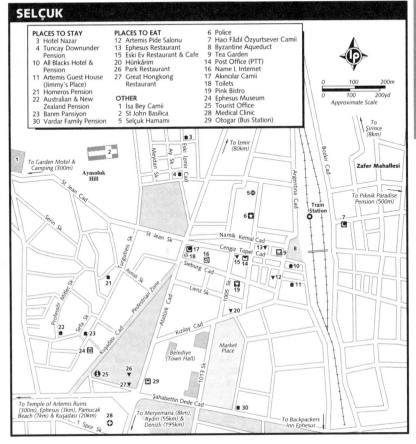

SELÇUK

PLACES TO STAY
3 Hotel Nazar
4 Tuncay Downunder Pension
10 All Blacks Hotel & Pension
11 Artemis Guest House (Jimmy's Place)
21 Homeros Pension
22 Australian & New Zealand Pension
23 Barım Pansiyon
30 Vardar Family Pension

PLACES TO EAT
12 Artemis Pide Salonu
13 Ephesus Restaurant
15 Eski Ev Restaurant & Cafe
20 Hünkârim
26 Park Restaurant
27 Great Hongkong Restaurant

OTHER
1 İsa Bey Camii
2 St John Basilica
5 Selçuk Hamamı

6 Police
7 Hacı Fâdıl Özyurtsever Camii
8 Byzantine Aqueduct
9 Tea Garden
14 Post Office (PTT)
16 Name L Internet
17 Akıncılar Camii
18 Toilets
19 Pink Bistro
24 Ephesus Museum
25 Tourist Office
28 Medical Clinic
29 Otogar (Bus Station)

the train station; on the west side behind the Ephesus Museum are a number of pensions.

The tourist office (☎ 892 6328) on the west side of Atatürk Caddesi, opposite the Ephesus Museum, can provide a handy map of the town and information on the area.

Internet access is available at, among other places, the Australian & New Zealand Pension, Artemis Guest House, the Pink Bistro, and Name L Internet on Sieburg Caddesi, which has fast connections.

Things to See & Do

The renowned archaeological site of Ephesus (described later in this chapter) is 3km down the road, but the town of Selçuk has the excellent **Ephesus Museum**. Highlights of this striking collection include the small, exquis-

ite figure of the boy on the dolphin, the several marble statues of Cybele (also known as Artemis) with rows of egg-like breasts representing fertility, and several effigies of Priapus, the phallic god (one was found near the supposed brothel in Ephesus). The museum is open from 8.30 am to noon and 1 to 5.30 pm daily; admission is US$3.50.

On Selçuk's Ayasoluk hill there are a few important sites. The **St John Basilica** was erected by Justinian and his wife Theodora in the 6th century AD. It is believed that St John came to Ephesus near the end of his life and wrote his gospel here. The supposed site of St John's grave, represented by a large flat marble slab, is often covered in flowers. The basilica is open from 8 am to 5.30 pm daily (later in summer); admission is US$2.

TURKEY

At the foot of Ayasoluk hill is the impressive **İsa Bey Camii** (1307), built by the Emir of Aydın in a transitional style somewhere between post-Seljuk and pre-Ottoman.

The foundations of the **Temple of Artemis**, between Ephesus and Selçuk, are all that is left of one of the seven wonders of the ancient world. A single column has been re-erected. To get an idea of what the temple once looked like, visit Didyma (on the coast south towards Bodrum), where the temple is thought to be similar.

Another spot on the pilgrimage itinerary is **Meryemana**, near the summit of Bülbül Dağı and about 8km south-west of Selçuk. A German nun, Catherine Emmerich (1774–1824), had a vision of the stone house in which she believed the Virgin Mary lived towards the end of her life. The nun had never left Germany, so in the late 19th century, when searchers found a house matching Emmerich's description near Selçuk, her vision became all the more intriguing. In 1967 the Pope visited and declared the vision authentic. You'll see rags attached to tree branches by Muslims – Mary is an Islamic as well as a Christian saint. The site is open from 9 am to 5 pm daily; admission costs US$4. A taxi from Selçuk to Meryemana should cost no more than US$27, including waiting time; consider sharing the trip with a group of fellow travellers.

Pamucak Beach, 7km from Selçuk, is the best beach option in the area, although it has suffered from pollution in recent years. Turks favour it on summer weekends but at other times it is relatively deserted (especially in comparison to beaches around Kuşadası).

You can escape the crowds of the coast by heading inland to a number of **hill villages**. One of the prettiest, with cobbled streets and Byzantine churches and monasteries, is **Şirince**, 8km from Selçuk. It's frequented by tour groups during the day but neglected at night. It has a couple of pensions and several restaurants.

Places to Stay

The number of Anzac-sounding names of pensions here attests to the volume of Aussies and Kiwis who pass through. Don't let that put you off. Also be aware that if you stay at a pension attached to a carpet shop you're likely to receive a sales pitch.

Garden Motel & Camping (☎ 892 2489) is west of Ayasoluk hill, the hill that bears St John Basilica; walk past the basilica, down the hill, then turn right at the İsa Bey Camii. Quiet tent and caravan sites among fruit orchards cost US$4 per person.

Dereli Camping (☎ 893 1206) near Pamucak Beach, 7km from Selçuk, charges US$4 per person for a pitch.

There are many pensions up the hill behind the Ephesus Museum, costing about US$7 to US$12 per room. One of the nicest is *Homeros Pension* (☎ 892 3995, fax 892 8393, e homerospension@yahoo.com, Asmalı Sokak 17) which has friendly owners, quirky decor and a carpeted rooftop terrace bar. Rooms start at US$5 per person and there's a more upmarket section across the road for US$7 per person. The owners can lend you a bike for getting around.

Barım Pansiyon (☎ 892 6923, Turgutreis Sokak 34) has a lovely vine-covered courtyard and neat singles/doubles for US$5/10.

The *Australian & New Zealand Pension* (☎ 892 6050, fax 892 1594, e oznzpension@superonline.com, 1064 Sokak 12) is well organised, family run, and a real backpacker scene. Singles cost US$6 and a comfy double with private bathroom is US$11; there is an excellent rooftop lounge, bar and restaurant. It also offers an all-in special that includes bed, breakfast, dinner and all the tea you can drink for US$10 per person.

Just west of the train station you'll find several good options. A current favourite, and part of the No 1 network of pensions and hostels, is *Artemis Guest House* (☎ 892 6191, e jimmy@egenet.com.tr, 1012 Sokak 2), also known as Jimmy's Place. It offers the world and is actually not a bad place. The rooms are simple but clean and tidy and the hostel provides towels. Tim Tams, Vegemite and Milo are provided for those homesick for down under, and good-quality meals (about US$5) for other nationalities. The owners also run the simple, but appealing, *Tuncay Downunder Pension* (☎ 892 6260, 2015 Sokak 1), which is all dorm beds for US$6 set around a whitewashed courtyard.

Around the corner from Jimmy's, the *All Blacks Hotel & Pension* (☎ 892 3657, e abnomads@egenet.com.tr, 1011 Sokak 1) is a tidy place with rooms from US$9 to US$14 and a rooftop bar.

Also worth considering is *Vadar Family Pension (☎ 892 4967, fax 892 0099, Şahabettin Dede Caddesi 7)*, which has no-frills rooms all with bathroom and a warm welcome for US$4 per person.

The spacious and quiet *Backpackers Inn Ephesus (☎ 892 3736, fax 892 6589, Kobuleti Caddesi 40)* is south-east of the town centre. Dorms are US$5; singles/doubles with bathroom are US$10/16.

Piknik Paradise Pansiyon (☎ 892 2129, Bademlik Caddesi 33) is certainly worth the effort of climbing the hill east of the train station. The views from the rustic rooms (US$10 per person) are smashing and it's well away from the tourist crowds.

A fine mid-range option is the friendly and comfortable *Hotel Nazar (☎ 892 2222, fax 892 0016, ℮ nazarhotel@yahoo.com, Eski İzmir Caddesi 14)*, which has good singles/doubles with private bathroom (some with balconies) for US$9/18. There's a fine rooftop bar and restaurant, and bike rental for US$2.50 per day.

Places to Eat

Most of the bigger hostels serve meals or organise barbecues.

Restaurants Cengiz Topel Caddesi has many outdoor restaurants and cafes. The *Artemis Pide Salonu*, about a block south of the tea garden at the eastern end of the street, has Turkish-style pizza for US$1.20 to US$2.20. Try the *kaşarlı* (cheese) and *karişik* (mincemeat) varieties. *Hünkârim (Kızılay Caddesi)* is similar and also serves beer.

The *Park Restaurant* east of the tourist office is expensive but the food is well prepared – the kebabs, especially *çöp şiş* (pieces of grilled meat on a skewer), are delectable.

For a change from the usual Turkish fare, try the fine Chinese cuisine at *Great Hongkong Restaurant (Agora Çarşisi 1)*, which has set menus from US$7.

The *Eski Ev Restaurant & Cafe (1005 Sokak 1/A)*, just behind the post office, gets many readers' recommendations; it has a pleasant courtyard, and serves wine, beer and reasonable pasta dishes.

Ephesus Restaurant (Namik Kemal Caddesi) has a good range of vegetarian options, including delicious *kabuk köfte* (fried courgette patties) and *kuru fasulye* (white bean stew).

Self-Catering The *market* behind the *belediye* (town hall) has all the essentials, and there are plenty of bargains at the Saturday *street market* (in the street that runs due south from the market). In particular, the local apples and figs are cheap and delicious.

Entertainment

Apart from some bars in the pedestrianised part of town, including the lively *Pink Bistro*, there's little nightlife in this small town.

The easy option is to enjoy a beer at one of the hostels. The rooftop bars at the *Australian & New Zealand Pension* and the *All Blacks* or the courtyard bar at *Artemis Guest House* (see Places to Stay) are all fine and charge US$1.25 for a large beer.

For something wilder, head for Bar Street in Kuşadası, but plan to stay over or factor in the cost of a taxi back to Selçuk after midnight.

Getting There & Around

Buses stop at the old otogar on the corner of Şahabettin Dede Caddesi. (The unfinished new otogar south of the centre on the Aydın road is a white elephant that might now become a shopping centre.)

Minibuses leave frequently for Kuşadası (US$1.10, around 30 minutes) and Pamucak (US$0.70, 10 minutes), passing the Ephesus turn-off (US$0.50). Taxis to Ephesus charge at least US$2.50. Many pensions arrange for carpet-shop-owning friends to take you to Ephesus – when they pick you up the hard sell starts. End this practice by saying 'no'.

You can make a day trip to Pamukkale (US$8, three hours) on a direct bus leaving before 9 am and returning by 5 pm. Tours are offered from several Selçuk hostels; a minibus tour should cost about US$12 per person (with five hours at Pamukkale).

Buses to İzmir leave regularly between 6.30 am and 7 pm (US$2.50, one hour). Buses go hourly to Bodrum (US$7, two hours).

EPHESUS (EFES)

Ephesus (Efes), the best preserved classical city on the south Aegean, is quite simply one of Turkey's 'must sees'. It really does give you a feel for what it must have been like in Roman times.

In high season, you will be shocked by the hundreds of tourists crammed into the streets and ruins from about 10 am to 4 pm, so try to visit outside these times. We suggest that you get here as early as possible and walk uphill from the lower entrance, have a rest, then resume a downhill stroll from the upper entrance. Thus you will see the ruins from two different angles. Coach groups generally only pass through in one direction. Half a day is sufficient unless you're really into your ruins, in which case hiring a guide is a good idea (around US$15 an hour).

History

In ancient times the sea came much farther inland, almost as far as present day Selçuk. Keep this in mind and it makes more sense that by 600 BC a prosperous city existed on the northern slope of Mt Pion (Panayir Dağı). The area was also a centre for the cult of Cybele, the Anatolian fertility goddess who later became known as Artemis.

In 356 BC the Temple of Artemis was razed by a pyromaniac intent on a stab at immortality. The Ephesians then started rebuilding the temple, which caught Alexander the Great's eye when he arrived in 334 BC. Fortunately he didn't destroy it, so the temple was completed and made it on to the list as one of the seven wonders of the ancient world.

When Alexander died, one of his generals, Lysimachus, assumed control of Ionia. Because the old city's harbour was silting up, Lysimachus forced the Ephesians to move to the west side of Mt Pion so that the city would still have direct shipping access to the sea – this is roughly where the current Roman ruins stand today.

When the Romans finally took over the city they developed it into their Asia Minor capital; it had a population of around 250,000 (huge for those days). Various emperors added their touches and for a considerable time Ephesus hosted Christian notables – St Paul's Letter to the Ephesians is directed to its inhabitants. (Paul was later encouraged to leave after upsetting local silversmiths.)

It wasn't an earthquake or conquering forces that led to the decline of Ephesus. Slowly the harbour silted up again and all attempts to keep it open failed. Ephesus lost its wealth and Selçuk took over as the regional centre.

Information

Ephesus is open from 8 am to 5.30 pm daily (until 7 pm in summer). Admission costs US$5. There are stalls at both the lower and upper gates where you can buy all manner of guidebooks for the site, or hire a guide. The nearest accommodation is at Selçuk, but you can also easily visit from Kuşadası.

Walking Tour

As you approach the ticket booth at the lower entrance you'll pass the 2nd-century **Gymnasium of Vedius** and the **stadium**. Also just outside the gates, near the teahouses and souvenir stalls, is the **Church of St Mary** (or Double Church) with its intact baptistry.

Once through the gates, walk down the tree-lined road to the **Arcadian Way** (Harbour St) – this was once the city's grandest street. Turn left past the **Gymnasium of the Theatre**, currently undergoing excavation. Ahead is the magnificent 25,000-seat **Great Theatre**. It has been insensitively restored with the wrong materials but is still worth visiting for the view.

From the theatre turn left right the **Sacred Way**, also called the Marble Way. Note the remains of the once-elaborate water and sewer systems, and the ruts made by wheeled vehicles on their way to the **commercial agora**. On the left at the end of the way is a **brothel**, which features a dusty mosaic of the four seasons in its main hall.

The crowds really gather at Embolos, which is the centre of Ephesus, at the end of the Sacred Way. To the right is the monumental Gate of Augustus, which was once a favourite public urinal. Just left of that is the **Library of Celsus**, definitely the most photographed of Ephesus' constructions. The library commemorates Gaius Julius Celsus Polemaeanus, a 2nd-century governor of Asia Minor. A dutiful son, Consul Gaius Julius Aquila, erected the library in dad's honour. There were once 12,000 scrolls in niches in the library's walls. The Austrian Archaeological Institute helped restore the library, so the signs here are in Turkish and German. The statues representing the virtues – goodness, thought, knowledge and wisdom – which once adorned the niches on the library's facade are stashed away in Vienna's Ephesus Museum.

Heading uphill is the **Curetes Way**, named after a group of priests from the

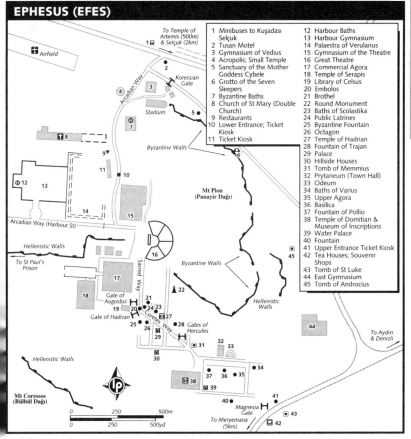

EPHESUS (EFES)

To Temple of Artemis (500m) & Selçuk (2km)

Airfield

Kor,ession Gate

Acradian Way

Stadium

Byzantine Walls

Mt Pion (Panayir Dağı)

Arcadian Way (Harbour St)

Hellenistic Walls

To St Paul's Prison

Sacred Way

Byzantine Walls

Hellenistic Walls

Gate of Augustus

Gate of Hadrian

Curetes Way

Gates of Hercules

Hellenistic Walls

Mt Coressos (Bülbül Dağı)

0   250   500m
0   250   500yd

Magnesia Gate

To Meryemana (5km)

To Aydın & Denizli

1	Minibuses to Kuşadası Selçuk	12	Harbour Baths
2	Tusan Motel	13	Harbour Gymnasium
3	Gymnasium of Vedius	14	Palaestra of Verulanus
4	Acropolis; Small Temple	15	Gymnasium of the Theatre
5	Sanctuary of the Mother Goddess Cybele	16	Great Theatre
6	Grotto of the Seven Sleepers	17	Commercial Agora
7	Byzantine Baths	18	Temple of Serapis
8	Church of St Mary (Double Church)	19	Library of Celsus
9	Restaurants	20	Embolos
10	Lower Entrance; Ticket Kiosk	21	Brothel
11	Ticket Kiosk	22	Round Monument
		23	Baths of Scolastika
		24	Public Latrines
		25	Byzantine Fountain
		26	Octagon
		27	Temple of Hadrian
		28	Fountain of Trajan
		29	Palace
		30	Hillside Houses
		31	Tomb of Memmius
		32	Prytaneum (Town Hall)
		33	Odeum
		34	Baths of Varius
		35	Upper Agora
		36	Basilica
		37	Fountain of Pollio
		38	Temple of Domitian & Museum of Inscriptions
		39	Water Palace
		40	Fountain
		41	Upper Entrance Ticket Kiosk
		42	Tea Houses; Souvenir Shops
		43	Tomb of St Luke
		44	East Gymnasium
		45	Tomb of Androcius

Temple of Artemis. Directly on your left are the **public latrines**. They were for men only and we are told that in winter slaves went there an hour before their masters to warm the marble seats.

Farther up is the impressive **Temple of Hadrian**, dedicated in 118 AD to Hadrian (of the Wall fame). Across the street is a row of shops from the 4th century with a large mosaic in front of them. Behind the temple are the **Baths of Scolastika**, named after the lady whose beheaded statue is at their entrance.

The many hillside houses opposite the temple are still being excavated and are only periodically open to the public (in order to preserve the frescoes and mosaics).

Next along the Curetes Way is the **Fountain of Trajan** (Trajan was Roman emperor

from AD 98 to 117). Of the statues that guarded the entrance, only Trajan's feet remain. The Curetes Way ends at the **Gate of Hercules**, which was constructed in the 4th century and depicts the mythical hero Hercules cloaked in the skin of a lion on both its main pillars. At the top of the hill, before the upper entrance, there are a number of other points of interest including the **Temple of Domitian and Museum of Inscriptions**, an **Upper Agora**, an **Odeum** (for musical performances), the **Baths of Varius** and the **Magnesia Gate**.

The much vaunted **Grotto of the Seven Sleepers** is in fact likely to induce slumber. More exciting is its legend: Seven Christian youths took refuge in the cave, which was sealed by Romans. Two centuries later the sealed wall crumbled in an earthquake. Out walked the youths who returned to Ephesus to find all their mates long gone. You pay to peep into the grotto.

Getting There & Away

Ephesus is a 2km 35-minute walk west from central Selçuk along a shady road. Alternatively, there are frequent minibuses (US$0.75) between Kuşadası and Selçuk that will drop you at the marked turn-off, leaving you just a 1km walk.

KUŞADASI

☎ 256 • pop 50,000

There is no getting away from it, Kuşadası is a blatant tourist trap pitched at package tourists 'doing' Turkey in a week. There is none of the atmosphere that made it one of Turkey's laid-back ports in the 1970s. The street touts and traders are positively voracious. The main reasons to come here are to catch a boat to the Greek island of Samos, to organise a tour to some of the more interesting ruins south along the coast, or just to party.

Orientation & Information

The centrepiece of Kuşadası is the Ökuz Mehmet Paşa Kervansarayı, an old Ottoman caravanserai converted into an upmarket hotel. Elsewhere the condominium-covered hillsides exhibit all the geometry of a perfect Turkish carpet.

West of the harbour is Güvercinada (Pigeon Island), connected to the mainland by a causeway. The small island sports a little fort and a restaurant.

The tourist office (☎ 614 1103, fax 614 6295) is close to the pier where the cruise ships disgorge their passengers. It's open from 8 am to noon and 1.30 to 5.30 pm daily in July and August, an hour or so less at other times, and is closed on weekends during the winter. The post office is near the caravanserai, as is Kismet Internet.

Beaches

If you like wrestling for that small piece of sand to sun yourself on then you have the choice of Yılancı Burnu (on the peninsula 1km to the south); the northern beach near the marina; the beach opposite the Tur-yat Mocamp; or, most famous of all, Kadinlar Denizi (Ladies' Sea), which is about 2.5km south of town and choked with hotels.

Cruises to various beaches between 9.30 am and 4 pm cost US$25 including lunch – for details call Diana Tours (☎ 612 8888).

Places to Stay

With over 350 places to stay it's not surprising that Kuşadası has a few reasonable hostels and hotels. The cheapest are pricier than those in Selçuk, at US$10 to US$12 per person, including private bathroom. Many can be found uphill behind the Akdeniz Apart-Otel near or along Aslanlar Caddesi.

The *Önder* (☎ 618 1590) and *Tur-Yat Mocamp* (☎ 618 0809) camping grounds, north of town on the waterfront near the marina, charge about US$7 for two people in a tent.

Sammy's Palace (☎ 612 2588, e sammy@ superonline.com, Kibris Caddesi 14) has a good bar, a restaurant, Internet facilities, double rooms with bathroom (US$14), and a good travel information service. Call the staff from the otogar; they will pay for your taxi to the hostel. The hostel's 'free' trip to Ephesus involves a trip to Ali Baba Carpet Shop.

The rooms at *Özhan Pansiyon* (☎ 614 2932, Kibris Caddesi 5) have a quaint, villagey feel and cost US$7/14 for singles/ doubles.

Pension Golden Bed (☎ 614 8708) is just off Aslanlar Caddesi (follow the signs). This quiet place is run by a Turkish-Australian couple. They have the best view from their terrace cafe and charge US$16 for a double with bathroom.

Hotel Sezgin (☎ 614 4225, fax 614 6489, e sezgin@ispro.net.rt, Zafer Sokak 15) off Kahramanlar Caddesi has been recommended by many readers; dorms are US$5 (US$3 on the roof) and singles/doubles are US$10/15.

The warmest welcome in Kuşadası has to be from Hassan (AKA Mr Happy) at the mid-range *Hotel Liman* (☎ 614 7770, fax 614 6913, Buyural Sokak 4). Very comfortable rooms in this block right by the harbour cost from US$15 to US$25 including breakfast, depending on the season. There are dorm beds here for US$5, too.

Places to Eat

The *Avlu Restaurant* (Cephane Sokak 15/A), just off Barbaros Hayrettin, serves good seafood for about US$4 per person.

TURKEY

Green Garden (Kaleiçi Kişla Sokak 12), between Sağlik and Atatürk Bulvarıs, has received rave reviews from readers; it's in a nice setting and a huge meal of several courses will cost about US$6.

The restaurant at *Sammy's Palace* (see Places to Stay) is run by Sammy's mum; a three-course dinner costs US$6.

Good, but expensive, *seafood places* along the waterfront charge US$8 to US$20 for a fish dinner, depending on the fish and the season. Try *Kazim Usta* opposite the tourist office. Cheaper meals (US$3 to US$6) are served on Sağlık Caddesi between Kahramanlar Caddesi and İnönü Bulvarı.

Entertainment

The Kaleiçi district shelters several charming cafes, a million miles away from the crass offerings of so-called Bar Street (Barlar Sokak), where you'll find the usual Irish and Brit pub experiences. This place heaves at the height of summer.

There is a *disco* on Güvercin Ada; entry is free but the place recoups this in the cost of drinks. *Hotel Kervansaray* hosts a pricey Turkish night (around US$25), complete with belly dancing, most summer nights.

There is an outdoor cinema, *Doğan Sinemasi*, on Kemal Arikan Caddesi across from the Fisher Harbour; films are screened in English (US$1.50).

Getting There & Away

Bus & Dolmuş The otogar is 1.5km southeast of the town centre on the highway; several bus companies have ticket offices on İnönü Bulvarı. There are buses to Bodrum (US$6, 2½ hours) and İzmir (US$3, 1½ hours). Dolmuşes regularly depart for Selçuk from the centre of town on Adnan Menderes Bulvarı.

Boat From Kuşadası, two lines sail to Samos (Sisam) daily in summer for US$30 (one way), US$35 (same-day round trip), or US$63 (open round trip); both have ticket offices near the tourist office. In spring and autumn there are irregular weekly services; in winter there are only special excursions.

For information on Mar Lines' ferry service from Kuşadası to Crete (Greece) and Ancona (Italy) contact Karavan in İzmir (☎ 232-463 7967).

PRIENE, MILETUS & DIDYMA

South of Selçuk and Kuşadası, down the Aegean coast, are three important archaeological sites. **Priene** is the first, 35km south of Kuşadası, overlooking the River Menderes (once the Meander). The town's heyday was around 300 BC. The best preserved part of the site is the **Bouleuterion**, the city council meeting place. From the Temple of Athena Polias you get the best views (especially late in the afternoon). The site is open from 8.30 am to 7 pm daily in summer (to 5.30 pm in winter); admission is US$1.50.

In contrast to Priene, **Miletus** is in a state of neglect and generally a disappointment – skip it if you don't have time. Believed to have been founded in the 6th century BC, Miletus' most impressive feature is the 15,000-seat **Great Theatre**, reconstructed by the Romans in the 1st century AD. The site has the same hours as Priene (entry US$1).

Didyma (Didim in Turkish) was once the residence of a great oracle said to rival in importance the oracle of Delphi in Greece. A temple dedicated to Apollo was constructed here in the 4th century BC. Much of the elaborate statuary from the road leading to the temple ended up in the British Museum in the 1850s. The site has the same hours as Priene and Miletus (entry US$1). The best time to visit is late afternoon, when the setting sun catches the masonry.

PAMUKKALE
☎ 258

Over 200km east of Selçuk, Pamukkale – famous for its white travertine terraces – is well off our main overland route, but is a handy stop if you want to skip the Mediterranean coast and head straight to Cappadocia.

It's worth knowing before you set off here that the promotional photos of visitors bathing in the pools were taken decades ago. Sadly, tourism has taken a heavy toll on the travertines. The authorities now ask walkers to remove their shoes and you can no longer bathe in the travertines themselves. Still, in the midday sun the calcium-covered terraces sparkle brilliantly and they can look equally dramatic just before dusk.

The hot springs above the travertines, used since Roman times as a therapeutic spa, are still open to the public. The most famous baths (and the most expensive, at US$4 per hour), complete with sunken

TURKEY

Roman columns, are at the Pamukkale Motel. The water is quite hot at 95°F.

There's a tourist office on the ridge above the travertines (☎ 272 1077). Safety lockers are available for US$2.

Hierapolis

On the plateau at the rear of the travertines is a fascinating ancient site. Hierapolis, also known as Pamukkale Örenyeri (Ruins District), was a Roman spa city. It was founded around 190 BC by Eumenes II, king of Pergamum. The city was occupied by Romans, then Byzantines, and lasted until an earthquake struck in 1334.

The centre of Hierapolis is believed to have been the **Sacred Spring** (where the Pamukkale Motel now stands), which flowed into the **Roman Baths** (the site of Pamukkale Museum). At the site are temples, a well-preserved 7000-seat **Roman theatre** dating from the 2nd century and the 5th-century octagonal **Matyrion** of the Apostle St Philip, who was martyred here in AD 80.

Places to Stay & Eat

The budget places are below the travertines in Pamukkale Köyü; the mid-range places are on the plateau above the travertines in Pamukkale Örenyeri. When you arrive at the lower village be prepared for an onslaught of touts.

Kervansaray Pension (☎ 272 2209) offers cheerful service, a rooftop bar, and clean singles/doubles with bathroom and balcony for US$14/20. The nearby *Aspawa Pansiyon (☎ 272 2094)* costs about the same.

The *Meltem Motel Backpackers Inn (☎ 272 2413)* is a decent hostel and part of the No 1 network. It has a pool, Internet service and a bar and restaurant. Dorm beds cost US$4.50, doubles with private bathroom are US$15.

Taking meals in your pension or hotel is usually the best option here, but ask prices in advance. *Mustafa's* has been recommended by several readers, and some vegetarian dishes are available.

Of the restaurants in the town, the *Gürsoy*, opposite the Yörük Motel in the village centre, has the nicest terrace, but the *Han*, around the corner facing the square, offers the best value for money. Meals at either place cost US$4 to US$6.

The Pizzeria, between the highway and the Yörcük Motel, seems to undergo the odd metamorphosis but the pizzas stay pretty much the same.

There are bars near the main square.

Getting There & Away

Many travellers make a long day trip to Pamukkale and Hierapolis from Selçuk or Kuşadası, or visit en route to the coast from Cappadocia; see those sections for transport details.

Alternatively take a train or bus to Denizli, the nearest major town, and then a bus or dolmuş the final 19km to Pamukkale. From Denizli, if you're heading east, you can take a bus to Isparta (US$5, 4½ hours) or Eğirdir.

AFRODISIAS

If time permits, on your way back to Selçuk or Kuşadası detour to Afrodisias, south-east of Nazilli near Karacasu. This beautiful ruined city is thought by many to rival Ephesus. The name comes from Aphrodite, the Greek goddess of love. It's a particularly rich site with an exquisite marble odeon, an agora, the Baths of Hadrian, a colonnaded palaestra (playing field), the Portico of Tiberius and a fine white marble theatre.

BODRUM

☎ 252 • pop 30,000

Bodrum, 151km south of Kuşadası, has one of the most beautiful settings along this coast. As ancient Halicarnassus, the town was the site of the monumental tomb of King Mausolus (hence the word 'mausoleum'), one of the seven wonders of the ancient world. Bodrum was also the birthplace of Herodotus, the 'Father of History', and home to the crusading Knights of St John, who in the 13th century holed up in the Castle of St Peter, one of Turkey's most impressive fortresses.

Nowadays, the picturesque harbour beneath the castle shelters yachts from many foreign ports, and the ritzy quayside reverberates in summer to the pounding beat of scores of bars and discos. Of course, Bodrum has been 'discovered' by package tourism, but visit out of season and you're likely to find it one of the most appealing of the Turkish Mediterranean resorts. Ferries ply the routes from here to the Greek islands of Kos and Rhodes.

BODRUM

PLACES TO STAY
6 Yenilmez Pansiyon; Menekşe Pansiyon
12 Şenlık Pansiyon; Sedan Pansiyon
20 Melis
39 Emiko
42 Merhaba Pension

PLACES TO EAT
13 Buğday
23 Körfez
24 Lunch Box Cafe & Restaurant; Palmiye Patisserie
27 Babadan

29 Meyhaneler Sokak Tavernas
37 Nazilli
38 Karadeniz
41 Cafe Penguen
43 Golden Plate Restaurant; Red Lion Bar; Sensi Bar

OTHER
1 Ancient Theatre
2 Migros Supermarket
3 Hospital
4 Mausoleum of Halicarnassus
5 Tepecik Camii

7 Mola Internet
8 Küba Bar
9 Medical Clinic
10 Temple of Mars
11 Türkkuyusu Camii
14 Marketplace
15 Tanşas Supermarket
16 Petrol Station
17 Otogar & Gümbet Dolmuş
18 Petrol Station
19 Fruit Market
21 Post Office (PTT)
22 Belediye (Town Hall)

25 Boat Excursion Departures
26 Adliye Camii
28 Net Room Internet Cafe
30 Tourist Office
31 Chez Ahmet
32 Passport Police
33 Ferries to Datça & Greece
34 Castle of St Peter; Museum of Underwater Archaeology
35 Police
36 Fora Bar
40 Hamam
44 Halikarnas Night Club

Orientation & Information

The otogar is 500m inland along Cevat Şakir Caddesi from the Adliye Camii, a small mosque at the centre of the town. The post office and several banks are on Cevat Şakir.

The tourist office (☎ 316 1091) is beside the Castle of St Peter but it's pretty useless.

The Net Room Internet cafe is upstairs on Yeni Çarşı, Mah 9, the pedestrian area immediately east of the Adliye Camii. Mola Internet is on Neyzen Tevfik Caddesi.

Castle of St Peter & Museum of Underwater Archaeology

Sited commandingly on an outcrop that splits Bodrum's twin bays is the Castle of St Peter, built in 1402 by the Knights of St John of Jerusalem, who captured the port from their base on the Greek island of Rhodes. The Gothic fortress was rebuilt in 1522 by the Crusaders, using stones from the mausoleum of Halicarnassus.

The castle is one of the highlights of a trip down the Turkish coast, both for its imposing appearance and because it houses the fascinating Museum of Underwater Archaeology. Visit early morning and you'll probably be able to walk the Hollywood-epic-style battlements in splendid isolation.

In the castle's main courtyard, which is populated by preening peacocks, is the former chapel. The chapel now houses a full-sized reconstruction of the stern half of a 7th-century **Roman ship** discovered off Yassıada (Flat Island) in 1958. On 6 June 626, Georgios, the ship's captain, recorded:

We were driven onto the reef that runs out from the western end of the island even before we could cast an anchor, and the ship has sunk in over 100 feet of water.

Equally interesting is the **glass shipwreck exhibit**. This ship sank in 1025 BC. It was carrying a load of glass, hence the name. Found in 1973, it is the oldest wreck discovered in the Mediterranean. The exhibit is open from 10 to 11 am and 2 to 4 pm. A separate exhibit of glass discovered in various wrecks can be seen in the base of the **Italian tower**.

Farther up, there are various turrets to explore. The **Snake Tower**, so called because of the bas-relief near its entrance, houses a display of amphorae recovered from wrecks. The **Gatineau Tower** has an inscription over its inner gate: *Inde deus abest* (Where God does not exist) – appropriate, as the dungeons are beneath. The **English Tower**, built during the reign of Henry IV of England, bears his coat of arms. It is now arranged like a medieval refectory; look for the artful Latin graffiti around the window niches.

Inside the **French Tower**, the castle's highest point, are the remains and sarcophagus of Queen Ada, a Carian princess. Her intact **tomb** was only discovered in 1989. Ada died somewhere between 360 and 325 BC and was probably the sister of Mausoleus, the tomb builder. This exhibit is open from 10 am to noon and 2 to 4 pm.

The castle is open from 8.30 am to noon and 1 to 5 pm Tuesday to Saturday. Admission is US$3, with another US$2 each for the glass shipwreck exhibit and the Carian princess' tomb. (Note that you don't have to pay extra to see the glass exhibit in the base of the Italian tower.)

Mausoleum of Halicarnassus

There is little left of the actual mausoleum of Halicarnassus, but you may want to visit the site as there are many interesting exhibits including a gallery where archaeologists have attempted to show what the tomb looked like before it was plundered to build the Castle of St Peter. The site is closed on Monday; on other days it is open from 8 am to 5 or 6 pm. Admission is US$1.75.

Up behind the mausoleum site is the **theatre**, which was built by Mausoleus and expanded to 13,000 seats by the Romans. The views from here over the town are splendid.

Bodrum Peninsula

From the town centre, you can walk west past the marina and over the hill to **Gümbet**, which has a nicer beach than Bodrum proper, though it's a bit polluted. It is very popular with the English and many come here to eat fish and chips.

Turgutreis, a small town 20km west of Bodrum, is expanding and can almost be afforded 'resort' status. Every Saturday there's a large market selling local produce. A dolmuş runs from Bodrum regularly throughout the day and the trip takes 25 minutes.

The ruins of ancient **Mindos**, some under water, are on a rocky islet south of the village of Gümüşlük.

Boat Excursions

By the time you reach Bodrum you will have heard the term 'blue voyage' (after Cevat Şakir Kabaağaç's book *Mavi Yolculuk*). This now basically means sailing on the Aegean or Mediterranean. Bodrum is as good a place as any to make such a trip as there are dozens of yachts (many of them *gulets* or traditional wooden yachts) moored along Neyzen Tevfik Caddesi. Popular destinations from here include **Karaada** (Black Island), where there are hot springs and a meteor crater; the **Akvaryum**, a small cove near Gümbet that's good for snorkelling; **Bitez** and **Akyarlar** beaches, where it's possible to windsurf (US$20 an hour); and **Camel Beach** (Kargı Bay) for bungee jumping. A typical excursion runs from 11.30 am to 6.30 pm and costs US$8 to US$10 from a pension or travel agency.

Places to Stay

Some of the smaller villages on the peninsula, such as Bitez Yalısı and Ortakent Yalısı, have camping grounds. There are more on the peninsula's north shore.

Bodrum has plenty of pensions and hotels costing US$5 to US$10 per person; prices rise steeply as you approach the waterfront but they drop in the off season.

Melis (☎ 316 1487, *Türkkuyusu Caddesi 50*) has plain, reasonably priced rooms with bathroom for US$7 per person. *Sedan Pansiyon* (☎ 316 0355, *Türkkuyusu Sokak 121*) and *Şenlik Pansiyon* (☎ 316 6382), nearby, charge slightly less but are not as nice.

The *Yenilmez Pansiyon* (☎ 316 2520, *Menekşe Çıkmazı 30*) and the *Menekşe*

TURKEY

Pansiyon (☎ *316 0537, Menekşe Çıkmazı 34)* are two nearly identical quiet, modern places offering doubles with showers for US$20. At the Menekşe you can use the kitchen and arrange diving trips with the owners. Both places are on an alley between Neyzen Tevfik 84 and 86.

Emiko (☎ *316 5560, Uslu Sokak 11)* is a Japanese-run place with a good reputation. It was being renovated when we visited, but expect to pay around US$10 per person.

Uphill from the Halikarnas Night Club (and occasionally suffering from the sounds that emanate from it) are two reasonable places. *Bambi Pension* (☎ *316 9014, İçmeler Yolu)* has a nice rooftop bar with a sea view; clean comfortable doubles cost US$16 in summer (US$12 off season).

Merhaba Pension (☎ *316 3978, Akasya Sokak 11)*, a family-run place, is down the hill closer to the disco. It doesn't look much from the outside but the doubles are reasonable for US$16 and there's a rooftop bar.

Places to Eat

For very cheap eats, buy a *dönerli sandviç* (roast lamb sandwich) for less than US$2 at a street-side *büfe* (buffet). In July and August, you'll get the best-value meals at simple local eateries, without menus in English and German, well inland. Most do not serve alcohol.

Buğday (*Türkkuyusu Caddesi 72*) is a cheap vegetarian and vegan place with tofu, salads and vegetable stir-fries.

Facing the quay, the *Lunch Box Cafe & Restaurant* is a nice place to relax with a predinner drink. Next door, *Palmiye Patisserie* fits the bill perfectly for breakfast or a snack, while north-west along Neyzen Tevfik Caddesi, *Körfez* does a good-value dinner deal for US$6 including a glass of wine.

Heading into the grid of small streets east of the Adliye Camii, you'll find *Babadan* patronised by locals as well as foreigners, serving döner kebap for about US$2.75 and beer for US$1.25.

Meyhaneler Sokak (also known as Taverna St) is wall-to-wall with tavernas.

Farther on is a little plaza with several open-air restaurants serving pide and kebap. The *Nazilli* is a favourite; a pide topped with meat or cheese costs about US$3.

There are plenty of options on Cumhuriyet Caddesi, including the 24-hour *Karadeniz* selling delectable pastries, desserts and decent sandwiches that all make up a perfect picnic. Farther along, *Cafe Penguen* is a good choice for Italian-style pizza (about US$5), burgers, and a slap-up English breakfast for US$4.

The *Golden Plate* between the Red Lion and Sensi bars is a friendly family-run place that does fish'n'chips just like those at home.

Self-caterers will be greeted with a smile at the many halk pazarı in this town, as few westerners venture from the restaurants and pubs of the beach strip. For supermarkets, there is a *Tanşas* near the otogar and a *Migros* near the Gümbet turn-off.

The *fruit market* is 300m north of the waterfront on Cevat Şakir Caddesi. The main *marketplace* is near the eastern end of Külcüoglu Sokak.

Entertainment

Come the summer season and it's party, party, party along Cumhuriyet Caddesi; every year outraged local citizens call for a stop to the all-night din, but every year it continues. Among the many bars to check out are *Sensi*, *Red Lion* and *Fora*.

Even if you hate discos, *Halikarnas Night Club* is an experience you shouldn't miss. Its position at the western end of Kumbahçe Bay, overlooking the castle, is unsurpassed, and you can dance alfresco till 6 am with lasers bouncing off this dramatic backdrop. There's a different theme each night (Monday admission is half price for women, Tuesday has a belly dancer, Wednesday it's free beer until 1 am...). Entry costs US$20 including your first drink.

A classier yachting crowd gathers by the harbour. *Chez Ahmet* near the castle has beers for US$1.25. The stylish *Küba* (*Neyzen Tevfik Caddesi)* is where the beautiful people hang out.

Getting There & Away

Air Turkish Air has several flights daily from İstanbul to Milas international airport (1¼ hours). During the summer season (May to September) there are also charter flights from the UK and other European cities.

Bus There are frequent buses to all points in the region, including Fethiye (US$7, 4½ hours), Kuşadası and Selçuk (US$9, three hours) and Marmaris (US$5, three hours).

Boat From May to September there are hydrofoils to Marmaris (US$25, 1¼ hours) and ferries to Datça and Didyma (US$10).

Hydrofoils and boats go from Bodrum to Kos (İstanköy) frequently in summer for US$20/30 one way/return. A high-speed ferry sails to Rhodes on weekdays (US$40 one way).

Getting Around

The Milas international airport is 25km from Bodrum; a shuttle from Milas to Bodrum costs US$6.

Bodrum itself is compact enough to get around by walking. For travelling around the peninsula, you might want to rent a scooter (about US$20 for 24 hours); there are several rental outlets along Cevat Şakir Caddesi.

Mediterranean Coast

The seas along Turkey's Mediterranean shoreline are so blue that east of Marmaris is known as the Turquoise Coast – ideal for boat excursions, with many secluded bays, sandy coves and photogenic ruins. The terrain becomes more rugged from Fethiye to Antalya – an area that once was the ancient kingdom of Lycia and which today can be explored on foot along the Lycian Way (see 'The Lycian Way' boxed text). The stylish resort of Kaş is carving a name for itself as adventure sports central for the region, while weary travellers in search of a place to chill out won't do much better than Olimpos, near the legendary flames of the Chimaera. The wild Taurus Mountains east of Antalya provide an unforgettable backdrop to the last sea views on our main route to Kathmandu.

MARMARİS
☎ 252 • pop 18,000

Turkey's premier yachting port, Marmaris, 165km east of Bodrum, is sited on a gorgeous bay at the edge of a hilly, pine-clad peninsula. The shameless way it courts package tourism, however, makes this one resort you can safely skip unless you're contemplating a gulet cruise or hopping over to the Greek island of Rhodes.

Orientation & Information

Marmaris has a small castle (kale) overlooking the town centre. İskele Meydanı (the main square) and the tourist office (☎ 412 1035) are by the ferry pier just north-west of the castle. The centre is mostly a pedestrian precinct, and new development stretches many kilometres to the south-east around the marina.

The otogar is 1.5km north of the marina on Mustafa Münir Elgin Bulvarı. The post office is on Fevzipaşa Caddesi, and there are ATMs on Kordon Caddesi, near İskele Meydanı.

Internet access is available at MS Internet behind the Pamukkale bus company office on Ulusal Egemenlik Bulvarı and at the Interyouth Hostel.

Things to See & Do

The **castle** has a few unexciting exhibition rooms but offers fine views. It's open from 8 am to noon and 1 to 5.30 pm daily except Monday; admission is US$1.25

All kinds of daily **boat trips** are available in summer to nearby islands and farther afield to **Dalyan** and **Caunos** (about US$30). The marina is also a good place to take a berth or bareboat charter, or hire a crewed boat and enjoy a 'blue voyage'; prices vary according to numbers, so negotiate at the harbour.

The beach at **İçmeler**, 10km away by minibus, is marginally better than the scrappy bit of gravel at Marmaris. There are several places in Marmaris that offer diving courses (US$40 for a one-day dive excursion). The Professional Diving Centre (☎ 412 9989), next to the tourist office, runs five-day learn-to-dive courses including nine dives, exams and food for around US$375.

Places to Stay

Marmaris has hundreds of lodgings, but finding a small, cheap room here is a task – it's easier to track down and kill the voracious mosquitoes that abound here.

About 1km east of Marmaris is the Günnücek Forestry Reserve and the basic *Dimet Camping* (☎ *413 3905*). For beachside camping try *Berk Camping* (☎ *412 4171*), with tent sites for US$5 and cabins for US$16. To get there, take a 'Siteler-Turban' minibus along the waterfront road to the last stop at the Türban Marmaris Tatil Köyü holiday village, 4km south-west of the main square.

TURKEY

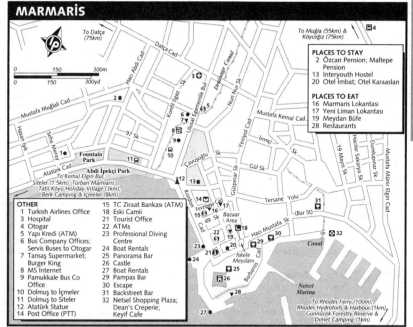

MARMARİS

To Datça (75km)

To Muğla (55km) & Köyceğiz (75km)

0   150   300m
0   150   300yd

Mustafa Muğlalı Cad

Hasan Işık

Seha Meray

Datça Cad

Hacı Abdi Cad

Konfi İlgaz Sk

Ulusal Egemenlik Bul

Drahinge Canal

Nuri Nur Sk

Mustafa Kemal Cad.

Yenyol Cad

İrmiçi Sk

Hacılar Sakarya Sk

19 Mayıs Sk

Dumlupınar Sk

Mustafa Münir Elgin Cad

Fountain Park

Atatürk Cad.

Abdi İpekçi Park

To Kemal Elgin Bul, Siteler (1.5km), Türban Marmaris Tatil Köyü Holiday Village (3km), Berk Camping & İçmeler (8km)

97 Sk

Çavuşoğlu Sk

Gül Sk

Güzpınar Sk

Kordon Cad

Tersane Yolu

Fevzipaşa Cad

49. Sk

Bazaar Area

Hacı Mustafa Sk

İskele Meydanı

Barbaros Cad

Canal

(Bar St)

Netsel Marina

To Rhodes Ferry (100m), Rhodes Hydrofoils & Harbour (1km), Günnücek Forestry Reserve & Dimet Camping (1km)

PLACES TO STAY
2 Özcan Pension; Maltepe Pension
13 Interyouth Hostel
20 Otel İmbat; Otel Karaaslan

PLACES TO EAT
16 Marmaris Lokantası
17 Yeni Liman Lokantası
19 Meydan Büfe
28 Restaurants

OTHER
1 Turkish Airlines Office
3 Hospital
4 Otogar
5 Yapı Kredi (ATM)
6 Bus Company Offices; Servis Buses to Otogar
7 Tansaş Supermarket; Burger King
8 MS Internet
9 Pamukkale Bus Co Office
10 Dolmuş to İçmeler
11 Dolmuş to Siteler
12 Atatürk Statue
14 Post Office (PTT)
15 TC Ziraat Bankası (ATM)
18 Eski Camii
21 Tourist Office
22 ATMs
23 Professional Diving Centre
24 Boat Rentals
25 Panorama Bar
26 Castle
27 Boat Rentals
29 Pampas Bar
30 Escape
31 Backstreet Bar
32 Netsel Shopping Plaza; Dean's Creperie; Keyif Cafe

Ask at the tourist office about *ev pansiyonları* (home pensions), where double rooms cost US$8 to US$12. Some are inland from Abdi İpekçi Park on 97 Sokak, including the *Cihan* (☎ 412 4312).

Within the bazaar is the town's premier budget option, *Interyouth Hostel* (☎ 412 3687, fax 412 7823, @ interyouth@turk.net, 42 Sokak 45), which is packed to the gunwales in summer. Dorm beds are US$4.50, doubles with shared bathroom US$6 per person. It's nothing fancy, but well set up for travellers and is part of the No 1 network.

With more character, and in a quieter position, is the family-run *Maltepe Pension* (☎ 412 1629), with small rooms with bathroom for US$8/16. It's possible to use the kitchen for self-catering. The nearby *Özcan Pension* (☎ 412 7761), is a bit more expensive but the rooms are bigger and some have recently been renovated.

If you're stuck, there are a couple of tiny, old hotels near the tourist office. *Otel Karaaslan* (☎ 412 1867) is cleaner than the *Otel İmbat* (☎ 412 1413). Both charge around US$8 per person for rooms with shared bathroom.

Places to Eat

The 'resort rule' applies: The farther you go inland from the water, the higher the quality and the lower the price. Have some delicious Marmaris honey while you're here.

The *Marmaris Lokantası* is one of the best of the open-air restaurants along Fevzipaşa Caddesi (the street with the PTT), offering İskender kebap for US$4. The nearby *Yeni Liman Lokantası*, in an arcade just off Fevzipaşa Caddesi, also has a good, if somewhat greasy, selection of meze and other traditional dishes; a meal here costs around US$5.

Opposite the Eski Camii, the *Meydan Büfe* is a cheap place for a sandwich in a convivial spot. From here you can trawl Hacı Mustafa Sokak (also known as Bar St), harbouring all sorts of possibilities for cheap eating from filled baked potatoes and roasted corn cobs through to pizzas.

Across the marina in the upmarket Netsel Shopping Mall are several options including *Dean's Creperie* and the *Keyif Cafe*, which has a lovely view, sandwiches for US$2 and full meals for around US$10.

TURKEY

By the harbour, Barbaros Caddesi is wall-to-wall restaurants, *Pizza Tat* just about summing up the quality of cuisine on offer.

Self-caterers should go to the Tansaş supermarket on Ulusal Egemenlik Bulvarı.

Entertainment
Marmaris' infamous 'Bar Street' (Hacı Mustafa Sokak) is probably the most densely packed group of watering holes in Turkey. Work your way from *Pampas Bar* to *Backstreet Bar*, via scores of interchangeable others. On the waterfront, *Escape* is a current favourite.

The best spot for a sundowner is *Panorama Bar*; follow the signs from the castle end of the bazaar. Plenty of the restaurants along Barbaros Caddesi screen English football matches as well as other sporting events on big screen TVs.

Getting There & Away
There are frequent direct buses and minibuses around the region, including Antalya (US$14, eight hours), Bodrum (US$6, three hours), Dalyan via Ortaca (US$3, two hours), Datça (US$4, 1¾ hours), and Fethiye (US$6, three hours). Many of these buses drop off at the bus company offices in the centre on Ulusal Egemenlik Bulvarı; you can usually get a free service bus to the otogar from the bus company offices.

Ferries to Rhodes Small car-ferries run from Marmaris to Rhodes daily except Sunday in summer (less frequently in the off season around October to May) for US$40 one way or US$55 return (plus US$10 port tax at Rhodes and US$10 to re-enter Turkey). The hydrofoil (☎ 412 6486) departs for Rhodes twice daily at 9.30 am and 4.30 pm (US$40), while another departs Rhodes for Marmaris at 8 am and 4.30 pm. See the Web site at www.yesil-marmaris .com for details.

AROUND MARMARIS
Datça Peninsula
The Datça Peninsula is a mountainous finger of land stretching 100km west of Marmaris. It's a scenic drive and there are several pleasant places to hole up, including the small villages of Bozburun and Knidos. **Datça** (75km from Marmaris) is beginning

to develop as resort but remains quieter and more relaxed than Marmaris. The post office, banks and tourist office are on the town's main street, İskele Caddesi.

There are about 50 small pensions in and around town (especially along Bruxelles Caddesi) and several fish restaurants down near the harbour. The *Kücük Ev* has been recommended by readers. There are hourly buses to Marmaris (summer only) for US$2.50.

KÖYCEĞİZ
☎ 252 • pop 6,500
The road north from Marmaris climbs into the mountains, affording sweeping panoramas of the fertile valleys below, where cotton, tobacco and fruit orchards grow. The small, quiet resort town of Köyceğiz, 75km east of Marmaris, stands at the northern edge of the great placid lake **Köyceğiz Gölü** – it was once a bay, but silt deposited over the centuries has cut it off from the sea. At the lake's southern end is the better-known resort of Dalyan.

At the western end of the lake are the **Sultaniye Kaplıcaları** (hot springs), reached by a sealed road from Köyceğiz, 28km away, or 30 minutes by boat (open from 6 am to 10 pm, US$0.75, water about 40°C).

There are walks in the mountains to the east of Köyceğiz and from the base of the lake to Dalyan – inquire at the Tango Pension (see Places to Stay in this section). They can also direct you to the nearby **waterfall**. It's about US$2 per hour to hire a bike, a good way to see this region.

Köyceğiz can also be used as a base for visiting attractions around Dalyan (see Dalyan later in this chapter). The Tango Pension organises excellent one-day boat trips that take in the mud baths, Lycian tombs, the ruined city of Kaunos and İztuzu beach. The cost is around US$15.

Places to Stay & Eat
Set back from the lake, the *Tango Pension* (☎ 262 2501, fax 262 4345, Ali İhsan Kalmaz Caddesi) is a classy, spotlessly clean place with a TV room, oodles of hot water, a restaurant and an agency for booking tours (including ones on their boat *Şahin*). All rooms have bathroom and tiny balcony and are superb value at US$7 per person, US$9 with breakfast. You can also

sleep on the roof (US$3). Dinner is provided for about US$4, less than you'll pay at the waterfront and better quality. They'll also pick you up at the otogar.

On the waterfront is *Hotel Kaunos* (☎ *262 4288, fax 262 4836, Cengiz Topel Caddesi 37*), a fine mid-range option. The architecture is very 1970s but there's a pool, restaurant and the rooms are excellent value for US$14/28 including breakfast (ask for a room overlooking the lake).

Fiskos Bar is an ideal place for a beer by the lake. Stick to the beers, too, at the rustic *Çiçek Pansiyon* (☎ *262 3038, Çarsi Meydanı*), which has cheap but shabby rooms and poor food. *Aperatif Kafeteriya*, next to the Çiçek is a better option for the usual kebaps.

On the way out of town towards Ortaca are a couple of restaurants with good Turkish food, the *Yuvarlarçay* and the *Yeşil Vadi*.

Getting There & Away

From Marmaris there are frequent buses and minibuses in summer to Köyceğiz (US$2, one hour).

Dolmuşes and buses will drop you at Köyceğiz's otogar, which is 2km from the town centre. From the otogar there are regular services to nearby towns and cities, and farther afield.

DALYAN & KAUNOS
☎ 252

Set in lush river-delta farming country, Dalyan offers dramatic ruins, excellent fishing and, to the south at İztuzu, fine **beaches** that are the nesting ground of *Caretta caretta*, or loggerhead turtle (a species estimated to be 95 million years old). In 1986 conservationists (including David Bellamy) succeeded in stopping a building project at İztuzu that would have threatened one of the turtles' few remaining Mediterranean nesting sites.

The unmissable **Lycian tombs**, on the cliff facing Dalyan, and the nearby ruined city of **Kaunos** are both within easy reach by boat excursion downriver. Kaunos was founded around the 9th century BC and by 400 BC was an important Carian city. The influence of Lycian culture can be seen in the design of the tombs (Kaunos bordered the kingdom of Lycia). The site includes a well-preserved

theatre, a ruined acropolis, baths and a basilica. It's open from 8.30 am to 5.30 pm daily and admission is US$2.

The **mud baths** and **thermal pool**, near where Dalyan Çayı joins the lake (Köyceğiz Gölü), are good fun (even the likes of Dustin Hoffman and Sting have visited here), but come early before the tour groups arrive. Entry is US$1.

Day-long **boat excursions** take in all these attractions; boats leave the Dalyan dock at 10 am (US$10 per person). A group can rent a whole boat for about US$50 to US$60 and set their own itinerary. The local boaters' cooperative, on the riverbank by the dock, sets rates.

There is a river dolmuş from Dalyan dock to İztuzu Beach (US$1.50 return, up to five boats daily in summer between 9 am and 5 pm). There are also river dolmuşes to Kaunos (US$5, three daily) and the mud baths (US$1.75, early evening).

The tourist office (☎ 284 4235) is behind the boaters' cooperative. The post office (PTT) is close to the central Atatürk and turtle statues; nearby is a Yapı Kredi ATM. The otogar is behind the post office.

Places to Stay & Eat

Dalyan Camping, with an attractive tea garden on the river, has clean toilets and bathrooms; a tent site for two is US$3. It's on a dirt side road, Ada Sokagı, in the Maraş Mahallesi area.

Çinar Sahil Pansiyon (☎ *284 2117, fax 284 2262, Yali Sokak*) is one of the nicest pensions, with clean, attractive rooms and a lovely terrace overlooking the tombs. It charges US$9 per person including breakfast. On the same road, *Onur Motel* (☎ *284 3074*) has air-con rooms for US$16 a double including breakfast.

Loggerhead turtles nest on the beaches of Turkey's Mediterranean coast.

Göl Motel (☎ *284 4022, Kordon Boyu)* is above a cafe facing the river and has reasonably OK rooms for US$5 per person.

In the centre of town, facing the river, are *Köşem* and *Kordon* – two pleasant restaurants with open-air dining. *Gerda's Cafe (Karakol Sokak)* whips up a respectable cappuccino, sandwiches and delicious homemade apple cake for US$1.25. *Sofra* and *Nektar* are two convivial bars along the main party street Maraş Caddesi.

Getting There & Away
The airport at Dalaman, 23km south-east of Dalyan, is served by international flights in summer. The airport is 5km out of town.

In summer there are morning buses from Dalyan's otogar to Marmaris, Fethiye and Muğla; otherwise catch a minibus to Ortaca (US$0.25) and then connect with another bus there.

FETHİYE
☎ 252 • pop 25,000

Yet another resort town with a superb coastal setting is Fethiye, 65km east of Dalyan. This is the site of ancient Telmessos, with giant Lycian stone sarcophagi from about 400 BC littered about, and the rock-cut Tomb of Amyntas looming above the town.

Telmessos was not part of the Lycian federation but it must have been defeated by Lycia in around the 4th century BC because Lycian inscriptions in the city date from then. Alexander the Great took it in 333 BC. It was lost soon after but recaptured with a Trojan-horse-like ruse – this time weapons were concealed inside the instrument cases of musicians. It underwent several name changes until settling upon Fethi Bey, a Turkish WWI hero.

Many budget travellers skip Fethiye and head straight for nearby Ölüdeniz, the area's best beach, and the secluded Butterfly Valley. The local resorts of Çalış, Hisarönü and Ovacık are all swamped with package tourists in summer – avoid them at all costs.

Orientation & Information
The otogar is 2km east of the centre. As you come into town along Atatürk Caddesi you will pass the post office, before the road hits the marina and arrives at the tourist office (☎/fax 614 1527).

There is Internet access at Internet 2000 by the footbridge over Atatürk Caddesi, at the small cafe opposite Şehut Fethi Bey Parkı and at Ferah Pension (Monica's Place).

Things to See & Do
It doesn't take long to tick off the fragments of ancient Telmessos. Carved into the cliffs above Fethiye is the **Tomb of Amyntas**, open from 8 am to 7 pm (US$1), and some **Lycian rock tombs**. At the western end of town is a small **Roman theatre**.

There's a rather touristy **hamam** in the bazaar where US$11 gets you the full treatment. It's open from 7 am to midnight.

Boat Excursions
If you stay in Fethiye longer than one night, take the '12-Island Tour' **boat excursion**. Prices are around US$13 per person including lunch, for a cruise around Flat Island, Dockyard Island, Cleopatra's bath (built for Antony's lover) and the Step Cave. There are plenty of opportunities for a swim and all up it's a very relaxing way to spend a day.

Fethiye is a popular starting point for three-day **yacht cruises**. Recommended boats offering much the same itineraries and activities are *Pinar 3* (☎ 542-311 0817, ✉ bulent@raksnet.com); *Murat 4* (☎ 532-425 0786); *Çelebi* (☎ 614 4604); and *Garfield* (☎ 614 9312). The trips range from US$70 to US$110 depending on the time of year.

Places to Stay
There's a cluster of pensions near the stadium on the way into town from the otogar. The *Göreme Pansiyon* (☎ *614 7586, fax 614 6944, Stadyum Yanı 25)* has spotless rooms for US$5/10 a single/double. Around the corner, *Olympiyat Pansiyon* (☎ *614 3444, 527 Sokak)* charges US$15 a double, breakfast included; out of season you may find it full of students.

Other budget pensions are uphill from the yacht marina along Fevzi Çakmak Caddesi. *İdeal Pension* (☎ *614 1981, Zafer Caddesi 1)* has superb views from its roof terrace and a laid back atmosphere and is on the No 1 network's route. Rooms are bit pokey, but many have balconies and they're comfortable for US$7 per person with bathroom or US$5 for rooms with shared bathroom.

Its main competitor is *Ferah Pension (Monica's Place; ☎ 614 2816, fax 612 7398,*

The Lycian Way

The Lycian Way is a 30-day, 500km walk through the pine and cedar covered mountains of Lycia, the stubby peninsula starting at Fethiye and finishing near Antalya. The route gets progressively more difficult as it winds around the coast and into the mountain ranges, finishing at a height of 1500m with a spectacular view of the tourist beaches of Antalya. However, it's easy to walk a bit at a time and the whole length of the path is marked every 100m with red-and-white paint flashes. Check out the Web site at www.lycianway.com.

Good places to hike parts of the route are Ölüdeniz, Kaş or Olimpos. From Ölüdeniz there's a stiff climb up the shoulder of Baba Dağı until you are looking down on the hang gliders. Around Kaş, you can choose level, but rocky, walking past overgrown ruined towers as far as Üçağız. From Çıralı to Ulupinar, via the flames of the Chimaera, is a well-known day walk.

The path from Olimpos to Adrasan leads you past hilltop ruins where orchids flourish and down a green gorge. Heading south from Adrasan, a tough day's hiking takes you to the lighthouse at Gelidonia – the southernmost part of the route. If you are staying in Antalya, day-walks up the Göynük Valley are a cool choice – you can splash in the clear waters of the canyon.

The peak attraction is the summit of Tahtali – Mount Olimpos (2388m). The path is way-marked from the main road near Ulupinar, or from Beycik village, right up and over the main pass at 1800m. Be warned – weather conditions on Tahtali can be dangerous. Don't climb in bad weather or alone; take waterproofs, food and water; mark your route or take compass bearings so you can return safely if cloud descends; and report in to the locals and take their advice.

Kate Clow, *The Lycian Way*
(UpCountry [Turkey] Ltd)

---

e *ferahpension@hotmail.com, 2 Karagözler Ordu Caddesi 21)* farther west along the bay. Dorm beds at this cosy place with a funky courtyard garden are US$6. Towels are provided, there's Internet access and the manager has a deal for free use of the pool at the upmarket Ata Park Hotel.

Ülgen Pension *(☎ 614 3491, fax 614 2911)* is the heart of town, above the bazaar. The owner is a charming old gent, and the terrace views and spotless rooms make it a good choice. It's US$5/6 per person for rooms without/with bathroom.

İrem Pansiyon *(☎ 614 3985 1 Karagözler Mahalles 45)* near the marina is more upmarket but not as well set up for travellers. Make sure you get a room with a sea view to justify the US$15 a double charge.

Places to Eat

For cheap food look along and around Atatürk Caddesi just past the post office; ***Sofra 2000*** and ***Saray Lokantası*** are both very popular options with locals.

Meğri, at the west end of the market, is an excellent choice for mezes with plates for around US$5. (There's another branch specialising in fish in the nearby tourist bazaar area.) ***Cafe Rihtim***, next door, is pleasant place to while away some time.

The bazaar, full of touristy shops and bars, is packed with options, but be on your guard for overcharging. The pretty ***Duck Pond Cafe*** has just that – a pool with real ducks – and a reasonably priced menu. ***Restaurant Güneş*** *(Likya Caddesi 4)* is more expensive, but has a wonderful choice of mezes; a good meal should cost between US$8 and US$12.

On the corner at the end of the bazaar ***Pizza 74***, a budget travellers' favourite, serves freshly baked pide. There are pricier restaurants and tea gardens beside the marina.

For self-caterers, there's a good *food market* between Çarşı Caddesi and Tütün Sokak, which really buzzes on Tuesday when local farmers flock to town to sell their produce.

Entertainment

The cafes overlooking the harbour are a good place to enjoy the sunset and a pre-dinner drink. The bazaar area has a liberal sprinkling of bars, including the convivial ***Car Cemetery Bar***, a good place for music and boozing, the ***Otantik Bar***, which sometimes has live Turkish music, and ***Ottoman Cafe Bar*** next door. ***Yasmin Bar*** *(Liman*

TURKEY

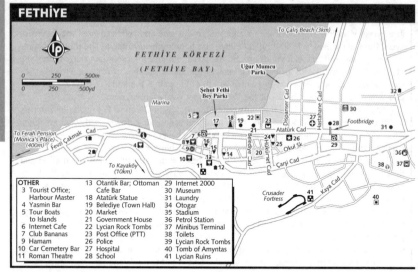

FETHİYE

To Çalış Beach (3km)

FETHİYE KÖRFEZİ
(FETHİYE BAY)

Uğur Mumcu
Parkı

Şehut Fethi
Bey Parkı

Marina

To Ferah Pension
(Monica's Place)
(400m)

To Kayaköy
(10km)

Atatürk Cad

Crusader
Fortress

OTHER	13	Otantik Bar; Ottoman	29	Internet 2000
3	Tourist Office;		Cafe Bar	30	Museum
	Harbour Master	18	Atatürk Statue	31	Laundry
4	Yasmin Bar	19	Belediye (Town Hall)	34	Otogar
5	Tour Boats	20	Market	35	Stadium
	to Islands	21	Government House	36	Petrol Station
6	Internet Cafe	22	Lycian Rock Tombs	37	Minibus Terminal
7	Club Bananas	23	Post Office (PTT)	38	Toilets
9	Hamam	26	Police	39	Lycian Rock Tombs
10	Car Cemetery Bar	27	Hospital	40	Tomb of Amyntas
11	Roman Theatre	28	School	41	Lycian Ruins

Caddesi) has the advantage of a view across the marina.

Club Bananas, near the hamam in the bazaar, is the current clubbing hot spot.

Getting There & Away
If you're going nonstop to Antalya, note that the *yayla* (inland) route is far shorter and cheaper (US$8) than the *sahil* (coastal) route (US$12). Buses from the otogar also serve Kalkan (US$2.50) and Kaş (US$3). Also note that Fethiye's otogar is notorious for touts – ignore them and make your own choices about accommodation.

Minibuses depart from their own terminal, 3km west of the otogar towards the centre, making short hops to other points along the coast, like Patara (US$2.75), Kınık (for Xanthos, US$2), Hisarönü (for Kayaköy) and Ölüdeniz (US$1).

AROUND FETHİYE
Kayaköy
The most interesting (and energetic) way to spend a day is to walk to the 'ghost town' of **Kayaköy** (also known as Karmylassos or Levissi), a 10km walk south of Fethiye. On the road up through the hills, you'll pass the ruins of a **Crusader fortress**, built by the Knights of St John. Kayaköy was predominantly inhabited by Greeks until 1923 when there was an exchange of peoples between

Greece and Turkey after the War of Independence. Totally deserted, save for a few tourist cafes, the abandoned village is very atmospheric. Entry is US$1.25. If you don't fancy the long walk, take a bus from the otogar to Hisarönü, then hike for 2km from there.

In Kayaköy, climb up to the Panayia Piryiotissa basilica, the village's main church, and you'll see signs pointing to a track over to Ölüdeniz (see the Ölüdeniz section later in this chapter). The 5km track down through the pine forests is fantastic, affording swooning views of the coast and famous beach. (It's part of the Lycian Way – see the boxed text 'The Lycian Way' earlier in this chapter.) You need to take care, though, as the route isn't always clear and is quite uneven in places.

Tlos, Letoon & Xanthos
Lycia was heavily populated in ancient times, as shown by the large number of wonderful old cities easily accessible by bus or dolmuş from Fethiye. The roads on the Lycian Peninsula are always being improved so get the free, recent map from the tourist office.

Tlos, 40km east of Fethiye and far up into the mountains on the inland route to Antalya, was an important citadel city in ancient Lycia. Today it is possible to see the ruins of an Ottoman fortress on the acropolis, Lycian rock-cut tombs (including that of Bellerophon), a theatre and necropolis. At

FETHİYE

To Kaş (110km) &
Antalya (295km)

To Hisarönü (11km),
Ölüdeniz &
Kayaköy (15km)

PLACES TO STAY
1   İrem Pansiyon
2   Ideal Pension
12 Ülgen Pension
32 Göreme Pansiyon
33 Olympiyat Pansiyon

PLACES TO EAT
8   Pizza 74
14 Meğri; Cafe Rihtim
15 Duck Pond Cafe
16 Restaurant Güneş
17 Restaurants; Tea Gardens
24 Saray Lokantası
25 Sofra 2000

Bellerophon's tomb, look for the bas-relief that depicts him riding Pegasus, the winged horse. The site is open from 8 am to 5 pm daily and admission is US$1.

In a fertile valley filled with tomato greenhouses, the **Letoön**, shrine of the goddess Leto, is 63km east of Fethiye and then a few kilometres off the highway. It can be reached by dolmuş from Fethiye; you are dropped off in Kumluova village, a short walk from the ruins. The site has excellent Lycian mosaics, a good theatre and a sacred pool used as the place of worship of Leto (open daily from 8.30 am to 5 pm, US$1).

Xanthos, a few kilometres east of Letoon above the village of Kınık, is among the most impressive archaeological sites along this coast, but the view is marred by more of those tomato greenhouses. It has a Roman theatre, Harpy Tomb and Lycian pillar tombs. The site is open during daylight hours and admission is free. Many of Xanthos' finest artefacts were carted off to the British Museum – the inscriptions and decorations you see are copies.

Saklıkent Gorge

About 12km after the turn-off to Tlos the spectacular 18km-long **Saklıkent Gorge** is a must for the adventurous. You approach the gorge along a boardwalk suspended above the river, then you have to wade the river,

which is icy cold because it sees no sun. The boardwalk is open from 8 am to 5 pm daily and costs US$2. You can hire plastic sandals for US$0.50. Excursions are available from pensions in Fethiye, Kaş and Kalkan. During the busy tourist season there are regular dolmuşes (about US$2) from Fethiye – these are marked 'Kayadibi/Saklıkent.

ÖLÜDENİZ
☎ 252

South of Fethiye, 17km over the mountains, is the gorgeous blue lagoon of Ölüdeniz (Dead Sea), too beautiful for its own good and now one of the most famous beach spots on the Mediterranean. This said, the beach – like many in Turkey – is rather gravelly and looks much better from afar than up close. It also gets hideously busy in summer and you have to pay to use the best strip inside the 'national park' (US$0.60 per person, US$2.50 per car).

Inland from the beach are moderately priced bungalows and camping areas, as well as some hotels. During the day Belcekız/Ölüdeniz, as the town is called, is chocker with package tourists, most of whom head back to Hisarönü when the sun sets. It still has good nightlife.

Budget travellers usually head to Butterfly Valley (see Butterfly Valley later in this chapter) for a few days.

Places to Stay & Eat

Around the beach there are some 50 different accommodation options; the tourist department cooperative office by the dolmuş stop can help you locate somewhere if the following are full.

Ölüdeniz Camping (☎ 617 0048, fax 617 0181, e mmsbar@hotmail.com) north around the bay from the main beach, is a relaxed place with clean toilets and showers, cabin and tent accommodation, a book exchange and the *M&M Bar* (which has a happy hour and Internet facilities). Rates are around US$5 per person in a cabin.

The family-run *Oba Camping* (☎ 617 0470, fax 617 0522, e obamotel@superonline.com), set back from the main beach, is also a well-run operation with cabins for two without/with showers for US$8/10. There's also a smart *restaurant*, Internet access and a laundry service.

The Best View in Turkey

Baba Dağı, the 1969m mountain that looms over Ölüdeniz, is the highest commercial tandem paraglider launching site in the world. All I can suggest is that, if you can afford it (and the prospect doesn't frighten you), then jump! It's the most exciting thing I did while in Turkey and the view on the way down of the Mediterranean, the islands, the hinterland and Ölüdeniz is unsurpassed.

The ride up the mountain along a narrow track in a 4WD vehicle is frightening to say the least and after surviving that, the flight is almost an anticlimax.

The superb pilots took me up as high as 2800m (sometimes through cloud). They videoed the flight, carried on a conversation, put the glider into controlled spiral turns and, finally, performed an effortless landing. You can even smoke or drink a beer on the way down.

There are several operators along the beach at Ölüdeniz, including the competent Focus (☎ 617 0401) next to the Sun Cafe which has a great group of pilots, Aventura (☎ 617 0391) and Sky Sports (☎ 617 0511). In season you'll pay around US$110 a flight (plus US$30 for a video and essential 'I did it' T-shirt); out of season you'll be able to bargain this down to around US$80.

Be warned: There have been fatal paragliding accidents here, so if you're at all unsure about the reputation of an operator or its pilots, don't risk it.

Jeff Williams

Closer to the beach, but more basic, is *Deniz Camping* (☎ *617 0045*); attached to the perennially popular *Buzz Bar* serving an amazing range of cocktails.

The open-air *Sun Cafe* next to the dolmuş stop by the beach serves superb wood-fired pizzas. Along the beach, several other places offer cheap meals and snacks. More upmarket restaurants are along the pedestrian mall that runs perpendicular to the beach. Also give the attractive *Grapevine Restaurant & Bar* next to Deniz Camping a look.

At the height of the season, Ölüdeniz can get really busy at night. Popular bars, apart from Buzz Bar, are *Crusoe's*, which has US$2 beers, and the everlasting *Underground* on the road to Fethiye.

Getting There & Away

Dolmuşes (US$2) regularly ply the route from Fethiye to Ölüdeniz via Hisarönü, departing from the minibus terminal in Fethiye, south of Çarşı Caddesi, and east of the market area.

Dolmuşes for Fethiye congregate in Belcekız/Ölüdeniz, where the road meets the beach, beside the Sun Cafe.

BUTTERFLY VALLEY

This secluded getaway, 8km south of Ölüdeniz, has become a firm fixture on the backpacker circuit. The butterflies, including the Jersey Tiger, are there in profusion from June to September but they aren't the main attraction. Travellers come here to enjoy the waterfalls and trekking opportunities and to drop out, away from the package crowds (who only visit during the day).

The boat trip over from Belcekız/Ölüdeniz is US$5 return and, in season, it leaves five times daily. At other times of year rough seas makes taking the dolmuş to the village of Faralya and hiking down into the valley a preferable option.

In season for US$10 you can get accommodation in a *treehouse* (basically a wooden shack on stilts) with all meals and a beer (camping is US$2 less). If you are budgeting, take your own water, food and beer. The only other basic accommodation is at *George's House*, a family-run place in Faralya that serves good food. There are three dolmuşes daily from Fethiye to Faralya, from where it's a long hard walk down into the valley.

PATARA & KALKAN
☎ 242

If you're still desperate for a beach after Ölüdeniz, Patara's 50m wide, 20km long strip is the one to head for. Patara was also the birthplace of St Nicholas, the 4th century Byzantine bishop of Myra (farther east) who achieved posthumous international fame as Santa Claus. Long before Santa, Patara was famous for its Temple of Apollo (open daylight hours; US$1).

Lodgings in Patara village (aka Gelemiş), 2.5km inland from the beach, range from camping to cheap pensions and hotels. The *Flower Pansiyon (☎ 843 5164)*, *Rose Pension (☎ 843 5165)* and *Golden Pansiyon (☎ 843 5162)* all charge about US$10 for a double room (some have private showers).

To get to Patara, take a dolmuş from Kaş (US$1.50, one hour) or from Fethiye (US$2, 1½ hours).

Tumbling down a steep hillside to a marina is **Kalkan**, 11km east of the Patara turnoff. It's a pretty place, but Kaş farther around the coast is nicer and has more to offer. If you do decide to stay, look for cheap pensions at the top of the town. The simple *Çelik Pansiyon (☎ 844 3022, Yalıboyu 9)* charges US$9/16 for rooms with bathroom, breakfast included. *Akın Pansiyon (☎ 844 3025)* towards the harbour has doubles without/with showers for US$16/22, breakfast included. *Pension Patara (☎ 844 3076)* close to the waterfront is an atmospheric old Greek mansion with doubles with bathroom for US$22; it has a nice rooftop terrace.

On the road between Kalkan and Kaş is the impressive mountain gorge of **Kaputaş**, crossed by a small bridge. Below the bridge, steps lead to a beautiful sandy cove (take a dolmuş from Kalkan or Kaş, US$0.50). Not far after the gorge is the **Blue Cave** (Mavi Mağara), which is visited by many tour boats.

There are frequent minibuses to Fethiye (US$1.50), Kaş (US$1) and Patara Beach in summer. The bus stop is on the north-west edge of town near the main coastal road.

KAŞ
☎ 322 • pop 5000

Kaş is without question the choicest resort on the Turquoise Coast. Farther in its favour is the wide range of adventure activities on offer, including diving, sea kayaking, mountain biking and jeep trips into the rocky hinterland. Known as Antiphellos in ancient times, Kaş also has a picturesque quayside square, friendly people, a big market on Friday, and, at nearby Kaputaş, a lovely beach. What more could you want?

The otogar is north of the town centre and up the hill a walkable distance on Kaş Antalya Yolu. The helpful tourist office (☎ 836 1238) at Cumhuriyet Meydanı is open from 8.30 am to noon and 1 to 7 pm weekdays, and from 10 am to noon and 1 to 7 pm weekends. There's a Yapı Kredi ATM one block back from the waterfront.

Things to See & Do

A few hundred metres west of the town centre is a well-preserved **theatre**. Lycian stone **sarcophagi** are dotted about the streets, and tombs are cut into the cliffs above the town. Two to look out for are the **Monument Tomb** uphill east from the tourist office and the 3rd-century-BC **Doric Tomb**, which is over the hill behind the theatre (entry is free).

The Greek island of **Kastellorizo** (Meis Adası) is visible a short distance across the water. Day trips, leaving at 10 am and returning at 4 pm, cost around US$30. You need to book these the night before and leave your passport details with the agent you book your ticket through.

Day boat tours to Kekova (see Kekova later in this chapter) are around US$20 including lunch, but a far better way to tour this area is on a kayaking trip organised by Bougainville Travel (☎ 836 3142, fax 836 1605) at İbrahim Serin Caddesi, which is well worth US$45 including a hearty lunch in Üçağız. If you're an experienced kayaker, Bougainville can rent you a kayak for your own trip.

Bougainville Travel is also one the most reputable of Kaş' nine diving operators. Barakuda Diving Centre (☎/fax 836 2996, **e** info@barakuda-kas.de) is also good. A single dive in the bay, including all equipment, costs around US$25, more for longer trips.

If you fancy mountain biking down from the foothills of the Akdağ range to Kaş (a thrill-and-a-half ride), the guys at Bougainville Travel are again the ones to see. You can take an organised trip in season or rent a bike for around US$7.50 a day.

Other adventure options include canyoning trips to Saklıkent Gorge for around US$25, including lunch.

Places to Stay

Kaş Camping, in an olive grove 1km west of town past the theatre, costs US$5 per pitch and also has simple bungalows for around US$8.

At the otogar you'll be accosted by pension touts; expect to pay no more than US$8/12 for singles/doubles. It's not the

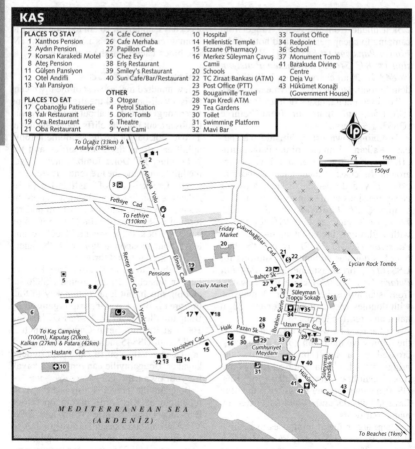

KAŞ

PLACES TO STAY	24	Cafe Corner	10	Hospital	33	Tourist Office
1 Xanthos Pension	26	Cafe Merhaba	14	Hellenistic Temple	34	Redpoint
2 Aydın Pension	27	Papillon Cafe	15	Eczane (Pharmacy)	36	School
7 Korsan Karakedi Motel	35	Chez Evy	16	Merkez Süleyman Çavuş	37	Monument Tomb
8 Ateş Pension	38	Eriş Restaurant		Camii	41	Barakuda Diving
11 Gülşen Pansiyon	39	Smiley's Restaurant	20	Schools		Centre
12 Otel Andifli	40	Sun Cafe/Bar/Restaurant	22	TC Ziraat Bankası (ATM)	42	Deja Vu
13 Yalı Pansiyon			23	Post Office (PTT)	43	Hükümet Konaǧi
		OTHER	25	Bougainville Travel		(Government House)
PLACES TO EAT	3	Otogar	28	Yapı Kredi ATM		
17 Çobanoǧlu Patisserie	4	Petrol Station	29	Tea Gardens		
18 Yalı Restaurant	5	Doric Tomb	30	Toilet		
19 Ora Restaurant	6	Theatre	31	Swimming Platform		
21 Oba Restaurant	9	Yeni Cami	32	Mavi Bar		

best area to stay, but just north of the otogar there is a collection of reasonable pensions including the **Xanthos** (☎ 836 1509, *Otogar Karşısı*) and **Aydın** (☎ 836 1624, *Yeniyol Caddesi 47*), which is run by a friendly family and is clean; the rooms have bathrooms and balconies.

There are lots of places near the mosque (Yeni Cami). **Otel Andifli** (☎ 836 1042, *Hastane Caddesi 7*) has tidy rooms and sea views for US$16/20, breakfast included. Nearby are **Gülşen Pansiyon** (☎ 836 1171, *Hastane Caddesi 23*) and **Yalı Pansiyon** (☎ 836 1132, fax 836 3487, *Hastane Caddesi 11*), both of which have rooms with great sea views for around US$10 a double.

Although you have to go to the rooftop terrace of **Ateş Pension** (☎ 836 1393,

ⓔ *ates_pension@hotmail.com*) for the views, the rooms have character and are good value at US$7/9 including breakfast. It's north-west of Yeni Cami and part of the No 1 network.

The cheapest deal in Kaş is to be found at **Smiley's Restaurant** (☎ 836 2812, *Günsoy Sokak*). The deal is that provided you eat in the restaurant (where mains go for around US$4), you get to sleep on an aged mattress in the large dorm rooms upstairs for free.

A good mid-range option is **Korsan Karakedi Motel** (☎ 836 1887, fax 836 3086, *Yeni Cami Sokak 7*) which has rooms for US$8/16. For more upmarket accommodation hike up the hill east of Cumhuriyet Meydanı.

Places to Eat

Cafe Corner at the post office end of İbrahim Serin Caddesi has been a meeting spot for ages and is ever popular; it serves juices or a vegetable omelette for US$1 and yogurt with fruit and honey for US$1.50. *Cafe Merhaba* across the street is good for cakes, juices and coffee.

The *Papillon Cafe (Bahçe Sokak)* is a bit more expensive (and tends to play very loud Turkish music) but has an interesting menu featuring European and Turkish dishes. *Oba Restaurant (Çukurbağlilar Caddesi 26)* is more relaxing and serves decent meze – a mixed plate is US$4.

Ora Restaurant just north of the market square has some outdoor tables and serves a good range of Turkish cuisine at reasonable prices.

The *Yalı* (Elmalı Caddesi) is one of the best cheapies in town and very popular. Across the road, satisfy your sweet tooth at *Çobanoğlu Patisserie*.

The *Eriş (Gürsoy Sokak 13)*, in a courtyard behind the tourist office, is another popular place, as much for its setting as its food.

Save your lira for a meal at *Chez Evy (Terzi Sokak 2)*, where you can eat fantastic French countryside cuisine in an interior decked out like the old Turkish curiosity shop. In summer there's a delightful courtyard. It's worth dropping by for a glass of wine and one of Evy's delicious crepes, if nothing else.

Entertainment

The *Sun Cafe/Bar/Restaurant* is a lively, stylish place on Hükümet Caddesi. Farther up the hill you'll find *Deja Vu*.

Mavi Bar facing onto Cumhuriyet Meydanı has a bit of a rockers' vibe and is a haunt for locals. By the end of the night everyone ends up at the funky *Redpoint (Süleyman Topçu Sokağı)*, which rocks on till 3 am.

Getting There & Away

From the otogar up the hill on Kaş Antalya Yolu, there are regular buses to/from Fethiye (US$3, 2½ hours), Patara (US$1.50, one hour) and Antalya (US$5, four hours). To reach Olimpos, take an Antalya bus and ask to be dropped off at the turn-off from the highway, where you can wait for a dolmuş or hitch a lift.

KAŞ TO ANTALYA

From Kaş, the highway heads east, hugging the coast and backed by pine clad mountains, then north to Antalya, passing the ruins of a dozen ancient Lycian cities.

The area has great secluded beaches, areas of rugged forest ideal for walking and ruins galore. The best place to stop is Olimpos from where you can walk to see the flames of the Chimaera.

Üçağiz & Kekova

☎ 242

Going up into the hills, 33km east of Kaş, the road leads south to Üçağız, a village set amid scattered Lycian ruins. To reach this quaint farming and fishing hamlet you need to take the turn-off from the highway and travel another 19km. The village is built atop the ruins of the 4th century BC Lycian **Teimiussa**. The name means 'three mouths', which refers to the three points of entry to the harbour.

This is an idyllic place in which to cosy up, with a handful of simple pensions and a few waterfront restaurants. Try *Flower Pension (☎ 874 2043)*, which has doubles for US$18 including breakfast, and the *Ibrahim Liman Marina Restaurant* which serves a delicious plate of mixed meze for US$4 and fresh fish dishes.

There are occasional minibuses from Kaş to Üçağız, but the usual way to get there is by boat tour. Check with the tourist office in Kaş for details.

Across the water to the east is the even prettier village of **Kale**, site of the ancient city of **Simena** and the dramatic Crusader **castle** of the Knights of St John, built on the base of an even older fortress. Take a boat here from Üçağız (around US$9 return). The village also has some appealing pensions.

The slender island of **Kekova**, across the bay, has a beach and interesting Byzantine ruins, some of which earthquakes have caused to slip into the Mediterranean. The submerged ruins are referred to as Batık Şehir (Sunken City) – you're not allowed to swim here so the ruins are best viewed up close on the kayaking tours run by Bougainville Travel (see Kaş earlier in this chapter).

Tours of the bay depart from Üçağız (US$10 to US$16 per person) but most visitors to the region come on boat tours from Kaş or Kalkan. If you can't afford a glass-bottom boat for viewing the underwater ruins, get a smaller boat and make sure the owner has a glass-bottom bucket!

Demre (Kale)

Demre (ancient Myra, also known as Kale), set in a rich alluvial plain, is another place associated with the 4th-century bishop who, later canonised as St Nicholas, was the original Father Christmas or Santa Claus (Noel Baba in Turkish). You can visit the restored 12th-century **Church of St Nicholas**, which houses his tomb. It's open from 8 am to 5.30 pm daily (admission US$3).

Some 2km inland from the church at Demre are the ruins of **Myra**. Here you can find a rock face honeycombed with ancient **Lycian tombs**, right next to a large **Roman theatre**. The ruins are accessible from 8 am to 5.30 pm daily for a charge of US$1. It costs US$5 to get a taxi to the ruins from the otogar. There are frequent buses and dolmuşes between Demre and Kaş (US$2, one hour, 45km).

Olimpos & The Chimaera
☎ 242

After climbing into the Beydağları, the mountains which form a natural barrier between the Finike Körfezi (Finike Bay) and Antalya Körfezi (Antalya Bay), you reach a turn-off marked for **Olimpos**. From here it's just over 8km down a winding unpaved road to Olimpos village, and a farther 3.5km on an ever-worsening road along a riverbed to the site of Olimpos and a pebbly beach. There's a US$1 entry charge to the ruins and the beach, but the admission booths are not always staffed.

Wild and abandoned, the 2nd-century-BC Olimpos ruins peek out from forest copses, rock outcrops and the riverbank. Along with other Lycian coastal cities, Olimpos went into decline in the 1st century BC. It recovered somewhat when the Romans arrived in the 1st century AD, but was finally abandoned in the 15th century. It's a truly beautiful spot and has long been a fixture on the backpacker circuit. At the height of summer this means the place heaves with visitors, and the treehouse complexes, for which the valley is famous, take on the feel of a hippy Butlins holiday camp. We've also received reports of theft and sexual assaults. Out of season, though, Olimpos can be idyllic – no wonder visitors seem incapable of leaving.

According to legend, **the Chimaera**, a natural eternal flame, is the hot breath of a subterranean monster killed by Bellerophon riding the winged horse Pegasus. The job wasn't done properly, hence the flames.

In reality, the flames licking from between rocks in the foothills of Tahtalı Dağı (Mt Olimpos) are caused by natural gas igniting when it meets the air. To walk here from Olimpos takes a couple of hours at a leisurely pace, slightly less from the nearby village of Çıralı – the trail from the car park off the main road is clearly marked. It's best to set off late afternoon and reach the flames at dusk, when they look their most dramatic. Take care not to add to the rubbish that, sadly, is scattered around the area.

Places to Stay In addition to the treehouse camps of Olimpos, there are many hotels and pensions at Çıralı on the next cove to the east. It is much closer to the Chimaera than Olimpos, more popular with Turks, and there are plenty of places to eat and stay. Çıralı beach is a nesting site for loggerhead turtles.

Olimpos Although Olimpos is famous for its treehouses, the only operation that actually has houses in trees is Kadir's. The rest are simple log cabins that more often than not look like POW camps. Don't let this put you off, but nor should you come with romantic notions of living like Tarzan either. One more word of warning – we've received a steady stream of reports of theft in the treehouses. If you want security, ask the manager for a padlock for your cabin.

Prices at all the treehouses tend to be around US$9 per night, including breakfast and a generally vegetarian evening meal.

The first major complex you'll come to on the 2km strip down to the beach is **Kadir's Yörük Top Tree House** (☎ 892 1250, fax 892 1110, e treehouse@supe ronline.com.tr). The original treehouse operation, it certainly remains the funkiest, if not necessarily the best. Dorms are US$6, treehouse doubles/triples US$7 and cabins without/with bathroom US$9/12. This place is the Disneyland of Olimpos, with a happening bar, bike rental, an unreliable Internet service and room for 200 plus (there are only six shared showers and toilets, so you do the maths).

Around 1km farther on, *Bayram's* (☎ 892 1243) was the most popular venue when we visited, partly because of its affiliation with the No 1 network of hostels. It's a laid-back, attractive place, able to house around 70 people, and apart from cabins on stilts has concrete double rooms for US$10.

Next door, a tad closer to the beach, is *Zeus Treehouses* (☎ 892 1347, e zeusolympos@hotmail.com), which has friendly management and lots of cabins set amid orange groves.

Sheriff's (☎ 892 1301), run by the local personality of the same name, has rows of wooden cabins (US$7) around a field of maize and some sturdier ones with concrete floors for US$10.

Orange Pension (☎ 892 1317) is another good option that comes recommended by several readers. Take your pick from treehouses (US$7), cabins with bathroom (US$10), or rooms in the actual pension (US$12). *Şaban* (☎ 892 1265) charges much the same, is popular with German and Dutch travellers and has a quieter vibe than other places.

Kadir's, Bayram's and Sheriff's all have bars, with beers around US$2. If you tire of these, then there's also *Gypsy's*, next to Zeus Treehouses. Apart from drinking, playing cards and backgammon, and chewing the cud with fellow travellers, all the treehouses offer night-time trips to see the Chimaera.

Çıralı There are lots of good cheap pensions, a camping ground and a few restaurants at Çıralı. Accommodation tends to be quieter and more secure than at Olimpos, but there's not the same atmosphere.

Green Point Caravan & Tent Camping, at the northern end of Çıralı Beach, is clean and well situated and discourages free camping on the beach, which endangers nesting turtles. Don't sleep on the beach unless you've a hard shell, flippers and weep profusely as you squeeze out 50-plus eggs.

Karakuş (☎ 825 7061, fax 825 7060) is one of the cheapest places with fine rooms with private bathroom for US$7 per person including breakfast.

Çıralı Pension (☎ 825 7122), on the road to the Chimaera, is a bit more upmarket. It has a *restaurant* and comfortable singles/doubles with bathroom for US$14/24 including breakfast.

Aygün Pension (☎ 825 7146), 200m before Çıralı Pension, is an appealing family-run place serving excellent meals; it's well worth the US$12/20 charge (breakfast included). Air-con doubles, including the fab breakfast, are US$20.

Çıralı is a good place to come for lunch if you're staying over at Olimpos; there are plenty of cafes inland, including the small *Inca Restaurant*, which offer better deals than the beachside operations.

Getting There & Away Dolmuşes and buses from Kaş and Antalya stop on the coastal highway near the Çavuşköy and Olimpos turn-off – here dolmuşes wait until they are at least half full before leaving the main road for Olimpos. It can cost from US$1 to US$2 to get to the treehouses.

There is no dolmuş from here to Çıralı; hitch up to the highway if you can, or catch a cab (at least US$10). From Olimpos you can walk around to Çıralı but you may have to pay entry to the ruins on the way.

Every day except Sunday there is one direct minibus from Antalya to Çıralı; it departs Antalya in the late afternoon, returning the following morning at 6.30 am. There are occasional buses to/from Kumluca (10km back west along the coastal road, where you can connect with buses to Kaş or Antalya) especially on Friday, market day. If you get dropped on the main coastal highway, the bus to Antalya is US$2.

ANTALYA
☎ 242 • pop 600,000

Antalya sprawls around the bay beneath the Taurus (Toros) Mountains. It is the chief city on Turkey's central Mediterranean coast and although it has a population of over half a million, it is worth a day or two of your time.

At the centre of the historic city is the Roman harbour, now the yacht marina. The Kaleiçi area overlooking the harbour is packed with pensions. The Antalya Archaeological Museum is a fine introduction to the spectacular nearby ruins, including Termessos, Perge and Aspendos. Skiing is also possible at the tiny resort of Saklıkent on Bey Dağları.

The city was founded in the 1st century BC and named Attaleia after its founder

TURKEY

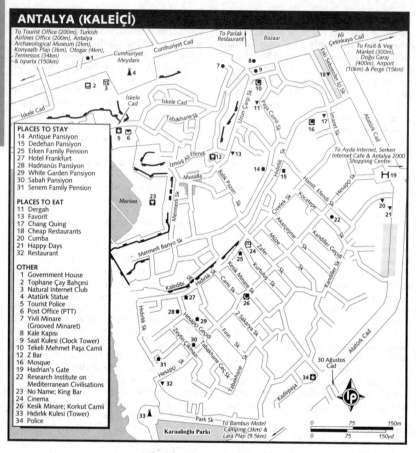

ANTALYA (KALEİÇİ)

To Tourist Office (200m), Turkish
Airlines Office (200m), Antalya
Archaeological Museum (2km),
Konyaaltı Plajı (3km), Otogar (4km),
Termessos (34km)
& Isparta (150km)

To Parlak
Restaurant
Bazaar
Ali
Çetinkaya Cad

Cumhuriyet Cad

Cumhuriyet
Meydanı

To Fruit & Veg
Market (300m),
Doğu Garaj
(400m), Airport
(10km) & Perge (15km)

İskele
Cad
İskele Cad

Tabakhane Sk

To Ayda Internet, Serken
Internet Cafe & Antalya 2000
Shopping Centre

İzmirli Ali Efendi

Musalla

Marina

Mermerli Banyo Sk

Kaledibi Sk

Hıdırlık Sk

To Bambus Motel
Camping (3km) &
Lara Plajı (9.5km)

Karaalioğlu Parkı

30 Ağustos
Cad

Atatürk Cad

PLACES TO STAY
14 Antique Pansiyon
15 Dedehan Pansiyon
25 Erken Family Pension
27 Hotel Frankfurt
28 Hadrianüs Pansiyon
29 White Garden Pansiyon
30 Sabah Pansiyon
31 Senem Family Pension

PLACES TO EAT
11 Dergah
13 Favorit
17 Chang Quing
18 Cheap Restaurants
20 Cumba
21 Happy Days
32 Restaurant

OTHER
1 Government House
2 Tophane Çay Bahçesi
3 Natural Internet Club
4 Atatürk Statue
5 Tourist Police
6 Post Office (PTT)
7 Yivli Minare
   (Grooved Minaret)
8 Kale Kapısı
9 Saat Kulesi (Clock Tower)
10 Tekeli Mehmet Paşa Camii
12 Z Bar
16 Mosque
19 Hadrian's Gate
22 Research Institute on
   Mediterranean Civilisations
23 No Name; King Bar
24 Cinema
26 Kesik Minare; Korkut Camii
33 Hıdırlık Kulesi (Tower)
34 Police

0 ___ 75 ___ 150m
0 ___ 75 ___ 150yd

Attalus II. In 1207 the Seljuks of Konya
took over and gave the city a number of its
current landmarks.

Orientation & Information

The city centre is at Kale Kapısı, a major intersection right next to Cumhuriyet Meydanı, with its dramatic equestrian statue of
Atatürk. Kaleiçi, the old town, is south of
Kale Kapısı down the hill. The main otogar
is 4km north of the centre on the D650 Hwy
to Burdur. There are service buses from the
otogar to Kaleiçi. The Doğu Garaj (eastern
otogar), for buses to local beaches, is 600m
east (left) of Kale Kapısı along Ali
Çetinkaya Caddesi.

The tourist office (☎ 241 1747) at
Cumhuriyet Caddesi 2 is 350m west of Kale

Kapısı (look for the sign 'Antalya Devlet
Tiyatrosu' on the right-hand side; it's in this
building). The Turkish Airlines office
(☎ 243 4382) is in the same building. The
central post office is east of Kale Kapısı,
where İsmet Paşa Caddesi meets Atatürk
Caddesi.

Several Internet cafes are located just off
Atatürk Caddesi, near Hadrian's Gate, including Ayda Internet and Serken Internet
Cafe. The Natural Internet Club is beside
the fountain, just beneath the Atatürk statue.

Things to See

Behind the **Saat Kulesi** or clock tower is
Antalya's hallmark, the Seljuk-period **Yivli
Minare** (Grooved Minaret), which rises
above a former mosque, now the **Fine Arts**

Gallery. On nearby Uzun Çarşı Sokak, the street by the clock tower, is the **Tekeli Mehmet Paşa Camii**, which has beautiful Arabic inscriptions in the coloured tiles above the windows and doors.

From Kale Kapısı, go east 100m along Ali Çetinkaya Caddesi to Atatürk Caddesi, then south to the impressive triple-arched **Hadrian's Gate**, built for the Roman emperor's visit in AD 130. Farther along, perched on cliffs above the sea, is the pleasant **Karaalioğlu Parkı**.

Heading back from the park into Kaleiçi, the fenced-off **Kesik Minare** (Broken Minaret), marking a ruined Roman temple, is on Hesapçi Sokak.

There are handsome restored Ottoman buildings all around the old quarter. Particularly worth searching out are the two housing the **Research Institute on Mediterranean Civilisations** (Kocatepe Sokak 25). Here you'll find an interesting exhibition of medieval flags and old photographs in the beautifully restored Agios Georgios Church. It's open from 9 am to 6 pm daily; admission is US$2.

Before returning to Cumhuriyet Caddesi take a closer look at the picturesque old harbour, an atmospheric place to stroll at night.

The excellent **Antalya Archaeological Museum** is 2km west from Kale Kapısı at the end of Kenan Evren Bulvarı. Apart from the usual Roman artefacts the fascinating Tomb Room has a collection of Christian art, including the bones of St Nicholas. It's open from 9 am to 5 pm Tuesday to Sunday; admission is US$2. Take a dolmuş here from Cumhuriyet Caddesi.

Places to Stay

Bambus Motel Camping (☎ 321 5263) on the Lara Plajı road has modern facilities on the beach – it's 3km east of the centre and is only suitable if you have your own vehicle.

The quiet, cobbled streets of Kaleiçi are the best place to base yourself. Go to the far west end of the central Hesapçi Sokak to find *Senem Family Pension* (☎ 247 1752, fax 247 0615, Zeytingeçidi Sokak 9), run by a charming lady. Tidy singles/doubles start at US$10/14 including breakfast and there's a rooftop bar/restaurant with fine views.

Another winner is *Sabah Pansiyon* (☎ 247 5345, fax 247 5347, Hesapçı Sokak 60), a friendly place with rooms to suit all budgets; sleep on the roof for US$3.50, in the older section for US$5 or in smart aircon doubles with bathroom for US$18.

Erken Family Pension (☎ 247 6092, fax 248 9801, Hıdırlık Sokak 5) is a reasonable cheapie, a bit dusty, but with character. Rooms are US$6/12.

Hadrianüs Pansiyon (☎ 244 0030, Zeytin Çikmazı Sokak 4/A) has old-fashioned rooms with fridges and TV, and a pleasant garden dining area where you can get a buffet breakfast. It charges US$8 per person. Nearby is the clean, well-maintained *White Garden Pansiyon* (☎ 241 9115, fax 241 2062, Hesapçı Geçidi), a good mid-range choice. It has a courtyard and large doubles for US$20.

Antique Pansiyon (☎ 242 4615, fax 241 5890, Paşa Camii Sokak 28) has bags of character, soft beds and a garden. Rooms are US$8/12. Also worth checking out is *Dedehan Pansiyon* (☎ 248 3787, Mescid Sokak 29), a tastefully decorated place opposite.

The prettily decorated *Hotel Frankfurt* (☎/fax 247 6224, Hıdırlık Sokak 7) is a spotless place with rooms for US$20/30 including breakfast.

Places to Eat

Many pensions serve good meals at decent prices. Eski Sebzeciler İçi Sokak, a short street just south-west of the junction of Cumhuriyet and Atatürk Caddesis, is filled with open-air restaurants where a kebap, salad and drink can cost as little as US$3. The local speciality is *tandır kebap* (mutton cooked in an earthenware pot), which tends to be expensive for what you get.

Chang Quing is an unmissable Chinese restaurant, south of Eski Sebzeciler İçi Sokak. Fried noodles are US$3, vegetable rice US$1.20. Along Atatürk Caddesi there are several Western-style fast-food places, the local option being *Happy Days* which has a salad bar, as well as pizza and burgers.

Cumba, near Hadrian's Gate, serves excellent Turkish food including *hibeş,* a spicy paprika meze, and İnegöl köfte. It has courtyard dining and live music. Expect to pay around US$7 a head including wine.

Parlak, in a courtyard just north of Kale Kapisi and off the south end of Kazım Özalp Caddesi, does great spit-roasted chicken with rice for US$3. A beer here is also cheap at US$1.

Favorit (Uzun Çarşı Sokak 19) is a bit touristy, but does serves a reasonably priced tandır kebap as well as a wider range of other dishes. *Dergah (Paşa Camii Sokak)* is a cheap kebap and pide joint with a garden.

The overpriced restaurants near or on the marina cater for tourists on cruises. One exception is the *restaurant* just north of the Hıdırlık Kulesi. It is not actually on the marina, but overlooks the sea and Mermeli Beach. It's superbly sited, friendly and has good food.

For self-caterers, there are many little *pastry shops* on Eski Sebzeciler İçi Sokak (Old Inner Street of the Greengrocers Market), at the intersection of Cumhuriyet and Atatürk Caddesis. The *fruit and vegetable* market is 300m east of the intersection of Cumhuriyet and Atatürk Caddesis.

Entertainment

Antalya is a popular package tourist destination and as such has plenty of nightlife. The *Tophane Çay Bahçesi* overlooking the marina is a lovely spot to while away the early evening over a beer or cup of tea.

At night, locals saunter around the marina and Karaalioğlu Parkı listening to music, watching sculptors or sipping coffee or tea in the *çay bahçesi* (tea gardens). By the marina, *No Name* and *King Bar* are both expensive watering holes; the more studenty *Z Bar* up the hill is cheaper and smokier and churns out rock and blues.

In the Antalya 2000 shopping centre, just off Atatürk Caddesi near Hadrian's Gate, there is a multiplex cinema. There's also a cinema in the heart of Kaleiçi at the top of Hıdırlık Sokak.

Getting There & Away

Turkish Airlines has daily nonstop flights from Antalya to Ankara and İstanbul. The airport bus for the Turkish Airlines office costs US$1, a taxi US$10.

From the otogar (4km north of the city) hourly buses go to Ankara (US$15, eight hours); other destinations include İstanbul (US$22, 12 hours), Nevşehir (for Cappadocia, US$18, 10 hours), Eğirdir (US$5.50, 2½ hours) and Konya (US$12, six hours), among other places.

AROUND ANTALYA

There are so many interesting ruins around Antalya that unless you've got bags of time

you're going to have to make some hard choices on what to visit. Using public transport to see them all quickly just isn't practical, so it makes sense to club together with a few other travellers to take a guided taxi tour for around US$30 (organise this at your pension or the many travel agencies in Kaleiçi) – this way you can easily see Perge and Aspendos and possibly even Termessos in a day, if you get an early start.

Termessos

Some 34km inland and west from Antalya is the ancient city of Termessos, once home to the Termessians, a Pisidian people. High in the mountains off the Korkuteli road, Termessos deserves a day and demands some vigorous walking and climbing, especially to the **necropolis**, 3km from the entrance. The **theatre** is in a grand position with a mountain behind and gorge to one side. The site is open from 8 am to 7 pm daily, until 5.30 pm in winter; admission is US$3.

At Termessos you can camp near the **National Park Museum**. There's a toilet and electricity, but no shower (US$1.50). Entry to the national park is US$0.25 (US$0.75 for cars). From Antalya you can get a dolmuş towards Korkuteli. From the turn-off to the park, you'll have to hitch or walk uphill 8km (two hours).

Perge & Aspendos

The impressive ruins of Perge lie about 15km east of Antalya and just north of Aksu. The once great Pamphylian trading city, founded perhaps in 1000 BC, includes a 12,000 seat stadium, a theatre for 15,000 and huge Hellenistic and Roman gates (open from 8 am to 6 pm in summer, US$2.50). Catch an Aksu dolmuş to the Perge turn-off, then hitch or walk the last 2km to the gate.

About 32km farther east is **Aspendos** (Belkis), with Turkey's best preserved ancient theatre, dating from the 2nd century AD and still used for performances during the Antalya Festival in September. This amazing site is open from 8 am to 7 pm daily in summer (shorter hours at other times). Admission is US$2. Take a minibus from Antalya that passes the Aspendos turn-off, get out here and walk (40 minutes) or hitch the 4km to the gate.

Köprülü Kanyon

Some 96km from Antalya and 44km north of the Antalya-Alanya highway is **Köprülü Kanyon Milli Parkı** with a number of Roman bridges. In the mountains, 12km to the west, are the Roman ruins of **Selge**, scattered among the houses of Altınkaya village (1050m). It is an incredible setting and the perfect getaway for the independent traveller. Of ancient Selge only the theatre is intact. The villagers can arrange **hikes** up the Köprülü Kanyon along the original Roman road or to Bozburun Dağı (2504m) in the Kuyucuk Range.

You can also organise half-day **rafting** trips through the canyon and along the Köprülü River at a number of travel agencies in Antalya, including through Sabah Pansiyon (☎ 242-247 5345). The cost is around US$30 including lunch. *Camping* in the national park is possible; you may also be able to get a *misafir odası* (guest room) in the village.

Inland to Central Anatolia

From Antalya our main route turns inland, cutting through awesome mountains to the attractive Lake District. The first lake you'll pass is Kovada Gölü; near here is Sagalassos, an ancient city still undergoing excavation, but shaping up to be the next Ephesus. Isparta is the region's major town, but it's better to stay in the tranquil resort of Eğirdir on Eğirdir Gölü. Heading east you'll come to the religious centre of Konya, with its striking Seljuk architecture. You're now on the edge of central Anatolia and fascinating Cappadocia – one of Turkey's not-to-be-missed highlights.

Another option worth considering is to head north to Ankara, Turkey's capital, from Konya before swinging back down to Cappadocia.

SAGALASSOS

You might feel you've had your fill of ancient ruins by now, but Sagalassos is something special. This Pisidian city, dating from at least 1200 BC, lies about 40km south of Isparta. Although the city is still being excavated, its position alone, 1400m above sea level, jammed against a limestone escarpment, sets the imagination racing.

There are two agoras in good condition and a fully restored library with a fine mosaic floor. The theatre is as yet untouched, and there are several temples. See it now before the coach tours arrive.

To get there, take any bus from Antalya heading for Isparta (or onwards) and ask to be dropped off at Ağlasun; the site is about 7km from this intersection. Alternatively, you could arrange a day trip here from Eğirdir.

EĞİRDİR

☎ 246 • pop 18,000

Coming over the mountains, 32km from Isparta, you drop down to Eğirdir Gölü, Turkey's fourth-largest lake, and the charming resort of Eğirdir, nestling quietly on its windswept shores. The small fishing and holiday community's tranquil atmosphere makes this a good place to recharge your batteries before getting into more serious travel. Most people stay on the island of Yeşilada, connected to the mainland by a short causeway.

The tourist office (☎ 311 4388) is on the mainland at 2 Sahil Yolu 13, 500m northwest of the otogar; it's open from 8.30 am to noon and 1.30 to 6 pm (closed on weekends). The post office and banks are also on the mainland. The Bengaz Internet Cafe is on the waterfront next to the belediye and is packed with off-duty soldiers on weekends.

Things to See & Do

Eğirdir has few sights. The **Dünder Bey Medresesi**, opposite the otogar, is now a market, but you'll see better stuff on sale at the Thursday street market. There's a **hamam** (US$8 for bath, scrub and massage) that has seen better days. The Byzantine citadel has all but crumbled away, while over on Yeşilada the 12th-century Greek Orthodox church **Ayios Stefanos** is also in ruins.

If you're up for an early start, many pension owners will offer to take you out **fishing**. Ask at your pension about organising boat trips on the lake and hiking excursions, as well as a trip to Sagalassos (around US$20).

A good spot for hiking is **Kovada Gölü Milli Parkı**, 35km to the south, which is noted for its flora and fauna. From here it's another 25km to the **Çandır Canyons**,

TURKEY

whose frigid waterfalls and pools are best appreciated in warm weather.

Places to Stay & Eat

Yeşilada is packed with pensions; most provide meals and all can organise boat tours.

Ali's Pension (☎ 312 3954, fax 312 2547), one of the best places, is on the east side of the island facing the lake. You'll receive a warm welcome and fine home cooking. Cosy rooms with wooden floors are US$8 per person. Next door, *Sunrise* (☎ 311 3032) charges the same price for big rooms and has a terrace overlooking the lake and a restaurant.

Up the hill from Sunrise and inland is the rustic *Sefa Sega Pansiyon* (☎ 311 4877), run by an eccentric old woman – she charges US$10 per person for bed and breakfast.

Paris Pension & Restaurant (☎ 311 5509) is on the west side of the island; all rooms have a bathroom, and three rooms have a large balcony facing the water's edge. A double costs US$20 including breakfast. Good meals are available for around US$12 for two (drinks included).

Göl Pension (☎ 312 2370) on the southern shore of Yeşilada also gets rave reviews from travellers (US$22 for a double).

On the mainland, *Lale Pension* (☎ 312 2406, fax 311 4984, ⓔ lalehostel@ho tmail.com, 2 Sokak 6) is a family-run place that has great views from its terrace; the small rooms have a shower and toilet. One of the owners speaks French and English, and they can take guests on walks to the canyons. Doubles are about US$16. It's part of the No 1 network (an accommodation and transport deal run by an association of hostels).

The *Melodi Restaurant* on Yeşilada is good value with most dishes costing around US$2; the *Eğirdir Hotel* on the mainland has an evening buffet; and the *Derya Restaurant* on the waterfront has a good reputation.

Getting There & Away

From Eğirdir there are direct services to Antalya (US$5, 2½ hours), Konya (US$9, four hours) and Nevşehir (US$18, eight hours). If you're stuck, catch a minibus to Isparta otogar and then take a bus onwards from there.

KONYA

☎ 332 • pop 680,000

The conservative town of Konya, 236km east of Eğirdir, is an important place of pilgrimage for Muslims. This one-time capital of the Seljuk Turks was where, in the 13th century, the poet and Sufic mystic Mevlâna Rumi founded the Mevlevi or whirling dervishes, one of Islam's mystical orders.

Today Konya's population of 680,000 remains staunchly Muslim – finding an alcoholic drink can be tricky and there's an initial frostiness among some (but far from all) locals towards foreigners. The reasons to stop here are to experience this other side of Turkey and to admire Konya's impressive Seljuk architecture, particularly the beautiful Mevlâna Museum (Mevlâna Müzesi), which brightens up an otherwise dour city.

Because it is such a religious place you should take special care not to upset the pious especially when you enter mosques and the Mevlâna Museum. Women should dress conservatively, and be prepared to cover their head and shoulders when entering the museum or mosques; no-one should eat or smoke in public during Ramazan. Also be aware that being hassled by touts around the Mevlâna Museum is unfortunately common.

Monday isn't a good day to visit because many of the museums are closed. Don't come to Konya expecting a show of whirling dervish dancing either. This only happens during the **Mevlâna Festival** every

Whirling to ecstasy...the ritual dance of the whirling dervishes.

TURKEY

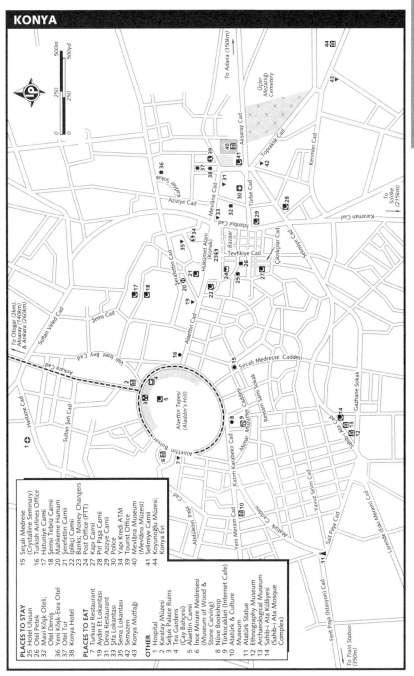

KONYA

PLACES TO STAY
25 Hotel Ulusan
26 Otel Petek
32 Mavi Köşk Oteli;
   Otel Derviş
36 Yeni Köşk-Esra Otel
37 Otel Tur
38 Konya Hotel

PLACES TO EAT
7 Turkuaz Restaurant
19 Aydın Et Lokantası
31 Deva Restaurant
33 Piri Paşa Camii
35 Sema Lokantası
42 Semazen
43 Konya Mutfağı

OTHER
1 Hospital
2 Karatay Müzesi
3 Seljuk Palace Ruins
4 Tea Gardens
   (Çay Bahçesi)
5 Alaettin Camii
6 İnce Minare Medresesi
   (Museum of Wood &
   Stone Carving)
8 Tüve Bookshop
9 Türkocakları (Internet Cafe)
10 Atatürk & Culture
   Museum
11 Atatürk Statue
12 Ethnography Museum
13 Archaeological Museum
14 Sahib-i Ata Külliyesi
   (Sahib-i Ata Mosque
   Complex)
15 Sırçalı Medrese
   (Crystalline Seminary)
16 Turkish Airlines Office
17 Hatuniye Camii
18 Şemsi Tebriz Camii
20 Mahkeme Hamam
21 Şerefettin Camii
22 İpilçi Camii
23 Banks; Money Changers
24 Post Office (PTT)
27 Kapı Camii
28 Piri Paşa Camii
29 Aziziye Camii
30 Police
34 Yapı Kredi ATM
39 Tourist Office
40 Mevlâna Museum
   (Mevlâna Müzesi)
41 Selimiye Camii
44 Koyunoğlu Müzesi;
   Konya Evi

TURKEY

December 10 to 17, and takes place in the less than inspiring surroundings of a modern stadium. It's much better to catch the monthly show at the Galata Mevlevihanesi in İstanbul (see İstanbul earlier in this chapter).

History
Konya is one of the oldest settlements in the world. About 50km to the south of Konya is Çatal Höyük, believed to be the oldest known human community, dating back to 7500 BC. In the town centre, Alaettin Tepesi (Aladdin's Hill) has ruins dating from as far back as the Hittites. During the Roman era the Christian saints Paul and Barnabas visited Konya and preached here.

Konya was at its most influential during the 13th century when it was the capital of the Seljuk Sultanate of Rum (Rome). A number of spectacular buildings were constructed under the aegis of Alaettin Keykubad (1219–31), the most famous of the Seljuk sultans. The styles of this time influenced later Ottoman forms of art and architecture.

Konya was for a long time a refuge for people fleeing from the Mongols and Crusaders. One such refugee was Celaleddin Rumi, later known as Mevlâna (Our Guide), who was born in what is now Afghanistan in 1207. In the 1250s Rumi started writing a monumental opus of Persian devotional poetry that set out his beliefs. The dance of the whirling dervishes is perhaps the most famous remnant of his teachings – in the ritualistic, ecstatic dance, repeated four times, the dervish seeks to attain mystical union with God.

Orientation & Information
The centre of the city stretches from Alaettin Tepesi, along Alaettin Caddesi and Mevlâna Caddesi to the tomb of Mevlâna, now part of the site of the Mevlâna Museum. The otogar is about 2km due north of the centre, and is connected to it by regular minibuses. The train station is about 1km due west of the hill.

Konya's tourist office (☎ 351 1074) is at Mevlâna Caddesi 21, across the square from the Mevlâna Museum. Opening hours are from 8.30 am to 5 pm, Monday to Saturday in summer. Plenty of banks and ATMs, as well as the post office, are found in and around Hükümet Alanı (Government Plaza, also known as Konak).

For Internet access, try Türkocaklari, on the top floor of Mimar Muzaffer Caddesi 56. For books and magazines in English, Nüve has a reasonable selection.

Mevlâna Museum
This museum (Mevlâna Müzesi) is a must-see. The turquoise tiles of its towers are splendid. Beyond the picturesque courtyard is the Seljuk-era **Mevlâna Türbesi**, which contains the sarcophagi of Rumi, his father and several other illustrious members of the sect. Many of the sarcophagi have large symbolic turbans on them. In an adjoining room, the *semahane* (dance floor), there is a small display of exquisite examples of Islamic art including illuminated Qurans and possibly the most expensive silk carpet in the world.

In the cloisters around the courtyard you can see various displays about the dervishes, including some cheesy waxwork setups. Just outside the complex is the **Selimiye Camii**, a 16th-century mosque, with a beautifully decorated interior and grand chandelier.

The complex is open from 9 am (10 am on Monday) to 5.30 pm daily; admission is US$2.50.

Seljuk Architecture
Near Alaettin Tepesi (Aladdin's Hill) is a ceramics museum called the **Büyük Karatay Müzesi**, housed in a building that was once a Muslim theological seminary (the Great Karatay Seminary). The strikingly tiled interior is worth the entrance fee. Built in 1251–52 by the Seljuk statesman Celaleddin Karatay, it also has a beautiful sculpted stone doorway. It's open from 9 am to noon and 1.30 to 5.30 pm daily except Monday; admission is US$1.25.

The **İnce Minare Medresesi** (Seminary of the Slender Minaret), now the Museum of Wood & Stone Carving, is on the western side of Alaettin Tepesi. Again, the elaborate doorway is the drawcard here. It is open the same hours as the Karatay Müzesi; admission is US$1.

Alaettin Tepesi is topped by the **Alaettin Camii**. This rambling 13th-century mosque's exterior is fairly plain, but the interior is a forest of old marble columns surmounted with recycled Roman and Byzantine capitals, with a fine, carved wooden *mimber* (pulpit) and an old marble mihrab (prayer niche) framed by beautiful modern Seljuk-style blue and black calligraphy. You can visit from 8.30 am to 6 pm, but remember that it's still in use as a place of worship.

Other examples of Seljuk architecture to look out for are the **Sırçalı Medrese** (Crystalline Seminary), the **Sahib-i Ata Külliyesi** (Sahib-i Ata Mosque Complex) and the **Şemsi Tebrizi Camii**, a mosque housing the tomb of Rumi's spiritual teacher. A fine baroque-style mosque is the **Azizye Camii** south-east of the bazaar.

Also worth a look is the **Koyunoğlu Müzesi**, around 750m south-east of the Mevlâna Museum. This collection of ethnographic bits and pieces – including some striking carpets, clothes and bits of pottery – was donated to the city by the Koyunoğlu family, whose charming Ottoman home, the **Koyunoğlu Konya Evi** stands next door. Opening hours are from 9 am to 5 pm; admission costs US$1.

The **Mahkeme Hamam** behind the Şerefettin Camii, is a clean, traditional place for a Turkish bath; the full works are around US$10 and it's open daily until 11 pm.

Places to Stay

The cheapest of the cheapies, and not a bad choice, is *Hotel Ulusan (☎ 351 5004)* behind the post office and signposted; basic but spotless singles/doubles with sink cost US$6/12.

Nearby is the *Otel Petek (☎ 351 2599, Çıkıkcılar İçi 40)* upstairs between a shop selling *helva* (a traditional sweet made with sesame oil, cereals and syrup or honey) and another selling nuts and dried fruit. Reasonably large rooms with clean sheets and shower cost US$11/14 with breakfast, a little less without the showers. The breakfast room has a view over the bazaar.

Between the bazaar and the Mevlâna Museum, the welcoming *Otel Derviş (☎/fax 351 1688, Bostançelebi Sokak 11/D)* is serviceable, with shower-equipped rooms going for US$13/16, subject to negotiation. The neighbouring *Mavi Köşk Oteli (☎ 350 1904, Bostançelebi Sokak 13)* is dingier, but charges about the same.

A notch up in quality is *Yeni Köşk-Esra Otel (☎ 352 0671, fax 352 0901, Kadılar Sokak 28)*. Rooms with showers and TV are US$14/20, with the newer rooms in the Esra Otel the most comfortable. It also has car parking.

Otel Tur (☎ 351 9825, fax 352 4765, Eş'arizade Sokak 13) charges US$17/20 for large, simply furnished rooms with TV and small bathroom. There's a car park at the rear. Rooms at the nearby *Konya Hotel (☎ 353 0672, fax 352 1003)* have more character but are pricier at US$20/35 with negotiation. There's a magnificent view of the Mevlâna Museum from the rooftop terrace restaurant.

Places to Eat & Drink

Şifa Lokantası (Mevlâna Caddesi 30) is very popular and only a short stroll west of the Mevlâna Museum. They'll serve you a *fırın baked kebap* and cold drink for US$4.50 and they do a mean yogurt soup (US$1) too.

Deva Restaurant (Mevlâna Caddesi 3), across from the Hotel Dergah, serves an assortment of Turkish dishes including *tandır kebap* (roasted in an oven). Expect to pay around US$4 for a meal.

Semazen (Topraklık Caddesi) is a clean fırın kebap and pide joint handily close to the Mevlâna Museum.

Sema Lokantası (İstanbul Caddesi 107), near the Hotel Çeşme, is welcoming and serves exotic dishes like *aşure* (Noah's Ark Pudding) as well as the usual kebaps and stews.

For Italian-style pizzas try *Aydın Et Lokantası (Tolunay Sokak 5)*, just off Alaettin Caddesi near the İmar Bankası.

The upmarket *Konya Mutfağı (☎ 352 8547, Akçeşme Mahallesi, Topraklık Caddesi 66)*, or Konya Kitchen, is in a restored house down towards the Koyunoğlu Museum. It's very popular with locals and service is polite. Although there's no English menu they'll let you peek at what's on offer in the kitchen. A traditional meal costs around US$8 per person.

A great night out is promised at the low-lit, first-floor *Turkuaz Restaurant (☎ 357 9474, Adliye Bulvarı)*, beside the İnce Minare. By 10.30 pm the place is packed with locals downing beers and joining in with the live music. A meal of mezes together with a main course like lamb chops costs around US$7.

Pleasant places for a snack are the *çay bahçesi* (tea gardens) on Alaettin Tepesi.

For self-caterers, the local thin-crust bread is good with jam for breakfast, or with other fillings for lunch. There are several *halk pazarı* (small supermarkets) in the side streets off Alaettin and Mevlâna Caddesis.

Getting There & Away

Air Turkish Airlines (☎ 351 2000, fax 350 2171), at Alaettin Caddesi 9, has daily flights to and from İstanbul. An airport bus (US$1.75) leaves from Alaettin Caddesi near the Turkish Airlines Office to connect with flights but you should check the time carefully.

Bus Konya's otogar or Otobüs Terminali is 2km north of Alaettin Tepesi. To get to the town centre take a minibus (US$0.30) from the rank outside the otogar. To get to the otogar, there are service buses from the bus company booking offices on Mevlâna Caddesi.

From the otogar there are regular services to Ankara (US$9, three hours), Antalya (US$10, six hours), Eğirdir (US$7, four hours), İstanbul (US$17, 10 hours), İzmir (US$12, eight hours) and Nevşehir (for Cappadocia; US$8.50, 2½ hours).

Train To get to Konya from İstanbul take either the *İç Anadolu Mavi Tren* (20 hours), *Meram Ekspresi* (seven hours 20 minutes) or the *Toros Ekspresi* (seven hours 10 minutes) from the Haydarpaşa station. There's no direct rail link across the plateau between Konya and Ankara. The best way to make this journey is by bus.

Getting Around

The city centre sights are easily reached on foot, so you only need public transport to get to the bus and train stations. Trams run from the otogar to Alaettin Tepesi but don't continue down Alaettin Caddesi; buses do.

Cappadocia

Heading east from Konya into the heartland of Central Anatolia, you'll reach the region of Cappadocia (Kapadokya), famous for its fantastic natural rock formations of soft volcanic stone. This is one of the most amazing landscapes anywhere in the world, into which, over the centuries, people have carved houses, churches, fortresses, even complete underground cities. Much is now protected in open-air museums.

The surreal landscape of Cappadocia had its beginnings some 30 million years ago with the eruptions of the three volcanoes that dominate the region – Melendiz Dağı, Erciyes Dağı and Göllü Dağı.

The eruptions poured a thick layer of volcanic ash over Cappadocia and this later hardened into a soft, porous stone called tuff. Down the ages, erosion by the elements has worn the tuff into extraordinary shapes. Where a boulder, usually basalt, protected the tuff beneath from farther erosion, columns and cones remained with the boulder perched precariously on top. The result are the phallic *peribacası* or 'fairy chimneys' that you see today.

There are many orchards and vineyards in these valleys and Cappadocian wine is among the best you can taste in Turkey.

Attractions include the Göreme and nearby Zelve Valleys; rugged Ihlara Valley dotted with ancient churches; Soğanlı with its scores of stone-cut chapels; and the huge underground cities at Kaymaklı and Derinkuyu. There's so much to see and do that you should allow yourself at least three days, and preferably longer, to do the area justice. It is also a great place for hiking and cycling.

The region is bounded roughly by the towns of Hacıbektaş in the north, Aksaray to the west, Kayseri in the east and Niğde in the south. The best all-round bases, with a decent range of pensions, hotels, restaurants and travel agencies are Göreme, backpacker central for Cappadocia, or nearby Ürgüp, which is slightly more grown-up. If you're looking for a less tourist-intensive experience, the charming villages of Çavuşin and Mustafapaşa are recommended. You can camp almost everywhere – most conveniently in the gardens of pensions.

HISTORY

Cappadocia was first settled by the Hatti, a Bronze Age people, in the area near Nevşehir. By about 2000 BC the Hatti had succumbed to Western European settlers, the Hittites, and the cultures were fused.

The Hittite empire waned around 1200 BC and a succession of different neighbouring kingdoms exercised control over the region. Around this time many underground cities such as Kaymaklı and Derinkuyu were thought to have been excavated. In the 6th century BC the Persians under Cyrus the

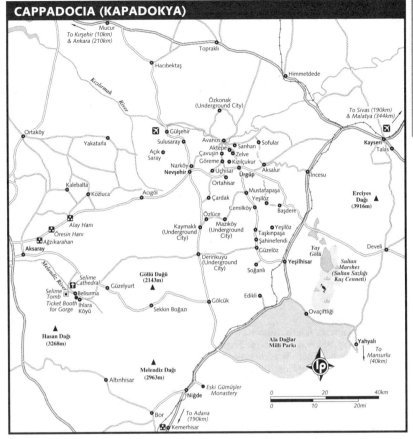

CAPPADOCIA (KAPADOKYA)

Great took control until Alexander the Great liberated the region in 333 BC. It remained independent for 350 years until the Romans annexed it in AD 18. The Cappadocians went on with their troglodytic existence, relatively undisturbed.

Christianity was introduced to Cappadocia in the 1st century AD by St Paul. As a defence measure against persecution, the Christians burrowed deeper into the soft tuff, fashioning elaborately decorated churches, monasteries and storage areas. As each threat swept through the region, such as the Arab invaders in the 7th century, the Christians shifted underground, hiding themselves by rolling stones in front of the entrances to their cave dwellings and cities.

From 726 to 843, the Christian church was split by the Iconoclastic Controversy. During this time, images other than the cross were forbidden, but in Cappadocia the defiant monks responded by taking their art underground, continuing to decorate churches and monasteries throughout the period. This also helped protect their art during Arab raids.

The Seljuks arrived in the 11th century, establishing caravanserais along the Silk Route and bringing two centuries of stability. Later the Mongols came, then the Ottomans. The Cappadocians continued their cave living as they had done for aeons. The last of the area's Christian Greeks left in the 1920s after the establishment of the Turkish republic.

Getting There & Away

Air The region's main airport is at Kayseri, which has two daily nonstop flights to İstanbul – see the Kayseri section later in this chapter for details. There are also two flights a week between İstanbul and Nevşehir international airport at Tuzköy near Gülşehir, 20km north of Nevşehir.

Bus The bus terminal in Nevşehir has buses and dolmuş services for the whole region. If you're planning on staying in Göreme or Ürgüp, double check when you buy your ticket that the bus continues on from Nevşehir; there are service buses but many intercity buses will just dump you at Nevşehir, or even worse, just on the highway. Also, when leaving Göreme you're likely to find yourself ferried to Nevşehir to pick up the main service, which can add a good half-hour to your travelling time. There are regular services from Nevşehir to Ankara (US$9, four hours), İstanbul (US$17, 11 hours), Kayseri (US$3.50, 1½ hours), and Konya (US$9, three hours).

Getting Around

There are minibuses hourly from Nevşehir to Niğde (US$3, 85km, 1½ hours) and half-hourly to Göreme. There is an hourly bus plying the tourist circuit from June to September (Ürgüp, Göreme, Zelve, Avanos etc) that costs US$0.35 for each leg.

NEVŞEHİR

☎ 384 • pop 55,000

The provincial capital is an ugly modern town where you're unlikely to want to linger. The otogar is 1.5km north of the town's main intersection, on the road towards Gülşehir, but buses and dolmuşes to most local towns and villages leave from near the tourist office (☎ 213 3659) on Atatürk Bulvarı, the main drag. Nevşehir hotels cater mainly for the business fraternity. Almost everyone else heads straight on to the prettier Cappadocian villages.

With time to spare you might visit the 18th-century mosque complex **Damat İbrahim Paşa Külliyesi**. The hamam is still in business. Bath hours are from 7.30 am to 9 pm (Wednesday for women). The big **tea garden** in front of the Park Bostan Restaurant is a good place to kill time, popular with local families at weekends.

GÖREME

☎ 384 • pop 2000

Just 12km east of Nevşehir is Göreme, a magical village of 2000 people set amid towering tuff cones and honeycomb cliffs and surrounded by vineyards. It's deservedly popular with backpackers because the beds and meals are cheap and good, and its sights are within walking distance.

Since the tourism boom of the 1980s and 1990s, life in Göreme has become an odd mixture of the modern and the ultra-conservative, with veiled women in traditional dress rubbing shoulders with scantily clad tourists throughout the summer.

Orientation & Information

Buses and minibuses drop you off at the otogar-cum-shopping mall. Across from the bus ticket offices in the otogar is a booth with information on local accommodation options. There are also several travel agencies where you can change money.

There's an ATM in front of the belediye. The post office, beyond the SOS Restaurant, tends to offer the best exchange rates as well as providing phone and fax services.

The Nese Internet Cafe, midway along Bilal Eroğlu Caddesi, is popular and busy; you can have a drink and read the papers while you wait. Also try Cafedoci@ which is 50m north of the bus station.

Göreme Open-Air Museum

Many **murals** can be seen in the rock-hewn monastery, nunnery and several dozen cave churches of the Göreme Open-Air Museum (Göreme Açık Hava Müzesi), 2km east of the village. Some murals date from as early as the 8th century, though the best are from the 10th to 13th centuries. Unlit for many centuries, they've hardly faded at all, though vandals have left indelible marks. The best murals are in the **Karanlık Kilisesi** or Dark Church.

It's easy to spend most of the day exploring the museum, but, to be honest, you can see cave churches and frescoes that are just as good if you're hiking through Rose Valley, without having to pay the hefty admission of US$5 (students US$3) plus another US$6 for the Karanlık Kilisesi. The site is open from 8.30 am to 5.30 pm (4.30 pm in winter), but it's best to get there early in the morning in summer before the tour groups.

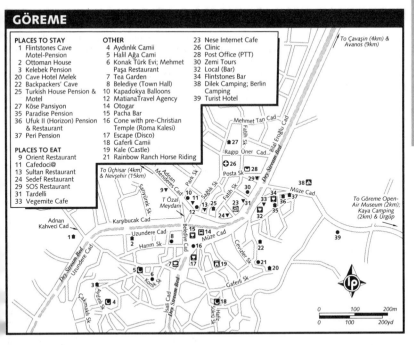

GÖREME

PLACES TO STAY
1 Flintstones Cave Motel-Pension
2 Ottoman House
3 Kelebek Pension
20 Cave Hotel Melek
22 Backpackers' Cave
25 Turkish House Pension & Motel
27 Köse Pansiyon
35 Paradise Pension
36 Ufuk II (Horizon) Pension & Restaurant
37 Peri Pension

PLACES TO EAT
9 Orient Restaurant
11 Cafedoci@
13 Sultan Restaurant
24 Sedef Restaurant
29 SOS Restaurant
31 Tardelli
33 Vegemite Cafe

OTHER
4 Aydınlık Camii
5 Halil Ağa Cami
6 Konak Türk Evi; Mehmet Paşa Restaurant
7 Tea Garden
8 Belediye (Town Hall)
10 Kapadokya Balloons
12 MatianaTravel Agency
14 Otogar
15 Pacha Bar
16 Cone with pre-Christian Temple (Roma Kalesi)
17 Escape (Disco)
18 Gaferli Camii
19 Kale (Castle)
21 Rainbow Ranch Horse Riding

23 Nese Internet Cafe
26 Clinic
28 Post Office (PTT)
30 Zemi Tours
32 Local (Bar)
34 Flintstones Bar
38 Dilek Camping; Berlin Camping
39 Turist Hotel

Göreme Village

Set amid cones and pinnacles of tuff, Göreme village is its own biggest attraction. At its centre is the so-called **Roma Kalesi**, a tall volcanic column with the remains of a rock-cut Roman temple facade high up. Also look at the **Konak Türk Evi** or Turkish Mansion House (1826), tucked away in the maze of cobbled streets to the east of the village. Once the home of Mehmet Paşa, the local Ottoman grandee, it has two beautifully decorated rooms, the *selamlık* (men's room) and *harem* (women's room). The frescoes on the walls were apparently created by the artist responsible for the paintings in the dining room of İstanbul's Topkapı Palace.

Walks Around Göreme

Valleys with gorgeous scenery and a mixture of ancient pigeon houses and even more ancient rock-cut churches fan out around Göreme village, which is surrounded by the magnificent Göreme National Park.

Particularly popular valleys are **Güllüdere Vadısı** (Rose Valley) connecting Göreme and Çavuşin; **Güvercinlik Vadısı** (Pigeon Valley), connecting Göreme and Uçhisar; **Ballıdere** (Honey Valley), running behind Göreme village; **Swords Valley**, running off the road to the Open-Air Museum; and **Zemi Valley**, behind the Turist Hotel, east of the centre, home to some spectacular rock formations.

Most of the valleys have signposts directing you to them but nothing to keep you on the straight and narrow once you get inside them. Nor are they all particularly easy to walk. Mehmet Güngör (☎ 271 2064, e mehmethashmet@yahoo.com) is a local guide with an encyclopaedic knowledge of the area. For US$10 a head he will lead you through any of the local valleys, usually together with Hashmet the famous walking dog – see the boxed text 'One Man and his Dog'.

Organised Tours

Prices are fixed at the start of each season among Göreme's many tour agencies and vary little from shop to shop. The agencies tend to offer a standard daily tour that takes in an underground city and a stretch of the Ihlara Valley, as well as various photogenic

One Man and his Dog

Hashmet, nose to the ground, is trotting ahead along the serpentine tracks leading through vineyards and apricot and apple orchards immediately outside Göreme. His master Mehmet says he's the best guide because 'he knows the way, and doesn't talk, so won't try to sell you a carpet.' I have to admit it's more than a novelty to be led on a trek through Cappadocia's gorgeous scenery by an amiable dog with floppy ears.

My afternoon walk with the dynamic duo of Hashmet and Mehmet takes me into the beautiful Rose Valley, so called because of the pink colour of the rock. On the way we pass many of the area's famous fairy chimneys, some pitted with the honey-bearing hives of bees, others carved with pigeon houses, where the pigeon droppings used to be collected to fertilise the fields. We also climb up into the Kizlar Kadesi (Monastery of Girls), a small but impressive cave chapel painted with intriguing red geometric designs.

Reaching the top of the hill overlooking Rose Valley, the only response is to gasp in awe at the serene, melted-ice-cream landscape before me. Mehmet aptly calls this 'the wow point'. We dive into the valley and pause at the shady refreshments stall of Ali, a local farmer.

Farther along the valley you could easily pass the White Church (also known as the Column Church) without realising it. The hidden interior is astounding, and I wonder how on earth such perfectly balanced columns and domes were achieved from this carved tuff. In the nearby Hagli Kilise, the intact frescoes of Jesus blessing a puzzling 16 disciples are the main attraction. Without my guides I'd have been lucky to stumble across such gems.

A walk with Mehmet and Hashmet is well worth the money, but Hashmet will let you tag along for free on Sundays as long as you help Mehmet clean up the rubbish that less conscientious visitors leave along the tracks.

Simon Richmond

viewing points and one of the caravanserais, with perhaps a final stop in Avanos to shop for pottery.

Most of the pensions either operate their own tours or work with one of the travel agencies. Expect to pay US$20 to US$25 for a day tour by minibus inclusive of lunch. To save arguments, check whether any visits to carpet shops or onyx factories are scheduled. Reliable agencies that have been in business for years include Ötüken Voyage (☎ 271 2588), Neşe Tour (☎ 271 2525), Zemi Tour (☎ 271 2576), Turtle Tours (☎ 271 2388) and Hiro Tour (☎ 271 2542); however, others may well be equally good. If you're planning on going on to Nemrut Dağı it's worth checking with some of these agencies for details of tours (see the Nemrut Dağı section later in this chapter).

Given the prices of day tours, you may well consider it better to get around the region under your own steam – which is much more fun and just as easily organised. See Getting Around later in this section for details of scooter hire.

Adventures@Altitude offers longer, more intrepid tours into the surrounding mountain areas. Contact Greg O'Leary at Paradise Pension (@ info@adventuresaltitude.com).

Horse riding is a good way to see the valleys. Rainbow Ranch (☎ 271 2413), uphill on the road to Cave Hotel Melek, rents horses for US$15 for two hours, but doesn't supply hard hats, so ride at your peril.

For the ride of a lifetime (one that your wallet won't forget in a hurry either), Kapadokya Balloons (☎ 271 2442, @ fly@kapadokyaballoons.com) offers US$200-plus daybreak balloon flights, weather and wind permitting.

Places to Stay

Camping The best camp site is *Kaya Camping* (☎ 343 3100, fax 343 3984), uphill from the Göreme Open-Air Museum. It has spectacular views, as well as a swimming pool, solar-heated showers and a restaurant. It costs US$3.50 per person plus US$1.75 per tent.

Dilek Camping (☎ 271 2395) and *Berlin Camping* (☎ 271 2249), side by side across from Peri Pension on the Open Air Museum road (Muze Caddesi), are less fancy but more convenient if you don't have a car. Two people can pitch a tent for US$6. Even if you're not staying you can use the Berlin's pool for US$3.50.

Pensions & Hotels The pension cooperative sets prices at the start of the season, so wherever you go you should get quoted roughly the same rates: US$4 to US$5 for a dorm bed, US$6 for a bed in a waterless room and US$7 or US$8 per person in a room with private facilities. Some pensions have areas where you can camp for even less.

A long time backpackers' favourite, although it has no cave rooms, is *Köse Pansiyon* (☎ *271 2294, fax 279 2577,* e *dawn2@turk.net)* north-west of the post office. The cafe is a major travellers' hangout and the management are very clued up.

Heading into town from the Open-Air Museum, *Peri Pension* (☎ *271 2136, fax 271 2730)* deservedly gets lots of fan mail and has rooms in fairy chimneys. Next door *Ufuk II (Horizon) Pension* (☎ *271 2157, fax 271 2578)* is also very good and has a stylish restaurant where the owner often plays traditional music.

Paradise Pension (☎/fax *271 2248,* e *mbuzlak@hotmail.com),* behind the Flintstones Bar, is well run and has friendly staff. Their cave rooms are better than the concrete rooms.

The rustic *Turkish House Pension & Motel* (☎ *271 2613),* not far north of the otogar, has a nice garden and rooms with or without bathroom. Although it's a hike to the far west of town *Flintstones Cave Motel-Pension* (☎ *271 2555, fax 271 2233)* is a really good choice with cave rooms, a swimming pool, volleyball court and reputedly the best chocolate cake in Turkey. You can also camp here for US$3 per person.

It's best to call the excellent *Kelebek Pension* (☎ *271 2531, fax 271 2763,* e *ali@kelebekhotel.com)* in advance so that you don't hike up the steep hill only to find the place full. You'll understand why when you've seen the terrace with spectacular views and the tastefully decorated rooms, which go for US$12 a double with shared bathroom, and US$20 with private bathroom. The food here is fab, too.

Another charming option is *Cave Hotel Melek* (☎/fax *271 2463,* e *melekhotel@hotmail.com),* high on the south-eastern valley wall. It has rock-cut double rooms without bathroom for US$10, or US$15/25 for single/doubles with bathroom, breakfast included.

Nearby is the *Backpacker's Cave* (☎/fax *271 2705,* e *backpackers50@hotmail.com),* a new operation that's part of the No 1 network (an accommodation and transport deal set up by an association of pensions). The dorms and rooms here are fine, as is the view from its terrace. There's also a bar.

At most of the places listed here you'll be getting real value for money accommodation of a high standard, but if you must have a bona fide hotel, go for *Ottoman House* (☎ *271 2616, fax 271 2351,* e *ottoman@indigoturizm.com.tr, Orta Mahalle 21)* which boasts near-luxury for just US$15/30.

Places to Eat

Most Göreme pensions provide good, cheap meals and may well serve wine and beer as well. There are also plenty of options for eating out.

The restaurants lined up along the main Avanos road are mainly geared towards the tour-bus trade but offer pleasant terraces where you can sit and eat while gazing at the fairy chimneys. The *SOS Restaurant*, just before you reach the post office, is the least flashy, and a bit cheaper as a result; it also gets rave reviews.

The *Sultan* is popular with locals for its excellent *domates çorbası* (tomato soup) for US$1. The *Sedef* does good pizzas and a long list of mezes; the *Tardelli* is similar. A full dinner with drinks (which are relatively expensive) might cost around US$10 in any of them.

Orient Restaurant, on the left-hand side of the road heading out towards Uçhisar (Adnan Menderes Caddesi) is one of the best places to eat in town. An excellent, filling four-course meal with soft drink costs US$4.75, but you can also pick and choose from the main menu.

Closer into town on the same road is the hip *Cafedoci@*, offering hearty portions of burgers, salads and other Western-style dishes alongside Internet terminals, movies on a big-screen TV and a range of beers and spirits.

The friendly *Vegemite Cafe* serves the famous Aussie spread on toast, as well as *gözleme* (Turkish pancakes), fruit juices and a range of sandwiches.

The most atmospheric place to dine is *Mehmet Paşa Restaurant* (☎/fax 271 2207) in the Konak Türk Evi. It also has an open-air terrace with fine views and a bar. The menu offers a fairly standard range of mezes and kebaps, for which you should expect to pay around US$8 a head.

Well worth the splurge is the delicious US$10 four-course set menu at the *Ottoman House* served in the hotel's tastefully decorated basement restaurant, with a carpeted bar attached.

You don't have to walk far from town to be able to buy all manner of produce from local farmers – apples, grapes, walnuts, dried fruit and fresh vegetables. Dine on *pastırma* (pressed meat preserved in spices), bread and a local wine – perhaps a Peribaca light red, or Tekel's Ürgüp white.

Entertainment
For a small village Göreme isn't short of watering holes. First off there's the homely *Pacha Bar*, right beside the otogar, with big-screen TV, decent music and a good range of drinks. Then there's *Flintstones Bar* at the start of the Open Air Museum road, which is cut right into the rockface, has an open fire for cold nights and a warm welcome all the time. Very close to it is the big new *Local*, with indoor and outdoor tables and good food to soak up the alcohol. Then there's *Cafedoci@*, which screens recent Hollywood movies to go with its drinks. Finally, there's *Escape*, a disco in a converted donkey stable behind the otogar, which has occasional performances by a transvestite belly-dancer.

Getting There & Away
Half-hourly dolmuşes connect Göreme with Nevşehir year-round (US$0.30, 15 minutes). There are also hourly buses to Çavuşin and Avanos, and two-hourly buses to Ortahisar and Ürgüp (US$0.45).

There are several places to hire mountain bikes, mopeds and motor scooters. Bikes cost around US$8; while mopeds and scooters go for US$15 for four hours, US$25 for 12 hours, or US$30 for 24 hours. For a couple, two scooters will cost about the same as a rental car. You must leave your passport as a security deposit.

To avoid argument later, take only a machine that's in good repair, even if it's more expensive. Beware of rental places that rent bikes with dents in them, then charge you for causing the dents when you return the machine. Ötüken Voyage (☎ 271 2588) and Zemi Tours are reputable places to hire bikes.

Since Göreme doesn't have any petrol stations and the rental companies will hike petrol prices, fill up the tank in Nevşehir, Avanos or Ürgüp before returning the bike.

ÇAVUŞİN & ZELVE
☎ 384
Although it is only 4km north of Göreme, Çavuşin feels a world away – it's much more your sleepy Cappadocian village, with horse-drawn carts clattering past a looming cliff honeycombed with former cave dwellings. The cathedral-sized **Church of John the Baptist**, near the top of the cliff, is one of the oldest in Cappadocia. Right beside the main road, up a steep iron stairway, is the **Church of St John** (also known as the Great Pigeon House) with fine frescoes. It's open from 8 am to 5.30 pm daily; admission is US$1.75.

The *İn Pension* (☎ 532 7070, fax 532 7195) on the main road between the two churches is a very nice place with rooms set around a courtyard. The owner speaks good French and is a knowledgeable hiking guide to the area. Half board (breakfast, dinner and a bed) is US$15. There are hourly buses to Çavuşin from Göreme.

Far less touristed than Göreme are the three valleys that converge at **Zelve** on the road to Avanos. Zelve was a monastic retreat and there are many chapels in the valleys. The **Balıklı Kilise** (Fish Church) has fish in some of the paintings and the **Üzümlü Kilise** (Grape Church) has (you guessed it) bunches of grapes. Clambering around some parts of the valley you'll need nerves of steel, a head for heights and a torch (flashlight). Zelve's opening hours are from 8 am to 6 pm (last admission at 5.30 pm) and admission costs US$2.50.

About halfway between the Göreme Avanos road and Zelve are the much photographed three-headed fairy chimneys of **Paşabağı**. It's a lot of fun climbing up inside the 10th-century chapel of Saint Symon by way of footholds cut into the walls of a vertical shaft.

Another popular spot for sunsets is **Aktepe** (Yeni Zelve). Nearby is the **Peribacalar Vadisi** (Valley of the Fairy Chimneys), one of the best concentrations of these odd volcanic cones. The cones here are capped with darker, harder rock cones.

AVANOS
☎ 384 • pop 12,000

Set on the north bank of the fast flowing Kızılırmak (Red River), Avanos is a proper town (ie, not just one that revolves around tourism), known principally for its pottery. Apart from shopping for pottery (virtually every other shop sells the stuff and at many you can try your hand at the potter's wheel), the cobbled streets of the old village up the hill are worth exploring.

The Avanos tourist office (☎ 511 4360) is on the north bank of the river as you come into town; it's open from 8 am to noon and 1.30 to 7.30 pm Monday to Friday in summer (5.30 pm in winter).

Things to See & Do
The most memorable pottery shop to visit is **Chez Galip** (☎ 511 4240, fax 511 4543, e info@chez-galip.com) which includes a distinctly eerie collection of over 20,000 locks of female hair plastered over a cave wall. (*The Silence of the Lambs* comes to Cappadocia!) The collection started years ago when one of Mr Galip's students left behind a lock of her hair – bizarrely many visitors have chosen to follow suit. Mr Galip, who looks like Albert Einstein, and his wife also organise pottery workshops (US$10 a day) and run a pension.

Çeç Horse Riding (☎ 511 4240) has hard hats and offers two-hour (US$8) to full-day rides. The most popular ride is at sunset through Rose Valley. Tell the outfitters your true level of experience otherwise you may end up with a feisty horse.

Places to Stay & Eat
Pensions here tend to be cheaper than in Göreme. *Kirkit Pension* (☎511 3148, fax 511 2135, e kirkit@gediknet.com) comprises several converted sandstone houses; beds cost US$9 in waterless doubles, US$11 with shower (breakfast included). From the tourist office, walk east and bear left at the first alley. Many readers recommend the meals here; you must order the three-course meal in the morning (US$5).

The nearby *Venessa Pansiyon* (☎ 511 3840, Hafızağa Sokak 20) comprises two old Armenian houses and an Ottoman-era Turkish house and has charming doubles with bathroom for US$11 including breakfast.

Tuvanna and *Tafana Pide Salonu* are two good restaurants close by each other on the main road west of the central square. *Sofra Restaurant*, opposite the post office east of the square, is another decent option, with a variety of meals for around US$3.

Just north of the main bridge is *Bizim Ev* is a multilevel restaurant in a converted Ottoman house, with a roof terrace overlooking the river. The four-course set meal here is good value at US$9. They also serve sandwiches and drinks.

There are hourly buses to Avanos from Göreme.

AROUND AVANOS
The underground city of **Özkonak** (open daily from 8 am to 7 pm in summer, 8 am to 5 pm in winter; US$2), 14km north of Avanos, is much less frequented than its southern counterparts. It has 10 floors to a depth of 40m, but only five floors are open at present.

UÇHİSAR & ORTAHİSAR
☎ 384

About 4km south-west of Göreme is Uçhisar, a picturesque town built around, and into, a prominent peak. A room-to-room scramble through its rock *kale* (citadel) leads to fine views over Cappadocia from the summit (open 8 am to sunset daily, US$1.25). Keen walkers will enjoy the pleasant walk to Göreme along the Güvercinlik Vadisi (Pigeon Valley).

Popular with French tourists, Uçhisar is in some ways less spoilt than Göreme and makes a good alternative base for exploring Cappadocia, although many pensions don't open until May. A bed with a view at the clean, simple *Kilim Pansiyon* (☎ 219 2774, fax 219 2660) costs US$20 per double including breakfast. *Les Terrasses d'Uçhisar* (☎ 219 2792, fax 219 2762) has attractive rooms with modern decor for US$25 a double including breakfast, and there's a great restaurant and terrace bar for soaking up the views in the evening.

In the main square the *Uçhisar 96* restaurant has a large garden in which to tuck into a range of mezes and kebaps. For a quick drink in an atmospheric *cafe* look out for the converted six-storey fairy chimney in front of Le Jardin de 1001 Nuits.

Another village dominated by its kale is **Ortahisar**, 3km south-east of Göreme. The 18m-high rock was used as a defence in Byzantine times. It's a great place to come for sunset panoramas provided you have a good head for heights (US$1.75).

To get to Uçhisar from Göreme, take any Nevşehir-bound bus. Services to Ortahisar from Göreme run every two hours.

ÜRGÜP
☎ 384 • pop 13,500

The small town of Ürgüp, 7km east of Göreme Valley, has some magnificent old houses left over from the pre-1923 days when it still had a large Greek population. There are several large tour-group hotels on its eastern outskirts, but the centre of town retains many honey-coloured stone buildings that are slowly being converted into fine hotels and pensions.

The otogar is behind Kayseri Caddesi, the main drag, which has most of the shops and restaurants. The helpful tourist office (☎ 341 4059) at Kayseri Caddesi 47 is in the park. It's open daily from 8 am to 6 pm (8 pm in summer). Asia Teras, next to the tourist office, has an Internet terminal as well as pool tables.

The Tarihi Şehir Hamamı (1902) is touristy, but still a good place for a bath (US$6).

Places to Stay & Eat
You can camp at the back of the *Pinar Hotel* (☎ 341 4054, Kayseri Caddesi 24) or at the shady *Çamlik Campsite* (☎ 341 1146) on the Kayseri road, near where it crosses the Damsa River.

Bahçe Hostel (☎ 341 3314, fax 341 4878, e bahce@altavista.net), across the road from the hamam, has basic waterless rooms for US$4.50 a head and pension rooms with bathroom for US$7/13 per single/double, which are set round a pleasant courtyard.

Up the hill is the homely *Hotel Elvan* (☎ 341 4191, fax 341 3455), with nicer rooms around a small courtyard, a comfy lounge and a roof terrace. Rooms cost US$15/25, breakfast included.

The *Born Hotel* (☎ 341 4756), heading up the hill towards Nevşehir, is an old pasha's house fallen on hard times. The big

rooms are pleasant enough for US$4.50 a head.

The *Asia Minor Hotel* (☎ 341 4645, fax 341 2721, e cappadocia50@hotmail.com) is a fine mid-range option with a pleasant garden, frescoes in the hall and stylishly decorated double rooms (no singles) for US$40 including breakfast.

Ürgüp's speciality is *kiremit kebap* (minced lamb or chicken made into patties and baked on a tile) – it's a bit of an acquired taste but it's just the thing if you like your food a little greasy.

The *Cappadocia Restaurant*, just off Dumlupınar Caddesi, has good food at reasonable prices (US$4 to US$5 for three courses). *Şölen Restaurant & Pide Salonu (Dumlupınar Caddesi)* specialises in kebaps and good cheap pide and pizza – including vegetarian – for under US$2.

The long-standing *Merkez Pastanesi* is the best in town. A large glass of tea and a portion of cake costs less than US$2.

Han Çirağan, at the far end of the main square, is a restaurant and wine bar in an old stone house. In summer you can dine outside in a pleasant small courtyard and sample their good range of local wines.

The traditionally furnished *Kaya Bar*, above the Süküroğllari pastry shop near the otogar, is a popular spot for a beer.

Getting There & Away
From Göreme there are buses to Ürgüp every two hours.

Ürgüp's otogar has a good range of services in summer, but not as many in winter. There's a daily service that runs every couple of hours to Kayseri (US$2.50, 1½ hours) and Mustafapaşa (US$0.30, 15 minutes).

MUSTAFAPAŞA
☎ 384

This delightful tiny village, 5km south of Ürgüp, is an ideal place to chill out. Right in the town centre is the imposing 19th-century **Church of Sts Constantine & Helena**, with a stone grapevine running round its entrance. Sadly, it's rarely unlocked.

It's a lovely walk to Monastery Valley, where you'll find three cave churches: **Ayios Stefanos Church** (St Stephen's), with fine carving and painted decoration; **Ayios Nikolaos Manastırı** (Monastery of St Nicholas); and the partially collapsed **Sinasos Church**.

The *Monastery Pension* (☎ 353 5005) has a big cave bar and restaurant and charges US$9 per head for simple rooms. The warm atmosphere at the *Old Greek House* (☎ 353 5306, fax 353 5141), which still bears some of the original 19th-century painting and decoration, makes it worth the US$25/35 for singles/doubles. Even if you don't stay, you should at least come to sample their tasty home cooking.

Hotel Pacha (☎/fax 353 5331) is a runner-up in the charm stakes with a flower-filled courtyard and terrace with lovely views. They charge US$7 a head for rooms with showers, including breakfast. Also pleasant is the refurbished *Hotel Cavit* (☎ 353 5186), with a nice garden shaded by grapevines. Rooms cost US$13/22.

The tour-group focused *Otel Sinasos* (☎ 353 5009, fax 353 5435) is a fantastic deal for US$13. The real gem is the restaurant, situated in a painstakingly restored old house.

GÜLŞEHİR & HACIBEKTAŞ

Gülşehir, 23km west of Avanos, is surrounded by impressive rock formations such as **Açık Saray** with its churches. It also has the **Karşı Kilise** (St John Church); an unexcavated underground city; and in the village, the **Karavezir Mehmet Paşa Camii & Medrese** (1778), an Ottoman seminary. There are no cheap places to stay in town.

About 28km north of Gülşehir is Hacıbektaş, the home of the founder of the Bektaşi order of dervishes. The only site of importance is the **Hacı Bektaş Müzesi**; it's open from 8.30 am to 12.30 pm and 1.30 to 5.30 pm daily except Monday, and admission is US$1.

Hacı Bektaş Veli, born in the 13th century in Iran, established a religious order that combined aspects of Islam (Sunni and Shi'ite) with orthodox Christianity. Hacıbektaş is the site of a haj (pilgrimage) in early August when half a million adherents come to the town.

There are buses to both Gülşehir (US$0.75, 20 minutes) and Hacıbektaş from Nevşehir, and there are minibuses between Gülşehir and Hacıbektaş (US$0.85, 30 minutes).

SOĞANLI

The Soğanlı Valley, 35km south of Ürgüp, is much less visited than Zelve or Göreme. It is a beautiful, tranquil place and well

worth seeing. The Aşağı Soğanlı and Yukarı Soğanlı (Lower Onion and Upper Onion Valleys, respectively) were once occupied by monks.

There are many fine churches in the valley (open daily from 8.30 am to 5.30 pm; admission US$1) including the **Tokalı Kilise** (Buckle Church), reached by a steep flight of steps; the twin-naved **Gök Kilise** (Sky Church); the **Karabaş Kilise** (Black Head Church) with its frescoes depicting the life of Christ; the **Kubbeli Kilise** and **Saklı Kilise** (Cupola and Hidden Churches); and the **Yılanı Kilise** (Snake Church) with a painted serpent just to the left of the entrance.

Soğanlı's isolation makes it an attractive destination. You should have no trouble finding somewhere to camp.

It's not easy to get to Soğanlı by public transport. You can take a bus from Kayseri to Yeşilhisar and then change for a bus to Soğanlı. If you are based in Göreme it's easier to visit here on a tour.

IHLARA GORGE
☎ 382

This is Cappadocia with a physical challenge – the remote Ihlara (Peristrema) Gorge has carved and painted churches dating from medieval times to the 14th century, and a river shaded by poplars and olive trees. It's a fantastic spot for hiking; the 16km walk from Ihlara Köyü (Ihlara Village) to Selime along the Melendiz Suyu stream can be done in a day if you're fit, or two days if you take it easy.

On the rim of the gorge near Ihlara Köyü is a ticket booth and a flight of stairs leading down into the valley (open daily from sunrise to sunset, US$2). At the bottom of the stairs and to the right is the **Ağaçaltı Kilise** (Beneath a Tree Church), which has fine frescoes. The **Yılanı Kilise** (Serpent Church) is well worth visiting. Its herpetological delights include female sinners being punished in hell by serpents.

At the northern end of the valley is **Selime**. The backdrop to the village is very surreal. On the cliffside north of the village, the **monastery** is one of Cappadocia's highlights. It is a labyrinth of tunnels, rock-cut rooms and sunken alleyways. A guide is recommended as there are many collapsed floors and gaping holes to trap the unwary.

TURKEY

The rustic village of Ihlara Köyü is 85km south-west of Nevşehir and 40km south-east of Aksaray. In the village, *Star Otel & Restaurant* (☎ 453 7676) was undergoing a refit at the time of writing. What was a simple place may well reopen as something a bit smarter. *Pansion Anatolia* (☎ 453 7440, fax 453 7439) is on the road running between the village and the entry to the gorge. Pleasant rooms with bathroom cost US$16 a double, or you can camp in the grounds for US$3 per person.

Ihlara buses run several times daily from Aksaray's otogar for US$0.50 one way. Aksaray can be reached from either Konya, 130km west, or Nevşehir, 70km north-east.

UNDERGROUND CITIES

To date about 40 underground cities have been discovered in Cappadocia. The most visited of them is Derinkuyu. Kaymaklı and Mazıköy are also quite popular, but there are at least 10 others periodically open to the public. Derinkuyu and Kaymaklı are open from 8 am to 5 pm, 6.30 pm daily in summer; admission costs US$2.50.

Some portions of the cities have been dated by archaeologists to 4000 years ago,

KELLI HAMBLET

Going underground – a network of rooms and tunnels in a Cappadocian underground city.

others say they were occupied by the 8th and 7th centuries BC. Xenophon (430–355 BC), the Greek historian, mentions them in his *Anabasis*.

At **Kaymaklı** a little cave in a mound leads down into a labyrinth carved four levels deep. There are signs of occupation everywhere, including smoke-blackened kitchens, deep wells and stables. It is believed that Kaymaklı was connected by a communication tunnel with Derinkuyu, 10km to the south.

Derinkuyu is the most popular of the underground cities, perhaps because it goes down eight levels. Some people are overwhelmed by claustrophobia when they look back up to the open air (70m above) through the ventilation shaft. Look for the huge circular stone doors used to block off levels from each other.

The entrance to the **Mazıköy** tunnels is just off the main square of Mazıköy (admission is US$2).

Although you can most easily visit one of the cities on a day tour out of Göreme, Avanos or Ürgüp, it's also easy to see them on your own by taking a Niğde-bound bus out of Nevşehir.

NİĞDE
☎ 388 • pop 68,700

Niğde, 85km south of Nevşehir, was built by the Seljuks. Backed by snowcapped mountains, it's a farming centre with a small but impressive selection of historic buildings.

The tourist office (☎ 232 3393) is on İstiklal Caddesi, just off the main square. It is open from 8.30 am to noon and from 1.30 to 5.30 pm daily except Sunday. The otogar is 1km north of the centre, and the train station 1km south-east.

The Seljuk **Alaeddin Camii** (1223) is a grand mosque, but the **Süngür Bey Camii**, built by the Seljuks and restored by the Mongols in 1335, is even better.

There are frequent buses from Niğde to Adana (US$6, three hours), Aksaray (US$2, 1½ hours), Kayseri (US$4.25, 1½ hours) and Konya (US$8.50, 3½ hours). Minibuses to Nevşehir (US$2.50, one hour) depart every hour on the hour from 5 am to 6 pm.

AROUND NİĞDE
About 10km east of the Niğde clock tower is the rock-hewn **Eski Gümüşler Monastery**

(open from 9 am to noon and 1.30 to 6.30 pm daily in summer; 8 am to 12.30 pm and 1.30 to 5.30 pm in winter; US$1.20). The main church has the best-preserved Byzantine frescoes in Cappadocia, painted between the 7th and 11th centuries.

The **Sultan Sazlığı Kuş Cenneti** (Sultan Marshes Bird Paradise), 60km north-east of Niğde, is a bird-watchers' paradise. There is an observation tower on the road to Yahyalı that affords views across Eğri Gölü. To the north is **Yay Gölü**, noted for its population of flamingos. The marshes are best visited if you have your own transport; otherwise take a bus from Kayseri to Yeşilhisar and change to a service to Ovaçiftliği.

KAYSERİ
☎ 352 • pop 425,000
In the shadow of snowcapped mountains, Kayseri, 80km east of Ürgüp, is rapidly metamorphosing into a bustling city of modern, apartment-lined boulevards. Something lingers of its old conservative soul, though, and after 9 pm many restaurants shut, and lone female visitors seem to be viewed with wholly unnecessary suspicion.

Many travellers whip through Kayseri en route to Nemrut Dağı or Cappadocia, but the city and surrounding area, which have a long history spanning from Hittite times, do have enough interesting sights of their own to fill at least half a day or more.

The basalt-walled citadel at the centre of the old town just south of Cumhuriyet Meydanı, the huge main square, is a good landmark. The otogar is just under 2km north-west of the citadel along Osman Kavuncu Caddesi. If there's no servis bus, walk out of the front of the otogar, cross the avenue and board any bus marked 'Merkez' (Centre), or take a dolmuş marked 'Şehir'. The train station is at the northern end of Atatürk Bulvarı, over half a kilometre north of the centre.

The helpful tourist office (☎ 222 3903, fax 222 0879), beside the Hunat Camii Medresesi, is open from 8.30 am to 5.30 pm daily in summer (closed winter weekends). Along Sivas Caddesi you'll find several Internet cafes including Unimed and Teknet.

Things to See
The black volcanic stone **citadel**, the Hisar or İç Kale, was originally built by Emperor

Justinian in the 6th century. Inside you'll find a lively bazaar. Opposite is the starkly handsome 13th-century **Mahperi Hunat Hatun Camii & Medresesi**. The hamam here is still in use (open from 8.30 am to 5 pm daily, longer for men).

More prime examples of Seljuk architecture are found north-west of the citadel around the Mimar Sinan Park, including the **Sahibiye Medresesi** (built in 1267) with its beautiful gateway, the **Çifte Medrese**, which houses the rather dull **Museum of Medical History**, and **Ulu Cami**, Kayseri's Great Mosque.

Don't miss the atmospheric **Vezirhanı** – an 18th-century courtyard where wool and cotton are traded on the ground floor, and carpets on the upper. It's at the southern end of the covered market. Also worth a look is **Güpgüpoğlu Konağı**, south-east of the citadel, a fine stone 18th-century mansion housing an interesting **Ethnographic Museum**. It's open from 8 am to 5 pm daily except Monday. Admission costs US$1.75.

Places to Stay
The basic **Hunat Oteli** (☎ 232 4319, Zengin Sokak 5), behind the Hunat Mosque near the tourist office, is quiet and clean, with waterless rooms for US$7 per person.

The smart and reliable **Hotel Turan** (☎ 222 5537, fax 231 1153, Turan Caddesi 8) has very spacious singles/doubles, some with bathtubs instead of showers. They usually cost US$18/28, but the staff may be ready to haggle. The top-floor breakfast room has good views.

The tidy **Hotel Çamlıca** (☎ 231 4344, Bankalar Caddesi, Gürcü Sokak 14) offers serviceable rooms for US$12 per head with sink, US$16 with shower.

Hotel Sur (☎ 222 4367, fax 231 3992, Talas Caddesi 12), just inside the city walls, is modern with double glazing to keep out the noise. Rooms with bathroom cost US$20/30.

At a pinch the **Hotel Terminal** (☎ 330 1120) next to the otogar will do. Rooms here have seen better days and cost around US$15/20 with bathroom, less without.

Places to Eat
Local delicacies include pastırma (salted sun-dried veal coated with *çemen*, a spicy garlic and pepper mixture, and allowed to

age for a month), *sucuk* (spicy sausage) and *tulum peynir* (hard cheese cured in goatskin).

İskender Kebap Salonu (Millet Caddesi 5), just inside the city walls and one floor above street level, serves good Bursa-style döner kebap for around US$4 a meal. The kebabs at *Beyazsaray (Millet Caddesi 8)* across the road are just as good, and they do a mean pizza as well. For dessert, try the sophisticated *Divan Pastanesi* opposite. A *şam fıstıklı baklava* (baklava with pistachio nuts) and a large glass of tea costs about US$2. There's a second branch on Sivas Caddesi.

Behind the post office, facing Cumhuriyet Meydanı, is a block of fast-food and take-away kebap places. Upstairs is the attractive *Tuana (Sivas Caddesi)*, whose big, bright dining room offers a great view towards Erciyes Dağı (Mt Argeus).

Getting There & Away
Air There are two daily flights from İstanbul to Kayseri's Erkilet airport. Tickets can be bought at the Turkish Airlines office (☎ 222 3858, fax 222 4748) at Sahibiye Mahallesi, Yıldırım Caddesi 1. An airport bus (US$1.50) connects the ticket office with the airport. Local bus No 2 also runs to the airport from Atatürk Caddesi.

Bus On an important north-south and east-west crossroads, Kayseri has lots of bus services. Daily services from Kayseri include Ankara (US$9.50, 4½ hours), Malatya (US$9, five hours), Nevşehir (US$3.50, 1½ hours), Şanlıurfa (US$15, eight hours), Sivas (US$5, 3½ hours) and Ürgüp (US$2, 1½ hours).

Train The *Vangölü/Güney Ekspresi,* the *Doğu Ekspresi* and the *Yeni Doğu Ekspresi* from İstanbul stop at Kayseri. The *Çukurova Ekspresi* and the 1st-class-only *Mavi Tren* stop in Kayseri on their way between Ankara and Adana.

AROUND KAYSERİ
The **Sultan Han**, built in the 1230s, is a striking old caravanserai, 45km north-east of Kayseri and 1km off the new highway. Besides being a fine example of a Seljuk royal caravan lodging and the second-largest in Anatolia (after the Sultan Hanı near Aksaray), it has been beautifully restored. It is open from 9 am to 1 pm and from 2 to 6 pm

daily except Monday; admission costs US$1.75. To get here, take any bus or dolmuş heading along the Sivas road and ask to get off at the Sultan Han turn-off.

Another fine caravanserai is the 13th-century **Karatay Han**, some 40km east of Kayseri. Take any bus to Pinarbaşi and get off when you see the han.

The 3916m extinct volcano **Erciyes Dağı** (Mt Argeus), 26km south of Kayseri, is a ski centre from December until the end of March. It has a chairlift and a beginners' lift. Accommodation is available at the *Dedeman Erciyes Ski Centre (☎ 352-324 2114, fax 342 2117)*, which has a swimming pool and offers singles/doubles/triples for US$90/120/150 half board. To get there take a Develi dolmuş (US$1, 30 minutes) from Talas Caddesi in Kayseri.

At İncesu, 35km south-west of Kayseri, you can wander the ruins of an old Ottoman town, with a magnificent complex consisting of a vast caravanserai, a mosque and a hamam. Take a bus or dolmuş from opposite the Kayseri otogar (US$0.75, 30 minutes).

Kayseri to Şanlıurfa

For many overlanders the really exciting part of Turkey begins after Cappadocia, and not just because this was the part of the country most affected by the Kurdish insurgency of the last 16 years. The tourist industry, so prevalent on the coast and around Cappadocia, gives way to a less developed, predominantly rural way of life which is also more traditionally Islamic.

This said, the next obvious destination on the overland route – the enigmatic ancient ruins atop Nemrut Dağı (Mt Nimrod) – are far from a tourist-free zone. It's possible to take round-trip tours from Göreme and Şanlıurfa, but for most travellers the choice will be either to make the ascent from Malatya to the north or Kahta to the south-west – we weigh up the pros and cons later in this chapter. Malatya is the transport hub for the area so you'll likely pass through here first whatever you decide to do. Even if you skip Nemrut Dağı (it's buried in snow in winter), do not miss Şanlıurfa, a truly exotic place redolent of the Middle East.

Since the capture of the Kurdistan Workers Party (PKK) leader Abdullah Öcalan in

Driving in Eastern Turkey

East of Cappadocia, you need to be aware that petrol stations are fewer, roads can be significantly worse and you will have to run the gauntlet of innumerable police and army roadblocks. Approaching a roadblock, slow right down and be sure you interpret the signals correctly (a red sign reading 'DUR' means stop, a green one reading 'GEÇ' means pass). If you're in the slightest doubt, always stop. Misreading a signal and running a roadblock could have serious consequences.

Fill your petrol tank before setting out, carry bottled water and snacks, and expect the ride to be longer than you think. Do most of your travelling in the earlier part of the day, so that you reach your destination by mid-afternoon. Avoid driving in the evening or at night. Roads in the extreme east and particularly in the north-east, are often riddled with potholes that break tyres and dent rims if hit at speed. When they're filled with rainwater it's impossible to judge their capacity to damage. Potholes occur at random in otherwise smooth roads and necessitate slow driving even on good stretches.

1999 (see The Region Today in the Facts About the Region chapter), the terrorist threat in the east has eased considerably. The atmosphere is now much more hopeful and less dangerous. Nonetheless it remains wise to check on the latest situation before setting out, and to be prepared for minor security hassles.

MALATYA
☎ 422 • pop 395,500

Malatya, the apricot capital of Turkey, offers one of the approaches to Nemrut Dağı. If you have time you could also visit the remains of the old city 11km to the north. Otherwise there's little to detain you in the modern centre unless you happen to be around in July when the apricot festival is in full swing.

The city stretches for many kilometres along İnönü/Atatürk Caddesi. The centre is around the *vilayet* (provincial government

headquarters) building, by the statue of former president İnönü. The new otogar, MAŞTI, is 4km to the west. The train station is a little closer to town, also to the west.

The helpful tourist office (☎ 323 3025) is on the ground floor of the vilayet – it's closed at weekends. The tourist office also organises tours to Nemrut Dağı (see Nemrut Dağı later in this chapter). Yeşil Net is an Internet cafe in the Yeşil cinema complex just west of the vilayet. There's also an Internet facility at MAŞTI.

Things to See
The **Malatya Museum** (Malatya Müzesi), south of the vilayet along Fuzuli Caddesi, offers a dimly lit collection spanning Palaeolithic to Byzantine times. The ethnography section upstairs contains some fine carpets and embroidery. It's open from 8 am to 5.30 pm (closed Monday) and admission costs US$1.75.

The vibrant **bazaar** sprawls north from PTT Caddesi and the Malatya Büyük Otel. The large undercover area specialising in food is fascinating, and there's an even livelier metal-working area (watch out for welders in the middle of the road).

The ruins of **old Malatya** 11km north in the village of Battalgazi include remains of the city walls and towers; the Seljuk-era **Ulu Cami**, which has a fine *eyvan* (vaulted hall) with an Arabic inscription; the ruined **Sahabiye-i-Kubra Medrese**, with a broken brick minaret; and the restored **Silahtar Mustafa Paşa Hanı** an Ottoman caravanserai dating from the 17th century. Buses to Battalgazi (US$0.25) leave from the northern side of Buhara Bulvarı at the junction with Turgut Temeli Caddesi.

Places to Stay & Eat
Otel Tahran (☎ 324 3615, PTT Caddesi) offers basic singles/doubles with sinks for US$5/9, but at the time of writing it was undergoing restoration (which could mean a price rise). The nearby *Merkez* is considerably less appealing but even cheaper.

Noisier but more cheerful is *Park Otel* (☎ 321 1691, Atatürk Caddesi 17), across from the belediye. Rooms with shower cost US$8.50/10.

The best deal in town is the *Malatya Büyük Otel* (☎ 321 1400, fax 321 5367), which faces the Yeni Cami, a block north of the vilayet. The rooms are very comfortable, with proper bathrooms and some even with TVs. Rates can go as low as US$17/21 per room (breakfast included).

The *Yeni Kent Otel* (☎ *321 1053, fax 324 9243, PTT Caddesi 33*) is a useful fall-back, with modern rooms for US$20/25.

For food try the spotless *Lokanta (PTT Caddesi 29)*. On Atatürk Caddesi, near the Park Otel, the popular *Beyaz Saray* serves excellent İskender kebap for around US$2. Even more popular is *Kent Lokantası (Atatürk Caddesi 137)*, serving great soups and stews.

VIP Melita Restaurant (☎ *322 5412)*, which is just off Atatürk Caddesi, offers a tempting range of mezes and some well-cooked kebaps and other dishes. At night there's music to accompany the delicious food.

Among the town's many good cake shops is *Sevinç Pastanesi*, opposite the Otel Kantar on Atatürk Caddesi, and the *Biricik Pastanesi* on Fuzuli Caddesi.

Before hiking up to Nemrut Dağı, stock up on dried fruit and nuts at the shops along Atatürk Caddesi, in the bazaar or at the otogar.

Getting There & Away

Air Turkish Airlines (☎ 324 8001) has daily flights to Ankara and İstanbul. The airport bus costs US$1.50 and leaves from the Turkish Airlines office 1½ hours before the flight departure time.

Bus From the new otogar MAŞTI, there are services to Adıyaman (for Kahta; US$5, three hours), Ankara (US$20, 11 hours), Diyarbakır (US$7, four hours), İstanbul (US$25, 18 hours), and Kayseri (US$12, four hours) among other places. There are service buses into town. To get to the otogar, take a bus from opposite the vilayet.

Train There are daily express trains from İstanbul (Haydarpaşa; US$11) and Ankara (US$7) via Kayseri (US$3) and Sivas (US$5). The 1st-class-only *Mavi Tren* to Ankara (US$9.50) also passes through Malatya.

Travelling out of Malatya, there are also daily services to Elazığ (US$5) and to Diyarbakır (US$2).

ADIYAMAN
☎ 416

There's no reason to stay in Adıyaman. The provincial capital is a booming oil town with canyons of faceless high-rises – accommodation options either on Nemrut Dağı or even in Kahta are better.

The new airport (☎ 216 1436) has twice-weekly flights to Ankara, with connections to İstanbul, İzmir, Antalya and Bodrum. Frequent buses and dolmuşes run the 35km to Kahta (US$0.85) throughout the day.

KAHTA
☎ 416 • pop 75,000

Plainly speaking, Kahta is a dump and you'd do well to spend as little time here as possible. Sadly, it is also the most convenient base from which to organise tours to all the sites around Nemrut Dağı (see Nemrut Dağı later in this chapter).

That said, the new hotels that have opened in the last few years are perfectly comfortable and the vast lake formed by the Atatürk Dam that laps at the edge of the fly-blown town is a good place to come for a meal, especially if you have your own wheels.

Mahmut Arslan at the tourist office (☎/fax 725 5007), on Mustafa Kemal Caddesi, 200m west of the otogar, speaks good English and is a mine of useful local information.

Places to Stay

In town, it will be baking hot in summer but few cheap hotels provide air-con or fans. Conversely, on the mountain it will be cold at night even in August so bring warm clothing and check that adequate blankets are provided. For details of accommodation on the mountain, see Places to Stay & Eat in the Nemrut Dağı section later in this chapter.

Anatolia Pension (☎ *725 6483, Adliye Karşısı)*, east of the otogar, has extremely basic singles/doubles for US$5/8.50. *Hotel Kommagene* (☎ *725 5548, fax 725 7614)*, at the junction with the Nemrut Dağı road, west of the otogar, is a more pleasant option, with comfortable rooms with bathroom for US$12/18 (slightly less without breakfast). Self-caterers can use the restaurant kitchen, and you can camp in the grounds for US$9 per van or US$6 per tent. We've had reports, though, that the food is awful and the manager can be very pushy with regards to tours.

Many tour groups stay at *Hotel Nemrut Tur* (☎ 725 6881, fax 725 6880, Mustafa Kemal Caddesi), 100m west of Hotel Kommagene. Some rooms here have air-con; if you don't like the first room you're shown, ask to see another. The food in the restaurant is surprisingly good. Individual travellers are charged about US$15/25 per room.

Opposite is the *Hotel Mezopotamya* (☎ 725 5112, Mustafa Kemal Caddesi 18) with cheerful, air-conditioned rooms for US$9 per person. Beside it, *Zeus Camping* (☎ 725 5695, fax 725 5696) charges US$9 for a van or a tent although, until nearby building work is finished, it's not particularly inviting.

Hotel Hans Bardakçı (☎ 725 8060, fax 725 5385, Mustafa Kemal Caddesi 24), opposite the tourist office, has air-con and a variety of rooms, some better than others, for US$25/45.

Places to Eat

At *Yudum*, upstairs on Mustafa Kemal Caddesi, east of the otogar and near the police station, a standard range of kebaps are at least well cooked and presented. A few doors away, the smaller *Kent Restaurant* turns out decent, cheap fare at low prices. Across the road is the friendly *Şafak Lokantası*, which serves (you guessed it) kebaps. At any of these places a meal and soft drink costs about US$3.50.

At the end of Baraj Yolu, the continuation of Mustafa Kemal Caddesi, the first restaurant you'll come to is *Akropolian* (☎ 725 5132). Here you can dine on good food on a terrace overlooking the lake, or dine indoors if the weather is bad. A plate of mezes, salad and fish will come to about US$4. Dolmuşes pass this way, or you can phone and ask to be picked up in town.

Closer to the small ferry on the lake is *Neşetin Yeri*, which serves a range of kebaps for about US$3.

Getting There & Away

The otogar is in the centre of town with the dolmuş and taxi stands right beside it. There are services to Ankara (US$17, 12 hours), İstanbul (US$25, 20 hours), Kayseri (US$13, seven hours), Malatya (US$5, 3½ hours) and Şanlıurfa (US$3.50, two hours).

Buses to Diyarbakır travel via Adıyaman and the south of the lake (US$6, five hours).

A more interesting way to travel to Diyarbakır is to take one of the five-daily dolmuşes to Siverek, which are timed to meet the ferries across the lake. In Siverek you may have to wait an hour or so for a connection to Diyarbakır but the bazaar is fun enough to fill in the time (US$5, four hours).

KAHTA TO NEMRUT DAĞI

On the way to Nemrut Dağı Milli Parkı (Mt Nimrod National Park) from Kahta you'll pass more than 100 oil wells producing around 60% of Turkey's petrol. The park is entered at **Karakuş**, 10km from Kahta, via a road to the left off the highway. Like that on Nemrut, the Karakuş mound is artificial, created to hold the graves of royal ladies of Commagene. An eagle tops one of the columns ringing the site. The summit of Nemrut is clearly, if distantly, visible from Karakuş; it's the highest point on the horizon to the north-east.

At Cendere, 19km from Kahta, the road crosses a **Roman bridge**. Unfortunately a heavy petrol truck caused the collapse of the original bridge, which has since been reconstructed. From here a sign points to the right for Nemrut Dağı; you can also reach the summit via the road to the left going to the village of Kahta Kalesi, opposite which are the ruins of a 14th-century Mamluk castle called **Yeni Kale**. You can climb up to look at the castle but only if you're reasonably fit and wearing sensible shoes. It's still possible to engage a guide in Kahta Kalesi to lead you up a trail to the summit.

About 1km farther along the main road, a road to the left takes you the 2km to **Eski Kale**, the impressive remains of the ancient Commagene capital of **Arsameia**. Admission costs US$1.75. This is a good spot for a picnic. A new 8km road makes it possible to drive from Arsameia to Nemrut Dağı, via the route from Malatya. If you return to the old road, you'll pass several villages before reaching Narince, where the road becomes rougher and steeper. Another 7km east of Narince is a turn-off to the left that takes you to Karadut and the summit.

Places to Stay & Eat

It's well worth staying in the mountains – the stunning views and peaceful settings make up for any lack of mod cons.

Karadut Pension (☎ *737 2169*), in the hamlet of Karadut, is nothing flash, but it's a very friendly place with excellent home cooking. Simple rooms cost US$7 per person. You can camp here for US$3.50. A passing minibus may charge US$2 or more to the summit; to rent an entire minibus for a trip to the summit and back to Karadut costs about US$13. This is a great place to stay if you want to experience life in a tiny mountain village.

North of Karadut, the last half-hour's travel (12km) to the summit is on a steep road paved with black basalt blocks and still fairly rough. On the way you'll pass the ugly *Hotel Euphrat* (☎ *737 2175, fax 737 2179*), which charges US$30/44 for singles/doubles with breakfast and dinner, and the smaller *Hotel Kervansaray* (☎ *737 2190*), which has a shady garden with swimming pool and charges US$20/35 for half-board. We have received an account from a reader about a problem with security at the Kervansaray. As always, it is a good idea to lock your valuables up. *Apollo Pansiyon* (☎ *737 2041*), is a converted village house with a garden restaurant. Bed and breakfast here costs US$7.50, dinner US$3.50. Finally there's the *Çesme Lokantası* (☎ *737 2032*) which has a few dorm beds for US$12.50 in a rear annexe.

NEMRUT DAĞI

One of the wonders of eastern Turkey is the colossal ancient statues atop Nemrut Dağı (not to be confused with the mountain on the shores of Lake Van), between the Malatya to the north and Kahta to the south.

The 50m-high crushed-rock tumulus on Nemrut Dağı's 2150m summit was built in the 1st century BC under the orders of the megalomaniac Antiochus, ruler of the tiny Commagene kingdom. Around the tumulus were set huge statues of himself and the gods (his 'relatives'). The king's tomb is thought to lie beneath those tonnes of rock. Nobody knows for sure.

Earthquakes long ago toppled the 2m-high heads from most of the statues, but the cracked faces that stare out enigmatically at the magnificent surrounding scenery retain a spellbinding power. The authorities are planning on placing the heads back on the bodies so anticipate some disruption at the site for the next few years.

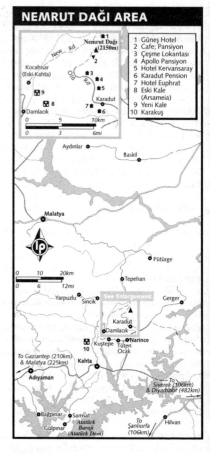

NEMRUT DAĞI AREA

1 Güneş Hotel
2 Cafe; Pansiyon
3 Çeşme Lokantası
4 Apollo Pansiyon
5 Hotel Kervansaray
6 Karadut Pension
7 Hotel Euphrat
8 Eski Kale (Arsameia)
9 Yeni Kale
10 Karakuş

History

Antiochus I Epiphanes (64–38 BC) was the son of Mithridates I Callinicus, who founded the Commagene kingdom, an offshoot from the Seleucid Empire. Treaties with both Rome and the Parthians allowed Antiochus to prosper, but the wealth fed his delusions of grandeur (the king claimed decent from both Darius the Great of Persia *and* Alexander the Great), hence the building of the funerary mound on top of Nemrut.

Only 26 years into his reign Antiochus mistakenly sided with the Parthians in a squabble with Rome, and in 38 BC the Romans deposed him. From then on Commagene was ruled either directly from Rome or by puppet kings until AD 72, when Emperor Vespasian incorporated it into Roman Asia.

The world had apparently forgotten about the monument until 1881, when Karl Puchstein, a German engineer, was astounded to come across it while charting these remote mountains. Archaeological work didn't begin until 1953, when the American School of Oriental Research undertook the project.

When to Visit

Plan to visit Nemrut Dağı between late May and mid-October, or (preferably) in July or August; the road to the summit becomes impassable in snow. Remember that at any time of year, even in high summer, it will be chilly and windy on top of the mountain. This is especially true at sunrise, the coldest time of the day. Take warm clothing on your trek to the top, no matter when you go. Turks in the know will be found on the summit swaddled in their hotel blankets.

At the Summit

Beyond the cafe near the car park you must hike 500m (15 or 20 minutes) uphill to the two sets of statues either side of the broken rock tumulus; make sure you're wearing sensible shoes. At the **western temple** Antiochus and his fellow gods sit in state, although the bodies have partly tumbled down along with the heads. But at the **eastern temple** the bodies are largely intact, except for the fallen heads, which seem more badly weathered than the western heads. On the backs of the eastern statues are inscriptions in Greek.

Both terraces have similar plans, with the syncretistic gods, the 'ancestors' of Antiochus, seated in this order, from left to right: First comes Apollo, the sun god – Mithra to the Persians, Helios or Hermes to the Greeks; next is Fortuna, or Tyche; in the centre is Zeus-Ahura Mazda; to the right is King Antiochus; and at the right end is Heracles, also known as Ares or Artagnes.

Low walls at the sides of each temple once held carved reliefs showing processions of ancient Persian and Greek royalty, Antiochus' 'predecessors'. Statues of eagles represent Zeus.

A helipad (to save VIPs the hassle of walking) occupies the site of an ancient altar next to the eastern temple. Nearby is a cabin with 'müze' written on its door which serves cups of çay and sells souvenirs. There's also a *pansiyon*, described accurately by one reader as 'two cement boxes', for around US$5 a dorm bed.

Admission to the archaeological site costs US$2.50.

Organised Tours

The most obvious base for ascending the southern slopes of Nemrut Dağı is Kahta. It costs about the same to use Malatya as a base, but it's not as convenient to see the sights on the other side of the mountains from here. There are also more expensive tours from Şanlıurfa and Cappadocia.

From Kahta Agencies offer two sorts of minibus tour. The short tour (US$35 per group, five hours, 106km) takes you from Kahta to the summit and back again, allowing about an hour for sightseeing. The long tour (US$45 per group, 140km, eight hours) takes you to the summit, and on the trip down stops at Arsameia, Cendere and Karakuş. Kahta has long had a reputation as a rip-off town so check exactly what type of tour you'll be on before handing over the cash.

Although it may be more enjoyable to go up the mountain in the middle of the day when it's warmer and you can enjoy the scenery in both directions, most tours are timed to capture the drama of sunrise or sunset; without enough people to make your own arrangements you're likely to travel either up or down in darkness.

From Malatya Malatya tourist office organises minibus tours to Nemrut Dağı from late April to mid-October. It's a four-hour ride through dramatic scenery to the summit. The last 30km of road is unpaved but goes right to the top, unlike the road from Kahta. After enjoying the sunset for two hours, you descend 2km to the forlorn, run-down Güneş Hotel. Here you have dinner and pass the night before taking the minibus back up to the summit for sunrise. After breakfast at the Güneş you return to Malatya for around 10 am.

The per person cost of US$30 includes transport, dinner, bed and breakfast, and you pay another US$2.50 for admission to the national park. In theory there are tours every day but if you turn up alone you have to be prepared to pay substantially more. Some readers have negotiated a transport-only fare, and taken a sleeping bag and food

Colossal stone heads up to 2m high sit atop remote Nemrut Dağı near Malatya.

to the summit with them. If you want to do this, remember that the mornings are freezing cold even in July.

If you prefer to descend via Kahta, hike across the summit to the car park and cafe building, and ask around for a minibus with an empty seat; or hitch a ride with someone going down to Kahta.

By taking this route you miss seeing other sites like Arsameia along the Kahta-Nemrut road. Be warned that if you are driving yourself, the road is extremely steep and very rough – certainly not for novices.

From Şanlıurfa Two-day tours to Nemrut (US$40/50 depending on accommodation) are available from Harran-Nemrut Tours in Şanlıurfa (see Şanlıurfa later in this chapter for details). You may stop at the Atatürk Dam along the way. Another option is to group together with other travellers and hire a taxi for the day; you'll need an early start and you should reckon on at least US$25 per person.

From Cappadocia Several agents in Göreme offer minibus tours to Nemrut Dağı, despite the distance of almost 600km. Two-day tours cost about US$125 and involve many hours of breakneck driving. If time allows, it's better to opt for a three-day tour (costing about US$150), which breaks the journey into more manageable chunks and also allows you to see the other ancient sites around Nemrut.

One reliable operator is Ötüken Voyage (☎ 384-271 2757), with regular Tuesday and Friday departures. Tours take in the Karatay Han near Kayseri and a visit to the bazaar in Karamanmaraş, before arriving in Kahta. On the second day you visit Nemrut Dağı for sunrise and then take in Arsameia, Cendere and Karkuş. Afterwards you continue to Harran, before stopping for the night in Şanlıurfa. On the last day you drive back to Göreme via Gaziantep, following the road through Adana and over the Taurus Mountains to Niğde. Neşe Tour offers similar packages departing on Wednesday and Saturday.

Getting There & Away
Taxi & Dolmuş From Kahta, taxi drivers charge about US$25 to run you up to the heads, but you shouldn't expect anything in the way of guidance.

One dolmuş a day leaves Kahta at about 3 pm to go up the mountain as far as the Çeşme Lokantası, stopping at Karadut village (US$1.50) on the way.

Car Driving to the summit from Kahta is no problem since all the sites are clearly indicated with English signs; either take the old road via Narince and Karadut or the shorter new route via Karakuş, Cendere, Eski Kahta and Arsameia. Though the return trip is only about 110km by the old road (70km by the new road), much of that will be driven in low gear, which uses more fuel, so make sure you fill up in Khata before setting out. Also pack a bottle of water and some food since the return journey can take between four and six hours and services along the way are limited.

ŞANLIURFA (URFA)
☎ 414 • pop 295,000
Fabled birthplace of Abraham, the great pilgrimage town of Şanlıurfa, 106km south of Kahta, shouldn't be missed. Although it's

ŞANLIURFA (URFA)

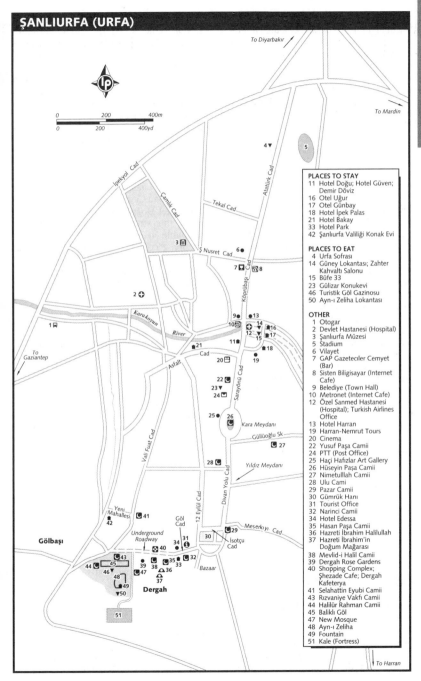

To Diyarbakır

To Mardin

4▼

5

0 — 200 — 400m
0 — 200 — 400yd

İpekyol Cad

Çamlık Cad

Tekal Cad

Atatürk Cad

Ş Nusret Cad 6●

3 🏛

7 🖬 Köprübaşı Cad 🖬 8

2 ✪

Karakoyun

River

9● ●13
10🖬 14
12 ▼ ●16
15 ▼ ●17
11🛆 ●18
21🛆
Cad 20🏢 ●19

22 🔵
23▼
24 🖸

25● 26 🔵
Kara Meydanı

Gülüöğlu Sk
🔵 27

28 🔵
Yıldız Meydanı

To Gaziantep

Asfalt

Sarayönü Cad

Vali Fuat Cad

12 Eylül Cad

Divan Yolu Cad

Yeni Mahallesi
42 🔵 41

Gölbaşı

Göl Cad

Underground Roadway
🔵 40
34 31
38 🔵
39 35🔵 🔵 32
44 🔵 45 33
46▼ 🔵 47 36
48 ▲ 37
🔵 49
▼50
43
🔵 29
30 İsotçu Cad
Meserkıyı Cad
Bazaar

Dergah

51

To Harran

PLACES TO STAY
11 Hotel Doğu; Hotel Güven; Demir Döviz
16 Otel Uğur
17 Otel Günbay
18 Hotel İpek Palas
21 Hotel Bakay
33 Hotel Park
42 Şanlıurfa Valiliği Konak Evi

PLACES TO EAT
4 Urfa Sofrası
14 Güney Lokantası; Zahter Kahvaltı Salonu
15 Büfe 33
23 Gülizar Konukevi
46 Turistik Göl Gazinosu
50 Ayn-ı Zeliha Lokantası

OTHER
1 Otogar
2 Devlet Hastanesi (Hospital)
3 Şanlıurfa Müzesi
5 Stadium
6 Vilayet
7 GAP Gazeteciler Cemyet (Bar)
8 Sisten Biligisayar (Internet Cafe)
9 Belediye (Town Hall)
10 Metronet (Internet Cafe)
12 Özel Sanmed Hastanesi (Hospital); Turkish Airlines Office
13 Hotel Harran
19 Harran-Nemrut Tours
20 Cinema
22 Yusuf Paşa Camii
24 PTT (Post Office)
25 Haçi Hafızlar Art Gallery
26 Hüseyin Paşa Camii
27 Nimetulllah Camii
28 Ulu Cami
29 Pazar Camii
30 Gümrük Hanı
31 Tourist Office
32 Narinci Camii
34 Hotel Edessa
35 Hasan Paşa Camii
36 Hazreti İbrahim Halilullah
37 Hazreti İbrahim'in Doğum Mağarası
38 Mevlid-i Halil Camii
39 Dergah Rose Gardens
40 Shopping Complex; Şhezade Cafe; Dergah Kafeterya
41 Selahattin Eyubi Camii
43 Rızvaniye Vakfı Camii
44 Halilür Rahman Camii
45 Balıklı Göl
47 New Mosque
48 Ayn-ı Zeliha
49 Fountain
51 Kale (Fortress)

TURKEY

ringed by highways and high rises, at its heart is a delightful area of sand-coloured mosques and buildings set around carp-filled pools, overlooked by an ancient fortress and adjacent to an exotic bazaar. It's a scorching hot place where Turks mix with Kurds and Arabs to create a truly Middle Eastern atmosphere.

Allow at least one night and a full day here. If you make an excursion south to Harran, the biblical town of beehive houses near the Syrian frontier, and to the surrounding archaeological sites, you'll need at least another day. To see the Atatürk Barajı (Atatürk Dam), en route to Adıyaman add another half day.

History

It's thought that a fortress stood on the hill where the existing kale now is more than 3500 years ago. The people built a powerful state called Hurri and through an alliance with the Pharaohs adopted many Egyptian customs, among them (rather surprisingly given the weather) sun worship. The Hittites took over in 1370 BC, then after a period of Assyrian rule, Alexander the Great marched through and renamed the town Edessa, after a former capital of Macedonia.

The Romans eventually took over, but before this Edessa adopted Christianity (circa AD 200). The religion was so new that the liturgical language was Aramaic, the language of Jesus. The city's position on the outer edge of the Roman Empire meant it was constantly fought over, with the Persians and later the Turks, Arabs, Armenians and Byzantines all battling for the city.

In 1098, the First Crusade arrived to set up a feudal state, which lasted until 1144 when it was conquered by a Seljuk Turkish emir. Edessa was renamed Urfa in 1637 when the Ottomans finally claimed the city and became Şanlıurfa (Glorious Urfa) little more than a decade ago, in recognition of its resistance to French occupation after WWI. Many people still call it Urfa.

Orientation & Information

The modern centre of town is near the belediye on Köprübaşı Caddesi, around 1km east of the otogar beside the Gaziantep-Diyarbakır highway. Gölbaşı, where the mosques, pools, fortress and bazaar are located, is 1.5km south of the otogar. The city's main thoroughfare is confusingly

called Atatürk, Köprübaşı, Sarayönü and Divan Yolu Caddesis along different stretches, but it provides an easily walkable link between Urfa's ancient and modern quarters.

The tourist office (☎ 215 2467) is in a building above the underground roadway on Göl Caddesi, near the Hotel Edessa; there's also an information booth in the Dergah rose garden. Also helpful is Özcan Arslan at Harran-Nemrut Tours (☎ 215 1575, mobile 0542-761 3065, fax 215 1156), just off Sarayönü Caddesi, who runs tours to local sites, including Harran and Nemrut Dağı.

You can change money at Demir Döviz, on Sarayönü Caddesi between Hotel Güven and Hotel Doğu. There are several ATMs along this street, too. Internet access is available at Metronet downstairs in the shopping complex near the Hotel Güven, and at Sisten Biligisayar farther north along Köprübaşı Caddesi near the intersection with Ş Nusret Caddesi.

Gölbaşı

Head to the extraordinarily picturesque quarter of Gölbaşı first. The focus of this carefully landscaped area, centred around the cave where the Prophet Abraham is believed to have been born and spent the first 10 years of his life, are two pools filled with sacred carp, **Balıklı Göl** and **Ayn-ı Zeliha**.

On the northern side of Balıklı Göl is the handsome **Rızvaniye Vakfı Camii** and **Medresesi**, while at the western end is the small 17th-century **Halilür Rahman Camii**. The two pools are fed by a spring at the base of Damlacık hill, on which the magnificent **kale** is built. The fortress is reached by going up a flight of stairs which then cascade back down again via a tunnel cut through the rock.

On the top of Damlacık hill you'll find a few sheep and goats and a pair of towering Corinthian columns dubbed the **Throne of Nemrut** after the supposed founder of Urfa, the biblical King Nimrod. Come up here for the spectacular views, worth the US$1.75 entry fee.

After the climb, there are shady cafes beside the pools where you can relax and enjoy the ambience of the **Dergah rose gardens** and the sympathetically designed shopping complex, before continuing to Abraham's birth cave, **Hazreti İbrahim'in Doğum**

Mağarası. There are separate entrances for men and women. A large Ottoman-style mosque stands to the west of the cave.

Next door is an attractive complex of mosques and medreses called **Hazreti İbrahim Halilullah** (Prophet Abraham, Friend of God). To the east, on Göl Caddesi, is the **Hasan Paşa Camii**, an Ottoman work. The **Mevlid-i Halil Camii** holds the tomb of a saint named Dede Osman. All of these places of worship are open to visitors, but remember this is a conservative city, so dress and act appropriately.

Other Attractions

Urfa's splendid **bazaar** spreads east of the Hasan Paşa Camii. It's a jumble of streets, some covered, some open, where everything from sheepskins and pigeons to jeans and handmade shoes is sold. Dive in and take your time exploring. In the old **Bedesten**, an ancient caravanserai, you'll find carpets, second-hand kilims and silk scarves. The **Gümrük Hanı** is a delightful courtyard where men sit sipping çay and playing chess and cards beneath plane trees.

Urfa's Syrian-style, 12th-century **Ulu Cami** on Divan Yolu Caddesi has a spacious forecourt with a tower topped by a clock with Ottoman numerals. More interesting is the beautifully restored **Selahattin Eyubi Camii** on Vali Fuat Caddesi, which leads up from behind Gölbaşı. Once a church, it is now liberally adorned with Arabic inscriptions. Nearby you can explore Urfa's evocative crumbling back streets. Elsewhere, some of the traditional mud-brick architecture has been restored, notably **Hacı Hafızlar**, opposite the Hüseyin Paşa Camii; the old house's fine carved stonework is much better than the art on show in the gallery.

The **Şanlıurfa Müzesi**, up the hill to the west of the vilayet building, off Atatürk Caddesi, is worth a look. Here you can see mosaics, artefacts from as far back as the Neolithic period and some incredibly intricate wooden doors and window shutters from old Urfa houses. It is open from 8.30 am to noon and 1.30 to 5.30 pm daily except Monday. Admission costs US$1.75.

Places to Stay

A good place to start looking is Köprübaşı Caddesi behind the Özel Sanmed Hastanesi. The best of the cheapies is *Otel Uğur*

(☎ 313 1340), up an uneven flight of steps at the end of the street, opposite the upmarket Hotel Harran, where basic, but clean singles/doubles cost US$5/9. The *Otel Günbay* (☎ 313 9797) nearby charges the same but isn't as nice.

The *Hotel İpek Palas* (☎ 215 1546), just south of Otel Günbay, has decent rooms from US$12/20, but at busy times single travellers may have to put up with the worst rooms, or pay extra for a double.

Hotel Güven (☎ 215 1700, fax 215 1941, Sarayönü Caddesi 133) has pleasant enough rooms for US$17/25 with shower but the reception staff can be surly. The nearby *Hotel Doğu* (☎ 212 1528) has much more basic rooms for US$9/14.

Around the corner on Asfalt Caddesi, a good option is *Hotel Bakay* (☎ 215 2689, fax 215 1156, Asfalt Caddesi 24). It has newly renovated rooms with air-con, TV and balcony for US$14/20.

Hotel Park (☎ 216 0500) upstairs at Göl Caddesi 4 only has its location going for it. Waterless rooms here are as basic as they come for US$5 per person.

Şanlıurfa Valiliği Konak Evi (☎ 215 9377, fax 215 3045, Vali Fuat Caddesi) is a six-room hotel in a delightfully restored 19th-century stone building near the Selahattin Eyubi Camii. The rooms are comfortable and modern and cost US$32/50, although prices are expected to rise soon.

Places to Eat

In the evenings at street stalls along Köprübaşı and Sarayönü Caddesis men sit chopping salads on wooden boards and wrapping charcoal-grilled pieces of liver *(ciğer)* in flaps of bread. Just remember to be careful what you eat here because the heat encourages the speedy incubation of microbes.

Güney Lokantası just off Köprübaşı Caddesi is reliable and sells kebaps, stews, vegetable dishes, pilavs and soups. A simple meal should cost around US$3. Next door is *Zahter Kahvaltı Salonu* where a breakfast of honey and fresh cream spread on flat bread and washed down with a large glass of çay, costs around US$1.

A good place to sample the local delicacy *içli köfte* (a deep-fried croquette with a mutton filling) is *Urfa Sofrası* on Atatürk Caddesi. A blowout meal will come to around US$6.

The various çay bahçesis at Gölbaşı all serve simple grills. The *Turistik Göl Gazinosu* and the *Ayn-ı Zeliha Lokantası* are both good. Also worth a look are *Şhezade Cafe* and *Dergah Kafeterya* on the terrace of the shopping complex, both with great views of the kale. Tea and snacks are also available at the bazaar's Gümrük Hanı.

For a meal in traditional surroundings try the lovely *Gülizar Konukevi (☎ 215 0505, İrfaniye Sokak 22)*, tucked away behind the main post office, and the restaurant at *Şanlıurfa Valiliği Konak Evi* (see Places to Stay).

If you feel like a beer, your choices are *Büfe 33*, more or less opposite Hotel İpek Palas, which sells canned Efes Pilsen, the restaurant at *Hotel Harran*, or the rooftop restaurant *GAP Gazeteciler Cemyet*, on Köprübaşı Caddesi. Although it has the feel of a dodgy club, also has an outdoor terrace.

Getting There & Away

Air Turkish Airlines (☎ 215 3344) has daily nonstop flights to and from Ankara with connections to İstanbul and İzmir. There are also two weekly nonstop flights to İstanbul. Service buses to the airport stop outside the Turkish Airlines office on Sarayönü Caddesi near the hospital.

Bus You can catch dolmuşes to the otogar outside the belediye. There are daily services to Ankara (US$20, 12 hours), Diyarbakır (US$7, three hours), Gaziantep (US$5, 2½ hours), İstanbul (US$29, 18 hours), Malatya (US$9, seven hours) and Van (US$14, nine hours).

Minibuses to Adıyaman (US$3, 1½ hours) leave from the minibus terminal next to the otogar.

HARRAN & AROUND

Parched Harran, 47km south of Urfa on the road to Syria, also has a biblical pedigree. With its crumbling beehive houses, fortress and ruined walls it really looks as if Abraham and his family could have lived here.

The most impressive monument is actually the kale which looms over the modern village. Locals have long since abandoned the beehive houses to their livestock in favour of more conventional dwellings. Entrance to the kale is US$1.75, but there may not be anyone in the ticket booth to collect the money. If anyone in the kale tries to charge you, insist on being given the official ticket. If they don't find you first, guides hang out in the tent that serves as a cafe on the summit of the kale. They'll probably want around US$6 for their services.

Should you wish to stay, the new *Bazda Motel* (☎ 414-441 3590, fax 441 2145) is on the approach road into town and has been designed to mimic the beehive houses. Airy rooms are good value at US$20 a head.

About 20km east of Harran is the Seljuk Han cl Ba'rur Caravanseral. Another 25km north-east of the caravanserai are the extensive remains of **Şuayb City**, including a network of subterranean rooms. Villagers will probably be happy to show you around and point out the more accessible caves. Bring a torch (flashlight) and wear sturdy shoes. In and around the poverty-stricken village of **Soğmatar**, 15km north, are ancient temples to the sun and moon gods.

Getting There & Away

From Sanlıurfa catch an Akçakale dolmuş (US$1) and get off at the junction 10km west of Harran. From here either hitch or take a taxi; bear in mind there's little shelter against the boiling sun.

Tours are offered by Harran-Nemrut Tours (see Orientation & Information under Şanlıurfa). Provided there are at least four people, tours depart at 9 am and 4 pm daily and cost US$10 per person. You'll spend two hours in Harran and be back in Urfa by either 1 or 8 pm.

To get to the sites beyond Harran without your own transport is time consuming. Even with your own car the roads are rough and poorly signed. The longer tours offered by Harran-Nemrut Tours, which include Han el Ba'rur, Şuayb City and Soğmatar, are therefore worth considering. They cost US$20 per person (assuming there are four people), leave at 6 am and last around 12 hours.

Şanlıurfa to Doğubayazıt

Heading east through the basin of the Euphrates and Tigris Rivers (known as the Fırat and the Dicle in Turkish) you'll be following in the footsteps of millennia of invaders and traders. Arabic culture, already evident in Urfa and Harran, is supplemented by that of the Kurds and Armenians in towns such as Diyarbakır and Van.

The dams and irrigation schemes of the South-East Anatolia Project or Güneydoğu Anadolu Projesi (GAP) are bringing fertility to the area's once barren deserts, but also obliterating communities and unique archaeological sites such as Hasankeyf. With time to spare you could explore the Tür Abdin plateau from towns such as Mardin and Midyat.

Our main route heads from the medieval old city of Diyarbakır via rocky, sheep-grazed plains, to the gorgeous alpine scenery surrounding Van Gölü (Lake Van). On the way you could stop off at the towns of Bitlis and Tatvan. In Van itself you can visit magnificent ruined fortresses and old Armenian churches before crossing the border into Iran. Although it is possible to cross at Esendere, some 200km east of Van (see the 'Van to Orūmīyé' boxed text), we recommend you head north to the main border crossing at Gürbulak, close to the town of Doğubayazıt at the foot of the twin-peaked Mt Ararat.

DİYARBAKIR
☎ 412 • pop 2 million
On the banks of the Tigris River (Dicle Nehri), 190km north-east of Urfa, is Diyarbakır, once notorious as the centre of the Kurdish resistance movement. Don't let this put you off. Since the PKK ended 15 years of armed rebellion, the atmosphere in this ancient city of 2 million is much more relaxed. The security forces are nowhere near as conspicuous and, although life remains tough for the many people who fled here from the countryside over the recent turbulent decades, you'll find most locals more hopeful for the future.

The main attraction is the medieval warren of streets within Diyarbakır's old town, framed by brooding basalt walls. These date from Roman times (when the city was called Amida), but as far back as 1500 BC there was a settlement here, part of the Hurrian Kingdom of Mitanni. Because of its strategic position, Diyarbakır has been much fought over. It gained its present name during the Arab occupation in the 7th century and was later ruled by the Seljuks, Turkomans and Ottomans. The brutal clampdown

on Kurdish insurgency in the mid-1920s by republican Turkish forces kicked off the round of troubles that has only recently abated.

Orientation & Information
Everything of interest is within the walls of the old city. Broad avenues radiate from the main north, south, east and west gates to a central crossroads. Beyond this the city is a maze and you'll probably find yourself having to use the services of a guide (there's always someone hanging around) to show you the way to specific sites. Agree a price in advance.

The train station is at the western end of İstasyon Caddesi which heads east to the Urfa Kapısı, the city's western or Edessa gate. The otogar is north-west of the city where Elazığ Caddesi (also called Ziya Gökalp Bulvarı) intersects the highway.

The tourist office (☎ 221 2173) is inside the Dağ Kapısı but has little useful information. Most banks have branches with ATMs on İnönü Caddesi. At the time of writing you needed to go into the new city of Diyarbakır, west of the old walled city, to find an Internet cafe. This may well have changed by the time you read this.

Things to See
Almost 6km in length Diyarbakır's monumental Roman walls, with their four main gates (kapısı) and 72 bastions, were rebuilt in the 11th century and are said to be second in extent only to the Great Wall of China. From the air, the shape of the walls resembles a turbot, with the fish's head at the İç Kale (citadel or keep) in the north-eastern corner. This fortress is now a military zone but if you ask nicely, the soldiers are likely to let you look around – the views from the battlements across the river are panoramic. The other best spot for climbing the walls is from the southern Mardin Kapısı towards the western Urfa Kapısı. Because of reports of theft in the past, it's a good idea to walk the walls in the company of others.

There are scores of mosques in Diyarbakır, the most important and visually striking being Ulu Cami (1091), which has a huge courtyard and some beautiful interior decoration. On one side of the courtyard is the Mesudiye Medresesi, while across Gazi Caddesi from the complex is

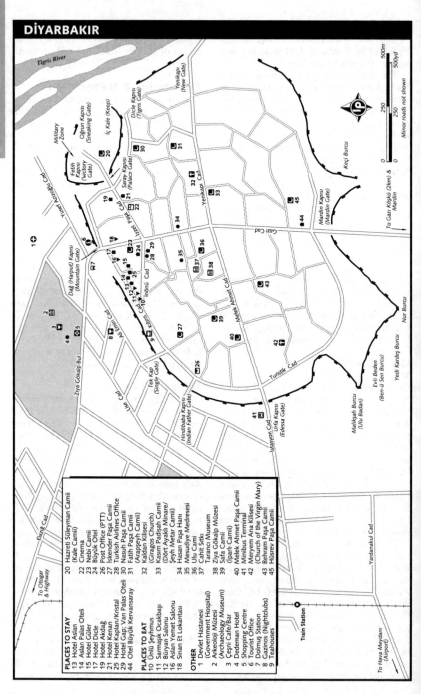

DİYARBAKIR

PLACES TO STAY
13 Hotel Aslan
14 Aslan Palas Oteli
15 Hotel Güler
17 Hotel Dicle
19 Hotel Akdağ
21 Hotel Kenan
25 Hotel Kaplan/Kristal
29 Hotel Gap; Van Palas Oteli
44 Otel Büyük Kervansaray

PLACES TO EAT
10 Ünlü Şeyhmus
11 Sarmaşık Ocakbaşı
12 Büryan Salonu
16 Aslan Yemet Salonu
18 Sinan Et Lokantası

20 Hazreti Süleyman Camii
   (Kale Camii)
22 Cinema
23 Nebi Camii
24 Büyük Otel
26 Post Office (PTT)
27 İskender Paşa Camii
28 Turkish Airlines Office
30 Nasuh Paşa Camii
31 Fatih Paşa Camii
32 Kaldan Kilisesi
   (Giragos Church)
33 Kasım Padişah Camii
   (Dört Ayaklı Minare/
   Şeyh Metar Camii)
34 Hasan Paşa Hanı
35 Mesudiye Medresesi
36 Ulu Cami
37 Cahit Sıtkı
   Tarancı Museum
38 Ziya Gökalp Müzesi
39 Safa Camii
   (İparlı Camii)
40 Melek Ahmet Paşa Camii
41 Minibus Terminal
42 Meryem Ana Kilisesi
   (Church of the Virgin Mary)
43 Behram Paşa Camii
45 Hüsrev Paşa Camii

OTHER
1 Devlet Hastanesi
   (Government Hospital)
2 Arkeoloji Müzesi
   (Archaeology Museum)
3 Çeşni Cafe/Bar
4 Dedeman Hotel
5 Shopping Centre
7 Tourist Office
8 Dolmuş Station
9 Gazinos (Nightclubs)
9 Teahouses

Hasan Paşa Hanı, a picturesque 16th-century caravanserai, occupied by carpet sellers and souvenir vendors.

Near the Ulu Cami are two small house museums whose traditional architecture, incorporating bands of black and white stone, is more interesting than the exhibits. Check out the 19th-century **Cahit Sıtkı Tarancı Museum,** formerly the home of a poet, and the **Ziya Gökalp Müzesi** commemorating a sociologist. Both are open from 8 am to noon and 1.30 to 5 pm daily (closed Monday); admission is US$1.75.

Deep in the maze of alleys south of Melek Ahmet Caddesi, is the spectacular **Behram Paşa Camii** (1572), Diyarbakır's largest mosque, and the wonderful **Meryem Ana Kilisesi,** the Church of the Virgin Mary, still used by the city's tiny community of Orthodox Syrian Christians. Hammer on the high basalt wall that surrounds the lovingly maintained church to be let in.

If you have more time, there's the large **Arkeoloji Müzesi** (Archaeology Museum), near the Dedeman Hotel off Ziya Gökalp Bulvarı, open from 8.30 am to noon and from 1.30 to 5 pm daily (closed Monday); admission is US$1.75. Although built in the early 20th century, the small **Gazi Köşkü,** 2km south of Mardin Kapısı, is a good example of a rich person's summer home.

Places to Stay

All of Diyarbakır's budget accommodation is conveniently clustered around Dağ Kapısı (also known as Harput Kapısı) – it shouldn't take you long to find something that suits, but bear in mind the stifling heat of summer when choosing a room.

The hospitable *Hotel Kenan (☎ 221 6614, Hz. Süleyman Caddesi 20)* offers clean, basic rooms, for US$7/12 a single/double, and is perhaps the best budget choice. Opposite, *Hotel Akdağ (☎ 229 1267)* is grubbier but charges slightly less.

Hotel Gap (☎ 223 6419), in an alley just off İnönü Caddesi, charges just US$5 per person for extremely basic rooms and has a pleasant courtyard. The *Van Palas Oteli (☎ 221 1218)* next door is similar.

Kıbrıs Caddesi has a whole string of hotels starting with *Hotel Dicle (☎ 223 5326, Kıbrıs Caddesi 3)* with rooms for US$9/15. Moving along, *Aslan Palas Oteli (☎ 221 1227, Kıbrıs Caddesi 21)* charges US$6/9

for very basic rooms, while *Hotel Aslan (☎ 224 7096)* next door has more comfortable rooms with bathroom for US$14/20.

Tucked down a quiet alley off Kıbrıs Caddesi, *Hotel Kristal/Kaplan (☎ 224 9606, fax 224 0187, Yoğurtçu Sokak 10),* two places side by side and run by the same management, are very good value. Rooms with bathroom and satellite TV cost US$14/20, breakfast included. The reliable and recently renovated *Hotel Güler (☎/fax 224 0294, Yoğurtçu Sokak 7),* opposite, has a friendly atmosphere and large rooms for US$25/35, breakfast included.

A smart mid-range option is *Büyük Otel (☎ 228 1295, fax 221 2444, İnönü Caddesi 4),* with modern rooms with bathroom for US$30/45 including breakfast. Some rooms have fine views over the old town, as does the roof terrace and restaurant.

Places to Eat

Along Kıbrıs Caddesi are several cheap, reliable places for a meal including *Aslan Yemet Salonu, Büryan Salonu* and *Sarmaşık Ocakbaşı.* The latter specialises in *ocakbaşı* (grills); you can sit right beside the grill, the chef handing you skewers of meat. Expect to pay US$3 to US$5. The *Ünlü Şeyhmus* pastry shop sells baklava and chewy Maraş-style ice-cream for US$1.25.

Sinan Et Lokantası, south of Dağ Kapısı has a vine-shaded terrace, a reasonable selection of dishes and serves beer; if there's live music you'll have to pay a cover charge but the casual atmosphere makes it worth it.

Although drinks and meals at *Otel Büyük Kervansaray (☎ 228 9606, fax 223 9522, Gazi Caddesi),* in the 16th-century Deliller Han, are way overpriced, it's worth sticking your head around the door to inspect the conversion job of a caravanserai that once had room for 800 camels.

In the evenings men set up kebap stands on the street beside the Dağ Kapısı and there are lots of fruit and veg vendors for self-caterers.

Entertainment

There's a string of *teahouses* by the walls along Kıbrıs Caddesi. There are plenty of dodgy looking *gazinos* (nightclubs) along the streets immediately west of Dağ Kapısı just off Ali Emiri Caddesi. A more convivial, though pricey, venue is the contemporary

Çeşni Cafe/Bar (☎ 229 5641) immediately behind the high-rise Dedeman Hotel. The restaurant upstairs at the Çeşni serves fine Western-style dishes and downstairs is a bar with live music.

Getting There & Away

Air There are daily nonstop flights to and from Ankara and İstanbul. A service bus from the Turkish Airlines office (☎ 223 5373, fax 223 3415), on İnönü Caddesi near Hotel Gap, goes to the airport; a taxi costs about US$8.

Bus Many bus companies have ticket offices in town near the Dağ Kapısı. Service buses will ferry you to the otogar, from where there are daily services to Ankara (US$25, 13 hours), Batman (US$2.50, 1½ hours), Erzurum (US$13, eight hours), Kahta (for Nemrut Dağı, US$6, three hours), Malatya (US$5, five hours), Şanlıurfa (US$5, three hours) and Van (US$10, seven hours).

There's a minibus terminal outside Urfa Kapısı, with services to Mardin, Malatya and Siverek (to get to Kahta without going right round the lake via Adıyaman). Other local buses leave from the Selahaddin-i Eyubi Çarşısı, the precinct across from the Dağ Kapısı; come here for dolmuşes to the otogar (US$0.25).

Train The *Güney Ekspresi* connects Diyarbakır with İstanbul, but it's neither speedy nor reliable. You're better off taking a bus.

MARDİN & MİDYAT
☎ 482

Few travellers come to the beautiful ancient town of **Mardin**, about 175km east of Urfa and 100km south of Diyarbakır, which is part of its appeal. A castle of some sort has stood on the hill above the town long before Assyrian Christians settled here during the 5th century.

In Mardin everything you'll need is along or just off Birinci Caddesi. The tourist office (☎ 212 7406, fax 212 5845) is at Cumhuriyet Alanı 515.

Check out the rambling **bazaar**, the secluded **Ulu Cami**, an 11th-century Iraqi Seljuk structure, the **post office**, housed in a carefully restored 17th-century caravanserai and the town's prime architectural attraction, the **Sultan İsa Medresesi** (1385).

The area's most interesting sight is the 7th-century **Deyrul Zafaran**, 6km east of Mardin. This monastery, once the seat of the Syrian Orthodox patriarchate, is now an orphanage. It's open daily between 8.30 and 11.30 am and 1.30 and 3.30 pm (the orphans will show you around for a small fee). There's no public transport; a return taxi ride from Mardin costs around US$9.

The sprawling settlement of **Midyat**, 65km east of Mardin, harbours some wonderfully carved stone houses. Dolmuşes from Mardin will drop you off at a crossroads, with the old town tucked away behind the shops in front of you.

About 18km east of Midyat, the 5th-century **Morgabriel** (Deyrul Umur) monastery rises like a mirage from its desert-like surroundings. To get here, either arrange a taxi (very scarce) in Midyat or take a Cizrebound bus from Madin and ask to be dropped off at the junction for Morgabriel.

Places to Stay & Eat

In Mardin the very sorry-looking *Hotel Bayraktar* (☎ 212 1338), on the main street facing Cumhuriyet Alanı, has singles/doubles for US$7/9. Rooms at the tiny *Otel Başak* (☎ 212 6246, Birinci Caddesi 360) have the advantage of being clean and fan-equipped and cost US$9 a head. The only other alternative is *Otel Bilen* (☎ 212 5568, fax 212 2575), 1.5km out of town near the highway, which has spacious rooms with TV and bathroom for US$20/33.

Midyat's sole option is *Otel Yuvam* (☎ 462 2531, Dörtyol Caddesi 1), with basic doubles with fan and shared bathroom for US$9. It's beside the roundabout in new Midyat where the Mardin dolmuşes first stop.

As for meals, in Mardin try *Pınay Kafeterya* upstairs in the shopping block immediately behind the Hotel Bayraktar, or the *Turistik Et Lokantası* on the other side of the hotel. At both you can sample *sembusek* (a folded pide sandwich) and *kaburga dolması* (lamb and rice with almonds). East along Birinci Caddesi are several *tea gardens*, the best of them with a fine view of the beautiful post office across the road.

Getting There & Away

Minibuses run every hour between Mardin's Belediye Garajı and the minibus terminal just outside Diyarbakır's Urfa Kapısı

(US$2.50, 1½ hours). Most other buses leave from just east of Cumhuriyet Meydanı, including services to Şanlıurfa (US$8.50, three hours). Minibuses to Midyat (US$2.50, one hour) and Nusaybin near the Syrian border (US$1.75) also leave from this area.

BİTLİS

The bleak pastoral landscape around Diyarbakır becomes more ruggedly dramatic as you head directly east towards Van Gölü (Lake Van). On the way, around 100km east of Diyarbakır, look out for the restored humpbacked **stone bridge**, Batman Suyu, originally built in 1146 and thought to have the longest span (37m) of any such bridge in existence.

Another 150km from the bridge brings you to the old town of Bitlis, squeezed into a narrow, high-walled valley and dominated by a evil-looking **castle**. This was the capital of a semi-autonomous Kurdish principality in late-Ottoman times. Its sights, which include the **Ulu Cami** (1126), the **Şerefiye Cami** and **Saraf Han**, a 16th-century caravanserai, can easily be visited in a day from Tatvan.

The **El-Aman Han** is a striking black stone caravanserai 13km out of town on the road to Tatvan; by this time though you're eyes will be feasting on the snow-capped mountain scenery surrounding Van Gölü.

The bus from Diyarbakır to Tatvan and Van passes through Bitlis and El-Aman Han.

TATVAN

☎ 434 • pop 54,000

The western port for Van Gölü steamers, Tatvan, 23km north-east of Bitlis, is not much to look at, but has a magnificent setting. Most people pass through quickly on their way to Van but it's well worth stopping to visit the pristine crater lakes of Turkey's other Nemrut Dağı (see The North Shore later in this section) to the north.

Hotels, restaurants, the PTT, Internet cafes, and the bus company offices huddle together in the town centre along Cumhuriyet Caddesi. The tourist office (☎ 827 6301, fax 827 6300) is around the corner from the Hotel Tatvan Kardelen.

The cheapest accommodation here is awful. Two of the better options are *Hotel Üstün* (☎ 827 9014, fax 827 9017, Hal Caddesi 23), which has cleanish rooms with

washbasin for US$7 per person, and *Akgün Otel* (☎ 827 2373, Hal Caddesi 51), which charges US$5/9 for waterless rooms, US$10/15 for rooms with bathroom.

On the main road *Hotel Altılar* (☎ 827 4096, fax 827 4098, Cumhuriyet Caddesi 164) has beds for US$10 per person (including breakfast) in presentable rooms. The *Tatvan Kardelen* (☎/fax 827 9500) is fairly comfortable, but you'd be mad to pay the posted prices of US$39/60.

King Hotel Restaurant & Campsite (☎ 462 5988, fax 827 7111), by the lakeside around 1km east of the centre, is worth considering. Bed and breakfast is US$10, a caravan for two with hot showers US$6 and the manager speaks English.

For a quick bite to eat try *Kösem*, *Şimşek Lokantası* and *Aşkin Pastanesi 2*, both on Cumhuriyet Caddesi.

Getting There & Away

At the time of writing the *Vangölü Ekspresi* train service from İstanbul to Tatvan was still not running east of Elazığ because of security worries. There's talk that passenger services will soon resume (possibly all the way to Tehrān). Should the situation change Tatvan's train station is about 2km northeast of the centre.

The Turkish Maritime Lines ferry from Tatvan to Van crosses the lake to a schedule known only to its captain, now that there is no need to fit in with any train timetable. Unless you've got endless time for hanging about, forget it and take the bus from Cumhuriyet Caddesi around the southern shore of the lake (US$3.50, two hours). Tatvan can be reached by bus from Diyarbakır.

VAN GÖLÜ

The largest lake in Turkey, Van Gölü was formed over 2 million years ago when lava from the Nemrut Dağı volcano north of Tatvan blocked its natural outflow. The water level is now maintained by evaporation, which results in a high mineral concentration and extreme alkalinity: Clothes washed in the lake come clean without soap. However, *darek*, members of the carp family, have adapted to life in the lake and there's even rumours of a Loch-Ness-type monster (*canavar*)!

Near Van itself the water is polluted, but the beaches at Gevaş and Edremit are good

TURKEY

for a swim. Don't go in if you have sunburn or open cuts or sores as the alkaline water will burn them intensely.

The South Shore & Akdamar

Travelling south around the lake from Tatvan to Van, the scenery is awe inspiring, but there's little reason to stop except to visit the 10th-century **Akdamar Kilisesi** (Church of the Holy Cross). This marvel of Armenian architecture is perched on Akdamar Island 3km out in the lake, and motorboats ferry sightseers back and forth. There's an entry fee for the island (US$2) but this is usually included in the ferry fare (see Getting There & Away).

Little remains of the palace and monastery that were once also on the island, but the church walls are in superb condition and the biblical-themed relief carvings are among the masterworks of Armenian art. Climb the rocky hill behind the church for a fantastic view.

Camping is free at *Akdamar Camping ve Restaurant* (☎ 432-622 2525) immediately opposite the ferry departure point for Akdamar island. The restaurant has a terrace with lake views and an indoor saloon in case of bad weather. For around US$3.50 you can get a good meal of fish kebaps, salad and drinks.

Getting There & Away It's around 85km from Tatvan to Akdamar; any bus headed to Van will drop you by ferry landing, and it's a simple matter of flagging one down when you want to return. It's more common, though, to visit Akdamar as a day trip from Van (see Van later in this chapter). Dolmuşes run the 44km from Van to Akdamar (usually going via Gevaş) for US$1.25. If the dolmuş stops in Gevaş either walk the last 8km or hire a taxi (around US$3).

Boats to the island run as and when traffic warrants it; except at the height of the season your best bet is to come on Saturday or Sunday when Vanlıs head to Akdamar to picnic. Provided others are there to share the cost, a return ticket for the 20-minute voyage and admission to the island costs US$5.

The North Shore

If anything, the journey around the lake's north shore from Tatvan to Van is more beautiful than the trip around the south shore. The road is rough in parts, and security checks become more frequent once you pass Erciş.

The **Nemrut Dağı** rising to the north of Tatvan should not be confused with the more famous one near Kahta with the giant heads on top. This Nemrut Dağı (3050m) is an inactive volcano with five crater lakes on its summit. A trip here is an unforgettable experience, not least for the fine views back over Van Gölü.

Weekends, when locals come to picnic, are the best bet for catching a dolmuş from Tatvan up the mountain. Otherwise a taxi from Tatvan will cost US$35 return including waiting time. The taxi driver will be able to point out a natural hot water bath; an ice cave *(buz mağarası)* in which a bottle of water will freeze in half an hour; the curious 'chimneys' of steam, said to be good for rheumatism *(buhar bacası)*; and the various different lakes.

With your own transport, leave Tatvan by the road around the lake, turn left towards Bitlis and then immediately right following a sign saying 'Nemrut 13km'. The road is rough but should be passable in an ordinary car except in wet weather. Bear in mind there are no facilities of any kind on the mountain.

Continue along the lakeshore for 42km and you'll come to the small town of **Ahlat**, famous for its Seljuk Turkish tombs and graveyard. The fortress on the shore was built during the reign of Süleyman the Magnificent. About 25km east of Ahlat is **Adilcevaz**, once an Urartian town but now dominated by a great Seljuk Turkish fortress, the **Kef Kalesi**, and the even greater bulk of **Süphan Dağı** (4434m).

If you continue around the lake for another 64km, you'll pass through Erciş, a forgettable modern town. Here the road splits – head south for Van (98km) or north for Doğubayazıt (137km).

Getting There & Away The major bus companies take the shorter southern route from Tatvan to Van. If you want to travel around the north shore, you'll have to break your journey into sections. Regular dolmuşes run from opposite the PTT in Tatvan to Ahlat (US$1.25, 45 minutes). From Ahlat to Adilcevaz takes just half an hour and costs US$0.75. From Adilcevaz to Erciş takes one hour and costs US$1.75. Buses run between Erciş and Van, taking

1¼ hours and charging US$2.75. Most travel in the morning.

VAN
☎ 432

The first thing you'll notice on arriving in Van, almost 100km from Tatvan directly across Van Gölü, is the bizarre giant statue of a white cat and kitten each with weird coloured eyes. These Bond-villain moggies, unique to the area, fetch so high a price that their owners keep them under lock and key.

Sprawling modern Van was completely rebuilt 4km inland from the lake following WWI. The area's history of settlement, however, dates back to the kingdom of Urartu, which flourished from the 13th to the 7th centuries BC. Evidence of Urartian culture can be found at Van's principal attraction, the amazing Van Kalesi (Van Castle or the Rock of Van) lording it over the lake and the bitterly poignant remains of old Van, a thriving city of Armenians until the massacres of 1915 (see Population & People in the Facts about the Region chapter).

Van is handy as a base for day trips to Akdamar and to the ancient Urartian city at Çavuştepe and the craggy mountain fortress of Hoşap.

Orientation & Information

Van's main commercial street is Cumhuriyet Caddesi, where you'll find banks with ATMs, hotels and restaurants. At the northern end, where Cumhuriyet Caddesi meets four other streets, is Ferit Melen

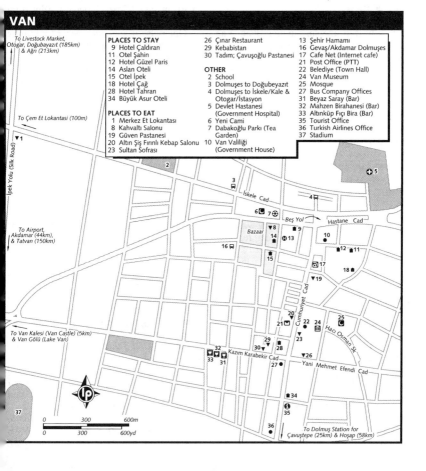

VAN

PLACES TO STAY
9 Hotel Çaldıran
11 Otel Şahin
12 Hotel Güzel Paris
14 Aslan Oteli
15 Otel İpek
18 Hotel Çağ
28 Hotel Tahran
34 Büyük Asur Oteli

PLACES TO EAT
1 Merkez Et Lokantası
8 Kahvaltı Salonu
19 Güven Pastanesi
20 Altın Şiş Fırınlı Kebap Salonu
23 Sultan Sofrası
26 Çınar Restaurant
29 Kebabistan
30 Tadım; Çavuşoğlu Pastanesi

OTHER
2 School
3 Dolmuşes to Doğubayazıt
4 Dolmuşes to İskele/Kale & Otogar/İstasyon
5 Devlet Hastanesi (Government Hospital)
6 Yeni Cami
7 Dabakoğlu Parkı (Tea Garden)
10 Van Valiliği (Government House)
13 Şehir Hamamı
16 Gevaş/Akdamar Dolmuşes
17 Cafe Net (Internet cafe)
21 Post Office (PTT)
22 Belediye (Town Hall)
24 Van Museum
25 Mosque
27 Bus Company Offices
31 Beyaz Saray (Bar)
32 Mahzen Birahanesi (Bar)
33 Altınküp Fıçı Bira (Bar)
35 Tourist Office
36 Turkish Airlines Office
37 Stadium

To Livestock Market, Otogar, Doğubayazıt (185km) & Ağrı (213km)

To Çem Et Lokantasi (100m)

İpek Yolu (Silk Road)

To Airport, Akdamar (44km), & Tatvan (150km)

To Van Kalesi (Van Castle) (5km) & Van Gölü (Lake Van)

İskele Cad

Beş Yol

Hastane Cad

Bazaar

Cumhuriyet Cad

Hacı Osman Sk

Kazım Karabekir Cad

Yani Mehmet Efendi Cad

To Dolmuş Station for Çavuştepe (25km) & Hoşap (58km)

0   300   600m
0   300   600yd

Meydanı, otherwise known as Beş Yol (Five Roads). Here you'll find several dolmuş and bus stops.

The otogar is north-west of the centre, just off (İpek Yolu), part of the old Silk Road; servis buses run from here to Cumhuriyet Caddesi. The train station, from where passenger services once ran into Iran, is near the otogar. The airport is 6km south of the centre.

The tourist office (☎ 216 2018, fax 216 3675) is at Cumhuriyet Caddesi 127; no-one speaks English but they can rustle up a street plan. There are several Internet cafes in and around Kazım Karabekir Caddesi; a reliable one is Cafe Net upstairs at Cumhuriyet Caddesi Örnek İşhanı 71/1.

Van Kalesi

Sited atop a slender finger of land rising dramatically from the surrounding plain, Van Kalesi (Van Castle or Rock of Van) is a must-see for which you should allow plenty of time to explore. If you come here for sunset, do so in a group for safety. Also be prepared for some hassles from local kids.

Approaching from the city centre, on the northern side of the rock, is the **tomb** of Abdurrahman Gazi, a Muslim holy man, visited by pilgrims. Rough steps beyond the ticket office and car park at the north-western corner lead to the top of the rock, where you can explore the fortifications, including the **Sardur Burcu** or Sardur Tower (840–830 BC) with several cuneiform inscriptions in Assyrian.

On the southern side, a narrow walkway with an iron railing leads to several rock-cut **funeral chambers**, including that of King Argishti I (786–764 BC), and a lengthy **cuneiform inscription** that recounts the high points of his reign. If there's a guide around, ask to be shown the tunnel through the rock that leads down to the scant remains of **old Van**, south of the rock.

Old Van is so ruined that it's easier to believe you're looking at the remains of 3000-year old Tushpa, the Urartian capital that once stood on this spot, than at a city destroyed in 1915. Of the Seljuk **Ulu Cami** only a broken brick minaret remains, but the **Hüsrev Paşa Külliyesi** (1567), has been restored and you may be able to get inside to see the fine brick dome and fragmentary murals.

To get here take a 'Kale' dolmuş from Beş Yol (US$0.15). These are frequent at weekends but if there are no direct dolmuşes, take an 'İskele' dolmuş and get out at the road junction leading to Van Kalesi. Even the direct Kale dolmuşes drop you 500m short of the ticket office. Van Kalesi is open daily from 9 am to 6 pm. Admission costs US$1.75.

Other Attractions

In the town centre, the only other very minor attraction is the **Van Museum** which has a small display of Urartian artefacts and an insulting exhibit on the WWI massacres, implying Turks suffered more than the Armenians who were practically wiped out. It's open from 8 am to noon and 1.30 to 5.30 pm daily (closed Monday). Admission costs US$1.75.

Otherwise it's an eye-opener to drop by the livestock market which takes place from early in the morning every day except Sunday just north of the otogar.

Places to Stay

Van has a good range of accommodation. The cheapies are in the bazaar area where, despite the lingering smell of fish, you'll find clean rooms at *Otel İpek* (☎ 216 3033, Cumhuriyet Caddesi 1, Sokak 3) for US$5 person including bathroom, and at the more basic *Aslan Oteli* (☎ 216 2469) for US$4.50 a head (even cheaper without bath). The Şehir Hamamı is near these two hotels.

Hotel Çaldıran (☎ 216 2718, Sıhke Caddesi, Sokak 176), a short walk west of Beş Yol, is handy and charges US$7/10 for basic singles/doubles. *Hotel Tahran* (☎ 216 2541, PTT Caddesi, Türkoğlu Sokak 44) has freshly painted rooms with small bathrooms for the same price.

On İrfanbaştuğ Caddesi beside the Van Valiliği (government building), *Hotel Güzel Paris* offers big, comfortable rooms with shower and TV for US$15/23 including breakfast. *Otel Şahin* (☎ 216 3062) is similar and a bit cheaper at US$10/19.

Hotel Çağ (☎/fax 214 5713, Hastane 2 Caddesi) is in a quiet location east of Cumhuriyet Caddesi and has pleasant enough rooms for US$10/15.

It's worth paying a bit more at the *Büyük Asur Oteli* (☎ 216 8792, fax 216 9461, Cumhuriyet Caddesi, Turizm Sokak 5), which has spacious, well-furnished rooms for US$18/25. There's a comfortable lobby and restaurant, and the English-speaking manager, Remzi Boybay, who is a great source of local information and can organise tours to local attractions.

Places to Eat

Kahvaltı Salonu opposite the Hz Omer Cami offers two choices of cheese with honey for breakfast as well as other staple dishes like *sucuk ve yumurta* (garlic sausage fried up with eggs).

Sultan Sofrası on Cumhuriyet Caddesi facing the post office is deservedly popular. Open 24 hours a day it serves soups, stews and delicious spit-roasted chicken. Another good choice, farther towards Beş Yol, is *Altin Şiş Fırınlı Kebap Salonu*.

Çınar Restaurant (Yani Mehmet Efendi Caddesi), attached to Hotel Bayram, offers reliable kebap meals for around US$2 in a pleasant dining room.

On Kazım Karabekir Caddesi, *Tadım* offers a routine choice of kebaps and stews; turn down the lane beside it for *Kebabistan* which serves pide and has some outdoor tables. The rest of the lane is filled with teahouses and on a summer's evening you can hardly move for men sipping tea and clicking backgammon pieces.

Take a dolmuş west along İskele Caddesi for about 1km to the *Çem Et Lokantası*, which offers a big buffet of cold mezes for a set US$3, no matter how high you pile your plate. Watch the final bill for fiddling, though. At the junction with İpek Yolu, *Merkez Et Lokantası* is a popular family place specialising in grilled meats.

Van has a good selection of *pastanes* for cakes and sweet snacks at US$1 per portion. Try *Çavuşoğlu Pastanesi*, near Tadım, or *Güven Pastanesi*, just north of the Vakıfbank on Cumhuriyet Caddesi, which has floor cushions at the back and tables in the sun at the front.

Entertainment

There's precious little nightlife in Van. For a beer, try *Altınküp Fıçı Bira (Kazım Karabekir Caddesi 53)* or the nearby *Mahzen Birahanesi*, downstairs at the rear of Kazım Karabekir Caddesi 37. Both are exclusively male hang-outs. The *Beyaz Saray* upstairs at Kazım Karabekır Caddesi,

Akdamar Oteli Karşışı, is a gazino serving food and drink, with a floorshow that encompasses singers and a belly dancer. Prices can mount up quickly – especially if you tip the belly dancer the seemingly standard US$6.

Getting There & Away

Air Turkish Airlines (☎ 215 5354, fax 215 5353), Cumhuriyet Caddesi 196, has two daily nonstop flights to/from Ankara, and another to/from İstanbul. A taxi from the airport will cost about US$5.

Bus Many bus companies have ticket offices at the intersection of Cumhuriyet and Kazım Karabekir Caddesis. They provide servis minibuses to and from the otogar, from where there are regular services to Ankara (US$25, 22 hours), Diyarbakır (US$12, seven hours), Erzurum (US$10, six hours), Hakkari (US$4.50, four hours), Malatya (US$12, 10 hours), Şanlıurfa (US$12, nine hours) and Tatvan (US$5, two hours, 150km).

For Doğubayazıt, it's best to catch a dolmuş from the terminal a couple of blocks west along İskele Caddesi from Beş Yol (US$5, 2½ hours). For details of getting to the Turkey-Iran border at Esendere see the 'Van to Orūmīyé' boxed text later in this chapter.

Ferry With no connecting passenger train service to keep it to schedule, the ferry across Van Gölü from Tatvan to Van leaves only when there's enough freight to justify it. 'İskele' dolmuşes ply up and down the main road to the harbour (US$0.25) but unless you're a glutton for punishment, stick with the buses.

AROUND VAN

A day excursion south-east of Van along the road to Hakkari takes you to **Çavuştepe**, 25km from Van. The narrow hill on the left side of the highway was once crowned with the fortress-palace **Sarduri-Hinili**, home of the kings of Urartu, built between 764 and 735 BC. Climb the hill to the car park where there's a guardian to collect the US$1.75 entrance fee and perhaps show you around.

Another 33km farther along, the Kurdish fortress **Hoşap Kalesi** (1643) perches photogenically on top of a rocky outcrop beside the village of Güzelsu. Cross the bridge into

Van to Orūmīyé

The Best Van bus company runs services from Van in Turkey to Orūmīyé in Iran via the border at Esendere (US$8.50). Buses leave around 10am and take about 10 hours to reach Orūmīyé, less if passengers are processed quickly through the border.

If you're travelling here in your own transport, aim to cross as early in the day as possible. Expect frequent security stops on the 300km route from Van.

On both the Turkish and Iranian (Serō) sides of the border there is nowhere to stay, eat or officially to change money.

The road to Orūmīyé, 50km west on the shore of Lake Orūmīyé (Daryāché-é Orūmīyé), passes through stark, gorgeous scenery. In Orūmīyé you'll be able to change money at Bank Melli on Enghelāb or on the street with black marketeers. There are several good hotels and onward bus transport to Tabrīz, Takab, or Tehrān, to join up with our main overland route, is easy to arrange.

the village and follow the signs around the far side of the hill to reach the castle entrance (US$1.75).

To get to Çavuştepe and Hoşap, catch a dolmuş heading to Başkale (US$5) from the dolmuş station 250m south of the tourist office, and say you want to get out at Hoşap. After seeing the castle, catch a bus back to Çavuştepe, 500m off the highway, and then catch a third bus back to Van. Pack lunch and water, and plan to be gone for most of the day as buses are scarce.

DOĞUBAYAZIT

☎ 472 • pop 36,000

The road to Doğubayazıt, 185km northeast of Van, takes you through more eye-catching scenery, particularly the vast frozen lava flow from Temdürek Dağı. Arriving in this dusty, scrappy frontier town crawling with soldiers is an anticlimax, but Doğubayazıt does have a couple of things going for it – snow-capped Mt Ararat (Ağrı Dağı, 5137m) and the beautiful fortress-palace-mosque complex İshak Paşa Sarayı.

The border at Gürbulak is only 35km from Doğubayazıt, making the town the main kicking-off point for the overland trail through Iran. If you don't have a visa the nearest place to arrange one is Erzurum, 285km west (see İstanbul to Iran via Ankara & Erzurum later in this chapter).

Orientation & Information

Dolmuşes from Van will drop you on Ağrı Caddesi at the junction with Belediye Caddesi, which just about qualifies as the town's main street. Here you'll find most hotels and restaurants. The otogar is on the continuation of Belediye Caddesi as it heads towards the hills and the İshak Paşa Sarayı.

There's no official tourist office. Try Doğuandolu Tourism Travel Agency (☎/fax 312 3620, e salihbasboga@hotmail .com) near the intersection of Ağrı and Belediye Caddesis for information; it can also arrange tours of the area and climbing permits for Mt Ararat.

The banks are not enthusiastic about changing money, whether cash or travellers cheques, but most have ATMs and it's easy to change money on the street, including getting Iranian rials at a decent rate.

The Sentim Internet Cafe is upstairs on Belediye Caddesi opposite Hotel Erzurum. Özgüneş Bilgisayar Internet Cafe, upstairs on the alley behind, has a nonsmoking section and fast machines.

İshak Paşa Sarayı

Perched spectacularly amid jagged hills 6km east of town, the picturesque İshak Paşa Sarayı is one of the most impressive buildings you'll come across on this overland route. This 366-room palace/fortress was completed in 1784 by a Kurdish chieftain named İshak (Isaac).

A mishmash of architectural styles, the palace had its gold-plated front doors nicked by the Russians in WWI (they're now in St Petersburg's Hermitage Museum). The largely restored ruins, however, pack as powerful a punch as the sweeping views from the roof and many windows.

Across the valley from the palace are an Ottoman **mosque**, the 18th-century **tomb** of a popular Kurdish writer, and the ruins of a **fortress**, possibly dating from Urartian times. The faint ruined foundations of **Eski Beyazıt**, a city dating from Urartian times (circa 800 BC), rise from the dusty plain below.

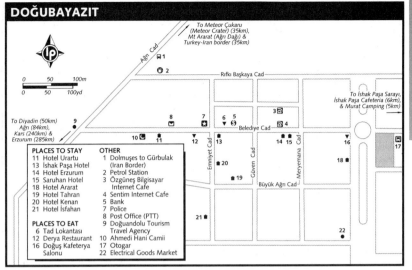

DOĞUBAYAZIT

To Meteor Çukaru
(Meteor Crater) (35km),
Mt Ararat (Ağrı Dağı) &
Turkey-Iran border (35km)

Ağrı Cad

Rıfkı Başkaya Cad

To İshak Paşa Sarayı,
İshak Paşa Cafeteria (6km),
& Murat Camping (5km)

To Diyadin (50km),
Ağrı (84km),
Kars (240km) &
Erzurum (285km)

Belediye Cad

Emniyet Cad

Güven Cad

Büyük Ağrı Cad-

Meryemana Cad

PLACES TO STAY	OTHER
11 Hotel Urartu	1 Dolmuşes to Gürbulak
13 İshak Paşa Hotel	(Iran Border)
14 Hotel Erzurum	2 Petrol Station
15 Saruhan Hotel	3 Özgüneş Bilgisayar
18 Hotel Ararat	Internet Cafe
19 Hotel Tahran	4 Sentim Internet Cafe
20 Hotel Kenan	5 Bank
21 Hotel İsfahan	6 Belediye Cad
	7 Police
PLACES TO EAT	8 Post Office (PTT)
6 Tad Lokantası	9 Doğuandolu Tourism
12 Derya Restaurant	Travel Agency
16 Doğuş Kafeterya	10 Ahmedi Hani Camii
Salonu	17 Otogar
	22 Electrical Goods Market

At weekends dolmuşes often run from the town up here; otherwise a taxi driver will want about US$5 for a return trip, waiting time included. Walking is pleasant (particularly going down), although women might feel rather isolated. Admission to the site costs US$4 and it's open from 8 am to 5.30 pm (closing slightly earlier in winter). Sunset is a particularly beautiful time to visit.

Other Attractions

After İshak Paşa Sarayı all other attractions around Doğubayazıt feel like also-rans, even the twin-peaked **Mt Ararat** (Ağrı Dağı), which much of the time is shrouded in clouds anyway. It is once again possible to climb Mt Ararat; you'll need permits (see Orientation & Information) and guides and must plan on spending at least five days for the ascent and descent. It's possible to drive around 3000m up the left-hand peak, Büyük Ağrı (Great Ararat). The best time to view the mountain is an hour or two after sunrise, before the clouds obscure it.

Local travel agents can arrange tours of İshak Paşa Sarayı, Mt Ararat and other sights, including the current candidate for the resting place of Noah's Ark, Musa Dağı, 8km east of Doğubayazıt; **Meteor Çukuru** (Meteor Crater), a giant crater caused by a meteor crash in 1920; and the unhygienic looking **Diyadin Hot Springs**. The tours cost around US$25. Save your money and just visit the palace.

Places to Stay & Eat

Murat Camping (☎ 312 3434, mobile 0542-527 5481), in a prime position just beneath İshak Paşa Sarayı, has spartan rooms for US$5 or you can pitch a tent for US$1. The genial owner is currently building better cabins on the site and plans to include a kitchen and shower block. They'll come and pick you up from the town centre if you give them a call. All the overland tour groups stay here, so it's *the* place for the latest on what's happening down the line. What's more, the food in the restaurant/bar is excellent and the place really rocks in the evening, as locals join overlanders sinking their last/first drink before/after Iran.

The atmosphere at the *İshak Paşa Cafeteria* overlooking the palace just isn't the same, but you can get a beer here and roll out your sleeping bag in the dining room for US$1.

Doğubayazıt itself has plenty of cheap, no-frills hotels, but women travelling alone may not feel comfortable in all of them. We can recommend the following, however. *Hotel Erzurum* (☎ 312 5080, Belediye Caddesi) is basic but fine for US$3.50 a head. *Saruhan Hotel* (☎ 311 3097), next

Doğubayazıt to İstanbul

Cycling days: 18
Approx distance: 1800km

From Doğubayazıt to Ağrı (100km), incredibly strong winds meant travelling at only 11km/h. Cyclists travelling east to west must be prepared for the winds to affect speed. I was filmed cycling for a Turkish TV program with my riding partners in crime, Ken and Gerald, who were travelling in an Indian autorickshaw! There's one pass to cross on the Ağrı to Horasan leg (105km), but it's not too strenuous. Accommodation in Horasan is not great – I discovered a mouse eating my next day's lunch at 3 am! From Horasan to Erzurum ('100km) can be done in one day.

The trip from Erzurum to Tercan (100km) becomes very green and beautiful after Aşkale (about 40km from Erzurum). Tercan is a good place to break the journey. Tercan to Erzincan is 95km, then it's a short day from Erzincan to Refahiye (75km) with one pass to climb. Here I was invited to stay at the local hospital, and had dinner with the resident doctors, nurses and dentist! From Refahiye to İmranlı (75km) involves two big passes but it's a great ride in fine weather.

İmranlı to Gemerek (240km) can be done in two days with a break at Sivas. From Gemerek to Ürgüp (155km) was a difficult day of cycling; the final 50km is up and down steep, short hills as you approach Cappadocia, so it would be the same whichever direction you're travelling. It's only another 8km from Ürgüp to Göreme.

They say the hills in Turkey are biggest in the east but it's not necessarily true! From Göreme to Edirne is a hilly 950km stretch (I cycled it in eight days) – but still good cycling.

Göreme to Ankara (285km) took three days via Kırşehir and Kırıkkale. There were no problems cycling into and out of Ankara. It took two more days to cycle the 265km to Sakarya (Adapazarı) via Gerede. Sakarya had been hit by the earthquake 10 months earlier, but I could still see the aftermath of the destruction. The area was very dusty, with a lot of roadworks and construction going on. The people seemed depressed but I experienced great hospitality. The final leg was 110km from Sakarya to İstanbul. Traffic builds up as you approach the city, but even the Turkish drivers are better than the Indians!

Continuing on from İstanbul towards Europe (two days), it was 130km to Lüleburgaz then 70km to Edirne, a pleasant town only 15km from the Bulgarian border.

Sue Cooper

door, is pretty much the same, although some rooms have decent views.

Hotel Tahran (☎ *311 2223, Büyük Ağrı Caddesi 124*), has clean singles/doubles with shower for US$5/9 and is popular with devout Muslims.

Hotel Ararat (☎ *312 4988, fax 312 4982, Belediye Caddesi*), across from the otogar, is in reasonable nick but not so grand as it first looks. Rooms are US$12/20 with bathroom and breakfast.

İshak Paşa Hotel (☎ *312 7036, fax 312 7644, Büyük Ağrı Caddesi*) offers reasonable comfort for US$9/14. The *Hotel Kenan* (☎ *312 7869, fax 312 7571, Emniyet Caddesi 39*) is similar, but slightly cheaper, and has a licensed *restaurant*.

The *Hotel Urartu* (☎ *312 7295, 311 2450, Belediye Caddesi*) looks pricier than it actually is. Pleasant modern rooms with room and TV cost US$14/25 including breakfast. The *Hotel İsfahan* (☎/*fax 312 5289, İsa Geçit Caddesi 26*), with a bar and restaurant, is also worth considering if you can get them to lower their rates to US$15/25.

Along Belediye Caddesi are several pastry shops and three decent places to eat, which are packed out with soldiers on weekends: *Tad Lokantası*, which does döner sandwiches for US$1.50, *Doğuş Kafeterya Salonu* near the otogar, which does a fine pide as well as more substantial meals and the *Derya Restaurant* near the post office, for meat dishes and pide.

Getting There & Away

Buses from Doğubayazıt are relatively limited and mostly go via Erzurum or Iğdır. There are services to Ankara (US$24, 16 hours), Erzurum (US$5, four hours), Iğdır (US$2, 45 minutes) and Van (US$5, 2½ hours).

İstanbul to Iran via Ankara & Erzurum

For those overlanders in a hurry to get to Iran, the most direct route, followed by buses from İstanbul to Tehrān, heads east through Ankara, Sivas and Erzurum to the border near Doğubayazıt. If you've failed to get an Iranian visa in İstanbul, then the Iranian embassy at Ankara and the Iranian consulate at Erzurum offer a couple more chances. The modern capital of Turkey might not have the history and spectacle of İstanbul, but there are a couple of sights that make it worth any traveller's while.

ANKARA

☎ 312 • pop 4 million

Sprawling over grassy hills in central Anatolia, Ankara, 450km south-east of İstanbul, is overwhelmingly modern, planned in the fashion of Brasilia (Brazil) and Canberra (Australia). Government ministries, embassies, universities and light industry predominate here, not tourist attractions. Ankara's cheap hotels are very poor value in comparison to other places, which doesn't encourage you to linger either.

The capital's connections with the past are well summed up by the Museum of Anatolian Civilisations, which appropriately is beside the citadel or Hisar of old Angora, the original settlement that dates back to the Hittites nearly 4000 years ago.

Modern Ankara was only established in 1923, after Atatürk's victory in the War of Independence. Atatürk exhibited his absolute faith in the new capital by not setting foot in İstanbul between 1919 and 1927. His reward was the monumental mausoleum Anıtkabir, Ankara's other top sight.

And, of course, with all those diplomats and politicians to entertain, Ankara can roll out some pretty classy restaurants and bars – though few fall into the budget category.

Orientation

The city has two distinct parts. Ankara's *hisar* (fortress) crowns a hill 1km east of Ulus Meydanı (Ulus Square), centre of 'old Ankara', and near most of the cheap hotels. 'New Ankara' (Yenişehir) is 3.5km to the south, centred on Kızılay Meydanı (Kızılay Square).

Atatürk Bulvarı is the city's main north-south axis. Ankara's mammoth otogar is 6.5km south-west of Ulus Meydanı and 6km west of Kızılay Meydanı.

Information

Tourist Office The tourist office (☎ 231 5572) is at Gazi Mustafa Kemal Bulvarı 121, opposite the Maltepe underground station. It is helpful and in addition has a good selection of souvenir arts and crafts from around Turkey.

Embassies & Consulates The diplomatic area is Çankaya, 5km south of Kızılay, and the adjoining districts of Gaziosmanpaşa and Kavaklıdere. Opening hours for visa applications are generally from 9 to 11 am. See the Regional Facts for the Visitor chapter for visa information.

Australia (☎ 446 1180, fax 446 1188)
  Nenehatun Caddesi 83, Gaziosmanpaşa
Canada (☎ 436 1275, fax 446 4437) Nenehatun
  Caddesi 75, Gaziosmanpaşa
France (☎ 468 1154, fax 467 9434) Paris
  Caddesi 70, Kavaklıdere
Germany (☎ 426 5451, fax 426 6959) Atatürk
  Bulvarı 114, Kavaklıdere
India (☎ 438 2195) Cinnah Caddesi 77A,
  Çankaya
Iran (☎ 427 4320) Tahran Caddesi 10,
  Kavaklıdere
Japan (☎ 446 0500) Reşit Galip Caddesi 81,
  Gaziosmanpaşa
New Zealand (☎ 467 9054, fax 467 9013) İran
  Caddesi 13, 4th Floor, Kavaklıdere
Pakistan (☎ 427 1410) Iran Caddesi 37,
  Gaziosmanpaşa
Syria (☎ 438 8704) Sedat Semavi Sokak 40,
  Çankaya
UK (☎ 468 6230, fax 468 3214) Şehit Ersan
  Caddesi 46/A, Çankaya
USA (☎ 468 6110, fax 467 0019) Atatürk
  Bulvarı 110, Kavaklıdere

Money Most of the major banks are concentrated in the districts of Kavaklıdere and Kızılay.

Post & Communications The main post office is on Atatürk Bulvarı just south of Ulus Meydanı, although there's a handy branch beside Ankara Garı (the train station), where you can also change cash and travellers cheques.

Many Internet cafes can be found in Yenişehir, particularly Kızılay, around Karafil and Olgunlar Sokaks. The one in the Atatürk Evi bookstore at Gazi Mustafa Kemal Bulvarı 133, near the tourist office, is useful if you're staying in Ulus.

Bookshops For a wide choice of foreign-language books try D&R Konur (☎ 419 7946), Konur Sokak 8/A–B, Kızılay, which has a pleasant cafe and the Esra Internet Cafe upstairs. Döst Bookstore in the pedestrianised street behind the post office in Kızılay also has a great English-language selection including newspapers and periodicals.

Medical Services The city's most up-to-date medical facility is the private Bayındır Hospital (☎ 428 0808), Atatürk Bulvarı 201, Kavaklıdere. The City Hospital (☎ 466 3346), Büklüm Sokak 53, near Tunalı Hilmi Caddesi, is also good.

Museum of Anatolian Civilisations

The Museum of Anatolian Civilisations (Anadolu Medeniyetleri Müzesi) on Hisarparkı Caddesi is Ankara's most worth-while attraction. With the richest collection of Hittite artefacts in the world, it's an essential supplement to visiting central Turkey's Hittite sites. It's uphill from Ulus Meydanı, next to the citadel (hisar).

The Neolithic (7000–5500 BC) section has a reconstructed room from Çatal Höyük, believed to be the oldest known human community. The Old Hittite section (1700–1450 BC) has lots of finds from Boğazköy and Alaca Höyük, including several bronze statues. Equally interesting is the Phyrgian section (1200–700 BC) with items from the tomb of a Phrygian king found at Gordion. It's open from 8.30 am to 5 pm, 'closed' on Monday in winter unless you pay twice the $3 entry fee.

Hisar (Citadel)

After the museum, go to the top of the hill and wander among the evocative old streets of the Hisar, entered by the Parmak Kapısı (Finger Gate). Several of the Ottoman houses have been restored as restaurants. Also look for the **Til Tur Kultur House**, a private residence that's a kind of museum. Climb up to the **eastern tower** (Şark Kulesi) for the view. Just below the Hisar is the traditional **bazaar** area.

Anıtkabir

The national shrine Anıtkabir (Mausoleum of Atatürk), 2km west of Kızılay Meydanı, is a striking memorial to the founder of modern Turkey. The best way to approach it is from Anıt Caddesi from Tandoğan Meydanı. You will have to leave bags with the guards at the main gate, but cameras are allowed. There are guards and security everywhere – do not even attempt to sit on the steps or grass; standing upright as a mark of respect is what's required here.

A colonnade leads to the huge courtyard, at the southern end of which is the **Sarcophagus of İsmet İnönü** (1884–1973), war hero and second president of the republic. On the east side of the courtyard is a **museum** that holds a fascinating collection of Atatürk memorabilia, while on the west is a **souvenir shop** celebrating the first president's personality cult with a wide variety of merchandise. Before entering the neoclassical mausoleum itself you must remove your hat. The changing of the guard is a good photo opportunity.

The mausoleum of Atatürk, Turkey's national hero, is one of Ankara's key attractions.

TURKEY

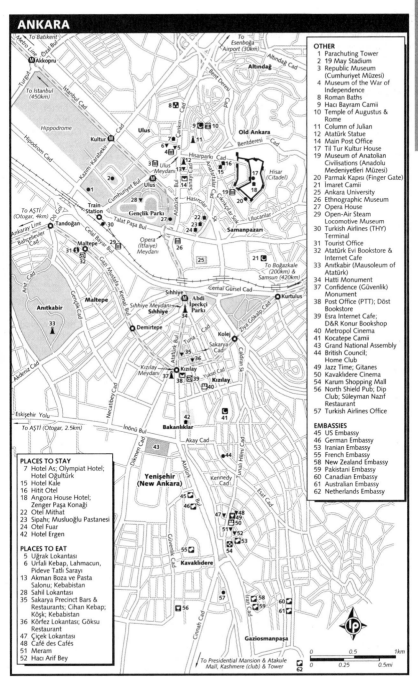

ANKARA

OTHER
1 Parachuting Tower
2 19 May Stadium
3 Republic Museum (Cumhuriyet Müzesi)
4 Museum of the War of Independence
8 Roman Baths
9 Hacı Bayram Camii
10 Temple of Augustus & Rome
11 Column of Julian
12 Atatürk Statue
14 Main Post Office
17 Til Tur Kultur House
19 Museum of Anatolian Civilisations (Anadolu Medeniyetleri Müzesi)
20 Parmak Kapısı (Finger Gate)
21 İmaret Camii
25 Ankara University
26 Ethnographic Museum
27 Opera House
29 Open-Air Steam Locomotive Museum
30 Turkish Airlines (THY) Terminal
31 Tourist Office
32 Atatürk Evi Bookstore & Internet Cafe
33 Anıtkabir (Mausoleum of Atatürk)
34 Hatti Monument
37 Confidence (Güvenlik) Monument
38 Post Office (PTT); Döst Bookstore
39 Esra Internet Cafe; D&R Konur Bookshop
40 Metropol Cinema
41 Kocatepe Camii
43 Grand National Assembly
44 British Council; Home Club
49 Jazz Time; Gitanes
50 Kavaklıdere Cinema
54 Karum Shopping Mall
56 North Shield Pub; Dip Club; Süleyman Nazıf Restaurant
57 Turkish Airlines Office

EMBASSIES
45 US Embassy
46 German Embassy
53 Iranian Embassy
55 French Embassy
58 New Zealand Embassy
59 Pakistani Embassy
60 Canadian Embassy
61 Australian Embassy
62 Netherlands Embassy

PLACES TO STAY
7 Hotel As; Olympiat Hotel; Hotel Oğultürk
15 Hotel Kale
16 Hitit Otel
18 Angora House Hotel; Zenger Paşa Konaği
22 Otel Mithat
23 Sipahı; Musluoğlu Pastanesi
24 Otel Fuar
42 Hotel Ergen

PLACES TO EAT
5 Uğrak Lokantası
6 Urfali Kebap, Lahmacun, Pideve Tatlı Sarayı
13 Akman Boza ve Pasta Salonu; Kebabistan
28 Sahil Lokantası
35 Sakarya Precinct Bars & Restaurants; Cihan Kebap; Köşk; Kebabistan
36 Körfez Lokantası; Göksu Restaurant
47 Çiçek Lokantası
48 Café des Cafés
51 Meram
52 Hacı Arif Bey

Opening hours are from 9 am to 5 pm (4 pm in winter) daily, although the museum closes from noon to 1.30 pm; admission is free. The nearest station on the Ankaray line is Tandoğan, which is 1500m north.

Other Attractions

Both the **Ethnographic Museum**, at the junction of Atatürk Bulvarı and Talat Paşa Bulvarı, and the **Museum of the War of Independence** (Kürtülüş Savaş Müzesi), in the first Grand National Assembly building, were closed for renovation at the time of research.

The **Republic Museum** (Cumhuriyet Müzesi), on Cumhuriyet Bulvarı, was the second headquarters of the Grand National Assembly and its history appears in photographs and documents; the captions are in Turkish. It's open from 8.30 am to noon and from 1 to 5 pm (closed Monday); admission costs US$1. North of Ulus Meydanı, on the east side of Çankırı Caddesi (the continuation of Atatürk Bulvarı north of Ulus Meydanı), are some Roman ruins, including the **Column of Julian** (Jülyanüs Sütunu), erected in 363 AD, and the **Temple of Augustus & Rome**. Right next to the temple is the **Hacı Bayram Camii**, a sacred mosque commemorating the founder of a dervish order established in 1400. On the west side of Çankırı Caddesi are some **Roman Baths** (Roma Hamamları).

At the far southern end of Atatürk Bulvarı in Çankaya is the **Presidential Mansion**, a quaint chalet that was Atatürk's country residence, set amid pretty gardens. It's only open Sunday afternoons from 1.30 to 5.30 pm, and on holidays from 12.30 to 5.30 pm, free of charge. Bring your passport.

Within walking distance of the Presidential Mansion is **Atakule**, the thin tower with a revolving restaurant on top which dominates views of Ankara. From 10 am to 2 am daily a lift whisks you to the top; admission is US$1.50.

Places to Stay

Most budget hotels are in Ulus, which is a dingy part of town with accommodation to match; prices get significantly higher as you head to the ritzier southern districts.

There's little to choose between the *Sipahı* (☎ 324 0235, Kosova Sokak 1) and the *Otel Fuar* (☎ 312 3288, Kosova Sokak 11). Both have grim but clean singles/doubles, some with their own showers for US$8/11. *Otel*

Mithat (☎ 311 5410, fax 310 1054, e akman@otelmithat.com.tr, Tavus Sokak 2) is the smartest place along this strip, with good shower-equipped rooms for US$13/19.

North of Ulus and one street west of Çankırı Caddesi is a noisy area with a few options. *Hotel As* (☎ 310 3998, fax 312 7584, Rüzgarlı Sokak 4) has better rooms than you'd expect from the lobby. They go for US$15/24. The nearby *Olympiat Hotel* (☎ 324 3331, fax 324 5585, Rüzgarlı Eşdost Sokak 18) could be cleaner, but is friendly and a bit cheaper at US$13/22 including breakfast. *Hotel Oğultürk* (☎ 309 2900, fax 311 8321, Rüzgarlı Eşdost Sokak 6) is the best on the street, but pricey at US$40/60, breakfast included.

Two decent places convenient for the Hisar are *Hotel Kale* (☎ 311 3393, Alataş Sokak 13), which has clean, spacious rooms with TV and bathroom for US$15/26, and the mid-range *Hitit Otel* (☎ 310 8617, fax 311 4102, Hisarparki Caddesi 12), which, with a bit of bargaining, offers rooms for US$30/50 including breakfast.

The best option by far though is the *Angora House Hotel* (☎ 309 8380, fax 309 8381, Kalekapısı Sokak 16–18), a beautifully decorated, restored Ottoman house tucked inside the Hisar. There are only five rooms priced from US$40 to US$60 a single and US$55 to US$75 a double.

If you want to stay in the smart Kızılay Meydanı district, *Hotel Ergen* (☎ 417 5906, fax 425 7819, Karanfil Sokak 48) is a bit old fashioned but charges a reasonable US$35/47 including breakfast.

Places to Eat

Old Ankara For the cheapest food, again stick to Ulus. On Kosova Sokak, *Musluoğlu Pastanesi*, next to the *Sipahı* serves big glasses of tea and pastries for breakfast.

The *Akman Boza ve Pasta Salonu* (Atatürk Bulvarı 3), in a courtyard behind a block of offices and shops at the southeastern corner of Ulus, is a good place for snacks and light meals. It has terrace tables around a trickling fountain.

Kebabistan (Sanayi Caddesi) overlooks the Akman from an upper storey. It's a family place with good food costing about US$3 to US$5 for a meal of roast lamb, less for pide. There's another *Kebabistan* (Karanfil Sokak 15/A) in Kızılay.

Along Çankırı Caddesi, *Uğrak Lokantası* is one of several places serving hearty portions of grilled chicken for just US$2.50. Round the corner on Rüzgarlı Sokak is a branch of the popular *Urfalı Kebap, Lahmacun, Pide ve Tatlı Sarayı* where a decent İskender kebap and drink costs US$2.50.

Within the citadel, several old houses have been converted into atmospheric restaurants serving traditional cuisine and alcohol. *Zenger Paşa Konağı (☎ 311 7070, Doyran Sokak 13)* near Angora House Hotel started off this trend and is still the best. A virtual museum of old-time Ankara, a meal here costs US$8 to US$12.

In Gençlik Parkı, *Sahil Lokantası,* on the north side of the lake near the open-air theatre, has pleasantly shaded tables. Inexpensive mezes cost around US$1.25, kebaps around US$2.50.

New Ankara The Sakarya precinct in Kızılay is lined with places to eat and drink. The ground floor of the big Sakarya Süper Marketi is devoted to snack stands. Just to the right of the market are more stands (try the *Otlangaç)* selling *midye tavası* (fried mussels on a stick), *bodrum lokması* (sweet fritters), *kuzu kokoreç* (grilled sheep's intestines) and similar treats.

Cihan Kebap (Selanik Caddesi 3/B), between Sakarya and Tuna Caddesis serves good kebaps with all the trimmings for US$4 to US$6. Even better is the spotless *Köşk (İnkilap Sokak 2),* just round the corner, a veritable kebap palace at unbeatable prices.

The reliable, rustic *Körfez Lokantası (Bayındır Sokak 24)* specialises in fish at between US$5 to US$9 per plate, but many kebaps cost less than US$4. Meals come with plentiful *lavaş* (freshly made unleavened village bread). Next door the *Göksu Restaurant* is a bit fancier.

There are many more expensive restaurants in Kavaklıdere and Çankaya; one bargain is *Hacı Arif Bey (Güniz Sokak 48),* near the Hilton Hotel and the Iranian Embassy, where a traditional meal costs US$6 or so. On Tunalı Hilmi Caddesi, *Meram* is a tempting pastry shop and cafe, while *Café des Cafés* is a classy Parisian-style contender. Cross the road and turn left down Bülten Sokak to find the reputable *Çiçek Lokantası.* A full meal here costs US$6 to US$10.

Self-Catering Ulus has several grotty-looking *corner stores* around Konya Caddesi, and a fresh *vegetable market* (Yeni Haller) just south-west of the intersection of Konya and Hisaparkı Caddesis. In Kızılay, Bakanlıklar, Kavaklıdere and Çankaya there are many Western-style supermarkets (even a Marks & Spencer) with myriad imported goodies.

Entertainment

Politicians on the make, go-ahead bureaucrats and Ankara's gilded youth all make the capital's nightlife much livelier than you'd expect. The in places change with the times, so check with locals as to what's hot before heading off.

The Sakarya district of Kızılay is lined with bars, among them *Forza* and *Kırmızı İskele,* which usually have live Turkish pop music and beers for little more than US$1.50.

South of the pool in Gençliki Park are several more gazinos (nightclubs) with live entertainment, drinks and food at low to moderate prices; to the north are mostly *teahouses* which vie with one another to advertise the lowest-priced beer.

From Kuğulu Park in Kavaklıdere, go north on Tunalı Hilmi Caddesi one block to Bilir Sokak and turn right to find *Jazz Time (Bilir Sokak 4/1),* which usually has live Turkish pop or folk artists, and, behind it, the quieter *Gitanes* bar.

The heaving *North Shield (Güvenlik Caddesi 111)* is a British-style pub. Nearby is the late-night *Dip Club (Güvenlik Caddesi 97)* underneath the popular Süleyman Nazıf restaurant in Ayrancı (entry US$8.50).

Cult (Uğur Mumcu Caddesi) in Gaziosmanpaşa gets going from 10 pm onward. Other clubs to check out are *Home (Esat Caddesi 37)* next to the British Council (entry US$10, free entry for women on Fridays) and *Kashmere (Farabı Sokak 34)* in Çankaya.

For more refined entertainment visit the *Opera House (☎ 324 2210)* on Atatürk Bulvarı, which features classical concerts, recitals and opera at bargain prices (around US$3 a ticket).

Several cinemas show recently released Western films, usually in the original language with Turkish subtitles. Try *Akün*

Sineması (Atatürk Bulvarı 227, Kavak-lıdere); the **Kavaklıdere** *(Tunalı Hilmi Caddesi 105)*, and the **Metropol** *(Selanik Caddesi 76, Kızılay)*. See the *Turkish Daily News* for program details.

Getting There & Away

Air Turkish Airlines (☎ 428 0200, 398 0100 at Esenboğa airport), at Atatürk Bulvarı 154, Kavaklıdere, has daily nonstop flights to most Turkish cities.

Bus Ankara's huge otogar, known as AŞTİ, (☎ 224 1000), 6km west of Kızılay, is the vehicular heart of the nation, with over 100 coach companies heading to all places day and night. Buses to İstanbul (US$8 to US$18, seven hours; express buses US$12 to US$21, six hours) leave every 15 minutes at least. Other sample fares are: Antalya (US$12, 10 hours), Bodrum (from US$12, 13 hours), Bursa (US$10, 5½ hours), Diyarbakır (US$20, 13 hours), Erzurum (US$18, 12 hours), İzmir (US$13 to US$18, 8½ hours), Konya (US$8, three hours) and Ürgüp/Cappadocia (US$8, 4½ hours).

Train Seven daily express trains, some with sleeping cars, connect İstanbul and Ankara. There are also useful services to İzmir, Kayseri, Sivas and a few other cities. See the Getting Around chapter for more information. For details call the train station (☎ 311 0620).

Getting Around

To/From the Airport Ankara's Esenboğa airport is 33km north of the city centre. Havaş buses (US$3, 40 minutes in light traffic) depart the Turkish Airlines city terminal at the train station 1½ hours before domestic flights and two hours before international Turkish Airlines flights. A taxi costs US$20 or more.

Local Transport Ankara's underground train system is made up of the east-west Ankaray line running from AŞTİ (the otogar) to Dikimevi, and connecting with the north-south Kızılay to Batıkent line at Kızılay.

EGO *karts* (sold in units of 5, 10 and 20 rides for US$1/2/4) can be used on both the metro and city buses. Buy them at the metro stations, kiosks by bus stops, or from a shop with the sign 'EGO Bilet(i)'.

Many city buses run the length of Atatürk Bulvarı; Nos 112, 114 and 603 travel from Ulus Meydanı to the embassy enclaves. Buses marked 'AŞTİ' go to the otogar, those marked 'Gar' go to the train station. City bus No 198 usually departs the otogar for the train station and Ulus; bus No 623 goes via Kızılay to Gaziler.

Taxis are multitudinous, metered, often suicidal and charge about US$3 for an average ride, US$5 to US$6 from one end of the city to the other.

ERZURUM
☎ 442 • pop 300,000

The largest city on the eastern Anatolian high plateau, Erzurum, 925km east of Ankara, has always been a transportation centre and military headquarters. There are few sights here and for most overlanders Erzurum is a merely a transit point and the last chance in Turkey to get an Iranian visa.

Orientation & Information

The Havuzbaşı roundabout with a large statue of Atatürk joins Erzurum's main roads, Cumhuriyet Caddesi and Cemal Gürsel Caddesi. It's almost 2km from the otogar to the roundabout. These roads are lined with everything you'll need as well as many older mosques and medreses.

Most of the cheap hotels are a little way to the north, downhill along Menderes Caddesi around Gürcü Kapı, once the 'Georgian gate' in the city walls and marked by a chunky stone fountain at a traffic intersection, 600m uphill from the train station.

You can walk to everything in old Erzurum, including the train station, but will need transport to get to and from the otogar (3km west of the centre) and the airport. The train station is 2.5km east of the otogar.

The tourist office (☎ 218 5697) is on the southern side of Cemal Gürsel Caddesi at 9/A, one block west of the Havuzbaşı traffic roundabout.

The Iranian consulate (☎ 218 2285) on Atatürk Bulvarı is open daily except Friday from 8 am to 1 pm and 2 to 4 pm. You can only apply for a transit visa here, for which there is a nonrefundable US$60 application fee. Some people wait less than a day for the visa, others weeks. Visas will not be granted to American applicants; apparently the British aren't too popular either.

There are lots of Internet cafes, several of them, including the Çağ and the Blue White, on Cumhuriyet Caddesi.

Things to See

There are several medieval monuments around Erzurum worth searching out. At the eastern end of Cumhuriyet Caddesi is the 13th-century **Çifte Minareli Medrese**, or Twin Minaret Seminary, where you can take tea. Next door, the architecture of the **Ulu Cami** (1179) is more restrained and elegant.

The citadel, or **kale**, erected by the Emperor Theodosius around the 5th century AD, is on the hilltop to the north. It's open from 8.30 am to 5.30 pm daily and admission costs US$0.30.

The Yakutiye Medresesi (Yakutiye Seminary), a Mongol theological seminary dating from 1310, now serves as Erzurum's best museum, the **Türk – İslâm Eserleri ve Etnoğrafya Müzesi** (Turkish & Islamic Arts & Ethnography Museum). It's open daily except Monday from 8.30 am to 5 pm for US$1.75.

Places to Stay & Eat

The *Hitit Otel (☎ 218 1204, Kazım Karabekir Caddesi 27)* and *Örnek Otel (☎ 218 1203, Kazım Karabekir 8)* are rock bottom but reliable, and offer singles/doubles with bathroom for US$9/12, marginally less for rooms without bath.

Otel Polat (☎ 218 1623, fax 234 4598, Kazım Karabekir Caddesi 4) is a longtime favourite which, despite a recent makeover, charges US$13/21 for rooms with decent bathroom and breakfast.

Another good choice just round the corner is the renovated *Hotel Sefer (☎ 218 6714, fax 212 3775, İstasyon Caddesi)*. It

charges US$15/25, breakfast included, for a reasonably modern room with bathroom and TV.

For the best choice of places to eat just stroll down Cumhuriyet Caddesi and take your pick. *Salon Çağın* and *Salon Asya* are two we can recommend. *Dönerci Hacıbey*, opposite the Yakutiye Medresesi, is welcoming to female diners.

Traditional decor and decent prices make *Sultan Sekisi Şark Sofrası (Ebuishak Sokak 1)*, on the narrow street across Cumhuriyet Caddesi from the Çifte Minareli Medrese, a good choice. The nearby *Üçler Kebap Salonu (Osmanpaşa Sokak 2)* serves *kuşbaşı* (lamb kebaps) for US$1.50 as well as the usual range of pides (US$1).

Getting There & Away

Air Turkish Airlines (☎ 234 1516, fax 233 1070), on Kazım Karabekir Caddesi, has two daily flights to Ankara, with connections to Antalya, İstanbul and İzmir. There's another branch on Cumhuriyet Caddesi from where buses to the airport depart two hours before each flight (US$1.75).

Bus The otogar, 3km from the centre along the airport road, handles most of Erzurum's intercity traffic. It has services to Ankara (US$20, 12 hours), Diyarbakır (US$14, eight hours), Doğubayazıt (US$7, four hours), İstanbul (around US$25, 18 hours) and Van (US$9, six hours).

Train There are good rail connections to Ankara via Kayseri, Sivas, Divriği and Erzincan. The *Yeni Doğu Ekspresi* covers the distance between Erzurum and Ankara in 21 hours; the *Doğu Ekspresi* takes about 25 hours – if it's on time.

TURKEY

Turkey Border Crossings

Turkey to Iran

The border at Gürbulak, 34km east of Doğubayazıt, is unmissable; a line of trucks seems permanently encamped here, and it's the same on the Iranian side (Bāzārgān). Dolmuşes leave Doğubayazıt from the petrol station on Ağrı Caddesi on a fairly regular basis (US$1.25). The bus driver is likely to offer you rials – check the exchange rate with other travellers in town first. if it's favourable, there's no problem doing a deal here rather than on the Iranian side.

The border is open 24 hours but it's safer to cross during daylight and early, to avoid being delayed behind a bus load of local travellers having their passports checked. It's quite a walk from the gate past the long line of trucks to the Turkish customs house, where you're unlikely to have your bags checked. In the immigration hall, all hell may be let loose depending on whether that bus load of travellers is trying to get through too. It looks worse than it is and, generally, the kindly locals will push you to the front of the scrum to hand your passport over to Iranian officials to be checked.

If all goes smoothly, the crossing may take less than an hour. You *must* have a visa for Iran as they're not issued here. Women should be dressed according to the Islamic code; you should have your head covered and be wearing a loose, reasonably full-length coat. Some people have told us of attempts by Iranian officials to extract a small fee. This is a bribe and you don't have to pay it, but if you're travelling in your own transport you might want to consider co-operating to save time and a full vehicle search (although this is rare). There's a tourism office here, too, but don't expect much in the way of advice.

Once out of the customs hall you'll be approached by money changers; ignore them – there are plenty outside the compound who'll give you a better rate.

Iran to Turkey

There are no direct buses from Tabrīz to the border town of Bāzārgān, but you can either take a shared taxi from the terminal, or the cheaper option of a bus to Mākū (6000 rials, 3½ hours) and a share taxi to Bāzārgān (around 3000 rials) from there.

Bāzārgān is little more than a collection of shops and black market moneychangers. You can off-load your rials here (bargain up from their starting figure) but you should get a better rate for US dollars on the other side of the border. Walk through the gate at the end of the road where there's a shuttle bus (500 rials) to take you the 1.5km to the customs and immigration post. If you're in a hurry or want to beat the crowds, you could also take a taxi (1500 rials), or you could walk, but it's all uphill. It's a bit confusing finding the Iranian passport control. Go around to the right of the buildings where the bus drops you off, through a customs point (sometimes unmanned – just walk through) and back out into the open yard, where the passport control is on the left. It's supposedly open 24 hours. If your visa is in order, going through seems to be a very straightforward procedure – we passed through in about five minutes but the time it takes will depend on the number of people crossing when you do. If you've had a visa extension in Iran, you may have to point this out to them. Make sure you still have the disembarkation card you were given when you entered Iran.

Things get a bit more complicated on the Turkish side, as you have to get a Turkish visa stamp. This means lining up at the Police Control window, where you will be given a payment voucher. You take this outside (not the way you came in) to the bank, where you pay for your visa and receive a sticker. Back at the Police Control this is inserted into your passport and stamped. Finally you can wander the 300m down to the main gates into Turkey, past the parade of parked trucks, through the duty-free liquor store and onto a waiting dolmuş for the 34km trip to Doğubayazıt (about US$1.25).

IRAN

Tehrān

Esfahān

Persepolis

MARTIN MOOS

Gombad-é Soltānīyé, Soltānīyé

MARTIN MOOS

Masjed-é Emām, Esfahān

SIMON RICHMOND

Masjed-é Jāme', Yazd

PAUL HARDING

Arg-é Bam, Bam

چایخانه

JOHN BORTHWICK

Taking Tea

IRAN
highlights

Takht-é Soleimān (Throne of Solomon)
A remarkable walled citadel surrounding a small lake in a remote, scenic location south of Tabrīz. Nearby is the dormant volcano Zendan-é Soleimān (Solomon's Prison).

Castles of the Assassins, Alamūt
Set in magnificent countryside are the impressive ruined castles of Lambersan and Gāzor Khān – hilltop fortresses of a medieval Islamic sect.

Gombad-é Soltānīyé, Soltānīyé
The huge dome of this 14th-century Mongol sultan's mausoleum is what puts it on the map, but it's the mausoleum's exquisite decoration that is most memorable.

Esfahān
The magnificent mosques Masjed-é Emām, Masjed-é Sheikh Lotfollāh and Masjed-é Jāme' are a visual textbook of Islamic architecture.

Masjed-é Jāme', Yazd
With its soaring minarets and lovely mosaics, this superb mosque towers over the fascinating old city – a warren of sunbaked adobe buildings.

Āstān-é Ghods-é Razavī, Mashhad
The Āstān-é Ghods-é Razavī (Holy Shrine of Emām Rezā) is a dazzling architectural wonder of the Islamic world, and the holiest place in Iran.

Arg-é Bam, Bam
Constructed in clay, this amazing medieval walled city looks all the better for its incomplete restoration, particularly at sunrise and sunset. Tea is served in the citadel gatehouse.

Taking Tea
Relax in a *chaykhāné* (teahouse) over sweet tea and a fragrant *qalyan* (water pipe). Esfahān has Iran's best teahouses, but there are good teahouses to be found in all major cities and towns in Iran.

Iran

Put aside the ranting clerics, polluting oil wells and women clad head to toe in black. Believe it or not, post-revolutionary Iran is one of the most fascinating, visually dazzling and welcoming countries in the Middle East. And, despite relatively high 'foreigner' prices for sightseeing attractions, it's also one of the cheapest. The only slight problem is getting in (but we've covered that in the Facts for the Visitor chapter).

Down the ages, plenty of people have just barged in; old Persia attracted some of the region's more gruesome invaders and eccentric explorers. Only in the past few years has Iran recovered from the excesses of the Islamic Revolution and the aftermath of the Iran-Iraq War, and the government is again (tentatively) promoting tourism.

Once you're there, getting around is no problem with Iran boasting excellent and absurdly cheap transport. Share a taxi to those remote ruins? No problem. A flight across the desert? That'll be US$10 please. Accommodation is not bad and while the arid landscape often leaves something to be desired, you're seldom short of ancient ruins, glorious mosques and labyrinthine bazaars *(bāzārs)* to explore. If activities are more your bag then consider hiking, mountain climbing and skiing.

Yes, it's still very much a fundamentalist Islamic country (don't expect much to be happening on a Friday or for there to be any nightlife), but Iran is nowhere near as forbidding a place as it once was. Safety is rarely an issue and the locals have hospitality in their blood. Women should hold no fears: If you dress and act according to (admittedly strict) local rules, you will be treated well, and suffer little, if any, of the hassles women often endure in Pakistan and Turkey.

THE ROUTE

Our route starts at the border crossing of Bāzārgān. If you want to visit the beautiful Armenian church of Ghara Kelīsā, then stop the night in Mākū; if not, then head to Tabrīz, western Iran's major city with one of the country's best bazaars. We then head

Iran at a Glance

Capital: Tehrān (population approx 12 million)

Population: approx 70 million

Area: 1,648,195 sq km

Head of state: Āyatollāh Alī Khameneī is the Supreme Leader; the elected president is Hojjat-ol-Eslām Seyed Mohammed Khatamī

Currency: Iranian rial

Country telephone code: ☎ 98

Exchange rates:

country	unit		rial
Australia	A$1	=	4425
EU	€1	=	7510
UK	£1	=	11,880
USA	US$1	=	7995

into the stark countryside to the ruins of Takht-é Soleimān and the huge domed mausoleum at Soltānīyé. Ghazvīn, the next stop east, is a good base from which to visit the remote, but fascinating ruined Castles of the Assassins.

Although it is possible to avoid it, Iran's frenetic capital Tehrān, with its concrete and freeways, is worth spending a couple of days in. Its fine museums are the best you'll find in the country. Tehrān is also the easiest place from which to make a long, but worthwhile, detour to the holy city of

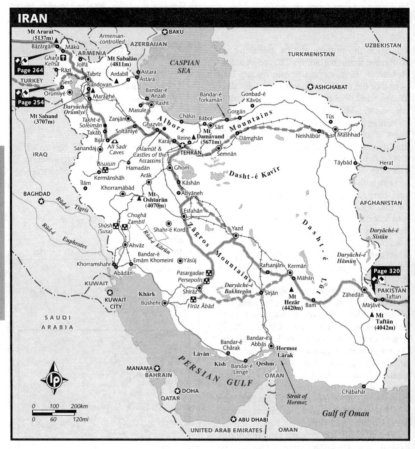

Mashhad – a place you'll want to visit if you're heading to the Central Asian republics.

From Tehrān, the route turns south to the laid-back desert town of Kāshān and Esfahān, the country's loveliest city, with beautiful mosques, palaces, bridges and teahouses. We then head to Shīrāz, city of poets, and the base for the great archaeological site of Persepolis. The route zips back north to the ancient Zoroastrian city of Yazd and continues directly east to another interesting oasis town, Kermān. Finally we reach Bam, home to the amazing mud-brick citadel Arg-é Bam. The border crossing into Pakistan is at Mīrjāveh, close to the deadbeat Balūchestān desert town of Zāhedān.

Bāzārgān to Tehrān

BĀZĀRGĀN

From the Iran-Turkey border crossing, either walk down the hill to the exit or take a two-minute ride in a minibus (500 rials). Bāzārgān is a tiny service community for the scores of truck drivers passing through each day; there's absolutely no need to linger here. If you do turn up late at night and want to wait until morning to continue, the spartan, but clean *Hotel Jafapour* (☎ 04634-2058), next to the border gate, costs 30,000 rials per person. The manager speaks English.

Shared taxis regularly go to Mākū (1000 rials or 3000 rials for the entire taxi, 22km).

From Mākū, there are several buses daily direct to Tabrīz, which, given an early start, you could easily make in a day from the border.

MĀKŪ
Boxed in by a soaring gorge, down which the main road runs, Mākū is worth considering as a pitstop before, or after, crossing the border with Turkey, 22km west. Apart from exploring the striking rocky landscape, the town is an ideal base from which to visit the old Armenian church Ghara Kelīsā, around 60km from Mākū.

Everything you'll need, including hotels, *kabābīs* (kebab restaurants) and money-changers, is along the main road. The bus station is around 2km from the centre, on the western edge of town.

Places to Stay & Eat
Hotel Alvand (☎ *04634-234 91*), close to the town's main square, has friendly management and acceptable singles/doubles with shared bathroom for 20,000/26,000 rials. *Hotel Lalah* (☎ *04634-234 41*), opposite, has larger rooms, some with private bathroom, for 20,000/30,000 rials.

The only upmarket option is the *Mākū Inn* (☎ *04634-232 12*) about 300m up from Alvand and off the main road. It's quiet and good value for 70,980/106,470 rials, and also boasts the only proper *restaurant* in town. A meal here will cost around 15,000 rials.

Amir is a decent kabābī about 200m down the road from the Hotel Lalah; a kabāb with a drink and salad is 13,000 rials. Even cheaper is the *Enghelāb* teahouse, on the square near the Alvand, where a bowl of *ābgūsht* (stew with thick chunks of potatoes, fatty meat and lentils) is 5000 rials.

Getting There & Away
There are six buses daily to Tabrīz (at 6.30, 7 and 8 am and noon and 1 and 2.30 pm), 300km east and a three- to four-hour journey. The fare is 5100 rials. Direct buses to Tehrān run at 4 and 5 pm daily, take 13 hours and cost 16,000 rials.

Shared taxis to Bāzārgān leave from outside Hotel Alvand; and to Tabrīz and Orūmīyé, from outside the bus station.

GHARA KELĪSĀ
The fortified Church of St Thaddaeus is probably the most remarkable Christian monument in Iran. (It's often called Ghara Kelīsā, but its proper name is Kelīsā-yé Tādī – the Church of St Thaddaeus.)

The period of construction is unknown, and very little remains of the original church. It was largely rebuilt after extensive earthquake damage in 1319, but there are some older parts, perhaps from the 10th century. It's notable for its surrounding walls, fine exterior decoration and attractive mixture of black and white stone.

The church has one service a year, on the feast day of St Thaddaeus in mid-June, when Armenian pilgrims from all over Iran attend the ceremonies. The church is open daily during daylight hours and costs 10,000 rials for entry.

If you don't have your own transport, the easiest way is to reach the church is to charter a taxi from Mākū or Bāzārgān, for around 45,000 rials return. Take a picnic, since the surrounding countryside is very pretty and worth exploring.

TABRĪZ
☎ 041 • pop 1.6 million
A dusty 300km south-east of Mākū, Tabrīz will be many overlanders' introduction to an Iranian city. Although it had a spell as the Persian capital during the Safavid period (1502–1722), there's little to show for it these days and many people pause no longer than one night.

However, there are reasons to stop, not least the excellent bazaar and the chance to arrange trips to nearby attractions such as Marāghé, Kandovan, Jolfā and Takht-é Soleimān. The people are very friendly and it's possible to meet with the local Armenian community, which has several churches in the city centre.

Orientation
The main street is Kheyābūn-é Emām Khomeinī, with most budget hotels between the Bāgh-é Golestān park to the east and the bazaar to the north-west. The train station is 4km west of the centre and the bus station 3km south, just off Kheyābūn-é Sharīatī.

Information
Tourist Offices The tourist office (☎ 5530 952) is at Kheyābūn-é 17 Shahrīvar 75 and is open from 7.30 am to 2 pm Saturday to Thursday. There's a free map of the city and

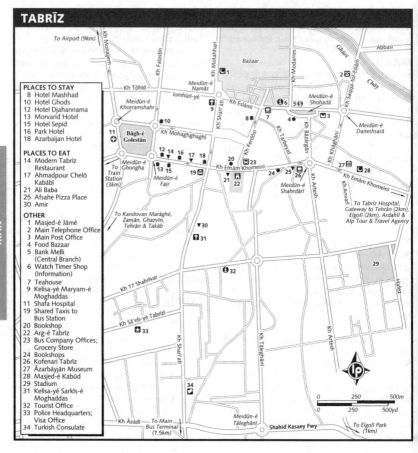

TABRĪZ

To Airport (9km)

Bazaar

Abbasi

PLACES TO STAY
8 Hotel Mashhad
10 Hotel Ghods
12 Hotel Djahannama
13 Morvarid Hotel
15 Hotel Sepid
16 Park Hotel
18 Azarbaijan Hotel

PLACES TO EAT
14 Modern Tabrīz
    Restaurant
17 Ahmadpour Chelō
    Kabābī
21 Ali Baba
25 Afsahe Pizza Place
30 Amir

OTHER
1 Masjed-é Jāmé
2 Main Telephone Office
3 Main Post Office
4 Food Bazaar
5 Bank Melli
   (Central Branch)
6 Watch Timer Shop
   (Information)
7 Teahouse
9 Kelisa-yé Maryam-é
   Moghaddas
11 Shafa Hospital
19 Shared Taxis to
    Bus Station
20 Bookshop
22 Arg-é Tabrīz
23 Bus Company Offices;
    Grocery Store
24 Bookshops
26 Kofenari Tabrīz
27 Āzarbāyjān Museum
28 Masjed-é Kabūd
29 Stadium
31 Kelisa-yé Sarkīs-é
    Moghaddas
32 Tourist Office
33 Police Headquarters;
    Visa Office
34 Turkish Consulate

Meidūn-é
Namāz

Meidūn-é
Khorramshahr

Bāgh-é
Golestān

To
Train
Station
(3km)

Meidūn-é
Ghongha

Meidūn-é
Fajr

To Kandovan Marāghé,
Zanjān, Ghazvīn,
Tehrān & Takāb

Meidūn-é
Shohadā

Meidūn-é
Daneshsarā

Meidūn-é
Shahrdāri

To Tabrīz Hospital,
Gateway to Tehrān (2km),
Elgolī (2km), Ardahil &
Alp Tour & Travel Agency

Kh 17 Shahrīvar

Kh Sā'eb-yé Tabrīzī

Kh Āzādī

To Main
Bus Terminal
(1.5km)

Meidūn-é
Tāleghānī

Shahid Kasaey Fwy

To Elgolī Park
(1km)

0   250   500m
0   250   500yd

some information on local attractions, but a better source of information is the local guide Nasser Khan and his colleagues who can be found at the Watch Timer shop (☎ 5229 151) at the entrance to the bazaar on Kheyābūn-é Eslāmī. Information is provided free of charge and they can also arrange excellent tours of the bazaar and trips to Kandovan, Jolfā and Takht-é Soleimān.

Visa Extensions Tabrīz is a good place to arrange visa extensions, which are available at the police headquarters (☎ 875 786) on Kheyābūn-é Sā'eb-yé Tabrīzī.

Money Bank Melli near the bazaar accepts travellers cheques. If you want to change money at the 'street rate', make discreet inquiries in the bazaar, or at your hotel.

Travel Agencies More expensive tours and other travel services are available from Alp Tour & Travel Agency (☎ 310 340), at Meidūn-é Bozorg, in the rich eastern suburbs of the city.

Things to See & Do
Don't miss the 3km-long **bazaar**, which includes sections for carpets, spices, shoes, hats and gold. Founded more than 1000 years ago and visited by Marco Polo, most of the current maze-like structure dates to the 15th century. Search out the *tīmché* (hall) where the main carpet wholesalers gather. Upstairs you can watch carpet

repairers at work. Since few foreigners come here, this is a good place to shop for reasonably priced souvenirs without the hard sell you'll encounter at other bazaars.

Although badly damaged by earthquakes, the 15th-century **Masjed-é Kabūd**, around 1km east of the bazaar, is still notable for its intricate tilework. You can watch restorers at work inside the mosque, painting in the gaps between the tiles. Entry is 10,000 rials. The nearby **Āzarbāyjān Museum**, has some mildly interesting exhibits, but the entry charge is steep at 15,000 rials.

Back in the centre of town, the huge, crumbling citadel **Arg-é Tabrīz**, built in the early 14th century, is worth a quick look. One of the more interesting Armenian churches is the old, but substantially rebuilt, **Maryam-é Moghaddas Church**, near the bazaar; inquire here if you want to find out more about their community.

Should you wish to escape the city, **Elgolī** is a large, pleasant park with a lake and camp site – take a shared taxi from Meidūn-é Shahrdārī.

Places to Stay

The cheapest places, clustered along Kheyābūn-é Emām Khomeinī, are rock-bottom basic and not particularly clean. *Hotel Sepid* (☎ 5552 099) offers dirty sheets and shared bathrooms for 12,000/19,000 rials a single/double. Across the road similar prices and standards of housekeeping are available at the otherwise friendly *Hotel Djahannama* (☎ 555 2419). It also has a car park at the back for 3000 rials per night.

Hotel Mashhad (☎ 5558 255, Kheyābūné Ferdōsī), a favourite with traders from neighbouring Azerbaijan, has slightly better standards, a shower under lock and key and singles/doubles for 12,000/20,000 rials.

Going up a notch, the *Morvarid Hotel* (☎ 5531 433, fax 5560 520, Meidūn-é Fajr) is clean and friendly, and charges 35,300/50,200 rials. Rooms have private bathroom, fridge and B&W TV, but the rooms at the front get the street noise. They allow guests to keep their motorcycles or bicycles in the lobby.

Park Hotel (☎ 5551 852, Kheyābūn-é Emām Khomeinī) has good value singles/doubles for 30,000/40,000 rials with shared bathrooms, doubles for 60,000 rials with

their own bathrooms. Some rooms are musty, though.

Hotel Ghods (☎ 5550 898, Kheyābūn-é Mohaghghaghī) is a bit more pricey at 41,500/62,500 rials a single/double, but the rooms are fine and the management welcoming.

The well-furnished *Azarbaijan Hotel* (☎ 5559 051, fax 5537 477 Kheyābūn-é Sharī'atī), recognisable by the red and white columns on the outside, is worth a splurge for 53,000/74,000 rials.

Places to Eat

Again head to Kheyābūn-é Emām Khomeinī. An excellent choice for both ābgūsht and *Tabrīz kūfte* (giant meatballs containing a boiled egg and walnuts), is *Ali Baba*. There's no English sign – look for the cartoon chef with a plate of kabābs. The manager speaks some English and the bill shouldn't be more than 10,000 rials.

For fancier surroundings, try the *Modern Tabrīz Restaurant*, downstairs and signposted in English; a meat kabāb with all the trimmings and drinks costs around 16,000 rials and you're likely to have the place to yourself. Up the road is *Ahmadpour Chelō Kababī*. It's not signposted in English, so look for the words 'Chelō Kabāb' and 'Chicken Kebab' on the window. A meal here is 15,000 rials.

For fast food you can't go far wrong with *Afsahe Pizza Place* (Kheyābūn-é Emām Khomeinī), which has decent pizzas from about 10,000 rials. Also try *Amir*, on Kheyābūn-é Sharī'atī, a bright burger and pizza joint.

The food bazaar is opposite the main bazaar, on the way to the post office; you can get fresh vegetables and fruit here. There's also a grocers along Kheyābūn-é Ferdōsī where you can buy mineral water, cheese and other deli-type items.

Teahouses

Near Afsahe Pizza Place is *Kofenari Tabrīz*, a traditional teahouse where men gather to smoke the *qalyan* (water pipe). Women will probably feel more comfortable at the convivial upstairs *teahouse* opposite the bazaar on Kheyābūn-é Eslāmī; look for the stairs after the cake shop. Tea costs 250 rials and a pipe 500 rials for ordinary tobacco, 1500 rials for flavoured tobacco.

IRAN

Getting There & Away

Air Iran Air (☎ 343 515) flies several times a day to Tehrān (113,000 rials) and less regularly to Rasht and Mashhad.

Bus, Minibus & Shared Taxi The bus and minibus station is to the south of the city – to get there, take a taxi from the intersection of Kheyābūn-é Emām Khomeinī and Kheyābūn-é Sharī'atī. On arrival, some buses will drop you closer to the centre from where you can catch a shared taxi to a hotel.

Buses regularly go to Esfahān (19.500 rials or 35,000 rials by Volvo, 16 hours), Ghazvīn (12,000 rials, eight hours), Jolfā (4500 rials, three hours); Māku (5000 rials, 3½ hours); Orūmīyé (5000 rials, three hours); Rasht (10,000 rials, eight hours); and Tehrān (12,000 rials or 30,000 rials by Volvo, nine hours). From the bus station, shared taxis go to Orūmīyé, Māku and Bāzārgān.

There's also a daily service to Baku in Azerbaijan (40,000 rials, 12 hours), but you must already have a visa for the country and have checked that it's valid for use across this heavily policed border.

Tickets can be booked at offices on Kheyābūn-é Ferdōsī.

Train Trains leave at 5.40 and 7.10 pm daily for Tehrān (12 hours); the earlier train has 1st-class air-con sleeper cabins for four people costing 31,000 rials. The later train has 2nd-class six-sleeper cabins without air-con for 26,500 rials. The trains stop at Zanjān and Ghazvīn but there's no discount on the fares if this is where you hop off. Tickets should be booked at least one day in advance at the station (sales from 8 am to 2 pm and 4 to 7 pm).

On Saturday and Monday there is also an 8.30 am service to Jolfā; it's slightly cheaper than the bus at 3600 rials and takes the same time.

AROUND TABRĪZ
Kandovan & Marāghé

A day trip to both these places is possible if you have your own transport or hire a taxi in Tabrīz. **Kandovan**, 50km south-west of Tabrīz, is a mini-Cappadocia, with the villagers living in caves hollowed out from the soft, volcanic rock on the slopes leading to **Mt Sahand**, a favourite hiking and skiing spot with Tabrīzīs. It's a rustic spot with none of its Turkish cousin's tourist gloss, although locals flock here to enjoy the scenery and take home mineral water, considered a health tonic.

There's not much to show that **Marāghé** was once the capital of the Mongol dynasty (1220–1380) – even the four ancient brick **tomb towers**, that make the town archaeologically interesting, predate the Mongols. The most easily accessible of the four towers is **Gunbad-é Surkh**, also known as Qermez (Red Tower) because of its colour. It's decorated with carved terracotta panels and few blue glazed tiles. The tombs are difficult to find which is where a taxi and guide comes in handy.

Jolfā

Occupying a sensitive spot near the border with Azerbaijan and Armenia, Jolfā, 135km from Tabrīz, is the closest town to **Kelīsa Darré Shām**, a magnificent 14th-century Armenian monastery otherwise known as the Church of St Stephanos. Said to have been founded as early as AD 62 by St Bartholomew, an early Christian apostle to Armenia, the building's beauty – it has fine exterior reliefs – is enhanced by its remote and spectacular location in the hills bang on the border. For this reason you need military permission to visit the site. While it's possible to arrange this independently, by far the easier option is to take an organised tour from Tabrīz.

TAKHT-É SOLEIMĀN

At least 250km south of Tabrīz, in remote and starkly beautiful landscape, stands the enigmatic citadel Takht-é Soleimān (Throne of Solomon). Although it has nothing to do with the biblical king, the citadel, surrounding a small natural lake, has an epic atmosphere. It contains ruins from the Achaemenid (559–330 BC), Parthian (190 BC–AD 224), Sassanian (AD 224–637) and Arab (637–1050) periods.

The lake is remarkable in itself. About 100L of water per second bubbles up from its 100m depths, the run-off feeding channels that flow through the citadel's walls to the plains below. Why the place was abandoned is a mystery, but since its rediscovery in 1819 by British explorer Sir Robert Ker Porter, there's been extensive excavation and parts – such as a section of the outer walls – have been rebuilt to give an idea of its former glory. There's usually an archaeologist on hand in the site offices to point out the Mongol-period assembly hall, the Sassanian palace, with its harem and adjoining fire temple – all are signposted. It is open from 7 am to 7 pm daily, entrance is 25,000 rials and there's a bookshop, with some English volumes, inside the site.

On your journey here you will not miss the conical **Zendan-é Soleimān** (Prison of Solomon) volcano, about 2.5km west of the ruins. Climb it not only for the superb **views** of the countryside and ancient city but also to stare inside its hollow mouth. This area is great for **hiking**.

Places to Stay & Eat

It's possible to rough camp near the citadel (there's a village, Nosratabad, here with a restaurant catering for tour buses), but if you want a hotel the only option is in the sleepy town of **Takāb**, some 40km south. The **Hotel Randji** (☎ 04837-231 79, fax 246 50) is not too bad, the rooms being well furnished and comfortable. The management prefers to be paid in dollars, the quoted rate being US$21 per person including breakfast. You can, however, negotiate to pay in rials and, if you cry poverty, the price is likely to drop to US$15. The hotel's *restaurant* is fine, which is just as well since there's not much else in town beyond the usual kabābīs.

Getting There & Away

You can reach Takht-é Soleimān by a series of buses and taxis from either Tabrīz, Orūmīyé – handy if you've crossed the border at Serō (see the boxed text 'Van to Orūmīyé' in the Turkey chapter) – or Zanjān. By far the easiest option is to charter a taxi for the whole journey, or get to Takāb and take the bus or a taxi from there.

From Tabrīz, there are frequent buses to Meyāndo'āb (4000 rials, 2½ hours) and less-frequent minibuses to Shāhīn Dezh (2000 rials, one hour), which is where buses from Orūmīyé also arrive. From here you'll have to hire a taxi to Takāb or to the site (10,000 rials, one hour). Alternatively, a taxi from Tabrīz to Takāb is around US$20 including a couple of hours waiting at the citadel.

From Takāb, a minibus runs to the village of Nostratabad daily at 7 am. From

here you can walk to the citadel. A return taxi journey including waiting time should cost around 50,000 rials.

From Zanjān, there is a direct rough road through the hills to Takht-é Soleimān, but you need a 4WD to negotiate it. The safer way is go via Bījār and Takāb. Separate buses connect each town (you'll have to walk between different stations in Bījār for the services to Takāb and Zanjān), but each journey takes a couple of hours and costs 2000 rials. There are also direct buses daily from Takāb to Zanjān.

SOLTĀNĪYÉ

The next major town on our route east is **Zanjān**, 280km south-east of Tabrīz. There's nothing to keep you in this lacklustre provincial capital longer than figuring out the most convenient way to reach the village Soltānīyé, 37km farther south, where you'll want to stop to visit the huge domed mausoleum **Gombad-é Soltānīyé**.

The last resting place of the Mongol Soltān Oljeitū Khodābandé was originally built for Alī, the son-in-law of the Prophet Mohammed (who was never buried here). It has one of the largest domes in the world – 48m high, and nearly 25m in diameter – but it is the fine exterior decoration of the outside gallery that is most arresting. Entrance is 20,000 rials and there's likely to be an English-speaking guide on hand to show you around.

While in the village there are a couple more monuments you could check out: the blue-domed **tomb** of Mullah Hassan Kashi and the Dervish monastery **Khanegah**.

Soltānīyé is 3km from the main road between Zanjān and Ghazvīn, 150km east; you'll easily spot the mausoleum dome. Take any bus, minibus or shared taxi between the two towns, get off at the junction and catch another shared taxi or bus to the village. There are also direct buses to Soltānīyé from Zanjān (1000 rials).

GHAZVĪN

☎ 0281 • pop 400,000

Mention Ghazvīn (also spelled Qazvin) to some Iranians and they may whisper about it being a den of homosexuality, rather than mention its fine carpets or seedless grapes. Gay or not, Ghazvīn is certainly a pleasant city, with several lovely buildings, plus a

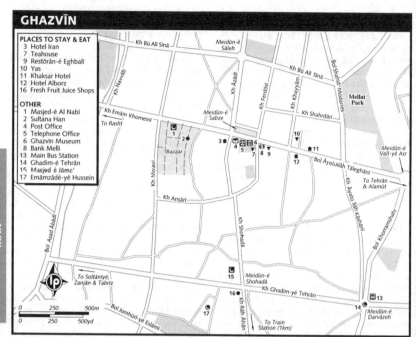

GHAZVĪN

PLACES TO STAY & EAT
3 Hotel Iran
7 Teahouse
9 Restōrān-é Eghbalī
10 Yas
11 Khaksar Hotel
12 Hotel Alborz
16 Fresh Fruit Juice Shops

OTHER
1 Masjed-é Al Nabī
2 Sultana Han
4 Post Office
5 Telephone Office
6 Ghazvīn Museum
8 Bank Melli
13 Main Bus Station
14 Ghadim-é Tehrān
15 Masjed é Jāme'
17 Emāmzāde-yé Hussein

good bazaar. Also it's the best base for a visit to Soltānīyé and the amazing ruins of the Castles of the Assassins. You might also want to use it as a stopover en route to the Caspian and the picturesque hillside village of Māsūlé.

Founded in the 3rd century BC, Ghazvīn prospered under the Seljuk rulers (1051–1220). Around 350 years later the Safavid Shāh Tahmāsb I transferred his capital here from Tabrīz, but it's glory days didn't last long – his successor Shāh Abbās I set up court in Esfahān in 1598.

Earthquakes have damaged much of Ghazvīn's architectural heritage, but today everything that is still worth seeing, and all the facilities that travellers need, are within easy walking distance of the town centre, Meidūn-é Sabze.

Things to See
The most beautiful of Ghazvīn's monuments, about 1km south of Meidūn-é Sabze, is the **Emāmzāde-yé Hussein**, a dazzling 16th-century mausoleum. Its facade is a riot of polychrome tiles and the main shrine is plastered with mirrors. More sedate is the

11th-century **Masjed-é Jāme'**, just off Kheyābūn-é Shohodā, which has some features dating even farther back to the Arab period (637–1050), including an exquisitely decorated prayer hall. Fridays and holidays aside the courtyard is a quiet place to linger.

Spend some time wandering through the extensive **bazaar**, west of Sabze. Here you'll find the **Sultana Han**, a courtyard dedicated to the making of furniture, and another impressively-tiled mosque, **Masjed-é Al Nabī**, built mainly during the Safavid period (1502–1722). The compact, pretty **Ghazvīn Museum**, set in pleasant gardens beside Meidūn-é Sabze, is also worth a visit. Its small collection of exquisite applied arts is on view from 8 am to 1 pm and 4 to 7 pm daily, except Friday. Entry is 10,000 rials.

Places to Stay & Eat
Hotel Iran (☎ 288 77, *Meidūn-é Sabze*) is the best place. It has clean singles/doubles with private bathrooms (some rooms have a shared toilet) for 20,000/27,000 rials, and a cafe. Kamil Nourzi, the manager, is a jolly chap who speaks some English and can

Buses depart from Tehrān's Southern Bus Terminal for southern destinations such as Esfahān.

MARTIN MOOS

Giddy Up!

MARTIN MOOS

Last petrol station before Pakistan!

MARTIN MOOS

Riding the chairlift at Darband

SIMON RICHMOND

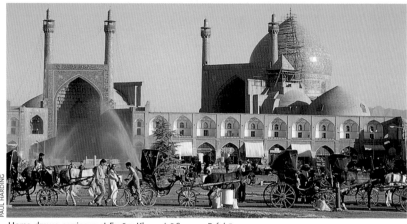

Horse-drawn carriages at Emām Khomeinī Square, Esfahān

Overland on two wheels

A cyclist takes a break in the Iranian desert.

Motorcycle riding, Iranian-style

arrange a taxi tour to the Castles of the Assassins.

Khaksar Hotel (☎ *242 39, Bolvār-é Āyatollāh Tāleghānī*), about 300m east of Sabze, has decent, no-frills rooms for 25,000/35,000 rials. The upmarket option is *Hotel Alborz* (☎/fax *266 31*), almost opposite the Khaksar, which has comfortable rooms with all mod-cons for US$25/35. It also has a small *coffeehouse*.

Restōrān-é Eghbalī (☎ *233 47, Bolvār-é Āyatollāh Tāleghānī*) about 200m east of Sabze is the best place in town – try the tasty *khōresht* (meat in a thick sauce with vegetables and chopped nuts with boiled rice). A meal here is around 15,000 rials. Farther down the road, just across Kheyābūn-é Khayyām, is the rather glitzy family restaurant *Yas* (☎ *228 53*), which does a full range of kabābs with all the trimmings. Expect to pay around 12,000 rials. A fine spot for breakfast, or just whiling away the afternoon, is the *teahouse* in the garden beside the Ghazvīn Museum. Fried eggs, bread and a pot of tea come to 2500 rials. There are also a couple of tempting *fresh juice shops* on Meidūn-é Shohadā, near the Emāmzādé-yé Hussein, that are worth a look.

Self-caterers will find plenty of fresh fruit and veg sellers in the bazaar and along Kheyābūn-é Shohadā.

Getting There & Away

Buses and shared taxis to Zanjān, Tehrān (3500 rials, two hours), Rasht (for Māsūlé) and Tabrīz leave from the bus station near Meidūn-é Darvāzeh in the south-eastern suburbs; shared taxis (12,000 rials per person) to Tehrān also leave from Meidūn-é Valī-yé Asr, east of the centre.

Ghazvīn's train station is 3km south of Meidūn-é Sabze; there are several departures a day to/from Tehrān, the journey taking around 1¾ hours and costing 5900 to 2300 rials, depending on the class. There are a couple of services to Tabrīz, too, departing at 8.20 and 9.06 pm nightly.

ALAMŪT & THE CASTLES OF THE ASSASSINS

Drive up into the foothills of the Alborz Mountains, 80km north of Ghazvīn, towards the area known as Alamūt and it's like entering another world. Secluded, timeless villages nestle in broad valleys beneath awe-inspiring snowcapped peaks. No wonder the Hashīshīyūn, an Ismaili cult founded in the 11th century by Hasan Sabbah, built their fortresses here. The cult's warriors carried out murders of political and religious figures, which is where we get the word assassin from. They were called assassins because of al-Sabbah's recruitment methods; candidates were doped on hashish, then transported to the mountain castles where they were further seduced in lush gardens by attentive maidens.

Little remains of the castles today, but what does is certainly worth making the effort to see. The most extensive ruins are at **Lambersan**, towering above the village of Rāzmīyān, while in the opposite direction, some 20km past the small town of Alamūt, is **Gāzor Khān**, perched in the most spectacular location. Steps have built up to this lair and there are ongoing excavations and magnificent views. This is also a marvellous trekking area, with many clear paths trod by villagers and their donkeys.

The ideal way to tour the area is by taxi; charter one for the day through Hotel Iran in Ghazvīn and it should cost around US$25. There is a village bus which takes five hours to reach Gāzor Khān leaving Ghazvīn daily around 1 pm and returning at 7 am. In the village, at the foot of the stronghold, is the spotless and charming *Hotel Koosaran* (☎ *0281-554 004*). This is basically a family home, which charges 8000 rials per person in shared rooms, sleeping on cotton mattresses on the floor. The owner speaks a little English, there's a lovely roof terrace and reasonably priced meals are available, if you call ahead. On the way to the castles, drop by the *Gastin Lar* teahouse, for refreshments and great views.

MĀSŪLÉ

On the Caspian Sea side of the Alborz Mountains is another charming village, Māsūlé. This is a favourite relaxation and hiking spot for many overland travellers, not to mention Iranian city dwellers in search of greenery and the cool climate at 1050m above sea level. The village is distinctive because of the pale cream painted and grey slate roofed houses which are layered on top of each other up the hillside. There are easy hiking trails nearby.

Māsūlé can be visited as a day trip from Rasht, another popular weekend retreat for Tehrānīs. From both Tehrān, 325km south-east, and Ghazvīn, 173km south-east, there are buses and shared taxis to Rasht. From Rasht to Māsūlé (56km) either charter a taxi for around 40,000 rials return, including waiting time, or take shared taxis to Fūman and then Māsūlé for around 5000 rials. If you fancy stopping over in the village, then the **Monfared Masooleh Hotel** (☎ 01864-3250) is the only option; singles/doubles cost US$20/30. It also has a stupendous rooftop **restaurant**.

Tehrān

☎ 021 • pop 12 million

Think of Tehrān as the LA of the Middle East, rather than an exotic crossroads steeped in Persian splendour (which it certainly isn't), and you'll just about have its measure. It's understandable why many overland travellers try to avoid this sprawling, freeway-dominated, chronically polluted and overcrowded capital, but if you do the same, you'll be missing out on some great museums, the country's best range of restaurants, pleasant parks and the buzzy atmosphere that, 20 years on from the revolution, is beginning to percolate. A couple of days here will give you a good insight into what is making modern Iran tick. Tehrān is also the obvious base for hiking or skiing trips into the Alborz Mountains, or for making a worthwhile diversion to the holy city of Mashhad.

HISTORY

As late as the 13th century, visitors were describing the unimportant village of Tehrān as a place of half-savages and highway robbers who lived in caves. It began its rise to prominence with the arrival of the Mongols in the late 12th century, who developed the village into a trading centre. This process continued for the next several hundred years, until in the 18th century European visitors were waxing lyrical about Tehrān's enchanting vineyards and gardens.

The Ghajar dynasty's Agha Muhammed Khān proclaimed Tehrān the capital when he was crowned as shāh of all Persia in 1789. At this time it had a population of

15,000. In the 1920s, as oil wealth started to accrue, the city was extensively modernised on a grid system and the population began to boom, leaping from less than 500,000 to 1.8 million in 1956 and then more than doubling to 4.5 million in the mid-1970s. Today, official figures put the population at around seven million, but the reality is that it is significantly higher.

ORIENTATION

Tehrān is vast, but thankfully about 90% of the streets that you're likely to use are marked in English. If you need landmarks, the Alborz Mountains are to the north, and the huge telephone office at Meidūn-é Emām Khomeinī dominates inner southern Tehrān, with the train and bus stations a farther 3km south. The Āzādī Monument marks the western end of town where you'll find the airport and Tehrān's Western Bus Terminal. Most of the longer north-south roads slope down as they head south, such as Kheyābūn-é Valī-yé Asr, which runs for more than 20km from Tajrīsh to the train station, and is claimed by Tehrānīs as the longest street in the world.

If you're using public transport, get to know the names and locations of the main squares as soon you can, and if you're staying a while, pick up the excellent *A Tourist Guide to Tehrān* map, published by Gita Shenasi (see Maps in the Facts for the Visitor chapter).

INFORMATION
Tourist Offices

There is no tourist office in Tehrān. The tourist information booths at the train station and both airport terminals have English-speaking staff but are no good for any general information.

Visa Extensions

It speaks volumes that the place you need to go for visa extensions is in the building occupied by the Disciplinary Force of the Islamic Republic of Iran, on Kheyābūn-é Khalantarī, just off Kheyābūn-é Nejātol-lāhī. Don't let this put you off; here the Department of Foreign Affairs (☎ 936 555) will issue extensions generally within 24 hours. The staff are friendly and speak English. It's open from 8 am to 1.30 pm daily, except Friday.

GREATER TEHRĀN

PLACES TO EAT
1 Jamshidiyé Park & Restaurants
6 Tamashagah Zaman
7 Sayad Mehdi
8 Elma Tajrīsh
17 Alighapū
25 Baghcheh

EMBASSIES
5 Ireland
9 Switzerland
10 Egypt & Yemen
13 Syria
14 Turkmenistan
16 Jordan

OTHER
2 Teahouses
3 Sa'd Ābād Garden Museum
4 Niyāvarān Palace Museum
11 International Trade Fair Ground

12 Enghelāb Sports Complex
15 Aux Livres Anciens Bookshop
18 ASP Shopping Centre; Noor Bookshop; Gipa Restaurant
19 Gāndi Shopping Centre; Monsoon; Gāndi Internet Café
20 Rezā Abbāsī Museum
21 Western Bus Terminal
22 Āzādī Monument
23 Mehrābād International Airport
24 Domestic Airport
26 Southern Bus Terminal

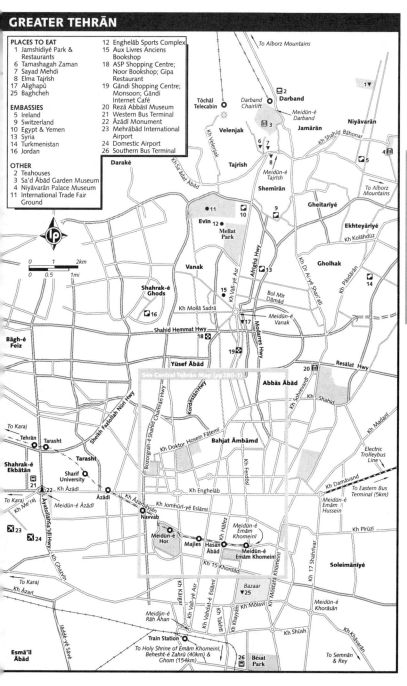

IRAN

Embassies & Consulates

It's a good idea to register with your embassy before heading off to the west of the country; this can be done over the telephone. If you need to arrange onward visas, you'll need to visit your own embassy first to secure a letter of recommendation. Most are open from around 8 or 9 am to 2 or 3 pm Sunday to Thursday; Islamic countries' missions, such as Pakistan, are also closed Thursday.

Armenia (☎ 6704 833) 1 Kheyābūn-é Razī
Australia (☎ 8724 457, fax 8720 484) 13 Kheyābūn-é 23, Kheyābūn-é Khalid Eslambuli
Azerbaijan (☎ 2215 191, fax 2217 504) 30 Kheyābūn-é Vatanpour, Kheyābūn-é Shahid Salehi
Canada (☎ 8732 623, fax 8733 202) 57 Kheyābūn-é Shahid Sarafraz
France (☎ 6706 005, fax 6706 544) 85 Kheyābūn-é Nōfl-Lōshātō
Georgia (☎ 2211 470, 2206 848) Kheyābūn-é Agha Bozorgāh
Germany (☎ 3114 111, fax 3119 883) 324 Kheyābūn-é Ferdōsī
India (☎ 8755 103, fax 8755 973) 46 Bolvār-é Mirdāmād
Ireland (☎ 2286 933, fax 2297 918) 8 Bombast Nahid, Kheyābūn-é Shahid Bāzdār (also called Kāmrāniyeh)
Italy (☎ 6496 955) Kheyābūn-é Nōfl Lōshātō
Japan (☎ 8713 396, fax 8713 515) Kheyābūn-é Ahmad-é Ghosavr
Netherlands (☎ 2567 005) 1st East Lane, Kheyābūn-é Kamasale
New Zealand (☎ 8757 052, fax 8757 056) 57 Kheyābūn-é Javad Sarafraz
Pakistan (☎ 934 332, fax 935 154) 1 Kheyābūn-é Ahmad Eitemad Zadeo, Jamshid Abad Shomali
Russia (☎ 6701 676) Kheyābūn-é Nōfl Lōshātō
Turkey (☎ 3115 299, fax 3117 928) 314 Kheyābūn-é Ferdōsī
Turkmenistan (☎ 2542 178, fax 2580 432) 39 Kheyābūn-é 5th Golestān
UK (☎ 6705 011, fax 6710 761) 143 Kheyābūn-é Ferdōsī
USA (☎ 8782 964, fax 8773 265) US Interests Section in the Swiss embassy, 59 Kheyābūn-é West Farzan

Money

Most of the banks along Kheyābūn-é Ferdōsī and around Meidūn-é Ferdōsī change money. The best is Bank Melli on Kheyābūn-é Ferdōsī; it also changes travellers cheques and gives cash advances on Visa and MasterCard, but don't expect the service to be speedy.

The better places to change money are the official money exchange offices along northern Kheyābūn-é Ferdōsī. Here and on Kheyābūn-é Jomhūrī-yé Eslāmi you'll constantly be approached by black marketeers, many literally waving cash in your face. Changing money with these guys *is* a risk; check exactly what exchange rate you'll be getting, minus any commission charges, and do the actual deal somewhere away from the street.

Post & Communications

If you're based in southern Tehrān, the most convenient post office (which has a poste restante) and telephone office are close by Meidūn-é Emām Khomeinī. The entrance to the telephone office is on the Kheyābūn-é Lālezār side of the square. Other post offices and telephone offices are located around major squares in the city.

Email & Internet Access Internet cafes are popping up all over Tehrān, and it's a sign of the times that the city's first now proudly flaunts itself with a large English sign, rather than hiding, as it once did, behind the front of an office furniture shop. Rahe Ayandeh or Future Way (☎ 8865 423, ⓔ cybercafe @neda.net), 84 Bolvār-é Keshāvarz, is still one of the most reliable places to surf the Internet, with cluey, English-speaking staff and plenty of reasonably speedy machines. Charges are 25,000 rials per hour (including one free drink) and it's open from 9 am to 8 pm daily, except Friday.

Slightly cheaper (20,000 rials per hour), but with only one machine is Online Internet (☎ 6497 508), on the 4th floor of Reza Passage, on Kheyābūn-é Valī-yé Asr. Hotel Khayyam, just off Kheyābūn-é Amīr Kabīr, also has slow Internet facilities and charges 20,000 rials per hour.

In the trendy hangout Gāndi Shopping Centre, on Kheyābūn-é Gāndi in the north of the city, is, naturally enough, the Gāndi Internet Cafe (☎/fax 8791 959). It charges 25,000 rials per hour, with a minimum charge of 5000 rials and rather pricey drinks.

Travel Agencies

One thing Tehrān isn't short of is travel agencies. Lachine Seyr (☎ 8727 561), 202 Bolvār-é Keshāvarz, has friendly English-speaking staff. We also received good service at Bon Tour (☎ 8780 915), 20 Kheyābūn-é Gāndi.

Agents specialising in tours and who can also help secure visas include:

Caravan Sahra Co (☎ 833 622, fax 833 623, ⓔ caravan@caravansahra.com)
Kheyābūn-é Ghaemmagham-é Farahani 29
Web site: www.carvansahra.com
Iran Tours Corporation (☎ 2255 440, fax 2254 330, ⓔ itcorp@sama.dpi.net.ir) 242 Kheyābūn-é East Vahid Dastgerdi
Iran Way Travel Agency (☎ 439 729, fax 246 926, ⓔ ftnamin@mail.dci.co.ir) Kheyābūn-é Navabi 17

Bookshops & Publications

As you'd imagine, Iran is not overflowing with opportunities to buy English-language books. However, in Tehrān you'll find a reasonable selection of old and generally uncontroversial titles at Gulestan on Kheyābūn-é Manūcherhī and the Ferdōsī Bookshop on Kheyābūn-é Ferdōsī.

One of the classiest selections can be found at Noor Bookshop (☎ 8055 319), Unit 3, ASP Building, where Bozorgrāh-é Shahid Hemmat meets Bozorgrāh-é Kordestān. For books in French, German and English try Aux Livres Anciens (☎ 8776 568), 28 Shahid Khoddāmi, near Meidūn-é Vanak; it's best to call all these places before setting off. The National Museum of Iran also has a decent range of tourist-oriented books.

For recent editions of *Time*, *Newsweek*, *National Geographic* and other overseas magazines, try the kiosk outside the Hotel Naderi, Kheyābūn-é Jomhuri-yé Eslāmi.

Medical Services

Standards of medical care in Tehrān are high and you shouldn't have problems finding a reliable, foreign-language speaking doctor should you need one. Clean, reputable hospitals include:

Emām Khomeinī Hospital	☎ 9380 819
Pārs Hospital	☎ 6500 519
Tehrān Clinic	☎ 8728 113

Your hotel or embassy should also be able to recommend a doctor and hospital.

Emergency

The following emergency numbers are available, however don't expect anyone to speak English. It might be preferable to call your embassy.

Emergency assistance line	☎ 198
Police	☎ 129

THINGS TO SEE & DO

Tehrān is definitely not a city made for walking and its main sites are so spread out that tackling them is a mammoth task that requires several shared-taxi journeys and plenty of stamina. If you're pressed for time and/or cash we recommend that you restrict your visits to the National Museum of Iran and the Islamic Arts Museum, either the Carpet or the National Jewels Museum, the bazaar, the gardens of the Golestān Palace or recreation areas such as the parks, Shahr, Lālé and Jamshidyeh. Forget the mosques – there are much better mosques in other cities along the route. Also allow time to escape into the foothills of the Alborz Mountains at Darband or Tōchāl – see the Around Tehrān section.

National Museum of Iran & Islamic Arts Museum

These neighbouring institutions are covered on the same ticket, making this the city's best-value museum. The excellent, but unimaginatively displayed, archaeological collection at the National Museum includes some choice pieces from Persepolis and Shūsh (Susa). Also look out for the eerily preserved Salt Man (with beard still clinging to the skull), the body of a 3rd- or 4th-century AD miner discovered near Zanjān.

The Islamic Arts Museum, sometimes called the Museum of the Islamic Period, is even better – two floors of thoughtfully displayed examples of carpets, textiles, ceramics, pottery, wood and metalwork, and excellent examples of tiles and stucco work from various mosques throughout the country. The calligraphy and miniatures are particularly fine. This is where you'll also find a good book and souvenir shop.

The museums are located just off Kheyābūn-é Emām Khomeinī and are open from 9 am to 6 pm daily, except Monday. Entrance is 30,000 rials.

Carpet Museum

Not to be missed by anyone who has even the slightest interest in Persian carpets, kilims

IRAN

and rugs. Scores of woollen and silk masterpieces dating from the 16th century to the present, hang in the spacious gallery. You can see prime examples of styles from major carpet-making centres including Esfahān, Kāshān, Kermān, Kordestān and Tabrīz. There's a small bookshop, cafe and a good library with several English reference books – handy for mugging up before scouring the bazaars. The museum is open from 9 am to 5 pm daily, except Monday. Entrance is 20,000 rials.

A visit here can be combined also with a stroll through the adjacent Lālé Park and the **Tehrān Museum of Contemporary Art**, which contains some intriguing works by modern Iranian artists, as well as temporary exhibitions featuring Iranian and foreign photographers and calligraphers. It's open from 9 am to 6 pm daily, except Friday when it's open from 2 to 6 pm. Entry is 2000 rials.

National Jewels Museum

An eye-popping display of the wealth of the shāhs, deep in the Fort Knox-like vaults of Iran's Central Bank. First up is the famous Peacock Throne, now, for all its dazzle, looking a bit poorly – one leg is patched up with brown tape. Other star attractions sit in the middle of the main darkened display hall, including the matchbox-sized 182 carat Daryā-yé Nūr (Sea of Light) pink diamond, and a globe plastered with 51,366 precious stones. Look out also for the Samarian Spinel, a red stone of 500 carats said to have hung around the neck of the biblical Golden Calf.

The museum is on Kheyābūn-é Ferdōsī and opening hours are limited to 2 to 4.30 pm Saturday to Tuesday, with entry 30,000 rials.

Glass & Ceramics Museum

Not far from the National Jewels Museum, on Kheyābūn-é Sī Tir, this restrained, elegant collection of glass and ceramics is housed in an interesting Ghajar period (1779–1921), building surrounded by a small, peaceful **garden**. Each piece in the museum is labelled in English and there are good explanations in English about, for example, Persian traditions of glass blowing. There's also a small bookshop. It's open from 9 am to 5 pm daily, except Monday, and entrance is 20,000 rials.

Golestān Palace & Gardens

This complex, next to the Tehrān Bāzār, has seven separate museums and galleries. With each one requiring a 10,000 rials ticket, you need to be choosy about which bits you see. The tranquil surrounding gardens are free and provide a vantage point from which you can admire the tiled palace buildings, some of which date from the 18th century and have been recently restored. There's also a nicely decorated, if somewhat pricey, **teahouse**.

Going in a clockwise direction from the entrance gate, the first building – the **audience hall** for the shāh – is one of the best. There are beautiful wall paintings in a side gallery as well as an impressive green marble throne. The **art gallery** has some fine paintings by local artists including the late 19th-century master Kamal al-Molk. It is more interesting than the **Hozkhane** where European artworks and presents from Victorian monarchs are stored. The **Shams al-Emāra**, has a dazzling mirror-tiled interior and some fine works of calligraphy. The **Ethnographical Museum** is livened up by some kitsch wax dummies wearing ethnic costumes and holding traditional cooking implements and musical instruments. The complex is open from 9 am to 3 pm daily, except Sunday and Thursday.

Sa'd Ābād Garden Museum

At the opposite end of town from the Golestān Palace lies what used to be the shāh's summer residence. Again there are several small museums within the complex, including the European-style **National Palace (White) Museum**, the last shāh's palace (with 54 rooms); the interesting **Military Museum**, with a collection of armoury; the enormous **Green (Shahvand) Palace**, with its collection of carpets, furniture and other oddments; and the **Museum of Fine Arts**, with some charming Persian oil paintings.

The grounds are open from 8 am to 5 pm daily but the museums have different opening times and separate entrance fees. A free minibus from the gates runs around the museums. To get to the gardens take a taxi from Meidūn-é Tajrīsh, or walk about 1.5km from the square, along Kheyābūn-é Shahīd Ja'afarī.

Rezā Abbāsī Museum

If you have time, this less-visited museum contains fine examples of Islamic painting and calligraphy from ancient Qurans, and galleries with delicate pottery and exquisite jewellery from several dynasties. It's set well apart from the pack, at the northern end of Kheyābūn-é Dr Ali-yé Shari'ati, and is not signed in English. Opening hours are from 9 am to 1 pm and 2 to 6 pm daily, except Tuesday. Entry is 20,000 rials.

Parks

It won't take you long to appreciate why Iranians love gardens and parks, especially in Tehrān, where they provide a refuge from the city's noise and pollution. For the visitor, the parks are also a window on modern Iranian manners and culture; here you'll see shyly courting couples, families enjoying picnics, even rollerbladers! The atmosphere in the northern Tehrān parks, where the middle-class and wealthy live, is notably relaxed.

Near Meidūn-é Emām Khomeinī, **Shahr Park** is well worth a stroll. It includes pleasant fountains, a small lake on which you can skate in winter, and an excellent teahouse (see Places to Eat). In the middle of town **Lālé Park** is also a favourite, particularly with students from nearby Tehrān University. There are some craft kiosks here. Moving farther north, **Sā'ī Park** has a pleasant atmosphere especially at dusk when many people visit. **Mellat Park,** alongside the northern reaches of Kheyābūn-é Valī-yé Asr, is one of the largest recreation areas with a central lake with pedalos and a sports complex.

The prettiest park of all is **Jamshidiyé**, north of Tajrīsh in the foothills of the Alborz Mountains. Expert landscaping has combined footpaths, trickling streams and rockeries with the boulders of the hills to seamless effect. The paths climb up to three restaurants (see Places to Eat), all with great views of the city; come at night to experience the cool breeze and see Tehrān laid out below like a diamond-studded carpet.

Other Attractions

Surprisingly, Tehrān has few mosques worth visiting. A short walk north-east of Meidūn-é Emām Khomeinī, the **Madrasé va Masjed-é Sepahsālār** is the city's largest and most important mosque and seminary.

It was built between 1878 and 1890, after the golden age of Persian architecture, so it's ungainly and gaudy, but the eight minarets are impressive, and the poetry, inscribed in several ancient scripts in the tiling, is famous.

If you're visiting the **bazaar**, which is an atmospheric place to wander whether you want to shop or not, then drop by the busy **Masjed-é Emām Khomeinī**. The place to catch Friday prayers is actually not a mosque but **Tehrān University**, the grounds of which you're free to wander any day; naturally it's a good place to meet students, many of whom will want to speak English with you.

Arriving in Tehrān from the west, you won't miss the giant upturned Y-shaped **Āzādī Monument**, marooned in traffic-isolated Meidūn-é Āzādī. Built in 1971 to commemorate the 2500th anniversary of the Persian Empire, the tower includes a missable museum and a viewing platform from where there's a bird's-eye perspective of the mad traffic below.

Finally, for its notoriety, you may want to wander by the old US embassy, on Kheyābūn-é Āyatollāh Tāleghāni, now known as the **US Den of Espionage**. Revolutionary Guards are trained here and the compound is closed to visitors, but there are fascinating, anti-American **murals** on the southern walls.

PLACES TO STAY – BUDGET

For a couple of real cheapies, head to the bazaar area. *Shams Hotel*, along Marv Alley, off Kheyābūn-é Nāser Khosrō, has bare cells around a central courtyard. The manager's friendly and charges 10,000 rials per person. *Hotel Pirooz* (☎ 3901 366, *Kheyābūn-é 15 Khordād*) is also very basic and costs 12,000 rials; ask for the top-floor rooms at the back – they have excellent city and mountain views. Neither hotel has a shower.

The main area for budget accommodation, Meidūn-é Emām Khomeinī, is also home to the city's motor spare parts bazaar; it's a noisy, grubby, chaotic place that becomes a ghost town at night, much like the rest of downtown Tehrān. We list some of the better places – there are more along Kheyābūn-é Amīr Kabīr and Kheyābūn-é Lālezār. *Farvadin Guest House* (☎ 3912 777, *654 Meidūn-é Emām Khomeinī*) has its entrance on Kheyābūn-é Ferdōsī. The cheapest

IRAN

CENTRAL TEHRĀN

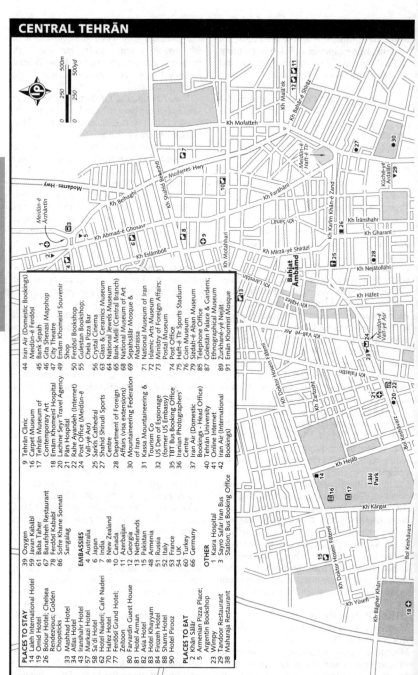

PLACES TO STAY
14 Laleh International Hotel
19 Omid Hotel
26 Bolour Hotel; Chelsea
   Rendezvous; Golden
   Chopsticks
33 Mashhad Hotel
34 Atlas Hotel
43 Iranshahr Hotel
57 Markazi Hotel
58 Sa'di Hotel
62 Hotel Naderi; Cafe Naderi
70 Hafez Hotel
77 Ferdōsi Grand Hotel;
   Zeitoon
80 Farvardin Guest House
81 Hotel Arman
82 Asia Hotel
83 Hotel Khayyam
84 Firozeh Hotel
88 Shams Hotel
90 Hotel Pirooz

PLACES TO EAT
2 Khān Sālār
5 Armenian Pizza Place;
   Argentin Bookshop
23 Wimpy
29 Tandoor Restaurant
38 Maharaja Restaurant
39 Oxygen
59 Javan Kababi
61 Baba Taher
67 Banafsheh Restaurant
78 Ferdōsi Kababi
86 Sofre Khane Sonnati
   Sangalaj

EMBASSIES
4 Australia
6 Japan
7 India
8 New Zealand
10 Canada
11 Azerbaijan
12 Georgia
13 Netherlands
15 Pakistan
48 Armenia
51 Russia
52 Italy
53 France
54 UK
60 Turkey
66 Germany

OTHER
3 Kasra Hospital
3 Sayro Safar Iran Bus
   Station; Bus Booking Office
9 Tehrān Clinic
16 Carpet Museum
17 Tehrān Museum of
   Contemporary Art
18 Emām Khomeini Hospital
20 Lachine Seyr Travel Agency
21 Pārs Hospital
22 Rahe Ayandeh (Internet)
24 Post Office (Meidūn-é
   Valī-yé Asr)
25 Sarkīs Cathedral
27 Shahid Shirudi Sports
   Centre
28 Department of Foreign
   Affairs (visa extensions)
30 Mountaineering Federation
   of Iran
31 Kassa Mountaineering &
   Tourism Co
32 US Den of Espionage
   (former US Embassy)
35 TBT Bus Booking Office
36 Iranian Photographers'
   Centre
37 Iran Air (Domestic
   Bookings) – Head Office
40 Tehrān University
41 Online Internet
42 Iran Air (International
   Bookings)
44 Iran Air (Domestic Bookings)
   Meidūn-é Ferdōsi
45 Bank Sepah
46 Gita Shenasi Mapshop
47 City Theatre
49 Emām Khomeini Souvenir
   Shop
50 Ferdōsi Bookshop
55 Gulestan Bookshop;
   Chela Pizza Bar
56 Crystal Cinema
63 Glass & Ceramics Museum
64 National Jewels Museum
65 Bank Melli (Central Branch)
68 National Museum of Art
69 Sepahsālār Mosque &
   Madrassa
71 National Museum of Iran
72 Islamic Arts Museum
73 Ministry of Foreign Affairs;
   Postal Museum
74 Post Office
75 Haft-é Tīr Sports Stadium
76 Coin Museum
79 Sizdah-é Aban Museum
85 Telephone Office
87 Golestān Palace & Gardens;
   Ethnographical Museum
89 Zurkhané-yé Nejāt
91 Emān Khomini Mosque

CENTRAL TEHRĀN

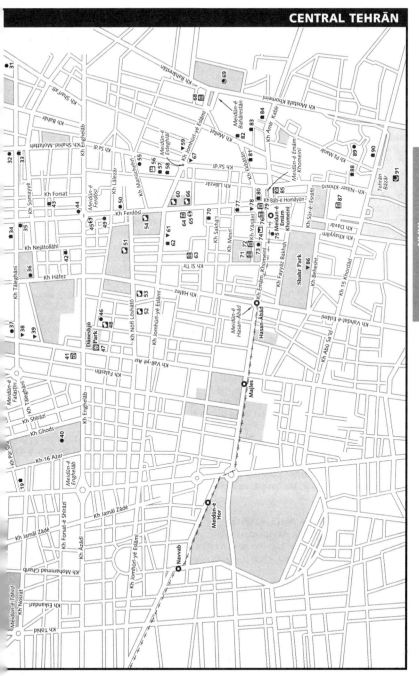

rooms – 35,000/50,000 rials for a single/double – have shared bathrooms.

Better is *Hotel Arman (☎ 3112 323, Kheyābūn-é Ekbātān)*, which has clean rooms, with private bathroom and air-con, for a reasonable US$10/12 – and staff will probably want US dollars. It's just off the main road, and fairly quiet.

Asia Hotel (☎ 3118 551, Kheyābūn-é Mellat) is central, clean and newly decorated, and good value for 25,000/50,000 rials. It has been recommended by several readers, and staff are friendly. Akbar, the manager, speaks English.

Also worth a look is *Firozeh Hotel (☎ 3113 487, Dolat Abadi Alley)*, just off Kheyābūn-é Amīr Kabīr. The compact, neat rooms all have private bathrooms for 50,000/60,000 rials.

Moving away from the din of the square, the cheapest rooms at the friendly *Hafez Hotel (☎ 6709 063, Kūché-yé Bank)* are 40,000 rials, but very small. Better to go for the larger ones for 60,000 rials. Showers are communal and not always clean.

One of our favourites, in an excellent location, is *Hotel Naderi (☎ 6701 872, fax 6720 791, Kheyābūn-é Jomhūrī-yé Eslāmī)*. For US$10 a night per person you get spacious rooms, full of character with private large bathrooms; ask for a room overlooking the garden at the back. Next door is the happening Cafe Naderi (see Places to Eat).

Also in a quieter central location is *Sa'di Hotel (☎ 3113 047, fax 3930 422, 402 Kheyābūn-é Lālezār)*. It's clean, pleasant and has a cafe. Rooms are good value at 35,000/50,000 rials and in better nick than at the less appealing *Markazi Hotel (☎/fax 3914 798)* up the road, which charges the same.

PLACES TO STAY – MID-RANGE

At some of these hotels payment is expected in US dollars. You may be able to negotiate lower rates at times when it's not too busy.

Sneaking into this category, but worth the extra money, is *Hotel Khayyam (☎ 3113 757, fax 3911 497, e hotelkhayyam@hotmail.com, Kheyābūn-é Amīr Kabīr)*. Off the main road, and therefore quiet, it has parking. The single rooms are small, but are as nicely furnished as the rest. For a single without/with bathroom it's US$15/25 and a double is US$25/35. There's also a decent *restaurant* and Internet facilities.

Ferdōsī Grand Hotel (☎ 6719 991, fax 6711 449, 24 Kheyābūn-é Mesrī) is stylish and central, and the service is good. Singles/doubles cost US$30/45, including breakfast. Charging the same, but a little less grand, is *Iranshahr Hotel (☎ 8846 650, fax 8821 924, e iranshahr@pegah.net, 75 Kheyābūn-é Īrāshahr)*. Apart from other mod cons, the rooms also have a small kitchen area.

Atlas Hotel (☎ 8800 408, fax 8800 407, e atlas@mavara.com, 206 Kheyābūn-é Tāleghānī) costs US$25/35. The rooms are quiet and have huge baths, and some have views over a pleasant courtyard.

Bolour Hotel (☎ 8829 881, 191 Kheyābūn-é Gharanī) has cosy rooms, the staff are friendly and it has two good *restaurants*. Rooms cost US$30/40, including breakfast.

Near the US Den of Espionage, *Mashhad Hotel (☎ 8825 145, fax 8822 681, 190 Kheyābūn-é Shahīd Mofatteh)* has large, nicely furnished rooms, for US$25/40. It's a favourite of tour groups and has a decent restaurant.

Within walking distance from Lālé Park, *Omid Hotel (☎/fax 6414 564, Kheyābūn-é East Nosrat)*, just off Kheyābūn-é Kārgar, has friendly staff, a quiet location and large modern rooms for US$35/40, including breakfast.

PLACES TO EAT

Take advantage of the relatively wide variety of cuisines available in Tehrān; you won't find as good a selection elsewhere. Many upmarket restaurants are closed on Friday; it's best to check opening times by phone first.

Restaurants

The traditional teahouses (see Teahouses & Cafes following) all serve food and are excellent options for a lunch of ābgūsht and possibly other dishes. If you're looking for a wider range of Iranian cuisine, then head to the ornately decorated, atmospheric *Alighapū (☎ 8777 803, 55 Kheyābūn-é Gāndi)*, open daily from 7.30 pm. A meal will cost around 30,000 rials and there's a salad bar for 6000 rials.

Jamshidiyé Park has three restaurants; the first is supposed to be *Azerbaijan/Turkish*, the second – the best – *Kurdish*, the third, at the very top of the hill, **Turkoman**. In reality, it's kabābs all the way with the possibility of khōresht. The views and atmosphere make up for the food. While in the north of the city also consider **Tamashagah Zaman**, near the Sa'd Ābād Garden Museum, a very fancy pizza and pasta restaurant in a mansion like a wedding cake that also houses a clock museum.

For Indian cuisine try the excellent **Tandoor Restaurant** (☎ 8825 705, *Kūché-yé Ardalān*) in the Hotel Tehrān Sara, popular with expats. **Maharaja Restaurant** (☎ 6462 765, *Kheyābūn-é Valī-yé Asr*) in the Jahan Hotel also has tasty curries from about 15,000 rials.

Among hotel restaurants, reliable options include Ferdōsī Grand Hotel, which does a bargain buffet at lunch and dinner at its **Zeitoon** restaurant for 20,000 rials. Bolour Hotel has the **Chelsea Rendezvous** on the 6th floor serving Iranian and Western food, and the small Chinese-Korean **Golden Chopsticks** on the 1st floor. **Omid Hotel** is very good, with dishes from 10,000 rials, and excellent service.

For contemporary Iranian and oriental dishes try the hip **Monsoon** (☎ 8791 982) in the Gāndi Shopping Centre or the stylish **Gipa** (☎ 8052 087, *53 ASP Shopping Centre*) beside Bozorgrāh-é Kordestān, which specialises in Chinese dishes.

Teahouses & Cafes

Traditional teahouses, complete with polychrome tiles, qalyans and carpeted sitting platforms, are dotted all over the city. Generally open from 9 am to 9 pm daily they are excellent places for relaxing in the evening as well as for snacks and lunch.

The spacious **Sofre Khane Sonnati Sangalag**, in Shahr Park, tastefully decorated with Persian knick-knacks, is a favourite with tour groups. While songbirds twitter in cages, sip on a pot of tea for 3000 rials or eat ābgusht for 12,000 rials. There's sometimes live traditional music here.

Baba Taher, on Kheyābūn-é Jomhūrī-yé Eslāmī, near the Hotel Naderi, is also a good choice, with outdoor seating and occasional live music. Ābgūsht or pizza is served for lunch and the tea is served with a few dates.

Join the market traders for *dīzi* (ābgūsht) at **Baghcheh** at the southern end of the bazaar on Hesam-al Lashkar, an excellent spot for a break if you're exploring this area. The courtyard has shaded platforms and, incongruously, wall paintings of what look like Norse gods. It's only open for lunch and closed Friday. Also near the bazaar, in the Golestān Palace, is a fancy, but pricey *teahouse*.

Near Meidūn-é Ārzhāntīn, **Khān Sālār** (*Kūché-yé Alvānd*), opposite the Kasra Hospital, has some traditionally inspired surroundings, though the food is not exceptional.

A perennial favourite with customers ranging from Tehrān's gilded youth to their gossiping grandparents is the **Cafe Naderi** , Kheyābūn-é Jomhūrī-yé Eslāmī. There's a restaurant, too, but it's the cafe, serving good cakes and ice cream, that lures the crowds. Sadly, the adjoining garden stands unused (there's nothing to stop you taking your drink out there, but you'll miss the buzz inside). It's a fine spot for breakfast, but closed at night.

You can also slum it with the rich kids at several trendy cafes in the **Gāndi Shopping Centre**. And, even if you're not up for walking, don't miss out on the fine teahouses and restaurants of Darband – see the Around Tehrān section.

Fast Food

There are dozens of interchangeable *kabābīs* between Meidūn-é Emām Khomeinī and Kheyābūn-é Jomhūrī-yé Eslāmī. **Ferdōsī Kabābī**, downstairs at the southern end of Kheyābūn-é Ferdōsī, is a good choice. Some staff speak English, and a full chicken kabāb meal costs about 15,000 rials.

With a touch more class, **Javan Kabābī** (*Kheyābūn-é Saf*), just off Jomhūrī-yé Eslāmī, is an old favourite. A *chelō kabāb* (a kabāb, usually of lamb or mutton, with boiled rice) is 21,000 rials, and there's a khōresht deal at lunch for 7000 rials. Nearby is **Banafsheh**, a popular fast-food joint with good pizzas for 14,000 rials, burgers for 7000 rials and chips for 35,000 rials.

Along Kheyābūn-é Valī-yé Asr you'll also find many cheap eating options. **Oxygen**, just south of Kheyābūn-é Tāleghānī, is a big fast-food operation which is expanding to include the neighbouring cake and coffee shops. It does the usual range of pizzas and burgers.

IRAN

More Western-style fast food is available in the classy upper reaches of Valī-yé Asr, around Meidūn-é Tajrīsh. *Elma Tajrīsh Restaurant* serves scrumptious pizzas, plus salad and drink, for about 15,000 rials. For dessert, walk back down Kheyābūn-é Valī-yé Asr to *Sayad Mehdi*, which serves excellent *fālūdé* (sugar vermicelli in lime juice) and saffron ice cream.

Armenian Pizza Place (Meidūn-é Ārzhāntīn) is also worth a visit and is convenient if you're catching a bus from the Sayro Safar bus station opposite.

For nostalgia freaks, the *Wimpy*, Meidūn-é Valī-yé Asr, referred to in the very first Lonely Planet guidebook, *Across Asia on the Cheap,* is still dishing out Iranian-style burgers. Look for it near the Kīsh Shopping Centre.

Self-Catering
Self-caterers should head to the bazaar area or to the food shops along Kheyābūn-é Jomhūrī-yé Eslāmī. An evening picnic in one of the parks is certainly worth organising.

ENTERTAINMENT
If you're looking for evening entertainment, the best places to head for are the parks – see Parks earlier in this chapter. Also join the locals window shopping along the main shopping streets, such as Valī-yé Asr, or the Petticoat Lane-like Kheyābūn-é Manūchehrī.

Tehrān has plenty of cinemas, but they predominantly show (often violent) Iranian films – go to witness a slice of Iranian life, not for the quality of the film. If you're desperate for a Western movie, heavily censored and dubbed versions are screened at the *Crystal Cinema*, Kheyābūn-é Lālezār.

One of the few inner-city *theatres* that features cultural events and traditional performances where foreigners are welcome is the *City Theatre*. The English-language newspapers normally advertise upcoming events.

To catch practice sessions of the fitness program *zurkhané*, search out the *Zurkhané-yé Nejāt*, east of Kheyābūn-é Pā Manār, and north of the bazaar.

SHOPPING
Not nearly as architecturally impressive as its counterparts in Esfahān, Tabrīz and Shīrāz, Tehrān Bāzār is still a fascinating place. If you can't buy something here, you probably can't buy it anywhere. It's a good place for haggling over carpets, textiles and souvenirs such as pottery and glass. You're also likely to get hopelessly lost. The main entrances are along Kheyābūn-é 15 Khordād.

Kheyābūn-é Ferdōsī is also excellent for shopping, particularly around the intersection with Kheyābūn-é Manūchehrī, where there are many antique and curio shops and people selling knick-knacks on the street.

GETTING THERE & AWAY
Bypassing Tehrān – by, say, a long direct bus service from Tabrīz to Esfahān – is possible. But since the capital is the hub for the vast majority of buses, and all train and air services, you're almost certain to find yourself passing through on an overland trip either east or west. With many Iranians also looking to escape the city, it pays to book any onward journey as soon as you arrive to be sure of getting the ticket you want.

Air
Iran Air flies daily between Tehrān and most cities and larger towns in Iran. Services are less frequent on the other smaller airlines, such as Iran Asseman and Kīsh Airlines. Both domestic and international flights leave from Mehrābād International Airport near Meidūn-é Āzādī. A taxi between here and Kheyābūn-é Ferdōsī is around 15,000 rials.

Most international airline offices (and many travel agencies) are along, or very near, Kheyābūn-é Nejātollāhī, but it's often easier to purchase a ticket on a domestic flight at a reputable travel agency.

Iran Air The head office for international flights (☎ 9112 591, 6001 191 reservations) is on Kheyābūn-é Nejātollāhī. The main office for domestic flights (☎ 9112 650 reservations) is on Kheyābūn-é Tāleghānī. A smaller office (☎ 8826 532) on Meidūn-é Ferdōsī handles domestic flights only.

Iran Asseman (☎ 8895 567) Kheyābūn-é Nejātollāhī. At the crossing with Kheyābūn-é Somayyé.

Bus
There are four bus stations. You can pre-book tickets at the TBT office on Kheyābūn-é Gharanī, or at The Union of Countrys Travelling Companies at the Sayro Safar Iran bus station.

Carpet Bagging in Iran

The best range of carpets and rugs – but not the cheapest prices – can be found in the bazaars in Tehrān, Esfahān, Tabrīz and Shīrāz. In many cases the name of a carpet or rug indicates where it is made, or from where the design first originated.

If you have the time and interest, you may wish to hunt down something special from the following regions and cities:

Āzarbāyjān
The *heriz* and *mehriban* carpets found near the Azerbaijan border have bold designs. They often feature hunting scenes and tales from Ferdōsī's poem *Shah-nama*, usually on a mud-coloured background, with bizarre fringes.

Ghom (Qom)
In the holy city of Ghom, you are more likely to see *gul-i-bulbul* carpets, made from goat wool, and featuring a variety of designs with birds and flowers. The best are gorgeous, thin and strong, but these days many carpets are mass produced for pilgrims.

Kermān
Kermān province is renowned for its soft and, often, very large carpets. They are very colourful, often containing shades of green (but not too much, as green is sacred to Islam), and usually made from locally grown cotton. Designs feature local flowers, nuts and fruit, as well portraits of famous Iranians and foreigners.

Kordestān
The centre for production, and sale, of carpets and rugs made by Kurds in western Iran is the capital, Sanandaj, and also Bījār where particularly hard-wearing rugs are made.

Lorestān
The Lors make *gabbeh*, very thick, vividly coloured carpets and rugs with sometimes quite abstract designs that nonetheless often tell a story about local life.

For more information about carpets and rugs, visit the annual Grand Persian Carpet Exhibition & Conference in Tehrān, usually held in August, or contact the Export Promotion Center of Iran (☎ 212 896, fax 2042 858), PO Box 1148, Tajrīsh, Tehrān, which organises the carpet fair.

There's an exquisite collection in the Carpet Museum in Tehrān (plus an extensive library with many books in English). The *Iran Carpet* map, available at the Gita Shenasi map shop in Tehrān, indicates the location of carpet weaving centres, but is of little additional use.

Buying Tips
You might be able to pick up a bargain in Iran but dealers in Western countries often sell Persian carpets for little more than you'd pay in Iran (plus postage), and you're less likely to be ripped off by your local warehouse dealer than a savvy Iranian bazaar merchant. Unless you're an expert, never buy a carpet as an investment.

Before buying anything, lay the carpet on the floor and check for any bumps or imperfections. Small bumps will usually flatten out with wear, but large bumps will remain. To check that a carpet is handmade, turn it over. The pattern will be distinct on the underside – the more distinct, the better the quality.

Posting a carpet/rug home adds about 33% to the cost. Currently, each foreigner can take out of Iran (by air, land or sea) one Persian carpet or two small Persian rugs totalling 12 sq metres. However, one traveller recently needed special permission from the post office in Tehrān to post a carpet home, so check the regulations (with the post office and not the carpet salesman!) before forking out any money.

The Western Bus Terminal, near Meidūn-é Āzādī, caters for all places west of Tehrān, including Ghazvīn (3500 rials, 2½ hours) and Tabrīz (14,000 rials or 30,000 rials by Volvo, nine hours) and anywhere along the Caspian Sea west of, and including, Chālūs. To get to the terminal, take a shared taxi, or if you haven't not got much luggage, try the new underground train; Tehrān station, around 1km north of the Āzādī Monument, is the closest.

The Southern Bus Terminal has services to the south and south-east of Iran, including Ghom (Qom; 2000 rials, 1½ hours), Kāshān (5000 rials or 9000 rials by Volvo, 2½ hours), Esfahān (11,000 rials or 20,000 by Volvo, seven hours) and Shīrāz (21,000 rials, 16 hours). Take a shared taxi heading south from the south-western corner of Meidūn-é Emām Khomeinī.

The small Eastern Bus Terminal serves destinations to the east; it's most useful if you're heading towards Kūh-é Ďamāvand. Take a shared taxi to Meidūn-é Emām Hussein, then another taxi to the station and hop on the electric trolleybus.

The private station run by Sayro Safar Iran at Meidūn-é Ārzhāntīn has buses to Esfahān, Kermān (27,000 rials, 18 hours), Mashhad (21,000 rials, 14 hours), Rasht (5000 rials, six hours), Shīrāz, and Yazd (15,000 rials, 10 hours).

Train

All train services around the country start and finish at the impressive train station in southern Tehrān. Destinations, and times of arrivals and departures, are helpfully listed in English on a huge board at the entrance, and the knowledgeable staff at the information booth (☎ 5122 556) speak English.

There are services between Tehrān and Bandar-é Abbās (56,600 rials, 1st class only, daily), Esfahān (16,900, 1st class; 10,000 rials, 2nd class; 1 and 8 pm, daily), Ghazvīn (5900 rials, 1st class; 2300 rials, 2nd class; five daily) Ghom (31,000 rials, 1st class; 12,000 rials, 2nd class; three daily), Kāshān (8000 rials, 1st class; 5000 rials, 2nd class; daily), Kermān (36,000 rials, 1st class; 20,000 rials, 2nd class; 6.25pm, Monday, Wednesday and Friday), Mashhad (34,000 rials, 1st class; 18,000 rials, 2nd class; up to nine daily), Tabrīz (31,000 rials, 1st class; 26,500 rials, 2nd

class; twice daily) and Yazd (29,000 rials, 1st class only; twice daily).

If you ask at the information booth, the assistants will help you buy a ticket at an office upstairs in the main building or direct you to the ticket office outside the station. Tickets can also be booked through travel agents. The train station is easy to reach by any shared taxi heading south from the south-western corner of Meidūn-é Emām Khomeinī.

Shared Taxi

Most towns within about four hours by car from Tehrān are linked by shared taxi. Shared taxis leave from specially designated sections inside, or just outside, the appropriate bus terminals, depending on the destination (refer to the Bus section earlier in this chapter). For example, shared taxis to Ghom leave from around the Southern Bus Terminal.

GETTING AROUND
To/From the Airport

Avoid the taxi drivers who huddle immediately outside the domestic and international terminals, and walk for about two minutes towards the main gates and catch a chartered taxi (about 15,000 rials), or shared taxi, to the city centre. At either airport, the driver will avoid paying the car park entrance fee and drop passengers off about 200m from the international terminal, or about 50m from the domestic terminal. If travelling by public transport, catch bus No 511 or 518 from Meidūn-é Enghelāb to the domestic (not international) terminal, or take a shared taxi to Meidūn-é Āzādī and another to either terminal.

Bus

Extensive bus services cover virtually all of Tehrān. They're often crowded, but cheap – 100 rials across most of central Tehrān. Some useful routes include:

No 126 Meidūn-é Tajrīsh – Meidūn-é Ārzhāntīn
No 127 Meidūn-é Tajrīsh – Meidūn-é Valī-yé Asr
Nos 128 & 144 Meidūn-é Valī-yé Asr – Meidūn-é Emām Khomeinī

Taxi

Shared taxis travel every nano-second along the main roads, linking the main squares: Emām Khomeinī, Vanak, Valī-yé Asr,

Tajrīsh, Ārzhāntīn, Āzādī, Ferdōsī, Enghelāb, Haft-é Tīr, Rāh Āhan and Emām Hussein. Any shared taxi can be hired for a private trip; anything from a private taxi agency will cost more. Always check the price before getting into a taxi.

Underground

The first stage of Tehrān's long-awaited underground system has finally opened. Running from Tehrān station, 1km north of Meidūn-é Āzādī to Meidūn-é Emām Khomeinī, one trip costs 500 rials. At the time of research, trains were only operating between 8 am and 4 pm, but it's planned to extend this in the future. When the proposed north-south line will open (if ever) is anyone's guess.

Around Tehrān

Many Tehrānīs head for the hills when it gets too hot and polluted in the city, either to relax at the many teahouses or to get some exercise trekking and rock-climbing. This is also their winter playground, providing excellent powder snow **skiing** at resorts such as Dīzīn, Darbansar (good for beginners) and Shemshak. South of Tehrān, heading into the desert, are the last resting place of Āyatollāh Khomeinī and the cemetery for the thousands who died in the Iran-Iraq War. Visits here can also be combined with a day trip to Ghom (Qom) – see the Tehrān to Esfahān section.

ALBORZ MOUNTAINS

Tehrān boasts two telecabins (chair lifts). The Tōchāl telecabin is long, and has restaurants at both chairlift stations, the highest being at 2900m; skiing here is possible in the winter. The rest of the year the rocky landscape is unbearably stark, but a hike to the summit of **Tōchāl** (3730m) can be combined with a walk to or from the pretty mountain area of **Darband**. Take plenty of water. A return ticket to the top is 25,000 rials or 18,000 rials one way.

The shorter combined elevator and open-air chairlift from Meidūn-é Darband provides access to prettier scenery, many more drink stalls and cafes along the way, and is cheaper (2500 rials, one way). If you want to walk, the trail up from Darband is far eas-

ier. Both telecabins are only open on Thursday and Friday. To both, take a shared taxi from Meidūn-é Tajrīsh. From the Tōchāl car park you'll then need to take the service bus (500 rials) up to the telecabin station.

You can visit Iran's tallest peak, the magnificent conical volcano **Kūh-é Damāvand** (Mt Damāvand, 5671m) in a day trip from Tehrān, but if you intend to do some serious walking (see the boxed text 'Climbing Damāvand') it's better to stay overnight. Mountain climbers should contact:

Ahmad Faramarzpour (☎ 0122-3253 270) The local guide
Kassa Mountaineering & Tourism Co (☎ 021 7510 463, ⓔ kassa@intelirnet.net)
9 Naghdi Alley, Kheyābūn-é Sharī'atī, Tehrān
Mountaineering Federation of Iran (☎ 021-8839 928) 15 Kheyābūn-é Varzandeh, Tehrān

Even if you're not a mountain climber, there are plenty of gentle hiking trails in the area, and the village of **Reine** is pretty. Take a shared taxi or minibus from Tehrān's Eastern Bus Terminal towards Āmol, get off at the junction to Reine, and take another shared taxi up the hill. It's worth chartering a taxi from Tehrān.

HOLY SHRINE OF EMĀM KHOMEINĪ & BEHESHT-É ZAHRĀ

The Āyatollāh asked that his shrine become a public place where people can enjoy themselves, rather than a mosque – and that's exactly what he got. The huge golden-domed complex is yet to be completed, but already there are several decent restaurants as well as some shops. It's open every day, but avoid mourning days when the place is swamped by thousands of the faithful.

About 500m away is the Behesht-é Zahrā, the main military cemetery for those who died in the Iran-Iraq War. It's an extraordinary, but eerie place. All comers are welcome to walk around, but again it's best to avoid mourning days and their attendant crowds.

The shrine and cemetery are on the southern outskirts of the city, on the road to Ghom – take a bus, minibus or shared taxi from the Southern Bus Terminal. A return trip by taxi should be around 40,000 rials including waiting time.

Climbing Damāvand

We started at Reine, where we met Ahmad Faramarzpour, a renowned guide who has two thick books of climbing reports. The next day we walked to Gusfan Sarah (3040m); driving here is possible, but altitude adaptation is better if you walk from the start. The route was along green, rocky slopes with sheep grazing and flowers blossoming. Clean water is available from a piped supply for the cattle. It took four to five hours to reach Gusfan Sarah.

Guests are housed in a mosque. When women are there they have their own sleeping area fenced off with a piece of cloth. There are a couple of families in the village who keep goats and sheep and mules for carrying luggage up and down the mountain. You can buy bread, yogurt and cheese from the people and fill up your water bottles from a clean piped supply (do this in the evening before the climb because the water freezes at night).

The next day we walked four to five hours to Dargah-é Sevvom (4150m), also known as the 'third shelter'. There's a hut here (but bring a tent in case it's full) and clean piped water – the last safe chance to refresh supplies before the summit. At night it's freezing, so a good sleeping bag, warm clothes and a camping stove are also necessary. Although most of the time the pathway to the summit is clear and sparsely marked by yellow flags, at crucial points it becomes lost in snow. Even in summer the weather can suddenly turn very cold and dangerous and everything on the volcano is loose, even the big, seemingly fixed rocks; for these reasons I was hiring a guide is essential.

I was the only woman on the climb. I was wearing a scarf and a Moroccan *djellaba* up to 4150m. After that I made a jacket out of the djellaba, leaving my trousered legs free for anybody to see. I was always treated in a dignified and attentive manner by the men.

Marie-José Wijntjes

Mashhad

☎ 051 • pop 1,964,489

There's only one reason for detouring 894km to the holy city of Mashhad – not near Tehrān at all, but most easily visited from the capital – but it's a compelling one. Meaning 'The Place of Martyrdom', Mashhad is where the 8th grandson of the Prophet Mohammed, Emām Rezā, died after eating grapes in AD 817. The story spread that Emām Rezā had been poisoned, so his tomb became a major pilgrimage site. It helped that it was said one visit here equalled 70,000 pilgrimages to Mecca. That the shrine became such a hit is not surprising – it's drop-dead gorgeous (once you get past the ugly concrete ring encircling it). What's more, unlike Mecca and Medina in Saudi Arabia, and Ghom in Iran, the precincts of Āstān-é Ghods-é Razavī are open to non-Muslims.

A short trip here isn't as crazy as it sounds. A return flight from Tehrān is around US$36, while an overnight berth on the train is even less. The only times you should hesitate visiting are on Friday, when it can be difficult to gain access to the shrine precincts without an official guide, and during the Iranian New Year (about 21 March) and the peak pilgrimage season (mid-June to late July), when Mashhad staggers under the pressure of millions of visitors.

There are also a few attractions near Mashhad, and the city serves as a natural staging post if you're travelling to/from Turkmenistan.

INFORMATION
Tourist Offices

The tourist office (☎ 717 057) is more concerned with visiting pilgrims than foreign tourists, so don't waste time searching it out; the information booth at the train station (☎ 246 81) is more helpful. There's also a useful left-luggage office here (2000 rials for three hours, 500 rials per hour thereafter).

Visa Extensions

It's relatively easy to get a visa extension from the visa/passport office at Meidūn-é

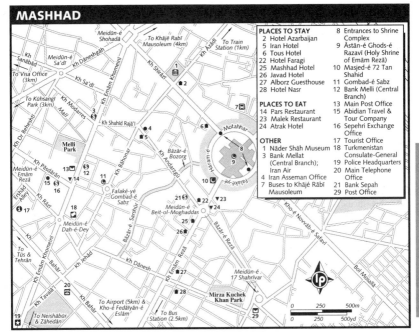

MASHHAD

PLACES TO STAY
2 Hotel Azarbaijan
5 Iran Hotel
6 Tous Hotel
22 Hotel Faragi
25 Mashhad Hotel
26 Javad Hotel
27 Alborz Guesthouse
28 Hotel Nasr

PLACES TO EAT
14 Pars Restaurant
23 Malek Restaurant
24 Atrak Hotel

OTHER
1 Nāder Shāh Museum
3 Bank Mellat
(Central Branch);
Iran Air
4 Iran Asseman Office
7 Buses to Khājé Rābī
Mausoleum

8 Entrances to Shrine
Complex
9 Āstān-é Ghods-é
Razavī (Holy Shrine
of Emām Rezā)
10 Masjed-é 72 Tan
Shahid
11 Gombad-é Sabz
12 Bank Melli (Central
Branch)
13 Main Post Office
15 Abidian Travel &
Tour Company
16 Sepehri Exchange
Office
17 Tourist Office
18 Turkmenistan
Consulate-General
19 Police Headquarters
20 Main Telephone
Office
21 Bank Sepah
29 Post Office

Rāhnamā'ī in the north-west of the city (take a taxi there).

Money

The central branches of Bank Melli, Bank Mellat and Bank Sepah will change money, and there's a foreign exchange counter in the departure lounge at the airport. Black marketeers hang around Bank Melli, but it's best to change money at the Sepehri Exchange Office.

ĀSTĀN-É GHODS-É RAZAVĪ

The Holy Shrine of Emām Rezā, and the surrounding buildings, are known collectively as the Āstān-é Ghods-é Razavī, and comprise one of the marvels of the Islamic world. The original tomb chamber of Emām Rezā was built in the early 9th century, but later destroyed, restored and destroyed again. The present structure in the centre of the complex was built under the orders of Shāh Abbās I at the beginning of the 17th century.

As well as the shrine, the complex contains two mosques, four museums, 12 lofty *eivāns* or halls (two of them coated entirely

with gold), six theological colleges, several libraries, a post office, refectory and a bookshop. Everywhere, beautiful coloured tiles catch the eye. The remarkable **Azīm-é Gōhar Shād Mosque** has a 50m blue dome and cavernous golden portal. The **Moghaddas Museum** houses a 16th-century gold bas-relief door, and a vast collection of gifts given to Emām Khomeinī by various world leaders. Next door, the less-interesting **Markazī Museum** has many Islamic ornaments and writing implements, a huge 800-year-old wooden door and a one-tonne stone drinking vessel made in the 12th century. Downstairs from the Markazī Museum is the fascinating **Stamp and Coin Museum**. The **Ghods-é Razavī Museum** has a display of carpets, calligraphy and hand-inscribed Qurans – probably the largest public display in Iran.

The Holy Shrine itself is strictly closed to non-Muslims, but it's generally fine to visit the rest of the complex. Please dress extremely conservatively and behave impeccably, and avoid large religious gatherings and the main pilgrimage season. All visitors have to deposit bags and cameras at the gates. Non-Muslims may feel more comfortable with a Muslim guide or friend, but it's not mandatory – ask around outside the shrine or at your hotel. If you go alone, report to the Foreigners' Registration Office (closed Friday) in the Administration Office, in the far west of the complex.

The complex is open daily from about 7 am to late in the evening. The museums are open from 7 am to 5 pm, closed Friday. During the renovations to the outer walls (ongoing since 1983!), the main entrances are located where Kheyābūn-é Shīrāzī and Kheyābūn-é Novvāb-é Safavī reach the complex.

OTHER ATTRACTIONS

After the shrine, all else in Mashhad pales into insignificance. If you're determined to make the most of a visit, check out the small, well-preserved **Gombad-é Sabz** (Sabz Dome), originally built in the Safavid period (1502–1722) and containing the tomb of Sheikh Mohammed Hakīm Mo' men. Unfortunately, it's usually closed.

The fine 16th-century **Khājé Rabī Mausoleum**, 4km north of central Mashhad, contains several famous inscriptions by Alī Rezā Abbāsī, one of the greatest Persian calligraphers, and stands in the midst of the large **martyrs' cemetery**. Take a shared taxi from the train station or a bus from just north of the holy shrine.

Mashhad has several **bazaars**, including the 700m long **Bāzār-é Rezā**. Among the range of tacky souvenirs, the bazaars sell gorgeous fabrics, rugs, turquoise (but beware of fakes) and saffron.

On the edge of the city, the tranquil **Kūhsangī Park** has a restaurant, a small lake and some hiking opportunities – take a shared taxi from Meidūn-é Shohadā.

PLACES TO STAY

There is a vast range of hotels in Mashhad. All cater for pilgrims, so most are within a few minutes walk of the shrine complex, and some will not accept foreigners at any time. In the off-season, the prices of mid-range hotels are negotiable.

There are a few cheapies near the corner of Kheyābūn-é Emām Rezā and Kheyābūn-é Dānesh. **Hotel Nasr** (☎ 979 43) charges 20,000/40,000 rials for singles/doubles, and is cleaner and quieter than most. **Alborz Guesthouse** (☎ 825 097) charges a bargain

10,000/15,000 rials, although it's in a nosier location.

Tous Hotel (☎ 229 22) might be a stone's throw from the shrine complex but is quiet and worth paying a little extra for; it's 25,000 rials per room. Also near the shrine is **Hotel Faragi** (☎ 541 12, Kheyābūn-é Andarzgū); it's recently had a paint job, but many rooms – 16,500/24,200 rials – remain stuffy.

Around the intersection of Kheyābūn-é Shīrāzī and Kheyābūn-é Āzādī the best option is **Hotel Azarbaijan** (☎ 540 01), which charges US$15/20, including breakfast.

Javad Hotel (☎ 221 642, fax 650 080) is not as comfortable as other mid-range places in the immediate area, but is good value for US$10/20, including breakfast.

The more upmarket **Mashhad Hotel** (☎ 2222 701, fax 2226 767, Meidūn-é Beitol-Moghaddas) is central, modern and remarkably good value for US$20/35. The rooms have air-con, fridge and colour TV. Another good top-end deal is the **Iran Hotel** (☎ 2228 010, fax 2228 583, Kheyābūn-é Andarzgū), charging US$19/28.

PLACES TO EAT

There are plenty of cheap eating houses around the shrine complex, especially along Kheyābūn-é Emām Rezā. **Malek Restaurant** is one of the best. A set menu comprising a tasty chelō morgh (chicken and rice), cola, bread, soup and salad costs about 15,000 rials.

Pars Restaurant, on the corner of Kheyābūn-é Emām Khomeinī and Kheyābūn-é Pāsdārān, serves tasty Iranian food (about 10,000 rials a plate) in a friendly atmosphere. The best restaurants are in the mid-range hotels. **Atrak Hotel** is elegant, but you can still get a burger for 8000 rials plus 15% tax. **Mashhad Hotel** is the best, with Iranian meals for about 16,000 rials, and excellent buffet breakfasts.

GETTING THERE & AWAY

A return flight to Mashhad is the preferred option (if you've flown into the country on Iran Air this is a good way of using your two complimentary internal flights), although taking the overnight train is fun. If you're looking to rationalise the cost, consider that by taking the train from Tehrān one night and back the same day and you've saved yourself a couple of nights accommodation.

Because of its popularity with local pilgrims, it's important to make advance bookings for transport in and out of Mashhad, if you want to be sure of a seat for a particular day.

Air
Iran Air (☎ 514 92) flies at least five times daily to Tehrān (150,000 rials); three or four times weekly to Esfahān (166,000 rials) and five times weekly to Shīrāz (188,000 rials). There are less frequent services to Tabrīz, Yazd, Zāhedān and a few other major cities.

Bus
From the bus station (easy to reach by shared taxi along Kheyābūn-é Emām Rezā), a plethora of buses go to every major city, and regional town, but most trips to/from Mashhad are *very* long and generally *very* boring. Two popular destinations include Tehrān (21,000 rials, 14 hours) and Zāhedān (12,500 rials, 15 hours).

Train
Up to nine trains daily travel between Tehrān and Mashhad for 18,000/34,000 rials (2nd/1st class). All offer sleeping accommodation – the 1st-class section is very comfortable – and there's usually a buffet car serving reasonable meals. If you're on an 'express' service, the journey time is around 13 hours.

GETTING AROUND
The Mashhad Taxi Agency has a counter outside the airport; the 20-minute ride into town costs 13,000 rials. A public bus travels regularly between the airport and the corner of Kheyābūn-é Emām Rezā and Kheyābūn-é Fedā'īyān-é Eslām, for 300 rials. From the train station you can either walk the 2km to the shrine, or take a taxi for around 3000 rials.

Tehrān to Esfahān

Our route south from Tehrān heads through the religious centre of Ghom to Kāshān, a pleasant oasis town that's the ideal base for visiting the pretty village of Abyāneh, another splash of greenery in an otherwise arid landscape. The former capital Esfahān, still the most architecturally impressive of Iran's cities, is our goal.

GHOM
After Mashhad, Ghom (also spelled Qom) is the holiest city in Iran; it's where Āyatollāh Khomeinī studied and it remains an important theological centre. The main attraction is the blue-and-gold domed **Hazrat-é Masumeh**, the tomb of Fātemé (sister of Emām Rezā), who died and was buried here in the 9th century. This extensive complex was built under Shāh Abbās I, and the other Safavid kings, all anxious to establish their Shi'ite credentials. You can walk around the perimeter of the complex, but unless you're a Muslim, you are not allowed inside. If you're short of time, it's best to push on to Kāshān.

Minibuses and shared taxis regularly travel to Tehrān (154km north), Kāshān (104km south) and Esfahān (285km south). There are also several train services daily to/from Tehrān, taking two hours; tickets cost between 12,000 and 31,000 rials depending on the class.

KĀSHĀN
☎ 0361 • pop approx 120,000
Baking hot Kāshān is a compact oasis town that so captured the heart of Shāh Abbās I that he asked to be buried here. Archaeologists reckon there's been settlements near central Iran's Kavir and Karkas Mountains since the Archaemenian period (559–330 BC) and it's said that the Three Wise Men set out from here for Bethlehem. Despite being destroyed by invading Arabs and Mongols, and rocked by earthquakes, Kāshān survived and prospered due to the quality of its textiles and pottery. The low-rise concrete centre of the town today looks like many others in Iran, but in the old quarter, near the remains of the city walls, you can glimpse what a place Kāshān once was.

Things to See
Head first to the mud-brick warren of streets around 1km south of the central square Meidūn-é Kamāl-ol-Molk. Here you'll find a small blue-tiled mosque with a conical dome, an ancient bathhouse (under restoration) and a couple of restored mansions: the ornately decorated **Khan-é Tabatabaee** and the **Khan-é Borujerdī**, cooled by tall wind-catching towers, or *bādgīrs*. The most impressive building, when renovations are finished, will be cavernous **Khan-é Abbassi**, which has

IRAN

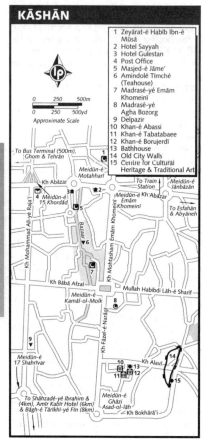

KĀSHĀN

1 Zeyārat-é Habīb Ibn-é
   Mūsā
2 Hotel Sayyah
3 Hotel Gulestan
4 Post Office
5 Masjed-é Jāme'
6 Amindolé Tīmché
   (Teahouse)
7 Madrasé-yé Emām
   Khomeinī
8 Madrasé-yé
   Agha Bozorg
9 Delpazir
10 Khan-é Abassi
11 Khan-é Tabatabaee
12 Khan-é Borujerdī
13 Bathhouse
14 Old City Walls
15 Centre for Cultural
   Heritage & Traditional Art

0   250   500m
0   250   500yd
Approximate Scale

To Bus Terminal (500m),
Ghom & Tehrān

Meidūn-é
Motahharī

Kh Abāzar

To Train
Station

Meidūn-é
Jānbāzān

Kh Mohammad Alī-yé Raja'ī

Meidūn-é
Khordād

Bāzāar

Kh Abāzar
Meidūn-é
Emām
Khomeinī

To Esfahān
& Abyāneh

Kh Mohtasham Emām Khomeinī

Kh Bābā Afzal

Mullah Habibdi Lāh-é Sharif

Meidūn-é
Kamāl-ol-Molk

Kh Fāzel-é Nardāqī

Meidūn-é
17 Shahrīvar

Kh Alavi

Meidūn-é
Ghāzi
Asad-ol-lāh

Kh Bokhārā'ī

To Shāhzadé-yé Ibrahim &
(4km), Amīr Kabīr Hotel (6km)
& Bāgh-é Tārīkhī-yé Fīn (8km)

---

parts that are more than 400 years old. Entry
to each mansion is 10,000 rials and all are
open from 7.30 am to 7.30 pm daily. Nearby,
take a look at the city walls, parts of which
are said to date back 1000 years; there are a
couple of natural cold rooms here and the
**Centre for Cultural Heritage & Traditional
Art**, open from 9 am to noon, where you can
see textile weavers at work, making velvet,
brocade, silk and cotton.

Returning to Meidūn-é Kamāl-ol-Molk,
check out the nearby **Madrasé-yé Agha
Bozorg**, a mosque and theological school,
which has lovely tiled portals and minarets,
before ducking into the shade of the covered **bazaar**, which threads its labyrinthine
way towards Meidūn-é Motahharī. Apart
from the famous carpet sellers, you'll also

find the entrance to the tranquil **Madrasé-yé
Emām Khomeinī**, formerly the Soltaniye
Mosque, a working **bathhouse** and the impressive **Amindolé Tīmché**, a lofty domed
hall, in the upper reaches of which carpet
designers work.

Shāh Abbās I's understated black marble
tomb lies in the **Zeyārat-é Habīb Ibn-é
Mūsā**, about 100m north of Meidūn-é
Emām Khomeinī, a short walk from the end
of the bazaar.

Kāshān's famous gardens, the **Bāgh-é
Tārīkhī-yé Fīn** (where the wily politician
Amīr Kabīr came to a sticky end in 1852)
are about 8km south-west of the centre.
Designed for Shāh Abbās I, this shady,
walled enclosure, cooled by bubbling natural springs, is a classical Persian vision of
paradise, but leaves something lacking to
modern eyes. Still, it's a pleasant place to
hide from the heat, and has a bookshop, so-
so teahouse and a missable museum. Several other teahouses line the road to the
gardens along which you can also visit the
delightful **Shāhzadé-yé Ibrahim**, a Ghajar
period (1779–1921) shrine with exquisite
tilework and a pretty courtyard. To get to
the gardens, charter a taxi (around 2000
rials), or catch a bus (200 rials) from Meidūn-é Kamāl-ol-Molk.

Places to Stay & Eat
The cheapest place is the basic, but friendly
Hotel Gulestan (☎ 446 793), which charges
25,000 rials per person for clean rooms with
shared bathrooms. It's upstairs on the south
side of Meidūn-é Motahharī; look for the
red sign next to the vegetable shop.

Hotel Sayyah (☎ 444 535, Kheyābūné
Abāzar) about 100m west of Meidūn-é
Emām Khomeinī costs a negotiable
US$20/25 for small, pleasant singles/
doubles. It has an attached *restaurant*, serving the usual kabābs. *Amīr Kabīr Hotel*
(☎ 300 91) about 2km before the Fīn gardens has decent, but overpriced, rooms for
US$35/ 45, and a reasonable *restaurant*.

The best place to eat is the classy *Delpazir*
(☎ 253 22, Kheyābūn-é Mohammad Alī-yé
Raja'ī), run by an Englishwoman and her
Iranian husband. Many tour groups stop here
and get treated to the 30,000 rial per person
buffet. Independent travellers are advised to
tuck into the excellent *fesenjān* (duck, goose,
chicken or quail in pomegranate and walnut

sauce) or one of the rarely found vegetarian dishes, for around 25,000 rials. Also good for lunch is the *teahouse* in the bazaar's Amindolé Tīmché, serving ābgūsht and tea for 6000 rials.

Getting There & Away

Buses run reasonably regularly to Esfahān (8500 rials, 3½ hours), Ghom (3000 rials, one hour) and Tehrān (9000 rials, four hours); there's a station on Kheyābūn-é 22 Bhaman and many other services leave from Meidūn-é 15 Khordād, about 600m west of Meidūn-é Emām Khomeinī.

One train leaves Tehrān at 1.40 pm daily arriving in Kāshān three hours later. A 1st/2nd-class ticket is 8000/5000 rials. The train from Kāshān to Tehrān leaves at 5 am.

AROUND KĀSHĀN
Abyāneh

A fine half-day trip from Kāshān, particularly if you've got your own transport, is the rustic village of Abyāneh, nestling in a fertile gorge, away from the arid deserts around. Recognised for its antiquity and uniqueness by Unesco, parts of the village dates back to the Safavid period (1502–1722). The closely packed houses, built on the hillslope facing into the sun, are fascinating to wander around. It's not difficult to locate the **Emāmzādé-yé Yahya**, a picturesque mosque with a pool and veranda with views across the valley, and the **Masjed-é Jāme'**, which has a beautiful carved wooden door behind a metal grille. Climb to the top of the jagged hills to inspect the remains of fortifications and for the grand views.

There's a *grocery store* on the outskirts of the village where you can get something to eat and buy souvenirs, but it's best to bring food and drink with you. The village is 74km south of Kāshān; take the road to Natanz. The best way to get here is charter a taxi for around US$10 return.

ESFAHĀN
☎ 031 • pop 1,220,595

If you visit only one place in Iran, make it Esfahān. Here you'll find the blueprint for Shāh Abbās' grand renaissance capital pretty much intact. The ornately tiled architecture is superb, particularly that surrounding Meidūn-é Emām Khomeinī, a

square that rivals St Mark's in Venice for beauty and which you'll return to time and again. There's plenty that's modern about the city, but if you're looking for the romance of old Persia, you'll find it here.

Nestling at the foothills of the Zagros Mountains, on the banks of the fast-flowing Zāyandé River, Esfahān has a pleasant climate and a relaxed, faintly cosmopolitan atmosphere compared with other Iranian cities. It's a place in which to walk, get lost in the bazaar, drink tea, doze in beautiful gardens, and meet people.

History

Esfahān's central location and natural attributes made it an important trading centre long before Shāh Abbās I proclaimed it his capital in 1598. There are the remains of a Sassanian period (AD 224–637) fire temple 9.5km west of the city. By the 10th century Esfahān was renown for its silks and cottons. During the Seljuk period (1051–1220) the city expanded and was briefly a capital. In 1235 the Mongols ploughed through and, in 1397, it's recorded that Tamerlane massacred 70,000 citizens and made minarets of their skulls.

Shāh Abbās, having united his country and freed it from foreign influence, had more humane plans for the city. Under his rule, Esfahān flourished to become a wonder of the renaissance world. Visitors reported 137 royal palaces, beautiful gardens, large caravanserais and a city planned out in 40 districts. The famous half-rhyme *Esfahān nesf-é jahān* ('Esfahān is half the world') was coined at this time to express its grandeur. However, its glory would last little more than a century. An invasion from Afghanistan forced the Safavid rulers' attentions away from architecture, and by the time of the rule of Karīm Khān Zand, the capital had shifted to Shīrāz and Esfahān's decline had set in.

The Ghajar rulers probably did the most damage to the city's architectural heritage, but by the mid-20th century, as tourism started to take off and oil wealth rolled in, restoration of the main monuments began and is still ongoing.

Orientation

The main road is Kheyābūn-é Chahār Bāgh, built in 1597 and once lined with many palaces – present-day needs are catered for

IRAN

ESFAHĀN

PLACES TO STAY
3 22 Bahman Hotel
4 Pardis Apartment Hotel
5 Persia Hotel
7 Amir Kabir Hotel
9 Piroozy Hotel; Naghsh-é Jahan Hotel; Nobahar Restaurant
25 Shad Hotel
28 Aria Hotel
30 Pars Hotel
35 Tous Hotel
36 Sahel Hotel; Bame Sahel
42 Pol & Park Hotel
45 Julfa Hotel

PLACES TO EAT
8 Hengāmé
27 Abbāsī Hotel; Chehelsotoun Restaurant
31 Restaurant Shahrzad
32 Hotel Alī Ghapū
34 Hamshahri
37 Maharaja

OTHER
1 Masjed-é Jāmé
2 Darvazeno Zurkhané
6 Stadium
10 Bank Mellat (Central Branch)
11 Money Exchange Office
12 Bank Melli (Central Branch)
13 Natural History Museum
14 Contemporary Arts Museum
15 Police Headquarters
16 Main Post Office
17 Decorative Arts Museum of Iran
18 Kish Airlines Office
19 Chehel Sotūn Palace & Park
20 Main Telephone Office
21 Local Bus Station
22 Esfahān Hospital
23 Hasht Behesht Palace; Shahid Raja'i Park
24 Second-Hand Book Bazaar
26 Madrasé-yé Chahār Bāgh
29 Shopping Centre; Iran Handicrafts Organization; Iran Travel & Tourism Agency; Iran Air Office (International & Domestic Bookings); Bookshops
33 Iran Air Office (Domestic Bookings)
38 Train Ticket Office
39 Teahouse
40 Teahouse
41 Paddleboat Hire
43 Bethlehem Church
44 Vānk Cathedral
46 Teahouse
47 Teahouse

along here and the road terminates at Sī-o-Sé Bridge, the picturesque bridge crossing the Zāyandé River. Meidūn-é Emām Khomeinī is a short walk to the east of this road, from Meidūn-é Emām Hussein.

Information
Tourist Offices Esfahān has a helpful tourist office (☎ 228 491) on the ground floor of the Alī Ghāpū Palace, on Meidūn-é Emām Khomeinī; pick up a good free city map here. The office is open from 8 am to 2.15 pm and 4 to 6 pm Saturday to Wednesday and from 8 am to 1.15 pm Thursday; closed Friday.

Visa Extensions Visa extensions can be obtained in less then 24 hours from the 2nd floor of the Foreign Affairs Branch (☎ 688 644) opposite Esfahān University. Take a shared taxi from the southern end of Sī-o-Sé Pol, and keep your eye out for a sign in English.

Money The central branches of Bank Melli and Bank Mellat have foreign exchange facilities, but it's better to change money at the 'street rate' in the official money exchange office on Kheyābūn-é Sepāh, which also accepts travellers cheques. A few souvenir shops along Kheyābūn-é Chahār Bāgh Abbāsī, and around Meidūn-é Emām Khomeinī, may also change money, but be discreet.

Post & Communications The main post office is along Kheyābūn-é Neshāt; if you want to post parcels you'll need to go here, otherwise there's a far more convenient office on Meidūn-é Emām Khomeinī. The main telephone office is easy to find on Kheyābūn-é Beheshtī. Internet facilities are available at the Amir Kabir Hotel, and Alī Ghāpū Carpets and Internet Daliran, both in the Spedana Carvan Sara off the east side of Meidūn-é Emām Khomeinī. Rates are around 25,000 rials per hour, but connections aren't great.

Travel Agencies A reliable travel agency is Iran Travel & Tourism Agency (☎ 223 010), in the shopping complex opposite the Abbāsī Hotel on Kheyābūn-é Amadegh. You can book international and domestic flights here and arrange guided tours around Esfahān.

Bookshops In the same complex as Iran Travel & Tourism Agency you'll find several bookshops, although none have a great selection of English-language titles. The widest range of offerings are found at the bookshop in the Abbāsī Hotel.

Medical Services If you need medical attention, the most central and reputable hospitals are:

Dr Shāri'atī Hospital   ☎ 272 001
Esfahān Hospital   ☎ 230 115
Esiā Ebn-é Maryam Hospital   ☎ 239 012

Meidūn-é Emām Khomeinī
Still sometimes known as Meidūn-é Naghshé Jahān, this huge square is one of the largest in the world (510m by 164m). Built in 1612, and originally used as a polo field, it is a majestic example of town planning. Apart from admiring the architecture, you can relax at one of the city's best teahouses, ride a horse and buggy around the square (5000 rials), go shopping at scores of souvenir shops or just watch Esfahānīs go about their business. Open-air prayer services are held here on Friday, and religious holidays, and the square is often (but not always) beautifully illuminated at night. At the time of research, plans were advanced to make the entire square a pedestrian-only zone.

Masjed-é Emām
Previously known as the Shāh Mosque, this magnificent building is one of the most stunning mosques in Iran. It is completely covered, inside and out, with the pale blue patterned tiles that are an Esfahānī trademark. The mosque was built over a period of 26 years by an increasingly impatient Shāh Abbās I, and eventually completed in 1638.

The main dome (54m high) is double-layered and though the entrance, flanked with its twin minarets (both 42m high), faces the square, the mosque itself is angled towards Mecca. The tiles of the mosque take on a different hue according to the light conditions, and the magnificent portal (about 30m tall), is a supreme example of architectural styles from the Safavid period (1502–1722).

Through a short corridor, a hallway leads into an inner courtyard, surrounded by four

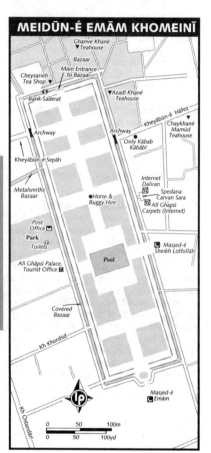

MEIDŪN-É EMĀM KHOMEINĪ

Ghanve Khané ▼Teahouse

Bazaar

Main Entrance to Bazaar

Cheysarieh Tea Shop ▼

Bank Saderat

▼Azadi Khané Teahouse

Archway

Kheyābūn-é Hāfez

Archway

Chaykhané Mamūd Teahouse

Only Kābab Kābābi

Kheyābūn-é Sepāh

Internet Daliran

Metalsmiths Bazaar

●Horse & Buggy Hire

Spedana Carvan Sara

Ali Ghāpū Carpets (Internet)

Post Office

Park Toilets

Masjed-é Sheikh Lotfollāh

Ali Ghāpū Palace, Tourist Office

Pool

Covered Bazaar

Kh Khorshid

Masjed-é Emām

Kh Ostandāri

| 0 | 50 | 100m |
| 0 | 50 | 100yd |

eivāns (rectangular halls). Three lead into vaulted sanctuaries; the largest to the south. In the east sanctuary, stamp your foot under the dome to hear the marvellous echo – an ingenious natural loudspeaker system. East and west of the mosque are two *madrasés* (theological schools).

The best time for photographs is around 11 am. The mosque is open to visitors from 7 am to 7 pm Saturday to Thursday and from 3 to 7 pm Friday. Entry is 20,000 rials.

Masjed-é Sheikh Lotfollāh

This small mosque, on the east side of the square, is known as the jewel in the ring (that being the square) of Esfahān. It was also built by Shāh Abbās I for the exclusive use of his entourage, and was dedicated to his father-in-law, Sheikh Lotfollāh, a holy preacher. Beautifully proportioned and decorated, the mosque boasts some of the best mosaics from the era and took nearly 20 years to complete. An unusual feature of this mosque is the absence of a minaret or courtyard, but there is an underground prayer room used in winter.

As you enter the main prayer room, look up from the right side of the door to see a shaft of light create the tail of a peacock from the middle of the dome. Outside, the dome's pale tiles change colour from cream to pink, depending on the time of day. The mosque was once called the 'Women's Mosque', because there is apparently a tunnel between this mosque and the Alī Ghāpū Palace, which allowed women from the old dynasties to attend prayers without being seen in public.

The mosque is open from about 8 am to 7 pm daily and entry is 20,000 rials.

Alī Ghāpū Palace

This six-storey palace was built in the 18th century as a functioning seat of government. Most of the murals and mosaics which once decorated the many small rooms, corridors and stairways have been destroyed, but the fretwork stalactites on the top floor, chiselled out in the shapes of musical instruments, are beautiful, as is the roof of the entrance dome, patterned like a Nā'īn carpet. The views of the square from the fourth floor covered pavilion are superb; the best time to visit is late afternoon to dusk.

The palace is open 8 am to 7 pm Saturday to Thursday and 3 to 7 pm Friday. Entry is 20,000 rials.

Masjed-é Jāme'

Easily combined with a walk through the fascinating nontouristy sections of the bazaar (see the Shopping section), this large and ancient mosque is a museum of Islamic architecture: It displays styles from the simplicity of the Seljuk period (1038–1194), through the Mongol period (1220–1380) and on to the more baroque Safavid period (1502–1722). The building's history is written in English (well, sort of) on a notice board at the entrance of the mosque. It's open from 7 am to 7 pm daily and entry costs 20,000 rials.

Chehel Sotūn Palace

After Meidūn-é Emām Khomeinī, this is the most beautiful place to hang out in Esfahān. At the centre of the shady gardens is a marvellous building constructed as a reception hall by Shāh Abbās I. There are 20 graceful 110m tall wooden columns holding up the grand portico, while the reflection in the long pool in front doubles the number, hence the palace's name which means '40 columns'. Inside the palace, the small collection of ceramics, old coins, pottery, and Qurans is overshadowed by amazing wall friezes – gory, frenetic battles between Shāh Abbās and the Uzbeks, alternate with scenes of celebration from the royal court.

If you bring your own food and drink, you can enjoy a picnic in the extensive gardens or beside the large pool. There's also an excellent *teahouse* by the entrance. The best time for photos is early morning, and it's usually lit up (but rarely open) at night. The grounds and museum are open from about 8 am to 7 pm Saturday to Wednesday and from 3 to 7 pm Friday. Entry is 15,000 rials.

Hasht Behesht Palace & Shahīd Raja'ī Park

This small palace and garden, just off Kheyābūn-é Chahār Bāgh Abbāsī, was built in the 17th century under Shāh Soleiman. It has some charming and impressive mosaics and stalactite mouldings, but has been *very* slowly undergoing renovation for at least 20 years. It's possible to admire the palace from the surrounding Shahīd Raja'ī park without paying the entry fee (15,000 rials). There is a second-hand **book bazaar** bedie the palace every Friday. The park is also popular with Esfahāni families for evening picnics.

Nearby is the covered **Bāzār Honar**, once full of artists' shops, but since the revolution most have been taken over by jewellers and goldsmiths. Along the bazaar is a closed entrance to the **Madrasé-yé Chahār Bāgh**, the city's largest theological college. This, and the walls of the college along Kheyābūn-é Chahār Bāgh Abbāsī, are about as close as you'll get to the renowned tilework decoration inside. It's firmly off limits to non-Muslims.

Museums

The best is the **Decorative Arts Museum of Iran**, Kheyābūn-é Ostand-Ari, which has small, but fine displays of calligraphy, miniatures, lacquer, metal and wooden works, pottery, glass, textiles and carpets. Most exhibits are antiques, but there are some interesting contemporary pieces too. The building in which it is housed – a former store for the finery of royal horses – has been well restored, and in the basement you can see brocade being made. It's open from 8 am to 1 pm and entry is 15,000 rials.

Next door is the **Contemporary Arts Museum** which has changing exhibitions of modern works and is missable. The **Natural History Museum** is housed in a building dating from the Timurid period (1380–1502), which is quite interesting in itself. However, the displays of molluscs, stones and stuffed animals are ordinary and there are few English captions.

Bridges

One of your lasting impressions of Esfahān will be of the old pedestrian bridges that cross the Rūd-é Zāyandé. Several have charming teahouses.

Sī-o-Sé Bridge links the upper and lower halves of Kheyābūn-é Chahār Bāgh-é, and was named because it has 33 arches. It was built in 1602 and is the largest bridge across the river. **Khājū Bridge** is shorter, but more attractive. It doubles as a dam, and you can still see the original 17th-century paintings and tiles. In the nearby park look for the tiny mausoleum of the American Professor Arthur Pope, who asked to be buried here in his favourite spot.

Mārnān Bridge is not that interesting, but serves as a finishing point for a pleasant stroll along the banks of the river. **Shahrestān Bridge** is the oldest – most of its present stone and brick structure is believed to date from the 12th century. The short **Chubī Bridge** was built by Shāh Abbās II, primarily to help irrigate palace gardens in the area; it has one of the city's nicest teahouses in its middle.

Jolfā

On the south side of the Rūd-é Zāyandé is the Armenian quarter of Jolfā, dating from the time of Shāh Abbās I and home to 10,000 Armenian Christians. It's an interesting area, the focal point of which is the **Vānk Cathedral**, built between 1655 and 1664. Set within a courtyard, the cathedral

IRAN

is a fascinating mixture of architectural styles, with a bell tower, a mosque-like dome, topped with a cross, and a richly decorated interior, with vivid frescos of the Last Judgement, biblical stories and the sufferings of St Gregor, founder of the Armenian faith. The attached **museum** contains fascinating handwritten books (including one weighing less than 1g), and other ethnological displays relating to Armenian culture and religion. There's even a small drawing by Rembrandt. The cathedral and museum are open from 8 am to noon and 2 to 5 pm daily, except Sunday. Entry is 20,000 rials.

Places to Stay – Budget

Amir Kabir Hotel (☎/fax 296 154, *Kheyābūn-é Chahār Bāgh-é Pā'īn*) has neat rooms and shared bathrooms around a pleasant courtyard, where you can take breakfast and meet fellow travellers. The brothers who run the place are friendly and speak English and there's Internet access. Singles/doubles/triples cost 25,000/40,000/ 60,000 rials, and dorm beds are 18,000 rials per person. Laundry service is available for 10,000 rials per kilogram.

Shad Hotel (☎ 236 883, *Kheyābūn-é Chahār Bāgh-é Abbāsī*) is also a friendly, central option. Small, clean twin rooms cost 40,000 rials with shared bathroom, but it's often full. A few blocks south, *Tous Hotel* (☎ 260 068) is basic, but the rooms have their own bathroom and are good value for 36,500/52,000 rials.

Sahel Hotel (☎ 234 585, *Meidūn-é Enghelāb-é Eslāmī*) is in a noisy, but very handy, part of town. The rooms are clean, and reasonable value for 40,000/80,000 rials.

Pars Hotel (☎ 261 018, *Kheyābūn-é Chahār Bāgh Abbāsī*) is friendly, and staff speak some English. Cosy rooms with fridge and TV, but shared bathroom, cost 50,000/100,000 rials for a single/double, including breakfast.

The large *Persia Hotel* (☎ 204 062, *Meidūn-é Chahār-é Takhti*), is a fall-back if others are full; the rooms are clean and acceptable at 41,860/60,640 rials.

A bit more expensive is the *Naghsh-é Jahan Hotel* (☎/fax 282 148, *Kheyābūn-é Chahār Bāgh-é Pā'īn*). It's nicely decorated and has old-fashioned rooms for 85,000/115,000 rials, including breakfast

with shared bathroom, but discounts are often possible.

Places to Stay – Mid-Range

Aria Hotel (☎ 227 224, *Kheyābūn-é Amadegh*) might not be as fancy as the Abbāsī opposite, but it's in an excellent location, the manager speaks English, and the rooms are fine. Singles/doubles with private bathroom and sometimes a balcony are good value for US$15/20 rials, including breakfast.

At the Kaveh bus station, *Kaveh Hotel* (☎ 420 531, fax 425 441) is ideal for late night or early morning departures, and is still reasonably close to town. Large doubles, with TV and bathroom, cost 70,000/ 120,000 rials, including breakfast.

Closer to town is *22 Bahman Hotel* (☎ 203 953, *Kheyābūn-é Masjed-é Sayyed*), which has spacious rooms with TV and fridge but shared bathroom for US$10/20, or US$24 for a double including bathroom. Avoid the rooms at the front overlooking the noisy road. *Pardis Apartment Hotel* (☎ 200 308, fax 227 831, *Meidūn-é Chahār-é Takhti*) is a good longer-term option since the rooms all have kitchens and cost US$21 per night.

Pol & Park Hotel (☎ 612 785, fax 612 788, *Bolvār-é Ā'īné Khūné*) is a fine choice, nicely positioned beside the river, with big rooms and huge bathrooms. Singles/ doubles/triples are US$21/31/38.

Julfa Hotel (☎ 244 442, fax 249 446), close to the Vānk Cathedral, has some rooms with views of the church for US$20/30. Much more central is the *Piroozy Hotel* (☎ 290 193, fax 290 179), a more upmarket option with comfortable rooms harbouring funky 1970s decor for US$45/65, including breakfast.

Places to Eat

Nobahar Restaurant (*Kheyābūn-é Chahār Bāgh-é Pā'īn*), downstairs next to the Naghsh-é Jahan Hotel, is signposted in English. It's one of the best Iranian restaurants along the main road. There's a menu in English, the service is good and the food is tasty; a meal costs around 20,000 rials.

Hengāmé is a decent pizza/hamburger joint a few doors south of the Amir Kabir Hotel. It offers tasty chips (French fries; 2000 rials), hot dogs (2500 rials), pizzas

(10,000 rials) and scrumptious Western-style hamburgers (3000 rials). Much flashier is **Hamshahri**, on the corner of Kheyābūn-é Abbās Ābād, closer to the river, which serves pizza for 9000 rials and sandwiches for 4500 rials. Another cheapie just east of Meidūn-é Emām Khomeinī is the **Only Kabāb Kabābī**.

Several of the teahouses (see Teahouses following) are good options for lunch. Try **Ghanve Khané** downstairs off one of the courtyards near the gold section of the bazaar. A tasty bowl of ābgūsht with sour pickles, yogurt and drinks costs a bargain 7000 rials. The comfortable **Bame Sahel** teahouse in the Sahel Hotel, also has a cheap menu including ābgūsht and lamb kabābs for 7500 rials. It also does a breakfast of eggs and bread for 2500 rials.

Restaurant Shahrzad (*Kheyābūn-é Abbās Ābād*) is well worth a splurge and is great for classic Iranian dishes such as fesenjān (17,500 rials). Bread and herbs are complimentary, but you'll pay for all the other salads and side dishes the waiters bring to your table. Service is good and the decor is charming.

The restaurant beneath the **Pardis Apartment Hotel** isn't bad and has a reasonably priced menu. Expect a meal here to cost around 20,000 rials. It's also worth checking out the much fancier restaurant in **Hotel Alī Ghapū** on Kheyābūn-é Chahār Bāgh-é Abbāsī.

About the only fully-fledged non-Iranian option is **Maharaja**, Kheyābūn-é Chahār Bāgh-é Pā'īn, which serves Indian food (although you can still get kabābs!); chicken curry is 16,000 rials, and there's a range of vegetarian dishes, but you need to give them 24 hours notice.

Don't overlook the **Chehelsotoun Restaurant** in the glorious Abbāsī Hotel (☎ 226 009, fax 226 008, Kheyābūn-é Amadegh) – a visit here is a must for the sheer elegance and Persian grandeur of the decor. Prices are not outrageous – about 30,000 rials for a main course. The buffet breakfast is also good value.

Head to the bazaar around the Masjed-é Jame' for the best range of fruit and vegetables. Esfahān is also famous for *gaz*, a chewy nougat confection mixed with chopped pistachios and other nuts – it's sold all over town.

Teahouses

You cannot leave Esfahān without enjoying a pot of tea (or two) and a qalyan at one of its many teahouses. The cost is generally 2000 rials for a pot of tea and 5000 rials for a pipe. There are teahouses at either end of the Sī-o-Sé Bridge; the one at the north end is particularly lively at night. The Khājū Bridge also has a pleasant teahouse at its north end, but far nicer is the cosy one in the middle of the Chubī Bridge, festooned with knick-knacks.

Another Aladdin's Cave of Persian 'whatnots' is **Azadī Khané**, just east of the north end of Meidūn-é Emām Khomeinī. Every surface of the vaulted room is covered with photos of sports stars, daggers and swords and lamps. More intriguing decoration is at **Chaykhané Mamūd** on Kheyābūn-é Hāfez; the hand-held chains are used for flagellation on the anniversary of the martyrdom of Emām Hussein.

The **teahouse** in the gardens of the Chehel Sotūn Palace is charming. The one facing onto the old caravanserai at the Abbāsī Hotel is also recommended, and sometimes has poetry readings or music performances at night. And for the Esfahān version of a sundowner, take tea and cakes at dusk at **Cheysarieh Tea Shop**, upstairs at the entrance to the bazaar; it has a fantastic rooftop view across Meidūn-é Emām Khomeinī.

Entertainment

Apart from soaking up the atmosphere of the teahouses, the most interesting way to spend an evening is to watch a zurkhané practice session at the **Darvazeno Zurkhané** on Kheyābūn-é Sombolestān. The sessions start around 9 pm and you should leave a donation of 10,000 rials.

Shopping

The bazaar, linking Meidūn-é Emām Khomeinī with Masjed-é Jāme', about 2km away, is a highlight of Esfahān – walking its full length is recommended although the sections close to and around the square (including the noisy metalsmiths bazaar) will be of most interest to souvenir hunters. Also worth checking out is the Honar Bāzār, a smaller arcade next to the Hasht Behesht Palace.

Esfahān is one of the best places to buy miniatures, picture frames, carvings and inlaid boxes, metalwork and carpets. Prices will be higher at shops around the main square; remember to haggle.

Getting There & Away

Air Iran Air has two offices, one (☎ 228 999) on Kheyābūn-é Chahār Bāgh Abbāsī and the other (☎ 228 200) in a nearby shopping complex along Kheyābūn-é Amadegh. Iran Air flies several times daily to Tehrān (91,000 rials), once daily to Shīrāz (91,000 rials) and less regularly to Bandar-é Abbās (159,000 rials), Kermān (118,000 rials), Mashhad (166,000 rials) and Zāhedān (178,000 rials). It also flies weekly to Kuwait City (US$118), while Kish Airlines (☎ 204 477) goes to Dubai (US$96).

Bus Although there are two major bus stations, every bus you'll need leaves from the more convenient Kaveh bus station, about 4.5km north of Meidūn-é Emām Hussein. Among other places, buses regularly go to Kāshān (8500 rials, four hours); Kermān (21,000 rials by Volvo, 12 hours); Shīrāz (16,000 rials, nine hours); Tehrān (10,500 rials or 20,000 rials by Volvo, seven hours); Tabrīz (22,500 rials by Volvo, 16 hours); and Yazd (7000 rials, five hours).

Train Express trains leave Esfahān for Tehrān (10 hours) at 11 pm daily (16,900 1st class; 10,000 rials 2nd class). From Esfahān, *all* trains go north towards Tehrān; there is no direct train to Yazd or beyond.

The train station is around 10km east of the centre, on the way to the airport, but there's a ticket booking office (☎ 224 425) on Meidūn-é Enghelāb-é Eslāmī. Passengers with prebooked train tickets can catch a special bus from outside the Kowsar International Hotel on Bōlvār-é Mellat, to the west of the southern end of the Sī-o-Sé bridge – check this with the ticket office.

Getting Around

To get to/from the airport, 12km from the city centre, catch a shared taxi from Meidūn-é Takhtī and another from Ghods or Lalé squares; *from* the airport, plenty of shared taxis head to the city. Hiring a whole taxi costs 20,000 rials.

Central Esfahān is compact enough to walk around. Many shared taxis ply the streets, but always check the prices before

---

Esfahān to Doğubayazıt

Cycling Days: 12
Distance: 1425km

Don't take the main road from Esfahān to Tehrān; turn off at the first junction and head to Natanz, 125km north. There's one hotel in town. It's around 80km to Kāshān through lovely cycling country. From Kāshān, I went to Ghom (105km) and then to Tehrān (150km); the traffic is *hell* when you get into the city. I cycled along the hard shoulder of the old highway out of Tehrān to Ghazvīn (130km) and then on to Zanjān (165km) – not very inspiring. This road runs parallel to the new autobahn which cyclists are not allowed on.

The scenery starts to improve from Zanjān towards Tabrīz. It took me a day to reach Miyaneh, 140km all uphill. The green, rolling hills make pedalling through here in May like cycling through Yorkshire. I stopped next at Bostān Ābād (105km) before entering Tabrīz (a farther 55km). Khoy, 165km west of Tabrīz, was the best place to break the journey next, before cycling on to Mākū (145km), the last stop in Iran before the border. Cyclists shouldn't be afraid to go to the front of the queue at immigration – otherwise you'll be waiting all day. From Mākū to Doğubayazıt, the first town across the border in Turkey (65km), can easily be done in half a day.

Sue Cooper

---

getting in; going one 500m block shouldn't cost more than 500 rials.

AROUND ESFAHĀN

If you have spare time, or want to escape the crowds, there are some interesting sights around Esfahān. **Golestān-é Shohadā**, the cemetery for those who died in the Iran-Iraq War, is an unforgettable sight. Foreigners are welcome to walk around, but avoid Fridays and mourning days. The cemetery is about 1.5km south of the Khājū Bridge.

In Kaladyn, about 7km west of the city centre, is **Manār Jombān**, the small tomb of the revered holy man Abu Abdollah, built in 1311. This otherwise unexceptional building is famous for its shaking minarets – which really do shake when pushed by one of the guards. It's a strange phenomena, but not really worth paying 15,000 rials to watch. To get here take a shared taxi along Kheyābūn-é Tāleghānī.

If you're up for some exercise, climb to the **Āteshkādé-yé Esfahān**, the ruins of a Sassanian fire temple, perched on top of a small hill, 1.5km farther west along the same road from the Manār Jombān. There are good views from here. Another popular spot for hiking is **Kūh-é Soffeh** (2240m), the crag that lords it over the southern end of Esfahān. If you feel like company, visit on a Friday when hundreds of locals go hiking; it takes around two hours to reach the peak.

Esfahān to Shīrāz

From Esfahān, there's a choice of route – either directly south to Shīrāz, the jumping off point for the ancient ruins of Persepolis, then returning north to the Zoroastrian town of Yazd; or south-east to Yazd then to Shīrāz. We opt for the former route, which allows for a handy flight between Esfahān and Shīrāz, if you're getting tired of desert landscapes and overnight bus journeys. If you were to go Yazd-Shīrāz-Kermān, cover the final leg during daylight as the scenery between Shīrāz and Kermān is particularly dramatic.

SHĪRĀZ
☎ 071 • pop 1,042,801

Shīrāz is the most pleasant large Iranian city after Esfahān. It is the birthplace of several important Persian poets and was capital during the Zand period (1747–79), when many of its beautiful buildings were built or restored. The atmosphere is relaxed and cultivated, the people generous (see the boxed text 'An Invitation to Lunch'), and, amid the ugly concrete blocks and freeways, enough old monuments remain to make it worth stopping for a day or two. It's also the obvious base for visiting the amazing ruins at Persepolis, for which you'll need a full day.

History
People have been living around Shīrāz since prehistoric times, but its foundation as a city dates from AD 684 when the conquering Arabs built their capital here. By the 12th century the city was an important artistic as well as commercial centre. It was spared by the Mongol and Timurid invaders, but fell on hard times after the Safavid period (1502–1722) when it was rocked by earthquakes and looted by Afghan armies.

The enlightened rule of Karīm Khān Zand brought Shīrāz back to glory. Karīm Khān, a great patron of the arts, commissioned many of the city's fine buildings. This period of prosperity was short-lived. The succeeding Ghajar dynasty shifted the capital to Tehrān and demolished Shīrāz's fortifications for good measure. The opening of the trans-Iranian railway in the 1930s took away trade from the city. Today Shīrāz is largely an administrative centre for the south.

Orientation
Most of the things to see, and many of the tourist facilities, are along, or near, the wide, tree-lined Bolvār-é Karīm Khān-é Zand – often simply called 'Zand'. The city centre is Meidūn-é Shohadā, still widely known as Meidūn-é Shahrdārī.

Information
Visa Extensions Shīrāz is a great place for visa extensions. The 'Aliens Bureau' is uphill behind the Hāfez Hospital – it's a little difficult to find so ask for directions. The tourist office (☎ 220 791) has brochures (in German and English) and a good (free) map, but the office itself is not particularly useful. It's opposite Melli Park and is not well signposted.

Money The central branches of the major banks will change money. The best is Bank Melli, which also gives cash advances on MasterCard and Visa, and accepts travellers cheques. The Bank Melli branch at the airport will also change money. To obtain the 'street rate', go to one of the money exchange offices along Zand. The black marketeers hang around Bank Melli and the Arg-é Karīm Khān.

Post & Communications The telephone office is along Kheyābūn-é 22 Bahman, and the well-organised post office is easy to find along a laneway off 22 Bahman. Access to the Internet is available at Gasht Tours

IRAN

IRAN

SHĪRĀZ

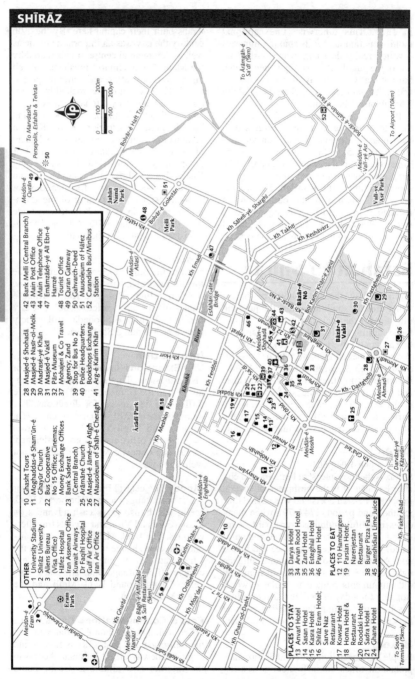

OTHER
1 University Stadium
2 Shirāz University
3 Aliens Bureau
   (Visa Office)
4 Hāfez Hospital
5 Iran Asseman Office
6 Kuwait Airways
7 Dr Faqihi Hospital
8 Gulf Air Office
9 Iran Air Office
10 Ghasht Tours
11 Moghaddas-é Sham'ūn-é
   Ghayūr Church
22 Bus Cooperative
   No 15 Office; Cinemas;
   Money Exchange Offices
23 Bank Saderat
   (Central Branch)
25 Ārāmané Church
26 Masjed-é Jāmé'-yé Atigh
27 Mausoleum of Shāh-é Cherāgh

28 Masjed-é Shohadā
29 Moghaddas-é Sham'ūn-é
30 Madrasé-yé Khān
31 Masjed-é Vakil
32 Pārs Museum
37 Mohajeri & Co Travel
   Agency; Zand
39 Stop for Bus No 2
40 Police Headquarters;
   Bookshops Exchange
41 Arg-é Karim Khān

42 Bank Melli (Central Branch)
43 Main Post Office
44 Main Telephone Office
47 Emāmzāde-yé Ali Ebn-é
   Hamzé
48 Tourist Office
49 Quran Gateway
50 Gahvarch-Deed
51 Mausoleum of Hāfez
52 Carandish Bus/Minibus
   Station

PLACES TO STAY
13 Anvari Hotel
14 Sasan Hotel
15 Kasra Hotel
16 Shirāz Eram Hotel;
   San6 Niaz
   Restaurant
17 Kowsar Hotel
18 Homa Hotel &
   Restaurant
20 Roodaki Hotel
21 Sadra Hotel
24 Ghane Hotel

33 Darya Hotel
34 Arvan Rood Hotel
35 Zand Hotel
36 Esteghlal Hotel
46 Payam Hotel

PLACES TO EAT
12 110 Hamburgers
19 Parsian Hotel;
   Narenjestan
   Restaurant
38 Burger Pizza Fars
45 Jamshidian Lime Juice

(☎ 301 900) on Kheyābūn-é Asad Adādī; it's closed Friday and not particularly reliable when it comes to organising tours – try one of the several travel agents along Bolvār-é Karīm Khān-é Zand instead.

Things to See & Do

It's easy to walk between the main sites in the city centre. Start at the impressive **Arg-é Karīm Khān**, a well-preserved citadel with four circular towers, one curiously leaning. During the Zand period, it was part of a royal courtyard that Karīm Khān planned to rival that of Esfahān. There is little to see inside, but restoration is continuing. It's open from 8 am to 1 pm and 3 to 7 pm daily with entry at 15,000 rials.

Opposite the citadel, the small **Pārs Museum**, set in pretty gardens, contains a mildly interesting exhibition on the life of Karīm Khān, along with other historic artefacts. Opening hours are erratic and it costs 15,000 rials. If time is limited, you're better off exploring the nearby **bazaar** (see Shopping later in this section), where you'll also find the majestic **Masjed-é Vakīl**. The 'Regent's Mosque' has a lovely inner courtyard surrounded by beautifully tiled alcoves and porches. English-speaking guides hang out by the entrance, and it costs 15,000 rials to go in.

If you don't want to pay to enter a mosque, head south to **Bogh'é-yé Shāh-é Cherāgh**, the tomb of the 'King of the Lamp' housing the remains of Sayyed Mīr Ahmad (a brother of Emām Rezā of Mashhad fame), who died, or was killed, in Shīrāz in AD 835. A mausoleum was erected over the grave in the mid-14th century, and it's now an important Shi'ite place of pilgrimage. You can enter the shrine, but you must take off your shoes. In the complex, there's also a small, unmarked **museum** with displays of fine china and glassware, a post office, telephone office and bookshop. The mausoleum is located just south of the bazaar, and is open from about 7 am to 10 pm daily. Women can borrow a chādor from the bookshop outside the gate.

Also worth a quick look is **Masjed-é Shohadā**, the 'Martyrs' Mosque', one of the largest and oldest in Iran, dating from the 13th century. It has little in the way of decorations, but it does boast some impressive barrel vaulting and a huge courtyard (more

An Invitation to Lunch

Iranian hospitality is legendary and it's rare for visitors not to experience some, if not many, engaging and humbling instances of it during their travels. One of the most memorable happened to me in Shīrāz.

It was noon and I was cooling down with a tub of *falūdé*, Shīrāz's favourite dessert, when Mohsen, a lime-juice maker, asked me what I was doing in town. Plenty of Iranians approach foreigners, eager to practice their English, but Mohsen was more proficient than most and very courteous. After five minutes chatting I was invited back to his nearby home. On the way I stopped to buy cantaloupe melons – Mohsen insisted on paying.

Going beyond the high walls and forbidding metal gates that shield Iranian homes is a fascinating experience. This large, elegant home was shared by Mohsen's parents and his brother's family as well as his own family. Sitting on carpets and cushions beneath an awning in the courtyard I was offered lime juice and introduced to the family members, including Sanah, Mohsen's six-year-old daughter, and Mohsen's mother, who insisted I stay for lunch.

The women ate indoors while I sat with the men and children outside, enjoying a delicious vegetable stew and a mountain of fluffy rice. Our conversation covered all topics, from national politics to how the family all pitched in to make the lime juice that they sold in their shop.

After a couple of hours I reluctantly had to leave to continue my research, but I returned the next day with a couple of small presents for Sanah and Mohsen's brother, a stamp and coin collector. He was so pleased that he rushed into the house and returned with a present for me.

Simon Richmond

than 11,000 sq metres). The only time you'll be able to look around is Friday.

Always open is one of the city's most beautiful mosques – the **Emāmzādé-yé Alī Ebn-é Hamzé**. It has a distinctive onion dome and a dazzling mirror-tiled interior –

you'll pass it while walking north along Kheyābūn-é Hāfez to **Ārāmgāh-é Hāfez**, the tomb of the celebrated poet (open from about 8 am to 9 pm daily; entry is 20,000 rials). The marble tombstone, engraved with verse, is surrounded by a small neat garden and pools. At the back of the garden is an atmospheric *teahouse*, a library and bookshop.

You'll need to take taxis to reach Shīrāz's other attractions. **Ārāmgāh-é Sa'dī**, the tomb of local poet Sa'dī, is set in tranquil gardens with a *teahouse*, about 5km north of the centre. A similar distance west of the centre are the picturesque **Bāgh-é Afīf Ābād**. The gardens, surrounding a former palace that now houses an interesting **military museum**, are only open from 4.30 to 7.30 pm daily. Entry is 20,000 rials.

Eram Park, known as the 'Garden of Paradise' has shady rows of cypress trees and many rose plantations. It's open daily during daylight hours with entry 20,000 rials. The palace in the centre of the park is closed to the public.

On the hillside at the north of Shīrāz, is the **Darvazé-yé Quran**, a monumental gateway first built in the 10th century – the present structure is much more modern, but still impressive. There are great **views** and **hikes** in the area, and a couple of good *teahouses*. It's particularly pleasant in the evening. Stop here if you've chartered a vehicle to Persepolis or beyond.

Places to Stay – Budget
Zand Hotel (☎ 229 49, Kheyābūn-é Dehnadī) is one of the best budget options. The owners don't speak English, but they're very friendly and the carpeted rooms are set around a quiet courtyard. Most have showers inside, but toilets outside and singles/doubles cost 13,900/24,340 rials.

The basic *Arvan Rood Hotel (☎ 420 41, Kheyābūn-é Pīrūzī)* has grim rooms for 14,000/24,000 rials. Better is *Darya Hotel (☎ 217 78)*, across the road, which has rooms with bathroom and an English-speaking manager. Singles/doubles/triples are 22,000/30,000/40,000 rials.

Esteghlal Hotel (☎ 277 28, Kheyābūn-é Dehnadī) is well set up for budget travellers, with money exchange, laundry, and an English-speaking manager who can arrange reasonably cheap tours to Persepolis. Small, clean singles/doubles/triples,

with private bathroom, cost 35,000/40,000/60,000 rials.

Payam Hotel (☎ 279 94, Kheyābūn-é 22 Bahman) is another convivial place on a quiet street. Doubles with shared bathroom cost 25,000 rials.

Kasra Hotel (☎ 334 957, Kheyābūn-é Anvarī) has basic rooms with shared bathrooms for 24,000/30,000 rials, but it's often full. Farther down the street and a step up in quality is *Anvarī Hotel (☎ 337 591)*. The rooms, with private bathroom, TV and fridge, are clean and comfortable. Doubles/triples are 50,000/60,000 rials. There's a handy car park (10,000 rials per night) across the road.

Places to Stay – Mid-Range
Sasan Hotel (☎ 337 830, Kheyābūn-é Anvarī) has acceptable but overpriced rooms with TV, fridge and towels, for US$15/18 a single/double, including breakfast.

A couple of options along Kheyābūn-é Rūdakī worth checking out are *Sadra Hotel (☎/fax 247 40)* and *Roodaki Hotel (☎/fax 269 09)*. Both have comfortable rooms for US$20/30, including breakfast. At Roodaki Hotel the prices are negotiable.

Among the better choices on Bolvār-é Karīm Khān-é Zand is *Kowsar Hotel (☎ 335 724, fax 333 117)*. Large rooms with a fridge and TV cost US$20/30. The staff speak English, but some travellers have complained about overcharging on bills. Up the road, *Shīrāz Eram Hotel (☎/fax 337 201)* is a popular tour-group haunt, with well-furnished rooms for US$25/35, including breakfast. It also has a restaurant and 24-hour coffeehouse.

If you're stuck, try the less glamorous *Ghane Hotel (☎ 247 40, Kheyābūn-é Tōhid)*. It's set back from the main road, and quieter than other places. The rooms are small, but decent enough, and cost US$20/25.

Places to Eat
Crowds gather daily around *110 Hamburgers (Kheyābūn-é Anvarī)* and for good reason. Chunky Western-style burgers, Iranian-style chips (French fries) and cola costs about 6000 rials. Pizzas (10,000 rials) take a bit longer but are worth the wait.

You can also get burgers at *Burger Pizza Fars* on the corner of Bolvār-é Karīm

Khān-é Zand and Kheyābūn-é Sa'dī, but the scrumptious pizzas are its speciality. For dessert, try *Jamshidian Lime Juice*, which sells mouth-watering falūdé and ice cream. The pickle shops along this road are great places for self-caterers; put together some spicy bits and pieces from here with fruit, veg and bread from the bazaar for a picnic in one of the parks.

If you're looking for something a bit classier, try *Sarve Naz Restaurant* on the 1st floor of the Shīrāz Eram Hotel. The menu is in English, and includes dishes such as fish (14,500 rials), chicken schnitzel (14,000 rials) and steak (18,000 rials). *Narenjestan*, the restaurant at the Parsian Hotel, isn't bad either, though pricier. At the time of research *Roodaki Hotel* was building a traditional Persian restaurant in its basement.

For a splurge, try either branch of the *Sufi Restaurant*, worth visiting for good food and atmosphere. The original one, near the Bāgh-é Afīf Ābād garden is on Kheyābūn-é Zagarī, while the second branch is on Kheyābūn-é Affif Ābād. Expect to pay about 25,000 rials per person, including soup and the mandatory visit to the salad bar.

The *teahouses* in Shīrāz are not as charming as those in Esfahān, but there are some pleasant places for a cuppa at the Hāfez and Sa'dī mausoleums, and at the Quran Gateway and Bāzār-é Vakīl.

Shopping

The **Bāzār-é Vakīl** (Vakil Bazaar) built by Karīm Khān is one of the finest in Iran. It's a great place to look for carpets and handicrafts; you'll find a good selection in the picturesque courtyard, **Saray Marshir**. The bazaar also has a **bathhouse** and a few *teahouses*. The **Bāzār-é Nō** (New Bazaar) is also worth a stroll around. Shīrāz is a good place to buy printed fabrics, tea sets and qalyans made from copper and bronze.

Getting There & Away

Air Iran Air (☎ 330 041) flies several times daily to Tehrān (138,000 rials) and Mashhad (188,000 rials) and daily to Esfahān (91,000 rials). There are also flights to the Gulf cities. Iran Asseman (☎ 308 841) has services to Tehrān only, at the same price. Gulf Air (☎ 301 962) has an office along Zand. There are also international flights to Abu Dhabi, Bahrain, Dubai and Qatar.

Bus & Minibus The main Carandish bus/minibus station is also known as the Termīnāl-é Bozorg. Bus tickets can also be bought in advance at one of the bus company offices along Zand. There are regular daily services for Esfahān (11,000 rials or 20,000 rials by Volvo, eight hours); Kermān (13,500 rials, eight hours); Tabrīz (32,000 rials, 24 hours); Tehrān (20,000 rials or 35,000 rials by Volvo, 16 hours); Yazd (10,000 rials, eight hours); and Zāhedān (28,000 rials, 17 hours).

Shared Taxi From the Carandish bus station, shared taxis leave for regional towns, including Marvdasht (for Persepolis), and occasionally travel all the way to Esfahān.

Getting Around

Bus No 10 travels between the airport, 10km east of the centre, and a stop behind the Arg-é Karīm Khān. Shared taxis for the airport leave irregularly from Meidūn-é Valī-yé Asr; from the airport, a private taxi will cost 10,000 rials.

The handy bus No 2 starts from the corner of Zand and Kheyābūn-é Sa'dī, and passes the tourist office, the Ārāmgāh-é Hāfez and Meidūn-é Golestān (for the Carandish bus station).

AROUND SHĪRĀZ

It makes sense to combine visits to Naghsh-é Rostam and Pasargadae with Persepolis. The archaeologically linear way to do this is to visit Pasargadae first (it's also the sight with the least-impressive ruins), but bear in mind the later in the day you arrive at Persepolis, the hotter and busier with tour groups it's likely to be.

Naghsh-é Rostam

Hewn out of a cliff, the four tombs of Naghsh-é Rostam are believed to be those of Darius I, Artaxerxes, Xerxes I and Darius II (from right to left as you look at the cliff). There are also eight **reliefs** from later in the Sassanian period (AD 224–637) depicting scenes of imperial conquests and royal investitures, and what is probably a **fire temple** from the Achaemenid period (559–330 BC). The best time for photos is before mid-afternoon.

[Continued on page 310]

PERSEPOLIS

A visit to the ruins of the ancient city of Persepolis (Takht-é Jamshīd) is certainly a highlight of Iran. It is the best preserved of Persia's ruined cities and the finest legacy of the great Achaemenian Empire, which ruled Persia between 559 and 330 BC. The most impressive feature of what remains are the splendid bas-reliefs adorning many of the staircases and palaces on the site.

Entry costs 50,000 rials and the site is open from 7.30 am to 7.30 pm. A sound-and-light show takes place at around 8.30 pm some Thursdays and Fridays. It is in Fārsī only and often goes on for hours, but it can be a great way to get another perspective on this spectacular site.

History

The first capital of the Achaemenian Empire was farther north at Pasargadae, but in about 512 BC Darius I started constructing this massive palace complex to serve as the summer capital. Some historians believe that the site was chosen by Cambyses II, son of Cyrus the Great. It was completed by a host of subsequent kings over a period of 150 years.

In its heyday the city spread over an area of 125,000 sq metres, and it was the place where all the peoples of the empire came to pay homage to the kings over Nō Rūz (the New Year); at other times of year it was probably deserted. For a city at the heart of such a great empire, Persepolis was rarely mentioned in foreign records, fuelling speculation that the existence of the city was kept a secret from the outside world.

Persepolis stands on the slopes of Mt Rahmat and at one time it was surrounded by an 18m-high wall. Its original name was Pārsā; the first known reference to it by its Greek name of Persepolis came after its sacking.

Inset: Detail from the Apadana Stairway (Photo by Patrick Syder)
Left: Bas-relief on the gateway of the Palace of Darius I (the Tachara) depicting the king doing battle with a lion.
Right: Bas-relief showing the king and bearers of the royal throne, Palace of 100 Columns.

SIMON RICHMOND

PATRICK SYDER

Persepolis was burned to the ground during Alexander the Great's visit in 331 BC, although historians are divided about whether this was accidental or in retaliation for the destruction of Athens by Xerxes. The ruins you see today are a shadow of Persepolis' former glory, even though they are more revealing than the less well preserved traces of the Achaemenian administrative capital at Shūsh or farther north at Pasargadae. The ancient city was lost to time for centuries, covered by dust and sand, before excavations began to reveal its full glory in the 1930s.

Entering the City

From the outside, much of the city is obscured by the high walls. The entrance to the site is, as it orignally was, via the monumental Grand Stairway carved from massive blocks of stone but with shallow steps. The arrival of important delegations was once heralded by trumpeters at the top of the staircase; acolytes then led the dignatories through **Xerxes Gateway**, or the Gate of All Nations, still a wonderfully impressive

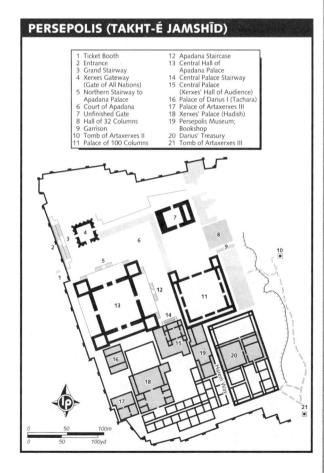

PERSEPOLIS (TAKHT-É JAMSHĪD)

1 Ticket Booth	12 Apadana Staircase
2 Entrance	13 Central Hall of
3 Grand Stairway	Apadana Palace
4 Xerxes Gateway	14 Central Palace Stairway
(Gate of All Nations)	15 Central Palace
5 Northern Stairway to	(Xerxes' Hall of Audience)
Apadana Palace	16 Palace of Darius I (Tachara)
6 Court of Apadana	17 Palace of Artaxerxes III
7 Unfinished Gate	18 Xerxes' Palace (Hadish)
8 Hall of 32 Columns	19 Persepolis Museum;
9 Garrison	Bookshop
10 Tomb of Artaxerxes II	20 Darius' Treasury
11 Palace of 100 Columns	21 Tomb of Artaxerxes III

monument today. Modern graffiti now scars the stone panels, although some of those scrawls have become footnotes of history themselves, with many left by British soldiers posted here in the 19th and 20th centuries.

The gateway was built during the time of Xerxes I and guarded by bull-like figures, strongly reminiscent of the statues of Assyria.

Palace of 100 Columns

Visitors from nations of lesser importance were sometimes led to the Palace of 100 Columns where the king would receive them. As you follow in their footsteps through the **Court of Apadana**, look for the **Unfinished Gate**, the **Hall of 32 Columns** and the impressive double-headed eagles, or griffins. This was the largest of the Persepolis palaces and was where subject nations came to restate their loyalty and bring tribute in a ritual reassertion of the power of the Achaemenian Empire.

Apadana Palace & Staircase

Important Persian and Median notables were more likely to be ushered to the Apadana Palace to the south. Constructed on a terrace of stone by Xerxes I, the palace was reached via another staircase; the more important people were, the higher they had to be physically. The bas-reliefs along the northern wall depict the scenes of splendour that must have accompanied the arrival of delegations meeting with the king.

Most impressive of all, however, are the bas-reliefs along the Apadana Staircase of the eastern wall. The northern panels recount the reception of the Persians in their long robes and the Medes in their shorter robes, and the three tiers of figures are amazingly well preserved. Each tier contains representations of the Imperial Guard or the Immortals. On the upper tier they are followed by the royal procession, the royal valets and the horses of the Elamite king of chariots, while in the lower two they precede the Persians with their feather headdresses and the Medes in their round caps. The stairs themselves are guarded by Persian soldiers.

The central panels of the staircase are dedicated to symbols of the Zoroastrian deity, Ahura Mazda. God is symbolised by a ring with wings, flanked by two eagles with human heads and guarded by four Persian and Median soldiers; the Persians carry the indented shields.

The panels at the southern end are for many the most interesting, showing 23 delegations bringing their tributes to the Achaemenian King.

PATRICK SYDER

Left: Spectacular bas-reliefs provide archaeologists with a narrative of the Achaemenian Empire.

Providing a rich record of the nations of the time, the southern panels are arguably most evocative of the power of the great Achaemenian Empire.

The Royal Palaces & Central Palace

The south-western corner of the site is dominated by the palaces attributed to each of the kings. The **Palace of Darius I** (also known as the Tachara or Winter Palace) is the most striking, with its impressive gateways and bas-reliefs and cuneiform inscriptions around the perimeter. The palace opens onto a royal courtyard, which is also flanked by an unfinished **Palace of Ataxerxes III** and **Xerxes' Palace** (Hadish).

Central Palace is also referred to as the Tripylon or Xerxes' Hall of Audience and stands at the heart of Persepolis. Its location enabled the king to receive his notables in an area shielded from outside view and it was here that many important political decisions were taken. On the columns of the eastern doorway are reliefs showing Darius on his throne, borne by the representatives of 28 countries. The crown prince Xerxes stands behind his father.

Persepolis Museum

Immediately to the east of Central Palace is the museum. Despite the depictions around the door of the king defeating evil, the original purpose of this structure is not known. The museum contains a stone foundation tablet and a range of artefacts discovered during excavations: alabaster vessels, cedar wood, lance and arrow tips. Look also for the small representation of a Sassanian king on a horse. Entry to the museum costs 20,000 rials, which is part of the initial fee paid when entering the site (it sometimes closes for an hour at lunch time).

The Treasury & Tombs

The south-west corner of the site is dominated by Darius' Treasury,

where archaeologists found stone tablets in Elamite and Akkadian detailing the wages paid to the unsung (and underpaid) labourers who built Persepolis. Little more than a few bas-reliefs and some of the foundations of the hundreds of columns remain. On the hill above the treasury are the rock-hewn tombs of Ataxerxes II and III, each with Zoroastrian carvings. The view from the tombs over Persepolis and the plain extending to the west is quite beautiful.

Getting There & Away

To reach Persepolis from Shīrāz take a bus from the back of Carandish Bus Terminal to Marvdasht, from where you can catch a shared taxi the 14km to Persepolis. Alternatively, catch a Shīrāz to Esfahān bus and ask to be let off at Persepolis junction; from here it is a 4km walk.

Right: Bull-like figures stand sentry at the Gate of All Nations. (Photo by Patrick Syder)

Anthony Ham

[Continued from page 305]

The tombs are worth seeing close up, but if you want to avoid paying the 10,000 rial entry fee, you can see most of them from outside the fence. Naghsh-é Rostam is 6km along the road north from Persepolis and best reached by taxi. There's no charge for inspecting Naghsh-é Radjab, four good Sassanian bas relief carvings that are hidden from the road at the turn-off to Naghsh-é Rostam.

The only restaurant in the area is *Laneh Tawoos* (☎ 07283-5022) on the road between Persepolis and Naghsh-é Rostam. It's a pleasant shady place and serves good kabābs, stews and salads for around 15,000 rials per meal. The management has plans to build cabins here and *camping* is possible.

Pasargadae

Begun under Cyrus (Kouroush) the Great in about 546 BC, the city of Pasargadae was superseded soon after Cyrus' death by Persepolis. It's nowhere near as visually stimulating as Persepolis, and what remains is widely scattered, so you'll need a guide.

The first structure you'll see is the six-tiered **Tomb of Cyrus**, the best preserved of the remains. Within walking distance of the tomb are the insubstantial remains of three **Achaemenid Palaces**; and the ruins of a tower on a plinth, known as the **Prison of Solomon**. Other remains are farther afield.

Pasargadae is 130km north of Shīrāz. If you haven't chartered a taxi directly, get a minibus to Marvdasht from Shīrāz, another minibus or shared taxi to Sā'adatshahr, and another shared taxi to Pasargadae. Alternatively, catch a bus between Shīrāz and Esfahān, and hitch a ride to Pasargadae from the turn-off. Entry to the site is 10,000 rials.

YAZD
☎ 0351 • pop 400,000

Yazd, wedged between the northern Dasht-é Kavīr desert, and the southern Dasht-é Lūt, boasts Iran's finest inhabited ancient mud-brick city. An important centre for Zoroastrianism, Yazd is also the best place to find out more about this fascinating religion. It's strongly Islamic too, so there are some excellent mosques. The atmosphere is relaxed and friendly, making Yazd a good base to chill out and explore the surrounding desert.

Orientation & Information

The adjacent bus and train station are 2km south of the town's focal point, Meidūn-é Beheshtī, around which you'll find budget accommodation. The old city is another 1km north of here.

The large, unsignposted building opposite the bus station is responsible for visa extensions.

You can change money at Bank Melli at the Shohadā crossroads, or, more conveniently, at Amin Money Exchange, on Kheyābūn-é Emām Khomeinī.

Women in Iran

Those Iranian women who choose not to wear the chādor (and there are many) make up for their pious sisters by piling on make-up, exposing as much hair as possible without actually removing their veils altogether and wearing the most opulent stack heels available on the Iranian shoe market. These attitudes to dress are found in the provincial capitals as well as Tehrān, all of which leads the visitor to conclude that the moral police are not nearly as strict about dress codes as they used to be.

While female tourists are not encouraged to bend Islamic law, should they choose to do so their eccentricity will be tolerated for the simple reason that they are foreigners. Iranians are getting used to the increasing number of foreign tour groups which (thanks to the security of numbers) often include women only cursorily observing hejāb requirements.

Independent travellers will feel equally comfortable as long as they wear a loose kaftan or *roupush* (light manteau), trousers and a headscarf. Plain colours need not be worn, either on the headscarf or the coat; and a chādor is only required when it is handed over at the entrance to a shrine. Looking smart and well presented will earn the tourist infinitely more respect than wearing a chādor (girls will be ogled in Tehrān even if they wear bags on their heads for the simple reason that they are foreign and female).

Barunka O'Shaughnessy

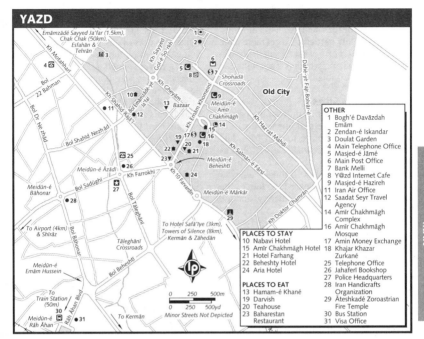

YAZD

Emāmzādé Sayyed Ja'far (1.5km),
Chak Chak (50km),
Esfahān &
Tehrān

Shohadā
Crossroads

Old City

Bazaar

Meidūn-é
Amīr
Chakhmāgh

Meidūn-é
Beheshtī

Meidūn-é Āzādī

Kh Farrokhi

Meidūn-é
Bāhonar

Meidūn-é Mārkār

To Airport (4km)
& Shīrāz

Tāleghānī
Crossroads

To Hotel Safā'īye (3km),
Towers of Silence (8km),
Kermān & Zāhedān

Meidūn-é
Emām Hussein

To
Train Station
(50m)

Meidūn-é
Rāh Āhan

To Kermān

0   250   500m
0   250   500yd
Minor Streets Not Depicted

OTHER
1 Bogh'é Davāzdah Emām
2 Zendan-é Iskandar
3 Doulat Garden
4 Main Telephone Office
5 Masjed-é Jāmé
6 Main Post Office
7 Bank Melli
8 Y@zd Internet Cafe
9 Masjed-é Hazireh
11 Iran Air Office
12 Saadat Seyr Travel Agency
14 Amīr Chakhmāgh Complex
16 Amīr Chakhmāgh Mosque
17 Amin Money Exchange
18 Khajar Khazar Zurkané
25 Telephone Office
26 Jahaferī Bookshop
27 Police Headquarters
28 Iran Handicrafts Organization
29 Āteshkadé Zoroastrian Fire Temple
30 Bus Station
31 Visa Office

PLACES TO STAY
10 Nabavi Hotel
15 Amīr Chakhmāgh Hotel
21 Hotel Farhang
22 Beheshty Hotel
24 Aria Hotel

PLACES TO EAT
13 Hamam-é Khané
19 Darvish
20 Teahouse
23 Baharestan Restaurant

IRAN

The main post office is next to Bank Melli, and there's a handy telephone office just north of Meidūn-é Āzādī.

The best place for information and the Internet is Y@zd Internet Cafe (☎ 238 32, e touristicplace@yahoo.com), near the entrance of Masjed-é Jāmé; the friendly English-speaking guys can arrange trips around the town and into the desert, as well as bicycle rental and vegetarian dinners. It is open from 8.30 am to 9 pm daily.

The staff at Saadat Seyr Travel Agency (☎ 660 693), 21/1 Bolvār-é Emāmzādé Jafar, speak English and can arrange train as well as flight tickets.

Note that the bazaar, many shops and all museums in Yazd shut for the 1 to 4 pm siesta.

Old City

Wandering through the Unesco-recognised Old City of Yazd, a warren of mud-brick wall-lined streets, is like stepping back in time. Look for the *bādgīrs* (wind towers) on rooftops, which are designed to catch even the lightest breeze to cool the dark interiors of the houses.

If you need something to aim for, ask directions to Zendan-é Iskandar (Alexander's Prison), an underground jail supposedly built by the Greek general – it's beside the 10th-century Bogh'é Davāzdah Emām (Tomb of the 12 Emāms). The prison has been renovated and there are a few ethnographic displays inside; entry is 10,000 rials.

Islamic Monuments

Among Yazd's many mosques, the most magnificent is the beautifully tiled 14th-century **Masjed-é Jāme'**. Its remarkably high, tiled entrance portal, flanked with two towering minarets, dominates the Old City; see if you can find a caretaker to show you the stairs up to the roof.

The pretty **Masjed-é Hazireh**, on Kheyābūn-é Emām Khomeinī, is worth a look. The impressive twin-minareted entrance to the **Amīr Chakmāgh Complex** was built as a grandstand for the annual religious passion plays held on 9 and 10 Moharram (usually in April). Behind the entrance is a small **bazaar**.

If you have time, 1.5km north-west of the centre is **Emāmzādé Sayyed Ja'far**, a shrine decorated inside with tens of thousands of mirror tiles, and exquisite mosaics. It also has lovely **gardens**. To get there, take a shared taxi north-west along Bolvār-é Jomhūrī-yé Eslāmī, which is a continuation of Kheyābūn-é Motahharī.

Zoroastrian Sites

On the edge of Yazd, 7km from the centre, are the striking **Towers of Silence**, a particularly atmospheric place to visit from late afternoon to dusk. Known to Zoroastrians as *dachme*, 'the place the dead go free', corpses were left in these hilltop citadels to be picked dry by vultures. At the foot of the hills is the current walled cemetery, and the crumbling buildings where bodies were once prepared before being carried to the citadels. It's a great spot for **hiking**, but take plenty of water and food since there's nothing out here. It's possible to cycle here from the centre, or you could take a good tour with the local Zoroastrian archaeologist Dinyar Shahzadi (☎ 204 04, 478 06) for 20,000 rials per hour including transport.

On the way to the towers drop by the **Āteshkadé**, a small Zoroastrian fire temple. The sacred flame, apparently burning since about AD 470, was transferred here from its original site in 1940. There's some English information about the religion, but it's better if you have a guide. The building is open from 7 am to noon and 4 to 7 pm daily; although a sign says entrance is free, a small donation will be appreciated.

About 50km from Yazd, **Chak Chak** is another important **fire temple** which attracts thousands of pilgrims for Nō Rūz, the Iranian New Year around mid-March. The temple is part of the desert tour organised by Y@zd Internet Cafe. Chartering a taxi here will cost around 80,000 rials return.

Places to Stay

Amīr Chakhmāgh Hotel (☎ 669 823), upstairs on the south side of the Amīr Chakmāgh Complex, is the best budget option, with clean singles/doubles/triples for 20,000/40,000/45,000 rials. Bathrooms are shared, there's air-con and the management speak a little English.

Beheshty Hotel (☎ 247 17, Kheyābūn-é Emām Khomeinī) has some rather grubby rooms, but is a friendly place. It's a little back from the road and easy to miss.

Singles/doubles/triples are 40,000/50,000/65,000 rials all with shared bathrooms. There are dorm beds for 25,000 rials and you can sleep on the floor for 18,000 rials.

Aria Hotel (☎ 660 411, Kheyābūn-é 10 Farvadīn) has bare bones rooms (many in need of renovation). If you get a room with private shower (but a shared toilet) for 60,000 rials a double it's worth it, otherwise bargain hard for a reduction.

Hotel Farhang (☎ 665 012, Kheyābūn-é Emām Khomeinī) is overpriced at US$30 a double, including breakfast, but is Yazd's best mid-range option. The rooms, all with bathroom, are reasonably decorated; some have three beds making sharing with fellow travellers an option. *Nabavi Hotel* (☎ 661 289, Kheyābūn-é Sayyed Gol-é Sorkh) is a bit cheaper at US$25 per double, but gets more mixed reports for its service.

Places to Eat

Many budget options are clustered around Meidūn-é Beheshtī. Here you'll find *Baharestan Restaurant*, where a kabāb meal costs 10,000 rials. Up the road, along Kheyābūn-é Emām Khomeinī is *Darvish*, a popular place for pizza (8000 rials) and burgers (3000 rials). Look for the black-and-yellow neon sign. For a tasty breakfast, tea and the qalyan, try the great *teahouse* near Hotel Farhang.

Don't miss out on *Hamam-é Khané*, a well-restored bathhouse in the south of the bazaar that's now a restaurant and teahouse. Ābgūsht is 12,000 rials, meatballs is 16,000 rials and *kashk-é bādenjūn* (aubergine, yogurt and mint dip) is 8500 rials. The *Y@zd Internet Cafe* can rustle up a vegetarian stew dinner if given four hours notice.

Hotel Safā'iye (☎ 842 812) in southern Yazd on the way to the Towers of Silence, has the best restaurant of the upmarket hotels, with excellent service and a charming setting. The hotel's Persian style *coffeehouse* is also very pleasant and serves pizza and other light dishes.

Entertainment

You can watch practice sessions of zurkhané at the Khajar Khazar, just off Kheyābūné Emām Khomeinī, between 6 and 7 pm and 8.30 and 9.30 pm Saturday to Thursday.

Yazd Internet Cafe offers night tours of the town.

Shopping

An important caravan station on the trade routes from Central Asia and India (Marco Polo visited here in 1272 en route to China), Yazd remains a renowned weaving centre, known for its silks and brocades – you can buy these in and around the bazaar. Yazd is also famous for intricate glassware and leather bags. There are some interesting antique shops beside the Masjed-é Jamé.

Getting There & Away

Air Iran Air (☎ 283 79) flies twice daily to Tehrān (111,000 rials); and twice weekly to Mashhad (140,000 rials). Iran Asseman (at Saadat Seyr Travel Agency – see Orientation & Information earlier in this chapter) also has flights five times weekly to Tehrān.

Bus & Minibus Many bus companies have offices along Kheyābūn-é Emām Khomeinī. Buses leave from the bus station, accessible by shared taxi from Meidūn-é Beheshtī. Yazd is well connected to all major cities, including Esfahān (7000 rials, five hours), Kermān (8000 rials, six hours), Shīrāz (10,000 rials, seven hours) and Tehrān (15,000 rials or 25,000 rials by Volvo, 10 hours).

Train Trains from Yazd to Tehrān (1st class only, 24,250 rials) depart at 10 pm and midnight daily. Services for Kermān leave at 2.25 am Saturday, Tuesday and Thursday (1st class 15,700 rials; 2nd class 8150 rials). Tickets can be booked at the station and Sadaat Seyr Travel Agency.

Getting Around

Bicycle rental is available from Yazd Internet Cafe for 4000 rials per hour. A shared taxi from the centre of town to the airport is around 1000 rials or 5000 rials for the entire taxi.

Yazd to Mīrjāvé

From Yazd our route crosses the arid Dāsht-é Lūt, punctuated by a few distant jagged mountains and the oasis town of Rafsanjān (the pistachio capital of Iran), heading towards Kermān. This is the last major city before Quetta in Pakistan and you'd do well to stock up on any necessities here before

continuing through the desert. You'd be mad not to break your journey at Bam to visit its astounding citadel. With an early start from Bam, you can reach the border easily in a day, which means avoiding the lacklustre town of Zāhedān.

Along the road from Bam to the border at Mīrjāvé there is a heavy army presence to combat the tribal gangs smuggling drugs from Afghanistan. Foreigners have been kidnapped in this area, so it's highly likely that if you're driving your own vehicle, you'll be required to take an army escort from one check point to the next. On buses, have your passport ready for frequent checks.

KERMĀN

☎ 0341 • pop 340,000

Kermān is a pleasant desert city with an excellent bazaar and other attractions to justify a stopover for a day or more. However, there's nothing extraordinary here and if you've seen Esfahān and Yazd you may choose to push on to Bam.

As with Yazd, Kermān's livelihood depended on its place along the Asian trade routes, but from about the beginning of the Safavid period (1502–1722) the city has increasingly relied on the production of carpets – still one of the major local industries.

Orientation & Information

Most of what you'll want to see or avail yourself of as a visitor is along the main road that links Meidūn-é Shohadā, at the east end of town, with Meidūn-é Āzādī at the west. The bus station is 2km south of Meidūn-é Āzādī and west are the train station (8km) and the airport (4km).

The tourist office (☎ 210 635), on Bolvār-é Jomhūrī-yé Eslāmī, can provide some pamphlets and free city maps but is of little help otherwise.

Visa extensions can be obtained in two hours at the 'Aliens' Bureau' (☎ 222 240); check at the Akhavan Hotel as to its current whereabouts since it moves around.

The central branch of Bank Melli will change money and give cash advances on MasterCard, but you'll get a better rate if you ask the manager at your hotel.

The main post office is next to Bank Melli with the telephone office close by to the north. Internet access is available at the Akhavan Hotel and the Internet Cybercafe,

IRAN

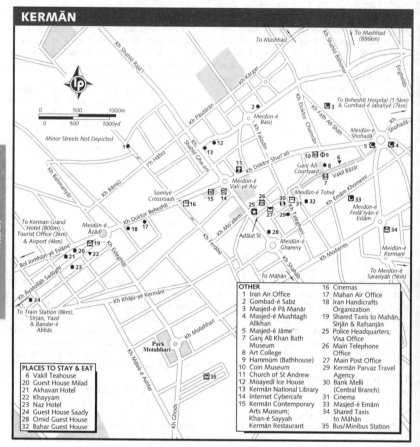

KERMĀN

To Mashhad
To Mashhad (886km)

Minor Streets Not Depicted

To Beheshtī Hospital (1.5km) & Gombad-é Jaballyé (7km)

Meidūn-é Basij

Meidūn-é Shohadā

Ganj Alī Courtyard

Vakīl Bāzār

Meidūn-é Vali-yé Asr

Meidūn-é Tohid

Somīyé Crossroads

Meidūn-é Fedā'īyān-é Eslām

To Kerman Grand Hotel (800m), Tourist Office (3km) & Airport (4km)

Meidūn-é Āzādī

Adālat St

Meidūn-é Ghareny

Meidūn-é Kermāni

To Māhān

To Meidūn-é Sarasīyāb (5km)

To Train Station (8km), Sīrjān, Yazd & Bandar-é Abbās

Park Motahharī

PLACES TO STAY & EAT
6 Vakīl Teahouse
20 Guest House Milad
21 Akhavan Hotel
22 Khayyam
23 Naz Hotel
24 Guest House Saady
28 Omid Guest House
32 Bahar Guest House

OTHER
1 Iran Air Office
2 Gombad-é Sabz
3 Masjed-é Pā Manār
4 Masjed-é Mushtagh Alīkhan
5 Masjed-é Jāme'
7 Ganj Alī Khan Bath Museum
8 Art College
9 Hammūm (Bathhouse)
10 Coin Museum
11 Church of St Andrew
12 Moayedi Ice House
13 Kermān National Library
14 Internet Cybercafe
15 Kermān Contemporary Arts Museum; Khan-é Sayyah Kermān Restaurant
16 Cinemas
17 Mahan Air Office
18 Iran Handicrafts Organization
19 Shared Taxis to Māhān, Sīrjān & Rafsanjān
25 Police Headquarters; Visa Office
26 Main Telephone Office
27 Main Post Office
29 Kermān Parvaz Travel Agency
30 Bank Melli (Central Branch)
31 Cinema
33 Masjed-é Emām
34 Shared Taxis to Māhān
35 Bus/Minibus Station

3rd floor Ansar Al Rasūl Building, on Meidūn-é Vali-yé Asr, open from 8 am to 1 pm and 4 to 9 pm Saturday to Thursday. One hour is 30,000 rials.

A couple of local guides who can help set up trips to nearby attractions and show you around town are Ali Mobini (☎ 2716 361) and the German-speaking Jallal Mehdizade (☎ 2702 185). Note that the bazaar, many shops and all museums in Kermān shut for the 1 to 4 pm siesta.

Things to See
Starting on the east side of Meidūn-é Shohadā, the twin domed **Masjed-é Mushtagh Alīkhan**, which has a small but tranquil walled garden with roses, weeping willows and pools, is worth a look. Opposite, is Ker-

mān's most impressive mosque, **Masjed-é Jāme'**. Built in 1349 it has four lofty eivāns, shimmering blue tiles and a clock tower. You can exit from here directly into the covered **Vakīl Bāzār**, most of which dates from the Safavid period (1502–1722); you'll need a couple of hours for exploration.

One of the bazaar's *hammūms* (steam-baths) has been well restored as the **Ganj Alī Khan Bath Museum**, a slightly tacky museum with a small collection of wax dummies indicating the purpose of a bathhouse. Entry is 10,000 rials. For the same price you can experience the real thing, a working **hammūm**, which is across the **Ganj Alī Courtyard** through the gold bazaar. Around the courtyard also peep into the **art college** on the north side to see some fine mosaics; ask the old caretaker to let you see the attached **mosque**.

A short walk south of the bazaar, the **Masjed-é Emām** dates from the 11th century, and includes remains of the original mehrāb *(mihrab)* and minaret, though much of the building has been rebuilt. You might well find the **Kermān Contemporary Arts Museum** more diverting – it displays the eclectic works of Sayyed Alī Akbar San'atī, a famous 20th-century artist born in Kermān. Entry is 500 rials.

Also worth a quick look, especially at night when it's dramatically lit up, is the **Moayedī Ice House**, an ingenious pre-electricity way of storing ice over the summer – the central storehouse is now used as a children's library. The **Kermān National Library** converted from an old factory is a very attractive building with pleasant gardens that will do nicely for a picnic.

Heading to the eastern edge of town, the rocky area around the **Gombad-é Jabalīyé** a small, octagonal dome of unknown age or purpose, is excellent for hiking. Take a shared taxi from Meidūn-é Shohadā.

Places to Stay
The basic *Bahar Guest House* (☎ 224 59) just south of Meidūn-é Tohid is one of the cheapest in town – only 10,000 rials per person – but is extremely reluctant to take foreigners.

Guest House Saady (☎ 438 02) just off Kheyābūn-é Āyatollāh Sadūghī – look for the painted sign in English on the corner – is more welcoming. It has a number of good, quiet singles/doubles for 14,000/24,000 rials. More central is *Omid Guest House* (☎ 220 571, Meidūn-é Ghareny) with decent enough rooms set around a courtyard that's also a handy parking space for overlanders with a vehicle. Rooms here are 25,000 rials per person, all with shared bathroom.

Guest House Milad (☎ 458 62, Kheyābūné Āyatollāh Sadūghī) has pokey rooms but the management speak English and are friendly enough. Doubles start at 30,000/50,000 rials for shared/private bathroom.

The best mid-range option is *Akhavan Hotel* (☎ 414 11, fax 491 13, e akhavanh otel@yahoo.com, Kheyābūn-é Āyatollāh Sadūghī). It has large, well-furnished rooms, Internet, laundry service, and an excellent restaurant. The tourist-savvy managers speak good English and can arrange all your transport needs. The high-season rate is US$20/30, including breakfast, but it gets down to 60,000/90,000 rials at other times.

Naz Hotel (☎ 467 86, fax 504 98), opposite the Akhavan, is much more come-as-you-are; if you can rustle up a manager you may get to see the large double rooms which are around US$20 (negotiable).

Places to Eat
There are several fast-food options around Meidūn-é Āzādī and Meidūn-é Vali-yé Asr, where you'll also find some excellent ice-cream shops. If you're looking for something more substantial the *Akhavan Hotel* has a set menu of fish/meat/chicken, soup, bread, salad, rice and a drink, for about 20,000 rials.

Khan-é Sayyah Kermān Restaurant in the grounds of the Kermān Contemporary Arts Museum has traditional decor and furniture, and tasty but overpriced food, from about 15,000 rials for the most basic kabāb. At lunch there's a salad bar that's worth 15,000 rials, but check the bill for overcharging. The same goes at the atmospheric *Khayyam* teahouse, where you'll need to double check prices before ordering. A bowl of ābgūsht is, again, overpriced at 12,000 rials.

All the prices are honest at the *Vakīl Teahouse* inside the bazaar because you pay at the door. Because you also have to pay a 5000 rial entrance fee, this beautifully decorated old bathhouse, with elegant brickwork is an expensive indulgence; if you've already seen these in Esfahān you won't need to see this. In its favour, there is live music, the ābgūsht is a reasonable 6000 rials and the tea (1000 rials) is spiced with cardamom, which makes a change.

For self-catering head to the east end of the bazaar where you'll find the fruit-and-veg sellers.

Getting There & Away
Air Iran Air (☎ 588 71) flies to Tehrān daily (165,000 rials), less often to Esfahān (118,000 rials) and Zāhedān (91,000 rials). Mahan Air (☎ 251 542) has several flights a week to Tehrān (165,000 rials) and a twice-weekly service to Mashhad (151,000 rials).

Bus & Minibus More a collection of bus company offices along a street, than a regular station, you'll have to hunt around Kermān's bus station (accessible by shared taxi from Meidūn-é Shohadā and Meidūn-é Āzādī) for the best service – Bus Company No 4 and Saryro Safar are both good options, the latter specialising in the more comfy Volvo services. Service for Bam (4800 rials, three hours) are run by Bus Company No 1 and leave at 4 and 7 pm daily – you can also use the more frequent Zāhedān bus (12,000 rials, eight hours). Other destinations available include Esfahān (14,500 rials or 20,000 rials by Volvo, 12 hours); Shīrāz (13,500 rials or 18,000 rials by Volvo, eight hours); Tehrān (23,000 rials or 38,000 rials by Volvo, 18 hours); Yazd (8000 rials, six hours).

Train Kermān is the end of the line for Iran's railway. To Tehrān (15 hours) trains leave Kermān on Tuesday, Thursday and Saturday afternoons. Tickets are 22,000/35,000 rials for 2nd/1st class. The train station (☎ 587 61) is 8km south-west of town – take a shared taxi from Meidūn-é Āzādī.

Shared Taxi To Māhān you're best off catching a shared taxi from Meidūn-é Fedā'īyān-é Eslām. To Bam, and sometimes Zāhedān, taxis leave from Meidūn-é Sarasīyāb, about 5km east of Meidūn-é Kermānī. For Bam you should pay around 14,000 rials.

AROUND KERMĀN
Māhān
A recommended half-day trip is to Māhān, 35km east of Kermān. The main attraction is **Ārāmgāh-é Shāh Ne'matollāh Valī**, a large mausoleum dedicated to a well-known local poet and mystic. It dates from the early 15th century, and has beautiful tilework and wooden doors, not to mention stunning carpets casually thrown about the interior. Pay the caretaker 10,000 rials and you can climb up to the roof for a magnificent view. There's also a pleasant *teahouse* near the entrance.

An easy 5km walk up the main road through the village from the mausoleum leads to the **Bāgh-é Shāhzāde**, a charming oasis garden and palace (entry 5000 rials). There's a reasonably priced restaurant here

with a lovely terrace overlooking the cascading pools and paddling ducks.

At the entrance to the town, *Māhān Inn* (☎ 0342-6222 700) is comfortable and clean, and costs US$11 per person. The attached *restaurant* is good. Shared taxis regularly travel between Meidūn-é Fedā'īyān-é Eslām in Kermān, and the mausoleum in Māhān. A private return taxi trip from Kermān, including waiting time, should be around 30,000 rials. If you've got your own transport Māhān is on the way to Bam; all buses to Bam and Zāhedān also pass through.

BAM
☎ 0344
As a grand finale (or spectacular start) to your trip through Iran, you cannot fault Bam. This laid-back oasis town's wealth is based on the date palms that flourish all over town and you'll find an incredible mud-brick citadel and walled city – Arg-é Bam – unquestionably one of the country's archaeological highlights.

Bam is easy enough to walk around, and the ancient city is about 2km from Meidūn-é Emām Khomeinī, the town centre, where you'll find a post office and the bazaar.

Arg-é Bam
Bam was probably founded in the Sassanian period (AD 224–637) but most of the remains date from the Safavid period (1502–1722). Between 9000 and 13,000 people once lived in this 6 sq km city until it was abandoned after an invasion by the Afghans in 1722. A lot has been restored (some would say too much) but for now, the balance between crumbling buildings and the freshly appointed give the place the mysterious and appealing air of a developing photograph.

Climb the stairway behind the main entrance to the ramparts of the outer wall for a definitive outlook over the old and new towns. On the way to the inner citadel check out the **bazaar square**, once a covered, busy market; the **Masjed-é Jāmé**, originally constructed in the 9th century, but rebuilt numerous times since; and the **zurkhané** house of strength or gymnasium where the ancient wrestling sport was practised.

The **inner citadel**, at the foot of which you find a restored **caravanserai** with bādi-

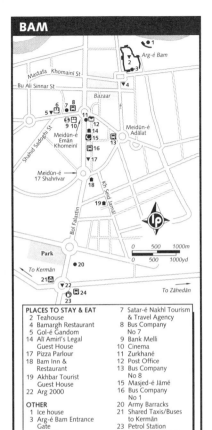

BAM

PLACES TO STAY & EAT	7 Satar-é Nakhl Tourism
2 Teahouse	& Travel Agency
4 Bamargh Restaurant	8 Bus Company
5 Gol-é Gandom	No 7
14 Alī Amirī's Legal	9 Bank Melli
Guest House	10 Cinema
17 Pizza Parlour	11 Zurkhané
18 Bam Inn &	12 Post Office
Restaurant	13 Bus Company
19 Akhbar Tourist	No 8
Guest House	15 Masjed-é Jāmé
22 Arg 2000	16 Bus Company
	No 1
OTHER	20 Army Barracks
1 Ice house	21 Shared Taxis/Buses
3 Arg-é Bam Entrance	to Kermān
Gate	23 Petrol Station
6 Cinema	24 Buses to Zāhedān

late afternoon and early morning are best. There is a wonderful teahouse above the inner citadel gatehouse and a good bookshop, too.

Places to Stay & Eat

Akhbar Tourist Guest House (☎ 5842, Kheyābūn-é Seid Jamāl) is a homely, relaxed place with a pleasant courtyard and comfortable rooms; the effusive Akhbar (a former English teacher) is the main attraction. Doubles, with shared bathroom, cost 50,000 rials and 70,000 rials with private bathroom. There are air-con dorm beds for 20,000 rials, a kitchen, library and good meals for 10,000 rials.

Alī Amirī's Legal Guest House (☎ 4481, fax 900 85) is more central, just down a lane from Meidūn-é Emām Khomeinī, but not as convivial. It has many spotless rooms without natural light, and is a strictly smoke-free zone, where one shower per day is allowed (extra washes are 3000 rials). Dorm beds are 20,000 rials with other rooms ranging from 30,000 to 50,000 rials. The vegetarian meals served up by Alī's mother in the family home still get rave reviews.

Bam Inn & Restaurant (☎ 3323, Meidūn-é 17 Shahrīvar) is the mid-range option at US$24 a spacious double with a balcony, though some rooms could be cleaner. It does have a decent ***restaurant*** where dinner is 10,000 rials.

Bamargh Restaurant opposite the Arg-é Bam entrance gate has a charming setting but is pricey (around 25,000 rials for a full lunch) besides getting mixed reviews for its food; better to enjoy the delicious date biscuits at the ***teahouse*** inside the Arg-é Bam. ***Gol-é Gandom***, Kheyābūn-é Shariati, next to the Shahre Tamasha cinema, is nicely decorated, air-conditioned and reliable; lamb kabābs are 13,000 rials and khōresht 10,000 rials. There's also a ***pizza parlour*** with outdoor tables near Meidūn-é 17 Shahrīvar.

There's the bazaar and shops around it for self-catering; try some of the local dates and sour cherries.

For nightlife you could try ***Arg 2000***, the unmissable ersatz citadel in the midst of the roundabout on the Zāhedān road; apart from kabābs (15,000 rials) you can get tea (2000 rials) and a qalyan (35,000 rials) here. There's also a zurkhané practice hall beside Meidūn-é Emām Khomeinī.

gar wind towers, contains the **garrison** and 17th-century governor's palace known as the **Chahār Fasl**. In the garrison, shout something and listen to the extraordinary echo – archaeologists believe this is an ancient loudspeaker system. Nearby are the 14th-century **stables**, which once housed 200 to 300 horses.

On the way up to the palace, there are some very dark and scary **dungeons**; take a torch (flashlight) if you want to see anything. The views from the palace are awesome; to the east of the outer walls you'll see an **ice house** shaded from the sun by curved walls.

The ancient city is open from 7 am to 6 pm daily. The main entrance is at the historic (southern) **gatehouse**. Allow at least two hours to look around, and try to visit twice –

IRAN

Bam to Esfahān

Cycling days: 6
Distance: 840km

Having transported my bicycle by pick-up truck from the border to Zāhedān, I took the bus to Bam; with past kidnappings this area isn't safe for solo cyclists. Setting out for Kermān from Bam, the wind was incredible and I covered just 75km in 6½ hours. I gave up and accepted a lift to Kermān. The landscape is undulating desert with nothing much to see. You could ride from Bam to Kermān (about 170km) in two days, though Māhān, 140km out of Bam, is the only place to stop in between so you need to ensure that the wind is behind you.

On the way to Rafsanjān from Kermān (110km), I'd stopped for a break when a jeep pulled up and I started chatting with a family. After 10 minutes I was invited to stay in their home in Rafsanjān. In the small town of Anār, a farther 100km away en route to Yazd, I also ending up staying in a family's home. Anār to Yazd was another day's ride (140km).

I'd planned to cover Yazd to Esfahān (320km) in two stages, but the wind was against me; I was blown off the bicycle six times, once directly into the middle of the road. After riding 130km, I eventually accepted a lift for the final 50km to Nā'in.

Still cycling against the wind, the final 150km to Esfahān took 11 hours, with the road gradually inclining towards the city.

Carry plenty of water through eastern Iran (I started out with 5L each day and filled up at every opportunity) as it can be difficult to find places to fill up in the desert.

Sue Cooper

Getting There & Away

Iran Asseman flies between Bam and Tehrān twice weekly (198,000 rials). Satar-é Nakhl Tourism & Travel Agency sells tickets.

There are two main bus companies, No 7 and 8, with No 7 offering frequent services to Kermān (4600 rials, three hours). There are daily services to Tehrān (26,900 rials by Volvo, 21 hours); Esfahān (25,000 rials, 15 hours); Mashhad (27,300 rials, 20 hours); Shīrāz (17,000 rials, 11 hours); and Yazd (12,600 rials, nine hours). No 8 has four daily services to Zāhedān (7900 rials, five hours). You can also flag down a passing bus near the roundabout on the Zāhedān road.

Shared taxis to Kermān also leave from the roundabout on the Zāhedān road.

ZĀHEDĀN
☎ 0541 • pop 400,000

There's no reason for lingering in dusty, drab Zāhedān, the nearest major town to the Pakistan border. With an early start from either Bam (or Taftan in Pakistan), you should easily be able to pass through the town.

Information

The 'Police Dept of Alien Affairs', at the visa office on the way to the airport, handles Iranian visa extensions.

There's also an Indian consulate (☎ 221 721), just off Kheyābūn-é Emām Khomeinī, which is open from 8.30 am to 1 pm and 2 to 5 pm Saturday to Thursday, but it can take up to a week to get a visa here.

You can pick up a visa within 30 minutes at the friendly Pakistani consulate (☎ 223 389), off Kheyābūn-é Pahlavanī. It is open from 8 am to 2 pm Saturday to Thursday.

The Bank Melli central branch changes money. There's a small black market for Pakistani and Afghan currency (and foreign passports) in the bazaar – but be *very* discreet. It's easier to change money with a black marketeer at the border.

The upmarket Esteghlal Grand Hotel (☎ 238 052, fax 222 239), Meidūn-é Āzādī, might have Internet facilities – at least they told us they would.

Places to Stay & Eat

Hotel Momtazhirmand (☎ 222 827) is the best cheapie. Basic but acceptable rooms with shared bathroom cost 15,000/18,000 rials a single/double. It's along the first laneway on the left heading north from the intersection of Kheyābūn-é Emām Khomeinī and Kheyābūn-é Doktor Sharī'atī.

Hotel Kavir (☎ 224 010, fax 220 059) has rather cramped air-con rooms with private bathroom for 52,000/80,000 rials.

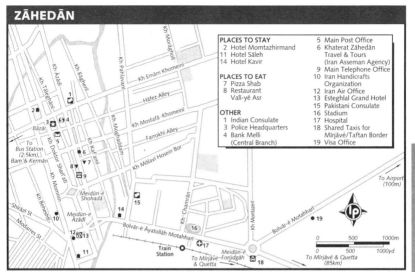

ZĀHEDĀN

PLACES TO STAY
2 Hotel Momtazhirmand
11 Hotel Sāleh
14 Hotel Kavir

PLACES TO EAT
7 Pizza Shab
8 Restaurant
  Valī-yé Asr

OTHER
1 Indian Consulate
3 Police Headquarters
4 Bank Melli
  (Central Branch)
5 Main Post Office
6 Khaterat Zāhedān
  Travel & Tours
  (Iran Asseman Agency)
9 Main Telephone Office
10 Iran Handicrafts
  Organization
12 Iran Air Office
13 Esteghlal Grand Hotel
15 Pakistani Consulate
16 Stadium
17 Hospital
18 Shared Taxis for
  Mīrjāvé/Taftan Border
19 Visa Office

Hotel Sāleh (☎ *231 797, fax 226 330*)
just south-west of Meidūn-é Āzādī is the
best in the mid-range bracket. It charges
100,000/150,000 rials for a double without/
with bathroom, but you may be able to negotiate a cheaper rate.

All these hotels have restaurants. The
restaurant in the *Esteghlal Grand Hotel* is
amenable and not much more expensive.
Pizza Shab, Kheyābūn-é Āzādī, is worth
checking out, but it's only open in the
evenings. Across the road, *Restaurant Valī-
yé Asr* is popular with locals, with decent
kabāb meals for 10,000 rials.

Getting There & Away

Air Iran Air (☎ 220 812) flies daily to Tehrān
(208,000 rials); twice weekly to Esfahān
(178,000 rials), Kermān (91,000) and Mashhad (153,000 rials). Iran Asseman also has
twice weekly flights to Tehrān; its representative is Khaterat Zāhedān Travel & Tours
(☎ 0541-225 001) on Kheyābūn-é Āzādī.

Bus The bus station is a grotty, sprawling
mess in the west of the city. The bus companies have offices all over the station area, so
you'll have to ask around. Buses leave many
times a day to Bam (7900 rials, five hours)
and less often to Esfahān (28,000 rials, 21
hours), Kermān (19,000 rials, six hours),
Mashhad (33,000, 15 hours), Shīrāz (28,000
rials, 17 hours), Tehrān (30,000 rials, 24
hours) and Yazd (19,000 rials, 14 hours).

Train From Zāhedān station (☎ 226 024)
you can catch a twice-weekly service to
Quetta – but given that it takes far longer
than going by bus, we *don't* recommend it.
Services are scheduled for 7 am Thursday
and 8.30 am Monday, but times and dates
are a movable feast. You'll need to buy a
ticket to the border (around 1700 rials) then
another ticket from Taftan to Quetta
(around 500 rupees).

MĪRJĀVÉ

Mīrjāvé, 85km east of Zāhedān is the closest village to the border. The *Mīrjaveh Inn*
(☎ *05448-4386)* is the only accommodation
option; it costs a negotiable 40,000 rials
per double. To get here your best bet is taking a shared taxi from Meidūn-é Forūdgāh
in Zāhedān.

Iran Border Crossings

Iran to Pakistan

Shared taxis, and occasional minibuses, from Zāhedān to the Iran-Pakistan border leave from the bus station. If you can't get a realistic price for a taxi here (10,000 rials per person, or 40,000 rials for the entire taxi), take a shared taxi to Meidūn-é Forūdgāh, on the way to the airport, where you can then pick up another shared taxi to the border.

Both sides of the border are open from around 8 am to 7 pm daily. From the gates on the Iranian side you can take a free minibus to the customs block; on the Pakistani side of Taftan, you walk straight out of immigration and customs into the village. There are plenty of moneychangers on both sides; check exchange rates with fellow travellers before doing a deal here.

Clearing customs on both sides can take anything from 10 minutes to several hours depending on whether your bags and transport are searched. On the Iranian side there's a separate immigration queue for men and women.

Since November 2000, foreign tourists arriving at Taftan without a Pakistani visa could get a 30-day landing permit on the spot, free of charge. This is not a visa and cannot be extended, so if you intend to stay longer than 30 days you must obtain a visa in advance.

Direct buses for Quetta (Rs 300, 14 hours) depart from immediately outside the Pakistani customs shed. There is also a twice-weekly train service from Zāhedān to Quetta. However, it's far quicker and much more comfortable to take the bus, not least because of the prolonged delay of processing all the passengers through border procedures before the train can continue.

Pakistan to Iran

Unless you have your own vehicle, you're most likely to arrive in Taftan mid-morning on an overnight bus from Quetta (which stops right outside the border post). Exiting on the Pakistan side is a breeze. Officials will probably want to look in your bags but it's pretty cursory and foreigners tend to get special treatment when it comes to stamping passports.

If it's crowded it can be frustrating getting through immigration on the Iran side because there's little concept of queuing, and there's nothing more depressing than seeing the person in front of you clutching 40 Pakistani passports! There's a separate queue for men (crowded and chaotic) and women (orderly and relatively sparse in numbers). Surprisingly, customs officials don't seem interested in checking the bags of foreigners, but if you have a vehicle, expect a thorough search. We've received accounts from drivers that when entering Iran from Pakistan in a diesel engine car *and* on a transit visa you will be required to pay a hefty fuel tax of US$174.

A shuttle bus takes you the short distance to the main gates and the roads to Mīrjāvé and Zāhedān. There's no reason to go to Mīrjāvé, so either wait for one of the occasional minibuses to Zāhedān, or a better option is to take a shared taxi or pick-up, which shouldn't cost more than 10,000 rials per person. (We rode on the back of an open pick-up, wedged in among our luggage, for 5000 rials.)

Note that Zāhedān is the first place in Iran where you can change money, so you should get enough rials from the moneychangers on the Pakistan side of the border to tide you over. They'll want your US dollars but will change Pakistani rupees into rials.

PAKISTAN

Uch Sharif

Khyber Pass

Lahore Old City

Pilgrims at Badshahi Mosque

Kandahari Bazaar, Quetta

PAKISTAN
highlights

Uch Sharif
Off the beaten track and a destination mostly for pilgrims, the exquisite Sufi shrines make Uch Sharif well worth the trip.

Lahore Old City
In addition to the imposing Lahore Fort and beautiful Badshahi Mosque, the Old City of Lahore has a remarkable maze of ancient alleyways.

Taxila
A rich archaeological site dating back 8000 years, Taxila was once the centre of the famous Gandharan dynasty and a repository for Graeco-Buddhist art.

The Khyber Pass
Bridging Pakistan and Afghanistan, the not-to-be-missed Kyber Pass is steeped in Asian overland history and intrigue; it's well worth securing a permit and armed escort to venture out to this rugged frontier.

Qawwali
Trance-like qawwali (devotional singing) is a uniquely Pakistani form of all-night entertainment, held at Sufi shrines in Lahore, Uch Sharif, Multan and Islamabad.

Buzkashi
This wild Afghan sport, which literally means 'goat grabbing', was brought to Pakistan by the Afghan refugee population.

Cricket
A national obsession, with Pakistan's home games held in Lahore, Rawalpindi and Peshawar; if you miss one of these, there's always the impromptu local matches that take place on the streets.

Bazaar Hopping
Some of your most abiding memories of Pakistan will be of the people and the colourful bazaars. Quetta's Kandahari Bazaar, Multan's Hussain Agahi Bazaar, Rawalpindi's Rajah Bazaar or the bazaars in Peshawar's Old City are great places in which to get lost.

Pakistan

Drugs, guns, military coups…Pakistan is often regarded as the 'mystery country' by travellers crossing Asia, a view not helped by media portrayals of a volatile nation with a wobbly law-and-order situation. It's seen as the place you have to pass through on the way to India but don't know much about; a nation that was once part of British India but now trades nuclear tests and teeters on the brink of war with India over the disputed Kashmir region. Bordering war-torn Afghanistan and taking in many of that country's refugees in the past 20 years has only enhanced its reputation for intrigue and the diversity of its people.

But be prepared to adjust some of your stereotypes: Pakistan *is* a wild and woolly place in parts (see the boxed text 'Safe Travel in Pakistan'), but in the Muslim tradition the Pakistani people are generally friendly, hospitable, curious and will go out of their way to help foreigners. Travel within the country is cheap and easy (despite the long distances you'll have to cover to get anywhere in the west of the country). There are some wonderful historic sites such as the Sufi shrines at Uch Sharif, the ancient site of Taxila, and Derawar and Rohtas Forts. Lahore is one of the world's great Mughal cities and Peshawar oozes excitement and provides the opportunity to visit the legendary Khyber Pass (with armed escort in tow!). And although not covered in this book (our route has to end *somewhere*), continuing north along the Karakoram Highway will take you through some of the world's finest mountain scenery.

Pakistan has only existed as a political unit since 1947, when the Partition of British India created a 'homeland' for India's Muslims. Since then, the military has played a big part in national politics, which has led to frequent spells of martial law – most recently in October 1999, when Prime Minister Nawaz Sharif was deposed by army chief General Pervez Musharraf.

Tourism isn't well developed in Pakistan (although 2001 has officially been declared Visit Pakistan Year), nor does the country seem as 'modern' as Turkey or Iran. But given the effects of tourism on parts of India, that's not a bad thing and the sense of adventure is enhanced by the fact that you'll meet fewer westerners here than elsewhere on the route. Nightlife as we know it in the West is virtually nonexistent, but much of the entertainment can be found in the bazaars and old cities. Chances are you'll find your encounters with the tribal cultures of Pakistan some of the most rewarding on this route.

Pakistan at a Glance

Capital: Islamabad (population 524,500)

Population: 130.58 million

Area: 803,940 sq km

Head of state: President Mohammed Rafiq Tarer. Since late 1999, Pakistan has been under military rule, with General Pervez Musharraf as Chief Executive.

Currency: Pakistani rupee (Rs)

Country telephone code: ☎ 92

Exchange rates:

country	unit		Pakistani rupee (Rs)
Australia	A$1	=	32
EU	€1	=	52
UK	UK£1	=	86
USA	US$1	=	58

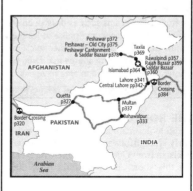

Safe Travel in Pakistan

In general, Pakistan is a safe country in which to travel, and its people are hospitable to visitors. However, for political and tribal reasons, there is restricted access to a number of areas which are either off limits altogether for travellers, or you need a permit and possibly an armed escort to visit them.

The main areas of concern to our route are Baluchistan and the North-West Frontier Province (NWFP). Unrestricted travel in Baluchistan is only possible in the provincial capital Quetta (and its environs) and on the main roads, ie, west to Taftan, east to Dera Ghazi Khan and Lahore and south to Sukkur (although the latter road runs through Sind and is not recommended if you are travelling independently). To travel anywhere else you need permission from the Home & Tribal Affairs Office in Quetta and you will need to hire an armed escort. In NWFP, most of the area outside Peshawar is essentially outside the control of the Pakistan government. Travel here is restricted to Peshawar and the main highways. To visit the Khyber Pass, for example, you need a permit and an armed escort. If you intend to leave the main towns in either of these provinces, check first with the local Pakistan Tourist Development Corporation (PTDC) office. Its staff are usually quite knowledgeable and can advise on requirements and safety issues.

Some travellers find Quetta and Peshawar, with their tribal and Afghan refugee populations, quite daunting. It is a male-dominated, conservative society and solo women in particular may feel uncomfortable as there are very few local women around in public. But these towns are quite safe, provided you dress modestly and avoid wandering around alone after dark – which you probably wouldn't do in New York or London either.

Lahore has had its share of bad press over the years and has been the scene of politically motivated bombings, anti-American demonstrations and sectarian murders. Tourists have never been targeted and expats living in Lahore consider it to be quite safe. Lahore has been notorious for scams such as drug peddlers working as police informers, con men impersonating police officers, and police in league with criminals. Never hand over your passport or show cash or valuables to someone claiming to be with the police. And it goes without saying that you're taking a huge risk if you buy drugs from anyone. Reports of theft from cheap hotels in the train station area have eased in recent years.

THE ROUTE

If you look on a map, there appears to be a fairly straightforward route slicing through Pakistan from Quetta to Lahore. But by taking this short cut you would miss many of the country's interesting sights. Instead, our journey takes a longer route, roughly following the railway line from Quetta to Peshawar, via Lahore.

There's only one place to cross the border from Iran into Pakistan, which is at the Mīrjāvé-Taftan crossing. Our route therefore begins in Taftan before making the long desert crossing to Quetta, a cool city thanks to its 1700m elevation, with a 'Wild West' feel.

From here there are three options. Many overland travellers with their own vehicle choose to drive straight up to Peshawar, a long trip via Loralai and Dera Ghazi (DG) Khan.

Another option is to cut straight across the country via Multan to Lahore. This is really only worthwhile if you have your own vehicle and want to take the shortest possible route, since there are no direct buses from Quetta to Multan, although you can easily break the journey at Ziarat, Loralai and DG Khan.

A third option, and the one described in this chapter, is the train journey from Quetta to Lahore, which continues on to Peshawar. It heads south through the Bolan Pass and across the stark Baluchistan Desert to Bahawalpur (for Uch Sharif and Derawar Fort) and Multan.

From there you can continue on the train or take a bus to Lahore, then detour to Rawalpindi, Islamabad, Peshawar and the Khyber Pass. Finally, it's an easy return trip to Lahore and the border crossing into India at Wagah.

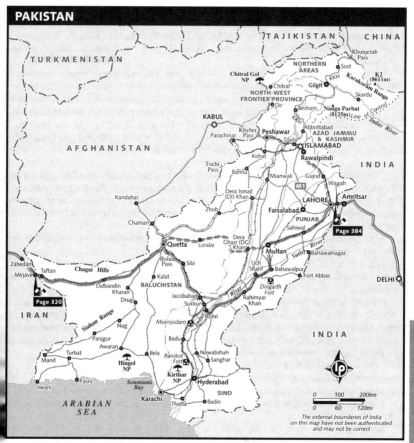

PAKISTAN

TAJIKISTAN   CHINA

TURKMENISTAN

Khunjerab Pass
NORTHERN AREAS
Sost
KKH
Karakoram Range
K2 (8611m)

Chitral Gol NP
Chitral
Gilgit
Skardu

NORTH-WEST FRONTIER PROVINCE
Dir
Besham
Nanga Parbat (8125m)
Line of Control
Indus River

KABUL
Khyber Pass
Peshawar
Abbottabad
AZAD JAMMU & KASHMIR

Parachinar
Taxila
ISLAMABAD

AFGHANISTAN
Kohat
Rawalpindi
INDIA

Tochi Pass
Bannu
Mianwali
Gujrat
Wagah

Kandahar
Dera Ismail (DI) Khan
M1
LAHORE
Amritsar

Zhob
Faisalabad
PUNJAB

Chaman
Sahiwal
Page 384

Dera Ghazi (DG) Khan
River
Multan
Sutlej River
Bahawalnagar

Quetta
Loralai
Uch Sharif
Bahawalpur
Fort Abbas

Zāhedān
Taftan
Chagai Hills
Bolan Pass
Sibi
Dingarth Fort
DELHI

Mirjāveh
Kalat
Rahimyar Khan

Dalbandin
Kharan
BALUCHISTAN
Jacobabad
River

Page 320
Drug
Sukkur
Rohri

IRAN
Moenjodaro
Indus River
INDIA

Siahan Range
Nag
Badu

Panjgur
Awaran
Bela
Ranikot Fort
Nawabshah
Sanghar

Turbat
Hingol NP
Kirthar NP
Hyderabad

Mand
Pasni
Sonmiani Bay
Karachi
SIND

Jiwani
Thatta
Badin

ARABIAN SEA

0   100   200km
0   60   120mi

The external boundaries of India on this map have not been authenticated and may not be correct

PAKISTAN

Taftan to Lahore

TAFTAN

Taftan is a hot, dusty border town with a collection of mud-walled buildings and not much to recommend it. If you miss the last bus to Quetta or arrive late and want to break your journey here, there's decent, though overpriced, accommodation at the *PTDC Motel* (☎ *0886-510302*) which has dorm beds for Rs 200 and singles/doubles for Rs 400/600. You could also ask about pitching a tent here.

There's a National Bank of Pakistan here but if you want to buy or sell Iranian rials or Pakistani rupees, make use of the money-changers lurking around the bus stand;

bargain up from their starting rate and count your money carefully. The rates are generally better at the moneychangers in Quetta, but if you're travelling west into Iran you'll need some rials to get you to Zāhedān.

Buses leave from a dusty area outside immigration control several times a day while the border remains open (the last one departs around 6 pm). The 14-hour journey costs Rs 250, or Rs 300 for an air-con bus.

There's also the direct train service from Zāhedān in Iran to Quetta – for more details, see Getting There & Away in the Quetta and Zāhedān sections.

DALBANDIN

If you're driving your own vehicle and you start early from Taftan you can make it to

Driving East

British traveller Nigel Croft made his way by Land Rover from London through Turkey, Iran, Pakistan and India. We bumped into him a couple of times en route and quizzed him about the long drive east.

Nigel found the roads through Turkey and Iran to be well maintained, though the drivers in Turkey are notably insane. In eastern Turkey there are frequent roadblocks manned by the *jandarma* (military police) and similar military checks in Iran, particularly between Yazd and the border. The police were, by and large, friendly and polite, although Nigel was hauled in for interrogation at one point in eastern Turkey after being 'reported' by a passing truck driver for acting suspiciously. He had been leaning out of the window looking at overflying birds with his binoculars. After some hurried explanations through an interpreter, Nigel was released with apologies from the policemen in charge.

'The roads in Iran were superb throughout and the only real problem was finding my way through the cities. The simple expedient of sticking a compass in between the front seats and the relevant Lonely Planet city map to hand proved to be pretty effective. An amazing sight was nomads driving their flocks through downtown Shīrāz in the early hours of the morning on their migration northward.'

Nigel had no problems filling his Land Rover with diesel – it was 90 times cheaper than in the UK!

Acting on advice, he crossed the border into Pakistan in the late afternoon, passed the customs checks without problem and stayed at the PTDC Motel in Taftan (which has a secure compound) in order to start early and get to Quetta in one hit.

'I set off at about 7 am and the first 280km or so to Dalbandin is a good, clear, fast road. After Dalbandin, which has a distinctly frontier air to it, the road narrows to slightly wider than single-track. Watch out for the speed bumps just outside Dalbandin. A German rider I met hit one at about 70km/h and wrecked the front end of his bike. It took about eight hours to get to Quetta, where a very welcome cold beer was quaffed in no time flat.

'Ignoring all advice that the route south via Sibi and Jacobabad, while farther, was a far better road and thus quicker than going north via Loralai to DG Khan, I decided to go to Ziarat to spend the night at this pleasant little hill station. The road to Ziarat is paved all the way, but from Loralai to Multan it was similar to the bad sections of the Dalbandin-Quetta road, only slower.'

Nigel said that most of the roads leading from Multan east to Lahore and Islamabad/Rawalpindi, or north to Peshawar are broad and well surfaced, offering plenty of room to move in emergencies – in theory.

'The donkey carts, horses, oxen and bicycle riders, all of whom like their fair share of the road, still make for slow driving, especially if you're not able to overtake immediately. Don't expect to average more than 50km/h over longer distances except on the fabulously empty toll road from Islamabad to Lahore.'

Paul Harding

Quetta in one day (eight to 10 hours driving), but travel at night is not recommended.

The road is in good condition between Taftan and Dalbandin (280km), the logical place to break the journey. The Baluchistan Culture & Tourism Cell (CTC) has a *resthouse* with rooms for Rs 250/300. Phone the CTC in Quetta (☎ 081-835298) for book-

ings. There are also government resthouses in Nushki, Padag, Yakmach and Notkundi, with basic rooms for around Rs 100.

After Dalbandin the road narrows and deteriorates for the 350km from there to Quetta – watch out for the speed bumps. Banditry may be a problem along this stretch; camping by the side of the road is not recommended.

QUETTA
☎ 081 • pop 560,000

Coming from Iran, Quetta is the first town of any size you reach in Pakistan, and it's likely to be a mild shock to the system, with the Middle East abruptly giving way to the subcontinent.

A meeting point for numerous tribal groups, Quetta is unlike most other Pakistani cities and exudes the air of a wild frontier town. There are few 'sights' here, but simply wandering around the hectic bazaars is an eye-opener. Here you'll see a colourful parade of people buying, selling, haggling and touting for business. Some 70% of the population are Pashtuns (Pathans), the original indigenous inhabitants, and much of the balance is made up of ethnic Baluchis and Brahuis. In recent decades many Mohajirs and Punjabis have settled here, while over the last few years Afghan refugees have added yet more variety to this ethnic melange.

Baluchistan's capital and only town of any size, Quetta is a fertile oasis surrounded by bleak, dry mountains. At an altitude of 1700m it is relatively cool in summer (unlike most of Pakistan) and is at its best from May to August. Winter (November to March) gets extremely cold and you can expect snow in January.

Quetta is pretty much an essential stop on the journey east, so it's worth allowing a bit of time here to relax, recharge and explore. Although the main township is quite safe for tourists, occasional tribal clashes do spill onto the streets.

History
The town takes its name from the ancient fort (*kwatta* in Pashto) that protected the roads to Afghanistan, Persia and India. Quetta didn't come into its own until the British era and even then was little more than a small arsenal until the late 19th century.

In 1730 it came under the Khan of Kalat, who made it his northern capital. In 1876 the British administrator Sir Robert Sandeman signed a treaty with the Khan of Kalat which handed over administration of the strategic Quetta region to the British. The town grew in importance, becoming the largest garrison in British India and the focus of British attempts to regulate the interior. But its position on a major and unstable seismic

fault almost reduced Quetta to rubble in 1935. The devastating earthquake of 31 May killed around 20,000 people.

These days Quetta is fast becoming a Central Asian town; strategically positioned near the Afghan border, it proved an important logistical springboard for the Taliban movement which swept through Afghanistan from its base in Kandahar in southern Afghanistan in 1996.

Orientation
Quetta has a dramatic setting in a mountainous amphitheatre; its centre is graced with wide, tree-lined boulevards and sturdy British architecture.

For travellers, there are three focal points in Quetta: the cheap hotels clustered around the train station in the south of town; the mid-range hotels and shops a couple of kilometres north along Mohammed Ali Jinnah Rd (commonly referred to as just Jinnah Rd); and finally, the colourful bazaar district to the east around Mizan Chowk. The general bus stand is 3km south of the train station.

Information
Tourist Offices The helpful Pakistan Tourist Development Corporation office (PTDC; ☎ 825826) at the Muslim Hotel in Jinnah Rd is open from 9 am to 3 pm (closed Friday afternoon and Sunday). This is probably your most reliable first source of current information on Baluchistan. The staff can also help book PTDC Motels in Ziarat, Taftan and Chaman.

The Culture & Tourism Cell (CTC; ☎ 835298), in the Baldia Plaza (2nd floor) on Iqbal Rd, promotes provincial tourism and operates some resthouses in Ziarat, Loralai, Gaddani, Gwadar and Dalbandin, but isn't much good for local tourist information.

Visa Extensions & Permits The Home & Tribal Affairs section of the Baluchistan Civil Secretariat deals with visa extensions and permits. Contact the Section Officer Political II (☎ 920 1878), Room 61, 1st floor, New Secretariat Block (the building at the back of that complex); the office is open daily from 8 am to 2 pm, except Friday afternoon and Sunday. Bring a photocopy of your passport and visa (and several passport photos just in case). This is also the place to come for official permission to visit the interior of Baluchistan (ie, anywhere outside Quetta or off the main highways).

Money Banks offering foreign exchange include the main branch of the National Bank of Pakistan on Jinnah Rd and the Habib Bank further north; both are open mornings only. Standard Chartered Grindlays Bank (SCB Grindlays), at the northern end of Jinnah Rd, changes travellers cheques efficiently but with a high commission of Rs 350. It can also give a cash advance on a Visa card (Rs 300 or 2% commission). The Muslim Commercial Bank (MCB) on Iqbal Rd has an ATM connected to the Cirrus/Maestro network.

The moneychangers give the best rates (usually without commission) and there are plenty of them, mostly around Jinnah and Iqbal Rds; the carpet shops give good rates and will often take travellers cheques. Iranian rials are available in the bazaars along Iqbal Rd. Take special care when dealing with street moneychangers on Iqbal Rd – they are adept at sleight-of-hand tricks that can leave you short-changed.

Post & Communications Poste restante is at the philatelic counter of the main post office (☎ 920293) on Zarghoon Rd. This is also the central telegraph office for domestic or international telegrams, telex and telephone calls and fax.

Net2Net Internet Cafe, on the 1st floor of the Engineers Building on Zarghoon Rd, charges Rs 100 per hour but guests at several popular hotels get a discount (Rs 75 per hour), so ask first. It's open from 9.30 am to 11 pm daily. There's also Internet access in the Serena Bazaar craft shop at the Quetta Serena Hotel for Rs 100 an hour (don't use the expensive business centre though).

Consulates The Iranian consulate on Hali Rd (☎ 843527) is always busy but claims to issue transit visas within 48 hours to citizens of most countries except the UK and the USA. The cost is Rs 1650 (about US$30). It's safer to try to organise a visa in Islamabad or Lahore.

The Taliban-controlled Afghan consulate (☎ 843364) on Prince Rd was not routinely issuing visas at the time of research.

Bookshops & Newspapers There are several bookshops along Jinnah Rd. Book Centre and the Quetta Book Stall are the best. There's a small book exchange in the Gul Carpet Market (Shop 13), below Gul's Inn Hotel. The province's English-language daily newspaper is the *Balochistan Times*.

Medical Services & Emergency The main hospitals are Lady Dufferin Hospital (☎ 836537) on McConaughay Rd, south of Mizan Chowk, and the Christian Hospital (☎ 842697) on Mission Rd, also known as Mission Hospital.

The city police station (☎ 920 2277) is on Liaquat Rd.

Dangers & Annoyances Although central Quetta is safe enough for travellers, there's not much going on after about 9 pm so it's not a great time to be out walking alone.

Things to See

Quetta's main attractions are its frontier atmosphere and colourful tribespeople, both of which you'll find in the bustling **bazaars**. From Mizan Chowk, spokes run north-west to the cloth markets of Kandahari Bazaar, west to the fruit and nut market, south-east to the vegetable and bird markets of Kansi Rd and north-west to Suraj Ganj Rd for Sindhi caps and shawls. Liaquat Rd is also worth a wander, though it's more modern.

On Fifal Rd, the **Archaeological Museum of Baluchistan**, has exhibits from the prehistoric period to the 20th century, some labelled in English. Among the displays are figurines from Moenjodaro, pottery pieces from sites in Baluchistan, a sword – bloodstains still visible – used in 1919 to kill a British commander, and a Quran handwritten by the great Mughal emperor Aurangzeb.

Places to Stay

Lourdes Hotel has a pleasant garden where you can pitch a tent for Rs 80 per person. Parking is an extra Rs 250 for a van or Rs 150 for a motorcycle. This is where most overland tour groups stay and is one place to pick up information on the road to Iran or India. There's cheaper camping in the garden of *Hotel Bloom Star* for Rs 65 per person and free parking. For contact details of both these hotels, see later in this section.

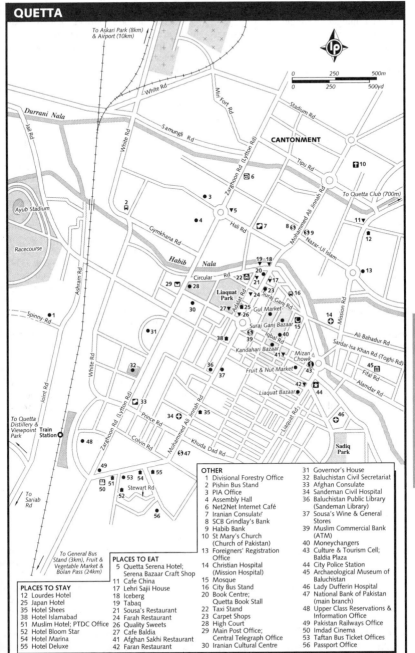

QUETTA

To Askari Park (8km) & Airport (10km)

Durrani Nala

White Rd

Min Fort Rd

Stadium Rd

CANTONMENT

Samungli Rd

Zarghoon Rd (Lytton Rd)

Tipu Rd

To Quetta Club (700m)

Ayub Stadium

Gymkhana Rd

Hali Rd

Mohammed Ali Jinnah Rd

Nazar-Ul Islam

Racecourse

Ashram Rd

Habib *Nala*

Circular   Rd

Spinny Rd

White Rd

Joint Rd

Adalat Rd

Liaquat
Park

Suraj Ganj Bazaar

Gul Market

Suraj Ganj Bazaar

Iqbal Rd

Kandahari Bazaar

Mizan
Chowk

Mission Rd

Ali Bahadur Rd

Sardar Isa Khan Rd (Toghi Rd)

Filal Rd

Fruit & Nut Market

Liaquat Bazaar

Alamdar Rd

To Quetta
Distillery &
Viewpoint
Park

Train
Station

Zarghoon Rd (Lytton Rd)

Prince Rd

Mohammed Ali Jinnah Rd

Khuda Dad Rd

Colvin Rd

Liaquat Rd

Sadiq
Park

To
Sariab
Rd

Stewart Rd

To General Bus
Stand (3km), Fruit &
Vegetable Market &
Bolan Pass (24km)

PAKISTAN

OTHER
1 Divisional Forestry Office
2 Pishin Bus Stand
3 PIA Office
4 Assembly Hall
6 Net2Net Internet Café
7 Iranian Consulate
8 SCB Grindlay's Bank
9 Habib Bank
10 St Mary's Church
   (Church of Pakistan)
13 Foreigners' Registration
   Office
14 Christian Hospital
   (Mission Hospital)
15 Mosque
16 City Bus Stand
20 Book Centre;
   Quetta Book Stall
22 Taxi Stand
23 Carpet Shops
28 High Court
29 Main Post Office;
   Central Telegraph Office
30 Iranian Cultural Centre

31 Governor's House
32 Baluchistan Civil Secretariat
33 Afghan Consulate
34 Sandeman Civil Hospital
36 Baluchistan Public Library
   (Sandeman Library)
37 Sousa's Wine & General
   Stores
39 Muslim Commercial Bank
   (ATM)
40 Moneychangers
43 Culture & Tourism Cell;
   Baldia Plaza
44 City Police Station
45 Archaeological Museum of
   Baluchistan
46 Lady Dufferin Hospital
47 National Bank of Pakistan
   (main branch)
48 Upper Class Reservations &
   Information Office
49 Pakistan Railways Office
50 Imdad Cinema
53 Taftan Bus Ticket Offices
56 Passport Office

PLACES TO EAT
5 Quetta Serena Hotel;
   Serena Bazaar Craft Shop
11 Cafe China
17 Lehri Sajji House
18 Iceberg
19 Tabaq
21 Sousa's Restaurant
24 Farah Restaurant
27 Cafe Baldia
41 Afghan Sakhi Restaurant
42 Faran Restaurant

PLACES TO STAY
12 Lourdes Hotel
25 Japan Hotel
35 Hotel Shees
38 Hotel Islamabad
51 Muslim Hotel; PTDC Office
52 Hotel Bloom Star
54 Hotel Marina
55 Hotel Deluxe

Surprisingly, Quetta has some of the best-value budget accommodation in Pakistan, with decent cheap hotels all along Jinnah Rd.

Muslim Hotel (☎ 824269) is easily the most popular with backpackers so it's a good place to meet other travellers. The rooms are grubby and basic but you can't argue with the price at Rs 70/120 for singles/doubles with bathroom (squat toilet). Hot water is only available in the morning. Ask for an upstairs room facing the central courtyard, since those facing Jinnah Rd are small, dark and noisy.

Hotel Deluxe (☎ 831537), on the corner of Jinnah and Quarry Rds, is a big step up in cleanliness and comfort, and charges Rs 150/200 for furnished rooms with heaters and hot water. **Hotel Marina** (☎ 824796), opposite, is also good value with small singles for Rs 150, and clean doubles/triples for Rs 250/350.

Japan Hotel (☎ 839161), just off Jinnah Rd near the bazaar, is not the most welcoming place in the world but it's superb value. Large, immaculate rooms – with such hitherto unheard of delights as spring mattresses – cost only Rs 150/250. The singles are as big as the doubles.

Moving up the scale, **Hotel Bloom Star** (☎ 833350, Stewart Rd), just off the train station end of Jinnah Rd, is spotlessly clean, comfortable and popular with travellers, from backpackers to businesspeople. The leafy courtyard garden, where you can take breakfast, is a real bonus. Cosy rooms with clean bathrooms cost Rs 280/350 on the ground floor or Rs 220/270 upstairs. A gas heater costs an extra Rs 80.

Hotel Islamabad (☎ 824006, Jinnah Rd) is centrally located and a pretty good choice (although it doesn't have a garden). Clean, comfortable rooms with hot water, heater and TV cost Rs 265/370.

Hotel Shees (☎ 823015, Jinnah Rd) is also reasonable with large, bright rooms for Rs 298/359, or Rs 595 for the deluxe suite.

Lourdes Hotel (☎ 829656, fax 841352, Staff College Rd) is fading a bit these days and is very overpriced at Rs 1699/2181 (including tax). Still, it's a Quetta institution, seemingly unscathed by the 1935 earthquake, and combines old-style charm with satellite TV, fridge, air-conditioning and heating.

Places to Eat

Quetta may not be a gourmet's paradise, but there are some great Afghan restaurants, superb fresh fruit, and the local speciality, *sajji*, which you should definitely try (unless you're vegetarian).

Sajji is a whole roast leg of lamb (a whole chicken is sometimes substituted) lightly spiced and eaten in the hands with paper-thin bread and goat's milk yogurt. Enough sajji for two people (and you need at least two people to eat one serving) costs about Rs 160 for chicken, Rs 190 for lamb. There are several restaurants serving sajji around Jinnah Rd, but the best is **Lehri Sajji House**, just off Jinnah Rd near Circular Rd, which serves nothing but sajji. Even if it looks like no-one's there, it's probably open – the sajji will be roasting across the road.

Kandahari Bazaar is the place to go for Afghan restaurants offering sweet Kabuli *pulau* (rice), kebabs and roast lamb. The **Afghan Sakhi Restaurant** is recommended for both food and atmosphere, with tasty kebabs and fresh naan bread the size and thickness of doormats.

The **Faran Restaurant** on Liaquat Rd is a cheap place popular with locals, but it doesn't have much in the way of charm. **Tabaq**, on Circular Rd just off Jinnah Rd, does good, cheap Pakistani food and kebabs, while the restaurant at the **Muslim Hotel** is a convenient place to meet other travellers.

Moving upmarket, the **Farah Restaurant** on Jinnah Rd has Continental cuisine and curries for under Rs 100. The best restaurants in Quetta are in the Cantonment, a stiff walk from central Jinnah Rd. **Cafe China**, on Staff College Rd, has tasty Chinese food at around Rs 90 to Rs 140 with cheaper noodle and rice dishes. The portions are very generous. The **Quetta Serena Hotel** has an evening barbecue buffet in the garden for an extravagant Rs 400.

There are a couple of decent bakeries on Jinnah Rd, including **Quality Sweets**. For locally made ice cream, try **Iceberg** on Jinnah Rd (it doubles as a telephone office).

Cafe Baldia, on the corner of Adalat and Iqbal Rds, is a wonderful place to sit and drink tea or have a light snack among the locals. It's mostly hidden from view from the road and is open from 7 am to 8.30 pm. Don't expect a big meal here but you can get cheap soups, chips and naan. *Sousa's* on Adalat Rd is another good place for a snack, with pastries, sweets and small pizzas on offer.

There's a fruit and vegetable *market* south of Mizan Chowk, where you can get dried fruit and nuts. The peaches, grapes, cherries, musk melons and apples of Quetta are especially delicious and are often sold by mobile vendors. Look out for *chiku* – a bit like a cross between a date and a bitter kiwi fruit.

Alcohol

If you've just come from Iran, or even from elsewhere in Pakistan, you'll be pleased to know that you can get alcohol here quite easily.

Although the sale of alcohol is technically illegal in Baluchistan, there are at least three places in town where you can walk in and buy cold beer or spirits without a permit. Two are 'under-the-counter' grog shops but *Sousa's Wine & General Stores* on Jinnah Rd is hardly clandestine. The owner is also the manager of the Quetta Distillery on Quarry Rd, which produces Cossack vodka. You can get various types of Murree beer (brewed in Rawalpindi) from Rs 80 to Rs 120 and Cossack vodka for Rs 450, as well as other spirits. If you can be bothered getting a permit from the Excise Department on Sariab Rd (about Rs 30), prices are 20% cheaper. If you buy alcohol, be discreet about it. Carry it in a bag or backpack and don't consume it in the open, even at your hotel (except in your room).

Entertainment

Askari Park is a family entertainment complex with restaurants and a cinema but it's quite a way out on Chaman Rd near the airport. *Imdad Cinema* on Jinnah Rd sometimes shows English-language films.

Quetta has quite a sociable little expatriate community of volunteers, teachers and medical workers and they're worth seeking out if you plan to be in town for a few days. In summer you can often find people at the swimming pool at the Quetta Serena Hotel. It costs Rs 300 a day for nonguests to use the pool, tennis courts and squash courts.

Although the qualifications for membership are still feudal, even the most plebeian of foreigners can visit the historic *Quetta Club* (☎ 74661), on Club Rd in the Canton-ment. If you are the guest of a member, you can use the squash courts, restaurant and attached golf course.

The rise in the Afghan population has prompted the occasional game of *buzkashi*, a wild Afghan sport which is something like rugby on horseback, played with a goat's head or carcass (or sometimes a replica); the name literally means 'goat grabbing'. Matches are occasionally played on a Friday, often at the Ayub Stadium, but dates are never fixed – ask at the PTDC office.

Shopping

Baluchistan produces some of the finest, or at least most distinctive, carpets in Pakistan, typically with bold colours and striking geometric patterns. Embroidery follows similarly psychedelic designs and is often inlaid with tiny mirrors. Bags, bed sheets, cushions, pillow cases, jackets and shirts are common examples. Tribal caps are worth looking out for.

Start shopping anywhere along the north end of Jinnah Rd. A couple of Afghan-owned carpet places aggressively hustle for custom here too. Other places to try include the Gul Market and in the Kandahari, Suraj Ganj and Liaquat Bazaars.

Getting There & Away

Quetta is far from any major towns and is not ideally set up for long-distance road travel. The main highways lead from Quetta to Taftan, Karachi, Jacobabad and DG Khan. Off these roads there are few services, and travel is restricted without official permission.

Air Given the distances to Peshawar and Lahore, this may be one of those occasions when you break the overland creed and fly. Pakistan International Airways (PIA; ☎ 820901), 17 Hali Rd, has four direct flights a week to/from Islamabad (Rs 2920), three to Lahore (Rs 2740), four to Peshawar (Rs 2620, or Rs 1960 in a smaller Fokker Friendship) and 13 to Karachi (Rs 2440).

Most flights are filled days ahead so try to book in advance.

Bus & Minibus Long-distance services operate from the general bus stand, the New Quetta Bus Stand (locally known as 'Bus Adda'), about 3km south of the train station. Buses (Rs 4) and rickshaws (about Rs 20) to the bus stand go from Jinnah Rd and from near the train station.

To Peshawar At the time of writing only one company, Sadabahar (☎ 444312), was operating a direct service to/from Peshawar (Rs 450, 24 hours, twice a day) from the general bus stand. The non-air-con buses go via DG Khan and Dera Ismail Khan (DI Khan).

To Taftan Several private companies do the 14-hour, 640km desert run to Taftan in reasonably comfortable buses for Rs 250 (Rs 300 with air-con). Most departures are between 4 and 6 pm and there are a couple of agents on Jinnah Rd near the Muslim Hotel that sell tickets for the same price as the companies at the bus stand. Book at least a day in advance if you want an air-con bus, and ask if they include a free ride to the bus stand (whatever they say, the buses do not pick up from their offices – only Karachi-bound buses leave from Jinnah Rd). New Wali and Mushtaqa Taftan (☎ 824029) both have departures at 4, 5 and 6 pm. Buses are invariably quicker than the train.

Other Destinations Heading east is more problematic as there are no direct buses to Multan. There are a couple of direct buses to DG Khan from the general bus stand, but these take a long, circuitous route and cost Rs 250. You're better off taking a bus to Loralai, then another to DG Khan. Minibuses to Loralai (Rs 100, four hours) leave regularly from the Pishin Bus Stand on White Rd. From here you can also get buses to Ziarat (Rs 45, 2½ hours).

Travelling to and from Bahawalpur you're better off taking the train as there are no direct buses. There are overnight buses to Sukkur and Saqitabad (Rs 150, both 12 hours) where you can change for Bahawalpur, but the journey through the Sind is not recommended as banditry is still a problem, especially at night.

For Karachi (Rs 250, 15 hours) there are bus companies on Jinnah Rd. The main Karachi terminal is about 1km south of the train station, although some buses leave from Jinnah Rd.

Train The train station (☎ 920 1066) is very orderly compared with most in Pakistan.

First-class and air-con seats and sleepers can be reserved at the separate building opposite the train station, which is also where you go for information. Second-class seats can be booked at the ticket offices just inside the station. For a sleeper, try to book ahead at least a couple of days before you want to travel. To get a concession on your ticket, go to the commercial department of the Pakistan Railways office, on the corner of Zhargoon and Jinnah Rds, the first building to your right as you walk out of the station. You'll need your passport and, if applicable, a student card.

Train fares in Pakistan are calculated by distance, so different routes to the same destination can mean slightly different fares. You need to add 12.5% tax to 1st-class and air-con fares.

Heading east by train, the *Quetta Express* leaves in the morning for Bahawalpur (Rs 180/360/925 economy/1st-class sleeper/air-con, 16 hours) but inconveniently through the night from Bahawalpur, Multan (Rs 200/400/1025, 18 hours), Lahore (Rs 270/525/1325, 26 hours, 28 hours in the opposite direction) and finally Rawalpindi (Rs 260/505/1285, 32 hours). The *Abbaseen Express*, with only 1st class (without air-con) and economy, leaves in the evening for Bahawalpur (17 hours), Multan (19½ hours), via Faisalabad to Rawalpindi (34 hours) and finally Peshawar (Rs 365/695, 38 hours). The *Chiltan Express* (1st class and economy) leaves at lunch time for Lahore (28 hours), via Jacobabad, DG Khan (16½ hours) and Multan (19½ hours). Expect all of these times to run at least three hours over as most long-distance trains are invariably held up.

Since the direct Peshawar train, the *Abbaseen Express*, follows a long, circuitous route, it makes sense either to break your journey or to take the bus or plane. The fare for a 1st-class sleeper is higher than that for the bus and the trip takes almost twice as long. For Lahore, Multan, Bahawalpur and Rawalpindi, take the train or a combination of train and bus.

Heading south-west, the *Taftan Express* departs on Saturday only at 11.45 am for Zāhedān in Iran, via Dalbandin and the border at Taftan. In actual travel time it's supposedly a 14-hour trip but the inevitable border delay means the train is stationary more often than not – expect about 30 hours. Coming from Iran, it departs Zāhedān on Monday at 12.25 pm. It costs Rs 205/410 in economy/1st class.

Car & Motorcycle The road to Peshawar via Zhob and Bannu is currently off limits to foreigners. The quickest way is the road to Loralai (212km) then DG Khan (a further 282km), and north via DI Khan and Kohat – a total distance of around 1060km. From DI Khan you can also branch off to the north-east on reasonably good roads to Islamabad/Rawalpindi.

From DG Khan it's about 94km on to Multan, from where you can turn off to Bahawalpur (two hours, 95km) or continue on to Lahore (five hours, 335km).

Independent travel to many parts of Baluchistan off the main highways (including Sibi) requires official permission from the Civil Secretariat and usually an armed escort (for which you must pay). Ask at the PDTC in Quetta for information before going anywhere.

Getting Around

There's no airport bus. Taxis to the airport charge around Rs 100, rickshaws around Rs 50. The taxi stand (☎ 844031) is on Adalat Rd.

It's a five-minute walk from the train station to the cheap hotels at the south end of Jinnah Rd. Buses run from the general bus stand to the train station and then up Zarghoon Rd. They then head south down Jinnah Rd before returning to the bus stand. Short trips cost about Rs 3. Off these roads the best way to get around is by autorickshaw. With the exception of those outside the train station, Quetta's rickshaw drivers tend to start off with reasonable prices so only a little bargaining should be required (wait till you get to India for the hard stuff!) but you should still agree on a fare before getting in.

Regular minivans depart from the city bus stand near Suraj Ganj Rd for Urak and the turn-off for Hanna Lake (Rs 10), and Askari Park (Rs 4).

AROUND QUETTA
Hanna Lake & Urak Tangi

Hanna Lake, 10km east of Quetta, is a popular weekend destination for locals though travellers may find it a bit dull. The tiny artificial island in the lake can be reached by pedal boat, but there's no swimming. From the lake it's an 11km drive up the Urak Valley to the nicer picnic site of **Urak Tangi**. The countryside is beautiful in spring and autumn.

In summer there are minibuses direct to Hanna Lake from Quetta's city bus stand, otherwise take the year-round Urak minibus and get off at the turn-off 2km before the lake (Rs 10). You can hire a taxi in Quetta for an afternoon trip to Hanna Lake and Urak Tangi for about Rs 500.

Hazarganji-Chiltan National Park

This little known, 15,555-hectare national park in the mountains 20km south-west of Quetta has a wide range of flora and fauna, including the Chiltan markhor (a large wild goat), wild sheep, leopards, cobras, pythons, birds and over 200 species of plants. Permission to visit must be obtained from the Divisional Forestry Office, Spinny Rd, Quetta, where you can also book accommodation at the park's *resthouse*. There's no public transport to or from here, but the park entrance is only a couple of kilometres from the main Quetta-Mastung road. The PTDC can provide more details.

Ziarat

The main hill station of Baluchistan, Ziarat is 120km north-east of Quetta at an altitude of 2600m.

The British were attracted to Ziarat by its setting among ancient juniper forests and mild climate, and they made it their Baluchistan summer headquarters in the 1880s. Mohammed Ali Jinnah, the Quaid-i-Azam (Great Leader), spent his final days here, at the former residency of the agent to the governor general. The **Quaid-i-Azam residence** survives with furniture left as it was when he died.

Pilgrims come to visit the **ziarat** (shrine) of the famous Muslim saint Mian Abdul Hakim (also known as Kharwari Baba), who fled here from Kandahar in Afghanistan.

Refreshingly cool in summer and almost invariably snow-clad in winter, Ziarat is a restful destination and if you're heading towards Loralai it makes an easy stopover. The main attraction is **hiking** in the surrounding forests and valley. The PTDC office (☎ 0833-356) at the PTDC Motel

Women on Horseback

The Turkey-to-India overland route has always attracted travellers of a certain intrepid ilk, and few can rack up the miles that Isabella Bird (1831–1904) did. When this indomitable Englishwoman turned up in Persia in 1889, she'd already travelled to the Sandwich Islands, been romanced by a frontiersman in the Rocky Mountains and lived with the inhabitants of Hokkaido. Isabella's increasingly compulsive and arduous journeys were made in defiance of Victorian social strictures and the concern of men for her wellbeing. Her tenuous object, to found mission hospitals in Muslim lands in memory of her husband and sister, gave some social legitimacy to her journeys.

Journeys in Persia and Kurdistan (1891) describes her travels from Baghdad to Tehrān and Esfahān, through Bākhtiārī country to Trebizond (present-day Trabzon in Turkey). She travelled alone on horseback through blizzards of snow and seas of mud, staying in leaking accommodation shared with pack animals and being held to ransom by her own muleteers. Isabella's most exacting journeys were still to come – riding a tricycle through Morocco at 70 – and her final illness struck as she was packing her trunks for China.

Fellow horsewoman Christina Dodwell is an equally intrepid 20th-century successor. Like Isabella, her motivation for travel is the inexorable 'movement is all'. In *A Traveller on Horseback* (1987) she travels from central Turkey through Kurdistan, Persepolis, Kermān and Baluchistan to Quetta and Karachi. She describes the difficulty of travelling during Ramadan, the joy of Eid and the indignities of being bossed around by Iran's Revolutionary Guards. Arrested countless times simply for being a woman travelling alone, she presses on to achieve her journey's goal, riding from Erzurum to Mt Ararat, her route decided by the flip of a coin. Christina is the ideal companion, never complaining, never boring and travelling for the sole reason of 'Why ever not?'. Why ever not indeed.

Janet Austin

is open throughout the tourist season from May to October and has information on various walks.

The **PTDC Motel** (☎ 0833-356) has a choice of villa or motel accommodation and a restaurant. There are other budget hotel options in the village.

There are morning and afternoon buses to/from Quetta, plus numerous minibuses. Direct minibuses go from the Pishin bus stand in Quetta (Rs 45, 2½ hours).

QUETTA TO BAHAWALPUR

The railway line heads south via Sibi towards Sukkur, passing through the dramatic **Bolan Pass** which begins at Kolpur, 24km south of Quetta. This famous pass is a vital link in the main route between Afghanistan and lower Sind. It stretches for 87km from Kolpur to Rindli.

On their way to fight in the two Anglo-Afghan Wars, British troops crossed the pass from Sind in 1839 and 1878, but only at the cost of great physical hardship and loss of life. Work on the Bolan Pass, which started in 1885, was an enormous challenge. The

route from Sibi to Kolpur had to climb from 120m to 1800m through 20 tunnels, with a gradient as steep as 1 in 25 between Mach and Kolpur. To protect the line from marauding tribespeople, many fortresses were built overlooking tracks and tunnel entrances.

In spring, long processions of nomads and camel caravans wind through the pass, bringing livestock and wares to sell in Quetta, before returning in winter. Beyond this is a vast expanse of Baluchistan Desert – hot as a furnace in summer, but with temperatures plummeting at night in winter.

BAHAWALPUR

☎ 0621 • pop 403,000

The southern Punjab town of Bahawalpur is nondescript, even by Pakistani standards, but it's a friendly place and is the best base for visiting a number of attractions including Uch Sharif, Derawar Fort and Lal Suhanra National Park. For this reason, if you're planning to make only one stop on the route between Quetta and Lahore, this should be it.

The present town traces its name and origins to 1748 when it was made capital of the

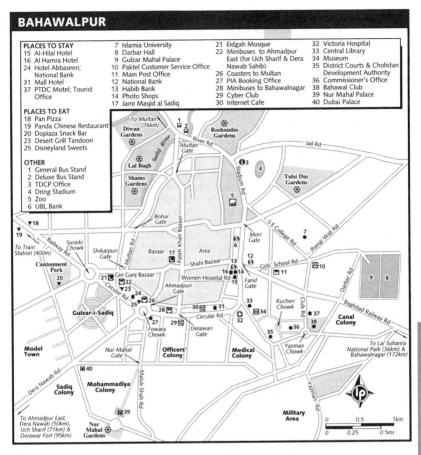

BAHAWALPUR

PLACES TO STAY
15 Al-Hilal Hotel
16 Al Hamra Hotel
24 Hotel Abbaseen;
   National Bank
31 Mall Hotel
37 PTDC Motel; Tourist
   Office

PLACES TO EAT
18 Pan Pizza
19 Panda Chinese Restaurant
20 Dopiaza Snack Bar
23 Desert Grill Tandoori
25 Disneyland Sweets

OTHER
1 General Bus Stand
2 Deluxe Bus Stand
3 TDCP Office
4 Dring Stadium
5 Zoo
6 UBL Bank

7 Islamia University
8 Darbar Hall
9 Gulzar Mahal Palace
10 Paktel Customer Service Office
11 Main Post Office
12 National Bank
13 Habib Bank
14 Photo Shops
17 Jami Masjid al Sadiq

21 Eidgah Mosque
22 Minibuses to Ahmadpur
   East (for Uch Sharif & Dera
   Nawab Sahib)
26 Coasters to Multan
27 PIA Booking Office
28 Minibuses to Bahawalnagar
29 Cyber Club
30 Internet Cafe

32 Victoria Hospital
33 Central Library
34 Museum
35 District Courts & Cholistan
   Development Authority
36 Commissioner's Office
38 Bahawal Club
39 Nur Mahal Palace
40 Dubai Palace

newly founded state of Bahawalpur, headed by Nawab Bahawal Khan Abbasi I, of a dynasty claiming descent from the Prophet Mohammed's uncle, Abbas. The state was ruled by the Abbasi nawabs with little outside interference until the 20th century, when it was merged into Pakistan by treaty in 1954.

Bahawalpur is at its best between October and March, but avoid it in summer when temperatures frequently exceed 40°C.

Information
Tourist Offices The PTDC office (☎ 82835), in the nifty bullet-shaped (and air-conditioned) building at the PTDC Motel on Club Rd, has local brochures, information on getting to nearby attractions, and can organise guides and transport given a bit of notice.

It's open from 9 am to 1 pm and 2 to 4.30 pm (closed Sundays and Friday afternoons). The Tourist Development Corporation of Punjab (TDCP; ☎ 871144) on Stadium Rd can also book local tours, transport and accommodation at Lal Suhanra National Park.

Money The Farid Gate branches of UBL, Habib and National Banks change cash and travellers cheques.

Post & Communications The main post office is a five-minute walk east of Farid Gate. Paktel customer service office, 1km east of Farid Gate, is the best place to make international calls.

There are a couple of Internet cafes (clubs) on Circular Rd just south of the bazaar. The Internet cafe near the Mall Hotel charges Rs 50 per hour. Cyber Club, further west opposite Derawari Gate, charges Rs 60 per hour but has a better setup.

Things to See
The **palaces** of the former rulers are now 'rented' out to the army by the Abbasi family, and military permission is required to visit them (which you're unlikely to get).

In the heart of the bazaar, **Jami Masjid al Sadiq** serves as Bahawalpur's main Friday mosque. Non-Muslims can enter the courtyard whenever it is unlocked to get a closer look at the black-and-cream marble and alabaster facade.

The small **museum** on CMH Chowk has several galleries, including one containing handicrafts from Cholistan and Bahawalpur. It's open from 9 am to 1 pm and 2 to 4 pm, but closes on Saturday and Friday afternoon. Entry is free. Next door, the **Central Library** is said to be one of the best in Pakistan and is open to all.

Places to Stay
Bahawalpur doesn't have a great range of budget accommodation, but the standard tends to be higher than in Multan and places are clean though still pretty basic.

Hotel Abbaseen (☎ 877592, Circular Rd), near Fowara Chowk, is about the best of the cheapies. Basic singles/doubles with fan and bathroom cost Rs 200/300; air-con rooms are Rs 350/450.

There are a couple of good, cheap places near Farid Gate. The *Al-Hilal Hotel* (☎ 875942, Circular Rd) has clean, cool rooms and 24-hour checkout for Rs 170/300. There's no sign in English. The *Al Hamra Hotel* (☎ 883348), back from the main street, has basic singles/doubles around a pleasant courtyard for Rs 130/240, or Rs 278 for a double with an air cooler. To find the Al Hamra, go through Farid Gate and take the first left.

The new *Mall Hotel* (☎ 874032, Circular Rd) is very clean and reasonably priced at Rs 500/650 with air cooler. Forget about using the cooler if you want to sleep, though – it sounds like a pack of horses running around in a tumble dryer. The management intends to install air-conditioning in some rooms and no doubt will double the prices accordingly.

The *PTDC Motel* (☎ 84750, Club Rd), next to the Bahawal Club, is expensive at Rs 1450/1850 plus tax, but the individual cottages arranged around a garden are pleasant and well appointed.

Places to Eat
The *Desert Grill Tandoori*, just up from the Hotel Abbaseen, is a modern, refurbished place serving chicken *karai* (braised chicken in a spicy sauce; Rs 190), rice dishes (around Rs 60) and sandwiches and burgers from Rs 50. The popular *Dopiaza Snack Bar* in Cantonment Park is good for barbecued chicken. It's open evenings only from about 7 pm.

You can get decent pizza at *Pan Pizza* on Railway Rd; a little further up, on the opposite side, is *Panda Chinese Restaurant*, probably the best in town. There are plenty of cheap food stalls and fruit juice stands at both Farid and Ahmadpuri Gates, and further inside the bazaar. *Disneyland Sweets*, also at Ahmadpuri Gate, has excellent takeaway sweets, puddings and cakes.

Shopping
The Bahawalpur region is known for its handicrafts, especially textiles. Items to look out for in the bazaar include shoes known as *khussas* (woven with gold and silver thread and worn by both sexes at weddings, Friday prayers and other special occasions); embroidered *puttas* and skirts; hand-woven carpets from the villages; brocades; painted terracotta; and brassware. Tasselled felt caps (like soft Turkish fezzes) traditionally worn by nawabs and nawabzadas can be bought at hat shops in the bazaar.

Getting There & Away
Bus & Minibus Colourful, windowless old-style Pakistani buses and minibuses leave from the chaotic dustbowl known as the general bus stand at the northern edge of town, while the 'deluxe' buses, ie, more modern, air-con ones, congregate at a separate stand about 50m south. Ordinary buses go to Lahore (Rs 100, eight hours) and Multan (Rs 25, two hours). There are also frequent minibuses to Multan from a separate part of the general bus stand.

Companies operating from the deluxe bus stand include New Khan Road Runners (☎ 887065), Friends (☎ 887418) and the

TDCP (☎ 871144) and all have makeshift offices here. Between them they have regular services to Lahore (Rs 160) as well as buses to Sukkur (Rs 200) and Saqitabad (Rs 100) to the south. There are no direct buses to Quetta, 770km away.

Coasters to Multan sometimes leave from Ahmadpuri Gate. Minibuses to Bahwalnagar and Rahimyar Khan leave from a stand 400m east, while minibuses to Ahmadpur East (Rs 12; change here for Uch Sharif) leave from a stand outside Eidgah Mosque.

Train Almost all long-distance trains pass through Bahawalpur but it can be difficult trying to book anything better than an economy ticket here and the staff are unhelpful. Try to book at least a day or two in advance. Trains heading north-east include the evening *Awam Express* to Lahore (Rs 110/235 for economy/1st-class sleeper, eight hours), Rawalpindi (Rs 175/355, 15 hours) and Peshawar (Rs 165/335, 19½ hours), and the afternoon *Shalimar Express* to Lahore. You can also catch the *Zulfiqar Express* to Lahore at midnight (Rs 235 for 1st class sleeper), or the even more inconvenient *Quetta Express* and *Tezgam Express*. There are two more trains to Peshawar and one to Rawalpindi. There are eight trains daily to Multan (Rs 32 in economy, two hours).

Heading west, there are only two services to Quetta (Rs 360/925 for 1st class/air-con sleeper, 18 hours); the *Abbaseen Express* in the afternoon and the *Quetta Express* in the evening. Book ahead for these.

Getting Around
Passenger Suzukis and tongas loop around Circular Rd, connecting the bus and train stations for a few rupees. An autorickshaw from the train station to the centre costs around Rs 15.

AROUND BAHAWALPUR
Uch Sharif
With its name meaning 'holy high place', the small town of Uch Sharif (or just Uch) is built around a hill overlooking the confluence of the Sutlej and Chenab Rivers. Famous for its exquisite Sufi shrines, which are open and free to all, Uch is well worth a visit. Other than pilgrims, however, few travellers make it here.

Believed to date from around 500 BC or earlier, Uch was under Hindu rule when Alexander the Great invaded India, and there are claims he spent a fortnight here during which time he renamed it Alexandria.

Uch became an important base for the spread of two of the most important Sufi sects, the Sunni Qadiriya school of Syed Mohammed Ghous Jilani Hallabi and the Shia Suhrawardiya school, popularised by Jalaluddin Bukhari.

The town has a carnival feel to it during *urs* festivals (the death anniversaries of saints; see below for approximate dates) and on Thursday nights when devotional *qawwali* singing takes place at the shrines.

Minibuses from Bahawalpur and Ahmadpur East drop passengers at the entrance to the atmospheric bazaar. To get to the shrines, head west through the bazaar for about 1.5km until you exit near the tomb of Jalaluddin Surkh Bukhari. Although the shrines and tombs are within easy walking distance of each other, they're not easy to find without a guide; local boys will happily offer their services for a small reward.

The 14th-century flat-roofed **Shrine & Mosque of Jalaluddin Surkh Bukhari** is surrounded by a brick wall decorated with blue tiles. The saint's urs is held on 19 Jamad Sahri (approximately 8 September 2001, 28 July 2002).

The **Shrine of Jalaluddin Bukhari** is dedicated to Hazrat Jalaluddin Bukhari (1303–83), the grandson of Jalaluddin Surkh Bukhari, who was a prominent member of the Suhrawardiya Sufi sect. The saint's urs is held on 10–12 Zilhaj (approximately 6–8 March 2001, 23–25 February 2002). The tomb lies south-east of the **Mausoleum of Bibi Jawindi**, Uch Sharif's most impressive monument, only half of which remains, having been partially destroyed by a flood in 1817. The octagonal tomb was built at the end of the 15th century and still has some beautiful blue and white tiles inside.

The **Shrine of Sheikh Saif-ud-Din Ghazrooni** is the oldest shrine in Uch, and said to be the oldest Muslim tomb on the subcontinent, but it's in a bad state of repair with no outer ornaments surviving.

Getting There & Away There's nowhere to stay in Uch, but the site can be easily seen in a day from Bahawalpur (71km away),

PAKISTAN

preferably arriving in the morning before it gets too hot. Regular minibuses go from Bahawalpur's Eidgah Mosque to Ahmadpur East (Rs 12) from where you can pick up another to Uch bazaar (Rs 8). Less frequent buses (Rs 22) go direct from Bahawalpur's general bus stand and from Eidgah Mosque. Either way the trip takes at least 1½ hours. Hiring a car and driver through the PTDC will cost around Rs 1500 for a day but you should be able to bargain a taxi down to less.

Derawar Fort

This dramatic fort sits on the edge of the Cholistan Desert, 45km south of Dera Nawab. The vast square structure was built in 1733 as the headquarters of Sadiq Mohammed Khan I, the first nawab of Bahawalpur.

Visible for many kilometres, the fort has 40 enormous bastions, most of them intact, and it stands more than 30m high with a circumference of 1.5km. Most of the interior is in need of renovation. The fort remains the property of the Abbasi family and you must apply to either Prince Salahuddin or Prince Falhouddin Abbasi at Sadiq Garh Palace in Dera Nawab (☎ 72999) for permission to enter. There isn't much to see inside, however – the vast exterior alone warrants a visit. The fort is best visited early in the morning or evening to avoid the heat and midday glare, and since this probably won't be possible from Bahawalpur (at least not by public transport), it may be best to avoid it altogether in summer.

Bahawalpur PTDC may be able to arrange overnight accommodation and camel safaris around the fort given one or two days notice.

Getting There & Away The cheapest way to visit the fort from Bahawalpur is to take a bus to Dera Nawab and from there hire a minivan (seating six) for about Rs 400 for the half-day return trip. A taxi from Bahawalpur works out at about Rs 1200 for the day. The Bahawalpur PTDC can arrange a car for a little more.

Lal Suhanra National Park

Covering a lake and a large tree plantation 36km east of Bahawalpur, this 51,588-hectare park is an important wildlife reserve

and Pakistan's only listed biosphere. If you have the time, it's worth a visit and is a pleasant place to relax for a day or so.

There's a small zoo, and animals found wild in the park include wild boars, hares, jackals, mongooses, desert foxes, porcupines, larks, owls, hawks, nilgais (a type of antelope), and ravine and hog deer. Entry is Rs 5.

If you want to stay here, there's a *TDCP Motel* inside the gates with comfortable doubles for Rs 600 (Rs 1000 with air-con), restful gardens, a swimming pool and a restaurant. Any TDCP office, including the one in Bahawalpur, can book it for you. There are also *resthouses* and a *camp site* in the park; contact Lal Suhanra National Park office (☎ 0621-80696), 3-A Trust Colony in Bahawalpur for information and bookings.

Getting There & Away You can take either a local bus (Rs 8) from Bahawalpur's general bus stand, or any Bahawalnagar-bound minibus from Derawari gate, to the park turn-off, some 30km from Bahawalpur. From here, it's a 4km tonga or rickshaw ride to the park. For information on tours ask at PTDC, TDCP or the Lal Suhanra National Park office in Bahawalpur.

MULTAN
☎ 061 • pop 1.18 million

The largest town in lower Punjab, Multan has some interesting Sufi shrines and a lively bazaar. Since it's on the main east–west highway, it's also an easy stopover on the way to or from Lahore, about 335km away.

One commonly quoted Persian saying is that Multan abounds in four things: *garm, gard, garra* and *goristan* – heat, dust, beggars and burial grounds. Not exactly a ringing endorsement, but this is one of the hottest, driest and dustiest towns in Pakistan – absolutely stifling and best avoided between May and September.

Little is known of Multan's pre-Islamic history, although it's thought to date back some 4000 years, which would make it the oldest surviving city on the subcontinent. Multan was the first town of Punjab to be captured by Mohammed bin Qasim (in 711). Since then it has attracted more mystics, holy men and saints than anywhere else in the subcontinent and today is dominated by their shrines and tombs.

Buses milling at a Pakistani bus stand.

The love of trucks starts at a young age.

A riot of colour adorns this Pakistani vehicle.

Pakistani truck art (detail)

Rail worker, Quetta train station

Vehicles of all types ply the streets of Peshawar.

Autorickshaws queue for customers in Peshawar.

MULTAN

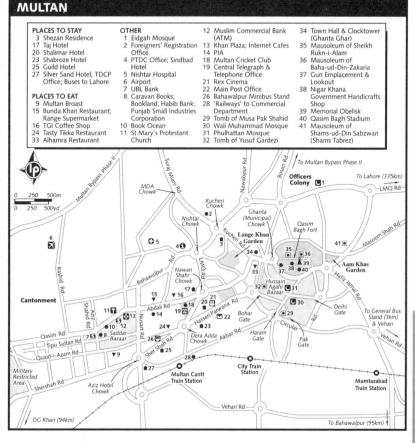

PLACES TO STAY	OTHER	12 Muslim Commercial Bank	34 Town Hall & Clocktower
3 Shezan Residence	1 Eidgah Mosque	(ATM)	(Ghanta Ghar)
17 Taj Hotel	2 Foreigners' Registration	13 Khan Plaza; Internet Cafes	35 Mausoleum of Sheikh
20 Shalimar Hotel	Office	14 PIA	Rukn-i-Alam
23 Shabroze Hotel	4 PTDC Office; Sindbad	18 Multan Cricket Club	36 Mausoleum of
25 Guild Hotel	Hotel	19 Central Telegraph &	Baha-ud-Din-Zakaria
27 Silver Sand Hotel; TDCP	5 Nishtar Hospital	Telephone Office	37 Gun Emplacement &
Office; Buses to Lahore	6 Airport	21 Rex Cinema	Lookout
	7 UBL Bank	22 Main Post Office	38 Nigar Khana
PLACES TO EAT	8 Caravan Books;	26 Bahawalpur Minibus Stand	Government Handicrafts
9 Multan Broast	Bookland; Habib Bank;	28 'Railways' to Commercial	Shop
15 Bunda Khan Restaurant;	Punjab Small Industries	Department	39 Memorial Obelisk
Range Supermarket	Corporation	29 Tomb of Musa Pak Shahid	40 Qasim Bagh Stadium
16 TGI Coffee Shop	10 Book Ocean	30 Wali Muhammad Mosque	41 Mausoleum of
24 Tasty Tikka Restaurant	11 St Mary's Protestant	31 Phulhattan Mosque	Shams-ud-Din Sabzwari
33 Alhamra Restaurant	Church	32 Tomb of Yusuf Gardezi	(Shams Tabrez)

Following almost two centuries of rule under the Mughals, Multan passed through various rival dynasties into the hands of the Sikhs, until the British stormed the citadel in 1848–49 after scoring a direct hit on the city ammunitions dump. The two-week Siege of Mooltan later became known as the Second Sikh War.

Information

Tourist Offices The PTDC, inside the Sindbad Hotel (☎ 512640), is open from 9 am to 1 pm and 2 to 4.30 pm daily except Friday afternoon and Sunday. Staff can be quite helpful if you have particular queries and can organise a city guide (Rs 500 a day) if given a bit of notice. Check out www.multan.com for more background information.

Money UBL and Habib Bank in the Cantonment change cash and travellers cheques before 1.30 pm. There are moneychangers in Saddar Bazaar. Muslim Commercial Bank (MCB) on Qasim Rd, Saddar Bazaar, has an ATM linked to the Cirrus/Maestro network.

Post & Communications The main post office is on Hassan Parwana Rd, but there's no poste restante service. The central telegraph & telephone office on LMQ Rd is open 24 hours a day and has an international fax service.

There are several Internet cafes in Khan Plaza on the north side of Saddar Bazaar (Qasim Rd). They're in the basements on either side of the plaza entrance and charge around Rs 45 an hour.

Qasim Bagh Fort

Multan's most prominent landmark, the fort is now largely in ruins except for its gate and part of the outer walls and bastions. The area does, however, include some of the most important sights in Multan – if you only have a few hours in town, this is the place to spend them.

Apart from the shrines, most of the fort was destroyed by the British in 1849 to avenge the death of Lieutenant Alexander vans Agnew, killed in Multan by order of the Sikh governor. Agnew's **memorial obelisk** stands on a plinth at one of the highest points of the fort mound. The most impressive remains are by the main entrance from Kucheri Rd.

Mausoleum of Sheikh Rukn-i-Alam

Lying just inside the main entrance to the fort, this masterpiece of Mughal architecture is the most important and most attractive of Multan's shrines and tombs.

A pious and widely loved scholar, Ruknud-Din Abul Fatah (1251–1334), commonly known as Sheikh Rukn-i-Alam (Pillar of the World), became head of the Suhrawardiya Sufi sect introduced to the region by his father Baha-ud-Din Zakaria, and is regarded as the patron saint of Multan. His tomb attracts large numbers of devotees and is the focal point for holy men, qawwali musicians and Multan's famous beggars.

Inside, the air is thick with incense, pilgrims are often in a semihypnotic trance, and this is as good a place as any to observe Islam at work, Pakistani-style. The saint's urs is held on 3 Jamaldi ul Awal (approximately 23 July 2001, 12 July 2002).

Mausoleum of Baha-ud-Din Zakaria

Some 300m north, the *mazar* (mausoleum) of Baha-ud-Din Zakaria (1182–1262), father of Rukni-Alam, was built in 1263. A disciple of the Sufi mystic Hazrat Shahabuddin Umar Suhrawardy of Jerusalem, he introduced the Suhrawardiya sect to the subcontinent and founded a university at Multan.

The urs of Baha-ud-Din is held on 27 Safar (approximately 22 May 2001, 11 May 2002).

Mausoleum of Shams-ud-Din Sabzwari

On the dry bed of the River Ravi, 1km northeast of the fort, the shrine of Shamsud-Din Sabzwari (Shams Tabrez) was founded by his grandson in 1330 and rebuilt by more distant descendants in about 1780. One of the most enduring legends about the many miracles of Shams Tabrez is that he moved the sun closer to himself, hence making Multan the hot and dusty city it is today (*shams* means 'sun' in Arabic). Whether or not the saint has been forgiven for this action, his tomb attracts vast numbers of devotees on his urs, held on 14–16 Rabusani (approximately 5–7 July 2001, 24–26 June 2002).

Hussain Agahi Bazaar

At the base of the fort mound is the sprawling bazaar and old town, connected to the rest of the town by seven medieval gates. The main market is the uncovered Hussain Agahi Bazaar, one of the most colourful in Pakistan, flanked by antique wooden merchant houses.

Eidgah Mosque

The vast Eidgah Mosque was built in 1735 and was later used by the Sikhs as a military garrison. In turn, the British used it as a courthouse (it was here that Vans Agnew was murdered) but it was restored to its original use in 1891 and today has some of the finest blue tilework in Multan.

Places to Stay – Budget

Cheap hotels in Multan are pretty dire – many simply can't be recommended. The area to look is on the main road either side of Dera Adda Chowk, only about a 10-minute walk up from the train station and close to the Bahawalpur minibus stand.

The basic *Guild Hotel* (*no phone*) on Sher Shah Rd has dirty singles/doubles for Rs 110/150 (Rs 200 with air cooler). The *Shabroze Hotel* (☎ 544224, *Hassan Parwana Rd*) is a better bet. A single without bathroom is Rs 135 and a single/double with bathroom is Rs 175/324. Rooms are average but at least the staff are friendly and there are pleasant courtyards to which you can retire.

Taj Hotel (☎ 549319, *Nawan Shahr Chowk*) has poky rooms behind its restaurant for Rs 125/224.

Places to Stay – Mid-Range

The *Silver Sand Hotel (☎ 511461, 514 Railway Rd)*, just off Aziz Hotel Chowk, is easily the best in this range with air-con rooms (essential if you're here in summer) for Rs 603/741. The rooms are clean, carpeted and have TVs, and there's a restaurant downstairs. The *Shalimar Hotel (☎ 583245, Hassan Parwana Rd)* isn't a bad choice either. Clean, good-value rooms with fan cost Rs 250/450, but the air-con rooms are overpriced at Rs 850/1000.

One of Multan's better hotels is the peaceful *Shezan Residence (☎ 512235, fax 512238, Kucheri Rd)*. Comfortable air-con rooms for Rs 1000/1600 (plus tax) are arranged around a pleasant garden.

Places to Eat

Local specialities include *faluda* (a kind of vermicelli sorbet flavoured with rosewater), *sohan halvah* (a nut brittle made in round tablets) and some of Pakistan's best mangoes. Bottles of milk mixed with soda water (available in a range of neon colours) have an unusual taste but are refreshing in summer and a bargain at Rs 5.

Cheap snacks can be found around Dera Adda Chowk, Ghanta (Municipal) Chowk and the bazaar. The *Alhamra Restaurant* (no English sign), on Ghanta Chowk, is a simple local dhaba with cheap vegetable dishes for around Rs 15. *Tasty Tikka* is recommended for its tasty chicken karai and pleasant garden. For the best *kheer* (rice pudding) head for the Bohar and Haram Gates of the old town. *Multan Broast*, south of Saddar Bazaar, has snacks for Rs 25.

Bunda Khan Restaurant, on Abdali Rd, is a bright air-con restaurant, popular with middle-class Pakistani families. It's a good place for a mild splurge with Pakistani dishes from Rs 60 to Rs 250, as well as Chinese (from Rs 150) and Continental food. There's a pleasant garden with tables set up al fresco amid neon palm trees.

If you arrive late, the *TGI Coffee Shop* at the Holiday Inn is open 24 hours. Prices are what you'd expect from a five-star hotel but the surroundings are pleasant and the food is good.

For self-caterers, the modern *Range Supermarket*, next door to Bunda Khan Restaurant, stocks all sorts of tinned and packet foods and other essential supplies.

Shopping

For handicrafts, the Nigar Khana government shop by Qasim Bagh is inexpensive and reliable, as is the Punjab Small Industries Corporation on Aziz Shahid Rd in the Cantonment.

Many types of clothing are unique to Multan, including embroidered *cholas* and kurtas for men, silk shirts and *khussa* shoes. Multan is also famous for camel skin lamps (the skin is stretched over a mould until it dries hard, then painted), blue glazed pottery, carpets, lacquered wooden objects, and earthenware vases, sometimes inlaid with tiny mirror tiles.

For handicrafts and local produce, the main shopping areas are Hussain Agahi Bazaar and nearby; and for imported and luxury consumer goods, Saddar Bazaar.

Getting There & Away

Bus & Minibus The best way to get to/from Lahore is on one of the TDCP buses; if only because in Lahore they leave from the city centre. The TDCP office (☎ 580951) is at 517-A Railway Rd, near the Silver Sand Hotel. Seven daily air-con services depart from here for Lahore (Rs 140, six hours) between 9.30 am and 11.30 pm. There's also a bus to Karachi (Rs 370) at 3.45 pm. For more regular buses, the general bus stand is about 6km east of the town centre. From here New Khan Road Runners (☎ 563055) has air-con services to Lahore roughly every half hour (Rs 135), three overnight buses to Rawalpindi (Rs 240, 11 hours), and a few services to DG Khan (Rs 40, two hours) and Bahawalpur (Rs 25, two hours).

Ordinary buses (without air-con) go to many destinations from the general bus stand, including Lahore (Rs 75).

For Bahawalpur, minibuses leave frequently from the stand just west of Dera Adda Chowk. They cost Rs 25 and may be able to drop you off at Farid or Ahmadpuri Gates, not just at Bahawalpur's northern bus stand. There are no direct buses to Quetta – the train is a better option.

Train Nine trains a day depart for Lahore (Rs 85/185/500 economy/1st-class/air-con sleeper, six hours) and Rawalpindi (Rs 155/315/820, 12 to 15 hours) and four go on to Peshawar (Rs 190/385/985, 17 to 20 hours).

PAKISTAN

There are another three to Quetta (Rs 200/400/1025, 20 to 23 hours) and 10 to Bahawalpur (Rs 32 economy seat, two hours) each day.

Trains originating in Multan have the most reliable departure times. Of these, the afternoon *Musa Pak Express* and overnight *109 Nonstop* go to Lahore; the afternoon *Multan Express*, *Meher Express* and the early morning *Bilal Express* depart for Rawalpindi. Only through trains from Lahore and Peshawar go to Quetta. Sleeper reservations for these popular services should be booked days in advance.

All trains leave from Cantonment station (Multan Cantt station). To get a tourist or student concession you must go to the Commercial Department, a few hundred metres east of the station. First you have to get past the security gates, then look for the door marked 'For Officers Only' – it's in there. You don't need a letter from the PTDC but you will need your passport and/or student ID.

Getting Around
Minibus Nos 1 and 3 run from Dera Adda Chowk to Nawan Shahr Chowk, Nishtar Chowk, Kucheri Chowk, the Eidgah Mosque and finally the general bus stand. Others run from Ghanta Chowk to Dera Adda Chowk. Fixed-route tongas run from Aziz Hotel Chowk to Dera Adda Chowk and then on to Bohar and Haram Gates for a few rupees.

An autorickshaw or tonga from the train station costs around Rs 10 to Dera Adda Chowk, Rs 25 to the fort and Rs 50 to the bus stand. You should definitely agree on a fare before getting in.

Lahore

☎ 042 • pop 5.13 million

Lahore may not be Pakistan's largest city, nor is it the capital, but it is the cultural, educational and artistic focus of the country. Lahore was for a time the centre of the Mughal Empire and many of its most beautiful monuments date from that period. The town also has many attractive buildings from the British era.

Lahore has become a crowded and heavily polluted metropolis with growing social problems, but it also has some of the most defiantly serene architecture, parks and gardens on the subcontinent, and there are plenty of places to escape from the clamour of the city. It takes more than a few days to appreciate, but at the very least you should allow a couple of days in Lahore to poke around in the Old City and the grand Mughal fort.

HISTORY
Lahore has been the capital of the Punjab for most of the last millennium. Lying on an important trade route between the subcontinent and Central Asia, but with little natural protection, its history is a repeating pattern of capture, destruction and rebuilding. Its origins and most of its pre-Islamic history are shrouded in legend.

Mahmud of Ghazni, the first Muslim ruler, invaded in 1021, making Lahore the capital of the Ghaznavid empire until 1186. For over three centuries Lahore passed through the hands of a succession of rival dynasties and was in constant danger of attack by Mongol hordes. Relative peace came when the Mughals under Babur captured Lahore in 1524. Akbar, the third Mughal emperor, made his headquarters here from 1584 to 1598, rebuilt the fort, walled the town and built several palaces. He also persuaded many leading cultural figures to come here, and established the city's reputation as a centre of learning and the arts.

The later Mughal emperors Jehangir and Shah Jahan also held court here, added to the fort and founded many of the city's most famous buildings and gardens. Shah Jahan was born here; Jehangir is buried in a northwest suburb. Aurangzeb, the last great Mughal emperor, was patron of the famous Badshahi Mosque in the north of the city, but he didn't spend much time in Lahore and the empire was already beginning to crumble when he died in 1707. The city was then fought over by feuding Mughal remnants, invaded by Afghans and finally sold by Ahmad Shah Abdali to the Sikh ruler Lahna Singh in 1770.

The Sikhs plundered many of the Mughal monuments and built almost nothing of worth in their place. After the death of Sikh ruler Ranjit Singh in 1839 the region fell into a power vacuum, soon filled by the British who captured it in 1846. Lahore has

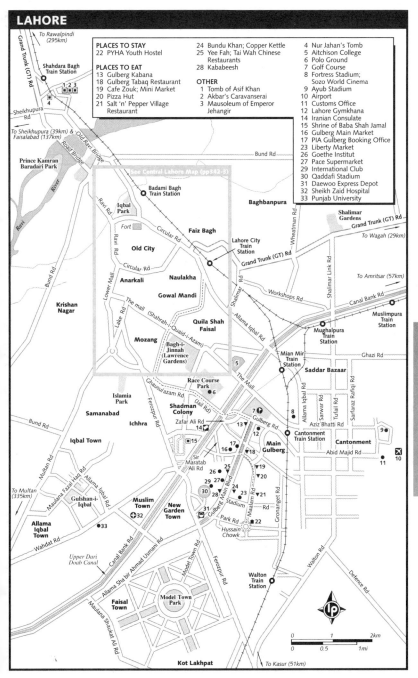

LAHORE

PLACES TO STAY
22 PYHA Youth Hostel

PLACES TO EAT
13 Gulberg Kabana
18 Gulberg Tabaq Restaurant
19 Cafe Zouk; Mini Market
20 Pizza Hut
21 Salt 'n' Pepper Village Restaurant

24 Bundu Khan; Copper Kettle
25 Yee Fah; Tai Wah Chinese Restaurants
28 Kababeesh

OTHER
1 Tomb of Asif Khan
2 Akbar's Caravanserai
3 Mausoleum of Emperor Jehangir

4 Nur Jahan's Tomb
5 Aitchison College
6 Polo Ground
7 Golf Course
8 Fortress Stadium; Sozo World Cinema
9 Ayub Stadium
10 Airport
11 Customs Office
12 Lahore Gymkhana
14 Iranian Consulate
15 Shrine of Baba Shah Jamal
16 Gulberg Main Market
17 PIA Gulberg Booking Office
23 Liberty Market
26 Goethe Institut
27 Pace Supermarket
29 International Club
30 Qaddafi Stadium
31 Daewoo Express Depot
32 Sheikh Zaid Hospital
33 Punjab University

PAKISTAN

CENTRAL LAHORE

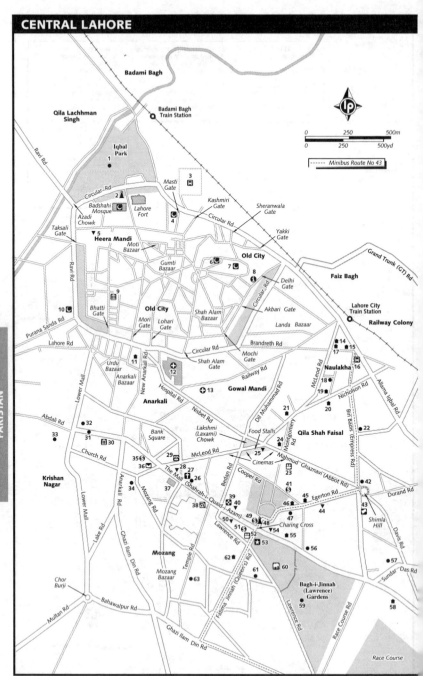

Badami Bagh

Qila Lachhman
Singh

Badami Bagh
Train Station

Iqbal Park
1

Circular Rd

Qila Lachhman

2

Badshahi
Mosque

Lahore Fort

Masti
Gate

3

Kashmiri
Gate

Sheranwala
Gate

Circular Rd

Yakki
Gate

Azadi
Chowk

4

Taksali
Gate

5

Heera Mandi

Moti
Bazaar

Gumti
Bazaar

6

7

Old City

8

Delhi
Gate

Faiz Bagh

Grand Trunk (GT) Rd

9

Bhatti
Gate

Old City

Akbari Gate

Lahore City
Train Station

Railway Colony

10

Purana Sanda Rd

Lahore Rd

Mori
Gate

Lohari
Gate

Shah Alam
Bazaar

Landa Bazaar

Circular Rd

Brandreth Rd

14

17

15

16

Naulakha

Urdu
Bazaar

11

Anarkali
Bazaar

Shah Alam
Gate

Mochi
Gate

Railway Rd

McLeod Rd

18

19

20

Nicholson Rd

12

13

Gowal Mandi

21

Anarkali

Nisbet Rd

Dil Muhammad Rd

Qila Shah Faisal

22

Birj Balois (Empress) Rd

Allama Iqbal Rd

Abdali Rd

32

33

31

30

Church Rd

Bank
Square

Lakshmi
(Laxami)
Chowk

Food Stalls

Montgomery Rd

29

35

36

The Mall

28 27

26

McLeod Rd

24

25

Cinemas

Mahmud Ghaznavi (Abbot) Rd

23

42

Krishan
Nagar

34

37

(Shahrah-i-Quaid-i-Azam)

38

Bedan Rd

Cooper Rd

39

40

41

45

46

Egerton Rd

44

43

Shimla
Hill

49

48

47

Charing Cross

Durand Rd

Davis Rd

Lawrence Rd

50

51

52

53

54

55

56

Mozang

Mozang
Bazaar

62

63

61

60

59

58

Chor
Burji

Multan Rd

Bahawalpur Rd

Ghazi Ilam Din Rd

Bagh-i-Jinnah
(Lawrence)
Gardens

Sundar Das Rd

57

Race Course Rd

Race Course

0   250   500m
0   250   500yd

Minibus Route No 43

PAKISTAN

PLACES TO STAY
11 Queen's Way Hotel
14 Parkway; Shabistan Hotel
15 Clifton Hotel
17 Asia Hotel
19 Shobra Hotel
20 Shah Taj
21 Orient Hotel
24 National Hotel; National Hotel Restaurant
45 Holiday Inn
46 Faletti's Hotel; PTDC Office;
    Arts & Oriental Books; Din's Tours
55 Avari Hotel
58 Pearl Continental
62 YWCA

PLACES TO EAT
5 Cooco's Cafe
25 Tabaq
28 Salt & Pepper
40 Kim Mun Chinese Restaurant
44 McDonald's
50 Pizza Hut
54 Salooss Restaurant; Wapda House

OTHER
1 Minar-i-Pakistan
2 Cenotaph of Maharajah Ranjit Singh
3 Badami Bagh Bus Stand
4 Begum Shah Mosque
6 Sunehri Masjid (Golden Mosque)
7 Wazir Khan Mosque
8 TDCP Office; Buses to Rawalpindi
9 Faqir Khana Museum
10 Data Darbar Mosque;
    Mausoleum of Data Ganj Bakhsh Hajveri
12 Lady Aitchison Hospital
13 Mayo Hospital
16 Minibus Stand
18 Eastern Carpets & Curios
22 Pakistan Railways Headquarters;
    Reservation Office; Commercial Department
23 Gulistan Cinema
26 Vanguard Books
27 Cathedral Church of the Resurrection
29 Central Telegraph & Telephone Office
30 Lahore Museum
31 Kim's Gun (Zamzama)
32 Punjab University (Old Campus)
33 Commissioner's Office; Punjab Civil
    Secretariat; Anarkali's Tomb
34 Excise & Taxation Department
35 National Bank
36 Main Post Office
37 High Court
38 Regale Internet Inn; Regal Cinema
39 Panorama Shopping Plaza
41 Moneychangers; Duty Free Shop
42 Ali Complex (Airline Offices;
    Travel Walji's)
43 US Consulate
47 PIA
48 Summit Minar
49 Citibank (ATM)
51 American Express; Moneychangers
52 Plaza Cinema
53 Police
56 Alhamra Arts Centre
57 Governor's House
59 Jinnah Library
60 Lahore Zoo
61 British Council
63 Adventure 'n' Culture Tours

expanded considerably since Partition and its relative prosperity and stability have attracted ever-growing and unmanageable numbers of migrants.

ORIENTATION

The main street is the British-era Mall, also known as Shahrah-i-Quaid-i-Azam, crossing the city north-west to south-east. The main post office, American Express, most bookshops, travel agents, government offices, banks, and many restaurants and shops are on or near The Mall.

The main crossroads, officially nameless but often called Charing Cross, is at the intersection of The Mall with Fatima Jinnah Rd (also known as Queen's Rd) and has the Summit Minar, the Islamic Summit Conference Building, as its tallest landmark. Just north of here, the old city is a tangle of narrow streets and contains most of Lahore's interesting sights. South-east, across the city canal, is the suburb of Gulberg, a rapidly developing secondary commercial centre and one of the smartest residential areas; most consulates and many of the best restaurants are here.

INFORMATION
Tourist Offices

The helpful PTDC office (☎ 631 1961, fax 636 4819) at Faletti's Hotel, Egerton Rd, is open from 9 am to 1.30 pm and 2 to 4.30 pm Monday to Saturday (closed from noon on Friday). Opening hours are slightly longer in summer.

The TDCP (☎ 636 9687, 636 0553, fax 758 9097), at 4A Lawrence Rd, south of The Mall, runs city tours (see Organised Tours later in this section) and intercity aircon buses, but doesn't give out general tourist information.

Foreigners' Registration Office

If you're staying in the country more than 30 days and Lahore is your base, you can register at the Foreigners' Registration Office (FRO) at 63 Kucheri Rd, near Lower Mall.

Consulates

Some countries have honorary consulates in Lahore but most are of little help and will usually direct you to Islamabad.

There's no Indian mission here: You must apply for a visa in Islamabad. The Iranian consulate (☎ 870274) doesn't normally issue visas except to Pakistani citizens or residents, though travellers have reported getting a transit visa here (in some cases subject to long waits).

The US consulate (☎ 636 5530) is at Sharah-e-Abdul, Hamid Bin Badees (50 Empress Rd), New Shimla Hills.

Money

Two places which accept travellers cheques without much hassle are American Express (1% on non-AmEx cheques) at 1121 Rafi Mansion, The Mall, and National Bank, Regal Chowk, The Mall.

Citibank, on The Mall at Charing Cross, changes cash and travellers cheques and is the only bank open during lunch time. It also has two 24-hour ATMs accepting most international debit and credit cards. There's a Muslim Commercial Bank ATM at the Avari Hotel. Legal moneychangers will readily accept cash or travellers cheques and they can be found on The Mall (near AmEx) and bunched around Cooper Rd, north-west of the Holiday Inn.

Post & Communications

The main post office (☎ 724 3580) is near the National Bank on The Mall (ask for poste restante at the inquiries desk), and the central telegraph & telephone office is across the road.

Regale Internet Inn, near the Regal Cinema at the western end of The Mall, is open 24 hours a day and charges Rs 50 an hour. If it's hot, head for the air-conditioned British Council library (☎ 111-424 424), 65 Mozang Rd, where Internet access is also Rs 50 an hour. It's open from 9.30 am to 6.30 pm Monday to Saturday.

Libraries & Cultural Centres

The British Council (☎ 636 2497), 65 Mozang Rd, opposite the Ganga Ram Hospital, is open from 9.30 am to 6.30 pm, Monday to Friday, and has an excellent library open to all.

The Goethe Institut (☎ 877113) is at 92-E/1 Gulberg III. Alliance Française (☎ 876043) is at 20-E/2 Gulberg III.

The Jinnah Library in the Bagh-i-Jinnah, open daily from 8 am to 8 pm, has a newspaper room open to the public, with Pakistani and foreign titles.

Travel Agencies

There are useful travel agencies all over town, especially on The Mall, at Wapda House and around Shimla Hill. Travel Walji's (☎ 636 7845), 23 Empress Rd, is the best for tours and can book flights.

Bookshops

Arts & Oriental Books (☎ 636 7027) at Faletti's Hotel is probably the best bookshop in Pakistan and stocks many books almost impossible to obtain in other countries. Travel and the arts are especially well represented. There's another small branch next to the Lahore Museum. Other good book and map shops are Ferozson's Vanguard Books and Lion Art Press, both on The Mall.

Medical Services

Two hospitals with good reputations are the Sheikh Zaid (☎ 586 5731) on Canal Bank Rd and the Mayo (☎ 732 0419) in Gowal Mandi. There are 24-hour pharmacies outside the Mayo.

Emergency

Police emergency numbers are ☎ 636 1239 and 583 8655. The police station is on Fatimah Jinnah Rd near Charing Cross.

CENOTAPH OF MAHARAJA RANJIT SINGH

Outside the fort and beside the Badshahi Mosque, this *samadhi*, or brick mausoleum, commemorates the founder of the short-lived Sikh Empire. The ashes of the maharaja lie in a lotus-shaped urn inside a small brick pavilion, along with those of his son Naunihal Singh. Normally, only Sikhs and Hindus are allowed to enter.

OLD CITY

Old Lahore is at the foot of the fort, covering 1 sq km of narrow twisting alleys surrounded by a 9m-high wall with 13 gates, looking in parts almost as it must have done in Mughal days. It's a fantastic place in which to get lost, as you probably will; the best way to relocate yourself is to go back to one of the main gates. When entering the Old City, **Delhi Gate** in the east leads past the 17th-century Royal Baths (now a TDCP tourist information centre) to the Wazir Khan Mosque, Brass Bazaar and the Sunheri

Masjid (Golden Mosque); **Bhatti Gate** in the south leads to the Faqir Khana Museum and eventually to Heera Mandi, the dancing girl's quarter; **Masti Gate** in the north leads to the Begum Shah Mosque (1614), named after one Maryam Zamani, the mother of Emperor Jehangir.

The **Sunehri Masjid** or Golden Mosque, in the centre of the Old City, was built in 1753 and is famous for its three gilded domes and gold-plated minarets, still shining as brightly as ever. Friday prayers bring the surrounding streets to a standstill.

At the east end of the Old City, 250m inside Delhi Gate, is the beautifully tiled **Wazir Khan Mosque**, founded in 1634 by Sheikh Ilm-ud-Din Ansari (also known as Wazir Khan), the royal physician and later governor of Punjab during the reign of Shah Jahan.

About 500m inside Bhatti Gate on the right-hand side, the small **Faqir Khana Museum** displays treasures of the Faqir family, who have lived in Lahore since the 18th century. It is said to be the largest private collection in south Asia, with over 13,000 pieces of art. Visiting it is like rummaging through someone's attic.

Items include relics of the Prophet Mohammed (on public display for one day during the Muslim month of Muharram), early Qurans, miniature paintings, carvings, clothes worn by the Mughal emperors, a small armoury of Sikh weapons and carpets from the royal courts.

It's best to phone the curator (☎ 765 8429) in advance to make sure someone is there to show you around the eight rooms.

West of Bhatti Gate, just outside the Old City is the **Mausoleum of Data Ganj Bakhsh Hajveri**. Author of a famous book on mysticism, the 11th-century Data Ganj Bakhsh, originally from Ghazni in Afghanistan, was one of the most successful Sufi preachers on the subcontinent and is today probably the most important Sufi saint in Pakistan. A modern mosque, the Data Darbar Masjid, has been built around the shrine.

This area attracts large numbers of devotees on Thursday nights, with qawwali singers and ceremonies continuing until late. Non-Muslim visitors may feel self-conscious but it's fascinating to watch the activities from a distance.

The saint's urs celebrations on 18–20 Safar (approximately 13–15 May 2001, 2–4 May 2002) are attended by tens (if not hundreds) of thousands of pilgrims.

LAHORE MUSEUM

The superb Lahore Museum (☎ 732 2835), on The Mall, has exhibits spanning the recorded history of the subcontinent. It was founded in 1887 in commemoration of Queen Victoria's Golden Jubilee (fittingly, there's a large brass statue of Queen Vic inside).

The museum has 17 galleries with items dating from the Stone Age to the 20th century. It is famous for its display of Gandharan sculpture (especially the haunting Fasting Buddha), manuscripts, Qurans, miniatures, carpets and other art of the Islamic period, articles from Moenjodaro, Harappa and other Indus Valley civilisation sites, and its collection of coins from the Achaemenian period onwards. The entry hall features a huge mural on the ceiling and, in a glass case to one side, the 'object of the month'.

The museum is open from 9 am to 5 pm (4 pm in winter) daily except the first Monday of each month. Admission for foreigners is Rs 50 (students Rs 25) and photography permits are Rs 10 (Rs 50 for video). It takes at least a few hours to explore it properly. Free guided tours are available by appointment on Monday and Thursday from 11 am.

KIM'S GUN

This mighty cannon, made famous at the start of Rudyard Kipling's classic novel *Kim*, was originally named Zamzama meaning 'Lion's Roar', and was used in various battles by the Afghan Durranis and then the Sikhs, before being brought to Lahore by Ranjit Singh as a symbol of his conquests. Kipling's father was the first curator of the Lahore Museum.

MINAR-I-PAKISTAN & IQBAL PARK

Soaring into the sky in Iqbal Park, Minar-i-Pakistan was built in 1960 to commemorate the signing in 23 March 1940 of the Pakistan Resolution by the All-India Muslim League, which paved the way for the founding of Pakistan. You can climb the 60m-high fluted concrete needle for a fine view

[Continued on page 349]

LAHORE FORT

The Shahi Qila, or Lahore Fort, is the star attraction of the Old City. It was built, damaged, demolished, rebuilt and restored several times before being given its current form by Akbar in 1566, when he made Lahore his capital. The fort was later damaged by the Sikhs and the British, although it has now been partially restored.

Within it is a succession of stately palaces, halls and gardens built by the Mughal emperors Akbar, Jehangir, Shah Jahan and Aurangzeb. The fort is comparable to and contemporary with the other great Mughal forts at Delhi and Agra.

Lahore Fort is entered on its western side through the colossal **Alamgiri Gate**, built by Aurangzeb in 1674 as a private entrance to the royal quarters and large enough to allow several elephants carrying members of the royal household to enter at one time. The iron studs were to deter elephant charges. The small **Moti Masjid** (Pearl Mosque) was built by Shah Jahan in 1644 for the private use of the ladies of the royal household and was restored to its original delicacy in 1904.

The **Diwan-i-Aam** (Court of Public Audience) was built by Shah Jahan in 1631 and features an upper balcony where the emperor would make a daily public appearance, receive official visitors and review parades.

Khawabgarh-i-Jehangir (Jehangir's Sleeping Quarters), a white pavilion on the north side of Jehangir's quadrangle, now houses a small museum of Mughal antiquities. Another graceful pavilion, the **Diwan-i-Khas** (Hall of Private Audience) was built by Shah Jahan for receiving guests. The sleeping quarters of Shah Jahan and a museum are at the southern end of the courtyard.

PATRICK HORTON

Inset: Minaret detail, Lahore Fort (Photo by Paul Harding)

Bottom: Looking across the Alamgiri Gate, Lahore Fort, towards the minarets of Badshahi Mosque and the tomb of Maharaja Ranjit Singh

LAHORE FORT

1	Shish Mahal (Palace of Mirrors)	18	Khawabgarh-i-Shah Jahani (Shah Jahan's Sleeping Quarters)
2	Kala Burj (Black Tower)	19	Hamman (Bathhouse)
3	Lal Burj (Red Tower)	20	New Museum
4	Ruined Arzgah	21	Daulat Khana (Throne Room)
5	Diwan-i-Khas (Hall of Private Audience)	22	Diwan-i-Aam (Court of Public Audience)
6	Khawabgarh-i-Jehangir (Jehangir's Sleeping Quarters)	23	Archaeological Offices
7	Akbar's Court	24	Masti Gate
8	Jehangir's Quadrangle	25	Clerk's House (Maktab Khana)
9	Shah Jahan's Quadrangle	26	Moti Masjid (Pearl Mosque)
10	Khilwat Khana (Ladies' Court)	27	Musamman Burj Gate
11	Paien Bagh (Women's Gardens)	28	Alamgiri Gate
12	Naulakha (Marble Pavilion)	29	Roshnai Gate
13	Tomb of Guru Arjan	30	Tomb (Samadhi) of Maharaja Ranjit Singh
14	Hathi Paer (Elephant Path)	31	Hazuri Bagh Baradari
15	Shah Burj Gate	32	Badshahi Mosque
16	Snack Bar & Toilets	33	Tomb of Allama Mohammed Iqbal
17	Baths	34	Royal Kitchens & Archaeology Dept
		35	Stables

The well-preserved **Shish Mahal** (Palace of Mirrors), built by Shah Jahan in 1631, is decorated with glass mirrors set into the stucco interior. The view from here over the rest of the fort and Badshahi Mosque is superb.

Naulakha, the marble pavilion on the west side of the quadrangle, lavishly decorated with *pietra dura* (inlaid detail) – studded with tiny jewels in intricate floral motifs – was erected in 1631. Several underground chambers were being restored at the time of writing, but they may be open to visitors by the time you read this.

You can exit the fort from here, down the Elephant Path and through the **Shah Burj Gate**; look behind to see the fine painted tilework of the outer wall.

The fort is open from 7 am to 6.30 pm daily in summer and 8 am to 4.30 pm in winter (Rs 4). The museums are closed from 12.30 to 2.30 pm. A guide costs around Rs 100.

BADSHAHI MOSQUE

The impressive Badshahi Mosque is opposite the main gateway to the fort. Completed in 1676 under Aurangzeb, it was the Mughals' final architectural fling. It is one of the largest mosques in the world, with huge gateways, four tapering minarets of red sandstone, three vast marble domes and an open courtyard capable of holding at least 60,000 people. It was damaged and later restored by the British. The rooms above the entrance gate (not open to the public) are said to house hairs of the Prophet Mohammed and other relics of his daughter, Fatima, and his son-in-law and cousin, Ali.

In the courtyard stands the **Tomb of Allama Mohammed Iqbal**, a modest memorial in red sandstone to the philosopher-poet who, in the 1930s, first postulated the idea of an independent Pakistan. In a small gallery to the right as you enter the main gate is a Quran hand-embroidered with thread of gold and silver. It was the work of a single goldsmith who spent 12 years on the project after losing his family in a fire and dedicating his life to religion.

CHRISTINE OSBORNE

GRANT DIXON

PAUL HARDING

Top Left: The arched entrance to the imposing Badshahi Mosque

Top Right: Ornate interior passage, Badshahi Mosque
Bottom: Badshahi, the largest and last of the Mughal mosques

[Continued from page 345]

of the fort and city. The lift seems to be permanently out of order, but those without a serious heart condition can walk the 255 steps to the top for Rs 10.

Iqbal Park is a good place to wander in the evenings when hundreds of people gather on every spare patch of ground to play cricket, fly kites or just hang around.

BAGH-I-JINNAH (LAWRENCE GARDENS)

This extensive park on The Mall, open daily from 8 am to 9 pm, is one of central Lahore's most pleasant places to unwind or meet people. The attractive British building in the centre of the park now houses the Jinnah Library.

ZOOLOGICAL GARDENS

West of the Bagh-i-Jinnah, Lahore Zoo (☎ 630 4682) is one of the oldest on the subcontinent and is quite well-maintained as zoos in this part of the world go. It was founded in 1872 and includes three birdhouses along with lions, elephants, monkeys, leopards, giraffes and tigers. The zoo and gardens are open from 8 am to 7 pm (Rs 7) daily.

SHALIMAR GARDENS

On Grand Trunk Rd to the north-east of town, about 4km from the train station, this was one of three gardens of that name built by Shah Jahan in the mid-1640s. It's also the only surviving Mughal garden of several built in Lahore. The gardens are run-down now and a little dull but are a good place to meet locals.

JEHANGIR'S MAUSOLEUM

The elaborately decorated sandstone mausoleum of Emperor Jehangir is in a garden outside Lahore on the right bank of the Ravi River. It was built in 1637 by Jehangir's son Shah Jahan, although it's believed to have been designed by Jehangir's widow, Nur Jahan. The tomb is made of marble with Trellis decorations of pietra dura bearing the 99 attributes of Allah in Arabic calligraphy.

The tomb was damaged by the Sikhs and then by summer flooding for years. Many roof tiles are missing and the marble is discoloured, but it is still an impressive sight and the large gardens are delightful. It's open from 8 am to 5 pm daily (Rs 4).

NUR JAHAN'S TOMB

Just over the train line from Jehangir's Mausoleum, the tomb of Nur Jahan has not been as well preserved. Most of it was supposedly plundered to decorate the Sikhs' Golden Temple at Amritsar.

After the death of her first husband, an Afghan prince, Nur Jahan was carted off to Delhi, destined for captivity, but Emperor Jehangir fell in love with her and they married in 1611. He gave her the name Nur Jahan meaning 'Light of the World' and allowed her to rule alongside him. She died aged 72 in 1645, 18 years after Jehangir, and her tomb was completed in the same year. The site is open from 8 am to 5 pm daily.

ORGANISED TOURS

Adventure 'n' Culture (☎/fax 637 2700, ⓔ actos@brain.net.pk) runs two very good city tours daily. The morning tour is run twice, starting at 7 and 8.30 am and includes the Badshahi Mosque, Lahore Fort, Jehangir's Mausoleum, Nur Jahan's Tomb and Lahore Museum.

The afternoon tour starts at 3.30 pm and visits Shalimar Gardens, a tour of the Old City, Shahi Hamam, Wazir Khan's Mosque, the Golden Mosque and a carpet shop. Both tours cost Rs 300 and pick up from Faletti's Hotel, Holiday Inn, Ambassador Hotel, Pearl Continental and Avari Hotel (in that order).

TDCP (☎ 636 9687) runs similar tours (also Rs 300) starting from their office at 4-A Lawrence Rd.

PLACES TO STAY

Lahore doesn't really have a travellers' scene, so there are no budget areas to head for like Sultanahmet in İstanbul or Paharganj in Delhi. What's more, the cheap hotels in the streets immediately opposite the train station don't enjoy the best of reputations, although horror stories of travellers being ripped off in this area have eased in recent years.

PLACES TO STAY – BUDGET
Camping

If you want to camp, you can pitch a tent at the *YWCA*, the *PYHA Youth Hostel* and *Faletti's Hotel* (for contact details, see later in this section).

PAKISTAN

Hostels & Hotels

The *YWCA Hostel* (☎ 630 4707, 14 Fatima Jinnah Rd), next to the Caltex station, is the most popular hostel among backpackers, although it's no longer dirt cheap. At the time of research the kitchen was not in use, but the management claimed to be building new facilities and rooms. Until then you can choose from a crowded, basic dormitory for Rs 125 or a double room at Rs 150 per person. Camping is Rs 70 and parking costs Rs 80 (Rs 20 for a motorcycle). Gates close at 10 pm so call ahead if you're arriving any later.

The *PYHA Youth Hostel* (☎ 878201, 110-B/3 Firdous Market), just off Hussain Chowk in Gulberg, would be fine if it wasn't so inconveniently located. It has dorm beds in two- to six-bed rooms with bathroom at Rs 60 if you're a HI/IYHF member. If you're not a member, you have to join up at a cost of Rs 510. Minibus No 43 runs direct to the door from The Mall and the train station.

Near the train station, the *Asia Hotel* (☎ 636 6450), off Brandreth Rd, is clean and reasonable value at Rs 150/250 for a single/double, or Rs 400 for a four-bed room. *Clifton Hotel* (☎ 636 6740), around the corner on Brandreth Rd, is nondescript but secure. Singles/doubles cost Rs 260/350. The *Parkway* (☎ 631 5647), on McLeod Rd, is another reasonable option with plain but clean rooms for Rs 275/350 and overpriced air-con rooms for Rs 700/800. The *Shabistan Hotel* (☎ 636 6292), also on McLeod Rd, is slightly cheaper at Rs 220/230.

The hotels listed in this section should be reliable but we've had lots of reports of rip-offs from cheap hotels in this area over the years. Wherever you stay, take sensible precautions. Don't leave any valuables in your room; use your own padlock on the door if possible; and be wary of hotel staff who try to engage you in conversation in your room.

Tucked away near the walls of the Old City, the *Queen's Way Hotel* (☎ 722 9734, 42 New Anarkali Rd) is pretty basic and some of the rooms are small and windowless, but it's friendly enough and cheap at Rs 150/300 for singles/doubles.

PLACES TO STAY – MID-RANGE & TOP END

The *National Hotel* (☎ 636 3011, 1 Abbott Rd) is the best in this range, with modern, spacious singles/doubles with TV, fridge and air-conditioning for Rs 750/950. Staff can be a bit off-hand.

The *Orient Hotel* (☎ 722 3906, 74 Macleod Rd) is an older-style place with narrow rooms arranged around a courtyard. The ordinary rooms are quite good value at Rs 270/420 (plus tax), and air-con rooms are Rs 680/950. The *Shah Taj* (☎ 631 3821, 13 Nicholson Rd) doesn't look very impressive but the rooms are OK with TV, fridge and air-conditioning. Ordinary rooms cost Rs 575/775 and bigger deluxe rooms are Rs 775/975.

The centrally air-conditioned *Shobra Hotel* (☎ 636 4959, 55 Nicholson Rd) has fairly standard rooms with bathroom for Rs 600/783.

The PTDC-run *Faletti's* (☎ 636 3946, fax 636 4819, Egerton Rd) was Lahore's grandest hotel in colonial days. The large ground-floor rooms are a bit threadbare and musty these days but still comfortable. Rooms with small TV and fridge cost Rs 1600/2000 plus 20.5% tax. You can also camp in the hotel grounds for Rs 50.

PLACES TO EAT

Lahore is Pakistan's gourmet capital and caters to almost every taste and budget. Some of the better restaurants are quite a way south in Gulberg.

The city is famous for its Mughal cuisine. Local specialties include lassi, *kheer* (rice pudding), *chapli kebabs*, *dahi bhaley* (fried grams in savoury yogurt and onions), *taka-tuk* (fried meat and egg), faluda (vermicelli, ice and ice cream), samosas, *halim* (pulses, wheat and rice mix), *alu chana* (potato and chickpeas), *nihari* (chunks of meat in a spicy sauce), fruit *chat* (spicy fruit salad) and *siri-paae* (goat's head stew). The Old City is the best place to search for such delights. You can get some of the best kheer and faluda at a shop opposite the Wazir Khan Mosque.

Tuesday is meatless day everywhere, which means no beef or mutton, but chicken is still served.

Restaurants

Central Lahore *Cooco's Cafe*, on Fort Rd in the Old City, should top your list of restaurants to visit in Lahore. Housed in a wonderful restored *haveli* (palace) and adorned with paintings by the owner, Iqbal Hussein, people eat here as much for the surroundings as for the food. Hussein is a well-known artist in Pakistan and most of the paintings depict girls from the Heera Mandi, the Dancing Girls Quarter, in which the restaurant is situated. The service is quick, the food is good and the menu is diverse. As well as a wide range of Pakistani food from *dhal* (Rs 20) to chicken karai (Rs 250), there are burgers and salads from around Rs 55.

The *National Hotel Restaurant* on Abbott Rd is reasonably good for Pakistani and international food but the service is painfully slow. Most dishes are under Rs 100 and simple, filling rice dishes are around Rs 65. Across the road, *Tabaq* is an incredibly busy place serving good *churgha* (steam roasted) whole chicken for Rs 155 (Rs 80 for half). It also does mutton and fish dishes.

The *Kim Mun Chinese Restaurant* on The Mall is fairly good and has a pleasant 1st-floor view, but it isn't great value at around Rs 120 a head.

The *Salooss Restaurant* (☎ 636 7137, Wapda House, The Mall) isn't as fabulous as its reputation suggests, but it makes a fairly good job of international food at around Rs 180 a head.

The *Avari Hotel* (☎ 631 0646, 87 The Mall) has no fewer than five restaurants and a coffee shop and is a good place for a splurge. These include *Fujiama*, Lahore's only Japanese restaurant – it's authentic but you'll be lucky to get away for under Rs 400 a head; *Dynasty* (Chinese); *Tollington* (barbecue); and the *Fort Grill* (Pakistani). 'Musical T', every evening from 6 pm at *Kim's* is good value. For Rs 100 you get entertained by a band and help yourself to the buffet.

The *Holiday Inn* and *Pearl Continental* also have flash cafes and restaurants. Check menu prices before committing yourself to a meal at a five-star hotel and don't forget the extra 20.5% tax.

Gulberg Gulberg has plenty of excellent, reasonably inexpensive restaurants, especially on Gulberg Main Blvd. This area is popular with Lahore's expat community.

Yee Fah and *Tai Wah* are passable Chinese restaurants side by side on Gulberg Main Blvd.

Gulberg Kabana is one of the best restaurants in town and has live Punjabi music most

nights. There's an extensive menu of international and Pakistani dishes and most are good value; you can eat well for under Rs 200. The open-air *Kababeesh*, further south, is also good and is recommended for its barbecues. A half chicken costs around Rs 100.

Salt'n'Pepper Village Restaurant, where local specialities are cooked in front of you, is very popular and recommended by travellers and expats. *Bunda Khan* and *Copper Kettle* near Liberty Market are also recommended for grilled Pakistani dishes and curries. The No 43 minibus route is close to most of these restaurants.

Fast Food
Good places to look for cheap food include Anarkali Bazaar, Mozang Bazaar, the alleys running off The Mall, and along McLeod Rd.

For barbecued meat, chicken and takatuk try the 24-hour stalls along Abbott Rd. The chicken is guaranteed fresh as the birds are kept alive in cages on the street until required; there are even goats tethered outside a few places. At night more stalls appear all along McLeod Rd (Lakshmi Chowk), between Bedan Rd and Abbott Rd, with tables and chairs set up at the front. As with any meat dish in Pakistan, you take your chances here, and expect chilli to feature heavily in the preparation.

If you're desperate for some recognisable fast food, *McDonald's* has four outlets in Lahore, the most convenient on Egerton Rd, about 300m east of Faletti's (a 'Maharaja Mac' meal costs Rs 89); and *Pizza Hut* is on The Mall. A large pan pizza (serving three) costs Rs 480 plus tax so it's certainly no cheap meal.

Salt & Pepper, at the western end of The Mall, is a good local burger restaurant.

ALCOHOL
Liquor permits are issued by the Excise & Taxation Department from room 47 on the 2nd floor of a squalid building near Farid Court House, just off The Mall on Mozang Rd, but it's nothing short of a nightmare even finding the place. Unless you are going to be in Lahore for a while, you will probably be better off making discreet inquiries at Faletti's or the Avari Hotel where you may be able to fill out a form on the spot and purchase alcohol even if you're not a guest.

Otherwise, ask around to find the Excise & Taxation Department (the building is not marked in English). You need photocopies of your visa, entry stamps and the front pages of your passport. The Excise & Taxation Department is open from 9 am to 12.30 pm Monday to Thursday, 9 am to around 11 am Friday; go early if you want the permit issued the same day. The monthly charge is Rs 45.

There are 'permit rooms' at Faletti's, Pearl Continental and Avari Hotels, open 8 am to 8 pm daily. Guests of these hotels can get permits on the spot. A bottle of Murree beer costs around Rs 80.

ENTERTAINMENT

For details on some traditional forms of Lahori entertainment, see the boxed text 'Dancing Girls & Qawwali Singers'.

The **Alhamra Arts Centre** (☎ 636 0040, 68 The Mall), just east of the Avari Hotel, has three theatre halls and is the main centre for musical, dramatic and other cultural activities.

The **International Club** (☎ 576 4276), near Qaddafi Stadium in Gulberg III, is an expat club with a bar, restaurant, music and a pool table. It's supposed to be open to members and guests only, but if you call ahead you may be able to wangle an invitation. It's a great place to meet westerners living in Lahore.

There are plenty of **cinemas** around Abbott and McLeod Rds. Most of the films are in Urdu, but it's worth coming here just to check out the garish and phenomenally oversize hoardings, some of them taller than three-storey buildings. The **Gulistan** (Abbott Rd), **Plaza** (Charing

---

Dancing Girls & Qawwali Singers

By day the Heera Mandi, or Dancing Girls Quarter, is just another tangle of streets overshadowed by the huge Lahore Fort in the Old City. At night (after about 11 pm) these streets begin to come to life.

Although this is Lahore's red-light district, it's not particularly seedy. Along with the ladies of the night beckoning from upper-floor windows, there are perfectly legitimate dancing girls plying their trade here. The streets develop a mini-carnival atmosphere, with food stalls and bright lights and crowds of people (mostly male), while the shuttered facades of homes open to reveal traditionally dressed girls in dancing rooms (kotha), complete with three-piece musical accompaniment, awaiting clients.

What happens if you step inside? First you need a lot of small change (such as Rs 5 notes), which the change dealers on the street will oblige you with for a commission. Inside, you sit on a couch and throw money while the girl sings and dances her heart out just for you, backed by a tabla, harmonium and shenai (a kind of oboe). She stops singing if you stop throwing money, and gets pretty miffed if you decide to leave halfway through a song. This goes on all night. The girls wait, then perform, then wait again.

In another part of town, on Thursday nights, another form of Lahori entertainment is taking place. Trance-like qawwali or devotional singing begins well after dark at Sufi shrines all over Pakistan on a Thursday, and continues through the night. Usually one or two singers take centre stage and are surrounded by devotees from all walks of Pakistani life. The singing is often accompanied by drumming, and an aromatic haze of smoke fills the air. There are two places to see this in Lahore: at the Mausoleum of Data Ganj Bakhsh Hajveri, just outside the Old City west of Bhatti Gate; and at the Shrine of Baba Shah Jamal in Shadman Colony. The latter is where renowned performer Pappu Saein works himself into a trance while beating a rhythm on his dhol (large drum).

Visiting both the Heera Mandi and the qawwali performances can be unnerving for westerners, as they both take place late at night and are both very traditional and male-dominated. The best advice is to ask a local to take you along, but at the very least you should remain as unobtrusive and discreet as possible. Autorickshaw drivers will be able to take you to the shrines of Data Ganj and Shah Jamal.

Cross) and *Regal (The Mall)* show international movies in English, as does *Sozo World* at Fortress Stadium in Gulberg (preceded by a spectacular light show with fountains and lasers).

The five-star hotels have *swimming pools* which nonguests can use for a fee. The best is at the Avari Hotel but the cost is a whopping Rs 490.

SPECTATOR SPORTS
The two main venues for football (soccer) are Qaddafi Stadium (☎ 871031) on Ferozpur Rd and Fortress Stadium (☎ 371803) in the Cantonment.

Important domestic and international cricket matches are played at the Qaddafi Stadium and Bagh-i-Jinnah. You can attend polo matches in season at the Race Course Park south of the Pearl Continental Hotel. PTDC may be able to help with information about sporting fixtures, otherwise consult *The News* and *Frontier Post*.

SHOPPING
Lahore isn't a great handicrafts centre, and prices are generally higher than elsewhere, but there are a few worthwhile places for souvenirs. Anarkali and the Old City are the places to look for bargains such as brass and copperware, but good quality is hard to find. Tailors in the Old City will make you a *salwar kameez* (traditional Pakistani shirt and loose trousers) for around Rs 250 (plus material).

Although Lahore isn't the best place to look for carpets, Eastern Carpets & Curios (☎ 6365380) has a fantastic range of Pakistani, Afghani, Iranian and Baluchi rugs, and friendly, knowledgeable owners, so it's worth a look. The showroom is just off Nicholson Rd, around the corner from the Shobra Hotel.

Hall Rd (or Hall Bazaar) is a must if you're in the market for electronic equipment – or even if you just want to see how many TVs, hi-fi systems, satellite dishes and ghetto blasters can be crammed into one street.

The Panorama Shopping Centre on The Mall is filled with shops selling gold jewellery, saris and leather garments, but it's not cheap.

The highest concentration of shops with imported goods – from food to CDs – is in

Amritsar to Quetta

Cycling days: 10
Distance: 950km

The first part of this journey was getting from Amritsar in India to Lahore in Pakistan (62km, three hours cycling). The border crossing here was no problem with helpful authorities on both sides. Pakistan proved to be a pleasant surprise: The drivers were more considerate and Lahore had a modern feel. There was no problem cycling through the streets here. However, it did take 30 days to get a 14-day Iranian tourist visa in Lahore for a total cost of US$155, including a letter of recommendation from the British High Commission in Islamabad – US$50.

It took three days from Lahore to reach Multan (350km) on flat terrain and bumpy roads that were being resurfaced at the time. The lush countryside around Multan is great for cycling. We enjoyed staying at Sahiwal along the way. From Multan to Quetta was another six days on the road. This area becomes mountainous, reaching a height of almost 3000m just before Ziarat, so riding time is slower. Make sure you start early to avoid being still on the road at dusk – it's quite isolated and there is little traffic along here. We stayed at DG Khan (plenty of hotels), then at government resthouses and small villages on the way up to Ziarat. The final night was spent at a police post about 60km east of Quetta.

The cycling from DG Khan to Quetta was probably the most enjoyable of the entire journey. The landscape is beautiful, the Baluchi culture is interesting and the people hospitable (if you ignore the village children who occasionally threw rocks at us!).

Sue Cooper

(From Quetta, Sue's partner, Wim, headed down to Karachi. Recognising she was approaching a more wild and isolated region, Sue stowed her bike as luggage and took a bus to Bam in Iran.)

PAKISTAN

Gulberg, especially Gulberg Main Market and Liberty Market. Pace Supermarket on Gulberg Main Blvd sells all sorts of imported grocery items, canned food and toiletries.

GETTING THERE & AWAY
Air
PIA has regular domestic flights between Lahore and Islamabad, Multan, Bahawalpur, Peshawar, Quetta and Karachi. PIA (flight inquiries ☎ 627 0599; reservations 630 6411) is on Egerton Rd, opposite Faletti's Hotel.

Lahore is served on direct international routes by PIA, Saudi Arabian Airlines, Kuwait Airways and Thai Airways International.

Bus & Minibus
Buses to everywhere operate from the Badami Bagh bus stand on Circular Rd about 2km north of the main train station (across from Iqbal Park). Luxury (air-con) buses and Coasters are lined up in a series of bays, each one representing a different destination (labelled only in Urdu). Despite this apparent orderliness, it can be a bit confusing since there's no central ticket or information office – individual ticket sellers will soon approach and ask where you want to go. Several reliable companies operate buses on long-haul trips for almost identical fares. Cheaper (less comfortable and without air-con) buses gather at the rear of the stand.

To Rawalpindi & Islamabad This trip takes (in theory) four hours on the motorway (350km) in either direction and up to six on the more direct Grand Trunk Rd (295km). In reality, even buses on the motorway take around five hours. Luxury buses use the motorway, cheaper buses tend to use the GT Rd. Services go to Rawalpindi or Islamabad but usually not to both – ask where you're going to get dropped off. New Khan Road Runners (☎ 6367330) has Coasters and buses from bay No 1 (Rs 182) to Committee Chowk in Rawalpindi. Minibuses without air-con leave from bay No 2 to Committee Chowk (Rs 100).

Skyways buses (☎ 631 1463; bay No 3) drop off at their depot in Faizabad, a transport junction about 5km south of central Islamabad (Rs 135). New Abasin Flying Coaches (bay No 5) drops off at the inconvenient Pir Wadhai bus stand.

The TDCP (☎ 636 9687), at 4-A Lawrence Rd, runs four daily coaches (Rs 200, 4½ hours) between its Lahore and Rawalpindi offices. These are a slightly more expensive than other buses but the pick-up and drop-off points are very central.

Daewoo Express (☎ 111-007008) has state-of-the-art luxury buses to Rawalpindi (Rs 280 or Rs 360 for super-luxury buses, four hours). These are the fastest, most comfortable and most expensive buses on the road, but the offices in both cities (from where the buses depart and arrive) are inconveniently located.

To Peshawar Regular buses make the eight- to 10-hour trip to/from Peshawar, although that time will be reduced when the motorway is completed. The standard fare in an air-con bus or Coaster is only Rs 150.

Skyways and New Abasin have buses to Peshawar via Rawalpindi from bay Nos 5 and 7 respectively. •

To Multan New Khan Road Runners has regular deluxe buses to Multan departing from bay No 10 (Rs 135, six hours). Non-air-con buses cost Rs 75. It's worth noting that Multan's general bus stand is way out of town, and it will cost you another Rs 50 to get into the centre by autorickshaw. A better option is the TDCP buses (Rs 140), which leave from their Lahore office and drop off near the Silver Sand Hotel in central Multan. There are seven services daily and these should be booked ahead.

To Wagah & India Regular buses (No 4) operated by New Khan Metro depart from the front of Badami Bagh bus stand (closest to Circular Rd), via the train station, to the border crossing at Wagah. The 30km trip takes almost an hour (Rs 10), so if you're heading out to see the flag-lowering ceremony (or to cross into India) you'll need to leave in plenty of time. Since the buses congregate at the train station waiting for passengers, it's more convenient to get on there.

If you're in a hurry and want to get all the way to Delhi, the PTDC operates a direct air-con bus service from Faletti's Hotel on Tuesday, Wednesday, Friday and Saturday at

6 am (Rs 950, 12 hours). This is the only direct public land transport between the two cities.

Other Destinations From Badami Bagh bus stand there are services to Swat Valley (Rs 220), Faisalabad (Rs 55), Bahawalpur (Rs 160, eight hours) and DG Khan (Rs 160, 10 hours).

Train

All trains stop at the impressive, fortress-like Lahore City station, also known as Lahore Junction, although a few also stop at Cantonment station.

Getting a tourist or student concession is a tedious procedure. Take your passport, and student card if applicable, to PTDC at Faletti's Hotel for a standard letter confirming that you are who you say you are. Take this to the Commercial Department at the Pakistan Railways headquarters building, 1km south of the station on Empress Rd and only open until about 1 pm. With the concession voucher, go to the railway reservations office at the rear of the same building. If possible, make long-distance reservations days ahead, particularly if you want a sleeper.

Lahore lies on the main national line between Peshawar and Karachi, and there are frequent direct services to all major destinations. Intercity trains run several times daily between Lahore and Rawalpindi (Rs 75 in economy; five hours) and are more reliable than long-distance trains. There are nine trains a day to Rawalpindi (Rs 75/160/440 economy/1st-class sleeper/air-con, 5–6 hours). Of these, the 6.30 am *Subuk Rafter* and the 4.30 pm *Subuk Kharam* originate in Lahore. Three trains, including the *Khyber Mail* and the *Awam Express* continue on to Peshawar (Rs 115/245/650, 10 hours).

Heading west, nine trains go daily to Multan (Rs 85/185/500, six hours), with seven continuing on to Bahawalpur (Rs 110/235/620, eight hours). Two trains go all the way to Quetta. These are the *Chiltern Express* which departs at 10.15 am and the *Quetta Express* (from Rawalpindi) which departs at 11.45 am (Rs 270/525/1325, 28 hours).

There's a direct daily train between Lahore and Amritsar in India but most travellers give it a big thumbs down. It departs at 11.30 am and is supposed to arrive at 3 pm but because of border delays it invariably pulls in much later.

GETTING AROUND
To/From the Airport

A new airport terminal was being built in Lahore at the time of writing. Bus No 24 runs from the airport to The Mall daily until about 9 pm. From the airport, a taxi to or from the train station or The Mall is around Rs 140, while the journey in an autorickshaw costs around Rs 80.

Bus

Cramped buses and minibuses (wagons) run almost everywhere every few minutes from a minibus stand opposite the Lahore City train station on Allama Iqbal Rd. Conductors shout the destinations at each stop, and the usual fare is around Rs 4.

Minibus No 43 runs from the minibus stand to Faletti's Hotel, Charing Cross, the YWCA Hostel, Gulberg and the PHYA Youth Hostel near Hussain Chowk. No 25 follows the same route up to Charing Cross and then continues north-west up The Mall. No 1 runs along Gulberg Main Blvd to The Mall, the Mausoleum of Data Ganj and the Fort. New Khan Metro operates big buses from Lahore City station to Charing Cross then east along The Mall to Saddar Bazaar and back to the station. Any bus heading north-west along Circular Rd from the train station will get you (eventually) to Iqbal Park, Lahore Fort and Badami Bagh bus stand.

Taxi & Autorickshaw

Taxis congregate at the train station and can be hailed from the street. Autorickshaws hang out at the station and next to the Regal Cinema on The Mall (among other places). Tongas and motorcycle rickshaws (slightly different from autorickshaws) also ply the route between the train station and Iqbal Park along Circular Rd. Typical fares from the train station to The Mall are Rs 50 by taxi and Rs 30 by rickshaw.

Car Rental

Din's Tours (☎ 631 1130), next to PTDC at Faletti's Hotel, can organise a car with a driver for Rs 70 an hour, plus Rs 9 per km. Book a day ahead if possible.

Lahore to Peshawar

If you're heading east, this part of the route takes you in the other direction, via the national capital and into the heart of the North-West Frontier Province. Transport by bus or train is good along this stretch and it's worth devoting a week or so to it (more if you want to continue up into the Northern Areas). At the end you come to the border with Afghanistan (with your armed escort by your side), at the legendary Khyber Pass.

LAHORE TO RAWALPINDI

By road there are two direct routes to Islamabad or Rawalpindi. These are the Grand Trunk (GT) Road and the new motorway (M2). The controversial motorway, completed in 1997 at a staggering cost of US$1 billion, is longer than the GT Rd at about 350km but cuts two hours off the journey – most of the time it's six lanes of completely deserted road. There are numerous toll booths along the motorway, which is probably one reason why it's not as well patronised as it could be, as well as modern service stations and roadside restaurants. If not for the bleak desert scenery, dearth of traffic and the heat, you could easily be on Britain's M1. The main reason for taking the GT Rd is to visit Rohtas Fort along the way.

Rohtas Fort

About 16km north-west of Jhelum and 8km south of Dina, colossal Rohtas Fort is one of the most extraordinary examples of military architecture on the subcontinent. It was started at vast expense in 1543 by the Pashtun ruler Farid Khan, better known as Sher Shah Suri, to protect the strategic Peshawar to Calcutta road from the Mughals and their allies. The fortifications were abandoned only a few years later when the Mughal emperor Akbar moved his frontier to Attock and built a new fort there.

The fort is now in ruins except for the crenellated outer walls and most of its 12 gates and 68 bastions, but the site is vast enough to warrant a visit of three or four hours. Not much remains of the interior buildings, but there are still two pavilions of the two-storey haveli (palace) of Man Singh

(governor of Lahore and a general in the time of his son-in-law, Akbar the Great), which you can climb for a view over the whole fort. To the west, at the pinnacle of the outer wall, a high stone platform marks the *burj* (execution tower) from where victims would be thrown into the ditch below. Two gates in the northern wall lead down to freshwater wells and the River Kahan. It's a great place to explore.

Places to Stay & Eat There's no accommodation in Rohtas village, but if you want to make an early morning or evening visit it's worth staying the night in Dina. The *Iqbal Hotel* (*☎ 0541-630624*) has decent rooms with bathroom for Rs 150/300. Next door, the *Al-Kousar* charges Rs 200 for a double and Rs 400 for air-con. Both are on the GT Rd about 200m north of the bus drop-off point. Both have reasonable *restaurants* and there are food stalls and restaurants further south where the buses drop off and pick up.

Getting There & Away From Lahore, take any bus heading to Rawalpindi on the GT Rd (not the motorway) and get off at Dina. Ordinary buses cost Rs 40, but deluxe buses will charge the full fare to Rawalpindi (Rs 100). From Rawalpindi take a Jhelum-bound minibus (Rs 25/50 ordinary/air-con). Several trains a day stop in Dina bound for Rawalpindi or Lahore but timings are not as convenient as buses.

From Dina you can take a high-clearance bus (a public bus with a high axle for crossing stream beds) for the half-hour drive to Rohtas, crossing the shallow Kahan River near the fort entrance. The last bus back to Dina officially leaves Rohtas at 3 pm but it's normally possible to hitch a lift back after this. You can take a taxi direct from Dina to Rohtas; for a return trip of three or four hours expect to pay at least Rs 200.

If you're driving, the turn-off to Rohtas is about 2km north of Dina, off to the left just past a service station.

RAWALPINDI
☎ 051 • pop 1.4 million
Rawalpindi and nearby Islamabad are very much twin cities and most travellers choose to base themselves in one and take a day trip to the other. For clarity we've given them separate entries, but you'll probably only

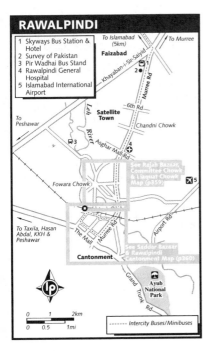

RAWALPINDI

1 Skyways Bus Station & Hotel
2 Survey of Pakistan
3 Pir Wadhai Bus Stand
4 Rawalpindi General Hospital
5 Islamabad International Airport

To Islamabad (5km)
To Murree
Faizabad
Khayaban-i-Sir Sayyid
Murree Rd
To Peshawar
6th Rd
Satellite Town
Leh River
Chandni Chowk
Asghar Mall Rd
See Rajah Bazaar, Committee Chowk & Liaquat Chowk Map (p359)
Fowara Chowk
Airport Rd
To Taxila, Hasan Abdal, KKH & Peshawar
The Mall
Murree Rd
See Saddar Bazaar & Rawalpindi Cantonment Map (p360)
Cantonment
Ayub National Park
Grand Trunk Rd

0   1   2km
0   0.5   1mi
------ Intercity Buses/Minibuses

need to use the services (banks, post office and hotels, for instance) of one or the other.

The Sikh army garrison town of Rawalpindi (City of Rawals) came into its own in the 1840s when the British made it Asia's largest cantonment or military camp. The Cantt, as the Rawalpindi Cantonment area is known, is still the headquarters of the Pakistan army, while the rest of the city is a patchwork of sprawling, vibrant bazaars connected by busy spoke roads.

Only 15km from ever-expanding Islamabad, Rawalpindi (or just 'Pindi'), was Pakistan's interim capital from 1959 to 1970 and is still the main transport junction between Lahore and northern Pakistan.

Orientation & Information
The main axes are Murree Rd and The Mall (also called Shahrah-i-Quaid-i-Azam). The cheaper hotels are in Saddar Bazaar and along Murree Rd at Liaquat (**lyah**-kut) Chowk and Committee Chowk.

South of Saddar, the Cantonment has top-end hotels, military camps and traces of the colonial years, and the Ayub National Park. At Rajah, the biggest bazaar, Fowara Chowk

has six roads radiating out to Saddar, Pir Wadhai (for the bus stand) and Murree Rd.

Tourist Offices The PTDC has a small and not particularly useful office (☎ 551 4672) in room No 7 at Flashman's Hotel. It's open from 8 am to 3 pm, Monday to Saturday (closed Friday afternoon). The PTDC-run Pakistan Tours (☎ 556 5449), also at Flashman's Hotel, is better for information (especially on their own tours and transport). The tourist offices in Islamabad are better.

Foreigners' Registration Office If you're staying in Pakistan longer than 30 days, you can register here (if you're staying in Islamabad, register there). Rawalpindi's office is in the Civil Courts beside the Senior Superintendent of Police. Catch an airport Suzuki on Adamjee Rd and get off just past Kucheri Chowk.

Money Most banks in Saddar Bazaar do foreign exchange. SCB Grindlays, on the corner of Canning and Haider Rds gives cash advances on a Visa card at 5% commission but don't bother changing travellers cheques here – the fee is Rs 500! The Muslim Commercial Bank (MCB) on the Mall in Saddar has an ATM accepting Cirrus and Maestro. In Rajah Bazaar try Habib's city branch in Bara Bazaar.

Moneychangers are grouped around the corner of Kashmir Rd and The Mall in Saddar Bazaar. They keep longer hours than the banks, offer better rates and will usually change travellers cheques without too much hassle.

Post & Communications The Rawalpindi main post office is on Kashmir Rd; poste restante is in the rear building. The post office is supposed to be open until around 9 pm but poste restante is locked up at 5 pm.

The Rawalpindi central telegraph & telephone office is on Kashmir Rd south of The Mall. Telephone numbers for Rawalpindi and Islamabad have recently changed. If you are having trouble accessing any number, call directory inquiries on ☎ 120.

Most of Rawalpindi's Internet centres are in Saddar Bazaar, on or near Bank Rd. Internet Cafe, upstairs next to the Karim Samosa Centre on Bank Rd, is open from 11 am to 11 pm and charges Rs 30 an hour.

The Cyber Cafe, above the Idress Book Shop on Bank Rd, is air-conditioned and also charges Rs 30 an hour.

Bookshops The Book Centre (☎ 556 5234) on Saddar Rd has maps, overseas periodicals, used books and lots of Lonely Planet titles. For cheap second-hand books and selected international magazines try the Old Book Bank, just off Kashmir Rd. To really appreciate Rawalpindi's obsession with old books and magazines, check out the huge book market that fills the streets (particularly Kashmir Rd) every Sunday.

Things to See & Do
Rajah Bazaar is a kaleidoscope of people and merchandise spreading out in every direction from Fowara Chowk. You could spend hours exploring the side streets and busy alleys off these main roads, although you might find yourself getting an unnerving amount of attention at times. In among the jewellers, cloth merchants and prize bonds stalls are street dentists flogging false incisors, watch-sellers crouched under sun shades and turbaned men sipping tea. Passenger Suzukis run regularly to Fowara Chowk from Kashmir Rd in Saddar or from Committee Chowk.

Beyond Rajah Bazaar, on Railway Workshop Rd, you'll find the 'truck art' workshops where you can watch the men who create these mobile masterpieces at work. From Fowara Chowk, take the Ganj Mandi Rd to the tonga stand and turn left over the wooden bridge. It's about another five-minute walk along this road to reach the painting depots on the left. Also along this road are stores selling chrome hubcaps, fenders, mirrors and all the other tassels and ornaments that adorn Pakistan's trucks and buses.

If you're interested in the implements of war, the Pakistan Army Museum on Iftikhar Rd makes a worthwhile diversion. Well-presented displays in a series of spacious galleries include everything from Stone-Age killing tools up to modern weaponry and memorabilia relating to conflicts such as the Indo-Pakistani wars. You can't miss the building – it's got tanks, cannons and anti-aircraft guns mounted out front. It's closed on Friday afternoon and Tuesday; admission (for foreigners) is the equivalent of US$1.

Places to Stay
There are four main areas for accommodation in Rawalpindi. Saddar Bazaar is the handiest location with a good mix of budget and mid-range places. At Liaquat Rd near Rajah Bazaar you'll find some good mid-range options. There's also busy Liaquat Chowk (and Gordon College Rd leading from it) and Committee Chowk, which is handy for buses to Lahore and Peshawar but noisy.

Places to Stay – Budget
Of the several cheap hotels around Hathi Chowk on Adamjee Rd, *New Shah Taj* (☎ 556 8528) has basic, noisy singles/doubles for Rs 90/120. *Al-Falah Hotel* (☎ 558 0799, Adamjee Rd) is the best of this bunch with bright, airy rooms with bathroom for Rs 100/190. There's a restaurant on the 1st floor.

New Kamran Lodge (☎ 558 2040, Kashmir Rd) is an old-style place with reasonable, clean rooms for Rs 250/350 and a large double with air cooler for Rs 450. It's a friendly enough place and there's a small restaurant.

One of the best places for backpackers in Pindi is the *Rawalpindi Popular Inn* (☎ 553 1884, G-261 Gordon College Rd) near Liaquat Chowk. It's well set up for travellers though dorm beds are pricey at Rs 125; singles/doubles with bathroom are Rs 175/300 and a double with shared bathroom is Rs 250. There's a laundry service, international telephone, helpful management and a convivial snack bar. The main downfall is the location, which isn't particularly convenient for anything, although it's only a short walk to Murree Rd. The nearby *Snow Ball Inn* (☎ 555 3327, H-40 Gordon College Rd) is cheaper at Rs 150/200 for large rooms with bathroom, but it's a bit grim and not as well set up.

Many of the cheap hotels in Rajah Bazaar won't take foreigners, which is no great loss. The *Hotel Al-Falah* (☎ 555 3206) on Fowara Chowk is an exception but has pretty basic, cell-like rooms for Rs 100/170. The *Seven Brothers Hotel* (☎ 555 1112) is better value with bright rooms for Rs 170/240 and a 4 pm checkout. The friendly *Hotel City Inn* (☎ 553 0218, Liaquat Rd) is cheaper but also good value, with clean rooms for Rs 130/200.

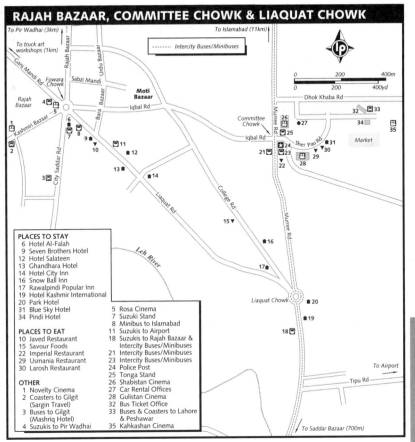

RAJAH BAZAAR, COMMITTEE CHOWK & LIAQUAT CHOWK

To Pir Wadhai (3km)

To truck art workshops (1km)

To Islamabad (11km)

------- Intercity Buses/Minibuses

Ganj Mandi Rd

Rajah Bazaar

Urdu Bazaar

Fowara Chowk

Sabzi Mandi

Rajah Bazaar

Kashmiri Bazaar

City Saddar Rd

Bara Bazaar

Moti Bazaar

Iqbal Rd

Dhok Khaba Rd

Committee Chowk

Murree Rd

Iqbal Rd

Sher Pau Rd

Market

College Rd

Liaquat Rd

Murree Rd

Leh River

Liaquat Chowk

To Airport

Tipu Rd

To Saddar Bazaar (700m)

0   200   400m
0   200   400yd

PLACES TO STAY
6 Hotel Al-Falah
9 Seven Brothers Hotel
12 Hotel Salateen
13 Ghandhara Hotel
14 Hotel City Inn
16 Snow Ball Inn
17 Rawalpindi Popular Inn
19 Hotel Kashmir International
20 Park Hotel
31 Blue Sky Hotel
34 Pindi Hotel

PLACES TO EAT
10 Javed Restaurant
15 Savour Foods
22 Imperial Restaurant
29 Usmania Restaurant
30 Larosh Restaurant

OTHER
1 Novelty Cinema
2 Coasters to Gilgit
   (Sargin Travel)
3 Buses to Gilgit
   (Mashriq Hotel)
4 Suzukis to Pir Wadhai

5 Rosa Cinema
7 Suzuki Stand
8 Minibus to Islamabad
11 Suzukis to Airport
18 Suzukis to Rajah Bazaar &
   Intercity Buses/Minibuses
21 Intercity Buses/Minibuses
23 Intercity Buses/Minibuses
24 Police Post
25 Tonga Stand
26 Shabistan Cinema
27 Car Rental Offices
28 Gulistan Cinema
32 Bus Ticket Office
33 Buses & Coasters to Lahore
   & Peshawar
35 Kahkashan Cinema

PAKISTAN

The **Pindi Hotel** (☎ 555 8809) near Committee Chowk is perfectly located if you stumble off a late night bus from Lahore or Peshawar. Clean, spacious rooms cost Rs 190/270. Some have small balconies but the rooms facing the bus stand are very noisy.

Places to Stay – Mid-Range

It may be possible to camp at PTDC's **Flashman's Hotel** (☎ 558 1480, The Mall) in Saddar Bazaar but otherwise it's no bargain with worn air-con rooms from Rs 1100/1400 and newer rooms from Rs 1600/2000.

The centrally air-conditioned **Hotel Marhaba** (☎ 556 6021, 118 Kashmir Rd) is a bargain if it's hot, but other than the air-con and the central location it's a gloomy, windowless place. Rooms with TV cost Rs 421/542, including tax. There's a restaurant downstairs.

The **Paradise Inn** (☎ 556 8594, Adamjee Rd) has comfortable but overpriced rooms for Rs 965/1085 with TV and air-con, as well as more luxurious rooms. There's a great rooftop terrace and parking is available.

Hotel Kashmir International (☎ 550 0495, Murree Rd) at Liaquat Chowk has its fair share of old-fashioned charm and is well worth the Rs 250/350 charged for rooms with bathroom and TV. A larger double with cooler is Rs 450. The location isn't thrilling but it's easy enough to pick up transport on Murree Rd.

SADDAR BAZAAR & RAWALPINDI CANTONMENT

PLACES TO STAY
14 New Shah Taj
15 Marhaba Hotel
16 Al-Falah Hotel
38 Paradise Inn
40 New Kamran Hotel
46 Pearl Continental Hotel; Front Page Cafe

PLACES TO EAT
5 Taste Hunt; Archies; Photographic Shops
10 Kim Fah Chinese Restaurant
18 Data Kabana Restaurant
20 Goher Ali Restaurant
33 Kamran Cafe; Burger Express
34 Anwar Cafe
37 KFC; Suzukis to Airport
41 Jehangir Inn

OTHER
1 Railway Commercial Dept
2 Railway Booking Office
3 Police Station
4 Log Inn Internet Club; Cinema
6 Variety Book Store
7 Book Centre
8 PIA
9 Pharmacy & General Store
11 Ciroz Cinema
12 National Bank
13 Cantonment General Hospital
17 Old Book Bank; Internet Cafe
19 Bus to Taxila, Wah & Hasan Abdal
21 Habib Bank; Moneychangers
22 Central Telegraph & Telephone Office
23 TDCP; Buses to Lahore; Moneychangers
24 Muslim Commercial Bank (ATM)
25 Army Stadium
26 PTDC Tourist Information Centre; Pakistan Tours; Flashman's Hotel
27 Bhatti Studio
28 Main Post Office
29 Minibus Nos 1 & 6 to Islamabad
30 SCB Grindlays Bank
31 Shakil Express Travel Agency
32 Cyber Cafe; Idress Bookshop
35 Internet Clubs
36 Rohtas Travel Agency
39 Mosque; Suzukis to Rajah Bazaar
42 Minibuses to Murree & Taxila
43 American Express Travel
44 Citibank
45 St Paul's Church
47 Christ Church
48 Pakistan Army Museum
49 Foreigners' Registration Office; Excise & Tax Office

The **Ghandhara Hotel** (☎ 553 0279, G-176 Liaquat Rd), a five-minute walk from Fowara Chowk, has very small but clean and comfortable rooms with TV for Rs 300/500, or Rs 600/700 with air-con. The new **Salateen Hotel** (☎ 555 5217, Liaquat Rd) is the best option along here with sparkling rooms from Rs 300/500 or Rs 800 for a large triple. Most of the rooms are carpeted and all are well-lit and ventilated. Parking is also available.

The Committee Chowk area is noisy, nondescript and not too appealing unless you want to be close to the buses. Of the numerous options here the **Blue Sky Hotel** (☎ 555 7629) is probably the best. It's clean, well run and someone has a sense of humour – the checkout sign reads 'Goodbye Time is 3 pm'. Pleasant air-con rooms cost Rs 663/784.

Places to Eat

Saddar Bazaar is your best bet for finding a good bite to eat in Rawalpindi. **Data Kabana**, in an alley off Haider Rd (opposite the Ciroz Cinema), is one of the best cheap restaurants around. Kebabs sizzle on braziers at the front and there's a rooftop dining area. Mutton tikka kebabs are only Rs 10 each.

Kamran Cafe on Bank Rd is part local restaurant, part fast-food joint with a good selection of Pakistani dishes, sandwiches, kebabs and ice creams. Around the corner on Kashmir Rd, **Burger Express** is one of several fairly insipid American-style fast-food places. It may come as a slight surprise to see *KFC* in Rawalpindi, but there it is on the corner of Adamjee and Murree Rds. It's open till midnight weekdays and till 1 am on weekends. Two pieces of chicken costs Rs 91.

The north end of Bank Rd has a small cluster of eateries. *Taste Hunt* has standard chicken and mutton dishes from Rs 80, a few curries from Rs 50 and a great rooftop terrace. The restaurant at the *Paradise Inn* is a good place for a reasonably priced Western-style breakfast and they do a barbecue on the rooftop terrace every evening at 7 pm. *Jehangir Inn*, at the north end of Kashmir Rd, is a recommended restaurant with a good range of Pakistani food such as chicken karai.

Of the flash restaurants, *Kim Fah* on the Mall is an elegant Chinese place with attentive staff. Mains aren't cheap at Rs 110 to Rs 200. The *Front Page Cafe* at the Pearl Continental is the place for a minor splurge if you're after a fancy dessert or an expensive snack. It's open 24 hours.

Near Liaquat Chowk, *Savour Foods* on Gordon College Rd is a hugely busy place pumping out cheap barbecue chicken for Rs 17 and chicken pulau (rice) from Rs 35 to 50.

Larosh Restaurant, attached to the Blue Sky Hotel at Committee Chowk, isn't cheap but the Pakistani dishes are varied and good; chicken and mutton dishes are around Rs 100. The *Imperial Restaurant*, around the corner on Murree Rd, has cheaper Pakistani staples. You can pick up a cheap burger or egg roll snack for Rs 10 from the *stalls* along Murree and Liaquat Rds.

Alcohol
You can get a liquor permit from the Excise & Tax Office, beside the Foreigners' Registration Office in Rawalpindi or Islamabad and then buy beer and spirits from the permit room at Flashman's Hotel. The top hotels (Flashman's or Pearl Continental) might let you buy alcohol directly (without a permit) if you sign the appropriate forms stating you're a non-Muslim, but unless you're a guest, don't count on it.

Entertainment
The *Ciroz Cinema* in Saddar shows international films (Rs 35). There are plenty of other cinemas around – easily located by the oversized, painted hoardings – but most show Pashto and Urdu films.

Regular international cricket matches, including Test matches, are played at the Rawalpindi Cricket Stadium (☎ 572 4717) in Satellite Town. Fast bowler Shoab Ahktar – nicknamed the Rawalpindi Express – is one of the city's more recent stars.

Shopping
The main shopping areas are Saddar Bazaar and Rajah Bazaar. You'll find cloth merchants, tailors and clothing stores everywhere. Head down Iqbal Rd and along the Bara Bazaar from Fowara Chowk, or along Bank Rd in Saddar. A salwar kameez off the rack starts at about Rs 350 but you could get one made up for you for less, depending on the material.

Sarafa Market in Rajah Bazaar is a good place to shop for jewellery and brasswork, while pottery can be found at the Bara Bazaar. For spices, head for the streets around Ganj Mandi Rd at Rajah Bazaar.

Getting There & Away
Air The nearest airport is Islamabad airport – see Getting There & Away in the Islamabad section for flight information. PIA's Rawalpindi booking office (☎ 556 8071, or 567011 for Northern Areas) is on The Mall.

Bus & Minibus The most convenient regular buses to Lahore and Peshawar leave from Committee Chowk, although there are some services from Saddar Bazaar.

Pir Wadhai bus stand is inconveniently situated in north-west Rawalpindi, but you shouldn't need to use it unless you get dropped there coming from somewhere else. It's about a 30-minute ride from Saddar Bazaar by passenger Suzuki (change at Fowara Chowk).

To Islamabad Numbered minibuses (wagons) are the quickest way between the two cities. Nos 1 and 6 from Haider Rd in Saddar Bazaar go via Aabpara to Super Market in Islamabad then east to the Secretariat for around Rs 8. Gaudy Bedford buses link Saddar Bazaar (Haider Rd), the train station, Liaquat and Committee Chowks, Aabpara and Islamabad's markets in one tedious line; this trip can take up to 1½ hours.

Black-and-yellow taxis rarely use their meters, so fix a price before you get in; Rawalpindi to Islamabad is at least Rs 120.

To Lahore TDCP (☎ 556 5824) runs four daily air-con coaches (9 am, 1.30, 4 and 7 pm) from the corner of Kashmir Rd and The Mall (Rs 200, 4½ hours). You can book ahead at the office at 44 Mall Plaza. New Khan Road Runners at Committee Chowk has air-con minibuses (Rs 182) and big buses (Rs 155) to Lahore roughly every half hour. There are also cheaper non-air-con minibuses leaving from alongside the Pindi Hotel (Rs 100), most of which go via the GT Rd.

The fastest, most comfortable and most expensive buses to/from Lahore are run by Daewoo Express (☎ 111-007008). Unfortunately the office, where the buses arrive and depart, is about 5km from Saddar Bazaar at Fazalabad on the road to the motorway (head north-west along The Mall). If you're taking an autorickshaw or taxi, the local pronunciation seems to be 'Deevo'. Luxury buses cost Rs 280 and super luxury is Rs 360.

Skyways (☎ 445 5242) in Faizabad has half-hourly departures in air-con buses (Rs 135, five hours). Any minibus running between Rawalpindi and Islamabad will drop you here.

To Peshawar Minibuses and Coasters go at least hourly to Peshawar (170km) from Committee Chowk (Rs 60, 3½ hours). Abasin Flying Coaches (☎ 555 7330) is the main operator. There are also buses from Pir Wadhai (Rs 55).

Other Destinations Mashabrum Tours (☎ 573 387) runs a daily Coaster to Gilgit at 3 pm from the Mashriq Hotel south of Fowara Chowk. Nearby, Sargin Travel (☎ 553 1776) runs an identical service departing at 4 pm. Both cost Rs 350 and take 14 to 17 hours. There are also buses to Gilgit in summer from Pir Wadhai.

A minibus stand at Marir Chowk, in northern Saddar Bazaar, has half-hourly departures to Jhelum (for Rohtas Fort). You can also take one of the Lahore-bound buses that run on the GT Rd and get off at Dina for Rohtas Fort, but you'll probably be charged the full fare to Lahore (Rs 100).

For Murree there are several bus stands. In Saddar Bazaar there are minibuses from Railway Rd (Rs 30, two hours); there are also buses from a stand just off Murree Rd between Saddar and Liaquat Chowk, and from Pir Wadhai. Daewoo Express has luxury buses every two hours from its depot on the Peshawar Rd (Rs 70). Minibuses (wagons) to Taxila, Wah Gardens and Hasan Abdal leave from the stand on Railway Rd and from Haider Rd in Saddar (Rs 10, 40 minutes).

Train There's a railway booking office 300m south of the train station in Saddar Bazaar. For a concession, go first to the pink Commercial Department directly opposite the main station. A letter from PTDC is not necessary.

There are nine trains a day to Lahore (5 to 6 hours). The fare is Rs 75 in economy, Rs 160 for a 1st-class sleeper and Rs 440 for an air-con sleeper. The best services are the ones that originate in Rawalpindi; these include the 5.45 am *Quetta Express* (which carries on to Quetta); the 6.30 am *Subuk Kharam*; the 8 am *Tezgam Express*; and the 11.45 pm *Night Coach*, which arrives in Lahore at 4.30 am.

To and from Peshawar there are five daily trains (Rs 48/100/300, four hours). The best is the *Awam Express* at 11 am, but expect long-distance trains from the south (ie, from Karachi or Quetta via Lahore) to arrive in Rawalpindi hours late. All trains to and from Lahore stop at Jhelum, while two day-time services to and from Peshawar stop at Taxila.

Getting Around
Suzukis to the airport go from Adamjee Rd in Saddar Bazaar (next to KFC) and from Fowara Chowk in Rajah Bazaar. They cost Rs 5 and take under half an hour in normal traffic.

Transport from the airport to Rawalpindi can be picked up from outside the main gate. A taxi will cost about Rs 75 to Rawalpindi, more at night.

Fixed-route passenger Suzukis cost only a few rupees; you can wave them down and jump on board, or look for a congregation of them waiting for passengers. The main starting points are next to the mosque on Kashmir Rd in Saddar Bazaar (for Suzukis to Rajah Bazaar); Fowara Chowk; Haider Rd in Saddar; and along Murree Rd at Liaquat and Committee Chowks. Autorickshaws buzz around and are OK for short trips; Saddar to Rajah Bazaar costs around Rs 20. In Saddar Bazaar taxis tend to congregate on the Mall and Haider Rd, near the corner with

Canning Rd. Horse-drawn tongas and three-wheel motorbikes hang out around Committee Chowk and in Rajah Bazaar.

ISLAMABAD
☎ 051 • pop 524,800

Islamabad may be Pakistan's capital city, but it's not exactly a thrilling destination. The grid-like streets and scattered suburban shopping centres give it a structured but dull quality. There are a few interesting things to see here, notably the modern Shah Faisal Mosque and the Lok Virsa Museum, but it's probably more fun to stay in Rawalpindi and commute.

However, if you have business to attend to, such as applying for visas to neighbouring countries, extending your Pakistan visa or getting trekking permits, this is the place to do it. The city also has some good shopping and is very clean.

Islamabad is classed as a district in its own right, not a part of Punjab or any other province.

History
Where Islamabad now stands there was nothing 40 years ago. Karachi being too far from everything, it was decided in the 1950s to build a new capital near Rawalpindi and the summer hill stations. To avoid urban chaos and decay, architect-planner Konstantinos Doxiades' idea was to let the city grow in only one direction, sector by sector across a grid, each sector having its own residences, shops and parks. Construction began in 1961 and will go on for decades. Though totally different in character, Rawalpindi may eventually be swallowed up by the encroaching capital.

Orientation & Information
Islamabad has no axis or centre. Each sector, built around a *markaz*, or commercial centre, has a letter-number designation (eg, F-7), with quarters numbered clockwise (eg, F-7/1 in the south-west corner, F-7/2 north-west etc). Each letter also has a name; F and G are Shalimar and Ramna, so, for example, F-7 is Shalimar-7 and so on. This can seem confusing, but it's handy if you need to take a taxi somewhere. Taxi drivers may not know the name of a place but they'll certainly drop you at the right place if you give them a number.

For practical reasons, sectors are called by their markets. The main ones, in sequence on the bus line, are Aabpara (**ah**-para; south-west G-6), Melody or Civic Centre (G-6), Sitara Market (G-7), Super Market (F-6), Jinnah or Jinnah Super (F-7) and Ayub Market (F-8). Other important landmarks are Karachi Company (G-9) and Peshawar Mor (G-8/1) in the west of the city.

Between the Fs and Gs is a commercial belt called the Blue Area.

Tourist Offices There are three PTDC offices in Islamabad, plus the head office of the Ministry of Tourism. The main office for general information (☎ 2921 2706) is on Aga Khan Rd in Super Market (F-6). It's open from 8 am to 3 pm (closed Friday afternoon and Sunday). There's another small office tucked away on Bhitai Rd in Jinnah Market (F-7/2). If you need a permit for trekking (required for certain restricted areas), the only place in Pakistan you can independently get this is at the Ministry of Tourism (☎ 2920 3509) in the Islamabad Sports Complex south of Aabpara. Permits cost US$50 a month for specified trekking routes.

Embassies & Consulates Most embassies are in the Diplomatic Enclave (G-5) at the east end of Islamabad. From Aabpara, Suzukis to Quaid-i-Azam University pass the American, Chinese, Russian, and French embassies. Minibus Nos 3 and 120 to Bari Imam (Nurpur Shahan village) pass near the Australian, Indian, German, Canadian, Iranian, and British embassies. If you're applying for visas here it's best to go early, usually before 9 am. Major foreign missions include:

Australia (☎ 282 4345, fax 282 0112) Ispahani Rd, G-5/4
Canada (☎ 227 0103, fax 227 9110) Diplomatic Enclave G-5
China (☎ 282 2540, fax 282 1116) Ramna-4; issues visas
India (☎ 281 4375, fax 222 4286) Diplomatic Enclave G-5; issues six-month tourist visas, usually within four days
Iran (☎ 227 6271, fax 282 4839) Street 2, G-5/1; the most reliable place in Pakistan to get a transit visa, but the wait can be long depending on your country of origin. A letter of recommendation from your home country is required.
UK (☎ 282 2135, fax 282 3439) Ramna-5
USA (☎ 282 6179, fax 221 4222) Ramna-5

PAKISTAN

ISLAMABAD

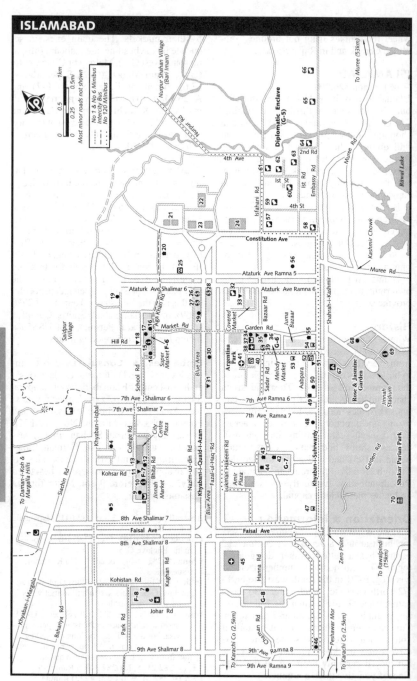

0   0.25   0.5   1km
0   0.5   0.5mi

Most minor roads not shown
No 1 & No 6 Minibus
Intercity Bus
No 120 Minibus

Nurpur Shahan Village
(Bari Imam)

Diplomatic
Enclave
(G-5)

To Muree (53km)

66

65

64   2nd Rd

4th Ave

62   63

61   Ist St   Ist Rd

Isfahani Rd

59   60   4th St

57   58

Embassy Rd

Muree Rd

Rawal Lake

Kashmir Chowk

Muree Rd

22

21   23   24

Constitution Ave

20   25

56

Ataturk Ave Ramna 5

Ataturk Ave Shalimar 6

19

27 26
28

Ataturk Ave Ramna 6

32

33

Covered
Market

Garden Rd

Juma
Bazaar

Market Rd

17
16
15
14
18

Bazaar Rd

Shahrah-i-Kashmir

Hill Rd

Super
Market F-6

29

38 37 34
35 36
39   G-6
40

55
54   52
53   50
49   51

68

69

67

Rose & Jasmine
Garden

Saidpur
Village

Aga Khan Rd

School Rd

Blue Area

30

Argentina
Park

41

Sadar Rd

Melody
Market

Aabpara

Jinnah
Stadium

7th Ave Shalimar 6

31

7th Ave Ramna 6

Garden Rd

7th Ave Shalimar 7

7th Ave Ramna 7

48

Shakar Parian Park

Khyaban-i-Iqbal

2

3

Khyaban-i-Suhrwardy

4

College Rd

City
Centre
Plaza

13
11 12
F-7

Nazim-ud-din Rd

Khyaban-i-Quaid-i-Azam

Fazal-ul-Haq Rd

Lukman Hakeem Rd

43
44   42
G-7

Kohsar Rd

Jinnah Bhitai Rd

Jinnah
Market

10
9   F-7
8

Amir
Plaza

5

47

70

8th Ave Shalimar 7

Faisal Ave

Blue Area

Faisal Ave

Zero Point

To Daman-i-Koh &
Margalla Hills

8th Ave Shalimar 8

1

45

Hanna Rd

To Rawalpindi
(15km)

Khyaban-i-Margala

Bahariya Rd

Kohistan Rd

Kaghan Rd

F-8

7

6

Johar Rd

G-8

Park Rd

Chaman Rd

To Karachi Co (2.5km)

Peshawar Mor

To Karachi Co (2.5km)

9th Ave Shalimar 8

9th Ave Ramna 8

9th Ave Ramna 9

PAKISTAN

ISLAMABAD

PLACES TO STAY
20 Marriott Hotel (permit room)
42 Simara Hotel
43 Al Hujurat Hotel
44 Blue Sky Hotel
49 Ambassador Hotel
55 Pakistan Youth Hostel
67 Tourist Campsite

PLACES TO EAT
11 Kabuli Restaurant
13 Pappasalli's Italian Restaurant;
    Bistro Alfredo
18 Luna Caprese
31 Omar Khayam
33 Satellite Centre
35 French Bakery
51 Kamran Restaurant

EMBASSIES
32 Afghan Embassy
57 Australian High Commission
58 French Embassy
59 German Embassy
60 Indian High Commission
61 Canadian High Commission
62 Iranian Embassy
63 British High Commission
64 US Embassy
65 Chinese Embassy
66 Russian Embassy

OTHER
1   Shah Faisal Mosque
2   Daman-i-Koh
3   Marghzar Zoo
4   Hot Spot
5   Alliance Française
6   Senior Superintendent of
    Police (SSP)
7   Foreigners' Registration
    Office
8   International Mail Office;
    Cyber Spider
    Internet Cafe
9   Nomad Gallery
10 PTDC office
12 Book Fair
14 Vanguard Bookstore
15 PTDC
16 Mr Books; Munchies
    Snack Bar
17 Shaheen Chemist &
    Cosmetics; Maharaja
    Handicrafts
19 London Book Company
21 Secretariat
22 Presidency
23 National Assembly
24 Supreme Court
25 Central Telegraph &
    Telephone Office
26 Société Générale

27 American Express
28 Bank of America
29 American Centre
30 PIA
34 British Council
    Library
36 Pakistan Railways
    Booking Office
37 Main Post Office
38 Police Station
39 UBL; National Bank;
    Holiday Inn
40 Internet
41 Capital Hospital
45 Pakistan Institute of
    Medical Science (PIMS)
46 Regional Passport
    Office
47 Bus Stop
48 Capital Development
    Authority (CDA)
50 Travel Walji's
52 Internet Club
53 Minibuses to Sitara &
    Peshawar Mor
54 Minibus/Suzukis to
    Diplomatic Enclave
56 US Consular Office
68 Liaquat Gymnasium
69 Ministry of Tourism
70 Lok Virsa

New Zealand citizens should contact the British high commission.

Visa Extensions Islamabad is officially the only place in Pakistan deal with expired visas, visa extensions and lost documents. For a tourist visa extension, start at the Passport Office at Peshawar Mor (G-8/4). A one-month extension is usually granted free; a maximum stay of three months is allowed. The office accepts applications from 9 am to noon Monday to Saturday (11 am on Friday).

After this you will need to go to the Foreigners' Registration Office (FRO) by the Senior Superintendent of Police in Ayub Market (G-8) and register (just as if you were staying over 30 days, even if you aren't).

Money American Express, in the Blue Area, cashes travellers cheques. Also try UBL beside the Holiday Inn, or the National Bank behind it. There's a Citibank branch at Amir Plaza (G-7/2) and the Muslim Commercial Bank has branches with ATMs accepting Cirrus/Maestro cards; try Hameed Chambers in Aabpara Market or the Blue Area.

There are private moneychangers clustered in the Blue Area near the corner of Kabir Avenue.

Post & Communications Islamabad's main post office is at the north end of Melody Market (G-6); there's a branch for international mail in Jinnah Market. The poste restante is open from 9 am to 2 pm (if the attendant can't find the key, tell him to look *under* the box) and the post office itself is open until 8 pm (closed Friday afternoon and Sunday). The central telephone & telegraph office on Ataturk Ave is open 24 hours.

Islamabad's Internet cafes are scattered. You'll find them at Aapbara and Melody Markets (G-6; on Municipal Rd), at Super Market (F-6) and at Jinnah Market (F-7). The average charge is Rs 30 an hour.

Try www.islamabad.net for information on all aspects of the city.

Bookshops The London Book Company in Super Market (F-6) has a big Pakistan section, maps, periodicals and used books. To get there from Super Market walk north on 14th St and turn right at 10th St to Kohsar Market. Mr Books and Vanguard Books, also in Super Market, have a good selection of international newspapers and books.

Cultural Centres The British Council Library (☎ 282 9041) in Melody Market (G-6) has week-old British papers, reference books and Internet access (Rs 60 an hour). The Alliance Française (☎ 282 2176) is at House 15, 18th St, F-7/2.

Medical Services The Shifa International (☎ 225 2509) in H-8/4 and the Capital (☎ 282 5691) are two good hospitals, although in an emergency you might want to call your embassy for advice first.

Shaheen Chemist & Cosmetics, on School Rd, Super Market (F-6) is a well-stocked pharmacy where you can replenish your medical kit.

Shakarparian Park & Lok Virsa Museum

Shakarparian Hill has sculpted gardens, an arboretum and panoramas of both Islamabad and Rawalpindi from the east viewpoint. Down below is the 20-hectare **Rose & Jasmine Garden**, site of several annual flower shows.

On Garden Rd is **Lok Virsa**, the National Institute of Folk & Traditional Heritage (☎ 281 2675), with a first-rate ethnographic museum including traditional handicrafts, best of which are the textiles and carved wood. The museum has an intricate facade, in the style of an old haveli. It's open from 10 am to 1.30 pm and 2 to 5 pm daily (closed Friday afternoon and Tuesday); admission is Rs 10. Next door, **Gallery Virsa** has changing local exhibitions and books and tapes for sale. Also in the complex is an open-air theatre which is used for performances during festivals, usually in October.

To get to Lok Virsa, get off the bus at the Zero Point stop, cross the road and follow the uphill path for about 30 minutes. Alternatively, bear right and enter the woods on a path where an approach road joins the Rawalpindi road, a 15-minute walk. A taxi from Aabpara costs about Rs 40.

Shah Faisal Mosque

This opulent, sleekly modern mosque is said to be Asia's biggest, with room for 100,000 worshippers. Most of its US$50 million cost was a gift of King Faisal of Saudi Arabia. Non-Muslims are free to enter and marvel at the spaciousness of it all, though you may feel a bit self-conscious. You must leave your shoes at a counter before entering. Get off an intercity bus at 8th Ave.

Nurpur Shahan & Bari Imam Shrine

North of the Diplomatic Enclave at Nurpur Shahan village is a shrine to Shah Abdul Latif Kazmi, also known as Bari Shah Latif or Bari Imam, a 17th-century Sufi teacher and Islamabad's unofficial patron saint. Thursday evening is quite festive, with pilgrims and trance-like qawwali music. The carnival-like urs (death anniversary) of Bari Shah Latif is celebrated here in the first week of May. To get here, take No 3 minibus from Aabpara or No 120 from Karachi Co, via Sitara Market and Aabpara.

Margalla Hills National Park

The hills north of Islamabad are full of hiking trails and resthouses. The PTDC has information on treks. One trail into the park goes from behind the Shah Faisal Mosque.

Daman-i-Koh is a popular picnic spot in the Margalla Hills with great views over Islamabad. Get off the intercity bus at 7th Ave and catch a Suzuki at Khayaban-i-Iqbal, or walk up the nearby path near the zoo. Just east is a road to **Saidpur**, 1km away, a village known for its pottery shops and workshops.

Places to Stay

The *Tourist Campsite*, on the busy Shahrah-i-Kashmir south of Aabpara Market, is a popular stop for overlanders and anyone else lugging a tent. It's no longer the bargain it once was and is not worth considering unless you have your own vehicle and camping gear. It costs Rs 100 to park a vehicle and Rs 50 per person to camp or doss in a basic concrete 'bungalow' (no beds). There's a kitchen with a few sinks but no cooking equipment. The site is reasonably shady and it's usually a good place to meet other overlanders.

Pakistan Youth Hostel (☎ 282 6899) is not a bad option if you're a member of Hostelling International (if not you have to pay a Rs 510 membership fee on the spot). It's a big place with dozens of four-bed (and larger) rooms, communal toilets and cold showers; however, there are no cooking facilities and no camping is allowed. Beds are Rs 60.

The best cheap hotels can be found in Sitara Market (G-7), a short ride on minibus Nos 105 or 120 from Aabpara. *Blue Sky Hotel* (☎ 220 4746) is probably the pick of the bunch, with clean, bright singles/doubles with bathroom for Rs 200/250 and friendly service. *Al Hujurat Hotel* (☎ 220 4403) also has clean rooms for Rs 225/300, plus Rs 50 if you want an air cooler. *Simara Hotel* (☎ 220 4555), next door, is similar at Rs 270/320.

If you want something a little more up-market, Islamabad has dozens of guesthouses hidden in the residential backstreets. These charge from around Rs 700/800 upwards and are popular with visiting businesspeople. The PTDC can give you a list, or look up www.islamad.net/guest.htm for more information.

Places to Eat

Aabpara, Sitara and Melody Markets all have kebab stands and cafes with cheap curries and fast food. It's simply a matter of wandering around and finding something you like. *Kamran Restaurant* in Aabpara is not too expensive and serves good Pakistani food. The *French Bakery* in Melody Market whips up all sorts of appealing sweets and pastries.

The best restaurants can be found around Jinnah Market (F-7) and along College Rd and in the Blue Area, while both Super and Jinnah Markets are crammed with fast-food cafes. *Kabuli Restaurant* near the PTDC office in Super Market is a good Afghan place. There's another one at Jinnah Market. Filling, meat-heavy dishes cost from Rs 75 to Rs 160. *Omar Khayam* is an Iranian restaurant in the Blue Area, recommended by expats. Mains start at Rs 155.

Pappasalli's Italian Restaurant in the City Centre Plaza at Jinnah Market (just off College Rd) is an expensive but trendy restaurant that does decent pizza (from Rs 175) and pasta (from Rs 250). Phone ☎ 2265 0550 for delivery. *Bistro Alfredo* next door is livelier and more informal but has the same menu.

The *Satellite Centre* is hard to find, tucked away in a guarded private house off Ataturk Ave. But don't let that put you off – it's run by expats and you can have lunch here between 11.30 am and 2.30 pm. The menu is mostly pizzas, burgers, baked potatoes and soups, which are good but not particularly cheap at around Rs 100 to Rs 150. It's at No 68, 89th St, G-6/3. *Luna Caprese* is a flash Italian restaurant on School Rd, Super Market, where you can bring your own beer or wine (if you have any).

Islamabad is a good place to pick up grocery supplies if you're self catering. There are well-stocked grocery stores in Jinnah and Super Market – the best is *Kohsar* at F-6/3.

Alcohol

If you have a permit to buy alcohol, there's a permit room at the Marriott Hotel on Aga Khan Rd.

Entertainment

The *Australian Club* (☎ 282 2115) at the Australian High Commission has a social night for all Australian visitors (and guests by permission) on most Thursdays from 6 to 10 pm; bring your passport. They also have an international night on the last Thursday of the month that is open to all visitors.

Hot Spot is a cool place in a converted railway carriage north of Jinnah Market. It's primarily an ice-cream parlour with a huge range of flavours (from Rs 60), but it also shows video movies at 9 pm (for a steep Rs 150). It's a popular hangout for young locals and a good place for some social observation. It's in the quiet residential streets at F-7/3, 7th St.

Shopping

Juma Bazaar, the block between Municipal and Garden Rds in Aabpara (G-6), comes to life on Sunday as a huge handicrafts market with carpets, leather, jewellery, clothing and Afghan curios.

Tourist shops in the shopping centres and the arcades of top-end hotels have pricey carpets, brasswork, jewellery, Kashmiri shawls, carvings and antiques. If you prefer hunting in the bazaars, head for Rawalpindi. The Nomad Gallery, in Jinnah Market, has Afghan and Pakistani handicrafts made by a local women's' group. Maharaja Handicrafts in Super Market (F-6) has been recommended for shawls and carpets.

PAKISTAN

Getting There & Away

Islamabad is not, perhaps a little surprisingly, the hub for onward transport. The airport is closer to Rawalpindi (although it is called Islamabad Airport), the train station is in Rawalpindi and most of the main bus companies operate from Rawalpindi.

Air The Islamabad office of PIA (☎ 281 6051) is at 49 Blue Area. PIA and several other carriers, including British Airways, operate direct international flights from Islamabad. For international tickets, you'll do better through a good travel agency.

PIA has multiple direct connections daily to/from Lahore (Rs 1300), Peshawar (Rs 725) and Karachi (Rs 3400), and four a week to Quetta (Rs 2920).

Weather permitting, there are daily flights north to Gilgit and Skardu which can be booked at the Northern Areas desk, around the side of PIA's Rawalpindi office. These flights can be booked solid in summer and they're usually not confirmed until the day of travel, so plan ahead. Foreigners pay a higher fare – Rs 2500 for both destinations.

Bus The only intercity bus station in Islamabad itself is in Karachi Company (Karachi Co), G-9, about 3km west of Aabpara Market. From here Islamabad Liners operates regular air-con buses along the motorway to Lahore (Rs 170, five hours). There are also Coasters to Peshawar (Rs 60, three hours) every half hour between 6 am and 8 pm. Minibus No 105 runs out to Karachi Co from Aabpara Market; a taxi should cost about Rs 30.

Train The train station is in Rawalpindi but there's a Pakistan Railways booking office (☎ 292 07474) on Garden Rd, Melody Market. It's open from 8.30 am to 4.30 pm daily with a half-hour break for lunch from 1 pm.

Getting Around

The dispersed nature of Islamabad makes walking around difficult. Minibus No 105 links Karachi Co, Peshawar Mor, Sitara Market, Melody Market and Aabpara. No 120 follows a similar route, but only as far as Peshawar Mor in the west, continuing to the Bari Imam shrine via the French, Australian and Canadian embassies. Coasters run up and down the Blue Area along Fazal-ul-Haq Rd. You can also use the Intercity minibuses to get from Aabpara to Super and Jinnah Markets. Short trips cost around Rs 3.

There are plenty of taxis around and, with wide streets and traffic lights, it's not as chaotic as Rawalpindi. You'll have to haggle for a decent fare though – from Aabpara to Jinnah Market shouldn't cost more than Rs 25. There are no autorickshaws in Islamabad.

For details of getting to Rawalpindi, see Getting There & Away in the Rawalpindi section.

AROUND ISLAMABAD
Taxila
☎ 0569

Only 28km north-west of Rawalpindi, Taxila is not to be missed, particularly if you have an interest in the growth of Buddhism in Asia. Gandhara is the historical name for the Peshawar Plain and its extension east across the Indus. Under Gandhara's various rulers, Takshasila or Taxila has always been one of its most important cities, and today it is one of south Asia's richest archaeological sites.

In the 6th century BC, the Achaemenians made it the Gandharan capital, at a site now called Bhir Mound. The Mauryan emperor Ashoka, a patron of Buddhism, built a university here, to which pilgrims and scholars came from all over Asia. About 180 BC, Bactrian Greeks developed a 'new' Taxila, at the site called Sirkap.

In the 1st century AD came the Kushans, building their own city at the Sirsukh site. Until the 3rd century this was the cultured capital of an empire stretching across the subcontinent and into Central Asia, the birthplace of a striking fusion of Greek and Indian art, and the place from which Buddhism spread into China and Central Asia. Monasteries and stupas (repositories for holy relics) were erected everywhere. The city fell into obscurity after it was destroyed by White Huns in the 5th century. The excavation of the site was led by Sir John Marshall between 1913 and 1934.

The ancient city excavations are open to the public, along with dozens of smaller sites over a 25 sq km area. You could cover the main sites in a day (half a day if you hire transport to get around), but it's a pleasant place to spend the night and have the site to yourself early in the morning.

Taxila Archaeological Museum This excellent museum is open from 8.30 am to noon and 2.30 to 5.30 pm daily (except the first Monday of each month) in summer, and 9 am to 4 pm in winter (Rs 4). Most of the statues, sculptures, friezes and artefacts on display here have been excavated from the Taxila site. Exhibits include bronze and copper jewellery and tools, semi-precious stones, huge earthenware water jugs, exquisite Buddha figures with Mediterranean faces and a fascinating coin room with coins dating from as far back as 350 BC.

The information centre (☎ 2344) at the PTDC Motel opposite the museum has some useful books for sale, and there's another book stall at the museum ticket counter.

Taxila Excavations Most of the main sites are within about 8km of the museum. There's a large map of the site outside the museum and each place of interest is signposted (in English) from the main road.

Just south of the museum, **Bhir Mound** dates from the 6th to 2nd centuries BC and is mostly unexcavated. What has been uncovered shows twisting streets and tiny stone houses or shops. Continuing east along the road between the museum and Bhir Mound brings you to **Dharmarajika**, the most important Buddhist site. Within the main stupa is an original, smaller stupa built by Emperor Ashoka, possibly to house ashes of the Buddha. Around it are the bases of statues and small votive stupas and the remains of a monastery complex. In one alcove are the stone feet of what must have been an immense Buddha statue. Most of what you see is Kushan work.

Back towards the main road, **Sirkap** is the remains of an orderly walled city started by the Bactrian Greeks in the 2nd century BC. It was later adapted by Scythians and Parthians. Along 500m of the wide main street are foundations of houses, stupas and a small Buddhist temple. South of the town are Kunala Stupa and the remains of two Kushan-era monasteries.

Further along on the opposite side of the road are the ruins of a classical Greek temple, **Jandial**, with Ionic columns in front and the base of what may have been a Zoroastrian tower in the rear. About 2km further, off the main road, is **Sirsukh**. Very little of this

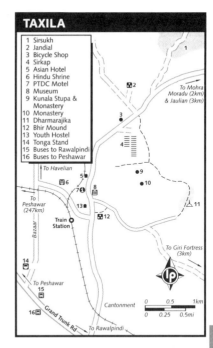

TAXILA

1 Sirsukh
2 Jandial
3 Bicycle Shop
4 Sirkap
5 Asian Hotel
6 Hindu Shrine
7 PTDC Motel
8 Museum
9 Kunala Stupa & Monastery
10 Monastery
11 Dharmarajika
12 Bhir Mound
13 Youth Hostel
14 Tonga Stand
15 Buses to Rawalpindi
16 Buses to Peshawar

Kushan city has been excavated, so there's not much to see – skip it if you're on foot.

The isolated **Mohra Moradu** monastery, dating from the 3rd to 5th centuries, is in a hollow about 5km north-east of the museum and 1km off the road. There is a small complete stupa in one monk's cell, looking like a wedding cake with multilevel base, spire and 'umbrellas'. This is a copy of the original, which is in the museum. An attendant might have to open some doors for you here.

At **Jaulian**, on a hill east of Mohra Moradu, the stupas are gone but the courtyard and foundations are in good condition. In a security enclosure near the entrance are the bases of several 5th-century votive stupas, ornamented with bas-relief Buddhas, elephants and nymph-like figures. The site caretaker will probably have to unlock some gates.

Places to Stay & Eat The *Youth Hostel*, just south of the museum, is cheap enough if you're a member of HI; a dorm bed is Rs 55. Nonmembers pay Rs 125. You may have to raise the manager from the outbuilding on the left. *Asian Hotel* (☎ 4442), on the main road just north of the museum, is a bit musty but OK. Singles/doubles with bathroom cost Rs 250/300.

There are fruit stalls and drink stands along the main road, and *restaurants* at the PTDC Motel and the Asian Hotel.

Getting There & Away From Rawalpindi, Taxila is 40 minutes from Saddar Bazaar (Haider Rd or Railway Rd) by frequent bus or minibus. The one-hour train ride (Rs 10) is more pleasant and puts you within walking distance of the site. Four daily trains stop at Taxila but the most reliable are those originating in Rawalpindi at 6.30 am and 2.30 pm. Two trains return to Rawalpindi in the afternoon.

Buses and wagons drop you off at the GT Rd near the start of the permanently congested Taxila Bazaar (made worse by the whacking great concrete pylons supporting a new overpass). From here, Suzukis and tongas pass Taxila train station en route to the museum. Going back to Rawalpindi, ask whether your bus is going to Saddar, Rajah or Pir Wadhai. Some Saddar-bound minibuses start from Taxila Bazaar; otherwise take a minibus or tonga south to the GT road and pick up transport there.

Getting Around Some buses and Suzukis go on up the road past Sirsukh, Mohra Moradu and the Jaulian turn-off (this road crosses the border between Punjab and North-West Frontier Province). Alternatively you can hire a tonga to take you around the site. With a bit of bargaining you should be able to arrange a three-hour tour for about Rs 200.

It would be a long day of walking to get around to the main sites on foot, which can dampen your appreciation of the place. A bicycle would be the answer but the concept of bicycle hire hasn't caught on here. There are a couple of second-hand bicycle shops along the main road but the owners will probably want a hefty deposit.

Murree
☎ 0593

Murree, 53km north-east of Islamabad, is the best-known of a series of hill stations developed here by the British as summer retreats. Beyond Murree there are several smaller villages known as the Galis.

It's possible to make a day trip up to Murree since there are plenty of buses, but that won't allow much time for hiking, which is the main attraction. There's plenty of accommodation in colonial bungalows and ramshackle guesthouses in the town. It's probably worth making a trip up here in summer simply to get away from the heat down on the plains. The air is cool and clear, and the scenery around the town is fine. But many travellers will find it over-developed, overloaded with middle-class Punjabi tourists and generally disappointing. What's more, it lacks the colonial elegance of larger hill stations such as Shimla in India. A faint colonial air lingers along The Mall – there's the old Cecil Hotel, several Christian churches and a convent – but it's pretty modern and touristy now.

Snow falls during winter (late December to late February) but the main road up to Murree is usually passable and weekends are still quite busy at this time. May to September is the busiest tourist season, when accommodation prices rise and it gets pretty crowded.

TDCP (☎ 411050) has an office below the Blue Pines Hotel on Cart Rd and a kiosk (☎ 410729) on The Mall where you can get tourist information and maps. No banks offer foreign exchange, so you will need to change money in Islamabad or Rawalpindi.

Things to See & Do There's not a lot to do in Murree town except wander along The Mall like everyone else. There are several pleasant **walks**. Head north up The Mall, past the post office and onto Bank Rd. After about 500m a trail branches off to the left and descends for an hour through woods to the Jhikagali road. From Jhikagali another forest trail climbs to **Kashmir Point** (2260m), the highest place in Murree. Alternatively you can walk or take local transport along Bank Rd straight to Kashmir Point (2km).

From **Pindi Point**, about 2km south-west of town, you can look out towards the Punjab or ride a chairlift 3km down to the road and back (Rs 70).

Places to Stay & Eat Prices are high on summer weekends, but out of the main season and on weekdays you should be able to find some bargains. Simply standing around on The Mall with a backpack on your shoulder will draw hotel touts from all directions. Prices noted here are approximate, depending on supply and demand.

There are a number of choices along the main shopping area of The Mall. *Waqar Hotel (☎ 410209)* has decent, clean double rooms (with no views) for Rs 200, or Rs 100 in the off season. *Chinnar Hotel (☎ 410244)* has singles/doubles from Rs 200/250, some overlooking The Mall. The *Al-Qamar (☎ 470311, Mount View Rd)* further up the hill is better value, with a variety of rooms from Rs 200/250 (Rs 100/150 off season). Most rooms have access to wide balconies commanding a fine view.

There are more hotels down on Cart Rd near the bus stand. The TDCP *Blue Pines Hotel (☎ 410230)* has clean singles/doubles for Rs 200/300, dropping to Rs 150/200 off season.

Cart Rd has cheap curries, braised chicken, *qeema* (minced mutton in sauce) and vegetables, as well as fruit and nut stalls. The Mall has fast-food shops and several decent, clean restaurants. Good places here include *Sam's Restaurant* and *Lintott's Cafe*. *Mr Food* is a pleasant little cafe serving coffee, sandwiches and burgers from Rs 60, and chicken dishes from Rs 80 to Rs 160.

Getting There & Away The main bus stand is down on Cart Rd. Minibuses shuttle between Murree and Rawalpindi (either to Railway Rd in Saddar Bazaar or to Faizabad) all day in summer (Rs 30, two hours). Dawdling buses go to Faizabad and Pir Wadhai for less, but avoid them if possible. Daewoo Express also has luxury buses to and from its Rawalpindi office (Rs 70). If you're heading to Islamabad, get off at Faizabad and take a passing intercity minibus from there.

In summer TDCP runs three buses direct to Lahore (Rs 270, six hours); book at its Cart Rd office. There are also cheaper Coasters to Lahore from a separate stand next to the Chambers Hotel on Cart Rd.

PESHAWAR
☎ 091 • pop 988,000

Peshawar (pi-**shar**-wur), capital of Pakistan's largely tribal North-West Frontier Province, oozes more colour, danger and romance than any other city in Pakistan. At the east end of the legendary Khyber Pass, this rough-edged trading town is a kaleidoscope of Asian peoples, dominated by the Pashtuns (Pathans). Its Mughal-era name means 'Frontier Town', and you'll soon get a feeling for why that still applies.

The civil war in Afghanistan has added a new ethnic mix in the form of Afghan refugees (unofficial sources say there are something like six million refugees in the Peshawar area alone). Several vast refugee camps lie beyond the city limits.

In the days of the overland hippy trail, Peshawar was the gateway into Pakistan, after crossing Afghanistan via Kabul and the Khyber. That avenue is now more or less cut off but recently the Peshawar-Khyber crossing has served as a revolving door to Afghanistan for journalists, aid workers and a few gung-ho, or simply curious, travellers.

For all its wild and woolly ways, Peshawar is religiously very conservative. Travellers should dress appropriately, avoid wandering around the refugee camps and avoid walking around alone after dark.

History
The early city, known as Pushapur or the City of Flowers, first came to prominence as the winter capital of the Kushans, whose empire rivalled those of Rome and Han China. It suffered heavily under a stream of invading armies who descended from the Khyber Pass, until the Mughals arrived in the 16th and 17th centuries AD. Aurangzeb lost the valley to an insurrection inspired by the Pashtun poet-warrior Khushal Khan Khattak in the 1680s.

Little architectural evidence remains of Peshawar's Mughal glory days, thanks to a Sikh army who in 1818 occupied the valley and trashed the city. Under Sikh governors the city was rebuilt and walled. The British were next to arrive, making Peshawar their frontier headquarters until Partition.

Orientation
Bala Hisar Fort is the main landmark on the GT Rd from Rawalpindi, with the Old City south and east of it. West of the railway is the Cantonment (Cantt), within which is Saddar Bazaar (referred to simply as Saddar).

Information
Tourist Offices The PTDC office (☎ 286829) in the Cantonment (in the Benevolent Fund Building) is open from 9 am to 1 pm and 2

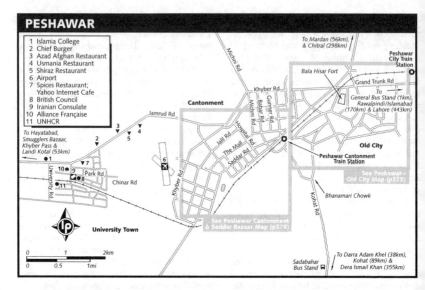

PESHAWAR

1 Islamia College
2 Chief Burger
3 Azad Afghan Restaurant
4 Usmania Restaurant
5 Shiraz Restaurant
6 Airport
7 Spices Restaurant;
  Yahoo Internet Cafe
8 British Council
9 Iranian Consulate
10 Alliance Française
11 UNHCR

To Mardan (56km), & Chitral (298km)

Peshawar City Train Station

Bala Hisar Fort

Grand Trunk Rd

To General Bus Stand (1km), Rawalpindi/Islamabad (170km) & Lahore (443km)

Khyber Rd

Cantonment

Michni Rd

Gunner Rd

Babar Rd

Hospital Rd

Jamrud Rd

Jalil Rd

The Mall

Saddar Rd

Old City

Peshawar Cantonment Train Station

See Peshawar – Old City Map (p375)

To Hayatabad, Smugglers Bazaar, Khyber Pass & Landi Kotal (53km)

Park Rd

Chinar Rd

University Rd

Khyber Rd

Kohat Rd

Bhanamari Chowk

See Peshawar Cantonment & Saddar Bazaar Map (p378)

University Town

0   1   2km
0   0.5   1mi

Sadabahar Bus Stand

To Darra Adam Khel (38km), Kohat (89km) & Dera Ismail Khan (355km)

to 4.30 pm, closed Friday afternoon and Sunday. It has current information on visits and permits to the Khyber Pass, Darra Adam Khel and other Tribal Areas, and can arrange tours (see Organised Tours later).

Foreigners' Registration Office If you're staying more than a month in Pakistan you can register at the FRO on Sahibzada Gul Rd; ask the rickshaw driver for Police Chowk No 2.

Consulates The American consulate (☎ 279801/3), 11 Hospital Road at the corner with Khyber Rd in the Cantonment, is the only Western diplomatic office in the city. British citizens can contact their embassy in Islamabad through the British Council Library in University Town.

The Taliban-run Afghan consulate (☎ 285962), on Mall Rd in the Cantonment, claims to issue visas within 10 days (US$30). The office is open from 9 am to 2.30 pm. To enter Afghanistan you'll need Taliban assistance, and a multiple entry visa to re-enter Pakistan (or you'll have to apply for another Pakistani visa in Afghanistan). We don't recommend it, but it can be done – see the boxed text 'Into Afghanistan'.

The Iranian consulate (☎ 41114) on the corner of Park and Sahibzada Abdul Qayyum Rds does not routinely issue visas.

Cultural Centres The British Council Library (☎ 111-424424), 17C Chinar Rd in University Town, has books, newspapers and Internet access. It's open from noon to 6 pm (closed Friday and Sunday). Alliance Française (☎ 843928), 1 Park Rd, just around the corner, stages French cultural events.

Money The National Bank of Pakistan on Saddar Rd changes US dollar and pound sterling travellers cheques for a Rs 100 commission. SCB Grindlays will give a minimum cash advance of Rs 5000 on a Visa card but charges Rs 350 commission. The Muslim Commercial Bank has a branch in Saddar and one in University Town with 24-hour ATMs accepting Cirrus and Maestro.

Moneychangers around Chowk Yadgar in the Old City, and along Saddar Rd near the Green's Hotel, will exchange cash and travellers cheques (both preferably in US dollars) at better rates than the banks and with no commission. Check bank rates first though and take care using these moneychangers – they won't be afraid to rip you off.

Post & Communications The main post office is on Saddar Rd. Poste restante can be collected here between 8 am and 1 pm Monday to Saturday. The central telegraph office (for overseas calls, fax and telex) is on the corner of Tariq Rd and The Mall in

Into Afghanistan

In better days, the traditional İstanbul to Kathmandu route would have passed through Afghanistan. Decades of war have put paid to this.

Although Lonely Planet, as well as many governments, advise against travelling in Afghanistan, we met several travellers along the way who had visited or planned to visit the country, which is now largely run by the extreme fundamentalist Muslim party, the Taliban. One such traveller was a Korean student, Yong Yoo Kyoung (Sona), who had travelled in Afghanistan on her own for 16 days.

'I met an Afghani in Delhi and when I looked into his face it was so sad', says Sona, explaining why she felt moved to undertake such a potentially dangerous trip. Sona easily secured a Taliban visa in Peshawar for US$30. She travelled around the country on buses, along roads which she described as 'horrible'. The average speed was little more than 10km/h.

Apart from the war-torn capital, Kabul, Sona visited Jalalabad, Ghanzi, Kandahar and Herat, staying with locals in places with 'no running water, no electricity, just a bed' for around US$10 a night. Needless to say, the food was bad. Despite all this, Sona said the people were kind and she didn't feel threatened during her time there.

A long-time American aid worker in Afghanistan, whom we also spoke to, confirmed the positive effect visits such as Sona's can have on Afghanis, who feel isolated and very much appreciate the chance to meet with foreign visitors.

If you have decided to visit Afghanistan, it's worth contacting the following organisations, who can give advice on security as well as accommodation:

Agency Coordinating Body for Afghanistan (ACBAR; ☎ 091-44392, fax 840471, e acbaar@radio.psh.brain.net.pk) 3 Rehman Baba Rd, University Town, Peshawar
United Nations Office for the Coordination of Humanitarian Assistance to Afghanistan (UNOCHA; ☎ 051-211451, fax 211450, e unocha@undpafg.org.pk) House 292, St 55, F-10/4 Islamabad

Simon Richmond

PAKISTAN

Cantonment. International calls from here are expensive, and there's no meter to monitor your call costs.

There are numerous Internet cafes (clubs), though the best ones are along Jamrud Rd towards University Town. Places such as Yahoo Internet Club and Cyberworld Centre, both on Jamrud Rd, are reliable and charge around Rs 35 an hour. The most central is Business Plus Internet, in an upstairs office opposite Green's Hotel in Saddar. The charge is only Rs 20 an hour but when we visited the server was down.

Bookshops & Newspapers Arbab Rd in Saddar Bazaar is the place to go for bookshops. Here you'll find London Books and Saeed Book Bank, as well as others, stocking postcards, international magazines and some English-language titles focusing on the North-West Frontier Province and Afghanistan.

The daily *Frontier Post* is Peshawar's English-language newspaper covering the North-West Frontier Province.

Old City

Raucous with the shouts of vendors and mule drivers, choked with tongas, rickshaws, motorcycles and bullock carts and a fascinating parade of Pashtun, Afghani and Chitrali men (and a few women, anonymous in their tent-like *burqas*) the meandering streets of the Old City lure you into dark passages full of tiny, overstuffed shops. Merchants sip *khawa* – frontier-style green tea, brought by runner from the fat samovar (urn) of a nearby teashop – and invite passing foreigners in for a cup.

From the Cantonment you approach the Old City through **Khyber Bazaar**, which consists mostly of sizzling kebab stands, cheap hotels and freelance carpet merchants. The city wall and its 16 gates were knocked down in the 1950s but many gates remain in name. Kabuli Gate is where Khyber Bazaar becomes **Qissa Khawani**, the old Street of Storytellers. This is the best-known bazaar, where hardy traders and travellers would gather to swap tales, though most of its teashops have given way to ready-made clothing stores and roaming caravans of traders no longer pull in here. Karakul fleece shops are faint echoes of former trade with Central Asia. Turn right about halfway along and you pass through a covered bazaar now mostly selling shoes, fabric and clothing and old Singer sewing machines. Take a right turn and get back on to Qissa Khawani, which turns into the brass and copperware bazaar in what used to be the old bird market. As you continue you'll smell the wonderful aroma of the tea and spice vendors. Turning right just before here will take you through the modern world of the electronics bazaar, piled high with radios, CD players and watches. Further along is the nut and grain market of **Pipal Mandi**.

Northwards is **Chowk Yadgar**, the heart of the Old City, now a redeveloped modern plaza dedicated to the heroes of the 1965 war with India. Running west from the plaza is **Ander Shahar**, the Jewellers' Bazaar. Here also is **Mahabat Khan Mosque**, the city's finest, built in 1630 by (and named for) the governor of Peshawar under the Mughal emperor, Shah Jahan, and renovated in 1898. Under Sikh rule, its minarets are said to have been used as gallows by the city's governor, a mercenary of Italian origin. You can enter the mosque here, and get a good view of its exterior from a small caravanserai to the east. In the alleys south-east of Chowk Yadgar are two more bazaars, **Mochi Lara**, the Leather Bazaar, and **Sabzi Mandi**, the busy Vegetable Market.

East from Chowk Yadgar the road forks beneath the four-tiered **Cunningham Clock Tower**, built at the turn of the 20th century for Queen Victoria's Diamond Jubilee. Bearing right at the tower, the main road features many two- and three-storey old houses with carved balconies, once the homes of rich merchants. Off to the right is **Meena Bazaar**, a labyrinth of shops for women, full of faceless, gliding *burqas*. Further up the street on the left is a collection of old Sikh havelis, one of which, **Sethi House**, has been restored and opened to the public. Ask PTDC to arrange a time for you to visit.

A further 500m, at the end of the main road, is a great gate into a run-down compound called **Ghor Khatri**. Now a police post, it was a caravanserai in Mughal times and the governor's mansion under the Sikhs. All that remains is a neglected Hindu temple to the south.

Back in the south of the old town is **All Saints Church** (1883), adapted from a former mosque and still oriented towards Mecca. Further east is a bird market and a decrepit but very traditional caravanserai-style teahouse.

Bala Hisar Fort

The imposing Bala Hisar Fort (High Fort) lives up to its name, looming large over the GT Rd. The Mughal emperor Babur built a fort here around 1526 after he first crossed the Khyber and took Peshawar. It later served as a royal residence during the Durrani dynasty before being captured, trashed and, in 1834, rebuilt by the Sikhs. It's now the headquarters of the Frontier Corps so is usually off limits, but visits can be arranged between 3 and 7 pm on Saturday and between 6 and 7 pm on Sunday (Rs 100). Once inside, access is still limited but there's a small museum and great views of the city from the ramparts. Sehrai Tours & Travel (see Organised Tours later) organises guided tours of the fort for Rs 385.

Peshawar Museum

In a large Victorian hall across the tracks from the Old City, the Peshawar Museum has an excellent collection of Gandharan art, which developed in the Peshawar Plain. Exhibits include statues and friezes depicting the Buddha's life, plus an ethnographic section with handicrafts, tools and clothing of North-West Frontier Province peoples. It's open from 8.30 am to 12.30 pm and 2.30 to 5 pm, closed on Wednesday. Entry is Rs 100 and photography is not permitted.

Islamia College

Islamia College on Jamrud Rd, University Town, is worth a look for its grand Victorian facade and clock tower, which is featured on the Pakistani Rs 100 note. It's hidden from the main road but anyone can

PESHAWAR – OLD CITY

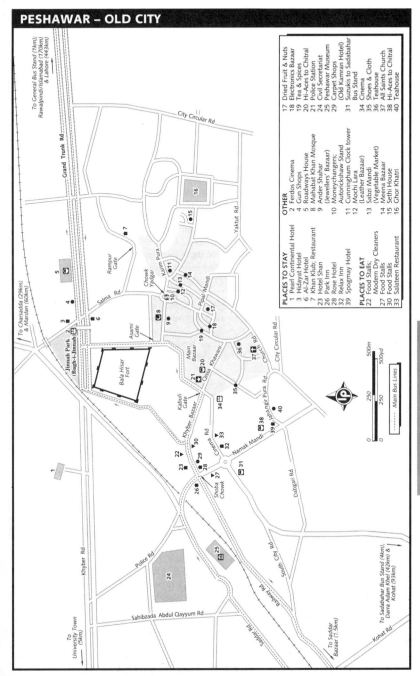

PLACES TO STAY
1 Pearl Continental Hotel
3 Hidayat Hotel
6 Al-Zar Hotel
7 Khan Klub; Restaurant
23 Hotel Shan
26 Park Inn
28 Rose Hotel
32 Relax Inn
39 Spogmay Hotel

PLACES TO EAT
22 Food Stalls;
   Modern Dry Cleaners
27 Food Stalls
30 Food Stalls
33 Salateen Restaurant

OTHER
2 Ferdos Cinema
4 Gun Shops
5 Roadways House
8 Mahabat Khan Mosque
9 Ander Shahar
   (Jewellers' Bazaar)
10 Moneychangers;
   Autorickshaw Stand
11 Cunningham Clock Tower
12 Mochi Lara
   (Leather Bazaar)
13 Sabzi Mandi
   (Vegetable Market)
14 Meena Bazaar
15 Sethi House
16 Ghor Khatri

17 Dried Fruit & Nuts
18 Electronics Bazaar
19 Tea & Spices
20 Hi-Aces to Chitral
21 Police Station
24 Civil Secretariat
25 Peshawar Museum
29 Carpet Shops
   (Old Kamran Hotel)
31 Suzukis to Sadabahar
   Bus Stand
34 Cinema
35 Shoes & Cloth
36 Teahouse
37 All Saints Church
38 Hi-Aces to Chitral
40 Teahouse

PAKISTAN

Strikes, Riots & Tear Gas

Qasim, the guide who was showing me around Peshawar's ancient bazaars, was deeply passionate about his city's history, but also a little sad that I should be seeing it on such a day.

'There are no shops open today', he said. 'They are all staying closed because of the strike.' I had arrived in Pakistan 10 days earlier, just as a nation-wide retail strike had virtually paralysed parts of the country. The strike was in protest at the general sales tax proposed by military leader Chief Executive General Pervez Musharraf, who only six months earlier had ousted Prime Minister Nawaz Sharif and tossed him in jail. This was nothing new for Pakistan – in the 50 years since Partition the military had frequently decided the democratically elected government wasn't up to scratch.

What worried the traders now was not the concept of a new tax, but that they might actually have to pay it. Musharraf had ordered a tax survey in preparation for the new tax and had deployed tax inspectors to gather information. In the frontier town of Peshawar, where so much of the merchandise is smuggled across from Afghanistan, such a survey would be disastrous. The result was a complete 'shutter down', referring to the roll-down shutters most traders use to lock up their shops. Almost two weeks with hardly any business was beginning to take its toll on the traders and street protests had started to flare up.

Emerging from a narrow lane into the main bazaar, Qissa Khawani, we were confronted by a swelling crowd of demonstrators – many of them teenagers – marching around, banging drums, yelling and setting tyres alight. At first it seemed to have more of a carnival atmosphere than a threatening one, but I sensed that my guide could see all hell breaking loose any minute. He hustled me into the serene Mahabat Khan Mosque just as the narrow street outside (the Jewellers' Bazaar) began to fill with people. We could hear growing noise, but much of it was muffled by the thick walls of the mosque and eventually silence fell. When we tried to leave the way we had come in, the entrance was blocked. Qasim had a hurried conversation in Pashto with a guard at the front, then explained that we would have to leave via the back exit.

All was quiet when we stepped from the mosque. Soon after we decided the tour was over and I farewelled Qasim.

Needing to change money, I took an autorickshaw to Chowk Yadgar, where the street moneychangers have stalls. It was deserted. As I wandered towards the street where less than an hour earlier I had been whisked into the mosque, I was hit by a sudden burning sensation. My eyes watered, my throat rasped, my nose felt like it was sucking in pepper. At first I could only think of the nearby spice market – a handful of paprika and chilli powder in the face wouldn't have felt much different. But the realisation soon dawned: The police had used tear gas at this spot to disperse the crowd.

As I stood there rubbing my eyes and trying not to breathe, a door opened slightly and a man waved me in. Once inside, away from the stinging residue of chemicals, he looked at me with sombre expectation and asked: 'You want change money?'.

Paul Harding

enter the gates and stroll around the immaculate lawn and gardens. Any bus heading west from Khyber Bazaar or the Cantonment will drop you there.

Smugglers Bazaar

Way out on the fringes of Peshawar – just before you enter the Tribal Areas on the road to the Khyber Pass – is the Karkhanai Bazaar, otherwise known as the Smugglers Bazaar. The place for contraband used to be Landi Kotal, at the border with Afghanistan, where smugglers from Afghanistan (which has few import duties) sold their foreign wares, safe behind the Tribal Areas' exemption from Pakistani law. Now this emporium of illicit goods has moved closer to the action, to Peshawar, where the goods can more easily be off-loaded to the buyers.

These days it's made up of bright, steel-shuttered shops full of refrigerators, VCRs, crockery, clothes, toiletries and toys. The far end (with its gun and hashish shops) is off limits to foreigners; a barrier and sign stop you wandering in. If you make the Khyber Pass trip up to the border you may notice goods being brought in: Look out for men riding brand new Chinese-built bicycles – still wrapped up in protective cardboard and plastic and bound for the Smugglers Bazaar!

The bazaar is safe enough in daylight – it's patronised by expatriates and Pakistani families. It closes down at dusk and, being close to the Kachagari refugee camp, this is *not* a good place to be at night. It's a 20-minute ride from Saddar on one of the old Afghan Mercedes buses (ask for Karkhanai) or take an ordinary bus as far as the stop before the Hayatabad turn-off (just past University Town) and take a Ford transit van from there.

Organised Tours

The PTDC can organise city tours (or a private guide), as well as a two-hour visit to a local Pashtun village (Rs 500) to see its *hujra* (guesthouse) and *zenana* (women's quarters). The PTDC can also arrange trekking and jeep safaris into the Northern Areas around Chitral and the Kailash Valley (minimum four days, around Rs 3000 for transport and a guide). Speak to the helpful Mr Salahuddin.

Peshawar is as good a base as any to arrange trips north to Chitral and the Shandur Pass, and also to Gilgit. Travel agents specialising in tours include Sehrai Tours & Travel (☎ 272085, e sehrai@psh.brain .net.pk) and Travel Walji's (☎ 274130), both on Saddar Rd in the Cantonment.

Places to Stay

There are three main areas for accommodation: Saddar Bazaar, convenient for shops and offices; Khyber Bazaar, noisier but close to the fascinating Old City; and the GT Rd, close to transport but noisy and not particularly pleasant.

Places to Stay – Budget

The *Tourists Inn Motel*, behind Jan's Bakery, is a real travellers' den and the most popular backpacker place, but we've had mixed reports about the management and at least one disturbing allegation. It has dorm beds,

At Your Service...

Making my way by bus to the Smugglers Bazaar, a middle-aged Pashto man sitting next to me struck up a conversation in limited English. You can almost guarantee this will happen on any bus trip anywhere in Pakistan. When he had established that I was going to Kharkhanai Bazaar he was concerned, telling me this bus didn't go all the way. At the next stop he hustled me off and into another waiting van before I knew what was happening.

A short time later we both got off, right outside the Smugglers Bazaar. 'Khakhanai!' he said simply. There followed a bit of an awkward silence. I wasn't sure whether he wanted payment for his time, to chat a bit more, or to come shopping with me. While I was considering this, he shook my hand and said: 'Please, can I be excused from your service now?' and disappeared onto a bus heading back the way we'd come. He just wanted my blessing that I was OK so he could go home!

Paul Harding

packed in like sardines, for Rs 100, double rooms for Rs 300 and a communal kitchen. Khyber Pass trips can be organised here.

Other Saddar places include the grotty *Hotel Shahzad* (☎ 275741, Saddar Rd) with singles/doubles for Rs 80/130 and a lobby that smells like old socks; and the extremely ambitiously named *Five Star Hotel* (☎ 276950, Sunheri Masjid Rd) with rooms for Rs 100/140 – not exactly spotless but probably worth that much. Rooms in both hotels have private bathrooms.

In Khyber Bazaar, the plain *Hotel Shan* (☎ 210668) is gloomy but pretty good value for the location at Rs 90/150. Deluxe (carpeted) rooms are slightly more. On Cinema Rd there are several cheapo options with doubles for around Rs 150 but most are real fleapits; *Relax Inn* (☎ 220241) is probably the least deplorable.

It would require a distinct lack of imagination to actually want to stay in the GT Rd area, but if you do, try *Al-Zar Hotel* (☎ 212531) opposite Ferdos Cinema. It's a friendly enough place with a 3 pm checkout; poky rooms with cold water cost Rs 100/150.

PAKISTAN

PESHAWAR CANTONMENT & SADDAR BAZAAR

Cemetery

To University Town;
Usmania; Shiraz;
Hayatabad &
Khyber Pass

Jamrud Rd

Khyber Rd

Qasim Rd

Khyber Rd

Hospital Rd

Jdd Rd (School Rd)

Si Syed Rd

Khyber Rd

Edwardes
College

Babar Rd

Fort Rd

Gunner Rd

Tariq Rd

Jheel Rd

Michni Rd

Khalid Rd

Kalid-bin-
Walid Bagh

The Mall

Railway Rd

Peshawar Cantonment
Train Station

The Mall

Fethi-Alam Rd

Sunehri Masjid Rd

Saddar
Bazaar

Arbab Rd

Saddar Rd

Fowara
Chowk

Khadim Shaheed Rd

Fruit &
Vegetable
Stands

Sahibzada Gul Rd

The Mall

Stadium Rd

Younus Rd

Arbab Niaz
Stadium

0   250   500m
0   250   500yd

------- Main Bus Lines

OTHER
1 American Consulate
2 Afghan Consulate
3 Central Telegraph Office
4 Commercial Department
5 PTDC Office
8 Jan's Arcade
9 State Bank
10 Habib Bank; Carpet Shops
11 Photo Shop
13 National Bank of Pakistan
14 Business Plus Internet;
    Sehrai Tours & Travel;
    Snooker Hall
15 General Post Office
17 PIA
19 St John's Cathedral
20 Foreigners' Registration Office
21 Dervish Mosque
22 Catholic Church
23 Muslim Commercial Bank (ATM)
24 Saeed Book Bank
25 London Books
28 Sunehri Mosque
29 Mosque
30 Falaksair Cinema
31 Aero Asia; Photo Shop
32 Khyber Political Agent's Office

PLACES TO STAY
6 Tourists Inn Motel
12 Green's Hotel;
    Lala's Grill
26 Hotel Shahzad
27 Five Star Hotel

PLACES TO EAT
7 Jan's Bakery;
    Outlet Venture
16 Hong Kong Restaurant
18 Honey Bakery;
    SCB Grindlays Bank

PAKISTAN

And the Mickey Mouse sheets dating back several years are still gracing the beds!

Hidayat Hotel (☎ 217839), set back from the main road, is several quantum leaps up in standard. The cheapest rooms are comfortable but nothing special at Rs 180/250, while the air-con rooms at Rs 550/650 are definitely mid-range. There's parking, a restaurant and good service.

Places to Stay – Mid-Range & Top End
Rose Hotel (☎ 250755) on the corner of Khyber Bazaar at Shoba Chowk is the best value of the mid-range places. It's very central, has parking for vehicles and a range of large singles/doubles/triples from Rs 195/300/400. Deluxe rooms (with TV) are

Rs 300/400/500 and air-con doubles cost Rs 700 (no singles). ***Park Inn*** (☎ 256 0048), diagonally opposite, has excellent value air-con rooms at Rs 590 for a double and Rs 850 for the deluxe room (no singles), including breakfast. All rooms have TV and some have a bathtub.

Spogmay Hotel (☎ 216961, Namak Mandi Chowk) isn't as well located but it has parking facilities, a restaurant and plenty of rooms, from plain doubles for Rs 200 to air-con singles/doubles for Rs 500/800. The entrance is around the corner from Namak Mandi on Jehangir Pura Rd.

Green's Hotel (☎ 276035) is a good upmarket choice in Saddar Bazaar. It has air-conditioned rooms with colour TV from Rs 900/1350.

The **Khan Klub** (☎ 214802, fax 256 1156, e khanclub@brain.net.pk, Nevey Darwaza), in the Old City near Rampur Gate, is Peshawar's most atmospheric hotel. The restored haveli has eight beautifully furnished and irresistibly romantic rooms from Rs 2500 to Rs 4000 (all doubles). The larger rooms have screen-fronted balconies facing the street, and there's a restaurant and teahouse here. It's expensive, but if you can afford one top-notch hotel in Pakistan, this should be it. Phone in advance to be sure of a room.

Places to Eat
Restaurants **Lala's Grill** at Green's Hotel has reasonably priced international and Pakistani dishes, and there's a wonderfully cool atrium area where you can enjoy a drink, meal or Western-style breakfast. The restaurant itself is more formal. Sandwiches, burgers and rice dishes cost around Rs 70, chicken tikka is Rs 105.

The best places for a quick kebab-style meal are in Khyber Bazaar – you can usually pick them by the blue and pink neon lights and the smoking braziers at the front. The unsigned **restaurant** next door to the Rose Hotel is good. The plain but clean **Salateen Restaurant**, on Cinema Rd near Khyber Bazaar, has a good selection of hearty meat dishes. Mutton tikka is Rs 100 and chicken karai is Rs 180.

For a splurge, don't miss dinner at the stylish, traditionally decorated **Khan Klub**. Seated on cushions at low tables you can listen to nightly *rabab* music from 7 pm while dining on Afghan and Pathan food from around Rs 75 to Rs 125. Expect a full meal to come to around Rs 200. There's also a teahouse upstairs, and Western-style breakfasts are served in the restaurant.

The best concentration of decent restaurants is out on Jamrud Rd in University Town, but it's no fun getting out here and back at night unless you prearrange a taxi, so they may be a better option for lunch.

Usmania and **Shiraz** are upmarket restaurants serving good Pakistani and international food, while **Spices** is a clean and casual place with a range of soups, salads, Chinese and Pakistani barbecue dishes. Half-chicken karai is Rs 80.

Fast Food A local Pashtun favourite is *chapli kebab*, a spicy mutton burger shaped

liked the sole of a *chappal* (sandal) and fried in what looks like engine oil.

Fowara Chowk in Saddar has many food stalls. There are several fast-food places on Arbab Rd, and out along Jamrud Rd on the way to University Town you'll find hamburger and pizza joints such as **Chief Burger**.

Khyber Bazaar is heaven for meat-loving snackers and many of the outdoor **stalls** have miniature wicker-top stools arranged at the front where you can squat with the locals; for less than Rs 25 you can fill up on *kaleji* (liver and tomatoes), wok-fried kebabs, grilled kebabs or *kalud* (kidney beans). For dessert there are stalls stacked with dates, melon slices, mangoes and kheer (rice pudding).

Self-Catering Saddar Bazaar's best bakeries are **Jan's**, near the tourist office, and the **Honey Bakery**, near SCB Grindlays Bank.

Jan's Shopping Arcade on Hospital Rd near the corner of Saddar Rd in Saddar Bazaar has a modern, well-stocked supermarket where you can pick up everything from toiletries to cornflakes.

Afghan-run **fruit and vegetable stalls** at the west end of Saddar Rd operate late into the evening, and individual fruit vendors are everywhere. Many of these vendors have blenders set up at the front of the stand for preparing delicious juice drinks (Rs 10). It's common to mix milk with these drinks (particularly with mango) so if you don't want it, ask for it *'bina dudh ki'* or *'dudh nahi'*. Some of the blenders look like they haven't been rinsed in years, but that's another story. Dried fruit and nuts can be found in Pipal Mandi in the old town.

Entertainment
The **Pearl Continental Hotel** claims to have the only public bar in Pakistan (open only to non-Muslims, of course). It's not the most atmospheric place in the world but you don't have to be a guest to drink there and if you haven't had a beer since Turkey, who cares about ambience? You'll have to fill out a permit form, and a bottle of Murree beer is a pricey Rs 120. The Pearl Continental also has a pool where nonguests can swim for a cool Rs 350.

Cinemas are regaining popularity with locals: In the 1970s and '80s they went out of fashion when they were a favourite target for a rash of tribal-influenced bombings. Cinema Rd is the place to go in the Old City where a couple of *cinemas* show English language (mainly American) films. Also try *Ferdos Cinema* on GT Rd and *Naz Cinema* near Asami Gate; most other cinemas screen Pashto films. There's a *snooker hall* upstairs above Sehrai Tours & Travel on Saddar Rd. It costs Rs 60 an hour to play on a full-size table and it's open till 11 pm.

Spectator Sports
Buzkashi, the wild version of no-rules rugby on horseback, came here with the Afghans but is now hard to find and is officially banned. Local Afghan players sometimes organise a match in winter. Ask at the PTDC.

First-class domestic cricket matches are played during the season (October to February) at the Arbab Niaz Stadium in the Cantonment. International tour matches are occasionally played here, although some teams (notably England on its 2000 tour) have expressed safety concerns at having to play here.

Polo in Pakistan is often associated with the Shandur Pass, between Chitral and Gilgit in the Northern Areas, where the highest polo ground in the world is the scene of an annual summer carnival. However, there's a polo ground behind the Pearl Continental Hotel in Peshawar where army teams often play. The PTDC may know if a match is coming up.

Shopping
If you're shopping seriously in the bazaars, good-natured haggling is essential, preceded by small talk over tea. Simply wandering around the Old City will turn up all sorts of interesting trinkets, clothing, electrical goods, tea and spices. There are standard shops, including carpet and handicraft merchants, along Saddar Rd, and Jan's Arcade stocks all sorts of items – if you want to buy a salwar kameez off the rack, this is a good place.

As elsewhere, there are street vendors who will follow you around in Peshawar; the merchandise you'll most commonly be assailed with here is the Afghan pocket knife, inlaid with semi-precious stone such as the blue lapis lazuli. These can be bargained down to around Rs 200 depending on the size.

The main shopping areas in the Old City are Qissa Khawani for copper and brass

items; Ander Shahar (Jeweller's Bazaar), running west from Chowk Yadgar, for jewellery; and the Mochi Lara (Leather Bazaar) near Chowk Yadgar for Pashtun chappals, leather bags or bandoliers.

There's a concentration of rug shops selling Afghani and Baluchi carpets above the Shan Hotel and in the old Kamran Hotel complex opposite. Pricier shops on Saddar Rd such as Carpet Palace, Kabul Carpets and the Lahore Carpet House accept credit cards and can help to arrange shipping.

Saddar is lined with handicraft shops offering marked-up versions of Old-City goods. A shop sponsored by the office of the United Nations High Commissioner for Refugees (UNHCR) in Saddar called Outlet Venture, next to the Tourists Inn Motel, has handsome but pricey refugee-made clothes, bags, jewellery and furnishings with Afghani motifs.

Getting There & Away
Air PIA (☎ 273082) has flights daily to/from Islamabad (Rs 725), Lahore (Rs 1865), Quetta (Rs 2645) and Karachi (Rs 3425). The flight to Quetta, with views over tribal territory and eastern Afghanistan, is not that much more expensive than an air-con sleeper on the most direct train.

If weather over the Lowari Pass is clear, PIA Fokker Friendships fly daily to Chitral. The one-hour flight costs Rs 2525 for foreigners. Even with a booking you must report to the PIA office at 11 am the day before the flight to get confirmation. At 3 pm that day any unconfirmed bookings are released to the public.

Bus There are several bus stands in Peshawar, as well as stands for minibuses and Coasters to outlying towns and to the Northern Areas.

The general bus stand is about 2.5km east of Bala Hisar fort along the GT Rd, but you shouldn't really need to use this. The newer bus stand (known as Roadways House), about 100m up from the fort, has buses to Islamabad, Rawalpindi and Lahore, and Coasters to just about everywhere. Buses coming into Peshawar may drop you off on the GT Rd opposite here.

To Rawalpindi & Lahore Ordinary buses to Rawalpindi (Rs 55, three hours) and Lahore (Rs 80, eight hours) depart regularly from Roadways House. Air-conditioned buses to/from Lahore cost Rs 150 and air-con Coasters to Rawalpindi cost Rs 60. Most Coasters go to Rawalpindi's Committee Chowk; buses go to Pir Wadhai.

The motorway linking Peshawar with Islamabad, and hence with Lahore, is expected to be completed some time in 2001. In that event, the journey time from Peshawar to Lahore will be cut to around 6½ hours.

To Quetta There are currently two buses without air-con a day to/from Quetta, via Kohat, DI Khan and DG Khan. They depart from the Sadabahar bus stand about 4km south of the Old City at 10 am and 12.30 pm (Rs 450, 24 hours). To get there take a tempo or minibus heading south along Kohat Rd from Cinema Rd, or bargain for an autorickshaw (Rs 30).

Other Destinations Hi-Ace minibuses go direct to Chitral from Roadways House, an exhausting 11- to 12-hour overnight trip (Rs 300).

Minibuses to Darra Adam Khel (Rs 12, 40 minutes) go from the Sadabahar bus stand south of town. There are two daily air-con buses direct to Karachi (Rs 500, 26 hours) from Roadways House.

Train The train is probably a better way to get from Peshawar to Rawalpindi or Lahore, at least until the motorway is completed. There are five trains a day to Rawalpindi (3½ hours), three of which continue on to Lahore (10 hours).

The best services to Lahore are the morning *Awam Express* and the overnight *Khyber Mail*. Fares are Rs 115 for an economy seat, Rs 245 for 1st-class sleeper, Rs 650 for air-con sleeper. For Quetta (38 hours) take the evening *Abaseen Express* at Rs 365/695 for economy/1st-class sleeper – at the time of writing, this train didn't have air-con carriages.

To get a student or tourist concession take a letter from the PTDC to the 2nd floor office of the Commercial Department at Cantonment station (this is the building on the left as you face the main station building). There's a separate reservations office in the main building; try to reserve a seat or berth for Lahore at least a day or two in advance.

Getting Around

Peshawar's local buses regularly run on a fixed route from GT Rd to Khyber Bazaar, Sunehri Masjid Rd, Khadim Shaheed Rd and along Jamrud Rd. This links the bus stands, Old City, museum, train station, Saddar, University Town and Hayatabad; a bus or minibus along the whole route is Rs 10 but most short trips (ie, Khyber Bazaar to Saddar) will cost less than Rs 5. Transport becomes infrequent after dark.

Autorickshaws charge about Rs 15 to points within the Cantonment. In the Old City you can hire a horse-drawn tonga for about Rs 100 an hour. The airport is pretty central, just west of the Cantonment. An autorickshaw from Khyber Bazaar shouldn't cost any more than Rs 50.

Taxis for hire – usually trying to drum up trips to the Khyber Pass – lurk along Hospital Rd near Jan's Arcade.

AROUND PESHAWAR
Khyber Pass

For centuries the Khyber Pass has divided and linked empires and peoples, marking a frontier between Afghanistan, Pakistan and Central Asia. The very name conjures up images of discovery, war and intrigue. The British have even used it in their rhyming slang parlance (don't ask).

Babur, Nadir Shah and Darius the Great, Buddhist travellers, Scythian warriors and Greek troops have all been drawn through the pass. In more recent times, overland travellers from the 1960s and '70s made their way through the Khyber when travelling from Afghanistan to Pakistan and on to India.

The Khyber isn't *at* the border but stretches through the Suleiman Ranges for many kilometres on both sides. It's long, mostly very broad, and barren; at the end you look over at Afghanistan – which at this point looks more or less like Pakistan – and then go back. It's not so much arriving at the end of the road that's exciting, but the trip from Peshawar to the border itself. From hiring your armed guard to entering the Tribal Areas and passing dozens of fortress-like Afridi homes, truckloads of Afghans (going in both directions) and the remains of British army forts, it's a trip not to be missed.

Near Peshawar you're in government-administered lands of the Khalid tribe. About 18km out is **Jamrud Fort**, built by the Sikhs

Guns for Hire

The Afridi village of Darra Adam Khel is one of those places you hear about long before you get there. It's the kind of place you would only expect to find in some lawless 'Wild West' like the Tribal Areas of Pakistan. Everyone in Darra is involved in just one thing: the manufacture of guns.

At the time of research the area was officially out of bounds to foreigners and the Home & Tribal Affairs Office was refusing to issue permits. But Darra is on the main road to Kohat, Dera Ismail Khan and beyond and there's no reason why travellers can't get on the bus. You're just not supposed to get *off* at Darra and the local *khussadars* (political agents) there have instructions to put foreigners back on the next bus.

The reality is that the local khussadars are happy to discreetly show you around the back-street workshops and let you fire off a round on an AK-47 for the requisite baksheesh. Darra is a dusty one-street town and, just like the gun-slinging wild west, a stranger is easily spotted. When I hopped off the bus it was only a matter of seconds before a guard, dressed in a black beret and a long, grey coat, materialised and hustled me away from prying eyes. I was taken straight to an open-sided shed full of rifles, and proudly shown a well-worn Russian-made Kalashnikov (safer for tourists to fire), a replica of a beretta shotgun, a modified Darra-built AK-47 and a cache of pistols.

After a short period of negotiation (in which I had little room to bargain, the inference being that they would be quite happy to put me on the next bus back to Peshawar) we settled on Rs 800 to shoot a clip from the Kalashnikov and two cartridges from the shotgun. Out on the testing range, I aimed the rifle at a large piece of distant sandstone where many a traveller had unloaded before me. 'Good shot!' cried my self-appointed guides, who were hovering at the sort of safe distance you'd allow anyone who was firing a military assault weapon for the first time. So what if my rock target was the size of a two-storey building? Flicking it to automatic, I sprayed the remaining 29 bullets all over the place and that was that. After almost dislocating a shoulder with the beretta, I'd had enough.

Less physical but more interesting was the free tour of the Darra workshops that followed. In simple wooden sheds with dirt floors and using basic tools, each component is carefully fashioned and made ready for mass assembly in another workshop. Here, someone concentrates on fashioning wooden stocks, there someone bores out barrels, and elsewhere trades-man carefully work on firing mechanisms. Darra isn't so much a village of gunsmiths, it's a factory. It's estimated that between 400 and 700 guns a day are finished in Darra.

Back out on the main street you may be allowed to quickly browse through the gun shops which display the finished product, before being bundled onto the next bus back to Peshawar. Don't be tempted to buy one of the nifty pen guns. Possession of an unlicensed firearm in Pakistan is illegal and penalties are stiff.

Paul Harding

in 1823 to mark the western edge of their empire. Its trademark stone arch (built in the 1960s) over the road marks the formal entrance to the pass. Here you will see ordinary men (not soldiers) wandering around the bazaar with rifles slung over their shoulders. By now you're in Khyber Agency, one of seven agencies that make up the Tribal Areas, populated here mainly by the Afridi tribe.

Small stone army forts, Pashtun houses and massive mud-walled Afridi homes pepper the hills. Pakistani law gives way to tribal law not far from the main road, which

is why you must travel with an armed Afridi escort. As the road forms a series of switch-backs, there are excellent views back east.

Near the narrowest point of the pass, about 15km from Jamrud, is **Ali Masjid** (Ali Mosque) with a large fort and British cemetery. The valley walls bear insignia of regiments that have served here. Before it was widened, the 3m-wide pass is said to have been too narrow for two fully laden camels to pass abreast.

Near the border is **Landi Kotal**, at 1200m. With the growth of the Smugglers Bazaar near Peshawar, this has lost its status as 'Contraband City', but it's still full of hashish and gun shops and the plush homes of rich smugglers. This is also the home of the Khyber Rifles Officers' Mess, with a small museum chronicling the Rifles' history and its many famous visitors. You should be able to talk your driver and escort into having a look around Landi Kotal and stopping here for *chai* (tea).

The last point foreigners can visit is **Michni checkpost**. From here you can see the Durand Line, once marked by pillars, as it snakes across the ridge marking the border. Down the other side is the border at Torkham, with an unused PTDC motel, 58km from Peshawar. The only thing to do other than admire the view is haggle with young boys trying to sell you wads of Afghani banknotes – which are worth nothing more than their souvenir value.

Getting There & Away At the time of research you could only go by hired car (or your own) so it's cheaper in a group. You need a permit from the Khyber Political Agent's Office on Stadium Rd. They want names, passport data and the date of the trip; the permit takes a few minutes and costs Rs 120. After you've sorted out transport, go back to the Khyber Political Agent's Office to arrange for your gunman, whom you pick up there on the day. Take your driver with you – without him you'll be denied permission.

The PTDC can do all of this for you if you arrange to hire a 4WD and driver through them. The cost is Rs 1900 for up to four people (plus your driver and armed guard). If you're on your own they'll do it for Rs 1600. Alternatively you could hire a taxi for the half-day round trip for around Rs 1200, but you'll have to organise your own permit. The Tourists Inn Motel arranges trips for Rs 400 per person. If you have your own vehicle you only need to arrange permits and an escort – even with a motorbike your gunman will be more than happy to ride on the back.

Khyber Railway

If you time your trip right and can afford it, you can ride up the Khyber Pass in style aboard a vintage steam train. In the 1920s the British built a 42km steam railway to Landi Kotal, but public services were shut down in 1985 because of fears about sabotage related to the Afghan war and tribal conflicts.

Sehrai Tours & Travel (☎ 272085, e sehrai@psh.brain.net.pk) runs the monthly Khyber Steam Safari, a steam-train journey from Peshawar up to Landi Kotal. The train travels with over 50 armed guards. There are stops at Peshawar airport (to cross the runway!) and at Shahgai Fort for tea, before arriving at Landi Kotal some four hours later. If four hours on a train is enough, you can return by minibus. The trip isn't cheap (Rs 3585 per person) but it's a unique opportunity. Monthly departure dates aren't fixed, so call ahead to check.

PAKISTAN

Pakistan Border Crossings

Pakistan to India

There are regular buses from Lahore to the border at Wagah, 30km to the east. The best place to pick one up is at the Lahore train station and the fare is Rs 10 (see Getting There & Away in the Lahore section for more information). The border, open daily from 9.30 am to 3.30 pm has a bank, a PTDC motel and (outside the main gate) a good second-hand book stall.

Around 500m of no-man's land separates the Pakistani passport and customs offices from the Indian facilities at Wagah. You must walk this; there are porters on hand to carry your bags. Your passport will be checked several times. Once in the Indian customs office you'll have to fill in several forms and it's quite possible that your bags will be thoroughly checked. The stadium seating outside is for the nightly border ceremony.

There's one more check of your passport and papers outside the customs hall, before you walk another 200m out of the compound into a slew of moneychangers, drink sellers and taxi drivers. Although the taxi drivers will say that it's a standard Rs 450 to Amritsar, this is the *maximum* they can charge – settle for around Rs 250 for the whole taxi to travel the 30km to Amritsar, or take a rickshaw the 4km to Attari from where there are frequent onward buses.

If you take the daily Lahore-Amritsar train, the customs and immigration checkpoint is at Attari. Travellers have reported that this train is held up for hours while everyone on board is cleared. It is better to use the above method.

India to Pakistan

There are regular buses from Amritsar to Attari, from where you can get a cycle-rickshaw to the Wagah border for a flat Rs 10. Here you'll find a hotel, food and drink stalls and moneychangers. It's illegal to take Indian currency into Pakistan, though you can get away with taking a small amount across; the moneychangers on the Pakistan side offer marginally better rates than those on the Indian side. It's also forbidden to take alcohol into Pakistan. The border closes at 4 pm. This is almost certainly the least busy border crossing on the route, so it shouldn't take too long to get through.

The Indian immigration and customs hall are inside the main gate on the left. Indian officials here have a reputation for being difficult and angling for (even demanding) baksheesh. Provided your passport and visa are in order, stand firm. There are no outgoing 'taxes' to pay and no bribes should be necessary. Travellers with their own vehicles have reported long waits while everything has been searched, seemingly in the hope that you'll get sick of waiting and bribe your way out. But things are changing – you are now asked to sign a visitors' book, commenting on whether the service from immigration staff has been good, bad or indifferent! Mysteriously, most of the previous comments state that everything was just fine.

Once out of customs (your bags will probably undergo a quick search) you walk along the road across about 500m of no-man's land; periodically someone will usher you over to check your passport again. There's even an unmanned metal detector which, when you walk through it, makes a cacophony of tinny beeps, but no-one seems to care. Formalities on the Pakistan side are straightforward, even laid-back (almost as if they're trying to show how much easier to deal with they are than the Indians!). Since November 2000, foreign tourists arriving at Wagah without a Pakistani visa can get a 30-day landing permit on the spot, free of charge. This is not a visa and cannot be extended, so if you intend to stay longer than 30 days you must obtain a visa in advance.

When you emerge through the gates there should be a bus waiting to take you straight to Lahore (Rs 10). Ask to get off at the train station, otherwise you'll end up at Badami Bagh bus station, which is a long way from the accommodation areas.

INDIA

Amritsar

Delhi
Agra

Kathmandu

Varanasi

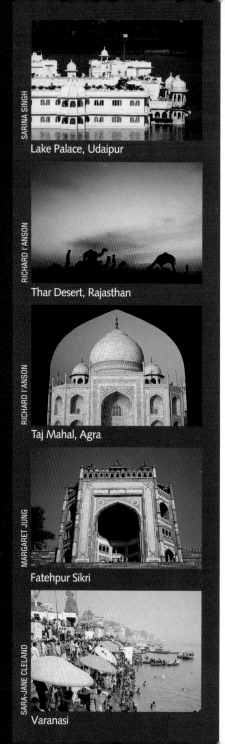

Lake Palace, Udaipur

Thar Desert, Rajasthan

Taj Mahal, Agra

Fatehpur Sikri

Varanasi

INDIA
highlights

Hiking
The walking is easy and the views are superb in the foothills of the beautiful Himalaya north of Dharamsala.

Masala Movies
The Raj Mandir Cinema in Jaipur is one of the plushest cinemas around, and it's packed to the rafters each night with punters out to catch a Hindi screen blockbuster.

Udaipur
The Lake Palace offers superb but expensive dining, but you can still enjoy a fine meal in one of the lakeside *havelis* that overlook Lake Pichola without breaking your budget.

Arabian Nights
There's nothing quite like the romance of a camel trek out into the Rajasthani desert, with a hearty meal as the sun sets over the dunes and the night spent sleeping under the stars.

Taj Mahal, Agra
The most cliched image of India imaginable, but this magnificent marble mausoleum is a sight not to be missed (even if it does cost two days' budget to get in!). Agra's huge Mughal fort makes a good follow-up.

Fatehpur Sikri
This extraordinary abandoned city is a perfectly preserved example of a Mughal city. It's often overlooked by travellers, but it's got more atmosphere than Delhi's Red Fort and a fascinatingly brief history.

Varanasi
This city of Shiva is one of the holiest places in India. A dawn boat ride on the Ganges River or meditating on the ghats among the bathers, pilgrims and priests is about as spiritual as it gets in India.

India

If you took all the colours, sights, sounds and smells you can think of, you'd probably still fall short of an adequate description of India.

Favoured destination of the overlanding hippies of the 1970s and still a place that draws travellers from all over the world for its rich culture, inexpensive living and sheer diversity, India is more a continent than a country, and it's always an eye-opener. Arriving overland, whether from Pakistan or Nepal, has its advantages since you'll be reasonably well prepared for the sensory onslaught. But while there are similarities between India and its neighbours, don't expect things to be the same. In fact, the only thing you can expect in India is the unexpected.

Travel in northern India can be hard work. There tends to be more poverty and squalor here than elsewhere, more pollution in the cities and a greater chance of eating a dodgy curry and ending up with Delhi belly. Indians have a passion for mind-numbing bureaucracy, and the grab for the almighty tourist dollar, particularly in places like Agra, Delhi and Rajasthan, can be very draining. But when you get under its surface (such as working out how to make those train reservations), India is one of the world's most rewarding countries for travel.

Looking for spirituality? You'll find it on the ghats at Varanasi and Pushkar and in temples all over the country. Maharajas' palaces and mammoth forts? They're everywhere in Rajasthan and in Delhi and Agra. Himalayan trekking and Tibetan culture? Head up to Himachal Pradesh and Dharamsala. Traces of the British Raj? Shimla is the place.

And while you're seeking out these tangible sights, the constant clamour of daily life unfolds all around you. Things are rarely 'normal' in India and you'll frequently find yourself scratching your head and asking 'Why?'. That's what makes the place so interesting.

Dive headfirst into this crazy, chaotic milieu, keep a cool head, and you'll come away with some amazing memories. Love it or loathe it, you can't ignore India.

India at a Glance

Capital: Delhi (population 9.4 million)

Population: 1 billion

Area: 3,287,263 sq km

Head of state: President Shri KR Narayanan. Elected prime minister in 2000 was Atal Behari Vajpayee.

Currency: Indian rupee (Rs)

Country telephone code: ☎ 91

Exchange rates:

country	unit		Indian rupee (Rs)
Australia	AUS$1	=	26
EU	€1	=	43
UK	£1	=	69
USA	US$1	=	46

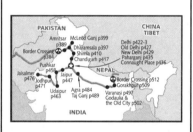

THE ROUTE

The route begins at the Wagah border crossing from where most travellers continue straight to Amritsar. From there we describe a 'northern route' which is best followed in summer (March to June) when it's very hot down on the northern plains but pleasant on the fringes of the Himalaya. Dharamsala, and the nearby village of McLeod Ganj, are easily reached from Amritsar; McLeod Ganj is popular with travellers for its Tibetan culture and cool mountain air. Shimla is favoured more by middle-class Indian tourists but the former British hill station makes an interesting Raj-era escape. From there the route drops down to Chandigarh and on to the seething capital of Delhi.

INDIA

INDIA

Indian Ocean

NEPAL
INDIA
PAKISTAN
SRI LANKA

The external boundaries of India
on this map have not been authenticated
and may not be correct

0   90   180km
0   150   300km

AFGHANISTAN

Peshawar

ISLAMABAD

PAKISTAN

Lahore

Multan

Sukkur

K2
(8611m)

GREAT HIMALAYA RANGE

Srinagar

JAMMU &
KASHMIR

Leh

Jammu

McLeod Ganj
Dharamsala

Pathankot

Amritsar
Wagah

Ludhiana

Bathinda

PUNJAB

Page 384

HARYANA

Hansi

Bikaner

Nagaur

Churu

Jaisalmer

Barmer

Thar
Desert

Jodhpur

RAJASTHAN

Mt Abu

Rann of Kutch

Bhuj

Jamnagar

Dwarka

Porbandar

Du

Veraval

Junagadh

GUJARAT

Rajkot

Bhavnagar

Gandhinagar

Ahmedabad

Ratlam

Udaipur

Kota

Bundi

Ajmer

Pushkar

Jaipur

Shivpuri

Gwalior

Mathura

Agra

DELHI

Hisar

Chandigarh

Shimla

HIMACHAL
PRADESH

Nanda Devi
(7816m)

Almora

Nainital

Dehra Dun
Haridwar

Ganges River

Bareilly

UTTAR
PRADESH

Lucknow

Yamuna River

Jhansi

Khajuraho

Satna

Katni

Jabalpur

Seoni

Nagpur

Amraoti

Jalgaon

Khandwa

Khargwa

Biaora

Bhopal

MADHYA
PRADESH

Indore

Ujjain

Dhule

Dindori

Ramnagar

Bilaspur

Raipur

Sagar

Chhattisgarh

Son River

Allahabad

Varanasi

Sarnath

Gorakhpur

Kushinagar

Ayodhya

Sultanpur

Kanpur

Kapur

Patna

Gaya

Bodhgaya

BIHAR

Ranchi

Jamshedpur

Sambalpur

ORISSA

Cuttack

Mahanadi River

Raigarh

Pokhara

Page 512

NEPAL

Mt Everest
(8848m)

KATHMANDU

CHINA
TIBET

GREAT HIMALAYA

SIKKIM

Gangtok

BHUTAN

THIMPHU

Darjeeling

Asansol

Kharagpur

Hooghly River

Kolkata

WEST
BENGAL

Digha

BAY OF BENGAL

BANGLADESH

DHAKA

MEGHALAYA

Shillong

Guwahati

ASSAM

Itanagar

ARUNACHAL
PRADESH

Dibrugarh

Brahmaputra River

NAGALAND

Kohima

MANIPUR

Imphal

MIZORAM

Aizawl

TRIPURA

Agartala

MYANMAR
(BURMA)

At this point you can either continue east or take a diversion west through Rajasthan, the state many consider to be quintessential India. This route is best tackled in winter (November to March) and includes Jaipur, Pushkar (via Ajmer), Udaipur, Jodhpur and the desert city of Jaisalmer. Returning to Delhi to resume the route, it's a shortish trip to Agra, home of the unmissable Taj Mahal, then to Varanasi on the sacred Ganges River. Finally the route turns north through Gorakhpur to Sunauli and the border with Nepal.

Wagah to Amritsar

WAGAH
The border village of Wagah is really only good for one thing – watching the flag-lowering ceremony and the bizarre antics of the Indian and Pakistani border guards

(see the boxed text 'Showtime at the Border').

There are food and drink stalls and moneychangers floating around, and if you must stay the night, there's the highly uninteresting *Niagra Falls Hotel* (☎ *0183-382646*) with doubles at Rs 300/400 for shared/private bathroom.

Cycle-rickshaws make the 4km trip to **Attari** for a flat Rs 10, autorickshaws (if you can find one) charge Rs 20 and taxis cost Rs 50; all will drop you at the bus stand. There are frequent buses from Attari to Amritsar (Rs 12, one hour). There are no direct buses from Wagah to Amritsar.

AMRITSAR
☎ 0183 ● pop 1 million
If not for one spectacular monument, Amritsar would be merely a pleasant but typical north Indian city. The presence of

Showtime at the Border

The one show you don't want to miss while in Amritsar is the official closing of the border at Wagah, enacted in full regimental silliness by the Indian and Pakistani armies.

If you cross the border into India late in the day (it closes to travellers at 3.30 pm Pakistan time, 4 pm Indian time), it's worth hanging around for a front-seat view of the proceedings. The actual ceremony, just 15-minutes long, starts nightly at around 6.45 pm (or just before sunset), but the crowds start arriving at least an hour before – and we do mean crowds. On the Indian side there is ministadium seating, and the soldiers do their best to keep the rowdy spectators in some kind of order.

If you arrive late, it's possible that a kindly officer will whisk you through to a front-row seat on the tarmac beside the guard house – this is the best vantage point from which to view and photograph the soldiers as they madly goosestep to the barrier and enact the curious flag-lowering and gate-closing procedure. Afterwards, you'll understand why there are so many kids selling snaps of the whole crazy performance.

Without wanting to overplay the event, it's worth seeing from both sides of the fence, since the point is for each side to outmarch, outsalute and outscream the other. The only way to do this is to make a special trip, which you can easily do from Lahore. On this side, the smaller and more subdued Pakistani crowd gathers to watch their soldiers – most of them very tall and very angry-looking – stomping around, snorting and screaming their lungs out. But this is serious business and every 10m of goose-stepping and pirouetting is greeted with heart-felt applause, while over the border the Indian crowds are going wild.

After more marching and yelling, a bugle sounds, the flags are simultaneously lowered and folded up, and the gates are slammed shut. It's a real fusion of orderly, colonial-style pomp and serious national rivalry.

This bizarre ceremony has been performed daily since it was first enacted (and presumably choreographed) in 1948, shortly after Partition. But don't let the Monty Pythonesque walks fool you into thinking this is all a game. These soldiers are trained to hate each other. Don't miss it!

Simon Richmond & Paul Harding

the exquisite Sikh Golden Temple in the heart of the old city, however, makes a stop in Amritsar an absolute must.

The original site for the city was granted by the Mughal emporer, Akbar. Founded in 1577 by Ram Das, the 4th guru of the Sikhs, Amritsar is both the centre of the Sikh religion and the major city of Punjab state. The name Amritsar means Pool of Nectar, referring to the sacred tank around which the Sikhs' Golden Temple is built.

The original site for the city was granted by the Mughal emperor, Akbar, but in 1761 Ahmad Shah Durani sacked the town and destroyed the temple. It was rebuilt in 1764, and in 1802 was roofed over with copper-gilded plates by Ranjit Singh and became known as the Golden Temple.

Aside from the temple, Amritsar has some pleasant gardens and a bustling old city. Sikhs are justifiably proud of their capital and are well known for their friendliness and hospitality.

Orientation

The old city is south-east of the main train station and is surrounded by a circular road that used to contain the massive city walls. There are 18 gates still in existence but only the north gate, facing the Ram Bagh gardens, is original. The Golden Temple and the narrow alleys of the bazaar area are in the old city.

The more modern part of Amritsar is north of the train station and over the busy GT Rd, where you will find most of the hotels. The bus station is 2km east of the train station on the road to Delhi.

Information

Tourist Offices The state tourist office moves around a bit but it's currently in the Hotel Palace (see Places to Stay – Budget later). There was no phone there at the time of writing (phone the hotel) and there's very little information there anyway. A better bet for information on the Golden Temple and the Sikh religion is the helpful, air-conditioned information office (☎ 553 954) at the temple itself. It's open from 8 am to 8 pm daily in summer (to 6 pm in winter).

Money There are numerous money changers on Link Rd, opposite the train station, but you'll have to shop around for decent rates. You can buy Pakistani currency here or exchange your Pakistani rupees for Indian. The Bank of Punjab branch office near the Golden Temple changes US dollars only but it has an ATM accepting MasterCard and Cirrus. The Bank of Punjab in the old city changes US dollars and pounds sterling, cash and travellers cheques.

Standard Chartered Grindlays Bank (SCB Grindlays, formerly ANZ Grindlays), on Mall Rd, changes travellers cheques for a Rs 200 fee and gives cash advances on Visa and MasterCard, again for Rs 200. All banks close at 2.30 pm weekdays and at noon Saturday.

Post & Communications A post office at the Golden Temple sells stamps (open from 9 am to 6.30 pm Monday to Saturday). The main post office is on Court Rd north of the train station (open from 9 am to 5 pm Monday to Saturday). Ask at the inquiry counter for post restante; mail is held for six months. It also has a Speedpost parcel service and there's a tailor shop next door to the main gate where you can have parcels stitched up. The Telecom office is attached to the post office, although it's easier and more convenient to use private phone offices.

For Internet access, Cyber Net is a convenient Internet cafe in Bikanerian Bazaar only about 100m from the Golden Temple. It's open to 11.30 pm and costs Rs 60 per hour.

Things to See

A five-minute walk north-east of the Golden Temple brings you to **Jallianwala Bagh**, an important park commemorating the 2000 Indians killed or wounded here, shot indiscriminately by the British in 1919 (see History in the Facts about the Region chapter). This appalling massacre was one of the major events in India's struggle for independence and was movingly re-created in the film *Gandhi*.

A section of wall with visible bullet marks is preserved, as is the well that some people jumped into to escape; 120 bodies were recovered from the well. You can follow some of the story in the **Martyrs' Gallery**, open from 9 am to 5 pm in summer

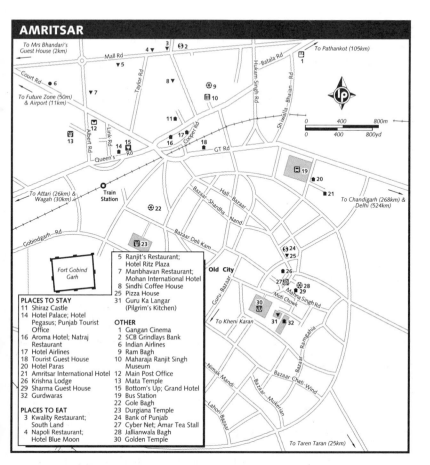

AMRITSAR

PLACES TO STAY
11 Shiraz Castle
14 Hotel Palace; Hotel
   Pegasus; Punjab Tourist
   Office
16 Aroma Hotel; Natraj
   Restaurant
17 Hotel Airlines
18 Tourist Guest House
20 Hotel Paras
21 Amritsar International Hotel
26 Krishna Lodge
29 Sharma Guest House
32 Gurdwaras

PLACES TO EAT
3 Kwality Restaurant;
   South Land
4 Napoli Restaurant;
   Hotel Blue Moon

5 Ranjit's Restaurant;
   Hotel Ritz Plaza
7 Manbhavan Restaurant;
   Mohan International Hotel
8 Sindhi Coffee House
25 Pizza House
31 Guru Ka Langar
   (Pilgrim's Kitchen)

OTHER
1 Gangan Cinema
2 SCB Grindlays Bank
6 Indian Airlines
9 Ram Bagh
10 Maharaja Ranjit Singh
   Museum
12 Main Post Office
13 Mata Temple
15 Bottom's Up; Grand Hotel
19 Bus Station
22 Gole Bagh
23 Durgiana Temple
24 Bank of Punjab
27 Cyber Net; Amar Tea Stall
28 Jallianwala Bagh
30 Golden Temple

and 10 am to 4 pm in winter. The park is open from 6 am to 7 pm in summer and 7 am to 6 pm in winter.

Buried in the old city to the west of the Golden Temple is the 16th-century Hindu **Durgiana Temple**, dedicated to the goddess Durga. A larger temple, built like the Golden Temple in the centre of a lake, is dedicated to the Hindu deities, Lakshmi and Narayan (Vishnu).

North-west of the train station is the Hindu **Mata Temple**, which commemorates a bespectacled 20th-century female saint, Lal Devi. Women who wish to have children come here to pray. It's notable for a Disneyesque series of grottoes and shrines featuring Hindu deities (take the stairs on the left).

Ram Bagh is a leafy park in the new part of town. From the southern end of the park you can enter a **museum** in the small summer palace of the Sikh Maharaja Ranjit Singh. The museum contains weapons dating back to Mughal times and some portraits of the ruling houses of the Punjab. It's open from 10 am to 4.45 pm Tuesday to Sunday (Rs 10).

Places to Stay – Budget
Amritsar has a few good accommodation options. Note that taking a rickshaw to the front door of most hotels (except the gurdwaras or pilgrims' resthouses at the Golden Temple) will result in you paying extra in commission.

To truly soak up the atmosphere of Amritsar, the place to stay is within the complex

Trouble in Amritsar

Amritsar has been at the centre of some of the most terrible events in India this century. It was here, at Jallianwala Bagh in 1919, that a mass of some 20,000 Indians gathered in a peaceful protest over the arrest of an Indian leader. British troops arrived and opened fire, indiscriminately killing almost 400 people and wounding many more. The Martyrs' Gallery at Jallianwala Bagh explains the story.

During the turmoil of the partition of India in 1948, Amritsar was a flash point for the terrible events that shook the Punjab, as Sikhs and Hindus fled eastwards (into Amritsar) and Muslims fled west to Lahore.

During unrest in the Punjab in the early 1980s, the Golden Temple was occupied by Sikh extremists, who were intent on expelling non-Sikhs from the state and creating a Sikh homeland. They were finally evicted, under the orders of Indira Gandhi, by the Indian army in 1984 in a military action that resulted in hundreds of Sikh deaths. Later that year Indira Gandhi was assassinated by her Sikh bodyguards. The temple was again occupied by extremists in 1986. The damage wrought on the Golden Temple by the tanks of the Indian army has now been repaired, and things are quiet again.

housing the Golden Temple itself. Hospitality is part of the Sikh faith, and every night hundreds of pilgrims – mainly Sikhs – bed down in one of several gurdwaras here. If you do stay here it is imperative that you respect this holy place – smoking, alcohol, drugs and any public display of familiarity between the sexes is grossly insulting to the Sikhs.

The gurdwaras *Sri Guru Ram Das Niwas* and *Sri Guru Nanak Niwas* are staffed by volunteers. Accommodation is free – there's an area set aside for foreigners – but you must pay a returnable deposit of Rs 50; you can stay for up to three days. There's a large dorm, bedding is provided and the toilets and shower block are in the centre of the courtyard. There's no pressure from any of the staff but a donation is expected, and you

shouldn't forget to make one – many travellers simply leave the deposit. If you prefer some privacy, there are three more gurdwaras offering private rooms at Rs 50 per person. *Sri Guru Hargobind Niwas* has singles with private bathroom; the 100-bed *Guru Arjan Dev Niwas* and *Sri Guru Nanak Niwas* have doubles and four-bed rooms. All these places are side by side, just past the community kitchen.

Sharma Guest House (☎ 551757, *Mahna Singh Rd*) is a small place conveniently close to the Golden Temple. Rooms vary, but the ones at the back overlooking a large garden are quite good. Singles/doubles with shared bathroom cost Rs 150/200, better rooms with private bathroom and TV are Rs 250/300 and there are 'deluxe' rooms for Rs 300/350. There's a small restaurant downstairs and Internet access is available.

Tourist Guest House (☎ 553830, *GT Rd*), east of the train station, is a former colonial guesthouse – a bit ramshackle but friendly and well set up for travellers. Dorm beds cost Rs 80, small doubles with shared bathroom are Rs 100 and larger doubles with private bathroom are Rs 200. Beware of touts directing you to inferior similarly named substitutes.

Hotel Palace (☎ 565111, *Queen's Rd*) is conveniently located opposite the train station. As with its twin, *Hotel Pegasus*, there's a wide range of rooms here from singles/doubles with private bathroom for Rs 150/250 to comfortable air-con rooms for Rs 500/750. The management is helpful and the Punjab tourist office is – at least temporarily – here.

Aroma Hotel (☎ 564079, *Queen's Rd*) greets you with a gloomy lobby but the rooms are huge, bright and good value at Rs 150/200 with hot water and air cooler. There's a bar and restaurant attached.

There's a string of cheap hotels across from the bus station, but none are much good. *Hotel Paras* (☎ 540208) charges a laughable Rs 150 for poky rooms.

Places to Stay – Mid-Range

The new *Krishna Lodge* (☎ 533978), down a quiet street near the Golden Temple, is good value. Doubles with private bathroom (hot water) and air cooler cost Rs 250; air-con doubles with cable TV are Rs 600. The front rooms are the brightest.

Amritsar International Hotel (☎ 555991), Punjab Tourism's multistorey centrally air-conditioned hotel, is a modern but non-descript building near the bus station. Room prices range from Rs 475/550 up to the deluxe rooms at Rs 750/1000. This is the only place in this category that doesn't add 10% tax.

Hotel Airlines (☎ 564848, Cooper Rd), near the train station, is an interesting place. The large but unexciting air-cooled rooms cost Rs 350/450. The air-con rooms, at Rs 600/750, are gaudily furnished and all feature – believe it or not – a swing. All have TV and there's a sun terrace and restaurant. Checkout is 24 hours. *Shiraz Castle (☎ 565157)* is down a quiet side street just off Queen's Rd. It's a small place with clean and comfortable rooms from Rs 290/425 and up.

Mrs Bhandari's Guest House (☎ 228509, 10 The Cantonment) is a delightful – though pricey – place to stay and a bit of an institution among overlanders and expats holiday-ing from Pakistan. About 4km north-west of the train station, it's set in a large, peaceful garden with a swimming pool, and campers can put up their own tent here for Rs 150. Clean rooms are stuck in a now very fashionable 1950s time warp; they vary in size and cost Rs 750/1250 (more with air-con). Meals can be pre-ordered: Breakfast is Rs 120, while lunch and dinner cost Rs 200/250 veg/nonveg. Parking is Rs 100.

Places to Eat

It's *de rigueur* to join the pilgrims for a basic meal of rice and vegetable curry at *Guru Ka Langar* at the Golden Temple. The huge hall is open (and meals are always served) 24 hours a day; there's no charge but you should make a donation.

Opposite the Golden Temple information office are several cheap *dhabas* (simple eateries). Further east in the bazaar towards Jallianwala Bagh are some good food stalls and ice-cream shops. The *stand* making 'potato cheesy chop' burgers and the *Amar tea stall* next door are worth a stop. Just around the corner, *Pizza House* is an air-con fast-food place doing pretty good all-veg pizzas and burgers for around Rs 50 to Rs 75. You can also get good south Indian *dosas* (lentil pancakes) for Rs 20 to Rs 35 as well as soups and shakes.

South Land, on Mall Rd diagonally opposite Ram Bagh, is a semi open-air place serving south Indian veg food such as dosas from Rs 15 to Rs 40. Next door, *Kwality Restaurant* is a comfortable, slightly fancy restaurant serving very good veg and non-veg dishes. It's not particularly cheap but the service is good and you can get a cold beer here.

The pink-fronted *Sindhi Coffee House*, opposite Ram Bagh, is a casual place where you can enjoy sandwiches and ice creams for less than Rs 35 and a few Indian and Chinese dishes under Rs 50.

Queen's Rd has numerous options, starting with cheap *dhabas* opposite the train station. Heading east, *Natraj*, in the Aroma Hotel, has inexpensive Indian and Chinese fare and a bar. *Napoli Restaurant*, at the Hotel Blue Moon on Mall Rd, has nothing remotely Italian on the menu but the Indian, Chinese and continental dishes from Rs 75 to Rs 130 are quite good.

For more upmarket dining, try *Manbhavan Restaurant (☎ 227801)* in the Mohan International Hotel on Albert Rd, which has international cuisine and live music in the evening, or *Ranjit's Restaurant (☎ 562836, 45 Mall Rd)*, at Hotel Ritz Plaza, with mains for around Rs 130 and a buffet on Friday and Saturday nights for Rs 200.

Entertainment

There are a few bars outside the old city in Amritsar, most attached to restaurants, but you could hardly call them places of entertainment. Places to try include the *Bottom's Up* bar at the Grand Hotel (open to 10.30 pm), or the bar at the Aroma Hotel's *Natraj Restaurant*, where a bottle of beer costs Rs 60.

There are several cinemas showing Hindi and English-language films. The best is the plush *Ganggan Cinema* on Batala Rd, north-east of the train station.

Another source of local entertainment are the small *pool halls* where you can mix with young Punjabis and even have a beer. A good one is *Future Zone*, just off Mall Rd in the north-west of the city.

You can *swim* in the pools at big hotels for a fee. Hotel Ritz Plaza on Mall Rd charges nonguests Rs 200.

[Continued on page 396]

INDIA

GOLDEN TEMPLE

The holiest shrine of the Sikh religion, also known as the Hari Mandir or Darbar Sahib, is in the centre of Amritsar's Old City. It's a place you'll find yourself returning to, and it should be seen in the dazzling light of day as well as illuminated at night. The temple itself is in the middle of the sacred pool Amrit Sarovar, which gave the town its name. Open and free to all, the temple is a beautiful place, especially early in the morning, though the weekends can get quite crowded.

Visitors must remove their shoes and cover their heads before entering the precincts (headscarves are available for Rs 10 from various vendors outside). No smoking is allowed. Photography is permitted from the **Parkarma**, the marble walkway that surrounds the sacred pool, but be discreet about photographing Sikhs in prayer. An English-speaking guide is available at the information office in the outer courtyard.

The Golden Temple is a two-storey marble structure reached by a causeway known as **Gurus' Bridge**. The lower parts of the marble walls are decorated with inlaid flower and animal motifs in the *pietra dura* (inlaid detail) style of the Taj Mahal. Once inside the temple, pilgrims offer sweet doughy *prasaad* (food offerings) to the attendants, who take half to distribute to everyone as they leave the temple. You should accept this even if you don't want to try it. The golden dome – said to be gilded with 100kg of pure gold – represents an inverted lotus flower. It is inverted, turning back to the earth, to symbolise the Sikhs' concern with the problems of this world.

RICHARD I'ANSON

Inset: Minaret atop the Golden Temple's lofty dome. (Photo by Richard I'Anson)

Bottom: A pilgrim rests in the peace of the Golden Temple.

RICHARD I'ANSON

Four priests at key positions around the temple keep up a continuous reading in Punjabi – broadcast by loudspeaker – from the Sikhs' holy book, the Guru Granth Sahib. The original copy of the Guru Granth Sahib is kept under a pink shroud in the Golden Temple during the day; at around 10 pm each day it is ceremoniously returned to the **Akal Takht** (Sikh Parliament) building. The morning processional ceremony takes place at 4 am in summer, at 5 am in winter.

The **Central Sikh Museum** is upstairs in the clock tower. It comprises a gallery of often-gruesome paintings which tell the story of the Sikhs and their martyrs; it also holds a collection of weaponry. The museum is open from 7 am to 7 pm daily.

Pilgrims are well provided for at the temple, with 400 basic rooms available free to travellers and pilgrims (ablutions are performed at washbasins in the central courtyard) and approximately 35,000 people are fed here daily. People from all walks of life, irrespective of colour, caste and creed, are welcomed; all sit on the floor and eat together. As well as accommodation, there is a community kitchen (open 24 hours), a good library, a medical centre, a post office, a bank and a railway-booking agency.

Top: Many thousands come to Amritsar's Golden Temple each day.

Bottom: A pilgrim framed by one of the temple's numerous ornate arches.

RICHARD I'ANSON

Illustrative Plan of the Golden Temple

According to tradition, the Buddha is believed to have journeyed through this region, and re-marked upon the suitability of the secluded site as one in which salvation could be attained. Guru Nanak, the founder of Sikhism, was also charmed by the site, and in the late 16th century a natural pool here was enlarged and named Amrit Sarovar – Pool of Nectar (centre). It is the pool in which Sikh pilgrims bathe.

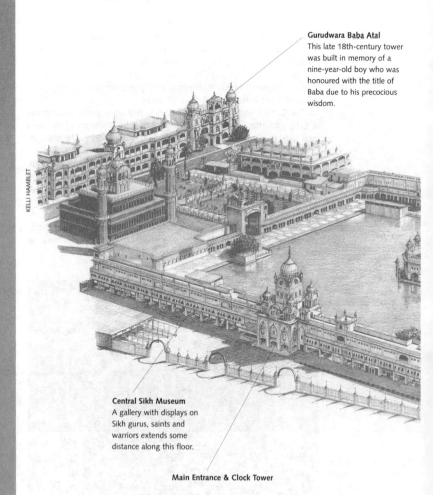

Gurudwara Baba Atal
This late 18th-century tower was built in memory of a nine-year-old boy who was honoured with the title of Baba due to his precocious wisdom.

Central Sikh Museum
A gallery with displays on Sikh gurus, saints and warriors extends some distance along this floor.

Main Entrance & Clock Tower

KELLI HAMBLET

GOLDEN TEMPLE

Hari Mandir/Golden Temple/Darbar Sahib
The Hari Mandir, also known as the Golden Temple or the Darbar Sahib, is the most sacred part of the temple complex. It is a two-storey marble structure featuring gold-plated domes and semiprecious stone-encrusted walls. The Hari Mandir enshrines the holy book, the Guru Granth Sahib. No formal rituals are conducted here, but hymns are sung throughout the day and night.

Gurus' Bridge
Pilgrims walk along this causeway to reach the Hari Mandir. The sacred Guru Granth Sahib is ceremoniously carried along the causeway each morning from the Akal Takht and installed in the Hari Mandir; it is carried back along the cause-way to the Akal Takht each evening.

Nishan Sahib
These Sikh flags are hoisted in the temple grounds and can be seen at all Sikh *gurdwaras* (temples).

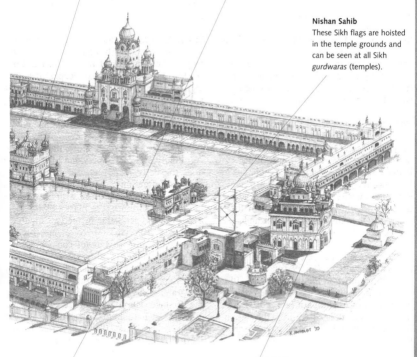

Parkarma
Pilgrims use this marble walkway, which surrounds the Sarovar, or sacred pool, to circumambulate the Hari Mandir.

Akal Takht
Built in 1609, this is the seat of secular power, where the Sikh parliament meets.

[Continued from page 391]

Shopping

Katra Jaimal Singh, near the telephone exchange in the old city, is a good area for locally made woollen blankets, shawls and sweaters. Hall Bazaar is a particularly good area to poke around for handicrafts. If you're in the market for footwear, Punjabi *juti* (wooden-soled shoes made with gold and silver thread) can be found in Moti Chowk, the street south-east of the Golden Temple entrance. Even if you don't want to buy, it's worth a stroll to see the shoemakers at work.

Getting There & Away

Air The Indian Airlines office (☎ 503780) is at 39A Court Rd. Amritsar is linked to Delhi (US$100) four times weekly.

Bus Amritsar has a vast and typically chaotic bus station with good connections to most parts of India and towards the Pakistani border. There's a useful information counter hidden around the back of the main terminal building, and ticket counters at the front. There are no direct buses to the Pakistani border, only to Attari.

To Dharamsala & Pathankot There is only one direct bus to Dharamsala at 11.50 am (Rs 98, eight hours), but you can easily take a bus or train 105km north to Pathankot and then change to another bus to Dharamsala or McLeod Ganj. Buses to Pathankot depart frequently throughout the day (Rs 43, three hours), and from there buses to Dharamsala cost Rs 60 and take another four hours or so.

To Chandigarh There are frequent ordinary buses to Chandigarh (Rs 99, five hours) and two deluxe buses in the morning (Rs 198). Agencies and guesthouses also sell deluxe bus tickets to Chandigarh (around Rs 200) but these buses don't leave from the station. Some leave from Hall Bazaar in the north of the old city.

To Delhi There are quite a few buses to Delhi (Rs 190, 10 hours), but this journey is much more comfortable and enjoyable by train. The only deluxe buses to Delhi (Rs 200) are run by private companies and tickets are sold through agents.

To Attari The journey to Wagah, about 4km beyond Attari, is much quicker by road than by taking the train. Buses from Amritsar only go as far as Attari (Rs 12, one hour) at least every 30 minutes until about 5.30 pm, but remember that the border closes at 4 pm. Buses usually leave from platform 23. You can easily get a rickshaw from Attari to Wagah.

Other Destinations There are regular buses to Jammu (Rs 70) and two morning buses to Shimla (Rs 170).

To get to Rajasthan it's easier to take a train to Delhi and go from there. If you're a masochist there are direct buses to Ganganagar (Rs 115, eight hours), where you can change for another bus to Bikaner (about another eight hours away), and then continue on to Jaisalmer (seven hours) – a lot of uncomfortable road travel.

Train If you're heading to Chandigarh, Delhi or Agra, the train is the best way to go. There are direct rail links to Delhi (Rs 99/154/446 in 2nd class/sleeper/air-con, eight to 10 hours, 447km), but the comfortable *Shatabdi Express*, which departs twice daily, does the journey in only 5½ hours. Tickets are Rs 610/1220 in chair car/executive class.

The *Nanded Express* goes through to Agra daily except Tuesday and Sunday, as does the daily *Dadar Express*, though it rolls in after midnight. The *Amritsar-Howrah Mail* links Amritsar with Lucknow (17 hours, 850km), Varanasi (23 hours, 1251km) and Kolkata, formerly Calcutta (38 hours, 1829km). There are no direct trains to Chandigarh, but you can change at Kalka or Ambala.

For Dharamsala, you can take a train to Pathankot and a bus from there. There are two trains a day (both in the morning) and the trip takes about 2½ hours (Rs 27 in 2nd class). The Pathankot bus stand is a 10-minute walk or Rs 10 rickshaw ride from the train station (turn left on the main road as you exit the station).

For Pakistan, the rail crossing point is Attari (26km). The daily *Samjhauta Express* leaves Amritsar at 9.30 am, reaching Lahore *theoretically* at 1.35 pm. This train gets delayed for hours at the border and travellers have reported depressingly long waits.

Getting Around

The airport is 11km from the city centre. An autorickshaw should cost around Rs 80 and a taxi is Rs 200.

Autorickshaws charge about Rs 30 from the train station to the Golden Temple. The same trip on a cycle-rickshaw will cost Rs 20.

Northern India

The term 'northern India' is used here to describe the part of the route through Himachal Pradesh. This state borders Punjab to the west, Uttaranchal to the south-west, Tibet to the east and Jammu & Kashmir to the north. The Indian Himalaya cuts through just north of Dharamsala, providing stunning scenery and some excellent, accessible trekking areas. Our route passes through Dharamsala, McLeod Ganj and Shimla, but it's easy enough to branch out here and visit the popular travellers' hangout of Manali or go trekking in the Kullu and Chamba Valleys.

The best time to visit is late September to November or April to June. Winter (December to March) gets very cold and you can expect snowfall.

DHARAMSALA

☎ 01892 • pop 19,200

When travellers talk of heading up to Dharamsala, they usually mean McLeod Ganj about 4km north (though closer to 10km by road). Essentially the two places are one – Lower Dharamsala and Upper Dharamsala (McLeod Ganj), but they are completely different in character and for clarity we've split them into separate sections. Since 1959, Dharamsala has been synonymous with the Tibetan Government in Exile, but the actual headquarters is about 2km above the town at Gangchen Kyishong.

Dharamsala itself is mostly Indian in character and is of little interest to travellers, although most find themselves either arriving or departing from here and coming down for business such as banking or shopping in the colourful Kotwali Bazaar.

Information

The Himachal Pradesh Tourist Development Corporation (HPTDC) has an office

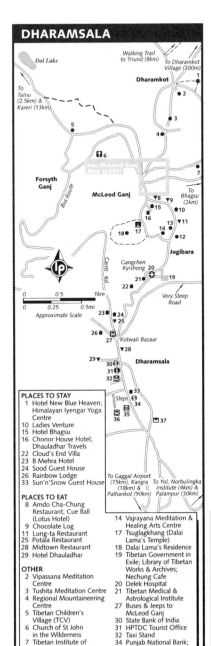

DHARAMSALA

PLACES TO STAY
1 Hotel New Blue Heaven;
   Himalayan Iyengar Yoga
   Centre
10 Ladies Venture
15 Hotel Bhagsu
16 Chonor House Hotel;
   Dhauladhar Travels
22 Cloud's End Villa
23 B Mehra Hotel
24 Sood Guest House
26 Rainbow Lodge
33 Sun'n'Snow Guest House

PLACES TO EAT
8 Amdo Cha-Chung
   Restaurant; Cue Ball
   (Lotus Hotel)
9 Chocolate Log
11 Lung-ta Restaurant
25 Potala Restaurant
28 Midtown Restaurant
29 Hotel Dhauladhar

OTHER
2 Vipassana Meditation
   Centre
3 Tushita Meditation Centre
4 Regional Mountaineering
   Centre
5 Tibetan Children's
   Village (TCV)
6 Church of St John
   in the Wilderness
7 Tibetan Institute of
   Performing Arts (TIPA)
12 Ekant Lodge
   (Yoga Classes)
13 Llamo's Kitchen

14 Vajrayana Meditation &
   Healing Arts Centre
17 Tsuglagkhang (Dalai
   Lama's Temple)
18 Dalai Lama's Residence
19 Tibetan Government in
   Exile; Library of Tibetan
   Works & Archives;
   Nechung Cave
20 Delek Hospital
21 Tibetan Medical &
   Astrological Institute
27 Buses & Jeeps to
   McLeod Ganj
30 State Bank of India
31 HPTDC Tourist Office
32 Taxi Stand
34 Punjab National Bank;
   Bank of Baroda
35 Kangra Art Museum
36 Bus Stand
37 Post Office

INDIA

(☎ 24212) with limited information but runs local tours (summer only) to Kangra, Jawalamukhi and Chamunda Devi, or to Palampur and Baijnath. The office is open from 9 am to 8 pm Monday to Saturday.

The main branch of the State Bank of India and the Punjab National Bank both accept major travellers cheques. The Bank of Baroda, nearby, can give cash advances on Visa and MasterCard within 24 hours.

Things to See

The **Kangra Art Museum**, a few minutes' walk south of the tourist office, has miniature paintings from the Kangra school of art, which flourished in the Kangra Valley during the 17th century. It also has elaborately embroidered costumes of the Kangra people, woodcarvings and tribal jewellery. It's open from 10 am to 5 pm Tuesday to Sunday (free).

Places to Stay & Eat

While new places are constantly appearing up the road in McLeod Ganj, Dharamsala's simple guesthouses remain quiet. Some of them are cheap enough and may be convenient if you have an early bus out of Dharamsala.

Sood Guest House (☎ 24269, Cantt Rd, Kotwali Bazaar) is clean and basic with doubles with bathroom for Rs 100 and triples for Rs 150. Bucket hot water is Rs 5.

B Mehra Hotel (☎ 23582) is a big, old place with singles/doubles with private bathroom for Rs 100. There are also triples and four-bed rooms for Rs 150. The bathrooms are not too clean and there's bucket hot water. The attached restaurant serves Tibetan, Chinese and Indian food.

Rainbow Lodge (☎ 22647, Old Charri Rd) is clean and quiet with just eight rooms. Singles with shared bathroom cost Rs 110 and doubles with private bathroom cost Rs 220 to Rs 275. Closer to the bus stand, *Sun'n'Snow Guest House* (☎ 22423), next to the Bank of Baroda, has reasonable doubles for Rs 100/150 with common/private bathroom.

There are plenty of *food stalls* in the bazaar whipping up samosas and fried curry potato. *Potala Restaurant*, up a narrow flight of stairs just north of the main intersection, has good veg and nonveg Tibetan and Chinese cuisine. *Midtown Restaurant*

in the middle of the bazaar serves very good Punjabi and Gujarati food.

HPTDC's *Hotel Dhauladhar* has a restaurant and bar with excellent sunset views.

Getting There & Away

Air Indian Airlines flies to Delhi (US$145) three times weekly. Gaggal airport is 15km south of Dharamsala; you can book tickets through travel agents in Dharamsala or McLeod Ganj.

Bus The bus stand is about 500m south of the Kotwali Bazaar. The quickest way to reach it is to turn right at the vegetable market and descend the steep flight of steps leading directly to the terminal. There's a booking office open from 5 to 11.45 am and 2 to 9 pm. Regular buses (every 30 minutes) make the trip up to McLeod Ganj from about 7.30 am, but they also stop in the village near the taxi stand, and on Cantt Rd at the Kotwali Bazaar crossroads, so you can pick them up there. They cost Rs 6 and take about 30 minutes. Cramped passenger jeeps also run a shuttle service for the same price.

There are six direct buses daily to Shimla (Rs 159/227 ordinary/deluxe, nine hours). There are around seven direct services to Delhi (13 hours), either early in the morning or after 5 pm. Costs vary according to the time of departure and type of bus, but ordinary services cost from Rs 236 to Rs 261; the deluxe bus at 8 pm is Rs 338. More deluxe services leave from McLeod Ganj.

There's one direct bus to Amritsar at 5 am (Rs 102, eight hours) but you can get on one of the frequent Pathankot buses (Rs 55, four hours) and take another bus or train from there.

There are several daily buses to Manali (Rs 151/194 ordinary/deluxe, 12½ hours); one to Dehra Dun at 9 pm (Rs 252, 14 hours), as well as services to Kullu, Chamba and other destinations in Himachal Pradesh.

MCLEOD GANJ
☎ 01892

A cool climate and fine mountain scenery combined with a strong Tibetan culture and laid-back atmosphere make this one of northern India's favourite travellers' hang-outs. Maroon-robed monks stroll around the ramshackle village, Western dharma students discuss Buddhist philosophies in cafes, and rows of shops offer Tibetan handicrafts, prayer flags, jewellery and *thangkas* (Tibetan paintings on fabric).

Some travellers find this all too much of a scene, but one of the great things about McLeod is that there's plenty to do here. Apart from opportunities for hiking in the hills, you'll see flyers around town advertising courses in yoga, meditation, reiki, spiritual healing, Tibetan language, cooking classes and more. It's also well set up for travellers, with plenty of Internet access, restaurant-bars and video halls, and travel agents dealing in everything from foreign exchange to organised treks.

Before Upper Dharamsala (named McLeod Ganj after the Lieutenant Governor of Punjab, David McLeod) was established in the mid-1850s as a British garrison, it was the home of the seminomadic Gaddi people. There are still Gaddi families in the villages around McLeod Ganj. The British developed the settlement as an important administrative centre for the Kangra region but, following a major earthquake on 4 April 1905, moved the centre to Lower Dharamsala.

Today McLeod Ganj is best known as the headquarters of the Tibetan Government in Exile and is the home of His Holiness the 14th Dalai Lama, Tenzin Gyatso. 'Dalai', which means 'ocean of wisdom', is a title that has been conferred on the rulers of Tibet since the 16th century.

In 1959, the Dalai Lama fled Tibet and was granted political asylum in India. In

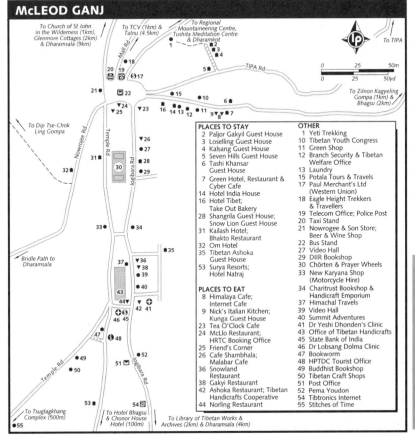

McLEOD GANJ

To Church of St John in the Wilderness (1km), Glenmore Cottages (2km) & Dharamsala (9km)

To TCV (1km) & Talnu (4.5km)

To Regional Mountaineering Centre, Tushita Meditation Centre & Dharamkot

To TIPA

TIPA Rd

To Zilnon Kagyeling Gompa (1km) & Bhagsu (2km)

To Dip Tse-Chok Ling Gompa

To TIPA

Mall Rd

Temple Rd

Nowrojee Rd

Jogibara Rd

To Tsuglagkhang Complex (500m)

To Hotel Bhagsu & Chonor House Hotel (100m)

To Library of Tibetan Works & Archives (2km) & Dharamsala (4km)

Bridle Path to Dharamsala

PLACES TO STAY
2 Paljor Gakyil Guest House
3 Loselling Guest House
4 Kalsang Guest House
5 Seven Hills Guest House
6 Tashi Khansar Guest House
7 Green Hotel, Restaurant & Cyber Cafe
14 Hotel India House
16 Hotel Tibet; Take Out Bakery
28 Shangrila Guest House; Snow Lion Guest House
31 Kailash Hotel; Bhakto Restaurant
32 Om Hotel
35 Tibetan Ashoka Guest House
53 Surya Resorts; Hotel Natraj

PLACES TO EAT
8 Himalaya Cafe; Internet Cafe
9 Nick's Italian Kitchen; Kunga Guest House
23 Tea O'Clock Cafe
24 McLlo Restaurant; HRTC Booking Office
25 Friend's Corner
26 Cafe Shambhala; Malabar Cafe
36 Snowland Restaurant
38 Gakyi Restaurant
42 Ashoka Restaurant; Tibetan Handicrafts Cooperative
44 Norling Restaurant

OTHER
1 Yeti Trekking
10 Tibetan Youth Congress
11 Green Shop
12 Branch Security & Tibetan Welfare Office
13 Laundry
15 Potala Tours & Travels
17 Paul Merchant's Ltd (Western Union)
18 Eagle Height Trekkers & Travellers
19 Telecom Office; Police Post
20 Taxi Stand
21 Nowrojee & Son Store; Beer & Wine Shop
22 Bus Stand
27 Video Hall
29 DIIR Bookshop
30 Chörten & Prayer Wheels
33 New Karyana Shop (Motorcycle Hire)
34 Charitrust Bookshop & Handicraft Emporium
37 Himachal Travels
39 Video Hall
40 Summit Adventures
41 Dr Yeshi Dhonden's Clinic
43 Office of Tibetan Handicrafts
45 State Bank of India
46 Dr Lobsang Dolma Clinic
47 Bookworm
48 HPTDC Tourist Office
49 Buddhist Bookshop
50 Tibetan Craft Shops
51 Post Office
52 Pema Youdon
54 Tibtronics Internet
55 Stitches of Time

INDIA

1989, he was awarded the Nobel Peace Prize, presented to him primarily for his endeavours to find a peaceful solution in his struggles for the liberation of Tibet.

Accommodation can be especially tight during Losar (Tibetan New Year), the Dalai Lama's birthday (6 July) and other Tibetan festivals.

Orientation

The heart of McLeod Ganj is the bus stand. From here roads radiate to various points around the township; the two main roads through the bazaar run parallel to the south towards the Tsuglagkhang Temple, 500m away. The main road back down to Dharamsala passes the church of St John in the Wilderness and the cantonment area of Forsyth Ganj. Other roads lead to the villages of Dharamkot and Bhagsu.

Further south (about a 20-minute walk via Jogibara Rd) is the administrative area of Gangchen Kyishong, including the Library of Tibetan Works & Archives.

Information

Tourist Offices The HPTDC office (☎ 21205), opposite Bookworm, is open from 10 am to 1.30 pm and 2 to 5 pm daily. The notice board next to Hotel India House on the Bhagsu road is worth a look for information on courses, local entertainment and coming events.

Money The State Bank of India, near the post office, is open from 10.30 am to 1.30 pm weekdays and from 10.30 to 11.30 am Saturday. It changes American Express, Thomas Cook and Visa travellers cheques in US dollars and pounds sterling only. Paul Merchants Ltd, near the bus stand, is a useful moneychanger and a Western Union representative; in theory you can have money wired from abroad within minutes. There are more moneychangers on Jogibara Rd in the bazaar.

Post & Communications The post office is on Jogibara Rd, just past the State Bank of India. To post parcels you need to complete a customs form, which you can get at the Office of Tibetan Handicrafts opposite the State Bank of India. This form is not required for posting books. There are several places offering a parcel-packing service, including a couple on Jogibara Rd. Letters

sent c/o poste restante, GPO McLeod Ganj are held for one month.

The telecom office is up a flight of stairs opposite the bus stand; however, none of the facilities were working when we visited. There are several private STD/ISD offices in the bazaar.

Several places, mostly guesthouses, offer reasonably reliable Internet access for Rs 90 per hour. One of the best places is the Internet cafe at the Hotel Himalaya on Bhagsu road. Also good is the Green Cyber Cafe at the Green Hotel, Skyline next to Tibetan Ashoka Guest House, and Tibtronics on Jogibara Rd.

Travel Agencies There are numerous travel agencies in McLeod Ganj, some attached to hotels or guesthouses. Reliable outfits include Potala Tours & Travels (☎ 21378), opposite the Hotel Tibet; Dhauladhar Travels (☎ 21158) Temple Rd; and Himachal Travels (☎ 21428, ℮ himachaltravels@vsnl.com), Jogibara Rd.

Bookshops & Publications McLeod Ganj is a good place to buy, sell or swap reading matter, as well as to look for books on Tibetan culture. There's an excellent selection of new books at Bookworm. The Department of Information & International Relations (DIIR) shop next to the Snow Lion Guest House on Jogibara Rd has a comprehensive selection of books as well as government publications on the Tibetan struggle for independence and Tibetan Buddhism. The nearby Charitrust Bookshop has probably the town's best collection of books on Tibetan travel, history and Buddhism. Buddhist Bookshop and Youtse Bookshop, on Temple Rd, are also worth a look.

Contact is a free monthly local magazine which has a useful 'what's on' listing, plus information on local courses and volunteer work. You can usually pick up a copy in guesthouses and cafes. Other journals published in McLeod include the *Tibetan Bulletin* and *Rangzen* (Freedom), published by the Tibetan Youth Congress.

Trekking Companies Eagle Height Trekkers & Travellers (☎ 21330), on Mall Rd, can organise porters and guides, as well as arrange treks in the Kullu, Chamba, Lahaul and Spiti Valleys and Ladakh from

Vehicles and pedestrians vie for space on India's city streets.

Scooters, a popular form of Indian local transport

Tata buses and trucks are seen all over India.

India's distinctive Ambassador taxis

Elephant and mahout below Amber Fort

Catching a deserved kip between jobs.

A novel school bus!

A well-laden cycle-rickshaw

US$40 per day. It also offers a three- to four-day trek over the Indrahar Pass.

Yeti Trekking (☎ 21887) also arranges tailor-made treks to most areas, with accommodation en route in huts and houses. It can be found in a fine old building, reached through a gate off the Dharamkot road. Summit Adventures (☎ 21679, e summit65@yahoo.com), in the bazaar on Jogibara Rd, also hires guides (Rs 600 per day) and organises treks of several days.

Regional Mountaineering Centre The Regional Mountaineering Centre (☎ 21787) is about a 15-minute walk north of McLeod Ganj on the Dharamkot road. You can get advice here on treks and mountaineering in the Chamba and Kangra Valleys, and staff can recommend local guides and porters. It's a good idea to advise the centre if you are planning a serious trek.

You may be able to hire basic equipment such as sleeping bags and tents from here. You can also purchase Survey of India trekking maps (Rs 45) and the paperback *Treks & Passes of Dhauladhar & Pir Panjal* (Rs 150) by SR Saini, the centre's director. The centre is open from 10 am to 5 pm daily, except Sunday.

Tibetan Organisations McLeod Ganj has numerous offices and organisations concerned with Tibetan affairs and the welfare of the refugee community. These include the Tibetan Welfare Office, the Refugee Reception Centre, Tibetan Youth Congress, Tibetan Children's Village and the Tibetan Women's Association. Interested visitors are welcome at many of these.

To find out when the Dalai Lama is to give a public audience (there's usually one a month while he's in residence), contact the Branch Security Office (☎ 21560) at the Tibetan Welfare Office on the Bhagsu road in McLeod Ganj. You should register two or three days in advance, and turn up at the temple one hour before the audience to get through security checks – make sure you have your passport. Cameras, bags and backpacks are prohibited and you should wear respectable dress.

Tsuglagkhang Complex

This complex, a five-minute walk south of McLeod Ganj, comprises the official resi-dence of the Dalai Lama, as well as the Namgyal Monastery, Tibet Museum, a bookshop and cafe and the Tsuglagkhang itself.

The **Tsuglagkhang**, or Central Chapel, is the exiled government's equivalent of the Jokhang Temple in Lhasa and as such is the most important Buddhist monument in McLeod Ganj. Although a relatively modest structure, it enshrines three magnificent images, including an enormous 3m-high gilt statue of Sakyamuni Buddha. To the left of this (and facing Tibet) are statues of Avalokitesvara (Tibetan: Chenresig), the Tibetan deity of compassion, of whom the Dalai Lama is considered an incarnation, and Padmasambhava (Tibetan: Guru Rinpoche), the Indian scholar who introduced Buddhism and Tantric teachings to Tibet in the 8th century. Inside the Avalokiteshvara statue are several relics rescued from the Jokhang Temple during the Cultural Revolution.

Also housed in the temple is a collection of sacred texts known as the *Kangyur*, which are based on the teachings of the Buddha, as well as the *Tangyur*, which are translations of commentaries based on the Buddha's teachings. The mural to the side depicts the trio of ancient Tibetan kings who oversaw the introduction of Buddhism into Tibet.

Next to the Tsuglagkhang is the **Kalachakra Temple**, built in 1992, which houses a stunning mural of the Kalachakra (Wheel of Time) mandala. Sand mandalas are created here annually on the 5th day of the 3rd Tibetan month. Photography is allowed in the Tsuglagkhang, but not in the Kalachakra Temple.

The **Tibet Museum**, just inside the entrance to the complex, was opened in April 2000. In a series of graphic black-and-white photos, videos and personal accounts it chronicles the Tibetan struggle from the Chinese army 'liberation' in 1950 through the Tibetan resistance to the Dalai Lama's exile. The museum is open from 10 am to 1 pm and 2 to 6 pm daily except Monday (Rs 5).

The remaining buildings form the **Namgyal Gompa**, where you can watch monks philosophise most afternoons. Most Tibetan pilgrims make a *kora* (circuit) of the Tsuglagkhang complex, which should be walked in a clockwise direction only. Take the road to the left, past the entrance to the temple, and after a few minutes a small path leads

Tibetan Medicine

'Take one urine sample and see me in the morning.' That could be the slogan for Dr Yeshi Donden, former physician to the Dalai Lama. Dr Yeshi now runs a thriving private clinic in McLeod Ganj, dispensing Tibetan herbal medicines to locals and tourists alike for everything from toothache to gangrene.

Consultations are free, although you might find yourself spending quite a while in the crowded waiting room. All you have to do is take along your first urine of the morning (before eating) and submit to a short examination and a few questions, made via a translator. Even if you don't think you have a physical ailment, Dr Yeshi has a knack of probing into your unknown aches and pains. And he has the urine. You'll be given a prescription for some traditional Tibetan medicine, which can be filled at the dispensary on the way out. The clinic is down a small side street off Jogibara Rd, just north of the Tibetan Handicrafts Cooperative.

The clinic of another Tibetan physician, Dr Lobsang Dolma Khangsar, is nearby.

off to the right, eventually looping all the way around the Dalai Lama's residence back to the entrance to the temple. The path is flanked by colourful *mani* stones (stones carved with a mantra) and prayer flags, and at one stage there is a series of small prayer wheels and two giant prayer wheels.

Library of Tibetan Works & Archives

The library (☎ 22467), halfway between Dharamsala and McLeod at Gangchen Kyishong (Tibetan Government in Exile complex) is the repository of Tibet's rich literary heritage. It contains about 40% of Tibet's original manuscripts, as well as an excellent general reference library, and is open to all.

There's also a **Tibetan Cultural Museum** on the 1st floor, with some excellent exhibits including fine statues, rare Tibetan stamps and a medal from the Younghusband mission to Lhasa. Entry costs Rs 5.

Also worth a visit near the library complex is the **Nechung Monastery**, which is home to the Tibetan state oracle. He occasionally conducts a public ceremony during which he slips into a trance. Word of mouth is the best way to find out if and when this is happening.

Tibetan Medical & Astrological Institute

This institute is at Gangchen Kyishong, about a five-minute walk below the main entrance to the library area. There's a museum, library, research unit and a college at which Tibetan medicine and astrology are taught.

Dip Tse-Chok Ling Gompa

The beautiful little Dip Tse-Chok Ling Gompa is at the bottom of a steep track leading off the lane past the Om Hotel. The main *du-khang* (prayer hall) houses an image of Sakyamuni and two enormous goat-skin drums made by monks at the *gompa* (monastery). There are some superb butter sculptures, made during Losar and destroyed the following year, and sand mandalas.

Church of St John in the Wilderness

Dharamsala was originally a British hill resort, and one of the most poignant memories of that era is the pretty Church of St John in the Wilderness. It's a 1km walk north of McLeod Ganj on the main road to Dharamsala.

Walking

The best day hike around McLeod Ganj is the walk to Triund and Ilaqa (see the boxed text 'Hiking in the Shadow of Dhauladhar' for details). Other interesting short walks include the 2km stroll east to **Bhagsu**. If you continue walking through Bhagsu, past the Shiva temple and the bathing pool there's a path leading to a waterfall (1km). A stiff 2km walk north-east of McLeod Ganj brings you to the little village of **Dharamkot**, where you can take in the lovely views. From Dharamkot, you can continue east down to Bhagsu and loop back to McLeod Ganj along the main Bhagsu road.

Longer hikes include the walk north-west to Dal Lake from where you can continue 13km to the village of Kareri. From here

Hiking in the Shadow of Dhauladhar

The best day hike from McLeod Ganj is the 9km ascent to Triund. You can continue on to Ilaqa and return to McLeod Ganj in a long day (about eight hours) but this walk is worth spreading over two days, camping at either Ilaqa or Triund.

Starting from McLeod Ganj, take the road up towards Dharamkot. Facing north from the entrance to the Vipassana Meditation Centre, take the back road on the left and then the rocky path immediately to the right. This takes you through a stand of pines, past a small quarry and up to the whitewashed Shiva temple and tea stall. Continue eastwards on the path (around the back of the tea stall) and along the ridge. After about 45 minutes of following the ridge, there's another drinks stall and good views down to McLeod Ganj, Bhagsu and Dharamkot. There's another 30 minutes of walking on a good path before the trail starts to get steeper for the final 45 minutes up to Triund (2842m). The view when you crest the ridge is superb, with the two main peaks of the Dhauladhar range smack bang in front of you. They're known locally as the Matterhorn Peak (5048m) and Moon Peak (4610m).

Triund isn't a village. It's merely a small, grassy plateau with a makeshift tea stall and the Forest Rest House. At a ridiculous Rs 1000 a night, you're better off bringing a tent. The beauty of camping overnight at Triund is rising to see the dawn on the Dhauladhar range. Although there is food available here, it might be wise to bring some supplies.

The 5km walk to Ilaqa takes about another 1½ hours. The trail is difficult to pick up at first, but if you walk up towards the prayer flags on the side of the valley above Triund, it soon becomes apparent. After you pass the tea stall at Ilaqa you can continue walking to the ice flow and up to some caves in the mountainside. Mist and clouds descend here after noon, so it's best to make it to Ilaqa in the morning.

To continue beyond Ilaqa, over the Indrahar Pass (4350m), requires a guide and mountaineering equipment.

---

ou can return to McLeod Ganj via Ghera nd Satobri. There's camping and a Forest Rest House at Kareri and a camp site at Jhera. Another option, if you have several ays to spare, is to continue beyond Kareri illage a further 13km uphill to Kareri Lake t 3300m, where there's another camp site. or this you should organise a guide in Kareri (around Rs 200 per day) or join an rganised trek from McLeod Ganj. For nore information on these hikes, ask at the Regional Mountaineering Centre or Eagle Height Trekkers & Travellers (see Information earlier).

Courses

here seems to be a limitless supply of Courses on offer in McLeod Ganj. In keeping with the scene here, most have an emphasis on spirituality and advancing the mind and body. Apart from asking around, he best place to find out what's on is the listings section of *Contact* magazine, or by necking notice boards in the bazaar or at Juesthouses.

Buddhist Philosophy & Meditation

Dhamma Sikhara Vipassana Meditation Centre (☎ 21309, ✉ dhsikhara@yahoo .com) in Dharamkot offers 10-day residential meditation courses, described as 'mental purification through self-observation'. The courses are free (costs are met by donation) but the rules are strict: Participants must stay on site and maintain a 'noble silence' – which means no communication with anyone except your teacher. Information and registration are available only between 4 and 5 pm Monday to Saturday. To get there, walk up the road past the Regional Mountaineering Centre and bear left. The entrance is at the top of the hill.

On the way up to Dharamkot is the Tushita Meditation Centre (☎ 21866, ✉ tushita@ndf.vsnl.net.in). One path heads off to the right near a small white *chörten* (Tibetan pagoda) just beyond the Regional Mountaineering Centre, another leads in from Dharamkot village. The centre has facilities for personal retreats, and also offers a regular 11-day introductory course in

Buddhist philosophy led by Western and Tibetan teachers. There's a suggested donation of Rs 300 per day to cover food and accommodation costs in this residential course. Again, participants observe a regime of silence and don't leave the site. The office is open for information and registration from 9.30 to 11.30 am and 1 to 4.30 pm Monday to Saturday, but courses usually need to be booked in advance. Both Dhamma Sikhara and Tushita are closed from December to the end of February.

Down at the library (☎ 22467, @ ltwa@ndf.vsnl.net.in) in Gangchen Kyishong, classes in specific aspects of Buddhist philosophy are led by Tibetan lamas and translated into English. Subjects are divided into two-week chunks, as outlined in the prospectus available from reception. They take place from 9 to 11 am weekdays, and cost Rs 100 per month, plus Rs 50 registration. It's possible to attend the first class for free.

Yoga There are several yoga courses held around McLeod Ganj and some guesthouses offer morning yoga sessions. The Himalayan Iyengar Yoga Centre (☎ 21312) in Dharamkot has five-day courses starting every Thursday in May, June, October and November (Rs 800). There are also intensive three-week courses which vary in price but can cost up to US$400.

There's meditation and Iyengar yoga classes (all levels) in the morning and evening at the Ekant Lodge (contact Shivam on ☎ 21593). Week-long courses start every Monday.

Language Courses The Library of Tibetan Works & Archives (☎ 22467) also runs Tibetan-language courses for beginners and advanced students. Classes are held on weekdays and are divided into three terms of three months. Beginner and advanced courses both cost Rs 200 per month, plus a Rs 50 registration.

There are several private Tibetan-language classes held in the village. Pema Youdon is a friendly Tibetan woman who teaches from her home opposite the post office. Some guesthouses also offer private classes: Check notice boards or listings in *Contact*. Hindi- and Chinese-language courses are also available.

Massage & Reiki Ayurvedic, Thai massage and reiki are all available. The School of Ayurvedic Massage (☎ 6192), next to the Spring Valley Hotel in Bhagsu, has pricey 10-day courses in the Kerala tradition at US$100. Vajrayana Meditation & Healing Arts Centre, off Jogibara Rd on a road leading to the Tsuglagkhang complex, has shiatsu massage training (from 9 am to 1 pm weekdays), as well as yoga and Buddhist meditation.

Tibetan Cooking You can learn Tibetan cooking at Llamo's Kitchen on the ground floor of the Tashi Choeling Monastery on Jogibara Rd. Classes are held for two hours every evening and a three-day course costs Rs 400. A short course (one day) is Rs 140.

Organised Tours
The Bhagsu taxi operators union (☎ 21034), which has a makeshift office near the bus stand in McLeod Ganj, has fixed-rate taxi tours to points of interest around McLeod Ganj and in the Kangra Valley:

• Bhagsunath Temple, Tsuglagkhang, Dal Lake St John's Church & Talnu (Rs 250, three hours)
• Norbulingka, Chinmaya ashram at Tapovan, Chamunda Devi, Kangra & Jawalamukhi temple (Rs 1000, eight hours)
• Norbulingka, Tapovan, Chamunda Devi, Palampur & Baijnath (Rs 1000, eight hours)

Travel agencies in McLeod Ganj can arrange similar tours.

Special Events
Each April the Tibetan Institute of Performing Arts (TIPA) convenes the **Shoton Festival**, an operatic event including folk dancing and contemporary and historical plays. There is also a three-day **TIPA Anniversary Festival** from 27 May, celebrating the foundation of the institute. Details of these and other performances are posted around McLeod Ganj.

Tibetan New Year (Losar), around late February/March (depending on the lunar calendar), when the Dalai Lama gives week-long **spring teachings**, is a great time to be in McLeod Ganj.

The Dalai Lama's birthday (6 July) is another popular time to be here; there are public celebrations and the Dalai Lama sometimes gives a public audience.

Voluntary Work

If you're interested in teaching English or computer skills to newly arrived refugees, check notice boards at the Library of Tibetan Works & Archives or look in *Contact* magazine. There are several schools in McLeod Ganj that welcome classroom helpers, as well as private groups seeking conversational English.

Places to Stay

McLeod Ganj has many guesthouses to choose from, mostly Tibetan-run and predominantly in the budget category with singles/doubles from as little as Rs 50/75. There's also a selection of mid-range hotels south of town past the tourist office. Most hotels and guesthouses have hot water, but not all supply heating in rooms, so winter can be pretty uncomfortable.

Some travellers find McLeod Ganj a bit crowded these days, especially from March to July, so quieter guesthouses in Bhagsu, 2km east, and Dharamkot, a stiff walk to the north, are an alternative. If you're planning on hanging around for a while, to complete a course or take a break from travelling, ask around about renting a room long-term. The tiny village of Dusallan, halfway between McLeod Ganj and Bhagsu, has several places where you can rent a room for around Rs 50 per day.

Places to Stay – Budget

McLeod Ganj Many of the budget guesthouses are just off the Bhagsu road, or in the streets around Jogibara Rd – all within easy walking distance of the bus stand.

Tibetan Ashoka Guest House (☎ 21763), tucked down a side street off Jogibara Rd, is clean and secure. Singles/doubles with shared bathroom start at Rs 55/90 and the better upper-floor rooms with private bathroom cost Rs 275/330.

Green Hotel (☎ 21200), on the Bhagsu road, is a long-time favourite with travellers – perhaps too popular these days judging by the level of indifference in the staff. Small, spartan basement rooms with shared bathroom cost Rs 50/80, or Rs 150 for a dingy double with private cold-water bathroom, up to Rs 350 for a reasonably comfortable upstairs room with balcony. *Kunga Guest House* (☎ 21180) is a friendlier place although the rooms are nothing special.

Doubles with shared bathroom cost Rs 100 and larger upper-floor rooms with private bathroom are Rs 250. The actor Richard Gere is rumoured to have stayed here!

Shangrila Guest House, opposite the chörten on Jogibara Rd, is a cheapie with doubles with shared bathroom (bucket hot water) for Rs 70. *Snow Lion Guest House*, next door, is friendly and has clean, well-maintained doubles for Rs 120/250 without/with private bathroom.

On the other side of the chörten, *Kailash Hotel* (☎ 21044, Temple Rd) has plain rooms for Rs 100, all with shared bathroom (24-hour hot water). Rooms at the back have great views, but are pretty rustic.

Om Hotel (☎ 21313, Nowrojee Rd), on a path leading down from the bus stand behind the Kailash, has ground-floor doubles with shared bathroom for Rs 80 and nicer upper-floor rooms with private bathroom for Rs 225 or Rs 250. There's a good restaurant and a terrace with lovely valley views.

There are several reasonable places along the road to the Tibetan Institute of Performing Arts (TIPA). *Seven Hills Guest House* (☎ 21580, TIPA Rd) has basic rooms but it's a well-equipped place with a beauty parlour, Korean restaurant, trekking guides and hot showers. Doubles with shared bathroom are Rs 80 or Rs 100, a double with private bathroom is Rs 175. Up a small set of steps to the left are three more places. *Kalsang Guest House* (☎ 21709) has large but threadbare doubles with private bathroom and hot shower for Rs 275, singles/doubles with shared bathroom for Rs 50/85 and a smaller double with bathroom for Rs 150. There are good views from the terrace.

Loselling Guest House (☎ 21072) has rooms with shared bathroom for Rs 50/85 (hot shower is Rs 10), or Rs 190 for a double with private bathroom. There's a good rooftop terrace but only breakfast is served here. *Paljor Gakyil Guest House* (☎ 21443), above the Loselling, has singles with shared bathroom for Rs 45, and doubles with bathroom for Rs 132. It's a clean, quiet place.

Heading south down Jogibara Rd past the post office you'll find a number of pleasant guesthouses away from the hustle of the main bazaar. *Ladies Venture* (☎ 21559), down past the Chocolate Log (see Places to Eat), is a very quiet and friendly place. Small rooms with bathroom but no view are

Rs 150/275; comfortable triples with a view cost Rs 400. Dorms cost Rs 50 but they are often full.

Bhagsu About 2km east of McLeod is the village of Bhagsu, or Bhagsunath, which has springs and a small Shiva temple built by the Raja of Kangra in the 16th century. There's a cluster of guesthouses and restaurants along the road to your left as you approach the temple.

Pink & White Hotel (☎ 21209) has doubles with private bathroom starting at Rs 200 (Rs 150 in off season), and better upperfloor rooms with balcony and views from Rs 300 to Rs 550. Next door, *Lucky House* (no phone) is a cheap but clean option attached to a family home and small cafe. The small single/double with outside toilet is Rs 40/50.

Directly across the road, *Oakview Guest House* had just opened when we visited (no phone) and is an immaculately new place. Carpeted rooms with balcony cost Rs 300 and a smaller single is Rs 250. There's a cafe and friendly management.

If you take the path leading uphill from the main bus/taxi stand you come to another clutch of backpacker places. *Seven Seas Lodge*, off the path to the left, has clean and spacious marble-clad rooms for Rs 200 (ground floor) and Rs 250 (1st floor). Further uphill is the *Omni Guest House* with five basic but pleasant double rooms with shared bathroom for Rs 100. These places both have restaurants attached and neither are connected to the telephone.

Dharamkot *Hotel New Blue Heaven (☎ 21005)* is one of several guesthouses down the hill below the entrance to the Vipassana Meditation Centre. Large but simple rooms with private bathroom cost Rs 175/225. There's also a restaurant here.

Places to Stay – Mid-Range
Hotel Tibet (☎ 21587), a few steps from the bus stand on the Bhagsu road, has standard doubles for Rs 550, semi-deluxe doubles for Rs 660 and deluxe rooms for Rs 990. All rooms are carpeted and have cable TV and bathroom. There's a very good restaurant and bar here.

Cloud's End Villa (☎ 22109) is a great place for a splurge. The residence of the Raja of Lambagraon-Kangra, it's inconveniently

located roughly halfway between Dharamsala and Gangchen Kyishong, but the five rooms have all the classic colonial trappings and range from Rs 770 to Rs 1250.

Other good mid-range places include the HPTDC's *Hotel Bhagsu (☎ 21091)* and *Chonor House Hotel (☎ 21006)*, both on the road heading south past the tourist office.

Places to Eat
The variety and quality of some of the food available in McLeod Ganj will come as a pleasant surprise to overland travellers who have just come from Pakistan and Iran. Here you can get Chinese, Japanese, passable Italian, continental, Indian and, naturally, Tibetan. Passing a few hours chatting in cafes is part of daily life here, and there are some fabulous sweets and desserts on offer.

Restaurants *Nick's Italian Kitchen* has some of the best cheap food around with a mix of Tibetan and Italian cuisine at around Rs 30 to Rs 50.

The nearby *Himalaya Cafe* also has good food and a wonderful rooftop balcony with views over the plains. You can get filter coffee here and refill your bottle with boiled and filtered water for Rs 5.

Friend's Corner and *McLlo Restaurant*, near the bus stand, are two popular restaurants in the evening, where you can get a reasonably priced beer and large portions of decent (though not outstanding) Indian or Chinese food.

Ashoka Restaurant, on Jogibara Rd, has perhaps the best Indian food in town. The tandoori chicken and chicken Mughlai (around Rs 100) are excellent. *Norling Restaurant*, opposite, is a simple place that does very good Tibetan.

Lung-ta, down past the Chocolate Log (see Cafes & Bakeries later) on Jogibara Rd, is McLeod's only Japanese restaurant, and the food is authentic and tasty. There's a filling set menu (Rs 100) and all other dishes are under Rs 40. Tuesday and Friday are vegetable sushi days. Profits here go to Gu-Chu-Sun, an NGO benefiting Tibetan prisoners of conscience. It's closed on Sunday.

Amdo Cha-Chung Restaurant on Jogibara Rd south of the post office does good Tibetan and Western food (all under Rs 40) and has a lovely terrace dining area with mountain views.

Hotel Tibet has one of the best restaurants in town and features Tibetan, Chinese and Indian cuisine. There's also a convivial bar here. The restaurant at *Hotel Bhagsu* is pricier but has very good food and cold beers. On sunny days, tables are set up in the gardens, and you can eat outside.

Cafes & Bakeries *Sunrise Cafe* on the Bhagsu road near Potala Tours & Travels is a popular dhaba where travellers congregate for a cheap *thali* (traditional 'all-you-can-eat' vegetarian meal), chai and a chat. Good places for snacks and Tibetan food in the bazaar include the hole-in-the-wall *Snowland Restaurant*, recommended for cheap, tasty Tibetan food; *Gakyi Restaurant* with a good range of vegetarian food and muesli; and the bright *Tea O'Clock Cafe*, opposite the bus stand, with good cakes, coffee and classical music. The restaurant at the *Snow Lion Guesthouse* does great garlic-fried potatoes and Tibetan meals. *Green Hotel* has a very popular restaurant, with a range of excellent home-made cakes, as well as vegetarian dishes and Tibetan standards such as *momos* (fried dumplings with vegetables or meat). It's also a good place for breakfast, and nothing on the menu is over Rs 40.

Malabar Cafe, opposite the chörten on Jogibara Rd, and the nearby *Cafe Shambhala*, are two more cosy little places serving good Indian, Chinese and continental dishes. There's another string of cafes along Temple Rd on the way to the Tsuglagkhang complex.

Nechung Cafe opposite the Library of Tibetan Works & Archives does filling lunches of rice and vegetable curry for Rs 20.

McLeod Ganj is heaven for anyone with a longing for coffee and cake. *Chocolate Log*, a short walk down past the post office on Jogibara Rd, is an old favourite serving Western dishes such as pizza and various types of cakes. *Namgyal Cafe* in the Tsuglagkhang complex also does superb cakes (especially anything with chocolate), great coffee and French-influenced light meals. It's open from 11 am to 8.30 pm daily except Monday.

There's a *bakery* beneath the Hotel Tibet in McLeod Ganj where you can buy freshly baked bread, cakes and doughnuts.

There are a handful of good cafes, dhabas and restaurants out at Bhagsu. *Oasis Cafe & German Bakery*, just past Hotel Pink & White, is a popular spot with outdoor seating and a menu featuring Indian, Chinese, Israeli, Mexican and Italian food, mostly under Rs 60. *Cafe Jaldara*, on the main road near the temple, has a range of south Indian dishes.

Entertainment

The travellers' scene in McLeod Ganj means there's always something going on. *McLlo Restaurant* and *Friend's Corner* near the bus stand both turn into drinking and music venues later in the evening. A bottle of beer costs Rs 60 to Rs 70 in either. Down in Bhagsu, there's a Saturday night *disco* at the Spring Valley Hotel, although this consists mainly of a lot of local boys lurking around in a darkened room. Entry is Rs 50. Open air 'full moon' parties are often arranged in season – you only need to ask around to find out where and when.

There are several *video halls* in the town centre on Jogibara Rd. They show new release movies and documentaries on Tibet all day and evening, with the program posted out the front. Tickets are usually Rs 10. *Namgyal Cafe* in the temple complex has a dinner and film night every Friday.

Pool (or billiards) is another popular pastime. *Cue Ball* at the Lotus Hotel on Jogibara Rd has plenty of tables and charges Rs 60 a game.

The Tibetan Institute of Performing Arts (TIPA) promotes the study and performance of the Tibetan performing arts, the most important being traditional *lhamo* (Tibetan folk opera). You may be able to attend practice sessions and concerts here. In addition, everything from dancing to contemporary theatre and Tibetan rock music is learned and performed here. Tibetan weddings are also held here and if you ask around it's usually no problem for visitors to come along and watch the ceremony.

Shopping

Tibetan textiles such as bags, *chubas* (dresses worn by Tibetan women), hats and trousers can be found at the Office of Tibetan Handicrafts, just north of the State Bank of India.

Just opposite is the Tibetan Handicrafts Cooperative. The co-op employs about 150 people, many of them newly arrived refugees, in the weaving of Tibetan carpets.

INDIA

Fine New Zealand wool carpets, with 48 knots per square inch, are Rs 2306 per square metre for a simple design, Rs 2487 for something more complex. The society can pack and post purchases home, and visitors are welcome to watch the carpet makers at work on traditional looms.

Stitches of Time, further downhill on Temple Rd, is run by the Tibetan Women's Association, and also makes chubas and other clothes to order.

The Green Shop, on the Bhagsu road, has hand-painted T-shirts and recycled hand made paper.

Getting There & Away

The Himachal Roadways Transport Corporation (HRTC) booking office is at the bus stand. You can also use the office to book buses leaving from Dharamsala. There are four daily buses from McLeod Ganj to Delhi, all travelling overnight and taking roughly 12 hours. The semi-deluxe is Rs 267 and the super-deluxe (7 pm) is Rs 346. There are also daily public buses to Manali and Dehra Dun. There are several daily buses to Pathankot (Rs 60, four hours) which go via Dharamsala. For other services, such as those to Shimla, you'll have to head down to Dharamsala (see that section earlier).

Several travel agents and guesthouses sell tickets for deluxe private buses to Delhi, Manali, Dehra Dun and even Leh. The Delhi bus (Rs 350, 12 hours) leaves at 6 pm. When booking a bus to Delhi check whether it goes to Connaught Place and/or Paharganj, or just to the Inter State Bus Terminal at Kashmiri Gate. The bus to Manali costs Rs 225 (some places charge Rs 250), takes 10 hours and leaves at 9 am.

There are buses for the 40-minute trip down to Dharamsala (Rs 6), departing every 30 minutes between 4.15 am and 8.30 pm. Cramped passenger jeeps also run when full for the same price.

Getting Around

McLeod's taxi stand (☎ 21034) is next to the bus stand and fixed rates apply to all destinations. Taxis cost Rs 40 to Bhagsu, Rs 50 to Dharamkot, Rs 50 to Gangchen Kyishong, Rs 80 to Dharamsala's Kotwali Bazaar, Rs 90 to Dharamsala bus station and Rs 200/300 one way/return to Norbulingka. It's an extra Rs 50 to continue to the Gyuto Ramoche Monastery. There's

---

An Audience with the Karmapa

On 5 January, 2000, the 17th Karmapa, spiritual leader of the Karma Kagyu tradition of Tibetan Buddhism, joined the Dalai Lama in exile in Dharamsala. The 14-year-old Urgyen Trinley Dorje had reportedly fled Tibet after Chinese officials refused to allow him access to important religious teachers in India.

Just like the Dalai Lama before him, he slipped out of his monastery in Lhasa (thoughtfully leaving a note to say he was just off to a religious retreat) and, with a small band of monks, trekked for at least five days over the Himalaya to Dharamsala – in the middle of winter! One of the interesting things about the Karmapa, from a lineage that has been going on since the 12th century, is that he is the only lama recognised by both China and Tibet, so the Chinese weren't particularly keen to lose him. The young lama was born in Tibet in 1985 and was 'discovered' and recognised as the reincarnate Karmapa in 1992, following the death of the 16th Karmapa in 1981.

When we visited, the Karmapa was installed in Gyuto Ramoche Monastery, about 2km from Norbulingka Institute, and was generously giving a public audience at 2 pm daily. To attend, simply turn up at the monastery about 15 minutes beforehand and register at a security desk outside (foreigners need to bring their passport). The audience takes place in the main hall of the monastery and each person in turn faces the Karmapa and is given a red ribbon or sash. Buddhist followers have the sash draped around their neck, others can take it in their hands. Dharma students can follow Buddhist tradition by offering a white scarf to the Karmapa.

The trip out to Gyuto Ramoche can be combined with a couple of hours at the Norbulingka Institute and lunch in the shady Norling Cafe.

another fixed-rate taxi stand at Gangchen Kyishong.

There are a few autorickshaws buzzing around the village. A ride to Bhagsu costs Rs 20 and to Dharamkot it's Rs 40.

Bicycles and motorcycles can be hired from a small shop (New Karyana) on Temple Rd. A 350cc Enfield costs Rs 350 per day; a scooter is Rs 300 per day.

AROUND DHARAMSALA
Norbulingka Institute

This complex, 14km from McLeod Ganj and 4km from Dharamsala, is set amid Japanese-influenced gardens with shady paths, wooden bridges across small streams and tiny waterfalls. Norbulingka was established to teach and preserve traditional Tibetan art, such as woodcarving, thangka painting, goldsmithing and embroidery. Craft shops display and sell the results of this work. The **Deden Tsuglakhang temple**, in the centre of the complex, has some impressive murals both in the entrance veranda, and in the large main hall. The library of the Academy of Tibetan Culture is also here.

Within the complex, *Norling Guesthouse (☎ 22664)* is pricey at US$20/25 for a single/double. The *Norling Cafe* is worth a stop for lunch though; the surrounding gardens are a very tranquil place to spend an afternoon and this can be combined with an audience with the Karmapa (see the boxed text).

To get here, catch a Yol-bound bus and ask to be let off at Sidhpur, near the Sacred Heart School. At this crossroad is a signpost to Norbulingka, from where it is about a 20-minute walk. A taxi from McLeod Ganj will cost Rs 200/300 one way/return.

SHIMLA
☎ 0177 • pop 123,000

Shimla, 235km south of Dharamsala, is up there with Darjeeling as the most famous of northern India's British-influenced hill stations. Full of colonial architecture and middle-class Indian tourists, it's worth the trip up here (preferably by toy train from Kalka) to see another side of Indian life.

Shimla was once part of the Nepalese kingdom and called Shyamala, another name for the goddess Kali, but it never gained any recognition until it was 'discovered' by the British in 1819. Three years later, the first 'British' house was erected, and in 1864 Shimla became the summer capital of India and remained an important retreat from the sweltering plains until 1939. Following independence, Shimla was initially the capital of the Punjab, then became the capital of Himachal Pradesh in 1966.

Today, Shimla is a pleasant, sprawling town, set among cool pine-clad hills with plenty of crumbling colonial charm. Some travellers find the place too 'touristy'; others who prefer the normal chaos and culture of India or the imported 'scenes' in McLeod Ganj and Manali may find it boring; but nostalgic history buffs will love it. In any case, at 2200m it's a pleasant place to be in summer and there are some nice walks in the surrounding hills.

High season is mid-April to mid-July, mid-September to late October and mid-December to mid-January (winter season). The best time to visit is mid-September to late November. In winter (December to February), the town and surrounding hills are blanketed in snow, but the main road usually remains open.

Orientation

There are only two roads in the central part of Shimla, but even so the town is scattered across a series of seven hills and getting around on foot can be demanding. The higher traffic-free Mall runs east–west, reaching its highest point at Scandal Point (or Scandal Corner). The large 'town square' known as The Ridge runs from Scandal Point up to Christ Church. Cart Rd circles the southern part of Shimla, and is where the bus and taxi stands and train station are; from here everywhere else is a steep hike away. The rest of Shimla is connected by a mass of lively bazaars and alleyways. Victory Tunnel goes under the western end of The Mall and links Cart Rd with Circular Rd.

Information

Tourist Offices The efficient HPTDC tourist office (☎ 252561) at Scandal Point provides local information and maps, and takes bookings for HPTDC buses and local tours. It's open from 8 am to 8 pm daily in the high season and 9 am to 6 pm in the low season. The other HPTDC kiosk down on Cart Rd can help with finding accommodation.

INDIA

SHIMLA

PLACES TO STAY
9 Ashoka Hotel; Hotel Uphar
    YWCA
26 YWCA
32 Vikrant Hotel
33 Hotel Ranjan
36 Hotel Fontaine Bleau
38 Hotel Dalzlel; Hotel Classic;
    Hotel Prakash
39 Bindu Raj Sood Dharamsala
43 The Cecil
45 Hotel Sangeet

PLACES TO EAT
13 City Point
14 Indian Coffee House; Devicos
    Restaurant; Hotel Loveena
    Palace
17 Dominoes Pizza
18 Baljee's Restaurant
21 Ashiana; Goofa; Quick Bite
23 Park Cafe
27 Food Dot.Com
28 Krishna Bakers
34 Local Dhabas

OTHER
1 Indira Gandhi Hospital
3 Rivoli Bus Station
4 Ice-Skating Rink; Rivoli Cinema

5 HPTDC Tourist Office (Main)
6 Rendezvous Restaurant
7 SCB Grindlays Bank
8 Main Post Office
10 UCO Bank
11 Central Telegraph Office
12 District Magistrate's Office
15 Punjab National Bank
16 Electronica Internet; Himachal
    Emporium
19 Town Hall
20 Gaiety Theatre; Trishool's
    Bakery
22 Himani's
24 Christ Church
25 Bandstand
29 Vishal Himachal Taxi Operators'
    Union Stand
30 Bank of Baroda; Gurdwara
    Sahib Shri Gura Singh Sabha
31 Kalka-Shimla Taxi Union Stand
35 Interstate Bus Terminal (ISBT)
37 State Bank of India
40 HPTDC Tourist Information
    Kiosk (Branch)
41 Himachal State Museum
42 Branch Post Office
44 Tibetan Refugee Handloom
    Shop
46 Jakhu Temple

Money The State Bank of India is in an impressive stone and mock-Tudor style building (once the home of the commander-in-chief of the British army) at the western end of The Mall. Don't bother going in though, as it charges Rs 20 per transaction, plus Rs 3 for every travellers cheque cashed. The UCO Bank and Punjab National Bank (the more easterly of the two branches on The Mall) change cash and travellers cheques with no fee. SCB Grindlays, at Scandal Point, charges an outrageous Rs 195 to change travellers cheques but is handy for cash advances on Visa and MasterCard, as is the Bank of Baroda, on Cart Rd. There are no ATMs.

Post & Communications The main post office, just west of Scandal Point, is open from 10 am to 6 pm Monday to Saturday and 10 am to 4 pm Sunday and public holidays. There's a reliable poste restante service located in a little cupboard at counter No 10. The central telegraph office (CTO), further west and on the other side of the road, is open 24 hours and is the cheapest place to make telephone calls and to send and receive faxes.

There's Internet access at the CTO (Rs 65 per hour), but the limited terminals are often busy. Electronica, on The Mall near Scandal Point, has more computers and charges Rs 20 for 15 minutes. The tourist office has Internet access for Rs 25 for 15 minutes.

Things to See & Do

The main attractions in Shimla are hiking in the surrounding forest and visiting the reminders of India's colonial past, notably the impressive **Viceregal Lodge**. Built in 1888, the lodge was formerly the residence of the British Viceroy Lord Dufferin, and is where many decisions affecting the destiny of the subcontinent were made, including the singing of the Partition agreement. Incredibly, every brick of the six-storey building was transported by mule (the railway wasn't built at that stage).

There are magnificent lawns, botanical gardens and a small cafe. Several rooms in the lodge, including the main hall and a small gallery, are open to the public, but the lodge's main role now is housing the Indian Institute of Advanced Study. The lodge is a pleasant 4.5km walk west of Scandal Point. It's open from 9 am to 1 pm and 2 to 7 pm

daily in summer, but closes a little earlier the rest of the year. Admission to the lodge and gardens, including a guided tour, costs Rs 10.

Only a brief sighting of a Monal pheasant (Himachal's state bird) can possibly make a visit to the **Himalayan Aviary** worthwhile. The rest of the wildlife (that isn't stuffed) seems to consist of geese and roosters. The aviary, on the road approaching the lodge, is open from 10 am to 5 pm daily except Monday (Rs 5).

The **Himachal State Museum** has a good collection of statues, miniatures, coins, photos and other items from around Himachal Pradesh and is worth a visit. It's open from 10 am to 5 pm daily except Monday (free). Photography is not allowed and you must check your bags in at the cloakroom. To get to the museum, take the middle of the three paths up the hill just past The Cecil Hotel.

Back at The Ridge, you can't miss **Christ Church** which, along with the black-and-white half-timbered house (a library) beside it, forms a surreal English backdrop. The church was built between 1846 and 1857 and is renowned for its stained-glass windows. You can discreetly have a look inside, or attend English-language services every Sunday morning during the tourist season.

If you start to feel like you're not in India any more, head down to the main **bazaar** or *mandi*, where twisting lanes packed with stalls and ringing with the cries of vendors will soon perk up your senses. The bustling Sabzi Mandi (Vegetable Market), also known as Lower Bazaar, is a maze of steep, circuitous lanes sandwiched between The Mall and Cart Rd. To get there, take any one of several alleys leading down from around Scandal Point. Cart Rd itself is more like India too – with traffic jams, exhaust fumes and dubious-looking dhabas, it seems a world away from the genteel Mall.

Walking

A popular early-morning walk is the 45-minute climb to the **Jakhu Temple** near Shimla Ridge (2455m). From Scandal Point, take the path up towards Hotel Dreamland and follow it around to the right. Bear left after this and you'll pass a crenellated wall on your left, and from there it's straight up, via some steps. The small temple is dedicated to Hanuman, the monkey god (appropriately, but not surprisingly, there are plenty of monkeys around). There are fine views over the surrounding valleys and, on a clear day, out towards snowcapped peaks.

Most of the other short walks to the west of Shimla are more like strolls in the countryside. **The Glen**, about 4km west of Scandal Point, is one of the former playgrounds of rich British colonialists. The turn-off is on the way to the state museum and goes through **Annandale**, another pretty area. This was the site of a famous racecourse, and cricket and polo are still played there. **Prospect Hill** is about 5km west of Shimla, and a 15-minute climb from Boileauganj. The hill is a popular picnic spot with fine views over the surrounding country. **Sankat Mochan**, 7km from Shimla, on the road to Chandigarh, has a Hanuman temple and fine views of Shimla. It can also be reached by taxi.

Freelance guides around Shimla will offer their services for around Rs 400 per day if you want to go on longer, overnight hikes. The tourist office can make recommendations for guides.

Organised Tours
The tourist office runs excellent 'Heritage Walks' at 11 am and 4 pm daily (Rs 50). They take about two hours and are led by informative English-speaking guides who explain Shimla's British heritage as you walk from Scandal Point to the Viceregal Lodge. You can book in advance or just turn up at the tourist office on the day.

HPTDC also organises the following daily sightseeing tours in the high season. Buses leave from Rivoli bus stand at 10 am.

- Kufri, Fagu, Mashobra & Naldehra (Rs 145)
- Fagu and Theog & Narkanda (Rs 180)
- Chail via Kufri (Rs 165)
- Naldehra & Tattapani hot springs (Rs 165)

Taxi unions offer similar, but more expensive, itineraries by private car.

The YMCA (see Places to Stay) arranges trekking, jeep safaris and camping trips in the region. These include a five-night trip into the Kullu Valley at Rs 1300 per person per day, all inclusive.

Places to Stay
Accommodation in Shimla is relatively expensive during the high season. In the low season, or when business is quiet, prices drop substantially, sometimes by as much as half, so always ask for a discount. Prices given here are for the high season. There are loads of places to stay in the mid-range and top-end categories but it's a bit more difficult to find good budget hotels.

Whether you arrive in Shimla by bus, train or taxi, expect to be greeted by touts wanting to lead you to a hotel. Unless you want their assistance, shake them off. By agreement, they get commission for taking you to a hotel, and you pay for it.

Places to Stay – Budget
The YMCA and YWCA both welcome men and women and are both reasonably good budget deals in high season, although you'll almost certainly do better at a private hotel in low season.

YMCA (☎ 252375) is popular and may be booked out (reservations are accepted by phone). There's a one-off Rs 40 membership charge. Singles/doubles with shared bathroom cost Rs 125/250, including breakfast. Hot water is available from 7 pm to 9 am. Doubles with hot bath cost Rs 430, including breakfast. Brand new rooms around the side are nice but expensive at Rs 700. There's no low-season discount but they might waive the membership fee. The hostel is clean and has a large common room with TV, plus a games room. It's not far past the Christ Church, up a laneway near a cinema.

YWCA (☎ 203081), above the main post office, isn't quite as good value but it's in a better location (with great views), has a garden and is a friendly old place. Small doubles with bathroom cost Rs 250/200 in high/low season (no singles), and bucket hot water is Rs 5. A four-bed room is Rs 350, and a large 'suite' with sitting room and attached hot-water shower is Rs 700/500 in high/low season. There's a Rs 20 temporary membership charge and cheap meals are available.

The friendly, family-run **Hotel Fontaine Bleau** (☎ 253549) has rooms in a cosy house for Rs 150 a single and from Rs 200 to Rs 500 for a double with bathroom. It's down a side road near the State Bank of India, at the western end of The Mall.

The cheapest areas are around the main bus station, and east along Cart Rd, but this is also the noisiest, dirtiest and least desirable part of town. Anything under Rs 100 here is usually a dive.

Hotel Ranjan (☎ 252818) is opposite the bus station and thus noisy, but the rooms are reasonable value. Clean, large doubles with bathroom cost Rs 200, triples are Rs 264 and a four-bed room is Rs 440. There are no singles.

Vikrant Hotel (☎ 253602), nearby, has singles with shared bathroom for Rs 165 and doubles with private bathroom for Rs 400; a bed in a five-bed dorm is Rs 73.

Around the Lakkar Bazaar area, a steep climb past The Ridge, are several reasonably priced places. *Hotel Uphar* (☎ 257670) is clean and used to backpackers. Threadbare doubles with hot shower are Rs 200; rooms for Rs 250 are nicer and the room with a view and minibalcony is Rs 425. All rooms have TV and there's a 50% discount during the low season. *Ashoka Hotel* (☎ 258166) is a reasonable place with doubles from Rs 300.

For the truly down and out, there are several *dharamsalas* (pilgrims' resthouses) and gurdwaras where you can sleep cheap, or even free (you should leave a donation). They include *Bindu Raj Sood Dharamsala* (☎ 20507) on Cart Rd west of the bus stand, and *Gurdwara Sahib Shri Guru Singh Sabha* (☎ 257336), next to Bank of Baroda on Cart Rd. These places are often full.

Places to Stay – Mid-Range

Mid-range rooms can be particularly good value in the low season, when a nice double with cable TV and hot water costs about Rs 250. Expect to pay double that in high season.

Just off The (western) Mall, a short walk up from the train station, are three reasonable places. *Hotel Prakash* (☎ 213321) has overpriced double rooms for Rs 440 and Rs 550 and a single for Rs 330. The friendly and comfortable *Hotel Classic* (☎ 253078) has poky singles but decent doubles for Rs 400 to Rs 500 with good views. *Hotel Dalziel* is the best of this bunch with doubles from Rs 350 to Rs 660, the latter being a comfortable, spacious room. You can get a 50% discount here during low season and they're open to bargaining any time.

Down at the far eastern end of The Mall, past the passenger lift, *Hotel Sangeet* (☎ 202506) is a good upper-end choice.

Clean, comfortable rooms with modern facilities (some with good views) cost Rs 700 to Rs 900 for doubles, and 50% discounts are given in low season.

Places to Eat

Shimla is well prepared to serve the holiday crowds so you'll find plenty of Indian, Chinese and continental restaurants and a burgeoning array of bright, Western-style fast-food places, particularly along The Mall. Down on Cart Rd, especially near the bus station, there are cheap dhabas and stalls serving the usual street food, and plenty of fruit and vegetable stalls.

Not many places open early for breakfast (most not until at least 9 am) but the *Indian Coffee House*, along The (western) Mall, throws open its doors at 8.30 am and serves reasonable breakfast fare (eggs, toast etc), south Indian snacks and good coffee. This is where traditionally dressed waiters hover around in fan-shaped head-gear. A *masala dosa* (curried vegetables inside a dosa) is Rs 20.

Park Cafe, just down The (eastern) Mall and up some stairs, is a cosy, ramshackle place popular with backpackers and young Indian tourists alike. It's laid-back with booth-style seating, has great music and is the perfect place to chill out in the evening. Good pizzas start at Rs 40 and most Indian meals (including a good veg thali) are less than Rs 50. There's an extensive breakfast menu and it opens at 9 am.

Devicos Restaurant, on The (western) Mall, near Scandal Point, is a clean, trendy place that does good, though a little overpriced, Indian, Chinese and Western food. Mains range from Rs 100 to Rs 200 and snacks start at Rs 50, including good sandwiches. There's a plush bar upstairs.

HPTDC has a building on The Ridge with three places to eat. *Ashiana* is about the best (and most expensive) for decor and service. *Goofa*, downstairs, serves a reasonable breakfast and *Quick Bite* has cheap pizzas and Indian food.

Good fast-food places to try include *Food Dot.Com* (it had to happen) down at the eastern end of The Mall, which has an open-fronted counter selling burgers (Rs 25) and pizzas (Rs 40); *Dominoes Pizza* with takeaway pizzas only (Rs 99 for a small with the lot); and *City Point* on The (western) Mall, great for pizzas, burgers and cakes.

There are several good bakeries in town, particularly on The Mall. *Trishool's*, next to the Gaiety Theatre, is recommended for mouth-watering sweets. *Baljee's* has a bakery counter at the front and *Krishna Bakers*, along The (eastern) Mall, does good cakes and pastries.

Entertainment

Probably the most popular entertainment in town is to stroll along The Mall and The Ridge and watch everyone else watching everyone else. On a summer evening it's like London's Oxford St at Christmas (minus the traffic and not as cold), with hordes of happy-looking tourists wandering back and forth. The views and lights in the early evening are quite atmospheric. There's a high bandstand at the eastern end of The Ridge (near Christ Church) where brass bands often play in summer. An ice-skating rink, down behind the tourist office, is open in winter – follow the signs from Scandal Point towards the Rivoli Bus Stand.

The lovely old *Gaiety Theatre* often has some shows or recitals, particularly in summer, but it's dressy in an English sort of way. The sign in the foyer advises: 'Sandals and casuals will not be worn by gentlemen after 7 pm'. Look out for notices about coming events or ask at the tourist office. *Rivoli Cinema* and *Ritz Cinema* sometimes show English-language films.

There are several restaurants that have bars where you can just go for a beer, but there's not much atmosphere. *Himani's* has a bar with big windows looking out over the valley, and (provided there are no families up there) you can drink out on the rooftop terrace. A beer costs Rs 75. Other places include the comfortable *Devico's*, and the rather dingy bar at *Rendezvous* on Scandal Point. Most top-end hotels have pricier bars.

Shopping

The Himachal Emporium on The (western) Mall has a reasonable collection of local handicrafts. The Tibetan Refugee Handloom Shop, at the other end of The Mall, is the showroom for a local development project and sells carpets, clothes and other Tibetan crafts. Woollen jumpers and carved walking sticks are popular items for sale in shops here.

Beyond The Ridge, the small but busy Lakkar Bazaar is the place for (cheap) souvenirs.

Getting There & Away

Air Indian Airlines flies three times weekly to/from Delhi (Rs 3000). Flights then continue on to Kullu (Rs 1500). Bookings can be made at the HPTDC office at Scandal Point. Shimla's airport is 23km south at Jubbarhatti.

Bus The large and chaotic Interstate Bus Terminal (ISBT) on Cart Rd might be difficult to make sense of if it wasn't for the very handy private computer booking booth (counter No 9). Staff here speak English, and you can book a ticket on any public bus up to a month ahead.

There are regular buses south to Chandigarh and Delhi, and north to Dharamsala and Manali. Buses to destinations east of Shimla depart from the Rivoli bus station, on the northern side of The Ridge, below the HPTDC office. Most private buses depart from the entrance to Victory Tunnel, about 500m west of the main bus stand on Cart Rd.

To Delhi & Chandigarh If you're in a hurry there are plenty of direct buses to Delhi, but if not, consider the toy train journey to Kalka and continue on from there (see Shimla to Kalka later).

There are daytime and overnight deluxe buses to Delhi (Rs 365, 10 hours), plus ordinary buses every hour (Rs 180 for day buses, Rs 191 overnight). Ordinary buses to Chandigarh leave every 30 minutes (Rs 70, four hours).

In the high season, HPTDC has an overnight bus to Delhi (Rs 325, 10 hours) which goes via Chandigarh. This bus drops you off conveniently at Janpath, near Connaught Place. It is best to book HPTDC buses at the tourist office at Scandal Point but the buses actually depart from the office at Victory Tunnel. In addition, travel agencies along The Mall offer private overnight 'deluxe' buses to Delhi (Rs 275). Prices and times change according to demand and the season but there's usually one bus in the morning and one overnight service. These buses also leave from the entrance to Victory Tunnel.

To Dharamsala & Manali There are several daytime buses to Dharamsala (Rs 148) and one overnight semi-deluxe bus (Rs 221, 10 hours).

To Manali there are two ordinary buses (Rs 204, 11 hours); all buses stop in Kullu. HPTDC offers daily deluxe buses in the morning to Manali (Rs 325, 10 hours). There are also private overnight buses to Manali (Rs 225) leaving from Victory Tunnel.

Local Buses Rivoli bus station has seven buses between 4 and 11.30 am to Rekong Peo (Rs 147, 10 hours) via Narkanda (Rs 40, three hours) and Rampur (Rs 80, six hours). There is one bus at 7.30 am to Sangla and a couple of buses around 9.30 am to Sarahan (Rs 106). There are also hourly buses to Naldehra.

For Tattapani, Kasauli and local destinations en route to Kalka or Narkanda such as Kufri and Theog, catch one of the regular local buses along Cart Rd.

Train There are two train stations in Shimla. All trains arrive at and depart from the main station on the western edge of town; some trains also depart from the central branch station. The train reservation office (☎ 252915) at the main station takes bookings for the Kalka and Delhi line. It's open from 10 am to 1.30 pm and 2 to 5 pm Monday to Saturday and 10 am to 2 pm Sunday.

Any train journey to Shimla involves a change from broad to narrow gauge at Kalka, a little north of Chandigarh. See the following Shimla to Kalka section for details of the toy train between these two towns, and for onward services to Chandigarh and Delhi.

Taxi There are two agencies with fixed-price taxis that are almost impossible to bagain down, even in the low season: the Kalka-Shimla Taxi Union (☎ 258225) on Cart Rd near the ISBT bus station, and the Vishal Himachal Taxi Operators' Union (☎ 205164), at the bottom of the lift on Cart Rd. Both are about the same price. Taxis are either Gypsy jeeps or 'multivans' that take three passengers plus the driver; or the Ambassador taxi that takes four passengers and costs about 10% more than the following prices.

Examples of one-way taxi fares from Shimla are: Kasauli (Rs 650), Chandigarh (Rs 810), Kalka (Rs 560), Manali (Rs 2200) and Dharamsala (Rs 2200). Note that the fare is higher coming up from Chandigarh (Rs 1100) or Kalka (Rs 780) to Shimla.

Getting Around
Getting around Shimla usually means a lot of walking as there are no rickshaws. The Mall is pedestrian and narrow Cart Rd is permanently clogged with cars and buses. At the eastern end of Cart Rd, next to the Vishal Himachal taxi stand, there is a passenger lift which goes up to the eastern end of The Mall between 8 am and 10 pm (Rs 5). It certainly saves a steep climb if you happen to be at that end of town.

AROUND SHIMLA
There are a few places of mild interest around Shimla. Most are served by local buses, but if you're in a group it's well worth using a taxi to get around. See the Shimla section for information on HPTDC tours to these places. The tourist office in Shimla can also give details of accommodation.

About 12km from Shimla on the main road to Kalka, **Kasauli** makes a pleasant day trip. There are some fine walks around the town, including to Sanawar and Monkey Point.

Chail, about 43km south of Shimla and accessible by local bus (Rs 28), was created by the Maharaja of Patiala as a summer capital after his expulsion from Shimla. The town is built on three hills – one is topped by the Chail Palace, one by the village itself and the other by the Snowview mansion. About 3km from the village is the **world's highest cricket ground** (2444m) – how can you miss the chance to see that? – built in 1893. There is also a **wildlife sanctuary** 3km from Chail with a limited number of deer and birds. This is good hiking country.

Beware the Persistent Porter

At the bus or train stations you'll be besieged by porters who will offer to carry your luggage for Rs 5 to Rs 20, depending on weight and distance. Some of these porters are little more than hotel touts, which means commission. If you use a porter, insist on going to the hotel of your choice.

INDIA

About 12km from Shimla, the small village of **Mashobra** has some pleasant walks, including one to Sipi, where there is a fair in May. About 15km further north, at an altitude of 2050m, **Naldehra** is a pleasant little village, mostly famous for having one of the oldest and highest golf courses in India. There is even a temple, the **Mahunag Mandir**, in the middle of the course.

Tattapani, 65km north of Shimla, is famous only for its hot sulphurous springs. They are not all that well developed, but the setting is great and the village is small and relaxed. The hot water is piped from a section of the Sutlej River to the two guesthouses on the bank.

The closest decent place to go **skiing** in winter is Narkanda, 62km from Shimla on the road up to Rampur. The season runs from early January to early April but the resort isn't terribly well set up by Western standards. You can book ski packages that include board, lodging and equipment hire through the tourist office in Shimla. Regular local buses (Rs 40) run up there from Shimla.

SHIMLA TO KALKA

Getting to or from Shimla is half the fun, especially if you have an interest in miniature trains. The toy train that runs between Kalka and Shimla takes longer than the bus but it's infinitely more enjoyable, particularly if you can get on early and get a good seat. Avoid it if possible on weekends in high season. If you can afford it, it's worth springing for a 1st-class seat on one of the luxury services, which you should book in advance.

The 96km narrow-gauge mountain railway was built in 1903 and is one of five vintage toy trains in India (Pathankot-Jogindernagar in the Kangra Valley is another). The line climbs roughly 1500m through the Shivalik ranges, passing through 103 tunnels (Barog, the longest, is more than 1km long), over 845 bridges and via 20 minor stations. The trip takes around five to six hours, so you'll want to make yourself comfortable.

There are three different services: the ordinary Shimla-Kalka Mail/Express trains; the faster 18-seat Rail Motor; and the deluxe *Shivalik Express*. On the ordinary trains, a 2nd-class ticket costs Rs 16 or Rs 32 (depending on the service) and 1st class is Rs 170 or Rs 198. On the Rail Motor it's Rs 191/340 (the latter for a luxury seat in a glass-sided carriage), and on the *Shivalik Express* it's Rs 340, which includes breakfast or dinner on board.

From Shimla, the *Shivalik Express* departs at 5.30 pm, arriving in Kalka at 10.15 pm. From Kalka it departs at 5.30 am, arriving in Shimla at 10.15 am. The Rail Motor departs from Shimla at 11.35 am, arriving at 4.25 pm; and from Kalka at 11.45 am, arriving at 4.10 pm. In season there are at least four more ordinary trains each way and three at other times.

From Shimla you can book a through-train to Delhi so that your Shimla-Kalka train connects immediately with a Kalka-Delhi service (the same can be done coming the opposite way from Delhi). The only way to do this from Shimla is to take the 10.40 am train to Kalka, which connects with the *Himalayan Queen*, arriving in New Delhi (via Chandigarh) at 10.35 pm.

To travel from Delhi to Shimla by train in one trip, the *Himalayan Queen* is again the most reliable. It departs from New Delhi station at 6.10 am, arriving in Kalka at 11.30 am. You then cross to another platform to take the 12.05 pm toy train which arrives in Shimla at 5.20 pm. If you make a reservation in Delhi, check that your ticket is valid all the way to Shimla, not just to Kalka.

Of course, you don't have to make the perfect connection. If you get off at Kalka, regular buses run to Chandigarh (Rs 17, one hour), where you can either stay the night or catch a bus or train to Delhi. The bus stand at Kalka is a 15-minute walk or Rs 20 autorickshaw ride from the train station. There are retiring rooms at the station if your need to stay the night, but there's nothing of interest in Kalka.

CHANDIGARH
☎ 0172 • pop 750,000
Chandigarh, 248km north of Delhi, is unlike any other Indian city you'll encounter on this route – if not in the entire country. Not many travellers have even heard of the place, let alone considered adding it to their itineraries, but apart from being the capital of Haryana state, it is interesting for two reasons.

The first is simply that it is a recently built planned city with an amazing amount of space by Indian standards. The streets are vast and free of congestion; shops, businesses and restaurants are organised in neat

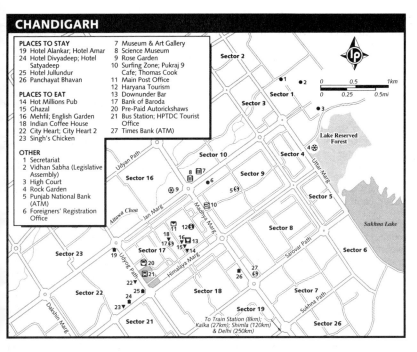

CHANDIGARH

PLACES TO STAY
19 Hotel Alankar; Hotel Amar
24 Hotel Divyadeep; Hotel Satyadeep
25 Hotel Jullundur
26 Panchayat Bhavan

PLACES TO EAT
14 Hot Millions Pub
15 Ghazal
16 Mehfil; English Garden
18 Indian Coffee House
22 City Heart; City Heart 2
23 Singh's Chicken

OTHER
1 Secretariat
2 Vidhan Sabha (Legislative Assembly)
3 High Court
4 Rock Garden
5 Punjab National Bank (ATM)
6 Foreigners' Registration Office
7 Museum & Art Gallery
8 Science Museum
9 Rose Garden
10 Surfing Zone; Pukraj 9 Cafe; Thomas Cook
11 Main Post Office
12 Haryana Tourism
13 Downunder Bar
17 Bank of Baroda
20 Pre-Paid Autorickshaws
21 Bus Station; HPTDC Tourist Office
27 Times Bank (ATM)

(albeit ugly) blocks; not a single stray cow can be seen wandering around; and it is generally clean and tidy. The second attraction is the bizarre 'rock garden' built almost single-handedly by a local engineer.

Chandigarh was conceived and born in the 1950s and was the master plan of the European modernist architect, Swiss-born Le Corbusier, who also designed many of the government buildings. Indians are very proud of it and it's one of the cleanest and most prosperous major cities in the country. It also has a thriving university and a youthful population.

Orientation

Very much like Pakistan's capital Islamabad, Chandigarh was designed on a grid system and is divided into 57 sectors, separated by broad avenues. Each sector is quartered into four zones, A–D, and each building within them has a unique number. Despite this logical breakdown, orientation can be tricky without a map, as only the broad separating avenues have street names. 'SCO' in business addresses, stands for 'shop-cum-office'. The bus station, modern shopping centre,

and many of the restaurants are in Sector 17. The train station is inconveniently located 8km out of Chandigarh.

Information

Tourist Offices The Chandigarh tourist office (☎ 704614), upstairs at the rear of the bus station, is open from 9 am to 5 pm weekdays and 9 am to 1 pm Saturday. Next door is Himachal Tourism (☎ 708569). One floor up is Punjab Tourism (☎ 711878) and UP Tourism (☎ 707649) and there's also Haryana Tourism (☎ 702955).

Money The major banks are in Sector 17B; the Bank of Baroda, SCO 62–63, does Visa cash advances. Private money exchange bureaus are nearby and there's a branch of Thomas Cook on Madhya Marg in Sector 9. Chandigarh has several ATMs accepting international cards, although most are a long way from the centre. Punjab National Bank in Sector 9D (SCO 46–47) has an ATM accepting Master-Card/Cirrus/Maestro, as does HDFC Bank, in Sector 8C, near Panchayat Bhavan (see Places to Stay later).

INDIA

Post & Communications The main post office is in Sector 17. STD/ISD booths with fax services can be found in sectors 17 and 22. There are numerous Internet cafes in sectors 9 and 17. Surfing Zone on Madhya Marg is open from 9 am to 11 pm daily and charges only Rs 35 per hour. World Net Cyber Cafe, near the post office in Sector 17, is also good.

Things to See & Do
The **Rock Garden**, built by Nek Chand, a roads inspector for Chandigarh's engineering department, is the city's premier tourist attraction. To call this strange and whimsical fantasy a 'rock garden' is underplaying things, but it is difficult to describe and has to be seen to be appreciated. The 10-hectare garden comprises a series of interconnected rocky grottoes, walkways and landscaped waterfalls. When you enter and wander around the first part of the garden you'll probably be nonplussed. But by far the most powerful aspect of the creation comes later when you discover the thousands of animal or humanoid figures made out of discarded materials, which stand in rigid rows like silent, static armies.

Nek Chand, who can still be found fiddling around in his garden, began creating his figures in 1958, using discarded materials such as broken ceramics and old machinery parts. Few people had a clue what was going on until 1972 when the garden (on government land) was inevitably discovered. Rather than demolish it, the authorities recognised the public interest this strange art form had created (what else did the brand-new Chandigarh have to call a tourist attraction?) and offered Chand the resources to continue his work.

This fine example of 'outsider' art is open from 9 am to 1 pm and 3 to 7 pm daily from 1 April to 30 September. The rest of the year it opens and closes an hour earlier. Entry is Rs 5.

To the south-east is the artificial **Sukhna Lake**, where you can rent rowboats or stroll around the 2km perimeter.

Three museums are clustered in Sector 10C. The **Museum & Art Gallery** contains a modest collection of Indian stone sculptures dating back to the Gandhara period, together with some miniature paintings and modern art (Rs 1). The adjacent **City Museum** gives an excellent rundown of the planning, development and architecture of Chandigarh. The nearby **Science Museum** covers the evolution of life on earth, and displays fossils and implements of prehistoric humans found in India. The city and science museums are both free. All three museums are open from around 10 am to 4.30 or 5 pm Tuesday to Sunday. Also worth seeing are Le Corbusier's **government buildings**; the Secretariat, the High Court; and the Vidhan Sabha (Legislative Assembly).

The **rose garden** in Sector 16 is claimed to be the biggest in Asia and contains more than a thousand varieties of roses. It's open daily (free).

Places to Stay
Chandigarh is clearly not set up for the likes of backpackers – budget accommodation is limited and any reasonably priced hotels are often full. But it's worth considering spending a night here on your way between Shimla and Delhi – apart from a visit to the rock garden, there are some reasonably lively bars to check out in Sector 17.

There are some cheap guesthouses in the residential streets around Sector 22, but at the time of writing these places weren't accepting foreigners, partly because of pressure from the government to close them down. There are also some dharamsalas in town; ask at the tourist office.

The cheapest option is ***Panchayat Bhavan*** (☎ *780701, Sector 18)*, but it's an institutional block with an old-fashioned youth hostel atmosphere. There's a huge dorm with endless camp beds for Rs 24, or there are large, bare doubles with private bathroom for Rs 200 (Rs 500 with air-con but you can do better elsewhere for that price). There are no singles.

Hotel Divyadeep (☎ *705191, Sector 22B, Himalaya Marg)* has simple singles/doubles with fan for Rs 300/350 and Rs 400/450 with air cooling and better rooms with air-con for Rs 450/550. All have private bathroom. ***Hotel Satyadeep*** (☎ *703103)* is a few doors away and has almost the same rooms and prices except that air-con rooms are Rs 50 cheaper. Both places have vegetarian restaurants.

Hotel Jullundur (☎ *706777, Sector 22B)* is opposite the bus station. Standard air-con rooms (for one or two people) with TV and private bathroom (hot water) start at Rs 550. *Alankar* and *Amar* hotels, at the other end of Udyog Path, are a bit more expensive but still affordable if the others are full.

Places to Eat

Chandigarh has many places to eat and, in keeping with its modern outlook and middle-class population, much of what's on offer is Western-style fast food and semi-upmarket restaurants. You don't have to go far from the bus station to find the restaurants and cafes – most are clustered in the Sector 17 shopping district, with a few scattered in Sectors 9 and 22.

Across the road from the bus stand on Udyog Path you'll find *City Heart* serving cheap Indian veg food. Nearby, *City Heart 2* is slightly more expensive, is nonveg, and also serves beer.

Singh's Chicken (Sector 22, Himalaya Marg) has a good range of chicken dishes for less than Rs 50.

Hot Millions Pub (SCO 74–75, Sector 17D) serves fast food and great sizzlers, and just along the road is *Domino's Pizza*. Across the plaza, *Indian Coffee House* serves very cheap south Indian fare such as masala dosas for Rs 20.

Mehfil (SCO 185, Sector 17C), and in the same street, *Ghazal (SCO 189–91)* are Chandigarh's top restaurants. Their menus are the standard mix of continental, Chinese and Indian, with main courses around Rs 100. Below Mehfil (entrance is at the side and down the stairs) is *English Garden*, a popular mid-range place where you can have a light meal for around Rs 90 and a beer.

Pukhraj 9, next to the Internet cafe on Madhya Marg, has good thalis from Rs 25, Chinese dishes from Rs 25 to Rs 60, as well as Indian standards and a few burgers. There's even a *Pizza Hut* out in Sector 26, but you'll need a rickshaw to get there.

Entertainment

Chandigarh doesn't have the nightlife of Delhi but it's more liberal and prosperous than many Indian cities. In Sector 17 there are numerous bars, cinemas and a couple of pool halls, and they generally have a friendly vibe. *Downunder Bar* has few concessions to Australianism, except loud music and lots of young people drinking and having a good time. *Hot Millions Pub* is another good place for beers and Indian/Western snacks, as is the more refined *English Garden*.

You can shoot some pool at *Pool Cafe* at SCO 8–9 in Sector 17, opposite Haryana Tourism.

Getting There & Away

Air Indian Airlines (☎ 704539), SCO 170, Sector 17C, is open from 10 am to 5 pm. It has flights on Wednesday and Friday to Delhi (US$75) and Amritsar (US$65) and one flight on Wednesday to Leh (US$80).

Bus Chandigarh has a huge and noisy bus station with good facilities and English timetables. Long-distance buses depart from the south side near the intersection of Himalaya Marg and Udyog Path.

A staggering number of buses depart for Delhi (five hours) around the clock. Ordinary buses cost Rs 108 and depart at least every 10 minutes. Express/deluxe buses cost Rs 215. Check where your bus will drop off – most terminate at the Kashmir Gate ISBT which is inconvenient for the city centre.

There are frequent buses to Kalka (Rs 17, one hour) for the train to Shimla. A direct bus to Shimla costs Rs 70 and takes about four hours on a good day. There are direct buses to Dharamsala (Rs 124, 10 hours) as well as night buses to Manali (Rs 185, 10 hours). You can get information on destinations to the north from the Himachal Roadways inquiry counter at window No 8. A new bus stand for buses to Manali and some other destinations is being established at Sector 43.

Train The train station is inconveniently situated 8km south-east of the centre, but the train is still a better way to get to Delhi, particularly if you're heading to New Delhi station. Fortunately, there's a rail reservation office upstairs in the main bus station, open from 8 am to 8 pm.

It is 245km by rail from Delhi to Chandigarh. The twice-daily *Shatabdi Express* does the journey in just three hours, and in air-con comfort (Rs 435/865 in chair car/executive class). Another option is the *Himalayan Queen* at 5.35 pm (Rs 207 in chair car, five hours), or the overnight *Kalka-Howrah Mail* at 1 am, which arrives

INDIA

at Delhi station at 6.25 am (Rs 97/279 in sleeper/three-tier air-con).

There are five daily trains to Kalka (Rs 18, one hour), just 25km up the line, and from there it takes almost six hours to reach Shimla on the narrow-gauge mountain railway (see the earlier Shimla to Kalka section for more details).

Getting Around

Chandigarh is far too spread out to walk around. The extensive bus network is the cheapest option. Bus No 13 runs along Himalaya Marg as far as the government buildings in Sector 1, and bus No 6 runs from the bus stand to the High Court. Both of these get you close to the Rock Garden. Bus No 37 runs to the train station from the bus station every 30 minutes (Rs 7).

Daring to be different, Chandigarh's autorickshaws are blue. There is a prepaid autorickshaw stand behind the bus station although it's not easy to find – it's in a small hut behind the area where local buses congregate. Set fares include: Rs 34 to the train station; Rs 19 to the Rock Garden. Autorickshaws on the street will demand much more, especially the ones that crowd around the car park outside the Rock Garden. You should be able to get better rates from cycle-rickshaws.

Delhi

☎ 011 • pop 8 million

Chaotic, congested, polluted, vibrant, frustrating and, at times, exciting, Delhi is India's capital and the industrial and transport hub of northern India.

For most Asian overland travellers, a stop in Delhi is par for the course. It's partly a necessary evil, partly a welcome opportunity to eat well (if you can afford to), meet up with other travellers and attend to business (banking, visas, parcels home etc). It's estimated that spending a day in Delhi's traffic is equivalent to smoking 20 cigarettes. It's also like being in the world's biggest rugby scrum, so understandably most travellers are keen to get in and out as quickly as possible.

Beyond the modern-day two-stroke engine fumes and aggressive touts, Delhi has a great deal of historic interest. Old Delhi was the capital of Muslim India between the 17th and 19th centuries and still contains many mosques, monuments and forts relating to India's Muslim history. New Delhi, relatively spacious and modern, was built as the imperial capital of India by the British.

The rise in entry fees to monuments has made sight-seeing in Delhi an expensive prospect but if you have the funds, spend your time exploring the Red Fort and Jama Masjid in Old Delhi, take a walk along Rajpath in New Delhi, and splurge on a restaurant meal. You could also try to get down to the Qutab Minar and some of the monuments in New Delhi such as Humayun's Tomb, Nizam-ud-din's Shrine and Purana Qila. There are also some good museums and the opportunity to see a cultural show.

HISTORY

Delhi hasn't always been the capital of India, but it has played an important role in Indian history. The settlement of Indraprastha, which featured in the epic *Mahabharata* more than 3000 years ago, was approximately on the site of present-day Delhi. The Mughal emperors made Agra the capital through the 16th and 17th centuries. Under the British, Calcutta (now known as Kolkata) was the capital until the inauguration of New Delhi in 1931.

There have been at least eight cities around modern Delhi, and the old saying that whoever founds a new city at Delhi will lose it has come true every time – most recently for the British, who lasted only 16 years.

The Mughal emperor, Shah Jahan, constructed the 7th Delhi in the 17th century, thus shifting the Mughal capital from Agra to Delhi; his Shahjahanabad roughly corresponds to Old Delhi today and is largely preserved, including the Red Fort and the Jama Masjid (Friday Mosque). Finally, the 8th Delhi, New Delhi, was constructed by the British – the move from Calcutta was announced in 1911 but construction was not completed, and the city officially inaugurated, until 1931. In 1947, it became the capital of truncated India, and Hindu and Sikh refugees poured in from Pakistan. Prior to Partition, Delhi had a very large Muslim population and Urdu was the main language. Now Hindu Punjabis have replaced many of the Muslims, and Hindi predominates.

ORIENTATION

Delhi is very spread out, but the area of most interest to visitors, on the west bank of the Yamuna River, is relatively compact. It's divided basically into two parts – the tightly packed streets of Old Delhi and the spacious, planned areas of New Delhi.

Old Delhi is the 17th-century walled city of Shahjahanabad, with city gates, narrow alleys, constant traffic jams and terrible air pollution, the Red Fort and Jama Masjid. Here you will find the Delhi train station and, a little further north, the main interstate bus station near Kashmiri Gate. Near New Delhi train station, and acting as a sort of buffer zone between the old and new cities, is the crowded market area of Paharganj, the budget travellers' ghetto.

New Delhi is a planned city of wide, tree-lined streets, parks and fountains and has little resemblance to Old Delhi. The centre of the business district is Connaught Place (the outer circle is called Connaught Circus) with the government areas around Rajpath to the south.

The Indira Gandhi International Airport is to the south-west of the city, and about halfway between the airport and Connaught Place is Chanakyapuri, the diplomatic enclave. Most of Delhi's embassies (and the prime minister's house) are concentrated in this tidy area.

INFORMATION
Tourist Offices

The Government of India tourist office (☎ 332 0008) at 88 Janpath is open from 9 am to 6 pm weekdays and 9 am to 2 pm Saturday. This busy office has a lot of information and brochures on destinations all over India. It has a good free map of the city, and can also help you find accommodation.

There's a useful Delhi Tourism Corporation office (DTC; ☎ 331 3637) around the corner in N-Block (36), Connaught Place, open from 7 am to 9 pm weekdays. It has a rail reservation counter for tourists and foreign exchange, and staff can book tours. You have to run the gauntlet of the touts trying to pull you into their bogus 'tourism information offices' first. The DTC also has counters at New Delhi, Old Delhi, and Nizamuddin train stations, as well as at the Interstate Bus Terminal at Kashmiri Gate. In the arrivals hall at the international air-

port terminal there is a tourist counter (☎ 566 5296) open 24 hours. Here, too, they can help you find accommodation although, like many other Indian tourist offices, they may try to steer you to their recommended (usually mid-range) hotels.

Note that many travel agencies, particularly opposite New Delhi train station, blatantly but falsely advertise themselves as 'official government tourist offices'. Don't believe a word of it.

Most of the state governments have information centres in Delhi. You'll find them all listed in the *Delhi City Guide* (see Bookshops & Publications later) but useful ones for this route include:

Haryana (☎ 332 4911) Chandralok Bldg, 36 Janpath
Himachal Pradesh (☎ 332 5320) Chandralok Bldg, 36 Janpath
Rajasthan (☎ 338 3837) Bikaner House (near India Gate)
Uttar Pradesh (☎ 332 2251) Chandralok Bldg, 36 Janpath

Visa Extensions & Other Permits

Hans Bhavan, near the Tilak Bridge train station, is where you will find the Foreigners' Regional Registration Office (FRRO; ☎ 331 9781). Come here for visa extensions and to get permits for restricted areas such as Mizoram. The office is open from 9.30 am to 1.30 pm and 2 to 4 pm weekdays.

Embassies & Consulates

Most foreign embassies, high commissions and consulates are located in New Delhi, generally in the Chanakyapuri district south-west of Connaught Place. This is the best place in India to get a tourist visa for Pakistan, a transit visa for Iran, or visas for Nepal or Bangladesh. If you're intending to apply for a transit visa for Iran, get your Pakistani visa first. Both missions will require you to provide a letter of introduction from your own embassy in Delhi (which you will probably have to pay a charge for). When applying for visas, remember to take in at least two recent passport photographs and photocopies of the relevant pages of your passport, just in case. Most embassies are open from around 9 am to 4 pm weekdays, but the visa section often closes at noon or 2 pm – it's best to arrive as early as possible.

INDIA

DELHI

Yamuna River

Mahatma Gandhi Marg

Shamnath Marg

Civil Lines

Qutab Rd

Sadar Bazaar

Sabzi Mandi

Kamla Nagar

Delhi University

The Mall

Model Town

Radio Colony

Parmanand Marg

Karol Bagh

Patel Nagar

New Rajendra Nagar

Shalimar Bagh

To Chandigarh (250km)

Vijay Ghat

Shanti Vana

Raj Ghat

Ring Rd

Red Fort

Bahadur Shah Zafar Marg

(Old) Delhi Train Station

Chandni Chowk

Old Delhi Train Station

New Delhi Train Station

Janpath

Grand Trunk Rd

Wazirabad Rd

Boulevard Rd

Outer Ring Rd

Vikas Marg

Sarai Rohilla Train Station

Ring Rd

Shalimar Rd

Patel Rd

Pusa Rd

New Rohtak Rd

Roshanara Rd

Desh Bandhu Gupta Rd

Gangaram Hospital Marg

Panchkuin Marg

Mandir Marg

Bahadur Shah Khari Singh Marg

See Old Delhi Map p.427

See Connaught Place Map p.434

See Paharganj Map p.435

PLACES TO STAY & EAT
12 Yatri Hotel
19 Master Paying Guest House
27 Dilli Haat

OTHER
1 Shalimar Bagh
2 Coronation Durbar Site
3 Roshanara Bagh
4 Hindu Rao Hospital;
   Ashoka Pillar
5 Mutiny Memorial
6 Kashmiri Gate
7 Kashmiri Gate Interstate
   Bus Terminal (ISBT)
8 St James's Church
9 Delhi Post Office
10 Satyam Cineplex
11 Karol Bagh Market
13 Gandhi Memorial Museum
14 Indira Gandhi Indoor
   Stadium
15 Feroz Shah Kotla
16 Hans Bhavan (Foreigners
   Regional Registration Office);
   Central Revenue Building
   (Income Tax Office)
17 Bengali Market
18 Lakshmi Narayan Temple
20 New Delhi Main Post
   Office; National Philatelic
   Museum
21 Jazz Bar; Hotel Maurya
   Sheraton
22 My Kind of Place; Taj
   Palace Hotel
23 Rail Transport Museum
24 Sarai Kale Khan ISBT (Bus
   Terminal)
25 Nehru Stadium
26 INA Market
28 All India Institute of
   Medical Sciences (AIIMS)
29 South Extension Market
30 Moth-ki Masjid
31 N Block Market
32 Bahai Temple
33 Kalkaji Devi Temple
34 M Block Market
35 Hauz Khas Village
36 Basant Lok Complex; Priya
   Cinema
37 Begumpur Masjid; Bijai
   Mandal
38 Khirki Masjid
39 PVR Anupam 4 Cinema
40 Qutab Minar Complex
41 Delhi Tourism Corporation
   Bus Stand
42 Tughlaqabad
43 Tomb of Ghiyas-ud-din

DELHI

To Apollo Hospital, Surajkund & Agra

42

43

Yamuna River

NH24

Ring Rd

Mathura Rd

Nizamuddin Railway Station

24

Sunder Nagar

Mathura Rd

Nizamuddin

Lajpat Nagar

Nehru Place

32

33

Kalkaji

Greater Kailash II

Outer Ring Rd

Delhi Golf Course

Lala Lajpat Pai Path

Lodi Rd

Defence Colony

25

Bhisham Pitamah Marg

Greater Kailash I

31

34

Josep Broz Tito Marg

Lal Bahadur Shastri Marg

41

Lodi Colony

Pitrival Rd

New Delhi

President's Estate

South Extension Part I

26

29

30

South Extension Part II

28

Siri

Khel Gaon Marg

Asian Games Complex

Outer Ring Rd

38

Malviya Nagar

Press Enclave Marg

Mehrauli Badarpur Rd

Sarojini Nagar

Ring Rd

27

Aurobindo Marg

35

Aurobindo Marg

Begumpur

37

Saket

39

21

22

Chanakyapuri

Sardar Patel Marg

23

Ramakrishna Puram

Parade Rd

Outer Ring Rd

Jawaharlal Nehru University

40

Mehrauli

To Gurgaon

Ring Rd

Vasant Vihar

36

Mehrauli Rd

Gurgaon Rd

Palam Rd

Indira Gandhi International Airport

To Jaipur

0 0.25 0.5 0.5mi
0 0.5 1km

N

Australia (☎ 688 8223, fax 688 5199) 1/50-G Shantipath, Chanakyapuri
Bangladesh (☎ 683 4065, fax 683 9237) 56 Ring Rd, Lajpat Nagar III
Canada (☎ 687 6500, fax 687 6579) 7/8 Shantipath, Chanakyapuri
China (☎ 687 1585, fax 688 5486) 50-D Shantipath, Chanakyapuri
Germany (☎ 687 1831, fax 687 3117) 6/50-G Shantipath, Chanakyapuri
Iran (☎ 332 9600, fax 335 4093) 5 Barakhamba Rd. Issues seven-day transit visas but not tourist visas. A letter of introduction from your embassy is required. Brits and Americans usually have to wait at least two weeks; other nationalities (Australians, New Zealanders) can get one in about four days. Approximately US$25 (payable in rupees at the State Bank of India).
Ireland (☎ 462 6733, fax 469 7053) 13 Jor Bagh Rd
Nepal (☎ 332 8191, fax 332 6857) Barakhamba Rd. Issues visas within 24 hours; US$25 for a one-month tourist visa.
Netherlands (☎ 688 4951, fax 688 4956) 6/50-F Shantipath, Chanakyapuri
New Zealand (☎ 688 3170, fax 687 2317) 50-N Nyaya Marg, Chanakyapuri
Pakistan (☎ 467 6004, fax 687 2339) 2/50-G Shantipath, Chanakyapuri. Issues 30-day tourist visas reasonably efficiently (next-day pick-up). A letter of introduction from your embassy is required.
UK (☎ 687 2161, fax 687 2882) 50 Shantipath, Chanakyapuri
USA (☎ 419 8000, fax 687 2028) Shantipath, Chanakyapuri

Money

The major offices of Indian and foreign banks operating in India are in Delhi. As usual, some branches will change travellers cheques, some won't. If you need to change money outside regular banking hours, SCB Grindlays (☎ 335 7000), at 10E Connaught Place, is open 24 hours, but charges Rs 200 commission on travellers cheques. There is a fast and convenient moneychanging office in Paharganj's Main Bazaar near Camran Lodge, open to 9 pm weekdays. There's an efficient, commission-free foreign exchange (cash and travellers cheques) at the Delhi Tourism Corporation office in Connaught Place, which is open from 7 am to 9 pm daily.

The ATM at SCB Grindlays is linked to Visa, MasterCard, Plus, Cirrus, Maestro and others. Another major bank with ATMs is Citibank (☎ 371 2484), in the Jeevan Bharati Building, Outer Circle, Connaught Place.

American Express (☎ 332 7602) has its office in A-Block, Connaught Place, and although it's usually crowded, service is fast. It's open from 9.30 am to 6.30 pm weekdays and 9.30 am to 2.30 pm Saturday. There's a 24-hour number (☎ 614 5920) for lost or stolen cheques that you should contact as soon as possible.

Thomas Cook (☎ 335 6575) has an office in Connaught Place at Block C33 and has a branch at the international airport.

The main branch of the State Bank of India (where you go to pay the fee for an Iran visa) is on Sansad Marg near the YWCA.

Post & Telephone

There is a small post office in A-Block at Connaught Place but the main post office is on the roundabout on Baba Kharak Singh Marg, 500m south-west of Connaught Place. Poste restante is in the main post office, open from 9 am to 5 pm weekdays. Poste restante mail addressed to 'Delhi' will go to the inconveniently situated Old Delhi post office, so ask your correspondents to specify 'New Delhi'.

Parcels can be sent from any of the previously mentioned post offices. If you have a major item that requires packing, it may be worth using one of the private agencies. They can pack your goods and send them via the post office for the normal postage plus a Rs 100 fee, or you can use one of the more expensive courier services. There are several agents in Paharganj: Parcel Packing at the Ankur Guest House (see Places to Stay) in Main Bazaar is a reliable operator.

There are many private STD/ISD phone offices around the city; some also have fax services and email. The directory inquiry number for Delhi is ☎ 197.

Email & Internet Access

Educated young Indians are obsessed with the Internet (chat rooms are incredibly popular), so it's not surprising that Delhi has the cheapest Internet access between İstanbul and Kathmandu. Along Main Bazaar in Paharganj, the standard charge is Rs 20 per hour. Despite this low cost, the machines are generally fast and reliable and most Internet cafes have a dozen or more terminals humming away. Several guesthouses in this area have their own Internet cafes. Outside Paharganj you'll pay more like Rs 60 per hour.

Internet cafes to try include:

Cyber Bar-Be-Que At Hotel Gold Regency, Main Bazaar, Paharganj. There's a few busy terminals in the lobby area and another Internet cafe through the restaurant, where you can even have a beer while you surf. Rs 20 per hour.
Cyber Cafe Next to Nirula Hotel in Sector L, Connaught Place. Rs 80 per hour.
Cyberstation Attached to Hotel Downtown, down an alley off Main Bazaar, Paharganj. Spacious set-up with loads of terminals and good connections. Rs 20 per hour.
DSIDC Cyber Cafe Next to Delhi Tourism in Sector N, Connaught Place. Air-conditioned and one of the cheaper places outside Paharganj at Rs 40 per hour.
Generation X Internet Cafe Below Ankur Guest House on Main Bazaar, Paharganj. The staff here know what they're doing. Rs 30 per hour.

Two useful Web sites are www.delhigate .com and www.thedelhicity.com.

Travel Agencies
Some of the ticket discounters around Paharganj and Connaught Place are real fly-by-night operations, so take care. Although many claim to be government-approved tourist offices, this is almost always false advertising. You'll often be approached by touts on the street in these areas making offers for onward transport or tours. Some of these offers are legitimate, but you should be aware that many travellers have been sold up the river. Before committing yourself to any seemingly attractive deals, check details with a genuine tourist office or reliable agent. Good budget agents to try include:

Aa Bee Travels (☎ 752 0117) Hare Rama Guest House, Paharganj
Hotel Namaskar (☎ 362 1234, e namaskarhotel@yahoo.com) Paharganj. Books flights and other transport and can arrange extended car hire.
Student Travel Information Centre (STIC Travels; ☎ 332 0239) Chandralok Bldg, Janpath 36 (opposite Imperial Hotel). Popular with travellers and is the place to buy or renew ISIC cards.
Tan's Travel (☎ 332 1490) 72 Janpath
Vin Tours (☎ 334 8571, e vintour@vsnl.com) Ashoka Rd (YWCA Blue Triangle Family Hostel)
Y Tours & Travel (☎ 371 1662) Ashoka Rd (YMCA)

Bookshops & Publications
There are a number of good bookshops around Connaught Place – a good place to look for interesting Indian books or to stock up with hefty paperbacks to while away those long train rides. Some of the better shops include:

The Bookshop Khan Market, Subramania Bharati Rd
Bookworm 29B Radial Rd No 4, Connaught Place
Delhi Book Co. M12, Connaught Circus
English Book Depot 17L Radial Road No 5, Connaught Place
New Book Depot 18 B-Block, Connaught Place
Piccadilly Book Store 64 Shankar Market (just off Connaught Circus)

The best places to buy Indian or international newspapers and magazines is from the vendors who lay their wares out on the pavement around Connaught Place (near the SGB Grindlays Bank in E-Block) and on Sansad Marg, near the Kwality Restaurant (see Places to Eat, Connaught Place & Janpath Area). You can also pick up second-hand novels and guidebooks. People Tree, on Sansad Marg, sells books about the environment and eco-friendly crafts. The largest stockist of Lonely Planet guides is Bahri Sons, opposite the main gate at Khan Market.

There are several handy guides available from newsstands, including *Delhi City Guide* (Rs 15) and *Delhi Diary* (Rs 10). *First City* (Rs 30) is a monthly magazine with gossip on what the city's upper-class 'tiger ladies' are up to, but also has good listings and reviews of cultural events and restaurants.

Libraries & Cultural Centres
The India International Centre (☎ 461 9431), by the Sikander Lodi Tomb, has lectures each week on art, economics and other contemporary issues by Indian and foreign experts.

The American Center (☎ 331 6841) is at 24 Kasturba Gandhi Marg and is open from 9.30 am to 6 pm. The British Council Library (☎ 371 0111), at 17 Kasturba Gandhi Marg, is open from 10 am to 6 pm Tuesday to Saturday. Alliance Française (☎ 625 8128) can be found at D-13 South Extension Part II.

INDIA

Photography

There are lots of places around Connaught Place to buy and process film, buy camera accessories or have repairs done. The Delhi Photo Company, at 78 Janpath, close to the Government of India tourist office, processes both print and slide film competently.

Medical Services & Emergencies

The East West Medical Centre (☎ 462 3738, 469 9229), near Delhi Golf Course, at 38 Golf Links Rd, has been recommended by many travellers, diplomats and expats. All rickshaw-wallahs know where it is. The Apollo Hospital (☎ 692 5858), Sarita Vihar, Mathura Rd, also has a good reputation.

Embassies have lists of recommended doctors and dentists. There is a 24-hour pharmacy at Super Bazaar in Connaught Place.

An ambulance service can be contacted on ☎ 102. The police emergency number is ☎ 100.

OLD DELHI

The old walled city of Shahjahanabad stands to the west of the Red Fort and was at one time surrounded by a sturdy defensive wall, only fragments of which now exist. The **Kashmiri Gate**, at the northern end of the walled city, was the scene of desperate fighting when the British retook Delhi during the 1857 Uprising (see History in the Facts about the Region chapter). West of here, near Sabzi Mandi, is the British-erected **Mutiny Memorial** to the soldiers who lost their lives during the Uprising.

Red Fort

The Lal Qila, or Red Fort, is Delhi's most impressive attraction. Shah Jahan started construction of the massive red sandstone fort in 1638 and it was completed in 1648. He never completely moved his capital from Agra to his new city of Shahjahanabad in Delhi because he was deposed and imprisoned in Agra Fort by his son Aurangzeb.

The Red Fort dates from the very peak of Mughal power. When the emperor rode out on an elephant into the streets of Old Delhi it was a display of pomp and power at its most magnificent. The Mughal reign from Delhi was a short one, however: Aurangzeb was the first and last great Mughal emperor to rule from here.

Today, the fort is a calm haven of peace after the frantic streets of Old Delhi, although on weekends and Fridays it can seem as though half of Delhi is inside. Entry to the fort is US$10 for foreigners, Rs 5 for Indians; pay at the kiosk opposite the main gate. There are three museums inside the fort; entry to each is Rs 2 and they're all closed on Friday.

Lahore Gate The main gate to the fort takes its name from the fact that it faces towards Lahore, now in Pakistan. If one spot could be called the emotional and symbolic heart of the modern Indian nation, this is probably it. During the struggle for independence, one of the nationalists' declarations was that they would see the Indian flag flying over the Red Fort in Delhi. After independence, many important political speeches were given by Nehru and Indira Gandhi to the crowds amassed on the *maidan* (open place or square) outside, and on Independence Day (15 August) each year, the prime minister addresses a huge crowd from the gate.

You enter the fort here and immediately find yourself in a vaulted arcade, the **Chatta Chowk** (Covered Bazaar). The shops in this arcade used to sell the upmarket items that the royal household might fancy – silks, jewellery and gold. These days they cater to the tourist trade.

The arcade leads to the **Naubat Khana** (Drum House), where musicians played for the emperor, and the arrival of princes and royalty was heralded from here. There's a dusty **Indian War Memorial museum** (Rs 2) upstairs. The open courtyard beyond the Naubat Khana formerly had galleries along either side, but these were removed by the British army when the fort was used as its headquarters.

Diwan-i-Am The Hall of Public Audiences was where the emperor would sit to hear complaints or disputes from his subjects. His alcove in the wall was marble-panelled and set with precious stones, many of which were looted following the 1857 Uprising. This elegant hall was restored as a result of a directive by Lord Curzon, the viceroy of India between 1898 and 1905.

Diwan-i-Khas The Hall of Private Audiences, constructed of white marble, was the

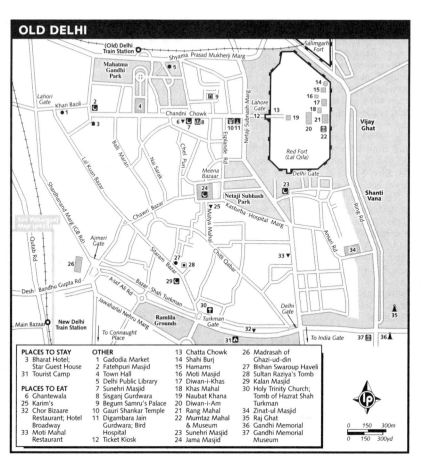

OLD DELHI

PLACES TO STAY	OTHER	13 Chatta Chowk	26 Madrasah of
3 Bharat Hotel;	1 Gadodia Market	14 Shahi Burj	Ghazi-ud-din
Star Guest House	2 Fatehpuri Masjid	15 Hamams	27 Bishan Swaroop Haveli
31 Tourist Camp	4 Town Hall	16 Moti Masjid	28 Sultan Raziya's Tomb
	5 Delhi Public Library	17 Diwan-i-Khas	29 Kalan Masjid
PLACES TO EAT	7 Sunehri Masjid	18 Khas Mahal	30 Holy Trinity Church;
6 Ghantewala	8 Sisganj Gurdwara	19 Naubat Khana	Tomb of Hazrat Shah
25 Karim's	9 Begum Samru's Palace	20 Diwan-i-Am	Turkman
32 Chor Bizaare	10 Gauri Shankar Temple	21 Rang Mahal	34 Zinat-ul Masjid
Restaurant; Hotel	11 Digambara Jain	22 Mumtaz Mahal	35 Raj Ghat
Broadway	Gurdwara; Bird	& Museum	36 Gandhi Memorial
33 Moti Mahal	Hospital	23 Sunehri Masjid	37 Gandhi Memorial
Restaurant	12 Ticket Kiosk	24 Jama Masjid	Museum

0   150   300m
0   150   300yd

luxurious chamber where the emperor would hold private meetings. The centrepiece (until Nāder Shāh carted it off to Iran in 1739) was the magnificent Peacock Throne. The solid-gold throne had figures of peacocks standing behind it, their beautiful colours achieved with countless inlaid precious stones. Between the peacock figures was a parrot carved out of a single emerald.

A masterpiece in precious metals, sapphires, rubies, emeralds and pearls was broken up, and the so-called Peacock Throne displayed in Tehrān's National Jewels Museum (see the Iran chapter) utilises various bits of the original. The marble pedestal on which the throne used to sit remains in place.

Royal Baths Next to the Diwan-i-Khas are the *hamams* or baths – three large rooms surmounted by domes, with a fountain in the centre – one of which was set up as a sauna! The baths are closed to the public.

Moti Masjid Built in 1659 by Aurangzeb for his own personal use and security, the small and totally enclosed Pearl Mosque, made of marble, is next to the baths. One curious feature of the mosque is that its outer walls are oriented exactly to be in symmetry with the rest of the fort, while the inner walls are slightly askew, so that the mosque has the correct orientation with Mecca.

Other Attractions The Khas Mahal, south of the Diwan-i-Khas, was the emperor's

INDIA

private palace, divided into rooms for worship, sleeping and living.

The **Rang Mahal** or Palace of Colour, further south again, took its name from the painted interior, which is now gone. This was once the residence of the emperor's chief wife, and is where he ate. The **Shahi Burj** is the three-storey octagonal tower at the north-eastern edge of the fort. It was once Shah Jahan's private working area, and from here water used to flow south through the Royal Baths, the Diwan-i-Khas, the Khas Mahal and the Rang Mahal. The tower is closed to the public.

There is a small but worthwhile Museum of Archaeology in the **Mumtaz Mahal**, still further south along the eastern wall. Another museum worth seeing is the **Svatantrata Sangrama Sangrahalaya** (Museum of the Independence Movement), located to the left before the Naubat Khana, among the army buildings. The independence movement is charted with newspaper cuttings, letters, photos and several impressive dioramas.

Sound-and-Light Show Each evening an interesting sound-and-light show recreates events of India's history, particularly those connected with the Red Fort. It consists of a commentary and strategic illumination of various parts of the fort. Shows are in English and Hindi, and tickets (Rs 30) are available from an office inside the fort (just outside the Naubat Khana). The English sessions start at 7.30 pm from November to January, 8.30 pm from February to April and September to October, and 9 pm from May to August. It's worth making the effort to see this show, but make sure you are well equipped with plenty of mosquito repellent and long-sleeve clothing.

Chandni Chowk

The main street of Old Delhi is the colourful shopping bazaar known as Chandni Chowk. It's hopelessly congested day and night and is a very sharp contrast to the open, spacious streets of New Delhi. At the eastern (Red Fort) end of Chandni Chowk, there is a **Digambara Jain Gurdwara** (temple). Traditionally, Jain monks of the Digambara, or Sky Clad, sect, wore no garments. There's an interesting **bird hospital** here, run by the Jains.

Next to the *kotwali* (old police station) is the **Sunehri Masjid**. In 1739, Nāder Shāh, the Persian invader who carried off the Peacock Throne, stood on the roof of this mosque and watched while his soldiers conducted a bloody massacre of Delhi's inhabitants.

The western end of Chandni Chowk is marked by the **Fatehpuri Masjid**, which was erected in 1650 by one of Shah Jahan's wives.

Jama Masjid

The great mosque of Old Delhi is both the largest in India and the final architectural extravagance of Shah Jahan. Begun in 1644, the mosque was not completed until 1658. It has three great gateways, four angle towers and two minarets standing 40m high and constructed of alternating vertical strips of red sandstone and white marble.

The eastern gateway was originally only opened for the emperor. It is now only open on Friday and Muslim festival days. The public can enter by either the north or south gate (Rs 10). You should remove your shoes, and those people likely to be considered unsuitably dressed (bare legs for either men or women) can hire robes at the northern gate.

The courtyard of the mosque can hold 25,000 people. You can climb the southern minaret – but only if you're a man or have one accompany you, and not at all during prayer times. The views in all directions are superb. You can also see one of the features that the architect Edwin Lutyens incorporated into his design of New Delhi – the Jama Masjid, Connaught Place and Sansad Bhavan (Parliament House) are in a direct line.

NEW DELHI
Jantar Mantar

Only a short stroll down Sansad Marg from Connaught Place, this strange collection of salmon-coloured structures is one of Maharaja Jai Singh II's observatories. The ruler from Jaipur constructed this observatory in 1725 and it is dominated by a huge sundial known as the Prince of Dials. Other instruments plot the course of heavenly bodies and predict eclipses. The entry fee is US$5. The observatory in Jaipur is larger and more interesting.

NEW DELHI

OTHER
1 Dr Ram Manohar Lohia Hospital
4 Max Mueller Bhavan
6 Rabindra Bhavan (Sangeet Natak Akademi; Lalit Kala Akademi; Shattiya Akademi)
7 Supreme Court
8 Crafts Museum
9 Sher Shah's Gate; Khairul Manzil Masjid
10 National Gallery of Modern Art
11 Pandara Market
12 Bikaner House (Rajasthan Tourist Office & Deluxe Buses to Jaipur)
13 Children's Park
14 National Stadium
15 Indira Gandhi National Centre for the Arts
16 CJ's Nightclub; Aloha; Hotel Le Meridien
17 Indian Airlines
18 Sansad Bhavan (Parliament House)
19 Gurdwara Rakab Ganj
20 Cathedral Church of the Redemption
21 Rashtrapati Bhavan
22 Secretariat (North Block)
23 Secretariat (South Block)
24 Vijay Chowk
25 National Museum;
26 Archaeological Survey of India
26 Captain's Cabin; Taj Mahal Hotel
28 Gandhi Smriti
29 Indira Gandhi Memorial Museum
30 Nehru Museum
31 Dandi March Sculpture
33 Nehru Planetarium
45 Santushti Shopping Centre (Basil & Thyme)
46 Safdarjang's Tomb
47 Indian Airlines (24 Hours)
48 Mohammed Shah's Tomb
49 Goa Tourist Office
52 Lok Nayak Bhavan (Ministry of Home Affairs)
53 Khan Market; The bookshop; Bahri Sons
54 East West Medical Centre
55 Sikander Lodi's Tomb
56 Bara Gumbad Masjid
57 India International Centre
58 World Wide Fund for Nature India
59 Indian Habitat Centre; Habitat World
60 Tibet House
61 Sunder Nagar Market
62 Zoo
63 Humayun's Tomb
64 Isa Khan's Tomb
65 Nizam-ud-din's Shrine

PLACES TO STAY
2 YWCA Blue Triangle Family Hostel
3 Ashok Yatri Niwas ITDC

EMBASSIES & CONSULATES
5 Nepali Embassy
27 Brazilian Embassy
32 Sri Lankan High Commission
34 Norwegian Embassy
35 British High Commission
36 Chinese Embassy
37 US Embassy
38 Australian High Commission
39 Pakistani High Commission
40 French Embassy
41 Dutch Embassy
42 Japanese Embassy
43 Canadian High Commission
44 German Embassy
50 Danish Embassy
51 Israeli Embassy

INDIA

Lakshmi Narayan Temple

Due west of Connaught Place, this garish modern temple was erected by the industrialist BD Birla in 1938. It's dedicated to Lakshmi, the goddess of prosperity and good fortune, and is commonly known as Birla Mandir (*mandir* means temple).

Rajpath

The Kingsway is another focus of Lutyens' New Delhi. It is immensely broad and is flanked on either side by ornamental ponds. The Republic Day parade is held here every 26 January, and millions of people gather to enjoy the spectacle.

At the eastern end of Rajpath lies the **India Gate**, a 42m-high stone arch of triumph. It bears the names of 85,000 Indian army soldiers who died in the campaigns of WWI, the North-West Frontier operations of the same time and the 1919 Afghan fiasco.

At the western end of Rajpath is the copper-domed **Rashtrapati Bhavan**, now the official residence of the President of India. This building was originally built for the viceroy. To the west of the building is a 130-hectare Mughal garden that's only open to the public in February and early March; book through the Government of India tourist office on Janpath. At the time of Mountbatten, India's last viceroy, the number of servants needed to maintain the 340 rooms and its extensive gardens was enormous. There were 418 gardeners alone, 50 of them boys whose sole job was to chase away birds!

The north and south **secretariat buildings** lie either side of Rajpath on Raisina Hill. These imposing buildings, topped with *chhatris* (small domes), now house the ministries of Finance and External Affairs respectively.

Sansad Bhavan

Although another large and imposing building, Sansad Bhavan, the Indian parliament building, stands almost hidden and virtually unnoticed at the end of Sansad Marg, just north of Rajpath.

Permits to visit the parliament and to sit in the public gallery are available from the reception office on Raisina Rd, but you'll need a letter of introduction from your embassy.

MUSEUMS & GALLERIES

Delhi has some good museums and galleries, but the admission price (for foreign tourists) at many shot up in 2000, in some cases from free to Rs 150!

National Museum

On Janpath, just south of Rajpath, the National Museum (☎ 301 9272) is Delhi's finest, with a good collection of Indian bronze, terracotta and wood sculptures dating back to the Mauryan period (2nd to 3rd centuries BC); exhibits from the Vijayanagar period in South India; miniature and mural paintings; and costumes of the various Adivasis (tribal peoples). The museum is open from 10 am to 5 pm daily except Monday, with free guided tours at 10.30 and 11.30 am, noon and 2 pm. There are film shows each afternoon. Admission is a steep Rs 150.

Next door is the Archaeological Survey of India office. Publications available here cover all the main sites in India.

National Gallery of Modern Art

This gallery (☎ 338 2835) stands near India Gate near the eastern end of Rajpath, and was formerly the Delhi residence of the Maharaja of Jaipur. It houses an excellent collection of works by both Indian and colonial artists.

It's open from 10 am to 5 pm daily except Monday (Rs 150).

Nehru Museum & Planetarium

The residence of Jawaharlal Nehru, Teen Murti Bhavan, on Teen Murti Rd near Chanakyapuri, has been converted into a museum. Photographs and newspaper clippings on display give a fascinating insight into the history of the independence movement. There's a planetarium in the grounds (shows are at 11.30 am and 3 pm).

The museum is open from 9.30 am to 4.45 pm daily except Monday (free).

Rail Transport Museum

This museum (☎ 688 1816) at Chanakyapuri will be of great interest to anyone fascinated by India's exotic collection of train engines. The exhibit includes an 1855 steam engine, still in working order, and a large number of oddities such as the skull of an elephant that charged a mail train in 1894, and lost.

The museum is open from 9.30 am to 5 pm daily, except Monday (Rs 5).

Indira Gandhi Memorial Museum

The former residence of Indira Gandhi at 1 Safdarjang Rd has also been converted into a museum (☎ 301 0094). On show are some of her personal effects, including the sari (complete with blood stains) she was wearing at the time of her assassination. Striking a somewhat macabre note is the crystal plaque in the garden, flanked constantly by two soldiers, which protects a few brown spots of Mrs Gandhi's blood at the location where she actually fell after being shot by two of her Sikh bodyguards in December 1984. It's open from 9.30 am to 5 pm daily (free).

OTHER ATTRACTIONS

There are numerous other sites of varying historical interest, including tombs and shrines and the remains of former cities, scattered around Delhi.

Coronation Durbar Site

This is a sobering sight for people interested in the Raj. It's north of Old Delhi and is best reached by autorickshaw (about Rs 150 return from Paharganj) or taxi. In a desolate field stands a lone obelisk where, in 1877 and 1903, the great theatrical *durbars* (royal courts) featuring the full contingent of Indian rulers paid homage to the British monarch. It was also here in 1911 that King George V was declared emperor of India – a statue of him rests nearby in an unkempt walled park.

Feroz Shah Kotla

Erected by Feroz Shah Tughlaq in 1354, the ruins of Ferozabad, the fifth city of Delhi, can be found at Feroz Shah Kotla, just off Bahadur Shah Zafar Marg between the Old and New Delhis. In the fortress-palace is a 13m-high sandstone **Ashoka pillar**. The remains of an old mosque and a fine well can also be seen in the area, but most of the ruins of Ferozabad were used for the construction of later cities. The entry fee is US5.

Raj Ghat

North-east of Feroz Shah Kotla, on the banks of the Yamuna River in Old Delhi, a simple square platform of black marble marks the spot where Mahatma Gandhi was cremated following his assassination in 1948. A commemorative ceremony takes place each Friday, the day he was killed.

Jawaharlal Nehru, the first Indian prime minister, was cremated just to the north at Shanti Vana (Forest of Peace) in 1964. His daughter, Indira Gandhi, who was assassinated in 1984, and grandsons Sanjay (1980) and Rajiv (1991) were also cremated in this vicinity.

The Raj Ghat area is now a beautiful park. The **Gandhi Memorial Museum** here is well worth a visit; a macabre relic is the pistol with which Gandhi was assassinated. It's open from 9.30 am to 5.30 pm daily except Monday (free).

Purana Qila

Just south-east of India Gate and north of Nizamuddin train station is the Purana Qila (Old Fort). This is the supposed site of Indraprastha, the original city of Delhi. Within the fort is the Qila-i-Kuhran Mosque, or Mosque of Sher Shar, which, unlike the fort itself, is in a reasonable condition. The entry fee is US$5. There's a sound-and-light show at Purana Qila each evening (Rs 25) but it's not as good as the one at the Red Fort.

Humayun's Tomb

Built in the mid-16th century by Haji Begum, the Persian-born senior wife of Humayun, the 2nd Mughal emperor, this is a wonderful early example of Mughal architecture. The elements in its design were to be refined over the years to the magnificence of the Taj Mahal in Agra. Haji Begum is also buried in the red-and-white sandstone and black-and-yellow marble tomb. Entry is US$10.

Nizam-ud-din's Shrine

Across the road from Humayun's tomb is the shrine of the Muslim Sufi saint, Nizamuddin Chishti, who died in 1325 aged 92. His shrine, with its large tank, is one of several interesting tombs here.

Other tombs include the later grave of Jahanara, the daughter of Shah Jahan, who stayed with her father during his imprisonment by Aurangzeb in Agra's Red Fort. Amir Khusru, a renowned Urdu poet, also has his tomb here, as does Atgah Khan, a favourite of Humayun and his son Akbar.

INDIA

Atgah Khan was murdered by Adham Khan in Agra. In turn Akbar had Adham Khan terminated and his grave is near the Qutab Minar.

It's worth visiting the shrine at around sunset on Thursday, as it is a popular time for worship, and *qawwali* (Sufi devotional singing) is performed after the evening prayers. This is one of Delhi's most important pilgrimage sites, so dress conservatively.

Delhi Zoo

The Delhi Zoo, on the southern side of Purana Qila, is a peaceful retreat and not bad as far as zoos in the developing world go. It's open from Saturday to Thursday (Rs 40) and is extremely popular at weekends with the denizens of Delhi, who seem to come here specifically to tease the animals.

Bahai Temple

This building, completed in 1987, is shaped like a lotus flower and set among pools and gardens. Adherents of any faith are free to visit the temple and pray or meditate silently according to their own religion. It looks pretty at dusk when it is floodlit, but is a bit disappointing close up. The temple is situated just inside the Outer Ring Road, 12km south-east of the city centre.

Qutab Minar

The buildings in this complex, 15km south of Delhi, date from the onset of Muslim rule in India and are fine examples of early-Afghan architecture. It's open from sunrise to sunset (US$5).

The Qutab Minar itself is a soaring 73m-high tower of victory that was started in 1193, immediately after the defeat of the last Hindu kingdom in Delhi. Although Qutab-ud-din began construction of the tower, he only got to the 1st storey. His successors completed it and, in 1368, Feroz Shah Tughlaq rebuilt the top storeys and added a cupola.

At the foot of the Qutab Minar stands the **Quwwat-ul-Islam Masjid** (Might of Islam Mosque), the first mosque to be built in India. Altamish, Qutab-ud-din's son-in-law, surrounded the original mosque with a cloistered court built between 1210 and

---

Five Hundred Metres of Madness

From fairly humble beginnings as a backstreet marketplace, Main Bazaar in Paharganj has become the heart of Delhi for most backpackers, and so it has naturally attracted every form of hustler, salesperson, beggar and budget hotelier.

Virtually anything you'd care to name – from incense to washing machines – is sold in this bustling market, but much of it is cheap tie-dye clothing that falls apart after two weeks. Although barely wide enough in some places for two autorickshaws to pass by, and constantly clogged with meandering people, Main Bazaar is not pedestrianised. Even cars will try to fit down here and it's not unusual to be sent reeling off the side of the road by an autorickshaw ploughing through from behind. The authorities' solution to this chronic problem is not to ban the traffic but to *widen* the street. This is partly because shops had been building outwards and encroaching on the street. When we visited, work was underway to achieve this, with unfinished ditches and piles of rubble threatening the unwary pedestrian at every turn.

A short walk down Main Bazaar will result in many offers. Catch the eye of the right (or wrong) person and you're in for plenty of attention. It could be an invitation to 'just look in my shop', an offer of a houseboat holiday in 'beautiful Kashmir' (not recommended), or a Bangladeshi beggar petitioning you for a Rs 500 donation. Smooth-talking young men will sidle up alongside and ask 'Where are you from?', 'How long have you been in India?', 'Is this your first time?', 'Do you like it here?'. Then comes the sales pitch. If you shrug it off, they act offended but soon move on to an easier target.

Offers of drugs or cash for travellers cheques with only one signature are made much more discreetly – ignore both.

It can be a hassle just getting from one end of Main Bazaar to the other, but it has a certain chaotic charm and you can't beat the location. Welcome to India!

1220. Ala-ud-din added a court to the east and the magnificent Alai Darwaza gateway in 1300.

The 7m-high **iron pillar** in the courtyard of the mosque has been there since long before the mosque's construction. Scientists have never discovered how this iron, which is of such purity that it has not rusted after 2000 years, could be cast with the lack of technology at the time. It was said that if you can stand with your back to the pillar and encircle it with your arms your wish will be granted, but the pillar is now encircled by a fence.

You can get out to the Qutab Minar on a No 505 bus from the Ajmeri Gate side of New Delhi train station, or from Janpath, outside the Chandralok building. Hiring a taxi is more convenient.

ORGANISED TOURS

Delhi is very spread out, so if you want to see a range of sights taking a city tour makes a lot of sense. Two major organisations arrange Delhi tours – beware agents offering cut-price tours. The Indian Tourism Development Corporation (ITDC), operating under the name Ashok Travels & Tours (☎ 332 0331), has tours that include guides and a luxury coach. Their office is in L-Block, Connaught Place, near Nirula's Hotel, but you can book at the Government of India tourist office on Janpath or at the major hotels. Delhi Tourism (☎ 331 3637), N-Block, arranges similar tours.

A five-hour morning tour of New Delhi costs Rs 140 with ITDC. Starting at 8 am, the tour includes the Qutab Minar, Humayun's tomb, India Gate, the Jantar Mantar and the Lakshmi Narayan Temple. The afternoon Old Delhi tour (Rs 120) starts at 2.15 pm and covers the Red Fort, Jama Masjid, Raj Ghat, Shanti Vana and Feroz Shah Kotla. If you take both tours on the same day (and a long day it will be, from 8 am to 5 pm) it costs Rs 220. These tour prices do not include entry fees to monuments. Some travellers complain that these tours are a bit rushed.

If you have a group, driving tours (in an Ambassador with driver) can be reasonable value. Almost any travel agent will organise tours to Agra and Rajasthan. A day tour to Agra costs around US$50 (US$60 if you include Fatehpur Sikri) and an eight-day tour of Rajasthan costs around US$400.

PLACES TO STAY

Whether you're arriving in Delhi by plane, train or bus, the biggest thing to be wary of is hotel touts and drivers of taxis or auto-rickshaws trying to con you into rip-off joints so that they can earn their fat commissions. We get an endless supply of mail from travellers who have fallen prey to these scams, or simply been taken by a driver to somewhere they didn't want to go. You'll be told the usual stories: That your hotel is closed or burnt down; there have been street riots and we can't take you to that part of town; there is a better, cheaper place nearby. Don't believe a word of it. One option is to make a booking by phone or fax in advance, or just call to check that a room is available from the airport/bus/train station. There are so many hotels and guesthouses in the backpacker hub of Paharganj that, preferably in daylight, you can simply be dropped off at the bazaar and find a place yourself.

During summer (May to August) discounts of up to 50% are often available and it's always worth asking for a discount if you intend staying for more than a couple of days.

PLACES TO STAY – BUDGET

Delhi is no bargain when it comes to cheap hotels. You can easily pay Rs 150 for the most basic single room – a price that elsewhere in India will generally get you a double with bathroom.

There are two main areas for cheap accommodation. Most travellers head for Paharganj near New Delhi train station, about midway between Old Delhi and New Delhi. It's a convenient location, has plenty of places to choose from and exudes a certain chaotic charm, but the pushy touts, heavy traffic and constant madness of the bazaar put some people off. It's set up for travellers with souvenir shops, Internet cafes and travel agencies – not unlike a shambolic version of Bangkok's Khao San Rd.

The alternative area is around Janpath at the southern side of Connaught Place in New Delhi; it's comparatively subdued but there's less choice (and still loads of touts).

There are also a number of rock-bottom hotels in Old Delhi, such as *Bharat Hotel* (☎ 395 5326) and *Star Guest House* (☎ 292 1127), both at the western end of Chandni

INDIA

Chowk and with double rooms for less than Rs 200. They're colourful but generally noisy, grotty and too far away from New Delhi's travel agencies, banks, restaurants and other facilities for most travellers, especially given the difficulties with transport. Many of the cheap hotels have 24-hour checkout, which is handy if you arrive late.

Camping

Tourist Camp (☎ 327 2898) is deservedly popular among overlanders or anyone with a vehicle. It's some way from Connaught Place but close to Old Delhi's sights. The camp is near Delhi Gate on Jawaharlal Nehru Marg, opposite the JP Narayan Hospital (Irwin Hospital). You can set up your own tent (Rs 50) on the hard ground, and there are basic single/double rooms with shared bathroom for Rs 125/200 and doubles with air cooler for Rs 250 (Rs 390 with bath). They're nothing flash and hot as hell in summer, but this place gets good recommendations from travellers and develops a real overlanding atmosphere when it fills up. There's a basic restaurant and a left-luggage room. Parking costs Rs 50 per day for a car or van and Rs 100 for a truck or bus.

Paharganj

Directly opposite New Delhi train station's front entrance is the start of Main Bazaar, a narrow road that stretches due west for about 1km. Because of its proximity to the station it has become a major accommodation centre for Indians and foreigners alike.

Hotel Namaskar (☎ 362 1234, ℮ namaskarhotel@yahoo.com, 917 Chandiwalan) is a good choice along here, mainly because of the management. It's very friendly, quiet, and well managed by two brothers who go out of their way to help. All rooms have windows and bath, and hot water is available on each floor. Guest's luggage (one bag per person) is stored free of charge if there is space, and there's a filtered water tank where you can fill your drink bottle for free. Singles/doubles cost Rs 150/250, and three- (Rs 300) and four-bed (Rs 400) rooms are available. An air-con double room is Rs 450. You can also arrange bus, train and plane tickets here and book car hire for extended trips. It's a five-minute walk from the train station (turn right down the small laneway just before Camran Lodge).

Hotel Sweet Dream (☎ 362 9801), next door, is not as well run but it's clean and the rooms are OK at Rs 200/250.

Anoop Hotel (☎ 352 1451, ℮ sent@ndf .vsnl.net.in, 1566 Main Bazaar) is very good value for this area. The marble-lined rooms, which have bathroom and hot water, are a decent size and cost Rs 180/250 (Rs 375/425 for air-con). A major attraction here is the rooftop terrace and snack bar.

Ankur Guest House (☎ 361 5102, 419 Main Bazaar), just inside a side lane almost opposite the Anoop, has plain but spotless rooms and good management. Smallish rooms with private bathroom and hot water are cheap at Rs 100/150 and a four-bed room is Rs 200. *Ajay Guest House (☎ 354 3125, 5084 Main Bazaar)*, further down the same lane, has a pleasant rooftop, a German bakery and a pool table in the foyer. All rooms have bathroom and cost Rs 170/220 or Rs 350 for an air-con double.

Hare Rama Guest House (☎ 352 1413, ℮ harerama@ndf.vsnl.net.in, 298 Main Bazaar) is opposite the Ajay and equally popular, particularly with Israeli travellers. There's a variety of rooms, some very small and windowless, from Rs 130/160 with shared bathroom, Rs 180/220 with private bathroom and Rs 350 for an air-con double. The restaurant is open 24 hours.

Traveller Guest House Inn (☎ 354 4849, 4360 Main Bazaar) is one of the first places you come to if you walk across from the train station. The rooms are clean, though some are without windows. There are no singles; doubles with bathroom are Rs 240. A decent triple with TV and bathroom (hot water geyser) costs Rs 330. It's not as good value as places further down the bazaar.

Kailash Guest House (☎ 367 4993, 4469 Main Bazaar), a little further along, is clean enough, although many of the rooms face inwards and can be a bit stuffy; those with windows are fine. It's not bad value at Rs 150/175 with shared bathroom, and Rs 225/250 with bathroom and cooler. *Kiran Guest House (☎ 352 6104, 4473 Main Bazaar)*, next door, is virtually a carbon copy of the Kailash, and prices are similar at Rs 120/175 with shared bathroom, Rs 150/225 with private bathroom.

Further on and down a side lane to the left are three reasonable places. *Hotel Star Palace (☎ 362 8584, ℮ starview@vsnl.com)*

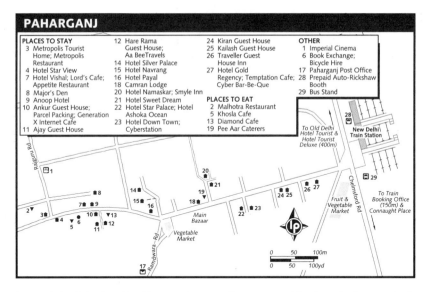

PAHARGANJ

PLACES TO STAY
3 Metropolis Tourist
   Home; Metropolis
   Restaurant
4 Hotel Star View
7 Hotel Vishal; Lord's Cafe;
   Appetite Restaurant
8 Major's Den
9 Anoop Hotel
10 Ankur Guest House;
   Parcel Packing; Generation
   X Internet Cafe
11 Ajay Guest House

12 Hare Rama
   Guest House;
   Aa BeeTravels
14 Hotel Silver Palace
15 Hotel Navrang
16 Hotel Payal
18 Camran Lodge
20 Hotel Namaskar; Smyle Inn
21 Hotel Sweet Dream
22 Hotel Star Palace; Hotel
   Ashoka Ocean
23 Hotel Down Town;
   Cyberstation

24 Kiran Guest House
25 Kailash Guest House
26 Traveller Guest
   House Inn
27 Hotel Gold
   Regency; Temptation Cafe;
   Cyber Bar-Be-Que

PLACES TO EAT
2 Malhotra Restaurant
5 Khosla Cafe
13 Diamond Cafe
19 Pee Aar Caterers

OTHER
1 Imperial Cinema
6 Book Exchange;
   Bicycle Hire
17 Paharganj Post Office
28 Prepaid Auto-Rickshaw
   Booth
29 Bus Stand

---

is the pick of the bunch. All rooms have private bathroom. Air-cooled rooms cost Rs 200/250 and good air-con rooms are Rs 450/500. There's a rooftop restaurant. *Hotel Down Town* (☎ 355 5815) is almost opposite. Some of the rooms are tiny but they're clean enough and pretty good value at Rs 125/150 with shared bathroom, and Rs 150/200 with private bathroom (and hot water). Larger air-con rooms cost Rs 350/400. *Hotel Ashoka Ocean* (☎ 362 8575, 4589 Main Bazaar) has air-cooled rooms with grubby bathrooms at the same price as the Down Town.

Camran Lodge (☎ 352 6053, 1116 Main Bazaar) at least has some character since it's built into the side of the old mosque, but the rooms are gloomy and cheap at Rs 80/160 for shared bathroom and Rs 180 for a double with private bathroom. Hot water by the bucket is free.

Hotel Navrang (☎ 352 1965, 6 Tooti Chowk) is one of the cheapest places in Paharganj and it's easy to see why. Five floors of shabby, basic rooms make it a depressing option. Dorm beds are Rs 50, singles with shared bathroom are Rs 80 and doubles with private bathroom are Rs 100. It's down a side street to the right off the vegetable market.

Further along this street, *Hotel Silver Palace* is well run and much better value.

Clean rooms with private bathroom (single or double) cost Rs 150.

Back on Main Bazaar and further west, *Hotel Vishal* (☎ 352 6314, 1575 Main Bazaar) is a bit of a rabbit warren but has good-sized rooms and two good restaurants on the ground floor. Rooms cost Rs 120/150 with shared bathroom and Rs 150/200 with private bathroom.

Still in Paharganj, there's another string of places on Arakashan Rd, just north of New Delhi train station, past the Desh Bandhu Gupta Rd flyover. They include *Hotel Soma* (☎ 752 1002) and *Tourist Inn* (☎ 777 7112). These are at the top end of the budget category with rooms from Rs 400 upwards, and are clean and well equipped.

Connaught Place & Janpath

There are a few cheap guesthouses near the Government of India tourist office. They're cramped and this area is not as lively as Paharganj, but you meet lots of fellow travellers.

Ringo Guest House (☎ 331 0605, 17 Scindia House), down a small side street near the tourist office, is an ageing travellers' institution, which hasn't even bothered to change its prices for a few years. Beds in crowded, 14-bed dorms are Rs 90; rooms with shared bathroom are Rs 125/250 and doubles with private bathroom are

INDIA

CONNAUGHT PLACE

PLACES TO STAY
1 Hotel 55
6 Nirula's Hotel
14 Hotel Alka; Vega
26 Hotel Blue
43 Sunny Guest House
44 Ringo Guest House; Don't
   Pass Me By Cafe; Don't
   Pass Me By Travels
57 YMCA Tourist Hotel;
   Y Tours & Travel
60 YWCA International
   Guest House

PLACES TO EAT
4 Ruby Tuesday
5 Nirula's Restaurant;
   Pegasus Tavern
8 Pizza Express
13 Cafe 100; Zen Restaurant
15 McDonald's
16 Keventers

17 Wenger's
19 Rodeo
21 Kovil; Pizza Hut
23 United Coffee House
24 Domino's Pizza
34 Nirula's (Branch)
38 Gaylord
39 Kwality Restaurant;
   People Tree
45 Kalpana Restaurant
53 Parikrama
55 Sona Rupa Restaurant;
   Royal Nepal Airlines
   Corporation (RNAC)

OTHER
2 Plaza Cinema
3 English Book Depot
7 Cyber Cafe
9 Odeon Cinema
10 Thomas Cook
11 Bookworm

12 New Book Depot
18 American Express
20 Post Office
22 SCB Grindlays Bank (ATM)
25 Piccadilly Book Store
27 Sita World Travels
28 Phat Phat Sewa
   (Jeeps to Red Fort)
29 EATS Airport Bus
30 Indian Airlines
31 Delhi Tourism Corporation
32 DSIDC Cyber Cafe
33 Blues Bar
35 Rivoli Cinema
36 Police
37 Regal Cinema
40 Citibank; Air India
41 Emirates; Wheels Rent a Car
42 American Center
46 Government of India
   Tourist Office; Delhi Photo
   Company

47 Tourist Police
48 Bank of Baroda
49 Standard Chartered Bank;
   Allahabad Bank
50 Someplace Else;
   Park Hotel
51 Tan's Travel
52 Prepaid Autorickshaw
   Stand
54 British Council
56 Map Sales Office
58 State Bank of India
   (Main Branch)
59 Free Church
61 Central Cottage
   Industries Emporium
62 Chandralok Building
   (Haryana, Himachal
   Pradesh & Uttar
   Pradesh Tourist
   Offices; STIC
   Travels)

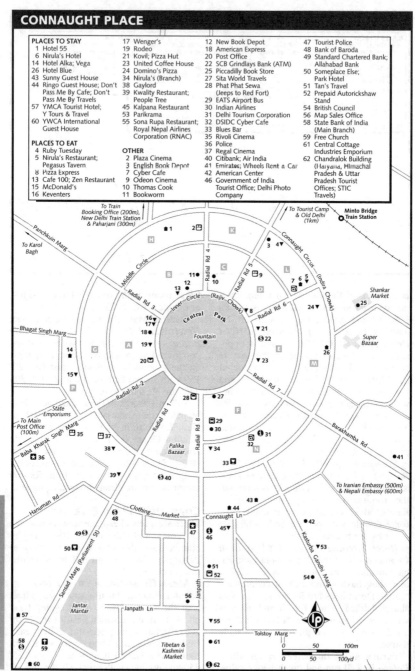

INDIA

Rs 350 to Rs 400. The rooms are small and flimsy and it could hardly be called top value. Meals are available in the rooftop courtyard. You can also store luggage for Rs 8 per item per day.

Sunny Guest House (☎ *331 2909, 152 Scindia House*), a few doors further along the same side street, is virtually a carbon copy and has exactly the same prices.

Hotel Blue (☎ *332 9123, 126 M-Block, Connaught Place*), opposite Super Bazaar, has singles/doubles for Rs 200/400 with shared bathroom and up to Rs 500/900 with private bathroom. There's a pleasant sitting area on the balcony overlooking Connaught Circus and you can get breakfast here. It's pricey for what you get, but par for the course in this area.

PLACES TO STAY – MID-RANGE

There's currently a luxury tax of 10% on rooms more than Rs 500 (not included in the following prices), and some places also levy an additional service charge of 5% to 10%.

Paharganj

The flash *Hotel Gold Regency* (☎ *354 0101, fax 354 0202,* e *goldregency@ hotmail.com, 4350 Main Bazaar*) sticks out a bit as the only mid-range place at the train-station end of Main Bazaar. It has a good restaurant, a busy email centre and a noisy disco. The rooms are large and clean, with possibly the biggest bathrooms in Paharganj, but have top-end price tags. Air-con singles/doubles cost Rs 870/1125, including breakfast, and 'executive deluxe' rooms are Rs 1300/1550. The hotel is open 24 hours.

At the other end of the bazaar, *Hotel Star View* (☎ *355 6301, 5136 Main Bazaar*) has a range of small but clean rooms from Rs 325/425, all with windows, bathroom and TV. Air-con rooms are Rs 575/675.

Metropolis Tourist Home (☎ *352 5492, fax 752 5600, 1634 Main Bazaar*) is a good mid-range choice. Clean and comfortable air-con rooms with bathroom cost Rs 550/ 660. There's a good restaurant here.

Connaught Place & Janpath

There are several mid-range hotels around Janpath and Connaught Place.

Ashok Yatri Niwas (☎ *332 4511*), on the corner of Ashoka Rd and Janpath, is just a 10-minute walk from Connaught Place.

Rooms in this high-rise, government-run hotel cost Rs 650/750/850 for singles/ doubles/four-beds (plus 10% luxury tax) with bathroom. The rooms are a reasonable size and some have been renovated recently, but none has a phone, TV or room service. It gets mixed reports from travellers – ask to see a few rooms before deciding.

The YMCA and YWCA places, which take either sex, are just south of Connaught Place. They're popular – though generally way overpriced – so you'll need to book ahead, and they have facilities such as travel agents, restaurants and parking.

YMCA Tourist Hotel (☎ *336 1915, fax 374 6032,* e *ymcath@ndf.vsnl.net.in, Jai Singh Rd*) is near the Jantar Mantar. Although it has an institutional (and pious) feel and is no great bargain, it's still popular with foreigners as it's well located, clean and has good facilities. There are gardens, a swimming pool, lounge and a restaurant. Despite what the touts may tell you, the hotel is open 24 hours, and credit cards are accepted. Rooms cost Rs 415/725 with shared bathroom, Rs 650/1150 with bathroom and Rs 800/1350 with air-con. There's also an additional 5% service charge, a 10% luxury tax on rooms over Rs 500 and a temporary membership charge of Rs 30, valid for one month. Breakfast is included.

YWCA International Guest House (☎ *336 1517, fax 334 1763,* e *ycaind@del3 .vsnl.net.in, 10 Sansad Marg*) has rooms for Rs 800/1000 (plus 10% service charge and the 10% luxury tax); all rooms have bathroom and air-con and breakfast is included. Car parking is available for Rs 50 per 24 hours.

There are a couple of excellent private guesthouses to the west of Connaught Place. Advance bookings are advisable during the high season.

Master Paying Guest House (☎ *585 0914,* e *urvashi@del2.vsnl.net.in, R-500 New Rajendra Nagar*) is a Rs 40 autorickshaw ride from Connaught Place, near the intersection of Shankar Rd and Gangaram Hospital Marg. This small, friendly place is in a quiet residential area and the owner has worked hard to create a homelike atmosphere. It has large, airy and beautifully furnished doubles from Rs 350 to Rs 750. Light meals are available, there's a pleasant rooftop terrace, and car hire for extended trips can also be arranged.

INDIA

PLACES TO EAT

Delhi has an excellent array of places to eat – from *dhabas* (snack bars) with dishes for less than Rs 15 up to top-of-the-range restaurants where a meal for two can top Rs 3500.

Paharganj

Main Bazaar in Paharganj has a compact strip of cheap restaurants that cater to foreign travellers, along with the usual Indian street-food stalls and fruit and vegetable vendors. Hotel rooftop restaurants are also popular places to sit and escape the street below. There are several local-style eateries where you can get a vegetable thali for Rs 15, though some are of dubious hygiene standards. Most restaurants are at the western end of Main Bazaar, past the central vegetable market.

Malhotra Restaurant is one of the best in this area and it has two branches in the street behind the Metropolis Tourist Home, one of which is air-conditioned. They're both clean and have large menus featuring reasonably priced Indian food. *Khosla Cafe* and *Diamond Cafe* both offer cheap travellers' fare with dishes like omelettes and mashed potato side by side with veg thalis. They also have a few tables at the front so you can enjoy some chaos while you eat.

Lords Cafe in Hotel Vishal, has passable cheap food and Sky sports on the TV, while the adjacent *Appetite Restaurant* is clean and gets good reports for its Indian and continental food. The *rooftop restaurant* in the Anoop Hotel is one of the best around for ambience and there's a German bakery here too.

Pee Aar Caterers, in the side street leading to the Hotel Namaskar, does excellent Rs 20 thalis (afternoons only).

Temptation Cafe at the Hotel Gold Regency is an upmarket place but the prices are reasonable and it's an air-con haven from the bustle outside. It's also one of the few places in Paharganj where you can sit back with a cold beer. There's Indian, Chinese and continental dishes on the menu with mains ranging from Rs 60 to Rs 225 plus snacks such as sandwiches and burgers from Rs 40.

Connaught Place & Janpath

There are many busy fast-food places in this area, both Western and Indian-style. Most have good food at reasonable prices and are clean, though some have no seating – it's stand, eat and run. They serve Indian food (such as samosas and dosas) and Western food (burgers and sandwiches).

Also in this area are some of the best restaurants in town – outside of the five-star hotels at least.

Restaurants *The United Coffee House (E-Block, Connaught Place)* is quite plush with a pleasantly relaxed atmosphere, traditionally dressed waiters, good food and some of the best coffee in Delhi.

Kwality Restaurant (Sansad Marg) is clean and very efficient and the standard nonveg food is good value. Main courses are around Rs 100.

Zen Restaurant (B-Block, Connaught Place) has mostly Chinese and Indian dishes at around Rs 150. It also has a bar and filter and espresso coffee.

Rodeo (A-Block, Connaught Place) is a lively restaurant serving good Mexican food (fajitas, tacos etc); it's worth visiting just for the sight of waiters in cowboy suits! You can have a drink at the bar here until 7.30 pm but after that you'll need to order a meal. Expect to pay more than Rs 200 per person.

Ruby Tuesday (L-Block, Connaught Circus) is a bright new neon-and-brass place with a range of pricey but well-presented Western-style snacks such as burgers and baked potatoes.

Gaylord (Connaught Circus) is one of the priciest, plushest restaurants on Connaught Place, with big mirrors, chandeliers and excellent Indian food. Main dishes are around Rs 200, but the high quality of the ingredients makes this a worthwhile splurge.

Parikrama (Kasturba Gandhi Marg), a revolving restaurant, is an interesting place to eat. Apart from the excellent views, the food here is pricey but very good. Main dishes are around Rs 170. It's open daily for lunch and dinner, and for drinks from 3 to 7 pm.

Budget Restaurants & Fast Food Well known for its wide variety of light snacks, both Indian and Western, is *Nirula's*. The ice-cream parlour is amazingly busy, and is open from 10 am to midnight. The main Nirula's is in L-Block on the outer circle. Above the ice-cream parlour, *Pot Pourri* is a busy sit-down restaurant. The smorgasbord salad bar is good value, though we've had mixed reports about the cleanliness. It's a good place for breakfast, which is served from 7.30 am. Also here is *Pegasus* (see Entertainment) which has a range of pricey bar snacks.

Keventers, on the corner of Connaught Place and Radial Rd 3, is a small corner store where you can order superb flavoured milk and ice-cold shakes (Rs 15) which come in pint milk bottles (returnable). You can't miss the place since there's always a crowd of people standing around the front slurping on a shake. It also does light snacks. *Wenger's* is a good little cake shop just around the corner in A-Block.

Cafe 100, in B-Block, is another very popular semi self-service place. There are Indian snacks, pizzas and burgers (less than Rs 50), a wide range of ice creams, and an excellent buffet upstairs (open from noon to 3 pm and 7 to 11 pm) for Rs 160.

Kovil is an excellent south Indian restaurant next to Pizza Hut in E-Block. The counter at the front has sandwiches, samosas and other light snacks for less than Rs 20. Inside, wonderful vegetarian food costs around Rs 150 for a full meal.

Sona Rupa Restaurant on Janpath does good north and south Indian vegetarian food; you can eat well for less than Rs 80 per person.

Don't Pass Me By, in the same lane as the Ringo and Sunny guesthouses, is a popular, cheap little place that caters to international tastes, including good breakfasts. Nearby, *Kalpana Restaurant* has Rs 20 thalis and cheap Western breakfasts but it's a real soup kitchen inside.

Connaught Place probably has more American fast-food joints than anywhere else in India and, judging by the number of westerners (and Indians) inside at any given moment, their popularity shows no signs of waning. These places are invariably air-conditioned, clean and have good toilet facilities. As for the food, you've probably tried it all before.

McDonald's is in P-Block, although their blanket advertising may give the impression they've taken over the entire area. A Maharaja Mac meal (lamb, not beef) costs Rs 87.

Pizza Hut is near SCB Grindlays Bank in E-Block. It's not cheap – a small veg pizza costs Rs 75 and a large supreme is Rs 395 – but the service is good and it's a bright

and comfortable restaurant. There are also branches of *Domino's Pizza* (☎ 373 4876), which does free delivery, and *Pizza Express* in Connaught Place; the former has take-aways only. Pizza Express has pizzas from Rs 140 to Rs 215 and a range of beers, wine and cocktails.

Old Delhi

In Old Delhi there are many places to eat at the western end of Chandni Chowk.

Ghantewala (Chandni Chowk), near the Sisganj Gurdwara (Sikh temple), is reputed to have some of the best Indian sweets in Delhi. The stalls along the road in front of the Jama Masjid are very cheap.

Karim's, down a lane across from the south gate of the Jama Masjid, is well known for its excellent nonveg food. There's everything from kebabs to the richest Mughlai dishes in this large restaurant, and prices are reasonable.

Chor Bizaare (Asaf Ali Rd) is located at Hotel Broadway, almost opposite the rear of the Tourist Camp. The decor is sort of 1930s Americana with an eclectic mix of bits and pieces including photographs, an old sports car (now used as a salad bar) and an old cello. The food is good but expensive, although you could get away with less than Rs 250 per person.

South Delhi

There are some good eating options in the area south of Connaught Place, but you'll need a taxi or similar transport to get to most of them.

Dilli Haat (Aurobindo Marg), opposite the INA Market, is a great place to sample food from all over India – many of the stalls devoted to particular states have restaurants which are very reasonably priced.

ENTERTAINMENT

There's always plenty going on in Delhi, but cultural entertainment, exhibitions, shows and favoured nightlife venues are constantly changing. The best place to check on current events is in *Delhi Diary*, *Delhi City Guide* or *First City* magazines.

For free social entertainment you can't beat a stroll down Rajpath (from the President's House to India Gate) on weekend evenings, especially in summer. Thousands of people line this 5km strip for what may be the world's biggest casual family gathering. Food stalls and ice-cream vendors make a killing, rich young Indians cruise up and down in flash cars, kids play games and many families are sprawled out on the lawn with their picnics.

Bars & Clubs

Delhi doesn't offer the sort of nightlife you might imagine of India's national capital. Although licensing laws have been loosened in recent years, most bars are either in top-end hotels or restaurants, and late-night discos are almost exclusively in five-star hotels. These are generally expensive to get into (not to mention the cost of drinks) and entry is sometimes restricted to members and hotel guests; couples and women stand a better chance of being admitted than unaccompanied men.

Still, there are a few reasonably lugubrious bars and 'pubs' around Connaught Place where you can have a few drinks and relax in a comfortable atmosphere. There are also beer and wine shops scattered around the city where you can buy a bottle of Kingfisher beer for as little as Rs 30 and take it back to your guesthouse (drinking in the open is illegal). There's one next to the Delhi Tourism Corporation office in Connaught Place.

Pegasus Tavern, a British-style pub at Nirula's Hotel in L-Block, is one of the most popular places around and it can be difficult to find a seat in the evening – but you can always stand at the bar. There's draught and bottled beer, but you can also get Indian wines, spirits and cocktails (Rs 110). *Blues Bar* on Connaught Circus also has draught beer; happy hour is from 4 to 7 pm but there's a Rs 250 cover charge after 8 pm.

Rodeo, the wild-west-theme bar-restaurant on Connaught Place (see Places to Eat), has a cover charge of Rs 150 after 7.30 pm if you only want to drink and not eat. Draught beer is Rs 70 and bottled beer Rs 135. Other places where you can have a drink include the *Zen Restaurant* and *United Coffee House* (see Places to Eat).

There are relatively few drinking spots in Paharganj, but *Hotel Gold Regency* in Main Bazaar provides 'upmarket' entertainment. As well as a bar-restaurant with live music, there's a disco from 10.30 pm every night. Entry is Rs 200 and it's not the funkiest

place in town – but it does have lights and loud music.

Delhi's five-star hotels have the rest of the city's best bars and nightspots, which are mostly patronised by wealthy young Indians. Most of the bars close at midnight, while the discos usually start up at about 10 pm and continue into the early hours. You'll need to dress up a little to get in.

Jazz Bar at Hotel Maurya Sheraton is good, with live jazz each evening, but drinks are expensive – more than Rs 200 for a beer. Theme bars with interesting decor and expensive drinks include *Captain's Cabin* at the Taj Mahal Hotel (decked out like the bar of a ship) and *Aloha* in Hotel Le Meridian (Pacific Islands theme).

Someplace Else is a bar-disco at Park Hotel starting around 10.30 pm. Entry is Rs 400 per couple (Rs 300 on Sunday, Monday and Wednesday). *CJ's* nightclub at Hotel Le Meridien charges Rs 500 per couple.

Cinemas

There are a number of cinemas around Connaught Place and Paharganj, but the fare is typically Hindi mass-appeal movies; seats range from Rs 25 to Rs 60.

The best cinemas are mostly in the southern suburbs, including *Priya Cinema* (☎ 614 0049), Basant Lok, Vasant Vihar, and *PVR Anupam 4* (☎ 686 5999), in the Saket Community Centre, Saket. *Satyam Cineplex* (☎ 579 7385) is on Patel Road, west of Karol Bagh. These cinemas regularly show Hollywood blockbusters tame enough to sneak past the Indian censors and tickets here are closer to Rs 100.

More central cinemas in Connaught Place include the *Regal* (☎ 336 2245) and the *Plaza* (☎ 332 2784). The *Rivoli* (☎ 336 2227), around the corner from the Regal, shows what passes for raunchy films in India, with titles such as *Naughty Girl* and *Secrets of Women*.

For something a little more cerebral, the *British Council* (☎ 371 0111, Kasturba Gandhi Marg) often screens good foreign films. *Habitat World* (see Theatre & Dance) also has a cinema concentrating on Indian documentaries and art-house films.

Theatre & Dance

Delhi is renowned for its dance and visual arts scene; check out *First City* magazine or

Delhi Diary for what's going on. Major dance and live-music venues include ***Habitat World*** (☎ *469 1920, Lodhi Rd*) at the India Habitat Centre; the nearby ***India International Centre*** (☎ *461 9431*); ***Kamani Auditorium*** (☎ *338 8084, Copernicus Marg*); and ***Triveni Chamber Theatre*** (☎ *371 8833, 205 Tansen Marg*) at Triveni Kala Sangam, near Rabindran Bhavan. They offer a mix of live theatre and dance.

SHOPPING

Good buys include silk products, precious stones, leather and woodwork, but the most important thing about Delhi is that you can find almost anything from anywhere in the entire country.

Two good places to start are in New Delhi, near Connaught Place. The Central Cottage Industries Emporium is on Janpath. In this building you will find items from all over India, generally of good quality and reasonably priced. Whether it's woodcarvings, brasswork, paintings, clothes, textiles or furniture, you'll find it here. Along Baba Kharak Singh Marg, two streets around (clockwise) from Janpath, are the state emporiums run by the state governments. Each of them displays and sells handicrafts from their state.

There are many other shops around Connaught Place and Janpath. By the Imperial Hotel are a number of stalls and small shops run by Tibetan refugees and rapacious Kashmiris selling carpets, jewellery and many (often instant) antiques.

In Old Delhi, Chandni Chowk is the famous shopping street. Here you will find carpets and jewellery, but you have to search the convoluted back alleys. Perfumes are made in the narrow street called Cariba Kalan.

Main Bazaar in Paharganj has a good range, although much of it is cheap clothing, footwear and bags. You can find an interesting variety of perfumes, oils, soaps and incense at two places (both signposted), one near Hotel Vivek and another near Camran Lodge. Take advantage of all the free testers. Monday is the official weekly holiday for the shops in Main Bazaar, and many are closed on that day, although a surprising number remain open seven days a week.

In recent years the Karol Bagh Market, 3km west of Connaught Place along Panchkuin Marg (Radial Rd No 3), has become even more popular than Connaught Place or Main Bazaar.

Hauz Khas Village in south Delhi has become a very interesting little shopping enclave, with an ever-changing collection of art galleries and boutiques catering for the upper end of the market.

GETTING THERE & AWAY

Delhi is a major international gateway and the centre for domestic transport in northern India, with extensive bus, rail and air connections.

Air

The domestic terminals (Terminals IA and IB of the Indira Gandhi International Airport) are 15km from the centre, and the international terminal (Terminal II) is a further 5km. There's a free IAAI bus between the two terminals, or you can use the Ex-Servicemen's Air Link Transport Service (EATS; see Getting Around later in this section).

Several airlines now require you to have your baggage x-rayed and sealed when you check in, so do this at the machines just inside the departure hall before you queue. Nearly all airline tickets include the departure tax in the price; if it's not included, you must pay at the State Bank counter in the departures hall, also before check-in.

International Delhi is the best place in India to pick up cheap flights. At certain times of the year international flights out of Delhi can be heavily booked so it's wise to make reservations as early as possible. Check and double-check your reservations – particularly those made through cut-price travel agents – and make sure you reconfirm your flight at least 72 hours in advance.

International flights are cheapest if purchased from a travel agent and there are plenty to choose from in Delhi (see Travel Agencies earlier under Information). You'll find budget travel agencies clustered around Janpath and around the corner in N-Block, and, of course, along Main Bazaar in Paharganj. You can find flights to Bangkok from US$260, İstanbul for US$340, London from around US$340, Singapore from US$320 and Sydney from US$500. The cheapest flights will usually be with less popular airlines such as Aeroflot and

Uzbekistan Air, but good agents will often be able to dig up cheap seats on better airlines, so shop around. Standard fares with Air India or Indian Airlines include: Bangkok US$345; London US$570; Singapore US$490; and Sydney US$1280.

Indian Airlines resumed its regular flights to Kathmandu in August 2000, nine months after the hijacking of one of its planes from Kathmandu airport. It costs US$142 one way. Royal Nepal Airlines also flies Delhi-Kathmandu at least twice daily for the same fare.

For reconfirming flights, check the *Delhi City Guide*, which lists the addresses and telephone numbers of most international and domestic airlines in the city.

Domestic Indian Airlines, the main domestic carrier, has a number of offices. The Malhotra Building office (☎ 331 0517) in F-Block, Connaught Place, is probably the most convenient, though busy at most times. It's open from 10 am to 5 pm daily except Saturday. The number for the main booking office is ☎ 141. For prerecorded flight-departure information, ring ☎ 142.

Indian Airlines has flights from Delhi to all the major Indian centres, including Bangalore (US$255), Kolkata (Calcutta, US$200), Dharamsala (US$145), Goa (US$235), Mumbai (US$135), Shimla (US$110) and Varanasi (US$125).

Jet Airways (☎ 685 3700) flies to Chandigarh (US$75), Goa (US$225), Jaipur (US$55) and Varanasi (US$125).

Bus

All the main roads leading out of Delhi are heavily congested so it's best to leave early in the morning. The main bus station is the huge Interstate Bus Terminal (ISBT) at Kashmiri Gate, north of the (Old) Delhi train station. It has 24-hour left-luggage facilities, a State Bank of India branch and a post office. City buses depart from here to locations all around Delhi.

To Rajasthan There are plenty of bus services to Jaipur and other destinations in Rajasthan and they're actually more convenient than trains (with the exception of the *Shatabdi Express*). The place to catch Rajasthan-bound deluxe government buses is Bikaner House (Rajasthan Tourist Office)

near India Gate, about 2km south-east of Connaught Place. Silverline buses (☎ 338 3469) depart for Jaipur every 45 minutes until 12.30 am (Rs 205, five hours). There are also six daily air-con services (Rs 330). Cheaper ordinary buses to Jaipur leave from the Kashmiri Gate ISBT (Rs 92, 5½ hours).

Also from Bikaner House, there are three buses daily to Ajmer (Rs 263, nine hours), one at 7 pm direct to Udaipur (Rs 430, 14 hours), and one at 11.40 pm to Jodhpur (Rs 363, 12½ hours).

Private buses to Jaipur and Ajmer also depart from near New Delhi train station; travel agencies and guesthouses can arrange tickets.

To Agra & Varanasi For Agra, Varanasi and other points south of Delhi, it's much easier and more comfortable to take the train. Government buses depart from the inconvenient Sarai Kale Khan ISBT, close to Nizamuddin train station. There are frequent departures for Agra (Rs 78 to Rs 120 depending on class, five hours), Mathura and Gwalior. There's a city bus link between this station and Kashmiri Gate ISBT.

Travel agencies and guesthouses sell tickets for tourist buses to Agra that pick up in Paharganj and Connaught Place. These are return services (Rs 200 or Rs 300 for air-con) that include a guided tour, but even if you don't want to come back to Delhi it may be worth taking this bus one way.

To Kathmandu Around Paharganj and the other travellers' hang-outs you'll see posters advertising direct buses to Kathmandu – these take between 38 and 50 hours and cost about Rs 850. It's a hell of a trip and most travellers will find it a lot more comfortable and better value to do it by train to Gorakhpur, and then take buses from there.

A number of travellers have also entered Nepal at the border crossing just east of the northern Uttar Pradesh village of Banbassa. There are daily buses to this village from New Delhi but the roads along here are in bad shape, so it's a rough ride. Travellers driving this route with their own vehicle generally give it the thumbs down.

To Northern India For Himalayan destinations, buses are the best option, but you can take a train for the first part of the journey, say to Chandigarh or Shimla. Shimla is accessible by both train and bus; direct day buses are Rs 145 (10 hours), and overnight deluxe buses are Rs 365. Alternatively you could take the bus to Chandigarh (Rs 108, five hours) and the narrow-gauge train to Shimla from Kalka. Buses to Chandigarh leave roughly every seven minutes from counter No 9. There are deluxe buses at 7.45 am and 2 pm (Rs 215; tickets from counter No 37).

There are also direct buses to Dharamsala (Rs 195, 13 hours), Manali (Rs 240, 16 hours) and Amritsar (Rs 192/382 ordinary/deluxe, 11 hours).

You can buy tickets for private buses to these destinations at agencies in Connaught Place and Paharganj. There are private overnight buses from New Delhi to Shimla (via Chandigarh; Rs 300), Dharamsala (Rs 375), Amritsar (Rs 250) and Manali (Rs 300).

The Delhi Transport Corporation runs a direct air-con bus to Lahore at 6 am on Tuesday, Wednesday, Friday and Saturday (Rs 800, 12 hours). It departs from the DTC terminal in Dr Ambedkar Nagar in south Delhi.

Train

Delhi is an important rail centre and a good place to make advance bookings. One of the best places to do this is the special foreign tourist booking office upstairs in New Delhi train station, open from 7.30 am to 5 pm Monday to Saturday. Ignore the touts lurking around the station who will try to tell you this office has moved, closed or doesn't exist. This is the place to go if you want a tourist-quota allocation, are the holder of an Indrail Pass or want to buy an Indrail Pass. It gets very busy, and it can take up to an hour to get served. A less-busy alternative – and more convenient if you're in Connaught Place – is the new rail reservation desk at the Delhi Tourism office in N-Block (open from 10 am to 5 pm daily except Sunday). This is also specially set up for tourist bookings. If you make bookings at either of these places, tickets *must* be paid for with rupees backed up by foreign exchange certificates (or ATM receipts), or in US dollars and pounds sterling with any change given in rupees.

The main ticket office is on Chelmsford Rd, about 150m south of New Delhi train station on the way to Connaught Place. This place is well organised, but it's also incredibly busy. There are dozens of ticket windows and an information window at the far end. Make sure you pick up a reservation form from the small booth outside the building first. It's best to arrive here first

Best Trains from Delhi

destination	train No & name	departure	distance	duration	fare (Rs)
Agra	2002 *Shatabdi Express*	6 am ND	192km	2 hr	390/760
	2180 *Taj Express*	7.15 am HN	186km	2½ hr	53/83
Amritsar	2903 *Golden Temple Mail*	7.35 pm ND	443km	10½ hr	99/154
	8237 *Chattisgarh Express*	9.05 pm ND		11½ hr	99/154
	2013 *Shatabdi Express*	4.30 pm ND		5½ hr	610/1220
Chandigarh	4095 *Himalayan Queen*	6.10 am ND	264km	5¼ hr	67/104
	2011 *Shatabdi Express*	7.35 am ND		3¼ hr	435/865
Gorakhpur	2554 *Vaishali Express*	7.45 pm ND	758km	13 hr	149/213
Jaipur	2413 *Jaipur Express*	5.15 am D	304km	5¾ hr	77/120
	2015 *Shatabdi Express*	6.15 am ND	308km	4¼ hr	495/985
Udaipur	9615 *Chetak Express*	2.10 pm SR	739km	20¼ hr	145/225
Varanasi	5206 *Lichchavi Express*	4.35 pm ND	788km	12½ hr	15/35

Abbreviations for train stations: ND – New Delhi; D – Old Delhi; HN – Hazrat Nizamuddin; SR – Sarai Rohilla.
Fares are for 2nd class/sleeper, except for *Shatabdi Express* which is air-con chair/executive class.

INDIA

thing in the morning. The office is open from 7.45 am to 9 pm Monday to Saturday. On Sunday it's open to 1.50 pm only.

Remember that there are two main stations in Delhi – Delhi train station in Old Delhi, and New Delhi train station at Paharganj. New Delhi is much closer to Connaught Place, and if you're departing from the Old Delhi train station you should allow adequate time (up to an hour in peak times) to wind your way through the traffic snarls of Old Delhi. Between the Old Delhi and New Delhi stations you can take the No 6 bus.

There's also the Nizamuddin train station south of the New Delhi area where some trains start or finish (including several trains to and from Agra). It's worth getting off here if you are staying in Chanakyapuri or anywhere else south of Connaught Place.

Some trains between Delhi and Jaipur, Jodhpur and Udaipur operate to and from Sarai Rohilla station rather than Old Delhi – it's about 3.5km north-west of Connaught Place. The one exception is the *Shatabdi Express* to Jaipur, which operates from New Delhi. If you take the *Shatabdi Express*, note that there are eight trains of this name departing daily, and some are timed confusingly close together. For instance, the New Delhi-Dehra Dun and New Delhi-Amritsar service leave about 10 minutes apart (from separate platforms). Hurrying to catch a last-minute train, one of our authors jumped on the 6 am *Shatabdi Express* bound for Agra – instead of the 6.15 am to Jaipur. Apart from the inconvenience of travelling to the wrong city, ticket inspectors in India aren't generally known for their compassion. They will not only expect you to cough up for the correct ticket (on top of the one you've already bought) but will fine you for ticketless travel!

The boxed text 'Best Trains from Delhi' gives good options for major destinations on our route, but there are many other trains to these and other destinations. For trains to Shimla, see the Shimla to Kalka section earlier in this chapter.

GETTING AROUND
To/From the Airport
Although there are a number of options, airport-to-city transport is not as straightforward as it should be, due to predatory taxi drivers who target unwary first-time

visitors and will say anything to steer you into their vehicle.

Bus The Ex-Servicemen's Air Link Transport Service (EATS; ☎ 331 6530) has a regular bus service between the airport (both terminals) and Connaught Place, operating between 4 am and 11 pm. The fare is Rs 50 from the international terminal and Rs 30 from the domestic terminal, plus Rs 5 per large piece of luggage; buses will drop you off at most of the major hotels en route and at the entrance to New Delhi train station (for Paharganj hotels). In Connaught Place the service leaves from near the Indian Airlines office, in F-Block, from 4 am to 11.30 pm.

When leaving the international terminal, the counter for the EATS bus is just to the right as you exit the building. This is probably the best, although not the quickest, way into the city if you arrive before 11 pm (see the warning about prepaid taxis in the following entry).

Taxi Look for the Delhi Traffic Police Prepaid Taxi Booth just outside the arrivals hall (but still inside the airport terminal), where you'll get the best prices (around Rs 200 to Paharganj). You'll be given a voucher that you have to present at the booth just outside the airport building. Even then you should ensure that you are shown to the right taxi. Other taxi drivers will try for a much higher fare, but worse than that, you can't always rely on them to take you where you want to go.

We've had reports of a number of travellers who have been given the run around by unofficial prepaid taxis in the middle of the night; they get taken to a hotel, told it's full, then on to another hotel (often in Karol Bagh) and intimidated into staying there at vastly inflated prices (up to US$150).

If you take a taxi from the airport late at night, before getting into the vehicle make an obvious point of noting down the registration number, and try to find a few companions in a similar predicament if you're on your own. If this is your first visit to Delhi, don't announce the fact. If the driver is not prepared to go where you want to go, find another taxi. If you're new to India it may be best to wait in the terminal building until daylight when there is much less risk of getting led astray, and more chance of finding a hotel open.

At the domestic terminal, the taxi booking desk is just inside the terminal and charges around Rs 180 to Paharganj, plus Rs 5 per bag. The taxi-wallahs outside will try for much more.

Bus

Avoid buses during the rush hours. There's a chance of being pickpocketed or (for women travellers) groped on a crowded bus where you're forced to stand. Whenever possible try to board (and leave) at a starting or finishing point, such as the Regal and Plaza cinemas in Connaught Place, or the bus stand at the rear of New Delhi station, as there is more chance of a seat. There are some seats reserved for women on the left-hand side of the bus. The Delhi Transport Corporation (☎ 335 4518) runs some buses, others are privately owned, but they all operate along the same set routes. Western embassies generally advise their staff not to take buses, but if you want to, the White Line and Green Line buses are slightly more expensive and thus a little less crowded. Private buses and minibuses also run on these routes. A short bus ride (like Connaught Place to Red Fort) is only about Rs 2, although fares are a flat Rs 5 on better buses.

Taxi & Autorickshaw

All taxis and autorickshaws are metered but the meters are invariably out of date or allegedly 'not working', or the drivers will simply refuse to use them.

If you're anywhere near Connaught Place or New Delhi station (ie, Paharganj) and need an autorickshaw, pick one up from the very useful police-run prepaid booths. There's one in the forecourt of New Delhi station, one at Nizamuddin station (but not at Old Delhi station), one at the Kashmiri Gate ISBT and one on Janpath just south of the Government of India Tourist Office. When you see what the prepaid fares are, you'll be amazed that almost every auto rickshaw driver on the street will simply turn in disgust and putt away if you try to negotiate down to the same fare for the same trip – they simply know they can get better from the next tourist! Unfortunately, even the prepaid drivers now seem to want a substantial 'tip' at the end of the journey, which you don't have to pay.

If you do happen to coax a metered journey out of a driver you will have to pay according to a perversely complicated scale of revised charges. Drivers are supposed to carry conversion cards but if you demand to see one, strangely enough they won't be able to find it. The fare charts are, however, also printed in the *Delhi City Guide* (Rs 15, available from newsagents). If the driver refuses to use the meter you must agree on a fare before getting in, otherwise an ugly scene is sure to follow.

Connaught Place to the Red Fort should cost around Rs 70 by taxi or Rs 40 by autorickshaw, although the traffic jams can make this a long trip. From Connaught Place to Paharganj should cost about Rs 8 according to the meter system, but Rs 20 seems to be the standard minimum fare for foreigners.

From 11 pm to 5 am there is a 20% surcharge for autorickshaws and 25% for taxis. If you're on your own at night make a show of writing down the licence plate number before setting off.

You will no doubt be asked if you want to go shopping (the driver will insist that 'just looking' is OK), as drivers get paid just for taking foreigners to stores – even if you don't purchase anything. You could arrange with your driver to make a show of looking around a few shops and in return get your sightseeing for free, although the hard-sell tactics at the shops can wear you down.

Jeep

The cheapest way to get from Connaught Place (south side) to the historic attractions of Old Delhi is with the regular jeeps that leave from a stand called Phat Phat Sewa near the Palika Bazaar, Inner Circle. These jeeps depart throughout the day to Chandni Chowk, opposite the Red Fort, and cost only Rs 5. You can also get them coming back the other way.

Motorcycle

If you are in the market for a new Enfield motorcycle, Karol Bagh is the place to look. Try Essaar on Jhandi Walan Extension and Nanna Motors at 112 Press Rd. For second-hand bikes and parts, try Madaan Motors at 1770/53 Naiwala Gali, Har Kishan Das Rd.

Bicycle & Cycle-Rickshaw

Although traffic and pollution are dreadful in Old Delhi and around Connaught Place, cycling is one option of getting around the sights to the south, though cyclists are an oppressed caste on Delhi's roads. There are very few places to hire bicycles but there's a small cycle-hire shop near Rajguru Rd in Paharganj.

Cycle-rickshaws are banned from the Connaught Place area and New Delhi itself, but they can be handy for travelling between Connaught Circus and Paharganj (around Rs 10), and around Old Delhi. It's a long trip by cycle-rickshaw from Paharganj to the Red Fort and it won't cost much less than an autorickshaw.

The Rajasthan Route

For many people, Rajasthan *is* India. Exotic cities perched on the fringes of the desert, imposing hilltop fortresses, brightly turbaned Rajput men sporting swash-buckling moustaches, romantic palaces, mirrored embroidery and women in saris so strikingly vivid in colour they take your breath away (or at least cause you to rummage in your bag for your camera).

Many of the sights and scenes you've seen in brochures come from Rajasthan and there's no denying that this is a picturesque region. The light seems brighter and the evening sky takes on a warm glow – not the hazy grey you see in Delhi and Agra. But the true colour is most apparent in the people. Iridescent greens and pinks, canary yellows, electric blues, vivid purples, oranges and reds seen in the turbans worn by men and the scarves and saris worn by women add astonishing colour to an otherwise uniformly golden brown or whitewashed landscape. The attraction for splashes of colour also extends to painting up the old parts of towns – Jaipur is often known as the 'pink city', Jodhpur the 'blue city', and Jaisalmer the 'golden city'.

Our route passes through Jaipur, then on to the holy town of Pushkar, a popular hang-out for travellers, before taking a sharp detour down to the romantic lakeside city of Udaipur. From there it's back up to Jodhpur, dominated by a massive hilltop fort, and finally to Jaisalmer, the mesmeric fortress city on the edge of the Thar Desert.

Rajasthan is also famous for the Keoladeo Ghana National Park, a World Heritage listed bird sanctuary near Bharatpur, which makes an easy side trip from Jaipur (four hours) or Agra (1½ hours).

The best time to visit Rajasthan is November to March. From May to September it is stiflingly hot, more so as you head west towards the desert. The monsoon approaches in late July but Rajasthan often misses out on the heaviest rains and the state is prone to severe drought. If you can stand the heat, the advantage of visiting between late March and June is that there are few tourists around and the attention from touts, vendors and rickshaw-wallahs drops considerably – presumably they're all too hot to be bothered. Hotel prices are slashed by up to 50%, which makes staying in a romantic Raj palace or *haveli* (traditional ornately decorated residence) an affordable prospect. Peak season is December to February when popular cities like Jaipur, Udaipur and Jaisalmer are crawling with tourists and sunset at the Sam sand dunes is like a three-ring circus. But the days are perfect and the nights cool.

Rajasthan has some of the most romantic palatial accommodation in India so if you're going to lash out at least once, why not consider the Lake Palace in Udaipur, Ram Bagh Palace in Jaipur or the Umaid Bhawan Palace in Jodhpur – and expect to pay at least US$200 a night for a double.

JAIPUR
☎ 0141 • pop 1.8 million

The vibrant capital of Rajasthan, 260km south-west of Delhi, is popularly known as the 'pink city' because of the pink-coloured buildings in its old city. As far as tourist numbers go, this is the most popular place in Rajasthan – part of the Delhi-Agra-Jaipur 'Golden Triangle' so revered by tour operators. Partly for that reason it's perhaps not the most alluring of Rajasthan's cities but you could easily spend a day or two exploring the old city and there are some good excursions from Jaipur – Amber Fort is a must.

The city sits on a dry lake bed in a somewhat arid landscape, surrounded by barren hills surmounted by forts and crenellated walls. Its centre is a busy cacophony of cars, rickshaws and tempos (large three-wheelers), sharing the streets with camel-drawn carts.

JAIPUR

PLACES TO STAY
1 Samode Haveli
8 Jaipur Inn
9 Umaid Bhawan Guest House; Saljan Niwas Guest House
10 Hotel Madhuban
12 RTDC's Hotel Swagatam
17 Jai Mangal Palace
19 Atithi Guest House;
Aangan Guest House
21 RTDC's Tourist Hotel;
Tourist Reception Centre
25 Evergreen Guest House;
Ashiyana Guest House
35 Hotel Arya Niwas
37 Hotel Sweet Dream
39 Hotel Kailash
47 Hotel Diggi Palace
51 Rambagh Palace;
Rajasthan Tours

PLACES TO EAT
20 Ganpati Plaza (Pizza Hut;
Celebrations; Baskin 31
Robbins)
23 Handi Restaurant
26 Chanakya Restaurant
27 Lassiwala

32 Bake Hut; Golden Dragon Restaurant
33 Niro's; Surya Mahal;
Natraj Restaurant
36 Indian Coffee House
40 LMB
41 Royal's Restaurant

OTHER
2 Govind Devji Temple
3 Jantar Mantar
(Observatory)
4 City Palace; Foreigners'
Registration Office
5 Hawa Mahal
6 Dr Vinod Shastri
(Astrologer)
7 Iswari Minar Swarga Sal
11 Sita World Travels
13 Government of India
Tourist Office
(Hotel Khasa Kothi)
14 Jaipur Towers (Thomas
Cook; Airline Agents)
15 Mewar Cyber Cafe
16 Main Bus Station
18 Polo Victory Cinema
24 Main Post Office;
Philatelic Museum
28 DHL Worldwide Express
29 Bank of Rajasthan; Andhra
Bank; Bank of Punjab
30 Raj Mandir Cinema
31 Cyber Cafe; Pool Club &
Cafe; Books Corner
34 Books & News Mart
35 Rajasthali Emporium;
Rajasthan Handloom House
38 Jama Masjid
42 Ram Niwas Public Gardens
43 Modern Art Gallery
44 Zoo
45 Central Museum
(Albert Hall)
46 Maharaja College
48 Statue Circle
49 Soma
50 Anokhi Showroom
52 Sawai Mansingh Hospital
53 Dolls Museum
54 Museum of Indology

INDIA

Jaipur owes its name, its foundation and its careful planning to the great warrior-astronomer Maharaja Jai Singh II (1693–1743). His predecessors had enjoyed good relations with the Mughals and Jai Singh was careful to preserve this alliance. In 1727, with Mughal power on the wane, Jai Singh decided it was time to move down from his hillside fort at nearby Amber to a new site on the plains. He laid out the city, with its surrounding walls and rectangular blocks, according to principles set down in the *Shilpa-Shastra*, an ancient Hindu treatise on architecture.

Orientation

The walled old city is in the north-east of Jaipur and contains most of the city's sights, while the new parts spread to the south and west. The principal shopping centre in the old city is Johari Bazaar, the jewellers' market. Unlike most bazaars in India, this one is broad and open.

There are three main interconnecting roads in the new part of town – Mirza Ismail Rd (MI Rd), Station Rd and Sansar Chandra Marg. Along or just off these roads are most of the budget and mid-range hotels and restaurants, the main train and bus stations, many of the banks and the modern shopping centre.

Information

Tourist Offices The Tourist Reception Centre (☎ 365256) is in the Rajasthan Tourism Development Corporation's (RTDC) Tourist Hotel compound on MI Rd and is open from 10 am to 5 pm daily except Sunday. It has a range of literature and the staff can be quite helpful. There's another tourist office (☎ 315714) on platform No 1 at the train station. It's open from 6 am to 6 pm daily and is a handy place to sit if you're waiting for a train. The Government of India tourist office (☎ 372200), in the Hotel Khasa Kothi, is less useful.

Money You can change money at Thomas Cook on the 1st floor of Jaipur Towers on MI Rd. It's open from 9.30 am to 6 pm daily except Sunday. There are three useful banks almost side by side on MI Rd. The Bank of Rajasthan has a foreign-exchange counter in a separate office next door. It's open from 10 am to 6 pm Monday to Friday

and 10 am to 3 pm on Saturday; it changes cash and travellers cheques in major currencies without commission. The nearby Andhra Bank will advance cash on Master-Card and Visa cards, and the Bank of Punjab also offers foreign exchange.

The Bank of Punjab branch on Station Road has an ATM accepting MasterCard and Cirrus.

Post & Communications The main post office (☎ 368740) on MI Rd is quite efficient and there's a man at the entrance who sews up parcels, sealing them with wax.

There are scores of round-the-clock STD/ISD telephone booths in Jaipur.

The Internet is gaining popularity here but it's not as cheap or widespread as in Delhi yet. There are a couple of places to access the Internet along MI Rd, near Niro's restaurant. Pool Club & Cafe (see Places to Eat later), down some stairs, has access for Rs 2 per minute or Rs 60 an hour. Hotels such as Evergreen Guest House and Jaipur Inn (see Places to Stay) have Internet access at Rs 2 per minute. Mewar Cyber Cafe, near the main bus terminal on Station Rd, charges Rs 75 an hour.

Bookshops There's a wide range of English-language books as well as magazines and maps at Books Corner, MI Rd (near Niro's restaurant). You can pick up a copy of the informative *Jaipur Vision* here, which contains useful information about the city.

Old City (Pink City)

In 1876, Maharaja Ram Singh had the entire old city painted pink, traditionally a colour associated with hospitality, to welcome the Prince of Wales (later King Edward VII), a tradition which has been maintained. It's lost its colour a bit and is more of a burnt ochre these days, but it still has a magical quality in the evening light. The old city is partially encircled by a crenellated wall with a number of gates – the major gates are Chandpol, Ajmeri and Sanganeri.

The major landmark in this part of town is the **Iswari Minar Swarga Sal** (Heaven Piercing Minaret), near the Tripolia Gate, which was built to overlook the city.

The main **bazaars** in the old city are interesting to wander around and include Johari Bazaar, Tripolia Bazaar, Bapu Bazaar and Chandpol Bazaar. Look out for the shop on Chaura Rasta that displays an extraordinary jumble of earthenware pots.

Hawa Mahal You'll probably know the facade of the Hawa Mahal, or Palace of the Winds, before you see it – it graces posters and postcards all over India. Constructed in 1799, this is one of Jaipur's major landmarks but it is little more than a facade and is smaller than it often appears in photographs. A stunning example of Rajput artistry, with its pink, delicately honeycombed sandstone windows, it was originally built to enable ladies of the royal household to watch the everyday life and processions of the city. You can climb to the top for a fine view over the city. The palace was built by Maharaja Sawaj Pratap Singh and is part of the City Palace complex. There's a small **museum** (closed Saturday) on the same site containing paintings, armoury and silver- and bronze-ware.

Entry to the Hawa Mahal is from the rear of the building. To get there, go back to the intersection on your left as you face the Hawa Mahal, turn right and then take the first right again through an archway. It's open from 9 am to 4.30 pm daily (Rs 2). It costs Rs 30/70 to bring in a camera/video.

City Palace Complex In the heart of the old city, the City Palace occupies a large area divided into a series of courtyards, gardens and buildings. Today, the palace is a blend of Rajasthani and Mughal architecture. The son of the last maharaja and his family still reside in part of the palace.

Before the palace proper you'll see the **Mubarak Mahal**, or Welcome Palace, which was built in the late 19th century by Maharaja Sawai Madho Singh II as a reception centre for visiting dignitaries. It now forms part of the **Maharaja Sawai Mansingh II Museum**, containing a collection of royal costumes and superb shawls including Kashmiri *pashmina* (goats' wool) shawls. One remarkable exhibit is a set of the voluminous clothing of Sawai Madho Singh I, who was a stately 2m tall, 1.2m wide and 250kg!

Other points of interest in the palace include the **Diwan-i-Am**, or the Hall of Public Audience, with its intricate decorations and manuscripts in Persian and Sanskrit, the **Diwan-i-Khas**, or Hall of Private Audience, with a marble-paved gallery, and the exquisite **Peacock Gate** in the Chandra Mahal courtyard.

Outside the buildings, you can see enormous silver vessels in which a former maharaja used to take holy Ganges water to England. There are several craft galleries in the complex and another museum in the **Maharani's Palace** which has an impressive display of weaponry, including a huge musket weighing 25kg.

The palace and museums are open daily between 9.30 am and 4.45 pm. Entry is Rs 130 (this includes entry to Jaigarh – see the Around Jaipur section – and the ticket is valid for two days). Photography is prohibited inside the museums. There are guides for hire inside the palace complex for Rs 150.

Jantar Mantar Next to the entrance to the City Palace is the Jantar Mantar, or Observatory, begun by Jai Singh in 1728. Jai Singh's passion for astronomy was even more notable than his prowess as a warrior and, before commencing construction, he sent scholars abroad to study foreign observatories. The Jaipur observatory is the largest and the best preserved of the five he built, and was restored in 1901. Others are in Delhi (the oldest, dating from 1724), Varanasi and Ujjain. The fifth, the Muttra observatory, is gone.

At first glance, Jantar Mantar appears to be just a curious collection of sculptures but in fact each construction has a specific purpose, such as measuring the positions of stars, altitudes and azimuths, and calculating eclipses. The most striking instrument is the sundial with its 27m-high gnomon. The shadow this casts moves up to 4m an hour.

The observatory is open from 9 am to 4.30 pm daily (Rs 4; free on Monday). Entry for a camera/video costs an excessive Rs 50/100.

Central Museum

This somewhat dusty collection is housed in the architecturally impressive Albert Hall in the Ram Niwas Public Gardens, south of the old city. Exhibits include a natural history collection, models of yogis adopting various positions, tribal ware, dioramas depicting Rajasthani dances and sections on

INDIA

SARAH JOLLY

Jantar Mantar, an extraordinary observatory built by Maharaja Jai Singh II in 1728, is still used by astrologers today. It has 13 different instruments to calculate the movement of celestial bodies.

decorative arts, costumes, drawings and musical instruments. The museum is open from 10 am to 5 pm daily (Rs 30). Photography is prohibited.

Other Attractions

Jaipur's **Modern Art Gallery** is on the 1st floor of the Ravindra Rangmanch Building (free, closed Sunday). The ramshackle **Museum of Indology** is an extraordinary private collection of folk art objects and other bits and pieces of interest – there's everything from a map of India painted on a rice grain, to manuscripts (one written by Aurangzeb), tribal ornaments, fossils, old currency notes, clocks and much more. The museum is actually a private house, and is signposted off J Nehru Marg, south of the Central Museum. It's open from 8 am to 6 pm daily (Rs 40; including a guide).

About 3km south-west of the old city is the **Rambagh Palace**, now one of India's most renowned hotels. Gayatri Devi, the glamorous third wife of the last maharaja of Jaipur, resides in part of this gracious palace. It's worth a trip down here to look around the gardens, take in a cultural show, or have a drink in the Polo Bar (see Entertainment).

Meditation & Yoga

The Dhammathali Vipassana Meditation Centre (☎ 641520) at Galta, 2km east of Jaipur, runs meditation courses for a donation. This is a sister operation to the one in McLeod Ganj.

Yoga courses are available at the Prakaritic Chikitsalya (☎ 510590), Bapu Nagar (near the Rajasthan University campus), the Sahaz Yoga Centre (☎ 204561) in Bani Park, and also at the Madhavanand Ashram (☎ 200317), C-19 Behari Marg, Bani Park.

Astrology

Dr Vinod Shastri (☎ 663338, 551117, e vshastri@jp1.dot.net.in) is the General Secretary of the Rajasthan Astrological Council & Research Institute and works from his shop near the City Palace on Chandani Chowk, Tripolia Gate. It costs Rs 300 for a 20-minute consultation and you will need to have your exact time of birth in order to get a computerised horoscope drawn up. A five-year prediction costs Rs 900 and a 30-year prediction costs a whopping Rs 3000. It's cheaper to get it done by a Tibetan lama in Kathmandu or a palmist in Varanasi!

Organised Tours

The RTDC offers half- and full-day tours of Jaipur and its environs. A full-day tour (9 am to 6 pm) costs Rs 135; there's a lunch break at Nahargarh. Half-day tours are a little rushed but otherwise OK. They cost

INDIA

Rs 90; times are 8 am to 1 pm, 11.30 am to 4.30 pm and 1.30 to 6.30 pm. Entrance fees to monuments are extra. Tours depart daily from the train station (according to demand), but you can also arrange to be collected from any of the RTDC hotels. Contact the RTDC transport unit (☎ 375466), the office on the left as you enter the Tourist Hotel compound, or the tourist office at the train station.

The RTDC offers various other tours on demand.

Special Events

Celebrating the onset of the monsoon is **Teej Fair**, also known as the Festival of Swings (a reference to the flower-bedecked swings which are erected at this time), held in honour of the marriage of Shiva and Parvati. It is celebrated with particular fervour in Jaipur. It's due to be held on 23 and 24 July in 2001, 11 and 12 August in 2002 and 1st and 2nd August in 2003.

There's an **Elephant Festival** held in March.

Places to Stay

Autorickshaw-wallahs and taxi drivers can be difficult about taking you to a hotel of your choice and they'll try for a commission even if they do. When you arrive, head straight to the prepaid autorickshaw stands which have been set up at both the bus and train stations.

Most of the budget and mid-range accommodation is clustered around MI and Station Rds and Bani Park, just north of the train station.

If you wish to stay with an Indian family, contact the Tourist Reception Centre, which has a list of places participating in Jaipur's Paying Guest House Scheme. You can find rooms from Rs 100 but the average is around Rs 300. They also sell a handy booklet listing all paying guesthouses in Rajasthan (Rs 5).

Places to Stay – Budget

Evergreen Guest House (☎ 363446, e evergreen@hotmail.com) is a rambling hotel just off MI Rd in the area known as Chameliwala Market. It's the best place to meet other backpackers, although the staff are a bit indifferent. You can't beat the swimming pool in summer, and the restau-

rant isn't bad. Nondescript singles/doubles with bathroom range from Rs 150/175 (free bucket hot water) to Rs 250/300 with air cooling and Rs 450/500 with air-con. It's difficult to locate on foot, but rickshaw-wallahs know where it is and it's only Rs 19 from the pre-paid booth at the train station.

Ashiyana Guest House (☎ 375414) is nearby if you find the Evergreen too much of a scene, but it's nothing to get excited about. The cheapest rooms (with shared bathroom and bucket hot water) go for Rs 70/150. It's behind Evergreen on the MI Rd side.

The concave high-rise **Jaipur Inn** (☎ 201121, fax 204796, e jaipurinn@ hotmail.com, B-17 Shiv Marg, Bani Park) is an old-time favourite with travellers and is well set up, although it looks more like a block of apartments at first sight. Beds in a cramped basement dorm cost from Rs 80, and you can camp on the lawn (Rs 50 per person) if you have your own tent. Accommodation ranges from spartan, makeshift rooms with shared bathroom for Rs 100/200 to good air-cooled rooms with private bathroom for Rs 250/350, rooms with balcony for Rs 300/400 and large air-con rooms from Rs 600/700. Bikes can be hired for Rs 25 per day. Meals are available and the rooftop terrace commands sensational views.

Hotel Diggi Palace (☎ 373091, e diggi htl@datainfosys.net, Shivaji Marg) is off Sawai Ram Singh Marg, less than 1km south of Ajmeri Gate. It's a popular hang-out with budget travellers and has plenty of character. Formerly the residence of the *thakur* (similar to a lord or baron) of Diggi, it has a lovely lawn area and relaxing ambience, though the cheaper rooms are very basic. Bare rooms with shared bathroom (free bucket hot water) cost Rs 125/250. Rooms with private bathroom and geyser are Rs 300; better air-cooled/air-con rooms are Rs 400/750.

Atithi Guest House (☎ 378679, fax 379496, e tanmay@jp1.dot.net.in, 1 Park House Scheme Rd), opposite All India Radio, between MI and Station Rds, is a well-kept, friendly place. Clean air-cooled rooms with private bathroom start at Rs 200/250 but the nicer rooms are Rs 300/350. Air-con rooms cost Rs 650/700. There's a pleasant rooftop garden and restaurant, and Internet access.

Angan Guest House (☎ 373449) next door has reasonable large rooms from Rs 175/250

INDIA

with air cooling and Rs 350/450 with air-con. There's a restaurant and Internet access here.

Hotel Kailash (☎ *565372, Johari Bazaar*), opposite the Jama Masjid, is well located – it's one of the few places to stay within the old city. Cramped corridors lead to reasonably spacious rooms with private bathroom for Rs 315/365. It's nothing flash. **Hotel Sweet Dream** (☎ *314409*) is another choice in the old city. Average rooms with private bathroom start at Rs 250/330; air-con is Rs 600/700. There's a veg restaurant on the rooftop.

RTDC's **Hotel Swagatam** (☎ *200595*), near the train station, has a rather institutional feel. Dorm beds are Rs 50; rooms with bathroom start at Rs 300/400 (including breakfast). RTDC's **Tourist Hotel** (☎ *360238*) is similar with rooms for Rs 150/250 and Rs 300/400 with air cooling.

Places to Stay – Mid-Range & Top End

The **Hotel Arya Niwas** (☎ *372456, fax 364376*, e *aryahotl@jp1.dot.net.in*), just off Sansar Chandra Marg, is an excellent mid-range choice. This large hotel in a converted haveli is made of Jaipur stone, is well maintained and has a nice front lawn and excellent self-service veg restaurant. Bright rooms with private bathroom range from Rs 300/400 up to Rs 600/750 for large air-con deluxe rooms.

The **Hotel Madhuban** (☎ *200033*, e *madhuban@usa.net, D-237 Behari Marg*) in Bani Park is recommended if you're after a homy ambience with no hassles. Standard rooms cost from Rs 450/550 to Rs 850/950, and deluxe rooms cost from Rs 700/800 to Rs 110/130 for a suite. The more expensive rooms have fine antique furnishings. They offer free pick-ups from the bus and train stations (ring ahead).

Umaid Bhawan Guest House (☎ *316184*, e *umaid-bhawan@yahoo.com, D1-2A, Bani Park*) is a stylish place with a pool and a relaxing atmosphere. Simple, comfortable rooms start at Rs 450/550 but go right up to the 'Regal Suite' at Rs 1300/1950. Next door, **Sajjan Niwas Guest House** (☎ *311544*) is excellent value with spacious, airy rooms from Rs 300/400.

If you're wondering how much for a room at the **Rambagh Palace** (☎ *381919, fax 381098, Bhawani Singh Marg*), standard rooms are US$185/205, but it's the Maharaja and Maharani suites at US$575 or US$775 a double you want if you're after real luxury!

Places to Eat

You'll find plenty of restaurants and fast food cafes along MI Rd. **Niro's** (☎ *374493*) is a favourite with Indians and westerners alike. It fills up fast (especially on weekends) but you can book ahead. There's an extensive menu offering excellent veg and nonveg Indian, Chinese and continental food. Mains range from Rs 125 to Rs 160 (half tandoori chicken is Rs 90) and there's a good range of frozen desserts. The nearby **Surya Mahal** serves good Indian food.

Don't miss trying a lassi at **Lassiwala**, opposite Niro's. It's just an open-fronted stall where thick, creamy sweet lassis are constantly churned out and served in throwaway earthenware cups (like little terracotta flower pots). If you haven't tried a real lassi yet (ie, not the banana lassis most restaurants do for tourists) this is the place to do it. A small cup costs Rs 10. It's so popular that another Lassiwala has opened up a couple of doors down.

Chanakya Restaurant, on the northern side of MI Rd, is highly recommended for its Indian and continental food, mostly under Rs 150.

Handi Restaurant, opposite the main post office, is tucked away at the back of the Maya Mansions building. It has great barbecue dishes for under Rs 130. In the evenings (from 6.30 pm), you can get takeaway kebabs (Rs 40) at the entrance to the restaurant.

There's a *Pizza Hut* in the Ganpati Plaza, along with a branch of the ice-cream chain **Baskin 31 Robbins**.

LMB (Laxmi Mishthan Bhandar), in Johari Bazaar, is still a popular cheap place in the old city. Out the front, a counter serves snacks and colourful Indian sweets. Nearby, **Royal's Restaurant** does cheap snacks such as burgers, sandwiches, dosas and ice cream.

Jaipur Inn (see Places to Stay earlier) boasts one of the city's only rooftop restaurants, with superlative views over Jaipur. The Indian veg buffet dinner is on every night at 7 pm and costs Rs 100 (nonguests should book in advance).

The **Empire Store** near Niro's has all sorts of takeaways such as sandwiches, cold coffee, candy floss and other weird sweets.

Bake Hut, down a nearby side street, offers a selection of sweet treats, and **Venus Bakery** *(Subhash Marg)*, just off MI Rd, also sells pastries.

Entertainment

Entertainment is limited, although many hotels put on some sort of evening music, dance or puppet show for tourists.

Raj Mandir Cinema (☎ 379372), just off MI Rd, is one of the plushest cinemas in India and a great place to see a Hindi blockbuster. It's incredibly popular and, despite its immense size, is usually booked out. Bookings can be made one day in advance (between 4 and 5 pm) and this is your best chance of securing a seat. Otherwise queue up when tickets go on sale half an hour before the screening. Tickets range from Rs 15 to Rs 47; avoid the cheaper seats, which are very close to the screen.

Bowling alleys are popular with young Jaipurians. The best alley is at **Dreamland** *(☎ 546608)*, a bit inconveniently located in Malviya Nagar at Gaurav Tower, Bardiya Shopping Centre. This complex also has the **Space Station** disco.

The **Polo Bar**, at the Rambagh Palace, is Jaipur's most atmospheric watering hole, with slightly modernist lounge furniture, a cool tiled interior and a fountain as its centrepiece; a bottle of beer is Rs 165 and cocktails are around Rs 250.

Polo matches are played at the **polo ground** next to Rambagh Palace during winter. Phone the polo club (☎ 383580) if you're interested in seeing one.

Shopping

Jaipur has a plethora of handicrafts ranging from grimacing papier-mâché puppets to exquisitely carved furniture. Shops around the tourist traps, such as the City Palace and Hawa Mahal, tend to be more expensive, and prices generally start high here, so bargain hard.

Jaipur is especially well known for precious stones and semiprecious gems. There are many shops which offer bargain prices, but you need to know your gems. Marble statues, costume jewellery and textile prints are other Jaipur specialities.

The Rajasthali Emporium on MI Rd, near Ajmeri Gate, sells an interesting range of handicrafts from around the state. Rajasthan Handloom House is next door, with a range of textiles. Another highly recommended place for textiles is the Anokhi showroom, at 2 Tilak Marg, near the Secretariat. It has high-quality products such as block-printed fabrics, tablecloths, bed covers and cosmetic bags.

Kripal Kumbh, B-18A Shiv Marg in Bani Park, is a great place to see Jaipur's famous blue pottery. There's also Neerja (closed Sunday), S-19 Bhawani Singh Rd at C-Scheme. For good quality *jootis* (traditional Rajasthani shoes), go to Charmica (opposite the Natraj restaurant) on MI Rd; a pair of jootis ranges from Rs 150 to Rs 350.

Getting There & Away

Air The Indian Airlines office (☎ 514500) is a little out of town on Tonk Rd, the southern extension of Sawai Ram Singh Marg, but you can book domestic flights through travel agents such as Satyam Travels & Tours (☎ 378794) on the ground floor of the Jaipur Towers building. Indian Airlines flies daily to/from Delhi (US$55), Jodhpur (US$80), Mumbai (US$155) and Udaipur (US$80).

Bus Rajasthan State Transport Corporation (RSTC) buses all leave from the main bus station on Station Rd, picking up passengers at Narain Singh Circle. There is a left-luggage office at the main terminal, and a prepaid autorickshaw stand. Deluxe buses all leave from platform No 3. These buses should be booked in advance; the reservation office is also at platform 3 and departure times are displayed on a board here.

Buses to Delhi depart throughout the day. Ordinary services cost Rs 101 and take around six hours. Deluxe (express) buses cost Rs 200 (five hours) and air-con buses are Rs 330.

There are numerous deluxe buses to Ajmer (Rs 65, three hours), where you can easily change for Pushkar, and there are a couple of direct ordinary buses to Pushkar (Rs 50, 3½ hours). There are also buses to Jodhpur (Rs 160/97 day/overnight, 7½ hours) and Udaipur (Rs 200, 9½ hours).

For the bird sanctuary at Bharatpur there are direct buses (Rs 87, four hours); you can also ask to be let off an Agra-bound bus.

INDIA

There are numerous private travel agencies in Jaipur that book services to major cities as well as Pushkar. There's a cluster along Motilal Atal Marg, near the Polo Victory Cinema.

Train The reasonably efficient computerised railway reservation office (☎ 201401) is in the building to your right as you exit the main train station. It's open (for advance reservations only) Monday to Saturday 8 am to 2 pm and 2.15 to 8 pm; Sunday 8 am to 2 pm. Join the queue for 'Freedom Fighters and Foreign Tourists' (counter 769). For same-day travel, you'll need to buy your ticket at the train station. For metre-gauge trains, the booking office is on platform No 6.

There are 12 trains daily to Delhi (305km) but four of these only go to Sarai Rohilla station and only two, the expensive *Shatabdi Express* and *Rajdhani Express*, go all the way to New Delhi station. The aircon *Shatabdi Express* is the best service, departing at 5.25 pm and taking less than five hours (Rs 495/985 in chair car/executive). Other good trains include the *Jaipur-Delhi Express* at 4.30 pm (Rs 120 in sleeper class); the overnight *Ahmedabad-Delhi Express* at 11.40 pm; and the *Gandhidam-Delhi Express* at 8.25 am.

There are plenty of direct trains to Ajmer (134km by rail), about 2½ hours away. The *Shatabdi Express* departs at 10.40 am (Rs 320/615 chair car/executive) but it's pricey for such a short trip. The *Jaipur-Ajmer Link Express* at 11.30 am is another good service (Rs 40/62 in 2nd class/sleeper).

For Jodhpur (314km), the overnight *Delhi-Jodhpur Express* departs at Jaipur 11.30 pm and gets into Jodhpur at 6.40 am (Rs 120/347 in sleeper/air-con three tier). There's also the *Jaipur-Jodhpur Intercity*, which departs at 5.30 pm, arriving at 10.45 pm. There are two trains to Udaipur (431km); the best is the overnight *Chetak Express* which departs at 10.10 pm and gets in around 12 hours later (Rs 149/692 in sleeper/air-con two-tier).

There's only one train direct to Agra at 3.20 pm. The *Marudhar Express* takes about seven hours – the bus is generally a quicker and easier way to go. Other trains go direct to Bikaner, Ahmedabad and Mumbai.

Jaipur to Amritsar

Cycling days: 14
Distance: 1400km

There were no major problems riding in Rajasthan and there was much less traffic here than in Uttar Pradesh.

The first day was from Jaipur to Ajmer (130km, 6½ hours), then a big, scenic hill climb over the Snake Mountain into Pushkar (15km, 1½ hours). It's a leisurely two-day ride from Pushkar to Jodhpur.

From Jodhpur to Jaisalmer is roughly 350km and three days of cycling into the increasingly barren desert. Traffic thins right out.

The ride from Jaisalmer up to Amritsar is around 800km, which you can ride over six to nine days depending on your level of fitness. If finding accommodation becomes a problem, ask at a village for the local *dharamsala* (pilgrim's lodging). They're usually clean and the friendly staff charge a small fee (or donation) for food and a room. I found the Jaisalmer to Amritsar stretch the most enjoyable in India. The roads were quieter, the people a lot more friendly. Once into Punjab the scenery becomes very green and fertile and the terrain more undulating. I found the Punjabis a particularly welcoming and friendly lot.

It's a three-day ride from Jaisalmer to Bikaner (approximately 350km) so this is a good spot for a rest day.

Sue Cooper

Getting Around

There are prepaid autorickshaw stands at the bus and train stations. Rates are fixed by the government, so there's no need to haggle. It costs Rs 19 to get to Bani Park or MI Rd from the train station and a similar rate from the bus station. If you want to hire an auto rickshaw for local sightseeing it should cost about Rs 200/300 for a half/full day (including a visit to Amber). Prices are often inflated for tourists, so be prepared to bargain. On the other hand, canny rickshaw-wallahs will offer very low fares and then proceed to take you to shops where they reap commission on any purchases you make. Cycle-rickshaws are a cheaper option.

An autorickshaw/taxi to the airport costs about Rs 180/220.

Bicycles can be hired from most bike shops, including the one to the right as you exit the main train station, a few steps past the reservation office. Some hotels, such as the Jaipur Inn and Hotel Arya Niwas, also hire out bikes for around Rs 20 a day.

AROUND JAIPUR

There are some interesting attractions around Jaipur and you can get to most of these places by bus, or on organised tours.

Amber

About 11km north of Jaipur, on the Delhi-Jaipur road, Amber is the ancient capital of Jaipur state. Construction of the fort-palace was begun in 1592 by Maharaja Man Singh, the Rajput commander of the Mughal emperor Akbar's army. It was later extended and completed by the Jai Singhs before the move to Jaipur on the plains below. The fort is a superb example of Rajput architecture, stunningly situated on a hillside and overlooking a lake which reflects its terraces and ramparts. There's a tribe of black-faced monkeys roaming around near the bridge as you cross over to the fort.

You can climb up to the fort from the road in about 10 minutes. A seat in a jeep up to the fort costs Rs 15 return. Riding up on traditionally painted elephants is popular, though daylight robbery at Rs 400 return per elephant (each can carry up to four people).

An imposing stairway leads to the **Diwan-i-Am**, or Hall of Public Audience, with a double row of columns and latticed galleries above. Steps to the right lead to the small **Kali Temple**.

The maharaja's apartments are on the higher terrace – you enter through a gateway decorated with mosaics and sculptures. The **Jai Mandir**, or Hall of Victory, is noted for its inlaid panels and glittering mirror ceiling. This leads to the **Sheesh Mahal**, a small mirrored chamber where, for a tip, guides will light a candle to demonstrate the eerie lighting effect. Opposite the Jai Mandir is the **Sukh Niwas**, or Hall of Pleasure, with an ivory-inlaid sandalwood door, and a channel running right through the

Stonework inlays in designs such as this are typical of the intricate work seen at Amber Fort.

room which once carried cooling water. From the Jai Mandir you can take in the fine views from the palace ramparts over the lake below.

Amber Palace is open from 9 am to 4.30 pm daily and entry costs Rs 50 plus Rs 25/100 for a camera/video). Guides can be hired at the tourist office (near the fort entrance) for Rs 75/230/380 for 1½ hours/half day/full day (maximum four people). There's an interesting art gallery near the fort entrance, open from 10 am to 5 pm daily except Sunday.

There are frequent buses to Amber from near the Hawa Mahal and from the train station in Jaipur (Rs 5, 30 minutes). You can catch the same buses back to Jaipur from the road opposite the bridge leading to the fort.

Jaigarh

Overlooking Amber Fort is the imposing Jaigarh, built in 1726 by Jai Singh. The fort was never captured and so has survived virtually intact through the centuries. It's within walking distance of Amber and offers a great view over the plains from the Diwa Burj watchtower. The fort, with its water reservoirs, residential areas, puppet theatre and the cannon, Jaya Vana, is open 9 am to 5 pm daily. Entry is Rs 15 (plus Rs 50 per car, and Rs 25/100 for a camera/video), but you can visit Jaigarh on the same entry ticket you used for Jaipur's City Palace, as long as it's within two days of purchase.

Nahargarh

Nahargarh, also known as the Tiger Fort, overlooks the city from a sheer ridge to the north. The fort was built in 1734 and extended in 1868. An 8km road runs up through the hills from Jaipur, and the fort can be reached along a zigzagging 2km path. The glorious views fully justify the effort. Entry is Rs 10, and a camera/video costs Rs 30/70. There's a small restaurant on the top.

Royal Gaitor

The **cenotaphs** of the royal family are at Gaitor, just outside the city walls. The cenotaph of Maharaja Jai Singh II is particularly impressive. Entry is free, but there's a charge of Rs 10/20 for a camera/video.

The cenotaphs of the maharanis of Jaipur are on Amber Rd, midway between Jaipur and Amber. Nearby is the **Jal Mahal** (Water Palace), in the middle of a lake. It used to be possible to reach the palace by a causeway but this has collapsed and at the time of research was yet to be fixed.

Sisodia Rani Palace & Gardens

Six kilometres from the city on Agra Rd (leave Jaipur by the Ghat Gate), and surrounded by terraced gardens, this palace was built for Maharaja Jai Singh's second wife, the Sisodia princess. The outer walls are decorated with murals depicting hunting scenes and the Krishna legend.

Vidyadharji ka Bagh, a garden built in honour of Jai Singh's chief architect and town planner, Vidyadhar, is about 200m before Sisodia Rani Palace on Agra Rd. These gardens and the palace gardens are open daily from 8 am to 6 pm.

JAIPUR TO PUSHKAR

There are a few direct buses from Jaipur to Pushkar, but an alternative is to take one of the more frequent services – or the train – to Ajmer and change there.

Ajmer

☎ 0145 • pop 477,000

Ajmer, 11km from Pushkar, is a busy, nondescript town with little of interest to visitors except as a stepping stone to Pushkar.

It is, however, a major centre for Muslim pilgrims during the fast of Ramadan, and has some impressive Muslim architecture. It also offers an alternative accommodation base if you can't get anywhere at Pushkar during the camel fair.

The tourist office (☎ 627426) is in the RTDC's Hotel Khadim compound, not far from the bus stand. There's also a small tourist information counter at the train station (both offices close on Sunday). You can pick up a map and information on Pushkar from either office.

The State Bank of India, opposite the Collectorate on Savitri College Rd, changes travellers cheques and currency. The Bank of Baroda on Prithviraj Marg, opposite the main post office, only changes travellers cheques, but also issues cash advances on MasterCard and Visa.

At the foot of a desolate hill in the old part of town, **Dargah Khwaja Sahib** is one of India's most important places for Muslim and, particularly, Sufi pilgrims. The Dargah is the tomb of a Sufi saint, Khwaja Muinuddin Chishti, who came to Ajmer from Persia in 1192.

Back in the city, not far from the main post office is **Akbar's Palace**. This imposing building was constructed by the Mughal emperor Akbar in 1570. Today it houses the government museum. Items on display include a collection of stone sculptures, some dating back to the 8th century AD, old weapons and miniature paintings. It's open from 10 am to 4.30 pm daily except Friday (Rs 4, free on Monday); a camera/video costs Rs 10/20.

Places to Stay & Eat *King Edward Memorial Rest House* (☎ 429936, *Station Rd*), known locally as KEM, is to the left as you exit the train station. It's a poorly maintained and unwelcoming flophouse with tiny singles/doubles with bathroom starting at Rs 65/150. Better rooms cost Rs 100/200.

Nagpal Tourist Hotel (☎ 429503), near the KEM, is better. Rooms with private bathroom range from Rs 175/300 to Rs 900/1200. Some of the cheaper rooms are a bit small but OK.

RTDC's *Hotel Khadim* (☎ 627490, *Savitri College Rd*) is near the main bus stand and its dorm beds are good value at Rs 50. Rooms with bathroom and geyser start at Rs 330/460 including breakfast. *Aravali Holiday Resort* (☎ 627089), next door, is cheaper and more homy (though not quite a holiday resort). Ordinary rooms with bathroom (bucket hot water) cost Rs 250/300.

Honeydew Restaurant, next to the KEM Rest House, has a good selection of veg and nonveg Indian, Chinese and continental food. *Madina Hotel* is handy if you're waiting for a train (it's opposite the station). This simple eatery cooks up cheap veg and nonveg fare.

There's a restaurant and bar at *Hotel Khadim*.

Getting There & Away Most travellers will pass through Ajmer on the way to or from Pushkar. The train station is in the centre of town on Station Rd. The main bus stand is about 2.5km north-east on Jaipur Rd. An autorickshaw between the two shouldn't cost more than Rs 15.

Bus There are plenty of state transport buses from the main bus stand. For Jaipur they leave roughly every 15 minutes (Rs 46, three hours). For Jodhpur there are buses every 30 minutes (Rs 70, four hours) until about 8 pm. There are also regular services to Udaipur (Rs 105, seven hours), Bikaner (Rs 97, 7½ hours) and Delhi (Rs 143, nine hours).

Private buses usually leave from Kutchery Rd or the northern end of Station Rd where most of the bus companies have offices. These can also be booked through agents in Pushkar.

Buses to Pushkar shuttle roughly every 20 minutes from the main bus stand. The trip takes about 30 minutes (Rs 6). There are also regular buses from a stand called Ghandi Bawan on Station Rd just north of the train station – you can easily walk here if you arrive by train. The last bus from Ghandi Bawan is about 9 pm, but if you arrive later than this you can still get a Bikaner-bound bus from the main bus stand. These usually drop off at the Marwar bus stand in Pushkar.

Train Ajmer is well connected by train to Jaipur (135km) and Delhi (444km) since it's on one of the main Delhi-Mumbai lines. However, there are no direct trains west from Ajmer to Jodhpur or Jaisalmer, or north to Bikaner. The comfortable *Shatabdi Express* departs at 3.30 pm, arriving in New Delhi at 10.15 pm. The fare to Delhi is Rs 630/1250 in chair car/executive class. The overnight *Ahmedabad-Delhi Mail* leaves at 12.45 am and arrives at 5.20 am (Rs 154/713 sleeper/air-con two-tier).

There are two daily trains to Udaipur, both with 2nd-class sleeper and air-con two-tier sleeper carriages: The overnight *Chetak Express* departs inconveniently at 1.50 am, arriving in Udaipur at 10.25 am (Rs 120/564 sleeper/air-con two-tier); the *Ahmedabad Express* departs at 8.45 am, arriving at 6 pm. Both trains originate in Delhi so you should try to book a day or two in advance if you want a sleeper berth.

The reservations hall is upstairs at Ajmer station. Agents in Pushkar will make reservations for around Rs 50.

PUSHKAR
☎ 0145 • pop 13,000

For centuries a place of holy pilgrimage for Hindus, Pushkar has also become a place of pilgrimage for travellers in more recent years. The tiny whitewashed village suffers from none of the grime, pollution and chaos of most north Indian cities, though it's distinctly touristy in the high season. You'll almost certainly be hassled for a donation on the ghats (see the boxed text 'Pushy Priests in Pushkar' later in this chapter), but it's still a very mellow, and a very holy, place. There are always scores of pilgrims down on the bathing ghats as well as sadhus (spiritual seekers) and priests performing ritual puja (offering or prayers).

On the fringe of the desert, the town is a crowded huddle of whitewashed and pale-blue buildings around a small lake. From some angles you could almost be in Greece, if not for the ghats that step down to the water and the temples dotted around. It's surrounded by hills: Nag Pahar, the Snake Mountain, separates Pushkar from Ajmer.

Pushkar is perhaps best known for its Camel Fair, which takes place here each October/November. This massive congregation of camels, cattle, livestock traders, pilgrims, tourists and film-makers is one of the planet's most incredible events. If you are anywhere within striking distance at the time, it's an event not to be missed. See Special Events later in this section.

As Pushkar is a holy place, alcohol, meat and even eggs are banned – but travellers

INDIA

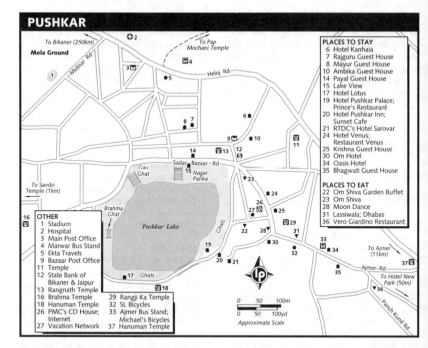

PUSHKAR

To Bikaner (250km)
To Pap Mochani Temple
Mela Ground
Motisar Rd
Heloj Rd
Sadar Bazaar Rd
Gau Ghat
Nagar Palika
To Savitri Temple (1km)
Brahma Ghat
Pushkar Lake
Ghats
Ghats
To Ajmer (11km)
Ajmer Rd
To Hotel New Park (50m)
Panch Kund Rd

PLACES TO STAY
6 Hotel Kanhaia
7 Rajguru Guest House
8 Mayur Guest House
10 Ambika Guest House
14 Payal Guest House
15 Lake View
17 Hotel Lotus
19 Hotel Pushkar Palace;
   Prince's Restaurant
20 Hotel Pushkar Inn;
   Sunset Cafe
21 RTDC's Hotel Sarovar
24 Hotel Venus;
   Restaurant Venus
25 Krishna Guest House
30 Om Hotel
34 Oasis Hotel
35 Bhagwati Guest House

PLACES TO EAT
22 Om Shiva Garden Buffet
23 Om Shiva
28 Moon Dance
31 Lassiwala; Dhabas
36 Vero Giardino Restaurant

OTHER
1 Stadium
2 Hospital
3 Main Post Office
4 Marwar Bus Stand
5 Ekta Travels
9 Bazaar Post Office
11 Temple
12 State Bank of
   Bikaner & Jaipur
13 Rangnath Temple
16 Brahma Temple
18 Hanuman Temple
26 PMC's CD House;
   Internet
27 Vacation Network
29 Rangji Ka Temple
32 SL Bicycles
33 Ajmer Bus Stand;
   Michael's Bicycles
37 Hanuman Temple

0   50   100m
0   50   100yd
Approximate Scale

usually find they can get their highs here in other ways.

Information

There is no tourist office in Pushkar (you can pick up a map and other information at either of the tourist offices in Ajmer; see the previous entry), but there are lots of travel agents and it's easy to find your way around. The State Bank of Bikaner & Jaipur changes travellers cheques (but strangely not cash) – the wait can be long and the staff brusque. It's easier to use the moneychangers scattered along Sadar Bazaar Rd, where you can exchange cash and travellers cheques at reasonable rates. On the same road are a number of places offering Internet services, STD/ISD phone calls and a couple of good bookshops.

Things to See & Do

The main attraction of Pushkar is the laid-back and devotional atmosphere, which is why many travellers find themselves kicking back here for a week or more, but there are a few interesting things to see, mainly Hindu temples. Few of these temples are as ancient as you might expect at such an important pilgrimage site, since many were desecrated by Aurangzeb and subsequently rebuilt. The most famous is the 14th-century **Brahma Temple**, said to be one of the few temples in the world dedicated to this deity. It's marked by a red spire, and over the entrance gateway is the *hans*, or goose symbol, of Brahma, who is said to have personally chosen Pushkar as its site.

The one-hour trek up to the hilltop **Savitri Temple** overlooking the lake is best made early in the morning; the view at sunrise is magical. To get there, walk around the lake (either on the southern side or past the Brahma temple) and pick up the trail leading south-west past a drinks stall. On the northern side of the lake, the **Pap Mochani Temple** sits on a smaller hill. It's only about a 20-minute walk from a road behind the Marwar bus stand. A leisurely circuit of the lake is a great way to spend an hour or two – the southern section (cross the bridge just past Sunset Cafe) is particularly interesting.

There are 52 **ghats** running down to the lake, and the waters around each are said to

Pushy Priests in Pushkar...

When you visit the ghats at Pushkar you'll almost certainly be approached by a priest who will want to bless you with *puja* (offerings or prayers). In fact, you'll probably notice other travellers with red ribbons tied around their wrists (known as 'Pushkar Passports') who have already had the treatment.

This is fine – it's a fundamental aspect of the Hindu religion – and a donation is always expected. But in recent years the priests (some genuine, some not) have used this as a scam to extract large amounts of money from newly arrived tourists. Demands for Rs 100, Rs 500 or even US dollars are not uncommon! At some point in the brief ceremony, the priest will ask you to tell Brahma how much you're going to give, and will probably suggest a figure. Don't fall for this emotional blackmail and don't be moved if he gets angry. Offering Rs 10 or Rs 20 is fine – the amount is up to you. As with any 'transaction' in India, it's probably best to say how much you're prepared to give beforehand, to avoid a scene later. Some travellers actually buy a red ribbon to wear around their wrists before going to the ghats, but puja is part of the Pushkar experience provided you know what to expect.

It doesn't end there. Priests or other locals may (forcibly) offer you a flower and ask you to throw it into the lake 'for karma'. Once you've done this, they'll demand payment – in this case it's better to avoid a scene and not accept any offerings of flowers.

Finally, the henna girls can be quite persistent in Pushkar. They will ask to see your hand, and once they've got hold of it will whip out the henna pens and start drawing! If you don't want a henna tattoo (which, of course, you will have to pay for), firmly say no. (Henna is a natural dye used to draw intricate patterns, or 'tattoos', on the skin and is especially popular among Rajasthani women.)

have particular powers of blessing. Pilgrims are constantly bathing in the lake's sacred waters. If you wish to go down to the ghats and mingle with the pilgrims, do it with respect – remember this is a holy place. Remove your shoes, don't smoke, refrain from kidding around and do not take photographs. Signs around the lake warn that photography is prohibited.

Pushkar is a good alternative to Jaisalmer for desert **camel safaris**. Although the landscape north-west of Pushkar doesn't offer great dunes, there's plenty of sand around and your group will probably have a little piece of desert all to itself. Several travel agents and guesthouses can arrange safaris from an overnight ride for around Rs 250 up to long-range treks as far as Jodhpur and Jaisalmer (around seven days).

Special Events
The **Pushkar Fair** is one of India's most incredible events, when every man and his camel descends on the tiny town – mainly congregating around the *mela* (fair) ground to the north-west. The atmosphere is intoxicating, the photo opportunities endless. It's worth arriving a few days before the actual fair in order to get settled in and search for accommodation (which should preferably be booked ahead). The exact date of the fair is not fixed but it falls on the full moon of the Hindu month of Kartik. In 2001 it will fall around 27–30 November; in 2002 it's 16–19 November; in 2003 it's 5–8 November.

During the Camel Fair, the RTDC and many private operators set up a sea of tents near the mela ground – but don't expect them to be a cheap option. Demand for tents is high so you're strongly advised to book well ahead (☎ 0141-202586, fax 201045).

If you miss this event, the **Nagaur Cattle Fair** is held around late January/early February and is a similarly chaotic trading spree with fewer tourists. Nagaur is about 90km north of Pushkar on the back road to Bikaner.

Places to Stay
Pushkar has a range of accommodation. There are dozens of budget places which are nothing fancy – often very basic – but are generally clean, family-run and freshly whitewashed. You should ask to see a few rooms before deciding, as many have a cell-like atmosphere and are poorly ventilated in

INDIA

summer. Prices blow sky high during the Camel Fair, when demand for rooms is exceptionally high, but you can certainly ask for discounts in the off season (April to September).

Places to Stay – Budget

RTDC's *Hotel Sarovar* (☎ *72040)* has a lakeside setting but the entrance is around the other side, just off Ajmer Rd. This impressive old building, set in its own spacious grounds with a murky swimming pool and a restaurant, has more character than most other RTDC places. Dorm beds cost Rs 50. Singles/doubles cost Rs 100/200 with shared bathroom and Rs 300/400 with private bathroom. There are also deluxe rooms with lake view for Rs 500/600 and air-con rooms for Rs 700/800. Nonguests can use the pool for Rs 50.

Hotel Pushkar Inn (☎ *72010),* also near the lakefront, is good value and well located. Rooms with shared bathroom are Rs 75/150 and air-cooled rooms with private bathroom cost Rs 250/350. Not far from the entrance to the Hotel Sarovar, *Hotel Om* (☎ *72762)* has a strange temple-like atmosphere. The rooms, all with private bathroom, are basic and cheap at Rs 75/150 (Rs 100/250 with air cooler) and there's a courtyard at the back.

Bhagwati Guest House (☎ *72423),* almost opposite the Ajmer bus stand, is a little away from the lake but it's friendly, clean and very cheap, with small rooms with shared bathroom for only Rs 40/60. There's a good rooftop restaurant here, and the owner, Chandu, is very helpful.

Oasis Hotel (☎ *72100),* next to the bus stand, is an ugly five-storey building but there's a swimming pool, a garden of sorts and a variety of rooms. Rooms start at Rs 150/200; with air-con they are Rs 800/900 in season but half that in the summer months.

There are several cheap guesthouses along the main Sadar Bazaar Rd. *Hotel Venus* (☎ *72323)* has rooms with bathroom for Rs 100/150. Set in a shady garden, there's also a popular restaurant upstairs overlooking the bazaar. *Krishna Guest House* (☎ *72461),* nearby, has some unexciting rooms around a courtyard for Rs 60/100 with shared bathroom and Rs 125/175 with private bathroom. There's an average restaurant upstairs.

Payal Guest House (☎ *72163),* right in the middle of the main bazaar, is a travellers' favourite, although the rooms are stifling in summer. It's a relaxed and homy place with rooms from Rs 50/100 with shared bathroom and Rs 100/150 with private bathroom. Meals are available (in season only) and there's even a small bakery. *Lake View Hotel* (☎ *72106),* across the road, fronts onto the lake and there are good views from the rooftop. Some of the rooms have balconies facing out to the bazaar. They range from Rs 60/100 for small rooms with shared bathroom to Rs 200/250 with private bathroom and balcony. The upper storey rooms are best.

In the backstreets north of the lake are a couple of unassuming but friendly places. *Mayur Guest House* (☎ *72302)* and *Rajguru Guest House* (☎ *72879)* both have rooms with shared bathroom from Rs 60/80 and with private bathroom from around Rs 100/125. The latter has a shady courtyard.

In the street running north from the bazaar post office are a few more cheap places. *Ambika Guest House* (☎ *73145)* is an interesting old place run by a friendly Brahmin family. Basic rooms with private bathroom cost Rs 50/100. *Hotel Kanhaia* (☎ *72146),* a little farther up, has rooms with shared bathroom for as little as Rs 40/ 50 and with private bathroom for Rs 90/150.

Hotel Lotus (☎ *72842),* on the southern side of the lake, is great for travellers who don't mind very basic facilities but like a 'spiritual' atmosphere. It's in a peaceful location surrounded by temples rather than other houses. Rock-bottom rooms in an overgrown garden cost Rs 50/100.

Places to Stay – Mid-Range

Hotel Pushkar Palace (☎ *72001, fax 72226,* e *hppalace@datainfosys.net),* close to the lake, is a landmark in Pushkar and one of the most popular hotels. It once belonged to the maharaja of Kishangarh. This hotel has a certain charm but it's a bit overpriced and the staff are indifferent. The cheapest rooms (Rs 150/200) have shared bathroom and are a bit cramped but they are right by the lake. The better rooms have private bathroom, although they are still quite small, and range from Rs 550/600 (with air cooling) to Rs 1210/1320 with air-con. The most expensive rooms have good lake views.

Hotel New Park (☎ 72464, Panch Kund Rd) is away from the lake but it's in a peaceful location which would suit some travellers. Rooms are well-kept, spacious and modern and there's a pool and restaurant here, but it lacks personality. Rooms start at Rs 300/350 with private bathroom and air cooling. Air-con rooms are great value in summer when there's a 20% discount on the usual rate of Rs 650/700. It's a 10-minute walk from the Ajmer bus stand, but you can call ahead for a free pick-up.

Places to Eat

Pushkar has plenty of reasonably priced eating places, many of them set up for travellers. Strict vegetarianism rather limits the range of ingredients, but in true Indian style the cooks attempt to make up for this with imagination. You can even get an eggless omelette in some places (only in India), but the pancakes tend to be a bit stodgy.

Buffet meals are popular and unbeatable value, with several places offering all-you-can-eat veg meals for around Rs 40.

Om Shiva Buffet in the main bazaar is the original, with a rooftop buffet for breakfast, lunch and dinner daily. *Om Shiva Garden Buffet*, on the road leading down to Hotel Pushkar Palace, offers the same thing for Rs 45. The garden needed a bit of sprucing up at the time of research but otherwise the setting is quite pleasant.

Sunset Cafe, attached to Hotel Pushkar Inn, has an open dining area with lake views as well as a courtyard at the back. This place has long been a popular hang-out with travellers and really is the perfect place to sit and watch the sun set – despite slow service. The menu features everything from dosas and sizzlers to *rosti*, good pizzas (Rs 40 to Rs 90) and pasta dishes (Rs 60 to Rs 90). It's also good for breakfast.

Venus Restaurant, at the Hotel Venus, has a good rooftop restaurant where you can look down on the activity in the bazaar. A veg thali is Rs 30.

Moon Dance has tables in a laid-back garden and serves a wide range of food, including good Indian, Mexican and Italian dishes.

Prince's Restaurant, in the Hotel Pushkar Palace, is a relatively upmarket place to dine, and you can eat in the restaurant or out in the garden. Most dishes are over Rs 60 and there's a good buffet lunch and dinner for Rs 120. There's also a small bakery here.

Vero Giardino Restaurant, on the road to Hotel New Park, has a peaceful garden setting, good food and an interesting menu with Indian and Italian dishes.

A couple of *dhaba*-style restaurants near the Ajmer bus stand offer Rs 20 thalis. Also here is a *lassi-wallah* where you can get excellent sweet lassis for Rs 10. Pushkar is one of many places in Rajasthan (and India for that matter) where you can try *bhang*, usually mixed in a lassi. It's a derivative of marijuana and can be quite potent so don't let the sweet taste of the drink fool you into having too much. See the boxed text 'Bhanged Up'.

Bhanged Up

Bhang is the name for a derivative of cannabis (usually made from hemp leaves). It's widely used in northern India and is often available mixed with a lassi in travellers' restaurants. This might appear on the menu as a 'special' lassi, or it may not appear at all but is still available if you ask. Although bhang is technically legal – there are government bhang shops in Varanasi, Udaipur, Jaisalmer and elsewhere – it's effects can be dangerously strong. Not surprisingly, it's like being stoned, so if you're not accustomed to this particular state of mind, it pays to be cautious.

Apart from the potential to make you ill, travellers have had bad experiences while under the influence of the drug, and India is no place to be experiencing paranoia! You also leave yourself open to being robbed or worse while in a state of delirium.

If you do intend to try a bhang lassi (or the bhang cookies and chocolate you can get in Jaisalmer), be aware that the effects aren't immediate (it can take up to an hour), so just because you feel fine after one bhang lassi, it doesn't mean it's time to have another. Only try it in the company of other people you can trust, and ensure that there's at least one person in the group who's not partaking.

INDIA

Shopping

Pushkar's main bazaar is a tangle of narrow lanes running off Saddar Bazaar Rd and lined with an assortment of interesting little shops – ideal for picking up gifts for friends back home. It's especially good for costume jewellery and embroidered fabrics such as wall hangings and shoulder bags. A lot of what is stocked here comes from the Barmer district south of Jaisalmer and other tribal areas of Rajasthan. There are also the inevitable clothing shops lost in a 1960s hippy time warp. You may find occasional timeless items, but much of it is pretty cliched.

The music shops are well worth a visit if you're keen to pick up some traditional, contemporary or fusion music. PMC's CD House, almost opposite Krishna Guest House, is a good place to start looking. There are also a number of bookshops in the main bazaar selling a tremendous range of second-hand novels and guidebooks, and they'll usually buy them back (or buy any books that are in good condition) for around 50% of what you pay.

Getting There & Away

To Pushkar, buses depart from Ajmer frequently for Rs 6 (although it's only Rs 5 when going from Pushkar to Ajmer – because of the road toll; for cars the toll is Rs 25). The 30-minute ride is a spectacular climb up and over the hills. These buses arrive and depart from the Ajmer bus stand on Ajmer Rd, about a five-minute walk from the lake.

Through buses that are heading from Ajmer to Bikaner, or from Pushkar to Jaipur or Delhi, use the main Marwar bus stand north of the lake, and skirt around the town along Heloj Rd. From Marwar bus stand there are numerous state transport buses to Jaipur (Rs 50, 3½ hours), two to Jodhpur (Rs 69, six hours), and one to Udaipur at 1.30 pm (Rs 70, eight hours). Private buses also leave from here for Jaipur (Rs 60, three hours), Delhi (Rs 140, 10 hours), Jodhpur (Rs 90, five hours), Jaisalmer (Rs 180, 11 hours), Udaipur (Rs 90, seven hours) and Bikaner (Rs 80, seven hours). There are only two or three private buses a day from Pushkar (via Ajmer), but many more leave from Ajmer only. Tickets can be bought through travel agents such as Ekta Travels (☎ 72131) opposite Marwar bus stand, or

Vacation Network (☎ 72863), on the road to Hotel Pushkar Palace.

When you buy a ticket from a travel agent, check whether the bus departs from Pushkar or Ajmer. Agents will also make train reservations for around Rs 50, which saves you the hassle of going into Ajmer and queuing up.

A taxi from Pushkar to Ajmer costs around Rs 150.

Getting Around

Fortunately there are no autorickshaws polluting Pushkar's air, nor are there any vehicles on the roads around the lake. Getting around on foot is easy and a pleasure, but you can also hire a bicycle for around Rs 30 a day (or Rs 5 an hour). Try Michael's Bicycles, next to the Ajmer bus stand, or SL Bicycles, farther along Ajmer Rd towards the lake.

UDAIPUR
☎ 0294 • pop 366,000

Getting down to Udaipur, 264km south of Ajmer and 670km from Delhi, requires putting quite a kink in the straight Delhi-Jaisalmer route, but it's well worth the effort. With its serene lakes, stunning palaces, restored havelis and wonderfully warm evening glow, this is surely the most romantic city in Rajasthan.

Udaipur was founded in 1568 by Maharana Udai Singh II following the final sacking of Chittorgarh by the Mughal emperor, Akbar. This picturesque city rivals any of the world-famous creations of the Mughals with its Rajput love of the whimsical and its superbly crafted elegance. It's also proud of its heritage as a centre for crafts and the performing arts and its school of miniature painting is noteworthy.

The city was once surrounded by a wall, but although the gates and much of the wall over the higher crags remain, a great deal of it has disappeared. The old city is still a jumble of tangled, cobbled streets. In common with most Indian cities, Udaipur's urban and industrial sprawl goes beyond the city's original boundaries, and pollution of various kinds can be discouraging. This will be your first impression of Udaipur if you arrive at the train or bus stations, but you'll find it much more pleasant closer to the lake.

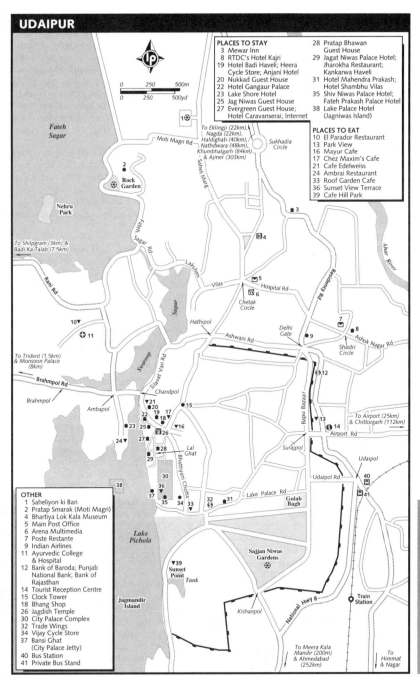

UDAIPUR

PLACES TO STAY
3 Mewar Inn
8 RTDC's Hotel Kajri
19 Hotel Badi Haveli; Heera
   Cycle Store; Anjani Hotel
20 Nukkad Guest House
22 Hotel Gangaur Palace
23 Lake Shore Hotel
25 Jag Niwas Guest House
27 Evergreen Guest House;
   Hotel Caravanserai; Internet
28 Pratap Bhawan
   Guest House
29 Jagat Niwas Palace Hotel;
   Jharokha Restaurant;
   Kankarwa Haveli
31 Hotel Mahendra Prakash;
   Hotel Shambhu Vilas
35 Shiv Niwas Palace Hotel;
   Fateh Prakash Palace Hotel
38 Lake Palace Hotel
   (Jagniwas Island)

PLACES TO EAT
10 El Parador Restaurant
13 Park View
16 Mayur Cafe
17 Chez Maxim's Cafe
21 Cafe Edelweiss
24 Ambrai Restaurant
33 Roof Garden Cafe
36 Sunset View Terrace
39 Cafe Hill Park

OTHER
1 Saheliyon ki Bari
2 Pratap Smarak (Moti Magri)
4 Bhartiya Lok Kala Museum
5 Main Post Office
6 Arena Multimedia
7 Poste Restante
9 Indian Airlines
11 Ayurvedic College
   & Hospital
12 Bank of Baroda; Punjab
   National Bank; Bank of
   Rajasthan
14 Tourist Reception Centre
15 Clock Tower
18 Bhang Shop
26 Jagdish Temple
30 City Palace Complex
32 Trade Wings
34 Vijay Cycle Store
37 Bansi Ghat
   (City Palace Jetty)
40 Bus Station
41 Private Bus Stand

Fateh
Sagar

Nehru
Park

To Shilpgram (3km) &
Badi Ka Talab (7.5km)

Rani Rd

To Trident (1.5km)
& Monsoon Palace
(8km)

Brahmpol Rd

Brahmpol

Ambapol

Moti Magri Rd

Saheli Marg

To Eklingji (22km),
Nagda (22km),
Haldighati (40km),
Nathdwara (48km),
Khumbhalgarh (84km)
& Ajmer (303km)

Sukhadia
Circle

Rock
Garden

Fateh Sagar Rd

Lakshmi

Vilas

Sagar

Hathipol

Swaroop

Chandpol

Ashwani Rd

Chetak
Circle

Hospital Rd

Delhi
Gate

Ahar River

Residency Rd

Ashok Nagar Rd

Shastri
Circle

Sajjat Vari Rd

Bapu Bazaar

To Airport (25km)
& Chittorgarh (112km)

Airport Rd

Lal
Ghat

Bhattiyani Chotta

Surajpol

Udaipol

Udaipol Rd

Lake Palace Rd

Gulab
Bagh

Lake
Pichola

Jagmandir
Island

Sunset
Point

Tank

Sajjan Niwas
Gardens

Kishanpol

National Hwy 8

Train
Station

To Meera Kala
Mandir (200m)
& Ahmedabad
(252km)

To
Himmat
& Nagar

0   250   500m
0   250   500yd

INDIA

Orientation

The old city, bounded by the remains of the city wall, is on the eastern side of Lake Pichola. Many intersections are still named for the old city gates ('pol' means gate): Important ones include Chandpol (where the road crosses to the western side of the lake), Hathipol, Delhi Gate, Surajpol (near the tourist office) and Udaipol (near the main bus stand).

Information

Tourist Offices The Tourist Reception Centre (☎ 411535) is in the Fateh Memorial Building near Surajpol, less than 1km from the bus stand. The office is open from 10 am to 1.30 pm and 2 to 5 pm, Monday to Saturday. There are also smaller tourist information counters at the train station, airport and the southern end of the City Palace complex.

Out & About Udaipur (Rs 10) is a new publication offering useful local information, event listings and articles. Pick up a copy at the tourist office.

Money The Bank of Baroda, just outside the old city in Bapu Bazaar, changes cash and travellers cheques reasonably efficiently and gives cash advances on Visa and MasterCard. Nearby, the Bank of Rajasthan and the Punjab National Bank also change money.

More convenient are the money changers (usually associated with travel agencies) in the old city. You'll find several around the intersection near the clock tower (near the road leading to the City Palace). There's a branch of Trade Wings exchange bureau in the Century Complex on Lake Palace Rd.

Post & Communications The main post office is directly north of the old city, at Chetak Circle, but poste restante is at the post office at Shastri Circle, opposite RTDC's Hotel Kajri. There's also a small post office in the quadrant outside the City Palace Museum.

Several hotels and travel agents in and around the old city offer Internet access for about Rs 80 an hour. The cheapest access is Arena Multimedia, 46 Madhuban, where you can log on for Rs 40 an hour, but it's well north of the old city, near the main post office.

Lake Pichola

Placid Lake Pichola was enlarged by Maharana Udai Singh II after he founded the city. It's still fairly shallow and can actually dry up in severe droughts, though this doesn't happen often. The City Palace extends a considerable distance along the east bank of the lake. North of the palace, you can wander along the lake shore, where there are some interesting bathing and *dhobi* (laundry) ghats.

Out in the lake are two islands, Jagniwas and Jagmandir. **Boat rides**, which leave regularly from the City Palace jetty (known as Bansi Ghat), are popular. These cost Rs 75 for half an hour and Rs 150 for one hour, the latter including a visit to Jagmandir Island.

Jagniwas Island Jagniwas, the island housing the Lake Palace, is about 1.5 hectares in size. The palace was built by Maharana Jagat Singh II in 1754 and covers the entire island so that it appears to be floating on the lake. Formerly the royal summer palace, today it is the ultimate in luxury hotels, with shady courtyards, lotus ponds and even a small mango-tree shaded swimming pool. Yes, this is the perfect place to fall in love, but casual visitors are not really encouraged. Nonguests can only come over for lunch or dinner – and then only if the hotel is not full, which it often is. Hotel launches cross to the island from the City Palace jetty. The Lake Palace, along with the Shiv Niwas Palace and Monsoon Palace (see later in this section) were used as sets in the James Bond movie *Octopussy*.

Jagmandir Island The other island palace, Jagmandir, was commenced by Maharana Karan Singh, but takes its name from Maharana Jagat Singh (1628–52) who made a number of additions to it. It is said that the Mughal emperor, Shah Jahan, derived some of his inspiration for the Taj Mahal from this palace after staying here in 1623–24 while leading a revolt against his father, Jehangir. Flanked by a row of enormous stone elephants, the island has an impressive *chhatri* (cenotaph) carved from grey-blue stone. The view across the lake, to the city and its glorious golden palace, is a scene of rare beauty.

City Palace & Museums

The imposing City Palace, towering over the lake, is the largest palace complex in Rajasthan. Actually a conglomeration of buildings added by various maharanas, it still manages to retain a surprising uniformity of design. Building was started by Maharana Udai Singh II, the city's founder. The palace is surmounted by balconies, towers and cupolas and there are fine views over the lake and the city from the upper terraces.

The palace is entered from the northern end through the Baripol (built 1600) and the Tripolia Gate (1725), with its eight carved marble arches. It was once a custom for maharanas to be weighed under the gate and their weight in gold or silver distributed to the populace.

The main part of the palace is now preserved as a museum. It includes the **Mor Chowk** with its beautiful mosaics of peacocks. The **Manak (or Ruby) Mahal** has glass and mirrorwork, while **Krishna Vilas** has a remarkable collection of miniatures. In the **Bari Mahal** there is a pleasant central garden. The **Moti Mahal** has beautiful mirrorwork and the **Chini Mahal** is covered in ornamental tiles. There's an armoury section downstairs. More paintings can be seen in the **Zenana Mahal**. There's a large tiger-catching cage near the Zenana Mahal entrance, and a tiny Worldwide Fund for Nature (WWF) shop nearby.

The museum is open daily from 9.30 am to 4.30 pm (Rs 35, or a hefty Rs 100 if you enter from the Lake Palace side). It costs Rs 75 to take in a camera and a whopping Rs 300 for a video camera. A guide (Rs 90) is worthwhile.

The other part of the palace is against the lake shore and has been partly converted into two luxury hotels: Shiv Niwas Palace and the Fateh Prakash Palace. To get through to this side, you have to pay another Rs 50 which allows you to see the Durbar Hall, and is deducted from your bill if you have lunch or dinner at either hotel.

There's a stunning **Crystal Gallery** at the Fateh Prakash Palace Hotel in the City Palace complex. This rare collection includes crystal chairs, tables and even beds! It's open from 10 am to 1 pm and 3 to 8 pm daily; entry (Rs 250) includes a soft drink, coffee or tea. No photography is allowed.

The Crystal Gallery overlooks the grandiose **Durbar Hall** with its massive chandeliers and striking portraits of former maharanas of Mewar. Historically, the durbar hall (or hall of audience) was used by India's rulers for official occasions such as state banquets, and formal or informal meetings. This is undoubtedly one of India's most impressive halls, with a lavish interior boasting some of the largest chandeliers in the country. The walls display royal weapons and striking portraits of former maharanas of Mewar. The illustrious Mewar rulers come from what is believed to be the oldest ruling dynasty in the world, spanning 76 generations.

Jagdish Temple

Only 150m north of the entrance to the City Palace, this fine Indo-Aryan temple was built by Maharana Jagat Singh in 1651 and enshrines a black stone image of Vishnu as Jagannath, lord of the universe. A brass image of the Garuda is in a shrine in front of the temple. The temple is open daily from 5 am to 2 pm and 4 to 10 pm.

Fateh Sagar

North of Lake Pichola, this lake is overlooked by a number of hills and is a hangout for young lovers. It was originally built in 1678 by Maharana Jai Singh but, after heavy rains destroyed the dam, it was reconstructed by Maharana Fateh Singh. In the middle of the lake is Nehru Park, a popular garden island with a boat-shaped cafe. You can get there by boat from near the bottom of Moti Magri Rd for Rs 5.

Bhartiya Lok Kala Museum

Exhibits at this small museum, which is also a foundation for the preservation and promotion of local folk arts, include dolls, masks, musical instruments, paintings and – the high point of the exhibits – puppets. It is open from 9 am to 6 pm (Rs 10). Regular 15-minute puppet shows (free) are staged daily. Longer puppet and cultural shows are held daily from 6 to 7 pm (Rs 30). Call ☎ 529296 for details.

Shilpgram

Shilpgram, a crafts village 3km west of Fateh Sagar, has displays of traditional houses from Rajasthan, Gujarat, Goa and

INDIA

Maharashtra. There are also demonstrations by musicians, dancers or artisans from these states. It's open 11 am to 7 pm daily (Rs 10). There's a good restaurant and a swimming pool (Rs 100) here.

Monsoon Palace (Sajjan Garh)

On a distant mountain range about 8km from Lake Pichola, this neglected palace was constructed by Maharana Sajjan Singh in the late 19th century. It is now owned by the government, and is closed to the public (although a little baksheesh to the caretaker may open doors). The main reason to come here is to take in the expansive and breathtaking views. An hour before sunset is a pleasant time to arrive. The palace is illuminated at night when it can easily be seen from Udaipur. The round trip takes about one hour and should cost about Rs 120 by autorickshaw (including 30 minutes at the site).

An enjoyable way of visiting the Monsoon Palace is to hire a motorcycle or scooter in Udaipur (see Getting Around). Once you get beyond the mild chaos of the city (about 2km beyond the Lake Pichola bridge along Brahmpol Rd), it's an easy and exhilarating ride to the top. The gates at the foot of the hill leading up to the palace are open from 8 am to sunset and admission is as steep as the road at Rs 40.

Gardens

The **Saheliyon ki Bari**, or Garden of the Maids of Honour, is in the north of the city. This small ornamental garden, with its fountains, kiosks, marble elephants and lotus pool, is open from 9 am to 6 pm daily. The **Sajjan Niwas Gardens** has pleasant lawns and a zoo. Not far from the Cafe Hill Park, **Sunset Point** is a nice place to watch the sun set (entry Rs 5). There's a musical fountain here, tinkling away each evening.

Organised Tours

Five-hour city tours leave daily at 8 am from the RTDC's Hotel Kajri (☎ 410501). Cost is exactly Rs 73.50 (excluding entry to sites). Depending on demand, an afternoon tour (2 to 7 pm) goes out to Eklingji, Haldighati and Nathdwara and costs Rs 105. There are also day tours to Ranakpur and Kumbhalgarh (Rs 262.50) and Chittorgarh (Rs 273). Contact the Tourist Reception Centre or the hotel for details.

Some travel agents and guesthouses offer jeep safaris.

Places to Stay – Budget

Udaipur pioneered the Paying Guest House Scheme in Rajasthan. The tourist centre has a list of places where you can stay with a local family for around Rs 100 to Rs 600 per night.

Hotels around the Jagdish Temple have the best location and range from very basic guesthouses to luxurious lakeside havelis. Lakeview rooms are usually a bit more expensive and should be requested when booking. Most hotels will cut their rates out of season (May to October).

Jagdish Temple Area Many places here have views over the lake; the area is away from the traffic and the central location is ideal. Since autorickshaw drivers will expect commission from these places, during the day you can ask to be dropped at the Jagdish Temple or Lal Ghat and walk to your hotel from there.

Jag Niwas Guest House (☎ 422067, 21 Gangaur Rd) is a small, family-run place (six double rooms). Rooms range from a smallish double with bathroom for Rs 150 up to a large air-cooled room for Rs 450 (no discounts for singles). There's a veg restaurant on the rooftop and the owner even offers cooking lessons.

Hotel Gangaur Palace (☎ 422303, 3 Gangaur Ghat) is a good choice in this area. Dingy rooms with shared bathroom are Rs 60/80. Large doubles (no singles) with bathroom range from Rs 150 to Rs 350 for lake view rooms. There's a rooftop restaurant.

Hotel Badi Haveli (☎ 412588, 85 Gangaur Ghat Rd) was once home to the astrologer to the maharana. These days it's a popular backpacker place with a bit of character and fine views over the lake. Plain but neat singles/doubles with shared bathroom are Rs 100/150, doubles with private bathroom are Rs 200 and the best room with a view is Rs 350. Some of the best upper-storey rooms are those with shared bathroom. Nearby is the *Anjani Hotel* (☎ 421770) with pretty grim rooms with bathroom from Rs 80/100 but better ones for Rs 350/450. You get breakfast (Rs 25) and veg thalis (Rs 40).

Evergreen Guest House (☎ *421585, 32 Lal Ghat)* has simple rooms around a small courtyard. Rooms are Rs 100/150 with shared bathroom, or Rs 200/250 with private bathroom. There's a rooftop restaurant.

Nukkad Guest House (*no phone, 56 Ganesh Ghati)* is a simple place run by a friendly, traveller-oriented family. Basic singles with shared bathroom cost Rs 40 and doubles with bathroom are Rs 80, but there are also larger rooms for Rs 60 and Rs 100. There's a rooftop with decent views and a restaurant.

Lake Palace Road & Elsewhere Lake Palace Rd is still central, about halfway between the bus station and Lake Pichola. *Hotel Mahendra Prakash* (☎ *419811, Lake Palace Rd)* has clean, spacious rooms with private bathroom and TV from Rs 250/300 to Rs 500/600. There's also a sparkling clean swimming pool, a restaurant and a rooftop with views of the City Palace. New rooms are currently being built overlooking the pool.

Hotel Shambhu Vilas (☎ *421921, Lake Palace Rd)*, a few doors away, is not as good but it has some interesting rooms (one has a mock Roman pillar in the middle). Air-cooled rooms cost Rs 400/500 and air-con Rs 600/800, with cable TV.

There are some decent budget options elsewhere in the city. *Mewar Inn* (☎ *522090, |e| mewarinn@hotmail.com, 42 Residency Rd)* is extremely cheap but it's not in a great location and the cost of autorickshaws into town must be considered. It's a hassle-free place though, and well set up for travellers with Internet, laundry, tours, yoga and left luggage. Basic rooms with shared bathroom are Rs 34/44. Rooms with bathroom and hot water start at Rs 75 for a double. A discount is given to YHA members. There's a rooftop veg restaurant and bicycles for hire (Rs 15 per day).

Lake Shore Hotel (*no phone)*, south of Chandpol near Ambrai Restaurant, faces the City Palace across Lake Pichola. It's a mellow place and has a terrace with marvellous views over the water. Basic but neat rooms with shared bathroom are Rs 100/200.

RTDC's *Hotel Kajri* (☎ *410501, Shastri Circle)* is handy if you're going on one of their city tours but is otherwise too far from

anything of interest. Dorm beds are Rs 50 and fairly ordinary rooms with bathroom are Rs 300/400.

Places to Stay – Mid-Range

Jagat Niwas Palace Hotel (☎ *420133, fax 520023, |e| jagat@jp1.dot.net.in, 24–25 Lal Ghat)*, on the lake shore, is a superb restored haveli that has long been popular with travellers. There are two sections: The front section has beautifully furnished lake-view double rooms (with air-con) for Rs 1250 and Rs 1695. Discounts of up to 50% are available out of season. The adjacent section has a range of stylish rooms from Rs 350 (with shared bathroom and four-poster bed) to Rs 750/950 with air-con and Rs 950/1190 with lake views. There's an excellent restaurant here (see Places to Eat).

Pratap Bhawan Guest House (☎ *560566, 12 Lal Ghat)* is a spotless new place run by retired Colonel NS Rathore and his wife. There are eight double rooms in this friendly place, from Rs 400 to Rs 700 for a large room with a view.

Hotel Caravanserai (☎ *411103, fax 521252, 14 Lal Ghat)* is a modern, marbled place which offers nice rooms from Rs 500/750 to Rs 1195/1300 with air-con and lake views. The food at the rooftop restaurant is average, but it has good views and live Indian classical music in the evening.

Places to Stay – Top End

Udaipur is one place where splashing out on an expensive hotel really is splashing out. We don't expect shoestringers to actually stay in these places, but they are included for interest's sake.

The *Lake Palace Hotel* (☎ *527961, fax 527974)* is one of the world's most spectacular hotels. The cheapest doubles in this swanky white palace are US$210 (no lake view); US$245 gets you a lake view. You don't even want to know about the suites.

Shiv Niwas Palace Hotel (☎ *528016, fax 528006, |e| resv@hrhindia.com)*, part of the City Palace complex, has 'cheap' rooms for US$100 but rooms around the pool start from US$250 a double. Rooms at *Fateh Prakash Palace Hotel* (☎ *528016, fax 528006, |e| gmfpp@udaipur.hrhindia.com)*, also in the City Palace complex, start at US$120, but the more ornate rooms furnished with traditional palace pieces cost US$200/250.

INDIA

Places to Eat

Udaipur has scores of rooftop cafes catering to budget travellers, as well as fine dining at the top-end hotels.

Reasonable cheap places in the old city with rooftop lake views (and *Octopussy* in the evenings) include *Natural City View Restaurant* at the Hotel Gangaur, not to be confused with the equally good *Natural View Restaurant* at the Evergreen Guest House. *Jagat Niwas Guest House* has a good veg restaurant.

Chez Maxim's Cafe is a tiny, inexpensive hole-in-the-wall place with Rajasthani miniature paintings decorating the walls. Indian veg dishes are under Rs 30, Western breakfast is Rs 50 and you can get apple pie and custard for Rs 40. *Mayur Cafe*, by the Jagdish Temple, has long been popular, but it has gone downhill these days, which shows in its service. There are south Indian dishes as well as Western alternatives.

Cafe Edelweiss, down near Chandpol, is a European-style bakery whipping up things like apple crumble and chocolate cake.

Sunset View Terrace, ideally situated on a terrace overlooking Lake Pichola, is worth visiting for the views alone. Live Indian classical music is played in the late afternoon and the menu offers a range of snacks such as pizzas (Rs 110), burgers (Rs 90) and milk shakes (Rs 50).

Ambrai Restaurant is equally worth visiting at sunset but for a completely different view. Unlike most other restaurants, it sits at water level and it faces the City Palace complex, which looks glorious in the late-afternoon light. It serves Indian, Chinese and continental dishes from Rs 75 to Rs 150, and is a great place to kick back with a beer.

El Parador, out in the Fateh Sagar area (opposite the Ayurvedic College & Hospital on Ambamata Rani Rd), is recommended. This is one of the only places in Rajasthan where you can get *real* percolated coffee. It's run by a friendly family who whips up a range of moderately priced Italian, Greek, Mexican and French cuisine. They also own the popular El Parador in Varanasi.

Roof Garden Cafe, around the corner from the Rang Niwas Palace Hotel, facing the City Palace, looks like the Hanging Gardens of Babylon. The setting is more exciting than the food.

Cafe Hill Park, south-west of the Sajjan Niwas Gardens on a hill overlooking Lake Pichola, is worth a visit just for the views. This rather ramshackle cafe offers Indian, continental and Chinese fare.

Park View is opposite the park on the busy main road just north of the tourist office. It's a dimly lit air-con place that's popular with Indian diners and is strong on north Indian curries. Fish curry is Rs 60, butter chicken Rs 160 and *rogan josh* (lamb curry) Rs 50.

Jharokha Restaurant (☎ 420133), in the Jagat Niwas Palace Hotel, is a great place to dine out, even on a budget. Named after the little Persian-style alcoves where you can sit and take lunch and dinner while looking over at the Lake Palace, this place is atmospheric *and* affordable. Indian veg dishes are around Rs 45, Chinese dishes are between Rs 55 and Rs 75 and continental dishes are around Rs 120. A beer is Rs 100 and there's a nightly puppet show here from 7.30 pm. It's wise to book ahead for dinner, as the place can fill up fast.

Shiv Niwas Palace Hotel is recommended for an unforgettable dining experience. There's seating indoors or in the pleasant open-air courtyard by the pool. You could just about get away with Rs 200 per head here if you don't drink. Indian classical music is performed each evening by the poolside.

Lake Palace Hotel is, of course, the ultimate dining experience, although there's no guarantee you'll get in, since it is usually only possible to get a table when the hotel is not full. The buffet lunch/dinner costs Rs 500/600 (including the boat crossing) and you can enjoy a drink at the pleasant bar. Reservations are essential, and reasonably tidy dress is expected.

Entertainment

Meera Kala Mandir (☎ 583176, Sector 11, Hiran Magari), near the Pars Theatre, south of the old city, has one-hour Rajasthani folk-dance and music performances daily except Sunday at 7 pm from July to April. It costs Rs 60 per person. An autorickshaw from the City Palace area costs Rs 25. You can buy tickets at some travel agents in the old city, and at Heera Cycle Store. Puppet shows are also held at the *Bhartiya Lok Kala Museum* (☎ 529296) from 6 pm each evening.

Many hotels and restaurants stage their own entertainment for patrons – usually puppet shows or Rajasthani music/dance performances. *Sunset View Terrace* is a good place to see some live music.

Many of the *budget restaurants* try to lure customers with a free nightly screening of the James Bond movie *Octopussy*, which, judging by the quality of the tapes, appears to have been played several million times. It's worth sitting through once though. It was partly shot in Udaipur, and features probably the best autorickshaw chase in film history. These days, contemporary cult movies are also screened.

Good places to enjoy a beer are *Ambrai Restaurant*, *Jharokha Restaurant* in the Jagat Niwas Palace Hotel, and, if your budget allows it, the bar at *Shiv Niwas Palace Hotel*.

Udaipur has no fewer than four *bhang shops* where you can order bhang lassis direct from the supplier. They come in light (Rs 30; a sensible place to start), medium and strong. The most convenient shop is near Heera Cycles in the old city.

Shopping

Udaipur has plenty of little shops selling a jumble of things, from funky Western clothing to traditional antique jewellery. The town is popular for its local crafts, and is famous for miniature paintings in the Rajput-Mughal style. There's a good cluster of shops selling these on Lake Palace Rd, next to the Rang Niwas Palace Hotel, and there are others around the Jagdish Temple. Be prepared to bargain hard or walk away, as most places have ridiculously inflated prices for tourists.

Getting There & Away

Air The Indian Airlines office (☎ 410999) is near Delhi Gate. There are daily flights from Udaipur to Delhi (US$110) and Mumbai (US$125), three a week to Jaipur (US$80) and four to Jodhpur (US$80). Jet Airways (☎ 561105) also flies daily to Delhi, Jaipur and Mumbai for the same fares.

Bus The main bus station is east of the old city. State transport buses arrive and depart from here, while private deluxe buses gather outside on Station Rd. There are hourly buses to Jaipur (Rs 135/200

ordinary/deluxe, nine hours) and Ajmer (Rs 98/144, six hours). Less frequent services go to Jodhpur (Rs 97/129, eight hours). There is a handful of express buses to Delhi (Rs 245, 14 hours) and ordinary buses to Chittorgarh (Rs 38, three hours) and Mt Abu (Rs 67, five hours).

Private bus companies operate to Jodhpur (Rs 90), Pushkar (Rs 100), Jaisalmer (Rs 170, 11 hours), Jaipur (Rs 150), Delhi (Rs 300) and Mumbai (Rs 350) among others. Tickets can be booked at travel agents in the old city or at the bus company offices on Station Rd. Shop around, as some places add extra commission on top.

There are *no* direct buses to Jaisalmer, deluxe or otherwise. You'll have to change at Jodhpur, but some unscrupulous agents have been known to sell travellers overpriced 'direct' tickets.

Train It's generally quicker to catch a bus, but a sleeper berth on a train is still a more comfortable option for the trip to or from Delhi (20 hours), Jaipur (12 hours) or Ajmer (8½ hours). Trains between Udaipur and Delhi run only to/from Delhi Sarai Rohilla station.

The *Chetak Express* to Delhi departs at 6.10 pm and costs Rs 225/1044 in sleeper class/air-con two-tier. This train goes via Chittorgarh, Ajmer (Rs 120/564) and Jaipur (Rs 154/713). Coming the other way, it departs from Delhi at 2.10 pm, arriving in Udaipur at 10.25 am. The *Ahmedabad Express* departs from Udaipur at 8 am, arriving in Delhi Sarai Rohilla at 7.05 am, also via Ajmer and Jaipur.

Getting Around

To/From the Airport The airport is 25km from the city. There's no airport bus; an autorickshaw/taxi will cost Rs 180/220.

Autorickshaw & Tempo The minimum fare for tourists anywhere within the city appears to be around Rs 20, but you'll really have to bargain and agree on a fare before you get in.

The commission racket is healthy in Udaipur and most rickshaw drivers will try to take you to a place of their choice rather than yours, especially if you want to go to the Lal Ghat area. You could ask for the Jagdish Temple, as all the guesthouses in that area are within easy walking distance of the temple. There are now prepaid autorickshaw booths at the bus and train station, so head for those when you arrive. Confusingly, the list of rates at the bus station is written only in Hindi. An autorickshaw from the train station to Lal Ghat is Rs 27 and from the bus stand to Lal Ghat is Rs 25. It costs Rs 150 to hire an autorickshaw for half a day of local sightseeing, although the prepaid booth posts fares of Rs 25 an hour.

Tempos run on set routes, including from the train station to the bus stand and Surajpol, but not to the old city. They're OK for short trips if you know where you're going.

Bicycle & Motorcycle You can hire bicycles from several places for around Rs 25 per day, and there are a couple of places where you can hire mopeds. Heera Cycle Store (☎ 523525), near the Hotel Badi Haveli in the old city, rents out bicycles/mopeds/motorcycles for Rs 25/150/250 per day (not including fuel). Vijay Cycle Store, next to Hotel Raj Palace, rents bicycles for Rs 20 a day (Rs 3 an hour) and mopeds for Rs 200 a day. With one of these you can get out to many of the sights within and around Udaipur, including the Monsoon Palace, Eklingji and Nagda.

AROUND UDAIPUR
The little village of **Eklingji**, 22km north of Udaipur, has a number of ancient temples. Avoid the main Shiva temple on Monday (an auspicious day for devotees), as it can get very crowded. There are three old temples at **Nagda**, about 1km off the road before Eklingji. Half-hourly local buses run from Udaipur to Eklingji (Rs 15, 40 minutes).

The exceptionally beautiful **Ranakpur** complex, 60km north of Udaipur, is one of the largest and most important Jain temples in India. Tucked away in a remote valley of the Aravalli range, it's certainly worth seeing if you have the time.

The main temple is the Chaumukha, or Four-Faced, Temple, dedicated to Adinath. Built in 1439, this huge, superbly crafted and well-kept marble temple has 29 halls supported by 1444 pillars, no two alike. Within the complex are two other Jain temples to Neminath and Parasnath and, a little distance away, a Sun Temple. One kilometre from the main complex is the Amba

Mata Temple. The temple complex is open daily (to non-Jains) from 11 am to 5 pm. Shoes and all leather articles must be left at the entrance.

RTDC's *Hotel Shilpi* (☎ 02934-85074) is conveniently located near the temple complex and has rooms with bathroom from Rs 200/250, deluxe doubles for Rs 400 and dorm beds for Rs 50. There's a *restaurant* here. The *dharamsala* (☎ 02934-85019) within the temple complex has very basic accommodation for a donation. From Udaipur there are frequent express buses to Ranakpur (Rs 31, three hours).

JODHPUR
☎ 0291 • pop 770,000
Dominated by a massive fort and with an old city radiating cobalt blue, Jodhpur is another of Rajasthan's gems but it receives much less interest from travellers than Udaipur or Jaisalmer. This is the second-largest city in Rajasthan (after Jaipur), hovering on the edge of the Thar Desert. Jodhpur was founded in 1459 by Rao Jodha, a chief of the Rajput clan known as the Rathores. His descendants ruled not only Jodhpur, but also other Rajput princely states. The Rathore kingdom was once known as Marwar, the Land of Death.

The old city of Jodhpur is surrounded by a 10km-long wall, built about a century after the city was founded. From the fort, you can clearly see where the old city ends and the new begins. It's fascinating to wander around the jumble of winding streets in the old city, out of which eight gates lead. Part of the film *Rudyard Kipling's Jungle Book*, starring Sam Neill and John Cleese, was shot in Jodhpur and yes, it was from here that those baggy-tight horse-riding trousers, jodhpurs, took their name.

Information
Tourist Offices The Tourist Reception Centre (☎ 545083) is in the RTDC's Hotel Ghoomar compound and is open from 8 am to 5 pm daily except Sunday.

There's an International Tourist Lounge (☎ 439052) at the main train station which provides information and has comfortable armchairs, a shower and a toilet.

Money The State Bank of India (High Court Rd branch) changes currency and

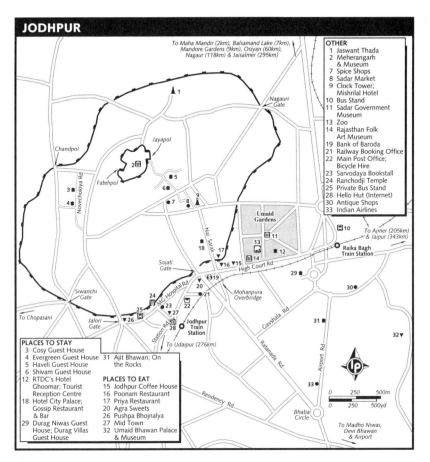

JODHPUR

To Maha Mandir (2km), Balsamand Lake (7km),
Mandore Gardens (9km), Osiyan (60km),
Nagaur (118km) & Jaisalmer (295km)

Nagauri Gate

Chandpol

Jayapol

Novechokiya Rd

Fatehpol

Umaid Gardens

To Ajmer (205km) & Jaipur (343km)

Raika Bagh Train Station

Nai Sarak

Sojati Gate

High Court Rd

Siwanchi Gate

MC Hospital Rd

Mohanpura Overbridge

To Chopasani

Jalori Gate

Station Rd

Jodhpur Train Station

To Udaipur (276km)

Cavshala Rd

Ratanada Rd

Airport Rd

Residency Rd

Bhatia Circle

To Madho Niwas,
Devi Bhawan
& Airport

0   250   500m
0   250   500yd

OTHER
1 Jaswant Thada
2 Meherangarh & Museum
7 Spice Shops
8 Sadar Market
9 Clock Tower; Mishrilal Hotel
10 Bus Stand
11 Sadar Government Museum
13 Zoo
14 Rajasthan Folk Art Museum
19 Bank of Baroda
21 Railway Booking Office
22 Main Post Office; Bicycle Hire
23 Sarvodaya Bookstall
24 Ranchodji Temple
25 Private Bus Stand
28 Hello Hut (Internet)
30 Antique Shops
33 Indian Airlines

PLACES TO STAY
3 Cosy Guest House
4 Evergreen Guest House
5 Haveli Guest House
6 Shivam Guest House
12 RTDC's Hotel Ghoomar; Tourist Reception Centre
18 Hotel City Palace; Gossip Restaurant & Bar
29 Durag Niwas Guest House; Durag Villas Guest House
31 Ajit Bhawan; On the Rocks

PLACES TO EAT
15 Jodhpur Coffee House
16 Poonam Restaurant
17 Priya Restaurant
20 Agra Sweets
26 Pushpa Bhojnalya
27 Mid Town
32 Umaid Bhawan Palace & Museum

travellers cheques. The Bank of Baroda, near the corner of Ratanada Rd and High Court Rd, changes travellers cheques.

Post & Communications The main post office is just north of the train station on Station Rd. There are plenty of STD/ISD phone offices around the train station area and along Nai Sarak.

Internet access is available in the small air-con 'Hello Hut' right in the middle of the train station forecourt (Rs 80 an hour) and at the Hotel Ghoomar on High Court Rd (Rs 100 an hour).

Meherangarh

Still run by the maharaja of Jodhpur, Meherangarh, or Majestic Fort, lives up to

its name. Sprawled across a 125m-high hill, this is the most formidable fort in Rajasthan. A winding road leads up to the entrance from the city, 5km below. The gates, of which there are seven, include the **Jayapol**, built by Maharaja Man Singh in 1806 following his victory over the armies of Jaipur and Bikaner, and the **Fatehpol**, or Victory Gate, erected by Maharaja Ajit Singh to commemorate his defeat of the Mughals.

The final gate is the **Lohapol**, or Iron Gate, beside which are 15 hand prints, the *sati* (self-immolation) marks of Maharaja Man Singh's widows who threw themselves upon his funeral pyre in 1843. They still attract devotional attention and are usually covered in red powder.

INDIA

Inside the fort, there is a series of court-yards and palaces. The **palace apartments** have evocative names such as the Sukh Mahal, or Pleasure Palace, and the Phool Mahal, or Flower Palace. They house a splendid collection of the trappings of In-dian royalty, including an amazing collec-tion of elephant howdahs (used when the maharajas rode their elephants in proces-sion through their capitals), miniature paint-ings from a variety of schools and the inevitable Rajput armoury, palanquins, fur-niture and costumes. In one room, there's even an exhibit of rocking cradles.

At the southern end of the fort, old can-nons look out from the ramparts over the sheer drop to the old town beneath. You can clearly hear voices and city sounds swept up by the air currents from the houses far below. It's interesting to hear the muezzin (the mosque official who calls the faithful to prayer) from up here, as there are several mosques in the old city. The views from these ramparts are fantastic – the box-like houses jumbled below look as if they've been powdered with blue chalk dust. The **Chamunda Devi Temple**, dedicated to Durga, stands at this end of the fort.

The fort is open from 9 am to 1 pm and 2 to 5 pm daily. Entry is Rs 50 and there's a Rs 50/100 camera/video charge. Guides are available at the entrance gate for around Rs 100. An elevator can whisk you from here to the top of the fort for Rs 10, but it's more interesting to walk around. There is an astrologer, Mr Sharma (☎ 548992), at the fort who charges Rs 100 for a short consultation.

If you're walking up to the fort, there's a short cut through the old city from the clock tower. It's just a matter of following the tangle of backstreets (walking north-east) until you come to the winding road and steps that lead up to the main gate (Jayapol).

Jaswant Thada

This white marble memorial to Maharaja Jaswant Singh II is a short distance from the fort, just off the fort road. The cenotaph, built in 1899, was followed by the royal crematorium and three other cenotaphs which stand nearby. There is some beauti-ful marble *jali* (lattice) work and fine views from the terrace in front of the cenotaph. Entry is Rs 10.

Umaid Bhawan Palace & Museum

Begun in 1929 and built of marble and pink sandstone, this immense palace was de-signed by the president of the British Royal Institute of Architects for Maharaja Umaid Singh, and took 15 years to complete.

Probably the most surprising thing about this grandiose palace is that it was built so soon before Independence, after which the maharajas, princely states and the grand ex-travagances common to this class became a thing of the past. It is said that the palace was built as a royal job-creation program to provide employment for thousands of local people during a time of severe drought.

Maharaja Umaid Singh died in 1947 but his successor still lives in part of the build-ing. The rest has been turned into a hotel. The palace (not including the museum) is closed to nonguests, unless you pay the fee of Rs 330, which is deducted from any food or drink you might purchase.

The museum is still worth a visit (Rs 50). On display is an amazing array of items be-longing to the maharaja – weapons, fasci-nating antique clocks, dainty crockery and hunting trophies.

Other Attractions

The pleasant **Umaid Gardens** contain the Sadar Government Museum (Rs 3, closed Friday), the library and the zoo (Rs 1, closed Tuesday). The museum's exhibits include moth-eaten stuffed animals, old weapons and sculptures. On High Court Rd you'll find the **Rajasthan Folk Art Museum** (Sangeet Natak Akademi) which has an in-teresting collection of traditional costumes, dolls, musical instruments and paintings. As with the Sadar Government Museum, there are few labels in English. Entry is Rs 5.

The **clock tower** is a popular landmark in the old city. The vibrant **Sadar Market** is close to the tower, and narrow alleys lead from here to bazaars selling vegetables, spices, Indian sweets, textiles, silver and handicrafts. It's a great place to ramble around at leisure.

Organised Tours

The Tourist Reception Centre conducts daily tours of Jodhpur from 9 am to 1 pm and 2 to 6 pm (Rs 85 per person; entry fees are extra). These take in all the local attractions including the Umaid Bhawan Palace, Mandore Gardens and Meherangarh.

Jodhpur is known for its interesting 'village safaris'. You can visit villages of the Bishnoi, a people whose belief in the sanctity of the environment and the need to protect trees and animals dates from the 15th century. Given a bit of notice, the tourist office can organise safaris for Rs 1050 per vehicle (up to eight people) including a guide. Not unlike the camel safaris of Jaisalmer, most of the traveller-oriented guesthouses also run village safaris.

Costs range from Rs 350 to Rs 800 per person for a day, usually taking in five villages and possibly a trip to Osiyan desert. Find out what you're getting before you book: Trips should include transport by jeep, lunch and water, and some include a short camel ride. Try Ajit Bhawan (☎ 437410), Durag Niwas Guest House (☎ 639092), Cosy Guest House (☎ 612066) or Madho Niwas (☎ 434486).

Places to Stay
Jodhpur operates the Paying Guest House Scheme with rooms ranging from Rs 100 to Rs 800. Contact the Tourist Reception Centre for details.

There are several very good cheap guesthouses inside the old city, from where you are in the thick of things and close to the fort. There's also a string of hotels along Nai Sarak leading out of the old city, and some more upmarket places in the southeast of town.

Places to Stay – Budget
Cosy Guest House (☎ 612066, Novechokiya Rd, Brahm Puri, Chuna ki Choki) is an atmospheric little place in the oldest and bluest part of the old city. It was once known as Joshi's Blue House (yes, it's blue), but the owner (Joshi) became discouraged by all the imitators. This friendly, family-run place is said to be 500 years old and is pretty authentic. Simple singles/doubles with shared bathroom start at Rs 90/150 (free bucket hot water) and rooms with private bathroom are Rs 175/250. There's also a three-bed dorm at Rs 55 per person. The rooftop offers a fine view, and village safaris and camel safaris can be arranged here.

Haveli Guest House (☎ 614615) is inside the walled city at Makrana Mohalla. Run by

a helpful family, it's good value and in a prime position only a few minutes' walk from the clock tower. Doubles with private bathroom start at Rs 200, better doubles with air cooler are Rs 300 and air-con rooms are Rs 600 (Rs 450 off season). Management were in the process of building 10 new rooms at the time of research. The rooftop veg restaurant offers good views of the fort and the old city.

Just before Cosy Guest House, *Evergreen Guest House* is a small place doubling as a local computer school. Poky rooms with shared bathroom are Rs 50/80 and there's an air-cooled double with private bathroom for Rs 150.

Shivam Guest House (☎ 610688), just around the corner from Haveli, is another family-run home (12 members of a family live here!). It doesn't look like much at first, but the rooms are fine and it's very homy. Rooms with shared bathroom are Rs 100/150, air-cooled rooms with private bathroom are Rs 150/300, and one air-con double is Rs 400. There's a restaurant and Internet access.

There are two reasonable places side by side on a small side street south of High Court Rd. *Durag Niwas Guest House (☎ 510692, 1 Old Public Park)*, at the far end of the street, is a family-run place with doubles with private bathroom for Rs 150 and Rs 250, and a huge air-cooled room for Rs 500. *Durag Villas Guest House (☎ 512298)*, next door, has clean rooms with private bathroom from Rs 150/250 and a larger room for Rs 400. Both places offer their own jeep and camel safaris: Durag Niwas has the cheaper of the two with village trips for Rs 350 and overnight camel safaris for Rs 800. Despite the similarities, these places are not associated.

RTDC's *Hotel Ghoomar (☎ 548010, High Court Rd)* has acceptable rooms with bathroom from Rs 300/400, air-con rooms for Rs 700/800 and dorm beds for Rs 50.

Places to Stay – Mid-Range
Hotel City Palace (☎ 649911, fax 639033, e hotel@nda.vsnl.net.in, 32 Nai Sarak) has fairly modern air-con rooms from Rs 990/1190.

Ajit Bhawan (☎ 437410, fax 637774, Airport Rd) is a stylish hotel that has long been popular with travellers, although it's

INDIA

getting way out of the reach of backpackers. It has a series of modern stone cottages arranged around a relaxing garden for Rs 1895/2295. There's a restaurant and sensational swimming pool (nonguests Rs 250), and village safaris (Rs 500 per person) are available.

Places to Eat
Mishrilal Hotel, at the clock tower, is nothing fancy to look at, but whips up the best lassis in town. A delicious glass of creamy special *makhania lassi*, a saffron-flavoured Jodhpur speciality, is Rs 12.

Agra Sweets, opposite Sojati Gate, also sells good lassis, as well as tasty Jodhpur dessert specialities such as *mawa ladoo*.

There are several decent restaurants conveniently located on Nai Sarak, the busy street leading from High Court Rd to the clock tower. *Priya Restaurant*, near the intersection with High Court Rd, is a veg 'fast food' place specialising in south Indian and Marwari food. Thalis are Rs 35 and masala dosas Rs 20, and there's a range of ice cream and kulfi (Mumbai-style pistachio ice cream). *Poonam Restaurant*, around the corner on High Court Rd, is also recommended for pure veg in Indian, Chinese and continental styles. Not far away is the *Jodhpur Coffee House*, with good coffee and snacks such as dosas.

Mid Town, near the train station, is clean and serves a good range of food. As well as Rajasthani thalis (Rs 80) and local specialities, there are Western-style desserts such as apple pie and ice-cream sundaes. Most mains cost between Rs 40 and Rs 80. *Kalinga Restaurant*, a little further up the same road at the Hotel Adarsh Niwas, is a pleasant place to eat. It has tasty veg and nonveg Indian, Chinese and continental food.

Gossip Restaurant, at the Hotel City Palace on Nai Sarak, has reasonably priced Indian and continental veg food (under Rs 100) and there's a bar here where you can get a cold Kingfisher for Rs 60.

Umaid Bhawan Palace has four restaurants, including *Kebab Konner*, an open-air restaurant which specialises in moderately priced barbecue Indian food (dinner only). The *Trophy Bar* is the classiest place in town for a drink, although the *bar* at Ajit Bhawan is also good.

The *refreshment room* on the 1st floor of the main train station is surprisingly good, with veg and nonveg Indian food available.

Shopping
The usual Rajasthani handicrafts are available here, but Jodhpur specialises in antiques. The greatest number of antique shops is along the road connecting the Ajit Bhawan with the Umaid Bhawan Palace. These shops are well known to Western antique dealers who come here with wallets stuffed with plastic cards. As a result, you'll be hard pressed to find any bargains. Many places also sell cheaper replicas based on original antique designs. However, it is important to remember that the trade in antique architectural fixtures is contributing to the desecration of India's cultural heritage (and is not condoned by Lonely Planet).

For excellent Indian spices, check out Mohanlal Verhomal (☎ 615846), shop 209B at the *sabzi* (vegetable) market, very close to the clock tower.

Getting There & Away
Air Indian Airlines (☎ 636757) is south of the centre on Airport Rd (open daily 10 am to 1.15 pm and 2 to 4.30 pm). It operates flights to/from Delhi (US$105), Udaipur (US$65) and Jaipur (US$80).

Bus The main bus stand for government-run buses is out near the Raika Bagh train station, about 2.5km from the city centre. From here there are buses to Jaisalmer at 5.30 am and 1.30 pm (Rs 80, five hours), frequent services to Ajmer (Rs 71, four hours), and around six buses a day to Udaipur (Rs 95, six hours).

A much better option is to use the private buses, most of which arrive and depart from a side street just off MG Hospital Rd, about five minutes' walk from the main train station. If you arrive in Jodhpur on a private bus, this is also the area you'll most likely be dropped off in. The most convenient place to buy tickets is from the agents on Station Rd and around the train station forecourt, although guesthouses can also book them. Most will probably try to add on Rs 10 commission.

To Jaisalmer the best bus to take is the Silverline service departing at 6 am and arriving at 11 am (Rs 82). There are other, less comfortable, buses hourly throughout the day (Rs 80 to Rs 90). There are also numerous services to Ajmer (Rs 80), Jaipur (Rs 100) and Udaipur (Rs 90).

Train The rail booking office is on Station Rd, between the train station and Sojati Gate. There's a tourist quota and the office is open from 8 am to 8 pm Monday to Saturday and to 1.45 pm Sunday.

The Tourist International Lounge inside the station is a spacious, comfortable place to sit and wait for a train. It's open from 5 am to midnight.

From Jodhpur there's one daily express train to Jaisalmer, five to Jaipur, three to Bikaner and two to Delhi. The overnight *Jodhpur-Jaisalmer Express* departs at 10.55 pm, arriving in Jaisalmer at 5.30 am. It has only 2nd-class and sleeper-class carriages (Rs 73/114). There's also a slower passenger train at 8.25 am. The *Jodhpur-Delhi Express* departs at 11 pm and arrives in Delhi (via Jaipur) at 11.25 am. The *Jodhpur-Delhi Mandore Express* makes the same trip at 7.30 pm, arriving in Delhi at 6.15 am. The fare to Delhi is Rs 204/944 in sleeper/air-con two-tier.

Getting Around

The airport is 5km from the city centre. It costs about Rs 60/110 from town in an autorickshaw/taxi.

There's a taxi stand near the main train station. Most autorickshaw journeys in town should cost no more than Rs 25. Jodhpur's autorickshaw owners are particularly proud of their vehicles. They're bigger, better maintained and more colourfully decorated than others in Rajasthan (and northern India for that matter). Taking autorickshaws through the narrow, crowded streets of the old city is not a great idea since it takes ages to get anywhere, and consequently it's difficult to bargain a reasonable fare.

You can hire a bike from several places near the main post office, for around Rs 20 a day.

JAISALMER

☎ 02992 ● pop 46,500

Nowhere else in India is quite like Jaisalmer. This captivating sandy outpost is often called the Golden City because of the honey colour imparted to its stone ramparts by the setting sun. Its desert fort, which resembles a gigantic sandcastle and is home to many locals, is like something out of *Arabian Nights*.

In high season you might find that Jaisalmer is a bit too much of a tourist scene – touts and rickshaw-wallahs battle to take you to a particular hotel, which in turn battles to sign you up for its camel safari. But most travellers find that a few nights spent out in the dunes around Jaisalmer is a highlight of a trip to Rajasthan.

Centuries ago, Jaisalmer's strategic position on the camel-train routes between India and Central Asia brought it great wealth. The merchants and townspeople built magnificent houses and mansions, all exquisitely carved from wood and golden sandstone. These havelis can be found elsewhere in Rajasthan, but nowhere are they quite as exquisite as in Jaisalmer.

Chivalric rivalry and ferocity between various Rajput clans were the order of the day, and the Bhatti Rajputs of Jaisalmer were regarded as a formidable force throughout the region. While Jaisalmer largely escaped direct conquest by the Muslim rulers of Delhi, it did experience its share of sieges and sackings with the inevitable *jauhar* (collective sacrifice) being declared in the face of certain defeat. There is perhaps no other city in which you can more easily conjure up the spirit of those times.

It was the rise of shipping trade and the use of the port of Mumbai (Bombay) that saw the decline of Jaisalmer. At Independence in 1947, Partition and the cutting of the trade routes through to Pakistan appeared to seal the city's fate, and water shortages could have pronounced the death sentence. However, the 1965 and 1971 India-Pakistan wars revealed Jaisalmer's strategic importance, and the Indira Gandhi Canal, to the north, is beginning to restore life to the desert.

Today, tourism rivals the military base as the pillar of the city's economy. However, there's a very real down side to Jaisalmer becoming one of Rajasthan's most popular tourist destinations: The number of hotels in the fort has significantly increased over the years and a major concern is that the poor plumbing and open drains have saturated the foundations, causing subsidence and collapse in buildings. The old open drains

JAISALMER

PLACES TO STAY
2 Hotel Renuka;
   Moomal; Indian Airlines
3 Hotel Pleasure
4 Hotel Jag Palace
11 Hotel Nachana
   Haveli; Kalpana
   Restaurant
13 Hotel Jaisal Palace
19 RTDC's Hotel
23 Hotel Jaisal Castle
25 Hotel Suraj
26 Deepak Rest House
27 Desert Boys Guest House
30 Hotel Paradise
35 Hotel Simla
45 Hotel Golden City

PLACES TO EAT
14 Trio; Top Deck
17 Slow Food Restaurant
31 Refreshing Point Rooftop
   Restaurant
32 8th July Restaurant
38 8th July Restaurant
39 Dhanraj Bhatia Sweets
40 Hotel Fort View
41 Natraj Restaurant; Metro
   Caffe; Salim Singh ki Haveli
42 Monica Restaurant

OTHER
1 City View; Sunset Point
5 Patwon ki Haveli
6 Nathmal ki Haveli
8 STD/ISD & Internet
8 Byas & Co
9 LPK Foreign Exchange
10 Jeep Hire
12 Bhatia News Agency; Beer
   & Wine Shop
15 Safari Tours & Internet;
   Bank of Baroda
16 Rajasthali
   (Government Emporium)
18 Hospital
20 Government Museum
21 Police Station
22 Main Post Office
24 Post Office
28 Jain Temples
29 Light of the East
33 Rajmahal (Maharaja's
   Palace & Museum
34 Laxminath Temple
36 Sahara Travels; Jai Bajrang
   Tea Shop; Bhang Shop
37 Joshi Travels
43 Bus Stand; Hotel Neeraj
44 State Bank of
   Bikaner & Jaipur
46 Tourist Reception Centre;
   Desert Culture Centre &
   Museum
47 Jaisalmer Folklore
   Museum
48 Main Roadways
   Bus Stand

were created to take a limited amount of water and waste, and cannot cope with the pressure being placed upon them today.

Orientation

Jaisalmer is a great place to simply wander. The streets within the old city walls are a tangled maze, but the city is small enough for this not to matter. The old city was once completely surrounded by an extensive wall, much of which has sadly been ripped away in recent times for building material. Some of it remains, however, including the city gates and, inside them, the massive fort which rises above the city and is the essence of Jaisalmer. The fort itself is a warren of narrow, paved streets complete with Jain temples and the old palace of the former ruler.

The main market area is directly below the hill, while the banks and several other shops and offices are near the Amar Sagar Gate to the west.

Information

Tourist Offices The Tourist Reception Centre (☎ 52406) is on Gadi Sagar Rd, 2km south-east of the First Fort Gate. It's open from 10 am to 5 pm Monday to Saturday. There's also a small tourist counter at the train station.

Money The Bank of Baroda at Gandhi Chowk changes travellers cheques and issues cash advances on Visa and MasterCard. The State Bank of Bikaner & Jaipur on Gadi Sagar Rd near the intersection with Shiv Rd changes travellers cheques and major currencies. There are several private moneychangers in the old city: the best is the efficient LPK Forex on Gandhi Chowk (opposite the Bank of Baroda), which changes cash and travellers cheques at reasonable rates but with Rs 30 commission.

Post & Communications The main post office (open from 10 am to 5 pm daily except Sunday) is on Hanuman Circle Rd south of Hanuman Chowk. There are plenty of STD/ISD phone booths around town, particularly in the market area.

Internet access is burgeoning in Jaisalmer, although connections are slow and the server frequently goes down. Many backpacker-oriented guesthouses (outside the fort) have Internet facilities, as do numerous travel agents and STD/ISD phone booths. The standard charge is Rs 2 a minute. Try Joshi Travels, near First Fort Gate.

Jaisalmer Fort

Jaisalmer Fort is the most alive of any museum, fort or palace that you're likely to visit in India. There are homes and guesthouses hidden in the laneways, and shops and stalls swaddled in the kaleidoscopic mirrors and embroideries of brilliant Rajasthani cloth. And yet, after the noise, activity and sales pressure of the bazaar outside, it's a haven of tranquillity and orderliness.

Built in 1156 by the Rajput ruler Jaisala, and reinforced by subsequent rulers, the fort crowns the 80m-high Trikuta Hill. About a quarter of the old city's population resides within the fort walls.

The fort is entered through a forbidding series of massive gates and an uphill zigzag walk leading to a large courtyard. The former maharaja's seven-storey palace, Rajmahal, fronts onto this. The square was formerly used to review troops, hear petitions and present extravagant entertainment for important visitors. Part of the palace is open to the public. There's a small museum, but little else to see inside. It's open from 9 am to 5 pm daily (from 8 am in summer); entry is Rs 10, plus Rs 20/50 for a camera/video.

Within the fort walls are a group of beautifully carved **Jain temples** built between the 12th and 15th centuries. They're dedicated to Rikhabdev and Sambhavanth.

Havelis

The impressive mansions built by the wealthy merchants of Jaisalmer are known as havelis, and several of these fine sandstone buildings are still in good condition. A visit to the following makes a good morning walking tour.

The **Patwon ki Haveli**, the most elaborate and magnificent of all the Jaisalmer havelis, stands in a narrow lane. It's divided into six apartments, two owned by the Archaeological Survey of India, two by families who operate craft shops here and two are private homes. There are remnants of paintings on some of the inside walls as well as some mirrorwork.

Salim Singh ki Haveli was built about 300 years ago and part of it is still occupied.

Salim Singh was the prime minister when Jaisalmer was the capital of a princely state, and his mansion has a beautifully arched roof with superb carved brackets in the form of peacocks. The mansion is just below the hill and, it is said, once had two additional wooden storeys in an attempt to make it as high as the maharaja's palace, but the maharaja had the upper storeys torn down! There's a Rs 15 entry charge at this haveli and it's open daily between 8 am and 6 pm.

The late-19th-century **Nathmal ki Haveli** was also a prime minister's house. The left and right wings of the building were carved by brothers and are very similar, but not identical. Yellow sandstone elephants guard the building, and even the front door is a work of art.

Museums

Next to the Tourist Reception Centre is the **Desert Culture Centre & Museum**, which has textiles, old coins, fossils and traditional Rajasthani instruments among other things. It's open from 9 am to 8 pm daily. The Rs 10 admission includes entry to the **Jaisalmer Folklore Museum**, on the road leading down to Gadi Sagar. There are many small temples and shrines around this lake and the hill nearby is a fabulous place to soak up the sunset.

The small **government museum**, near RTDC's Hotel Moomal, has a limited collection of fossils, and a stuffed great Indian bustard, the state bird of Rajasthan. The museum is open from 10 am to 4.30 pm daily except Friday (Rs 3, free on Monday).

Camel Safaris

Few travellers visit Jaisalmer without taking a camel safari into the desert. Just about every guest house or hotel in town can (and *will* try to) organise a camel safari for you. If you're happy with what they're offering, and are not put off by high-pressure sales tactics (which should be discouraged) most of these are perfectly legitimate, but don't get sucked into signing up the minute you check in. One advantage of going through your guest house is that if you're on your own they can more easily arrange a group of people who you can meet before you go. Most safaris require a minimum of two people and are more fun with four, provided the group chemistry is good. Otherwise, there are plenty of travel

agents and independent operators around town. Sahara Travels (☎ 52609) by the First Fort Gate, is recommended, but charges more than most. It's run by Mr Bissa, alias Mr Desert, Jaisalmer's 'Marlboro Man'. His tours cost Rs 450 a day, more if jeep transfers are required. Safaris offered by the hotels listed in the Places to Stay section should be fine (if not, let us know). For details, see the 'Have Camel, Will Travel' boxed text later in this section.

The Tourist Reception Centre (along with every other tour operator in Jaisalmer) has a sunset tour to the Sam sand dunes (Rs 125 per person), as well as half-day morning camel rides for Rs 150.

Special Events

In February, the **Jaisalmer Desert Festival** features camel races, dances, folk music, desert ballads and puppeteers. It's quite touristy and attracts a lot of visitors, but nothing on the scale of Pushkar's Camel Fair. It's due to be held 6–8 February in 2001, 25–27 February in 2002 and 14–16 February in 2003.

Places to Stay

Jaisalmer is a major tourist trap, and many hotels, both cheap and not so cheap, have sprung up to meet the demand. The touting and commission situation has gotten so out of hand that the district magistrate has set up a mobile Tourist Protection Force to keep the touts at a distance. Even so, tourists still get duped – touts have taken to stopping buses and getting on board before they even arrive in Jaisalmer. If you do encounter pressure from touts, especially around the bus station, don't believe any stories about the hotel you want being 'full', 'closed', 'burnt down' or 'no good any more', until you check it for yourself.

Check that you have in fact been taken to the hotel you asked for, as some cunning rickshaw drivers will hurry you into a different hotel where they get a commission and disappear. Many popular budget hotels now send their own vehicles to meet the bus or train, but some touts will lie and say they are from the hotel you want when they're not.

Unfortunately, some of the cheap places are really into the high-pressure selling of camel safaris. Some places can get quite ugly if you book a safari through someone else. Not only will they refuse to hold your baggage, but in many cases they'll actually evict you from the hotel! Before you check in, stress that you will only stay if you don't have to do a safari – if they hassle you, simply move to another hotel.

Prices are at their peak between December and February (particularly during the

Have Camel, Will Travel

It may be a bit cliched these days, but of all the things you can do in Rajasthan, nothing epitomises the desert experience more than an overnight camel safari. Plodding out into the dunes perched on one of these doe-eyed dromedaries takes a bit of getting used to – in fact it can be very painful – but once you ease into the rhythm there's little to do but sit back, relax and follow the leader.

The highlight of the camel safari is the evening on the dunes. After a long day of riding, the driver tends the camels while the cook lights a fire and whips up a simple but hearty meal of curried vegetables, rice and chapati. Over chai there's campfire stories until it's time to roll out the bedding and drift off to sleep under the stars. You wake at dawn, covered in six inches of sand, and after a breakfast of eggs, fruit and more chai, it's back on the camel for another day's desert exploration. Safaris typically last from one to four days – for some people four days is not enough, for others more than a few hours on a camel is all they can stand. To get to the most interesting parts of the desert from Jaisalmer by camel, three to four days is required, but if you're short on time you can arrange jeep transfers which take you out to meet the camel driver and pick you up again.

The easiest place to arrange a camel safari is Jaisalmer and the best time to do it is October to February. But this has become big business in this desert town and *everybody* is trying to sell a camel safari. Touts will accost you before you even get off the bus and everyone will tell you that everyone else's camel safaris are rubbish.

The reality is that few if any hotels or travel agents have their own camels – they are just intermediaries for the independent camel owners. But they will usually arrange things like food, additional transport if required, mineral water and bedding. Many travellers have complained that they didn't get what they were promised in terms of food and water, or even the route taken on the safari. If you pay what seems like a very low price, all you might end up with is the camel and a blanket. Expect to pay at least Rs 350 per person per day. This covers one camel per person (don't elect to share, it's not as much fun), three meals a day, bedding and (with good operators) plenty of mineral water. You'll pay more for luxuries such as tents, better food, beer etc. Competition is fierce and there are offers of cheaper safaris, but whichever operator you choose, make sure you know in advance exactly what you're getting and ensure it's all there before you go – asking for a refund if you're not satisfied later is a waste of time.

The question of whether you can bypass the agents and pay less by going straight to the camel owners is difficult. It can be done (ask around near Gandhi or Hanuman Chowks) but owners are reluctant to do it as it makes them unpopular with the operators. You also leave yourself open to a poorly organised tour.

A typical circuit takes in Amar Sagar, Lodhruva, Mool Sagar, Bada Bagh and Sam. It's not possible to ride to the Sam sand dunes in a day, but with a jeep drop-off and pick-up you could do it in 1½ days. Many operators now go to great pains to tell you that their safari *doesn't* go to Sam, which has become overcrowded and is close to the road. In many ways you're better off taking a sunset tour to Sam sand dunes and a camel safari elsewhere, but the chances of your operator having its own private set of dunes is unlikely!

Finally, words of caution. Watch your valuables – take your moneybelt with you and wear it at all times. And solo women should be wary; we've had reports of amorous camel drivers being overly friendly. Report any problems to the operator that booked the trip and to the police.

INDIA

Desert Festival) and outside these times it's worth asking for a discount. From May to September substantial discounts should be available, but Jaisalmer is like an oven at this time, camel safaris are scaled down and the idea of plodding out into the desert is pure madness!

Places to Stay – Budget

The two main areas for budget accommodation are in the old part of the city north of the fort, and within the fort itself.

In the town area, there's a good choice of budget hotels along the two streets that run parallel to each other north from Gandhi Chowk. Many have bucket hot water and squat toilets.

Hotel Swastika (☎ *52483, Chainpura St*) is a popular hang-out with travellers. It's clean, well-run and there's no great pressure, even though the usual camel safaris are on offer. Morning tea is served free and there are great views from the rooftop. There are dorm beds for Rs 60, singles/doubles with shared bathroom for Rs 150/220 and with private bathroom for Rs 220/250.

Hotel Pleasure (☎ *52323*) is another hassle-free place with some very cheap but good-value rooms which cost Rs 70/100 with shared bathroom or Rs 100/150 with private bathroom. Rooms with air-con are only Rs 150/200 in summer!

Hotel Renuka (☎ *52757*), nearby, is a pleasant family-run place with a reliable travel agency attached. Rooms with shared bathroom are Rs 70/100, or Rs 100/150 with private bathroom. There are two doubles with balconies for Rs 200.

Hotel Jag Palace (☎ *50438*) has tidy rooms with bathroom for Rs 150/200. Vegetarian meals are available on the roof terrace.

The *Hotel Golden City* (☎/fax 51664, e khangazi@hotmail.com) is a little removed from the old city, but it's quiet, well run and cheap. Dorm beds cost only Rs 15, clean, spacious rooms with private bathroom are Rs 55/110 and air-con rooms are Rs 200/275. There's a rooftop restaurant with a tandoor oven and cold beer. Call ahead for a pick-up from the bus or train station.

Within the fort, the *Hotel Simla* (☎ *53061*), a tastefully restored and furnished haveli, is a fine choice here. Rooms with shared bathroom are Rs 80/150. With private bathroom

they're Rs 200/250, and a pretty room with an alcove and balcony is Rs 550/750. It's also possible to sleep on the roof for Rs 30, which includes mattresses and blankets.

Hotel Paradise (☎ *52674*), on the far side of the main square from the palace as you come through the last gate into the fort, straddles budget and mid-range. This popular place has rooms arranged around a leafy courtyard and sensational views from the roof. Rooms with shared bathroom are Rs 80/150, or from Rs 400/500 to Rs 750/850 with private bathroom. The best rooms are huge with balcony, TV and air cooler.

Desert Boys Guest House (☎ *53091*) gets good reports. Doubles with private bathroom cost Rs 150 downstairs and Rs 250 for the upper rooms with view.

Deepak Rest House (☎ *52665*) is actually part of the fort wall and offers good views from its rooftop and from the upper rooms. Basic rooms with shared bathroom are Rs 30/120. Doubles with bathroom (but no view) start at Rs 150. Room No 9 (Rs 400) is the best.

There are several other small family guesthouses scattered around the fort, some of which close during the summer months.

Places to Stay – Mid-Range

In the town area, *Hotel Nachana Haveli* (☎ *52110, fax 52778, Gandhi Chowk*) is a charming old haveli with rooms around a courtyard. Rooms with air cooling and attached hot water bathroom range from Rs 650/750 to Rs 950/1150. Meals are available with advance notice, though they're not cheap (Rs 250 for dinner).

Hotel Jaisal Palace (☎ *52717, fax 50257*), not far from the Amar Sagar Gate, is a reasonably well-maintained place with a rooftop veg restaurant. The rooms are a little small but they all have attached hot bathroom and TV and cost Rs 500/600/900 per single/double/triple. An extra Rs 300 is charged if you want the air-conditioning turned on. Check-out is 9 am.

RTDC's *Hotel Moomal* (☎ *52392*) is a bit removed from the action and is nothing special. Thatched huts cost Rs 750 and there are conventional rooms from Rs 450/500. A dorm bed is Rs 50. There's a restaurant, bar and a beer shop.

Within the fort, the *Hotel Suraj* (☎ *51623*), near the Jain temples, is an interesting old haveli with rooms ranging from Rs 300/350 to Rs 550/650, all with private bathroom.

Hotel Jaisal Castle (☎ 52362, fax 52101) is a restored haveli in the south-western corner of the fort. Its biggest attraction is its position high on the ramparts looking out over the desert, but it's not the most welcoming place in Jaisalmer. The cheapest rooms are Rs 500/650.

Places to Eat

There are dozens of restaurants to choose from in the area immediately around the fort (and a few inside). Many of them churn out standard travellers fare but they're convivial places to hang out. Some of the smaller restaurants close out of season.

Monica Restaurant, not far from the First Fort Gate, is popular with travellers and has an extensive menu offering Indian, continental and Chinese food, as well as Rajasthani specialities.

Natraj Restaurant, not far away, has a fine view of the upper part of the Salim Singh ki Haveli next door. The food is good: Most Indian dishes are around Rs 40, while continental dishes run to about Rs 100. Next door, *Metro Caffe* is clean and has snacks such as dosas and ice creams under Rs 30.

There's a collection of reasonable restaurants around Gandhi Chowk, just past Bhatia Market. *Trio*, near the Amar Sagar Gate, is one of Jaisalmer's longest-running restaurants. The food is excellent and there's occasionally live music in the evenings. *Top Deck*, alongside Hotel Nachana Haveli, offers reasonably priced Indian, continental and Chinese cuisine.

Kalpana Restaurant, in the same area, is nothing special, but is a good place to watch the world go by and you can get a Kingfisher beer here for Rs 55. Other rooftop restaurants worth investigating are at *Hotel Fort View*, near First Fort Gate, and *Hotel Golden City*, which is south of the old city but has a great view and good tandoori dishes.

More upmarket, *Slow Food Restaurant* is in a quaint outdoor bamboo structure and has a good range of nonveg dishes. Half tandoori chicken is Rs 120, garlic chicken Rs 175 and roast lamb in garlic sauce Rs 165. A Rajasthani veg thali is Rs 110.

The *8th July Restaurant*, above the main square inside the fort, enjoys a prime location although the food is average and it's not particularly cheap. Indian vegetarian dishes range from Rs 40 to Rs 70 and small pizzas are around Rs 60. A mixed fruit lassi is Rs 35. Aussies can even get Vegemite on toast (Rs 35 for three slices) and Brits can opt for their equivalent, Marmite. There's another branch outside the fort but it's not as atmospheric and may be closed out of season.

Refreshing Point Rooftop Restaurant, nearby, is so popular that you may have to wait for a table. There's a phenomenal menu offering Indian, continental, Italian, Mexican, Tibetan, Chinese and even Greek cuisine, mostly under Rs 80. Hearty breakfasts are served as well.

Right outside First Fort Gate, *Jai Bajrang* is a pleasant little tea shop where you can sit outside with a chai or one of the best sweet lassis in town. Almost next door is Jaisalmer's government-authorised *Bhang Shop*. Lassis start from Rs 30 (mild) and bhang cookies can be baked with advance notice. You can even order a 'bhang pack' for your camel safari, which includes cookies and bhang chocolate!

Dhanraj Bhatia Sweets in Bhatia Market is a well-known producer of local confectionary. It's renowned in Jaisalmer for its speciality sweets such as *ghotua* and *panchadhari ladoos* (sweet balls made from chickpea flour). You can hang around outside and watch the sweets being made.

Shopping

Jaisalmer is renowned for embroidery, traditional Rajasthani mirrorwork, rugs, blankets, old stonework and antiques. Tie-dyed and other fabrics are made at the Khadi Gramodyog Bhavan (Seemagram), not too far from the fort. You can also pick up things like turbans and authentic Rajasthani saris here. There's a government handicrafts emporium, Rajasthali, just outside Amar Sagar Gate, where you can compare prices.

In the fort, on the laneway leading up to the Jain temples, is a fascinating shop called the Light of the East. It sells crystals and rare mineral specimens. Ask to have a look at the huge apophyllite piece which is kept in a closed box.

INDIA

Getting There & Away
Air Indian Airlines operates flights between Jaisalmer and Delhi three days a week in winter only (November to March). The cost is US$155.

Bus The main Roadways bus stand (☎ 51541) is some distance from the centre of town, near the train station. Fortunately, all buses start from (and drop off at) a more convenient depot just behind the Hotel Neeraj.

To Jodhpur there are deluxe buses roughly every hour during the day (Rs 80, 5½ hours). The best (fastest and most comfortable) service is the Silverline bus at 5 pm (Rs 82). This arrives in Jodhpur at around 10 pm – in plenty of time to catch the 11 pm *Jodhpur-Delhi Express* overnight train to Delhi. The Silverline continues on to Jaipur (Rs 172, 13 hours). There are several daily direct deluxe buses to Bikaner (Rs 120, seven hours).

You can book deluxe private buses through most of the travel agencies and guesthouses. Buses to Udaipur and Delhi will probably require a change in Jodhpur. For Delhi and Jaipur it's best to take a bus to Jodhpur and a train from there.

Train The train station is about 3km east of the fort. The reservations office is open from 8 am to 8 pm daily and is usually not too busy, but travel agents around the fort can save you an autorickshaw ride out and back by making bookings for you for a fee. The train from Jodhpur to Delhi should be booked as far in advance as possible, particularly if you want a sleeper in high season. Trains out of Jaisalmer are often full of soldiers taking leave from the military base.

Currently the only express train out of Jaisalmer is the *Jaisalmer-Jodhpur Express*, which leaves Jaisalmer at 10.30 pm and arrives in Jodhpur at 5.35 am (Rs 73/114 in 2nd/sleeper class). This doesn't provide you with any useful connections to Delhi – you either have to spend the day in Jodhpur, or take an afternoon bus from Jaisalmer to Jodhpur in time for one of the overnight services to Delhi.

Getting Around
Autorickshaws are the easiest form of motorised transport around the city, but they're not allowed inside the fort (thankfully).

You'll find them gathered outside the fort entrance touting for fares. They're rapacious in this touristy town – bargain hard.

There are a number of bicycle-hire places, including a cheap one at Gandhi Chowk in the lane opposite the Skyroom Restaurant (Rs 3/15 per hour/day), and another just outside the main gate of the fort (more expensive).

AROUND JAISALMER
There are some fascinating places to see in the area around Jaisalmer, although it soon fades into a barren sand-dune desert which stretches across the lonely border into Pakistan.

Due to alleged arms smuggling across the border from Pakistan, most of Rajasthan west of National Highway No 15 is a restricted area. Places exempted are Amar Sagar, Bada Bagh, Lodhruva, Kuldhara, Akal, Sam, Ramkund, Khuri and Mool Sagar. Many of the following places are included in jeep safaris or as part of camel safaris organised from Jaisalmer.

Sam Sand Dunes
A desert national park has been established in the Thar Desert near Sam village. One of the most popular excursions is to the sand dunes on the edge of the park, 42km from Jaisalmer. This is Jaisalmer's nearest real Sahara-like desert. It's best to be here at sunrise or sunset, and many camel safaris spend a night at the dunes. Just before sunset jeep loads of trippers arrive from Jaisalmer to be chased across the sands by young boys selling soft drinks and by tenacious camel owners offering short rides. Yes, this place has become a massive tourist attraction, so don't set your heart on a solitary desert sunset experience. If you want less touristy sand dunes, Khuri is a good alternative.

One tragic consequence of the rising tourist numbers is the discarded rubbish – please don't contribute to the problem. Encourage locals to keep the dunes clean.

There are just a few daily buses between Sam and Jaisalmer (Rs 15, 1½ hours).

Other Sites
About 7km north of Jaisalmer, **Bada Bagh** is a fertile oasis with a huge old dam. Above the gardens are royal **chhatris** with finely

carved ceilings and equestrian statues of former rulers. Entry is Rs 10.

The once-pleasant formal garden **Amar Sagar**, 7km north-west of Jaisalmer, has now fallen into ruin. The lake here dries up several months into the dry season. Nearby is a beautifully carved **Jain temple**. Farther out beyond Amar Sagar, 15km north-west of Jaisalmer, are the deserted ruins of **Lodhruva**, which was the ancient capital before the move to Jaisalmer. The Jain temples, rebuilt in the late 1970s, are the only reminders of the city's former magnificence. The main temple has an image of Parasnath, the 23rd *tirthankar* (one of the 24 great Jain teachers). In the temple is a hole from which a cobra is said to emerge every evening – it is considered auspicious to see it. Entry to the temple is free.

Nine kilometres west of Jaisalmer, **Mool Sagar** is another pleasant, but somewhat neglected, small garden and tank. It belongs to the royal family of Jaisalmer. Entry is Rs 5.

Kuldhara is a deserted village about 25km west of Jaisalmer. There's not much to see although its story is interesting. It's said that the villagers up and left about 400 years ago after a dispute with their prime minister, but they buried all their gold and silver, which they couldn't carry. Several years ago some Western tourists turned up with metal detectors and found hundreds of gold and silver coins. But their activity was noticed by locals and they were promptly apprehended and forced to hand over the treasure.

Agra to Sunauli

AGRA
☎ 0562 • pop 1,118,800

Few people visiting this part of India would consider bypassing Agra, as it contains India's most famous monument and one of the most recognisable sights in the world – the Taj Mahal. As the capital of India under the Mughals in the 16th and 17th centuries, Agra was endowed with this and other fine monuments, notably the magnificent fort.

Other than these sights there's little to distinguish Agra from any other northern Indian city, except for the density of marble shops and silk and gem emporiums you'll be hustled into the minute you let your guard down. Many travellers find Agra itself a real turn-off: Apart from terrible pollution, its status as the most touristy city in India means there's a constant hassle for your rupees by canny salesman and predatory rickshaw-wallahs. Some also find the Taj Mahal to be overrated and that feeling will only be exaggerated by the admission fee foreign visitors are now faced with – over US$20. This short-sighted dual pricing policy has affected Agra badly. If you visit all of the main sights listed here it will cost over US$40 – plus another US$10 if you make the day trip out to Fatehpur Sikri.

History
Badal Singh is credited with building a fort on the site of the present Agra Fort in 1475, but this didn't stop Sikander Lodi making his capital on the opposite bank of the Yamuna in 1501. Babur defeated the last Lodi sultan in 1526 at Panipat, 80km north of Delhi, and Agra then became the Mughal capital. The city reached the peak of its magnificence between the mid-16th and mid-17th centuries under the reigns of Akbar, Jehangir and Shah Jahan. It was

Agra to Jaipur

Cycling days: 7
Approx distance: 247km

Agra to Jaipur was our biggest stint of sightseeing, spending several nights at each place (over two weeks) with only 20km to 50km cycling in between.

The weather was getting warmer by now (mid-January) but the terrain in Rajasthan is still flat and there were fewer roadside hassles than we had experienced in Uttar Pradesh. We rode the first day from Agra to the beautiful Fatehpur Sikri. From there we rode to Bharatpur (25km, one hour). The bird sanctuary is well worth visiting.

From here were rode via Deeg (one hour), Alwar (1½ hours), Sariska National Park (two hours), Shapura (five hours) and finally to Jaipur (two hours). The road into Jaipur is very busy.

Sue Cooper

AGRA

PLACES TO STAY
11 Hotel Sakura; Hotel Sheetal; Buses to Jaipur
13 Lauries Hotel
14 Tourist Rest House
22 Hotel Pawan; Andhra Bank
25 Hotel Akbar Inn
29 Hotel Athithi; Pizza Hut; LPK Forex
33 Hotel Safari

PLACES TO EAT
16 Dasaprakash; Meher Cinema
19 Zorba the Buddha
23 Park Restaurant; Lakshmi Vilas
30 Only Restaurant

OTHER
1 Ram Bagh
2 Chini Ka Rauza
3 Itimad-ud-daulah
4 SN Hospital
5 Agra College
6 Gokalpura Market
7 Jama Masjid
8 Agra Fort Bus Stand
9 Foreigners' Registration Office
10 Idgah Bus Stand
12 District Hospital
15 Main Post Office
17 Agra Ashok Hotel
18 Government of India Tourist Office
20 Cyber Hut
21 Police Station
24 Telegraph Office
26 Archaeological Survey of India
27 State Bank of India
28 Trade Wings
31 Clarks Shiraz Hotel; Indian Airlines
32 UP Tourism Office

To Aligarh (83km)

To Dayal Bagh Temple (3km)

0   250   500m
0   250   500yd

Dayal Bagh Rd

National Highway 2 Bypass

Balkeshwar Rd

Karbala Rd

Aligarh Rd

Yamuna River

1

To Shikodabad (63km)

Chilli Int Rd

Nehru Rd

Belanganj Train Station

Pandit Kaliacharan Tiwari Rd

Kanpur Rd

To Sikandra (4km), Mathura (56km) & Delhi (204km)

Raja Mandi Train Station

Agra City Train Station

Belan Ganj

2

3

Yamuna Bridge Train Station

Ramratan Marg

Bhagat Singh Marg

Kinari Bazaar

Old Town Area

Strand Rd

Chhata Rd

To Bharatpur

Gokalpura

Panchkuiyan Rd

Gokalpura Rd

Capt Naresh Rd

4

5

Hospital Rd

Jama P Mandi Rd

Jama Masjid Rd

Ghalipura Rd

6

Mahatma Gandhi (MG) Rd

Mantola Road

7

Agra Fort Train Station

Katchpura Village

Saiyad Ali Nabi Marg

Fatehpur Sikri Rd

9

Fort

8

Chhipi Tola Rd

See Taj Ganj Map (p489)

To Fatehpur Sikri (40km)

Idgah Train Station

Yamuna Kinara Rd

Shahjahan Park

Taj Mahal

Kachahari Rd

Nammer Rd

Field Marshal - Cariappa Rd

Golf Course

10

11

12

14

13

To Kheria Airport (3km)

Ajmer Rd

15

16

17

25

26

Taj Rd

27

28

Fatehbad Rd

Mahatma Ghandi (MG) Rd

Gwalior Rd

18

19

24

The Mall

Gough Rd

30

29

Station Rd

To Bharatpur

Fatehpur Sikri Rd

Sadar Bazaar

20 22 23

31

Taj Rd

Agra Cantonment Train Station

Station Rd

Prithvi Raj Rd

21

32

33

Shamshabad Rd

Grand Parade Rd

To Gwalior (118km)

INDIA

during this period that the fort, Taj Mahal and Agra's major tombs were built. In 1638 Shah Jahan built a new city in Delhi, and Aurangzeb moved the capital there 10 years later.

In 1761 Agra fell to the Jats, who looted its monuments, including the Taj Mahal. It was taken by the Marathas in 1770, before the British wrested control in 1803. After heavy fighting around the fort during the Uprising of 1857, the British shifted the administration of the north-western provinces to Allahabad. Agra has since developed as an industrial centre with more coke-based (coal) industries than anywhere else in the country. In an attempt at lowering pollution levels (and thus protecting the Taj from further chemical damage), the government has put a stop to new industrial development and has ordered all coke-based industries to switch to gas or close down.

Orientation

Agra is on the western bank of the Yamuna River, 204km south of Delhi. (The river, incidentally, is like an open sewer. Scientists have declared it incapable of supporting any life form.) The old part of the city and the main marketplace (Kinari Bazaar) are north-west of the fort. The spacious British-built cantonment is to the south, and the main road running through it is called The Mall. The commercial centre of the cantonment is Sadar Bazaar.

The labourers and artisans who toiled on the Taj Mahal set up home immediately south of the mausoleum. This area of congested alleyways is known as Taj Ganj and today it contains most of Agra's budget and many marble shops.

Agra's main train station, Agra Cantonment (abbreviated as Agra Cantt), is west of Sadar Bazaar. The city's major bus stand, Idgah, is nearby.

Information

Tourist Offices The Government of India Tourist Office (☎/fax 363377), 191 The Mall, is open from 9 am to 5.30 pm weekdays and to 4.30 pm Saturday. It has maps of Agra and a good brochure on Fatehpur Sikri. There's also a helpful UP (Uttar Pradesh) Tourism office (☎ 360517) at 64 Taj Rd, open from 10 am to 5 pm daily (except Sunday and the 2nd Saturday in the

month). The tourist information counter (☎ 368598) at Agra Cantonment train station is open from 8 am to 8 pm daily.

Money The State Bank of India south of Taj Ganj and the Andhra Bank in Sadar Bazaar change money but they're predictably slow. Trade Wings, nearby on Fatehbad Rd, is more efficient and is open from 9 am to 9 pm daily. There's a Rs 40 commission. LPK Forex has a branch about 50m west along Fatehbad Rd.

Post & Communications The main post office is on The Mall, opposite the Government of India tourist office. It's open from 10 am to 6 pm Monday to Saturday.

Several guesthouses in the Taj Ganj area have Internet facilities. There are also Internet cafes in Sadar Bazaar. Cyber Hut, near Hotel Pawan (see Places to Stay – Mid-Range later), is one of the cheaper places, charging Rs 60 per hour. Cyberlink, in Taj Ganj, charges Rs 1.5 per minute.

Medical Services Some private clinics have been mixed up in medical insurance fraud, so stick with government hospitals: The District Hospital (☎ 364738) is on Namner Rd; SN Hospital (☎ 361318) is on Hospital Rd.

Taj Mahal

Described as the most extravagant monument ever built for love, this poignant Mughal mausoleum has become the de facto tourist emblem of India. It was constructed by Emperor Shah Jahan in memory of his 2nd wife, Mumtaz Mahal, whose death during childbirth in 1631 left the emperor so heartbroken that his hair is said to have turned grey overnight.

Construction of the Taj began in the same year and was not completed until 1653. In total, 20,000 people from India and Central Asia worked on the building (some later had their hands or thumbs amputated, to ensure that the perfection of the Taj could never be repeated). The main architect is believed to have been Isa Khan, who was from Shīrāz in Iran. Experts were also brought from Europe – Austin of Bordeaux and Veroneo of Venice both had a hand in the Taj's decoration – which allowed the British to delude themselves for some time

INDIA

Taj Tickets

The dramatic increase in the price of a ticket to see the Taj Mahal will unfortunately deter a few travellers from going beyond the gates to see this wonderful monument up close. In January 2000, the entry fee for foreigners shot up to Rs 505. Most of this money goes to the Agra Development Association (ADA), a municipal body established to improve the city's roads, gardens and environmental problems. In October 2000, the Archaeological Survey of India (ASI) decreed that foreigners should pay the equivalent of US$10 to enter all World Heritage-listed monuments in India (Indians pay Rs 10). This effectively put the cost of visiting the Taj up to US$21 (Rs 960) – enough for a night in flash hotel or 10 nights in a cheap Taj Ganj guesthouse! If you're going to bite the bullet and pay the entry fee, the best time to visit is early (between 6 and 8 am) or late (from about 5 pm) when it won't be too busy.

The planned abolition of free entry on Fridays was abandoned after violent demonstrations by Muslims who found they would be charged to enter the Taj to pray! However, there are plans to close the monument on Friday and offer free entry on Monday; ask about the current situation when you arrive in Agra. In addition, negotiations are currently underway to find an intermediate fee that reflects the differential wealth of Indian and foreign visitors without placing an unfair burden on international visitors.

The cheap option is to view the Taj from the outside. Take a rickshaw or cycle around past the fort to the road bridge crossing the Yamuna River. From there you can either walk east along the riverbank, or continue by rickshaw through Katchpura village until you emerge behind the Taj on the north bank of the Yamuna. The symmetry of the Taj means that the view from here is almost identical to the view from the front. The reflection of the Taj in the river on a clear day is a bonus. Previously, few people bothered to see the Taj from this angle, but with the price hike it's likely to become a popular way to do it. Bear in mind that this is no substitute for seeing the Taj up close – you miss out on going inside the mausoleum and you don't get to see the wonderful *pietra-dura* work – the inlaid semiprecious stone patterns that are the trademark of the Taj.

that such an exquisite building must certainly have been designed by a European.

The Taj is definitely worth more than a single visit (if you can afford it) as its character changes with the light during the day. Dawn is a magical time, and the grounds are virtually deserted.

There are three entrances to the Taj (east, south and west); the main entrance is on the western side. The Taj is open from 6 am to 7 pm daily except Monday (when it's closed all day for cleaning). Entry fees rose substantially early in 2000 (see the boxed text 'Taj Tickets').

The grand red sandstone gateway on the southern side of the interior forecourt is inscribed with verses from the Quran in Arabic. Depending on how busy it is, entry may be via a small gate to the right of here. Everyone who enters the Taj must undergo a security check. Food, tobacco, matches and other specified items (including, thankfully, the red-blotch-forming paan, but also things

like playing cards) are not allowed to be taken inside. There's a cloakroom nearby for depositing your belongings for safekeeping. Cameras are permitted, and there's no problem taking photos of the outside of the Taj. However, guards will prevent you from taking photographs inside the mausoleum.

Paths leading from the gate to the Taj are divided by a long **watercourse** in which the Taj is reflected. The ornamental gardens through which the paths lead are set out along classical Mughal *charbagh* (formal garden) lines – a square quartered by watercourses. To the west is a small **museum** that's open from 10 am to 5 pm daily, except Monday and Friday. It houses original architectural drawings of the Taj, information on the semiprecious stones used in its construction, and some nifty celadon plates, said to split into pieces or change colour if the food served on them contains poison. Entry to the museum is free.

The Taj Mahal stands on a raised marble platform, north of the ornamental gardens. The white minarets gracing each corner of the platform are purely decorative – the Taj Mahal is not a mosque. Twin red sandstone buildings frame the Taj; the western one is a mosque, the identical eastern one is purely for symmetry. (It can't be used as a mosque because it faces in the wrong direction.)

The central Taj structure has four small domes surrounding the bulbous central dome. The **tombs** of Mumtaz Mahal and Shah Jahan are in a basement room. Above them in the main chamber are false tombs, a common practice in mausoleums of this type. Light is admitted into the central chamber by finely cut marble screens.

Ironically, the perfect symmetry of the Taj is disrupted only by the tomb of the man who built it. When Shah Jahan died in 1666, Aurangzeb placed his casket next to that of Mumtaz Mahal. His presence, which was never intended, unbalances the mausoleum's interior.

Although the Taj is amazingly graceful from almost any angle, it's the close-up detail which is really astounding. Semi-precious stones are inlaid into the marble in beautiful patterns using a process known as *pietra dura*. As many as 43 different gems were used for Mumtaz's tomb alone. The precision and care which went into the Taj Mahal's design and construction is just as impressive whether you view it from across the river or from arm's length.

Agra Fort

Construction of the massive red sandstone Agra Fort on the bank of the Yamuna River was begun by Emperor Akbar in 1565, though additions were made up until the rule of his grandson, Shah Jahan. In Akbar's time, the fort was principally a military structure, but during Shah Jahan's reign it had partially become a palace.

The auricular fort's colossal double walls rise more than 20m in height and measure 2.5km in circumference. They are encircled by a fetid moat and contain a maze of buildings that forms a small city within a city. Unfortunately not all buildings are open to visitors, including the white marble Moti Masjid (Pearl Mosque), which is regarded by some as the most beautiful mosque in India.

The Amar Singh Gate to the south is the sole entry point. It's open from 6 am to 5.30 pm daily; admission is US$10 (Rs 510). If you have a Taj Mahal ticket you can visit the fort free on the same day (you still pay the Rs 5 Archaeological Survey of India charge). There's a lot to see in the fort, so you may find a guide useful.

Diwan-i-Am The Hall of Public Audiences was built by Shah Jahan and replaced an earlier wooden structure. This is where the emperor met officials and listened to petitioners. Beside the Diwan-i-Am is the small **Nagina Masjid** or Gem Mosque. A door leads from here into the **Ladies' Bazaar**, where female merchants came to sell goods to the ladies of the Mughal court. No males were allowed to enter the bazaar except Akbar, though according to one apocryphal story he still enjoyed visiting in female disguise.

Diwan-i-Khas The Hall of Private Audiences was also built by Shah Jahan, between 1636 and 1637. It's where the emperor received important dignitaries or foreign ambassadors. The hall consists of two rooms connected by three arches.

Musamman Burj The exquisite Musamman Burj (Octagonal Tower) stands close to the Diwan-i-Khas. Shah Jahan died here after seven years' imprisonment in the fort. The tower looks out over the Yamuna and is traditionally considered to have one of the most poignant views of the Taj, but Agra's pollution is now so thick that it's difficult to see. The Mina Masjid was Shah Jahan's private mosque during his imprisonment.

Jehangir's Palace Akbar is believed to have built this palace for his son. It was the largest private residence in the fort and indicates the changing emphasis from military to luxurious living quarters. The palace displays an interesting blend of Hindu and Central Asian architectural styles – a contrast to the unique Mughal style which had developed by the time of Shah Jahan.

Other Buildings Shah Jahan's **Khas Mahal** is a beautiful white marble structure used as a private palace. The rooms underneath it were intended as a cool retreat from the summer heat. The **Shish Mahal** or Mirror Palace is reputed to have been the harem dressing room and its walls are inlaid with tiny mirrors. The **Anguri Bagh** or Grape Garden probably never had any grapevines but was simply a small, formal Mughal garden. It stood in front of the Khas Mahal.

In front of Jehangir's Palace is the **Hauz-i-Jehangri**, a huge bowl beautifully carved out of a single block of stone. According to one traditional story Jehangir's wife, Nur Jahan, made attar (perfumed essential oil) of roses in the bowl; it's also fabled to have been used for preparing bhang.

The **Amar Singh Gate** takes its name from a maharaja of Jodhpur who slew the imperial treasurer in the Diwan-i-Am in 1644 and, in a bid to escape, reputedly rode his horse over the fort wall near here. The unlucky horse perished, though it is now immortalised in stone. Amar Singh survived the fall but not Shah Jahan's wrath. Justice tended to be summary in those days; there is a shaft leading down to the river where those who made themselves unpopular with the great Mughals were hurled without further ado.

Jama Masjid

Across the train tracks from the Delhi Gate of Agra Fort is the Jama Masjid, built by Shah Jahan in 1648. An inscription over the main gate indicates that it was built in the name of Jahanara, Shah Jahan's favourite daughter, who was eventually imprisoned with Shah Jahan by Aurangzeb. The mosque has no minarets but its sandstone domes have striking marble patterning.

Itimad-ud-daulah

On the opposite bank of the Yamuna, north of the fort, is the exquisite Itimad-ud-daulah– the tomb of Mirza Ghiyas Beg. This Persian gentleman was Jehangir's *wazir*, or chief minister, and his beautiful daughter, Nur Jahan, later married the emperor. Nur Jahan constructed the tomb between 1622 and 1628 in a style similar to the tomb she built for Jehangir near Lahore in Pakistan.

The Itimad-ud-daulah was the first Mughal structure totally built from marble and the first to make extensive use of pietra dura, the marble inlay work that is so characteristic of the Taj. Though small and squat compared to its more famous cousin

(it's known as the 'baby Taj'), its human scale is attractive. Extremely fine marble latticework passages admit light to the interior, and the beautifully patterned surface of the tomb is superb.

The Itimad-ud-daulah is open from around 6 am to 6 pm daily; admission is US$5 (Rs 235) for foreigners, Rs 5 for Indians.

Akbar's Mausoleum

The sandstone and marble tomb of Akbar, the greatest of the Mughal emperors, is situated in the centre of a peaceful garden grazed by deer at Sikandra, 4km north-west of Agra. Akbar began its construction himself, blending Islamic, Hindu, Buddhist, Jain and Christian motifs and styles, much like the syncretic religious philosophy he developed called Deen Ilahi. When Akbar died, the mausoleum was completed by his son, Jehangir, who significantly modified the original plans.

The stunning southern gateway is the most impressive part of the complex. It has three-storey minarets at each corner and is built of red sandstone strikingly inlaid with white marble abstract patterns. The ticket office is located here, to the left of the arched entrance. The mausoleum is open from sunrise to sunset; entry is US$5 (Rs 235) for foreigners, Rs 5 for Indians. A video-camera permit costs Rs 25.

Sikandra is named after Sikander Lodi, the Delhi sultan who ruled from 1488 to 1517, immediately preceding the rise of Mughal power on the subcontinent.

Local buses heading to Sikandra run along MG Rd from the Agra Fort bus stand (Rs 3).

Other Attractions

The alleyways of **Kinari Bazaar**, or old marketplace, start near the Jama Masjid. There are several distinct areas with names that are relics of the Mughal period, although they don't always bear relation to what is sold there today. The **Loha Mandi** (Iron Market) and **Sabji Mandi** (Vegetable Market) are still operational, but the **Nai ki Mandi** (Barber's Market) is now famous for textiles. Something entirely different is for sale in the **Malka Bazaar**, where women beckon to passing men from upstairs balconies. In the butcher's area next to the leather market, watch out for the festering bloody animal skins that are piled high in the streets.

The white marble **Dayal Bagh Temple** of the Radah Soami religion has been under construction since 1904 and is not expected to be completed until some time in the 21st century. If you're lucky, you may get to see pietra dura inlaid marblework in process, although the building itself is architecturally unremarkable. Dayal Bagh is 2km north of Agra and can be reached by bus or bicycle.

If you want to walk between Taj Ganj and Agra Fort *and* avoid the rickshaw-wallahs, **Shahjahan Park** is pleasant and peaceful. To the east of Taj Ganj is the **Taj Protected Forest**, an area of greenery with walking trails.

Swimming
You can use the pools at several large hotels for a fee. These include the Agra Ashok Hotel, Lauries Hotel, Hotel Atithi, and the Clarks Shiraz Hotel. The Agra Ashok has the best pool (Rs 200).

Organised Tours
Guided tours depart from the Government of India tourist office at 9.30 am and proceed to Agra Cantonment train station to pick up passengers arriving from Delhi on the *Taj Express*, which pulls in at 9.47 am. The tours include the Taj Mahal, Agra Fort and a hasty visit to Fatehpur Sikri. They finish at 6 pm so day trippers can catch the *Taj Express* returning to Delhi at 6.35 pm. Buy tickets (Rs 700, including entry fees) from the tourist information counter at the train station (you can board the bus at the Government of India tourist office beforehand).

Special Events
In February, the Taj Mahotsav Festival is held in Shilpgram, a crafts village and open-air emporium about 1km along the road running from the eastern gate of the Taj Mahal. The festival features live performances of music and dance.

Places to Stay
Agra's paying-guest scheme enables you to stay with local families for between Rs 200 and Rs 500. Contact the tourist information counter at the train station when you arrive.

Most of the budget accommodation is clustered in Taj Ganj, the area just south of the Taj Mahal. However, some travellers find that it's better – certainly more peaceful –

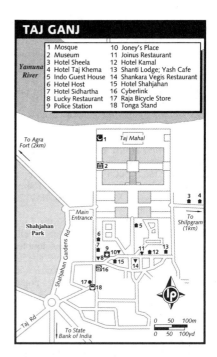

TAJ GANJ

1 Mosque	10 Joney's Place
2 Museum	11 Joinus Restaurant
3 Hotel Sheela	12 Hotel Kamal
4 Hotel Taj Khema	13 Shanti Lodge; Yash Cafe
5 Indo Guest House	14 Shankara Vegis Restaurant
6 Hotel Host	15 Hotel Shahjahan
7 Hotel Sidhartha	16 Cyberlink
8 Lucky Restaurant	17 Raja Bicycle Store
9 Police Station	18 Tonga Stand

to stay outside this area. Unless stated otherwise, rooms mentioned have private bathroom. In most cases you'll pay more than the rates given here if you are taken straight to a hotel by taxi or rickshaw as commission will be added on. In Taj Ganj you can pretty much get out anywhere and wander around until you find something.

Places to Stay – Budget
Tourist Rest House (☎ 363961, ⓔ trh@vsnl .com, Kachahari Rd) is an excellent place to stay. It's a little away from the popular Taj Ganj area, but it's a leafy oasis of peace, run by two helpful brothers. Comfortable, spotless, air-cooled singles/ doubles with hot water are Rs 120/150, with toiletries and towels provided. An air-con room is only Rs 200/250. Decent vegetarian food is served in the candle-lit courtyard or in the restaurant. You can also get good local information and book reliable tours here. Don't confuse this place with similarly named hotels (such as the Tourist Guest House near Agra Fort). Rickshaw drivers are generally not keen to take you here since they don't get commission, but you

could ask to be dropped at the Meher Cinema about 100m away.

There are plenty of surprisingly cheap hotels in the compact area immediately south of the Taj. Many have rooftop views of the famous building, but often it's just wishful thinking. Shanti Lodge and Hotel Kamal have uninterrupted views from their rooftops but they make surprisingly little use of this.

Indo Guest House (no phone), virtually on the doorstep of the Taj's southern gate, is nothing fancy but it's clean and run by a lovely family. There's just five basic rooms with hot water at Rs 60/80 or Rs 100/120 with air cooling.

Hotel Sheela (☎ 331194), near the Taj's eastern gate, is surrounded by a large well-kept garden and has good singles/doubles with soft beds and hot water for Rs 200/250. You can also camp on the lawn for Rs 50 and there's parking available so it's popular with overlanders.

Hotel Host (☎ 331010), on the road leading to the Taj's western gate, has comfortable rooms with phone, carpet, air cooling and hot water. Singles/doubles are a bargain at Rs 100/175. There's also a rooftop dining area from where you can just about see the Taj.

Hotel Sidhartha (☎ 331238), nearby, is a clean, friendly, spacious place built around a garden courtyard. Small rooms with bucket hot water cost Rs 80/100, or Rs 125/170 for larger rooms with air cooler.

Shanti Lodge (☎ 330900) gets mixed reviews, but it has a decent view of the Taj from its rooftop eating area. Cramped and slightly shabby rooms start from Rs 80/100. Some rooms are definitely better than others.

Hotel Shahjahan (☎ 331159) in the heart of Taj Ganj has all sorts of rooms, mostly in the basic mould, with squat toilets. A single with shared bathroom is Rs 50; plain singles/doubles with private bathroom start at Rs 120/150. There's a restaurant on the roof.

There are several more budget places outside Taj Ganj worth considering.

Hotel Safari (☎ 360110, Shamsabad Rd) is clean and good value. Air-cooled rooms with hot water cost Rs 150/200. There are also air-con rooms for Rs 300/350. Some rooms have bathtubs and all are supplied with towel, soap and toilet roll.

Hotel Akbar Inn (☎ 226836, 21 The Mall), midway between Sadar Bazaar and Taj Ganj, is set on a large, open property. It has some tiny rooms with shared bathroom from Rs 40/60, marginally better rooms with private bathroom and hot water from Rs 120/160 and reasonable air-con rooms for Rs 250/300. You can also camp here for Rs 50 per tent. There are extensive lawns and a pleasant terrace. All in all it's quite run down, but it's hassle free.

There are a couple of OK places close to Idgah bus stand, on Ajmer Rd.

Hotel Sakura (☎ 369793, e ashu.sakura@yahoo.com) has a variety of rooms (ask to see a few) from slightly grubby rooms with private bathroom for Rs 100/150 to larger rooms with air cooler for Rs 350/600. Private buses to Rajasthan depart from outside and you can buy tickets here. There's also a restaurant serving veg/nonveg food and Western breakfasts. *Hotel Sheetal (☎ 369420),* next door, is similar and its air-cooled rooms are reasonable value at Rs 150/175.

Places to Stay – Mid-Range

Hotel Pawan (☎ 363716, e khurana@vsnl.com, 3 Taj Rd), also known as Hotel Jaiwal, is on the main drag of Sadar Bazaar close to shops and restaurants. It's a big, friendly place with spacious air-cooled rooms from Rs 240/350. Air-con rooms are Rs 500/600. All rooms have private bathroom and 24-hour hot water, and they take great pride in telling you that their water is 'soft'.

Lauries Hotel (☎ 364536, e laurieshotel@hotmail.com, MG Rd) is an established hotel where Queen Elizabeth II's party stayed on a visit to India in 1961. It has some old-world charm and extensive gardens but it's pretty tatty and run down these days. Large rooms are asking a bit much at Rs 750/900, but you can camp for Rs 50. There's a swimming pool (Rs 50 for nonguests).

Hotel Taj Khema (☎ 330140) is a UP Tourism place in a good location east of the Taj. There's a viewpoint here on a grassy hillock in the back garden. They capitalise on this by charging a ridiculous Rs 50 for nonguests to have a look, and Rs 150 on Mondays (even though it's not *that* good). Cottage-style rooms cost Rs 600/700 or Rs 800/900 with air-con. There's a restaurant and bar here.

Places to Eat

Check out the local speciality, *peitha*: ultra-sweet candied pumpkin.

In the Taj Ganj area there are a huge number of makeshift eateries catering to budget travellers, many of them on rooftops or terraces. Their cooking facilities are minimal and hygiene is dubious, but they still manage to produce extensive, multicuisine menus. A very ugly side to eating out in Agra emerged a couple of years ago, which involved food deliberately being poisoned in order to extract medical insurance claims. There haven't been any further reports recently, but it pays to stick to places that are well-patronised.

Although these places are unlicensed, beer can be 'arranged' in most restaurants (sometimes served clandestinely in a teapot) and 'special' (bhang) lassis are widely available. The latter should definitely be treated with caution here, and probably avoided altogether. It only takes a few minutes to walk around this area and check out the latest 'in' places.

Joney's Place is tiny, like a lurid caravan, but it's one of the area's longest-running establishments and is still as popular as ever. It's too small to even have a kitchen – the food is prepared outside. It serves great Western breakfasts and good Indian and Israeli food, and its iced-banana lassis (while not tasting much like a true lassi) have reached legendary status.

Shankara Vegis Restaurant and *Joinus Restaurant*, opposite each other, have rooftop dining and menus featuring Indian, Italian, Chinese and Western breakfasts. Most dishes are between Rs 30 and Rs 60.

Lucky Restaurant has the usual have-a-go-at-everything menu but it's one of the more convivial places to hang out. Apart from the open-sided ground floor area, there are a few tables on the roof with views of the Taj.

Yash Cafe also has an enjoyable atmosphere, aided by Western music, comfy chairs and candlelight dinners. It has a long menu of veg and nonveg food and a pizzeria.

Zorba the Buddha in Sadar Bazaar rarely gets a bad word from travellers (except perhaps for its prices). This spotlessly clean, nonsmoking, Osho-run vegetarian restaurant has a very innovative menu. Excellent main dishes cost around Rs 70 to Rs 120,

and you can't leave without trying one of the ice-cream dishes (Rs 40) – Ginger Snow is a personal favourite! There's also a range of flavoured coffees. It can be difficult to get a table in the evening, but it's also a great place for lunch (open from noon to 3 pm). The restaurant is closed each year in May and June.

Although Agra has a fine tradition of Mughlai food, you would never know it from the food dished up in its cheaper restaurants. For quality Mughlai cuisine, you'll need to try the expensive luxury hotels.

Dasaprakash, in the Meher Cinema complex on Gwalior Rd, serves tasty and highly regarded south Indian food in air-con comfort. South Indian dishes cost from Rs 50 to Rs 75, spaghetti is Rs 90 and the Dasaprakash thali is Rs 100.

Lakshmi Vilas (Taj Rd) is a cheap south Indian veg restaurant, recommended for its 23 varieties of dosa from Rs 20. There's a pricey *Pizza Hut* on Fatehbad Rd.

Only Restaurant, at the Taj Ganj end of The Mall, is highly rated by locals but the food is nowhere near as fancy as the decor, and unless the place is at least half full, even the live Indian music can't rescue a dead ambience. Veg dishes start at Rs 50 and Murg Mughlai is Rs 90, but most mains are over Rs 100.

A better option for a minor splurge is the new *Park Restaurant* in Sadar Bazaar. This spotless air-con place does very good north Indian food as well as continental and Chinese, with most dishes less than Rs 150. Fish Amritsar is Rs 75 and a tandoori salad is Rs 55. It's open for breakfast, lunch and dinner (to 11.30 pm).

Shopping

Agra is best known for marble items inlaid with coloured semiprecious stones such as lapus lazuli and topaz, similar to the pietra-dura work on the Taj. These range from small ornamental pieces to plates, jewellery boxes, table tops and chess boards. Some of the work is extremely intricate and is carried out by skilled artisans but this will be reflected in the price. Tourist prices are always inflated, particularly around Taj Ganj, so shop around and bargain hard. One of the best places to look is in the workshops and showrooms of Gokalpura Market (opposite Agra College), where much of Agra's inlaid marble is produced (most of the best stuff comes from villages outside Agra).

Agra is also well known for leather goods, jewellery, and *dhurrie* (rug) weaving. Sadar Bazaar and the area south of Taj Ganj are full of emporiums of one kind or another, but prices here are higher than in the bazaars of the old part of the city. The best jewellery shops are around Pratapur, also in the old part of Agra, though you can still pick up precious stones cheaper in Jaipur.

About 1km along the road running from the eastern gate of the Taj is Shilpgram, a crafts village and open-air emporium. It has displays of crafts from all over the country. Prices are high, but the quality is good and the range hard to beat.

Agra is India's capital of scams and quite a few tourists manage to get ripped off here. The easiest way to avoid pitfalls is not to let rickshaw-wallahs persuade you to visit shops on the way to your destination – you'll pay inflated prices to cover the cost of commission. It's also best to avoid the cool young men on mopeds who claim to be students wanting to learn about your country. An invitation to visit their home will inevitably lead you straight to a craft shop, or worse. Common gem scams involve con-artists convincing you to buy jewellery or gemstones cheaply here which can sell at great profit back home. Not a chance. Lastly, don't be tempted by the unconvincing scams which promise handsome profits in return for helping a shop export goods to your home country – somewhere along the line your credit card will take a beating.

Getting There & Away

Air The Indian Airlines office (☎ 360948) is at the Clarks Shiraz Hotel. Agra's airport, 7km from the centre of town, is on the popular daily tourist shuttle from Delhi to Agra, Khajuraho, Varanasi and back again. It's a 40-minute flight from Delhi to Agra, leaving at 10 am. Fares from Agra are: Delhi US$55, Khajuraho US$80 and Varanasi US$105.

Bus If you're heading for Jaipur or elsewhere in Rajasthan, the bus is a good option, but for Delhi, Varanasi, or points south such as Gwalior the train is better.

Most buses leave from the Idgah bus stand. Buses to Delhi (Rs 84, five hours) depart every 30 minutes; to Jaipur (Rs 87, six hours) they depart hourly. Jaipur buses go via Bharatpur (Rs 24, 1½ hours). Buses to Fatehpur Sikri (Rs 15, 1½ hours) leave every 30 minutes from around 6.30 am. There's one bus to Khajuraho (Rs 120, 10 hours) at 5 am.

Rajasthan government buses depart from a small booth outside Hotel Sheetal, close to the Idgah bus stand. Deluxe buses leave here every hour for Jaipur (Rs 115, 5½ hours) and there are air-con services (Rs 200) at 6.30 am and 12.30 pm; you should book a day in advance, especially for air-con. Tickets can also be booked at Hotel Sakura.

Long-distance buses heading east (to Lucknow, Varanasi or Gorakhpur) leave from the Agra Fort bus stand on Chhipi Tola Rd.

Train Trains to/from Agra are very busy, especially those travelling between Delhi and Varanasi. Try to reserve as far in advance as possible, especially if you want a sleeper.

The reservation hall is to the right as you exit Agra Cantonment station. Reservation forms are available from counter No 2 and there's a foreign-tourist window.

To Delhi Agra Cantonment station is on the main Delhi-Mumbai line. The fastest train to Delhi is the daily air-con *Shatabdi Express* (Rs 390 in air-con chair class, two hours). It leaves New Delhi at 6.15 am and departs from Agra for the return trip at 8.18 pm, making it ideal if you only want to visit Agra for the day. A cheaper alternative is the daily *Taj Express* (Rs 53/83 in 2nd/sleeper class, 2½ hours). It leaves Delhi's Nizamuddin station at 7.15 am and departs from Agra for the return trip at 6.35 pm.

Plenty of other expresses operate between the two cities, most taking from three to four hours. Trains running between Agra and New Delhi station include: the 4.45 pm *Punjab Mail*, the noon *Kerala Express*, the 8.10 am *Karnataka Express* and the 3.53 pm *Chhatisgarh Express*. Numerous other trains terminate at Nizamuddin station in Delhi.

To Varanasi There are some direct trains to Mughal Serai near Varanasi, but most of the expresses running between Delhi and Kolkata (Calcutta) do not stop at Agra. If you're heading to or from Varanasi (which is on this line), you may have to use the Tundla or Firozabad stations, east of Agra, where most expresses stop. A bus between Firozabad and Agra takes 1½ hours and costs Rs 15; to Tundla it takes about an hour.

The exception is the *Marudhar Express,* which departs from Agra Cantonment at 10.15 pm and arrives at Varanasi Junction at 11.05 am (Rs 208/965 in sleeper/two-tier air-con). This is the ideal train to be on, so try to book ahead if you want a sleeper.

To Rajasthan Agra's train connections to cities in Rajasthan have been disrupted by Rajasthan's conversion from metre gauge to broad gauge. Currently, the only direct train heading west is the *Marudhar Express,* leaving Agra Fort at 4.40 am (Agra Cantonment at 5.25 am). It stops at Jaipur (Rs 120/564 sleeper/two-tier air-con) and terminates at Jodhpur (Rs 203/944) at 6.30 pm.

Getting Around

To/From the Airport Agra's Kheria airport is 7km from the centre of town and 3km west of Idgah bus stand. From Taj Ganj, taxis charge around Rs 90 and autorickshaws Rs 50.

Taxi & Autorickshaw Tempos operate on set routes: From the Agra Fort bus stand to Taj Ganj it's just Rs 2. Taxis and autorickshaws are unmetered so be prepared to haggle.

Prepaid transport is available from Agra Cantonment train station to Taj Ganj (Rs 38/82 by rickshaw/taxi), Sadar Bazaar (Rs 18/35) and to the Taj Mahal and back with an hour's waiting time (Rs 65/125). Some travellers are wisely choosing not to take motorised transport to the Taj in an effort to reduce harmful pollutants in the mausoleum's vicinity. A prepaid autorickshaw for local sightseeing costs Rs 250 for a full day or Rs 40 per hour; taxis cost Rs 500 for a full day locally, or Rs 650 if you also want to go to Fatehpur Sikri. Some drivers may show their own falsely inflated fare charts. In any case, the prepaid rates are quite high and you should be able to do better with a bit of bargaining.

Cycle-Rickshaw Agra is very spread out and not conducive to walking since hordes of cycle-rickshaw-wallahs pursue would-be pedestrians with unbelievable persistence. Many visitors get frustrated by this but the rickshaw-wallahs often speak English well, have a finely tuned sense of humour, and can be useful sources of local information. Don't take any nonsense from rickshaw-wallahs who offer to take you from A to B via a few marble or jewellery shops.

From Taj Ganj to Sadar Bazaar is less than Rs 15, and to Agra Cantonment less than Rs 20, which is the most you should pay to get anywhere in Agra. Although cycle-rickshaws are the most environmentally friendly way to get around they are not particularly suited to Agra's diffuseness. If you're heading from the fort to the Taj, it's almost quicker to walk (via Shahjahan Park) than catch a cycle-rickshaw since this stretch consists of a long, slow incline.

Bicycle The simple solution to Agra's transport problem is to hire a bicycle. The city is sufficiently traffic-free to make cycling an easy proposition and avoiding rickshaw-wallahs will increase your enjoyment, provided it's not too hot and smoggy. Raja Bicycle Store, near the Taj Ganj tonga and rickshaw stand, hires bicycles for Rs 5 per hour, Rs 15 for half a day and Rs 30 for a full day; a new bicycle will cost Rs 10/25/50 to hire. Some hotels also arrange bicycle hire.

FATEHPUR SIKRI

This magnificent fortified ghost city was the capital of the Mughal empire between 1571 and 1585, during the reign of Emperor Akbar. Fatehpur Sikri was thereafter quickly abandoned, but thanks to its durable red sandstone and a lot of work by the Archaeological Survey of India it remains a perfectly preserved example of a Mughal city at the height of the empire's splendour.

Most people visit Fatehpur Sikri as a day trip from Agra, but it can be an atmospheric place to spend the night, which allows you to watch the impressive sunset over the ruins – and you'll have the place virtually to yourself for a few hours in the morning. The best viewpoint is from the top of the city walls, a 2km walk to the south.

The deserted city lies along the top of a ridge 40km west of Agra. The village, with

INDIA

its bus stand and train station, is at the bottom of the ridge's southern face. A Rs 4.50 fee per car is payable at Agra Gate, the eastern entrance to the village.

The historic enclosure is open 6 am to 5.30 pm; entry is US$10 for foreigners, Rs 10 for Indians. A video-camera permit is Rs 25. There's no entry fee to visit the Jama Masjid and the tomb of Shaikh Salim Chishti as they are outside the city enclosure. The function and even the names of many buildings remain contentious, so you may find it useful to hire a guide. Licensed guides cost around Rs 85 and can be found near the ticket office; unlicensed guides solicit tourists at the Buland Darwaza.

Jama Masjid

Fatehpur Sikri's beautiful mosque, also known as the Dargah Mosque, contains elements of Persian and Hindu design and is said to be a copy of the mosque at Mecca. The main entrance is through the impressive 54m-high **Buland Darwaza**, the Gate of Victory, constructed to commemorate Akbar's victory in Gujarat. A Quranic inscription inside its archway quotes Jesus saying:

> The world is a bridge, pass over it but build no house upon it. He who hopes for an hour may hope for eternity.

This seems highly appropriate considering the city's fate.

In the northern part of the courtyard is the superb white marble **dargah (tomb) of Shaikh Salim Chishti**, built in 1570. Just as Akbar came to the saint four centuries ago looking for a son, childless women visit his tomb today. The carved marble lattice screens *(jalis)* are probably the finest examples of such work you'll see anywhere in the country. The saint's grandson, Islam Khan, also has his tomb within the courtyard. The eastern gate of the mosque, known as the **Shahi Darwaza** (King's Gate), was the one used by Akbar.

Palace of Jodh Bai

North-east of the mosque is the ticket office and entrance to the old city. The first building inside the gate is a palace, commonly but wrongly ascribed to Jodh Bai, Jehangir's Hindu mother and the daughter of the maharaja of Amber.

The architecture is a blend of Hindu and Muslim styles. The walls of the **Hawa Mahal** (Palace of the Winds) are made entirely of stone latticework.

Birbal Bhavan

Thought to have been built either by or for Akbar's favourite courtier, Raja Birbal, this elegant building provoked Victor Hugo, the 19th-century French author, to comment that it was either a very small palace or a very large jewellery box. Birbal, a Hindu noted for his wit and wisdom, unfortunately proved to be a hopeless soldier and lost his life, and most of his army, near Peshawar in 1586. The palace fronts onto the **Lower Haramsara**, which was once believed to be an enormous stable, with nearly 200 enclosures for elephants, horses and camels, but it's now thought to be where the palace maids lived.

Karawan Serai & Hiran Minar

The Karawan Serai, or Caravanserai, was a large courtyard surrounded by the hostels used by visiting merchants. Outside the fort grounds, the Hiran Minar (Deer Minaret) is said to have been erected over the grave of Akbar's favourite elephant. Stone elephant tusks protrude from the 21m-tower from which Akbar is said to have shot at deer and other game which were driven in front of him. The flat expanse of land stretching away from the tower was once a lake and still occasionally floods today.

Palace of the Christian Wife

Close to the Palace of Jodh Bai, this house was used by Akbar's Goan Christian wife, Maryam, and at one time was gilded throughout – giving it the name the Golden House.

Panch Mahal

This whimsical five-storey palace was probably once used by the court ladies and originally had stone screens on the sides. These have been removed, making the open colonnades inside visible. Like a house of cards, each of the five storeys is stepped back from the previous one until the top floor consists of only a tiny kiosk. The lower floor has 84 columns, no two of which are exactly alike.

Treasury

For a long time this building was known as Ankh Micholi, which translates roughly as 'hide and seek' – a game the emperor is supposed to have played here with ladies of the harem. However, current thinking suggests that the building was the imperial treasury – an idea supported by the curious struts carved with sea monsters who were believed to protect the treasures of the deep. Near one corner is a small canopied enclosure known as the Astrologer's Seat, where Akbar's Hindu guru may have sat while instructing him.

Diwan-i-Khas

The Hall of Private Audiences, known as the Jewel House, is unique for its interior design. A carved stone column in the centre of the building flares to support a flat-topped 'throne' which is 6m high. Narrow stone bridges radiate from the corners of the room and meet at the throne. The function of the building is disputed: Some think Akbar spent much time on the 'throne' (so to speak) discussing and debating with scholars of different religious persuasions; others believe it to be the perch from which he meted out justice.

Diwan-i-Am

Just inside the north-eastern gates of the deserted city is the Hall of Public Audiences, a large open courtyard surrounded by cloisters. Beside the Diwan-i-Am is the **Pachisi Courtyard**, set out like a gigantic game board. It is said that Akbar played the game pachisi here, using slave girls as the pieces.

Other Monuments

Musicians would play from the **Naubat Khana**, at one time the main entrance to the city, as processions passed beneath. The entrance road then ran between the mint and the treasury before reaching the Diwan-i-Am. The **Diwan Khana-i-Khas (Khwabgah)**, in front of the Daftar Khana (Record Office), was Akbar's own sleeping quarters. Beside the Khwabgah is the tiny but elaborately carved **Rumi Sultana** or Turkish Queen's House. Near the Karawan Serai, badly defaced elephants still guard the **Hathi Pol**, or Elephant Gate.

Outside the Jama Masjid are the remains of the small stone-cutters' mosque. Shaikh Salim Chishti's cave was supposedly at this site and the mosque predates Akbar's imperial city. There's also a **Hakim's (Doctor's) House** and a fine **hamam** beside it.

Places to Stay & Eat

The *Archaeological Survey Rest House* (☎ 882248) is the cheapest place to stay. It costs only Rs 10 but advance bookings must be made at the Archaeological Survey of India (☎ 363506), 22 The Mall, Agra.

Maurya Rest House (☎ 882348), below the Buland Darwaza (main gate of the Jama Masjid), is the most pleasant of the budget hotels in the village. There are basic singles with (grotty) shared bathroom for Rs 60 or with private bathroom (free bucket of hot water) for Rs 100. It's well run by a friendly family, and food is available in the small, shady courtyard or the rooftop restaurant.

You can camp on the lawn at *Goverdhan Tourist Complex* (☎ 882648), about 300m back from the bus stand on the Agra road, and there are cheap rooms here too.

There are plenty of snack and soft-drink vendors around all the entrances to the enclosures. Fatehpur Sikri's speciality is *khataie*, the biscuits you'll see piled high in the bazaar. UP Tourism's *Gulistan Tourist Complex*, back out on the Agra road, has a restaurant and a bar.

Getting There & Away

Bus to Fatehpur Sikri from Agra's Idgah bus terminal (Rs 15, 1½ hours) depart every 30 minutes between 6.30 am and 7 pm. It costs about Rs 400 to hire a car and driver (through a guesthouse or good travel agent) for the round trip to Fatehpur Sikri from Agra, including two or three hours at the site. The prepaid taxi rate for a half-day trip is Rs 500 (Rs 750 for air-con).

Don't encourage the villagers along the Agra road who force dancing bears to stop the passing traffic.

VARANASI

☎ 0542 • pop 2 million

Also known as Benares (or Banares), the city of Shiva on the bank of the sacred Ganges is one of the holiest places in India. Hindu pilgrims come to bathe in the waters of the Ganges, a ritual which is said to wash away all sins. Varanasi is an auspicious place to die, since expiring here ensures release from the cycle of rebirths and an instant passport to heaven. It's a magical city where the most intimate rituals of life and death take place in public on the city's famous ghats (steps which lead down to the river).

INDIA

For travellers, this is the place where you can most easily see the everyday processes of devout Hinduism, from ritual bathing and puja to funeral processions and cremations. An early morning walk along the sacred ghats or boat trip on the Ganges is an unforgettable experience.

In the past, the city has been known as Kashi and Benares. Its present name restores an ancient name meaning the city between two rivers – the Varuna and Assi.

It has been a centre of learning and civilisation for over 2000 years, and claims to be one of the oldest living cities in the world. Mark Twain famously said that:

> Benares is older than history, older than tradition, older even than legend, and looks twice as old as all of them put together.

The old city does have an antique feel but few buildings are more than a couple of hundred years old thanks to marauding Muslim invaders and Aurangzeb's destructive tendencies. The newer parts of Varanasi around the Grand Trunk (GT) Rd will probably be your introduction to the city. They are chaotic, crowded and polluted – typical of any large north Indian city. You have to head south into the Godaulia area and towards the river before you begin to appreciate its charm.

Orientation & Information

The old city of Varanasi is situated along the western bank of the Ganges and extends back from the riverbank ghats in a labyrinth of alleyways too narrow for traffic. Not even cycle-rickshaws can fit in here, which is nothing short of a blessing. Godaulia is just outside the old city, and Chautganj is north of here, separated from the cantonment by the train line.

One of the best ways to get your bearings in Varanasi is to remember the positions of the ghats, particularly important ones such as Dasaswamedh Ghat and Manikarnika (the Burning Ghat). The alleyways of the old city can be disorienting, but the hotels here are well signposted.

For a useful Web site on the city, look up www.vis itvaranasi.com.

Tourist Offices There's a helpful UP tourist information office (☎ 346370) at Varanasi Junction train station that has city and train information. This is a good place to go as soon as you arrive in Varanasi. The enthusiastic Mr Sankar is keen to make sure tourists don't get duped by autorickshaw and taxi drivers and he's full of information. It's usually open from 6 am to 8 pm (10 am to 5 pm on Sunday). A less useful UP tourist office (☎ 341162) is in the Tourist Bungalow.

The friendly Government of India tourist office (☎ 343744) at 15B The Mall in the Cantonment is open weekdays from 9 am to 6 pm, and 9 am to 4 pm on Saturday.

Money Probably the best places to change money are the agencies on Luxa Rd near Godaulia Crossing. Glorious Services has rates that are slightly lower than in the banks but it's quick, open 8 am to 8 pm daily, and changes all travellers cheques and 36 currencies. Radiant Services, nearby, is similar. In the cantonment area, the State Bank of India near the Hotel Surya changes cash and US dollar travellers cheques, but won't accept travellers cheques in pounds sterling.

The Bank of Baroda (near the Hotel Ganges and opposite the main post office) and the Andhra Bank on Dasaswamedh Ghat Rd, next to Yelchiko Restaurant, provide cash advances on major credit cards.

Post & Communications The main post office is a short walk or cycle-rickshaw ride north of the old city. The reliable poste restante here is open from 10 am to 6 pm Monday to Saturday. In the cantonment, there's a post office at the central telegraph office (CTO). You can make international and STD calls from the CTO 24 hours a day.

There are quite a few places providing Internet access for around Rs 50 per hour. Pathak Internet is just around the corner from Shanti Guest House, and there are a couple of places, including Vishal Internet, in the narrow alleys just behind Dasaswamedh Ghat.

There's also Internet access at Hotel Surya in the cantonment and at Glorious Services near Godaulia Crossing. Many guesthouses with Internet access charge closer to Rs 100 per hour.

Medical Services & Emergency The Heritage Hospital (☎ 313977) is close to the main gate of Benares Hindu University.

VARANASI

PLACES TO STAY
3 Hotel Surya;
   Canton Restaurant;
   State Bank of India
4 Hotel Clarks Varanasi
5 Hotel Varanasi Ashok;
   Nandi Bookshop
12 Hotel India; Palm
   Springs Restaurant
14 Nar Indra
15 Hotel Plaza Inn
16 Tourist Bungalow &
   UP Tourism Office;
   Hotel Amar
22 Hotel Buddha
23 Hotel Ajaya;
   Dawat Restaurant
24 Hotel Barahdari
36 The Nest

40 Sandhya Guest House;
   Hotel Sunshine

PLACES TO EAT
17 El Parador
20 Kamesh Hut Garden
   Restaurant
21 Poonam Restaurant
33 Shahi Restaurant
37 Sindhi Restaurant
38 Kerala Cafe
39 Bread of Life Bakery

OTHER
1 Private Buses to Sarnath
2 Civil Court
6 Indian Airlines
7 Government of India
   Tourist Office

8 TV Tower
9 Central Telegraph
   Office; Post Office
10 Cottage Industries
   Exposition
11 Hotel Vaibhav; Palki
   Restaurant
13 Buses to Sarnath
18 Bus Station
19 Autorickshaws
   to Godaulia
25 Weaver's Handloom
   Enterprises
26 Alamgir Mosque
27 Main Post Office
28 Police Station
29 Town Hall
30 Basant Bar &
   Restaurant

31 Bharat Mata
   Temple
32 Andhra Bank;
   Yelchiko Restaurant
34 Foreigners'
   Registration Office
35 Rama Krishna Ashram
41 Durga Temple
42 Tulsi Manas Temple
43 Hanuman Temple
44 Heritage Hospital
45 Autorickshaws
   to Godaulia
46 Malaviya Bhavan
47 Bharat Kala Bhavan
48 New Vishwanath
   Temple
49 Ram Nagar Fort &
   Museum

To Airport (21km) & Jaunpur

To Sarnath (10km)

Maqbul Alam Rd

Varanana River

Rishipattan Rd

Nadesar Park

Raja Bazar Rd

The Mall

Patel Nagar

Cantonment

Varanasi City Train Station

Raighat Rd

Aipur Rd

Kashi Train Station

Varanasi Junction Train Station

Chetganj

Kotwali

Keshava Ghat

Raj Ghat

Prahlad Ghat

Grand Trunk Rd

Vidyapeeth Rd

Kabir Chaura Marg

Nati Sarak Rd

Daranagar Rd

Kashi Station Rd

Trilochan Ghat
Gai Ghat
Panchganga Ghat

To Allahabad

Aurangabad Rd

Sigra Crossing

See Godaulia & the Old City Map (p502)

Rana Ghat
Scindia Ghat
Manikarnika Ghat; Jalsain Ghat
Lalita Ghat
Meer Ghat
Dasaswamedh Ghat
Rana Ghat

To Mughal Serai (12km)

Raja Moti Chand Rd

Guru Nanak Rd

Luxa Rd

Mandpur Rd

Kedar Ghat
Harishchandra Ghat
Hanuman Ghat
Shivala Ghat
Anandmayee Ghat
Bachraj Ghat
Tulsi Ghat
Assi Ghat

Durgakund Rd

Sonarpur Rd

Bhelpura

University Rd

Assi River

Nagwa Ghat

Ganges River

Panch Koshi Rd

Benares Hindu University

Ram Nagar Rd

Ferry

Pontoon Bridge

0   0.5   1km
0   0.25   0.5mi

INDIA

The closest police station (☎ 330653) to the old city is between the town hall and the main post office.

Dangers & Annoyances The main hassles are predatory rickshaw-wallahs and persistent touts, although it's not as wearying as in Agra. Varanasi suffers frequent power cuts, so if you stay in the old city, carry a torch to find your way in the labyrinthine alleys. The old city is also said to be potentially dangerous after dark, and you should avoid walking here alone late at night. Many hotels in this area lock their doors at 10 or 11 pm, although there are several 24-hour places.

Varanasi's Hindu and minority Muslim population can occasionally be a volatile mix – during our visit there was a strict police-enforced 'curfew' (basically a shutdown of the trouble spots, mostly around Godaulia and south along Sonarpur Rd) following an outbreak of violence. However, don't believe rickshaw-wallah stories that there is trouble without checking at the tourist office or asking other travellers first.

The Ganges is far from clean (at Tulsi Ghat the faecal coliform count was measured at a staggering 250,000 times the World Health Organization safe permitted maximum!) so avoid ghat chai-wallahs who rinse their glasses in river water. Better still, patronise the ones that use the nifty throwaway clay pots instead of glasses. The river is, of course, used for bathing by Hindu pilgrims and local people and is a source of great enjoyment for young children. Occasionally you'll even see westerners dousing themselves in there. This is not recommended for obvious reasons.

The Ghats of Varanasi

Few places in India represent the nation's religious traditions and devotional nature as perfectly as Varanasi. And the place to see it all unfolding is down on the ghats which line the western bank of the Ganges. Most are used for bathing but there are also several 'burning ghats' where bodies are cremated, the principal one being Manikarnika Ghat. The best time to visit the ghats is at dawn when the river and the ghats themselves are bathed in a magical light and pilgrims come to perform puja to the rising sun. Dusk is also a good time as there are often colourful torch-lit ceremonies held at Dasaswamedh Ghat.

There are around 100 ghats in Varanasi, but Dasaswamedh Ghat is the busiest and makes a convenient starting point. If the water level is low, you can simply walk from one ghat to the next: This way you're among the throng of people who come to the edge of the Ganges not only for a ritual bath, but to do yoga, offer blessings, buy paan (betel nut and leaves plus chewing additives such as lime), sell flowers, get a massage, play cricket, have a swim, get a shave, and improve their karma by giving money to beggars.

The city extends from Raj Ghat, near the major road and rail bridge, to **Assi Ghat**, near the university. The Assi Ghat is one of the five special ghats which pilgrims are supposed to bathe at in sequence during the ritual route called Panchatirthi Yatra. The order is Assi, Dasaswamedh, Adi Keshava, Panchganga and finally Manikarnika.

The **Bachraj Ghat** is Jain and there are three riverbank Jain temples. Many of the ghats are owned by maharajas or other princely rulers, such as the fine **Shivala Ghat**, owned by the maharaja of Varanasi. The **Dandi Ghat** is the ghat of ascetics known as Dandi Panths, and nearby is the popular **Hanuman Ghat**.

The **Harishchandra** or Smashan Ghat is a secondary burning ghat. It's one of the oldest ghats in the city. Above it, the crowded **Kedar Ghat** is a shrine popular with Bengalis and south Indians. **Mansarowar Ghat** was built by Raja Man Singh of Amber and named after the Tibetan lake at the foot of Mt Kailash, Shiva's Himalayan home. **Someswar** or Lord of the Moon Ghat is said to be able to heal diseases.

The name of **Dasaswamedh Ghat** indicates that Brahma sacrificed (*medh*) 10 (*das*) horses (*aswa*) here. Conveniently central, it's one of the most important and busiest ghats and a good place to linger and soak up the atmosphere. Note its statues and the shrine of Sitala, goddess of smallpox.

The **Meer Ghat** leads to the Nepalese Temple, which has erotic sculptures. The **Jalsain Ghat**, where cremations take place, virtually adjoins **Manikarnika Ghat**, one of the oldest and most sacred in Varanasi. Manikarnika is the main burning ghat and one of the most auspicious places that a

Hindu can be cremated. Bodies are handled by outcasts known as *doms*, and they are carried through the alleyways of the old city to the holy Ganges on a bamboo stretcher swathed in cloth. The corpse is doused in the Ganges prior to cremation. You'll see huge piles of firewood stacked along the top of the ghat, each log carefully weighed on giant scales so that the price of cremation can be calculated. There are no problems watching cremations, since at Manikarnika death is simply business as usual, but don't take photos and keep your camera well hidden.

Above the steps here is a tank known as the **Manikarnika Well**; Parvati is said to have dropped her earring here and Shiva dug the tank to recover it, filling the depression with his sweat. The **Charanpaduka**, a slab of stone between the well and the ghat, bears footprints made by Vishnu. Privileged VIPs are cremated at the Charanpaduka.

Scindia Ghat was originally built in 1830 but was so huge that it collapsed into the river and had to be rebuilt. The **Ram Ghat** was built by the raja of Jaipur. The **Panchganga Ghat**, as its name indicates, is where five rivers are supposed to meet. Dominating the ghat is Aurangzeb's smaller mosque, also known as the **Alamgir Mosque**. The **Gai Ghat** has a figure of a cow made of stone upon it. The **Trilochan Ghat** has two turrets emerging from the river, and the water between them is especially holy. **Raj Ghat** was the ferry pier until the road and rail bridge were completed here.

Temples

There are over 200 temples in Varanasi and, while few are visually or architecturally impressive, the following important shrines make an interesting diversion from life on the ghats. For around Rs 50 you should be able to hire a cycle-rickshaw to take you to the main temples south of the old city, as well as the university and Ram Nagar Fort.

Vishwanath Temple The Vishwanath Temple, or Golden Temple, tucked in the narrow alleyways of the old city behind Lalita Ghat, is the most sacred temple in Varanasi. It is dedicated to Vishveswara – Shiva as lord of the universe. The current temple was built in 1776 by Ahalya Bai of Indore, and the 800kg of gold plating on the towers, which gives the temple its colloquial name, was provided by Maharaja Ranjit Singh of Lahore some 50 years later. Non-Hindus are not allowed into the temple but you can view it from the upper floor of a house across the street.

Next to the Vishwanath Temple is the **Gyan Kupor Well** (Well of Knowledge). The faithful believe drinking its water leads to a higher spiritual plane, though they are prevented from doing so by both tradition and a strong security screen. The well is said to contain the Shiva lingam removed from the previous temple and hidden to protect it from Aurangzeb.

Durga Temple About 2km south of the old city, the Durga Temple is commonly known as the Monkey Temple because of the many frisky monkeys that have made it their home. Don't confuse it with the smaller Hanuman temple (dedicated to the monkey god), just south of Assi Ghat. The Durga Temple was built in the 18th century by a Bengali maharani and is stained red with ochre. Durga is the 'terrible' form of Shiva's consort Parvati, so at festivals there are often sacrifices of goats. Non-Hindus can enter the courtyard but not the inner sanctum.

Tulsi Manas Temple Only 150m south of the Durga Temple is the modern marble shikhara-style Tulsi Manas Temple, built in 1964. Its two-tier walls are engraved with verses and scenes from the *Ram Charit Manas*, the Hindi version of the *Ramayana*. Its author, poet Tulsi Das, lived here while writing it.

You can watch figures performing scenes from Hindu mythology on the 2nd floor. The temple is open 6 to 11.30 am and 3 to 9 pm.

New Vishwanath Temple This temple was planned by the great nationalist Pandit Malaviya and built by the wealthy Birla family of industrialists on the grounds of Benares Hindu University. Pandit Malaviya wished to see Hinduism revived without its caste distinctions and prejudices so, unlike many temples in Varanasi, this temple is open to all, irrespective of caste or religion. It's open from 5 am to noon and 1.30 to 9 pm.

Bharat Mata Temple Dedicated to 'Mother India', this unadorned temple has a marble relief map of India instead of the usual images of gods and goddesses. The map is said to be perfectly in scale, both vertically and horizontally. It's open daily from 7 am to 5 pm.

Benares Hindu University

Varanasi has long been a centre of learning and that tradition is continued today at the Benares Hindu University (BHU), built in 1917. It was founded by Pandit Malaviya as a centre for education in Indian art, music, culture and philosophy, and for the study of Sanskrit. The 5-sq-km campus houses the **Bharat Kala Bhavan**, which has a fine collection of miniature paintings, sculptures from the 1st to 15th centuries and old photographs of Varanasi. It's open Monday to Saturday from 11 am to 4.30 pm (7.30 am to 12.30 pm from May to June). To visit all sections costs Rs 40. BHU is a 20-minute walk or a short rickshaw ride from the Durga Temple.

Ram Nagar Fort & Museum

On the opposite bank of the river, this impressive 17th-century fort is the home of the former maharaja of Benares. During the monsoon, access is by ferry, at other times it's via a decrepit pontoon bridge. The interesting museum here contains old silver and brocade palanquins for the ladies of the court, gold-plated elephant howdahs (seats for carrying people on an elephant's back), an astrological clock, macabre elephant traps and an armoury of swords and old guns. The fort is open daily from 9 am to noon and 2 to 5 pm (Rs 4).

Activities

River Trips A boat ride on the Ganges is something you should do while in Varanasi, although you should be prepared to see the odd corpse or body part floating down the river. The best time to go out on the water is early in the morning when the light is particularly atmospheric. Even if you're not staying near the river, it's easy to organise a boat for sunrise as rickshaw-wallahs are keen to get a pre-dawn rendezvous arranged for the trip to the river. Get the rickshaw-wallah to take you to a large ghat such as Dasaswamedh, since there will be a number of boats to choose from. Travellers have reported being taken to smaller ghats where

there was only one boat, placing them in a poor bargaining position. Any of the main ghats between Scindia and Rana should be OK.

The government rate for hiring a boat capable of holding up to four people is supposedly set at Rs 50 per hour; for a boat that can seat up to 10 people it's Rs 75 per hour. You'll undoubtedly have to remind boatmen of these rates since tourists frequently pay much, much more. Be sure to agree on a price before getting into a boat.

Swimming If the sight of pilgrims bathing in the Ganges makes you want to have a splash yourself (perish the thought), there are several hotels that allow nonguests to use their pools for a fee. One of the best is the Hotel Clarks Varanasi (Rs 250), or try the Hotel Varanasi Ashok (Rs 150).

Yoga & Spirituality The Malaviya Bhavan (☎ 310291, fax 312059) at Benares Hindu University offers courses in yoga and Hindu philosophy, such as a four-week certificate course or a four-month part-time diploma. For the less committed, the Shanti Guest House runs morning and evening yoga classes for Rs 50. There are numerous 'hole-in-the-wall' places in the old city offering yoga instruction for around Rs 100 an hour. You'll see flyers pinned up around the place, or try the Bramheshwar Yoga Teaching Centre, behind Dasaswamedh Ghat, with hour-long hatha yoga lessons (Rs 100) every morning; or the All India Tantric Society (☎ 321257) near Chausatti Ghat, with teachings in yoga, tantra astrology and Indian philosophy (accommodation is available in the Brahmadeva Ashram for Rs 60 a double).

Varanasi is also well endowed with astrologers, palmists, mystics, spiritual healers and sadhus. The Rama Krishna Ashram on Luxa Rd offers free courses in meditation and spirituality. Yagik Bushan, an 'astrological guru' who claims Goldie Hawn as his most famous client, has an office below Sita Guest House at Chausatti Ghat. He charges around Rs 300 for a palm reading and horoscope.

Steam Baths & Massage The Hotel Surya offers steam baths for just Rs 35, and body massages for Rs 150. You can get a vigorous head-, neck- and back-massage at Dasaswamedh Ghat from about Rs 10.

Organised Tours

Government guides hired via the Government of India tourist office cost Rs 230/345 for a half/full day, or you can pay more to include road and/or boat transport. A three-hour tour including taxi/autorickshaw would cost about Rs 500/350. You can choose from set itineraries or construct your own.

Special Events

Many religious festivals take place on Varanasi's ghats throughout the year, including numerous 'bathing festivals'. Mahashivratri (Festival of Shiva), in early March, is one of the biggest, as is Ganga Dashahara (mid-June), which celebrates the descent of the Ganges from Heaven to Earth. The Ganga Boat Rally finishes in Varanasi (having come from Allahabad) on 8 February.

Burhwa Mangal, in March, is another riverside festival with music and dancing.

Places to Stay

There are three main accommodation areas in Varanasi: the old city and the area south along the ghats (including Bhelpura); Chetganj and Lahurabir (south of the train station); and the cantonment to the north. Wherever you intend to stay in Varanasi, be firm with the rickshaw-wallah when you arrive. The one thing he will say that's true is that he can't take you all the way to your guesthouse if it's in the old city proper, but everything is within easy walking distance of Godaulia or Dasaswamedh Ghat. Be aware that even if someone (eg, a young boy) leads you to a guesthouse, he will probably reap commission.

Contact the UP Tourism office at the train station for a list of Varanasi's paying guest accommodation, which enables you to stay with a local family. They average around Rs 50 to Rs 200 per person. *The Nest (☎ 360137)* is a good choice.

Note that many hotels will drop their rates by up to 50% in the low season (April to July), so ask about discounts.

Places to Stay – Budget

Old City & Ghats Area This area is certainly the city's most colourful and there are several good lodges right on the river with superb views along the ghats. Nearly all the hotels have rooftop terraces to relax on. Most are strictly budget options and rooms are often cramped and basic, but you can't beat the location.

Shanti Guest House (☎ 320950) is a little back from the river, just off an alleyway leading to Manikarnika Ghat. It's very popular and has a 24-hour rooftop restaurant with good views of the old city and the river. Spartan singles/doubles with shared bathroom start from a mere Rs 40/60 and there are dorm beds for Rs 25. Rooms with private bathroom and lukewarm water start from Rs 100/125 and you can even get an air-con room for a steep Rs 600. Unfortunately, there are few outwards-facing windows and the walls are paper-thin. This is an interesting area though, as funeral processions regularly thread their way through the alleys to Manikarnika Ghat.

Vishnu Rest House (☎ 450206, Panday Ghat) is a popular riverside place with terraces offering great views, and it has a nice little cafe. The rooms are extremely poky though. Dorm beds are Rs 35. Singles/doubles are Rs 70/120, all with bucket hot water. Phone ahead as it's often full. Rickshaw-wallahs may try to take you to other, similarly named places.

Alka Hotel (☎ 328445, fax 328445, ℯ hotelalka@hotmail.com, Meer Ghat) is newer and slightly more upmarket than other riverside places in the area – its best rooms are almost mid-range. There's hot water, and a pleasant terrace restaurant. Rooms with shared bathroom cost only Rs 110/150; doubles with private bathroom start at Rs 250 up to Rs 750 for air-con rooms with a balcony overlooking the river.

The *Kumiko Guest House (☎ 450308, D 24–26 Panday Ghat)* is a cosy little guesthouse in an atmospheric 400-year-old building. There are just a few suitably ancient rooms. A dorm bed costs Rs 30, rooms with shared bathroom cost Rs 100/130 and a double with private bathroom overlooking the ghats is Rs 200. Japanese food is served in the evenings.

Sita Guesthouse (☎ 450061, ℯ sita_guest_house@yahoo.com, D 22/16 Chausatti Ghat) is well located and some of the more expensive rooms have great views over the river. Doubles with balcony cost Rs 300 and comfortable upper-storey rooms are

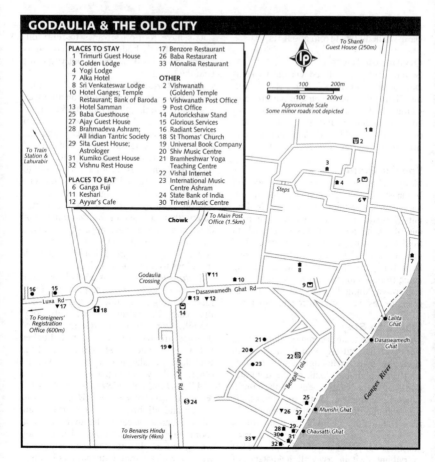

GODAULIA & THE OLD CITY

PLACES TO STAY
1 Trimurti Guest House
3 Golden Lodge
4 Yogi Lodge
7 Alka Hotel
8 Sri Venkateswar Lodge
10 Hotel Ganges; Temple Restaurant; Bank of Baroda
13 Hotel Samman
25 Baba Guesthouse
27 Ajay Guest House
28 Brahmadeva Ashram; All Indian Tantric Society
29 Sita Guest House; Astrologer
31 Kumiko Guest House
32 Vishnu Rest House

PLACES TO EAT
6 Ganga Fuji
11 Keshari
12 Ayyar's Cafe

17 Benzore Restaurant
26 Baba Restaurant
33 Monalisa Restaurant

OTHER
2 Vishwanath (Golden) Temple
5 Vishwanath Post Office
9 Post Office
14 Autorickshaw Stand
15 Glorious Services
16 Radiant Services
18 St Thomas' Church
19 Universal Book Company
20 Shiv Music Centre
21 Bramheshwar Yoga Teaching Centre
22 Vishal Internet
23 International Music Centre Ashram
24 State Bank of India
30 Triveni Music Centre

To Shanti Guest House (250m)

0   100   200m
0   100   200yd
Approximate Scale
Some minor roads not depicted

To Train Station & Lahurabir

Chowk

To Main Post Office (1.5km)

Godaulia Crossing

Dasaswamedh Ghat Rd

Luxa Rd

To Foreigners' Registration Office (600m)

Mandapur Rd

Bengali Tola

Lalita Ghat

Dasaswamedh Ghat

Ganges River

Munshi Ghat

Chausatti Ghat

To Benares Hindu University (4km)

Steps

Rs 250. There are also basic rooms with shared bathroom for Rs 60/100.

Yogi Lodge (☎ 392588, *Kalika Gali*), in the alleys back from the ghats, has long been a favourite with budget travellers. It's very basic but is well run by a friendly family. Dorm beds cost Rs 50, and small rooms with shared bathroom cost from Rs 80/100/150 for a single/double/triple. Like many other popular hotels in the old city, its success has spawned countless similarly named, inferior places.

Golden Lodge (☎ 323832), nearby, is a quiet place near the Vishwanath Temple, with basic rooms for Rs 60/75 with shared bathroom (hot water), Rs 80/100 with private bathroom, and Rs 150/200 with air cooling. You can sleep on the roof for Rs 10.

Baba Guesthouse (☎ 328672, *D 20/15 Munshi Ghat*) is basic but OK with dorm beds from Rs 30, and singles/doubles for Rs 80/100 with shared bathroom and Rs 100/150 with private bathroom.

Sri Venkateswar Lodge (☎ 393737), behind the Shiva temple on Dasaswamedh Ghat Rd, is a quiet place with hot water and rooms round a leafy courtyard. It charges Rs 70/110 with shared bathroom and from Rs 175 for doubles with private bathroom. Rooms are clean and have windows.

Trimurti Guest House (☎ 393554), near the Vishwanath Temple, has decent rooms with shared bathroom for Rs 50/80, doubles with private bathroom for Rs 120 and a few dorm beds for Rs 30. Yoga classes are offered for Rs 50.

Brahmadeva Ashram (☎ *321257*) at Chausatti Ghat has very basic accommodation – little more than a concrete box and a bed – at Rs 25 in a dormitory or Rs 60 for a double room, but you can receive free instruction in yoga, Indian philosophy and Tantric studies.

There are a couple of decent choices on Dasaswamedh Ghat Rd in Godaulia. They're a bit more spacious than those in the alleyways of the old city but try to avoid rooms that front onto the noisy main road. *Hotel Samman* (☎ *392241*) is cheap enough. Reasonable rooms with TV, windows and a grotty private bathroom start from Rs 100/150. Checkout is 24 hours.

Hugging the river midway between the old town and the university, the Bhelpura area is quieter and not as claustrophobic as the old city, but it's still close to the more sedate southern ghats. There are some good guest houses to choose from here.

The *Sandhya Guest House* (☎ *313292, Sonarpur Rd)* is a few minutes' walk from Shivala Ghat. It's run by a friendly, helpful manager and has a dining area on the roof. Clean rooms with shared bathroom cost Rs 70/100 and with private bathroom and geyser Rs 90/150. You can sleep on the roof on a bedroll for Rs 20. Some rooms were being refurbished when we visited and aircon should be available (Rs 400 a double). Nearby *Hotel Sunshine* (☎ *315134*) is another good place with clean rooms from Rs 100/150 with private bathroom (squat toilet), or Rs 200 for a small double with a balcony. There's a rooftop dorm for Rs 80 a bed.

Chetganj & Train Station Area While these areas offer nothing of particular interest, they may be to your liking if you want to keep out of the crush of the old city, or need to be close to transport options.

Hotel Buddha (☎ *343686, 26/35 Lahurabir)* is one of the best low-budget hotels in the area. It's back from the main street, so it's quiet, and the staff are helpful and friendly. You can call for a free pick-up from the train station or airport. There's a wide range of rooms that are plain but spacious. Rooms with attached hot-water bathroom range from Rs 140/200 to air-con rooms for Rs 450/550. There are also a few tiny rooms with shared bathroom for Rs 90/130. The hotel food is reasonable, and

served on a veranda overlooking a narrow garden. Early morning boat trips to the ghats can be arranged for Rs 75.

Hotel Ajaya (☎ *343707, Kabir Chaura Marg)* looks like a mid-range hotel at first glance but the rooms are cheap enough. Clean, pleasant rooms with private bathroom, air cooling and colour TV are Rs 150/200; air-con rooms are Rs 450/500. The checkout is open 24 hours, and there's a restaurant and bar here.

The UP *Tourist Bungalow* (☎ *343413, Parade Kothi)* has a pleasant garden but is otherwise typically institutional. Dorm beds cost Rs 75. Rooms with private bathroom go for Rs 175/225, deluxe air-cooled rooms with TV are Rs 325/400 and air-con rooms are Rs 550/625. Breakfast is an extra Rs 50 per person. The UP Tourism office is in this complex.

Most other places in this street are pretty basic. *Hotel Amar* (☎ *343509*) was doing some renovations when we visited (putting down the requisite marble floor) so it mightn't be too gloomy. Rooms with private bathroom and hot water cost Rs 130/175.

There's a string of hotels lining the Grand Trunk Rd opposite the station with rooms from Rs 150/200, but they're noisy and not too clean. Try *Nar Indra* (☎ *343586*). It has 24-hour checkout and a veg/nonveg restaurant.

Places to Stay – Mid-range

The *Hotel Plaza Inn* (☎ *348210, fax 340504)*, not far from the Tourist Bungalow, is a modern place with comfortable, air-con rooms and all amenities. It's good value at Rs 750/950.

The cantonment area, on the northern side of Varanasi Junction station, contains a sprinkling of budget hotels and most of the city's upmarket accommodation. It's the place to retreat to when the claustrophobia of the old city gets to you. If you stay here, you'll depend on hotel restaurants for sustenance since there are few independent eating places in the area.

Hotel Surya (☎ *343014, fax 348330, The Mall)* is the pick of the places to stay if you need to wind down from the rigours of being on the road. It's set around a pleasant garden and has rooms with bathroom and hot water for Rs 200/250, or Rs 500/650

INDIA

with air-con. The hotel is popular with overlanders, and you can camp on the lawn for Rs 50.

Hotel India (☎ 342912, fax 348327, 59 Patel Nagar) is more upmarket. Well-appointed air-con rooms with bathtubs and TV start from Rs 950/1200. The hotel has an excellent restaurant and a cellar bar.

Hotel Barahdari (☎ 330040, e baradari@ la1.vsnl.net.in) is not far from the main post office and within walking distance of the ghats. It's run by a friendly Jain family and has a vegetarian restaurant and a peaceful garden. Comfortable, smallish, air-cooled rooms with attached hot-water bathroom and TV cost Rs 350/400, Rs 550/600 with air-con.

Places to Eat
Godaulia & the Old City The food in the old city is pretty uninspiring. Cafes offer a standard travellers' menu consisting of Western breakfasts and snacks that mostly involve giving their jaffle (toasted sandwich) machine a serious work out. Varanasi is well known for its sweets and high-quality paan, and the alleyways of the old city are full of shops offering ample opportunity to indulge in either. Places in the old city are not supposed to serve alcohol, though in a few places you can get beer, usually not very cold and sometimes served in a teapot. There's also a government bhang shop not far from the Manikarnika Ghat, where a man sitting behind a grill window dispenses bhang cookies like cinema tickets at the box office!

Some of the places in Varanasi's old city were reported to have been involved in a food-poisoning scam aimed at extracting medical insurance from travellers in 1998. This seems to have stopped, but you should keep your ears open and eat where other travellers and locals are eating.

Shanti Guest House, *Yogi Lodge*, *Trimurti Guest House* and *Vishnu Rest House* all have restaurants popular with travellers. Shanti (open 24 hours) and Vishnu both have excellent views. The food at all these places is pretty dull, with vague attempts at continental as well as Indian and Chinese.

Ganga Fuji, not far from the Vishwanath Temple, is a snug place offering Western breakfasts as well as Indian, Chinese and Japanese meals for between Rs 25 and Rs 40, including nonveg. There's live classical Indian music in the evenings, starting at 7.30 pm.

In the backstreets behind Vishnu Restaurant, *Monalisa Restaurant* is 'restaurant of the moment' among travellers. It's a cosy little place with thalis for only Rs 15, chicken tikka (chicken marinated in spices then dry-roasted) for Rs 35, Japanese dishes for Rs 22, and reasonable attempts at Italian, Israeli and Chinese food.

Moving away from the river, *Ayyar's Cafe* is a modest veg eatery on Dasaswamedh Ghat Rd serving good masala dosas for less than Rs 20, and full thalis for Rs 30. *Keshari*, down a small alley opposite, is a clean, popular veg restaurant providing an extensive menu of meals and snacks. Main dishes are around Rs 25 to Rs 40.

Temple Restaurant in the Hotel Ganges offers a 1st-floor view of the hustle and bustle of Dasaswamedh Ghat Rd. It serves good veg/nonveg Indian fare, Chinese food and Western breakfasts. There's live Indian classical music in the evenings. On Luxa Rd, *Benzore Restaurant* at the Hotel Empire has a great rooftop dining area and the usual menu of Indian and Chinese for under Rs 80. *Shahi Restaurant*, about 1km further west, is highly recommended locally for some of the best dosas (Rs 16) in town, as well as soups (Rs 20) and veg biryani (Rs 36).

Sindhi Restaurant, by the Lalita Cinema, also prepares a range of good south Indian vegetarian food for less than Rs 30, and thalis for Rs 25. Even more popular is the *Kerala Cafe (Mandapur Rd)*, across the junction, which mostly specialises in dosas for only Rs 10 to Rs 20.

Bread of Life Bakery (Sonarpur Rd) is a haven for Western-style breads and biscuits. It also has a restaurant section with Western meals for Rs 95, plus breakfasts and baked potatoes. It's open 8 am to 9 pm, closed Monday.

Chetganj & Cantonment Areas There are several places to choose from in these areas.

El Parador, next to Hotel Sandona, is a long-standing place offering an eclectic menu with Greek, Mexican and Italian dishes, all chalked up on a blackboard.

There's a relaxed 'traveller' ambience here and it's run by a friendly family, but unfortunately the food is a bit overpriced these days with most mains around Rs 100.

Poonam Restaurant in the Hotel Pradeep, Jagatganj, has good service and decent Indian, Chinese and continental dishes. Half tandoori chicken is Rs 100 and fish tikka Rs 110, and you can get things like roast lamb (Rs 125) and vegetable au gratin (Rs 85).

Around the corner, the *Kamesh Hut Garden Restaurant* has a pleasant garden setting, attentive service, and excellent-value food. Butter chicken is Rs 180, vegetable fried rice Rs 30 and pizzas from Rs 40. Breakfast is served from 7 am.

Hotel restaurants are the best bet in the cantonment area. *Canton Restaurant* at the Hotel Surya serves good veg/nonveg fare and Western stand-bys. The restaurant overlooks the hotel garden and a lazy breakfast on the lawn makes a great start to the day.

Palm Springs Restaurant in the Hotel India has excellent Indian cuisine and a pleasant air-con dining room. Indian veg dishes cost around Rs 100, continental dishes are Rs 150 to Rs 200 and beer is reasonable at Rs 60.

Entertainment

Varanasi is not renowned for its nightlife. There are no bars in the old city. The best places to have a drink are the top hotels in the cantonment area (Hotel India and the Hotel Vaibhav next door have decent bars). Otherwise, there is only a handful of places you can go for a drink and they're usually darkened rooms with little atmosphere. Try *Yelchiko Bar & Restaurant (Vidyapeeth Rd)*, open from 11 am to 10.30 pm, *Basant Bar & Restaurant (Chaitganj Marg)* or the *Dawat Restaurant* at Hotel Ajaya. A bottle of beer costs Rs 70 to Rs 80.

Indian classical music recitals are held at several music-teaching centres in the old city, considerably covering every night of the week except Sunday. They include: the International Music Centre Ashram, south of Dasaswamedh Ghat Rd (at 8 pm on Wednesday and Saturday; Rs 40); the Sri Vaishnava Music Ashram (at 6.30 pm on Tuesday and Friday; free); and the Triveni Music Centre, near Panday Ghat (Monday at 7 pm and Thursday at 9 pm; free).

Shopping

Varanasi is famous throughout India for silk brocades and beautiful Benares saris. However, there are lots of rip-off merchants and commission people at work. Invitations to 'come to my home for tea' will inevitably mean to somebody's silk showroom, where you will be pressured into buying things. See the UP Tourism city map (free from the tourist offices) for addresses of government emporiums and 'recognised' souvenir shops. City tours (not run by the tourist office) will also involve numerous unscheduled stops in silk shops. Mohan Silk Stores, 5/54 Viswanath Gali, a few side streets south of the GT Rd near the train station, is a small shop with a good range of silk scarves (from Rs 200), saris (from Rs 500 to Rs 8000) and prints.

There's a market west of the main post office called Golghar where the makers of silk brocades sell directly to local shops. You can get cheaper silk brocade in this area than in the big stores in the chowk area, but you must be careful about the quality. Mixtures of silk and cotton can look very like pure silk to the untrained eye. The market is closed on Sunday. Pilikothi, a Muslim area north-east of the main post office (near the Yamuna Cinema), is another area worth visiting for silk. Here you'll find a silk factory called Weaver's Handloom Enterprises (☎ 331817) which has been operating – using handlooms – since 1890.

Varanasi is also renowned for its ingenious toys, musical instruments and expensive Bhadohi carpets. There's a superb range of local and national products (including Kashmiri carpets) in the fixed-price Cottage Industries Exposition in the cantonment, opposite the Hotel Taj Ganges. Its prices are high but a visit will give you an idea of the relative costs of various items.

Getting There & Away

Air Varanasi is on the popular daily tourist shuttle route linking Khajuraho (US$105), Agra (US$110) and Delhi (US$125) four times a week. There are also daily Indian Airlines flights to/from Mumbai. The Indian Airlines office (☎ 345959) is in the cantonment near the Hotel de Paris. Sahara India Airlines also flies to/from Delhi (US$110), Mumbai (US$234) and Kolkata (Calcutta).

INDIA

Indian Airlines flies direct to Kathmandu five times a week, but it can be difficult getting a seat.

Bus Varanasi's bus station is a few hundred metres north-east of Varanasi Junction train station. It's a fairly sleepy depot and there's no timetable information in English. Buses lined up on the street out front are mostly faster, private buses. For Gorakhpur there are frequent express buses (Rs 87, seven hours), mostly in the morning and evening (the last one is at 8.30 pm). Direct buses to Sunauli (Rs 123, 10 hours) are also frequent. There are also buses to Allahabad (Rs 50, three hours), Lucknow (Rs 110, 8½ hours), one service to Agra (Rs 225, 14 hours) and one overnight service to Delhi (Rs 218, 18 hours). The train is a much better option for Agra and Delhi.

There are no direct buses to Khajuraho so take a train to Satna and a bus to Khajuraho (four hours) from there.

To Nepal Touts and travel agents, particularly around the Tourist Bungalow, sell 'through tickets' to Kathmandu or Pokhara for around Rs 400. Whatever they claim, you will have to change to a Nepali public bus at the border as there are no direct buses on this route. The ticket usually includes a night in a cheap hotel in Sunauli (Nepal side). It's cheaper and just as easy to take public buses. You could also catch an express train to Gorakhpur and pick up a bus to Sunauli from there.

Train Varanasi Junction (also known as Varanasi Cantonment) is the main station. There is a separate reservation centre building on the left as you approach the station, but foreign tourist quota tickets must be purchased at the Foreign Tourist Assistance Bureau on the left as you enter the main station building. This office is rarely crowded and is open daily except Sunday between 8 am and 8 pm.

The best trains to catch to Gorakhpur are the *Kashi Express* at 3.20 pm (Rs 62/97, 2nd class/sleeper) or the 5.50 am *Intercity Express* (2nd class) only).

Not all trains between Delhi and Kolkata (Calcutta) stop at Varanasi Junction but most halt at Mughal Serai, 12km south of Varanasi – check this when buying your ticket. This station is a 45-minute ride away by bus (Rs 5), tempo (Rs 10) or autorickshaw (Rs 100) along a congested stretch of the Grand Trunk Rd. You can make reservations at Varanasi Junction train station for trains leaving from Mughal Serai. The trip to or from Delhi takes between 12 and 17 hours and the 788km journey (via Lucknow) costs Rs 15/35 in 2nd class/sleeper, Rs 680 for three-tier air-con and Rs 1088 for two-tier air-con. Trains via Tundla are slightly cheaper (767km). Useful trains are the daily *Kashi Vishwanath Express* at 2 pm and the *Shramjeevi Express* at 3.20 pm, which both run to New Delhi station; the *Poorva Express* departs from Varanasi at 8 pm on Wednesday, Thursday and Sunday, but from Mughal Serai on other days. Several other trains, including the *Farraka Express*, terminate at Old Delhi station.

The train to Agra (663km) takes around 13 hours and costs Rs 135/210 in 2nd class/ sleeper, Rs 608/972 in three/two-tier air-con. Only one train, the overnight *Marudhar Express*, runs directly from Varanasi to Agra Cantonment station, but you'll need to book ahead for this. Several others on the Delhi-Kolkata (Calcutta) line go via Tundla station, about an hour by bus from Agra. This is a slightly shorter trip so the trains are cheaper (Rs 185 in sleeper class).

There are also plenty of trains east to Kolkata, formerly Calcutta (Howrah station; 678km), which take from 15 to 20 hours, and to Patna. If you want to visit the outstanding temples of Khajuraho you'll first have to get to Satna on the overnight *Kurla Express* (Rs 97 in sleeper class) and take a bus from there.

Travellers should keep a close eye on their baggage while on trains heading into and out of Varanasi, as it's notorious for theft.

Getting Around

To/From the Airport Babatpur airport is 22km north-west of the city. A bus runs from the Indian Airlines office at 10.30 am and 2.30 pm, going via the Government of India tourist office. The fare is Rs 35 and it takes around 45 minutes. Rates at the prepaid booth at the train station are Rs 120 for an autorickshaw and Rs 200 for a taxi – you won't get better than this trying to bargain on the street. In the opposite direction, rickshaw-wallahs may charge much less since they assume they'll pick up a commission at the hotel where they drop you.

Bus Local buses are very crowded unless you can get on at the starting point – many start from outside the main train station. They cost Rs 2 to Rs 5, but they're irregular and you need to beware of pickpockets. A useful bus goes from Varanasi Junction train station to Lanka, which is close to Benares Hindu University.

Taxi & Autorickshaw Varanasi's autorickshaw drivers are hell-bent on commissions. If you arrive late at night and pick one up from the train station they can be downright dangerous because there's a good chance they won't take you where you want to go. Since no vehicles can enter the narrow streets of the old city, they dislike having to take you to a hotel near the main ghats. The best move if you intend to stay in this area is to ask to be taken to a major landmark such as Godaulia Crossing or Dasaswamedh Ghat.

The other problem is bargaining a fair price, but this has been made easier by the introduction of prepaid booths on the southern side of Varanasi Junction train station. When you arrive at the train station, ignore the touts and head straight for these booths, which are supposedly staffed 24 hours. Some of the displayed prepaid taxi rates from there are: Dasaswamedh Ghat Rs 75, Assi Ghat Rs 80, Benares Hindu University or Sarnath Rs 100, Mughal Serai Rs 150. Some prepaid autorickshaw rates are: Dasaswamedh Ghat or Godaulia Crossing Rs 30, Sarnath Rs 50 and Mughal Serai Rs 100.

Shared Autorickshaw & Tempo These operate along set routes with fixed prices (Rs 3 to Rs 5). They can be the best way to get around the city cheaply, although not when you have hefty baggage. From the stand outside the northern entrance of Varanasi Junction train station there are tempos to the cantonment. There's a stand outside the southern entrance for destinations including Lahurabir.

Cycle-Rickshaw Figures quoted for cycle-rickshaw trips typically start at five times the local price instead of just double. In theory, a trip between the train station and Godaulia should cost about Rs 15; from the cantonment hotels to Godaulia should be around Rs 25. However, these prices are what Indians would pay, and it is generally accepted locally that foreigners should pay more. Unless you want to spend half your visit haggling, expect to pay a bit higher, but bargain hard!

SARNATH
☎ 0542
The Buddha came to this hamlet, 10km north-east of Varanasi, to preach his message of the 'middle way' to nirvana after he achieved enlightenment at Bodhgaya. Later, the great Buddhist emperor Ashoka erected magnificent stupas and monasteries here.

Even if you're not particularly interested in Buddhist culture, Sarnath is an easy half-day trip and its monuments are set in tranquil landscaped gardens, making it a pleasant escape from the madness of Varanasi.

Between the 5th and 7th centuries AD, Sarnath was at its peak, boasting some 1500 monks, a stupa nearly 100m high, the emporer Ashoka's mighty stone pillar and many other wonders. Soon after, Buddhism went into decline and when Muslim invaders destroyed and desecrated the city's buildings, Sarnath was reduced to little more than a set of ruins. It was not until 1835 when British archaeologists started excavations that Sarnath regained some of its past glory. It's now a major Buddhist centre.

Lumbering Tata trucks and Ambassador taxis are among the many vehicles vying for space on India's crowded roads.

KIERAN MANGAN

INDIA

During the **Buddha Purnima Festival** in May, Sarnath celebrates the birth of the Buddha with a big fair and a procession. Although you may be able to arrange to stay in some of Sarnath's monasteries, you'd be better off going to Bodhgaya or Dharamsala if you're interested in studying Buddhism.

There's a UP Tourism office (☎ 586965) at the Tourist Bungalow in Varanasi which can provide a basic map of the site and arrange guides.

Things to See

The 34m **Dhamekh Stupa** dominates the site and is believed to mark the spot where the Buddha preached his famous sermon. In its present form it dates from around AD 500 but was probably rebuilt a number of times. The nearby **Jain Temple**, built in 1824, is thought to mark the birthplace of the 11th Jain tirthankar, Shreyanshnath.

Ashoka is said to have meditated in the building known as the **main shrine**. The foundations are all that can now be seen, and to the north of it are the extensive ruins of the monasteries. Standing in front of the main shrine are the remains of **Ashoka's pillar**. At one time this stood over 20m high, but the lion capital is now in the Archaeological Museum. Entry to this part of the site is free on Friday, otherwise you need to buy the Archaeological Museum ticket to get in.

The **Archaeological Museum** is airy and well presented, with the main attraction being the superb capital from the Ashokan pillar. The capital, with its four back-to-back lions, has been adopted as the state emblem of modern India and can be seen on every banknote. Other finds from the site include figures and sculptures from Sarnath's Mauryan, Kushan and Gupta periods. Among them is the earliest Buddha image found at Sarnath and many images of Hindu gods dating from the 9th to 12th centuries. The museum is open 10 am to 5 pm daily except Friday (Rs 2). Buy tickets from the booth across the road.

Mulgandha Kuti Vihar is a modern temple opened in 1931. A bodhi tree growing here was transplanted in the same year from a tree in Anuradhapura, Sri Lanka, which is said to be an offspring of the original tree under which the Buddha attained enlightenment. There's a group of statues here showing the Buddha giving his first sermon to his five first disciples. Inside there's a range of books on sale relating to Buddhism. The temple is closed between 11.30 am and 1.30 pm. North of the Mulgandha Kuti Vihar is the depressing **deer park**, where the deer inmates are accompanied by some Indian birds and waterfowl.

You can also visit the modern **temples** in the Thai, Chinese, Tibetan, Burmese and Japanese monasteries, as well as the ruined **Chaukhandi Stupa**.

Places to Stay & Eat

The *Hotel Mrigadava* (☎ 586965) is the UP Tourism place with basic dorm beds for Rs 70, air-cooled rooms with private bathroom from Rs 250/300 (Rs 450/550 with air-con) and a dull restaurant. It's on the right as you approach the main crossroads in town.

Anand is a small, inexpensive restaurant serving Indian and Chinese food. There's small open-air *restaurant* opposite the museum serving cheap fare.

Getting There & Away

Despite what the autorickshaw drivers will tell you, crowded local buses depart frequently from the southern side of Varanasi Junction train station (Rs 5, 45 minutes). Ask for the Mahenagar bus. An autorickshaw to the site costs Rs 50 and a taxi Rs 100 (prepaid rates). Only a few local trains stop at Sarnath.

GORAKHPUR
☎ 0551 • pop 575,000

Most travellers happily pass straight through Gorakhpur on their way to or from Nepal. There's not a great deal to detain you here, and the city is infamous for its annual plagues of flies and mosquitoes. It is, however, an essential junction if you've taken the train from Delhi or Varanasi.

Gorakhpur is named after the sage, Yogi Gorakhnath. The **Gorakhnath Temple** is a couple of kilometres north-west of the city centre and is worth visiting if you have time to fill in between transport connections. The city is also home to well-known Hindu religious publishers Geeta Press.

If India has become all too much for you, the **Arogya Mandir** (☎ 310469) is a natural healing centre about 6km north of

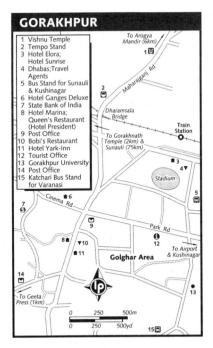

GORAKHPUR

1 Vishnu Temple
2 Tempo Stand
3 Hotel Elora; Hotel Sunrise
4 Dhabas; Travel Agents
5 Bus Stand for Sunauli & Kushinagar
6 Hotel Ganges Deluxe
7 State Bank of India
8 Hotel Marina; Queen's Restaurant (Hotel President)
9 Post Office
10 Bobi's Restaurant
11 Hotel Yark-Inn
12 Tourist Office
13 Gorakhpur University
14 Post Office
15 Katchari Bus Stand for Varanasi

the train station. It has a slightly sterile atmosphere – like a hospital – and dabbles in all sorts of natural cures including yoga, hydrotherapy, massage, mud packs and strict diets. Anyone can be admitted for a short residential course. There's a one-off charge of Rs 150 and dormitory accommodation costs Rs 90 a day. One traveller we met described it as 'an interesting cultural experience'. You can get there by cycle-rickshaw (Rs 25) or take a tempo from Dharamsala Bridge (Rs 5), about five minutes walk west of the train station.

Information

There's a helpful little tourist office in the train station where you can get train information and be pointed in the right direction for buying tickets. The main UP Tourism office (☎ 335450) on Park Rd can give you a map and local information on Gorakhpur and Kushinagar (see later in this chapter).

The State Bank of India on Bank Rd exchanges cash and AmEx travellers cheques (US dollars or pounds sterling). The Bank of Baroda, on Maharajganj Rd, gives cash advances on Visa and MasterCard.

Places to Stay & Eat

The most convenient hotels are the cheapies across from the train station on Station Rd. It's a slightly seedy area and can be very noisy (get a room at the back), but it's handy for the Sunauli bus stand, and buses coming from Sunauli will also drop you off here.

Hotel Elora (☎ 200647) is the best of this bunch. Rooms at the back have balconies and are sheltered from the worst of the noise. Singles/doubles cost from Rs 110/150 with private bathroom and there are doubles with air cooler for Rs 200 and air-con for Rs 425. Nearby, the *Hotel Sunrise* (☎ 337458) charges Rs 110/175 for reasonably clean rooms with private bathroom, Rs 175/225 with air cooler and Rs 300/425 with air-con. The checkout is open 24 hours.

The *retiring rooms* at the train station have dorm beds for Rs 50 and singles/doubles for Rs 90/140.

There's a better standard of hotels in the Golghar area, about a Rs 10 rickshaw ride from the train station. *Hotel Yark-Inn* (☎ 338233) is not one of them, but it has a range of passable rooms with private bathroom and (usually) TV. Prices go from Rs 120/200 up to Rs 500 for a large air-con double.

Hotel Marina (☎ 337630), tucked in behind the Hotel President, doesn't look too flash but the rooms are fine. Clean rooms with private bathroom and television start at Rs 195/245 and air-conditioned doubles at Rs 475.

The small outdoor eateries near the train station are cheap, quick with the food and not too bad, although you'll need plenty of mosquito repellent in the evenings.

The busy *Bobi's Restaurant* at the Ambar Hotel in the city centre has decent veg and nonveg fare and serves pastries and ice cream.

The austere *Queen's Restaurant* in the Hotel President is a better option if you want a sit-down meal or a Western breakfast in relative comfort. It's open late and serves reasonably cheap Indian and Chinese food. Chicken curry is Rs 45.

There's a bar at the *Hotel Ganges Deluxe*, but don't expect a raging night out. It's open till 11 pm.

INDIA

Getting There & Away

Bus There are several bus stands scattered around the city, but the most interesting are the Katchari bus stand (for Varanasi), about 2km south of the train station, and the Sunauli bus stand, only about 300m from the station. Buses to Kushinagar (Rs 19, 1½ hours) and Faizabad (for Ayodhya; Rs 54, four hours) also depart from the Sunauli stand every 30 minutes or so.

To Sunauli & Nepal There are regular departures for the border at Sunauli (Rs 33, three hours) from 5 am onwards from the bus stand just south of the train station. You'll need to be on an early bus from Gorakhpur (no later than 6.30 am) to be sure of catching a day bus from the border to Pokhara or Kathmandu. Travel agents along Station Rd offer 'express' tickets (Rs 325, 12 hours) to Kathmandu or Pokhara but you will still have to change buses at the border. Doing it yourself is cheaper and gives you a choice of buses.

To Varanasi Buses to Varanasi (Rs 86, seven hours) depart roughly every half hour from 6 am to 10 pm from the Katchari bus stand, a Rs 10 cycle-rickshaw ride southeast of the city centre. Travel agents opposite the train station sell 'deluxe' bus tickets for Rs 175 (six hours).

Train Gorakhpur has direct train connections south to Varanasi and Kolkata (Calcutta) and west to Lucknow and Delhi. There's a handy foreigner's ticket window (No 811) in the reservations hall. There are five daily trains to and from Varanasi (Rs 97/477 in sleeper/two-tier air-con), taking five to six hours. The overnight *Chaura Express* arrives in Varanasi at 4.30 am, so it's worth hanging out at the station until daylight if you take this train. The *Intercity Express* (express in name only) departs at 4.50 pm, takes closer to seven hours and only has 2nd-class seats (Rs 62). The early-morning trains are the best ones to get if you spend the night in Gorakhpur.

Trains into and out of Varanasi are particularly notorious for theft, so keep an eye on your luggage at all times.

Trains to Delhi (Rs 224/648/1037 in sleeper/three-tier air-con/two-tier air-con) take 14 to 19 hours via Lucknow. The *Vaishali Express* at 5.15 pm is one of the quickest, stops at New Delhi station and has all carriage classes.

KUSHINAGAR

If you're interested in the Buddhist trail, Kushinagar, 55km east of Gorakhpur, is worth a visit. The Buddha is reputed to have breathed his last words, 'Decay is inherent in all component things' and expired here. Now pilgrims come in large numbers to see the remains of his brick **cremation stupa**, the reclining Buddha figure in the **Mahaparinirvana Temple**, the modern **IndoJapan-Sri Lanka Buddhist Centre** and the numerous Buddhist monasteries here. The tourist office opposite the Myanmar monastery is helpful and open Monday to Saturday from 10 am to 5 pm, and sometimes on Sunday.

The *International Cultural Guesthouse* (☎ 05564-72164) is a cheap option opposite the Buddhist Centre. Bare doubles cost Rs 100. *Pathik Niwas* (☎ 05564-71038), UP Tourism's hotel, has a garden, dorm beds for Rs 100 and singles/doubles from Rs 400/500.

There are frequent buses from Gorakhpur (Rs 20, 1½ hours) so it's easy enough to make a day trip here (the last bus back is at around 6 pm). The Kushinagar bus stand is several kilometres from the temples and monasteries, so get off/on by the Kushinagar Police Post, and follow the southwards turn-off for the temples.

SUNAULI
☎ 05522

Straddling the India-Nepal border, this is little more than a bus stop, a couple of hotels, a few shops and a 24-hour border post. There's a much greater range of facilities on the Nepalese side, where the atmosphere is decidedly more upbeat. Indians and Nepalis are free to wander back and forth between the two parts of Sunauli (usually spelt Sonauli on the Indian side) without going through any formalities. Foreigners, however, must officially exit one country and acquire the requisite visa for the other (see the 'India Border Crossings' boxed text at the end of this chapter).

INDIA

Sunauli to Agra

Cycling days: 8
Distance: 910km

Ashley and I cycled to Varanasi in three days via Basti (seven hours) and Shahganj (five hours), avoiding Gorakhpur. It was scenic but this part of Uttar Pradesh (UP) is clearly not a tourist area. On some tea stops we would be surrounded by 50 or more people, causing minor chaos on the roads. The level of 'hassle' for cyclists in India is certainly greater than in Nepal or Pakistan.

Indian drivers were the worst we encountered, especially on the road from Varanasi to Agra, and especially the bus and jeep-taxi drivers. Cyclists are the lowest caste on the road (one up from pedestrians). The roads throughout UP are reasonably flat, and the traffic approaching Varanasi was not too bad.

On the five-day ride from Varanasi to Agra we alternated between the main trunk road (in reasonably good condition) and parallel minor roads (lighter traffic). From Varanasi, we rode to Allahabad (120km, six hours), a friendly university town worth a stop. Then to Fatehpur (five hours) and Etawah (eleven hours). The final 200km approaching Agra was particularly prone to hassle – mostly from offensive men. Reaching Agra, a tourist spot, was like finding an oasis, although that didn't last. The Taj was nice, but it was good to leave.

Sue Cooper

The State Bank of India in Sunauli does not change money, but there are numerous foreign-exchange offices on the Nepalese side offering competitive rates. Note that you can pay for bus tickets and just about anything else in Indian rupees on the Nepalese side of the border.

There are several hotels and restaurants along the road between the bus stand and the border, but there's no compelling reason to stay here unless there's a problem with your visa and the powers that be won't let you leave India. The better places to stay (although not by much) are across the border.

Hotel Niranjana (☎ 38201), about 600m from the border, is a UP Tourism hotel, and is a clean, friendly place with a garden. Dorm beds cost Rs 50; rooms with private bathroom, hot water and air cooler are Rs 275/350; air-con rooms with TV are Rs 450/500. There's also a *restaurant* here.

Getting There & Away

Buses to Indian cities depart from the Sunauli bus stand on the edge of town, about 800m from the border post. There are buses to Gorakhpur every half hour or so between 5 am and 7 pm (Rs 40, three hours) and direct buses to Varanasi (Rs 123, 10 hours). There are direct buses to Delhi but you're better off heading to Gorakhpur and taking the train (see the Gorakhpur section for details).

If you're entering India, be wary of touts and travel agents offering onward combined bus/rail tickets, since these are not 100% reliable. It's easy enough to arrange onwards train travel yourself at the Gorakhpur or Varanasi train stations.

To get to Nepal, you simply walk or take a cycle-rickshaw across the border, pausing at the immigration post on each side, then head for the bus stand.

India Border Crossings

India to Nepal

Buses from Varanasi or from Gorakhpur stop on the outskirts of Sunauli, about 1km from the actual border. Although the border is open 24 hours, if you arrive at dawn it's likely that you'll have to wake the Indian guard to stamp you out of the country. Having your bags checked is very unlikely.

You either walk or hire a rickshaw (around Rs 10) to take you to the border, literally a gate in the middle of the town. Don't forget to stop at the easy-to-miss Indian immigration checkpoint on your right, about 100m from the border. If you decide to rest and clean up before the onward journey, the hotels on the Nepali side of Sunauli offer better value.

The Nepali immigration office is on your right, just inside the gate. If you don't have a visa you can get a 60-day tourist visa here for US$30 (exact cash is best). You should have a passport photo with you for one of the two forms you'll need to fill in. There are moneychangers in the row of restaurants and hotels around 100m beyond the immigration office.

Buses to Kathmandu and Pokhara leave roughly at hourly intervals from 4.30 am onwards.

Nepal to India

Whether you've come from Kathmandu, Tadi Bazaar or Pokhara, the bus will drop you either at the Sunauli bus stand or (if you booked through a private agent) outside Hotel Buddha. Both are only a few hundred metres from the border, and close to cheap hotels if you arrive late and want to stay the night.

The Nepal immigration office, just inside the border (on the left as you face India) is open 24 hours. There's also a tourist office here. You have to fill out a form but it takes only a few minutes to be stamped out of the country. From here you walk into India (or take a cycle-rickshaw). Look out for the very informal Indian immigration checkpoint – it's just a couple of desks outside a nondescript building on your left about 100m from the border (look for the blue-and-red border sign). Again you fill out a form and you must already have a valid Indian visa in your passport.

The bus stand is another 800m further on; from there you can catch a bus to Gorakhpur (for train connections) or direct to Varanasi.

NEPAL

Kathmandu

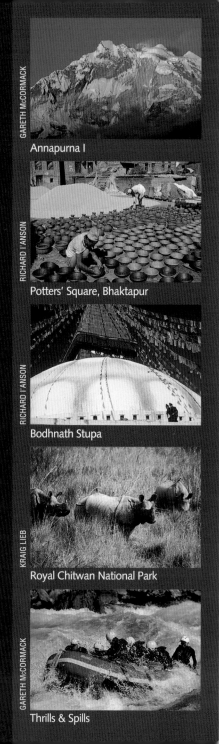

Annapurna I
GARETH McCORMACK

Potters' Square, Bhaktapur
RICHARD I'ANSON

Bodhnath Stupa
RICHARD I'ANSON

Royal Chitwan National Park
KRAIG LIEB

Thrills & Spills
GARETH McCORMACK

NEPAL
highlights

Mountain Views
From the south end of Pokhara the Annapurna skyline is impressive; a three-hour walk to Sarangkot offers an even better view. Ghorapani has one of the best mountain views in Nepal, and from Nagarkot catch the panoramic vista of the Himalayan range from Dhaulagiri to Everest.

Durbar Square, Kathmandu
The seat of Kathmandu's royalty until a century ago, this historic area contains the ancient royal palace and a stunning collection of temples and structures, including the fascinating Kumari Bahal, the house of the Kumari Devi, Kathmandu's living goddess.

Bhaktapur
Deserted in the early morning or the evening, the narrow cobbled streets of medieval Bhaktapur are a scene from another world. Potters' Square, the Peacock Window and the magnificent Golden Gate are all must-see sights.

Temples & Stupas
The wealth of religious architecture in the Kathmandu Valley is stunning. Pashupatinath and the huge Bodhnath stupa are just east of Kathmandu city, while the stunning hilltop Swayambhunath Temple is to the west.

Royal Chitwan National Park
The Royal Chitwan National Park offers the most likely chance of coming face to face with a two-tonne one-horned rhinoceros – best seen from the back of an elephant.

Thrills & Spills
Mountain biking, white-water rafting, trekking and bungee jumping – Nepal is something of a thrill seeker's dream.

Nepal

For such a small country (at least in length and breadth), Nepal commands a great deal of respect and wonder. Many experienced travellers regard this as their favourite destination: for its scenery, its people, its culture and its challenges.

Nepal's greatest attraction is the Himalaya, the string of mighty mountains draped across the north of the country. They offer not only breathtaking scenery, but some of the best trekking on earth. Travellers coming here to trek soon discover the warmth and friendliness of the Nepali people and the historical treasure trove that is the Kathmandu Valley.

In the valley you'll find not only the thriving city of Kathmandu, but the fascinating secondary royal cities of Patan and Bhaktapur, each a living museum in its own right. Scattered around are villages, terraced fields, Tibetan communities, age-old temples and walking trails that take you to the very rim of the valley from where you can clearly see the panorama of the Himalaya.

History and culture aside, Nepal is an outdoor enthusiasts' dream. As well as trekking, some of the world's finest white-water rafting rivers flow from the mountains and the sport is well developed and affordable by Western standards. Physically fit travellers can take to the hills on a mountain bike, flush travellers can take to the sky in a hot-air balloon and brave travellers can bungee jump into a 160m gorge. Finally, down on the subtropical lowland Terai, the Royal Chitwan National Park offers some of the finest wildlife watching in West Asia. A close encounter with a rhinoceros is to be expected.

Nepal is a developing country and is not without its environmental and social problems, but the upbeat nature of its people is infectious. Even on the well-trodden trails

Nepal at a Glance

Capital: Kathmandu (population 535,000)

Population: 24.7 million (2000 est)

Area: 147,181 sq km

Head of state: King Birendra Bir Bikram Shahar Dev

Currency: Nepali rupee (Rs)

Country telephone code: ☎ 977

Exchange rates:

country	unit		Nepali rupee (Rs)
Australia	A$1	=	40
EU	€1	=	68
UK	UK£1	=	107
USA	US$1	=	74

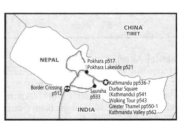

you won't walk far without being greeted with a smile and *'Namaste'*. After the rigours of travelling overland from İstanbul, stepping into Nepal is like stepping into another world. Make sure you leave enough time in your trip to appreciate it.

THE ROUTE

Nepal constitutes the shortest part of the İstanbul to Kathmandu route and, in fact, the route covers only a fraction of central Nepal. Some travellers will no doubt lurch straight out of India and onto a bus bound for Kathmandu, but there's plenty more to see and do in this tiny kingdom.

Starting at the border crossing at Sunauli (Sonauli on the Indian side) there's a road heading north to Pokhara at the foot of the

Money Matters

Prices in this chapter are either in Nepalese rupees (Rs) which, at the time of writing, was fixed at 0.625 Indian rupees (or INRs 1 = NPRs 1.60), or US dollars (US$).

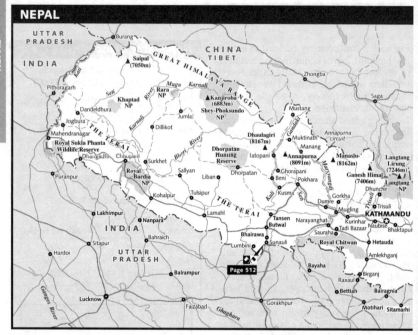

NEPAL

UTTAR PRADESH

INDIA

CHINA
TIBET

beautiful Annapurna range. From there it's a straightforward trip east to Kathmandu, but it's worth stopping on the way at the Royal Chitwan National Park. Alternatively, you can head straight from Sunauli to Kathmandu, via Tadi Bazaar, the jumping off point for Royal Chitwan.

Sunauli & Around

SUNAULI
☎ 071
The minute you cross the border at Sunauli, you know you've left India and entered Nepal. Things somehow feel calmer and less chaotic. Still, there's nothing in Sunauli worth staying for, but if you arrive late in the day you may need to spend the night here.

It's also the base for visiting Lumbini, birthplace of Siddhartha Gautama – better known as the Buddha. About 4km north of Sunauli, **Bhairawa** is a larger town with airline offices, banks and more hotels. There's nothing of interest here either but it's an alternative (and closer) base if you plan to visit Lumbini.

Orientation & Information
Sunauli itself straddles India and Nepal with the border marked by a gate in the middle of town. On the Nepal side you'll find the customs and immigration office just inside the gate (to the right as you enter Nepal), along with a friendly tourist office (☎ 20304). Less than 100m to the north is the bus park and farther along is a string of budget hotels, restaurants, travel agents and moneychangers. Indian rupees are accepted currency in Sunauli and Bhairawa, and you should get close to the official rate at the moneychangers. (Note: INRs 500 notes are not accepted anywhere in Nepal, even at banks.) If you're heading into India, change your Nepalese money here as it's not so readily accepted over the border.

Places to Stay & Eat
Hotel Plaza is probably the best of an average bunch with clean singles/doubles with hot-water shower for Rs 200/300. It's about 100m north of the bus park on the left-hand side of the road. Almost opposite, where the private buses from Pokhara drop off, *Hotel Buddha* has grim rooms but they're

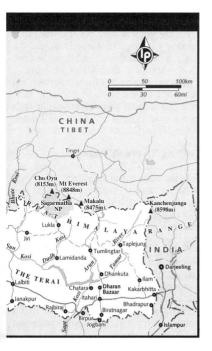

cheap at Rs 100 and Rs 150 for doubles with private bathroom. There's a travel agent and a very ordinary *restaurant* here.

Hotel Mamata (☎ 20312) is basic but a reasonable option if you're after a cheap bed. A place in a six-bed dorm is Rs 50 and a double with shared bathroom is only Rs 80. Singles/doubles with private bathroom are Rs 100/200.

There are rooftop or 'garden' *restaurants* attached to most guesthouses along here, as well as couple of independently run restaurants, but they all churn out pretty much the same stuff. Look for the one with the most patrons.

The hotels in Bhairawa are generally more expensive.

Getting There & Away

The bus park is about 100m north of the border. From here there are buses to Kathmandu, Pokhara and Tadi Bazaar (for Royal Chitwan National Park). There's a booking office here, so try to buy a ticket in advance rather than on the bus.

Travel agents in Sunauli also sell tickets for 'tourist' buses to Pokhara and Kathmandu, which are no different from public buses except that they pick up from hotels in Sunauli and Bhairawa. They cost Rs 200/240 for day/night buses to either destination. It's cheaper to buy tickets at the bus park.

To Pokhara There are two routes for the trip to Pokhara. The direct route on the Siddhartha Hwy (166km) takes about 7½ hours; the middle section is particularly narrow and winding and parts of the road are in very poor condition. There are some spectacular views of the Annapurnas as you descend into Pokhara, though, and you pass through the stark Mahabharat Range between Butwal and Tansen. There are frequent buses in the morning (from about 3.45 am to 12.30 pm) and a handful of afternoon buses. Tickets vary from Rs 120 to Rs 190, depending on the time. Travel agents advertise a morning minibus service along the Siddhartha Hwy for a steep Rs 280.

The longer route follows the Mahendra Hwy via Narayanghat and Mugling before joining the main Kathmandu-Pokhara road, the Prithvi Hwy. Since these are Nepal's two main highways, this is a much straighter and smoother ride and it takes eight to nine hours. Buses on this route cost between Rs 160 and Rs 190.

To Tadi Bazaar There are four public buses each day along the Mahendra Hwy to Tadi Bazaar (Rs 112, five hours). This is the jumping-off point for the village of Sauraha on the boundary of Royal Chitwan National Park. Travel agents in Sunauli sell tickets for Rs 140.

To Kathmandu Buses follow the Mahendra Hwy before joining the Prithvi Hwy at Mugling and heading east to Kathmandu. There are regular buses between 4.30 and 11.30 am (Rs 160, nine hours) or minibuses (Rs 215); and night buses (Rs 200, 12 hours) at 4.30, 5.30, 6.30 and 8 pm.

To India For buses to destinations in India you'll have to cross the border and walk or take a rickshaw to the bus park on the Indian side (see the India chapter for information). Travel agents on the Nepal side sell tickets for the same buses at inflated prices: Gorakhpur (NPRs 100), Varanasi (NPRs 280).

Getting Around

A rickshaw will take you the 4km to Bhairawa for about Rs 25, or you can take a shared jeep for only Rs 3.

LUMBINI

Regarded as the birthplace of Siddhartha Gautama – the founder of Buddhism – Lumbini makes an easy and enjoyable day trip from Sunauli or Bhairawa. The evidence that this is his birthplace (even back then it was just a forest and a pond) is the centrepiece of Lumbini, the inscribed **Ashoka pillar** that the great Mauryan emperor erected here in the 3rd century BC. Apart from a few scattered ruins there's not much to see and it requires a serious effort of the imagination to conjure up the ghosts of the past. But it's the absence of tourist hype and the peacefulness that make a visit worthwhile. Of course, a development project to turn Lumbini into a 'centre of international Buddhist culture' is on the drawing board.

Siddhartha Gautama was born a prince to Suddhodana, ruler of the republic of Kapilavastu, and Maya Devi. Although born in Lumbini in 563 BC, he grew up in Kapilavastu (present day Tilaurakot) 27km west. The story goes that at the age of 29, having led a privileged life of luxury within the palace walls, he came across an old man, a sick man, a corpse and a hermit. This confrontation with suffering caused him to renounce his princely life. He became a wandering ascetic but found that extreme self-denial did not provide him with the answers to the nature of existence. After meditating for 49 days under a bodhi tree at Bodhgaya, Buddha finally attained enlightenment and spent the rest of his life preaching the 'middle way' to nirvana.

The Indian emperor Ashoka visited Lumbini on a pilgrimage to Buddha's birthplace in 245 BC, and left a number of his famous inscribed pillars in the region. In AD 636 the Chinese pilgrim Hsuan Tang (Tripitaka) described 1000 derelict monasteries and Ashoka's pillar at Lumbini, shattered by lightning and lying on the ground. Today, the **pond** where Maya Devi is believed to have bathed can still be seen, although in much restored form. The brick foundations of stupas and *viharas* (dwellings for Buddhist monks) dating from the 2nd century BC can be seen around the pond.

The site of the **Maya Devi Temple** is now an archaeological dig, but the bas relief showing an image of Maya Devi and the newly born Buddha is enshrined nearby. It's also known as the nativity sculpture.

Most people day trip from Bhairawa, but there are a couple of cheap places to stay, including a very basic *dharamsala* (pilgrim's lodging) and the *Lumbini Village Lodge*, about 1km east of the main site.

Getting There & Away

From Bhairawa's Buddha Chowk, minibuses make the 22km trip to the village of Lumbini Mehalbar, about 1km from the main site (Rs 15, one hour). If you're in a group or can afford it, hiring a jeep is the way to go, especially if you intend to make this a half-day trip. From Sunauli or Bhairawa a taxi-jeep will charge between Rs 450 and Rs 700, with about a two hour waiting at the site. You can hire them direct from the roadside or organise it through a travel agent (and pay a little more).

Travel agents can also help you find a motorcycle for rent, which will cost about Rs 500 for the day.

Pokhara

☎ 061

At first glance Pokhara is a slightly shambolic town. Roads are potholed, many buildings appear derelict or in a state of unfinished construction, and even in the developed Lakeside area the place only looks half built. But on a clear day, you only have to look to the north to see the attraction – the snowy peaks of the Annapurnas and the jagged Machhapuchhare are tantalisingly close and spectacularly beautiful.

Not only is Pokhara closer to the high peaks of the Himalayan range than Kathmandu, but it doesn't have the steep valley sides obscuring the view. From many hotel rooftops and from the south of the lake, the mountain views here are awesome.

It's this natural beauty and easy access to some of the best village-inn trekking in Nepal that is Pokhara's main draw, since the town itself has little of the cultural or architectural heritage that makes Kathmandu so famous. It's also a relatively peaceful, laidback place with a mild climate and every

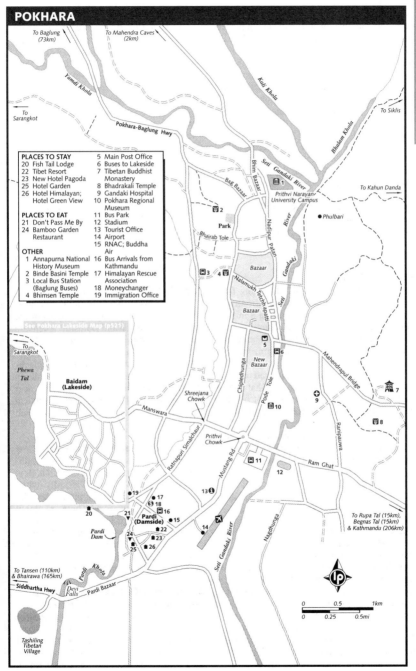

POKHARA

To Baglung (73km)
To Mahendra Caves (2km)
To Sarangkot
To Siklis
To Kahun Danda

Yamdi Khola
Kali Khola
Bhalam Khola
Pokhara-Baglung Hwy
Bhim Bazaar
Seti Gandaki River
Bag Bazaar
Prithvi Narayan University Campus
Nadipur Patan
Phulbari
Park
Bhairab Tole
Gandaki River
Seti Gandaki River
Bazaar
Nalamukh Tetchhapatti
Bazaar
Bazaar
Mahendrapul Bridge
New Bazaar
Chipledhunga
Pode Tole
Ranipauwa
Ram Ghat
Shreejana Chowk
Manswara
Prithvi Chowk
Ratnapuri Simalchaur
Mustang Rd
Nagdhunga
To Rupa Tal (15km), Begnas Tal (15km) & Kathmandu (206km)
Pardi (Damside)
Pardi Dam
Pardi Khola
Pardi Bazaar
Siddhartha Hwy
Devi Falls
To Tansen (110km) & Bhairawa (165km)
Tashiling Tibetan Village
Phewa Tal
Baidam (Lakeside)
To Sarangkot

See Pokhara Lakeside Map (p521)

PLACES TO STAY
20 Fish Tail Lodge
22 Tibet Resort
23 New Hotel Pagoda
25 Hotel Garden
26 Hotel Himalayan; Hotel Green View

PLACES TO EAT
21 Don't Pass Me By
24 Bamboo Garden Restaurant

OTHER
1 Annapurna National History Museum
2 Binde Basini Temple
3 Local Bus Station (Baglung Buses)
4 Bhimsen Temple
5 Main Post Office
6 Buses to Lakeside
7 Tibetan Buddhist Monastery
8 Bhadrakali Temple
9 Gandaki Hospital
10 Pokhara Regional Museum
11 Bus Park
12 Stadium
13 Tourist Office
14 Airport
15 RNAC; Buddha Air
16 Bus Arrivals from Kathmandu
17 Himalayan Rescue Association
18 Moneychanger
19 Immigration Office

0   0.5   1km
0   0.25   0.5mi

convenience you could want – a good precursor to Kathmandu and an excellent place to rest up if you've just come from India. Development in the popular travellers' area known as Lakeside has gone haywire in recent years, with hundreds of guesthouses, restaurants, cafes, bars, trekking outfits and shops crowding the eastern side of the lake, but around the lake, village life still persists in the form of rice paddy farms, dozy water buffalo and simple fishing boats.

The Pokhara Valley is inhabited mainly by Bahun and Chhetri people, although the hills around Pokhara are predominantly the home of the Tibeto-Burmese Gurung people. Only with the eradication of malaria in the 1950s did it become safe to live here and the roads to Kathmandu and the Indian border were only constructed in the 1970s. It may look shambolic, but Pokhara has come a long way in 30 years.

ORIENTATION

Pokhara is quite spread out, stretching for about 6km from north to south, but the areas of most interest to travellers are in a fairly compact 2km strip along the eastern shore of Phewa Tal. The main tourist area is Lakeside, also known as Baidam, which starts roughly at the Fish Tail. Lodge in the south and continues up until the road begins to peter out in the area known as Khaharey. Farther south is a secondary area of hotels called Damside, in between the Pardi Dam and the airport.

North of the airport is the main bus park, a busy area which will probably be your introduction to Pokhara. About 1km north of here is the start of the sprawling bazaar area, the oldest part of Pokhara. Here you'll find the post office, local shops and markets and a throng of activity.

INFORMATION
Tourist Office

Pokhara's tourist office (☎ 20028) is opposite the airport runway on Mustang Rd. Staff here are evidently instructed to hand out a poor-quality town map and nothing else, so it's difficult to think of a good reason to visit. The office is open from 10 am to 5 pm Sunday to Thursday and 10 am to 3 pm Friday. A new tourist office is rumoured to be opening between Damside (Pardi) and Lakeside.

Visa Extensions

The immigration office is at the southern end of the main Lakeside road. You can get a one-month visa extension here (US$50). The office is open from 10 am to 5 pm Sunday to Thursday and 10 am to 3 pm Friday, but you must apply before 1 pm (noon on Friday). Bring a passport photo.

Money

The Nepal Grindlays Bank in Lakeside is convenient. It changes cash and travellers cheques from 9.45 am to 4.15 pm Sunday to Thursday and 9.45 am to 1.15 pm Friday. It also has a new 24-hour ATM from which you can get cash using Visa and MasterCard. You can still make cash advances over the counter. There are numerous moneychangers in Lakeside and Damside that are open longer hours (usually 7 am to 8 pm daily) and will change cash and travellers cheques swiftly.

Post & Communications

The main post office is in the bazaar near Mahendrapul Bridge, a long way from the activity in Lakeside and Damside. There are convenient postal services at the Yak Book Store and Fish Tail Bookshop in Lakeside.

Private phone centres are the best places to make long-distance calls. There's plenty of them scattered around Lakeside and most have private booths with meters so you can monitor the call charge. A few stay open very late.

Email & Internet Access Internet access here is more than twice the cost of Kathmandu, and the connections are often slow or shut down completely, usually when you're in the middle of typing a lengthy message. Save your work! There are plenty of Internet cafes, or businesses with a few terminals set up, especially along the main road in Lakeside. They all charge Rs 7 per minute. Try the Pokhara Cyber Cafe, above the Pyramid Restaurant in Lakeside.

Annapurna Conservation Area Project Information Office

The Annapurna Conservation Area Project (ACAP) office in Lakeside (☎ 21102) is where you need to go to pay the Rs 1000 entry fee to the Annapurna Conservation Area before you head out trekking. Permits are not officially available on the trail, although you may be able to get one in Jomsom if you fly in. It's best to check first. The office is open from 9.30 am to 4.30 pm daily except Saturday. You need to fill out a form and provide one passport photograph.

Bookshops

There are numerous bookshops along the Lakeside road stocking new and second-hand books and trekking maps. The *Kathmandu Post* usually turns up at newsagents and bookstalls by mid-morning.

Yak Book Store and Fishtail Bookshop are worth a look but there are many others.

THINGS TO SEE & DO
Phewa Tal

Phewa Tal is the second-largest lake in Nepal. It's possible to walk or cycle part of the way around the lake, or you can hire one of the numerous *doongas* (boats) bobbing around at several spots along Lakeside. From Fewa Boat Hire in central Lakeside they cost Rs 140 per hour or Rs 400 for the day. You can paddle yourself around and jump overboard for a swim, or hire a boatman to take you to another part of the lake

(Rs 180 per hour). If you are boating near Damside, keep well away from the dam wall as currents can be strong, especially during and immediately after the monsoon. In the lake there's a small island with the double roofed **Varahi Temple**. It costs Rs 20 to get a boat to the temple and back.

Along Lakeside road are a number of banyan and pipal trees with *chautaras* (stone platforms which serve as shady places for porters to rest) built around them. These stone platforms were designed to provide a resting place for walkers, and building them was one good way of improving one's karma for future existences.

Museums & Temples

The **Pokhara Regional Museum**, set back from the main road north of the bus station, has a mildly interesting exhibition on local history and ethnography. There are models and displays showing village life and there are plans to add an archaeological wing. It's open from 10 am to 5 pm daily (except Tuesday) and to 3 pm Friday. Entry is Rs 5.

Annapurna Natural History Museum, at the northern end of town on the Prithvi Narayan University campus, has some

Pokhara's Snowy Skyline

The wonderful Annapurna panorama forms a superb backdrop to Pokhara. On a clear day you can see the mountains clearly from the lake and from many Lakeside hotel rooftops. Even better, you can climb to Sarangkot or one of the other viewpoints around the valley and enjoy a closer uninterrupted view. The view gets a bit hazy from the end of March to about October.

So which peaks does the Annapurna massif consist of? Viewing it from left to right, the main peaks are Annapurna South (7219m); Annapurna I (8091m); Hiunchuli (6441m); Machhapuchhare (6997m); Gangapurna (7455m); Annapurna III (7555m); Annapurna IV (7525m); Annapurna II (7939m); and Lamjung Himal (6986m).

The most impressive is the famous Machhapuchhare ('fish tail'), looking from this angle like a Himalayan Matterhorn. If you walk several days west along the Jomsom Trek route you'll see where it gets its name. A second peak gives it the appearance of a huge fish tail. It appears to be the tallest mountain in the range, but that's because it's quite close to Pokhara; at less than 7000m it's much smaller than Annapurna I. Machhapuchhare is a holy mountain and climbing it is forbidden. An attempt to climb it in 1957 got within 50m of the top, but was turned back when the Sherpas refused to conquer such a holy summit.

The ascent of Annapurna I, the highest mountain in the range and the first 8000m peak to be successfully scaled, is recounted in Maurice Herzog's classic mountaineering book *Annapurna*.

To the west of the Annapurnas is the impressive Dhaulagiri (8167m). The Kali Gandaki River, which cuts the deepest gorge in the world, flows between Dhaulagiri and the Annapurnas and actually predates the rise of the Himalaya. For a while, before more precise measuring methods were available, it was thought that Dhaulagiri was the world's highest mountain.

interesting though dated exhibits on the environmental problems of the area. There are also cement models of Nepali wildlife (which makes a change from stuffed animals), a large insect collection and an incongruous display of dolls and wooden models. The museum is open from 9 am to 12.30 pm and 1.30 to 5 pm daily except Saturday (entry is free).

On the main road in the old part of the bazaar the small, double-roofed **Bhimsen Temple** is one of Pokhara's few temples of any note and it makes a good landmark. Farther north, atop a small hill with a park at its base, the white Shikhara-style **Binde Basini Temple** is Pokhara's best-known temple. It's dedicated to Durga (Parvati) in her Binde Basini Bhagwati manifestation.

Devi Falls

About 1km south-west of Damside on the main Siddhartha Hwy, Devi Falls (also known as Patale Chango, Devin's or David's Falls) is where the Pardi Khola suddenly drops down into a hole in the ground and disappears. It's worth seeing when the water is high or as a quick stop if you're on your way to the Tibetan settlements. For some reason this is quite a big local attraction, with loads of souvenir stalls set up. There's a Rs 5 admission charge.

Tibetan Settlements & Buddhist Monastery

There are a number of Tibetan settlements around Pokhara and you see many Tibetans around the lake selling their crafts and artefacts. The **Tashiling Tibetan Village**, where they weave Tibetan carpets, is only a few hundred metres past Devi Falls, just off the Siddhartha Hwy. Visitors are welcome and it's as good a place as any to shop for Tibetan rugs and handicrafts.

There's also a larger settlement known as **Tashipalkhel** at Hyangja, a short drive or an hour or two's walk north-west of Pokhara on the start of the Jomsom Trek route. This is said to be the oldest and largest Tibetan settlement in Nepal.

The hilltop **Tibetan Buddhist Monastery** is a comparatively recent construction with a large Buddha statue and colourful wall paintings. To get there, cross Mahendrapul Bridge from the bazaar area and follow the road (paved at first) to the monastery.

ACTIVITIES

Trekking is ultimately what attracts most travellers to Pokhara and from here you can easily strike out on anything from leisurely walks around the valley to the three-week Annapurna Circuit. For details on treks around Pokhara see Trekking Around Pokhara later in this chapter.

Trekking & Rafting

Most guesthouses and many trekking and travel agencies around Pokhara can arrange guides and porters for short or long treks. Shop around and ask lots of questions. If you hire a guide very cheaply, you may only get someone to show you the way, as opposed to a knowledgeable guide with a good command of English who can enhance your trek. A licensed guide should cost US$8 to US$12 per day, and a porter costs around US$4 to US$6 per day. If you only want someone to show you the way, a porter can act as a guide and trekking companion. For the Jomsom Trek you don't need a guide and, in season, the Annapurna Circuit and Sanctuary treks are busy enough to ensure that you won't get lost. However, you should never trek alone.

Women trekkers can contact Three Sisters Adventure Trekking (☎ 24066, e sisters3@cnet.wlink.com.np). It specialises in organised treks for women and provides experienced female guides and porters, although they're a little pricier than most. Organised treks cost from US$30 per day and guides are US$20 per day.

There are plenty of rental shops in Pokhara where you can pick up any gear you might need – down sleeping bags and jackets cost around Rs 25 per day and a large deposit is required.

Popular **rafting** trips organised out of Pokhara (and approximate inclusive prices) are the Kali Gandaki (US$100, three days), the raging Marsyangdi (US$225, five days) and the Karnali (US$375, 11 days). Reliable outfits include: Drift Nepal (☎ 21423) at Hotel Monal; Ultimate Descents (☎ 23240) at Hotel Snowland; and Equator Expeditions (☎ 20688).

Yoga & Meditation

Sadhana Yoga, about 2.5km from Lakeside, has daily hatha yoga workshops and meditation retreats for Rs 700 for one day, Rs 2400

POKHARA LAKESIDE

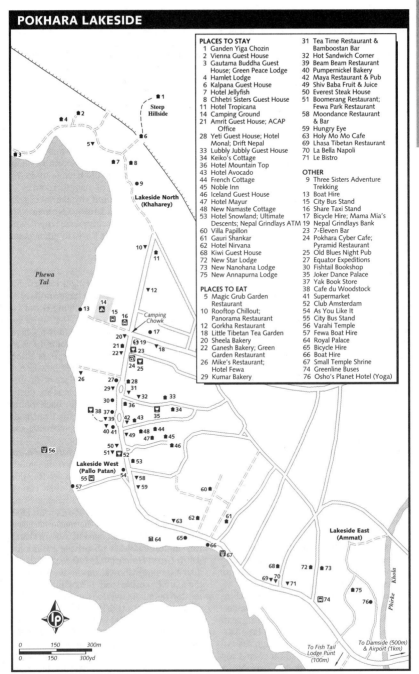

PLACES TO STAY
1 Ganden Yiga Chozin
2 Vienna Guest House
3 Gautama Buddha Guest House; Green Peace Lodge
4 Hamlet Lodge
6 Kalpana Guest House
7 Hotel Jellyfish
8 Chhetri Sisters Guest House
11 Hotel Tropicana
14 Camping Ground
21 Amrit Guest House; ACAP Office
28 Yeti Guest House; Hotel Monal; Drift Nepal
33 Lubbly Jubbly Guest House
34 Keiko's Cottage
36 Hotel Mountain Top
43 Hotel Avocado
44 French Cottage
45 Noble Inn
46 Iceland Guest House
47 Hotel Mayur
48 New Namaste Cottage
53 Hotel Snowland; Ultimate Descents; Nepal Grindlays ATM
60 Villa Papillon
61 Gauri Shankar
62 Hotel Nirvana
68 Kiwi Guest House
72 New Star Lodge
73 New Nanohana Lodge
75 New Annapurna Lodge

PLACES TO EAT
5 Magic Grub Garden Restaurant
10 Rooftop Chillout; Panorama Restaurant
12 Gorkha Restaurant
18 Little Tibetan Tea Garden
20 Sheela Bakery
22 Ganesh Bakery; Green Garden Restaurant
26 Mike's Restaurant; Hotel Fewa
29 Kumar Bakery

31 Tea Time Restaurant & Bamboostan Bar
32 Hot Sandwich Corner
39 Beam Beam Restaurant
40 Pumpernickel Bakery
42 Maya Restaurant & Pub
49 Shiv Baba Fruit & Juice
50 Everest Steak House
51 Boomerang Restaurant; Fewa Park Restaurant
58 Moondance Restaurant & Bar
59 Hungry Eye
63 Holy Mo Mo Cafe
69 Lhasa Tibetan Restaurant
70 La Bella Napoli
71 Le Bistro

OTHER
9 Three Sisters Adventure Trekking
13 Boat Hire
15 City Bus Stand
16 Share Taxi Stand
17 Bicycle Hire; Mama Mia's
19 Nepal Grindlays Bank
23 7-Eleven Bar
24 Pokhara Cyber Cafe; Pyramid Restaurant
25 Old Blues Night Pub
27 Equator Expeditions
30 Fishtail Bookshop
35 Joker Dance Palace
37 Yak Book Store
38 Cafe du Woodstock
41 Supermarket
52 Club Amsterdam
54 As You Like It
55 City Bus Stand
56 Varahi Temple
57 Fewa Boat Hire
64 Royal Palace
65 Bicycle Hire
66 Boat Hire
67 Small Temple Shrine
74 Greenline Buses
76 Osho's Planet Hotel (Yoga)

Steep Hillside

Lakeside North (Khaharey)

Phewa Tal

Camping Chowk

Lakeside West (Pallo Patan)

Lakeside East (Ammat)

Phirke Khola

To Fish Tail Lodge Punt (100m)

To Damside (500m) & Airport (1km)

0   150   300m
0   150   300yd

for three days, including meals and accommodation. Contact Raging River Runners (☎ 26839) in Lakeside for details.

Ganden Yiga Chozin (☎ gyc@mos.com .np) has short residential courses in Buddhist philosophy led alternately by a Tibetan lama and an Italian monk. There's also hatha yoga classes and meditation every morning. Non-residential courses cost Rs 500 per day (minimum three days) and residential courses including meals cost Rs 800.

Osho's Planet Hotel (☎ 22838) in Lakeside has yoga and meditation courses as well as massage and acupuncture, classes in Indian classical music, singing and tabla playing. Courses start from Rs 900 per day, including meals and accommodation. A standard six-day course costs US$75. The hotel itself is average but there's a relaxing garden at the back.

Massage

There are many private places in Lakeside offering massage, presumably to cater to all those aching post-trek muscles. Professional shiatsu or reflexology costs around Rs 800 per hour, but there are cheaper operators. Barbers will do vigorous head and neck massages for a negotiable price. If you're having a shave or haircut, they'll probably launch into a massage whether you ask for it or not.

PLACES TO STAY

In Pokhara, as in Kathmandu, you're more spoiled for budget accommodation choices than virtually anywhere en route since İstanbul.

Lakeside is still the preferred area with most travellers, and this is where you will find the majority of guesthouses and restaurants. Damside is quieter, which is what attracts some people. Touts may try to convince you that Damside is *the* place to go, and will probably exaggerate its charms. The reality is, unless you don't like being part of a tourist 'scene', Lakeside is a more interesting place to stay.

Prices are highest from October to February and lowest from May to September. However, with so many competing guesthouses, there's always room for a little bargaining. Prices quoted here are high season. Many places, especially mid-range and top end, quote prices in US dollars, payable in

rupees at current exchange rates. Where this is the case, we've also given prices in US dollars, rather than in rupees, which would probably be different by the time you turn up.

The Lakeside hotels stretch quite a long way from south to north. Those in the north are cheap backpacker places where you can escape the crowds, but it's a fair walk down to the restaurants and main action.

Camping

If you have a tent, you could make a deal with one of the guesthouses to camp in their garden, which you should be able to do for around half the price of a single room.

The *camping ground*, by the lake near Camping Chowk, is a large grassy area with basic facilities and plenty of parking if you have a vehicle. It costs Rs 40 to pitch a tent and Rs 80 for a vehicle.

Budget

Lakeside Many of the budget lodges and guesthouses along the lake have similar facilities and prices. The following is only a selection of what's on offer.

Keiko's Cottage (☎ 27007), down a lane running off the main road in central Lakeside (turn at Hotel Mountain Top), is at the upper end of the budget range pricewise but it's a friendly, family run place with immaculate rooms. The front rooms are fairly plain at Rs 300 a double, but the back rooms for US$8 are large and pleasantly furnished. There's also a room with a kitchenette for Rs 400, and a pleasant garden.

Across the road, *Lubbly Jubbly Guest House* (☎ 22881) is cheaper and quite good. Doubles with shared bathroom are Rs 100/150. There's a pleasant semi-open eating area.

Yeti Guest House (☎ 21423), around the corner, is set back from the road in a large garden. It's basic, but quite OK at Rs 200/300 for singles/doubles with private bathroom. *Amrit Guest House* (☎ 24240, fax 22201) is near Camping Chowk, on the west side of the main Lakeside road. It's plain, but has a rooftop restaurant overlooking the lake and is great value at Rs 100/150 with shared bathroom and Rs 250/300 with private bathroom.

One street farther south, *Hotel Avocado* (☎ 23617) has great rooftop views, but no garden. Doubles cost Rs 150/250 with shared/private bathroom. Across the road and tucked behind the large Hotel Starlight, *New Namaste Cottage* has a secluded garden with rooms around the outside in Indonesian losmen style. It's about as basic as they come (Asian-style toilet but hot water), but is friendly and cheap. Rooms, all with shared bath, cost Rs 70/120.

Farther along, *French Cottage* is another basic but friendly little place with seven rooms. Singles/doubles with shared bathroom are Rs 80/120 and there's a garden.

The road running east opposite Club Amsterdam has a few options. *Noble Inn* (☎ 24926, e pplazza@cnet.wlink.com.np) is a modern, grey monstrosity with a pleasant garden. The rooms are reasonably good value at Rs 250 for a double with shared bathroom and Rs 400 to Rs 800 with private bathroom. There's solar and electric hot water. *Hotel Mayur* (☎ 22285) is similar and has excellent top-floor views. Modern, well-kept rooms cost Rs 250/300 (shared bathroom) on the lower floor, Rs 400/500 (private bathroom) upstairs.

At the end of this road, *Iceland Guest House* (☎ 23082) is very clean and well kept. Singles/doubles with private bathroom are Rs 200/300. The deluxe upper-floor rooms with a view and a TV are US$20 per double.

New Annapurna Lodge (☎ 25011) is an interesting place to stay, especially if you're into self-sufficiency. The lovely family that runs it keeps a Friesian cow from which they get all their milk, they have a vegetable garden, fruit trees and a coffee bush from which they make superb home-made coffee. All of this is, of course, shared with the guests. The rooms aren't bad either at Rs 100/150 with shared bathroom and Rs 300/400 with private bathroom and hot water. It's hidden down a winding laneway opposite the road to the Fish Tail Lodge.

Back on the main Lakeside road, travel a little farther and you come to a pleasant village-like area on the right. *New Nanohana Lodge* (☎ 22478) is a modern place with a nice 1st-floor garden and a rooftop terrace. Pleasant doubles with private bathroom are US$5 downstairs and US$12 upstairs. Rooms with a Japanese bath are US$15. *New Star Lodge* across the road is a cheaper option under the same management. Basic double rooms with shared/private bathroom cost Rs 120/150.

On the next street north-west is a string of places with good mountain views, but not much atmosphere. *Kiwi Guest House* (☎ 22052, e kiwi@cnet.wlink.com.np), down a small lane, is decent. The garden is a bit cramped, but there are good views from the hotel roof. There's a range of clean rooms from US$3/4 to US$10/20. The cheapest have shared bath, the most expensive have air-con and TV.

There are a number of cheap places down the road past the small temple shrine on the lake's edge. One of these is *Gauri Shankar* (☎ 20422), with nice garden rooms with shared bathroom from Rs 120/180, and with private bathroom from Rs 150/200. If you want hot water it's Rs 350 for a double.

The second laneway heading inland has a couple of cheap and decent places, in pleasant surroundings. *Villa Papillon* (☎ 27030), in a leafy, private garden, has singles/doubles for Rs 150/250 with private bathroom and doubles for Rs 150 with shared bathroom.

North of Camping Chowk the hotels begin to thin out. *Hotel Tropicana* (☎ 22118) is a spotless, modern place with lake views. The basic downstairs single/double rooms go for Rs 150/200 with private bathroom or Rs 200/300 for a larger room. A huge upstairs double with lake view and balcony is US$10.

Farther north, the lakeshore becomes much closer, the atmosphere is more rural and the accommodation is generally basic and inexpensive.

Hotel Jellyfish (☎ 32194) has rooms facing the lake. It's clean and great value with large, simple rooms with private bathroom and hot water for Rs 150/200.

Following the trail up the hillside (past the cheap and cheerful Kalpana and Banana Lodge guesthouses) brings you to *Ganden Yiga Chozin* (no phone). It's a Buddhist meditation centre but anyone can stay here. There's a nice garden and it has a relaxed feel. Dorm beds are steep at Rs 100 and basic singles/doubles cost Rs 150/200.

Back on the Lakeside road, *Hamlet Lodge* (☎ 32293) is a relatively new place at the foot of the hills. The facilities are good, and double rooms cost Rs 350. It's partly made of local stone and has good facilities, including a pleasant rooftop veranda overlooking the lake. Large, clean rooms cost Rs 150 for a double with shared bathroom and Rs 200/300 for singles/doubles with private bathroom.

Vienna Guest House, above and behind Hamlet Lodge, has excellent lake views because of its elevated position and there's a rooftop terrace. The rooms are large and concrete box-like but are cheap at Rs 80/100 with shared bathroom and Rs 150/300 with private bathroom. If you really want some solitude, continue around to *Green Peace Lodge* (e *greenpeacelodge@hotmail.com*), which has very basic singles/doubles at Rs 100/120 (shared bath) and a great balcony restaurant overlooking the lake. Next door, *Gautama Buddha Guest House* is similar. Bicycles can be hired from Green Peace but at night it's a hassle (about a 20-minute walk) if you want to go into town.

Damside This area is much quieter than Lakeside and has more of a local 'village' feel, but is also slightly run-down looking.

Hotel Himalayan (☎ 21643) is one of the cheap options off the main road. It's a family run place with a nice garden. Small doubles with shared/private bathroom are Rs 150/200 and there are some better rooms from Rs 250 to Rs 400.

Hotel Garden (☎ 20870), closer to the dam, is a peaceful, well-run place that gets good reports from travellers. Singles/doubles with shared bathroom are US$3/4 but the cheapest rooms with private bathroom are US$8/10. Some of the deluxe rooms have excellent views.

New Hotel Pagoda (☎ 21802, *Pardi Rd*) is another quiet, friendly place with small but tidy rooms for Rs 200/250 with shared bathroom and Rs 500/650 with private bathroom and hot water. There are some larger rooms at the back.

Mid-Range

Lakeside *Hotel Monal* (☎ 21423, fax 20266), behind the Drift Nepal office on Lakeside road is a stylish, central place with well-appointed rooms from US$10/15 to US$18/25 a single/double. The more expensive rooms are on the 2nd floor.

Chhetri Sisters Guest House (☎ 24066, e *sisters3@cnet.wlink.com.np*) is a very friendly little place run by three sisters. It has been completely renovated to mid-range standard and has a good position at the north

end of the lake. There are dorm beds for US$4 (private bathroom) and private rooms ranging from US$8/10 to US$15/20 for rooms with a view. Most rooms have a private bathroom. The rooftop views are good and there's a nice restaurant here.

Hotel Nirvana (☎ 23332, fax 23736, e *nirvana@cnet.wlink.com.np*) is worth checking out. It's immaculately clean and well maintained, and there are good rooftop views. Basic ground-floor doubles start at Rs 400, better rooms are US$8/10 and 2nd-floor rooms with lake and mountain views are US$15. It's run by a switched-on Canadian-Nepali couple.

Damside *Tibet Resort* (☎ 20853, e *tibetres@cnet.wlink.com.np*) is a modern three-storey place with a big garden. It's fine if you want a bit of extra comfort although it's not exactly cheap at US$23/34 for standard rooms with TV and hot shower. There's a superb view of the mountains from the terrace and a good restaurant here.

Hotel Green View (☎ 21844) is a reasonably good choice, set back a little from the road with a pleasant garden at the front. There are fairly basic rooms at the back for US$8/12, but the comfortable new building in front has good rooms, some with mountain views and balconies, for US$15/25.

PLACES TO EAT

Pokhara doesn't quite have the variety of food and restaurants offered in Kathmandu, but you can certainly eat well here. If you've just come from India or from a trek, this is heaven! Menus in most restaurants will have a go at anything: Italian, Mexican, Chinese, continental (which is pretty much everything else) as well as Indian and Tibetan. Sometimes it seems the hardest thing to find is a plain old Nepali *dal bhat* (rice and lentil stew). As with any food on the subcontinent, you take your chances a little, especially with meat and anything uncooked such as salad.

Lakeside

Most dining possibilities are along the main road skirting Lakeside.

If you just fancy a quick snack, look out for the little sandwich stalls. *Hot Sandwich Corner*, down the side road past Tea Time Restaurant, does excellent sandwiches (rolls) from Rs 35 to Rs 80, which you can eat in or takeaway. A large beer is Rs 90. There's another one opposite the Old Blues Night Pub.

Gorkha Restaurant, north of Camping Chowk, is one of the few places you can get a cheap dal bhat (Rs 60) in Lakeside. The rest of the menu is cheap and simple Nepali and Tibetan and there's a pleasant garden. You can also get the Tibetan tipple *thong ba* (beer made from millet) for Rs 50 and a regular beer is a very reasonable Rs 85.

Little Tibetan Tea Garden, east of Camping Chowk, turns out consistently good food and gets rave reviews from travellers.

Tea Time Restaurant & Bamboostan Bar is a happening little place in the middle of Lakeside (opposite Hotel Mountain Top) with a cosy front veranda eating area in addition to an indoor section.

Maya Restaurant & Pub on the main Lakeside road is an ambient bamboo set-up with coloured lights, candles and complimentary popcorn. The menu runs the usual gamut of everything and the staff are friendly and quick. Set breakfast is Rs 65, Nepali set meal is Rs 175 and Vegemite cheese toast is Rs 35.

Moondance Restaurant & Bar is recommended for some of the best pizza in town (from Rs 120) and it has a warm and pleasant atmosphere. There's a fireplace inside, a popular bar, pool table, darts and the service is excellent. Steak dishes cost Rs 180, and for dessert try the rich choc-fudge brownie or the lemon meringue pie (Rs 70).

If you're just back from a trek and craving some iron, *Everest Steak House* is the place to go. Steak dishes aren't cheap at Rs 200 to Rs 275, but they are good and there's other less-expensive dishes on the menu. The rooftop restaurant overlooks the lake.

Boomerang Restaurant is one of a number of outdoor places on the west side of the road. There's a nice garden dotted with chairs, tables and thatched shelters and even a couple of small Norfolk Island pine trees. It's not the cheapest food around – a simple set breakfast is Rs 75 – but nothing beats sitting out on a fine morning with views over the lake. The dinner atmosphere (and food) isn't as good. There's also a German bakery here.

Heading south, *Hungry Eye* is a long-standing place that's quite fancy and pricey,

but the food is still good. Fresh fish dishes are a speciality (around Rs 285), and there's Nepali and Indian food on the menu. Farther down past the Royal Palace, you come to a string of restaurants including the very European sounding *Le Bistro* and *La Bella Napoli*. They both do a decent range of pizzas, pastas and anything else you'd care to ask for, but the food is fairly insipid.

Lhasa Tibetan Restaurant is a big outdoors place with a number of Tibetan specialities joining the usual international menu. *Thukpa* (noodle soup) is Rs 65 and a Tibetan meal for three is Rs 245. A cheaper option is *Holy Mo Mo Cafe*, which advertises the best *momos* (Tibetan dumplings) in town (they're OK) from Rs 40 and has beer for Rs 90.

Mike's Restaurant at the Hotel Fewa offers the best location in Lakeside. The open-air terrace is beside the lake (the only place with an actual lake frontage), and the food is good, although not as good as its reputation. It's quite pricey with sandwiches and burgers from Rs 130 and Cajun chicken at Rs 260.

If you're staying at the north end of Lakeside there are a few interesting places. *Magic Grub Garden* is an attractive place for lunch under thatched shelters looking out over the lake. The food is standard and the prices reasonable. Other places include the *Rooftop Chillout Restaurant* and *Panorama*, side by side with good lake views.

Bakeries Lakeside also has some decent bakeries that are especially good for breakfast or for takeaway pastries. *Kumar Bakery*, opposite Tea Time Restaurant, is a great little place with fresh bread and huge bowls of muesli (Rs 30). *Ganesh Bakery* also does good breads and cakes, and the views from the ramshackle upstairs eating area are excellent.

Pumpernickel Bakery is similar to the set-up in Kathmandu except it has a better garden. It's a popular place for breakfast and there's an impressive assortment of breads and pastries. Croissants are Rs 15, good coffee is Rs 18 and a yak cheese roll is Rs 40.

Fruit-Juice Stalls You can't miss the fruit-juice stalls lining the Lakeside road – they're the ones festooned with huge bunches of fruit. These places make the most amazing lassis and juices from freshly squeezed or blended mango, banana, papaya, pineapple, watermelon and oranges, but there are a couple of things to watch out for. One is to ensure they don't dilute the juice with water, which may not be safe to drink – the best thing is to watch them prepare it. The second is to ask for the size cup you want, otherwise you might end up with a pot the size of a small bucket and a bill for Rs 145!

Self-Catering There are several *convenience stores* in Lakeside where you can buy everything from a bottle of wine to a can of beans. Trekkers are certainly well catered for. Some also double as pharmacies, stationers etc. There's a good *supermarket* opposite the Maya Pub, and the well-stocked *As You Like It* (the perfect slogan) department store farther south.

Damside
There is not much of note in the Damside area; most people eat at their hotels or head up to Lakeside. *Don't Pass Me By* is a basic little restaurant on the edge of the lake. *Bamboo Garden*, wedged into a road junction near the dam, is also worth a try.

ENTERTAINMENT
Pokhara is gradually becoming more of a late-night place, although for many travellers entertainment doesn't stretch beyond watching a recent-release video over a few beers in one of the many restaurants on Lakeside road.

There are some reasonable bars in Lakeside with music blaring out until 10 or 11 pm most nights, and this area has a more relaxed feel than Thamel in Kathmandu. *Club Amsterdam* is one of the most popular, with a lakefront outdoor deck, pool tables and Sky sports on the big screen. Beer costs Rs 110 and cocktails from Rs 110 to Rs 150. Another good bar is the *Maya Restaurant & Pub*, which has a happy hour in the early evening with two cocktails for the price of one.

Cafe du Woodstock, on the lakefront in the middle of Lakeside, is the latest party spot but nothing really happens until after 11 pm. There are all-night dance parties here on Tuesdays and Fridays, with house, trance and rave music dominating. It's down a laneway behind Beam Beam. *Joker Dance Palace* is a strange local disco-style club

that appears to be empty most of the time. Entry is Rs 200, which includes a drink.

Cultural entertainment is not hard to find in Pokhara. It's all staged for tourists, but some of the shows are quite good. *Boomerang Restaurant* has Nepali folk dancing every Monday, Wednesday, Friday and Saturday and *Fewa Park Restaurant* next door has traditional dancers performing every evening between 7 and 9 pm. Both are free if you have dinner there. *Hungry Eye* also has a show every night.

Probably the best show is put on at the flash *Fish Tail Lodge*. It runs from 6.30 to 7.30 pm and costs Rs 150.

Moondance Restaurant breaks the mould with a rock band playing every Saturday and Sunday night from 7.30 to 10.30 pm. Other places also have bands from time to time.

SHOPPING
Pokhara's large Tibetan population sells many crafts and artefacts. Carpet-weaving is a major local industry. Saligrams, the fossilised sea creatures found north up the Kali Gandaki Valley, are a popular souvenir, but they are often radically overpriced. You shouldn't pay more than about Rs 100.

There's plenty of trekking gear, sleeping bags, Gore-Tex jackets and fleeces for sale along Lakeside road, although the range isn't as big as in Kathmandu.

GETTING THERE & AWAY
Be wary of travel agencies in Pokhara selling through tickets to cities in India, especially if they include onward train transport. We've heard about many rip-offs and broken promises. There are no tourist buses to India – you must change at the border – and you're better off arranging onward transport in India yourself.

Air
There are daily services between Kathmandu and Pokhara. Many private companies have sprung up and jumped on the domestic bandwagon; Buddha Air (☎ 21429) and Necon Air (☎ 20256) are recommended. The flight takes less than an hour and costs US$67 with private airlines, US$61 with Royal Nepal Airlines Corporation (RNAC). It costs the same whether you book your ticket directly with the airlines or with one

of the many travel agents at Lakeside, but check a few prices first to be sure. Flights to Jomsom cost US$50 with RNAC and US$61 with the private airlines.

There are great Himalayan views if you sit on the right-hand side of the plane on the flight from Kathmandu to Pokhara, and vice versa.

Bus

The main Pokhara bus park is a dusty (or muddy) expanse of chaos, about 3km east of Lakeside. The booking office is at the top of the steps that lead into the bus park on its western edge.

To Kathmandu The bus trip between Pokhara and Kathmandu takes seven or eight hours and most departures are early in the morning. The first stretch of road from Pokhara to Naubise is in excellent condition (with the exception of a 20km stretch around Dumre). From Naubise to Kathmandu it deteriorates a little, but this is still the best road in Nepal. From the Pokhara bus park there are regular services for Rs 125 (day) and Rs 142 (night).

Greenline (☎ 26562) offers daily air-con services to Kathmandu at 8 am; the fare is steep at Rs 600 but these are the most comfortable buses and it includes breakfast at Kurintar about halfway. There's a booking office in Lakeside, which is where the buses leave from.

There are also 'tourist buses', which are not strictly for tourists but which pick up in Lakeside at 7 and 9 am daily (Rs 200). There's also a minibus at 10.30 am (Rs 250, six hours) and a night bus at 6.30 pm (Rs 200, 10½ hours). The only real advantage of taking these buses is not having to go to the bus park, but they also drop off at Kantipath, near Thamel, which is much more convenient than the Kathmandu bus park. You can buy tickets from agents and guesthouses all over Lakeside.

At the time of research, tourist buses coming from Kathmandu terminated at a makeshift bus park at Rastaben Chowk (near Mustang Chowk), between the airport and Damside. However, this was due to be shut down, so the 'tourist buses' may have to go back to using the public bus park. That should relieve the irritating tout situation slightly. If you are besieged by hotel touts on arrival, don't have anything to do with them. Grab a taxi to somewhere central on Lakeside, have a drink and a bite to eat at one of the restaurants, then check out some hotels for yourself.

To Royal Chitwan National Park Public buses between Pokhara and Tadi Bazaar, the access point for Royal Chitwan National Park, depart from the bus park from around 5.30 am (Rs 90, five hours). Greenline buses to Kathmandu at 8 am go via here (Rs 480, 5½ hours) with breakfast included.

Minibuses that pick up in Lakeside at 6.30 and 7.30 am cost Rs 200 and should go all the way to Chitrasali (halfway between Tadi Bazaar and Sauraha) but check when you book.

To Sunauli Buses to the border with India at Sunauli/Bhairawa depart from the main Pokhara bus park (Rs 160/187 day/night, nine hours).

There are minibuses from outside Tea Time Restaurant in Lakeside at 6.30 am daily (Rs 220, seven hours) and via Narayanghat at 7.30 am (Rs 250, eight hours). A big bus also picks up here are 7.45 am (Rs 200 via Narayanghat). These are still public buses and they will pick up local passengers along the way.

To Trekking Routes To get onto the start of the Jomsom Trek, most trekkers take the bus as far as Nayapul (just before Baglung) from where it's just a 20-minute walk to Birethanti. The bus continues on to Baglung (Rs 57, three hours) where you can walk an alternative route via Beni. Buses for Nayapul/Baglung leave from the local bus station, west of the main bazaar, roughly every 15 minutes from early morning until mid-afternoon; the trip to Nayapul takes about two hours (Rs 35). From this bus station there are also regular buses to Phedi (Rs 25) for the start of the Annapurna Sanctuary (Base Camp) trek.

To Besi Sahar, for the start of the Annapurna Circuit, there are two buses at 7.25 and 8.25 am daily from the main Pokhara bus park (Rs 80, five hours).

GETTING AROUND

City buses run regularly to the main bus park and the bazaar (Rs 5) from two points

NEPAL

in Lakeside: from Camping Chowk and from the road leading down to Fewa Boat Hire. The best place to catch a return bus from the bazaar to Lakeside is from just south of the post office.

Bicycle is a good way to get around, although it's all uphill going north. The cheapest bicycle hire in Lakeside is next to Mama Mia's restaurant just up from Camping Chowk – you can get an old rattler for Rs 25 a day. Other places hire for Rs 40. You can rent a motorcycle or scooter for about Rs 400.

Taxi drivers are rapacious and hard to bargain with in Pokhara – avoid them if possible. They'll want Rs 100 to go from Lakeside to the airport or the bus park. It shouldn't cost any more than Rs 50 to get from the bus park to Lakeside.

TREKKING AROUND POKHARA

Pokhara is the closest starting point for some of Nepal's finest treks: the Annapurna Circuit, Jomsom Trek; and the Annapurna Sanctuary (Base Camp) trek. What makes

Following the Apple Pie Trail

The Jomsom Trek is sometimes called the 'Apple Pie Trail' because that dish appears on the menu of just about every lodge along the way. Of course, it's also a dig at just how Westernised and comfortable this popular route has become, but this is still one of the most interesting and enjoyable short treks in Nepal – with an airport in Jomsom it can be walked in only four or five days if you fly one way (from US$50).

Ideally, you should allow six days if you want to reach the village of Kagbeni (2810m) and the temples at Muktinath (3710m) and five days to walk back. If you intend to fly, it's best to fly from Pokhara to Jomsom and walk back – that way you won't arrive in Jomsom and have to hang around waiting for a flight out because of bad weather or overbooking. Allow yourself some time to acclimatise before heading up to Muktinath (spending the night in Kagbeni is a good idea).

The walk down from Jomsom to Pokhara is the same as the final third of the Annapurna Circuit, which is usually walked in an anticlockwise direction. The lodges along this part of the trek are among the most comfortable in Nepal, with welcoming pot-belly stoves, a surprising range of food on the menu, private rooms (some with private bathroom) and occasional hot water. Still, you'll pay less than Rs 100 for a double room with shared bathroom and less than half that for a dorm bed. From December to February it's a good idea to carry a sleeping bag.

Although you'll see plenty of Western trekkers walking in both directions, at times they're in the minority. You're likely to see more Nepali porters transporting all manner of goods up to villages in *dokos* (cane baskets carried on the back and supported by a strap around the head); local villagers going about their daily business; caravans of sure-footed mules being herded along the narrow trails; and Buddhist and Hindu pilgrims (often barefoot) making their way up to the holy temple at Muktinath.

From Jomsom it's only an hour to Marpha, a tightly packed village of whitewashed homes, which has some of the best lodges on the trail. This area is fairly bleak but it's surrounded by orchards (hence the apple pies). You can continue on to Kalopani, following the Kali Gandaki riverbed. The morning views of Tukuche Peak (6290m) and Dhaulagiri (8167m) are awesome, and the view of Dhaulagiri improves as you walk south towards Tatopani (unfortunately, you have to keep turning around to see it). The trail becomes more lush and scenic, and Tatopani is a good place to spend the night as there is a natural hot-water spring here. From Tatopani it's a steep climb up to the villages of Ghara and Sikha. You need to start early to comfortably make it to Ghorapani in a day. From Ghorapani you can make the early morning ascent to Poon Hill, one of the finest lookout points in Nepal. It's possible to walk down to the main road at Nayapul, via Ulleri and Birethanti, on the same day and catch a bus back to Pokhara.

If you have time at your disposal, take it much slower and spread the walk over a week – there are many other villages to stop at along the way. And definitely try a piece of apple pie at the end of a hard day on the trail.

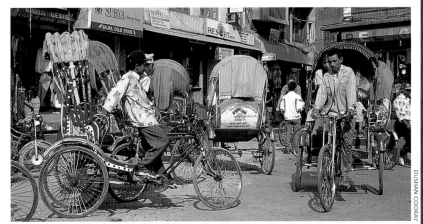
Colourful Nepali cycle-rickshaws

Enjoying the view from a rope suspension bridge.

Trekkers on horseback in the Himalaya foothills.

Diesel smoke, ever present in Kathmandu, belches from a bus.

A bullock cart crosses over one of Nepal's many rivers, which are usually dry in summer.

A great way to view Royal Chitwan National Park

Hardy mules tackle the tough Nepali terrain.

these so popular, apart from the superb concentration of mountains in the Annapurna-Dhaulagiri range, is the ease with which most people can walk these routes without the need to carry a tent or supplies. Dotted along the trails are tiny villages and tea-houses where you can enjoy a warm bed and a reasonably good meal every night. You rarely have to walk any more than a few hours before you come to a place to stop and eat or rest. Describing these treks is beyond the scope of this book, but there are many useful publications and maps available in Nepal. For more information, see Lonely Planet's *Nepal* or (even better) *Trekking in the Nepal Himalaya*. Nepa Maps publishes reasonably good maps of the Annapurna Circuit and Sanctuary Treks, the Royal Trek and the Ghorapani Trek for around Rs 175.

If your time is limited, there are some interesting day walks or short treks around Pokhara that take you closer to the mountain views.

Sarangkot

The trek up to the village of Sarangkot (1592m) takes about three or four hours on the Lakeside route, or around two hours if you head up to the Pokhara Bazaar and start from the Binde Basini Temple. Probably the best way to do it is walk *to* Sarangkot via Binde Basini Temple and back via the Lakeside route (it's easy to get lost on the way up from the lake but a straightforward walk down).

From the temple, head directly west and follow the vehicle track which runs most of the way up to Sarangkot. Where the track ends, there's a stairway to the top. Heading down, there's a steep descent through the forest via a stone stairway until you reach the lake, then an easy walk around the shore to the east which takes you back to Lakeside.

There are a few places to stay and eat, so you could go up to Sarangkot in the evening, stay overnight and see the views at dawn, then come back down.

Annapurna Skyline Trek

Also called the 'Royal Trek', after Prince Charles walked it some years ago, this can be walked in three or four days. The trek doesn't reach any great altitude but it provides good views as it follows a ridge for most of the way. As this is not a heavily

trekked route, there is no established tea-house accommodation along the way, but you pass through several villages where accommodation should be available if you ask around. Otherwise, take a tent.

Ghorapani & Poon Hill If you don't have time for the Jomsom Trek (and can't afford to fly), this option offers partial tea-house trekking to one of the best lookout points in the region. If you take the bus to and from Nayapul (as you would for the Jomsom Trek), this trek can be done in three days out of Pokhara. It could be done in two very long and very tiring days if you start early from Pokhara and walk all the way to Ghorapani on the first day, but it's a very steep climb. Four days would allow you to slow down and smell the rhododendrons.

From Nayapul, cross the river to Birethanti and continue on the trail for about three hours to Tikedungha where you can spend the night. The following day the trail climbs steeply to Ulleri (2070m) and up to Nangathanti (2460m), a walk of about three hours. Another hour brings you to Ghorapani (2775m) where there's plenty of accommodation. Rise at dawn for the one-hour walk up to the lookout at Poon Hill (3210m), which offers superb views of Dhaulagiri, Machhapuchhare and the Annapurnas. The walk back down to Nayapul can easily be managed in a day, allowing you to catch a bus back to Pokhara.

An alternative to backtracking is to take the trail from Birethanti to Ghandruk on the Annapurna Sanctuary Trek, then turn off to join up with the Jomsom Trek at Deorali, near Ghorapani. The loop trip starting and ending in Birethanti takes four to five days. To do either of these treks you'll need to pay the ACAP park fee of Rs 1000.

Royal Chitwan National Park

Stretching across the flat, subtropical Terai region, Royal Chitwan National Park is your best chance of spotting exotic wildlife on this route, so it shouldn't be missed. You'd be unlucky not to see a rhinoceros here and you may even spot a leopard lounging in a tree or a rare Bengal tiger.

The 932-sq-km national park was proclaimed in 1973. Nine years earlier a sanctuary had been established to halt the demise of the wildlife on the Terai – particularly tigers and rhinos, which were vanishing at an alarming rate thanks to oversettlement and the resulting loss of natural habitat. Chitwan now contains an estimated 465-plus rhinos and 80 tigers (up from 100 rhinos and 20 tigers in 1973), as well as 50 other species of mammals and more than 450 different types of bird. There's also an elephant breeding and training program in the park buffer zone.

The setting is a mixture of dense forest, long grass and narrow river flood plains. This makes sighting one of the elusive tigers or leopards difficult, but it also makes for interesting walking and the early morning elephant rides are unforgettable.

The best time to visit Chitwan is from October to February. From mid-January to the end of February, locals are allowed in the park to cut grass, so it's not a great time to visit. Late February to May is a prime time for wildlife watching as much of the grasscover has been removed, although it starts to get hot and sticky after April. Many lodges close during the May to August monsoon – the worst time to visit the park.

ORIENTATION & INFORMATION

The park's northern boundary is the broad Rapti River. Just north of here is the small village of Sauraha, which is accessible from the Mahendra Hwy at Tadi Bazaar 6km away. Most travellers stay here, although there are several expensive 'jungle lodges' south of the river, inside the park boundaries.

The ticket office and visitor centre are in Sauraha (open from 6 to 9.30 am and 1.30 to 4.30 pm daily). This is where you pay your park entry fee (Rs 650, valid for two days), and where you can independently organise an elephant ride. There's a small museum at the visitor centre, with exhibits about the park and its wildlife, and a community souvenir shop opposite. The park headquarters are farther west at Kasara.

See the Sauraha section later in this chapter for information on services in the village. One thing you shouldn't forget to bring to the Terai is insect repellent. There's a small risk of malaria and mosquitoes are out in force here after dusk.

ORGANISED TOURS

Many agents sell organised tours out of Pokhara and Kathmandu. This can be convenient, though it's never as cheap as doing it independently (the agent has to make his cut), and many travellers have found that they didn't get everything they were promised. Don't be conned into staying inside the park – you'll pay a small fortune for those lodges (at least US$90 a night, all inclusive) and if you don't pay this much you'll almost certainly end up in a lodge in Sauraha, outside the park.

Budget tours out of Kathmandu or Pokhara cost around US$55 for three days and two nights. This should include accommodation (in Sauraha), transport, park entry fee and activities such as an elephant ride, guided walk, canoe trip etc. Find out exactly what you're getting. When you take into account transport time, a package like this really only gives you one full day at the park. Two full days is better, and it's a relaxing and cheap enough environment to warrant longer. A three-day package at a mid-range place in Sauraha, such as Royal Park Hotel, costs US$120.

It's also possible to combine a **whitewater rafting** trip on the Trisuli River with a visit to Royal Chitwan. Trips usually begin at Mugling or farther down the Trisuli and take two days to get to Chitwan. Don't expect too many thrills: The Trisuli is the tamest of Nepal's rivers. When we passed, in April, it was a muddy brown ribbon of water with the occasional milky swell. Inclusive rafting/Chitwan packages from Kathmandu cost from US$150, but make sure you know what you're getting.

ACTIVITIES

When you arrive at Sauraha and check into a lodge or guesthouse, you'll be bombarded with all the possibilities: jungle walks, jeep safaris, elephant rides, canoe trips on the Rapti *and* they can sign you up for the lot right there and then. Many of the lodges charge low rates for rooms and rely on the extra business from booking these activities to make a profit. If you've come all the way from Istanbul you'll probably be familiar with this scenario.

There's nothing wrong with organising your activities through your guesthouse – it's very convenient to do so. The problem lies in how much commission (or service charge) is being added on, and in the quality and experience of the guides they use. So don't be pressured into booking everything the minute you walk in the door. Talk to other travellers, shop around at some of the agents in town and look into organising the elephant rides yourself at the government ticket office. You may find that what your guesthouse offers is perfectly reasonable, so go with it.

Try not to scare the wildlife by wearing bright colours when you go into the park – greens and browns are best; red, yellow and white are the worst.

Elephant Rides

An early-morning elephant ride is undoubtedly one of the highlights of a visit to Chitwan and should not be missed. This is your best chance of getting up close to a rhinocerous since they are accustomed to elephants and are generally unfazed by their presence. You can easily organise one of the government elephants yourself, but you'll need to get to the ticket office early and expect a queue. Agents and guesthouses send 'runners' down to book elephants for their guests or clients, so there's usually plenty of pushing and shoving. The ticket office opens at 6 am. It's not as busy later in the day if you're going on an afternoon ride.

A one-hour ride in the national park costs Rs 650 per person. Guesthouses shouldn't charge any more than Rs 50 extra to do the booking for you. Howdahs (wooden-railed seats) are generally used and four people ride on each elephant. Rides depart in the morning (about 7.30 am) and afternoon (4 pm); early morning, when a thin mist hangs over the forest and gradually evaporates, is the most atmospheric time, and perfect for wildlife viewing.

Some guesthouses have their own elephants, but these are restricted to the Baghmara Community Forest, a buffer zone a few kilometres west of the park. Although wildlife can roam freely in this area, the presence of villagers and livestock means that your chances of seeing anything interesting are reduced.

A good time to wander down to the Rapti River is around noon when the elephants are bathing.

Tree Climbing at Chitwan

Early morning walks in Chitwan National Park are exhilarating and can be heart-stoppingly exciting. You have to remember that what you're essentially looking for is a two-tonne Indian one-horned rhinoceros on its territory – and they will charge! Your guide should explain some emergency techniques in the event that you do get too close to a rhino – namely, run as fast as possible to the nearest tree and climb it. Another trick is to throw off a piece of clothing as you make your escape. Rhinos have very poor eyesight and may be distracted by another shape – maybe.

Our walk was nearing its end when the guide started spotting tell-tale rhino signs; mountainous droppings here, trampled undergrowth there. Then we saw another small group of walkers crouched in a clearing, eyes trained ahead. We crept closer, following their line of vision, and soon saw the object of interest – a tank-like rhino in the open grassland about 100m away. The guides had already pointed out climbable nearby trees and suggested we make our way towards one of them. When the rhino suddenly bolted and began its charge, people scattered in all directions, shinnying up trees and dangling from branches in an effort to make room for stragglers. The rhino's charge was short and sharp – more of a scare tactic or nervous reaction – and it soon turned and plodded off into the forest.

Although running up trees is an adrenaline-pumping experience, tourists and guides have been fatally injured by rhinos. It's a lot safer to view rhinos from atop an elephant.

Paul Harding

Jungle Safaris

Jungle walks and jeep safaris can easily be organised at Chitwan. The guided walks begin with a short canoe ride across the Rapti River before you head into the undergrowth. A knowledgeable and experienced guide with a good command of English can make the difference between a good walk and a relatively dull one (terrifying wildlife

NEPAL

encounters notwithstanding), so it's worth meeting your guide before booking the walk.

Most lodges employ their own naturalists, but there are quite a few independent guides around the village. Walking is a great way to see the park's birdlife, butterflies and flora, although short walks cover mostly grassland and riverine forest; you need a full day to get into the jungle.

Jungle walks booked in Sauraha cost around Rs 250 for a half day (about four hours, usually early in the morning) or Rs 400 for a full day. Overnight walks can also be arranged at around Rs 400 per day.

For nervous types, a jeep safari can take you deeper into the park and is a lot safer. The animals are surprisingly unperturbed by vehicles. A jeep safari of three hours or so costs Rs 650 and should include a visit to the park headquarters at Kasara and the gavial crocodile breeding program.

As well as looking out for *gaida* (rhinos) and the rare sighting of a *bagh* (tiger) or *chituwa* (leopard), you're likely to see several species of deer including the *chital* (spotted), *mirga* (barking) and *jarayo* (sambar). Also in the park are *bhalu* (sloth bears), *nilgai* (antelope), *bandar* (langur monkeys) and *sarpa* (snakes).

Canoe Trips

You can glide down the Rapti River in a dugout canoe, and combine it with a guided walk back to the village and a visit to the Elephant Breeding Centre about 3km west of Sauraha. With luck you might spot a gavial or mugger crocodile in the river, but there are also plenty of water birds around. The canoe trip costs around Rs 200 per person, if you get there on foot or by ox cart. A jeep transfer pushes the cost up.

Village Tours

Again most guesthouses can organise half-day tours of traditional Tharu villages, populated by the original Terai inhabitants. Some lodges in Sauraha host stick-dancing shows and cultural programs, which nonguests can attend for an admission of around Rs 50.

You can easily walk or hire a bicycle to explore nearby villages on your own. They're friendly places full of inquisitive children. The nearest Tharu village is Bachauli, about 1km east of Sauraha.

SAURAHA
☎ 056

Sauraha is a dusty village that might have remained very much a typical Terai farming community if not for its proximity and easy access to Chitwan. It's still business as usual in parts, with rickety ox carts rumbling down the main street, villagers tending to fields and livestock roaming around. Most of the villages around Sauraha still consist of mud huts with grass-thatched roofs and bamboo fences.

But tourism is making inroads in the form of dozens of lodges lining the main street, along with a small cluster of restaurants, tour agents and guides for hire, bookshops, moneychangers and telephone offices. Even the Internet has made it to Sauraha. It's still pretty low key and hopefully will stay that way.

There are no banks in Sauraha but there are a couple of moneychangers accepting cash and travellers cheques. You're better off changing money in Pokhara or Kathmandu. Internet access at an office in the middle of the village costs Rs 10 a minute.

Places to Stay

There are plenty of lodges in Sauraha. If you want to look at a few and choose your own, make that clear to the jeep drivers/touts who will besiege you at Chitrasali or Tadi Bazaar.

Many of the places in the southern part of the village have simple mud-and-thatch cottages arranged around a pleasant garden. Most should provide mosquito nets and have solar-powered hot water which might reach a luke-warm temperature on a nice day. You can usually bargain down to less than the prices given here.

Rainforest Lodge (☎ 80007, e *hello@ mos.com.np*) is one of the first places you come to. It's well managed and has a pleasant garden. You can camp in the garden for free if you book any park activities through them. Basic mud-and-thatch cottages with mosquito net and fan and shared bathroom cost Rs 100/150 a single/double. Brick cottages with private bathroom cost Rs 150/250, or Rs 200/300 with hot water, while the 'deluxe' room with bathroom and hammock goes for Rs 400. There's a slideshow on the park wildlife in the evening.

About 100m back towards Chitrasali, *Tiger Wildlife Camp (☎ 60272)* is a quiet, nondescript place with a pleasant garden and a rooftop area. Sturdy bungalows are very good value from Rs 100/150 with private bathroom and tepid water.

Farther down along the main road you'll find *Chitwan Resort Camp (☎ 80082)*, which has clean rooms with private bathroom at a higher standard than the real cheapies. They cost from Rs 350/400. Another place along here is *Travellers Jungle Camp (☎ 80013)* with mud huts for Rs 150 and more modern doubles with private bathroom and solar hot water for Rs 300.

There's a string of cheap places at the southern end of the village, not far from the ticket office and park entrance. *Annapurna View Lodge (☎ 80024)* is about 400m past the Chitwan Tiger Camp. Simple mud-and-thatch huts here cost Rs 50/100 with shared bathroom or Rs 200/250 with private bathroom. You can pitch your own tent in the garden for Rs 50 and they claim not to charge service fees (for ticket bookings) if you book activities with them. This place is popular with overland tour groups.

Sauraha Jungle Lodge (☎ 60560, e subediraj@hotmail.com) is in a relatively secluded spot in the middle of fields a little off the 'main' roads. It advertises 'real jungle rooms' and they certainly are cheap: Basic mud huts are Rs 30/60. If you want a better room with private bathroom it's Rs 200/300.

If you're female and feeling stressed, *Lun Tara (☎ 421210 in Kathmandu, e luntara@ hons.com.np)* is a relaxing place for women in a relatively isolated spot across the river from the elephant breeding centre (about 2.5km from Sauraha). Basic mud cottages with shared bathroom cost Rs 100/ 200, but most of the cottages are attractive doubles with private bathroom and furnishings for Rs 500. There's a restaurant here and park activities can be arranged, as well as interaction with village women and various workshops such as cooking and Nepali dance. They'll pick you up in a horse and cart from the Chitrasali bus stop.

Places to Eat & Drink

Practically every guesthouse has a restaurant but the food can be pretty bland. There are a handful of independent places clus-

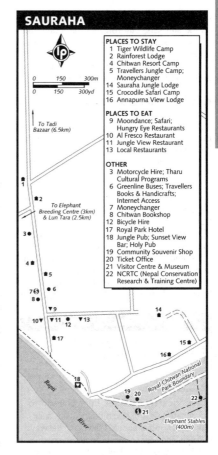

SAURAHA

0   150   300m
0   150   300yd

To Tadi
Bazaar (6.5km)

To Elephant
Breeding Centre (3km)
& Lun Tara (2.5km)

Rapti

Rapti River

Royal Chitwan National
Park Boundary

Elephant Stables
(400m)

PLACES TO STAY
1 Tiger Wildlife Camp
2 Rainforest Lodge
4 Chitwan Resort Camp
5 Travellers Jungle Camp;
   Moneychanger
14 Sauraha Jungle Lodge
15 Crocodile Safari Camp
16 Annapurna View Lodge

PLACES TO EAT
9 Moondance; Safari;
   Hungry Eye Restaurants
10 Al Fresco Restaurant
11 Jungle View Restaurant
13 Local Restaurants

OTHER
3 Motorcycle Hire; Tharu
   Cultural Programs
6 Greenline Buses; Travellers
   Books & Handicrafts;
   Internet Access
7 Moneychanger
8 Chitwan Bookshop
12 Bicycle Hire
17 Royal Park Hotel
18 Jungle Pub; Sunset View
   Bar; Holy Pub
19 Community Souvenir Shop
20 Ticket Office
21 Visitor Centre & Museum
22 NCRTC (Nepal Conservation
   Research & Training Centre)

tered in the middle of the village, which are great meeting places in the evening. Be warned though: Kitchen resources are often minimal and if a place is busy, service may be painfully slow!

Al Fresco is more expensive than some but the food is particularly good. Light meals are Rs 60 to Rs 100, mains are more like Rs 175. There's a range of Indian and Nepali dishes as well as pizzas from Rs 115. *Moondance* and *Safari*, side by side on the main road, have standard menus with mains for around Rs 120, beer for Rs 110, and rooftop dining areas.

Down on the sandy river floodplain, just before Chitwan Tiger Camp, are three bamboo and thatch bars, *Jungle Pub*, *Sunset View Bar* and *Holy Pub*. They're a great spot to prop yourself up and enjoy a beer (Rs 100) as the sun sets, but you may be wondering what happens to them during the monsoon when this area is under water. The owners simply clear out, let them get washed away, and build new ones the following season.

Getting There & Away

Tourist buses from Pokhara and Kathmandu should drop you off at Chitrasali, where the dirt road from Tadi Bazaar to Sauraha crosses a small river. Here you'll be besieged by touts wanting to drag you to 'their' lodge. Some offer free or cheap rides to Sauraha. The normal fare for a jeep is Rs 30. In the heat of the moment it can be difficult to extricate yourself from this onslaught. Some travellers choose to walk to Sauraha (about 3km) rather than be subject to it! It's easiest just to choose the lodge/tout you most like the sound of, pay the Rs 30, and then if you don't like it you're free to look elsewhere.

Public buses from Kathmandu, Pokhara or Sunauli will drop you at Tadi Bazaar, on the

Mahendra Hwy 6km from Sauraha. Touts also meet buses here and the jeep ride again is Rs 30. There may also be ox carts available to take you at marginally quicker than walking pace (about Rs 15). See the Sunauli, Pokhara and Kathmandu sections for details on buses to Tadi Bazaar and Chitrasali.

Going from Sauraha, guesthouses and private agents sell tickets to Kathmandu and Pokhara, with the jeep ride to Chitrasali or Tadi Bazaar included. There's a bus in both directions at 10.30 am. Ticket prices vary from agent to agent but should cost Rs 150 to Kathmandu (5½ hours) or Pokhara (five hours). Most places tack the jeep fare on, and some simply charge inflated prices. Public buses from Tadi Bazaar are cheaper: Rs 90 to Pokhara and Rs 77 to Kathmandu.

For Sunauli, take a jeep to Tadi Bazaar and a public bus (Rs 112, five hours) from there.

Greenline (☎ 60267) has an office on the main road in Sauraha. Air-con buses from Chitrasali depart for Kathmandu and Pokhara at 9.30 am and cost Rs 480.

Getting Around

Bicycles can be hired at a number of places in Sauraha for Rs 15 per hour or Rs 100 per day. Motorcycles can be hired for Rs 140/500 per hour/day. These are handy for getting out to places like Bishajaar Tal (20,000 Lakes) or the Elephant Breeding Centre.

Chitwan to Sunauli

Cycling days: 3
Distance: 192km

The first day's ride was from Chitwan to Somnath (120km, seven hours), with a surprise hill climb of about 800m along the way. Roads and scenery were good. Somnath is 20km east of Butwal where the main roads to Pokhara, Sunauli and Kathmandu meet. You can avoid Butwal and ride straight to Lumbini (50km, 2½ hours). Lumbini is a relaxing place to stay and it's an easy one-hour ride from here to the border at Sunauli (about 22km). Alternatively, you can ride from Chitwan to Butwal in a day (140km).

We decided to stay on the Nepali side (it was New Year's Eve!). I got into the habit of always spending the night on the side of the border of the country I had just been cycling in, rather than crossing over at the end of the day to find myself in a new country. It felt safer as I had familiarity on my side.

Sue Cooper

Kathmandu

☎ 01 • pop 535,000

Kathmandu is a place of legends – not only historically, but in the travellers lexicon of the past 30 years. Kathmandu is the capital and the largest city in the country and the main centre for hotels and restaurants. Combined with the towns of Bhaktapur and Patan, which each have an artistic and architectural tradition that rivals anything you'll find in the great cities of Europe, this is also one of the world's greatest open-air museums. At other times it can appear as just another developing capital catapulting into the modern age, pollution, poverty and all.

Arriving in Kathmandu from a long overland journey – or even fresh off the plane – can be a surreal experience. The tight, narrow streets of Thamel are packed with restaurants, bars, touts and tour operators, but it's not at all glitzy. It's chaotic and irresistible. The old city and Durbar Square are steeped in history and you could spend hours getting lost in this area.

Despite notions of pristine mountain air, pollution is a big problem. The combination of vehicle exhaust emission and the natural closed-in effect of the valley make this one of the most polluted cities in the world. Take the time to get out of Kathmandu city and explore the valley. As well as Bhaktapur and Patan, there's the Tibetan Buddhist centre of Bodhnath, the cremation ghats at Pashupatinath, the temples at Swayambhunath and Changu Narayan, and the superb mountain views from the valley rim at Nagarkot or Pulchowki.

Kathmandu is much more than just the end of the road; it's the beginning of a whole new experience. Relax, eat well, swap overland tales, but take the time to absorb this amazing place.

HISTORY

The Kathmandu Valley has long been a cultural and racial melting pot, with people coming from both east and west. This fusion has resulted in the unique Newari culture that is responsible for the valley's superb art and architecture.

The Newari golden age peaked in the 17th century when the valley consisted of small city-states, and Nepal was a vitally important trading link between Tibet and the north Indian plains. The valley's visible history is inextricably entangled with the Malla kings. It was during their reign, particularly in the 17th and 18th centuries, that many of the valley's finest temples and palaces were built. At one time, each of the three city-states in the valley – Kathmandu, Patan and Bhaktapur – had its own Malla king.

The unification of Nepal in 1768 by Gorkha's King Prithvi Narayan Shah signalled the end of the Kathmandu Valley's fragmentation.

ORIENTATION

Most of the interesting things to see in Kathmandu are clustered in the old part of town from Kantipath (the main north–south road) west towards the Vishnumati River. New Rd starts from the ornamental entrance

by Kantipath and goes straight into the heart of old Kathmandu, changing its name to Ganga Path before it comes to Durbar Square where the old Royal Palace is located. Freak St, Kathmandu's famous street from the hippy era, runs south off Basantapur Square.

Running north-east from Durbar Square is the thoroughfare that was once the main trading artery of the city and is still the busiest street in old Kathmandu. East of Kantipath is Durbar Marg, a broad, modern street flanked by travel agencies, airline offices and a number of restaurants and expensive hotels. It ends at the main entrance to the new Royal Palace. The Thamel area, west of Kantipath, is the brightly lit downtown Kathmandu for most travellers – the cheap accommodation and restaurant centre of the city.

INFORMATION
Tourist Offices & Information

The Nepal Tourism Board's office (☎ 256909, e info@ntb.wlink.com.np) on Bhrikutimandap Marg, in the city on the eastern side of Tundikhel, is the only official tourist office in Kathmandu. It can provide a free city map, answer queries and help with recommendations for trekking outfits and travel agencies (mainly by directing you to the various governing bodies such as the Trekking Association of Nepal). Also in the building is the tourism police (☎ 247041, e tourism@mos.com.np).

There are a number of good notice boards in Thamel that are worth consulting if you are looking for information on such diverse things as apartments, travel and trekking partners, yoga and meditation courses, language courses and cultural events. The Kathmandu Guest House has a good notice board, as do the Pumpernickel Bakery and the Fire & Ice restaurant.

Other useful notice boards are found at the Trekkers' Information Centre (run by Himalayan Rescue Association; ☎ 262746, e hra@aidpost.mos.com.np) in Jyatha opposite the Shree Guest House; and at the Travellers' Information Centre (run by Kathmandu Environmental Education Project; ☎ 259275, e tours@keep.wlink .com.np), next door. HRA gives lectures on altitude sickness at 2 and 3 pm Sunday to Friday. There are some useful notebooks with up-to-date information from other trekkers. KEEP and the HRA provide a

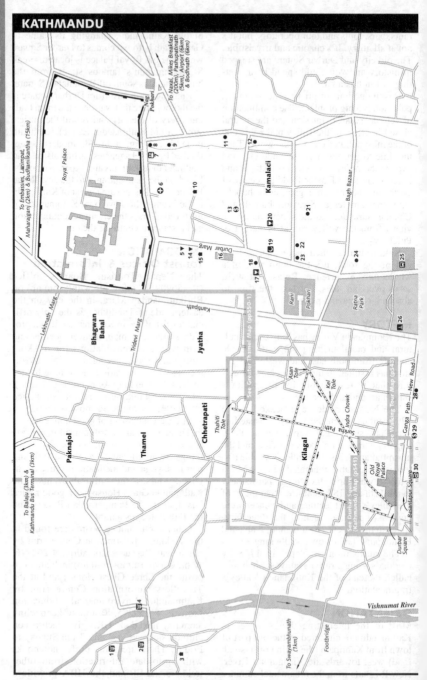

KATHMANDU

NEPAL

To Embassies, Lazimpat, Maharajganj (2km) & Budhanilkantha (15km)

To Naxal, Mikes Breakfast (200m), Pashupatinath (3km), Airport (6km) & Bodhnath (6km)

Royal Palace

Nag Pokhari

Bagh Bazaar

Kamalaci

Durbar Marg

Rani Pokhari

Ratna Park

Lekhnath Marg

Tridevi Marg

Kantipath

Bhagwan Bahal

Jyatha

See Greater Thamel Map (pp550-1)

Asan Tole

Kel Tole

See Walking Tour Map (p543)

Ganga Path

New Road

Paknajol

Thamel

Chhetrapati

Thahiti Tole

Kilagal

Indra Chowk

Sukhra Path

See Durbar Square (Kathmandu) Map (p541)

Old Royal Palace

Basantapur Square

To Balaju (3km) & Kathmandu Bus Terminal (3km)

Durbar Square

Vishnumati River

To Swayambhunath (1km)

Footbridge

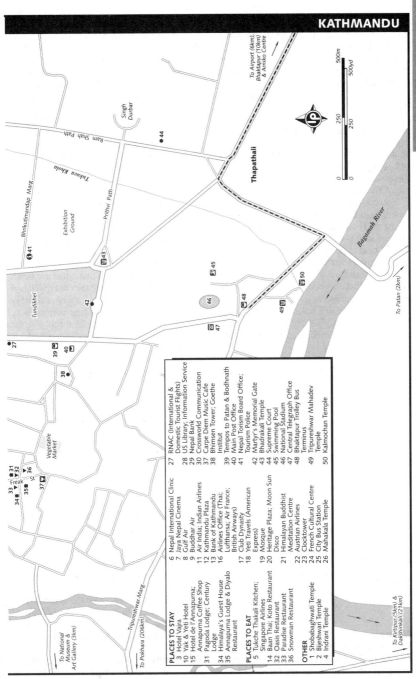

KATHMANDU

To Airport (6km),
Bhaktapur (10km)
& Arniko Centre

Singh
Durbar

Ram Shah Path

● 44

Bhrikutimandap Marg

Tukucha Khola

Prithvi Path

Thapathali

Exhibition
Ground

Bagmati River

🏠 41

🏨 43

To Patan (2km)

Tundikhel

42 ●

🏛 45

46

● 48

49 🏛 🏛 50

🏛
47

● 27

39 🏛
40 🏛

38 ●

Vegetable
Market

🏨 31
▼ 32
St. ▼ 36
33 ▼
Freak
34 ▲ ▼ 37
35 ●

Tripureshwar Marg

To National
Museum &
Art Gallery (3km)

To Pokhara (206km)

To Kirtipur (5km) &
Dakshinkali (21km)

PLACES TO STAY
3 Hotel Vajra
10 Yak & Yeti Hotel
15 Hotel de l'Annapurna;
    Annapurna Coffee Shop
31 Pagoda Lodge; Century
    Lodge
34 Himalaya's Guest House
35 Annapurna Lodge & Diyalo
    Restaurant

PLACES TO EAT
5 Tukche Thakali Kitchen;
   Singapore Airlines
14 Baan Thai; Koto Restaurant
32 Oasis Restaurant
33 Paradise Restaurant
36 Snowman Restaurant

OTHER
1 Shobabaghwati Temple
2 Bijeshwari Temple
4 Indrani Temple

6 Nepal International Clinic
7 Jaya Nepal Cinema
8 Gulf Air
9 Buddhar Air
11 Air India; Indian Airlines
12 Kathmandu Plaza
13 Bank of Kathmandu
16 Airlines Office (Thai;
    Lufthansa; Air France;
    British Airways)
17 Club Dynasty
18 Yeti Travels (American
    Express)
19 Mosque
20 Heritage Plaza; Moon Sun
    Disco
21 Himalayan Buddhist
    Meditation Centre
22 Austrian Airlines
23 Clocktower
24 French Cultural Centre
25 City Bus Station
26 Mahakala Temple

27 RNAC (International &
    Domestic Tourist Flights)
28 US Library; Information Service
29 Nepal Bank
30 Crossworld Communication
37 Carpe Diem Music Cafe
38 Bhimsen Tower; Goethe
    Institut
39 Tempos to Patan & Bodhnath
40 Main Post Office
41 Nepal Torism Board Office;
    Tourism Police
42 Martyr's Memorial Gate
43 Bhadrakali Temple
44 Supreme Court
45 Swimming Pool
46 National Stadium
47 Central Telegraph Office
48 Bhaktapur Trolley Bus
    Terminus
49 Tripureshwar Mahadev
    Temple
50 Kalmochan Temple

500m
500yd

250
250

mineral water refill service for Rs 10 per litre and iodine tablets for purifying water (Rs 500 for 50).

Travellers Nepal is a good-quality, free monthly magazine that covers a broad range of interesting topics and has a good section of practical information, with addresses and phone numbers.

Embassies & Consulates

Most of the foreign embassies and consulates in Kathmandu are north of the city in Lazimpat, Panipokhari and Maharajganj. *Tempos* (passenger taxis) heading north along Kantipur will take you into this area.

You can get visas for India (although some travellers have reported problems doing this), Pakistan, Thailand and Bangladesh. There's no Iranian mission here. The only visas for Tibet/China issued in Kathmandu are for organised groups; individuals wishing to travel to Tibet should get a visa before arriving in Nepal (Delhi is a good place to get them). Even with a Chinese visa you may not be able to travel overland to Tibet, since the border at Kodari is currently closed to independent travellers. Foreign embassies in Kathmandu include:

Australia (☎ 371678, fax 371533) Bansbari, just beyond the Ring Rd in Maharajganj
Canada (☎ 415193) Lazimpat
China (☎ 411740, fax 414045) Baluwatar. Open from 9 am to noon and 3 to 5 pm weekdays; visa applications from 10 to 11.30 am Monday, Wednesday and Friday.
France (☎ 412332, fax 419968, ⓔ ambafr@ mos.com.np) Lazimpat
Germany (☎ 416832, fax 416899) Gyaneshwar
India (☎ 410900, fax 413132, ⓔ indemb@ mos.com.np) Lainchaur. Open from 9 am to 1 pm and 1.30 to 5.30 pm weekdays; visa applications from 9.30 am to 12.30 pm weekdays – allow at least seven days for processing; 15-day to six-month (multiple-entry possible) visas available, cost varies according to nationality.
New Zealand (☎ 412436) Dilli Bazaar
Pakistan (☎ 374011, fax 374012) Ring Road, Maharajganj. Open from 9 am to 5.30 pm weekdays.
UK (☎ 410583, fax 411789) Lainchaur
USA (☎ 411179, fax 419963) Panipokhari

Money

The most convenient bank for travellers staying in the Thamel region is the branch of Nepal Grindlays Bank on Tridevi Marg.

It's open from 9.30 am to 7.30 pm weekdays and 10 am to 5 pm Sunday (closed Saturday). It will change cash and travellers cheques and give advances on Visa and MasterCard in Nepali rupees. Nepal Grindlays Bank has 24-hour ATMs accepting Visa and MasterCard at its Thamel, Kantipath and New Baneshwor branches.

The main Nepal Bank in Dharmapath near New Rd is handy if you're staying in Freak St and is open from 7 am to 7 pm daily. The Bank of Kathmandu in Kamaladi, just east of Durbar Marg changes cash and travellers cheques commission-free.

The American Express agent is Yeti Travels (☎ 227635, fax 226153), which has its office off the forecourt of the Hotel Mayalu on Jamal Tole, just around the corner from Durbar Marg. You can buy travellers cheques here, but you can't exchange them.

There are also a number of licensed moneychangers in Thamel. Their hours are much longer than the banks, and they are quick and efficient to use, but rates vary considerably so shop around. Some charge commission, others don't. Kathmandu also has a great number of 'change money' men and although this black market is officially illegal it is widely accepted; you'll soon get sick of hearing the words 'change money' every three minutes as you stroll around Thamel.

Post & Communications

The main Kathmandu post office is on the corner of Kantipath and Khichapokhari, close to Bhimsen Tower. The stamp counter (No 4) is theoretically open from 8 am to 7 pm Sunday to Thursday and from 11 am to 3 pm Saturday. Unless you have a lot of mail, it's better to take advantage of the hotels, bookshops and communication centres, which will tackle the bureaucracy for you for a nominal charge. Pilgrim's Book House offers a reliable postal service.

The poste restante section at the main post office is quite efficient and is open from 9.15 am to 3.30 pm (to 3 pm Friday and in winter).

Parcels can be sent from the separate foreign post office just north of the main post office. It's open from 10 am to 5 pm Sunday to Thursday and to 2 pm Friday.

Telephone & Fax International phone calls can be made and faxes can be sent from the central telegraph office (open 24 hours) about 500m south of the post office, opposite the National Stadium.

The dozens of 'communication centres' in Thamel and elsewhere offering fax, telephone and mailing services are more convenient, although slightly more expensive – it's worth shopping around. Phone calls and faxes cost around Rs 165 per minute to almost anywhere. Some places offer a callback service at Rs 10 per minute, plus the cost of the initial call. Several Internet cafes in Thamel offer Internet phone calls using dialpad. At the time of research the service was only available to the USA and the line was a bit scratchy but it's incredibly cheap at Rs 10 per minute. Try Centre Point Cyber Cafe.

Email & Internet Access Every second business in Thamel seems to offer Internet access. As well as the dedicated cyber cafes, providers range from hotels or travel agents to the ubiquitous telephone information centres. The network gets congested and the line often drops out, so it's worth typing up long email messages off-line and then sending them. Rates are a flat Rs 3 per minute at most places, but there are a couple of price-cutters in Thamel offering Rs 2 per minute and down in Freak St you'll find the cheapest access of all at Rs 60 per hour (or Rs 1.50 per minute). Try the following:

Anjan Overland Service Freak St; Rs 1.50 per minute or Rs 60 an hour
Centre Point Cyber Cafe Near Hotel Garuda, Thamel; Rs 3 per minute, has dialpad Internet phone
Crossworld Communication Freak St, just south of the Mountain Cafe; only Rs 50 per hour, and busy as a result
Cyber Club Cafe Below Les Yeux Restaurant, Thamel; Rs 3 per minute
Easy Cyber Club Brezel Bakery, Thamel; Rs 3 per minute

National Parks & ACAP Office

Trekking permits are no longer required for the major treks but national park conservation fees are levied and these can be paid at the National Parks & ACAP counter in the Sanchaya Kosh Bhawan building east of Thamel Chowk (below Fire & Ice restaurant). The fee for the Annapurna Conservation Area is Rs 1000 (this can also be paid in Pokhara); for Everest it's Rs 650 and for Langtang it's Rs 650. For the Annapurna Conservation Area you need to take along a passport photograph.

Travel Agencies

Kathmandu has hundreds of travel agencies, particularly along Durbar Marg, Kantipath and in Thamel. Travel agencies are the best places to go for airline tickets. For trekking, rafting and other specialist tours, it's worth going directly to the operators, especially if you want accurate information (see Activities later in this chapter).

We get varying letters from travellers who are happy/unhappy with certain travel agencies, so it's difficult to make recommendations. You should always shop around, and make sure you know what you're paying for. For straightforward travel and ticketing matters, try Wayfarers Travel Services (☎ 417176, fax 245875, ⓔ wayfarer@mos.com.np) in Thamel. Other agencies worth trying are Yeti Travels (☎ 221234, ⓔ yeti@vishnu.ccsl.com.np) on Durbar Marg and Red Lion Travel & Tours (☎ 260595, ⓔ rltt@wlink.com.np) in Thamel.

Bookshops

Kathmandu has a large number of excellent bookshops. Many have particularly interesting selections of books on Nepal including books that are not usually available outside the country. As well as shops with new books there are many shops with second-hand books for sale and trade.

Pilgrims Book House is a couple of doors north of the Kathmandu Guest House and has an extensive collection of books on Nepal and other Himalayan regions. The Kailash Bookshop, on the road from Durbar Marg to the Yak & Yeti Hotel, is also good and has an antiquarian section.

The Barnes & Noble Bookhouse just south of the Kathmandu Guest House has a good range.

Libraries & Cultural Centres

The British Council Library (☎ 222698) on Kantipath is open from 11 am to 6 pm Monday and Friday and from 11 am to 5 pm Tuesday to Thursday (closed weekends).

The French Cultural Centre (☎ 224326) is in Bagh Bazaar and has French publications and organises French film nights.

The German Goethe Institut (☎ 250871) in Ganabahal, near Bhimsen Tower, has film nights and occasional exhibitions as well as library facilities.

The Kaiser or Kesar Library (☎ 411318) is worth a visit just to see the building and gardens. It's part of the Department of Education compound on the corner of Kantipath and Tridevi Marg, and has an incredible collection of books on Buddhism, Tibet and Nepal.

Medical Services

The best bet in the Kathmandu Valley is the Patan Hospital (☎ 522266), which is partially staffed by Western missionaries and is in the Lagankhel district of Patan, close to the last stop of the Lagankhel bus. The Teaching Hospital (☎ 412808) in Maharajganj is reasonably well equipped and has also been recommended.

The CIWEC clinic (☎ 228531, Ⓔ advice@ciwecpc.mos.com.np) just off Durbar Marg is used by many foreign residents of Kathmandu. It's open from 9 am to noon and 1 to 4 pm weekdays and is staffed by westerners. With a single visit costing around US$30, it is hardly surprising the clientele is almost exclusively Western as well.

The Nepal International Clinic (☎ 434642, Ⓔ nic@naxal.wlink.com.np) is near the Jaya Nepal cinema, opposite the Royal Palace. It also has an excellent reputation and is a bit cheaper than the CIWEC clinic. It's open from 9 am to 5 pm daily. The Himalayan International Clinic (☎ 223197, Ⓔ amatya@hic.wlink.com.np) is conveniently located in Jyatha near the Himalayan Rescue Association.

DURBAR SQUARE

The centrepiece of old Kathmandu and the former seat of the Malla kings, this is undoubtedly Kathmandu city's main historical attraction. Durbar in Nepali means palace and this is where the old Royal Palace is located (the royal residence was moved to Narayanhiti about a century ago). Clustered around the Durbar Square are the old Royal Palace (Hanuman Dhoka), the Kumari Bahal (House of the Living Goddess), the Kasthamandap (House of Wood) and numerous interesting wooden temples. The large square to the south, arrayed with handicrafts and souvenirs, is Basantapur Square.

You could spend hours wandering around the Durbar Square area, but expect to get plenty of attention from potential guides, sadhus (wandering Hindu holy men) wanting you to take their photo, rickshawwallahs wanting to take you somewhere else, and children begging for money, pens and trying to get you to buy them powdered milk (at inflated prices). Official guides are available from the Sinha Swan Khala office in the south-eastern corner of Basantapur Square, and these can be very informative. They cost Rs 500 for a one-hour tour. You can talk freelance guides down to a bit less. Some are good, some aren't.

The following is a brief introduction to the principal temples and buildings in Durbar Square. For more information, see Lonely Planet's *Nepal*.

Hanuman Dhoka

The entrance to the old Royal Palace is on the north side and is marked by a Hanuman statue – which is what gave the palace its name (Hanuman is the monkey god and *dhoka* means entrance).

The present building was first constructed by King Pratap Malla in the 17th century, and it contains 10 *chowks* (courtyards). The most famous of these is **Nasal Chowk**, which takes its name from a small figure of the Dancing Shiva inside the whitewashed chamber on the eastern side of the square. This square is traditionally used for coronations: The present King Birendra was crowned here in 1975. **Mul Chowk**, to the east, was completely dedicated to religious functions within the palace and is configured like a vihara. **Mohan Chowk**, north of Nasal Chowk, is the residential courtyard of the Malla kings. It dates from 1649 and at one time a Malla king had to be born here to wear the crown. The richly sculptured water spout is where the Malla kings would ritually bathe each morning.

The part of the palace west of Nasal Chowk, overlooking the main Durbar Square area, was constructed by the Ranas in the late 19th century. Here the **Tribhuvan Museum** has an excellent exhibition on Nepal's modern history, celebrating King Tribhuvan's successful revolt against the Rana regime.

The palace is open from 9.30 am to 4 pm Tuesday to Friday (Rs 250). Photography is prohibited.

DURBAR SQUARE (KATHMANDU)

PLACES TO STAY	7 Kakeshwar Temple	22 Narsingha Statue	35 Kasthamandap (House of Wood)
49 Hotel Sugat	8 Great Drums	23 Panch Mukhi	36 Singh Sattal
51 Park Guest House	9 Krishna Temple	Hanuman Temple	37 Kabindrapur Temple
	10 Saraswati Temple	24 Dancing Shiva Statue	38 Garuda Statue
PLACES TO EAT	11 Stone Vishnu Temple	25 Tribhuvan Museum	39 Trailokya Mohan Narayan Temple
2 Festive Fare Restaurant	12 Great Bell	26 Degutaleju Temple	40 Kumari Bahal (House of the
47 Bakery Cafe	13 King Pratap Malla's Column	27 Seto (White) Bhairab	Living Goddess)
	14 Jagannath Temple	28 Bhagwati Temple	41 Gaddhi Baithak
OTHER	15 Kala (Black) Bhairab	29 Shiva-Parvati temple	42 Coronation Platform
1 Mahendreshwar Temple	16 Indrapur Temple	30 Narayan Temple	43 Kirtipur Tower
3 Tana Deval Temple	17 Vishnu Temple	31 Maju Deval	44 Basantapur Tower
4 Taleju Temple	18 Stone Inscription	32 Lakshmi Narayan Temple	45 Bhaktapur Tower (Lakshmi Bilas)
5 Mahavishnu Temple	19 Mohan Tower	33 Ashok Binayak (Maru	46 Patan (Lalitpur) Tower
6 Kotilingeshwar Mahadev	20 Hanuman Statue	Ganesh Shrine)	48 Anjan Overland Internet
Temple	21 Audience Chamber	34 Shiva Temple	50 Sinha Swan Khala Office

Taleju Temple & Makhan Tole

North-east of Hanuman Dhoka, the **Taleju Temple** is the square's most magnificent, but it's not open to the public. Even Nepalis can only visit the temple during the annual Dasain festival.

West of here is a cluster of temples and this is also the beginning of Makhan Tole, an interesting street that runs north-east to Indra Chowk. The **Kakeshwar Temple**, an odd mix of styles, was originally built in 1681 but was badly damaged in the 1934 earthquake. South of here are the small **Indrapur** and **Vishnu** temples, and behind them is the large **Jagannath Temple**, noted for the erotic carvings on its roof struts. This is the oldest structure in this part of the square and is a favourite haunt of colourfully dressed sadhus.

Opposite the Vishnu Temple, on the outside of the palace wall, is a **stone inscription** to the goddess Kalika, written in 15 languages. King Pratap Malla set this up in 1664 and a Nepali legend states that milk will flow from the spout in the middle if anyone can read all 15 languages.

Behind the Jagannath Temple is the **Kala Bhairab**, a large figure of the black Bhairab – Shiva in his most fearsome aspect. There's a corresponding **Seto Bhairab** (white) hidden away behind a grille opposite **King Pratap Malla's column**.

West of the Jagannath Temple is the easily recognised octagonal **Krishna Temple**, built by King Pratap Malla in 1648. It contains images of Krishna and two goddesses. Just beyond the Krishna Temple are the

Walking Tour

It's interesting to spend a few hours just wandering around the old city where daily life goes on largely unaffected by tourism. In the crowded tangle of streets around Durbar Square you'll find local markets, fruit and flower stalls, religious shrines, children playing in courtyards and people simply coming and going from their homes.

There are regular reminders of Kathmandu's museum-like quality in the ancient statues, sculptures, shrines and temples littering the old city. The following brief description leads you through some of the more interesting areas.

From the north-eastern end of Durbar Square, follow the busy, narrow **Makhan Tole** to **Indra Chowk**. This major square has a couple of interesting temples, the Akash Bhairab Temple and a Shiva Temple. Continuing north-east to **Kel Tole** you'll find the ornate Seto Machhendranath Temple in a large courtyard. Keep walking north-east to **Asan Tole**, one of the busiest junctions in Kathmandu and a popular and atmospheric marketplace full of spice and produce stalls. Also here is the Annapurna Temple and a two-storey pagoda.

Take the road leading directly west out of Asan Tole, passing the Ugratara Temple, to a square known as **Bangemudha** containing the Ikha Narayan Temple and a small Buddha statue. Just south of here you'll see a lump of wood into which thousands of coins have been nailed. Nailing a coin into the wood is supposed to cure toothache, but the string of dentists' shops along the alley to the north presumably finish the job! You can make a diversion along this northern street towards **Thahiti Tole**, to see the Kathesimbhu stupa, which is in a courtyard on the left. This is a miniature copy of the great Swayambhunath Temple west of Kathmandu.

Return to the street and turn right, retracing your steps back past the coin-studded lump of wood, and turn right at the next junction, opposite the **Jana Bahal Temple**. A short walk brings you to **Kilgal Tole** and just beyond this an opening to your left leads to the long rectangular **Yitam Bahal** (monastery) courtyard. There is a stupa and several sculptures here and, on the western side, is the Kichandra Bahal, one of the oldest *bahals* (monasteries) in the city. Back out on the street, turn left and walk to the next junction which has the **Nara Devi Temple** in the far right corner. Turn left here and walk south. Look out for the magnificently carved wooden window on the facade of an otherwise nondescript building on your left next to a triple-roofed pagoda. Continuing south you pass the **Yatkha Bahal** on your right, a large open courtyard with a stupa in the centre. Back on the road it's a short walk south to **Kot Square**, scene of the massacre which brought the Ranas to power in 1846, and then it's back to your starting point at Durbar Square.

Great Drums, to which a goat and buffalo must be sacrificed twice a year.

Bhagwati Temple

In the Durbar Square proper, this triple-storey, triple-roofed temple surmounts the building below it. The best view of this temple is from the Maju Deval across the square.

Shiva-Parvati Temple

Just across the way, this temple was built in the late 18th century by Bahadur Shah and contains an image of Shiva and his consort (again, best seen from the Maju Deval).

Maju Deval

Beloved of hippies and travellers for many years, this is the best place in the Durbar Square area to sit and watch the world go by. The nine-stage platform is probably the most popular meeting place in the city. The temple dates from 1690 and contains a Shiva lingam (though the roof is topped by a pinnacle, shaped like a Buddhist stupa). There are some interesting erotic carvings on the roof struts.

Kasthamandap

In the far south-western corner of Durbar Square, the Kasthamandap (or House of Wood) is the building which gave Kathmandu its name. It was possibly built in the 12th century and legend has it that the entire structure was built from a single sal tree. Originally it was a community centre where visitors gathered before major ceremonies,

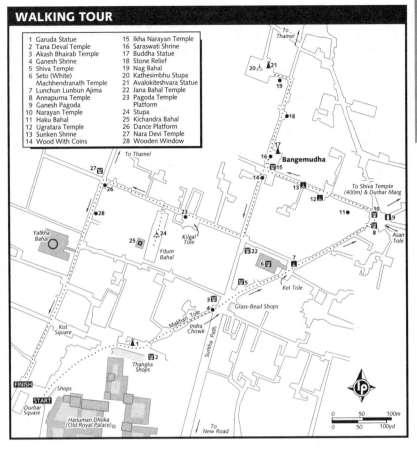

WALKING TOUR

1	Garuda Statue	15	Ikha Narayan Temple
2	Tana Deval Temple	16	Saraswati Shrine
3	Akash Bhairab Temple	17	Buddha Statue
4	Ganesh Shrine	18	Stone Relief
5	Shiva Temple	19	Nag Bahal
6	Seto (White)	20	Kathesimbhu Stupa
	Machhendranath Temple	21	Avalokiteshvara Statue
7	Lunchun Lunbun Ajima	22	Jana Bahal Temple
8	Annapurna Temple	23	Pagoda Temple
9	Ganesh Pagoda		Platform
10	Narayan Temple	24	Stupa
11	Haku Bahal	25	Kichandra Bahal
12	Ugratara Temple	26	Dance Platform
13	Sunken Shrine	27	Nara Devi Temple
14	Wood With Coins	28	Wooden Window

but later it was converted to a temple to Gorakhnath.

Trailokya Mohan Narayan Temple

Back towards the palace, this temple was built by Prithvibendra Malla in 1680 and is easily identified as a temple to Narayan or Vishnu by the fine kneeling Garuda in front.

Kumari Bahal

This is the structure that most captures the imagination, not so much because of its architectural beauty, but because of who lives here. The Kumari Bahal (House of the Living Goddess) faces Durbar Square and its entrance is flanked by stone lions. Inside lives the young girl (the Kumari Devi) who is selected to be the town's living goddess –

until she reaches puberty and is replaced by a new living goddess.

The selection of the Kumari Devi is complex. The candidate is taken from a particular caste of Newari gold and silversmiths and is usually somewhere between age four and puberty. She must meet 32 strict physical requirements and have a favourable horoscope. Once candidates are selected, they are placed in a darkened room and subjected to a frightening display of noises and men dancing in horrific masks. The child who remains most calm is thought to be the new Kumari – a reincarnation of the goddess Durga. She then goes with her family to live in the Kumari Bahal and is supported by the temple income. The Kumari emerges for several ceremonial events, the biggest

NEPAL

being the Indra Jatra Festival in August/September.

Inside the building, the three-storey courtyard is enclosed by superbly carved wooden balconies. This is as far as foreigners can go. Photographing the Kumari Devi is forbidden, but photography is allowed inside the courtyard when the goddess is not present.

OTHER ATTRACTIONS
Freak Street

Kathmandu's most famous street from the old hippy overland days of the late 1960s and early 1970s runs south from Basantapur Square. Its real name is still Jochne but since the early 1970s it has been far better known by the moniker 'Freak St'. In its hippy prime this was the place for cheap hotels, colourful restaurants, hashish shops, and the weird and wonderful 'freaks' who gave the street its name. In those days Freak St was one of the great gathering places on the road east.

For those people who find the ever-expanding Thamel too crowded, Freak St still offers a bit of nostalgia and cheap hotels in the heart of old Kathmandu, a stone's throw from Durbar Square.

People-Watching

The best place in Kathmandu to sit and watch the world go by is from the upper steps of the Maju Deval temple in Durbar Square. This is still known locally as the 'hippy temple' from the days when the 'freaks' used to gather here and contemplate life while passing around a joint. These days it's a good place to sit and watch the constant activity of Kathmandu taking place below, but you won't find much solitude. Within minutes you'll be approached by a young Nepali either wanting to practice his English or trying to sell you something.

National Museum & Art Gallery

Not far from Swayambhunath, the National Museum is a bit disappointing, but the art gallery has a fine collection of religious art. A visit can easily be combined with a trip to the ancient Buddhist stupa of Swayambhunath (see the 'Temples of the Kathmandu Valley' special section later in this chapter).

The museum has a rather eccentric collection that includes some moon rock, a number of moth-eaten stuffed animals, a vast number of uniforms and military decorations, swords and guns, and a portrait gallery. The most interesting exhibit is a leather Tibetan cannon.

The museum is open from 10 am to 5 pm in summer and 10 am to 4 pm in winter, except on Friday when it's open from 10 am to 2.30 pm (closed Tuesday). Entry costs Rs 10.

ACTIVITIES
Trekking

There are numerous specialist trekking agencies around Thamel and Durbar Marg, and just about every travel agency in town will be able to organise guided treks of one sort or another. If you're planning on trekking independently, or want to round up some trekking partners or join someone else's trek, check out the notice boards around town (see Information earlier).

Organised treks can vary greatly in standards and costs. Treks involving village accommodation or camping can cost from US$25 per person per day if you go through cut-price agencies, up to US$60 or US$70 per day with the top companies. Costs should include transport to and from the trek starting points (although flights will cost extra), guides and porters, meals, accommodation (in tents or lodges), water (boiled or treated) and possibly rental equipment such as sleeping bags and waterproof gear.

Some of the smaller agencies specialising in independent trekkers in Kathmandu include:

Asian Trekking (☎ 415506, 🖃 asiant@
asiantrekking.com) PO Box 3022
Himalayan Encounters (☎ 417426, 🖃 raf
tnepal@himenco.wlink.com.np) Kathmandu
Guest House compound, Thamel
Lucky Trek & Expedition Nepal (☎ 259415)
Thahity Chowk
Motherland Nepal Trekking (☎ 663079,
🖃 mother@mos.com.np) near Thamel Chowk

Mountain Biking

Could there be a better place for mountain biking than Nepal? You can hire a sturdy mountain bike (see Getting Around later in this section), grab a map and take off on your own, or you could join an organised

Trekking in Nepal – A Brief Introduction...

What & Where?

Trekking as a leisure activity began in Nepal in the 1960s after pioneering Himalayan moun-
taineers began using trails to reach base camps from where they could make their assault on
the great peaks. Most of the popular (and remote) trails in use today, however, have been
used by Nepali people as trade and communication routes for centuries, and still are. Walking is the only way to get to many villages in Nepal.

Trekking is not mountaineering, although you'll get up past 5000m if you walk the Annapurna Circuit (at Thorung La pass) or to the Everest Base Camp. On high treks like these, make
sure you know the affects of Acute Mountain Sickness (AMS) and the importance of acclimatisation. Often, though, you'll be passing through beautiful hill country with terraced fields,
ramshackle villages and rhododendron forests – with a few 8000m peaks thrown in for enhanced scenery! Although there are plenty of shorter walks around Kathmandu and Pokhara,
Nepal's most popular treks take at least a week, and for the Everest Base Camp and Annapurna Circuit treks you need to allow up to three weeks (although many travellers complete
the circuit comfortably in two weeks). A typical day's trekking starts early (around 7 am) and
finishes eight or nine hours later at a village lodge or camp site, with a couple of hours for
lunch in the middle of the day and regular rest stops.

When?

The best time to go trekking is October to May (the dry season) and the worst time is June
to September (monsoon). October and November are the busiest times, when the views are
crystal clear and the climate is mild. December and January are bitterly cold at altitude (the
Thorung La pass is often blocked by snow). By mid-March the views begin to get hazy as the
long dry spell causes dust to hang in the air.

How?

The question of independent trekking versus organised trekking is a very personal choice. Independent trekking gives you ultimate freedom to go at your own pace and choose your own
trekking partners (and is cheaper); an organised trek frees you from having to find a place to
stay and eat at the end of a long day, from carrying extra gear, and it means you have trekking
partners if you're travelling solo. In between is the option of simply hiring a local guide or
porter (around US$8 to US$12 and US$4 to US$6 per day respectively). For most reasonably
fit people, guides and porters are not necessary on the Annapurna and Everest treks, but a
good guide can enhance your experience and a porter can certainly take a load off your back.

More Information?

There's not enough room in this book to even begin to cover the main treks in Nepal: Everest Base Camp; Langtang; Helambu; Annapurna Circuit and Sanctuary; or the remote treks
of Dolpo, Mustang and Kanchenjunga.

However, piles of books, guides and maps are available from shops in Kathmandu, and
trekking and travel agencies are always keen to impart advice, although it may not always be
impartial since their main aim is to sign you up for a trek. There are a couple of excellent
sources of independent trekking advice in Kathmandu. The Himalayan Rescue Association
(HRA) and the Kathmandu Environmental Education Project (KEEP) both run useful information centres – see Information in this section for details. A number of trekking agencies offer
free slide shows outlining their treks. The regular talks and slide shows at the Kathmandu
Guest House cost Rs 250, but they are excellent and offer impartial advice and a question-
and-answer session.

tour which takes care of things like gear, equipment, accommodation and food. It also means you have a guide and support team.

Organised rides range from a one-day tour of the Kathmandu Valley (US$25) to a 12-day off-road adventure from US$550. Downhill rides from the valley rim at Nagarkot offer the thrills without the hard work. You get a shuttle up to Nagarkot and ride down to Bhaktapur (US$55).

The two main mountain-biking operators are: Dawn Till Dusk (☎ 418286, e dtd@wlink.com.np) in the Kathmandu Guest House compound; and Himalayan Mountain Bikes (☎ 437437, e bike@hmb.wlink.com.np) at the Adventure Centre Nepal, next to Northfield Cafe in Thamel.

White-Water Rafting

Regular trips are organised out of Kathmandu on most of Nepal's major rafting rivers, the most popular being the Trisuli, Bhote Kosi, Sun Kosi and the Seti (see the Pokhara section for rivers farther west). Trips on the Trisuli can be organised through various agents for US$15 per day, including transport, meals and camping on the riverbank. The better rafting companies charge double this. The advantage of the Trisuli is that it's easily accessible (it runs virtually parallel to the Prithvi Hwy), so you can have a two- or three-day rafting trip without having to travel far out of Kathmandu. It's a fairly leisurely experience, though, with few white-water thrills, except during or immediately after the monsoon when the water is high.

The best short trip is probably the exciting two-day Bhote Kosi (US$70 to US$80), which can be combined with a death-defying 160m bungee jump into a river gorge. Most of the professional rafting

Riding the Bhote Kosi

The first drama on our two-day jaunt down the Bhote Kosi occurred only about 20 minutes after we had put in. We'd been warned to brace ourselves for the 'big hole' and with the guide screaming 'Right back!', 'Left forward!', 'All forward!', 'Everybody DOWN!' in the space of three seconds it was surprising we got through OK.

It was the second boat that got stuck. As we looked back from our calm mooring, we saw them go in, paddles flailing everywhere, instructions being screamed. But in they stayed, bobbing and spinning like corks in a washing machine. In the midst of a difficult part of a Class 4 rapid, excitement turned to mild panic (for the rafters, not the leaders) as a rescue operation swung into action. Then the raft bucked once too often and out went the first casualty. He disappeared under the foam then surfaced seconds later, pop-eyed and spluttering, in classic feet-first man-overboard position. A safety kayaker deftly manoeuvred into position so the rafter could grab hold of his kayak, and managed to rescue a stray paddle and sandal. Another rafter popped out before the boat did, but the drama was over in a matter of minutes. Everyone was fine – and it made a great topic of conversation back at the camp.

With Class 3 and 4 rapids with names like 'Gerbil in the Plumbing', 'Frog in the Blender', 'John Holmes' (because it's long) and 'Midnight Special', the Bhote Kosi is one of the most exciting and technically demanding white-water rafting trips in Nepal, and certainly the best two-day trip. It's not for the faint-hearted, but it's exhilarating and you don't need any prior rafting experience to do it – Nepal's top rafting companies have professional and experienced guides to take you through it. When you're not battling rapids, the valley scenery and riverside villages add to the experience.

Also on the Bhote Kosi three hours from Kathmandu is the Last Resort camp, where thrill-seekers can bungee jump 160m from a purpose-built cable suspension bridge into the river gorge. A jump costs US$80 (including transport) or US$100 with a night at the Last Resort. Better still is to combine it with a day of rafting (US$125). Book through Wet Dreams (☎ 439525) in Thamel.

companies with offices in Thamel host regular slide shows and talks outlining their trips; it's well worth attending one or more of these to assess the various companies and get an idea of what you're in for.

Major rafting companies operating out of Kathmandu include:

Drift Nepal (☎ 425797, e driftnepal@wlink .com.np) Thamel
Equator Expeditions (☎ 415782) Thamel
Himalayan Encounters (☎ 417426) Kathmandu Guest House compound, Thamel
Ultimate Descents Nepal (☎ 419295) Adventure Centre Nepal, Thamel
Wet Dreams (☎ 439525) next to Kathmandu Guest House, Thamel

Hot-Air Ballooning
On a clear day this is probably the best way to view the vast expanse of the Himalaya – from more than 3000m above the ground.

The view of Kathmandu and the valley is equally breathtaking.

The balloon flights take place during the season at 6.30 am daily and fly either east to west or vice versa over the city, depending on the wind. It's an amazing experience, although crossing over the international airport is a little unnerving, and the landing in a rice field usually attracts a huge, excited and curious crowd of local villagers.

The cost of the one-hour flight is US$195 per person, which includes transport to and from your hotel, and a full buffet breakfast at a Thamel restaurant. For further information and bookings contact Balloon Sunrise Nepal (☎ 424131, fax 424157, e balloon@sunrise.mos.com.np).

Mountain Flights
Regular one-hour mountain flights – out to Mt Everest and back – take off daily

---

Riding the Bhote Kosi

The following is a snapshot of the other rafting rivers in Nepal, just to whet your appetite:

Trisuli
The least demanding and least-desirable river in Nepal. Easy access from Kathmandu and lack of thrills mean this can be paddled for just US$15 a day.

Kali Gandaki
At medium and lower flows, a fun and challenging three-day ride with great scenery to boot. Starts at Baglung (access from Pokhara) and costs US$70 to US$100.

Sun Kosi
The longest rafting trip in Nepal at 270km (US$300 to US$350, nine to 11 days) with rapids from Class 2 to 4. A great trip if you really want to spend some time getting to know a river.

Seti
Not a huge white-water trip, but an enjoyable two- or three-day ride with plenty of easy rapids and fine scenery (from US$150).

Karnali
A remote and challenging trip in the far west of Nepal, this is the largest river in the country and runs through some wonderful canyons and jungle. This is for true rafting devotees with up to 12 days spent on the water (US$400 to US$450).

Marsyangdi
Perhaps Nepal's wildest river, this five-day trip starts with a trek to the village of Ngadi, superb mountain scenery, then steep, technical and solid Class 4 and 5 white-water rapids. This is an excellent trip to do with an experienced company using top guides. It's around US$250.

MICK WELDON

Paul Harding

in the high season. They cost a fixed US$109 whether you buy your ticket through travel agents or through one of the numerous private airlines operating this flight. If you don't intend to trek to the Everest Base Camp, this is your only chance of seeing the 'Big One' up close. Even though seeing Everest is actually mildly disappointing, flying alongside the entire Himalayan range (at eye level) shows what a truly stunning chain of mountains this is. Everyone gets a window seat and you may even be summoned to the cockpit to get a decent view of Everest (rather than having to peer through the yellow-tinged porthole windows). If seeing mountains up close is a priority, it's worth the money. The early flights (7 am) are best and you should get a postponement to another day if the weather or visibility is poor. Note that there's also a Rs 100 airport tax.

Yoga & Meditation

Yoga and meditation courses are widely advertised around Kathmandu, especially on notice boards.

The Patanjali Yoga Centre (☎ 276670), Tahachal 13, next to the Hotel Shreshtha in Kalimati, has introductory yoga workshops from 11 am to 3 pm every Wednesday (including lunch), and daily classes in hatha yoga and meditation.

The Himalayan Buddhist Meditation Centre (☎ 221875) in Kamaladi, just east of Durbar Marg, has a regular program of mandala dance and meditation.

Other places to try are the Arogya Ashram at Pashupatinath; the Kopan monastery (☎ 226717) north of Bodhnath, which has a 10-day residential course introducing Buddhist philosophy; and the Shakti Healing Yoga Centre (☎ 222875) between Durbar Square and Swayambhunath.

ORGANISED TOURS

A few travel agencies offer tours to points of interest around the Kathmandu Valley. Red Lion Travel & Tours (☎ 260595) in Thamel has bus tours to Pashupatinath, Bodhnath, Swayambhunath and Patan for Rs 250. Any agent can arrange a car and driver for a tailored day of sightseeing, but if there's a group of you, it's just as easy and probably cheaper to hire a taxi for half a day.

PLACES TO STAY

Kathmandu has a huge range of places to stay. Backpackers are well catered for with cheap, comfortable and friendly lodges, but there are also plenty of mid-range and luxury places.

It's definitely worth looking around if you plan to stay for any length of time, and check more than one room in a particular hotel because they can vary widely. We can only give a small selection of what's on offer here.

For budget and mid-range places the Thamel area is the tourist ghetto. There is still a scattering of rock-bottom places along Freak St, and these are still very popular with backpackers and overlanders. In fact, when we visited in March there was hardly a bed available in Freak St.

During the peak times (October to November and February to early April) rooms in the most popular hotels can be in short supply. Generally, though, finding a room – and bargaining down the price – is easy. Prices given here are the high-season prices shown on hotel tariff cards. At all but the top-end hotels these are pure fiction, shown to you more in the hope that you might be silly enough to pay them. Prices are highly negotiable and 50% discounts are pretty standard.

PLACES TO STAY – BUDGET

Even the cheapest hotels often provide hot showers, although water is usually solar-heated and is only hot in the late afternoon. Toilets are usually Western style and many places have pleasant roof terraces or gardens.

Thamel & Paknajol

Kathmandu Guest House (☎ 413632, fax 417133, e ktmguest@ecomail.com.np) is Thamel's original and still one of the most popular places around. It also serves as a useful central landmark since it's so well known and is right in the thick of things, though it is set back in its own peaceful area. These days it's distinctly mid-range – and not the best value around – but we've included it in this category because it still has some cheap rooms and a lot of backpackers like to stay here for the atmosphere. There's always an interesting mix of people here, including overlanders and returning or departing trekkers. The budget rooms are pretty worn and cost US$6/8 a single/double with washbasin but shared bathroom (hot water shower) or US$10/12 with bath. In the newer wing pleasant, small rooms with bathroom are US$17/20. Add 12% tax to these prices.

Hotel Star (☎ *414000,* **e** *star@htp.com .np),* next door, featured prominently in Kim Stanley Robinson's *Escape from Kathmandu.* These days it has zero atmosphere but it's certainly central. Rooms start at Rs 150/200 with shared bath, and Rs 200/350 with private bathroom.

Pheasant Lodge (☎ *417415)* is a basic place tucked farther around the laneway past Hotel Star, so it feels removed from the Thamel bustle. Rooms with shared bathroom are Rs 100/150.

Hotel Potala (☎ *419159)* is a decent Tibetan-run cheapie down a small lane opposite KC's Restaurant. Basic but clean rooms, all with shared bath, cost from Rs 125/175.

Hotel California, just off Thamel's main north–south street, is a friendly, well-run place with reasonably clean rooms, although some are a bit gloomy. There are dorm beds for Rs 80, singles with shared bathroom for Rs 200 and doubles with private bathroom for Rs 350.

Hotel Horizon (☎ *220904, fax 252999),* farther along the same alley, has a range of rooms at reasonable prices. They start at US$4/5 for fairly spartan rooms with bathroom and go to US$10 for larger doubles, and US$15 for good luxury rooms. **Mom's House Lodge** (☎ *252492)* is a small place but centrally located and cheap. Singles/doubles with shared bathroom are Rs 100/150 and doubles with private bathroom are Rs 250.

Marco Polo Guest House (☎ *251914,* **e** *marcopolo@wlink.com.np),* on the busy street just east of Thamel Chowk, is popular. There's a convivial TV lounge and some surprisingly pleasant rooftop patios. Rooms with shared bathroom start at only Rs 100/150. With private bathroom they're Rs 200/250 or Rs 400 for larger doubles. The rooms at the back are particularly good, and there's usually hot water. The quiet and clean **Student Guest House** (☎ *251551,* **e** *krishna@student.wlink.com.np)* next door has decent-sized rooms with private bathroom and hot water from US$5/8. Despite the name, there's no student orientation or special discount here.

North of Hotel Garuda, **Mustang Guest House** (☎ *426053,* **e** *chitaure@mos.com .np)* is tucked down an inconspicuous laneway but is otherwise in the thick of things. Rooms are reasonably good value at Rs 150/200 with shared bath, or Rs 250/300 with private bath.

Holy Lodge (☎ *416265,* **e** *holylodge @wlink.com.np),* down the street past the Rum Doodle Restaurant, has neat and clean rooms from Rs 200/300 to US$9/12 with bathroom, and a nice courtyard at the back.

Not far from the steep Paknajol intersection (north-west of Thamel) there are a couple of pleasant guesthouses. They're away from traffic, a short walk from Thamel (but it could be a million miles), and they have beautiful views across the valley towards Balaju and Swayambhunath. The small and friendly **Tibet Peace Guest House** (☎ *415026)* has well-equipped rooms with lockers, bathrooms and telephones; singles/doubles cost from Rs 200/250.

At the end of the road **Kathmandu Peace Guest House** (☎ *439369,* **e** *ktmpeacegh@ visitnepal.com)* is a friendly, attractive place with doubles for US$6 with shared bathroom or single/doubles from US$8/12 with private bath. There's Internet access and great views from the roof terrace. **Kathmandu Garden House** (☎ *415239,* **e** *hmtql@ccsl.com.np),* across the road, is not as good but is still value for money at Rs 200/300 for doubles with shared/private bathroom.

Chhetrapati & Jyatha

The Chhetrapati neighbourhood is named after the important five-way intersection (with a distinctive bandstand) to the south-west of Thamel. The farther you are from Thamel, the more traditional the surroundings become.

Hotel Madhuban (☎ *252277,* **e** *hrt@ hardrock.wlink.com.np),* around to the east and just north of Chhetrapati Square, is an excellent choice. Clean, homely and quiet, it has large singles/doubles for US$6/10 or US$8/15. There's a TV lounge and a nice rooftop terrace. This area is away from the Thamel bustle but only a few minutes' walk from the action.

The neighbourhood to the south-east of Thamel has traditionally been known as Jyatha, but increasingly the word is used to

GREATER THAMEL

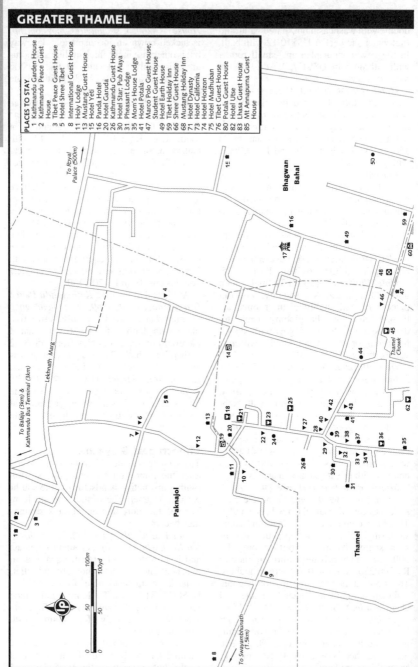

PLACES TO STAY
1 Kathmandu Garden House
2 Kathmandu Peace Guest
   House
3 Tibet Peace Guest House
5 Hotel Shree Tibet
8 International Guest House
11 Holy Lodge
13 Mustang Guest House
15 Hotel Yeti
16 Panda Hotel
20 Hotel Garuda
26 Kathmandu Guest House
30 Hotel Star; Pub Maya
31 Pheasant Lodge
35 Mom's House Lodge
41 Hotel Potala
47 Marco Polo Guest House;
   Student Guest House
49 Hotel Earth House
59 Tibet Holiday Inn
66 Shree Guest House
68 Mustang Holiday Inn
71 Hotel Dynasty
73 Hotel California
74 Hotel Horizon
75 Hotel Madhuban
76 Tibet Guest House
80 Potala Guest House
82 Hotel Utse
83 Lhasa Guest House
85 Mt Annapurna Guest
   House

GREATER THAMEL

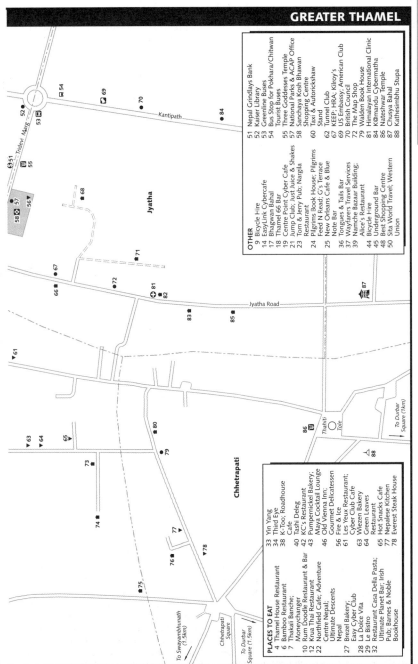

Kantipath

Tridevi Marg

Jyatha

Jyatha Road

Chhetrapati

Thahiti
Tole

To Durbar Square (1km)

To Swayambhunath (1.5km)

Chhetrapati Square

To Durbar Square (1.5km)

PLACES TO EAT
4 Thamel House Restaurant
6 Bamboo Restaurant
7 Thakali Banche; Moneychanger
10 Rum Doodle Restaurant & Bar
12 Krua Thai Restaurant
22 Northfield Cafe; Adventure Centre Nepal; Ultimate Descents Nepal
27 Brezel Bakery; Easy Cyber Club
28 La Dolce Vita
29 Le Bistro
32 Restaurant Casa Della Pasta; Ultimate Planet Bar; Irish Pub; Barnes & Noble Bookhouse
33 Yin Yang
34 Third Eye
38 K-Too; Roadhouse Cafe
40 Tashi Deleg
42 KC's Restaurant
43 Pumpernickel Bakery; Maya Cocktail Lounge
46 Old Vienna Inn; Gourmet Delicatessen
56 Fire & Ice
61 Les Yeux Restaurant; Cyber Club Cafe
63 Wiezen Bakery
64 Green Leaves Restaurant
65 Hot Snacks Cafe
77 Nepalese Kitchen
78 Everest Steak House

OTHER
9 Bicycle Hire
14 EasyLink Cybercafe
17 Bhagwan Bahal
18 Thamel 66 Bar
19 Centre Point Cyber Cafe
21 Jump Club; Just Juice & Shakes
23 Tom & Jerry Pub; Nargila Restaurant
24 Pilgrims Book House; Pilgrims Feed N Read; G's Terrace
25 New Orleans Cafe & Blue Note Bar
36 Tongues & Tails Bar
37 Wayfarers Travel Services
39 Namche Bazaar Building; Alice's Restaurant
44 Bicycle Hire
45 Underground Bar
48 Best Shopping Centre
50 Sita World Travel; Western Union
51 Nepal Grindlays Bank
52 Kaiser Library
53 Greenline Buses
54 Bus Stop for Pokhara/Chitwan Tourist Buses
55 Three Goddesses Temple
57 National Parks & ACAP Office
58 Sanchaya Kosh Bhawan Shopping Centre
60 Taxi & Autorickshaw Stand
62 Tunnel Club
67 KEEP; HRA; Kilroy's
69 US Embassy; American Club
70 British Council
72 The Map Shop
79 Walden Book House
81 Himalayan International Clinic
84 K@mandu Cybermatha
86 Nateshwar Temple
87 Chusya Bahal
88 Kathesimbhu Stupa

describe the main north-south road that runs into the western end of Tridevi Marg.

Shree Guest House (☎ 250615, ℮ djoshi@wlink.com.np), on Jyatha Rd, is basic and threadbare but it's a friendly place. Rooms here cost Rs 175/250 with private bathroom and there's hot water in the morning.

Lhasa Guest House (☎ 226147, ℮ dasel@ccsl.com.np) is another good place with rooms for US$8/12 with private bathroom or a single with shared bathroom for US$4. The bathrooms are spotless and there's a nice rooftop terrace and garden. Farther south, off Jyatha Rd, *Mt Annapurna Guest House* (☎ 225462) has well-kept, airy rooms for US$5/6 and a good view from its rooftop terrace. The best rooms are the two rooftop doubles for US$10 but they're often full.

Bhagwan Bahal
This area to the north-east of Thamel is much quieter than Thamel proper, with just a few scattered guesthouses.

Hotel Earth House (☎ 418197, fax 418436), just off Tridevi Marg, is a good budget hotel which is already starting to show its age. It has friendly staff, a nice rooftop garden and a variety of clean and decent rooms. Singles/doubles start at US$4/6 but can go as high as US$10/16. The rooms at the back are best.

Panda Hotel (☎ 424683, ℮ panda@wlink.com.np) has nice clean rooms, especially the front with balcony. Doubles with shared bathroom are Rs 200, with private bathroom it's US$6 to US$12.

Durbar Square & Freak Street
Hotel Sugat (☎ 245824, ℮ maryman@mos.com.np) is a bit run-down but you can't beat the location, overlooking the square. Dark but reasonably sized rooms cost Rs 11/33 with shared bathroom and Rs 300/400 with private bathroom.

Park Guest House (☎ 228572), almost next door, is cleaner and has some rooms overlooking Basantapur Square. The better rooms are reflected in the price: Rs 250/300 with shared bath, Rs 400 for a double with private bathroom.

On Freak St itself, *Century Lodge* (☎ 247641) is in a small courtyard to the left if you're walking south from the square.

It's one of Freak St's long-term survivors and remains a popular, atmospheric place. No frills singles/doubles cost Rs 125/150 with shared bath, or there are small doubles with private bathroom at Rs 250.

Pagoda Lodge (☎ 247629) is reached from the same courtyard. It's about as basic as they get, and rooms cost just Rs 90/165, all with shared bath, although even this is negotiable.

Just off Freak St (turn right opposite Oasis Garden Restaurant if walking down from the square) is the excellent *Annapurna Lodge & Diyalo Restaurant* (☎ 247684). This place is well kept and cheerful, in contrast to some of the Freak St dives. Doubles cost Rs 200 with shared bath, or Rs 300 with private bath. There are no singles.

Himalaya's Guest House (☎ 246555), a couple of short blocks west of Freak St, is a good choice. Clean, comfortable rooms cost from Rs 150/300 with shared bathroom and Rs 350 for a double with private bathroom. There's a good cafe here, and the rooftop views are great.

PLACES TO STAY – MID-RANGE
Mid-range in Kathmandu means from around US$10 to US$50 for a double. Many hotels blur the lines by offering a mixture of budget and mid-range rooms.

Thamel & Paknajol
Hotel Garuda (☎ 416340, fax 413614, ℮ garuda@mos.com.np) is one of the more sought after mid-range Thamel addresses. It's central, well run and good value. Singles/doubles are from US$9/13, up to US$29/36 with air-con, TV and balcony.

Tibet Holiday Inn (☎ 411453, fax 423426, ℮ hotelgnr@col.com.np), opposite the shopping centre east of Thamel Chowk, offers reasonably high standards and is set back from the noisy street. Large, clean rooms with hot water start from US$19/25, or deluxe (with TV) at US$25/30, but discounts of 60% are a matter of course.

Hotel Shree Tibet (☎ 419902, fax 425938, ℮ sritibet@ccsl.com.np), hidden down a laneway in Paknajol, is a clean place with good rooms, although some are gloomy due to the buildings being very close together. Singles/doubles go for US$10/15, although there's room to negotiate. The small restaurant serves decent food.

International Guest House (☎ 252299, fax 252999, **e** igh@wlink.com.np) is in an area known as Kaldhara and has standard singles/doubles for US$16/20, or deluxe rooms for US$20/25, but discounts up to 50% are offered. It's a pleasant hotel with one of the best rooftop views in the city. This area is quieter and less of a scene than Thamel but not too far away from the restaurants.

Chhetrapati & Jyatha

The popular *Potala Guest House* (☎ 220467, fax 223256) straddles budget and mid-range, with clean, well-kept singles/doubles with TV from US$10/15 and better suites for US$20. There's hot water, a small garden and a good notice board here.

Tibet Guest House (☎ 260556, **e** tibet@guesths.mos.com.np), down a laneway in Chhetrapati, has good-sized and well-maintained rooms with bathroom from US$16/21, and others ranging up to US$37/39, all plus 12% tax. There's a restaurant, a pleasant garden and good views from the rooftop garden.

Hotel Utse (☎ 226946, **e** utse@wlink .com.np), on Jyatha Rd, is a comfortable Tibetan hotel. The rooms are spotlessly clean and very comfortable, putting some of the more expensive hotels to shame. Singles/ doubles cost from US$15/21; deluxe rooms with carpet and TV are US$19/25. It's a very well-run hotel, with a good rooftop area, and is often full in the peak months.

Hotel Dynasty (☎ 263172, fax 250793, **e** hoteldyn@wlink.com.np), down a quiet lane, is an excellent mid-range choice. It's modern, with a flash marble lobby and a lift. The rooms are a good size and all have TV, phone and hot water. They cost US$40/50, or US$50/60 with air-con. The rooftop terrace offers a fine view and even has real lawn on it!

Mustang Holiday Inn (☎ 249041, **e** ntb@mhi.wlink.com.np), north of the Dynasty in a small enclave of hotels, has pleasant rooms and is well run. It's at the low end of the mid-range scale with rooms from US$8/10 with shared bath, or US$15/20 with private bath, though these are negotiable, even in the high season.

Bijeshwari

Across the river in the Bijeshwari area, on the way from Thamel to Swayambhunath, the *Hotel Vajra* (☎ 272719, fax 271695, **e** vajra@mos.com.np) is one of Kathmandu's most interesting hotels. Built partially in Newari style and with intricate ceiling and wall frescoes, it has a distinct style and a superb location looking across the river to Kathmandu. The hotel has an art gallery, its own theatre where classical Nepali dances are performed, a library with books on Tibet and Buddhism, a rooftop garden and the Explorer's Restaurant. Rooms in the old wing are small but full of character and cost US$14/16 with shared bathroom or US$33/38 with private bathroom. Rooms in the flashy new wing cost from US$53/61. If you're staying here it's wise to have a bicycle at the ready, since it's a fair walk into town and difficult to get a taxi at short notice.

PLACES TO EAT

After long months on the road, or a stint of trekking and subsisting on dal bhat, most travellers find Kathmandu a culinary paradise.

In the budget range, Kathmandu has numerous tea stalls and shops. Many may not even have a name but at these stalls, *dal bhat tarakari* – the lentil soup, rice and vegetable everyday meal of most Nepalis – will be the main dish on offer. By upcountry standards these places aren't cheap – dal bhat tarakari will cost around Rs 50 (much more in restaurants).

In Thamel, if you stay away from beer, you can eat very well for less than Rs 200. A good breakfast should cost less than Rs 100. A beer in a restaurant will cost around Rs 105, sometimes more. There are excellent bakeries and cake shops in Thamel and elsewhere, as well as cafes where you just sit back with a tea, coffee or beer and watch the world go by.

There is a growing number of restaurants around town which specialise in Nepali food. Most places offer a set meal, either veg or nonveg, and you sit on cushions at low tables.

Thamel

Thamel restaurants spill into Paknajol, Jyatha and Chhetrapati, just like Thamel hotels. The junction outside the Kathmandu Guest House is the centre of Thamel dining and you can find numerous budget-priced restaurants within a one-minute walk in either direction.

Italian, Chinese, Mexican, Indian and good old 'continental' feature heavily on most menus, but there are also some very good restaurants specialising in Thai, French, Japanese, Tibetan and Nepali. You'll find a lot of the food tastes pretty much the same though, and when looking at the 'homogenous' restaurants, what probably makes the difference is the prevailing, atmosphere, music (or absence of) and service.

KC's Restaurant was one of the Thamel originals, which hit the magic travellers' restaurant formula spot-on. The food is still good, though it's been superseded by other places and is a bit on the expensive side. Steak sizzlers cost Rs 230, burgers are Rs 100 and pasta costs from Rs 165. You can even get fondue for Rs 280 per person.

Alice's Restaurant in the Namche Bazaar building is a decent place with a well-positioned rooftop terrace. The food is excellent and the atmosphere is good. Along with all the steak sizzlers, pizzas, pastas, burgers and a fine range of north Indian dishes, you can get a pretty good Waldorf salad for Rs 95 and rum-and-raisin cheesecake for Rs 55.

Restaurant Casa Della Pasta is a flash place near the Kathmandu Guest House, with excellent Italian food, good service and a big movie screen.

Third Eye, lit up like a Christmas tree at the front, is a long-running favourite that retains something of the old Kathmandu atmosphere. There's a sit-down section at the front, and a more informal section with low tables and cushions at the back. Indian food is the speciality, and the tandoori dishes here are especially good.

Yin Yang (☎ 425510) does authentic Thai food. It's not particularly cheap, with starters around Rs 90 and main meals from Rs 200 to Rs 300, but the food is a definite cut above the imitation Thai food found elsewhere.

Green Leaves Restaurant has a pleasant rooftop eating area and prides itself on 'organic food'. It's quite good and reasonably priced with pasta dishes around Rs 80 and steaks around Rs 115.

La Dolce Vita (☎ 419612) probably makes the best attempt at true Italian cuisine and the menu is a bit more imaginative

than the standard Thamel offering, with delights such as tiramisu (Rs 110). Prices are a little higher than average, but the servings are generous and the quality high. Pizzas and pasta cost from Rs 185. You can also get Italian wine here including grappa and chianti (Rs 1300 a bottle!).

Out through the rear of the Pilgrim's Book House is *Pilgrims Feed N Read*. It's a relaxed place, with indoor and outdoor areas, snacks, light meals and thong ba (Tibetan millet beer; Rs 70). There's often Indian classical music (sitar and tabla) performed here.

Next door, the open-air *Northfield Cafe* is a place for serious breakfast devotees – eggs any way you like – and it specialises in Mexican (or Tex-Mex) for lunch and dinner. It's a bit pricey for Thamel with a pair of enchiladas at Rs 175, Rs 220 for fajitas or Nepali set meal for Rs 160, but the food and service are both very good. There's an ambient evening setting in the courtyard with bonfires providing the light.

Le Bistro has the familiar international menu with lots of pasta dishes. A prime attraction here is the large open courtyard, ideal for pleasant outdoor dining.

Rum Doodle Restaurant was named, of course, after the world's highest mountain, the 40,000½-foot Mt Rum Doodle. The conquest of Rum Doodle was dramatically described in that spoof on heroic mountaineering books, *The Ascent of Rum Doodle*. The restaurant is in the same side street as the Holy Lodge, and specialises in steak (from Rs 220) and pasta (around Rs 180). There's also a range of curries and vegetarian dishes. It's a favourite meeting place for mountaineering expeditions, particularly in the upstairs *40,000½-Foot Bar*. You can try Rum Doodle Rum Punch here (like mulled wine) and Nepali fruit wine.

Krua Thai is another good open-air Thai place. The food is authentic (spicy) although not that cheap: Tom yam is Rs 230, green curry Rs 230 and noodle dishes are Rs 180 to Rs 230. There's a good range of vegetarian dishes on offer.

Fire & Ice is an excellent open-air Italian place serving some of the best pizzas in Kathmandu (Rs 180 to Rs 290), imported Italian soft-serve ice cream (Rs 100) and seriously good coffee. It's always busy so you'll need to book for dinner in the high season, or eat early. It's in the modern Sanchaya Kosh Bhawan Shopping Centre on Tridevi Marg.

Utse Restaurant, in the hotel of the same name in Jyatha, turns out excellent Tibetan dishes, such as momo and *kothe* (fried pasta stuffed with meat/vegetables).

Old Vienna Inn, across from the Marco Polo Guest House, is the place to come if you're after Wiener schnitzel, goulash etc. It's one of the old Thamel haunts. Most mains are around Rs 200 to Rs 250. *Gourmet Delicatessen* in front of the restaurant is good.

Everest Steak House is very popular, especially with returned trekkers suffering from protein deficiency. The menu lists 20 excellent steak dishes (real beef) with a variety of sauces and preparations – most are around Rs 200 but the chateaubriand is a dazzling Rs 750 (it's enough for two). There are also some vegetarian alternatives, including pizza and pasta, but the sheer aroma of sizzling meat will be enough to keep most vegetarians out!

In Jyatha, just behind KEEP, *Kilroy's* is a stylish, highly regarded place owned and run by expat Thomas Kilroy. The sandwiches are great for lunch (Rs 80 to Rs 150), but most dinner mains are well over Rs 200 – beef and Guinness hot pot is Rs 345. It has a nice terrace and a sister operation, *K-Too*, has recently opened in the heart of Thamel.

One of the cheapest restaurants specialising in Nepali food is *Thakali Banche* in Paknajol. It's a simple 1st-floor restaurant with dishes from Rs 15 to Rs 65, Thakali set meals from Rs 70 and cheap beer (Rs 85).

Thamel House (☎ *410388*) is set in a traditional old Newari building, and so has bags of atmosphere. The food is also traditional Nepali, although they may try to lumber you with the set menu at Rs 550. Ask for the a la carte menu and choose individual dishes (most less than Rs 200).

Around the intersection near the Kathmandu Guest House are a couple of hot bread outlets which do a roaring trade in sandwiches, bread rolls, pizza slices (Rs 50) and pastries. These are really popular at lunchtime, and the ham-and-cheese rolls make a great lunch on the run.

Hot Snacks Cafe, down a small laneway off the street running south from the Kathmandu Guest House, does cheap Nepali food.

Just Juice & Shakes, tucked in a laneway near Hotel Garuda, does the best lassis in town. Nearby, *Lhasa Tibetan Restaurant* is an inexpensive place with fried momos at Rs 55 being about the most expensive thing on the menu. Beer is Rs 90 and thong ba Rs 40.

Breakfast Spots Eating breakfast out in a garden courtyard or on a rooftop terrace on a sunny morning is one of the great pleasures of Kathmandu. Just about every restaurant and cafe serves breakfast and you can get pretty much anything you want if it involves eggs, bread and muesli. There's usually a variety of set breakfasts (Rs 70 to Rs 100) or you can choose from the menu. The following are a few of the better Thamel breakfast spots.

Wiezen Bakery has a pleasant garden and is quiet, with newspapers to read, music playing in the background and fantastic muesli and curd. There's also a good range of cakes, breads and pastries.

Brezel Bakery, almost opposite Kathmandu Guest House, has a great two-tier rooftop terrace overlooking the Thamel activity. There's fresh brown bread and croissants, filter coffee (Rs 45) and eggs on toast costs Rs 30.

Pumpernickel Bakery is remarkably popular considering there's no service (you order at the counter). It's good for freshly baked bread and croissants (from Rs 20) and overland travellers rush in to get a courtyard table in the morning. Despite a reputation to the contrary, the filter coffee is terrible.

Tashi Deleg, almost opposite the Pumpernickel, is an unassuming Tibetan place that has good cheap breakfasts and friendly service. The various set breakfasts are excellent value from Rs 50 to Rs 80.

Other restaurants in Thamel that also do good set breakfasts include *Northfield Cafe* (with Granola, waffles, all types of coffee), *Alice's Restaurant*, *La Dolce Vita* and *Le Bistro* (see the Thamel section earlier in this chapter).

A mention should also be made of *Mike's Breakfast*, which is nowhere near Thamel (it's in Naxal east of the Royal Palace), but is a legendary breakfast spot. Meals are served in a leafy garden from 7 am.

Freak Street & Durbar Square

Freak St has a number of restaurants where you can find good food at low prices, although the choice is fairly limited.

Oasis Restaurant is good for burgers and snacks and the *Paradise Restaurant* across the road is a good vegetarian place.

Carpe Diem Music Cafe, at the southern end of Freak St, is a cosy place to hang out with a good atmosphere and good music. The food is inexpensive with Chinese meals less than Rs 50 and Nepali set meals from Rs 80.

Snowman has been around forever but it still has the best range of pies and cakes around and is a popular hang-out. Apple pie is Rs 40 and a lassi is Rs 30.

Bakery Cafe, on Ganga Path, just off Basantapur Square, is a good spot to go for a snack after you've finished sightseeing in Durbar Square. There's a pleasant, covered courtyard and the food ranges from burgers (from Rs 50) and sandwiches (Rs 75), to pizzas (from Rs 80) and momos (from Rs 70). At the front there's a counter selling sweets and cakes.

Durbar Marg

The restaurants in the glossier Kantipath and Durbar Marg areas are generally more expensive than around Thamel although there are a few lower-priced exceptions.

Annapurna Coffee Shop, beside the entrance to the Hotel de l'Annapurna, offers a standard 'big hotel' style menu with burgers from Rs 225, pizza from Rs 250, and Nepali dishes. It's popular but the food is only average.

Other possibilities include the moderately priced *Koto Restaurant*, which some say prepares the best Japanese food in town. There are plenty of dishes for around Rs 150 to Rs 200. *Baan Thai* serves excellent Thai food, and the service is very attentive. Expect to pay around Rs 400.

Also on Durbar Marg there's the small *Tukche Thakali Kitchen* (☎ 225890), which includes Tibetan dishes. The interior is a bit gloomy, but the food is good and reasonably priced at Rs 125 for a veg set lunch, or Rs 155 with meat. A three-course set meal is Rs 390. There's a cultural program of folk dancing here from 7 to 8 pm daily except Tuesday. It costs Rs 400 with a set meal.

ENTERTAINMENT

Nepal is traditionally an early-to-bed country but nightlife is a growth industry in Kathmandu, and not only among visitors. There are some bars in Thamel that claim to stay open to 6 am (though most close up at 11 pm by law), as well as some hip music clubs. There are also a couple of interesting new nightclubs which attract mostly well-heeled locals and a few curious westerners. The crowded travellers' restaurants and bars are great places to meet and talk with people.

Bars & Clubs

There are numerous bars scattered around Thamel, all within a short walk of each other. They vary in degrees of atmosphere, and a place that's jumping one night could be dead the next. Closing time for many is officially 10 or 11 pm, but some stay open much later, especially if they have a live band.

Maya Cocktail Lounge, in a lane opposite KC's Restaurant, is an intimate but very busy place that does great cocktails (Rs 110). Between 4 and 8 pm you can get two cocktails for the price of one.

Pub Maya, around the corner from the Kathmandu Guest House, is a small, long-running place that's good for a quiet drink. Happy hour is from 4 to 7 pm and there's satellite TV.

Blue Note Bar at New Orleans Cafe has a nice garden area and Nepali folk music on Thursday nights. It's open to 11 pm.

Jump Club, upstairs near Hotel Garuda, is a lively music club that gets going at about 10 pm and closes at 2 am. It's a good place to meet local people and other travellers and features a mix of hip-hop, techno and top 40. The best music nights are Wednesday and Saturday.

Tongues & Tails Bar, south of Kathmandu Guest House, regularly has live music, and it has a good atmosphere and cheap cocktails.

Close to Thamel Chowk is *Underground Bar*, which stays open to 2 am and always has the music cranked up pretty high. It has two-for-one cocktail deals between 7 and 10 pm but it's pretty quiet here before about 11 pm. A bottle of beer is Rs 120.

Tom & Jerry Pub, upstairs opposite Pilgrims, is a popular, rowdy place with pool tables.

Tunnel Club is a late-night drinking place that stays open to 6 am. It can get a bit rough and there's not a lot happening here before midnight.

Near the Yin Yang Restaurant is *Ultimate Planet Bar*. It's a very plush place with leather seating and a sophisticated sound and light system. There's a small dance-floor. Also in this building is the *Irish Pub*, with a pleasant terrace, draught Guinness and cheap drinks from 4 to 8 pm.

Carp Diem Music Cafe on Freak St is a good place to hole up and listen to some good world music.

Nightclubs are catching on in Kathmandu and a couple that have opened in the last few years are popular with young Nepalis who can afford it.

Club Dynasty (☎ 222686), near Durbar Marg, is regarded as the trendiest place around and is good for dancing. Admission is Rs 200 and it's open late. The clientele is mixed but it definitely leans towards men. *Moon Sun Disco* is a fairly average place at the Heritage Plaza in Kamaladi.

Casinos
Kathmandu has four casinos, all at the upmarket hotels – the Soaltee, Everest, de l'Annapurna and Yak & Yeti.

The casinos are open 24 hours a day, and they'll ply you with free beer if you're actually playing at the tables. The main games offered are roulette and blackjack. Nepalis are forbidden from entering altogether.

Nepali Music & Dance
There are regular performances of Nepali music and dancing in Kathmandu, including at the National Theatre. All the big hotels and some smaller restaurants (such as Tukche Thakali Kitchen – see Places to Eat) have nightly 'cultural shows', usually in their main restaurant around 7 pm.

Cinemas
There are plenty of cinemas, usually showing Indian Hindi films (not subtitled), although there are occasionally English-language films. In the Kathmandu Plaza in Kamaladi is *Kathmandu Minivision*, which shows Western films. Programs and screening times are usually published in the *Kathmandu Post*.

An easier way to veg out in front of a screen is in the numerous restaurants and parlours in Thamel where popular Western movies appear on pirated videos or laser discs almost as soon as they hit the cinemas in the West. You'll see the movies chalked up on pavement blackboards on the streets. DVD movies are shown several times daily at Kathmandu Guest House.

SHOPPING
Everything turned out in the various centres around the valley can be found in Kathmandu, although you may often find a better choice or more unusual items in the real centres – it's certainly more pleasant shopping for metalwork and crafts in Patan or woodcarvings and pottery in Bhaktapur. You'll also find there'll be less 'hard sell' away from the centres of Thamel and Durbar Square.

Typical items on sale include Tibetan prayer wheels and *thangkas* (religious paintings), *khukuri* knives (traditional curved knives of the Ghurkas), papier mache masks, pipes and colourful clothing.

There are numerous convenience stores in Thamel where you can buy cheap alcohol, trekking supplies, groceries, pharmaceutical products and just about anything else.

Bronze Statues & Curios
The best place to start looking for bronze or metalwork is on Durbar Marg, but there are also some shops worth visiting on New Rd. This is one area where research is vitally important, as quality and prices do not necessarily have any direct correlation. Curio Arts on Durbar Marg is a good place to start.

An endless supply of curios, stuff, knick-knacks, pieces, thingos and plain junk is turned out for tourists. If you shop around you can find creations that are beautifully made by craftspeople whose time is obviously not worth a lot of money. Basantapur Square is the headquarters for this trade, but before you match wits with these operators, visit the Amrita Craft Collection in Thamel. This relatively small shop has a wide collection, all with prices that are reasonably fair.

Thangkas
The main centre for thangkas is just off Durbar Square, and this is where you'll find the best salespeople (not necessarily the best thangkas). For modern work in Thamel, visit the Tibetan Thangka Treasure, near KC's restaurant.

Clothing

Kathmandu is the best place in the valley for clothes and many places have good-quality ready-to-wear Western fashions, particularly shirts. Amusing embroidered T-shirts are a popular speciality. There are lots of good tailors around Thamel and, apart from embroidered T-shirts, they'll also embroider just about anything you want on your own jacket or jeans.

Jewellery

The prices for silver jewellery are very low compared with what you'd pay at home, and many people have jewellery made to order. You buy the stones or draw the design and they'll have it made up, usually in just a day or two. The quality is usually excellent, but be sure to agree on a price before giving the go-ahead to have anything made.

Trekking Gear

Kathmandu is a good place to buy cheap trekking gear such as jackets, fleeces, tents, sleeping bags, backpacks, water bottles and camping stoves. There are shops all over Thamel specialising in this sort of gear and many also rent it out cheaply (with a hefty deposit required).

Much of the gear is manufactured in Kathmandu but labelled with well-known names such as North Face, Karimor, Lowe Pro and Gore-Tex. You'll know what's imported and what's not by looking at the price – the fake stuff is much cheaper but it's usually quite well made and will stand up to the rigours of trekking. You can pick up a Nepal-made day pack from around Rs 600 to Rs 900, or a larger pack from Rs 1000 to Rs 3000. A lined Gore-Tex jacket can be bought for Rs 800 to Rs 1000 and a North Face fleece from Rs 400 to Rs 900. A good-quality down jacket should cost more like Rs 5000 and a down sleeping bag around Rs 3000. Remember that these items are every bit as negotiable as crafts or souvenirs, although rental prices are usually fixed.

GETTING THERE & AWAY
Air

International Although many international airlines have offices in Kathmandu (most around Durbar Marg), the easiest way to buy cheap flights out of Nepal is through the travel agents around Thamel and Durbar Marg. There are plenty of airlines flying into and out of Nepal.

Royal Nepal Airlines (☎ 220757) has flights to Bangkok (US$220), Delhi (US$142), Dubai (US$260), Frankfurt (US$605), Hong Kong (US$310) and Singapore (US$310), London (US$630) and Paris (US$575).

Singapore Airlines (☎ 220759) flies to London (US$670), Los Angeles (US$669), New York (US$780), Sydney (US$676) and many Asian destinations.

The golden rule with flights out of Kathmandu, whether international or domestic, is to reconfirm, preferably more than once! This particularly applies to Royal Nepal Airlines. Even this may not guarantee you a seat – make sure you get to the airport early as people at the end of the queue can still be left behind.

There's a Rs 1000 international departure tax payable at the Nepal Arab Bank in the airport terminal.

Domestic RNAC has computerised booking on the main routes, and these are booked at the main RNAC office; all other domestic flights are booked in an utterly haphazard manner at a small office just around the corner.

With so many competing airlines, you shouldn't have too much trouble getting a seat if you book a few days in advance. Recommended airlines include Buddha Air (☎ 542494), Necon Air (☎ 473860), Cosmic Air (☎ 241052) and Yeti Airlines (☎ 421215). Standard fares from Kathmandu include: Pokhara (US$67) and Lukla (US$91). There's a domestic airport tax of Rs 100 on all flights, including mountain flights.

Bus

The main bus station is on the Ring Rd at Balaju, about 3km north-west of Thamel. It is officially called the Gongbu Bus Park, but is generally known as the Kathmandu Bus Terminal, or simply 'bus park'. All long-distance buses to Pokhara and destinations in the Terai or eastern Nepal depart from here, except the tourist buses. It's a huge and busy place, and there are no signs in English. There's at least one reservation counter for each destination, and there's an inquiry counter on the left as you enter;

bookings for long trips should be made a day in advance. Services include: Pokhara (Rs 105, seven hours), Tadi Bazaar (for Chitwan; Rs 77, five hours), Sunauli (Rs 135, eight hours), Birganj (Rs 130, seven hours) and Kharkabitta (Rs 365, 13 hours). There's a day bus to Pokhara at 7.30 am and an overnight bus at 7 pm. You can get from the bus park to Thamel on city bus No 23.

Buses for destinations within the Kathmandu Valley, and for those on the Arniko Hwy (Jiri, Barabise and Kodari at the Tibetan border), operate from the City Bus Station, in the centre of the city.

The more expensive tourist buses to Pokhara and Chitwan – heavily promoted in Thamel – conveniently depart from the Thamel end of Kantipath. Tickets can be bought from any travel agent in Thamel and guesthouses also often sell tickets. There's a bus to Pokhara at 8 am (Rs 200 or Rs 250 in a minibus), and to Chitwan (Chitrasali) at 7 am (Rs 175).

Greenline (☎ 253885, e greenline@unlimit.com) has its depot on the corner of Tridevi Marg and Kantipur, just around the corner from where the tourist buses depart. Air-con buses to Pokhara (seven hours) depart at 8 am and cost a steep Rs 600, but this includes breakfast along the way and, while not luxurious, they're about as comfy as you get in Nepal. The same bus goes to Chitwan (Chitrasali; Rs 480, 5½ hours).

To India Be cautious about booking through-tickets to India. Many agents offer a service of booking a bus to the border at Sunauli, then another bus on to Gorakhpur or Varanasi, then an onward train. This is pretty risky and many travellers have arrived in India and found that their tickets are useless or that no train has been booked. It's cheaper and easier to do the trip in three stages on your own, but if you prefer to prebook, agents in Thamel do bus and train tickets to Varanasi for around Rs 840 with 2nd-class train seat and Rs 2895 with air-con sleeper, and to Delhi for around Rs 1197/3517. Bus only (with a change at the border) costs around Rs 425 to Gorakhpur and Rs 650 to Varanasi.

See under Travel Agencies earlier for recommendations.

To Tibet At the time of writing, individual travellers could not enter Tibet from Nepal.

Even if you have a Chinese visa, border officials in Zhangmu are no longer issuing TTB (Tibetan Tourism Bureau) permits which allow you to enter Tibet independently. The only way to do it is on an organised tour through an approved agent, and these are expensive.

On the positive side, there are plenty of agencies in Kathmandu which offer fully organised trips to Lhasa (usually involving a flight back to Kathmandu) and if you have a Chinese visa, there's nothing to stop you leaving the tour in Tibet and continuing on into China. The cost of an eight-day tour to Lhasa is between US$400 and US$600 (plus around US$260 if you fly back).

Some agents offering tours include:

Explore Nepal Richa Tours (☎ 423064, e explore@enrtt.mos.com.np) Namche Bazaar Bldg, Thamel
Green Hill Tours (☎ 424968, e ghill@wlink.com.np) Thamel
Natraj Tours & Travels (☎ 222906) Kamaladi
Tibet Travels & Tours (☎ 249140, e kalden@tibet.wlink.com.np) Tridevi Marg

GETTING AROUND

The best way to see Kathmandu and the valley is to walk or ride a bicycle. Most of the sights in Kathmandu can easily be covered on foot. There are plenty of reasonably priced taxis and autorickshaws but the latter have long been contributing to Kathmandu's chronic air pollution. A better option for certain routes is the new electric tempos.

To/From the Airport

Getting into town is, or at least should be, quite straightforward. There is an organised taxi service on the ground-floor foyer immediately after you leave the arrivals section. The taxis, called Airport Taxi Services, have a fixed fare of Rs 200 to Thamel or Durbar Marg or Rs 400 to Bhaktapur. Once outside the international terminal you are confronted by hordes of hotel touts, who are often taxi drivers making commission on taking you to a particular hotel. Many hold up a signboard of the particular hotel they are connected with, and if the one you want is there, you can get a free lift. The drawback is that the hotel is then much less likely to offer you a discount as they will be paying a hefty commission to the taxi driver.

Kathmandu to Royal Chitwan

Cycling days: 4
Approx distance: 209km

The ride out of Kathmandu was an easy half day. Once out of the Kathmandu Valley at 1400m it's all downhill to Naubise at 600m. Then it's a steady climb up to 2500m on the old Rajpath road, where we stayed at the roadside village of Hapsechaur (no hotels but we were invited to stay with the head teacher and his family). From here it's a smooth run down to Hetauda and the Royal Chitwan National Park. There were spectacular views for the cycle over the Daman Pass on day two, and we spent the night at Lamidanda, before continuing on to Hetauda on day three. Kathmandu to Hetauda can easily be cycled in two days if you start early and break the journey about 20km before the Daman Pass.

The final 70km to Chitwan (Sauraha) is through typical flat Terai scenery, with reasonable road conditions. This is the warmest part of Nepal, although it can get cool in December/January.

An alternative is to take the main highway from Kathmandu to Mugling (mostly downhill) then head south to Narayanghat and Tadi Bazaar. This could be cycled in one or two days but is not as scenic as the Daman Pass.

Sue Cooper

If you don't want to be taken to a hotel of the driver's choice, a ride to Thamel or the city centre should cost no more than Rs 150. Bear in mind that even if you take a prepaid taxi from Airport Taxi Services, the driver will still want to take you to a hotel where he can get commission. The metered fare for a taxi from Thamel to the airport is about Rs 80, but most drivers will want at least Rs 100.

There are public buses which pick up from the main road – about 300m from the terminal – but they're only really usable if you have very little luggage and know exactly how to get to where you want to go.

To get to the airport by bus, catch one heading to Bhaktapur via Pashupatinath and ask to be let off on the main road.

Bus

While bus travel is very cheap, it is often unbelievably crowded and not very comfortable – no surprises if you've come from India. Nearly all buses to points around the valley operate from the City Bus Station. The station appears to be completely disorganised but it's just a matter of walking in and asking someone for the bus to your destination. Buses to Nagarkot cost Rs 15 and Rs 7 to Bhaktapur.

The dilapidated electric trolley buses to Bhaktapur leave from the southern end of Kantipath near the National Stadium. These cost Rs 5 and drop you off at about a 10-minute walk from the centre of Bhaktapur.

Taxi

The charge for a metered taxi is Rs 7 flagfall and Rs 2 for every 200m (Rs 10/3 at night), and drivers don't usually take too much convincing to use the meter for short trips within Kathmandu city. For trips around the Kathmandu Valley (including the airport), you will probably find you'll have to agree on a fare before getting in.

Many so-called taxis are just private vehicles. These don't have meters, so you will have to negotiate a fare. Licensed taxis have black licence plates while private cars have red plates. Taxis can be booked on ☎ 420987, or at night call ☎ 224374.

For trips out of town, taxi drivers will usually charge a return fare even if you only go one way. The metered fare to Bhaktapur is Rs 150, but the standard charge from Thamel is Rs 300 (coming the other way you might get the driver to charge only the metered fare since he will probably be returning to Kathmandu anyway). The standard fare to Patan is Rs 100, to Nagarkot Rs 800, to Bodhnath Rs 80 and to Pashupatinath Rs 70. A taxi from Thamel to the Kathmandu Bus Terminal is Rs 65.

Cycle-Rickshaw & Autorickshaw

Three-wheeled metered autorickshaws are quite common in Kathmandu and cost about two-thirds of what you would pay for a cab. Flagfall is Rs 3, plus Rs 6 per kilometre. Some refuse to use the meter, in which case establish a price. Most rides around town should cost less than Rs 40.

Cycle-rickshaws cost Rs 20 to Rs 50 for most rides around town – they can be more expensive than going by autorickshaw or taxi. The tourist rate from Thamel to Durbar Square is Rs 40 but the trip shouldn't really cost any more than Rs 25. The cycle-rickshaws hanging around Durbar Square are accustomed to tourists and will try to overcharge. You must be certain to agree on a price before you start.

Tempo

The white electric tempos, which are like large passenger autorickshaws, are a cheap and environmentally friendly way to get around on short set routes. The main tempo stand is just up from the post office on Kantipath. Tempos leave when full and can be hailed down on the street (assuming you know where it's headed!). They cost between Rs 2 and Rs 7 for short trips (ie, from the tempo stand to Pashupatinath costs Rs 7).

Motorcycle

There are a number of motorcycle rental operators around Freak St and Thamel. Officially you need an international driver's licence, but no-one ever checks. You are also required to leave a substantial deposit or your passport. For Rs 400 per day you'll get a 100cc or 125cc Indian-made Honda road bike, and will be restricted to the Kathmandu Valley (but also including Daman, Kakani, Nagarkot and Dhulikhel). For a 250cc trail bike the cost is around Rs 1000 per day.

Motorcycles can be great fun, once you master the traffic. However, think carefully before hiring, as you will be encouraging the proliferation of noisy, polluting machines. Most reasonably fit people will find that a mountain bike is a better option.

Bicycle

Once you get away from the crowded streets of central Kathmandu, cycling is a pleasure, and if you're in reasonable shape this is the ideal way to explore the valley. It costs around Rs 80 per day for a regular single-speed Indian or Chinese-made bicycle. Check the brakes before taking it out and be certain to lock it whenever you leave it. You can also hire multigeared mountain bikes in varying stages of dilapidation,

which should be fine for light use around the valley. They cost between Rs 120 and Rs 250 per day for older bikes, and up to Rs 400 per day for newer ones in reasonable condition. Imported bikes are available for rent but these cost considerably more. If you're planning to really explore the valley, paying a bit extra for a decent mountain bike is money well spent.

Dawn Till Dusk (☎ 418286), in the Kathmandu Guest House compound, rents out quality bicycles from Rs 350 to Rs 500 per day, including repair kit, lock and helmet. Himalayan Mountain Bikes (☎ 416596) rents quality bikes for US$10 per day.

Around Kathmandu Valley

PATAN

☎ 01 • pop 190,000

Patan is separated from Kathmandu only by the Bagmati River and is the second-largest town in the valley. It is often referred to as Lalitpur, which means 'city of beauty'. Patan has a long Buddhist history and the four corners of the city are marked by stupas said to have been erected by the great Buddhist emperor Ashoka around 250 BC. Later inscriptions refer to palaces in the city in the 5th century AD, although Patan's great building boom took place under the Mallas in the 16th, 17th and 18th centuries.

Patan's central Durbar Square is an architectural feast, with a far greater concentration of temples than in Kathmandu or Bhaktapur. It's a wonderful town to simply wander around, with temples, monasteries and craft workshops at every turn.

Orientation & Information

The Durbar (Palace) Square is the centre of Patan. From the square, four main roads lead to the four Ashoka stupas while the city radiates out in concentric circles.

Jawlakhel, to the south of the city, has a major Tibetan population and is the centre for carpet-weaving in the valley.

There's a moneychanger in Durbar Square but the rates are poor and the commission is high. You're better off using the Nepal Grindlays Bank in Jawlakhel. *Patan Walkabout* is a booklet detailing a signposted

NEPAL

KATHMANDU VALLEY

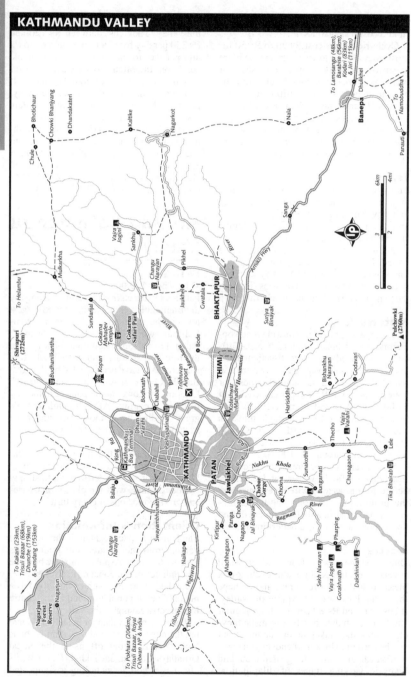

walk around Patan. It's available from the bookshop at Patan Dhoka.

The admission fee to enter Patan's old town is Rs 200.

Durbar Square

Patan's old **Royal Palace** forms the entire eastern side of the Durbar Square. Facing it on the western side is a large number of temples – undoubtedly the most stunning display of Newari architecture in Nepal.

The palace at Patan is older than those at Kathmandu and Bhaktapur. Parts of it were built in the 14th century, but the main construction was completed under the reign of the Mallas in the 16th and 17th centuries. Inside is a series of interconnecting courtyards, three temples dedicated to the valley's main deity, Taleju, and the superb Patan Museum.

The northern courtyard (Man Keshar Chowk) and museum are entered from the square by the **Golden Gate** (Sun Dhoka). Directly above is a window at which the king would make public appearances. The **Patan Museum** houses a series of well-presented galleries an amazing collection of cast bronze and gilt copper work, mainly of Hindu and Buddhist deities. The museum is open from 10.30 am to 5 pm daily, and is worth the Rs 120 admission. The central palace courtyard (Mul Chowk) contains the three **Taleju temples**: Taleju Bhawani, the five-storey Degutalle Temple and the triple-roofed Taleju Temple.

The southern courtyard (Sundari Chowk) features the sunken tank known as **Tusha Hiti**, with superbly carved stonework. The entrance to the courtyard from the main square is fronted by statues of Hanuman, Ganesh and Vishnu (as Narsingha).

Out in the main square is a plethora of temples, some elaborately decorated with stone statues and erotic carvings on the roof struts. From south to north, the main ones are the octagonal stone **Krishna Temple**; the three-storey **Hari Shankar Temple**, dedicated to the half-Shiva, half-Vishnu deity (between these is the large **Taleju Bell**); the two-storey **Jagannarayan Temple**, dating from 1565 and thought to be the oldest temple in the square; the stone **Krishna Mandir**; the elaborately decorated **Vishwanath Temple**; and, at the north end of the square, the **Bhimsen Temple**. The large open area to

the west of here is laid out with crafts and jewellery and in the centre is the sunken **Manga Hiti** tank.

Golden Temple

Also known as the Kwa Bahal, or the Suwarna Mahavihara (Golden Temple), this unique Buddhist monastery is only a few minutes walk north of Durbar Square. The simple entrance, flanked by painted guardian lion figures, gives no hint of the magnificent structure in the courtyard within.

Inside the shrine are images of the Buddha and Avalokiteshvara and a stairway leads to the 1st floor where monks will show you the various Buddha images and frescoes which illustrate the walls. The life of the Buddha is illustrated in a frieze in front of the main shrine.

The inner courtyard has a railed walkway around three sides. Leather shoes and other leather articles must be removed if you leave the walkway and enter the inner courtyard itself. In the centre of the courtyard is a small but very richly decorated three-storey temple crowned by a golden roof with an extremely ornate *gajur* (a bell-shaped top). Look for the sacred tortoises which potter around in the courtyard – they are temple guardians. The temple is open from 8.30 am to 6 pm (Rs 25).

Other Temples

Directly north of Durbar Square is the **Kumbeshwar Temple**, one of the valley's three five-storey temples. It's dedicated to Shiva, as indicated by the large Nandi, or bull, facing the temple inside the main entrance. Thousands of pilgrims visit the temple during the Janai Purnima festival in July and August each year to worship the silver and gold lingam which is set up in the tank.

South from Durbar Square and down a laneway is the brick **Bishwakarma Temple**, with its entire facade covered in sheets of embossed copper. The temple is dedicated to carpenters and craftspeople.

Continue south from Durbar Square for a few more minutes to the **Rato (Red) Machhendranath Temple**, on the western side of the road. Rato Machhendranath, the god of rain and plenty, comes in a variety of incarnations. Standing in a large, spacious

[Continued on page 568]

PASHUPATINATH

Nepal's most important Hindu temple stands on the banks of the Bagmati River, about 5km east of Kathmandu. There's not much to see of the temple itself – non-Hindus are not allowed inside – but there's plenty of activity along the riverbanks here and this is regarded as a very auspicious place. A trip to Pashupatinath can easily be combined with a visit to Bodhnath as the two sites are an interesting 20-minute walk apart.

Pashupatinath is one of the most important Shiva temples on the subcontinent and draws many pilgrims and sadhus. Although Shiva (the destroyer and creator) is often a bloodthirsty god, he is not so in his benevolent incarnation as Pashupati, and before making an important journey the king will visit the temple to seek the god's blessing.

Pashupatinath is a popular place for cremations, as the Bagmati, like the Ganges in India, is a holy river. The **burning ghats** directly in front of the temple are reserved for the cremation of royalty. The ghats on the west bank just south of the footbridge are for the common people. Visitors are permitted to watch cremations and photography is allowed from a discreet distance, but remember that these are funerals.

On the eastern side of the Bagmati River, facing the Pashupatinath temple, are 11 stone *chaityas* (small stupas), each containing a *lingam* (a phallic symbol of Shiva's creative power).

After crossing the footbridge, continue up the steps to the **Goraknath Temple** complex which contains an array of temples, tridents, lingams and sculptures dedicated to Shiva. Farther along the path is the **Guhyeshwari Temple**, but non-Hindus cannot enter and the high wall prevents you from seeing in. Past the temple is a footbridge over the river, from where you can clearly see the stupa at Bodhnath to the north. Continue north and turn right at the first track through the village; you'll eventually come out on the main road opposite the stupa.

The best times to visit Pashupatinath are during devotional activity, between 6 and 10 am and between 6 and 7.30 pm. The festival of **Shivaratri** (Shiva's birthday) in February/March is a great time to be here, when pilgrims come to attend a great fair.

Pashupatinath is an easy bicycle ride from Kathmandu or Thamel. Otherwise, an autorickshaw costs Rs 60 and a taxi is around Rs 70. Tempo No 2 leaves Kathmandu from the stand near the post office (Rs 7) and buses go from City Bus Station to Bodhnath via Pashupatinath (the stop is called Gosala).

BODHNATH

About 6km east of Kathmandu is the huge stupa of Bodhnath, the largest stupa in Nepal and one of the largest in the world. This is the religious centre for Nepal's substantial Tibetan population and one of the few places in the world where Tibetan culture is both accessible and unhindered. There are a number of thriving monasteries here, plenty of shops selling Tibetan crafts, and maroon-robed monks involved in daily activity. During the afternoon there are large numbers of tour

Inset: The pinnacle of the stupa at Bodhnath (Photo by Bill Wassman)

groups milling around, but in the afternoon they drift away and this becomes a Tibetan town again. In the evening the community turns out to circumambulate the stupa – this should always be done in a clockwise direction.

The current stupa was probably built in the 14th century. It is thought to stand on the site of a much earlier stupa, built some time after AD 600 by the Tibetan king, Songtsen Gampo. Stupas were originally built to house holy relics and they are never hollow. It's not certain whether anything is interred at Bodhnath, but some believe it holds a piece of bone from Gautama Buddha.

The base of the stupa takes the shape of a mandala (symbolising earth), on which sits the dome (symbolising water), the spire (symbolising fire), the umbrella (symbolising air) and the pinnacle (symbolising ether). On each side of the spire's square base are painted a pair of Buddha's eyes, each with a third eye between. The 'nose' is actually the Nepali number one, signifying the unity of all life. The brick wall around the stupa has 147 niches, each with four or five prayer wheels.

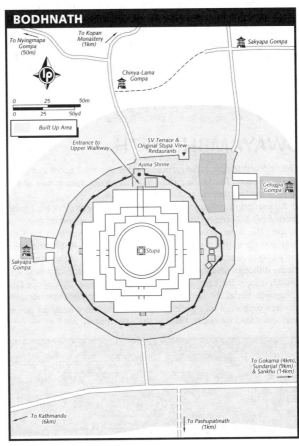

BODHNATH

To Nyingmapa Gompa (50m)

To Kopan Monastery (1km)

Sakyapa Gompa

Chinya-Lama Gompa

0   25   50m
0   25   50yd

Built Up Area

Entrance to Upper Walkway

SV Terrace & Original Stupa View Restaurants

Ajima Shrine

Gelugpa Gompa

Stupa

Sakyapa Gompa

To Gokarna (4km), Sundarijal (9km) & Sankhu (14km)

To Kathmandu (6km)

To Pashupatinath (1km)

There are a number of **gompas** (monasteries) in Bodhnath. These are decorated with *thangkas* (religious paintings), statues and prayer wheels and are worth visiting. Visitors must be respectful and discreet: Remove your shoes and hat before entering, avoid taking photos during services, do not step over or sit on monks' cushions and stand quietly during ceremonies. The Sakyapa Gompa is the only one that opens directly onto the stupa, but the Chinya-Lama Gompa (50m north of the stupa) and the Gelugpa Gompa (on the north-eastern edge) are close by.

About 1km north of the stupa is the **Kopan Monastery** where residential courses in Tibetan Buddhist philosophy are held.

Local buses go to Bodhnath, via Pashupatinath, from Kathmandu's City Bus Station (Rs 5), but you could cycle just as quickly. Or catch Tempo No 2 for around Rs 8. A taxi to Bodhnath costs around Rs 80.

SWAYAMBHUNATH

The Buddhist temple of Swayambhunath sits on a hill about 2km west of Kathmandu. The soaring stupa with its golden spire is one of the images most commonly associated with Nepal.

An inscription indicates that King Manadeva began work on the site around AD 460 and by the 13th century it was an important Buddhist centre. The great eastern stairway to the stupa was built by King Pratap Malla in the 17th century. Entry to the site is Rs 50, and there are plenty of potential guides willing to follow you all the way up those steps. Although you can reach the temple by vehicle, the best approach is from the east, either on foot or by bicycle. One of the first things you see at the top of the stairs is the huge **dorje** (thunderbolt symbol) supported on a pedestal. This is a symbol of Buddhist power and was added by Pratap Malla in the 17th century.

Top: Prayer flags adorn the massive stupa at Bodhnath.

Bottom: The eyes of the Buddha gaze across the Kathmandu Valley.

The central **stupa** is topped by a gold-coloured square block from which the eyes of the Buddha look out over the valley in four directions. Set around the base of the stupa is a series of prayer wheels which pilgrims, circumambulating the stupa, spin as they pass by, thus releasing the mantra *'om mani padme hum'*.

There are many interesting things to see around the stupa. To the right of the eastern stairway is a **gompa** containing a huge prayer wheel, and where a service takes place at 4 pm daily. On each side of the dorje are two white Shikhara temples erected by Pratap Malla in 1646. Behind the stupa is the pagoda-style **Hariti Temple**, dedicated to the goddess of smallpox. Near this temple are pillars on which figures of gods and goddesses are seated. There are also many stalls and vendors around the stupa selling crafts, souvenirs and jewellery.

To the west of Swayambhunath hill is the **Natural History Museum**, which has a large collection of butterflies, fish, reptiles, birds and animals (open from 10 am to 5 pm; entry is free).

If you visit Swayambhunath by taxi or autorickshaw, ask to be taken to the eastern stairway or you will be dropped at the car park on the western side, from where it's a short climb up the hill to the entrance. A taxi from Thamel to the car park costs around Rs 70.

It's an easy 15-minute bike ride to the eastern stairway from Thamel (although there's some uphill work after the bridge over the Vishnu-mati River), and you can combine a visit to Swayambhunath with a pleasant loop ride via the National Museum & Art Gallery.

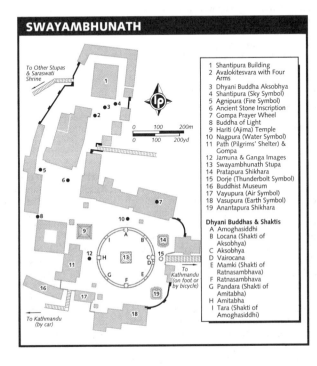

SWAYAMBHUNATH

To Other Stupas
& Saraswati
Shrine

To Kathmandu
(by car)

0   100   200m
0   100   200yd

To
Kathmandu
(on foot or
by bicycle)

1 Shantipura Building
2 Avalokitesvara with Four Arms
3 Dhyani Buddha Aksobhya
4 Shantipura (Sky Symbol)
5 Agnipura (Fire Symbol)
6 Ancient Stone Inscription
7 Gompa Prayer Wheel
8 Buddha of Light
9 Hariti (Ajima) Temple
10 Nagpura (Water Symbol)
11 Path (Pilgrims' Shelter) & Gompa
12 Jamuna & Ganga Images
13 Swayambhunath Stupa
14 Pratapura Shikhara
15 Dorje (Thunderbolt Symbol)
16 Buddhist Museum
17 Vayupura (Air Symbol)
18 Vasupura (Earth Symbol)
19 Anantapura Shikhara

Dhyani Buddhas & Shaktis
A Amoghasiddhi
B Locana (Shakti of Aksobhya)
C Aksobhya
D Vairocana
E Mamki (Shakti of Ratnasambhava)
F Ratnasambhava
G Pandara (Shakti of Amitabha)
H Amitabha
I Tara (Shakti of Amoghasiddhi)

[Continued from page 563]

courtyard the three-storey temple dates from 1673.

Despite its height, the Temple of the Thousand Buddhas, or **Mahabouddha Temple**, is not immediately visible because it is tightly surrounded by other buildings. It's about a 10-minute walk south-east of Durbar Square.

Rudra Varna Mahavihara

Also known as Uku Bahal, this Buddhist monastery near the Mahabouddha Temple is one of the best known in Patan. A large rectangular structure with two-storey gilded roofs encloses a courtyard absolutely packed with interesting bits and pieces. There are *dorjes* (thunderbolt symbols), bells, banners, peacocks, elephants, Garudas, rampant goats, kneeling devotees and a regal-looking statue of a Rana general.

Places to Stay & Eat

There are a few cheap places to stay close to Durbar Square. There's not a great advantage to staying here since it's so close to Kathmandu, but if you want peace and quiet and more traditional surroundings it makes a fine alternative.

Third World Guest House (☎ 522187, e *dsdp@wlink.com.np*) has the best location in town, with all rooms having views over the square, but you pay the price for it. Rooms cost US$15 with shared bath, and US$20 with private bathroom, although you should be able to get a 30% discount. The *restaurant* here is also quite good with Nepali set meals from Rs 110, burgers for Rs 80 and beer for Rs 105.

A short walk from Durbar Square, *Cafe de Patan* (☎ 537599) is a popular eating place and also has rooms. The position is excellent and the rooms are pleasant, although a little overpriced. Clean single/double rooms with shared bathroom are Rs 300/400; with private bathroom they are Rs 500/600.

South-east of Durbar Square, *Mahabuddha Guest House* (☎ 540575) is a comfortable little place. The rooms, at Rs 180/300, all have shared bath, but there is one bathroom for every three rooms.

There are several good cafes in the old town. *Cafe Pagoda*, in the north-eastern corner of the square, has good views from its rooftop and a fairly standard menu, as does *Cafe de Temple*. In the rear courtyard of the museum is the excellent open-air *Museum Cafe*. The garden setting is serene although the food is pricier than elsewhere. Pasta dishes are around Rs 170, a thali is Rs 180 and a lassi is Rs 70. You don't have to pay the hefty museum admission if you only want to eat here (and not visit the museum).

Shopping

Patan has many small handicraft shops and for certain crafts it is the best place in the valley. The Tibetan Jawlakhel area in the south of Patan is the place for Tibetan crafts and carpets. There is a string of carpet shops as you enter Jawlakhel, and a shop front, Khukuri House, is the official supplier of khukuri knives to the British Gurkha regiments.

Patan is the centre for bronze-casting and other metalwork and there are a number of excellent metalwork shops just north of Durbar Square.

An interesting souvenir or gift made in Patan is the Nepali game *bagh chal* (literally 'move the tigers'). This board game, often made in the form of a brass box which folds in half, is not unlike a stylised form of chequers. The pieces consist of four tigers and 20 goats. The player with the tigers wins if they can 'eat' all of the goats by jumping over them. The player with the goats tries to block this option, and wins if the goats can encircle a tiger and prevent it from moving. Nepalis love this game and are usually very good at it. You can pick up a small set in Patan for around Rs 200 and a larger set, with more intricately made pieces, for Rs 300 to Rs 500.

Getting There & Away

Buses from Kathmandu drop you at the city gate, Patan Dhoka, about a 15-minute walk from Durbar Square. There's another, larger bus stop directly south of Durbar Square, near the Southern (Lagan) Stupa. Tempos (route No 14) also operate from the Kathmandu main post office as soon as they have 10 passengers (Rs 8). A taxi from Thamel costs Rs 100 and an autorickshaw costs around Rs 80.

If you travel to Patan by bicycle a good route from Kathmandu is to take the track down to the river from opposite the big convention centre on the Bhaktapur road. A footbridge crosses the river and you enter Patan by the Northern Stupa near the Kumbeshwar Temple. It's an easy 5km ride from Thamel.

BHAKTAPUR
☎ 01 • pop 130,000
Bhaktapur, also known as Bhadgaon (pronounced 'bud-gown') or the City of Devotees, is the third major town of the valley and is in many ways the most medieval. Visiting Bhaktapur after the busy streets of Kathmandu is like being transported back in time.

The oldest part of the town is around Tachupal Tole (Dattatraya Square), to the east. Bhaktapur was the capital of the entire valley during the 14th to 16th centuries and during that time the focus of the town shifted west, to the Durbar Square area. Much of the town's great architecture dates from the end of the 17th century during the rule of King Bhupatindra Malla. An entire day could easily be spent wandering through Bhaktapur's narrow lanes and watching craftspeople at work, but it's also a pleasant place to spend the night, allowing you to explore at a more leisurely pace.

Orientation & Information
Bhaktapur is basically a pedestrian's city, which really adds to its timeless charm. Taxis and tour buses stop at the tour-bus park on the northern edge of Bhaktapur, a short walk from the heart of the city; public buses stop at Navpokhu Pokhari on the western edge of town. If you come to Bhaktapur by trolley bus, the stop is on the main road bypassing Bhaktapur, a 10- to 15-minute walk south of Taumadhi Tole.

All foreigners visiting Bhaktapur are charged a fee of Rs 300. This is collected at the various entrances to the city; on the larger streets there is a ticket booth; smaller streets have roaming ticket collectors. If you are staying overnight (or longer) in Bhaktapur, you only need to pay the entrance fee once.

Durbar Square
Bhaktapur's Durbar Square is larger than Kathmandu's, but not as packed with temples as Patan's. Unfortunately, the earthquake of 1934 destroyed many of the temples here.

The old **Royal Palace** is on the north side of the square and contains seven courtyards

(out of 99 the palace was once claimed to have). The palace is entered by the magnificent **Golden Gate** (Sun Dhoka), topped by a Garuda and generally considered the most important piece of art in the Kathmandu Valley. This leads to the **55 Window Palace** to the east. On the west side of the Golden Gate is an **art gallery** (open daily except Tuesday, Rs 20). The inner courtyards include the **Taleju Chowk** (closed to non-Hindus), **Kumari Chowk** and **Sundari Chowk**.

In the Durbar Square itself is a series of temples, with most significant being those on the eastern side of the palace. These include the large, white **Fasidega Temple**, dedicated to Shiva; the stone **Siddhi Lakshmi Temple**; and the **Pashupatinath Temple**, a replica of the main Shiva shrine at Pashupatinath.

Taumadhi Tole
A narrow street heading east from behind the Pashupatinath Temple leads you to Bhaktapur's second great square, Taumadhi Tole. The main feature here is the 30m-high **Nyatapola Temple**, the highest in the valley. The temple was built during the reign of King Bhupatindra Malla in 1702 and features erotic carvings on its painted roof struts. Also in this square is the triple-roofed **Bhairabnath Temple**. The enormous wheels and disassembled pieces stacked nearby make up the temple chariot in which the image of Bhairab is paraded around town during the Bisket Festival.

Tachupal Tole
It's only about a 10-minute walk from the Nyatapola Temple to the handsome, brick-paved Tachupal Tole. South from this square a maze of narrow laneways, passageways and courtyards runs down to the ghats on the river. Tachupal Tole, also called Dattatraya Square, was probably the original central square of Bhaktapur so this is the oldest part of the town.

The tall, square **Dattatraya Temple** on the eastern side was originally built in 1427. Like some other important structures in the valley, it was said to have been built using the timber from a single tree. At the other end of the square is the two-storey **Bhimsen Temple**, fronted by a platform with a small double-roofed Vishnu Temple and a pillar topped by a brass lion.

There are 10 buildings around the square which were originally used as *maths* (priests' houses). The best known was the **Pujari Math**, originally constructed in the 15th century during the reign of King Yaksha Malla, but restored in 1763. It is famed for the superb **peacock window**, in the small alley on its left-hand side, if you face it from the square. The window is reputed to be the finest carved window in the valley and is the subject of countless postcards and photographs. The building now houses a **Woodcarving Museum** which is open from 10 am to 5 pm daily, except Tuesday (to 3 pm Friday). Admission is Rs 20.

Directly across the square from the Pujari Math is the **Brass & Bronze Museum** with fine examples of metalwork from the valley. Its opening hours and admission price are the same as those for the Woodcarving Museum.

Potters' Square

Walking south from Durbar Square you come to **Potters' Square**, a remarkable area full of potters busy working at their wheels.

The square itself has two small temples, a solid-brick Vishnu Temple and the double-roofed Jeth Ganesh Temple. The latter was donated by a wealthy potter in 1646 and to this day its priest is a potter. In the square itself, literally thousands of finished pots sit out in the sun to dry, and are sold in the stalls around the square and between the square and Taumadhi Tole.

Places to Stay

A growing number of visitors to Bhaktapur stay overnight and for good reason. There's more than a day's worth of sightseeing here and one of the pleasures is that once evening falls most of the day trippers from Kathmandu disappear, and don't return until after breakfast the next day. There are a number of small guesthouses close to Durbar Square.

Golden Gate Guest House (☎ 610534, e *bcci@wlink.com.np*) is entered by a passageway from Durbar Square or from the laneway between Durbar Square and Taumadhi Tole. The owners are friendly, there are fine views from the roof and single/double rooms cost Rs 350/550, all with shared bath, or a steep US$10/15 with bath. Some of the rooms have balconies and there's also a restaurant downstairs. *Shiva*

Guest House (☎ 613912) has a better location fronting onto Durbar Square. The rooms, some with views over the square, have been renovated but are a bit cramped and overpriced at US$15/20 with private bathroom, or US$6/8 with shared bathroom. There's a good cafe downstairs.

Bhadgaon Guest House (☎ 610488, fax 610481) is just off the south-western corner of Taumadhi Tole and has excellent rooftop views. The rooms are large, clean and comfortable, and cost US$10/15 with bath.

Pagoda Guest House (☎ 613248), on the lane heading off from the north-western edge of the square, is clean and comfortable. There's a variety of rooms, all clean and well maintained but a bit cramped, which cost from US$7/8 with shared bathroom up to US$20/25 with private bathroom. There's also a rooftop restaurant here.

Nyatapola Guest House (☎ 612415) is one of the cheaper places in central Bhaktapur. Basic rooms with shared bathroom cost Rs 250/275, and there's a nice terrace restaurant.

Places to Eat

In the middle of Taumadhi Tole, *Cafe Nyatapola* is in a building that was once a traditional pagoda temple. From upstairs there are good views over the square but it's cramped and often dominated by large groups of tourists. Prices are comparatively high with soups at Rs 85 and a Nepali set lunch at Rs 495.

In the corner of the square is the small *Sunny Restaurant*, which has a terrace, great views over the square and no crowds.

On Tachupal Tole, opposite the Dattatraya Temple, *Cafe de Peacock & Soma Bar* is one of the best spots in the valley to while away an afternoon. The food is good and the views of the beautiful square are mesmerising.

Shopping

As in Patan there are a number of crafts for which Bhaktapur is the centre. There are plenty of shops and stalls catering to visitors around Durbar Square and Taumadhi Tole.

Bhaktapur is the pottery centre of the valley and a visit to Potters' Square is a must. Bhaktapur is also renowned for its woodcarving and you'll see good examples in the Handicrafts Centre on Tachupal Tole.

There are other shops around the squares and you will find unusual pieces in the alley beside the Pujari Math. One of the more unusual items you can buy here is a flexible wooden neck tie! Some of the best puppets, on sale in their thousands in all the valley towns, come from Bhaktapur.

Getting There & Away

Travelling by public bus or minibus to Bhaktapur you disembark near the walled water tank called Navpokhu Pokhari, a short walk from Durbar Square. The minibuses from Kathmandu's City Bus Station are crowded and can take more than one hour (Rs 4). The Chinese-built trolley buses are preferable (Rs 5). At the Bhaktapur end, you have a 10-minute walk to get to the town centre (by Ram Ghat and up into the town by Potters' Square). The trolley buses leave Kathmandu from Tripureshwar Marg and take around 35 minutes. They run until about 9 pm.

Buses for Nagarkot leave regularly from the north-eastern corner of the city (Rs 11).

If you're cycling from Kathmandu, the main road to Bhaktapur runs through to Dhulikhel, Barabise and finally to Tibet, so it carries a lot of traffic. Avoid peak hours. A better alternative for cyclists is to ride via Thimi. Take the Thimi turn-off – left at a T-junction after the Bhaktapur road crosses the Manohara River.

A taxi from Thamel costs around Rs 300, and it will drop you at the tour-bus park on the northern edge of the city, just a short walk from Durbar Square. Returning to Kathmandu, you may actually be able to get the taxi driver to use the meter.

NAGARKOT

☎ 01

Nagarkot is a resort village situated high on the north-eastern rim of the Kathmandu Valley. Getting up at dawn to see the sun rise over the Himalaya is a great experience, especially if you're not planning to go trekking on this trip but still want to take in the splendour of the mountains. There are other places on the valley rim that offer fabulous mountain views, but this is regarded as is the best.

There are panoramic mountain views from the ridge at the top of the village – from Dhaulagiri in the west, past Everest (a tiny dot on the horizon) to Kanchenjunga. A one-

Short Walks from Nagarkot

There are some good treks down into the valley from Nagarkot. One of the best is the return walk to Bhaktapur via Changu Narayan. The walking trail follows the road to Bhaktapur along a ridge but this first section is fairly dull and it's easier to take a local bus to the hairpin bend where the trail branches off and follows a long spur into the valley.

From here the trail climbs uphill through a pine forest for about 20 minutes and then follows the ridgeline before dropping down to Changu Narayan. The walk from the road takes about 1½ hours and passes through Chhetri villages with wonderful views down over the valley. From the temple you can continue on the walking trail south to Bhaktapur or take a bus from the car park. Alternatively you could also descend to the Manohara River to the north and take the road to Bodhnath and Kathmandu.

Another trail from Nagarkot leads to Sankhu in the north-east of the valley, which is a two-hour walk away. The picturesque Newari village can easily be seen from Nagarkot, or from the trail to Changu Narayan. The trail starts by following the same ridge to Changu Narayan, then drops steeply down the hillside in a north-westerly direction, joining the main Helambu to Sankhu trail and passing a group of teahouses. The main trail then descends to Sankhu, but you can make a diversion to the temple of Vajra Jogini to the west (ask directions at the teahouses). There are buses back to Kathmandu from Sankhu.

hour walk south from the village (past the army training base) takes you up to a lookout tower with a superb 360-degree view.

There's plenty of cheap accommodation but as there's little to do here most people stay one night, see the sunset and sunrise, and head back to Kathmandu. A road runs directly up to Nagarkot from Bhaktapur and there are good opportunities for trekking in the surrounding valleys. Taking a bus up one way and walking back to Bhaktapur via Changu Narayan is easy and enjoyable.

Although you should have clear views in the morning from October to March, it starts to get hazy from April and you're unlikely to see anything from about May to September.

Places to Stay & Eat

Most of Nagarkot's accommodation is strung out along the road leading uphill from where the bus drops you (take the left fork). Apart from those listed here, there are numerous mid-range places.

About a five-minute walk up from the bus stop, *Sherpa Guesthouse* (☎ 680015, e thupten@wlink.com.np) has just two simple double rooms (one is a separate cottage) with shared bathroom and mattresses on the floor for Rs 150. It's very rustic and run by a friendly family. Despite the simplicity of it all, there's Internet access here and Western movies are shown some evenings. Even if you can't get (or don't want) a room here, *Free Tibet Restaurant* is excellent. There's an atmospheric little dining area with cushions and low tables or you can sit outside in the terraced garden. The food is reasonably priced: A Nepali set meal is Rs 100, omelettes are Rs 30 and a bottle of beer is Rs 110.

If you take the track to the right where the road forks (just below Hotel Elephant Head), there are two decent places out on the edge of the ridge with great mountain views. *Hotel Milestone* (☎ 680088) is a pleasant little place with four cottages, all with private bathroom, warm water and squat toilets. The rooms are basic but cheap at Rs 150/200 a single/double. *Hotel Green Valley* (☎ 680878) has plain rooms (ask to see a few) but some face the mountains. They cost from Rs 150/200 with shared bathroom to Rs 400/600 with private bathroom and the promise of hot water.

A cheap option among the cluster of guesthouses near the Mahankali Temple is *New Pheasant Lodge* (☎ 680032). The rooms are basic, concrete-box style but cheap at Rs 100/150 with shared bath.

Hotel Galaxy (☎ 680122) has very pleasant rooms with north-east facing views and private bathroom (some with bathtub) for US$9/14. Discounts of 35% are available when it's quiet.

All of the hotels and guesthouses have restaurants and there are a couple of tea stalls and independent places (including a pizza place) down near the main intersection.

Getting There & Away

There are occasional buses to Nagarkot from the City Bus Station in Kathmandu (Rs 15, two hours). Local buses also depart roughly every hour from the Nagarkot bus stop in the north-east of Bhaktapur. The winding 15km trip from Bhaktapur takes one hour and costs Rs 11. A taxi from Kathmandu city costs around Rs 800.

CHANGU NARAYAN TEMPLE

The impressive temple complex of Changu Narayan stands on a hilltop about 4km north of Bhaktapur. The temple, dedicated to Vishnu in his incarnation as Narayan, is particularly beautiful and features some intricately carved roof struts depicting multi-armed deities.

The temple is relatively new, having been rebuilt in 1702 after a fire, but the site dates back to the 4th century and there are many important stone images and sculptures within the main courtyard that are much older than the temple itself. In the north-west corner is an image of Vishnu astride the Garuda, which is featured on the Nepali Rs 10 note. Fronting the main entrance is a kneeling Garuda figure said to date from the 5th-century Licchavi period, and flanking the gilded door of the temple are two stone lions. Entry to the temple is Rs 60.

There's a pleasant *cafe* near the temple entrance, a great place to recuperate if you've just walked up from Bhaktapur or down from Nagarkot.

There's a sealed road all the way up to Changu village (about 100m from the temple) and regular buses (Rs 5) run up from Bhaktapur, departing from a designated stop in the north of town. A taxi from Bhaktapur costs about Rs 170. The nicest way to reach here, however, is on foot (about two hours from Bhaktapur) or mountain bike (about one hour). You could save the steep walk up by taking the bus, then walk down via the fields and villages of Jaukhel and Gwatala; take the rear exit from the temple to pick up the trail.

Language

Farsi (Persian)

For a more comprehensive guide to Farsi (Persian), pick up a copy of Lonely Planet's new *Farsi (Persian) phrasebook*.

Transliteration

Transliterating from non-Roman script into the Roman alphabet is always a tricky affair. Formal transliterations of Farsi are overly complicated in the way they represent vowels and do not accurately represent the spoken language. In this language guide the system used is designed to be as simple as possible for spoken communication.

Elsewhere in this book, transliterations (especially of place names) use the more formal system, where vowels appear both with and without diatrical marks.

Pronunciation

This guide mostly uses colloquial expressions and pronunciations. Classical Farsi is not the language of everyday speech, but a literary form of the language, normally only used in books or speeches. Colloquial Farsi is the language of everyday speech, that spoken by most Iranians most of the time.

Hyphens have been used between compound words which are pronounced as one word but written as two, and where a combination of consonants would otherwise be mispronounced.

In general, the last syllable of a multisyllable word is stressed, unless the last vowel in the word is a short vowel, eg, em**ā**m but b**a**l-e (bolded 'a' indicates stress).

Vowels & Diphthongs

A macron over a vowel (ā) indicates a longer vowel sound. This is very important as the wrong vowel length can completely change the meaning of a word, or make it incomprehensible, eg, *māst* (rhyming with 'passed') means 'yogurt', while *mast* (rhyming with 'gassed') means 'drunk'.

a	as in 'father',
ā	as in 'far' (longer than a)
e	as in 'bed'
i	as in 'marine'
o	as in 'mole'
u	as in 'rule'

Consonants

The letters **b**, **d**, **f**, **j**, **m**, **n**, **p**, **sh**, **t** and **z** are pronounced as in English.

ch	as in 'cheese'
g	as in 'goose'
gh	a guttural sound like a heavy French 'r' pronounced at the back of the mouth
h	as in 'hot'
kh	as the 'ch' in Scottish *loch*
l	always as in 'leg', never as in 'roll' (see note below)
r	trilled
s	as in 'sin'
y	as in 'yak'
zh	as the 'g' in 'mirage'
'	very weak glottal stop, as the sound made between the words 'uh-oh' or the 'tt' in Cockney 'bottle'

Note: doubled consonants are always pronounced distinctly as in *hat trick* not *battle*; the sole exception is *Allāh* (God), in which the l's are swallowed as in English *doll*.

Be Polite!

When addressing a stranger, especially one older than you, it's polite to include *āghā* (sir) or *khānom* (madam) at the beginning of the first sentence, or after one of the standard greetings. *Āghā ye* and *Khānom e* are the equivalents of Mr, and Mrs/Miss/Ms. *Āghā* can be used before or after the first name as a title of respect, eg, *Mohammad Āghā* or, more likely, *Āghā Mohammad*.

The pronoun *shomā* is the polite form of 'you' singular, and should be used when addressing people you don't know well – *to* is only generally used when talking to close friends and relatives of the same generation or later, and to children and animals.

Essentials

The all-purpose greeting in Iran is *salām aleykom*, which does duty for good morning, good afternoon and good evening. The same expression is used throughout the Muslim world, so if you learn only one phrase in Iran, this is it!

Welcome.	*khosh āmadin*
Hello.	*salām*
Good morning.	*sob bekheyr*
Good day. (noon)	*rux bekheyr*
Good evening.	*shab bekheyr*
Goodbye.	*khodā hāfez*
How are you?	*hāletun chetor e?*
Fine. And you?	*khubam. shomā chetoin?*
Yes.	*bale*
No.	*na*
Please.	*lotfan*
Thank you.	*motashakkeram*
Thank you very much.	*kheyli mamnum*
Excuse me/ I'm sorry.	*bebakhshid*
What's your name?	*esmetun chi ye?*
My name is ...	*esmam ... e*

Signs – Farsi

Entrance	ورود
Exit	خروج
Open	باز
Closed	بسته
No Entry	ورود ممنوع
No Smoking	دخانیات ممنوع
Prohibited	ممنوع
Hot	گرم
Cold	سرد
Toilets	توالت
Men	مردانه
Women	زنانه

Language Difficulties

Do you speak English?	*shomā ingilisi baladin?*
Does anyone here speak English?	*injā kesi ingilisi balad e?*
I understand.	*mifahman*
I don't understand.	*na mifahman*
Please write it down.	*lotfan un o benevisin*

Getting Around

Where's the ...?	*... kojā st?*
airport	*furudgāh*
bus stop	*istgāh e utubus*
train station	*istgāh e ghatār*

What time does the ... leave/arrive?	*... che sā'ati harekat mikone/mirese?*
aeroplane	*havāpeymā*
boat	*ghāyegh*
bus	*utubus*
train	*ghatār*

What time is the ... bus?	*utubus e ... key miyād?*
first	*avval*
last	*ākhar*
next	*ba'di*

I'd like a	*... mikhām*
one-way ticket	*belit e ye sare*
return ticket	*belit e do sare*

1st class	*daraje yek*
2nd class	*daraje do*

Accommodation

Do you have any rooms available?	*otāgh khāli dārin*

I'd like a ... room	*ye otāgh e ... mikhām*
single	*taki*
shared	*moshtarak*

How much is it for ...?	*barāye ... cheghadr mishe?*
one night	*ye shab*
a week	*ye hafte*
two people	*do nafar*

Emergencies – Farsi

Help!	*komak!*
Stop!	*ist!*
Go away!	*gom sho!*
Call ...!	*... khabar konin!*
a doctor	*ye doktor*
an ambulance	*ye āmbulans*
the police	*polis o*
I wish to contact my embassy/consulate.	*mikham bā sefārat/ konsulgari khod am tamās begiram*
Where's the toilet?	*tuvālet kojā st?*

We want a room with a ...	*mā ye otāgh bā ye ... mikhāyim*
bathroom	*dastshuyi*
shower	*dush*
TV	*televiziyon*
window	*panjere*

Around Town

Where is the ...?	*... kojā st?*
bank	*bānk*
church	*kelisā*
city centre	*markaz e shahr*
consulate	*konsulgari*
embassy	*sefārat*
hotel	*hotel*
mosque	*masjed*
market	*bāzār*
police	*polis*
post office	*edāre ye post*
public telephone	*telefon e umumi*
public toilet	*tuvālet e umumi*
tourist office	*edāre ye jahāngardi*
town square	*meydun a shahr*

Is it far from here?	*un az injā dur e?*
Go straight ahead.	*mostaghim berin*
To the left.	*samt e chap*
To the right.	*samt e rāst*
here	*injā*
there	*unjā*

Health

Where is the ...?	*... kojā st?*
chemist	*dārukhune*
dentist	*dandun pezeshk*
doctor	*doktor*
hospital	*bimārestān*

I'm sick.	*mariz am*

I have ...	*... dāram*
anaemia	*kam khuni*
asthma	*āsm*
diabetes	*diyābet*

antiseptic	*zedd e ufuni konande*
aspirin	*āsperin*
condom	*kāndom*
contraceptive	*zedd e hāmelegi*
diarrhoea	*es-hāl*
medicine	*dāru*
sunblock	*kerem e zedd e āftāb*
tampon	*tāmpon*

Time & Dates

What time is it?	*sā'at chand e?*

today	*emruz*
tomorrow	*fardā*
yesterday	*diruz*
tonight	*emshab*
morning, am	*sob*
afternoon, pm	*ba'd az zohr*
day	*ruz*
month	*māh*
year	*sāl*

Monday	*dos hanbe*
Tuesday	*se shanbe*
Wednesday	*chahār shanbe*
Thursday	*panj shanbe*
Friday	*jom'e*
Saturday	*shanbe*
Sunday	*yekshanbe*

Numbers

1	*yek*
2	*do*
3	*se*
4	*chāhār*
5	*panj*
6	*shish*
7	*haft*
8	*hasht*
9	*noh*
10	*dah*
11	*yāzdah*

12	*davāzdah*
13	*sizdah*
14	*chāhārdah*
15	*punzdah*
16	*shānzdah*
17	*hifdah*
18	*hijdah*
19	*nuzdah*
20	*bist*
21	*bist o yek*
22	*bist o do*
30	*si*
40	*chehel*
50	*panjāh*
60	*shast*
70	*haftād*
80	*hashtād*
90	*navad*
100	*sad*
167	*sad o shast o haft*
200	*divist*
1000	*hezār*

| one million | *yek milyon* |

Food

restaurant	*chelo kababi*
teahouse	*chāy khune*
breakfast	*sobhune*
lunch	*nāhār*
dinner	*shām*
supper	*asrune*

| I'm a vegetarian. | *sabzikhār am* |

I don't eat ...	... *nemikhoram*
meat	*gusht*
chicken	*morgh*
fish	*māhi*

bread	*nun*
butter	*kare*
cheese	*panir*
eggs	*tokhm e morgh*
fork	*changāl*
honey	*asal*
knife	*chāghu*
pepper	*felfel*
salt	*namak*
yogurt	*māst*

Vegetables

cucumber	*khiyār*
eggplant	*bādemjun*
garlic	*sir*
lettuce	*kāhu*
olive	*zeytun*
onion	*piyāz*
peas	*nokhod*
potato	*sib zamini*
tomato	*goje farangi*
vegetables	*sabzijāt*

Meat & Poultry

beef	*gusht e gāv*
chicken	*morgh*
goat meat	*gusht e boz*
lamb/mutton	*gusht e gusfand*
meat	*gusht*

Fruit & Nuts

apple	*sib*
apricot	*zard ālu*
fig	*anjir*
fruit	*mive*
grape	*angur*
lemon	*limu*
melon	*kharboze*
orange	*porteghāl*
pomegranate	*anār*

almond	*bādum*
hazelnut	*fandogh*
pistachio	*peste*

Drinks

boiled drinking water	*āb e jush*
coffee	*ghahve*
drink	*nushābe*
fruit juice	*āb mive*
mineral water	*āb e ma'dani*
soft drink	*nushābe*
tea	*chāyi*
water	*āb*
yogurt drink	*dugh*

with/without ...	*bā/bedun e ...*
ice	*yakh*
milk	*shir*
sugar	*shekar*

Hindi & Urdu

Hindi and Urdu, official languages of India and Pakistan respectively, are very similar. They belong to the Indo-Aryan language family and evolved from the same dialect. The main difference between them is that Hindi is written from left to right in Devanagari script, while Urdu runs from right to left and is written in a modified form of the Persio-Arabic script. While the scripts may be unfamiliar, many of the grammatical features will be familiar to English speakers.

The unmarked words and phrases throughout this section should be understood by both Hindi and Urdu speakers. Differences are indicated by (H) and (U) for Hindi and Urdu respectively.

English is the second official language of India and is the language of government, business and the military in Pakistan, so if you get stuck you can always try English.

For a more comprehensive guide to Hindi and Urdu, get a copy of Lonely Planet's *Hindi & Urdu phrasebook*.

Pronunciation

Most of the sounds in Hindi and Urdu correspond to the Roman letters used to represent them in the transliteration.

Vowels & Diphthongs

It's important to pay attention to the pronunciation of vowels and especially to their length. A line over a vowel (eg, $\bar{a}$, $\bar{i}$, $\bar{u}$) indicates a longer vowel sound.

The symbol ~ over a vowel (eg, $\tilde{\bar{a}}$, $\tilde{i}$, $\tilde{\bar{i}}$, $\tilde{u}$, $\tilde{u}$,) indicates that it should be spoken through the nose.

a	as the 'u' in 'sun'
ā	as in 'father'
e	as in 'bet'
i	as in 'sit'
ī	as the 'ee' in 'feet'
u	as in 'put'
ū	as the 'oo' in 'fool'
ai	as the 'a' in 'bad'
o	as in 'both'
au	as the 'aw' in 'saw'
o	as in 'both'

Note that **ai** is pronounced as a diphthong when followed by **ya**, and **au** is pronounced as a diphthong when followed by **va**.

ai	as the 'i' in 'high'
au	as the 'ou' in 'ouch'

Consonants

Most consonants in the transliterations are pronounced as in English, with the following exceptions:

c	as the 'ch' in 'cheese'
g	always as in 'gun', never as in 'age'
ṭ	pronounced with the tongue further back than in English. Curl the tongue back towards the roof of the mouth.
ḍ	pronounced with the tonuge curled back towards the roof of the mouth.
r	slightly trilled
ṛ	an 'r' with the tongue placed near the roof of the mouth and flapped quickly down, touching the roof as it moves.
q	as the 'k' in 'king', but pronounced further back
y	as in 'yak'
kh	similar to the 'ch' in Scottish *loch*
gh	like the 'g' in 'go' but pronounced further back in the throat

Aspirated consonats are pronounced with a breath of air, represented by an **h** after the consonant (except for **sh**, pronounced as in 'ship', and **kh** and **gh**).

Essentials

Hello.	*namaste/namskār* (H) *assalūm alaikum /ādāb* (U)
Goodbye.	*namaste/namskār* (H) *khudā hāfiz* (U)
Yes.	*jī hã*
No.	*jī nahī*

Please – usually conveyed through the polite form of the imperative, or through other expressions. This book uses polite expressions and the polite forms of words.

Thank you.	*shukriyā/ dhanyavād* (H)
You're welcome.	*koī bāt nahī*

Signs – Hindi

प्रवेश/अन्दर	Entrance
निकार/बाहर	Exit
खुला	Open
बन्द	Closed
अन्दर आना [निषि/मना] है	No Entry
धूम्रपान करना [निषि/मना] है	No Smoking
निषि	Prohibited
गर्म	Hot
ठंडा	Cold
शोचालय	Toilets

Signs – Urdu

Entrance	داخلا/اندر
Exit	باہر
Open	بند
Closed	کھلا
No Entry	اندر آنا منع ہے۔
No Smoking	سگریٹ پینا منع ہے۔
Prohibited	منع
Hot	ٹھنڈا
Cold	گرم
Toilets	پاخانہ/بیت الخلا

| Excuse me/Sorry. | *kshamā kījiye* (H) |
| | *māf kījiye* (U) |

How are you?	*āp kaise/ī haĩ?* (m/f)
	āp khairiyat se haī? (U)
Fine, and you?	*bas āp sunāiye* (m/f)
	āp kī duā hai (U)
What's your name?	*āp kā shubh nām kyā hai?* (H)
	āp kā isme girāme kyā hai (U)

Language Difficulties

Do you speak English?	*kyā āp ko angrezī ātī hai?*
Does anyone here speak English?	*kyā kisī ko angrezī ātī hai?*
I understand.	*maĩ samjhā/ī*
I don't understand.	*maĩ nahī̃ samjhā/ī*
Could you speak more slowly?	*dhīre dhīre boliye* (H)
	āhista āhista boliye (U)
Please write it down.	*zarā likh dījiye*

Getting Around

| How do we get to ...? | *... kaise jāte haĩ?* |

When is the ... bus?	*... bas kab jāegī?*
first	*pehlā/pehlī*
next	*aglā/aglī*
last	*ākhirī*

What time does the ... leave/arrive?	*... kitne baje jāyegā/ pahũcegā?* (m)
	... kitne baje jāyegī/ pahũcegī? (f)
plane	*havāī jahāz* (m)
boat	*nāv* (f)
bus	*bas* (f)
train	*relgāṛī* (f)

I'd like a ... ticket.	*mujhe ek ... ṭikaṭ cāhiye*
one way	*ek-tarafā*
return	*do-tarafā*

1st class	*pratham shrēni* (H)
	pehlā darjā (U)
2nd class	*dvitīy shrēni* (H)
	dūsrā darjā (U)

Accommodation

Where is the (best/ cheapest) hotel?	*sab se (acchā/sastā) hoṭal kahā̃ hai?*
Could you write the address, please?	*zarā us kā patā likh dījiye*
Do you have any rooms available?	*kyā koī kamrā khālī hai?*

How much for ...?	*... kā kirāyā kitnā hai?*
one night	*ek din*
one week	*ek hafte*

I'd like a ...	*mujhe ... cāhiye*
single room	*singal kamrā*
double room	*ḍabal kamrā*
room with a	*ghusalkhānevālā*
bathroom	*kamrā*

I'd like to share a	*maĩ ḍorm mẽ ṭheharnā*
dorm.	*cāhtā/ĩ hũ* (m/f)
May I see it?	*kyā maĩ kamrā*
	saktā/ĩ hũ (m/f)
Where's the	*ghusalkhānā kahã*
bathroom?	*hai?*

Around Town
Where's a/the ...	*... kahã hai?*
bank	*baink*
consulate	*kaũnsal*
embassy	*dūtāvās* (H)
	sifāratkhānā (U)
Hindu temple	*mandir*
mosque	*masjid*
post office	*ḍākkhānā*
public phone	*sārvajanik fon* (H)
	pablik fon (U)
public toilet	*shaucālay* (H)
	pākhānā (U)
Sikh temple	*gurudvārā*
town square	*cauk*

| Is it far from/near | *kyā nvoh yahã se dūr/* |
| here? | *nazdīk hai?* |

Health
| I'm sick. | *maĩ bīmār hũ* |

Where's a/the ...?	*... kahã hai?*
doctor	*ḍākṭar*
hospital	*aspatāl* (H)
	haspatāl (U)
chemist	*davākhānā*
dentist	*ḍenṭisṭ*

antiseptic	*aintīseptik*
asprin	*(esprin) sirdard kī*
	davā
condoms	*nirodhak* (H)
	kāṇḍam (U)
contraceptives	*garbnirodhak* (H)
	kanṭrāsepshan (U)
diarrhoea	*dast*
medicine	*davā*

nausea	*ghin* (H)/*matlī* (U)
syringe	*sūī*
tampons	*ṭaimpon*

Time & Date
When?	*kab?*
What time is it?	*kitne baje haĩ?/*
	ṭāim kyā hai?
It's (ten) o'clock	*(das) baje haĩ*
half past two	*ḍhāī baje haĩ*

| today | *āj* |
| tomorrow/yesterday | *kal* |
| (meaning is made clear by context) |
| now | *ab* |

morning	*saverā*
evening	*shām*
night	*rāt* (H)/*shab* (U)
day	*din* (H)/*roz* (U)
week	*hafte*
month	*mahīnā*
year	*sāl/baras*

Days – Hindi
Monday	*somvār*
Tuesday	*mangalvār*
Wednesday	*budhvār*
Thursday	*guruvār/brihaspativār*
Friday	*shukravār*
Saturday	*shanivār*
Sunday	*itvār/ravivār*

Days – Urdu
Monday	*pīr*
Tuesday	*mangal*
Wednesday	*budh*
Thursday	*jume rāt*
Friday	*jumā*
Saturday	*haftā*
Sunday	*itvār*

Numbers
Whereas we count in tens, hundreds, thousands, millions and billions, the Hindi and Urdu numbering system goes tens, hundreds, thousands, hundred thousands, ten millions. A hundred thousand is a *lākh*, and 10 million is a *karoṛ*. These two words are almost always used in place of their English equivalents.

Emergencies – Hindi & Urdu	
Help!	*mada kījiye!*
Stop!	*ruko!*
Thief!	*cor!*
Call a doctor!	*ḍākṭar ko bulāo!*
Call an ambulance!	*embulains le ānā!*
Call the police!	*pulis ko bulāo!*
I'm lost	*maĩ rāstā bhūl gayā/ gayī hũ (f/m)*
Where's the ...?	*... kahã̄ hai?*
police station	*thānā*
toilet	*ghusalkhānā*
I wish to contact my embassy/consulate.	*maĩ apne dūtās ke sebāt katnā logõ cāhtā (f)/cāhtī (m) hũ (H)*
I wish to contact my embassy/consulate.	*maĩ apne safārat-khāne se rābitā karnā cāhtā (f)/ cāhtī (m) hũ (U)*

Once into the thousands, large written numbers have commas every two places, not three.

1	*ek*
2	*do*
3	*tīn*
4	*cār*
5	*pãc*
6	*chai*
7	*sāt*
8	*āṭh*
9	*nau*
10	*das*
11	*gyārah*
12	*bara*
13	*terah*
14	*caudah*
15	*pandrah*
16	*solah*
17	*satrah*
18	*aṭṭhārah*
19	*unnīs*
20	*bīs*
21	*ikkīs*

22	*bāīs*
30	*tīs*
40	*cālīs*
50	*pacās*
60	*sāṭh*
70	*sattar*
80	*assī*
90	*nabbe/navve*
100	*sau*
1000	*hazār*

one million (written 1,00,000)	*ek lākh*
10 million (written 1,00,00,000)	*ek karoṛ*

Food

breakfast	*nāshtā*
lunch	*din kā khānā*
dinner	*rāt kā khānā*
fork	*kā̃ṭā*
knife	*churī*
glass	*glās*
plate	*pleṭ*

I'm a vegetarian.   *maĩ shākāhārī hũ (H)*
                    maĩ sabzīkhor hũ (U)

food	*khānā*
bread	*roṭī*
fried bread	*parā̃ṭhā*
tandoori rounds	*nān or tandūrī roṭī*
sliced bread	*ḍabal (double) roṭī*
butter	*makkhan*
cheese	*panār*
chillies	*mārc*
without chillies	*mirc ke binā*
rice	*cāval*
fried rice	*pulāv*
salt	*namak*
spices	*masāle*
sugar	*cīnī (H)/shakar (U)*
yogurt	*dahī*

Vegetables

cabbage	*band gobhī*
lentils	*dāl*
peas	*maṭar*
potato	*ālū*

pumpkin	*kaddū*
spinach	*pālak*
vegetable	*sabzī/sāg*

Fruit

apple	*seb*
apricot	*khubānī*
banana	*kelā*
fruit	*phal*
mango	*ām*
orange	*nārangi*

Meat & Poultry

beef	*gāy kā māns*
chicken	*murgh*
fish	*machlī*
goat	*bakrī kā māns*
meat	*māns/gosht*
mutton	*ber kā māns*

Drinks

coffee	*kāfī*
milk	*dūdh*
soft drink	*sauft drink*
(cup of) tea	*cāy*
tea with milk	*dūdhvālī cāy*
tea with sugar	*cīnī ke sāth*
(boiled) water	*(ūblā) pānī*

Nepali

It's quite easy to get by with English in Nepal; most people the average visitor will have to deal with in the Kathmandu Valley and in Pokhara will speak some English. Along the main trekking trails, particularly the Annapurna Circuit, English is widely understood.

Nepali is quite an easy language to pick up. It's closely related to Hindi and, like Hindi, is an Indo-European language. If you want to know more Nepali than is included here, Lonely Planet's *Nepali phrasebook* is a handy introduction to the language.

Even if you learn no other Nepali, there's one word every visitor soon picks up – *namaste* (pronounced 'na-ma-stay'). Strictly translated it means 'I salute the god in you', but it's used as an everyday greeting, encompassing everything from 'Hello' to

'How are you?' and even 'See you again soon'. Properly used, it should be accompanied with the hands held in a prayer-like position, the Nepali gesture which is the equivalent of westerners shaking hands.

Pronunciation

Vowels

a	as the 'u' in 'hut'
ā	as the 'a' in 'father'
e	as the 'e' in 'best' but longer
i	as the 'i' in 'sister' but longer
o	as the 'o' in 'sold'
u	as the 'u' in 'put'
ai	as the 'i' in 'mine'
au	as the 'ow' in 'cow'

Consonants

Most Nepali consonants are quite similar to their English counterparts. The exceptions are the so-called retroflex consonants and the aspirated consonants. Retroflex sounds are made by curling the tongue back to touch the roof of the mouth with the tip as you make the sound; they're indicated in this guide by an underdot, eg, **t**, *Kathmandu*.

Aspirated consonants are sounded more forcefully than in English and are made with a short puff of air. They're indicated in this guide by an 'h' after the consonant, eg, **kh**, *khānuhos* (please).

Both retroflex and aspirated consonants are best learned by having a Nepali demonstrate them for you.

Essentials

Hello/Goodbye.	*namaste*
How are you?	*tapāilai kasto chha?*
Excuse me.	*hajur*
Please (give me).	*dinuhos*
Please (you have).	*khānuhos*
Thank you.	*dhanyabad*

Unlike in the West, verbal expressions of thanks are not the cultural norm in Nepal. Although neglecting to say 'Thank you' may make you feel a little uncomfortable, it's rarely necessary in a simple commercial transaction; foreigners going round saying *dhanyabad* all the time sound distinctly odd to Nepalis.

Essentials

I	*ma*
Yes. (I have)	*chā*
No. (I don't have)	*chhaina*
OK.	*theekcha*
Where?	*kahā?*

here	*yahā*
there	*tyahā*
good/pretty	*ramro*

Do you speak English?	*tapāi angreji bolna saknu hunchha?*
I only speak a little Nepali.	*ma ali nepāli bolchhu*
I understand.	*ma bujhchu*
I don't understand.	*maile bujhina*
Please say it again.	*pheri bhannuhos*
Please speak more slowly.	*tapāi bistārai bolnuhos*

Getting Around

bus	*bus*
taxi	*taxi*
boat	*nāu*
ticket	*tikaṭ*

How can I get to ...?	*... kolāgi kati paisā lāgchha?*
Is it far from here?	*yahābata ke tādhā chha?*
Can I walk there?	*hiḍera jāna sakinchhu?*
I want to go to ...	*ma ... jānchhu*
Where does this bus go?	*yo bus kahā jānchha?*
How much is it to go to ...?	*... jāna kati parchha?*
I want a one-way/ return ticket.	*jāne/jāne-āune tikaṭ dinuhos.*
Does your taxi have a meter?	*tapāi ko taxi mā meter chha?*

Accommodation

Where's a ...?	*... kahā chha?*
guesthouse	*pāhuna ghar*
hotel	*hoṭel*
camp site	*shivir*
lodge	*laj*

What's the address?	*thegānā ke ho?*
Please write down the address.	*thegānā lekhunuhos*

Can I get a place to stay here?	*yahā bās paunchha?*
May I look at the room?	*kothā herna sakchhu?*
How much is it per night?	*ek rātko, kati paisā ho?*
Does it include breakfast?	*bihānako khāna samet ho?*

room	*kothā*
clean	*safā*
dirty	*mailo*
fan	*pankhā*
hot water	*tāto pāni*

Around Town

I'm looking for (a/the) ...	*ma ... khojiraeko*
bank	*baink*
... embassy	*... rājdutāvas*
museum	*samgrāhālaya*
police	*prahari*
post office	*post afis*
tourist office	*turist afis*

Where's the market?	*bazar kata parchha?*
What time does it open/close?	*kati baje kholchha/ banda garchha?*
I want to change some money.	*paisā sātnu manlāgchha*

Trekking

Which way is ...?	*... jāne bato kata parchha?*
Is there a village nearby?	*najikai gaun parchha?*
How many hours/ days to ...?	*... kati ghanṭā/din?*
Where's the porter?	*bhariya kata gayo?*
I want to sleep.	*malai sutna man lagyo*
I'm cold.	*malai jado lagyo*
Please give me (water).	*malai (pani) dinuhos*

way/trail	*sāno bāṭo*
bridge	*pul*
downhill	*orālo*
uphill	*ukālo*

left	*bāyā*
right	*dāyā*
cold	*jāḍo*

Health

Where can I find a good doctor?	*rāmro dākṭar kaha pāincha?*
Where's the nearest hospital?	*yahā aspatāl kahā chha?*
I don't feel well.	*malāi sancho chhaina*
I have diarrhoea.	*dishā lāgyo*
I have altitude sickness.	*lekh lāgyo*
I have a fever.	*joro āyo*
I'm having trouble breathing.	*sās pherna sakdina*

medicine	*ausadhi*
pharmacy	*ausadhi pasal*

I have ...	*malāi ... lāgyo*
asthma	*damko byathā*
diabetes	*madhu meha*
epilepsy	*chāre rog*

Time & Date

What time is it?	*kati bajyo?*
It's one o'clock.	*ek bajyo*

minute	*minet*
hour	*ghantā*
day	*din*
today	*āja*
yesterday	*hijo*
tomorrow	*bholi*
now	*ahile*
week	*haptā*
month	*mahinā*

What day is it today?	*āja ke bār?*
Today is ...	*āja ... ho*

Monday	*som bār*
Tuesday	*mangal bār*
Wednesday	*budh bār*
Thursday	*bihi bār*
Friday	*sukra bār*
Saturday	*sani bār*
Sunday	*āita bār*

Emergencies – Nepali

Help!	*guhār!*
It's an emergency!	*āpaṭ paryo!*
There's been an accident!	*durghaṭanā bhayo!*
Please call a doctor.	*dākṭarlai bolāunuhos*
Where's the (public) toilet?	*shauchālaya kahā chha?*
I'm lost.	*ma harāye*

Numbers

1	*ek*
2	*dui*
3	*teen*
4	*chār*
5	*panch*
6	*chha*
7	*sāt*
8	*āṭh*
9	*nau*
10	*das*
20	*bees*
21	*ekkāis*
22	*bāis*
30	*tees*
40	*chālis*
50	*pachās*
60	*sāṭṭhi*
70	*saṭari*
80	*assi*
90	*nabbe*
100	*saya*
200	*dui saya*
500	*panch saya*
1000	*hazār*
100,000	*lākh*

one million	*das lākh*
ten million	*crore*

Food & Drink

I'm a vegetarian.	*ma sākāhari hun*
What's this/that?	*yo/tyo ke ho?*

bread (loaf)	*(pau) roṭi*
curd	*dhai*
drinking water	*khāna pāni*

egg	*phul/anḍā*
food/meal	*khāna*
fruit	*phala*
green leafy vegetable	*sāg*
lentils	*dāl*
meat	*māsu*
milk	*dudh*
pepper	*marich*
rice/cooked rice	*chāmal/bhāt*
salt	*nun*
sugar	*chini*
tea	*chiyā*
teahouse	*bati*
vegetable (cooked)	*tarkāri*

Turkish

Ottoman Turkish was written in Arabic script, but this was phased out when Atatürk decreed the introduction of Latin script in 1928. In big cities and tourist areas, many locals know at least some English and/or German. In the south-eastern towns, Arabic or Kurdish is the first language.

For a more in-depth look at the language, get hold of a copy of the new edition of Lonely Planet's *Turkish phrasebook*.

Pronunciation

The letters of the new Turkish alphabet have a consistent pronunciation; they're reasonably easy to master, once you've learned a few basic rules. The letter ğ is always silent, but all other letters are pronounced, and there are no diphthongs.

Vowels

A a	as in 'Shah'
E e	as in 'fell'
İ i	as 'ee'
I ı	as 'uh'
O o	as in 'hot'
U u	as the 'oo' in 'moo'
Ö ö	as the 'u' in 'fur'
Ü ü	as the 'ew' in 'few'

Note that ö and ü are pronounced with pursed lips.

Consonants

Most consonants are pronounced as in English, but there are a few exceptions:

Ç ç	as the 'ch' in 'church'
C c	as English 'j'
Ğ ğ	not pronounced – it draws out the preceding vowel
G g	as in 'go'
H h	as in 'half'
J j	as the 's' in 'measure'
S s	as in 'stress'
Ş ş	as the 'sh' in 'shoe'
V v	as the 'w' in 'weather'

Double consonants are held for longer and pronounced separately, as in *hat trick* not *battle*.

Essentials

Hello.	*Merhaba.*
Goodbye/ Bon Voyage.	*Allaha ısmarladık/ Güle güle.*
Yes.	*Evet.*
No.	*Hayır.*
Please.	*Lütfen.*
Thank you	*Teşekkür ederim.*
That's fine/ You're welcome.	*Bir şey değil.*
Excuse me.	*Affedersiniz.*
Sorry. (Excuse me/ Forgive me.)	*Pardon.*
How much is it?	*Ne kadar?*

Language Difficulties

Do you speak English?	*Ingilizce biliyor musunuz?*
Does anyone here speak English?	*Kimse Ingilizce biliyor mu?*
I don't understand.	*Anlamiyorum.*
Please write that down.	*Lütfen yazın.*

Getting Around

Where's the bus/ tram stop?	*Otobüs/tramvay durağınerede?*
I want to go to (Izmir).	*(İsmir)'e gitmek istiyorum.*
Can you show me on the map?	*Haritada gösterebilir misiniz?*

Signs – Turkish

Giriş	Entrance
Çıkış	Exit
Boş Oda Var	Rooms available
Dolu	Full
Danışma	Information
Açık/Kapalı	Open/Closed
Polis/Emniyet	Police
Polis Karakolu/	Police station
Emniyet	
Müdürlüğü	
Yasak(tır)	Prohibited
Tuvalet	Toilet

Go straight ahead.	*Doğru gidin.*
Turn left.	*Sola dönün.*
Turn right.	*Sağa dönün.*
near/far	*yakın/uzak*

When does the ...	*... ne zaman kalkar/*
leave/arrive?	*gelir?*
ferry/boat	*feribot/vapur*
city bus	*şehir otobüsü*
intercity bus	*otobüs*
train	*tren*
tram	*tramvay*

next	*gelecek*
first	*birinci/ilk*
last	*son*

I'd like a ... ticket.	*... bileti istiyorum.*
one-way	*gidiş*
return	*gidiş-dönüş*
1st class	*birincısınıf*
2nd class	*ikincısınıf*

Accommodation

Where is a cheap hotel?	*Ucuz bir otel nerede?*
Do you have any rooms available?	*Boş oda var mı?*

I'd like (a) ...	*... istiyorum.*
single room	*tek kişilik oda*
double room	*ikikişilik oda*
room with a bathroom	*banyolu oda*
to share a dorm	*yatakhanede bir yatak*
bed	*bir yatak*

How much is it per night?	*Bir gecelik nekadar?*
May I see it?	*Görebilir miyim?*
Where's the bathroom?	*Banyo nerede?*

Around Town

I'm looking for the/a ...	*... arıyorum*
bank	*bir banka*
city centre	*şehir merkezi*
... embassy	*... büyükelçiliğini*
hotel	*otelimi*
market	*çarşıyı*
post office	*postane*
public toilet	*tuvalet*
telephone centre	*telefon merkezi*
tourist office	*turizm danışma bürosu*

beach	*plaj*
castle	*kale/hisar*
church	*kilise*
hospital	*hastane*
mosque	*cami(i)*
old city	*tarihışehir merkezi*
palace	*saray*
ruins	*harabeler/kalıntılar*
square	*meydan*
tower	*kule*

Health

I'm ...	*Ben ...*
diabetic	*şeker hastasıyım*
epileptic	*saralıyım*
asthmatic	*astımlıyım*

I'm allergic to ...	*... alerjim var.*
antibiotics	*antibiyotiğe*
penicillin	*penisiline*

antiseptic	*antiseptik*
aspirin	*aspirin*
condom	*prezervatif*
contraceptive	*gebeliğiönleyici*
diarrhoea	*ishal/diyare*
medicine	*ilaç*
nausea	*bulantı*
sunblock cream	*güneş blok kremi*
tampon	*tampon*

Time & Date

What time is it?	Sāt kaç?
today	bugün
tomorrow	yarın
in the morning	sabahleyin
in the afternoon	öğleden sonra
in the evening	akşamda

Monday	Pazartesi
Tuesday	Salı
Wednesday	Çarşamba
Thursday	Perşembe
Friday	Cuma
Saturday	Cumartesi
Sunday	Pazar

January	Ocak
February	Şubat
March	Mart
April	Nisan
May	Mayıs
June	Haziran
July	Temmuz
August	Ağustos
September	Eylül
October	Ekim
November	Kasım
December	Aralık

Numbers

0	sıfır
1	bir
2	iki
3	üç
4	dört
5	beş
6	altı
7	yedi
8	sekiz
9	dokuz
10	on
11	on bir
12	on iki
13	on üç
14	on dört
15	on beş
16	on altı
17	on yedi
18	on sekiz

Emergencies – Turkish

Help!/Emergency!	İmdat!
There's been an accident!	Bir kaza oldu!
(There's a) fire!	Yangın var!
Call a doctor!	Doktor çağırın!
Call the police!	Polis çağırın!
Could you help us, please?	Bize yardım edebilir-misiniz lütfen?
Go away!	Gidin!/Git!/Defol!
I'm lost.	Kayboldum.

19	on dokuz
20	yirmi
21	yirmıbir
30	otuz
40	kırk
50	elli
60	altmış
70	yetmiş
80	seksen
90	doksan
100	yüz
100	yüz bir
200	ikıyüz
1000	bin
2000	ikıbin

one million	bir milyon

Food

breakfast	kahvaltı
lunch	öğleyemeği
dinner	akşamyemeği
restaurant	lokanta

I don't eat meat.	Hiç et yemiyorum.

bread	emek
butter	tereyağı
cheese (sheep's)	beyaz peynir
eggs	yumuta(lar)
fork	çatal
honey	bal
knife	bıçak
pepper	biber
salt	tuz
sugar	şeker
yogurt	yoğurt

Vegetables

cabbage	*lahana*
chickpeas	*nohut*
cucumber	*salatalık*
garlic	*sarmısak*
marrow/squash	*kabak*
onion	*soğan*
peas	*bezelye*
potato	*patates*
spinach	*ıspınak*

Meat & Poultry

beef	*sığır eti*
chicken (roasting)	*piliç*
chicken (stewing)	*tavuk*
goat meat	*keçi eti*
lamb (milk-fed)	*(süt) kuzu*
mutton	*koyun eti*
meat	*et*

Fruit

apple	*elma*
apricot	*kayst*
fig	*incir*
fruit	*meyva*
grapes	*üzüm*
orange	*portakkal*
peach	*armut*
watermelon	*karpuz*

Drinks

beer	*bira*
coffee	*kahve*
fruit juice	*meyva suyu*
milk	*süt*
mineral soda	*soda/maden sodası*
spring water	*memba suyu*
tea	*çay*
Turkish coffee	*türk kahvesi*
yogurt drink	*ayran*

Gazetteer

IRAN

Abyāneh	ابیانه
Āstān-é Ghods-é Razavī	آستان قدس رضوی
Bam	بم
Bāzārgān	بازرگان
Esfahān	اصفهان
Fīrūz Ābād	فیروز آباد
Ghara Kelīsā	قره کلیسا (کلیسای تادی مقدس)
Ghazvīn	قزوین
Ghom	قم
Jolfā	جلفا
Kandovan	کندجان (کندوان)
Kāshān	کاشان
Kermān	کرمان
Māhān	ماهان
Mākū	ماکو
Marāghé	مراغه
Mashhad	مشهد
Māsūlé	ماسوله
Naghsh-é Rostam	نقش رستم
Pasargadae	پاسارگاد
Shīrāz	شیراز
Soltānīyé	سلطانیه
Tabrīz	تبریز
Takht-é Jamshīd (Persepolis)	تخت جمشید
Takht-é Soleimān	تخت سلیمان
Tehrān	تهران
Yazd	یزد
Zāhedān	زاهدان

PAKISTAN

Amristar	امرتسر
Bahawalpur	باهاواپور
Cantonment	کنٹونمنٹ
Derawar Fort	دیراوار فورٹ
Hanna Lake	هنا لیگ

LANGUAGE

Islamabad	اسلام‌آباد	Peshawar	پشاور
Karachi	کراچی	Quetta	کوئٹہ
Khyber Pass	خیئ بر پاس	Rohtas Fort	روتاس فورٹ
Lahore	لاہور	Taftan	تفتان
Lal Suhanra	لال سوہانرا	Taxila	ٹاکسیلا
Multan	ملتان	Uch Sharif	اُچ شریف
Muree	مری	Urak	اُرگ

Glossary

Here, with definitions, are some unfamiliar words and abbreviations you may find in the text of this guide.

Abbreviations
In – India
Ir – Iran
N – Nepal
P – Pakistan
T – Turkey

acropolis – hilltop citadel and temples of a classical Hellenic city
ada(sı) (T) – island
ābgūsht (Ir) – a hearty soup/stew combination commonly served in teahouses and roadside cafes
agora – open space for commerce and politics in a classical Hellenic city
air-cooled rooms – rooms in guesthouses, generally with big, noisy waterfilled fans built into the walls
Anatolia – the Asian part of Turkey; also called Asia Minor
arg (Ir) – citadel
ashram – spiritual community or retreat
āstān-é (Ir) – sanctuary, threshold
āteshkādé (Ir) – a Zoroastrian fire-temple
autorickshaw – small, three-wheeled, motorised contraption for transporting passengers short distances
āyatollāh (Ir) – literally a 'sign or miracle of God'; Shi'ite cleric of the highest rank; used as a title before the name

bādgīr (Ir) – wind tower or ventilation shaft used to catch breezes and funnel them down into a building to cool it
bāgh (Ir) – garden
bahal (N) – monastery
baksheesh – tip or gratuity; bribe
bāzār (Ir) – bazaar; marketplace
bedesten (T) – vaulted, fireproof market enclosure where valuable goods are kept
belediye (sarayı) (T) – town hall; municipality
bhang (In) – dried leaves and flowering shoots of the marijuana plant
bolvār (Ir) – boulevard
bouleuterion – place of assembly; council meeting-place in a classical Hellenic city

Buddha – Awakened One; the originator of Buddhism; also regarded by Hindus as the ninth incarnation of Vishnu
büfe (T) – snack bar
bulvarı (T) – often abbreviated to 'bul'; boulevard or avenue
burqa (P) – a long, tent-like garment that completely hides the body shape and face, worn in public by women of conservative Muslim communities who are observing purdah
buzkashi (P) – a game brought by Afghani refugees to Pakistan; like rugby on horseback, it is played with a goat's head or carcass (or sometimes a replica)

caddesi (T) – often abbreviated to 'cad'; street
cami(i) (T) – mosque
cantonment (In, P) – administrative and military area of a Raj-era town
caravanserai (T) – large fortified waystation for (trade) camel caravans
çarşı (sı) (T) – market or bazaar
çay bahçesi (T) – tea garden
chādor (Ir) – literally 'tent'; a cloak, usually black, covering all parts of a woman's body except the hands, feet and face
chappals (In, P) – sandals
chāykhāné (Ir) – teahouse
chelō kabāb (Ir) – kebab served with rice
chelō kabābī (Ir) – place serving *chelō kabāb*; restaurant in general
chhatris (In) – literally 'umbrella'; cenotaph
chörten – Tibetan Buddhist stupa
chowk – term used in India, Pakistan and Nepal for town square, intersection, marketplace, and/or courtyard
chuba – dress worn by Tibetan women
Coaster (P) – type of minibus

dağ(ı) (T) – mountain
dal bhat (tarakari) (N) – rice and lentils (with vegetables)
dargah (In) – shrine or tomb of a Muslim saint
daryā (Ir) – sea
daryāché (Ir) – lake
dasht (Ir) – plain; plateau; desert, specifically one of sand or gravel

deniz (T) – sea
dervish – member of mystic Muslim brotherhood
dhaba (In, P) – hole-in-the-wall restaurant or snack bar
dhal – lentil stew/soup
dharma – the word used by both Hindus and Buddhists to refer to their respective moral codes of behaviour
dharamsala (In, N) – pilgrim's resthouse
dolmuş (T) – shared taxi; can be a minibus or sedan
döner kebap (T) – meat roasted on a revolving vertical spit
dosa (In) – paper-thin pancakes made from lentil flour
döviz (burosu) (T) – currency exchange (office)
du-khang – Tibetan prayer hall
durbar (In, N) – royal court or palace

eivān (Ir) – see *iwan*
Emām (Ir) – leader; title of one of the 12 descendants of Mohammed, who, according to Shi'ite belief, succeeded him as religious and temporal leader of the Muslims
eski (T) – old (thing not person)
eyvan (T) – see *iwan*

fālūdé (Ir) – vermicelli in rosewater syrup served with a dash of lime juice
Fārsī (Ir) – Persian language or people
feribot (T) – ferry
fesenjān (Ir) – traditionally a poultry stew, but sometimes served with beef or lamb, in a rich sauce of pomegranate juice and walnuts

ganj (In) – market
gavial – species of crocodile found in the Terai in Nepal which inhabits rivers and has a long, narrow snout
gazino (T) – Turkish nightclub
geyser – hot-water heater
ghat (In) – steps or landing on a river; range of hills or road up hills
golestān (Ir) – rose garden; name of poem by Sa'dī
göl(ü) (T) – lake
gompa – Tibetan Buddhist monastery
GT Road (P) – Grand Trunk Road
gulet – traditional Turkish yacht
gurdwara – Sikh temple; resthouses with an attached Sikh temple are also referred to as *gurdwaras*

hamam(ı) (T) – *(also hammam);* Turkish bath
hammūm (Ir) – see *hamam*
han(ı) (T) – inn or caravanserai
haveli (In) – traditional ornately decorated residences, particularly in reference to those found in Rajasthan
hejāb (Ir) – veil; the modest dress required of Muslim women and girls
hisar(ı) (T) – fortress or citadel
howdah (In, N) – seat for carrying people on an elephant's back
HPTDC – Himachal Pradesh Tourist Development Corporation
hükümet konaği (T) – government house, provincial government headquarters

imam – *(also Emām)* prayer leader; Muslim cleric
iskele(si) (T) – jetty or quay
iwan – *(also eivān, eyvan)* vaulted hall opening onto a central court in a mosque

Jainism – religion founded around 500 BC; Jains believe that only by achieving complete purity of the soul, through the practice of various austerities, can one obtain liberation
jali (In) – carved marble lattice screen
jama (jami) masjid (In, P) – a mosque used for Friday prayers
jootis (In) – traditional leather shoes of Rajasthan; men's jootis often have curled up toes

kabābī (Ir) – anywhere that sells kebabs; general term for snack bar
kale(si) (T) – fortress; citadel
kalīsā (Ir) – church (sometimes cathedral)
kapı(sı) (T) – door or gate
karai (P) – meat braised with vegetables, served in a pan
karma – Hindu-Buddhist principle of retributive justice for past deeds
kebapçı (T) – place selling kebaps
kheer (P) – rice pudding
kheyābūn (Ir) – street or avenue
khōresht (Ir) – thick meaty stew made with vegetables and chopped nuts, served with rice
khukuri (N) – traditional curved knife of the Ghurkas
kilise(si) (T) – church
köfte (T) – meatballs
köfteci – *köfte* maker

konak, konağı (T) – mansion; government headquarters
köprü (sü) (T) – bridge
köşk(ü) (T) – pavilion; villa
kotwali (In) – police station
köy(ü) (T) – village
kūh (Ir) – mountain
kule(si) (T) – tower
kulfi (In) – pistachio-flavoured sweet similar to ice cream

lahmacun (T) – an Arabic soft pizza made with chopped onion, lamb and tomato sauce
lama – Tibetan-Buddhist priest or monk
lassi (In) – yogurt and iced-water drink
lhamo – Tibetan folk opera
liman(ı) (T) – harbour
lingam (In) – phallic symbol; symbol of Shiva
lokanta (T) – restaurant

madrasé (Ir) – Islamic theological seminary or school, attached to a mosque
mahal (In) – house or palace
mahalle(si) (T) – neighbourhood or district of a city
maharaja, maharana, maharao (In) – Hindu princely ruler or king
maharani (In) – wife of a princely ruler or a ruler in her own right
mahout (In) – elephant rider/master
maidan (In) – open grassed area
mandala – design in Hindu and Buddhist art, usually circular, symbolising the universe
mandi (In) – bazaar or market
mandir (In) – Hindu or Jain temple
masala dosa (In) – curried vegetables inside a *dosa*
masjed (-é jāme') (Ir) – (Friday) mosque
masjid (In, P) – mosque
medrese(si) (T) – see *madrasé*
mehrāb (Ir) – see *mihrab*
meidūn (Ir) – town square; open space
mela (In) – fair
meydan(ı) (T) – see *meidūn*
meze (T) – appetisers
mimber – see *minbar*
mihrab – niche inside a mosque indicating the direction of Mecca; in Iran specifically, the hole cut in the ground before the niche
minare(si) (T) – minaret; tower from which Muslims are called to prayer
minbar – pulpit in a mosque

Moharram (Ir) – first month of the Muslim lunar calendar; Shi'ite month of mourning
momo – Tibetan fried dumpling with vegetables or meat
Mughal – Muslim dynasty of Indian emperors from Babur to Aurangzeb
müze(si) (T) – museum

namaste – traditional Hindu greeting (hello or goodbye), often accompanied by a small bow, with the hands brought together at chest or head level, as a sign of respect
nargileh (T) – traditional water pipe (for smoking)
nawab (In, P) – Muslim ruling prince or powerful landowner
nirvana – ultimate aim of Buddhists; final release from the cycle of existence
Nō Rūz – Iranian New Year's Day, celebrated on the vernal equinox (usually around 21 March)
NWFP (P) – North-West Frontier Province

Osho – Bhagwan Rajneesh, the guru who mixed Californian pop-psychology with Indian mysticism
otogar (T) – bus station
Ottoman – of or pertaining to the Ottoman Empire, which lasted from the end of the 13th century to the end of WWI

paan (In) – chewable preparation made from betel nut, betel leaves and lime
pagoda – multistoreyed Nepali temple
pansiyon (T) – pension, B&B or guesthouse
pastane, pastahane (T) – pastry shop or patisserie
pazar(ı) (T) – weekly market or bazaar
Persia – the former name for Iran
pide (T) – Turkish-style pizza
pideci (T) – *pide* maker
pietra dura – marble inlay work characteristic of the Taj Mahal
pol (Ir) – bridge
PTDC (P) – Pakistan Tourist Development Corporation
PTT (T) – Posta, Telefon, Telegraf (Post, Telephone, Telegraph) – the term is still widely used even though the telephone network has been privatised
puja (In) – literally 'respect'; offering or prayers

qalyan (Ir) – water pipe or hubble-bubble
qawwali – Sufi devotional singing
Quran – the holy book of Islam
raj (In) – rule or sovereignty
raja (In) – king
Rajput – Hindu warrior caste; royal rulers of central India
rakı (T) – alcoholic drink made with anise
Ramadan, Ramazān – ninth month in the Muslim lunar calendar; month of fasting
RTDC – Rajasthan Tourism Development Corporation

sadar, saddar (In, P) – main
sadhu (In) – ascetic or holy person; one who is trying to achieve enlightenment
salwar kameez (P) – traditional outfit for men and women comprising a long, dress-like tunic (kameez) and a pair of baggy trousers (salwar)
samsara – Buddhists and Hindus alike believe earthly life is cyclical; you are born again and again, the quality of these rebirths being dependent upon your *karma* in previous lives
saray(ı) (T) – palace
savārī (Ir) – private car; local word for a shared taxi
şehir (T) – city or municipality
Seljuk – of or pertaining to the Seljuk Turks; the first Turkish state to rule Anatolia from the 11th to the 13th centuries
servis (T) – a shuttle minibus service to and from the *otogar*
shāh (Ir) – king; the usual title of the Persian monarch
shikhara (N) – temple with a tapering, pyramidal tower; from the Sanskrit for 'mountain peak'
sokak, sokağı (T) – often abbreviated to 'sk'; street or lane
stupa (N) – hemispherical Buddhist religious structure
Sufi (T) – Muslim mystic, member of a mystic *(dervish)* brotherhood

takht (Ir) – throne
TDCP – Tourist Development Corporation of Punjab
tempo – three-wheeled public transport vehicle, bigger than an autorickshaw, used in India, Pakistan and Nepal
thali – traditional Indian 'all-you-can-eat' meal consisting of a variety of curry dishes, relishes, pappadams and rice, served on a metal plate
thangka – rectangular Tibetan painting on cloth
thong ba (N) – beer made from millet
THY (T) – Türk Hava Yolları, Turkish Airlines
tika – a mark devout Hindus put on their foreheads with *tika* (red sandalwood) powder
TIPA – Tibetan Institute of Performing Arts
tikka (In, P) – meat, usually beef, mutton or chicken, marinated in spices and then barbequed or grilled on a spit
tirthankars (In) – the 24 great teachers of Jainism
tōmān (Ir) – unit of currency equal to 10 *rials*
tonga – two- or four-wheeled horse-drawn carriage found in Pakistan and India
toy train (In) – narrow-gauge railway
tuff, tufa – soft stone laid down as volcanic ash

urs (P) – death anniversary of a revered person

vihara (N) – Buddhist religious buildings and pilgrim accommodation
vilayet, valilik, valiliği (T) – provincial government headquarters

wagon (P) – minibus
wallah (In) – man; added onto almost anything, eg, rickshaw-wallah

yol(u) (T) – road

zurkhané (Ir) – traditional wrestling venue; style of wrestling

LONELY PLANET

You already know that Lonely Planet produces more than this one guidebook, but you might not be aware of the other products we have on this region. Here is a selection of titles that you may want to check out as well:

Istanbul to Cairo on a shoestring
Turkey
World Food Turkey
Iran
Nepal
Nepali phrasebook
A Season in Heaven
India
Hindi & Urdu phrasebook
Istanbul City Map
Read This First Asia & India
Healthy Travel Asia & India
Pakistan
North India
Delhi
Istanbul
Middle East
Rajasthan
Central Asia
World Food India
Turkish phrasebook
Farsi phrasebook
Black on Black
Shopping for Buddhas
In Rajasthan
A Short Walk in the Hindu Kush
Trekking in the Indian Himalaya
Trekking in the Nepal Himalaya

Available wherever books are sold

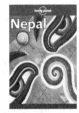

LONELY PLANET

Guides by Region

Lonely Planet is known worldwide for publishing practical, reliable and no-nonsense travel information in our guides and on our Web site. The Lonely Planet list covers just about every accessible part of the world. Currently there are 16 series: Travel guides, Shoestring guides, Condensed guides, Phrasebooks, Read This First, Healthy Travel, Walking guides, Cycling guides, Watching Wildlife guides, Pisces Diving & Snorkeling guides, City Maps, Road Atlases, Out to Eat, World Food, Journeys travel literature and Pictorials.

AFRICA Africa on a shoestring • Cairo • Cairo City Map • Cape Town • Cape Town City Map • East Africa • Egypt • Egyptian Arabic phrasebook • Ethiopia, Eritrea & Djibouti • Ethiopian Amharic phrasebook • The Gambia & Senegal • Healthy Travel Africa • Kenya • Malawi • Morocco • Moroccan Arabic phrasebook • Mozambique • Read This First: Africa • South Africa, Lesotho & Swaziland • Southern Africa • Southern Africa Road Atlas • Swahili phrasebook • Tanzania, Zanzibar & Pemba • Trekking in East Africa • Tunisia • Watching Wildlife East Africa • Watching Wildlife Southern Africa • West Africa • World Food Morocco • Zimbabwe, Botswana & Namibia
Travel Literature: Mali Blues: Traveling to an African Beat • The Rainbird: A Central African Journey • Songs to an African Sunset: A Zimbabwean Story

AUSTRALIA & THE PACIFIC Auckland • Australia • Australian phrasebook • Australia Road Atlas • Cycling Australia • Cycling New Zealand • Fiji • Fijian phrasebook • Healthy Travel Australia, NZ & the Pacific • Islands of Australia's Great Barrier Reef • Melbourne • Melbourne City Map • Micronesia • New Caledonia • New South Wales • New Zealand • Northern Territory • Outback Australia • Out to Eat – Melbourne • Out to Eat – Sydney • Papua New Guinea • Pidgin phrasebook • Queensland • Rarotonga & the Cook Islands • Samoa • Solomon Islands • South Australia • South Pacific • South Pacific phrasebook • Sydney • Sydney City Map • Sydney Condensed • Tahiti & French Polynesia • Tasmania • Tonga • Tramping in New Zealand • Vanuatu • Victoria • Walking in Australia • Watching Wildlife Australia • Western Australia
Travel Literature: Islands in the Clouds: Travels in the Highlands of New Guinea • Kiwi Tracks: A New Zealand Journey • Sean & David's Long Drive

CENTRAL AMERICA & THE CARIBBEAN Bahamas, Turks & Caicos • Baja California • Belize, Guatemala & Yucatán • Bermuda • Central America on a shoestring • Costa Rica • Costa Rica Spanish phrasebook • Cuba • Dominican Republic & Haiti • Eastern Caribbean • Guatemala • Havana • Healthy Travel Central & South America • Jamaica • Mexico • Mexico City • Panama • Puerto Rico • Read This First: Central & South America • World Food Mexico • Yucatán
Travel Literature: Green Dreams: Travels in Central America

EUROPE Amsterdam • Amsterdam City Map • Amsterdam Condensed • Andalucía • Austria • Baltic States phrasebook • Barcelona • Barcelona City Map • Belgium & Luxembourg • Berlin • Berlin City Map • Britain • British phrasebook • Brussels, Bruges & Antwerp • Brussels City Map • Budapest • Budapest City Map • Canary Islands • Central Europe • Central Europe phrasebook • Copenhagen • Corfu & the Ionians • Corsica • Crete • Crete Condensed • Croatia • Cycling Britain • Cycling France • Cyprus • Czech & Slovak Republics • Denmark • Dublin • Dublin City Map • Eastern Europe • Eastern Europe phrasebook • Edinburgh • England • Estonia, Latvia & Lithuania • Europe on a shoestring • Europe phrasebook • Finland • Florence • France • Frankfurt Condensed • French phrasebook • Georgia, Armenia & Azerbaijan • Germany • German phrasebook • Greece • Greek Islands • Greek phrasebook • Hungary • Iceland, Greenland & the Faroe Islands • Ireland • Italian phrasebook • Italy • Krakow • Lisbon • The Loire • London • London City Map • London Condensed • Madrid • Malta • Mediterranean Europe • Mediterranean Europe phrasebook • Moscow • Munich • Netherlands • Normandy • Norway • Out to Eat – London • Out to Eat – Paris • Paris • Paris City Map • Paris Condensed • Poland • Polish phrasebook • Portugal • Portuguese phrasebook • Prague • Prague City Map • Provence & the Côte d'Azur • Read This First: Europe • Rhodes & the Dodecanese • Romania & Moldova • Rome • Rome City Map • Russia, Ukraine & Belarus • Russian phrasebook • Scandinavian & Baltic Europe • Scandinavian phrasebook • Scotland • Sicily • Slovenia • South-West France • Spain • Spanish phrasebook • St Petersburg • St Petersburg City Map • Sweden • Switzerland • Tuscany • Ukrainian phrasebook • Venice • Vienna • Walking in Britain • Walking in France • Walking in Ireland • Walking in Italy • Walking in Spain • Walking in Switzerland • Western Europe • World Food France • World Food Ireland • World Food Italy • World Food Spain
Travel Literature: After Yugoslavia • Love and War in the Apennines • The Olive Grove: Travels in Greece • On the Shores of the Mediterranean • Round Ireland in Low Gear • A Small Place in Italy

INDIAN SUBCONTINENT & THE INDIAN OCEAN Bangladesh • Bengali phrasebook • Bhutan • Delhi • Goa • Healthy Travel Asia & India • Hindi & Urdu phrasebook • India • Indian Himalaya • Karakoram Highway • Kerala • Madagascar • Maldives • Mauritius, Réunion & Seychelles • Mumbai (Bombay) • Nepal • Nepali phrasebook • Pakistan • Rajasthan • Read This First: Asia & India • South India • Sri Lanka • Sri Lanka phrasebook • Tibet • Tibetan phrasebook • Trekking in the Indian Himalaya • Trekking in the Karakoram & Hindukush • Trekking in the Nepal Himalaya
Travel Literature: The Age of Kali: Indian Travels and Encounters • Hello Goodnight: A Life of Goa • In Rajasthan • Maverick in Madagascar • A Season in Heaven: True Tales from the Road to Kathmandu • Shopping for Buddhas • A Short Walk in the Hindu Kush • Slowly Down the Ganges

MIDDLE EAST & CENTRAL ASIA Bahrain, Kuwait & Qatar • Central Asia • Central Asia phrasebook • Dubai • Farsi (Persian) phrasebook • Hebrew phrasebook • Iran • Israel & the Palestinian Territories • Istanbul • Istanbul City Map • Istanbul to Cairo • Istanbul to Kathmandu • Jerusalem • Jerusalem City Map • Jordan • Lebanon • Middle East • Oman & the United Arab Emirates • Syria • Turkey • Turkish phrasebook • World Food Turkey • Yemen
Travel Literature: Black on Black: Iran Revisited • The Gates of Damascus • Kingdom of the Film Stars: Journey into Jordan

NORTH AMERICA Alaska • Boston • Boston City Map • Boston Condensed • British Columbia • California & Nevada • California Condensed • Canada • Chicago • Chicago City Map • Florida • Great Lakes • Hawaii • Hiking in Alaska • Hiking in the USA • Las Vegas • Los Angeles • Los Angeles City Map • Louisiana & the Deep South • Miami • Miami City Map • Montreal • New England • New Orleans • New York City • New York City City Map • New York City Condensed • New York, New Jersey & Pennsylvania • Oahu • Out to Eat – San Francisco • Pacific Northwest • Rocky Mountains • San Francisco • San Francisco City Map • Seattle • Southwest • Texas • Toronto • USA • USA phrasebook • Vancouver • Virginia & the Capital Region • Washington, DC • Washington, DC City Map • World Food New Orleans
Travel Literature: Caught Inside: A Surfer's Year on the California Coast • Drive Thru America

NORTH-EAST ASIA Beijing • Beijing City Map • Cantonese phrasebook • China • Hiking in Japan • Hong Kong • Hong Kong City Map • Hong Kong Condensed • Hong Kong, Macau & Guangzhou • Japan • Japanese phrasebook • Korea • Korean phrasebook • Kyoto • Mandarin phrasebook • Mongolia • Mongolian phrasebook • Seoul • Shanghai • South-West China • Taiwan • Tokyo • World Food Hong Kong
Travel Literature: In Xanadu: A Quest • Lost Japan

SOUTH AMERICA Argentina, Uruguay & Paraguay • Bolivia • Brazil • Brazilian phrasebook • Buenos Aires • Chile & Easter Island • Colombia • Ecuador & the Galapagos Islands • Healthy Travel Central & South America • Latin American Spanish phrasebook • Peru • Quechua phrasebook • Read This First: Central & South America • Rio de Janeiro • Rio de Janeiro City Map • Santiago de Chile • South America on a shoestring • Trekking in the Patagonian Andes • Venezuela
Travel Literature: Full Circle: A South American Journey

SOUTH-EAST ASIA Bali & Lombok • Bangkok • Bangkok City Map • Burmese phrasebook • Cambodia • Hanoi • Healthy Travel Asia & India • Hill Tribes phrasebook • Ho Chi Minh City • Indonesia • Indonesian phrasebook • Indonesia's Eastern Islands • Java • Lao phrasebook • Laos • Malay phrasebook • Malaysia, Singapore & Brunei • Myanmar (Burma) • Philippines • Pilipino (Tagalog) phrasebook • Read This First: Asia & India • Singapore • Singapore City Map • South-East Asia on a shoestring • South-East Asia phrasebook • Thailand • Thailand's Islands & Beaches • Thailand, Vietnam, Laos & Cambodia Road Atlas • Thai phrasebook • Vietnam • Vietnamese phrasebook • World Food Thailand • World Food Vietnam

ALSO AVAILABLE: Antarctica • The Arctic • The Blue Man: Tales of Travel, Love and Coffee • Brief Encounters: Stories of Love, Sex & Travel • Chasing Rickshaws • The Last Grain Race • Lonely Planet ... On the Edge: Adventurous Escapades from Around the World • Lonely Planet Unpacked • Not the Only Planet: Science Fiction Travel Stories • Sacred India • Travel Photography: A Guide to Taking Better Pictures • Travel with Children

Index

Abbreviations

In – India   N – Nepal   T – Turkey
Ir – Iran   P – Pakistan

Text

A

Abbasids 14
Abyāneh (Ir) 293
accommodation 105-6
Adilcevaz (T) 250
Adıyaman (T) 236
Afghanistan 373
Afrodisias (T) 196
Agra (In) 483-93, **484**, **489**
Agra Fort (In) 487-8
Ağrı Dağı (T), *see* Mt Ararat
Ahlat (T) 250
air travel 116-21, 127-8
Ajmer (In) 456-8
Akbar's Mausoleum (In) 488
Aktepe (T) 228
Akvaryum (T) 198
Akyarlar (T) 198
Alamūt (Ir) 273
Alborz Mountains (Ir) 287
alcohol 110-11
Alexander the Great 13
Alibey Adası (T) 183
Amber (In) 455
Amritsar (In) 387-97, **389**
Anatolian Civilisations,
    Museum of (T) 258
Anıtkabir (T) 258-60
Ankara (T) 257-62, **259**
    accommodation 260
    embassies 257
    entertainment 261-2
    medical services 258
    places to eat 260-1
    postal services 258
    to/from 262
    transport in 262
Annapurna mountains (N) 22,
    519
    Annapurna Natural History
    Museum (N) 519
Antalya (T) 213-16, **214**
Antalya Archaeological
    Museum (T) 215
Anzac battlefields (T) 179-80,
    179
Anzac Day 178

Bold indicates maps.

Arāmgāh-é Hāfez (Ir) 304
architecture 34-5
    Seljuk (T) 220-1
Arg-é Bam (Ir) 316-17
Archaeological Museum (T)
    160, 184
Armenians 30
Aspendos (T) 216
Āstān-é Ghods-é Razavī (Ir)
    289-90
Atatürk (Mustafa Kemal) 17,
    19, 148
Australia
    to/from 120
autorickshaws 141-3
Avanos (T) 229
Aya Sofya (T) 152-3
Ayvalık (T) 183-4
Āzādī Monument (Ir) 279

B

Badshahi Mosque (P) 348
Bahawalpur (P) 332-5, **333**
Bakhtegān National Park (Ir) 24
Ballıdere (T) 225
Baluchis 30
Bam (Ir) 316-18, **317**
Bandhavgarh National Park (In) 25
Bangladesh 17
bargaining 68
bars & clubs 111-12
Bāzārgān (Ir) 266-7
beaches 101, 180 183, 190,
    194, 198, 200, 203-4, 207-8
Behesht-é Zahrā (Ir) 287
Benares Hindu University (In)
    500
Bergama (T) 184-5
Bhairabnath Temple (N) 569
Bhairawa (N) 514
Bhaktapur (N) 569-71
Bhimsen Temple (N) 520, 569
Bhutto, Benazir 20
Binde Basini Temple (N) 520
Bishwakarma Temple (N) 563
Bitez (T) 198
Bitlis (T) 249
Black Sea (T) 124

boat travel 123
boat trips
    India 500
    Turkey 198, 200, 203, 204,
    209
Bodhnath (N) 564-5, **565**
Bodrum (T) 196-200, **197**
body language 38-9
Bogh'é Davāzdah Emām (Ir) 303
books 74-6
border crossings 121-3, 129
    Afghanistan 122
    Armenia 122
    Azerbaijan 123
    Bangladesh 123
    China 123
    Georgia 122
    India 384, 512
    Iran 264, 320
    Nepal 512
    Pakistan 320, 384
    Tibet 123
    Turkey 264
    Turkmenistan 122
Brahma Temple (In) 458
bridges
    Esfahān 297
British rule 15-17
Buddhism 42-3
    holy days 99
budgeting 52-3
Bursa (T) 173-8, **174-5**
bus travel 121-2, 128-33, *see
    also individual country
    entries*
business hours 97
Butterfly Valley (T) 208

C

camel safaris 459, 478, 479
Canada
    to/from 119-20
Çanakkale (T) 180-2, **181**
Çandır Canyons (T) 217
Cappadocia (T) 222-34, **223**
car travel 122, 135, *see also
    individual country entries*
caravanserais
    Karatay Han (T) 234

Karawan Serai (In) 494
Sultan Han (T) 234
carnets 136
carpets
    Carpet Museum (Ir) 277-8
    Pakistani 329
    Persian 285
Castle of St Peter (T) 197-8
Castles of the Assassins, the
    (Ir) 273
Caunos (T) 200
Çavuşin (T) 228-9
Çavuştepe (T) 253
Chail (In) 415
Chak Chak (Ir) 312
Chandigarh (In) 416-20, **417**
Changu Narayan Temple (N)
    572
Chehel Sotūn Palace (Ir) 297
children, travel with 93
Chimaera, the (T) 212
Church of St Nicholas (T) 212
cinema 36, 112
City Palace (In) 465
climate 22-3, 50-1
clubs, see bars & clubs
consulates 61-3
Corbett Tiger Reserve (In) 25
courses 104
cricket 113
culture
    considerations for 36-9, 459
customs regulations 63
cycle-rickshaws 143
cycling 101-2, 138-40
    India 454, 511, 483
    Iran 300, 318
    Nepal 534, 560
    Pakistan 353
    Turkey 171, 187, 209, 256

D

Dalyan (T) 200, 203-4
dance 112-13
Darband (Ir) 287
Dardanelles, the (T) 178-80
Darra Adam Khel (P) 382
Datça (T) 202
Dattatraya Temple (N) 569
deforestation 25-6
Delhi (In) 420-46, **422-3**,
    427, **429**, **435**, **436**
    accommodation 433-7
    embassies 421-4
    entertainment 439-41
    Internet services 424-5
    medical services 426
    places to eat 438-9
    postal services 424
    shopping 441
    to/from 441-4
    transport in 444-6

Demre (T) 212
Derawar Fort (P) 336
Derinkuyu (T) 232
Devi Falls (N) 520
Dharamsala (In) 397-8, **397**
Dhaulagiri (N) 528
Didyma (T) 195
Dil Burnu Park (T) 173
disabled travellers 92-3
diving 209
Diyarbakır (T) 245-8, **246**
Dolmabahçe Palace (T) 164-5
dolmuş, see minibus travel
Doğubayazıt (T) 254-7, **255**
dress 54, 92
drinks 109-11
driving permits 61
drugs 93-4, 461
Durbar Square, Kathmandu (N)
    540-4, **541**

E

eating, see etiquette, eating
Eceabat (T) 182
economy 29
Efes, see Ephesus
Eidgah Mosque (P) 338
Eklingji (In) 470
electricity 78
elephants 25
    elephant rides (N) 531
Elgolī (Ir) 269
email services 72-3
Emām Khomeinī, Holy Shrine
    of (Ir) 287
Emām Khomeinī Square, see
    Meidūn-é Emām Khomeinī
Emāmzādé Sayyed Ja'far (Ir)
    311
Emāmzādé-yé Alī Ebn-ē Hamzé
    (Ir) 303
embassies 61-3
entertainment 111-13
environmental issues 24-6
Ephesus (T) 191-4, **193**
Ephesus Museum (T) 189
equipment 54-5
Erzurum (T) 262-3
Esfahān (Ir) 293-300, **294**
Eski Gümüşler Monastery (T)
    232-3
etiquette, see also culture
    eating 38
Europe
    to/from 119, 121-2
Everest 22
Eğirdir (T) 217
Egyptian Bazaar, see Mısır
    Çarşısı

F

Fatehpur Sikri (In) 493-5
fax services 72

festivals 51-2, 100-1
    Festival of Swings (In) 451
    Jaisalmer Desert Festival (In)
        478
    Mevlâna Festival (T) 218
    Pushkar Fair (In) 459
    Taj Mahotsav Festival (In)
        489
Fethiye (T) 204-6, **206-7**
flora 26
food 107-9
    India 108-9
    Iran 107-8
    Nepal 109
    Pakistan 108
    Turkey 107
football 113
Freak Street (N) 544

G

Galata Bridge (T) 162
Galata Mevlevihanesi (T) 164
Galata Tower (T) 163-4
Gallery Virsa (P) 366
Gallipoli, see Anzac battlefields
    and Gelibolu peninsula
Gandhi, Indira 20, 390
Gautama, Siddhartha 516
gay & lesbian travellers 92
Gāzor Khān (Ir) 273
Gelibolu peninsula (T) 178-80
geography 22
ghats
    Varanasi (In) 498-9
Ghazvīn (Ir) 271-3, **272**
Ghods-é Razavī Museum (Ir)
    289
Ghom (Ir) 291
Ghorapani (N) 529
Gölbaşı (T) 242-3
Golden Temple
    Amritsar (In) 392-5
    Patan (N) 563
Golestān Palace (Ir) 278
Gombad-é Soltānīyé (Ir) 271
gompas
    Dip Tse-Chok Ling (In) 402
    Namgal (In) 401
Gorakhpur (In) 508-10, **509**
Göreme (T) 224-8, **225**
Göreme Open-Air Museum (T)
    224
government, see politics
Grand Bazaar, see Kapalı Çarşı
Gülhane Parkı (T) 160
Gülşehir (T) 231
Gümbet (T) 198

H

Hacıbektaş (T) 231
hamams 102, 153, 161, 162,
    175-6

Hanna Lake (P) 331
Hanuman Dhoka (N) 540
Harran (T) 244
Hawa Mahal (In) 449
Hazarganji-Chiltan National
   Park (P) 24
health 79-90
   diarrhoea 84-5
   food 81
   hepatitis 85-6
   HIV/AIDS 86
   insurance 60
   malaria 87
   vaccinations 79-80
   water 81
   women's health 89
Hierapolis (T) 196
highlights 45-7
hiking 102-3
   India 103, 402-3, 411-12
   Iran 102, 312
   Nepal 103, 520, 528, 545,
      546-7, 571
   Pakistan 102-3, 370
   Turkey 102, 217, 225, 226
Himalaya range 22
Hinduism 40-1
   holy days 98-9
Hippodrome (T) 153
history 13-21
hitching 140
holidays 51-2, 97-100
Holy Shrine of Emām Rezā, see
   Āstān-é Ghods-é Razavī
horse riding 229
Hoşap (T) 253
hospitality 38
Humayun's Tomb (In) 431
Hussain Agahi Bazaar (P) 338
Hussein, Saddam 18

I

İçmeler (T) 200
Ihlara Gorge (T) 231-2
India 385-511, **386**
   bus travel 132-3
   independence 16
   partition 16-17
   to/from 128
   train travel 134-5
   visa 58
insurance 60
Internet
   access 72-3
   resources 73-4
Iran 265-320, **266**
   bus travel 130
   revolution 18

Bold indicates maps.

to/from 127-8
train travel 133
visa 56-7
İshak Paşa Sarayı (T) 254-5
Islam 13-14, 39-40
   holy days 97-8
Islamabad (P) 363-8, **364-5**
   accommodation 366-7
   alcohol 367
   embassies 363
   entertainment 367
   medical services 366
   places to eat 367
   postal services 365
   shopping 367
   to/from 368
   transport in 368
İstanbul (T) 146-72, **149**,
   150-1, **154-5**, **158**, **163**
   accommodation 165-6
   emergency services 152
   entertainment 169-70
   Internet services 151
   medical services 152
   places to eat 167-9
   postal services 151
   to/from 170-2
   transport in 172
itineraries 49
İzmir (T) 185-8, **186**

J

Jaipur (In) 446-55, **447**
Jaisalmer (In) 475-82, **476**
   Desert Festival 478
   Fort 477-8
Jallianwala Bagh (In) 388
Jama Masjid (In) 428
Jamshidiyé (Ir) 279
Jantar Mantar (In) 428, 449
Jodhpur (In) 470-5, **471**
Jolfā (Ir) 270, 297-8

K

Kahta (T) 236-7
Kale, see Demre
Kalkan (T) 209
Kandahari Bazaar (P) 326
Kandovan (Ir) 270
Kangra Art Museum (In) 398
Kanha National Park (In) 25
Kapalı Çarşı (T) 160
Kaputaş (T) 209
Karaada (T) 198
Karawan Serai (In) 494
Kaş (T) 209-11, **210**
Kasauli (In) 415
Kāshān (Ir) 291-3, **292**
Kashmir 17, 21
Kashmir Point (P) 370

Kathmandu (N) 534-61, **536-7**,
   541, **543**, **550-1**
   accommodation 548-52
   embassies 538
   entertainment 556-7
   Internet services 539
   medical services 540
   places to eat 553-6
   postal services 538
   shopping 557-8
   telephone services 538-9
   to/from 558-9
   transport in 559-61
Kathmandu Valley (N) **562**
Kaunos (T) 203
kayaking 103
Kayaköy (T) 206
Kaymaklı (T) 232
Kayseri (T) 233-4
Kekova (T) 211
Keoladeo Ghana National Park
   (In) 24
Kermān (Ir) 313-16, **314**
Khomeinī, Āyatollāh 18, 19
Khyber Pass (P) 381-3
Khyber Railway (P) 383
Kızıl Adalar, see Princes' Islands
Konya (T) 218-24, **219**
Köprülü Kanyon (T) 217
Kovada Gölü Milli Parkı (T) 217
Köyceğiz (T) 202-3
Kūh-é Soffeh (Ir) 301
Kuldhara (In) 483
Kumari Devi 543-4
Kumbeshwar Temple (N) 563
Kurds 30
Kuşadası (T) 194-5
Kushinagar (In) 510

L

Lahore (P) 340-55, **341**, **342-3**
   accommodation 349
   alcohol 352
   consulates 343-4
   emergency services 344
   entertainment 351, 352-3
   medical services 344
   places to eat 350-2
   postal services 344
   shopping 353-4
   to/from 354-5
   transport in 355
Lahore Fort (P) 346-7, **347**
Lahore Museum (P) 345
Lake Palace (In) 464
Lake Pichola (In) 464
Lake Van, see Van Gölü
Lal Suhanra National Park (P)
   24, 336-7
Lambersan (Ir) 273
Landi Kotal (P) 382

language 43-4, 573-88
laundry 78-9
Line of Actual Control 17
literature 33-4
Lodhruva (In) 483
Lok Virsa Museum (P) 366
Lumbini (N) 516-18
Lycian Way, the (T) 205

M

magazines 76
Māhān (Ir) 316
Mākū (Ir) 267
Malatya (T) 235-6
maps 53-4
Mardin (T) 248-9
Margalla Hills National Park (P) 366
Markazī Museum (Ir) 289
Marmaris (T) 200-2, **201**
Mashhad (Ir) 288-91, **289**
Mashobra (In) 416
Masjed-é Emām (Ir) 295-6
Masjed-é Jāme' (Ir) 311
Masjed-é Sheikh Lotfollāh (Ir) 296
Masjed-é Vakīl (Ir) 303
Māsūlé (Ir) 273-4
Mausoleum of Halicarnassus (T) 198
Mazıköy (T) 232
McLeod Ganj (In) 398-409, **399**
Mediterranean Sea 123-4
Meidūn-é Emām Khomeinī (Ir) 295, **296**
Meryemana (T) 190
Mevlâna Museum (T) 220
Michni checkpost (P) 383
Midyat (T) 248-9
Miletus (T) 195
minibus travel 140-1
Mīrjāvé (Ir) 319
Mısır Çarşısı (T) 162
Mohammed, Prophet 13-14
monasteries
  Eski Gümüşler Monastery (T) 232-3
  Kelīsa Darré Shām (Ir) 270
  Khanegah (Ir) 271
  Morgabriel (T) 248
  Nechung (In) 402
  Rudra Varna Mahavihara (N) 568
  St George (T) 173
  Tibetan Buddhist (N) 520
money 63-70
  ATMs 65
  black market 66
  credit cards 65-6
Mongols 14
Monsoon Palace (In) 466

Mool Sagar (In) 483
mosques 34-5, 39
  Badshahi Mosque (P) 348
  Blue Mosque (T) 153
  Emāmzādé-yé Alī Ebn-é Hamzé (Ir) 303
  Jama Masjid (In) 428
  Masjed-é Emām (Ir) 295-6
  Masjed-é Jāme' (Ir) 311
  Masjed-é Sheikh Lotfollāh (Ir) 296
  Masjed-é Vakīl (Ir) 303
  Quwwat-ul-Islam Masjid (In) 432
  Selimıye Camii (T) 220
  Shah Faisal Mosque (P) 366
  Süleymaniye (T) 161
  Wazir Khan Mosque (P) 345
  Yeni Cami (T) 162
motorcycle travel 122, 135-6
Mountbatten, Louis 16
Mt Ararat (T) 255
Mt Sahand (Ir) 270
Multan (P) 336-40, **337**
Murree (P) 370-1
museums
  Annapurna Natural History Museum (N) 519
  Antalya Archaeological Museum (T) 215
  Archaeological Museum of Baluchistan (P) 326
  Arkeoloji Müzesi (T) 160, 184
  Āzarbāyjān (Ir) 269
  Bhartiya Lok Kala Museum (In) 465
  Büyük Karatay Müzesi (T) 220
  Carpet Museum (Ir) 277-8
  Central Museum (In) 449-50
  Contemporary Arts Museum (Ir) 297
  Decorative Arts Museum of Iran (Ir) 297
  Deniz Müzesi (T) 164
  Desert Culture Centre & Museum (In) 478
  Ephesus Museum (T) 189
  Eski Şark Eserleri Müzesi (T) 160
  Ethnographical Museum (Ir) 278
  Faqir Khana Museum (P) 345
  Ghazvīn (Ir) 272
  Glass & Ceramics Museum (Ir) 278
  Göreme Open-Air Museum (T) 224
  Himachal State Museum (In) 411

Indira Gandhi Memorial Museum (In) 431
Islamic Arts Museum (Ir) 277
Jaisalmer Folklore Museum (In) 478
Kangra Art Museum (In) 398
Kermān Contemporary Arts Museum (Ir) 315
Lahore Museum (P) 345
Lok Virsa Museum (P) 366
Maharaja Sawai Mansingh II Museum (In) 449
Malatya Museum (T) 235
Mevlâna Museum (T) 220
Mosaic Museum (T) 153
Museum of Anatolian Civilisations (T) 258
Museum of Indology (In) 450
Museum of Underwater Archaeology (T) 197-8
National Gallery of Modern Art (In) 430
National Jewels Museum (Ir) 278
National Museum (In) 430
National Museum (N) 544
National Musuem of Iran (Ir) 277
Natural History Museum (Ir) 297
Nehru Museum (In) 430
Pakistan Army Museum (P) 358
Pārs Museum (Ir) 303
Patan Museum (N) 563
Peshawar Museum (P) 374
Pokhara Regional Museum (N) 519
Rail Transport Museum (In) 430-1
Rajasthan Folk Art Museum (In) 472
Ram Nagar Fort (In) 500
Rezā Abbāsī Museum (Ir) 279
Sa'd Ābād Garden Museum (Ir) 278
Ram Nagar Fort (In) 500
Science Museum (In) 418
Tibet Museum (In) 401
Tibetan Cultural Museum (In) 402
Topkapı Palace Museum (T) 156-9
Tribhuvan Museum (N) 540
Turkish & Islamic Arts Museum (T) 153, 175
Umaid Bhawan Palace (In) 472

music 32-3, 112-13
Mustafapaşa (T) 230-1

N

Nagarkot (N) 571-2
Nagda (In) 470
Naghsh-é Rostam (Ir) 305-10
Naldehra (In) 416
Nangathanti (N) 529
National Jewels Museum (Ir) 278
National Museum (In) 430
National Museum (N) 544
National Museum of Iran (Ir) 277
national parks & reserves 24-5
    Bakhtegān NP (Ir) 24
    Bandhavgarh NP (In) 25
    Corbett Tiger Reserve (In) 25
    Hazarganji-Chiltan NP (P) 331
    Kanha NP (In) 25
    Keoladeo Ghana NP (In) 24
    Lal Suhanra NP (P) 336-7
    Margalla Hills NP (P) 366
    Royal Bardia NP (N) 25
    Royal Chitwan NP (N) 25, 529-34
    Termessos NP (T) 24
Nemrut Daği (T) 238-40, 238
Nepal 513-72, 514-15
    bus travel 132-3
    Internet services 73
    to/from 128
    visa 58-9
Nevşehir (T) 224
New Delhi (In) 428-30
New Vishwanath Temple (In) 499
New Zealand
    to/from 120
Newar pagoda temples 35
newspapers 76
Niğde (T) 232
Norbulingka Institute (In) 409
Nurpur Shahan (P) 366
Nyatapola Temple (N) 569

O

Old Delhi (In) 426-8
Olimpos (T) 212-14
Ölüdeniz (T) 207-8
Ottoman Empire 14-15

P

Pakistan 321-84, 323
    bus travel 131-2

foreigners' registration 58
    restricted-area permits 61
    to/from 128
    train travel 133-4
    visa 57-8
Pamukkale (T) 195-6
paragliding 208
Pasargadae (Ir) 310
Pashtuns 30
Pashupatinath (N) 564
passports 55
Patan (N) 561-9
Patara (T) 208-9
people 29-31
Perge (T) 216
Pergamum, see Bergama
Persepolis (Ir) 306-9, 307
Persian carpets 31
Persians 30
Peshawar (P) 371-81, 372, 375, 378
Phewa Tal (N) 519
photography 76-8
Pindi Point (P) 370
Pokhara (N) 516-29, 517, 521
    accommodation 522-4
    entertainment 526
    places to eat 524-6
    to/from 526-7
    transport in 527-8
politics 27-8
pollution 24
Poon Hill (N) 529
population 29-31
Portuguese 15
postal services 70-1
Potters' Square (N) 570
Priene (T) 195
Princes' Islands (T) 172-3, 173
Pujari Math (N) 570
Punjabis 30
Pushkar (In) 457-62, 458

Q

Quetta (P) 325-31, 327
Qutab Minar (In) 432-4

R

radio 76
Rajah Bazaar (P) 358
Ramadan 51, 97
Ranakpur (In) 470
Rawalpindi (P) 356-63, 357, 359, 360
Red Fort (In) 426-8
religious holidays 51-2
Rezā Abbāsī Museum (Ir) 279
rhinoceros 25
Rohtas Fort (P) 356
route planning 47-9

India 385-7
Iran 265-6
Nepal 513-14
Pakistan 322-3
Turkey 145-6
Royal Bardia National Park (N) 25
Royal Chitwan National Park (N) 25, 529-34
Rudra Varna Mahavihara (N) 568
ruins
    India 431, 482-3
    Pakistan 368-70
    Turkey 184, 195, 196, 206-7, 211, 216, 235, 238-40, 244

S

safaris 102
safe travel 93-7
Sagalassos (T) 217
St John Basilica (T) 189
St Nicholas, Church of (T) 212
Sajjan Garh, see Monsoon Palace
Saklıkent Gorge (T) 207
Sam sand dunes (In) 482
Şanlıurfa (T) 240-4, 241
Sarangkot (N) 529
Sarnath (In) 507-8
Sauraha (N) 532-5, 533
sea travel 123-4
Selçuk (T) 188-91, 189
Selimiye Camii (T) 220
Seljuks (T) 14
Shah Faisal Mosque (P) 366
Shāh Mohammed Rezā Pahlavī 18
Shikhara temples 35
Shilpgram (In) 465-6
Shimla (In) 409-15, 410
Shīrāz (Ir) 301-5, 302
shopping 114
Siddhartha Gautama 42
Sikhism 41
    holy days 99
Simena (T) 211
Sirkap (P) 369
Sirsukh (P) 369
skiing 101
    India 416
    Iran 101
    Turkey 176
Soltānīyé (Ir) 271
Soğanlı (T) 231
special events, see festivals
Spice Bazaar, see Mısır Çarşısı
Stamp and Coin Museum (Ir) 289
student cards 60

Bold indicates maps.

stupas 35
Süleymaniye (T) 161
Sultan Marshes Bird Paradise (T) 233
Sultanahmet (T) 152-61
Sultaniye Kaplıcaları (T) 202
Sunauli (In) 510-11
Sunauli (N) 514-16
Sunken Palace Cistern, see Yerebatan Sarnıçı
Swayambhunath (N) 566-7, **567**

T

Tabriz (Ir) 267-70, **268**
Taftan (P) 323-5
Taj Mahal (In) 485-7
Taj Mahotsav Festival (In) 489
Takht-é Soleimān (Ir) 270-1
tampons 55, 91
Tashiling Tibetan Village (N) 520
Tattapani (In) 416
Tatvan (T) 249
taxi travel 141
Taxila (P) 368-70, **369**
tea 109-10
teahouses 111
Tehrān (Ir) 274-87, **275**, **280-1**
  accommodation 279-82
  embassies 276
  emergency 277
  entertaiment 284
  Internet services 276
  medical services 277
  places to eat 282-4
  postal services 276
  shopping 284
  to/from 284-6
  transport in 286-7
Teimiussa (T) 211
telephone services 71-2
television 76
Artemis (T) 190
temples 34-5, 39, 516
  Apollo, Temple of (T) 208
  Artemis, Temple of (T) 190
  Bhairabnath Temple (N) 569
  Bhimsen Temple (N) 520, 569
  Binde Basini Temple (N) 520
  Bodhnath (N) 564-5
  Bishwakarma Temple (N) 563
  Brahma Temple (In) 458
  Changu Narayan Temple (N) 572
  Dattatraya Temple (N) 392-5
  Golden Temple (In) 392-5
  Golden Temple (N) 563
  Kumbeshwar Temple (N) 563

Maya Devi Temple (N) 516
New Vishwanath Temple (In) 499
Nyatapola Temple (N) 569
Pashupatinath (N) 564
Shiva-Parvati Temple (N) 542
Swayambhunath (N) 566-7
Taleju Temple (N) 541-2
Trailokya Mohan Narayan Temple (N) 543
Vishwanath Temple (In) 499
tempos 143
Termessos (T) 216
Termessos National Park (T) 24
theft 95
Tibetan Buddhist Monastery (N) 520
Tibetans 30
  holy days 99
tigers 25
time 78
tipping 67-8
Tōchāl (Ir) 287
toilets 79
Tomb of the 12 Emāms, see Bogh'é Davāzdah Emām
tongas 144
Topkapı Palace Museum (T) 156-9
tourist offices 55
tours 124-6
  India 450-1, 466, 472-3, 489, 501
  Nepal 530, 548
  Pakistan 349, 377
  Turkey 180, 225-6, 239-40
Towers of Silence (Ir) 312
train travel 122, 133-5, see also individual country entries
trekking, see hiking
Troy (T), 182
Truva, see Troy
Tsuglagkhang Complex (In) 401-2
Turkey 145-264, **146-7**
  bus travel 130, 131
  car travel 235
  consulates 148
  earthquake 19, 24
  to/from 127
  train travel 133
  visa 56
Turkish baths, see hamams
Turks 29-30

U

Üçağiz (T) 211-12
Uch Sharif (P) 335-6
Uçhisar (T) 229-30

Udaipur (In) 462-70, **463**
UK
  to/from 119, 121-2
Ulleri (N) 529
Uludağ (T) 176
Umaid Bhawan Palace (In) 472
Umayyads 14
Urak Tangi (P) 331
Urdu 43
Urfa, see Şanlıurfa
Ürgüp (T) 230
USA
  to/from 119-20

V

Vakīl Bazaar (Ir) 314
Van (T) 251-3, **251**
Van Gölü (T) 249-51
Van Kalesi (T) 252
Vānk Cathedral (Ir) 297
Varanasi (In) 495-507, **497**, **502**
video 76-8
vimana temples, see shikhara temples
visas 55-60
Vishwanath Temple (In) 499
visual arts 31-2

W

Wagah (In) 387
wagons, see minibus travel
walking, see hiking
walking tours
  Nepal 542
  Turkey 192-4
water sports 101
Wazir Khan Mosque (P) 345
weather 22-3, 50-1
weights & measures 78
white-water rafting 103
  Nepal 520, 547-8
  Turkey 217
wildlife 26-7
women
  status of 36
women travellers 90-2, 310
work 104-5

Y

Yazd (Ir) 310-13, **311**
Yedikule (T) 161
Yerebatan Sarnıçı (T) 153, 160
yoga 520-2, 546

Z

Zāhedān(Ir) 318-19, **319**
Zelve (T) 228
Ziarat (P) 331-3
Zoroastrianism 41-2

Boxed Text

Akbil 172
Anzac Day 178
At your Service… 377
Audience with the Karmapa, An 408
Bath Time 162
Best Trains from Delhi 443
Best View in Turkey, The 208
Beware the Persistent Porter 415
Bhanged Up 461
Braving the Baluchistan Desert 135
British Autorickshaw Overland Expedition, The 142-3
Buddha Trail, The 42
Buyer Beware 114
Carpet Bagging in Iran 285
Climbing Damāvand 288
Comparative Costs 68
Conflict in Kashmir, The 21
Dancing Girls & Qawwali Singers 352
Driving East 324
Driving in Eastern Turkey 235
Dual Pricing 67
Englishman Abroad, An 75
Esfahān to Doğubayazıt 300
Everyday Health 82
Fine Art of Bargaining, The 69
Five Hundred Metres of Madness 432
Following the Apple Pie Trail 528
Guns for Hire 382
Have Camel, Will Travel 479
Hiking in the Shadow of Dhauladhar 403
I've Just Got to Have That! 115
India at a Glance 385

Into Afghanistan 373
Invitation to Lunch, An 303
Is it Safe? 94
İstanbul Telephone Area Codes 151
İstanbul to Kathmandu and the Lonely Planet Story 48
Kathmandu Walking Tour 542
Lycian Way, The 205
Major Islamic Holidays 98
More Than Just a Floor Covering 31
National Parks 24-5
Nepal at a Glance 513
No 1 Network vs the Fez Bus 131
Nutrition 81
One Man and His Dog 226
Pokhara's Snowy Skyline 519
Pushy Priests in Pushkar… 459
Riding the Bhote Kosi 546-7
Safe Travel in Pakistan 322
Short Walks from Nagarkot 571
Showtime at the Border 387
Skiing at Uludağ 176
Strikes, Riots & Tear Gas 376
Taj Tickets 486
Tibetan Medicine 402
To Follow or Not to Follow 46
Tree Climbing at Chitwan 531
Trekking in Nepal 545
Trekking in Nepal – A Brief Introduction… 545
Trouble in Amritsar 390
Van to Orūmīyé 254
Walk Between the Bazaars, A 160
Walking Tour 542

Warning: Overland Dangers! 50
Women in Iran 310
Women on Horseback 332

Border Crossings

Border Crossings 129
India to Nepal Border Crossing 512
India to Pakistan Border Crossing 384
Iran to Pakistan Border Crossing 320
Iran to Turkey Border Crossing 264
Nepal to India Border Crossing 512
Pakistan to India Border Crossing 384
Pakistan to Iran Border Crossing 320
Turkey to Iran Border Crossing 264

Cycling

Agra to Jaipur 483
Amritsar to Quetta 353
Bam to Esfahān 318
Chitwan to Sunauli 534
Doğubayazıt to İstanbul 256
Esfahān to Doğubayazıt 300
İstanbul to İzmir 171
İzmir to Antalya 187
Jaipur to Amritsar 454
Kathmandu to Royal Chitwan 560
Sue's Long Ride 138
Sunauli to Agra 511

MAP LEGEND

CITY ROUTES

Freeway .... Freeway	Lane .... Lane
Highway .... Primary Road	= = = = Unsealed Road
Road .... Secondary Road	⊓⊓⊓⊓⊓⊓ .... Stepped Street
Street .... Street	⟩= = ... Tunnel

REGIONAL ROUTES

.... Tollway, Freeway	.... Minor Road
.... Primary Road	.... Described Route
.... Secondary Road	‒ ‒ ‒ ...Alternative/Side Route

HYDROGRAPHY

- .... River, Creek
- .... Lake
- ... Dry Lake; Salt Lake
- .... Waterfalls

BOUNDARIES

- .... International
- .... State
- .... Disputed
- .... Fortified Wall

TRANSPORT ROUTES & STATIONS

.... Train	.... Cable Car, Chairlift
... Underground Train	.... Ferry
.... Metro	.... Walking Trail
.... Tramway	.... Walking Tour

AREA FEATURES

.... Building	.... Market
.... Park, Gardens	.... Sports Ground
.... Beach	.... Campus
+ + + ... Cemetery	.... Urban Area

MAP SYMBOLS

✪ CAPITAL .... National Capital	▢ ... Church, Cathedral	⌢⌢ .... Mountain Range	▨ .... Ruins
◉ CAPITAL .... State Capital	▣ .... Cinema	▣ .. Museum or Gallery	▨ .... Shopping Centre
● CITY .... City	◙ . Embassy, Consulate	▣ .... National Park	▨ .... Sikh Temple
● Town .... Town	◉ .... Golf Course	▣ .... Pagoda	▣ .... Stately Home
● Village .... Village	▦ .... Gompa	▣ .... Parking Area	▣ .... Taxi Rank
▪ .... Airfield	◐ ... Hamam, Hammam	⇀ ......One-Way Street	▨ .... Telephone
▨ .... Airport	▨ .... Hindu Temple	)(............ Pass	▣ .... Temple
⊝ .... Bank	◍ .... Hospital	◐ .. Petrol/Gas Station	▣ ....Temple (Classical)
⟍ .... Bird Sanctuary	▣ .... Internet Cafe	▼ .... Place to Eat	▣ .... Theatre
◈ ▨◀ ...Border Crossing	● ... Islamic Monument	■ .... Place to Stay	◉ .... Toilet
▨ .... Buddhist Temple	※ .... Lookout	● ...... Point of Interest	▣ .... Tomb
▣▨ .. Bus Terminal, Stop	▲ .... Monument	▣ .... Police Station	❶ .. Tourist Information
▨ ... Cafe or Teahouse	◖ .... Mosque	▨ .... Post Office	▣ .. Transport (general)
▨ .... Camping Ground	▲ .... Mountain	▨ .... Pub or Bar	▣ .... Zoo

Note: not all symbols displayed above appear in this book

LONELY PLANET OFFICES

Australia
Locked Bag 1, Footscray, Victoria 3011
☎ 03 8379 8000 fax 03 8379 8111
email: talk2us@lonelyplanet.com.au

UK
10a Spring Place, London NW5 3BH
☎ 020 7428 4800 fax 020 7428 4828
email: go@lonelyplanet.co.uk

USA
150 Linden St, Oakland, CA 94607
☎ 510 893 8555 TOLL FREE: 800 275 8555
fax 510 893 8572
email: info@lonelyplanet.com

France
1 rue du Dahomey, 75011 Paris
☎ 01 55 25 33 00 fax 01 55 25 33 01
email: bip@lonelyplanet.fr
www.lonelyplanet.fr

World Wide Web: www.lonelyplanet.com *or* AOL keyword: lp
Lonely Planet Images: lpi@lonelyplanet.com.au